D1408457
LIBRARY
LAKELAND COLLEGE

MICHAEL G. HADJIMICHALAKIS
University of Washington and
Board of Governors of the Federal Reserve System

MODERN MACROECONOMICS

an intermediate text

PRENTICE-HALL, INC., Englewood Cliffs, New Jersey 07632

Library of Congress Cataloging in Publication Data

HADJIMICHALAKIS, MICHAEL G.
Modern macroeconomics.

Bibliography
Includes index.
1.Macroeconomics. I. Title.
HB172.5.H32 339 81-12024
ISBN 0-13-595074-0 AACR2

Editorial/production supervision by Linda C. Mason
Interior and cover design by Dawn L. Stanley
Manufacturing buyer: Ed O'Dougherty

Printed in the United States of America
10 9 8 7 6 5 4 3 2 1

ISBN 0-13-595074-0

PRENTICE-HALL INTERNATIONAL, INC., *London*
PRENTICE-HALL OF AUSTRALIA PTY. LIMITED, *Sydney*
PRENTICE-HALL OF CANADA, LTD., *Toronto*
PRENTICE-HALL OF INDIA PRIVATE LIMITED, *New Delhi*
PRENTICE-HALL OF JAPAN, INC., *Tokyo*
PRENTICE-HALL OF SOUTHEAST ASIA PTE. LTD., *Singapore*
WHITEHALL BOOKS LIMITED, *Wellington, New Zealand*

This book is dedicated to my parents—
Maria Palos Hadjimichalakis
and Gregory Hadjimichalakis

Contents

THE ECONOMICS OF FULL EMPLOYMENT, PRICES, AND INTEREST, 57

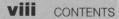

KEYNESIAN-NEOKEYNESIAN MACROECONOMICS AND THE NEOCLASSICAL SYNTHESIS, 159

V
THE BEHAVIORAL FUNCTIONS, 417

EXTENSIONS, 585

15

THE OPEN ECONOMY, 587

16

THE GROWING ECONOMY, 615

Preface

In writing this book I have tried to present a *modern* treatment of macroeconomics, that is, a treatment that includes in its basic framework all the recent advances in theory which have a direct bearing on the actual working of an entire economy and on the actual conduct of economic policy. This means that, in addition to the traditional classical and Keynesian approaches, we must examine recently advanced models, such as the monetarist, expectational, and supply-side macroeconomic models. My interest has been to present the various competing "schools" and the controversies surrounding them in a fair and objective manner.

My approach has been to write an account that is dynamic, that evolves historically, and that relies on microeconomic foundations. A dynamic approach, one capable of monitoring movements through time, is necessary since the broad magnitudes examined by macroeconomics, such as prices, national income, interest rates and employment, vary through time. We need a framework that evolves historically, since many raging controversies have their origins in the works of such great masters as Wicksell and Keynes. And we need the microeconomic foundations of macroeconomics since macro, the aggregate of individual decisions, must be consistent with those decisions of individual agents.

In addition, these microeconomic foundations of macroeconomics can dispel the most common complaint made by students (and teachers) of macroeconomics, namely that macroeconomics is "different," that it does not use concepts, ideas, and techniques learned in micro, such as maximization by individual agents or supply and demand. I hope that my approach can counteract the prevalent state of affairs in which students who have taken a course in microeconomics are unable to see the interrelationships between micro and macro. By establishing our macroeconomic analysis on a firm microeconomic foundation and by incorporating microeconomic terminology into our analysis, I hope to highlight the unity between these two areas of study.

I also intended to write a rigorous book, which is analytically precise, and which would, nonetheless, be accessible to both instructor and student. Furthermore, I was determined to write this book without using any college mathematics. In fact, one can understand the contents without a knowledge of high school mathematics.

My strategy is to employ an *all-inclusive, flexible* framework capable of generating, and consistent with, such disparate models as the neoKeynesian (i.e., Tobin-Modigliani) and the neoclassical, or monetarist (i.e., Friedman, Brunner-Meltzer), models. In order to do this we need only to insert, at the appropriate point, the particular assumptions. In this effort I hope that I have been objective in my treatment of all the competing theories and schools of thought.

I have designed this framework so that the exposition will be engaging and relevant to the reader; the essence of the book is found in the first ten chapters. This form permits examination of important, arresting issues very early, in fact, as early as Chapter 2. Monetary issues and other controversies appear as early as Chapter 3. In addition, we start by examining issues of the 1970s and 1980s, by strategically introducing and analyzing modern noeclassical macroeconomics with an emphasis on inflation, inflationary expectations, and interest rates, rather than on falling prices, the Great Depression, and the IS-LM curves.

To enhance the accessibility and relevance of the book each of the first four chapters is preceded by a summary section, or "bypass." These bypasses serve two purposes: For those who intend to read the entire chapter, they provide a solid summary; for those who prefer to exclude a chapter and proceed directly to the next chapter, they provide along with a summary, all the tools and information necessary to understand what follows. With the innovation of these bypasses the entire book becomes flexible and meets the needs of a wide range of audiences.

The relevance of the material is underscored by our insistence that the theories be applied to real-world situations. Economic policy *in practice* spans the last 50 years, from the haphazard application of monetary and fiscal policy in the 1930s, to the "New Economics" of the Kennedy-Johnson era, to the Nixon-Ford-Carter economic policies, and now to the "supply-side" policies of the Reagan administration. Furthermore, the recent, drastic change in the Federal Reserve's conduct of monetary policy, which now relies on reserves rather than on federal funds interest rates, and the change in the financial structure, which now permits the payment of interest on demand deposits, are examined in an appropriate practical framework.

Acknowledgments

This book is the outgrowth of eleven years of teaching both undergraduate and graduate macroeconomics courses at the University of Washington. For the first seven years, I asked the students to take notes and then to copy and recopy them, "until they wrote their own textbooks." At the end of the semester or quarter I asked five or six students to lend me their notes, which I read, searching for the points on which most or all of the student notes were unclear or incorrect. These lapses showed me where better explanations were needed in order to provide a clear, simple presentation of the material. During the last four years, photocopies of the manuscript were bound and distributed to the students in order to compile a textbook which was easy to test and was available for comments by both students and colleagues. I have benefited greatly from the comments of many of my undergraduate students, who are too numerous to mention; however, in this group, Daniel T. Slesnick stands out. I have also benefited greatly from the comments and suggestions of several of my graduate students. Special mention is due, chronologically, to Lewis O. Johnson, Eliot B. Bradford, Michael R. McMahon, Andrew R. Criswell, Beth Yarbrough, and Robert Yarbrough. Colleagues who taught and commented on the manuscript include, in addition to former graduate students, James R. Barth, Karma G. Hadjimichalakis, William Kaempfer, and Evan Koening.

I am grateful to several of my reviewers, especially to James R. Barth of George Washington University, John Z. Drabicki of the University of Arizona, and Kenneth A. Lewis of the University of Delaware. Their interest in the contents and exposition of the manuscript went beyond what is expected from or required of reviewers. For assembling this group of reviewers, and for the confidence and the support he gave me throughout this project, I am indebted to David C. Hildebrand of Prentice-Hall. For a truly smooth production process I am thankful to Senior Production Editor Linda Mason, and for the design to Dawn Stanley. I am also thankful to Lynn M. Caddey for superb typing and overall final preparation of the manuscript.

The exposition in this book was greatly improved by the numerous editorial suggestions on the entire manuscript made by my friend and editor, Dollmarvelene Flood Pardi. I am grateful for these suggestions and for her insistence that I avoid the use of "Econojargon" and concentrate, instead, on standard English.

To the extent that the exposition in this book is rigorous I have benefited from the teaching and the tradition established by my teachers at the University of Rochester, Ronald W. Jones and Lionel W. McKenzie. James Tobin has left his imprint throughout this book, especially on Chapters 7, 10, 13, and 14. I am also grateful to him for his generous permission to use unpublished material in Chapter 10.

To the extent that the framework employed in this book is successful, I owe a great deal to my mentor, Hugh Rose, whose influence on the entire text is apparent, but especially in Chapters 2, 3, 4, 5, and 16. It is to Hugh Rose that I owe my understanding of the Wicksellian model, a key ingredient in this book.

I am, however, most grateful to my wife and colleague, Karma G. Hadjimichalakis; it was she who first induced me to write this book by taking notes on my lectures and by persuading me that it would be easy for me to translate the lecture notes into a textbook. How little I knew! In addition, she tried the manuscript on several classes of business students, both at the undergraduate and the MBA level. And, finally, she made detailed comments on all versions of all chapters.

As I write this preface, I am concluding the first year of a two-year tenure at the Board of Governors of the Federal Reserve System. During this first year, a year of great upheaval in financial markets and a year of reappraisal of the conduct of monetary policy, I have benefited from learning the institutional aspects, both the old and new, of monetary policies. I have also been pleasantly surprised to discover how relevant the framework and analysis of this book—essentially completed by the day of my arrival here—is to actual conduct of monetary policy.

Michael G. Hadjimichalakis
Washington, D.C.

MODERN MACRO-ECONOMICS

Overview

Macroeconomics deals with models of an entire economy, that is, with scenarios capable of generating and explaining broad magnitudes such as employment and unemployment, national product, and the price level. Macroeconomics endeavors to explain not only why these and similar economy-wide variables have a particular magnitude at any moment but also why they change as they do. Most of these variables are recorded regularly in tables such as the National Product and National Income Accounts, and, in a sense, macroeconomic analysis brings to life the accounting framework of these tables.

We are interested in these economywide variables because they are good barometers of a nation's economic health; it is natural, therefore, that economists might want to influence some or all of these magnitudes. It is understandable, then, that almost every relation we unravel in macroeconomic models may have important policy implications, which is why macroeconomic analysis can be, and usually is, called the theory of economic policy.

It is primarily because of this strong policy orientation that macroeconomics abounds with controversies, a situation that is both understandable and, sometimes, even desirable. After all, a particular policy, say an increase in taxes, affects large masses or even an entire nation. At any rate, since the well-being of large masses is involved, it is advisable to undertake a thorough examination of all the implications of the suggested policy, whether the suggested policy can achieve its stated objective or whether it is the policy best suited for the job. This type of investigation, understandably, breeds controversy.

In this book we do not shy away from controversy. And although we find that some of these controversies are, in fact, inessential, sham disputes and that others emanate from faulty logic, we also discover that some are attributable to important differences in assumptions about economic behavior; in other words, some issues currently dividing macroeconomists are empirical in nature. We examine all these controversies by employing an *all-inclusive, flexible* framework, capable of generating, and consistent with, both neoclassical (Friedman) and neo-Keynesian (Tobin, Modigliani) models of macroeconomics: All that is needed is to insert, at the appropriate point, the particular assumptions.

Yet other controversies can be understood, and thus resolved, only in an *historical* context. In fact, most macroeconomic controversies revolve around interpretations of the work of the great masters; the most important sources are still the neoclassical economists, especially Wicksell, Fisher, and the younger Keynes (before 1936) on the one hand, and the Keynes of the *General Theory* on the other. Although the work of those authors is relatively recent, it was written before mathematics became the main tool of economic theory. Thus, those works were written using the techniques and economic language of their time. As a result, contemporary economists find those works almost impossible to penetrate, which, of course, helps create and perpetuate controversy. The need exists, then, for a modern macroeconomic framework, firmly rooted in an historical context and capable of generating the works of the masters. This will help not only to explain the evolution of our subject but also, and more important, to make the reader both *competent* and *willing* to study the original works to form his or her own opinion about these controversies.

If anything is known about the variables that macroeconomics seeks to explain, it is that they change. We need, therefore, a *dynamic framework,* one capable of examining movements of variables through time. We usually distinguish between short-run dynamics, or those changes in the variables over the short cycle, a period short enough to permit us to treat the economy's capital stock (i.e., its productive capacity) as fixed, and the *long-run* or *growth dynamics,* which deals with long-run trends in the variables examined, usually under the constraint of full employment of the continuously expanding capital stock and labor force.

Although substantial contributions to both branches of dynamics have been made during the last two decades, these contributions are usually absent from macroeconomics texts, which instead mention only a few aspects of growth dynamics. In general, *changes* in the variables are examined by comparative statics and not by a dynamic framework. This attitude seems to suggest to the reader that the profession suffers from fear of *motion sickness,* which, of course, is not true. It is imperative, therefore, that we make the reader immune to any potential motion sickness by designing a dynamic framework from the very beginning.

Macroeconomics is concerned with relationships between broad aggregates. This, however, does not mean that it ignores the body of knowledge about the behavior of individual agents, such as producers or households. On the contrary, during the last forty years there has been a concerted effort to make the aggregate relationships consistent with these considerations of microeconomics. For example, the aggregate consumption function has been restricted to the form of the consumption function of the individual household. And, similarly, the aggregate demand for money was made consistent with the demand of the individual agent.

Modern macroeconomics is related to microeconomics in other, yet equally important, ways. In fact, we can see that the younger field, macroeconomics, has been patterned after the older.

Of course, there is only one microeconomic theory, the general equilibrium (or disequilibrium) theory introduced in 1874 by Léon Walras: The effects of a change in a parameter (or an endogenous variable) in one market will affect all markets and the variables they determine. In other words, all endogenous variables are determined simultaneously by all markets. (This, of course, differs from the partial equilibrium approach where the strategy is to concentrate on a particular aspect, assuming that everything else remains the same. For example, we can take as given all prices but one and investigate supply and demand in the market in which that particular price is determined.) Macroeconomics has been established in modern times, in 1936, as a general equilibrium analysis, and since then its progress has paralleled that of microeconomics. (It is remarkable that Keynes, student and protégé of Marshall, the champion of *partial* analysis, had to reach outside his formal education to design the modern macroeconomic framework. In this sense, Walras, who was largely deleted from the Anglo-Saxon literature, got his revenge posthumously.)

Here, our macroeconomic framework is not only a *general,* rather than a partial, one but is also patterned after other aspects of microeconomics.[1] Within this self-contained book some of the required microeconomic knowledge is developed in Part I, where its inclusion emphasizes that microeconomic knowledge is necessary to the proper understanding of macroeconomics. Chapter 1 emphasizes that the economy is organized into the familiar units of *firms* (or producers) and *households* (or consumers), whose environment and behavior are scrutinized.

The first part of Chapter 1 examines briefly the theory of household choice and applies this theory to the problem of derivation of the household's supply of labor. Two features of both the theory and the application in this part of Chapter 1 are worth emphasizing. First, we note that the household is endowed with quantities of goods rather than given money income, a feature that is partly designed to highlight, in this work of National Income Analysis, that income is one magnitude that must be *determined* from within the system and not assumed as *given* from the outside. Another feature of this part of Chapter 1 is the elaborate treatment of *homothetic* preferences using only elementary techniques. Empirical work usually relies on the

---

[1] In particular, we define *equilibrium* by stipulating that markets are cleared and expectations fulfilled. The term *ex ante* refers to behavior planned on the basis of parametric prices, while the term *ex post* refers to the actual market situations where plans may not be accomplished and expectations not realized. Perfect flexibility of price is usually sufficient to guarantee that the corresponding market is cleared. Similarly, instantaneous adjustment of expectations to current reality means that expectations are realized, that is, that "myopic perfect foresight" exists. In order to describe the real world according to the equilibrium solution to a model, the minimum requirements must be the *existence* and *stability* of the equilibrium in that model. Therefore, we adhere strictly to these requirements of modern micro theory in this book on macroeconomics.

implications of homothetic preferences, and it is high time that these were incorporated into a book.

The second part of Chapter 1 examines production technology, the realm of the agents called firms, or producers. The rational behavior of the firm is examined in a manner analogous to that of households, and the firm's demand for labor is derived. Finally, the assumptions of the rational behavior of firms and of pure competition permit us to divide the national product among the owners of the factors of production. In this way we establish and also present the theoretical underpinnings of the National Product and National Income Accounts.

Chapter 1 explicitly examines maximization for only one period of time. In later chapters the time horizons for the household and the firm are enlarged to permit *intertemporal* maximization. And additional tools and techniques taken from microeconomic theory are introduced as they are needed.

So far we have established the need for a macroeconomic framework that is (a) unified and all-inclusive, (b) derived historically, and (c) dynamic. All these requirements are satisfied by the strategic choice of the first and simplest microeconomic model presented in Section I of Chapter 2. There we examine a barter economy where no borrowing or lending is permitted, and where the instantaneous adjustment of the real wage clears the *single* labor market, and thus continuously guarantees full employment of labor and prevents any insufficiency of, or an excess of, the demand for goods and services. The long-run version of this model is the neoclassical growth model introduced by Solow and Swan in 1956, the examination of which we undertake in Chapter 16. Thus, from the very beginning we present a dynamic framework.

In Section I of Chapter 2 the assumption of no borrowing or lending was responsible for guaranteeing that investment is identical to savings, which, in turn, implies that the goods market is always cleared. Beginning with Section II borrowing and lending are explicitly permitted. This inclusion, of course, increases the array of assets available to the wealth holder, which, in turn, implies that one can invest more than one saves and, vice versa, that one can invest less than one saves. On the other hand, we continue to be interested in the equality of investment and savings because only then can we guarantee clearance of the goods market. This interest, in turn, necessitates our citing in detail the underlying reasons for consumption-savings and investment decisions. While an extensive treatment of this topic is postponed until Chapters 11 and 12, we briefly examine this issue in Section II of Chapter 2, relying on household choice theory and profit maximization by firms. The remainder of Chapter 2 reexamines the more complicated model, still assuming barter and full employment. We find that this model has the same properties as the simpler model of Section I. Of course, it permits the posing and answering of more-interesting questions than does the earlier model. (The growth properties of this model are derived in Chapter 16.) The focus of Chapter 2 is on those assumptions that guarantee that the economy will always be at full employment or that it will gravitate naturally toward full employment. This belief, that the economy gravitates naturally toward full employment, which was held complacently by neoclassical economists, was effectively challenged by Keynes in 1936, but it has been revived in the 1960s and 1970s by the modern neoclassicists, or monetarists. The foundations of neoclassical macroeconomics, the new as well as the old, are completed in Chapters 3 and 4, which are concerned with monetary issues.

Beginning with Chapter 3, we relax the assumption of barter by introducing money into the system. This introduction of money permits us to talk about the price level, that is, the prices of goods and services, and about the value of money which is the inverse of the price level. We then examine the relation between the quantity of money and the level of economic activity, especially the prices of goods and services.

In Chapter 3 we introduce and examine two widely used formulations, the flow formulation and the stock formulation, of the quantity theory of money. Either of these versions of the quantity theory produces this result: that excess supply of money causes prices to rise and excess demand for money causes them to fall. Then we concentrate on the question of the monetary mechanism, that is, why and how, for example, an excess supply of money materializes as excess demand for goods and services, which, in turn, causes prices to rise. Of course, one way of transforming an excess supply of money into an excess demand for goods and services is to assume that when individuals hold more money than they desire, they eliminate this excess supply of money by buying goods and services. This we call Schema I.

On the other hand, a more realistic sequence of events appears in Schema II, which outlines the following process: When individuals find themselves with more money than they need, they lend part or all of this excess money supply, thereby increasing the supply of loans, which, in turn, lowers the interest rate, which increases investment and consumption demand, thereby causing excess demand for goods and services, which, finally, increases the prices of goods and services.

When investigating empirically the relation between changes in the money supply and changes in prices, modern quantity theorists dispense with the intermediate steps of Schema II, thereby giving the impression that they have adopted Schema I. However, we find that when modern quantity theorists examine the determination of interest rates and of prices, they actually adopt Schema II, a subject we take up in Chapter 4.

In Chapter 4 we examine the determination of both the interest rate and the price level in a fully employed economy. We develop an interdependent (i.e., general equilibrium and disequilibrium) system consisting of three distinct markets: a money market and a loanable funds market, which together comprise the financial sector, and a goods and services market, which comprises the real sector (given the assumption that factors are fully employed). Our analysis is dynamic, and the effects of the feedback between the financial and the real sectors play a crucial role in this analysis of movements in the interest rate and the price level.

The model is especially suited for analyzing the economic problems of the 1970s and the 1980s, known as the decades of inflation. We note that rising interest rates and inflationary expectations, as well as the effects of monetary and fiscal policies on these variables, have attracted more attention than ever before from policy makers and ordinary citizens alike.

Our aim in this chapter is to construct and apply a consistent general equilibrium framework in order to examine these issues. To focus more directly on these issues, we dispense with problems of unemployment in the neoclassical manner by assuming a continuously fully employed economy.

As a byproduct of our analysis, we show that this loanable funds model yields the quantity theory results as a special case. Of course, this model is richer than the strict quantity theory model of the preceding chapter, in the sense that it also explains, and in fact relies on, interest rates. We can say, therefore, that the usual quantity theory model is the reduced form of this fully specified general equilibrium (interdependent) system. In fact, we see that Friedman and other monetarists rely on this very model when they are confronted with interest rate determination and that these two aspects of our model taken together do indeed provide the foundation of monetarism.

A second byproduct of our analysis in this chapter is the insight we gain into historical doctrine. We see that this model, so useful in explaining the issues of the 1970s and 1980s, dates back to the turn of the century, to the work of the Swedish economist Knut Wicksell. We also see how this model was improved upon and popularized by Keynes and Fisher in the 1930s, and resurrected in a modern version by Friedman and Hugh Rose in the 1960s.

In Section I of Chapter 4 we construct the model from its individual components, that is, from the markets for loans, for money, and for goods and services. In Section II we see how the entire model can be reduced to one that yields the quantity theory results. The distinction between market and natural rates of interest, as well as the concomitant distinction between temporary and full equilibrium, is instrumental in analyzing the dynamic behavior of the system in Section III. In addition, the relation between interest rates and prices is clearly delineated.

In Section IV of Chapter 4 we examine the effects of a change in the money supply on the price level and on the interest rate, in the beginning of the process, at the end of the process, and also through time (i.e., we trace the trajectories of the price level and of the interest rate). Furthermore, we distinguish between a one-shot increase in the money supply and a (continuous) change in the rate of growth of the money supply, as well as the effects of these changes on the interest rate and on prices. We outline the three effects of changes in the money supply on the interest rate, which Friedman stressed: the "liquidity effect," the "price level effect," and the "price anticipation effect." Of course, continuous increases in the money supply cause continuous increases in the price level, which are eventually anticipated. This creation of inflationary expectations is further examined and applied to two important cases: namely, the Fisher hypothesis, or the effect of inflationary expectations on the real and on the nominal interest rates, zero and one, respectively, and the attempts by the monetary authorities to peg the nominal interest rate below its natural rate, which causes accelerating (cumulative) inflation.

In Section VI, the final section of Chapter 4, we trace the model back to Wicksell and Keynes and to their treatments of the cumulative process, both the inflationary and the deflationary. However, we note one crucial difference between the analyses of Wicksell and Keynes. Wicksell's strict quantity theory result, which states that prices rise if, and only if, the money supply rises, rests squarely on his assumption that the demand for money is independent of the interest rate. But when

Keynes assumed this dependency, he discovered that prices may change even though the money supply remains fixed. This discovery disillusioned Keynes and encouraged him to launch his revolution, a theme taken up in Chapter 5.

Part III of this book examines in detail the Keynesian macroeconomic framework from its inception to its most recent extensions. In the first section of Chapter 5, we see why Keynes was disillusioned with the prevailing orthodoxy. The two philosophies are, in fact, presented and contrasted in terms of their respective theorems. In effect, Keynes successfully demonstrated that in the neoclassical system both the interest rate and employment were indeterminate and that another crucial market, the money market, was necessary for a simultaneous determination of those two variables. Moreover, he proceeded to change the rules of the game, stating that investment and savings determine the employment level, and not the interest rate, which is then assumed to be determined by the money market. We demonstrate that the "employment adjustment mechanism"—the statement that employment increases (falls) if, and only if, investment is greater (lower) than savings—is consistent with basic microeconomic considerations (i.e., the law of supply and demand) if the money wage is fixed. We also demonstrate that the "interest rate adjustment mechanism," based on liquidity preference, that is, on the supply and demand for money, is consistent with the loanable funds theory, which we established and used in Chapter 4.

Of course, with investment greater (less) than savings, the goods market experiences excess demand (excess supply). In Section II of Chapter 5 we examine in greater detail the goods market and the role it plays in determining, *ceteris paribus*, the level of employment. Following the existing literature, we first translate the *employment* adjustment mechanism into the *income* adjustment mechanism. In other words, the goods market determines and changes income. Next we examine the role of particular components of aggregate demand in determining income. We begin by considering the roles of government demand and of taxation as separate entities and then as a net result, that is, as the *budget deficit* or *surplus*. Then we examine the role of foreign trade and, in particular, of beggar-thy-neighbor policies in increasing the income of a country. Finally, we introduce and examine a measure for the response of output to autonomous changes in aggregate demand, a measure of response that is termed a *multiplier*. And we derive in a simple fashion these multipliers for different changes, and we rank them according to their magnitudes.

We see that the transformation of Keynes's adjustment mechanism from one of employment determination to one of income determination reflected the keen interest in income as a key economic indicator in the 1940s and 1950s. But now the trend is reversed, and once again, employment, x, is the key variable. This is why, beginning with the next chapter, we conduct our explicit analysis in terms of employment.

Chapter 6 concentrates on the simultaneous determination of the interest rate and employment level, treating prices parametrically. Also, like Keynes, we assume fixed money wages. The money market and goods and services market are developed systematically and their interdependence, by means of the IS–LM framework, is highlighted and shown to be patterned after the microeconomic treatment of markets. (The modern intellectual father of both is, of course, J. R. Hicks.) Chapter

6 also examines tentatively both the dynamics of the interdependent markets and the comparative statics of monetary and fiscal policies. Although this analysis is tentative—that is, because the price level, a key endogenous variable, is treated as a parameter—nevertheless, a serious comparison of the efficacy of monetary and fiscal policies is undertaken.

In our comparison of monetary and fiscal policies we discover at the outset that they have different sectoral effects; they not only affect the interest rate differently but also have the same qualitative effects on employment. Second, we identify some extreme special cases, when only monetary policy or only fiscal policy is effective. However, we also show that these special cases lack empirical support and should be rejected. And, finally, we examine the Government Budget Restraint (GBR), which permits the exploration of alternative means of financing a government deficit, namely by increasing the money supply and/or by issuing new government bonds, that is, by government borrowing in the open market. The current controversy over whether this government borrowing, needed to finance a given budget deficit, crowds out any and all effects of fiscal policy is systematically explored.

Chapter 7 examines the rationality of fixed money wages, noting that inelastic price expectations may be the underlying factor. Prolonged periods of unemployment may, however, modify these expectations and thus persuade workers to accept money-wage cuts. This chapter, which is patterned after and updates Keynes's Chapter 19, entitled "Changes in Money-Wages," shows that in the absence of deflationary expectations, money-wage flexibility will eventually lead the economy to full employment. However, if deflationary expectations are formed during this period, the whole system may collapse. This phenomenon explains Keynes's own fear of "depression psychology" and his advocacy of an *activist* monetary and fiscal policy over a do-nothing policy, that is, waiting for the emergence of money-wage flexibility as a tool to fight recessions. And it is this advocacy of activist economic policies that is the hallmark of Keynesian economics.

Chapter 8 presents and examines the complete neo-Keynesian system that has emerged from the combined efforts of economists during the last forty years. We emphasize the determination and movements of the price level, as well as of money wages, employment, and the interest rate. The model and its implications are no longer tentative. In fact, the determination of the price level is imperative not only because it has always been the primary task of monetary macro theory but also because we cannot determine either the employment level or interest rates without knowledge of the price level; the difficulty arises since there is an infinity of such pairs, (employment level–interest rate), one for each level of prices. And, finally, since the prices of goods depend directly on supply and demand, determination of the price level brings into focus the role of *supply,* as well as that of demand, for goods and services.

In Section I of Chapter 8 we introduce the general framework. First we derive the "effective demand curve," which depicts all the combinations of prices and of employment, or income, that the market system can support. Next we introduce the supply curve, also known as the marginal cost or productivity curve, which is consistent with the profit-maximizing behavior of firms. In addition, we identify several "supply-side" factors, such as changes in factor (money) prices, in productivity, and in capacity utilization and changes in tax rates, which are capable of shifting this marginal cost curve.

In Section II we examine the special case of fixed money wages in order to familiarize ourselves with this new technique and also to relate our results to those previously derived. With money wages given we can determine the other three endogenous variables, a goal we were not able to achieve with our earlier framework. In Section III we determine the price level and *income,* along with the interest rate, in an analysis reminiscent of and consistent with standard price theory, in fact, with the theory of both the firm and the industry. And, finally, in Section IV we determine all four endogenous variables and also describe their equilibrating mechanism, tracing their dynamic behavior. Furthermore, we confirm our earlier results, especially those in Chapter 7.

Part IV focuses on the role of stabilization policies in the complete model. Chapter 9, utilizing the complete model of Chapter 8, examines how the proper authorities, by manipulating the money supply or the budget deficit, can achieve a permanently higher level of employment, accompanied by a permanently higher price level. This type of economic policy, called *comparative static stabilization,* is illustrated with examples from modern U.S. history, spanning the period from the Great Depression to the present. That higher employment levels can be achieved at higher prices gives rise to two philosophies, the first of which we shall call the Employment Stability, or ES, party, since it cares more about employment than prices. In particular, it objects to price stability if it is achieved at the expense of jobs. On the other hand, the Price Stability, or PS, party objects to employment stability if it is achieved at higher prices.

Although shades of these two philosophies exist in political parties all over the world, we shall examine real-world situations taken from modern American history. In fact, the *Great Recession* of 1974–75 is explained as the natural outcome of a relentless pursuit of the PS party philosophy. We shall find that the roots of this recession were disturbances on the supply side, such as (a) crop failure and the rise in grain prices; (b) devaluation of the dollar; (c) quadrupling of oil prices by OPEC; and (d) drastic wage increases, which followed the lifting of wage and price controls.

It is interesting to see that the 1978–80 recession, almost as severe as the one in 1974–75, also has its roots in supply-side shocks, such as (a) doubling of oil prices; (b) inflationary expectations fueled by the belief that the imposition of wage-price controls was imminent; and (c) a drastic productivity slowdown. We also note that the (new) administration and the Fed responded to these supply shocks in a manner reminiscent of the response by the earlier administration, in 1974–75.

In the same section, II, we examine several ways to favorably influence the supply side by reversing the effects of the shocks. One way is to provide incentives, mainly for capital formation, to improve the economy's productivity. A second way is the reduction in tax rates, which, by increasing after-tax wages and profits, improves the efficiency of both labor and capital. This is a modification, as well as a generalization, of the idea associated with the "Laffer curve." A third way is the deliberate reduction in market power, whether this power is attributed to natural monopolies or to government regulations. It should be mentioned that the outcome of these three measures, namely the decrease in prices and the rise in employment, meets with the approval of both political philosophies.

Section III examines the issues and problems associated with the use of *dynamic stabilization* policies, a term that refers to the manipulation of the money supply and of the budget deficit in order to reduce, or possibly eliminate, oscillations in key economic magnitudes, especially in employment and in the price level (or the rate of inflation). In the real world the most frequently used stabilization policies are of this dynamic variety and, for this reason, their use is controversial. Some economists argue that this conduct of economic policy should not be left to the *discretion* of *authorities,* but that the authorities should, instead, follow a set of predetermined *rules.* (This is the famous rules *versus* authorities debate.) Some of these same economists also argue that the *only* rule to be followed is a fixed rate of growth in the money supply, a prescription that is recommended in the belief that the economy is basically stable. In fact, they argue that if it were not for "bad" monetary policies, the economy would never experience any oscillations at all. The merits and demerits of all these assertions will also be explained in this section.

In Chapter 10 we examine the problem of the simultaneous existence of inflation and unemployment. This issue is relatively new—making its debut in the 1950s—although the problem is known to have existed for at least a century. The early analyses of the 1950s distinguished between "demand pull" and "cost push" inflation. The former results from increases in aggregate demand, while the latter originates in reductions in supply, because of rises in costs. The literature of the 1950s attributed cost push inflation to *market power,* which enables some firms to *administer* prices. Examination of the "cruel dilemma," faced by the policy maker, was intensified by the empirical research of A. W. Phillips, whose work established a negative relation between money-wage inflation and unemployment. This relation was soon established theoretically by Lipsey and others, who simply used the law of supply and demand for the labor market. Using a simple arithmetic formula, that the rate of price inflation is equal to the rate of money-wage inflation minus the rate of productivity change, we examine the wage-price guideposts used during the Kennedy-Johnson administrations. This same arithmetic is also used to derive the Price-Phillips curve.

We note that when expectations are incorporated into the system, there is an infinity of Phillips curves, one for each assumed expected rate of inflation. Furthermore, we see, based upon the above stipulation and the additional assumptions made by Friedman and Phelps, that when (a) workers correctly anticipate and fully take into consideration the exact rate of inflation, and when (b) there is a *natural* or *normal* rate of unemployment, no trade-off occurs between inflation and unemployment. And any attempt to keep the market rate of unemployment below its natural rate will produce *accelerated* inflation. In addition, we demonstrate that expectations that are not of this variety produce a trade-off, which, incidentally, also exists in a true long run when the capital intensity is influenced by inflation.

To test for the influence of expected inflation on the Phillips curve, we used a theory capable of explaining how expectations are formed and adjusted. One such prominent theory stipulates that the expectation of the rate of inflation for this period is a weighted average of the actual inflation for the last period and of its previous expectation. From this conclusion it follows that the expected rate of inflation is a weighted average of *all* past inflation rates (of course, with the weights of the distant past being negligible). Using postwar actual inflation rates for the United States economy, we find that as inflation became greater and more persistent, individuals revised their expectations of inflation more rapidly. We then use these estimates of expected inflation to find the expectation-ridden Phillips curve. Our results suggest that as we proceed through the post-war period, the effect of expectations on the Phillips curve increases. In fact, we find that for the period 1960–80 and for the period 1965–80, price setters take fully into consideration the expected rate of inflation. This is consistent with a vertical Phillips curve.

The influence of expectations is further examined using the modern concept of *rational* expectations, a view that dictates that expectations should be the same as the predictions of the model used. We show how the marriage of the natural rate hypothesis (NRH) and the rational expectations hypothesis (REH) precludes any trade-off between inflation and unemployment, even for a single period. We also show, however, that the practical relevance and applicability of this result is minimal.

In Chapter 10 we also extend the analysis to allow for heterogeneous labor and the simultaneous existence of unfilled vacancies and of unemployment. And, finally, the costs of additional inflation, or of additional unemployment, are examined and some remedies for the *cruel dilemma* are offered.

In Part V we derive formally and discuss extensively the behavioral relations we have employed in this book: the consumption and savings functions, the investment function, the demand for money, and the supply of money. In Chapter 11 we employ standard household choice theory to derive the household's consumption and, hence, its savings function. Beginning with the special case of given, *fixed,* endowments for each period's income, in Section I we show that when the substitution effect outweighs the income effect, there is a negative relation between consumption and the interest rate; under the same assumption there is a positive relation between the interest rate and savings. When the endowment for each period is *variable,* it is possible to have a positive relation between savings and the interest rate, even if the relation between consumption and interest rate is positive. Finally, by employing the assumption of homothetic preferences, we derive exact forms of the consumption and savings functions, forms that are useful for empirical research. Here we examine the *life-cycle* and the *permanent-income* hypotheses, associated, respectively, with the names Franco Modigliani and Milton Friedman. In addition, other empirical investigations are examined at some length here.

Chapter 12 examines the investment function. In Section I we employ the basic Fisherian, two-period production model to illustrate all the existing approaches to deriving investment, that is, the *present value* approach, the *marginal efficiency of investment* approach, and the approaches based on the *increasing cost* of investment. In Section II we use the present value criterion at an elementary level in order to derive the investment function. In Section III we derive the investment function from the marginal efficiency of investment viewpoint, and we highlight the basic shortcomings of this approach, as well as those of the preceding section. Section IV, which highlights the importance of increasing cost of investing at the firm level, contains the derivation of the investment demand based on increasing *subjective* costs. This method, which utilizes Kalecki's *principle of increasing risk*, has motivated the modern mathematical theories of increasing adjustment costs. Section V examines two approaches that view investment as a supply function and not as a demand function based on demand for capital by firms that are independent of households. The first of these approaches relies almost exclusively on the implications of efficient production, namely factor price equalization, and on the Stolper-Samuelson theorem and the Rybczynski theorem, while the second embeds the two-sector model in a stock-flow formulation. Finally, Section VI examines the empirical evidence with an emphasis on Jorgenson's work and Tobin's "q" theory.

In the remainder of Part V we examine money as an asset, alternative to other assets, and we derive its demand and supply. Using four alternative theories, we establish, in the first four sections of Chapter 13, a negative relation between the demand for money and the interest rate. (This relation is in addition to the positive one between the demand for money and the level of income.) First, in the Tobin-Baumol fashion, we show that even the transactions demand for money is dependent upon the interest rate. Second, we establish, in accordance with the theories of Keynes and Tobin, a negative relation between the demand for money and the interest rate, the case in which wealth holders have *certain*, but *differing, inelastic expectations* of bond prices (or interest rates). Among the shortcomings of this approach is the implication that investors hold either bonds or cash, but not both. The third theory, examined in Section III, is designed to derive the demand for money with the implication of a diversified portfolio, and it is based upon the *uncertainty* of expectations, along the lines of Tobin. The fourth theory, the topic of Section IV, also considers money as one of several alternative assets available to the wealth holder. The demand for these assets is derived using standard microeconomic tools, such as utility maximization, which is subject to the wealth constraint. The resulting demands (for all assets) are found to be functions of all the assumed parameters, that is, of wealth and of the prices, or yields, of the assets. And we see, once again, that the demand for money depends on the interest rate. This fourth approach is the one espoused by Friedman. In Section V we examine the empirical evidence, which shows, contrary to some earlier work, that there is substantial interest-elasticity of the demand for money. The recently observed instability (or shift) of the demand function for money is also examined and its impact on the conduct of economic policy explained.

In Chapter 14 we examine the process of money creation by comparing the traditional view of banking, one of mechanically applying the money multiplier, with the modern view, which relies on the rational behavior of banks. This new view treats money as an endogenous variable; the monetary authority can control the amount of currency and reserves, but the total amount of money, no matter how broadly or narrowly defined, is the outcome of the choice of all the agents in the economy and results from the interactions of the decisions of (a) the financial institutions (banks), (b) the nonbank public, and (c) the Federal Reserve System. In Section I we determine the money supply, M, and we see how it can be influenced by the standard tools of monetary policy. As a byproduct, we also determine an entire array of interest rates and rates of return. In Section II we examine the actual conduct of monetary policy, emphasizing its occasional reliance on monetary aggregates, on the federal funds rate, and on the recent move toward a direct control of the reserve, or monetary base. And, finally, in Section IV we examine the empirical investigations, concentrating on the size of the interest elasticity of the supply of money.

Part VI extends the model to cover other important issues. Chapter 15 extends the model to analyze open economies, so that the goods market now has additional components reflecting demand from abroad (exports) and demand for foreign goods (imports). Similarly, the market for loans is extended in order to finance (net) investment abroad. More important, a new financial market must be introduced, namely the market for foreign exchange. Consequently, in Chapter 15 we determine, in addition to the earlier variables, the exchange rate, and we derive the effects of monetary and fiscal policies on these variables.

Chapter 16 continues the analysis of the two models examined in Chapter 2 by allowing for growth in both the capital stock and the population of a society. Section I examines the no-borrowing-or-lending case, and it identifies the steady state, showing that output, income, consumption, savings, investment, and capital all grow at the natural rate of population growth. The dynamic approach to the steady state is also examined, as are the comparative dynamics of a parameter's change.

Section II reexamines the problem in the explicit presence of borrowing and lending. The model, in fact, is reduced to one that is indistinguishable from the no-borrowing-or-lending model. Of course, the new model is richer in that it permits the posing and answering of more-interesting questions than does the model in Section I.

A WORD ABOUT NOTATION

It is clear from this summary that the analysis in this book is rigorous. *Yet, we avoid using any college mathematics.* An occasional equation appears here and there, but only for the purpose of brevity. The reader, however, will be greatly aided by knowing at the outset that the symbol Δ represents, in our form of shorthand, the expression "change in." For example, Δx means "change in x." Of course, $\Delta x > 0$ means a positive change in x, that is, a rise in x. Similarly, $\Delta x < 0$ means a fall in x, and $\Delta x = 0$ means that x remains unchanged. Also, in our shorthand, we occasionally use the following compact form:

$$\Delta x \gtreqless 0 \quad \text{when} \quad y \gtreqless 0$$

This should be read as saying:

x rises (i.e., $\Delta x > 0$) when $y > 0$,
x remains unchanged (i.e., $\Delta x = 0$) when $y = 0$,
x falls (i.e., $\Delta x < 0$) when $y < 0$.

A WORD ABOUT THE USES OF THIS BOOK

The first ten chapters are the core of the book, while the last two (15 and 16) present extensions to cover the case of an open and of a growing economy. Chapters 11–14 provide a more-detailed treatment of the four key behavioral relations used throughout the book, the consumption-savings function, the investment function, the demand for money, and the supply of money.

Each of the first four chapters is preceded by a summary section, or "bypass." These bypasses serve two purposes: For those who intend to read the entire chapter, they provide a solid summary; for those who prefer to exclude a chapter and proceed directly to the next chapter, they provide, along with a summary, all the tools and information necessary to understand what follows. It is therefore possible for one to move immediately on to Chapter 5 and the remaining chapters in order to design a traditional "neo-Keynesian" course.[2]

These bypasses enhance the accessibility of this book. In fact, the entire book is designed to be flexible in order to meet the needs of a wide range of audiences. By a suitable choice of chapters, this book can be used for undergraduate economics courses, both for majors and nonmajors, and for business courses, both at the undergraduate and at the MBA level. It can also be used to provide the foundations for master's-level courses in economics, provided that supplemental readings are included.

For instance, a compact course aimed at providing only the analytical foundations necessary to expose the student to policy issues early on, can utilize all bypasses to reach Chapters 5 through 10, and to possibly use Chapter 14. Still, a policy-oriented, but more analytical, course, such as one for MBAs, with its strong interest in financial markets, could add Chapters 3 and 4, which examine money, interest, and prices, in the context of a loanable funds (credit) market.

A more thorough course, however, could add the microeconomic foundations, that is, Chapters 11–14. There is a choice here. One possibility is to round off the course with these chapters, following exactly the sequence of this text. On the other hand, this material can be studied early on and selectively. For example, the instructor of a business course, with a special interest in finance, may find Chapter 13, which discusses the demand for money, with an emphasis on portfolio choice, particularly useful. Or a course aimed at preparing the students for graduate study in economics might utilize Chapters 11 and 12, with their emphasis on intertemporal choice theory.

A final word on the last two chapters is in order. These chapters are an integral part of the book and not merely an addendum. These chapters can be used early on; Chapter 16, on growth, can be used immediately after Chapter 2, and Chapter 15, on the open economy, immediately after Chapter 4.

---

[2] However, experience has persuaded us that early treatment of the issues of inflation, inflationary expectations, and interest rates, such as the one undertaken in Chapters 3 and 4, which focus on the modern neoclassicists, especially Friedman, is more interesting and preferable to beginning the book with issues of falling prices, the Great Depression, and the IS–LM curves.

microeconomic foundations

To aid the reader and to ensure that the material meets the needs of a wide range of undergraduate courses, this book contains four summary sections, or bypasses, to its chapters. These bypasses serve two purposes: For those who intend to read the entire chapter, they provide a solid summary; for those who prefer to exclude a chapter and proceed directly to the next chapter, they provide, along with a summary, all the tools and information necessary to understand what follows.

chapter one bypass

The reader who wants only a brief overview of Chapter 1 should read the following.

First, we must distinguish between money wages and real wages. Money wages, W, are the number of dollars a unit of labor is paid, say dollars per man-hour. The real wage, however, is the number of goods, say corn, or GNP, that each unit of labor can command. To find the real wage, w, we simply divide the money wage by the price level, that is, the price of goods and services, or GNP:

$$w = \frac{W}{p} = \frac{\text{\$/Man-hour}}{\text{\$/Units of GNP}} = \frac{\text{Units of GNP}}{\text{Man-hours}},$$

which as we see, gives the real wage, that is, the number of units of GNP per man-hour.

Second, from the rational behavior of households, from their attempt to always choose the most preferred position, we can derive the supply curve of labor as a function of the real wage, w. Depending on the preferences, the supply curve of labor, N^s, can be upward sloping, as in Figure B.1-1a; downward sloping, as in Figure B.1-1b; both upward sloping and downward sloping, as in Figure B.1-1c; or independent of the real wage, as in Figure B.1-1d. However, in this book we shall use mostly the cases of B.1-1a and B.1-1d.

Third, from the firms' rational behavior (i.e., from their attempts to maximize profits), we can derive the result that firms hire labor up to the point where its marginal product, MP_N, is equal to the real wage, w, paid (to labor). This gives us the demand curve for labor, N^d, which is nothing but the marginal productivity of labor curve, as in Figure B.1-2, where we see that the lower the real wage, the higher the demand for labor. (Of course, by having a demand schedule and a supply schedule of labor, we also have a market for labor, a theme taken up in Chapter 2.)

Fourth, since firms produce the national product, we can examine the production technology, or the production function, of the economy. The production function exhibits constant returns to scale, which means that if we double, say, the quantity

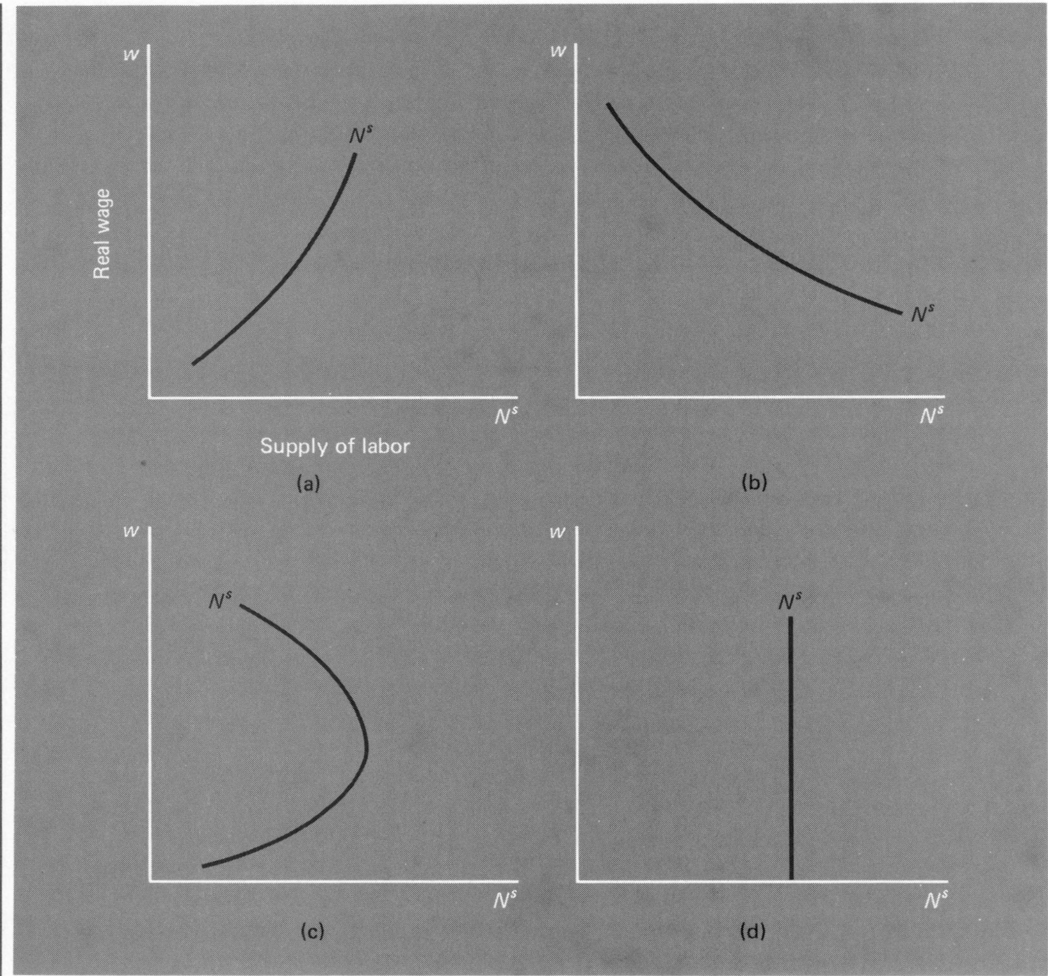

FIGURE B.1-1

of inputs, or factors, the national product also is doubled. Furthermore, we can depict this function, either in its absolute form, Y, or in per-unit-of-capital form, Y/K, as in Figure B.1-3.

Fifth, and the final point, the reader can see that profit maximization by firms, which happens when the marginal product of labor is equal to its real wage, also implies that the marginal product of capital is equal to the (percentage) rate of profit. This, in turn, shows that the national output is distributed to the owners of factors of production as income. A typical national income account (NIA) is shown in Table B.1-1. On the other hand, the national product, or GNP, accounts emphasize the allocation of this product to its users, domestic consumers, as consumption, *C;* domestic firms, as investment, *I;* government, as government expenditure, *G;* foreign

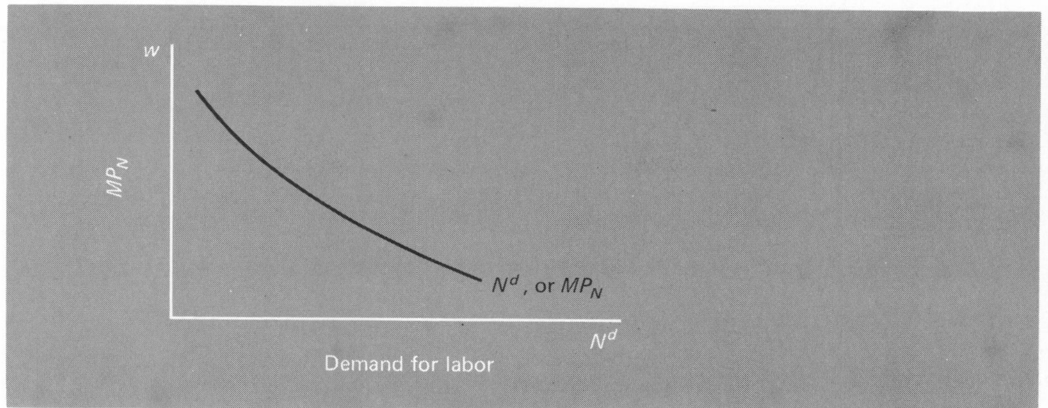

FIGURE B.1-2

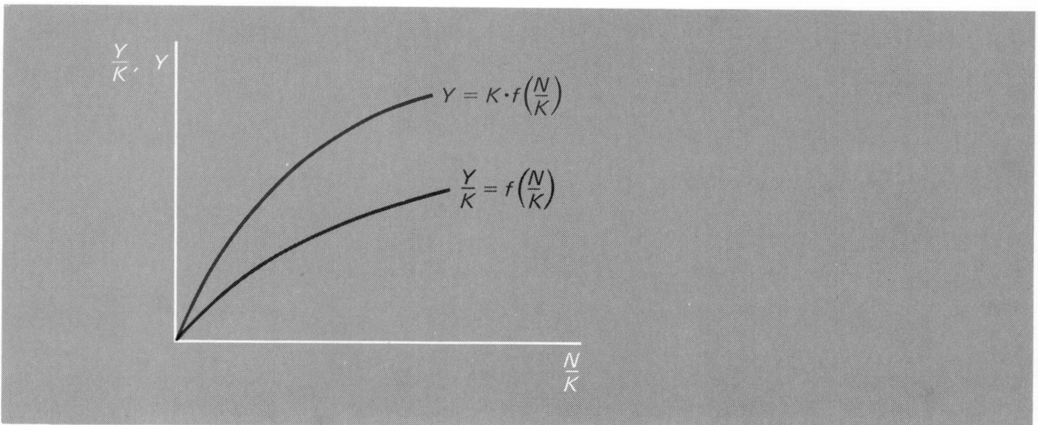

FIGURE B.1-3

TABLE B.1-1 NATIONAL INCOME (IN BILLION DOLLARS), 1980

National Income		2,121.4
Compensation of Employees		1,596.5
Wages and Salaries	1,343.6	
Supplements to Wages and Salaries	252.9	
Proprietors' Income		130.6
Rental Income of Persons		31.8
Corporate Profits		182.7
Net Interest		179.8

SOURCE: *Survey of Current Business,* April 1981, p. 14.

TABLE B.1-1 (continued) FROM GNP TO NATIONAL INCOME (IN BILLION DOLLARS), 1980 (OR, RELATION OF GNP AND NATIONAL INCOME)

Gross National Product	2,626.1
Less: Capital Consumption Allowances	287.3
Indirect Business Tax and Non-Tax Liability	212.3
Business Transfer Payments	10.5
Statistical Discrepancy	−.7
Plus: Subsidies Less Current Surplus of Government Enterprises	4.6
Equals: National Income	2,121.4

SOURCE: *Survey of Current Business,* April 1981, p. 14.

demanders, as export surplus, $\chi - \mu$. This allocation is represented in Table B.1-2 and in the following equation:

$$C + I + G + (\chi - \mu) = Y \tag{1}$$

Table B.1-2 is constructed using (1) as an *identity.* However, we are also interested in (1) as an *equality,* which means that the demand for goods and services is equal

TABLE B.1-2 GROSS NATIONAL PRODUCT (IN BILLION DOLLARS), 1980

Gross National Product	Y	2,626.1
Personal Consumption Expenditures	C	1,672.8
Durable Goods	211.9	
Non-Durable Goods	675.7	
Services	785.2	
Gross Private Domestic Investment	I	395.3
Fixed Investment	401.2	
Non-Residential	296.0	
(a) Structures	108.8	
(b) Producer's Durable Equipment	187.1	
Residential	105.3	
Changes in Business Inventories	−5.9	
Net Exports of Goods and Services	$\chi - \mu$	−23.3
Exports, χ	339.8	
Imports, μ	316.5	
Government Purchases of Goods and Services,	G	534.7
Federal	198.9	
State and Local	335.8	

SOURCE: *Survey of Current Business,* April 1981, p. 13.

to the supply, Y. But since output, Y, is always equal to income, and since income can be consumed (C), or saved (S), or paid in taxes (T), we have the identity

$$Y \equiv C + S + T \tag{2}$$

Combining (1) and (2), we have

$$C + I + G + (\chi - \mu) = C + S + T$$

or

$$I + G + (\chi - \mu) = S + T \tag{3}$$

When this equality holds, the market for goods and services is cleared; when the left-hand side (LHS) is greater (less) than the right-hand side (RHS), there is excess demand for (supply of) goods and services. In the special, or abstract, case, when government expenditures and taxes are zero and when there is no international trade, $\chi - \mu = 0$, the following equality must hold in order to clear the goods market: $I = S$, or $I - S = 0$. Similarly, if investment is greater than savings, $I - S > 0$, it means that the aggregate demand for goods and services is greater than the supply, $C + I > Y$.

1 households, firms, production Technology, and National Accounts

Since macroeconomics deals with scenarios, or models, of an entire economy, it is natural to begin this work by examining the *structure* of the economy at hand. In this chapter we shall emphasize that the economy is organized into the familiar units, or "agents": *households* (or consumers) and *firms* (or producers). To avoid problems of aggregation, we examine the *average* agent directly. Moreover, we assume that the average agent behaves *rationally*, in the sense that, when confronted with a particular set of data, the agent will always choose the most preferred position. And we examine, in turn, the particular criterion of rationality for the average household and for the average firm. Finally, we assume that households and firms operate in an environment of *pure competition*, which means that each agent is one of millions, and thus this agent cannot, by his own actions, influence the price of the goods or services he buys or sells. In other words, our average agent is a *price taker*.

I. HOUSEHOLDS AND THE SUPPLY OF LABOR

Let us begin by examining the problem of household's *choice*, focusing on one manifestation, namely, the derivation of its supply of labor. To examine *any* problem of household choice, it is sufficient to know (a) the quantities of the goods with which the household is endowed; (b) the terms of exchange of these goods; and (c) the *tastes*, or *preferences*, of the household. Knowing the first two permits us to determine a household's "income." Let us suppose that the household is endowed with $\bar{a}$ units of good A and $\bar{b}$ units of good B. To find a single number describing the income, we need the terms of exchange, or the *relative prices.*

The relative price of good B is the number of units of good A one must give up in order to obtain in the market, by exchange, one unit of good B. The relative price of A is the inverse of the relative price of B, or the number of units of good B one gives up (gets) in order to obtain (by giving up) one unit of A. In this section we concentrate primarily on the particular application when we designate good A as "leisure" and good B as "corn." Thus the relative price of leisure is the number of units of corn that the individual gets when he gives up one unit of leisure. Since giving up units of leisure means *offering* an equal number of units of *labor,* it follows that the relative price of leisure is merely the (real) wage rate, which we shall denote as w. And its inverse, $1/w$, is simply the relative price of corn.

If the household is endowed with $\bar{c}$ units of corn and $\bar{l}$ units of leisure, its "income," measured in units of corn, I_c, is $I_c = \bar{c} + w\bar{l}$ units of corn; or $I_l = (1/w)$ $\bar{c} + \bar{l}$ units of leisure as income, measured in units of leisure. (Usually it is assumed that an individual household is endowed with leisure only, namely, 24 hours of leisure per day.)

As an example, if we suppose that $\bar{c} = 100$ bushels per day, $\bar{l} = 24$ hours per day, and $w = 2$ bushels per hour, the individual's income, measured in corn, is

$$\frac{100}{\text{Day}} + \frac{2 \text{ Bushels}}{\text{Hour}} \cdot \frac{24 \text{ Hours}}{\text{Day}} = \frac{148 \text{ Bushels}}{\text{Day}}, \text{ or 148 bushels}$$

per day; on the other hand, in units of leisure, ½ · 100 + 24 = 74 hours of leisure per day.

Figure 1-1 illustrates the endowment point, E, with $\bar{c}$ units of corn and $\bar{l}$ units of leisure. The slope of the line through E is equal to the real wage, while the

FIGURE 1-1

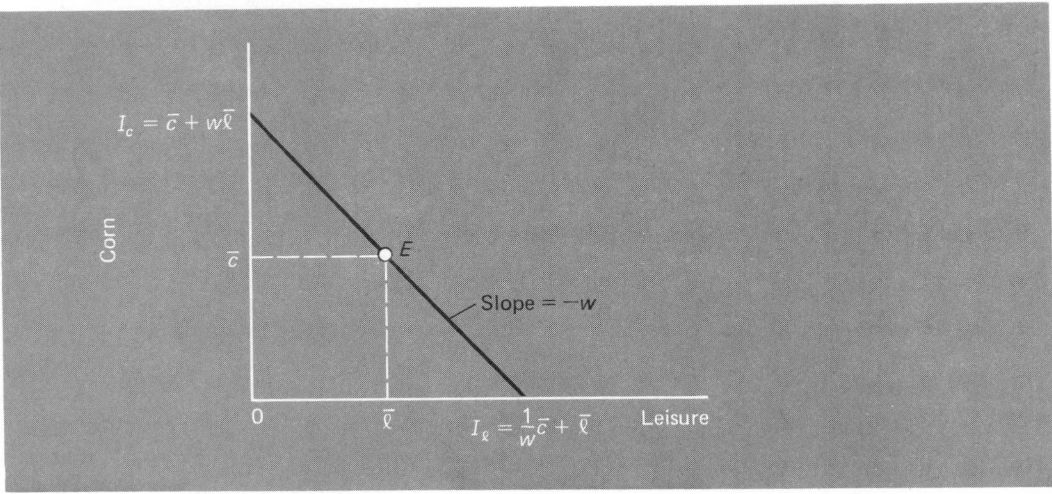

intercept of this line on the corn axis measures the income in corn units, $I_c = \bar{c} + w\bar{l}$, and the intercept on the leisure axis measures income in leisure units. Figure 1-2 illustrates the usual case, the implication of the assumption that the individual (household) is endowed with only leisure—24 hours per day. The line passing through the endowment point, E, with a slope equal to the assumed wage, is called the *budget*, or *consumption-possibilities* line. It shows all the "baskets," that is, the combinations of corn and leisure that the individual can afford to consume if he uses his entire income. Since the average household is a *net supplier* of labor, that is, since he consumes an amount of leisure that is less than his endowment, $\bar{l}$, it follows that, in Figure 1-1, the actual consumption point will lie northwest of point E. In Figure 1-2, however, it always lies to the northwest of E, since the individual does not possess any corn to begin with and will always be, therefore, a net supplier of labor (and a net demander of corn). For example, by deciding to choose (i.e., consume) point F, he decides to consume only OL hours out of the $OE = 24$ hours with which he is endowed. He supplies (offers) the difference, $OE - OL$, as labor. In return for this supply of labor he gets OK units of corn—at the wage rate, w. And it follows that when we know the actual consumption point, F, we can immediately determine the supply of labor.

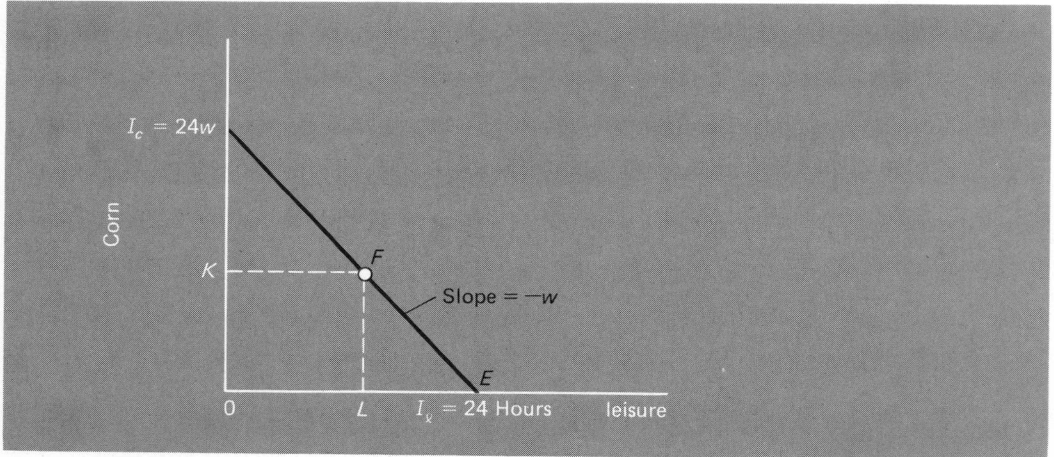

FIGURE 1-2

We shall now examine the procedure that the household uses to decide upon *one* of the infinite number of *potential* baskets, shown by the budget line, to *actually* choose. At this point the assumption that the average household is *rational* comes into play. Here it means that from the infinity of baskets that an individual can afford to consume, he will select the one he prefers above all others. Of course, this implies that the consumer is able to rank all possible baskets according to his preferences, which brings us to another postulate: the consumer possesses a *complete preference ordering* (or *ranking*) of the baskets that might be available to him. This means that the consumer, when confronted with two different baskets, is able to tell whether he prefers the first to the second, prefers the second to the first, or is indifferent between the two baskets. In the last case, we would term the baskets equivalent. (It should be noted that the ranking is consistent only if an additional property is assumed, namely, if an individual prefers the first basket to the second and, in turn, prefers the second to a third one, he must prefer the first to the third.)

One way to utilize the complete ranking is through the concept of *indifference curves.* The crux of this theory is the following: We subdivide the set of all possible baskets into many, in fact, into an infinity of, sets. All baskets belonging to a particular set are equivalent in the individual's estimate, that is, they are baskets toward which the individual is indifferent. These sets, then, are called *indifference sets,* and a curve depicting such a set is an indifference curve. Next, we can rank the indifference sets or the curves. If an indifference curve includes even one basket containing more of each of the (two) goods than a basket belonging to another indifference curve, the first curve is preferred to the second. Figure 1-3 depicts a few of the infinite number of these curves, which constitute the individual's *indifference map.* Note that the indifference curve labeled 2 includes a basket (represented by point G) that contains more of good A and more of good B than does basket H (included in the indifference curve labeled 1). Thus, indifference curve 2 is preferable to curve 1.

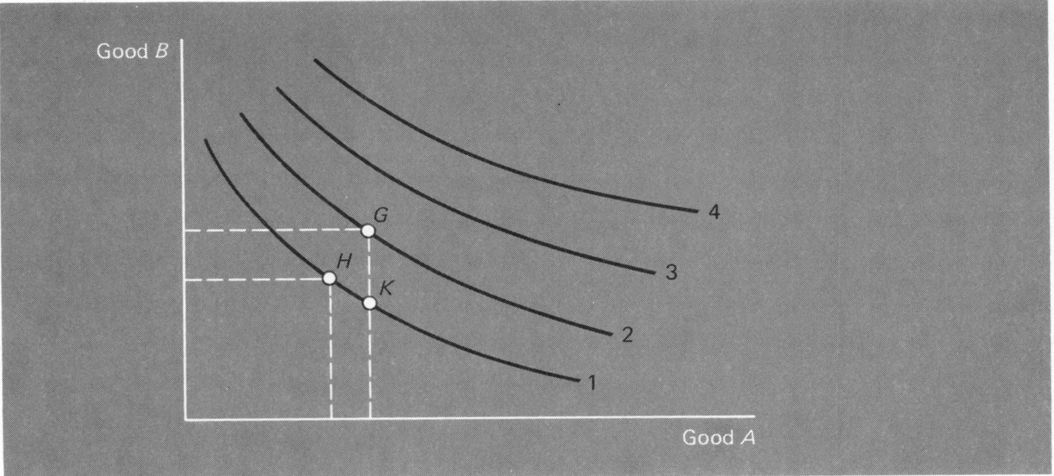

FIGURE 1-3

Indifference curves have three properties, all of which are illustrated in Figure 1-3: First, they are downward sloping; second, they are convex; and third, they are not intersecting. The slope of the tangent, at a particular point on an indifference curve, depicts the *marginal rate of substitution* (MRS), which measures the number of units of a good, say, of B, that the individual is *willing* to give up (obtain) to acquire (give up) one more unit of good A. Equipped with this definition, we can express the second property of indifference curves as the *principle of diminishing marginal rate of substitution.*

Having introduced an individual's tastes, as represented by this individual's indifference map, it is an easy matter to determine which basket (out of an infinite number, which lie on the individual's budget line) will be chosen. This is the point

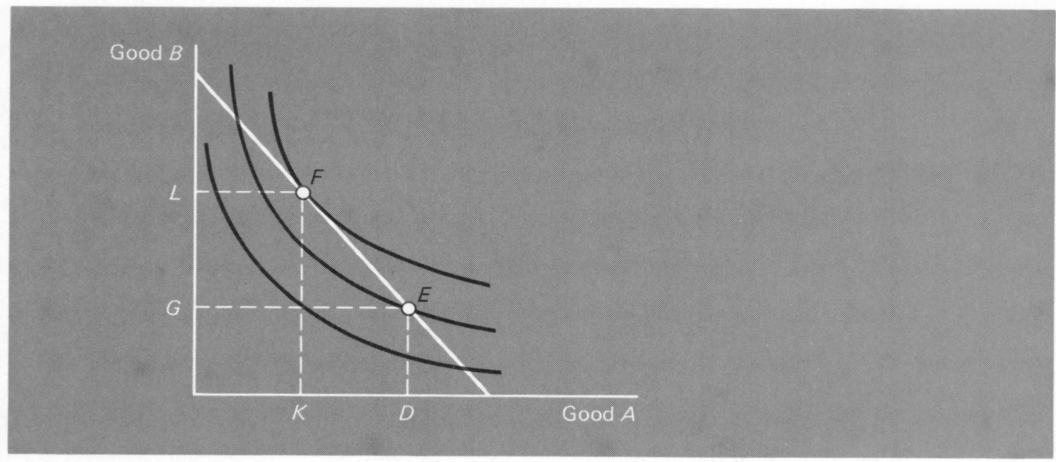

FIGURE 1-4

at which the postulate of rationality will come into play; individuals will choose the most preferred bundle, that is, the one that belongs to the highest indifference curve that their individual budget allows them to attain. Figure 1-4 shows that, in general, the most preferred basket is the one represented by point *F,* where we see that the highest indifference curve is the one that is tangent to the individual's budget line. This is the rule that individuals follow in deciding how much of each good they will consume. But we know that the slope of the budget line is equal to the relative price of good *A,* that is, to the number of units of good *B* that the individual *has* to give up (in the market) in order to get one more unit of good *A.* On the other hand, we know that the slope of the tangent to an indifference curve is equal to the MRS at the point of tangency, which, in turn, is equal to the number of units of good *B* that the individual is *willing* to give up in order to acquire one more unit of good *A.* Thus, at the most preferred point, *F,* the MRS is equal to the relative price of *A.* Of course, one can express the MRS in units of good *A* per unit of *B* by taking the inverse of the slope of the tangent. On the other hand, the inverse

FIGURE 1-5

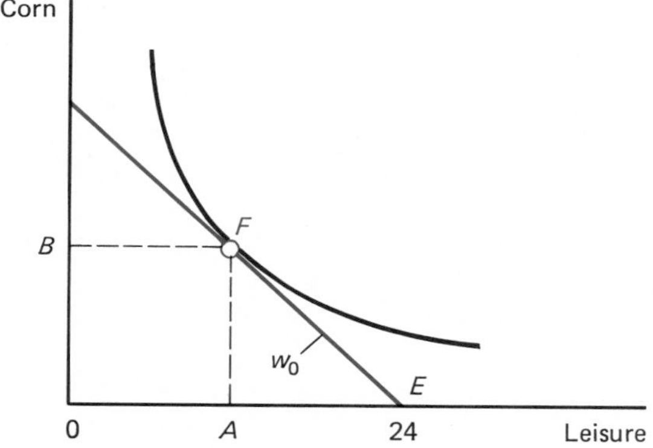

of the slope of the budget line is equal to the inverse of the relative price of *A*, which is the relative price of *B*. Thus, at *F*, the relative price of *B* is equal to the MRS (in units of good *A* per unit of good *B*). Clearly we have established this proposition: *A rational individual consumes the basket whose MRS is equal to the relative price.*

We shall now apply this analysis to the problem of labor-leisure choice. At point *F* of Figure 1-5, the MRS is equal to the real wage, *w*, assumed at the level w_0. Thus, when the wage is equal to w_0, the individual will demand and consume *OA* units of his 24 hours of leisure; he will offer the remainder, 24 − *OA*, in the marketplace as labor, for which he will get *OB* units of corn.

Figure 1-6 traces the quantity of leisure consumed and the quantity of labor

FIGURE 1-6

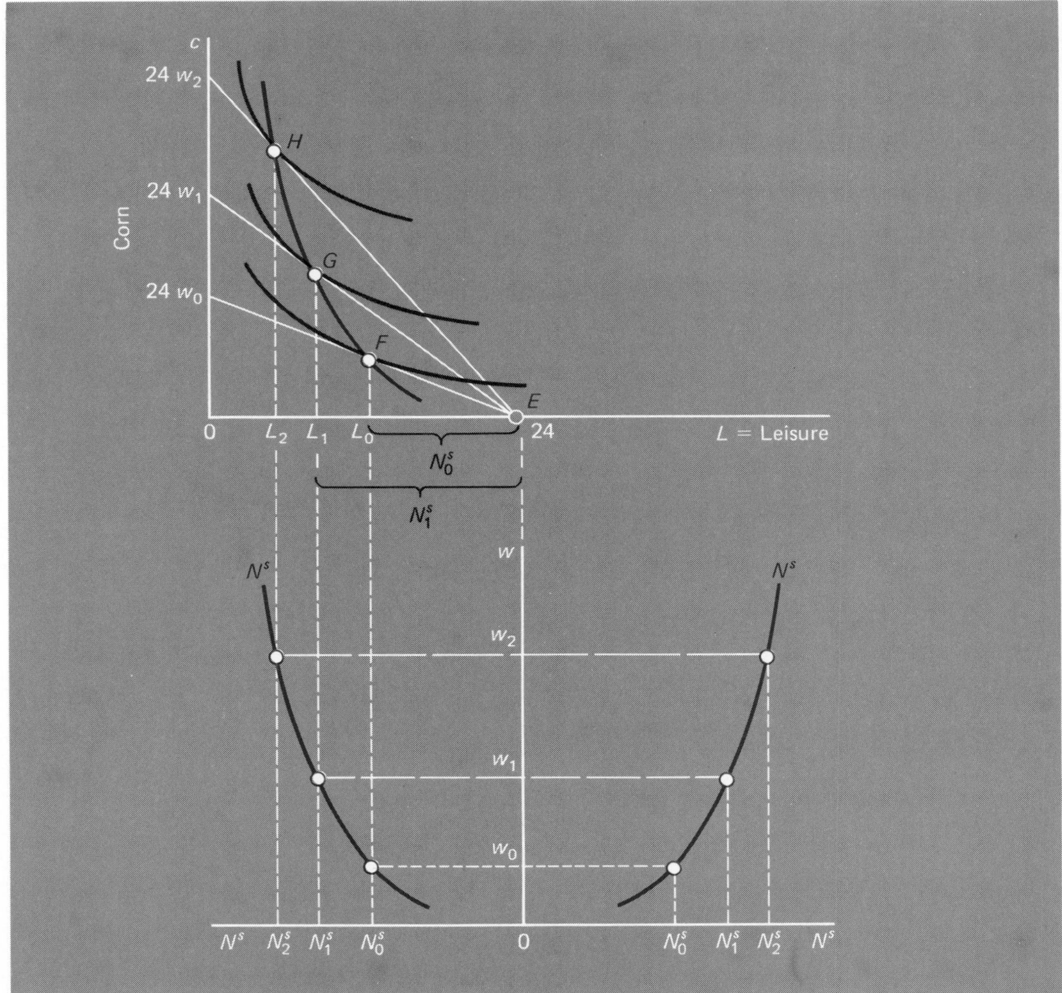

offered by this individual when the wage changes. In the upper panel we see that when $w = w_0$, the individual consumes OL_0 units of leisure, and he supplies 24 − OL_0 units of labor, denoted as N_0^s units. This direct information is given in the left part of the lower panel, while its mirror image is shown in the right part. When the wage rises to w_1, the individual consumes less of this leisure, OL_1, and supplies more, $24 - OL_1 = N_1^s$, which is similarly displayed in the two parts of the lower panel. In this lower panel we can connect all the combinations of wage and of supply of labor, (w, N^s), and derive the *supply curve of labor,* which traditionally is shown as a separate entity, in a graph like the right side of the lower panel of Figure 1-6. The supply curve of labor we derived here is upward sloping, which means that an increase in the real wage influences the household to offer more labor. Unfortunately

FIGURE 1-7

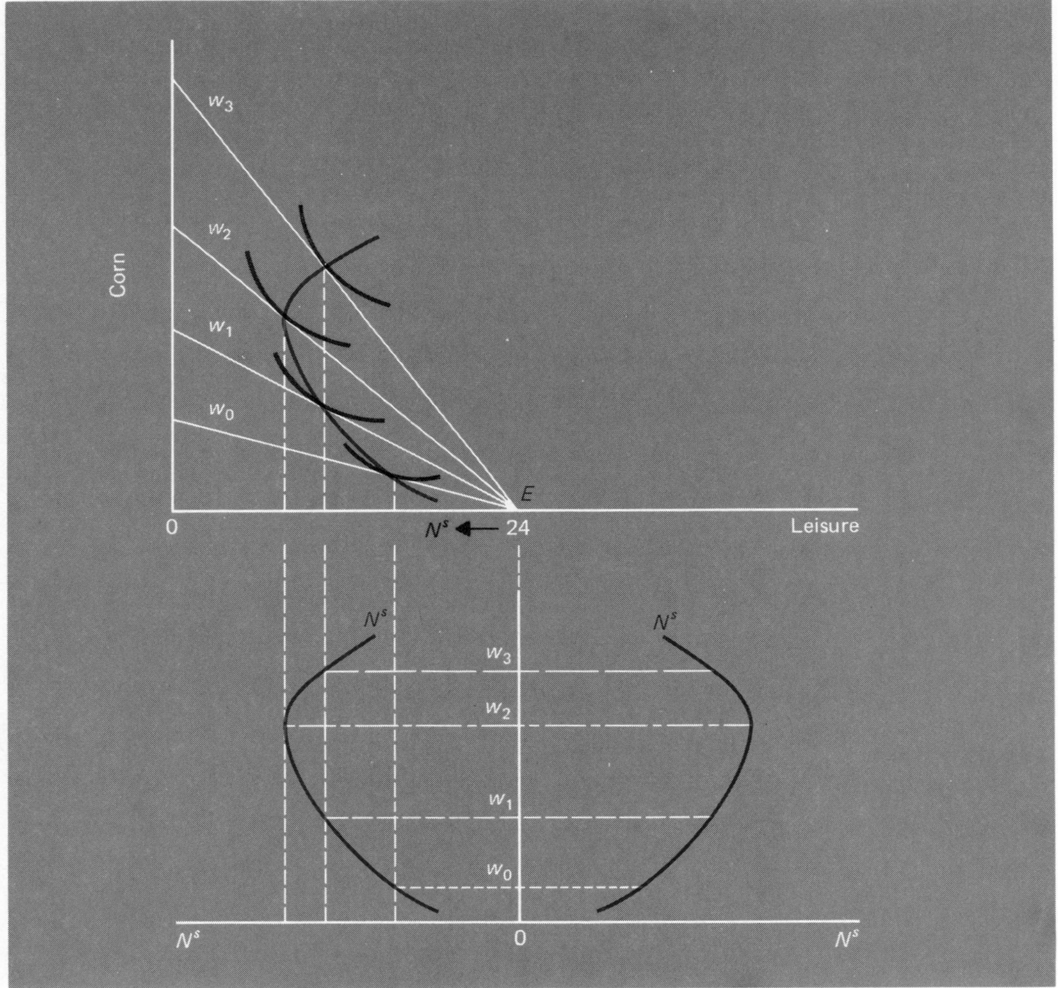

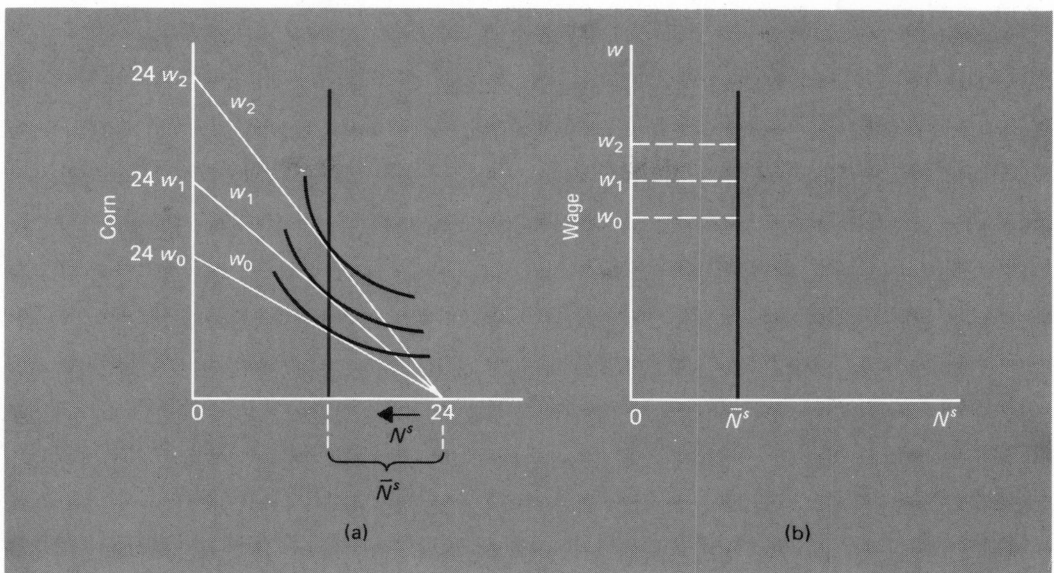

FIGURE 1-8

this is not the only implication of this exercise in household choice theory; it is conceivable that the household's tastes are such that the offer curve, in the (leisure, corn)-plane, is bending backward, as in the upper panel of Figure 1-7, which yields, in the lower panel, a backward-bending supply curve of labor. In fact, it is possible that the offer curve may be entirely vertical, yielding a totally inelastic supply curve of labor, as illustrated in Figure 1-8 where 1-8a reproduces a graph like the upper panels in Figures 1-6 and 1-7, and Figure 1-8b depicts only the right-hand section of the lower panels. Figure 1-9 shows that it is possible to have a supply curve of labor that is a decreasing function of the real wage.

Why, then, can the supply curve of labor, theoretically, be upward sloping, downward sloping, or even independent of the real wage? It can be all of these and yet not be a paradox; this ambiguity of results is another example of a reflection of a general economic principle that is always present when the individual is a *net supplier* of the good under consideration. In such a case an increase in the price of the good induces the individual to want to *consume less* of the good and to substitute for it another, less-expensive good; this is the *substitution effect.* However, since the individual is a net supplier of this good, the increase in price increases the individual's income (or wealth), which, in turn, induces (or permits) this individual to *consume more* of every good and, in particular, more of this same good; this is the *income effect,* which is in opposition to the substitution effect.

In our labor-leisure choice problem, an increase in the price of leisure, that is, an increase in the real wage, induces the individual to consume less of leisure and, therefore, to offer more as labor; this is the substitution effect. On the other hand, the increase in the real wage makes this individual wealthier, enabling him to consume more of everything, and, in particular, more of leisure, and, therefore,

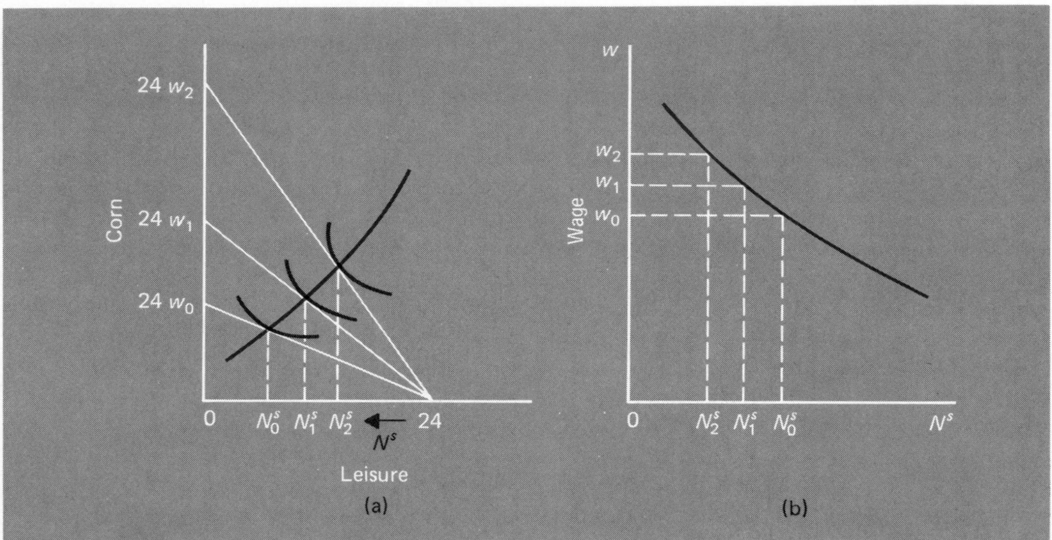

FIGURE 1-9

to supply less labor; this is the income effect. If the (absolute value of the) substitution effect is greater than the income effect, the supply curve of labor is upward sloping; if the income effect outweighs the (absolute value of the) substitution effect, the supply curve of labor is downward sloping. And if the two effects cancel out each other, the supply of labor is independent of the real wage. But the existence of the first, of the second, or of the third case depends entirely on the tastes, or preferences, of the household.

HOMOTHETIC PREFERENCES

A particular class of preferences, namely, *homothetic* preferences, has proved to be very useful in both theoretical and empirical work. On the theoretical level, these preferences help eliminate most of the above-mentioned ambiguity of results. On the empirical level, we have shown that they may indeed represent the tastes of the average household.

Homotheticity is not restricted to preferences; it can be a property of any function, whether this function depicts preferences, production technology (as we shall see in the next section), or any other relation. In general, a function is homothetic if its level curves (such as the indifference curves) have the same slope along any ray through the origin. For example, along the line *OK* in Figure 1-10, the slope of the tangents to all the indifference curves is equal to $1/P_1$, while along the ray *OL*, the slope is equal to $1/P_2$.

In the present application of homotheticity, such a ray through the origin, that is, an Engel curve, has a special meaning; its slope measures the ratio, *B/A*, of the quantities of the two goods consumed. Since this slope is constant when the relative price is given, it follows that *for given relative prices, the ratio of the quantities*

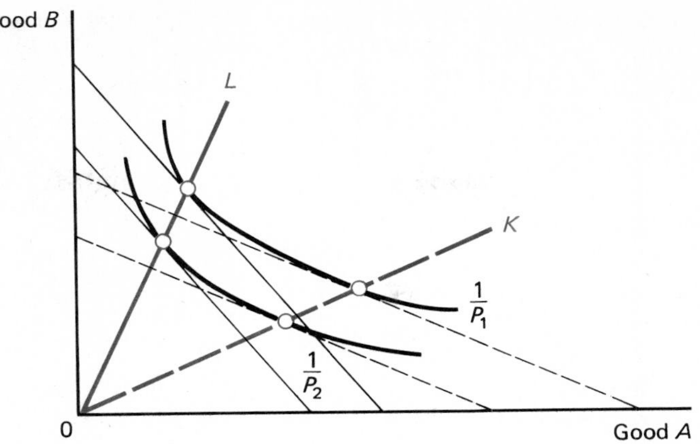

FIGURE 1-10

consumed is independent of the level of income if preferences are homothetic. On the other hand, we see from Figure 1-10 that a higher-ratio B/A is associated with a higher relative price of A. We can express these results directly in the $(1/P, B/A)$-plane where, for concreteness, P denotes the relative price of good B, and hence $1/P$ denotes the relative price of good A. Homotheticity dictates, then, that the ratio B/A is an *increasing* function of the relative price of A, that is, $1/P$, and that it also is independent of the level of income. Note that any one of the curves labeled 1, 2, 3 in Figure 1-11 represents homothetic preferences, since all of them are increasing functions of $1/P$.

Let us concentrate on the curve labeled 3. Because it is an upward-sloping curve, which passes *through the origin,* it can be represented, algebraically, by equation (i):

$$\frac{B}{A} = \lambda \cdot \frac{1}{P} \qquad \text{(i)}$$

FIGURE 1-11

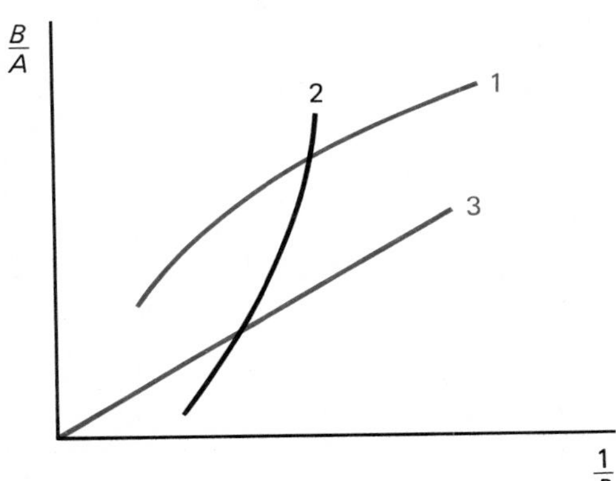

where λ is positive. It is well known, moreover, that the elasticity of an upward-sloping line, through the origin, is equal to one. In the $(1/P, B/A)$-plane, this elasticity is called the *elasticity of substitution.* Equipped with this terminology, we can say that (i) represents a *special case* of homothetic preferences, namely, one in which the elasticity of substitution is constant and equal to one.

When good A is leisure and good B is corn, (i) can be written as (i′):

$$\frac{c}{l} = \lambda \cdot w \tag{i′}$$

where c and l are the quantities of corn and leisure, respectively, that are consumed by the individual, and w is the real wage—the relative price of leisure or labor. We shall now use the special form of homothetic preferences, captured by (i) or (i′), to derive exact simple expressions representing the demand for and the offer of each good, concentrating on the application to the labor-leisure choice problem. We shall need some arithmetic, but only at the junior-high-school level.

We cannot derive the demand and offer functions of corn and leisure (or supplied labor) from (i′) alone. This equation represents only tastes. We also need the budget constraint

$$l + \frac{1}{w} \cdot c = \bar{l} + \frac{1}{w} \cdot c \tag{ii}$$

Equation (ii) states that the value of the basket, *(l, c),* of leisure and corn consumed, measured in units of leisure (i.e., the LHS of (ii)) must be equal to the value of the endowment basket $(\bar{l}, \bar{c})$, again measured in leisure units (i.e., the RHS of (ii)). Both (ii) and (i′) are needed to derive the explicit forms of demands and offers.

Rewriting (i′) as (iii):

$$c = \lambda \cdot w \cdot l \tag{iii}$$

and substituting it in (ii), we get

$$l + \frac{1}{w} \lambda w l = \bar{l} + \frac{1}{w} \cdot \bar{c}, \quad \text{or} \quad (1+\lambda) l = \bar{l} + \frac{1}{w} \cdot \bar{c},$$

and solving for l, we get

$$l = \frac{1}{1+\lambda} \left(\bar{l} + \frac{1}{w} \cdot \bar{c}\right) \tag{iv}$$

Substituting (iv) into (iii), we get

$$c = \frac{\lambda}{1+\lambda} \cdot (w\bar{l} + \bar{c}) \tag{v}$$

Denoting $1/(1+\lambda)$ as β, and since $1/(1+\lambda)+\lambda/(1+\lambda)=1$, it follows that $\lambda/(1+\lambda) = 1-\beta$. Moreover, income measured in leisure units, I_l, and income measured in corn units, I_c, are, respectively,

$$I_l = \bar{l} + \frac{1}{w} \cdot \bar{c} \tag{vi}$$

$$I_c = w\bar{l} + \bar{c} \tag{vii}$$

It follows that (iv) and (v) can be written as

$$l = \beta I_l \tag{viii}$$

$$c = (1-\beta) \cdot I_c \tag{ix}$$

Equation (viii) means that the demand for leisure is a constant fraction, β, of income measured in units of leisure; it is illustrated in Figure 1-12a. Similarly, by (ix), the demand for corn is a constant fraction of income measured in units of corn, as shown in Figure 1-12b. The constant β is the marginal propensity to consume leisure, MPC_l, and $(1-\beta)$ is the marginal propensity to consume corn, MPC_c. The average propensity to consume (APC) a particular good is found by dividing the consumption of the good under consideration by income, measured in the same units. It follows, then, that $\beta = APC_l$ and $(1-\beta) = APC_c$. The former, $MPC_l = APC_l = \beta$, is the slope of the line in Figure 1-12a, while the latter, $MPC_c = APC_c = 1-\beta$, is the slope of the line in Figure 1-12b.

So far we have derived the demands, l and c, as functions of the income of an individual. Traditionally, however, we have been interested in deriving the demand for a good as a function of *its* relative price. Let us concentrate on the demand for leisure as represented by (viii) or (iv) and note what happens to the demand for leisure, l, when its relative price, w, rises: An increase in the wage rate, w, will decrease I_l, as seen from (vi). Since β is given, the increase in w decreases the quantity βI_l, which is the demand for leisure, l, as we know from (viii). Thus (viii) implies

FIGURE 1-12

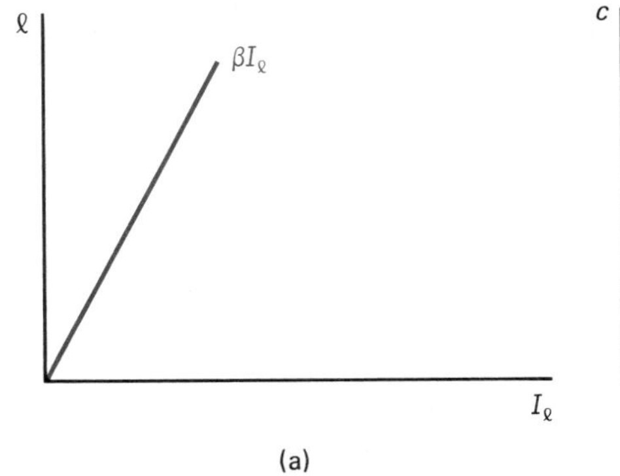

(a)

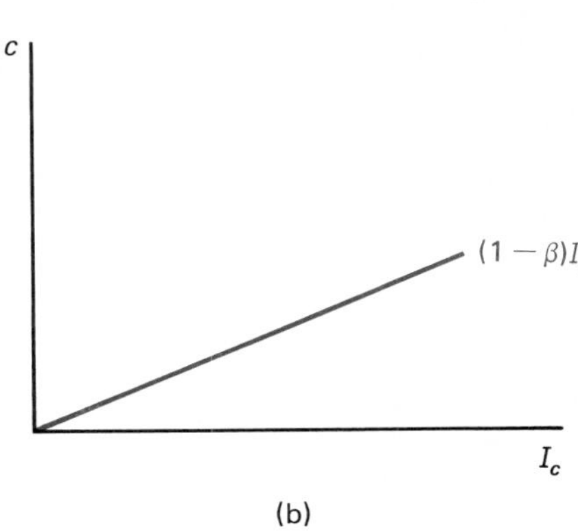

(b)

that the demand for leisure is a decreasing function of the real wage. Moreover, since the offer, or supply of labor, N^s, is found by subtracting the demand for leisure, l, from the endowment of leisure, $\bar{l}$,

$$N^s = \bar{l} - l$$

$$= \bar{l} - \beta I_l,$$

it also follows that the supply of labor is an *increasing* function of the real wage.

The careful reader must have noticed that these results depend on an additional assumption, not as yet mentioned. The increase in the real wage decreases income measured in units of leisure only if the individual is endowed with *some* amount of corn. When the endowment of corn is zero, that is, when $\bar{c} = 0$, the $I_l = \bar{l}$, which is independent of the real wage. In this case the demand for leisure is $l = \beta I_l = \beta \bar{l}$, a constant, independent of the real wage. And similarly the supply of labor is also independent of the real wage, $N^s = \bar{l} - l = \bar{l} - \beta \bar{l} = (1 - \beta)\bar{l}$.

This case suggests that claims associated usually with "supply-side" economists, that an increase in the "after tax" wages, brought about by a reduction in tax rates, will increase the supply of labor, are not generally valid. In this case, a reduction in the tax rate on wages will leave the supply of labor unchanged; and one can construct a case when the reduction in taxes on wages will decrease the supply of labor. The supply side thesis is true only when preferences—and endowments—are such that they yield an upward sloping supply curve of labor.

In summary, we have proved that when preferences are homothetic, with unitary elasticity of substitution, the demand for leisure depends negatively, and the supply of labor depends positively, on the real wage only when individuals are endowed with wealth in addition to their leisure. When individuals are endowed only with leisure, both the demand for leisure and the supply of labor are independent of the real wage: The tastes are such that the individual is willing to offer a given amount of labor for whatever the market will yield. These two cases are shown in Figures 1-13 and 1-14, respectively.

These results can be extended. For example, when individuals are endowed only with their leisure, the supply of labor is positively related to the real wage if the elasticity of substitution is greater than one. Obviously, this is the case represented by Figure 1-6. On the other hand, the supply of labor depends negatively on the real wage, as in Figure 1-8, when the elasticity of substitution is less than one.

Finally, the reader should be able to examine the abstract case of goods A and B. Using the preference equation, (i), and the budget constraint, (x),

$$A + PB = \bar{a} + P\bar{b} \tag{x}$$

one should be able to derive the demands

$$A = \beta I_a$$

$$B = (1 - \beta) I_b$$

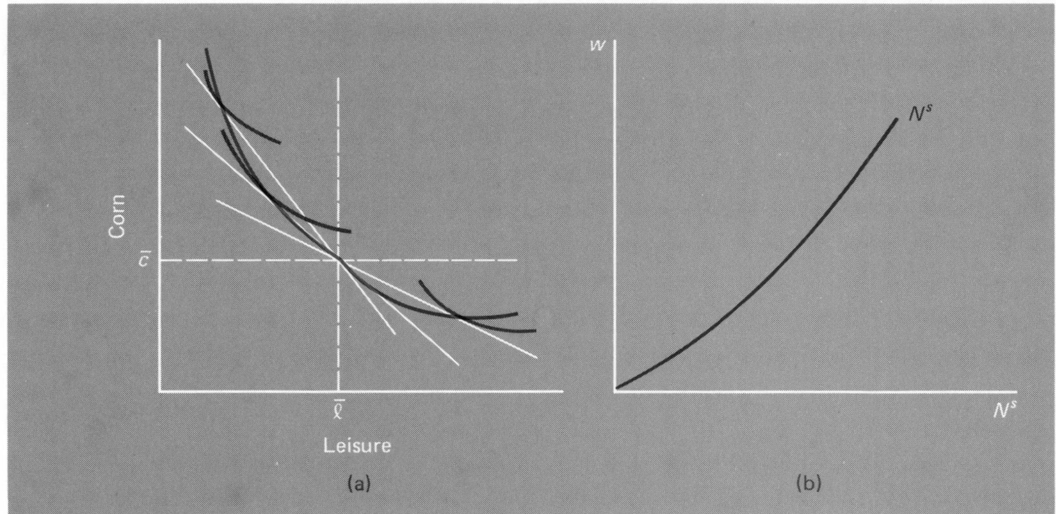

FIGURE 1-13

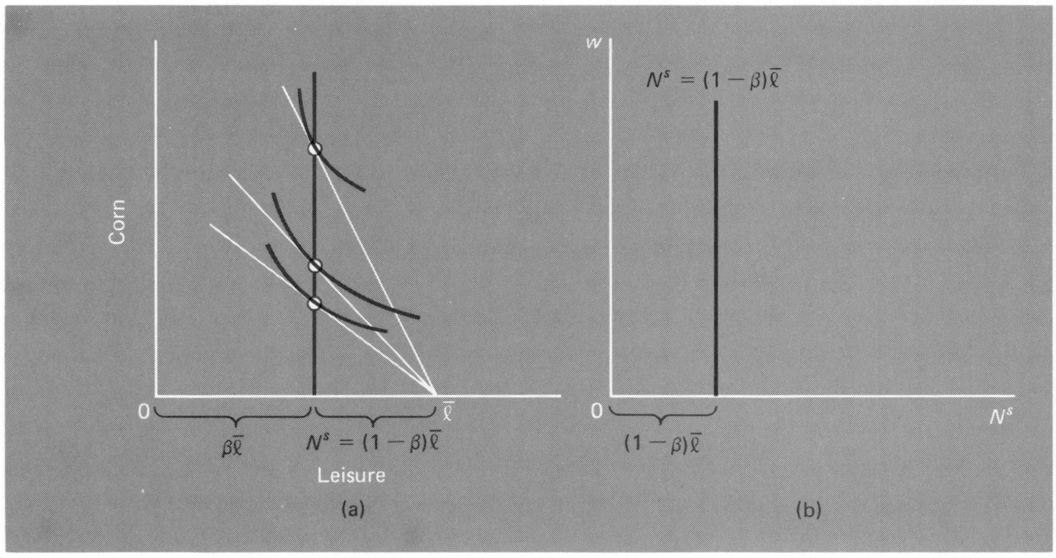

FIGURE 1-14

An arithmetical example

Let us suppose that the (average) household's preferences between corn, c, and leisure, l, are homothetic and of the form (i″). Furthermore, let us suppose that the household is endowed with only 24 hours of leisure per day and that it has no corn. In other words, we shall assume that $\bar{l} = 24$ hours per day; $\bar{c} = 0$; and $\lambda = \frac{1}{2}$.

$$\frac{c}{l} = \frac{1}{2} \cdot w \tag{i''}$$

Given these assumptions, we get $MPC_l = APC_l = 2/3$ and $MPC_c = APC_c = 1/3$. Moreover, income, measured in units of leisure, I_l, is 24 hours per day. It follows, therefore, that the demand for leisure is 16 hours and the supply of labor 8 hours per day, regardless of the level of the real wage, as shown in Figure 1-15a. We should also note that in the (w,N^s)-plane of Figure 1-15b, the N_0^s curve is the supply curve of labor derived from this case.

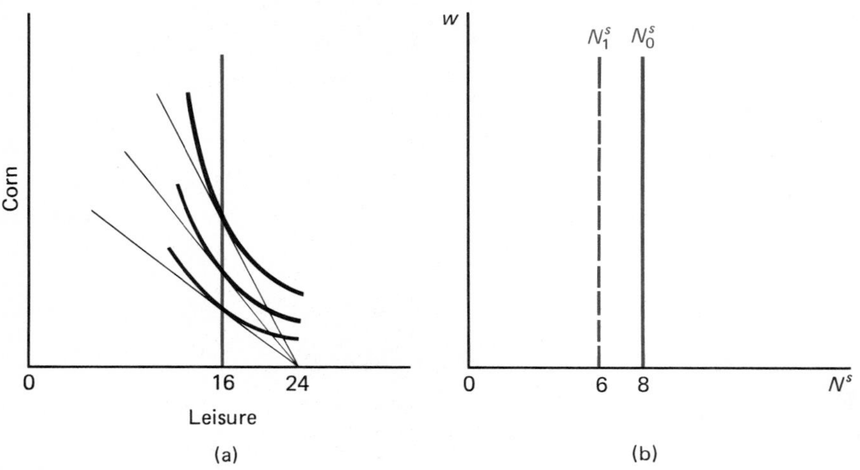

FIGURE 1-15

Let us now examine the case in which the endowment remains the same while the household's tastes, still homothetic, change, so that they are now represented by (i'''):

$$\frac{c}{l} = \frac{1}{3} \cdot w \tag{i'''}$$

At this point we have $MPC_l = APC_l = 3/4$, which, in turn, sets the demand for leisure at $l = (3/4) \cdot 24 = 18$ hours per day and the supply of labor at $N^s = 24 - 18 = 6$ hours per day. This means that the supply curve of labor, while still vertical, shifts to the left, to the position N_1^s in Figure 1-15b.

On the other hand, let us now suppose that while the homothetic preferences are still the ones represented by (i''), the endowments change so that, in addition to the 24 hours of leisure per day, the household is also endowed with 6 bushels of corn per day. In this case the supply of labor is upward sloping, as in Figure 1-16. Note that when the wage is 1 (bushel per hour), $I_l = 24 + (1/w) \cdot 6 = 30$; $l = (2/3)30 = 20$; and $N^s = 24 - 20 = 4$. And when the wage is 2, $I_l = 27$; $l = 18$; and $N^s = 24 - 18 = 6$. But when the wage rate is $1/2$, we have another noteworthy result: $I_l = 36$; $l = 24$; and $N^s = 24 - 24 = 0$! In other words, when the wage is

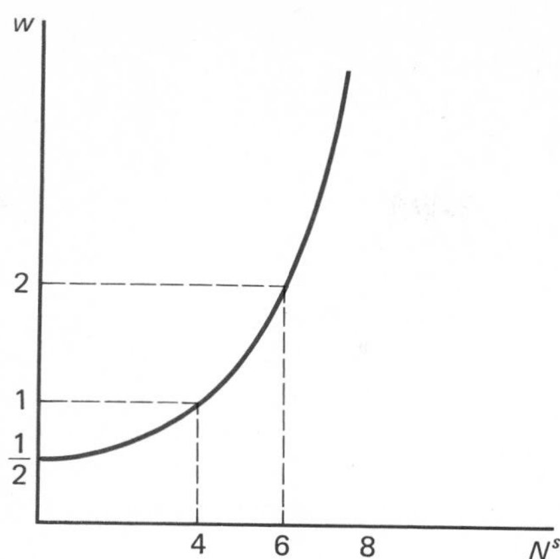

FIGURE 1-16

½, the household will not supply any labor. As the reader can see, if the wage rate is lower than ½, say at ¼, the household will become a net demander for labor (by 8 hours in this case) and a net supplier of corn. Obviously, this cannot be the average household, although some households do behave in this manner.

II. PRODUCTION TECHNOLOGY, FIRMS, AND NATIONAL ACCOUNTS

In the remainder of this chapter we shall focus on production to provide a convenient vehicle for examining (a) the production aspects of the national accounts, as one might surmise. And since production is within the realm of the agents called firms and producers, we shall examine (b) the firm's rational behavior in a manner analogous to that for consumers, or households. Furthermore, (c) we shall derive, as a byproduct, their demand for labor in a way similar to that of the derivation of the supply of labor by households. And, finally, (d) our assumptions, of rational behavior by firms and of a purely competitive market behavior, will permit us to divide the product between the owners of the two factors of production, which will provide us with the theoretical underpinnings of the national *income* accounts, which are the mirror image of the national product accounts.

PRODUCTION TECHNOLOGY

In any period of time, in say a year, thousands, or even millions, of different commodities and services are produced by the *firms* in an economy. These agents utilize a variety of *factors of production,* that is, several kinds of labor, several kinds of capital, land, or raw materials.

At the present level of abstraction, we shall simplify heroically by aggregating to a great degree; we shall assume that our economy produces a *single* good called GNP. Sometimes we shall refer to this good as corn. This good can be consumed immediately or added to the stock of the factor of production called capital. Only two factors of production, labor and capital, are needed to produce this single good. It is assumed that labor and capital are homogeneous unless it is explicitly stated otherwise. Production technology can be summarized by the production function

$$Y = F(K,N) \tag{1}$$

where Y is the total output of the single good (GNP), K is the economy's capital stock, and N is the labor force utilized.

For the economy as a whole, we assume that the production function *exhibits constant returns to scale,* which means that if we change *both* factors in the same proportion, output will change in that same proportion; for example, a doubling of both capital and labor will double total output. (It is true that some industries in our economy, such as public utilities, exhibit *increasing* returns to scale. No doubt there are other industries that operate under *decreasing* returns-to-scale technology. However, empirical studies seem to confirm that *for the economy as a whole,* the assumption of constant returns to scale approximates reality.) Symbolically, we say that the production function F is linear homogeneous (or homogeneous of the first degree):

$$\lambda Y = F(\lambda K, \lambda N), \ \lambda > 0 \tag{2}$$

that is, if we multiply both K and N by λ, total output Y will be multiplied by the same number.

If we want to represent the production function diagrammatically in a plane, it is obvious that we have to keep one factor of production constant. Figure 1-17a shows the relation between employment, N, and output, keeping capital constant at the level K_1. Figure 1-17b depicts the relation between output and capital for a given employment level $\bar{N}$.

The shape of these two curves should be noted; each of these curves is *concave,*

FIGURE 1-17

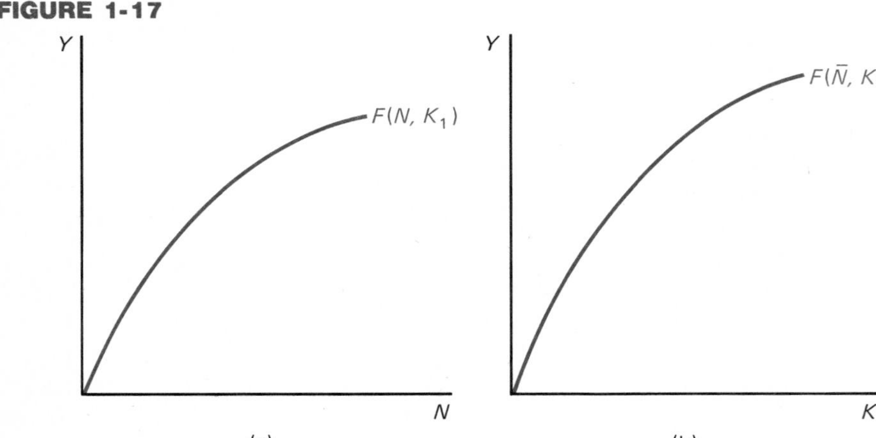

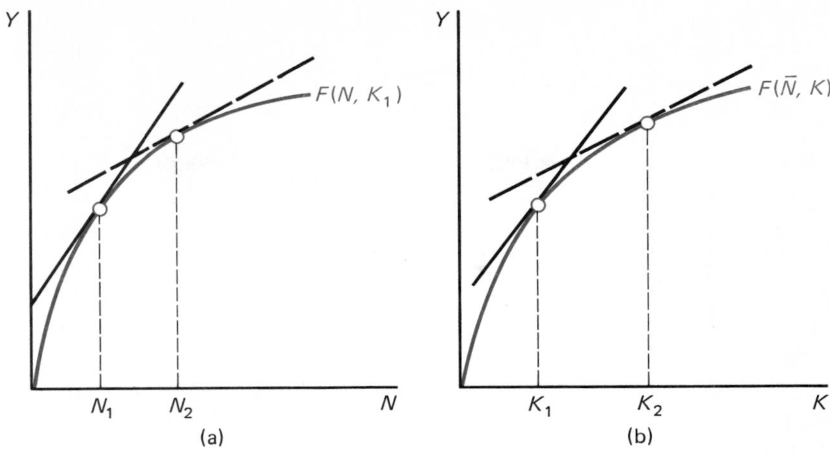

FIGURE 1-18

which means that increasing one factor (say N in Figure 1-17a) while keeping the other constant (K at K_1 in Figure 1-17a) *increases* output—but at a diminishing rate. The slope of a tangent to the curve $F(N,K_1)$ in Figure 1-18a gives us the marginal product of labor, MP_N. Note that the slope is smaller for N_2 than for N_1. Similarly, the slope of a tangent in Figure 1-18b represents the marginal product of capital, MP_K. Note also that the tangent for K_2 is flatter than for K_1. This property of the production function, namely, that output increases at a diminishing rate when one factor of production is successively increased while the other factor is kept constant, is a reflection of *diminishing returns.* This does not contradict our earlier assumption that the production function exhibits constant *returns to scale.* On the contrary, it is a consequence of that assumption. When we double, for example, the amount of labor, we also double the quantity of output—but only if the amount of capital is doubled. On the other hand, if we do not change capital at all, it is clear that output *cannot* be doubled; output will increase—but to less than double the original amount.

In the (N, Y)-plane, we can show the effect of an increase in K by shifting the curve upward, as in Figure 1-19a. For each fixed level of K, there is one such curve. Note that for N given at $\bar{N}$, the increase in K successively increases Y from Y_1 to Y_2 to Y_3. Of course, this is a reflection of the fact (shown in Figure 1-17b) that an increase in K, while keeping N constant, will increase output Y. Similarly, Figure 1-19b shows that an increase in N shifts the production curve upward in the (K, Y)-plane.

Figures like 1-19a and 1-19b are somewhat cumbersone. Fortunately, we can take advantage of the *constant returns-to-scale* assumption to simplify the graphical operations. We saw earlier (equation (2)) that if we multiply both K and N by a constant (and the same) number, output Y is also multiplied by the same number. We now choose to multiply by $1/K$, that is, we shall set $\lambda \equiv 1/K$ in equation (2). It follows that

$$Y/K = F(K/K,\ N/K) = F(1,\ N/K)$$

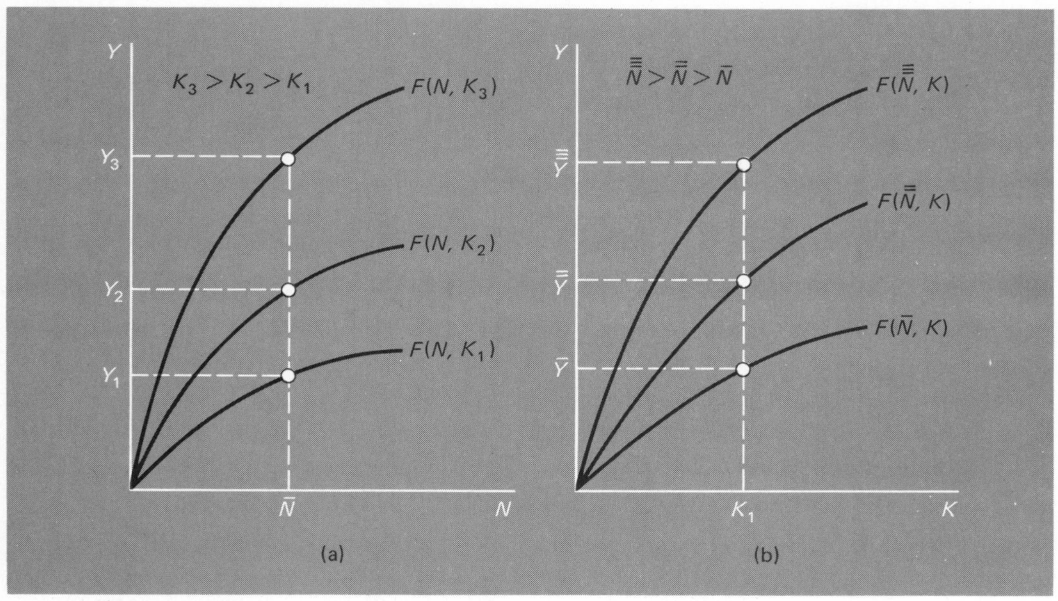

FIGURE 1-19

We see, therefore, that output per unit of capital (or *the average product of capital*) depends only on employment per unit of capital, which we write as

$$Y/K = f(N/K) \tag{3}$$

and depict graphically in Figure 1-20.

Since it happens that the marginal product of labor coincides with the slope of the $f(N/K)$ curve in this $(N/K, Y/K)$-plane, we can utilize this graph for additional results. Examine Figure 1-21. Take any employment/capital ratio, such as $(N/K)_1$. The slope of the tangent at C, which is equal to BC/AB, represents the marginal

FIGURE 1-20

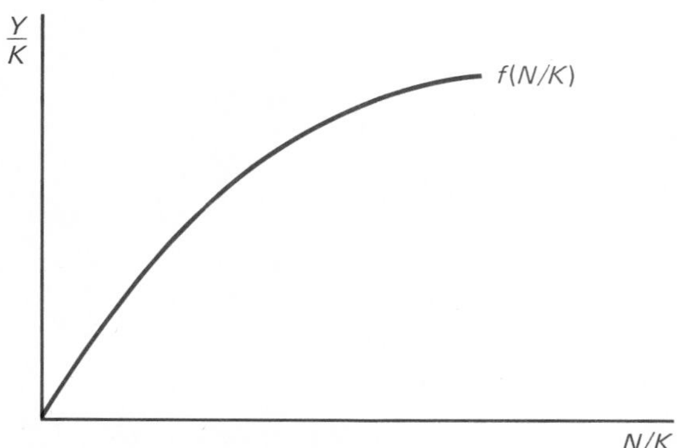

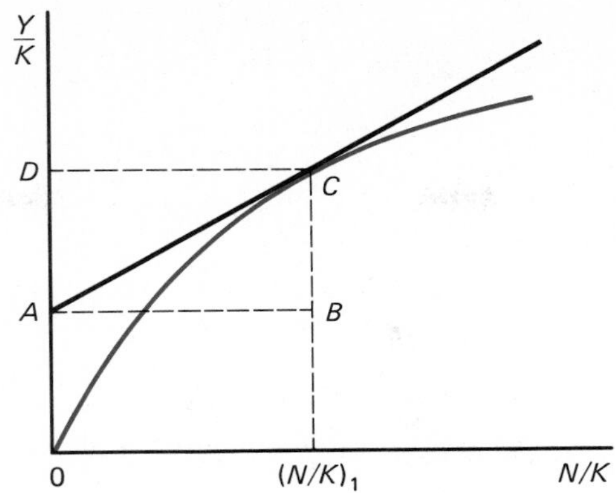

FIGURE 1-21

product of labor. Now, if we multiply this by the assumed employment/capital ratio (N/K), which is equal to AB, we have

$$(N/K) \cdot MP_N|(N/K)_1 = (BC/AB) \cdot AB = BC$$

But $BC = AD$. Also for $(N/K)_1$, the average product of capital equals OD. Subtracting AD from OD we have OA, which is the marginal product of capital.

$$MP_K = OA = f[(N/K)] - (N/K) \cdot MP_N \tag{4}$$

Thus, the marginal product of capital is equal to the intercept of the tangent to f at the given employment/capital ratio.

In what follows we shall denote N/K by x. With the new notation we have

$$Y/K = f(x) \tag{5}$$

We can see from Figure 1-22 that as the employment/capital ratio, x, rises, the marginal product of labor falls and the marginal product of capital rises. On the other hand, when the capital/labor ratio rises, the marginal product of capital falls and the marginal product of labor rises. Note that an *increase* in K/N is equivalent to a reduction in N/K. Thus x_0 corresponds to a higher K/N than does x_1; a reduction of N/K, from x_1 to x_0, is equivalent to an increase in the capital/labor ratio. It implies a fall in the MP_K and an increase in the MP_N. We can depict the relationship between the MP_N and the labor/capital ratio; since MP_N falls when x rises, we have a downward-sloping marginal product curve in Figure 1-23.

We have, therefore, reduced our system, which shows output per unit of capital, marginal product of labor, and marginal product of capital to a dependence on only one magnitude, namely, employment per unit of capital, x. This was a direct result of our using $\lambda \equiv 1/K$. Let us now suppose that we use, instead, $\lambda \equiv 1/N$ in equation (2). It follows that

$$Y/N = F(K/N, N/N) = F(K/N, 1)$$

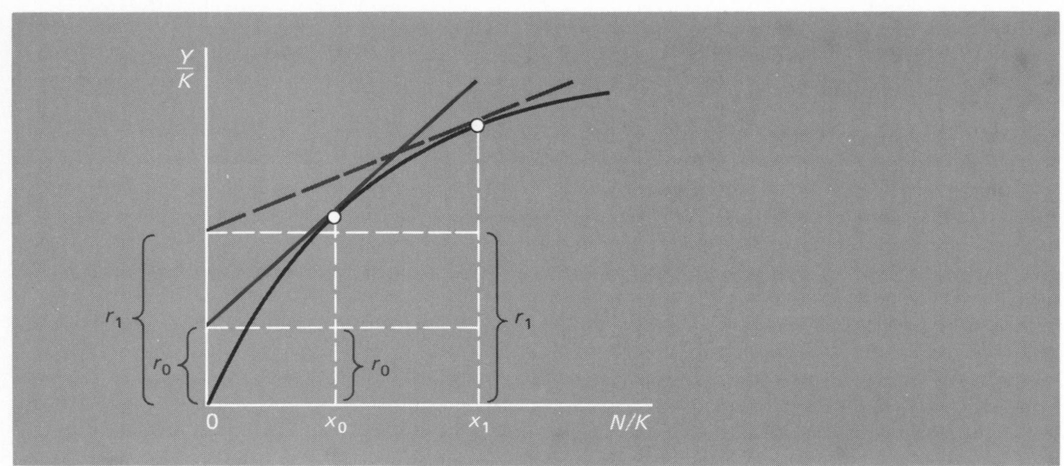

FIGURE 1-22

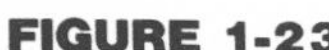

FIGURE 1-23

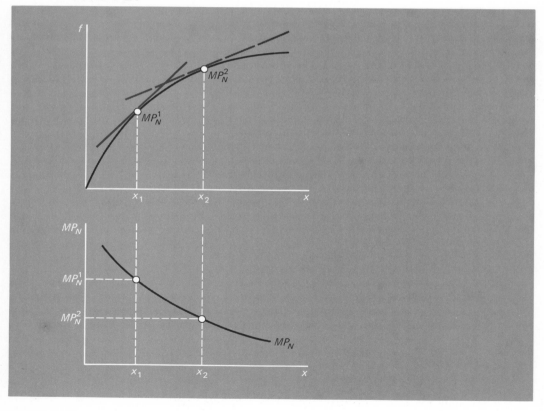

Thus, output *per capita* (assuming that N is both the population and the labor force) depends only on the capital per capita, or, in other words, on the capital/labor ratio. Denoting the latter as k, that is, $k \equiv K/N = 1/x$, we can write the above equation as

$$Y/N = \phi(K/N) = \phi(k) \tag{6}$$

We can depict this curve in the $(K/N, Y/N)$-plane, as in Figure 1-24. In this plane it happens that the slope of the $\phi(k)$ curve is the MP_K. It can, then, be shown that

$$MP_N = \phi(K/N) - K/N \cdot MP_K \tag{7}$$

Now (7) means that the intercept (on the Y/N axis) of the tangent to ϕ is the marginal product of labor. In Figure 1-24 the MP_K and the MP_N have been evaluated at the particular capital/labor ratio, k_0. Of course, we can utilize this graph in order to derive all the earlier results. In doing so, the reader should note the symmetricity of the two graphs, Figure 1-21 and Figure 1-24, as well as that of equations (4) and (7).

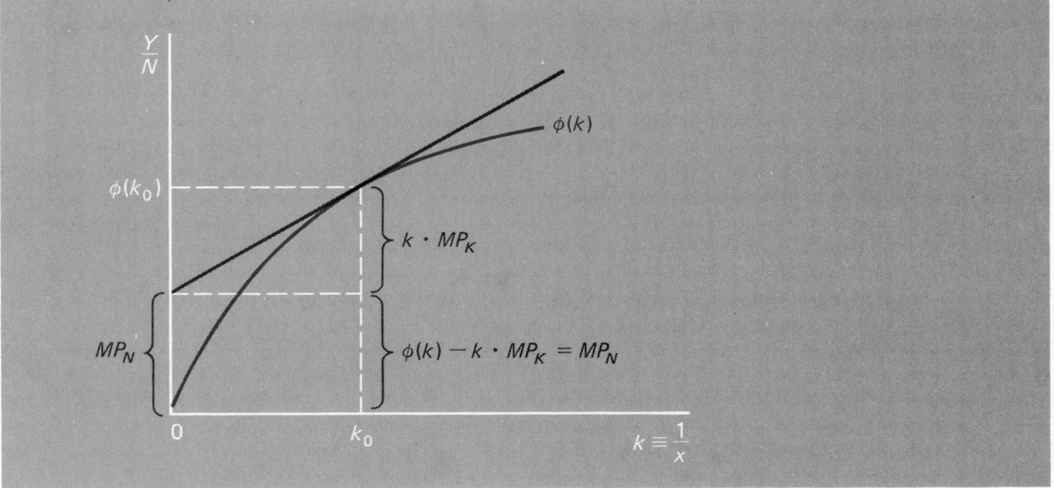

FIGURE 1-24

GROSS NATIONAL PRODUCT ACCOUNTS

We have examined in detail the technical characteristics of producing the GNP. It is now time to stipulate how it is used. The GNP can be bought, either to be consumed or to be added to society's capital stock. Economists refer to this latter "use" as *investment.* While these are the only two purposes for which GNP is bought, this demand can come from private sources, households (consumption), and firms (investment), or from government sources. We shall use the symbol C to denote private consumption and the symbol I for private investment. We shall lump government purchases together, using the symbol G without distinguishing between government consumption and government investment. Finally, residents of foreign countries can buy our GNP. We shall denote this foreign demand as exports, χ. Of course, residents of our country buy goods from abroad, which we shall denote as imports, μ. Here we shall concentrate on the *net* demand from abroad, that is, on the difference, either positive or negative, between exports and imports, $\chi - \mu$, without distinguishing between consumption and investment components of net foreign demand.

It is a tautology, or a truism to say that whatever was bought (by private individuals, by the government, and by foreigners) is precisely what was sold by the suppliers (producers). Thus we can write down the following identity:

$$C + I + G + (\chi - \mu) \equiv \text{GNP} \tag{8}$$

Although this equation, as an identity, is void of any theoretical connotation, it nevertheless serves a useful purpose; it is this identity that the Commerce Department (Office of Business Economics, OBE) utilizes regularly to construct the Table of Gross National Product. The actual numbers for 1980 are shown in Table 1-1.

A good deal of this book will be devoted to bringing to life the accounting framework of identity (8) and its numerical counterpart, Table 1-1. This translation of the framework, from one of *accounting* to one of *analysis* of GNP, will be achieved by assigning the variables on which each component depends. For example, the interest rate is a determinant of investment and, possibly, of consumption. On the other hand, political considerations usually lie behind government demand, whereas the exchange rate may be the most important determinant of foreign demand. We have

TABLE 1-1 GROSS NATIONAL PRODUCT (IN BILLION DOLLARS), 1980

Gross National Product	Y	2,626.1
Personal Consumption Expenditures	C	1,672.8
Durable Goods	211.9	
Non-Durable Goods	675.7	
Services	785.2	
Gross Private Domestic Investment	I	395.3
Fixed Investment	401.2	
Non-Residential	296.0	
(a) Structures	108.8	
(b) Producer's Durable Equipment	187.1	
Residential	105.3	
Changes in Business Inventories	−5.9	
Net Exports of Goods and Services	$\chi - \mu$	−23.3
Exports, χ	339.8	
Imports, μ	316.5	
Government Purchases of Goods and Services,	G	534.7
Federal	198.9	
State and Local	335.8	

SOURCE: *Survey of Current Business,* April 1981, p. 13.

a particular interest in guaranteeing *equality* (rather than identity) between aggregate demand $[C + I + G + (\chi - \mu)]$ and aggregate supply, GNP. This means that the market for corn (GNP) is cleared, that is, the quantities that the demanders of GNP want are matched exactly by the quantity that producers want to produce. Of course, this will happen *only if* the underlying determinants of each component of aggregate demand and supply are of precisely the "right" magnitude.

FIRMS, THEIR RATIONAL BEHAVIOR AND THE DEMAND FOR LABOR

In Section I of this chapter we defined the households' rational behavior. We stipulated that each household wants to reach its most preferred position. Now we can make the same stipulation regarding firms, whose most preferred position is attained when their profit is maximized. So profit maximization is assumed to be the rational behavior of firms. In this section we examine the average firm's behavior in *one period of time.* In later chapters we enlarge the firm's time horizon and, therefore, examine intertemporal maximization. It will be seen then that the results from this chapter will still be useful, but, of course, not sufficient.

One way of examining the firm's rational behavior as a producer is, diagrammatically, analogous to that of the household; we can introduce the concept of an isoquant, which has the same graphical properties as an indifference curve. An *isoquant* is defined as all the combinations (or "baskets") of labor and capital that yield the same number of units of the single product. Two of these isoquants are drawn in Figure 1-25a. These curves are homothetic because of the assumption of constant returns to scale. The straight lines in Figures 1-25b and 1-25c have a slope equal to (minus) the ratio of wages to profit (or relative wage). Profit maximization (or cost minimization) can be shown (as in Figure 1-25c) to occur when the MRS in production is equal to the relative wage.

In examining the firm's rational behavior here, we shall not pursue the graphical technique used above. Instead we shall *directly* examine profit maximization: first we identify it, and then we maximize it.

FIGURE 1-25

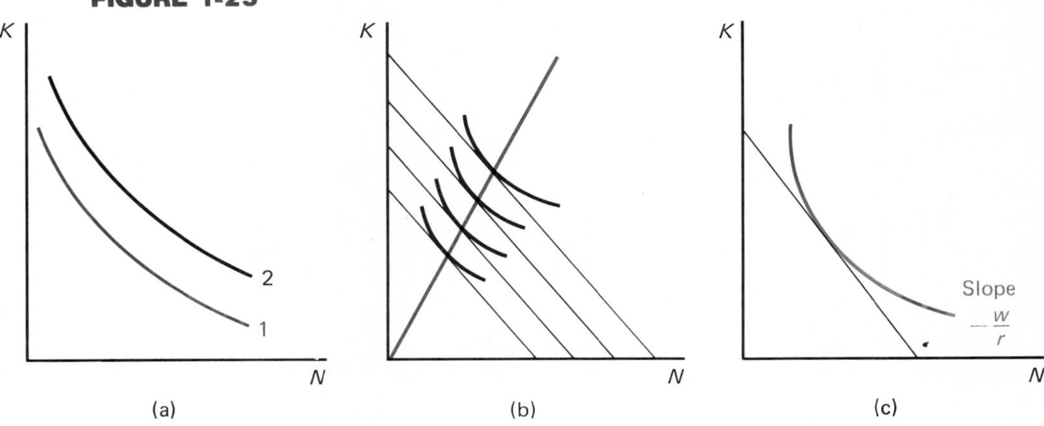

Our setting will be one of a "barter" economy in which there is only one good, "corn" or "GNP," called Y. Obviously, its relative price is equal to one. The number of units of "corn" that we get when we give up one unit of "corn" is, of course, one. To find profit, which we shall denote with the letter Π, we need to know revenue and cost. If the (average) firm produces Y units of output and sells it at the price of one, its revenue is equal to Y. Cost, on the other hand, is equal to the number of units of labor, N, that the firm utilizes multiplied by the (real) wage, w, or wN. Note that workers are paid in "corn," that is, w is units of corn per unit of labor. Thus

$$\Pi = Y - wN \tag{9}$$

and Π is the *absolute* profit, or so many units of "corn." A more interesting concept is the one expressed in percentage terms. Of course, if the firm has K units of capital (in corn) and it secures Π units of corn as profit, the rate of profit is Π/K. (It should be clear that when the firm maximizes the rate of profit, it follows that the firm maximizes absolute profit and that the converse is also true.) Dividing both sides of (9) by K and defining $\Pi/K \equiv r$, we have

$$r \equiv \frac{\Pi}{K} = \frac{Y}{K} - \frac{wN}{K}$$

Substituting (5), we have

$$r \equiv \frac{\Pi}{K} = f(x) - wx \tag{10}$$

To show r graphically is fairly simple. In Figure 1-26 we find first the (labor) cost (per unit of capital) wx. Here we see the importance of the assumption that the average firm (as well as any other agent, i.e., households) is a "price taker"; no matter how much labor the firm hires, the wage it pays does not change. Therefore

FIGURE 1-26

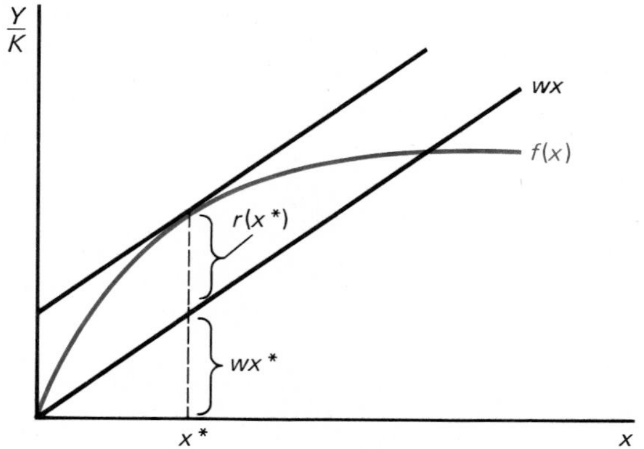

w is treated as a true parameter, fixed. *It follows that wx is a straight line through the origin with slope equal to w.*

The revenue per unit of capital is $f(x)$ or Y/K, that is, the average product of capital. It follows that the rate of return to capital, r, is found to be the *vertical* difference between $f(x)$ and wx. The firm is a profit maximizer, and thus its problem is to find the greatest difference between $f(x)$ and wx by appropriately choosing the variable(s) under its control. Of course, the variable under the firm's control is labor per unit of capital, x. In Figure 1-26 the greatest rate of return occurs if the firm chooses x equal to x^*. Of course, x^* (yielding the greatest difference between $f(x)$ and wx curves) is found by a well-known graphical rule: At such an x^*, the slope of the tangent to the $f(x)$ curve should be equal to the slope of the wx curve. But we know that the slope of the $f(x)$ curve is the marginal product of labor and that the slope of the wx curve is w, the real wage. Thus we have the rule that the firm should follow to maximize its profit: Hire workers up to the point where the marginal product of these workers is equal to their real (in terms of "corn") wage, that is, $MP_N = w$. Note that if $MP_N = w$, we can substitute the former for the latter in (10) and see that

$$r = f(x^*) - x^* MP_N \tag{11}$$

But the right-hand side of the equation is the marginal product of capital. Thus

$$r = MP_K \tag{12}$$

It follows, then, that if the firm maximizes its profit, the factors have to be hired up to the point at which their marginal products are equal to their respective rewards.

Returning to our diagrammatic analysis, note that we found that the maximum rate of profit (and thus the only one that can be sustained) is equal to the marginal product of capital. In Figure 1-26 this is equal to the distance between $f(x)$ and wx. However, in the preceding section we found that MP_K is equal to the intercept on the vertical axis. But is there any inconsistency involved here? The answer is no, since we can see in Figure 1-26 that $r(x^*)$ is *equal* to the intercept on the vertical axis.

Usually the *short run* is defined as a period short enough for the firm's capital stock, K, to be considered fixed. Thus if K is fixed at $\bar{K}$ and x is given from the maximizing solution, we can find the product $Y = \bar{K} \cdot f(x^*)$, which is what the firm produces and supplies in the market. Now every beginning student of economics knows the rule a firm must follow in *supplying* output (to the market) in order to maximize its profit: Supply must be carried to the point at which its marginal revenue is equal to its marginal cost, $MR = MC$. For a firm that is a price taker (like the one here), MR is equal to the price of the good. Thus the supply rule is that MC must be equal to the good's price.

Our rule, $MP_N = w$, in this chapter, is a rule for *hiring*. How do the two rules, the one for hiring labor and the one for supplying output, compare? Supposedly both rules have been derived from maximizing behavior. If this is so, the two rules have to be consistent. We can see this by writing the rule $w = MP_N$ as

$$1 = \frac{w}{MP_N} \tag{13}$$

The right-hand side of this equation is the *marginal cost* of output. But why is this so? One unit of labor produces (at the margin) MP_N units of output (corn); but one unit of labor costs w units of the same output. Therefore each of the MP_N units of "corn" costs w/MP_N at the margin. Q.E.D. Now the left-hand side is unity. But, as we mentioned above, in this one-good world the price of "corn" is equal to one. We have, therefore, proved that $MC =$ price and, consequently, that the $w = MP_N$ *rule of hiring* is consistent with (i.e., it implies) the *supply rule,* $MC = MR =$ price.

Until now our analysis has been conducted in a "barter" framework. Let us now suppose that there is money in the economy and that the firm receives p dollars per unit of output it sells and that workers are similarly paid in dollars, namely, W dollars per unit of labor. It follows that $w = W/p$ is the real wage, the number of units of corn that the worker gets for each unit of labor. The firm's problem is to

$$\text{Maximize } \tilde{\Pi} = pY - WN$$

where $\tilde{\Pi}$ is the dollar value of absolute profits. But the corn value of profits is found by dividing Π by p, that is, $\Pi = \dfrac{\tilde{\Pi}}{p}$. Thus

$$\Pi = \frac{\tilde{\Pi}}{p} = Y - \frac{W}{p}N$$

Note that by substituting w for W/p above, the equation becomes identical with (9). Now divide by K so that

$$r = \frac{\Pi}{K} = \frac{Y}{K} - \frac{W}{p}x$$

from which it follows that for maximum r, we need the rule that the marginal product of labor should be equal to the real wage, W/p:

$$MP_N = \frac{W}{p} \tag{14}$$

This hiring rule can, of course, be reduced to the familiar supply rule, $p = MC$. One unit of labor, costing W dollars, produces, at the margin, MP_N units of corn. At the margin, then, each of the MP_N units of corn costs W/MP_N dollars. Thus $MC = W/MP_N$. But if $p = MC$, it should be that $p = W/MP_N$. We can rewrite (14) exactly like that.

We can utilize the hiring rule of the firm in order to derive its demand for labor. Suppose that the real wage was originally equal to w_0 in Figure 1-27. Because

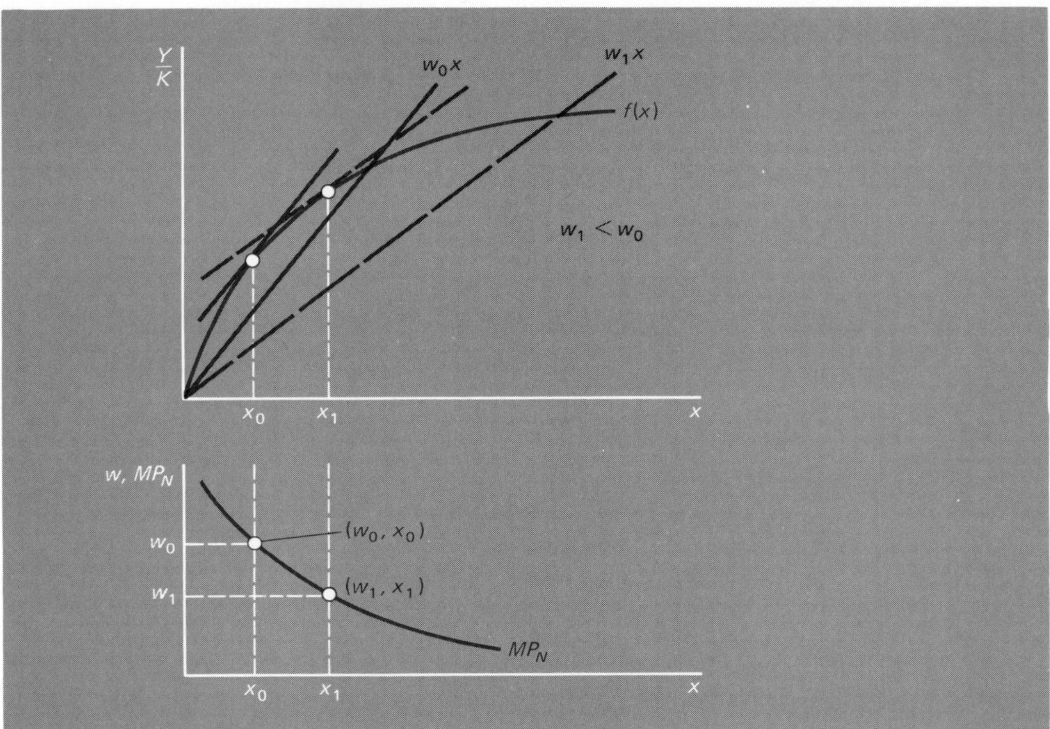

FIGURE 1-27

the firm has to hire labor until its (labor's) marginal product is equal to the real wage, it is clear that the labor demanded by the firm is equal to x_0. We depict this result in the lower panel of Figure 1-27 by the point $w = w_0$, $x = x_0$. Now suppose that the wage is lower, say $w = w_1$. The w_1x line through the origin is flatter than w_0x, as shown in the upper panel of Figure 1-27. The line tangent to the $f(x)$ curve and parallel to w_1x guarantees that the labor demanded is equal to x_1. We find this point in the (x,w)-plane, located in the lower panel of Figure 1-27. We repeat this procedure for all possible wage rates, we find the corresponding amounts of labor demanded, and we plot the (w,x) points in the lower panel of Figure 1-27. Finally, we connect all these points, thereby deriving the demand curve for labor. It should be clear that this demand curve for labor *coincides* with the marginal-product-of-labor curve; the reason, of course, is that at each real-wage rate, w, the marginal product of labor, MP_N, should be equal to w. Thus, the vertical axis of the lower panel of Figure 1-27 measures both w and MP_N.

In general, the economy's (aggregate) demand curve for labor is found by horizontally aggregating all the firms' demand curves. In this book, however, we need not perform this aggregation, since we assume that we are directly examining the average firm. Thus the economy's demand curve (for labor) behaves exactly as the average firm's demand curve does.

INCOME DISTRIBUTION AND NATIONAL INCOME-PRODUCT ACCOUNTS

We have seen that the profit-maximizing firms hire labor until its marginal product becomes equal to whatever real wage exists in the market. We have also seen that this implies that capital's marginal product is equal to the rate of profit:

$$MP_K = f(x) - x \cdot MP_N = r$$
$$MP_N = MP_N = w$$

We can show that when each factor is paid its marginal product, output, Y, is exactly exhausted:

$$\begin{aligned} wN + rK &= MP_N N + [f(x) - xMP_N]K \\ &= MP_N \cdot N + Kf(x) - (N\, MP_N/K) \cdot K \\ &= Kf(x) \\ &= Y \end{aligned}$$

This result enables us to use the terms *national product* and *national income* interchangeably; we can say that the national product gives rise to an equivalent income for the factors of production used to produce it—or that the marginal product rule divides total output between the factors so that it is all exhausted. This is characteristically depicted in Figure 1-28. It should be emphasized that this property is the direct outcome of the assumption of constant returns to scale in production. (If the returns to scale are increasing, that is, if the degree of homogeneity is greater than one, it can easily be shown that the marginal product rule would distribute to the factors of production *more* output than is produced. Similarly, with decreasing returns to scale, less output than is produced will be distributed.) This result is usually called Euler's theorem.

The equivalence of the value of total product with the value of total factor income has proved to be a potent weapon in the arsenal of economists. In microeconomics it provides the pillar for the dominant view in the theory of income distribution. Moreover, it is usually employed for finding the relation between commodity prices and factor prices, as well as for the relation (equalization) of factor prices between countries. In macroeconomics the equation

$$Y = wN + rk \tag{15}$$

is called the basic *national income accounting identity.* It is called an "identity" because it is self-evident. (Usually it is a tautology because of the definition of "profit" as a residual.) Needless to say, we have derived it here as a *theorem.*

The above equation is utilized in a variety of ways in macroeconomics. Of course, there is a table constructed regularly by the Department of Commerce dividing national income among the factors of production. In the real world, capital is subdivided into real estate capital and capital of corporations. Moreover, there are (small) owner-operated businesses whose "income" is partly the owner's own wages and partly profits, which are impossible to disentangle precisely and, therefore, remain

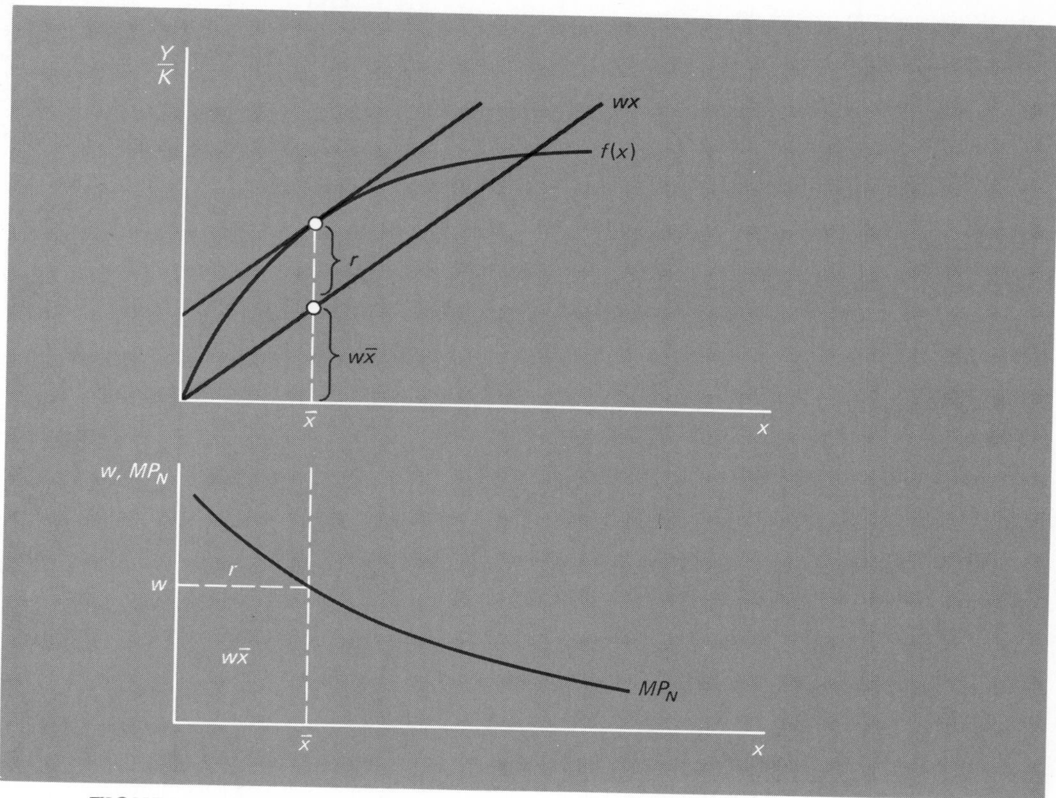

FIGURE 1-28

in these broad categories in the statistics. Table 1-2 depicts the official data for 1980.

The reader who has compared Tables 1-1 and 1-2 must be puzzled. Both tables depict data for 1980; the first deals with gross national product, GNP, and the second with national income, NI. Since we have stated that the two coincide, why, then, is GNP $2,626.1 billion while NI is only $2,121.4 billion? First, our production function deals with *net* product. We therefore have to subtract from GNP that amount that represents "depreciation of capital," or, in the official jargon, we have to subtract "Capital Consumption Allowances." Second, GNP is measured by adding the receipts of sellers. The receipts, however, include sales and other taxes which do not represent rewards to factors of production. These "Indirect Business Taxes" must also be subtracted. Table 1-3, using 1980 data, shows how we move from GNP to NI. Note that we have to take into consideration three additional, but insignificant, items.

Now that we have found what national income is, the introduction of another identity will prove instrumental. Income can be either consumed or saved. In the real world, taxes are also paid and, therefore, accounted. Thus we have

$$Y \equiv C + S + T \tag{16}$$

TABLE 1-2 NATIONAL INCOME (IN BILLION DOLLARS), 1980

National Income		2,121.4
Compensation of Employees		1,596.5
Wages and Salaries	1,343.6	
Supplements to Wages and Salaries	252.9	
Proprietors' Income		130.6
Rental Income of Persons		31.8
Corporate Profits		182.7
Net Interest		179.8

SOURCE: *Survey of Current Business,* April 1981, p. 14.

TABLE 1-3 FROM GNP TO NATIONAL INCOME (IN BILLION DOLLARS), 1980 (OR, RELATION OF GNP AND NATIONAL INCOME)

Gross National Product	2,626.1
Less: Capital Consumption Allowances	287.3
Indirect Business Tax and Non-Tax Liability	212.3
Business Transfer Payments	10.5
Statistical Discrepancy	−.7
Plus: Subsidies Less Current Surplus of Government Enterprises	4.6
Equals: National Income	2,121.4

SOURCE: *Survey of Current Business,* April 1981, p. 14.

where C is consumption (as before), S is savings, and T denotes taxes. In the real world another small item must be added on the right-hand side of the above identity, namely, transfers to foreigners. Table 1-4 is constructed in such a way that the above identity is preserved.

Summarizing, we have found that

$$Y \equiv C + I + G + (\chi - \mu) \tag{8}$$

$$Y \equiv wN + rK \tag{15}$$

$$wN + rK \equiv C + S + T \tag{17}$$

Combining all the information, we have

$$C + I + G + (\chi - \mu) \equiv Y \equiv wN + rK \equiv C + S + T \tag{18}$$

TABLE 1-4 DISPOSITION OF NATIONAL INCOME (OR, RELATION OF NI, PERSONAL INCOME, AND CONSUMPTION-SAVING)

National Income		2,121.4
Less: Corporate Profits	182.7	
Contributions for Social Security	203.7	
Plus: Government Transfer Payments	283.8	
Net Interest Paid by Government and Consumers	76.5	
Dividends	54.4	
Business Transfer Payments	10.5	
Equals: Personal Income		2,160.2
Less: Personal Tax Payments	338.5	
Equals: Disposable Personal Income		1,821.7
Less: Personal Outlays	1,720.4	
(a) Personal Consumption	1,672.8	
(b) Consumers Interest Payments	46.4	
(c) Personal Transfer Payments to Foreigners	1.2	
Equals: Personal Saving		101.3

SOURCE: *Survey of Current Business,* April 1981, p. 14 and p. 16.

This is a most important identity. We not only use it repeatedly in this book but also bring it to life as an equality.

As we said earlier, we are interested in the *equality* of (8):

$$C+I+G+(\chi-\mu)=Y \tag{8'}$$

that is, in the equilibrium of the market for goods and services. Since Y is identically equal to $C+S+T$, it follows that if the market for goods and services is cleared (i.e., if supply equals demand for the national product), we have the following equality:

$$C+I+G+(\chi-\mu)=C+S+T$$

Or, subtracting C from both sides,

$$I+G+(\chi-\mu)=S+T$$

This equality is to macroeconomics what the renowned Prince of Denmark is to the play *Hamlet!* Occasionally we shall abstractly examine an economy without a government (i.e., $G=T=0$) and without international trade (i.e., $\chi=\mu=0$). In such an economy, to say that the market for goods and services is cleared is equivalent to saying that investment is equal to savings:

$$I-S=0$$

To say that aggregate demand for goods and services is greater than aggregate supply means $C + I > Y$. It is equivalent to saying

$$I - S > 0$$

Excess supply, on the other hand, is shown as

$$I - S < 0$$

QUESTIONS

1. Examine an economy with only two goods, corn and leisure:
   a. If the average worker is endowed with only 24 hours of leisure and if this worker's tastes are such that both the marginal and average propensities to consume corn are equal to one-half, find the exact form of the supply curve of labor.
   b. If everything else is as in part *a* above, but tastes change so that $APC_c = MPC_c = 1/3$, what happens to the supply curve of labor?
   c. Suppose that the worker's tastes are as in part *a* above, but in addition to the 24 hours of leisure, this worker is also endowed with some corn. Is the supply curve of labor upward or downward sloping or simply independent of the real wage?
   d. If an individual's endowment of corn is permanently confiscated, what happens to this individual's total demand for corn and supply of labor?

2. Suppose that there is an increase in the labor force due to relaxation of immigration laws:
   a. What happens to total output?
   b. What happens to the wage and profit rates?
   c. What happens to total wages and total profits and their sum?

3. Suppose that an earthquake destroys some capital but without any loss of life. What happens to the following? Compare with question 2.
   a. Output
   b. Wage rate, profit rate
   c. Total wages, total profits, and their sum
   d. Interest rate

4. Suppose C denotes corn, L denotes leisure, and w is the real wage. If the average household is endowed with only 24 hours of leisure and its homothetic preferences are of the form

$$\frac{C}{L} = 0.5\,w$$

Find the supply curve of labor. Give exact numbers on the labor axis.

5. Evaluate the statement: "A backward-bending supply curve of labor implies that leisure is an inferior good."

6. Use the concepts of national income and product accounts to show that "Savings = Investment" is the condition for clearance of the goods market.
7. Even in Chapter 1 we have relied heavily on the assumptions of rationality and pure competition. Which steps in our analysis would we have been unable to take without one (or both) of these assumptions?
8. What are "relative prices" and why is this concept so fundamental to economics? How can we talk about "prices" in a model with no "money"?
9. The production technology developed in Chapter 1 is characterized by constant returns to scale and by decreasing returns. How is this possible?
10. Derive graphically the demand curve for labor from profit maximization by the firm.
11. Suppose that a household has preferences (between leisure and corn) represented by equation (i″) in the text (and question 4) and that it is endowed with only 24 hours of leisure per day. Suppose further that the prevailing wage is 2 bushels of corn per hour and that the government has been taxing wages at a rate of 50%:
    a. What is the exact amount of labor supplied by this household?
    b. Suppose that the government decides to give this household an outright gift of 4 bushels of corn per day. Assuming that the tax rate and wage remain, respectively, at 50% and 2 bushels per hour, what will the amount of labor, supplied by the household, be now?
    c. Suppose that instead of the above policy, the government decides to reduce the tax rate on wages to 25%. With the wage remaining at two bushels per hour, what will the household's supply of labor be? Show also that the tax gift of this policy is equal to the outright gift of the earlier policy, namely, 4 bushels per day.
    d. If you were a policy maker which policy would you choose? Would your decision depend on whether there is widespread unemployment? Relate this problem to the issues of "supply side" economics.

REFERENCES

HICKS, J. R., *Theory of Wages,* pp. 117–20, 244. London: Macmillan, 1932.

______. *Value and Capital* (2nd ed.), Chaps. 1–2. London: Oxford, 1946.

Federal Reserve Board, *Federal Reserve Bulletin,* Washington, D.C. (any recent issue).

MALINVAUD, E., *Lectures on Microeconomic Theory,* Chap. 1–3. Amsterdam: North-Holland Press, 1972.

ROBBINS, LIONEL, "On the Elasticity of the Demand for Income in Terms of Effort," *Economica,* 1930, p. 123.

RUGGLES, NANCY, and RICHARD RUGGLES, *The Design of Economic Accounts.* National Bureau of Economic Research, 1970.

United States Department of Commerce, *A Survey of Current Business,* 1976 Supplement: *The National Income and Product Accounts of the United States, 1929–1974* (and any recent issue).

The economics of full employment, prices, and interest

chapter two
bypass

The reader who wants only a brief overview of chapter 2 should read the following.

First one should note that we have provided the simplest possible description, or model, capable of reenacting and explaining the variables mentioned in the national accounts; we assume that firms of an economy produce one homogeneous output, called GNP, denoted by Y, by using a technology of *constant returns to scale.* The efforts of the firms to maximize their profits give us the demand-for-labor schedule, with the property that the lower the real wage, w, the higher the demand for labor, N^d. The supply-of-labor schedule, on the other hand, is derived from the efforts of households to reach *their* most preferred position; in general, we shall say that the higher the real wage, w, the higher the supply of labor, N^s. We also allow for the possibility that the supply of labor is independent of the level of the real wage, say eight man-hours per day—no matter what the real wage is.

Now that we know the demand for and the supply of labor, we also know the market for labor, which is described in Figure B.2-1. At the point of intersection of the demand and the supply curves, the real wage is determined at the level $\bar{w}$. Alternatively, we can say that when the real wage is equal to $\bar{w}$, the labor market is *cleared,* that is, the demand for labor is equal to the supply. In other words, at $\bar{w}$, everyone seeking a job can find one; there is no unemployment. Now, by applying the "law of supply and demand," we can say that whenever the real wage is not at its market-clearing level, $\bar{w}$, there are (market) forces to bring it back there. For example, if the wage happens to be at w_0, where the demand would fall short of

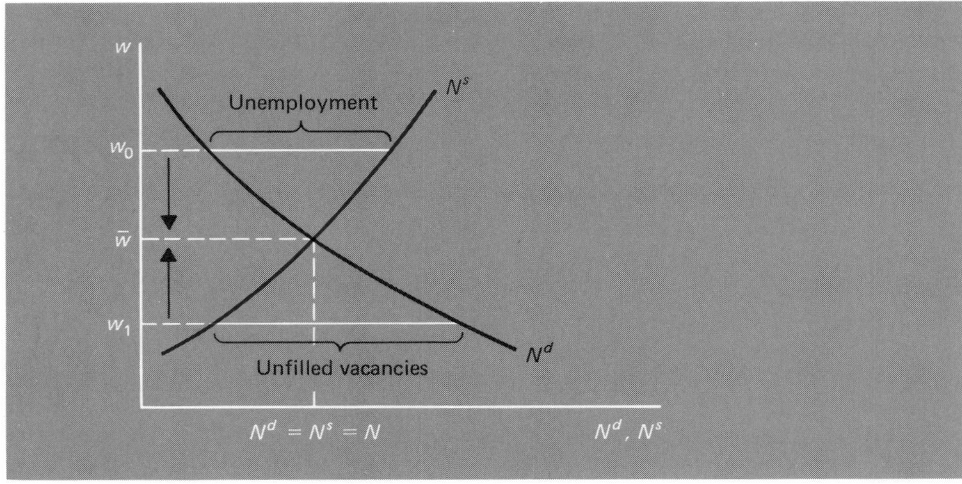

the supply and where there would be unemployment, the real wage will fall to $\overline{w}$ in order to eradicate this unemployment. Similarly, if the wage is w_1, it creates an excess demand for labor and thus unfilled vacancies, which drives the wage upward. If we assume that this wage movement is quick (i.e., instantaneous), we will always observe a market-clearing wage like $\overline{w}$, a circumstance that precludes involuntary unemployment; those who are not working will choose to "consume their time as leisure." Now the only question left is to inquire whether the output produced by this fully employed labor force will actually be demanded. At this point we introduce an important assumption: that we are examining not only a barter economy but also one in which borrowing and lending are nonexistent. In such a Robinson Crusoe economy, of course, the only reason for saving is to invest and the only way to invest is by saving. In other words, investment, I, is identically equal to savings, S (i.e., $I \equiv S$). But equality between investment and savings means equality between aggregate demand for goods and services, $C + I$, and aggregate supply. In other words, whatever is produced is demanded in the marketplace. There will never be insufficient demand, and therefore there will be no unemployment—as long as borrowing and lending are excluded and as long as the real wage moves quickly to clear the labor market.

Second, when borrowing and lending are permitted, intended investment is not necessarily equal to intended savings. But their equality is needed if aggregate demand for goods and services is to be equal to aggregate supply. Hence a method is needed to effect this equality, which bring us to the loans market. On the demand side of this market we have investment that is financed by borrowing. As Figure B.2-2 shows, investment is a decreasing function, I, of the interest rate, i. On the supply side, we have savings lent by households. It is usually stipulated that savings is an increasing function, S, of the interest rate, as in Figure B.2-2. The intersection of the demand and supply schedules for loans determines the interest rate, $\bar{i}$. In other words, at $\bar{i}$ the market for loans is cleared (i.e., $I = S$). By appealing to the extreme version of the law of supply and demand (i.e, when $i = i_0$ the interest rate

FIGURE B.2-2

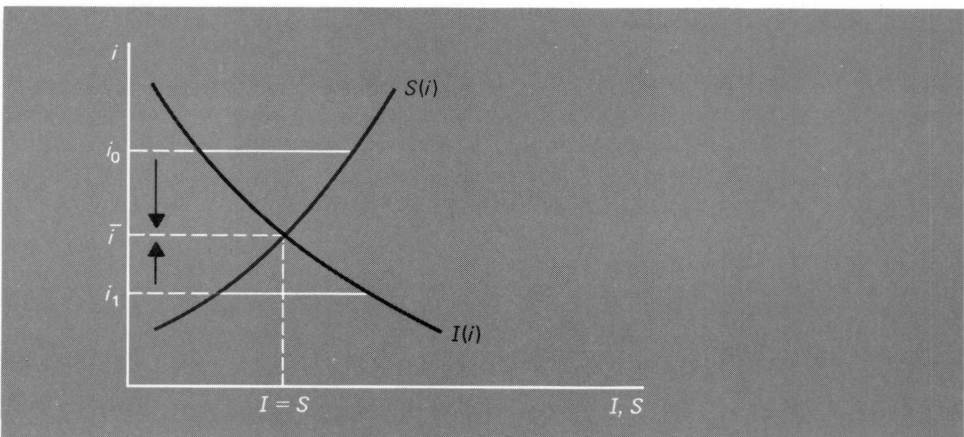

falls quickly to $\bar{i}$ and when $i = i_1$ it rises to $\bar{i}$), we guarantee continuous loans market clearance.

But the market interest rate does another job, though indirectly. Since $I = S$ indicates that the goods and services market is *also* cleared, and since the instantaneous movement of the interest rate produces the equality $I = S$, it follows that the interest rate also clears the goods and services market. If we continue to assume the extreme version of the law of supply and demand for the labor market, it always follows that all three markets—for labor, for loans, and for goods and services—will continuously clear. There is never a problem of unemployment or of insufficient demand. It remains to be seen, however, whether these "nice" results will remain true when the assumption of barter is dropped and money is introduced into the system. The rather complacent belief in continuous full employment, or in the natural tendency of the capitalistic economy to gravitate toward full employment, was effectively challenged by Keynes in 1936. In the 1960s and 1970s, however, the modern neoclassicists, or monetarists, instituted a revival of the pre-Keynesian belief.

2 The full-Employment Model

The purpose of this chapter is to provide the simplest possible economic description of the world around us. We are already familiar with the numbers usually mentioned in connection with the U.S. economy or with any other. We shall endeavor to find a theory, a scenario, capable of explaining some or all of those numbers mentioned in the *national income* and *national product* accounts: why, for example, the national income or the GNP is higher or lower than before; or why so many people are employed at certain wages. Economists use the word *model* for their scenario. Since our model here will be the simplest possible, our assumptions will necessarily be crude and unrealistic. We choose them strategically, however, to permit us to answer questions about the most important aspects of the economy. By stripping our model of all complications, we shall expose some of the fundamental relationships examined throughout this book. And we shall continuously revise our model by making the assumptions more realistic. More realistic assumptions, however, imply more complicated models, which are more difficult to analyze. Accepting the maxim that it is better to learn how to walk before you run, we examine the simplest case first, which is also the way our subject evolved in the literature.

This chapter focuses on the assumptions that guarantee that the economy will be always in full employment, or will gravitate naturally to full employment. This belief—which was held, rather complacently, by neoclassical economists—was effectively challenged by Keynes in 1936, but it was revived in the 1960s and 1970s by the modern neoclassicists, or monetarists.

In Section I we examine a barter economy where no borrowing or lending is permitted and where the instantaneous adjustment of the real wage clears the *single* labor market and, therefore, continuously guarantees full employment of labor and prevents any insufficiency of, or an excess of, the demand for goods and services.

In Section I the assumption of no borrowing or lending is responsible for guaranteeing that investment is identical with savings, which, in turn, implies that the goods market is always cleared. Beginning with Section II, borrowing and lending are explicitly permitted. This, of course, increases the array of assets available to the wealth holder, which, in turn, implies that one can invest more than one saves and, vice versa, that one can invest less than one saves. On the other hand, we continue to be interested in the equality of investment and savings because only then can we guarantee clearance of the goods market. This, in turn, necessitates citing in detail the reasons that lie behind consumption-savings and investment decisions. While an extensive treatment of this topic will be postponed until Chapters 11 and 12, we shall briefly examine this issue in Section II, relying on household choice theory and profit maximization by firms. The remainder of Chapter 2 reexamines the more complicated model, still assuming barter and full employment. We find that this model has the same properties as the simpler model of Section I. Of course, it permits the posing and answering of more interesting questions than does the earlier model.

I. THE SIMPLEST BARTER MODEL: NO BORROWING OR LENDING

In this section we assume that the economy produces one homogeneous and perfectly divisible good called GNP and that this good is corn. Let us use the symbol Y to denote this good. To produce this good, we need only two factors of production: labor, N, and capital, K. The technology of production exhibits constant returns, that is, if the quantities of utilized capital and labor are doubled or tripled, the quantity of output, Y, is also doubled or tripled. In general, we say that the production function

$$Y = F(K,N) \tag{1}$$

has the property that if K and N are multiplied by the same positive number λ, Y is also multiplied by this same number:

$$\lambda Y = F(\lambda K, \lambda N) \tag{2}$$

We have seen in Chapter 1 that by setting $\lambda \equiv 1/K$ in (2), we can reduce (1) to the statement that output per unit of capital, Y/K, depends only on labor per unit of capital, N/K. Defining x as N/K, we have

$$\frac{Y}{K} = f(x) \tag{3}$$

which is shown graphically in Figure 2-1. Knowing the economy's particular x, say x_0 in Figure 2-2, we can immediately find the marginal product; it is the slope of the tangent to the $f(x)$ curve. Similarly, the marginal product of capital is the intercept on the Y/K axis when that tangent is extended to meet the Y/K axis.

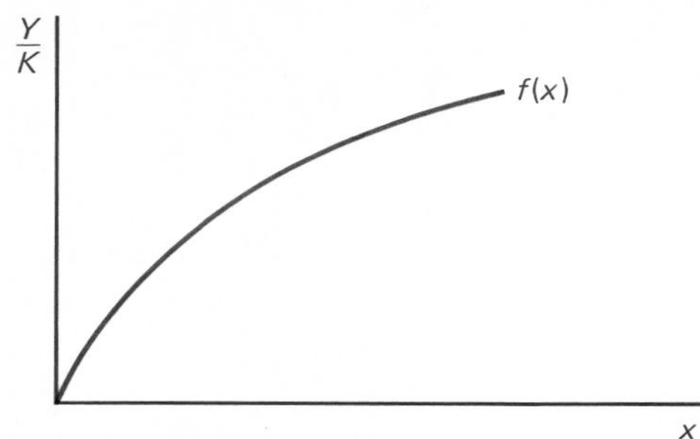

FIGURE 2-1

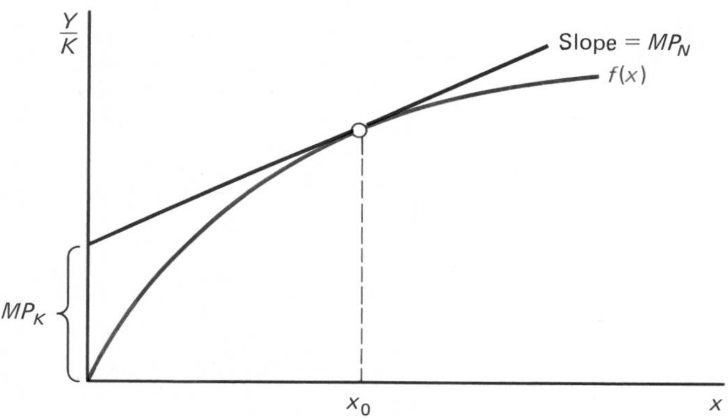

FIGURE 2-2

Production is undertaken by the agents called *producers,* or *firms,* whose aim is to maximize profits, and who operate in a *purely competitive* environment. This means that each firm is incapable of influencing the terms under which it trades. More specifically, we stipulate that no matter how many workers it wants to hire, the wage will not change. Similarly, the firm can sell as much as it wants to produce without having to accept a lower price than the prevailing one. In other words, the firm is a *price taker.*

The economy in which the firm operates is one of barter, which means that no money is used to carry out exchange. And since there is only one good, corn, it follows that the firm pays the labor it hires in terms of corn, namely, w units of corn for each unit of labor. It also follows that the price of corn is equal to one; it takes one unit of corn to acquire one unit of corn. Similarly, the firm's profits, Π, are also measured in units of corn, $\Pi = Y - wN$, and the rate of profit is, of course, $r = \Pi/K = f(x) - wx$. The firm's attempt to maximize its profit, Π, and therefore its rate of profit, r, forces it to produce and thus hire labor until the marginal product of labor is equal to the market's (real) wage, w. It follows, therefore, that the demand curve for labor coincides with the marginal-product-of-labor curve, MP_N, which is depicted in Figure 2-3.

There is a second set of agents in the economy called *households* or *consumers,* which are also rational individuals; they want to consume the most preferred basket of goods and services they can afford. These households are assumed to be endowed with their time, or leisure, which is an object of preference, as is corn. We know

FIGURE 2-3

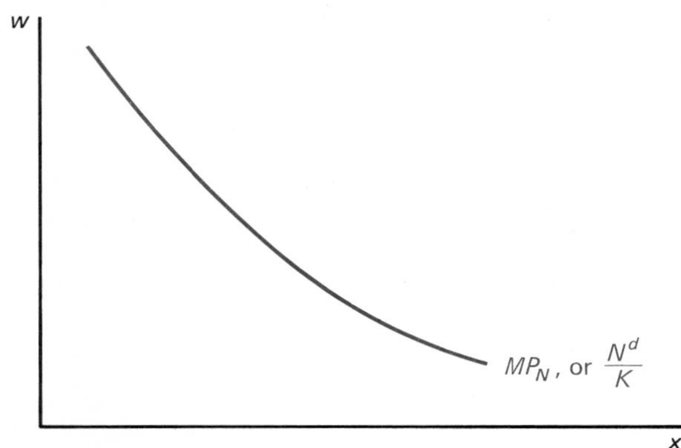

FIGURE 2-4

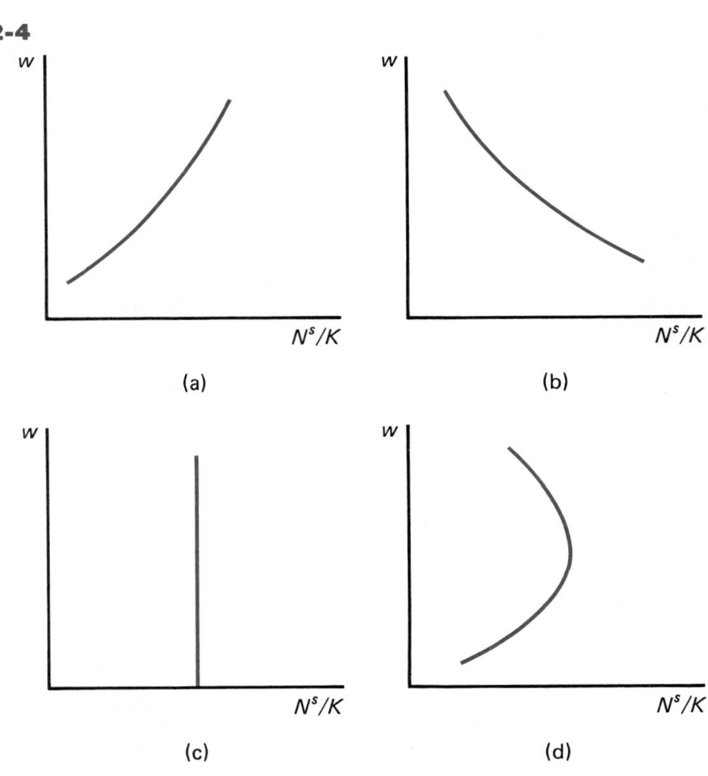

from Chapter 1 that the average household's attempt to consume the most preferred "basket" of corn and leisure gives us the economy's supply curve of labor, which can be upward sloping (curve (a) in Figure 2-4) or downward sloping with respect to the real wage, w (curve (b) in Figure 2-4). However, it can even be independent of the wage rate (curve (c) in Figure 2-4) if preferences are homothetic and the elasticity of substitution is unity. In most of our illustrations we shall utilize this latter, vertical supply curve of labor.

Some additional assumptions about our barter economy will be introduced as they are needed. We shall examine this economy both for the short run and the long run, beginning with the former.

SHORT RUN

The *short run* is defined as a period short enough to allow the economy's plant and equipment—the economy's capital stock, K—to be viewed as fixed or unchanged. We shall examine the economy described above (i.e., the model) in the short run, when the economy's plant and equipment cannot vary. Let us consider the capital stock as fixed, that is, $K = \bar{K}$. No change in our results will emerge if the fixed quantity of capital is assumed to be equal to one, $K = \bar{K} = 1$. Under these assumptions, employment demand per unit of capital, x, is identical with employment demanded; employment supplied is denoted by v; and the average product of capital is equal to total GNP. This dual role of the symbol x (and of v when they do not coincide) will be followed until Chapter 16, where growth of K, as well as of N, is explicitly considered.

THE LABOR MARKET

We are now ready to examine the economy's labor market. We have already derived the demand and supply curves, depicted in Figure 2-5, which describes the labor market.

To avoid confusion later, we shall restate the description of the labor market: We assume that there is one homogeneous kind of labor, which is offered by the

FIGURE 2-5

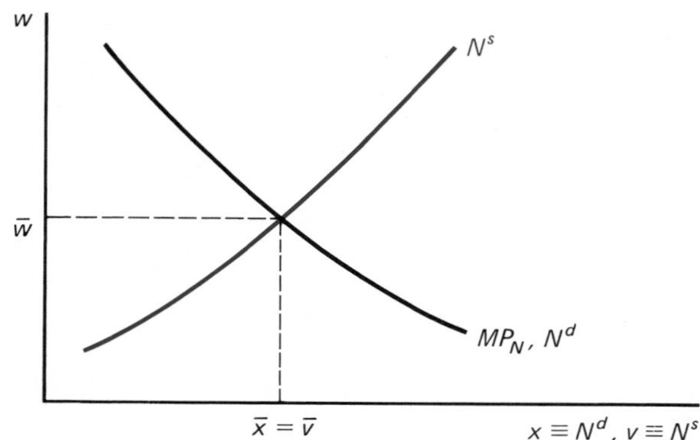

households and demanded by the firms for use in the production of Y. Furthermore, we should emphasize that the assumption of homogeneous labor is unrealistic; we shall see later that when we permit heterogeneity of labor, the results will be different.

Figure 2-5 shows the equilibrium of the labor market. When the wage rate is equal to $\bar{w}$, the demand for labor is equal to the supply. In other words, when the real wage is equal to $\bar{w}$, everyone who wants to be employed is, in fact, employed.

Now suppose that the real wage happens to be $\bar{\bar{w}}$, as in Figure 2-6. It is clear that the supply is greater than the demand. For the wage rate, $\bar{\bar{w}}$, that exists in the market, more labor is offered (by workers) than is demanded (by firms); the difference between the two is unemployment. If, on the other hand, the wage rate is $\bar{\bar{\bar{w}}}$, it is clear that the demand for labor is greater than the supply, and there is excess demand for labor (i.e., unfilled vacancies).

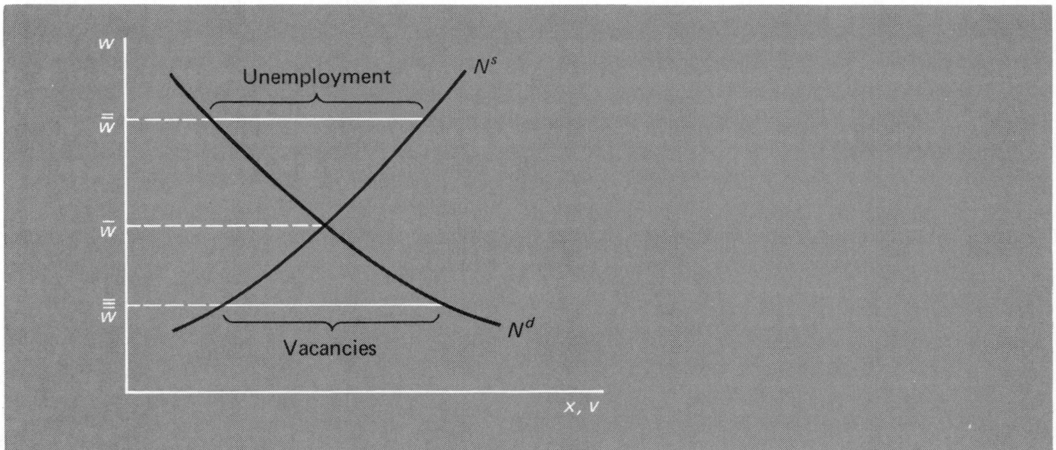

FIGURE 2-6

At this point we introduce the "law of supply and demand," which, in general, states that if the demand side of a market is greater than its supply side, the "price" (that is "determined" by this market) will increase. On the other hand, the "price" will fall if supply is greater than demand. In the present case we are dealing with the labor market, and the price in question is the real wage (in units of corn).

In a true barter economy, one expects that the real wage—the wage that is in units of corn—will fall if there is unemployment and that it will rise if there is excess demand for labor. One can envision applying this rule to the proverbial market for longshoremen, where the wage in kind will move until everybody willing to work finds a job. In a present-day monetary economy, the real wage is found by dividing the money wage, W, by the dollar price of corn (i.e., $w \equiv W/P$). To say, then, that w falls is no longer a straightforward statement. This will prove to be a major complication later on.

To complicate matters further, we mentioned that until 1936 most economists refused to admit the existence of involuntary unemployment. But what was the basis for this belief? It appears that they simply introduced an extreme form of the law of "supply and demand" for the labor market. Using Figure 2-6, they said that the real wage moves so fast that it *instantaneously* clears the labor market; if the wage were equal to $\bar{\bar{w}}$, so that unemployment occurred, w would fall back to $\bar{w}$ and unemployment would disappear immediately. And, similarly, if excess demand for labor were present, the real wage would move up at once to fill the unfilled vacancies! In this way they could maintain that anyone who was unemployed chose to remain so! After all, they had the theory of labor-leisure choice from which to derive the supply curve of labor.

In summary, pre-Keynesian economists relied on the real wage to move quickly in order to perpetuate full employment. But one more problem remains: How do we know that the output produced by the full-employment level of labor and the level of capital (assumed fixed in the short run) will all (and exactly) be demanded? We can illustrate this problem in the Figure 2-7 graph. In the upper panel of Figure 2-7, we find that the real wage will be equal to $\bar{w}$, which will equate the demand for and supply of labor. Knowing the amount of labor used and knowing the quantity of capital in the short run ($\equiv 1$), we find that $\bar{Y}$ units of output will be produced. The question is: How do we know that precisely this much corn will be demanded? In the absence of government and foreign trade, the demand for corn

FIGURE 2-7

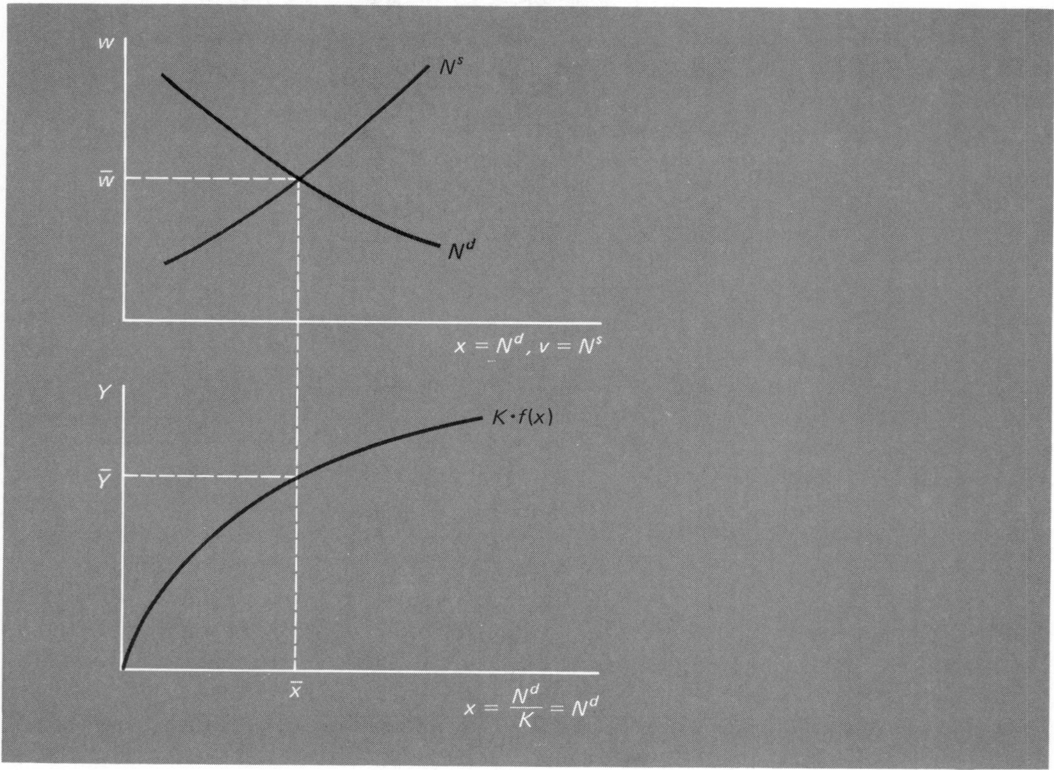

has only two components: consumption, C, and investment, I. But how do we know that intended consumption plus intended investment is equal to $\overline{Y}$?

$$C + I \stackrel{?}{=} \overline{Y}$$

Even here economists introduced a *deus ex machina;* they examined an economy in which *no borrowing or lending was permitted.* The only way, then, for a person to provide for future consumption is to store consumption goods for the future or to retain capital and later hire labor to produce. *In other words, the only way to invest is by saving and, conversely, the only way to save is by investing.* This means that society's saving is identically equal to investment:

$$S \equiv I \tag{4}$$

As we know from Euler's theorem of distribution, output is exactly equal to society's income, which, in turn, is either saved or consumed:

$$Y \equiv C + S$$

Therefore the question as to whether

$$C + I \stackrel{?}{=} \overline{Y}$$

reduces itself to this one:

$$C + I \stackrel{?}{=} C + S$$

or, eliminating C from both sides:

$$I \stackrel{?}{=} S$$

Of course, the answer is yes by equation (4). When investment is *identically* equal to savings, we say that Say's Law identity (or Say's Law in the strict sense of the term) holds.

J. B. Say, a classical French economist, argued that there is never a problem of lack of demand or of excess demand for goods and services because *supply creates its own demand.* Of course, if borrowing and lending are excluded, this version of Say's Law holds.

We can, therefore, summarize the results of our analysis so far: *Given a barter economy without borrowing and lending, if the real wage moves to instantaneously clear the labor market, neither underemployment nor overemployment will ever occur. And the economy will never be faced with the problems of insufficiency or excess demand in the product market. Since there is no other market in this simplified economy, all (both) markets are cleared all the time; in other words, the economy is in a state of perpetual full equilibrium.*

We should emphasize that knowing the real wage that clears the labor market permits us to find all the relevant magnitudes for this economy and, therefore, to

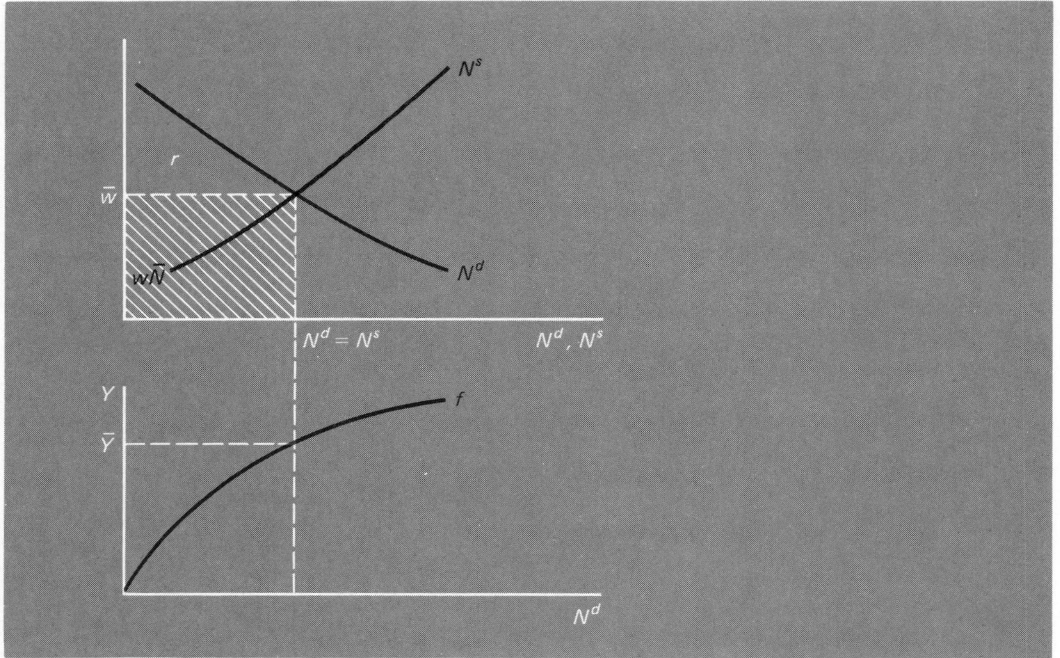

FIGURE 2-8

explain the national product–national income accounts. In the upper panel of Figure 2-8 we determine total wages, wN, and total profits, $r \cdot K = r \cdot 1 = r$. This corresponds to Table 1-2 in Chapter 1. According to Euler's theorem of distribution, their sum (i.e., the area under the N^d curve) is equal to $\overline{Y}$ (the lower panel of Figure 2-8).

To find the allocation of income between consumption and savings, and thus the allocation of output between consumption and investment demand, we need additional theorizing. Accordingly, we specify that consumption demand, C, depends on society's wealth and income. The only wealth in this simplified scheme is the capital stock, K. Income, of course, is equal to output, Y. Thus we specify that

$$C = C(K, Y) \tag{5}$$

with the further assumption that an increase in income (other things being equal) will increase consumption demand, or that the marginal propensity to consume, $\Delta C/\Delta Y$, is positive.

We know, of course, that part of income is consumed and that the rest is saved:

$$C + S \equiv Y \tag{6}$$

Savings, therefore, is income not consumed:

$$S = Y - C(Y,K)$$

It follows, then, that savings is also a function of income and wealth with the marginal propensity to save $\Delta S/\Delta Y > 0$. Note further that

$$\frac{\Delta C}{\Delta Y} + \frac{\Delta S}{\Delta Y} = 1 \text{ by (6)}$$

With this stipulation we can extend the earlier results. When $w = \bar{w}$, we know all the variables, namely, income and its division between wages and property income as well as GNP and its division between consumption and savings. Of course, income is identical with GNP. Since savings is identically equal to investment, we also know investment. Thus, all the relevant variables are accounted for.

We have just specified that savings depends on K and Y:

$$S = \tilde{S}(Y, K) \tag{7}$$

In what follows, we make the simplifying assumption that S is linear homogeneous. If, for example, we double Y and K, savings is also doubled:

$$\lambda S = \tilde{S}\ (\lambda Y, \lambda K)$$

If, as before, we specify λ as $\lambda \equiv 1/K$, we have

$$\frac{S}{K} = \tilde{S}\left(\frac{Y}{K}, 1\right)$$

or

$$\frac{S}{K} = T(Y/K) \tag{8}$$

And it follows that savings per unit of capital depends (positively) only on output per unit of capital, as seen in Figure 2-9. We know, however, that output per unit of capital, Y/K, depends positively (and uniquely) on employment per unit of capital,

FIGURE 2-9

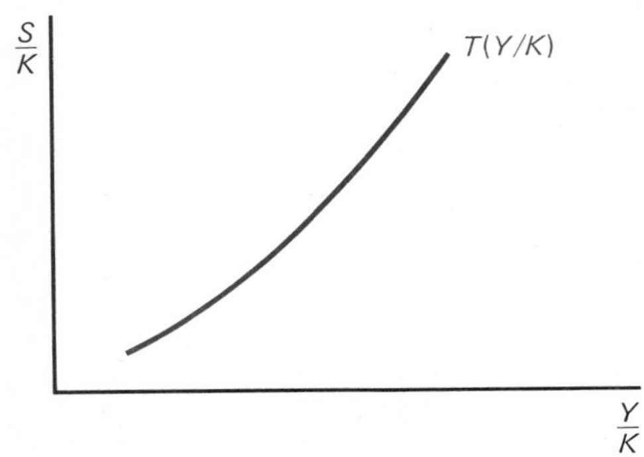

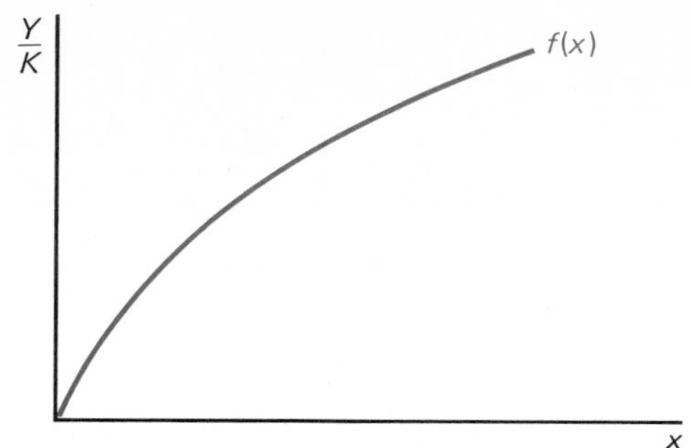

FIGURE 2-10

$N/K = x$, as in Figure 2-10. We depict these two facts in one graph, Figure 2-11. We can immediately prove that savings per unit of capital, S/K, ultimately depends only on employment per unit of capital and that this relationship is positive, as seen in Figure 2-11.

Suppose that $x = x_0$. In the first quadrant we find that $Y/K = (Y/K)_0$. But when $Y/K = (Y/K)_0$, we see in the second quadrant that $S/K = (S/K)_0$. Now, suppose further that x is higher, say $x = x_1$. Applying the same technique as before, we find that S/K is higher now, namely $(S/K)_1$. We can depict this result *directly* in the graph in Figure 2-12, and we can now use the new notation,

$$\frac{S}{K} = S(x) \tag{9}$$

Furthermore, we can now complete the graphical determination of all the relevant unknowns in the economic system.

We see that the model depends ultimately on only one variable, namely, x. When we know x, as in Figure 2-13, we can find all the other magnitudes. The

FIGURE 2-11

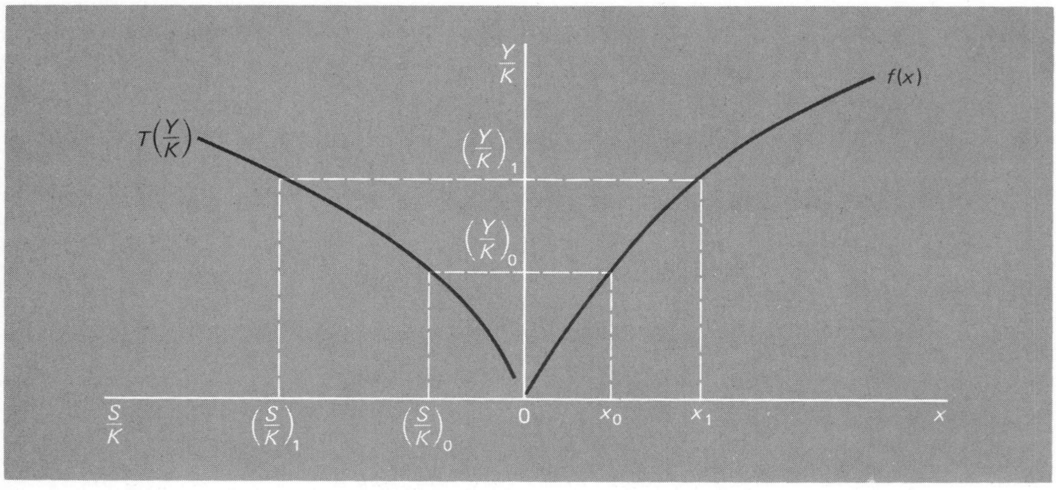

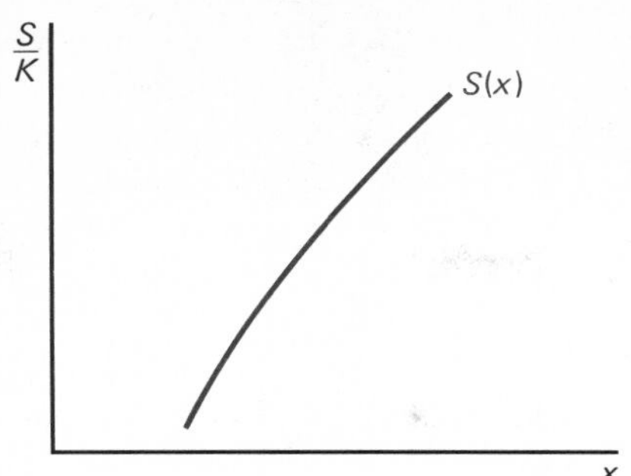

FIGURE 2-12

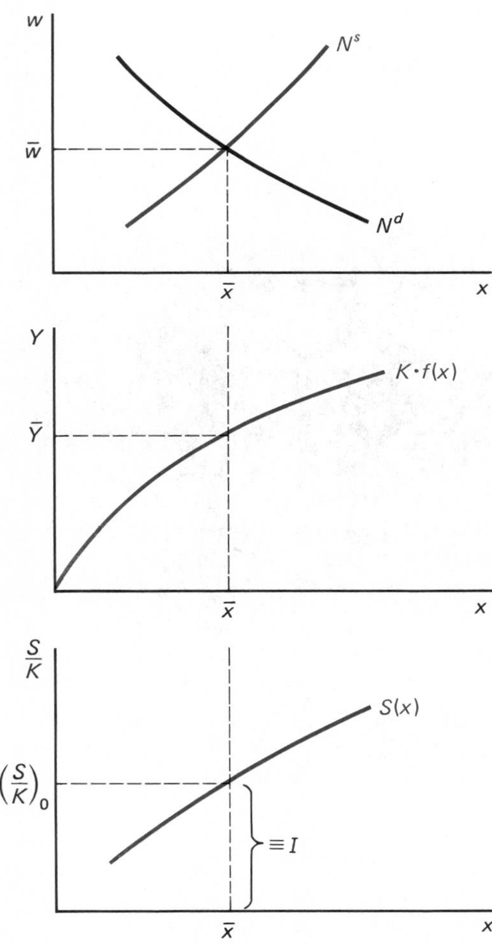

FIGURE 2-13

only problem remaining for this model of the economy is to determine the movement of the economy over time, a problem undertaken later.

Summarizing the results of this section, we should emphasize that our assumptions—that of a barter economy, that of an absence of borrowing or lending, and, finally, that of the instantaneous adjustment of the real wage to clear the single labor market—guarantee that no problem of insufficiency of or excess demand for goods and services will arise, and, furthermore, that the labor market will be cleared, that is, unemployment cannot exist in this system. Our model has generated all the other important magnitudes of the national product and national income accounts, but, of course, it cannot explain unemployment. It should be emphasized that, *at best,* this model was the one used by economists prior to 1936. This was both the beginning and the end of employment theory.[1] No wonder they could not explain unemployment!

In the remainder of this book we relax the strict assumptions listed above. The rest of this chapter introduces borrowing and lending. In Chapter 3 we move away from barter by introducing money. In Chapter 5 we permit noninstantaneous movements of wages. And in Chapter 10 more than one labor market is used. In this way we derive models and results that correspond better to reality. But the reader should not fail to notice that the problems become a lot more complicated. While the issues in this section were resolved in a few pages, the same issues, using more realistic assumptions, will take chapters.

II. BORROWING AND LENDING

In this section we permit borrowing and lending and thus remove one of the assumptions noted earlier. Occasionally we shall refer to *borrowing* as the supply of (privately issued) bonds and to *lending* as buying bonds. A *bond* is a promise to make payments of some good, say, of "corn" in a barter economy, or of "dollars" in a monetary economy, at specified times in the future.

The introduction of borrowing and lending, or of the financial asset called a "bond," has important implications. First, it increases the menu of assets available to the wealth holder (saver). We know from the preceding section that there was only one way for a person to provide for future consumption: to trade consumption goods or labor for capital goods. Then in the future he must either "consume" those capital goods or combine them with his own, or with purchased, labor services to produce consumption goods. With this new assumption he can now buy a bond that will yield a specified, previously agreed upon payment of consumption goods at some time in the future.

Second, it negates our earlier stipulation that savings, S, is *identically* equal to investment, I (i.e., $I \equiv S$), the strict form of Say's law and a corollary to the assumption of absence of borrowing and lending. Now, with the new assumption, it follows that one can invest more than one saves or, conversely, that one can invest less than one saves. And it is no longer the case that the only way to invest is to

[1] See the best treatment in J. R. Hicks, *Theory of Wages* (London: Macmillan, 1932).

save and, conversely, that the only way to save is to invest. Since there are now two assets available to the saver, we can stipulate that

$$S \equiv I + \text{Lending, and } \textit{not} \text{ that } S \equiv I$$

On the other hand, we continue to be interested in the *equality* between investment and savings, $I = S$, because only then can we guarantee the clearance of the market for goods and services. For this reason we need to examine, in greater detail, the determinants of savings (and thus consumption) and of investment. When this is done, we can begin to formulate the theory that allows this equality, $I = S$, to materialize.

The firm is the average agent responsible for investment demand, while consumption demand (and thus the supply of savings) emanates from the average household. It should be clear why the decisions of firms to invest may not always coincide with those of households to save. Each of these agents has different motives for its decision making: *The firm is assumed to maximize the present value of expected future profits, while the household's theory of choice requires maximization of intertemporal utility.* For concreteness, we shall assume that the average firm prefers buying capital rather than renting it. (This behavior may be due to its desire to minimize transactions costs.) The firm finances its capital purchases by issuing (supplying) bonds. Thus the average firm is assumed to be a net borrower. (Note that firms are owned by households and that all net cash flows into firms accrue, therefore, to households.) On the other hand, we assume that the average household is a net lender.

THE CONSUMPTION AND SAVINGS FUNCTIONS

Borrowing and lending (otherwise called "intertemporal exchange") make savings a function of the interest rate, i, in addition to being a function of current income, Y, and of wealth, that is, $\tilde{S}(i, Y, K)$ rather than $\tilde{S}(Y, K)$, as in the preceding section. Of course, consumption is also a function of the same three variables, that is, $C = C(i, Y, K)$.

It is easy to establish informally the dependence of savings upon the interest rate. The act of saving, that is, of not consuming part of the corn from the current period, is equivalent to exchanging present income (corn) for future income (corn). But at what terms? This is where the interest rate comes into play. This concept is related to that of relative prices. The relative price of today's income (i.e., of *present* income) of corn is the number of units of corn that an individual will receive *tomorrow* (i.e., in the *future*) if that individual gives up one unit of today's (present) corn. Obviously, this number of units is greater than one. This excess over unity (i.e., what the individual gets tomorrow *above* what that individual gives today) is defined as the *interest rate*. Denoting the interest rate by i, it is clear that the relative price of today's corn is $1 + i$; similarly, the relative price of tomorrow's corn is the number of units of corn that an individual gives up today in order to get one unit tomorrow; this is equal to $1/(1 + i)$ and is, of course, *less* than one.

Let us now examine whether the relation between savings and the interest rate is positive, negative, or nonexistent. It is important here to recall that we are examining the average household, which is assumed to be a *net saver*—a *net supplier* of today's corn. An increase in the interest rate, i, increases the relative price, $1 + i$, of today's corn. This increase in price has *two effects* on the demand (by the individual) for today's corn, that is, on (current) consumption. The higher relative price of current corn induces the individual to consume *less*, a phenomenon called the *substitution effect*.[2]

On the other hand, the increase in the price of the good for which the individual is a net supplier (i.e., of today's corn) makes this individual wealthier. The individual, in turn, will want to consume more of every noninferior good. Here we assume that both today's and tomorrow's corn are noninferior (i.e., "normal"). Hence the individual will want to consume, in particular, *more* of today's good. This is the *income*, or *wealth*, *effect*, which is in the opposite direction to the substitution effect.

If the substitution effect is greater (in absolute value) than the income effect, the increase in the interest rate will reduce consumption, or, in symbols, $\Delta C/\Delta i < 0$. Since savings, S, is current income (corn) not consumed currently (i.e., $S = Y -$

FIGURE 2-14

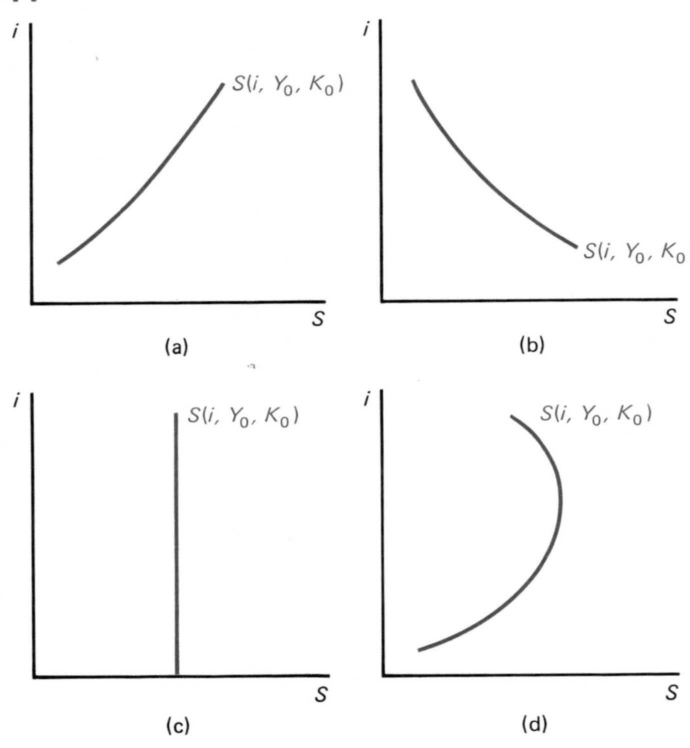

[2] Its name derives from the fact that the individual substitutes the inexpensive for the more expensive good. Current corn is the more expensive good. But what is the inexpensive good? In this simple example it is future corn, whose relative price, $1/(1 + i)$, falls when $1 + i$ rises.

C), it follows that the reduction in consumption, C (because of the increase in the interest rate), implies an increase in savings. Therefore we have just demonstrated that when the substitution effect outweighs the income effect, an increase in the interest rate increases savings, $\Delta S/\Delta i > 0$, and decreases consumption, $\Delta C/\Delta i < 0$.

A similar reasoning reveals that when the income effect outweighs the substitution effect, an increase in the interest rate increases consumption, $\Delta C/\Delta i > 0$, and thus decreases savings, $\Delta S/\Delta i < 0$. Of course, it is conceivable that the two effects cancel out each other, with the result that savings is independent of the interest rate. It is clear from the preceding discussion that any one of the four graphs in Figure 2-14 is a possible depiction of the relation between the interest rate and savings.

This is the appropriate point to mention that "supply side" economists recommend a reduction of tax rates on interest income so that the resultant increase in the "after tax" interest rate may stimulate savings, and hence, capital accumulation and growth. It is evident from our analysis that this policy will be successful only when tastes are such that the substitution effect outweighs the income effect.

Until now we have *assumed* that there is a positive relation between consumption and income and, similarly, a positive relation between savings and income. Following the technique used in this section, we can derive these relations as results emanating from the rational behavior of a household. We can easily establish that an increase in the household's current income (i.e., today's corn) will increase the value of its endowments (measured in units of either today's corn or tomorrow's corn), which will, in turn, induce the household to consume more from the current income. As long as both today's corn and tomorrow's corn are "normal" goods, we can show that the household will consume only part of the extra current corn, thereby saving some and increasing savings, as well as consumption.

Assume that the (average) household is endowed with $\bar{y}_1$ units of today's corn and with $\bar{y}_2$ units of tomorrow's corn, as seen at point $\bar{E}$ of Figure 2-15. With

FIGURE 2-15

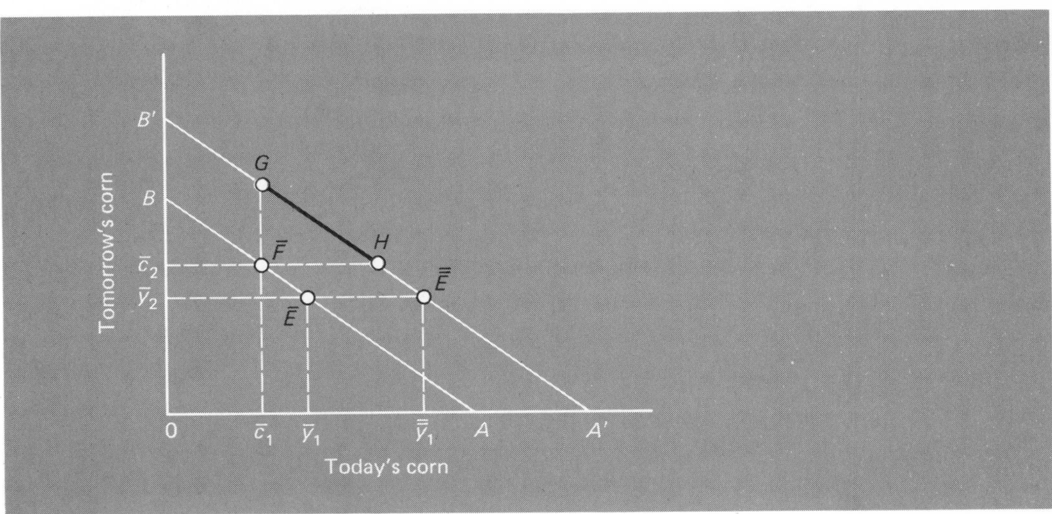

the interest rate equal to i_0, we can measure the value of this endowment in units of today's corn; it is equal to $\bar{y}_1 + \frac{1}{1 + i_0} y_2$, or equal to the distance OA in Figure 2-15. Similarly, the value of the endowment, in units of tomorrow's corn, is $(1 + i_0) \cdot \bar{y}_1 + \bar{y}_2$, or OB units in Figure 2-15. Since the household is a net saver, it must consume at a point on the budget constraint BA, northwest of $\bar{E}$, say at point $\bar{F}$. Since savings is current income not consumed currently (i.e., $S = \bar{y}_1 - \bar{c}_1$), point $\bar{F}$ indeed depicts positive savings.

Let us now suppose that, other things being equal, there is an increase in the amount of today's corn, from $\bar{y}_1$ to $\bar{\bar{y}}_1$, so that the new endowment point is $\bar{\bar{E}}$ and its value is equal to OA' units of today's corn or OB' units of tomorrow's corn. Since the household is better off—because its endowment has risen—it will consume more of both goods, more of today's corn and more of tomorrow's corn, an implication of the assumption that both goods are normal. But this assumption also implies that the new consumption point must lie on the segment GH, exclusive of the end points, that is, to the right of point G and to the left of point H. In other words, the increase in consumption will be less than the distance $\overline{FH}$ which is equal to the increase in current income. It follows, then, that savings also increases. Although $S = y_1 - c_1$, and although both y_1 and c_1 have risen, we can say, nevertheless, that their difference has definitely risen. In summary, we have seen that an increase in current income causes an increase in both consumption and savings.

Finally, we can see the response of consumption and savings to an increase in the endowment of tomorrow's corn, from $\bar{y}_2$ to $\bar{\bar{y}}_2$ in Figure 2-16, which also shows the new endowment point $\bar{\bar{\bar{E}}}$. The value of the endowment, whether this value is measured in units of today's corn or in units of tomorrow's corn, has risen. The household will consume more of each good, and it is immediately clear that (current) consumption will rise. But what about savings? It is easy to establish that savings

FIGURE 2-16

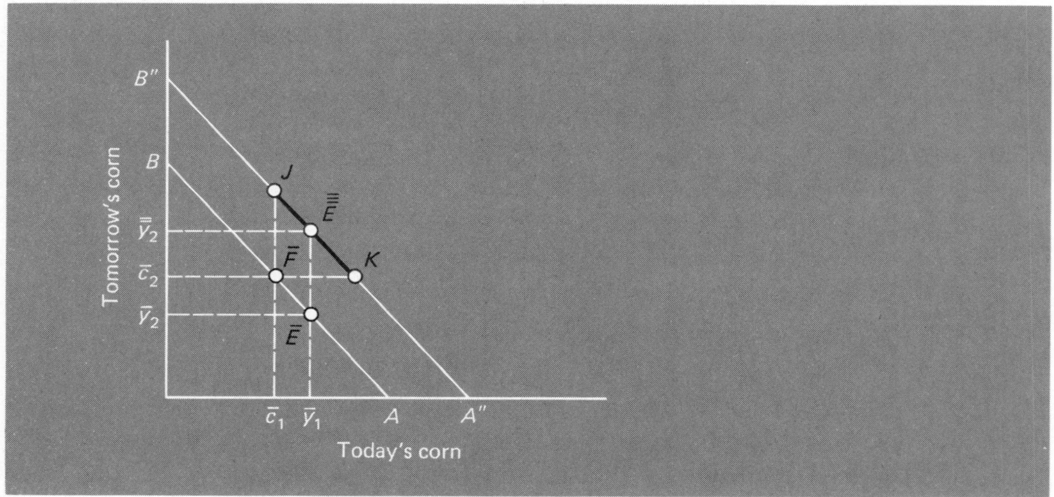

will *fall:* Since $S = y_1 - c_1$, and since c_1 rises while y_1 remains the same, their difference *decreases.* In Figure 2-16 the consumption point moves from $\bar{F}$ to a point on the segment *JK.* Whether it will end on $J\bar{\bar{E}}$ or $\bar{\bar{E}}K$, savings will fall. (Of course, if the new consumption point ends up between $\bar{\bar{E}}$ and *K,* savings not only will fall but will also become negative.)

We have just established that an increase in the endowment of future income will increase current consumption and decrease savings. We can now identify future income, y_2, with wealth, which is here capital, *K,* and state that an increase in wealth increases (current) consumption and decreases savings. While this negative relation between savings and wealth seems incongruous at first, even a cursory explanation can clarify it; people save, with a goal in mind, to reach a particular level of wealth. But if their wealth increases directly, they come closer to their goal, a situation that allows them to decrease their efforts to accumulate wealth, that is, to decrease their efforts to save.

Using our earlier notion (i.e., *Y* for y_1 and *K* for y_2), we can summarize our discussion with the following savings and consumption functions:

$$S = \tilde{S}(i, Y, K), \text{ where } \frac{\Delta\tilde{S}}{\Delta i} \gtreqless 0, \frac{\Delta\tilde{S}}{\Delta Y} > 0, \frac{\Delta\tilde{S}}{\Delta K} < 0 \tag{10}$$

$$C = C(i, Y, K), \text{ where } \frac{\Delta C}{\Delta i} \gtreqless 0, \frac{\Delta C}{\Delta Y} > 0, \frac{\Delta C}{\Delta K} > 0 \tag{11}$$

A formal derivation of these functions is undertaken in Chapter 11, where exact forms are also discussed. Here, as in the preceeding section, we simplify by assuming that savings is homogeneous of degree one, with respect to income, *Y,* and wealth, *K,* but not with respect to the interest rate. Multiplying *Y* and *K* by λ, we get

$$\lambda S = \tilde{S}(i, \lambda Y, \lambda K)$$

Setting $\lambda \equiv 1/K$, we have

$$\frac{S}{K} = \tilde{S}\left(i, \frac{Y}{K}, 1\right)$$

and since $Y/K = f(x)$:

$$\frac{S}{K} = \tilde{S}\,[i, f(x), 1]$$

that is, savings, per unit of capital, depends only on *i* and *x.* We shall denote this relation as *S:*

$$\frac{S}{K} = S(i, x), \text{ with } \frac{\Delta S}{\Delta i} \gtreqless 0 \text{ and } \frac{\Delta S}{\Delta x} > 0 \tag{12}$$

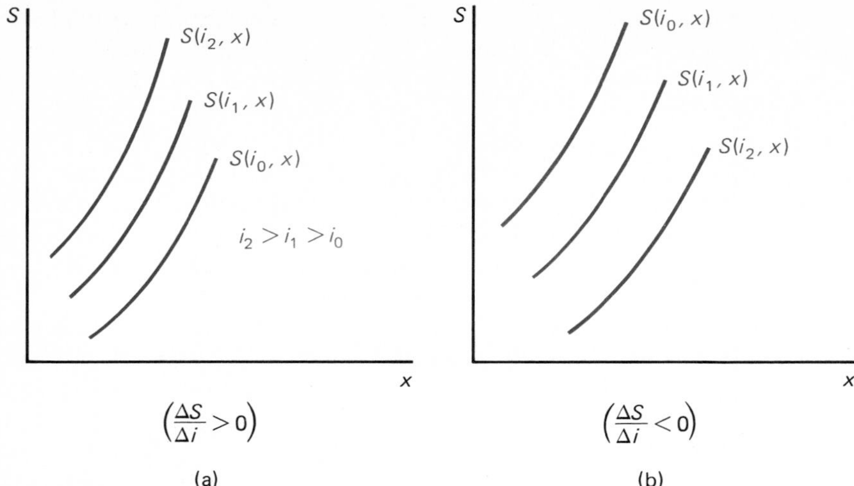

FIGURE 2-17

As before, the relation between x and S is positive, but the relation between i and S can be positive, negative, or nonexistent. It is clear, however, that there is an infinity of savings (per unit of capital) curves in the *(x,S)*-plane, one for each assumed level of interest rate. Figure 2-17a illustrates the case in which a positive relation exists between the interest rate and savings, while Figure 2-17b assumes a negative relation.

Similarly, there is an infinity of S curves in the *(i,S)*-plane, one such curve for each assumed x. The two opposite cases are illustrated in Figures 2-18a and 2-18b. Note that in the *(x,S)*-plane, Figures 2-17a and 2-17b, an increase in x is depicted as a movement *along* the (same) curve, whereas in the *(i,S)*-plane, the increase in x

FIGURE 2-18

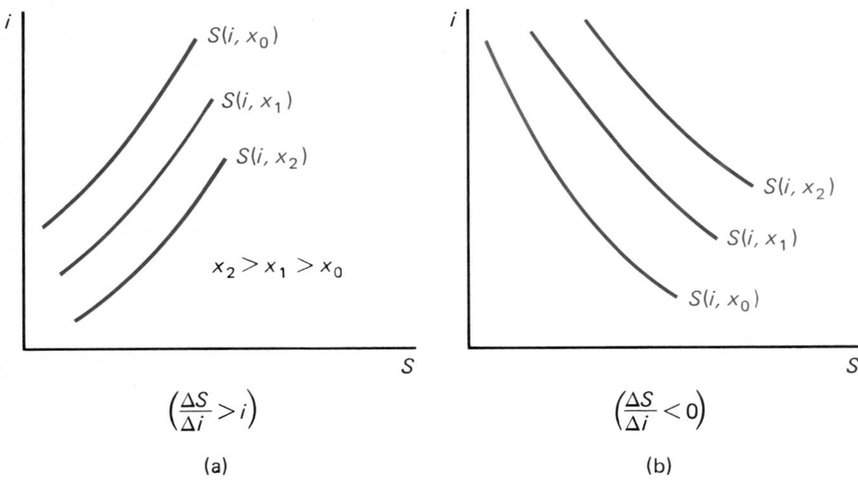

is depicted as a *shift* of the curve. Similarly, an increase in i is depicted as a shift of the curve in the (x,S)-plane (Figures 2-17a and 2-17b), and as a movement along the (same) curve in the (i,S)-plane (Figures 2-18a and 2-18b).

THE INVESTMENT FUNCTION

We noted earlier that the average firm is responsible for investment decisions, such as how much capital to *add* to the existing capital stock; in other words, how much to increase the plant and its equipment.

A decision by a firm to invest is a decision to increase its capacity to produce and to sell final output. Naturally, *prospective profit* in production influences investment. We assume further that the firm finances its investment by borrowing, either from the loans market or from itself. It follows, then, that the *cost of borrowing* (i.e., the interest rate) should also influence investment decisions.

Schematically, we can show that investment, I, is a function of the interest rate, i, and of the profit rate, r. In general we can say that investment per unit of capital, I/K, is a function of i and r:

$$\frac{I}{K} = \phi(i,r) \tag{13}$$

In particular, a higher profit rate will, *ceteris paribus,* increase investment (per unit of capital), $\Delta(I/K)/\Delta r > 0$. Similarly, an increase in the interest rate will, *ceteris paribus,* reduce investment, $\Delta(I/K)/\Delta i < 0$.

Before proceeding, we can note briefly that a recommendation by supply-side economists to reduce taxation or profits, in order to increase the after tax profitability of investment, can be explained directly by our analysis. At any rate, other things equal, this policy is generally valid, as opposed to a policy aimed at reducing interest taxation.

We have established in Chapter 1 that a one-to-one, positive relation exists between the rate of profit and employment, per unit of capital, x. Hence an increase in economic activity, x, increases the rate of profit, r, which, in turn, spurs an increase in investment. It follows, then, that ultimately investment, per unit of capital, is a function of the interest rate, i, and of employment, per unit of capital, x. We shall use the symbol I for this relation:[3]

$$\frac{I}{K} = I(i,x) \text{ where } \frac{\Delta I}{\Delta i} < 0, \frac{\Delta I}{\Delta x} > 0 \tag{14}$$

In the (i,I)-plane an investment curve is downward sloping. Moreover, since investment also depends (positively) on x, there must be an infinity of investment curves, one for each assumed level of x. In particular, the higher the assumed level

---

[3] Recall that in the short run the capital stock, K, is fixed and equal to one. Therefore $(I/K) = I$, and the symbol I/K stands for both investment per unit of capital and simply investment.

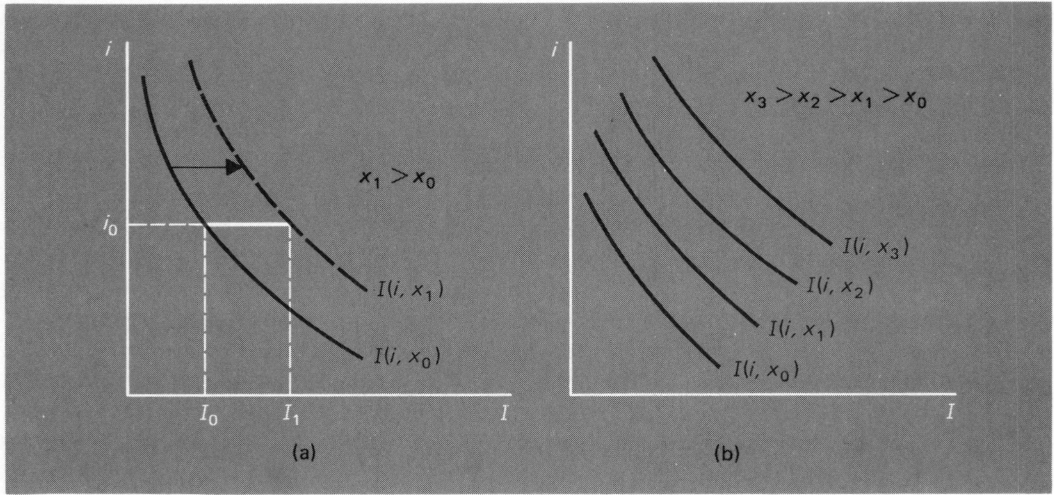

FIGURE 2-19

of x, the farther to the right the investment curve will lie, as in Figure 2-19b. This is an implication of the positive relation between x and I, and it shows that for the same level of the interest rate—say i_0 in Figure 2-19a—there is a correspondingly higher amount of investment (I_1, rather than I_0, in Figure 2-19a).

We can, alternatively, depict the investment function in the (x,I)-plane, where the interest rate enters implicitly (i.e., parametrically), since no axis is reserved for this variable. Thus, in Figure 2-20b I is upward sloping with respect to x, with an infinity of such curves, one for each assumed level of the interest rate. When the interest rate is lower, say $i_1 < i_0$, the I curve *shifts upward,* illustrating the property that for the same x, say x_0, investment *rises,* to I_1, when the interest rate falls, to i_0. Thus, in the (x,I)-plane, there is an infinity of investment curves, one for each assumed interest rate. Moreover, the lower the interest rate, the higher, and farther to the left, the investment curve, as depicted in Figure 2-20b, will be.

We have, so far, considered determinants of investment, namely, i and x, which are themselves market determined. There is, however, another important factor that influences investment, and this usually lurks in the background as a nonmarket "parameter." This factor is the *risk premium,* which the firms must subtract from their prospective profit, or the lenders must add to the cost of borrowing. Whichever procedure is followed, the end result is, qualitatively, the same: *An increase in the risk premium, denoted as σ, will lower the amount of investment undertaken by firms.*

Michael Kalecki was the first to derive, in 1937, a firm's investment demand.[4] For that derivation he relied on the *principle of increasing risk:* The risk premium increases as the size of the firm increases via investment. The original Kalecki contribution, as well as its modern extensions, will be examined in Chapter 12. For the

[4] Michael Kalecki, "The Principle of Increasing Risk," *Economica,* November 1937, pp. 440–47.

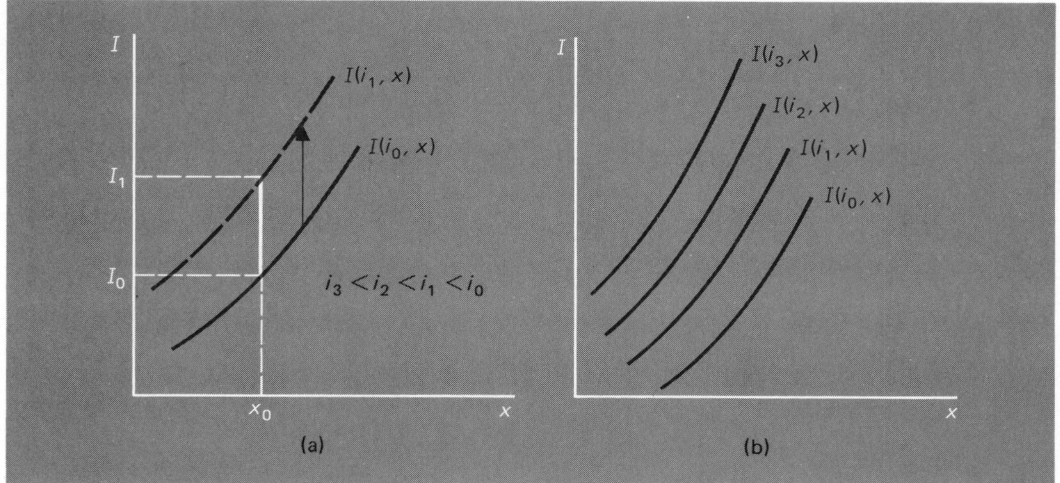

FIGURE 2-20

present analysis, it suffices to summarize the above heuristic discussion in the following abbreviated form: Investment demand, I/K, depends on the variables i and x, and the "parameter" σ:

$$\frac{I}{K} = I(i,x;\sigma) \tag{15}$$

where

$$\frac{\Delta I}{\Delta i} < 0, \frac{\Delta I}{\Delta x} > 0$$

and

$$\frac{\Delta I}{\Delta \sigma} < 0$$

The additional symbol, $\Delta I/\Delta\sigma < 0$, proposes that for the same interest rate and the same employment (and thus the same profit rate), an increase (decrease) in the risk estimate will lower (raise) investment demand. It is interesting to recall that Keynes attributed a rise (fall) in investment demand, while the interest rate and employment remains the same, to raised (lowered) "animal spirits" of entrepreneurs.[5] It is clear that, here, higher (lower) animal spirits are produced by lower (higher) risk estimates. Graphically, an increase in the risk estimate, from σ_0 to σ_1, is illustrated by an inward shift of *all* the investment curves in the (i,I)-plane, as in Figure 2-21,

[5] J. M. Keynes, *The General Theory of Employment, Interest and Money* (New York: Harcourt, Brace & Co., 1936).

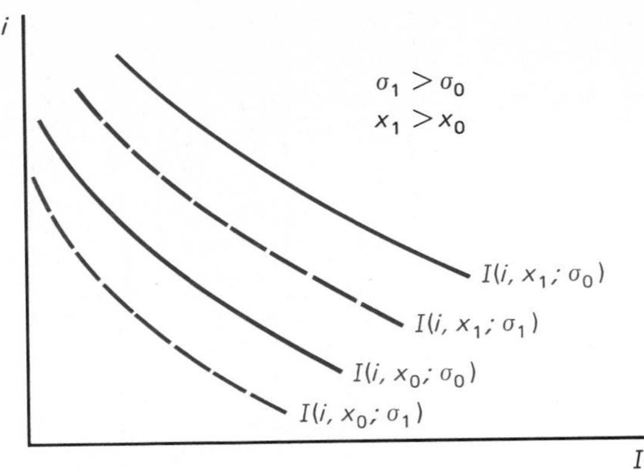

FIGURE 2-21

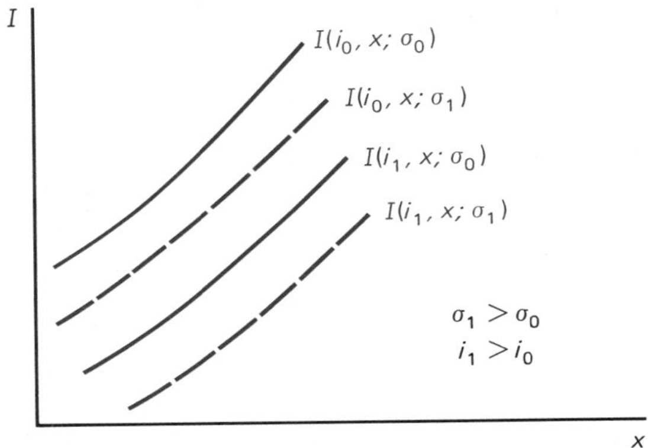

FIGURE 2-22

and by a rightward shift of all the investment curves in the *(x,I)*-plane, as in Figure 2-22.

THE LOANS MARKET AND FULL SHORT-RUN EQUILIBRIUM

In the preceding pages we introduced borrowing and lending, an assumption under which investment is *not* identically equal to savings; now one may invest more or less than one saves, which is, after all, the purpose of intertemporal exchange (borrowing and lending). Furthermore, the agent who is a saver is generally not the same as the investor. We have already assumed that the average household is a net lender, and that the average firm is a net borrower. Since the jth saver has the option of adding to his capital stock, that is, investing or lending, it is the case that

$$S^j \equiv I^j + \text{Lending}^j$$

where "lending" can be either positive or negative (i.e., borrowing).

For the individual, investment is no longer identically equal to savings, and thus, for the economy as a whole, investment is not identically equal to savings. And yet we need an equality between savings and investment for the entire economy, otherwise the market for goods and services will not be cleared. One may be tempted to argue that since the sum of lending, over all individuals, j, is zero (since some components are positive and some negative), on balance they cancel out, making I truly equal to S. However, this argument is correct only in the *ex post* sense, since there is no reason why planned net lending would be zero and the intentions of the savers to save would be identical with the decisions of the firms to invest. Instead we have to rely on some additional element to bring about the eqúality, $S/K = I/K$. This must be market forces. Thus the only element left to identify is the relevant market, and the "price" that this market determines.

We shall assume that firms finance investment, I, by borrowing, while households lend out their savings, S. Thus there is a market for loans in which the component on the demand side is investment, I, and that on the supply side is savings, S. It follows, then, that the difference, $I - S$, represents net borrowing for the entire economy.

Next we shall make the realistic assumption that the interest rate is the variable determined in the loans market, which means that the interest rate will rise or fall depending on whether the demand for loans is greater than or less than the supply, respectively. And the interest rate will remain stationary only when the demand for loans is equal to the supply. We can demonstrate this graphically in Figure 2-23, where both investment and savings depend on the interest rate. Let us assume that the proper conditions exist for savings to be positively related to the interest rate. At the rate of interest equal to i_*, investment, I, is equal to savings, S. If i is greater than i_*, say i_0, investment is less than savings, that is, the demand for loans is less than the supply. Therefore, if $i = i_0$, there is a tendency for i to fall. Similarly, if $i = i_1 < i_*$, investment is greater than savings, implying that there is excess demand for loans, which bids the interest rate upward.

FIGURE 2-23

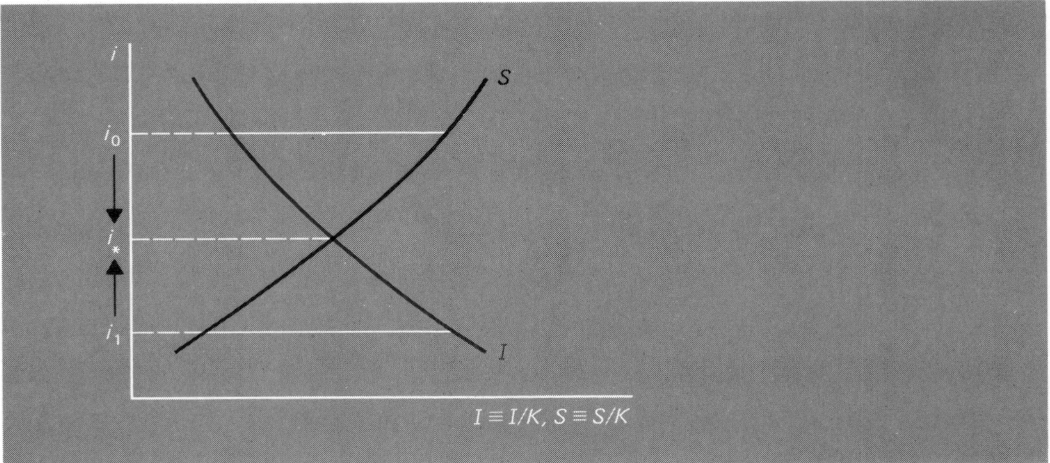

Now, assuming that savings is a *decreasing* function of the interest rate, are there forces in the market that will always force the interest rate toward equilibrium? In Figure 2-24a, assume that the interest rate is at $i_0 > i_*$. At this interest rate, investment, I_0, is less than savings, S_0, creating an excess supply of loans and forcing the interest rate downward toward i_*. On the other hand, if the interest rate is below i_*, at i_1, there is excess demand for loans, which will push the interest rate back to i_*. Equilibrium will be achieved in the case illustrated in Figure 2-24a. However, in the case of Figure 2-24b, there are no forces to bring about loans market clearance; when $i = i_0 > i_*$, $I_0 > S_0$. Thus, for $i = i_0$, the excess demand for loans will move the interest rate upward, away from equilibrium. Similarly, when $i = i_1 < i_*$, there is excess supply of loans ($S_1 > I_1$), which will lower the interest rate. Hence equilibrium point A cannot be achieved.

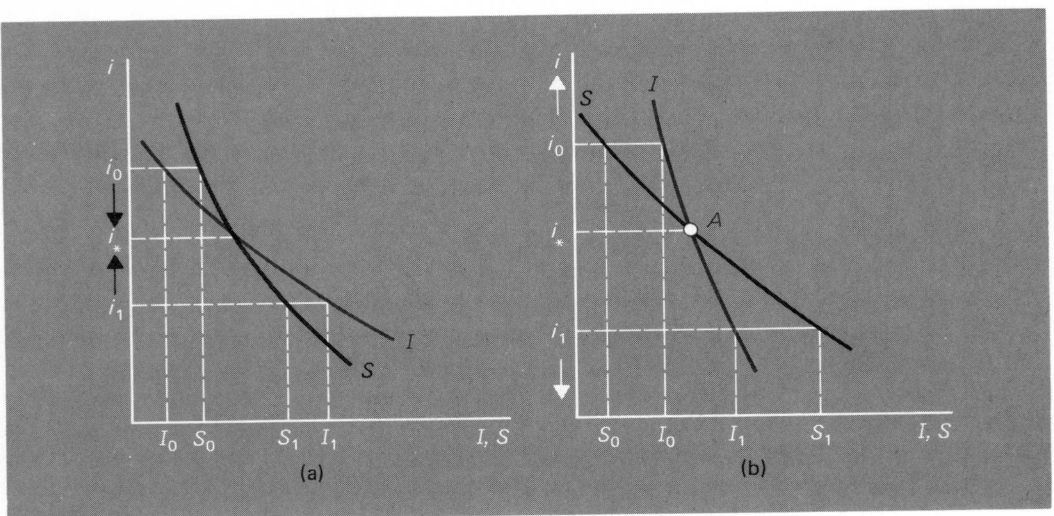

FIGURE 2-24

Since we are interested in guaranteeing the existence of market forces that act to clear the loans market, it is obvious that we want to exclude the case of Figure 2-24b. The only difference between Figures 2-24a and 2-24b is with respect to the slope of the investment curve vis-à-vis the slope of the savings curve. In Figure 2-24a the investment curve is flatter than the savings curve, while the opposite holds for Figure 2-24b. The lesson we can draw from a comparison of these two cases is the following: *When savings is a decreasing function of the interest rate, the loans market is stable if a rise in the interest rate decreases investment by more than it decreases savings.*

We can express this requirement, symbolically, by the condition that

$$\frac{\Delta I}{\Delta i} < \frac{\Delta S}{\Delta i} \tag{16}$$

(If the reader still has doubts, these should disappear as he or she recognizes that the independent variable, i, is on the vertical axis.)

It is clear that this stability condition is satisfied if savings is an increasing function of the interest rate, that is, if $\Delta S/\Delta i > 0$. Since there is no *a priori* reason why savings should be only an increasing function of the interest rate, we shall *not* make this assumption. Thus, by making the weaker assumption, $\Delta I/\Delta i < \Delta S/\Delta i$, our analysis is more general; it can be applied to more cases. Given this assumption, it is guaranteed that the market for loans will be cleared in every period of time.

We have emphasized that the loans market must be stable in order to talk about clearance of the (loans) market, or about the determination of the interest rate. We shall now demonstrate that stability of this market is needed for an additional reason, namely, for deriving comparative statics results. More specifically, the investment and savings schedules can be shifted, as a result of policy, by changing an underlying parameter. In this vein, let us assume that the Kalecki-type risk premium is lowered for each level of investment, which might account for the increased "animal spirits" of the entrepreneurs, often mentioned by Keynes. Under these circumstances, we know from our earlier discussion that the investment schedule I will shift to the right. The question arises about the level of the interest rate at the new market-clearing position, Will it rise or fall?

We can see from Figure 2-25a that as long as savings is an increasing function of the interest rate, the outward shift of the investment schedule will raise the interest rate. But what can we say when there is a negative relation between savings and the interest rate? In Figure 2-25b the rightward shift of the investment schedule *raises* the interest rate (as in the case of Figure 2-25a), whereas in Figure 2-25c this shift *lowers* it. Shall we say, then, that when savings is a decreasing function of the interest rate, an increase in the investment schedule may either increase or decrease the interest rate? The answer is no, since the case in Figure 2-25c can never materialize; the situation is unstable. Thus the stability of the loans market permits us to exclude the case of Figure 2-25c and, therefore, to derive this result: *An increase in the propensity to invest will increase the interest rate, a situation that is independent of either a positive or a negative relation between savings and the interest rate.* This use of stability

FIGURE 2-25

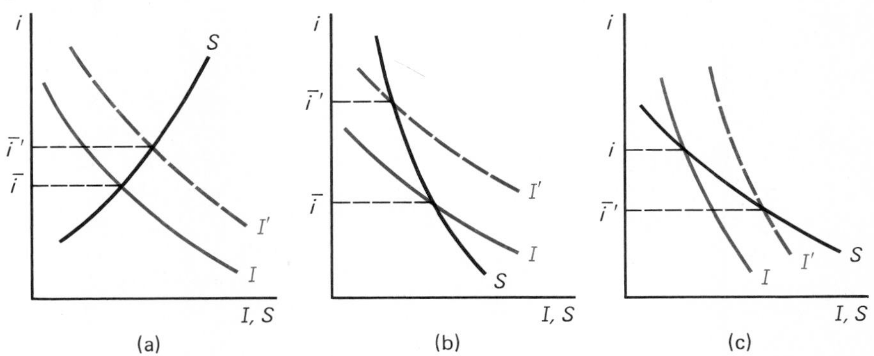

properties to derive determinate comparative statics results is called the (Samuelson's) *correspondence principle.*

In the literature before 1936, this comparative statics result commanded particular attention; it was interpreted to mean that the rate of interest could be safely relied upon to always clear the loans market and, therefore, also to clear the *goods market.* But this was not all. In the example above, the investment schedule shifted outward. Let us now suppose that this occurred because the government undertook investment expenditures, for example, in public works. Prior to 1936, economists in general would have said that this would not affect aggregate demand for goods and services or disturb full employment of labor because, according to the conventional wisdom of the time, the increase in investment would increase the interest rate, which, in turn, would lower *private* investment demand and probably lower (private) consumption (i.e., increase savings). Even if it increased consumption, the difference between private investment and private savings, $I - S$, would fall—this is the economic meaning of the stability condition $\Delta I/\Delta i < \Delta S/\Delta i$. At the new interest rate, there would be a fall in aggregate private demand, *precisely equal* to the government investment demand. In their terminology, government expenditure would "crowd out" private expenditure. Since total demand remains the same, there would be no net effect on the market for goods and services. And since the market for goods and services could originally support full employment of labor, it follows that it would continue to do so.

The phenomenon of crowding out can be clearly shown by using Figure 2-26 where I_p represents private investment and I_G government investment, assumed fixed, and indicated by the horizontal distance between the I_p and I curves. The initial equilibrium occurs at point (1) where all investment is private. The increase in the demand for loans to finance government investment creates excess demand for loans. Thus the interest rate rises to i_1 to clear the loans market with an increase in both savings and *total* investment equal to *CD.* However, because of the increase

FIGURE 2-26

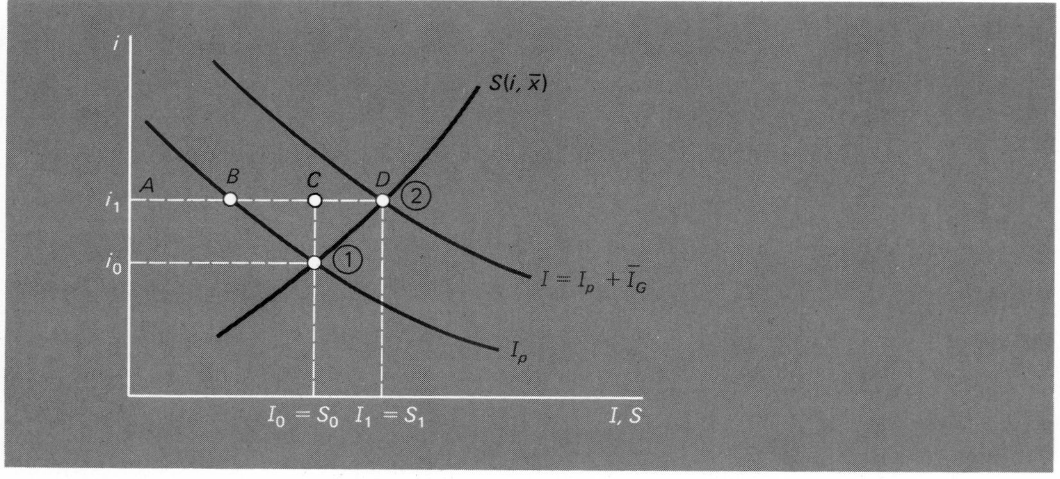

in the interest rate, *private* investment *decreases* by BC. Furthermore, with output fixed at the full-employment level, consumption decreases by the exact amount savings increases, namely CD. Thus the *total* decrease in *private* demand for goods and services is given by the distance $BD = BC + CD$, which is exactly equal to the increase in government investment demand. Hence, with an increase in government demand for loans to finance government investment, the interest rate rises to clear the loans market and, in so doing, reallocates the full-employment supply of output between private demand (consumption plus private investment) and government demand. And at the new equilibrium interest rate, government demand has "crowded out" private demand.[6] The reader should note the crucial role that the assumption of fixed output—at the full-employment level—plays in the above argument.[7]

So far in our analysis of the loans market and of the determination of the interest rate, we have ignored a crucial fact: In addition to the interest rate, both investment and savings are functions of employment per unit of capital, x. Thus there is an infinity of savings curves, one for each assumed x, as Figure 2-27a depicts. Similarly, it is shown in Figure 2-27b that there is an infinity of investment curves, one for each x. Figures 2-27a and 2-27b have been drawn under the assumption that $x_2 > \bar{x} > x_1 > x_0$.

Now suppose that we are examining a particular period of time. Since there are an infinite number of investment and savings curves, which *one* pair shall we use to examine the loans market and, therefore, to determine the interest rate? This is the point at which the assumption of perfect real-wage flexibility, which we intro-

FIGURE 2-27

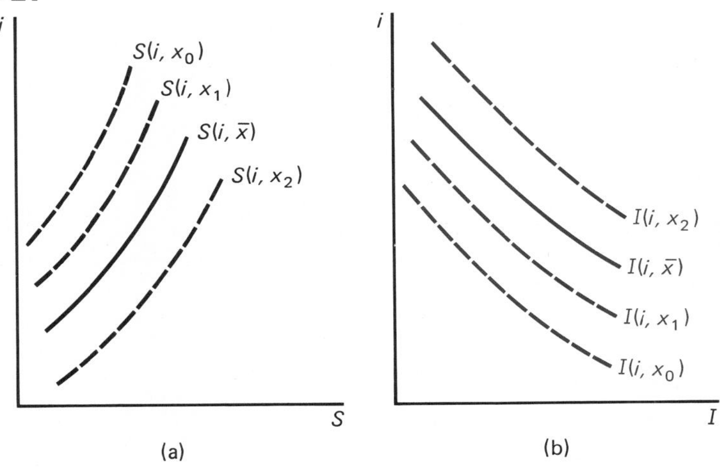

[6] In Figure 2-26 we assumed that savings is an increasing function of the interest rate. It is left to the reader to show that the results hold even when savings is a decreasing function of the interest rate.

[7] Earlier we noted the revival of neoclassical beliefs. It should not surprise us, therefore, when we see that the "crowding out" plays a prominent role in the debate between "monetarists" and "neo-Keynesians."

duced in Section I, will be instrumental; the instantaneous clearance of the (homogeneous) labor market, through an appropriate movement of the real wage, will produce the employment/capital ratio, x, that will prevail in the period considered.

This is shown in Figure 2-28 where, for simplicity, the supply curve of labor (per unit of capital) is assumed to be independent of the real wage. Thus the real-wage rate $\bar{w}$ gives the (full) employment (per unit of capital) level $\bar{x}$. And it is this $\bar{x}$ that will be used to identify the relevant pair of I and S curves. From Figure 2-27a we find the relevant savings curve, namely, $S(i,\bar{x})$, and from Figure 2-27b we find $I(i,\bar{x})$. These are the curves that are depicted in a single graph in Figure 2-29.

In Figure 2-29 the market rate of interest is instantaneously determined at the level $\bar{i}$, which clears the *loans market.* In other words, at the rate of interest $\bar{i}$, investment is equal to savings, that is, $I - S = 0$. But an excess of investment over savings, $I - S$, is precisely the excess demand for goods and services. Hence, when the interest rate is at the level $\bar{i}$, the *goods and services market* is also cleared. Furthermore, in the short run, the capital stock is fixed at $\bar{K}$. With employment per unit of capital equal to $\bar{x}$, the economy's output is equal to $\bar{Y}$, as in Figure 2-30. The clearance of the market for goods and services implies that this quantity is exactly demanded and sold for consumption and investment purposes, $C + I = \bar{Y}$. Of course, I is found in Figure 2-29 where $\bar{I} = \bar{S}$, from which it follows that we can find C and S. On the other hand, the wage and profit rates, w and r, are shown in Figure 2-28. These can also be found in our basic workhorse graph in Figure 2-31.

FIGURE 2-28

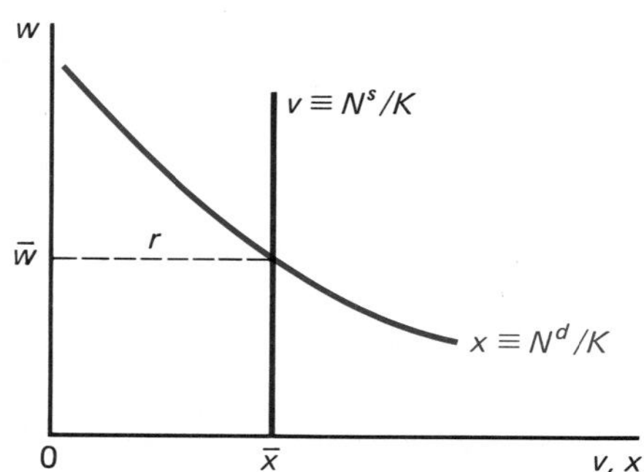

FIGURE 2-29

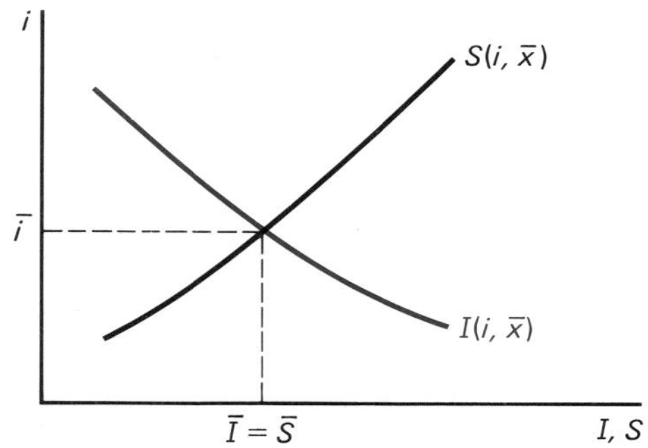

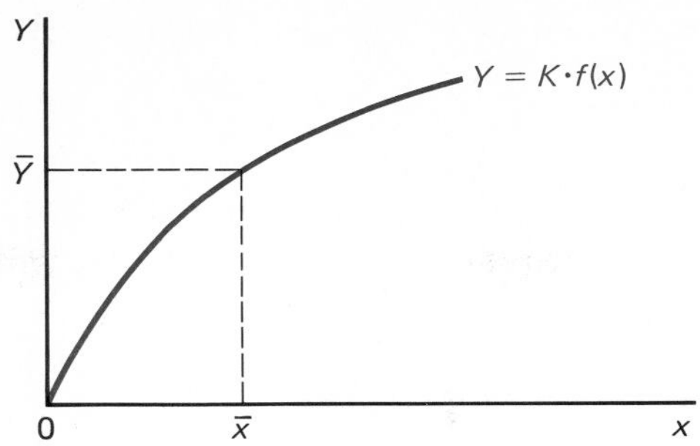

FIGURE 2-30

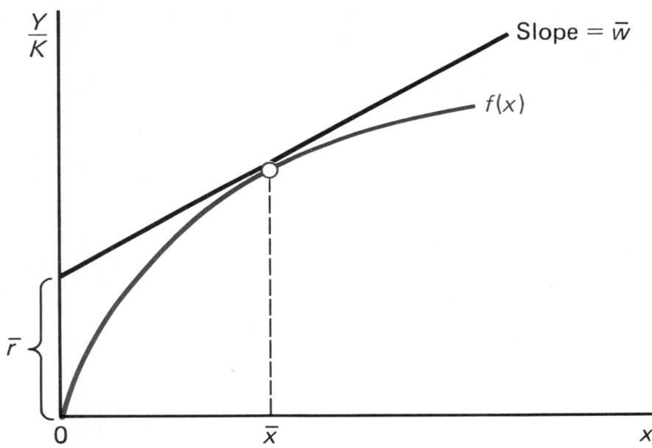

FIGURE 2-31

It is clear from the preceding analysis that under the assumptions of our model, in the short run, all markets—those for labor, loans, and goods and services—are cleared instantaneously. It follows that, under our assumptions, there is room for neither unemployment nor insufficiency of (nor excess demand for) goods and services. Moreover, we have been able to reproduce most magnitudes of the national product and national income accounts, such as GNP, consumption, savings, investment, the wage rate and total wages, and the profit rate and total profits, as well as the rate of interest. Thus, even though we relaxed one assumption by introducing borrowing and lending, the basic results remain identical with those of the simplest model in Section I.

QUESTIONS

1. Suppose that the "animal spirits" of the entrepreneurs rise:
   a. Explain what this means.
   b. Show what this implies for the investment curve.
   c. Show the ultimate effect on the interest rate.

d. Does your answer to part *c* change if the interest rate influences savings negatively? Why, or why not?

2. Suppose that the average household is endowed with 1,000 bushels of today's corn (per period) and zero bushels of tomorrow's corn.

a. If the preferences between present and future corn are homothetic and of the form

$$\frac{C_2}{C_1} = \frac{1}{4} \cdot (1 + i)$$

find the exact form of the savings curve, both with respect to current income and with respect to the interest rate. What are the marginal propensity to consume and average propensity to consume today's corn?

b. If tastes change and are now represented by

$$\frac{C_2}{C_1} = \frac{1}{3} \cdot (1 + i)$$

what will happen to the marginal propensity to consume, the average propensity to consume, and the interest rate?

3. In a barter economy with borrowing and lending, instantaneous movement of the interest rate implies continuous clearance of the market for goods and services. Why? If we also assume that wages are perfectly flexible, what can we conclude about unemployed laborers in this economy?

4. Comment on the following:

a. "An increase in the interest rate increases consumption."

b. "An increase in the real wage decreases the supply of labor."

c. "An increase in the price of oil increases the consumption of oil in Texas."

d. What do all the above statements have in common? Explain.

5. How is the requirement that "Savings = Investment" an example of the law of supply and demand?

6. Comment on the statement: "The most realistic model is always the best model."

7. Explain the relationship between Say's Law and the presence or absence of borrowing/lending in the model.

8. Under the assumptions of Chapter 2, if savings is a decreasing function of the interest rate, then a rise in the interest rate must lower investment by more than it lowers savings. What characteristic of the world allows us to make this inference?

9. If output is fixed at the full-employment level, show the effect of an increase in government investment demand when savings is a decreasing function of the interest rate.

10. Compare the results of the model involving borrowing and lending with the results of the model involving no borrowing or lending.

11. Advocates of "supply-side" economics recommend a reduction of tax rates on interest so that the resultant increase in the "after tax" interest rate may stimulate savings and, hence, growth. Construct an arithmetical example which supports this view and another which rejects it.

REFERENCES

(See Also the References for Chapters 11 and 12)

FISHER, IRVING, *Theory of Interest.* New York: Macmillan, 1930.

FRIEDMAN, MILTON, "The Role of Monetary Policy," *American Economic Review,* March 1968, pp. 1–17.

HICKS, J. R., *Theory of Wages.* London: Macmillan, 1932.

MALINVAUD, E., *Lectures on Microeconomic Theory,* Amsterdam: North-Holland Press, Chap. 10.

ROSE, HUGH, "Real and Monetary Factors in the Business Cycle," *Journal of Money, Credit and Banking,* May 1969, pp. 138–52.

———, "Unemployment in a Theory of Growth," *International Economic Review,* September 1966.

SOLOW, ROBERT M., "A Contribution to the Theory of Economic Growth," *Quarterly Journal of Economics,* February 1956, pp. 65–94.

———, "On Theories of Unemployment," *American Economic Review,* March 1980, pp. 1–11.

chapter three
bypass

The reader who wants only a brief overview of Chapter 3 should read the following.

To introduce money and determine the price level, that is, the price of goods and services, we shall apply the quantity theory of money, which stipulates that the value of money, $1/p$, which is the inverse of the price level, is determined by the supply of and demand for money. There are two formulations of the quantity theory: one, introduced by Irving Fisher, emphasizes *flows;* the other, introduced by the Cambridge economists, Marshall, Pigou, and Keynes, emphasizes *stocks.*

According to the flow formulation, the price level, p, is at whatever level is necessary for this equation, called the Fisher equation, to hold:

$$MV = pY \tag{1}$$

M is the stock of nominal money balances and V is the velocity of money, or the average number of times that money circulates per period. The left-hand side (LHS) of (1) is the flow supply of money (number of dollars per period) and the right-hand side (RHS) is the flow demand (number of dollars per period). Thus, according to (1), the price level is determined at the level that makes the demand for money equal to its supply. Furthermore, it is stipulated that the price level *rises* when there is excess flow supply and it falls when there is excess demand for money; the price level remains unchanged only when there is zero excess demand or excess supply of money. Or, in schematic form:

$$MV > pY \rightarrow \Delta p > 0$$

$$MV < pY \rightarrow \Delta p < 0$$

$$MV = pY \rightarrow \Delta p = 0$$

Similar statements can be made by using equation (2), or the Cambridge equation, where l is the inverse of velocity and denotes the proportion of income held in the form of money:

$$M = lpY \tag{2}$$

According to the Cambridge equation, the price level should be at the level that makes the stock demand for money, lpY (number of dollars), equal to the stock supply, M (number of dollars). A frequent variant of the Cambridge equation is (2a), which states that the supply of real balances (the LHS) is equal to the demand for real balances (the RHS of (2a)). The supply of *real balances* is the number of units of goods (and services) that the nominal money stock, *M,* can buy; it is found by dividing nominal money balances by the price level:

$$\frac{M}{P} = lY \tag{2a}$$

$$\frac{M}{P} = \text{Real balances} = \frac{\text{Nominal balances}}{\text{Price level}}$$

$$= \frac{\$}{\$/\text{Units of goods}} = \text{Units of goods}$$

In using (2a), both Keynes and Friedman emphasize that people demand real balances, *lY,* while the monetary authorities supply *nominal* balances, *M;* therefore the price level is the variable which changes to make the supply of real balances, *M/p,* equal to the demand. Moreover, the price level rises when there is excess supply of real balances, it falls when there is excess demand, and it remains unchanged when there is zero excess demand for or excess supply of real balances:

$$\frac{M}{p} - lY > 0 \rightarrow \Delta p > 0$$

$$\frac{M}{p} - lY < 0 \rightarrow \Delta p < 0$$

$$\frac{M}{p} - lY = 0 \rightarrow \Delta p = 0$$

Modern monetary economists have expended substantial effort in explaining the monetary mechanism, that is, *why* and *how* an excess supply of money materializes as excess demand for goods and services, which, in turn, causes prices to rise. To merely dismiss this process as a case of "too much money chasing too few goods" is either meaningless or tautological.

One way of transforming an excess supply of money into an excess demand for goods and services is to assume that when individuals hold more money than they desire, they eliminate this excess supply of money by buying goods and services.

This we call Schema I:

$$\text{Schema I: } \frac{M}{p} - lY > 0 \rightarrow \text{EDG} > 0 \rightarrow \Delta p > 0$$

On the other hand, a more realistic sequence of events is outlined in Schema II:

$$\text{Schema II: } \frac{M}{p} - lY > 0 \rightarrow S_L \uparrow \rightarrow i \downarrow \rightarrow \text{EDG} > 0 \rightarrow \Delta p > 0$$

This schema states that when individuals find themselves with more money than they need, they lend part or all of this excess money supply, thereby increasing the supply of loans, S_L; this, in turn, lowers the interest rate, which increases investment and consumption demand, $C + I$, thereby causing excess demand for goods and services, EDG > 0, which finally increases their prices.

When investigating empirically the relation between changes in the money supply and changes in prices, modern quantity theorists dispense with the intermediate steps of Schema II, thereby giving the impression that they adopt Schema I. However, we find that this does not have to be so: When modern quantity theorists examine the determination of interest rates and of prices, they explicitly adopt Schema II, a theme that will be taken up in Chapter 4.

3 Money and Prices: the quantity theory from Marshall and Fisher to Keynes and Friedman

In this chapter we introduce money into the system and examine the relation between the quantity of money and the level of economic activity, especially the prices of goods and services. First we introduce, in Section I, the general statement of the quantity theory of money, while in the next two sections, II and III, we examine two widely used formulations—the flow formulation and the stock formulation—of the quantity theory of money. Either of these versions of the quantity theory produces this result: Excess supply of money causes prices to rise and excess demand for money causes them to fall. Moreover, with the output assumed fixed at its full-employment level, and with the velocity of money assumed fixed by the payments habits of society, the price level rises (falls) if, and only if, the money supply is increased (decreased). In Section IV we sketch the proof of the dependence of velocity on the payments habits of society.

The bulk of this chapter—and its essence—is Section V, which is devoted to the monetary mechanism, namely, how an excess supply of money materializes as excess demand for goods and services, thereby causing a rise in their prices. Understanding the monetary mechanism is crucial to understanding the role of money in formulating (anti-inflationary) economic policy. It is not surprising, therefore, that this issue, which we shall explore, is at the center of current controversy.

I. MONEY AND ITS VALUE

Until now we have conducted our analysis under the assumption of barter, but we now drop this assumption by introducing money into our system. A major task of our analysis will be to examine whether, and under what conditions, our earlier results are still valid. Of course, this is not all, since money has peculiarities and problems of its own which we must also examine.

Initially we shall define *money* as anything that is generally acceptable as a means of payment. Of course, this definition implies that money is also acceptable as a store of value. These two properties—medium of exchange and store of value—are all that we need for the time being. Although it is not necessary for our analysis, we can be more concrete and say that money consists of notes, coins, and demand deposits in banks and that, in general, money is the indebtedness of some entity or entities. For example, coins and notes are the indebtedness of the federal government, whereas demand deposits are the indebtedness of banks. But we shall temporarily postpone our examination of these implications of alternative definitions of money. Also, we shall postpone examining the issue of how money can be increased or decreased. For now, it is enough to assume that there is something called money and that it can be changed at will by the monetary authority (government)—by merely pressing a button, as it were.

The introduction of money necessitates (and permits) stating prices in dollar terms. From now on, p will denote the money price of one unit of GNP, that is, p is the number of dollars per unit of GNP (corn). Furthermore, it will be beneficial if the reader identifies p with the Consumer Price Index. And since workers will be paid W dollars per unit of labor, W/p represents the real wage, that is, units of GNP per unit of labor. When we need, therefore, to refer to the real wage, w, we shall use W/p. It is immediately obvious that the moment we introduce money into the system, we must cope with the determination of and changes in prices, an issue that was nonexistent in the barter economy. Thus, with inflation as a characteristic of a monetary but *not* of a barter economy, one might advocate a return to the "good old days" of barter to eliminate inflation. While this would definitely cure inflation, it would be an extreme and costly remedy.

When p is the money price of GNP, it follows that its inverse, $1/p$, is the *relative price* of money, or the number of units of GNP that one unit of money (e.g., one dollar) can buy. This relative price is usually called the *value of money.* The determination of the value of money was nonexistent in our earlier analysis of the barter model. But now we must confront this issue and also examine whether our earlier results remain valid in a monetary economy.

Historically, the determination of the value of money was examined separately from the determination of the values of all the other variables, such as interest rate, rate of profit, real wage, and savings. According to this view, our earlier analysis should remain intact, even if we introduce money into the system. What we need, then, is a theory to *separately* determine the value of money. In the jargon of the time, the model of the economy can be dichotomized. In this standard approach, "Volume I" dealt with the determination of the *real* variables. Moreover, these variables can neither be influenced by money nor can they, in turn, influence the value

of money, which is relegated to "Volume II" and determined by the *quantity* of money. However, the quantity of money cannot influence any real variable.

The determination of the value of money by the quantity of money is referred to, somewhat inaccurately, as the *quantity theory of money.* The general version of this theory is merely an application of the *law of supply and demand* for money to the determination of the value of money:

> The value of money, like the value of any other good, is determined by supply and demand. When there is an excess demand for money, its value, $1/p$, rises, and when there is an excess supply of money, its value falls. Only when supply equals demand will the value of money remain unchanged.

We shall see how this original statement of supply and demand has been modified to emphasize the *quantity* of money as the *sole* determinant of the value of money.

There are two versions of the quantity theory. Each variant emphasizes a different attribute of money: The *flow* formulation emphasizes the medium-of-exchange property, whereas the *stock* formulation emphasizes the store-of-value property of money. We shall begin with the former.

II. FLOW FORMULATION OF QUANTITY THEORY—IRVING FISHER

The father of the flow formulation of quantity theory is the great American economist, Irving Fisher,[1] who emphasized the medium-of-exchange property of money, which is called a *flow* formulation, since the supply of and demand for money are measured in flows, the dollars *per period.* Toward this end, we shall define the flow demand for money as the extent to which people are *willing* to *acquire* money. We emphasize the word *willing* to show intentions. On the other hand, our emphasis on the word *acquire* connotes a movement, a crucial property of flows.

According to the predominant version of the flow formulation, the only way to acquire money is by selling something. This version focuses on goods and services, in particular, the period's output, Y. In dollar terms, the receipts are pY dollars per period. Note that $p = \$/\text{Output}$ and $Y = \text{Output/Period}$. Therefore

$$pY = \frac{\$}{\text{Output}} \cdot \frac{\text{Output}}{\text{Period}} = \frac{\$}{\text{Period}}$$

that is, pY has the dimension of a *flow.*

Formally, the *flow supply of money* is defined as the extent to which people are *willing* to *get rid of* money. The words *get rid of* again are meant to connote movements. If M denotes the quantity of money (i.e., the number of dollars), this

[1] Irving Fisher, *The Purchasing Power of Money* (New York: Macmillan, 1911).

cannot be the *flow supply of money* because M has the dimension of a stock. We need, therefore, something to transform stocks into flows. To do this, introduce an *operator* in the symbol V, whose dimension should be a number per period (i.e., so many times per period). It would follow, then, that MV has the dimension of a flow:

$$MV = \$ \cdot \frac{\text{Number}}{\text{Period}} = \frac{\$}{\text{Period}}$$

and MV depicts the flow supply of money. In the literature, V is called the *velocity* of money. A better name might have been the *frequency* of money, since V is defined as the number of times, on the average, that people want money to circulate—it is the average speed with which money circulates, hence the term *velocity.*

With the above definition of V at hand, we see that MV is the number of dollars per period that people want to get rid of—by buying goods and services. We are now ready to apply the law of supply and demand by comparing MV and pY.

$$\text{If } MV > pY, \tag{a}$$

that is, if the (flow) supply of money is greater than the demand, then $(1/p)$, the value of money, decreases. Of course, a decrease in the value of money can come about only through an increase in the price level, p. Note that $MV > pY$ means that the value of payments, MV, that people wish to make in order to purchase final output is greater than the value of final output. This is why the price of final output, p, rises.

$$\text{If } MV < pY, \tag{b}$$

that is, if the value of payments people wish to make is less than the value of output, the price level, p, falls, thereby increasing the value of money, $1/p$. And, finally,

$$\text{if } MV = pY, \tag{c}$$

the equality between supply and demand for money implies equality between supply and demand for output and thus no change in price, p, and the value of money, $1/p$.

It is clear that this theory stipulates that the excess supply of money materializes as excess demand for goods and services, while the excess demand for money surfaces as excess supply of goods and services. We are now ready to see how an increase, say, in the nominal quantity of money, M, will result in an increase in the price level, p. Let us suppose that this increase in M, from M_0 to M_1, is undertaken when the economy is initially at a position like (c) above, where the flow supply of money is equal to the flow demand. At the original price level, p_0, there is now excess flow supply of money (i.e., $M_1 V > p_0 Y$). This, of course, is case (a) above and reflects itself as excess demand for goods and services. As people attempt to get rid of more money than they want to acquire, they demand more goods and services, thereby creating excess demand for them and bidding prices upward. Eventually the price level, p_1, is higher than p_0 and at the new position of rest:

$$M_1 V = p_1 Y$$

Thus the increase in the nominal quantity of money, *M,* raises the price level.

We should note that this result depends on an implicit assumption of both fixed output, *Y,* and fixed velocity, *V.* Traditionally, this analysis has been carried out under the assumption of full employment. And we know from our analysis of the barter system that given this assumption, all other real magnitudes in our system are known. What is needed, then, is knowledge about the determination of *M* and *V.* We have already specified that *M* is under the absolute control of the monetary authority (government). On the other hand, the velocity of circulation is assumed to depend only on the payments habits of society. Now, these payments habits change very little, and very slowly. For all practical purposes, then, the velocity should be treated as a fixed number; in particular, it should be assumed that there is no correlation between *M* and *V.* In a later section we present a sketch of the derivation of *V* from the payments habits of society.

In summary, we have shown that with the assumptions of full employment and constant velocity, an increase in the quantity of money will increase only the price level. Since we assumed that *V* and *Y* were fixed, it follows, furthermore, that an increase (decrease) in the price level can occur *only if* the quantity of money is increased (decreased).

III. STOCK FORMULATION OF QUANTITY THEORY—CAMBRIDGE: MARSHALL, PIGOU, KEYNES[2]

The stock formulation of quantity theory, devised by Marshall and Pigou, was explained and elaborated by the young Keynes, both in his *Tract on Monetary Reform* and in his *Treatise on Money.* Even the name "Cambridge equation" was coined by Keynes.[3] The stock formulation emphasizes the *store of value* attribute of money. Money is regarded as an asset that yields convenience and security. According to Marshall, Pigou, and Keynes (of the *Tract*), money is considered an alternative to only one other asset, physical capital. In the *Treatise,* where Keynes also restated the Cambridge approach, there are *three* assets: money, bonds, and equity claims. The demand for money is, in either case, a consequence of choice theory.

---

[2] Alfred Marshall, *Money, Credit and Commerce* (London: Macmillan, 1923); A. C. Pigou, "The Value of Money," *Quarterly Journal of Economics,* November 1917, pp. 38–65; and J. M. Keynes, *A Tract on Monetary Reform* (London: Macmillan, 1923).

[3] See J. M. Keynes, *A Treatise on Money* (London: Macmillan, 1930), p. 205, of *The Collected Writings of J. M. Keynes,* Vol. V, *The Pure Theory of Money* (all references to the *Treatise* are from this last publication).

The *stock* formulation is sometimes called the (real) *cash balances approach*—a reflection of the fact that the stock demand and the stock supply are termed *cash balances.* Utilizing our earlier notation, M is now the stock supply of (nominal) cash balances. However, pY must be modified to be ready for use as the demand for (nominal) cash balances. Since pY is a flow, we need an operator to transform it into a stock. Such an operator is the famous "Cambridge k," whose dimension should be a period of time so that it will yield dollars when multiplied by pY, which is dollars per period of time. Now, since we have been using the symbol k to denote the capital/labor ratio, we need another symbol. We shall, therefore, use the letter l to represent the "Cambridge k"!! And we shall define l as the average period of time that people want a dollar to rest (in one's pocket) as cash balances. It follows, then, that $l \cdot pY$ is precisely the *stock* of dollars demanded:

$$lpY = \text{Period} \times \frac{\text{Dollars}}{\text{Units of corn}} \times \frac{\text{Units of corn}}{\text{Period}} = \text{Dollars}$$

Formally, l is precisely the inverse of V (i.e., $l \equiv 1/V$). Remember that V transforms stocks into flows. Now l is V's inverse and thus performs the inverse job, namely, transforming flows into stocks. Understanding this, one can consider the operator, l, as the fraction of income society wishes to hold as cash balances. *Thus $l \cdot pY$ is the total money balances that society wishes to hold,* that is, the *stock demand* for money. On the other hand, the *stock supply* of money is what society actually holds (i.e., M).

We are now ready to compare stock demand and stock supply to determine the value of money. We can make the comparison either in real terms or in nominal terms. However, we shall start with the latter, although Cambridge's main expositor, Keynes, emphasized the former.

$$\text{When } M > l \cdot pY, \tag{a}$$

that is, when the stock supply is greater than the stock demand, people want to get rid of the unwanted balances. In their attempt to do so, they buy more goods and services and thus bid the price level, p, upward. It follows that when there is an excess supply of money, its value, $1/p$ falls. Similarly,

$$\text{when } M < l \cdot pY, \tag{b}$$

that is, when people have less money than they desire, and they attempt to increase their cash balances, they curtail expenditure on goods and services and lower their aggregate demand for them. As a result the price level, p, falls. We have just shown that an excess stock demand for money causes its value, $1/p$, to rise. And, finally,

$$\text{when } M = l \cdot pY, \tag{c}$$

that is, when people have precisely the quantity of cash balances they desire, they do not intend to dispose of or to accrue any. Thus they neither increase nor decrease their expenditure for goods and services, which implies that the price level, p, and the value of money, $1/p$, remain the same.

We can examine the determination of the value of money in terms of real balances. Dividing both sides of (a), (b), and (c) by p, we get, respectively:

$$\frac{M}{p} > l \cdot Y \tag{a'}$$

$$\frac{M}{p} < l \cdot Y \tag{b'}$$

$$\frac{M}{p} = l \cdot Y \tag{c'}$$

In the case of (a′), at the existing price level, the supply of real balances is greater than the desired demand (for real balances). In such a case, people want to get rid of the excess real balances. But, as Keynes emphasized:

> Whenever depositors as a whole take steps to diminish the amount of their real balances, their behavior can only take the form of *an increased demand* [for goods and services] *on their part at the existing level of prices,* which must result in a tendency for the price level to rise. Thus the price level is the balancing factor which brings into appropriate relation the volume of real balances which results from the collective decisions of the bankers.[4]

It should be noted that the Cambridge approach, as explained by Keynes, emphasizes that holders of money demand *real* cash balances, whereas the suppliers of money (be they the monetary authority or bankers) furnish *nominal* cash balances. As Keynes said, "This [Cambridge] method sets out from the idea that what a holder of money requires is a quantity of *real balances* which bears the appropriate relationship to the quantity of real transactions upon which he employs his balances," which is $l \cdot Y$ in our notation.[5] Keynes summarizes the whole approach in the following *proposition:*

> *The volume of cash balances depends on the decisions of the bankers and is "created" by them. The volume of real balances depends on the decisions of the depositors and is "created" by them. The price level is the resultant of the two sets of decisions and is measured by the ratio of the volume of the cash balances created to that of the real balances created.*[6]

---

[4] Keynes, *Treatise,* p. 204, italics in original.

[5] Keynes, *Treatise,* p. 199.

[6] Keynes, *Treatise,* p. 201, italics in original.

This is how the old quantity theorists believed the value of money and thus the price level were determined. It turns out to be precisely how modern quantity theorists explain the determination of the price level, as we can see when we compare Keynes's remarks with those of the most famous modern quantity theorist, Milton Friedman:

> It is important to note at the outset an essential difference between the determinants of the nominal stock of money, on the one hand, and the real stock of money, on the other. The nominal stock of money is determined in the first instance by the monetary authorities or institutions and cannot be altered by the non-bank holders of money. The real stock of money is determined in the first instance by the holders of money.[7]

In summary, we have seen that as long as the supply of money is greater than the demand—either case (a) or case (a′)—the value of money will fall. Of course, this statement does not say how this inequality has been brought about. The initial force can be either an increase in M or a decrease in either l or Y. As Keynes said, however:

> The quantity theory of money has been too often enunciated in a one-sided way, so as to make it appear that the price level depends solely on the volume of money balances created by the bankers. But the price level can be affected just as much by the decisions of the depositors to vary the amounts of real balances which they (the depositors) keep, as by the decisions of the bankers to vary the amounts of money balances which they (the bankers) create.[8]

The emphasis on the supply side (i.e., on M only) results from additional assumptions that are usually made. First, it is assumed that the economy always produces the maximum output, that is, at the full-employment level. We noted this in our earlier analysis. The labor market clearance shown in the upper panel of Figure 3-1 determines x; given this x, the maximum Y is determined from the production technology, as shown in the lower panel of Figure 3-1. Of course, implicit also is the stipulation that the interest rate be such that it equilibrates savings and investment emerging from full employment x, as shown in Figure 3-2. This guarantees that the maximum output produced, $\bar{Y}$, will be demanded, and that $\bar{x}$ will be maintained.

The second additional assumption is that the velocity of circulation, V, and thus its inverse, l, are fixed. This is determined by the payments habits of society, which are usually assumed constant. In the next section we outline a method for deriving l (and thus V) from the payments habits of society, as well as a method for showing how a change in those habits will influence l and V.

---

[7] Milton Friedman, *The Optimum Quantity of Money* (Chicago: Aldine, 1969), p. 116.

[8] Keynes, *Treatise*, p. 204.

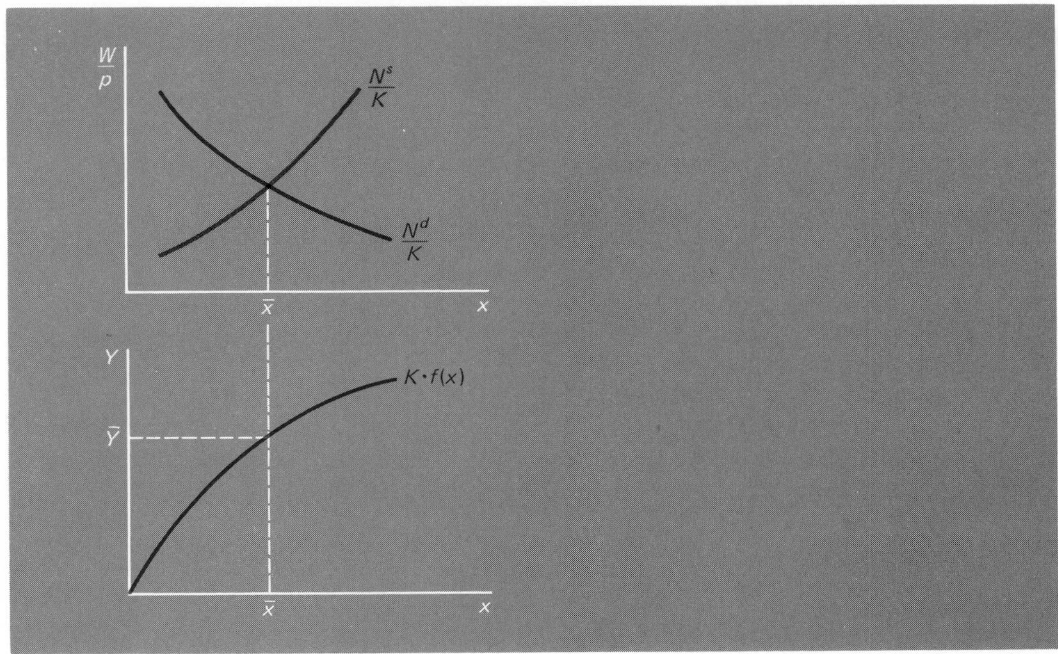

FIGURE 3-1

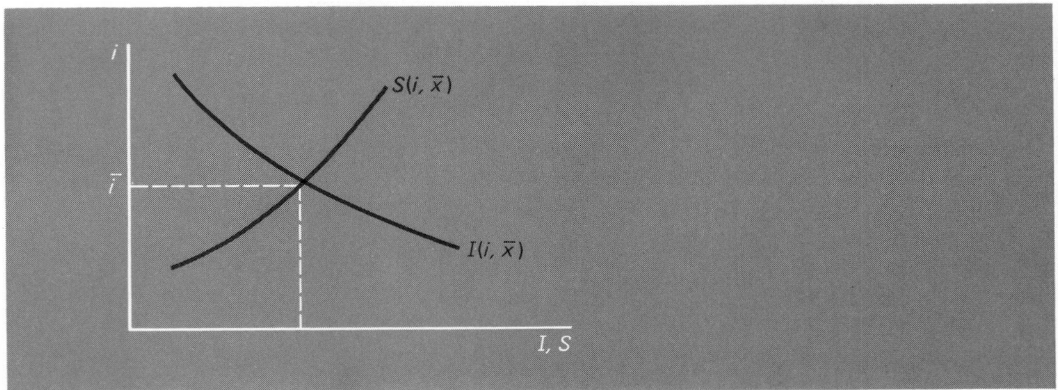

FIGURE 3-2

IV. DETERMINANTS OF VELOCITY, *V*, AND *I*

We mentioned earlier that the velocity and its inverse can be derived from the payments habits of individuals. Here we shall outline such a derivation. To begin, let us suppose that an individual is paid 300 dollars once a month and that he spends 10 dollars each day (for simplicity we shall examine only thirty-day months). In Figure 3-3

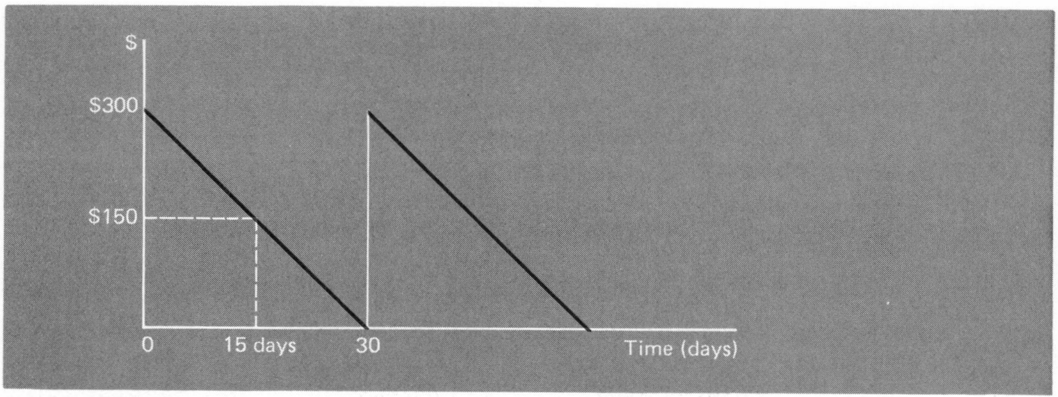

FIGURE 3-3

we represent the number of dollars that each individual holds at any moment of time.

The horizontal axis measures time and the vertical axis measures dollars. The moment the individual is paid his monthly income, at time 0, he has 300 dollars. The next day he has 290 (having spent ten dollars), the day after that he has 280, and so on, until the thirtieth of the month when he spends his 10 dollars. That is the moment he is paid again, and the process continues indefinitely.

It is obvious that, on the average, the individual holds 150 dollars, or one-half of his monthly income. Equivalently, looking at the horizontal axis now, the average dollar remains in each individual's possession for fifteen days, that is, one-half of the period, which is a month. We can say that each dollar rests for a period of one twenty-fourth of a year. This period, one twenty-fourth of a year, is exactly our l. Now, recall that l has to have the dimension of a period of time. Also, recall that sometimes l is interpreted as being the proportion of income held as money. We have just seen that this is correct: the individual wants to hold one-half of his *monthly* income, that is, one twenty-fourth of his *yearly* income (i.e., 150 dollars), as cash. Since the velocity of circulation, V, is the inverse of l, we also know that V is equal to twice per month, or twenty-four times per year.

We have seen from the above example how the payments-receipts habits determine the velocity of circulation and thus its inverse, l. Now we can show how V and l are influenced by a change in these habits. Let us suppose that a new law is enacted requiring that every person be paid once per week rather than once per month. Of course, it is assumed that each person receives the same wages as before. For simplicity, we shall assume that there are exactly four weeks in each month, and that the individual is paid seventy dollars each week, again spending ten dollars every day. This is shown in Figure 3-4, which also reproduces the earlier example.

It is clear from Figure 3-4 that the velocity of circulation is drastically increased, and that the proportion of income that is held as cash is drastically reduced. Now each dollar rests for only 3½ days, that is, ½ week, or $\frac{1}{104}$ of a year. Another way of interpreting this is to say that the individual wants to hold only $\frac{1}{104}$ of his

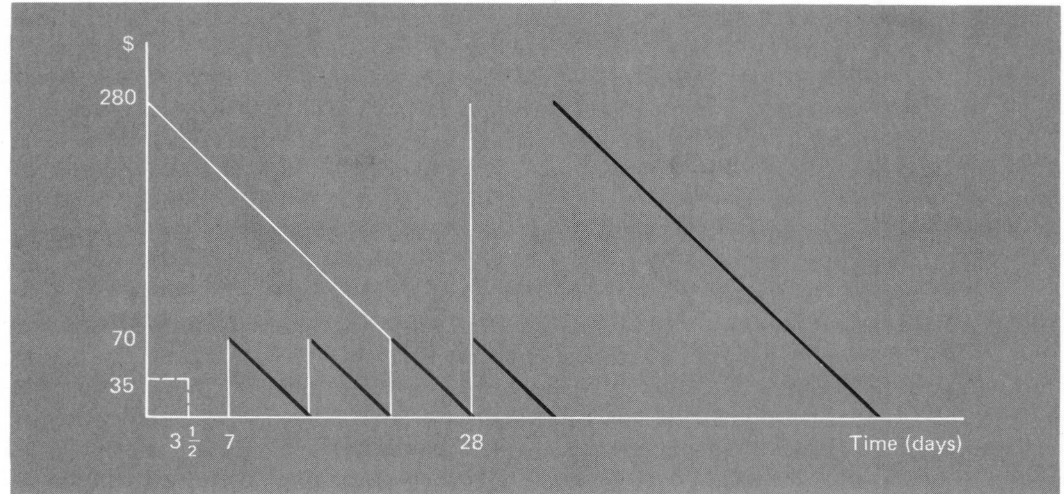

FIGURE 3-4

yearly income as cash, as compared with the $\frac{1}{24}$ of his income that he held earlier. Thus the more frequent payment of workers has diminished society's demand for money, $l \cdot pY$, by decreasing l (i.e., increasing V). Of course, this decrease in l may initiate the excess supply of real balances examined in case (a).

The neoclassical theorists assumed that the payments habits of society change only in the long run. Therefore they felt justified in assuming l and V as fixed. At any rate, they thought that there was no correlation between M and l (or V); l could change, as in our earlier example, but not because of a change in M. In this sense they considered l and V fixed.

V. THE MONETARY MECHANISM

In this section we want to examine critically, and in greater detail, the mechanism by which an excess supply of real balances drives the price level upward, while an excess demand brings it down. Despite the detailed description given in Sections I and II, the quantity theory results depend ultimately on one *crucial assumption:* that people reduce their excess supply of money by buying goods and services and, similarly, that they add to their real balances (in case they experience excess demand for them) by curtailing expenditures on goods and services. In the words of Keynes:

> Whenever depositors as a whole take steps to diminish the amount of their real balances, their behavior can only take the form of *an increased demand* [for goods and services] *on their part at the existing level of prices* which must result in a tendency for the price level to rise.[9]

[9] Keynes, *Treatise,* p. 204, italics in original.

And in the words of Friedman:

> If they want to hold a relatively small real quantity of money, they will individually seek to reduce their nominal cash balances by increasing expenditures.[10]

Thus the mechanism of transmission from, say, an excess supply of money to an increase in prices relies on the assumption that the alternative to holding money is buying goods and services. Many have called this assumption *unrealistic;* they claim that the real alternative to holding cash is holding some other financial asset, say, a bond (i.e., loans). Thus, if you have more money than you desire, you may modify your portfolio (i.e., reduce your real balances) by buying more bonds (i.e., by supplying more loans).

The critics can perhaps make their point best by using the following extreme example: Assume that an employee takes his monthly paycheck of one thousand dollars to the bank and deposits seven hundred dollars to his checking account (i.e., cash balances) and three hundred dollars to his savings account (i.e., loans). (Or he could use the three hundred dollars for his monthly mortgage payment. Note that a reduction of one's debts is really an increase in the supply of loans.) Upon his return home, however, he discovers that the entire one thousand dollars has been deposited to his checking account. Thus this individual finds himself with more cash balances than he desires. Is it realistic to say that he will go on a spending spree and, say, invite friends for a beer blast? Of course not. Most likely the individual will modify his portfolio, reducing his balances by three hundred dollars and increasing his loans by the same amount.

Suppose, instead, that a helicopter showers the individual's yard with money. In this case it is realistic to say that he may go on a spending spree. In earlier times, when the quantity theory was invented, this second analogy was more relevant; there were sharp increases in money through the discovery of gold. In modern times, however, the first analogy is the relevant one, since money is increased mainly through the purchase of government bonds.

Even if this crucial assumption—that an excess supply of money can be eliminated only by an increase in expenditure—is realistic, there is a second criticism against the traditional quantity theory approach. This concerns the *logical consistency* of the whole model; if it is true that an excess supply of real balances induces people to increase their aggregate demand, shouldn't this be reflected in the consumption (and thus savings) or in the investment functions, or in both? Yet, traditionally, neither real balances, M/p, nor excess real balances, $M/p - l \cdot Y$, are arguments in any of these functions. Thus what is said in Volume II, that $M/p - l \cdot Y > 0$ implies an increase in $C + I$, does not comply with the assumptions regarding the C and I functions.

During the fifties this second criticism, of *inconsistency* in the neoclassical system, was brought to the forefront of economic literature by Don Patinkin, whose

---

[10] Friedman, *Optimum Quantity of Money,* p. 116.

primary aim was to make the neoclassical system consistent.[11] The above explanation makes it clear that we need the introduction of the excess supply of real balances, $M/p - l \cdot Y$, as an argument in the consumption and savings functions. In particular, consumption should be an increasing function, and savings a decreasing function, of the excess supply of real balances. Symbolically, they would be in this form:

$$C\,(i, Y, K, \frac{M}{p} - l \cdot Y), \text{ with } (\frac{M}{p} - l \cdot Y) \uparrow \rightarrow C \uparrow$$

$$S\,(i, Y, K, \frac{M}{p} - l \cdot Y), \text{ with } (\frac{M}{p} - l \cdot Y) \uparrow \rightarrow S \downarrow$$

This specification of the consumption and savings function would be sufficient to accommodate (mechanically at least) the general quantity theory results. Patinkin introduced only the quantity of real balances, M/p, not excess real balances $[(M/p) - l \cdot Y]$, in the consumption function. This, of course, means that the theory can accommodate the strict quantity theory results, that is, when the excess supply of, or the excess demand for, real balances is brought about through a change in the money supply alone, and not through a change in demand, say, through a change in l.

Controversy still exists regarding Patinkin's way of introducing M/p into the consumption and savings functions. The controversy centers on his method of deriving the consumption and savings functions. However, we shall not be concerned further with the "Patinkin controversy." Here, and in the next chapter, we shall examine in detail a very appealing way of avoiding the two criticisms, the one about realism and the other about consistency. At the turn of the century the Swedish economist Knut Wicksell introduced this approach, which can, with only slight modifications, accommodate many crucial modern issues.[12]

Adapting Wicksell's approach, let us assume that holding bonds (i.e., supplying loans) is the alternative to holding real balances. It immediately follows that if there is an excess supply of real balances, the public reduces them by adding to the supply of loans. This increase in the supply of loans lowers the interest rate, which, in turn, increases aggregate demand for goods and services, $C + I$, and thereby raises the price level. It is through this indirect route that an excess supply of real balances raises the price level.

Schematically, the sequence of events, according to the original quantity theory approach, can be shown by Schema I:

Schema I:

$$\frac{M}{p} - l \cdot Y > 0 \rightarrow (C + I) \uparrow \rightarrow p \uparrow ,$$

---

[11] Don Patinkin, *Money, Interest and Prices,* 2nd ed. (New York: Harper & Row, Pub., 1965).

[12] Knut Wicksell, *Interest and Prices,* 1898, trans. R. F. Kahn (London: Macmillan, 1936).

that is, an excess supply of real balances increases aggregate demand for goods and services, which increases the price level. The new approach is shown by the more complicated representation of Schema II (where S_L denotes supply of loans):

Schema II:

$$\frac{M}{p} - l \cdot Y > 0 \rightarrow S_L \uparrow \rightarrow i \downarrow \rightarrow (C + I) \uparrow \rightarrow p \uparrow,$$

that is, an excess supply of real balances implies an increase in the supply of loans, S_L, which implies a fall in the interest rate, which, in turn, implies a rise in aggregate demand for goods and services, and hence a rise in the price level.

Note the importance of the loans market and the interest rate in Schema II. Since money plays a role in determining the interest rate, and since the interest rate influences aggregate demand for goods and services, the transmission mechanism is established. Since such a connection through the interest rate does not exist in Schema I, a logical inconsistency results. This is another reason why Keynes, in his Treatise on Money, abandoned the Cambridge approach (i.e., Schema I above) in favor of the connection through the interest rate (i.e., Schema II). Keynes stated:

> Formerly I was attracted by this [Cambridge] line of approach but it now seems to me that the merging together of all the different sorts of transactions—income, business and financial—which may be taking place only causes confusion, and that we cannot get any real insight into the price-making process without bringing in the rate of interest and the distinctions between incomes and profits and between savings and investment.[13]

We must point out that there is not unanimous belief in the superiority of II over I. In fact, some argue that since both schemata begin with an excess supply of money and end up with a rise in economic activity, and thus an increase in the price level, that is all that matters. And so, why not use the simpler Schema I? Modern quantity theorists prefer Schema I over Schema II for precisely these reasons. They point out that this preference does not necessarily mean that they believe that an individual with more money than he or she desires will actually go on a "spending spree." It merely means that they are not interested in the proximate reason why the increase in M increases economic activity and, therefore, prices.

The reliance on Schema I *versus* Schema II can perhaps be best illustrated by a controversy, in the 1950s, between two American economists, Professor Paul Samuelson of MIT and Professor Milton Friedman of Chicago. The controversy began when both were on the same panel testifying before a congressional committee on how money influences economic activity. According to Samuelson, who recounts the incident, he (Samuelson) "spelled out in great detail what [he] considered to be the mechanisms and sequences involved in attempts to affect the level of national income through use of monetary policy." In other words, Samuelson explained the

---

[13] Keynes, *Treatise,* p. 205.

process using Schema II. Later Friedman wrote to him that although he had no quarrel with his (Samuelson's) analysis, he considered it redundant. According to Samuelson, Friedman maintained the following:

> So long as a change in M can be counted upon to achieve the desired effect in the end why bother to elucidate the intermediate steps involving the interest cost and availability of credit? Friedman likened the discussion to a quarrel over whether it is the loss of blood, the bullet of the murder weapon, the gun itself, the finger that pulled the trigger, or the gunman who kills the victim. So long as we can be sure that death will "follow," the initial act—why quibble about the details? And the same goes for monetary policy: so long as an engineered change in M can be counted on not to induce an offsetting opposite change in the "velocity of circulation of money," Friedman prefers to skip the intervening stages.

Samuelson recounted this incident in his paper "Some Notions on Causality and Teleology in Economics," under a section entitled "Who Killed Cock Robin?"[14]

Of course, the thrust of Samuelson's argument, as well as the arguments of all those who prefer Schema II, is that knowledge of all the various linkages is necessary for two reasons. First, one or another of these linkages may occasionally be faulty, and thus an increase in M may not have the desired effect, an increase in economic activity. Only if we are aware of all these linkages can we remedy a potentially faulty one. Samuelson preferred to use another analogy, saying that "we face a sequence of switches in series." It should be clear that the circuit will be broken, even if only one of these switches is left open. The same is true for Friedman's analogy. If, for example, the ammunition is not live, nothing happens, even if one pulls the trigger. In the words of Samuelson, "Thus, I probably do not share Friedman's confidence that the gun will invariably kill the victim."

There is a second reason why knowledge of all the linkages, as in Schema II, is important. Suppose that we want to increase, say, the level of economic activity without engineering an increase in the quantity of money. How can we do it? It is obvious that we should intervene in one or more of the intermediate steps and influence one or more intermediate variables, for example, by using other means to lower the interest rate.

Modern quantity theorists concentrated their efforts on establishing empirically a relation between the quantity of money and economic activity. Foremost among these empirical works are those of Milton Friedman and some of his associates, especially Anna Schwartz, whose work culminated in the classic *A Monetary History of the United States, 1867–1960.*[15] Although Friedman and Schwartz are careful to point out that "the close relation between changes in the stock of money and changes in other economic variables, alone, tells nothing about the origin of either or the direction of influence" (p. 686), they believe that they have established a one-way

[14] *Collected Scientific Work of Paul A. Samuelson* Vol. 3 (Cambridge, Mass.: MIT Press, 1973).

[15] Milton Friedman and Anna J. Schwartz, *A Monetary History of the United States, 1867–1960* (Princeton, N.J.: Princeton University Press, 1963).

causality: Changes in money supply *cause* changes in economic activity. In other words, they carefully establish a special case of Schema II, but they show little interest in how it is brought about.

A considerable portion of the efforts of the monetarists has focused on elaborate reworking and testing of different versions of the quantity theory. For example, they have rewritten the Cambridge equation, $M = l \cdot p \cdot Y$, in percentage change form:

$$\frac{\Delta M}{M} = \frac{\Delta l}{l} + \frac{\Delta p}{p} + \frac{\Delta Y}{Y}$$

They have found the time paths of each of these percentages and related them to each other. Furthermore, they have distinguished between short-run and long-run variations: In the short run they usually assume that $\Delta l/l$ is zero, implying that a change in the rate of growth of the money supply, $\Delta M/M$, is split between changes in prices, $\Delta p/p$, and changes in output, $\Delta Y/Y$; in the long run, since they consider the ouput fixed and they allow for the trend in l, the rate of inflation, $\Delta p/p$, is exactly equal to the rate of monetary expansion, $\Delta M/M$, that is, $(\Delta p/p) = (\Delta M/M)$.

Perhaps the epitome of this monetary approach, of examining the ultimate relation between changes in the money supply and changes in economic activity, is the reduced-form model developed by L. C. Andersen and J. L. Jordan,[16] whose affiliation with the St. Louis Federal Reserve Bank accounts for the model's being dubbed the St. Louis model. This is an ambitious undertaking, which purports to describe and forecast the movements of the economy by using a reduced-form, two-equation model or even a one-equation model. It is designed to predict movements in prices (and money income) by relying exclusively on the movements of the money supply, M. The Andersen-Jordan statement is controversial, since it is stronger than the traditional quantity theory, or monetarist thesis; it claims not only that "money matters" but also that "only money matters" in affecting economic activity and hence in affecting prices.

On the other hand, the monetarists' emphasis is usually on the outcome of a change in the money supply and not on the reasons nor on the means by which the outcome is achieved. For this reason the late Harry Johnson, a colleague of Friedman's, attacked this application of the quantity theory and termed it a "black box" theory, or a sleight-of-hand maneuver. Johnson, usually a friendly critic of modern quantity theorists, made this scathing criticism of monetarism in his most important lecture:

> The general equilibrium and empirical revolutions of the recent past have taught economists to ask for explicit specification of the full general equilibrium system with which the theorist or empiricist is working, and to distrust

[16] L. Andersen and J. Jordan, "Monetary and Fiscal Actions: A Test of Their Relative Importance," *Federal Reserve Bank of St. Louis Review*, November 1968.

results that appear like rabbits out of a conjurer's hat—and an old-fashioned top hat at that.[17]

Within the profession there is an ongoing, lively debate about causality, whether changes in money alone cause changes in economic activity or whether there is, in addition, the converse causality, that money changes *because* economic activity changes.[18] If the latter view is correct, money is (partly) endogenous and, therefore, not an independent variable, that is, not a true parameter. But we shall postpone examining this and similar issues until Chapter 14, which deals explicitly with real-world changes in the supply of money. However, in the next chapter we shall *derive* the dependence of the price level on the excess supply of money from a fully specified, general (i.e., interdependent) equilibrium system and, in that way, make the quantity theory immune from Johnson's criticism. We shall see that this is the same model that Friedman used in the 1960s and later to examine the effect on the interest rate of growth of the money supply.

We shall identify the three effects, emphasized by Friedman, of a change in the rate of growth of the money supply on the interest rate: the "liquidity effect," the "price level effect," and the "price anticipation effect."[19] And we shall distinguish between the nominal and the (expected) real interest rate and note the effects of economic policy on them. Our model, developed to examine the role of monetary policy in an inflationary environment like the 1970s and 1980s, will also encompass the role of monetary policy in creating inflationary expectation and, in turn, the ability of these inflationary expectations to affect the interest rate and other economic variables. Throughout this analysis we shall assume full employment, an assumption compatible with the neoclassical (monetarist) tenet that the economy always gravitates toward full employment.

It is noteworthy that the analysis in the next chapter—the reduced-form quantity theory results and several of the monetarists' (especially Friedman's) propositions—is derived by an elaboration of Schema II. In effect, when Friedman and other monetarists examine the role of economic policy on economic activity, they dispense with intermediate steps; they examine only ultimate results. But when they confront the role of monetary policy on the interest rate, they rely on Schema II for deriving theses effects.

A final comment is in order in this chapter on the quantity theory. In 1956 Friedman undertook a "restatement" of the quantity theory.[20] In that restatement

---

[17] Harry G. Johnson, "The Keynesian Revolution and the Monetarist Counter-Revolution," *American Economic Review,* May 1971, p. 13.

[18] See, for example, James Tobin, "Post Hoc Ergo Propter Hoc?" *Quarterly Journal of Economics,* May 1970, pp. 301–17.

[19] Milton Friedman, "Factors Affecting the Interest Rates," in *Money and Finance: Readings in Theory, Policy, and Institutions,* ed. D. Carson (New York: John Wiley, 1972), pp. 319–30.

[20] Milton Friedman, "The Quantity Theory of Money—A Restatement," in *Studies in the Quantity Theory of Money,* ed. M. Friedman (Chicago: University of Chicago Press, 1956), pp. 3–21.

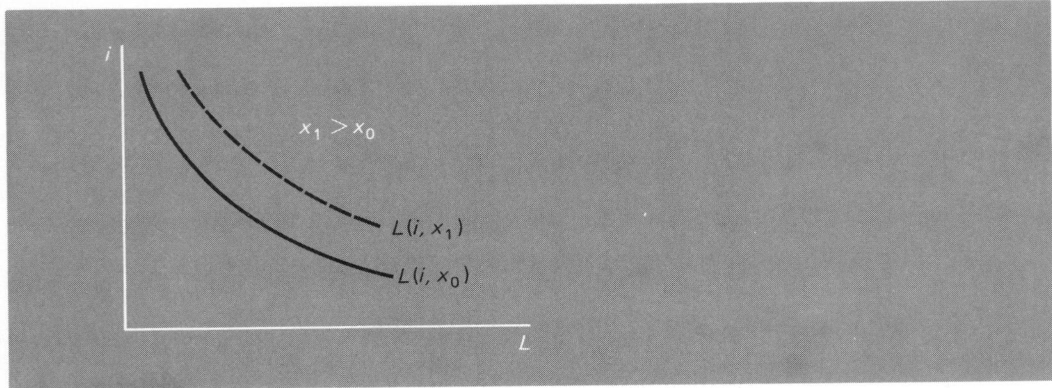

FIGURE 3-5

he transformed the quantity theory, reducing it from one of price determination to one involving merely a derivation of the demand for money. He showed that velocity, V, or the Cambridge "k" (i.e., our "l") is a function of several endogenous variables, including the interest rate, i, and the rate of inflation. The negative dependence of l on the interest rate was also established by William Baumol (1952) and James Tobin (1956).[21] Taking into account these recent developments, we can denote the demand for real balances by L and get

$$L = l(i) \cdot f(x) \equiv L(i,x)$$

where $\Delta L/\Delta i < 0$ and $\Delta L/\Delta x > 0$.

This makes the demand for real balances, L, a function of two variables. Thus, for a given x, there is a negative relation between the interest rate, i, and the demand for real balances, as shown in Figure 3-5. Moreover, when x rises, say from x_0 to x_1, as in Figure 3-5, the L curve shifts to the right. In other words, in the (i,L)-plane, there is an infinity of demand for real balances curves, L, one for each assumed x. Beginning with the next chapter and continuing throughout the book, we shall follow this notation and graphical depiction of the demand for real balances.

QUESTIONS

1. Show that "the value of money, as with any other good, increases with its demand and falls with supply."
2. Both Keynes and Friedman emphasize that people demand real balances while the monetary authorities supply nominal balances.
   a. Why do people demand real balances?

[21] See References in Chapter 13.

b. What variable must change to reequilibrate the demand for and supply of real balances?
c. Compare two possible scenarios for accomplishing this.

3. The Cambridge equation emphasizes the role of the price level in equating the stock demand to the stock supply of money.
a. Explain briefly the interpretation of *"l"* in this formulation.
b. What is assumed concerning the value of *"l"* in the adjustment of the stock demand to the stock supply?
c. How might the assumption of the Cambridge formulation be affected by innovations in credit cards, thrift institutions, and payments methods in an economy?
d. Would you expect *"l"* to be the same in all countries or in the same country at different points in history? If not, explain how *"l"* would take on the new values, and what might cause the change.

4. There have been at least three versions of the quantity theory.
a. Explain the differences between the quantity theory of Fisher and the Cambridge formulation. What are the advantages, if any, of the differences? What is the quantity theory all about?
b. In what way are the quantity theories similar? How would a researcher distinguish between them?

5. What is the flow demand for money? The flow supply?

6. A person is paid \$90 monthly and spends \$3 per day. What is *"l"?* Now the person is paid \$45 every two weeks. What is *"l"?*

7. What are two fundamental criticisms of the quantity theory?

8. What are the two schemata by which an excess supply of money generates a rise in the price level? Why is the distinction between the two schemata important?

9. Consider an economy with three goods that consist of one physical output (corn) and two currencies or monies. (For example, a bordertown where both dollars and pesos circulate.)
a. How many relative prices will exist? How many *independent* relative prices will exist? How would you decide whether to make purchases in dollars or in pesos?
b. How is your answer to part *a* an example of Gresham's law, which states that "bad money drives out good"?

10. Suppose that the nominal stock of money is \$100 billion, velocity is five times per year, and output is 10 billion units per year. What is the equilibrium price level? What percentage of income do individuals on average desire to hold in money balances?

REFERENCES

ANDERSEN, L., and J. JORDAN, "Monetary and Fiscal Actions: A Test of Their Relative Importance," *Federal Bank of St. Louis Review,* November 1968.

FISHER, IRVING, *The Purchasing Power of Money.* New York: Macmillan, 1911.

FRIEDMAN, MILTON, "The Quantity Theory of Money—A Restatement," in *Studies in the Quantity Theory of Money,* ed. M. Friedman, pp. 3–21. Chicago: University of Chicago Press, 1956.

———, "A Theoretical Framework for Monetary Analysis," *Journal of Political Economy,* March/April 1970, pp. 193–238.

FRIEDMAN, MILTON, and ANNA J. SCHWARTZ, *A Monetary History of the United States, 1867–1960.* Princeton, N.J.: Princeton University Press, 1963.

JOHNSON, HARRY G., "The Keynesian Revolution and the Monetarist Counter-Revolution," *American Economic Review,* May 1971, pp. 1–14.

KEYNES, J. M., *A Tract on Monetary Reform.* London: Macmillan, 1923.

———, *A Treatise on Money.* London: Macmillan, 1930.

MARSHALL, ALFRED, *Money, Credit and Commerce* (London: Macmillan, 1923).

PATINKIN, DON, *Money, Interest, and Prices* (2nd ed.). New York: Harper & Row, Pub., 1965.

PIGOU, A. C., "The Value of Money," *Quarterly Journal of Economics,* November 1917, pp. 38–65.

TOBIN, JAMES, "The Monetary Interpretation of History," *American Economic Review,* June 1965, pp. 464–85.

———, "Post Hoc Ergo Propter Hoc?" *Quarterly Journal of Economics,* May 1970, pp. 301–17.

WICKSELL, KNUT, *Interest and Prices,* 1898, trans. R. F. Kahn. London: Macmillan, 1936.

chapter four

bypass

The reader who wants only a brief overview of Chapter 4 should read the following.

First, the question of how the excess supply of money materializes as excess demand for goods and services, sketched in the preceding chapter as Schema II, is answered by examining the loans market in a true monetary economy. On the demand side of the loans market, we have the investment demand of firms, since investment is financed by borrowing. On the supply side of the loans market, we have savings plus a new component, namely, that portion of the excess supply of money that individuals decide to lend. And if $M/p - L$ is the excess stock supply of money, then $\lambda \cdot (M/p - L)$ is the flow excess supply of money and the part that is lent out.

Hence λ is an "operator" that transforms stocks into flows. It is the *fraction* of the excess stock supply of money that should be eliminated, by adding it (as a flow) to the supply of loans per period. For example, if the excess stock supply, $(M/p - L)$, is 1,000 million units, and λ is ¼ per year, then $\lambda(M/p - L) =$ (¼/yr) · 1,000 = 250 units, which will be added to the supply of loans per year. This also means that in four years the 1,000-unit discrepancy will disappear. Of course, four years is the inverse of λ.

Moreover, the interest rate is determined where the loans market is cleared, that is, when the demand for loans, I, is equal to the supply of loans, $S + \lambda(M/p - L)$:

$$I = S + \lambda\left(\frac{M}{p} - L\right)$$

Rewriting this equation as (1),

$$I - S = \lambda\left(\frac{M}{p} - L\right), \tag{1}$$

we have loan market clearance in a form that is particularly amenable to graphical depiction. In Figure B.4-1 the $I - S$ curve is downward sloping with respect to the interest rate, since I is decreasing and S is increasing with the interest rate. On the other hand, $\lambda(M/p - L)$ is upward sloping, since the money supply is independent of the interest rate, while the demand for real balances, L, is, in general, decreasing with the interest rate. The market rate of interest, i_m, is determined at the intersection, E, of the $I - S$ and $\lambda(M/p - L)$ curves. In the case depicted in Figure B.4-1, at the market interest rate, i_m^0, there is positive excess supply of money, equal to OA, as we see from the $\lambda(M/p - L)$ curve; on the other hand, for the interest rate that clears the loans market, this excess flow supply of money is identically equal to the

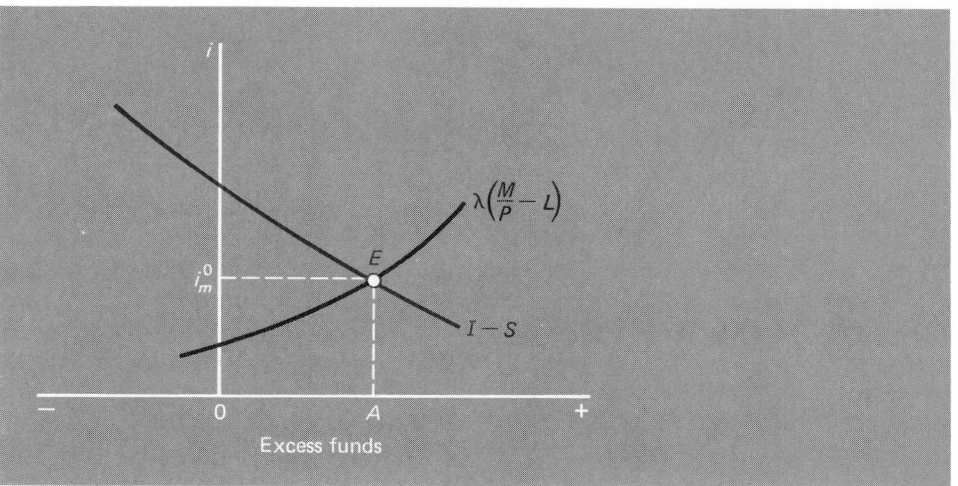

FIGURE B.4-1

excess demand for goods and services, $I - S$, or OA, as we see from the $I - S$ curve.

Figure B.4-1 depicts the case when the loans market is cleared but the goods and services and the money markets are not cleared. This is only a *temporary equilibrium:* The excess demand for goods and services, $I - S > 0$, implies that the price level will rise, say from p_0 to p_1, which, in turn, will shift the $\lambda(M/p - L)$ curve to the left, so that it intersects the $I - S$ curve at point F, as shown in Figure B.4-2. At F there is still excess flow supply of money and, therefore, excess demand for goods and services equal to OA', which will cause the price level to rise, say to p_2. This rise shifts the $\lambda(M/p - L)$ curve once again to the left and continues to do so

FIGURE B.4-2

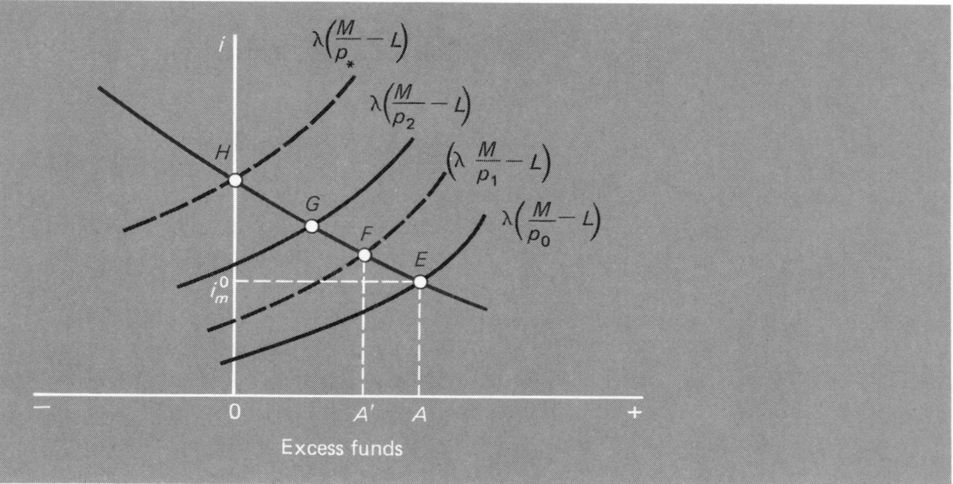

until the price level rises to p_*, whose corresponding excess flow supply-of-money curve, $\lambda(M/p - L)$, intersects the $I - S$ curve on the i-axis. In this case, which is also depicted separately in Figure B.4-3, we have *full* equilibrium: All markets—the goods and services and the money markets, as well as the loans market—are cleared. Hence there is no tendency for any variable to change.

Now, starting from a full-equilibrium position, such as the one depicted in Figure B.4-3, an increase in the nominal money supply, M, will shift the $\lambda(M/p - L)$ curve to the right, lowering the interest rate and creating a situation like point E in Figure B.4-2. This will set in motion the same mechanism we examined earlier: The price level and the interest rate will rise, shifting the $\lambda(M/p - L)$ curve to the left until the $\lambda(M/p - L)$ curve will intersect the $I - S$ curve at point H, where all motion stops. At this point it is clear that the interest rate returns to its original level, but that the price level will rise by the same percentage that the nominal money supply is increased.

The reader should note the self-liquidating nature of the excess supply of money and, therefore, the excess demand for goods and services. If left alone, all markets will eventually be cleared. But if the monetary authority wants to permanently keep the lower interest rate, corresponding to point E, it should keep increasing the money supply indefinitely. Of course, rising prices create anticipation of further rises, which complicate the picture: The $I - S$ curve itself will keep shifting to the right, necessitating an ever-increasing rate of growth in the money supply. Another application of this theory concerns the Fisher hypothesis, which states that a given percentage increase in the rate of growth of the money supply will increase actual and expected inflation by the same percentage, and that this, in turn, will increase the *nominal* rate of interest by the same percentage, thereby leaving the *real* rate of interest unchanged. The (expected) real rate of interest is found by subtracting the (expected) rate of inflation from the nominal interest rate, that is, from the *observed* interest rate.

As an historical point, we should note that although this analysis is quite

FIGURE B.4-3

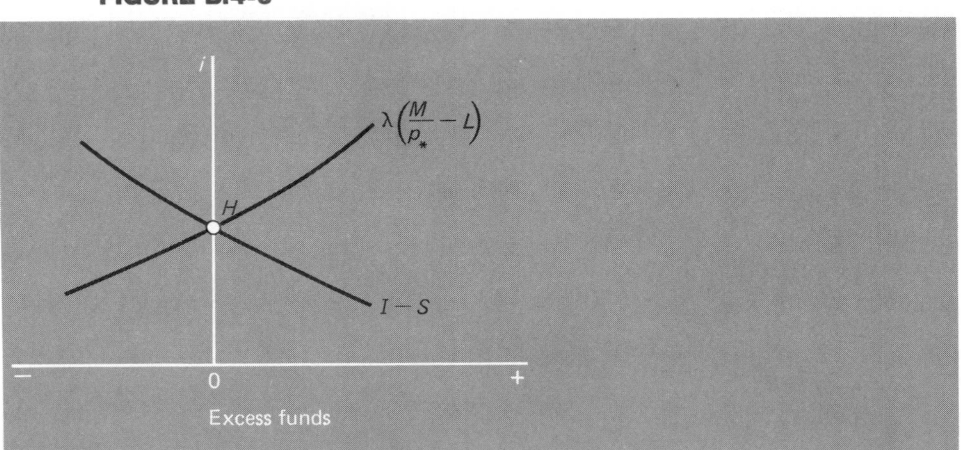

modern, its foundation was laid at the turn of the century by the Swedish economist Knut Wicksell. Wicksell, however, assumed that the demand for real balances, L, is $l \cdot Y$ and independent of the interest rate. But the extensions to this case, the interest-elastic demand for money, were undertaken by Keynes, while the distinction between the nominal and the real interest rate, a distinction required when inflationary expectations are present, was introduced by Fisher.

All the results of this analysis, except one, are independent of the interest elasticity of the demand for money. This one difference, however, is crucial: An increase in the propensity to invest, say, which shifts the $I - S$ curve to the right, as in Figures B.4-4 and B.4-5, will require only a rise in the interest rate and no

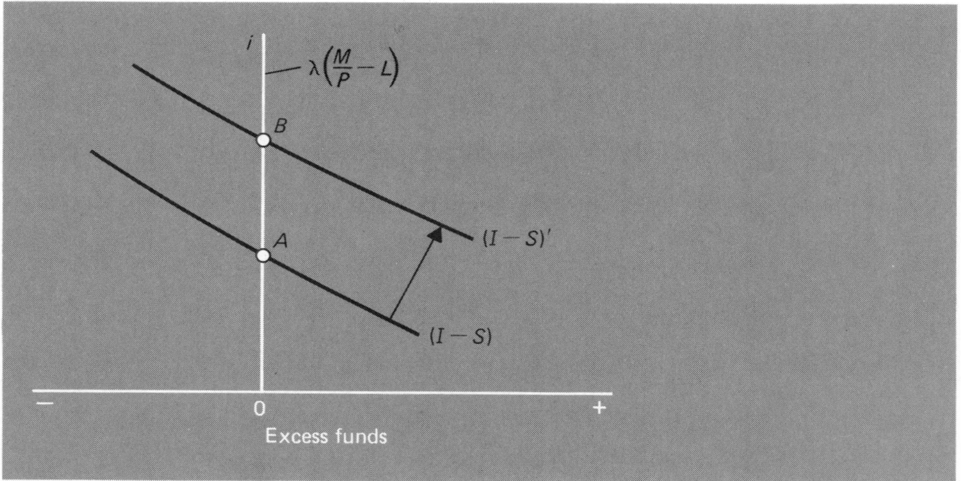

FIGURE B.4-4

FIGURE B.4-5

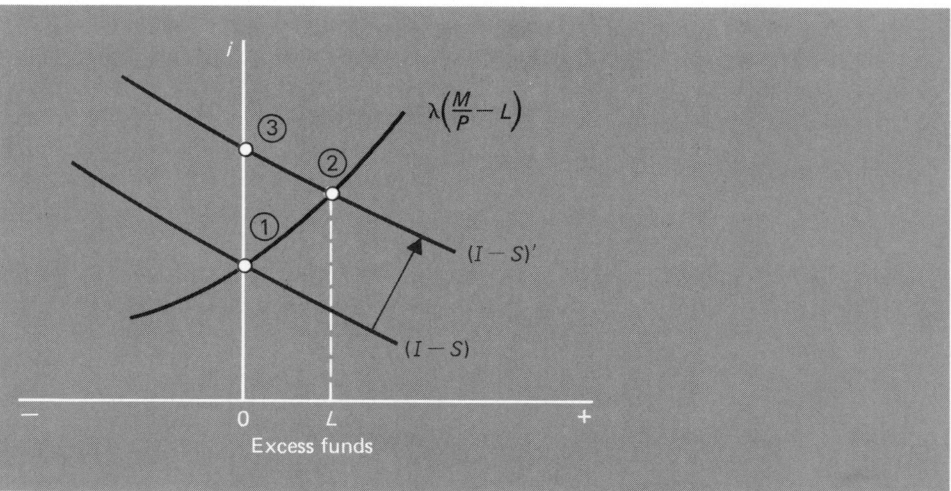

rise in the price level in order to bring about the new equilibrium. This is shown as a movement from point *A* to point *B* in Figure B.4-4, where the excess flow supply-of-money curve is vertical, coinciding with the *i*-axis. On the other hand, when the excess supply of money depends (positively) on the interest rate, the increase in the interest rate alone is not sufficient to eradicate excess demand. At point ② of Figure B.4-5 there is still excess demand for goods and services necessitating an increase in the price level. This proof, that prices can change even if the money supply remains fixed, disillusioned Keynes and induced him to launch his "revolution," a theme we take up in the next chapter.

4 Money, Interest, and Prices

In this chapter we examine the determination of both the interest rate and the price level in a fully employed economy. We shall develop an interdependent (i.e., general equilibrium and disequilibrium) system consisting of three distinct markets: a money market and a loanable funds market, which together comprise the financial sector, and a goods and services market, which comprises the real sector (given the assumption that factors are fully employed). Our analysis is dynamic, and the feedback effects between the financial and the real sectors play a crucial role in this analysis of movements in the interest rate and the price level.

The model is especially suited for analyzing the economic problems of the 1970s and the 1980s, known as the decades of inflation. Rising interest rates and inflationary expectations, as well as the effects of monetary and fiscal policies on these variables, have attracted more attention than ever before from policy makers and ordinary citizens alike.

Our aim in this chapter is to construct and apply a consistent general equilibrium framework in order to examine these issues. To focus more directly on these issues we shall dispense with problems of unemployment in the neoclassical manner, by assuming a continuously, fully employed economy.

As a byproduct of our analysis, we shall show that this loanable funds model yields the quantity theory results as a special case. Of course, this model is richer than the strict quantity theory model of the preceding chapter, in the sense that it also explains, and in fact relies on, interest rates. We can say, therefore, that the usual quantity theory model is the reduced form of this fully specified general equilibrium (interdependent) system. In fact, we shall see that it is on this very model that Friedman and other monetarists rely when they themselves are confronted with interest rate determination; these two aspects of our model taken together do indeed provide the foundations of monetarism.

A second byproduct of our analysis in this chapter is its rendering of insights into historical doctrine. We see that this model, so useful in explaining issues of the 1970s and 1980s, dates back to the turn of the century, to the work of the Swedish economist Knut Wicksell. We also see how this model was improved upon and popularized by Keynes and Fisher in the 1930s, and resurrected in a modern version by Friedman and Hugh Rose in the 1960s.

In Section I we construct the model from its individual components, that is, from the markets for loans, for money, and for goods and services. In Section II we see how the entire model can be reduced to one that yields the quantity theory results. The distinction between market and natural rates of interest, as well as the concomitant distinction between temporary and full equilibrium, is instrumental in analyzing the dynamic behavior of the system in Section III. In addition, the relation between interest rates and prices will be clearly delineated.

In Section IV we examine the effects of a change in the money supply on the price level and on the interest rate, in the beginning of the process, at the end of the process, and also through time (i.e., we trace the trajectories of the price level and of the interest rate). Furthermore, we distinguish between a one-shot increase in the money supply and a (continuous) change in the rate of growth of the money supply, as well as the effects of these changes on the interest rate and on prices. We also depict the three effects stressed by Friedman—the "liquidity effect," the "price level effect," and the "price anticipation effect"—on the interest rate of changes in the money supply. Of course, continuous increases in the money supply cause continuous increases in the price level, which eventually are anticipated. This creation of inflationary expectations will be further examined in Section V and applied to two important cases: namely, the Fisher hypothesis, or the effect of inflationary expectations on the real and on the nominal interest rates, zero and one, respectively. And, finally, we explore attempts by the monetary authorities to peg the nominal interest rate below its natural rate, which causes accelerating (cumulative) inflation.

In Section VI, the final section, we trace the model back to Wicksell and Keynes and to their treatments of the cumulative process, both the inflationary and the deflationary ones. However, we note one crucial difference between the analyses of Wicksell and Keynes. Wicksell's strict quantity theory result, which states that prices rise if, and only if, the money supply rises, rests squarely on his assumption that the demand for money is independent of the interest rate. But when Keynes assumed this dependency, he discovered that prices may change even though the money supply remains fixed. This is what disillusioned Keynes and encouraged him to launch his revolution, a theme taken up in Chapter 5.

I. THE REAL AND THE FINANCIAL SECTORS

The following analysis of a monetary economy is contemporary, and it can be used to examine many problems fruitfully, such as inflation facing our economy in the 1980s. While the tools and techniques that comprise this analysis are quite modern, the foundation for the analysis was laid at the turn of the century by Knut Wicksell.[1]

Wicksell decried the prevalent view that maintained that when we introduce money into the model, all that remains is to introduce the quantity theory equation (say $M/p = l \cdot Y$) and then to examine only this equation, separately from the rest of the model. He emphasized that money requires more respect; money is a store of value—an asset—and its introduction expands the selection of assets available to the wealth holder.

It is instructive to see how this selection of assets is extended as we move from the simplest barter model to the full-fledged modern monetary economy. In the simple barter model (i.e., the one without borrowing and lending), the only asset available to wealth holders is investment goods. In the barter model with borrowing and lending, there are two assets: investment goods and loans (bonds). In the present monetary model, however, there are three assets: investment goods, loans (bonds), and money. Furthermore, we can say that, alternatively, in a monetary economy an individual can hold one's wealth in (a) investment goods, (b) loans to nonbanks, and (c) loans to banks. Of course, in this schema, loans to banks are meant to represent demand deposits, that is, money. All the above information is summarized in Table 4-I.

TABLE 4-I

TYPE OF MODEL	ASSETS TO BE HELD		
Barter model without borrowing or lending	Investment goods		
Barter model with borrowing and lending	Investment goods	Bonds (loans to nonbanks)	
Monetary economy	Investment goods	Bonds (loans to nonbanks)	Money (loans to banks)

The minimum number of commodities that have to be examined in a modern monetary economy is three, namely, goods and services (often referred to simply as goods), bonds (or loans), and money. (A more realistic analysis should involve more than three commodities, since there are several kinds of bonds issued, not only by private individuals [as assumed here] but also by the government. To accommodate this

[1] Knut Wicksell, *Interest and Prices,* 1898, trans. R. F. Kahn (London: Macmillan, 1936); and Knut Wicksell, *Lectures on Political Economy,* Vol. II, *Money,* 1911, English trans., ed. Lionel Robbins (London: Routledge & Kegan Paul, 1934).

phenomenon, we shall extend the model in a later chapter.) Applying Walras' Law, we see that the sum of their excess *flow* demands should be zero.

$$EG + EM + EB = 0 \tag{1}$$

where EG is the excess demand for goods (and services); EM is the excess flow demand for money; and EB is the excess flow demand for bonds.

Since there are three markets, we need to examine explicitly only two of them, for if two of the markets are cleared, we know that the third is also cleared. We shall choose, then, to examine only the goods and bonds markets.

We shall often talk of loans rather than of bonds, since to demand bonds means to supply loans, to supply bonds means to demand loans, and therefore the excess demand for bonds, EB, is identical with the excess supply of loans, that is, minus the excess demand for loans, $(-EL)$. Thus we shall examine only the goods and loans markets, beginning with the former.

THE GOODS AND SERVICES MARKET

A market has a demand side and a supply side. Ignoring government demand and demand from abroad, there remain only two components of aggregate demand for goods and services, namely, consumption demand, C, and investment demand, I. The supply side has two components: first, the currently produced output, Y, plus whatever depletion of inventories, U, occurs. (The depletion of inventories, although *unplanned*, is *voluntary*.) Thus

	C		I
Demand Side:	(Intended demand by consumers)	+	(Intended investment demand)
	Y		U
Supply Side:	(Intended supply, i.e., production)	+	(Unintended depletion of stocks, disinvestment)

We assume that the monetary value of p (i.e., the price of goods and services) is determined when the demand for goods and services is exactly equal to their supply. In other words, p is *determined* by the equality

$$C + I = Y + U \tag{2}$$

Rearranging this equality, we get

$$I = (Y - C) + U$$

or

$$I = S + U, \text{ since } S \equiv Y - C$$

Finally, we can write it as

$$I - S = U \tag{3}$$

We see from (2) and (3) that the excess of investment over savings, $I - S$, is the difference between demand and production. But the former is intended, *ex ante* demand, while the latter is *ex ante* supply. Thus $I - S$ is the *ex ante* excess demand, and in (3) it is reflected as the decreasing of stocks. Therefore we can say that *the price of goods and services, p, is determined at the level at which the* ex ante *excess demand is exactly balanced by the voluntary decisions of firms to decrease inventories.*

We have specified that a positive value of U is a *reduction* of inventories, and that it reflects excess demand for goods and services (i.e., a positive $I - S$). It follows, therefore, that an ex ante excess supply of goods and services (i.e., $I - S < 0$) is reflected as a *piling up* of inventories (i.e., as a negative U). Thus we can write the excess demand for goods and services, EG, as

$$EG \equiv I(i,x) - S(i,x) \tag{4}$$

We have seen that although the price is determined at a level that clears the goods market, it is still possible to have either *ex ante* excess demand (i.e., $I - S > 0$) or *ex ante* excess supply (i.e., $I - S < 0$). But when $I - S$ is different from zero, this scenario does not end with the market determination of the price level. If, for example, the market clearance is brought about by the depletion of inventories, $U > 0$, firms will attempt to replenish them. (The *level* of inventories is a matter of rational decision making by firms. It is decided on the basis of the marginal cost of carrying the inventories and of the marginal revenue of losing them.)

To replenish the decreased inventories in the next period, more output is needed, which will put pressure on the resources (labor, raw materials, etc.) and raise the cost of producing this additional amount. In other words, output is assumed to be produced at an increasing cost, and, therefore, in the next period prices must rise to cover the higher cost. It follows, then, that if there is ex ante excess demand for goods and services, the price level will tend to rise. Similarly, if there is ex ante excess supply of goods and services, seen as an accumulation of inventories, there will be reduced production in the next period, lowered marginal cost, and, finally, a lowered price for goods and services.

Having provided a rough sketch of the price adjustment mechanism, we can summarize it as follows: The price level rises if, and only if, there is excess demand for goods and services ($I - S > 0$); it falls if, and only if, there is excess supply ($I - S < 0$); and it remains unchanged only if there is zero excess demand or supply ($I - S = 0$). Or, the price adjustment mechanism is the time-honored "law of supply and demand" applied to the market for goods and services, and it can be depicted by the following schema:

$$EG > 0 \rightarrow p\uparrow \text{ (i.e., } \Delta p > 0) \tag{5a}$$

$$EG < 0 \rightarrow p\downarrow \text{ (i.e., } \Delta p < 0) \tag{5b}$$

$$EG = 0 \rightarrow p \text{ unchanged (i.e., } \Delta p = 0) \tag{5c}$$

where, of course, $EG = I - S$.

We can, however, be a bit more explicit (although somewhat *ad hoc*) regarding the relation between excess demand (or excess supply) and changes in the price level. It seems reasonable to stipulate that the greater the excess demand, the greater the consequent rate of increase in prices, $\Delta p/p$. Symbolically, this is captured by the equation

$$\frac{\Delta p}{p} = \epsilon \cdot EG \qquad \text{where } \epsilon > 0, \tag{6}$$

which simply means that the percentage change in prices is *proportional* to the excess demand for goods and services.

We see that the constant ϵ has a special meaning; it is the "speed of adjustment" for the goods market, that is, the speed at which the market is cleared. Its inverse, $1/\epsilon$, denotes *the time it takes for the goods market to be cleared.* The smaller ϵ is, the longer it will take for this market to be cleared, since prices do not move fast enough to clear the goods market quickly. On the other hand, when ϵ is very high, it takes little time for the market to be cleared. At the limit, when ϵ tends to infinity, the market clears instantaneously. In effect, the goods market would *always be cleared* in this case. Obviously, at the other extreme, the case of price rigidity can be represented with ϵ equal to zero.

THE LOANS MARKET

The loans market, in the absence of money, was examined earlier in Chapter 2, where we saw that the demand side consisted of investment demand (only), that is, it was and is assumed that investment demand is financed by loans. The supply side also had only one component, namely, savings. And the interest rate was assumed to be determined by the equality of investment and savings. Later this theory was assumed valid even when money was introduced and examined in a dichotomized economy using the strict quantity theory of the succeeding chapter (Chapter 3).

The distinguishing feature of the loans (or loanable funds) theory introduced by Wicksell is that money, or, more precisely, the excess supply of it, plays a role in the determination of the interest rate. In other words, money enters as a component both on the demand side and on the supply side of the loans market.

On the supply side, in addition to the savings of the period, we have the component "dishoarding." To see how dishoarding occurs, we must first note that there are individuals whose supply of (nominal) cash balances, M, is greater than their demand, $p \cdot L$. These individuals add all of, or a part of, their excess supply of money, $(M - p \cdot L)$, to the supply of loans. And it is this part of an individual's excess stock supply of money that we call "dishoarding," which, of course, represents a *reduction* in individual money holdings.

Similarly, on the demand side of the loans market, we have a component in addition to investment demand—"hoarding"—which emanates from those individuals whose demand for money balances is greater than their supply (i.e., $p \cdot L > M$). These individuals, in order to increase their balances, decide to borrow all or a part of their stock excess demand for money. They borrow funds *to keep them in cash,* hence the term *hoarding.*

The components of the demand and the supply side are as follows:

Demand Side: Investment + Hoarding

Supply Side: Savings + Dishoarding

To avoid discussing both hoarding and dishoarding, we shall examine only the net outcome, and we shall speak only of dishoarding, which, if positive, assumes net excess supply of money, with the understanding that negative dishoarding is actually hoarding. More specifically, we shall consider that the demand side consists only of the investment component, while the supply side consists of savings *plus* net dishoarding. Of course, if net dishoarding is negative, it means, in effect, that we *subtract* this amount (which is truly hoarding) from the supply of savings. Thus

Demand Side: Investment

Supply Side: Savings + Net dishoarding

Whether we add net dishoarding to savings, or we add net hoarding to investment, we make two noteworthy points. First, since investment, I, is in real terms, hoarding should also be in real terms so that we can add them together. And we must express savings, S, and dishoarding in the same way.

Second, we should keep in mind that savings and investment are *flows.* Thus hoarding and dishoarding are also flows, while an excess supply of money, in real terms, $M/p - L > 0$, is a stock. We need, therefore, an "operator" to transform the real stock, $M/p - L$, into a (real) flow. Such an operator is λ, which is applied on $M/p - L$. Thus

$$\lambda\left(\frac{M}{p} - L\right)$$

is the flow called dishoarding. It is clear that λ should be a number *per period;* if we multiply a number per period by dollars, we get dollars per period, which is a flow.

Example

Suppose that an individual has \$1,000 ($\equiv M$) but desires to hold only \$800 ($\equiv p \cdot L$). His excess stock supply (in money terms), $M - p \cdot L$, is equal to \$200.

Suppose further that, for him, λ is equal to ¼ per period. This means that he wants to eliminate this discrepancy of \$200 between his demand for and supply of money at the rate of ¼ of the discrepancy per period:

$$\lambda\,(M - p \cdot L) = \frac{1/4}{\text{Period}} \cdot \$200 = \frac{\$50}{\text{Period}}$$

In other words, the individual wants to eliminate the discrepancy of \$200 at the rate of \$50 per period. As a corollary, we see that the individual will eliminate all the discrepancy in four periods, a reflection of the result that $1/\lambda$ is the time it takes to eliminate the discrepancy.

It should be clear that we can change the period in such a way that λ will become equal to one. Using the above example, let us suppose that the flows were measured using, originally, a period equal to one year. Since λ was equal to 1/4 *per year,* it would take four years to eliminate the discrepancy. If, instead, we choose our period of measurement for flows as equal to four years, it follows that the discrepancy would be eliminated in *one* period. This is the precise meaning of a λ equal to one. Note that we had

$$\lambda = \frac{1/4}{\text{Year}}$$

which we can rewrite as

$$\lambda = \frac{1}{4\ \text{Years}}, \text{ or, finally, as}$$

$$\lambda = \frac{1}{1\ \text{Period}}, \text{ since } 1 \text{ period} \equiv 4 \text{ years now.}$$

We have seen that by changing the period under consideration, we can change the value of the speed by which the individual transforms an excess supply of money into dishoarding (and thus into an addition to the supply of savings) or an excess demand for money into hoarding. However, *for the same period,* this speed could be higher or lower depending on the costs associated with the individual's efforts to change his excess demand for money into a supply of loans (i.e., demand for bonds). If, for example, there are increasing brokerage fees, one's speed might be lowered. The same would follow if, for example, one attempted to quickly transform billions from cash into bonds. In such a case the fear arises that this effort may actually increase the terms of purchasing the bonds. It would then seem prudent for the individual to space these purchases over several periods, that is, for the individual's λ to be smaller.

For the issues examined in this and in the following chapter, no loss of generality is involved if we assume that λ is a fixed number, independent of costs. In a later chapter, however, when the magnitude of this speed is crucial, we shall permit it to vary. Since we shall be assuming a fixed λ here, no great harm is done if we choose our period in such a way that λ becomes equal to one, which would mean, of course, that individuals would want to erase, during the period examined, the whole excess supply of money by adding it to the supply of loans.

Using dishoarding in real terms, using the production function, $Y = K \cdot f(x)$, and setting K equal to one, we can write:

$$\frac{\text{Dishoarding}}{\text{p}} = \lambda\left(\frac{M}{p} - L\right)$$

$$= \lambda\left[\frac{M}{p} - L(i,x)\right] \qquad (7)$$

And this is the term we shall add to the supply side of loans:

$$\text{Supply of loans} = S(i,x) + \lambda\left[\frac{M}{p} - L(i,x)\right]$$

It follows, therefore, that the excess demand for loans, EL, is

$$EL \equiv I(i,x) - S(i,x) - \lambda\left[\frac{M}{p} - L(i,x)\right] \qquad (8)$$

It should be clear that $\lambda\left[\frac{M}{p} - L(i,x)\right]$ is the excess *flow* supply of real balances (i.e., *minus* the excess flow demand for real balances). In the notation of equation (1), that is, of Walras' Law:

$$EM = -\lambda\left[\frac{M}{p} - L(i,x)\right] \qquad (9)$$

The excess demand for loans, EL, as represented by (8), has been derived from first principles, but we can test its correctness by inquiring whether it satisfies Walras' Law, equation (1). By (1), we get

$$-EB = EG + EM$$

$$\text{But } -EB = EL.$$

Therefore we have

$$EL = EG + EM \qquad (10)$$

Now, substituting (4) and (9), respectively, in the right-hand side of (10), we get (8). We see that our analysis *is* consistent with Walras' Law—in flow terms.

As with the goods market, we can now apply the "law of supply and demand" for the loans market and say: The interest rate will rise when there is excess demand for loans; the interest rate will fall if there is excess supply of loans; and it will remain the same only if the loans market is cleared. The "interest adjustment mechanism" can be represented schematically as follows:

$$EL > 0 \rightarrow i\uparrow \text{ (i.e., } \Delta i > 0) \tag{11a}$$

$$EL < 0 \rightarrow i\downarrow \text{ (i.e., } \Delta i < 0) \tag{11b}$$

$$EL = 0 \rightarrow i \text{ remains unchanged (i.e., } \Delta i = 0) \tag{11c}$$

As before, we shall assume that the rate of change (or simply the change) in the interest rate is proportional to the excess demand for (or excess supply of) loans. This is captured by the equation

$$\Delta i = \delta \cdot EL, \ \delta > 0 \tag{12}$$

The positive constant δ is the speed of adjustment for the loans market, and $1/\delta$ is, therefore, the time it takes to clear the loans market.

In what follows we shall work with an extreme version of the law of supply and demand for loans; we shall assume that the interest rate moves rapidly to instantaneously clear any excess demand for or excess supply of loans. Thus, at all times, the market for loans is cleared (i.e., $EL = 0$). The economic meaning of this assumption becomes clear when we examine the determinants of the speed of adjustment of a market.

For any market, the speed of adjustment, and thus the time it takes for market clearance, depend on the availability and the cost of information: The less costly the information regarding a market, the faster that market clears. At the extreme, if the information is plentiful and costless, the market clears instantaneously. However, we should note that we did not make such an assumption when we examined the adjustment mechanism for the goods and services market. But now, comparing the two markets, our view is that information is more plentiful, more easily accessible, and less costly in the financial market than in the goods and services market, because the latter is a proxy for a myriad of different markets. Thus the loans (financial) market clears a lot faster than the goods market. Our graphical analysis becomes a lot easier if we assume that one of the two markets clears instantaneously. We choose, of course, the loans market for this role. But for the issues we shall examine here, this assumption is not restrictive. However, we shall relax this assumption when, in a later chapter, it becomes crucial for the results. Note that in what follows, this equality always holds:

$$EL = I(i,x) - S(i,x) - \lambda \left[\frac{M}{p} - L(i,x) \right] = 0 \tag{13}$$

II. THE COMPLETE SHORT-RUN MODEL

In this chapter we examine only the short run, a period during which the quantity of capital, K, can be taken as fixed. Often, without loss of generality, we shall assume that this fixed K is equal to one (i.e., $K = \overline{K} \equiv 1$).

We shall also continue the approach followed in Chapters 2 and 3, the assumption that in each period of time, because of perfect real-wage flexibility, the market for labor is always cleared, as in Figure 4-1. Thus, for the short-run period under consideration, we shall assume that the employment/capital ratio is fixed at its full-employment level, $\bar{x}$. This, in turn, permits us to identify the one relevant investment curve out of the infinity of such curves in the (i,I)-plane. In Figure 4-2a this is labeled the $I(i,\bar{x})$ curve and is depicted by a heavier line. In Figure 4-2b we can identify the relevant savings curve, which is labeled $S(i,\bar{x})$ and is also depicted by a heavier line.

Schematically, the complete description of the economy is given by equation (13), which denotes the continuous clearance of the loans market; the law of supply and demand for goods and services, as represented by (5a)–(5c); and the definition of excess demand for goods and services, EG, as given by (4). In addition, we must also specify the fixity of both the capital stock and the employment/capital ratio at

FIGURE 4-1

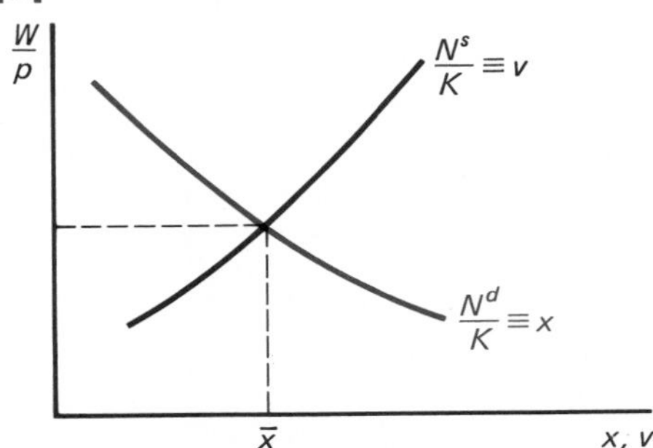

FIGURE 4-2

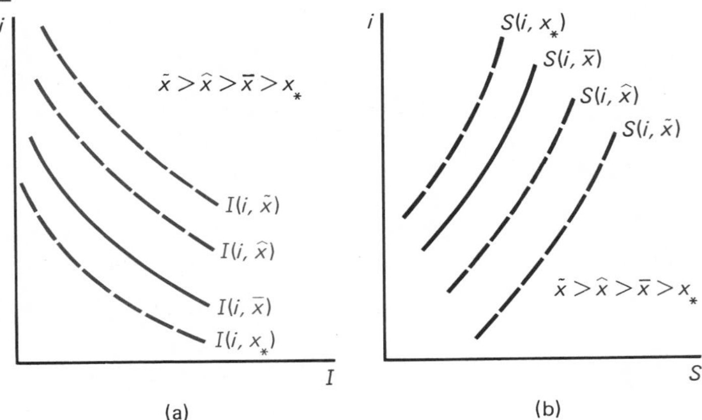

$K = \overline{K} \equiv 1$ and $x = \overline{x}$, respectively. We can condense all this information in the following "model":

$$EL = I(i,x) - S(i,x) - \lambda \left[\frac{M}{p} - L(i,x) \right] = 0 \tag{14}$$

$$EG > 0 \rightarrow p\uparrow \text{ (i.e., } \Delta p > 0) \tag{15a}$$

$$EG < 0 \rightarrow p\downarrow \text{ (i.e., } \Delta p < 0) \tag{15b}$$

$$EG = 0 \rightarrow p \text{ unchanged (i.e., } \Delta p = 0) \tag{15c}$$

$$K \equiv \overline{K} \equiv 1 \tag{16}$$

$$x = \overline{x} \tag{17}$$

We are now ready to depict diagrammatically the economy represented by (14)–(17). Since we are examining the case for which the loans market is always cleared, we can rewrite the $EL = 0$ equation, (14), as

$$I(i,\overline{x}) - S(i,\overline{x}) = \lambda \left[\frac{M}{p} - L(i,\overline{x}) \right] \tag{18}$$

Note that the left side of (18) is the excess demand for goods and services and the right side is the excess supply of real balances, both of which are expressed in flow terms. Employing the $I(\cdot)$ and $S(\cdot)$ curves in the left panel of Figure 4-3, we first derive the $I(i,\overline{x}) - S(i,\overline{x})$ curve in the right panel of Figure 4-3. We see in the left

FIGURE 4-3

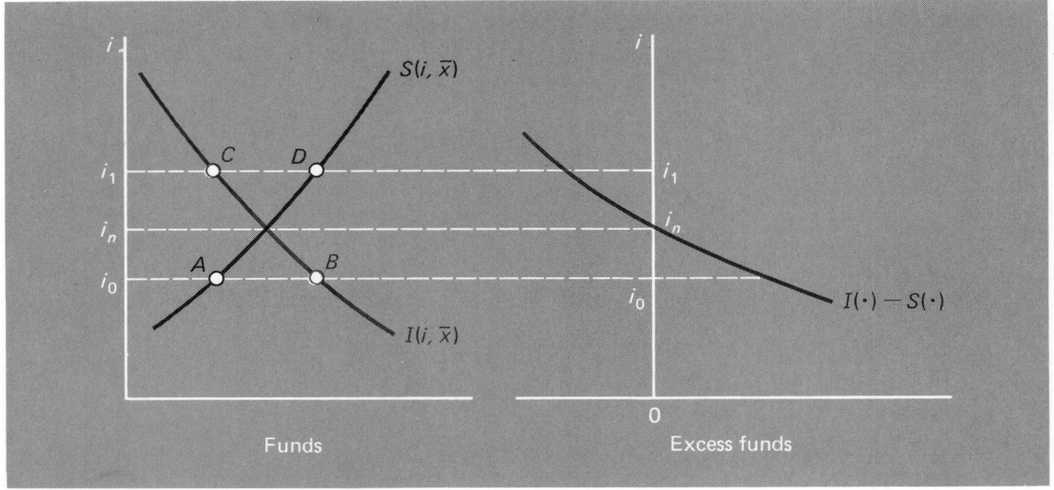

panel that when the interest rate is equal to i_n, $I - S$ is zero, and that we can depict this in the right panel as a point on the i-axis. On the other hand, if $i = i_0$, $I - S = \overline{AB} > 0$, as depicted in the right panel. Then, for each i, we find what the magnitude, positive or negative, of $I - S$ is, and we depict it in the right panel. For example, if $i = i_1$, $I - S < 0$ and equal to CD. It follows, therefore, that the $I - S$ curve is downward sloping, as shown in the right panel of Figure 4-3. In this same panel the horizontal axis measures *excess funds* (to emphasize the excess of I over S and vice versa).

Now we proceed to derive the excess supply-of-money curve, that is, the right side of (18). In Figure 4-4a we can draw the demand for real balances when x is at its full-employment level, $\bar{x}$. We can also draw the supply of real balances for a given price level, P_0, and for a given nominal quantity of money, M_0. In Figure 4-4b we can plot the excess supply of real balances curve, $M/p - L$. At the level of interest rate i_*, $L = M_0/P_0$; therefore $M_0/P_0 - L = 0$, which is shown as a point on the vertical axis (denoting zero $M/p - L$). At levels higher than i_*, there is excess supply of real balances, $M_0/P_0 - L > 0$. For example, at $i = i_0$ there is positive excess supply of real balances equal to AB. On the other hand, an interest rate lower than i_* shows a negative excess supply of real balances (i.e., excess demand). Thus, at $i = i_1$ the excess supply is *minus DC*. Now, for each level of the interest rate, we find the excess demand or excess supply and plot these points. Connecting them, we find the excess supply curve, such as the one labeled $M_0/P_0 - L(i,\bar{x})$. This curve is upward sloping with respect to the interest rate because an increase in the interest rate, while leaving the supply constant, decreases the demand for

FIGURE 4-4

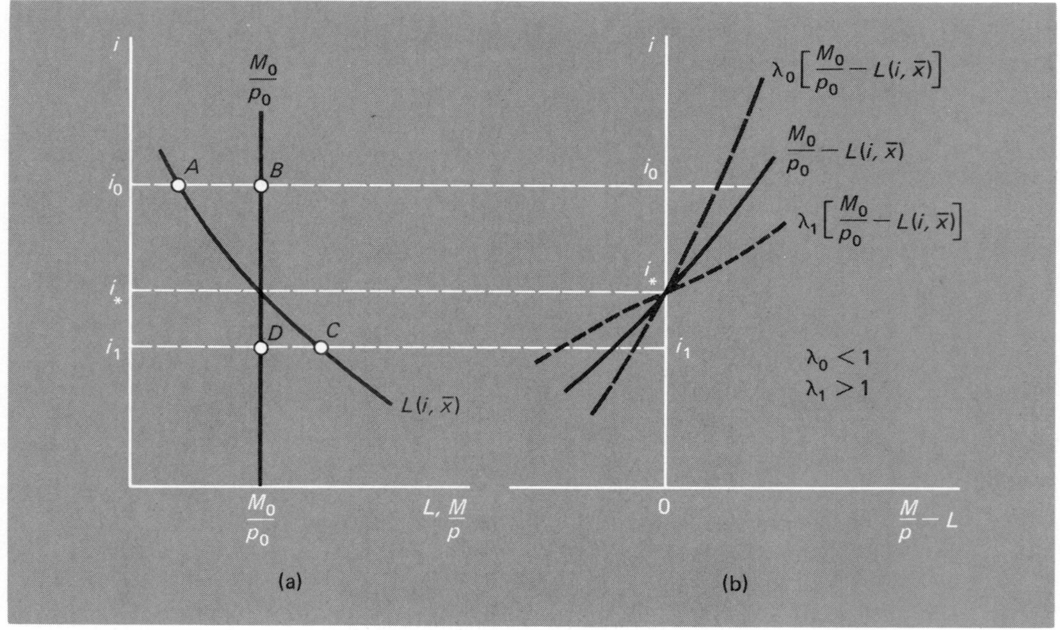

money and, therefore, increases the excess of supply over demand if it is positive and decreases excess demand if excess supply is negative.

At this point we are interested in deriving the *flow* excess supply-of-money curve. If we assume that λ is equal to one, the curve labeled $M_0/p_0 - L(i,\bar{x})$, in Figure 4-4b, is the relevant curve. If, however, λ is different from zero, the flow curve will be steeper or flatter than that curve. If $\lambda = \lambda_0 < 1$, the flow curve will be steeper, as shown in Figure 4-4b by the curve $\lambda_0[M_0/p_0 - L(i,\bar{x})]$. If $\lambda = \lambda_1 > 1$, the curve is flatter, as shown by $\lambda_1[M_0/p_0 - L(i,\bar{x})]$. Note that all three curves cross the i-axis at $i = i_*$, since at i_*, $M_0/p_0 - L(i,\bar{x}) = 0$ and is independent of the magnitude of λ. As before, we shall assume a fixed λ—until further notice.

Suppose that, keeping x and p at their assumed levels (i.e., $x = \bar{x}$ and $p = p_0$ in Figure 4-4), we *increase* M, from M_0 to M_1. What will happen to the flow excess supply of real balances? The answer to this question is seen in Figure 4-5, where the supply of real balances is greater than before, $M_1p_0 > M_0/p_0$. It follows, therefore, that the interest rate, i_*^1, for which $M/p - L = 0$, is lower than before, $i_*^1 < i_*^0$, and that the $M/p - L$ curve shifts from $M_0/p_0 - L(i,\bar{x})$ to $M_1/p_0 - L(i,\bar{x})$, that is, to the right, as shown in Figure 4-5b. Now, no matter which fixed λ we assume, the flow excess supply curve, $\lambda[M_1/p_0 - L(i,\bar{x})]$, will also shift to the right. Figure 4-5b was drawn under the assumption that the fixed λ is greater than one, as the reader can easily verify.

We can generalize our result by saying that an increase in the nominal quantity of money, M, shifts the flow excess supply curve to the right (and a decrease in M shifts the same curve to the left). On the other hand, it is easy to verify that we can shift the flow curve to the right if we *lower* the price level from p_0 to p_1 $(p_1 < p_0)$ while keeping the quantity M unchanged, as shown in Figure 4-6, whose

FIGURE 4-5

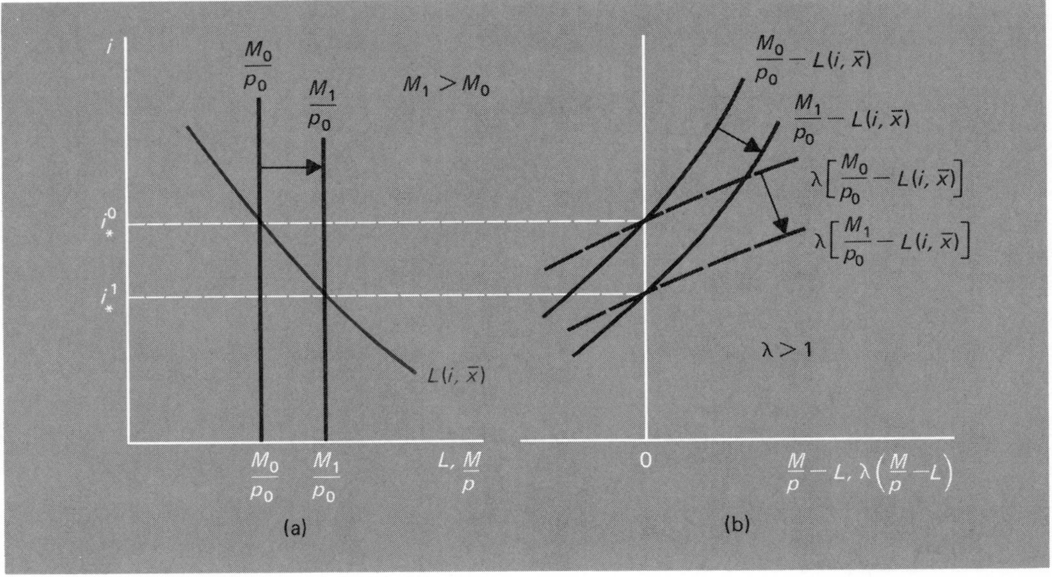

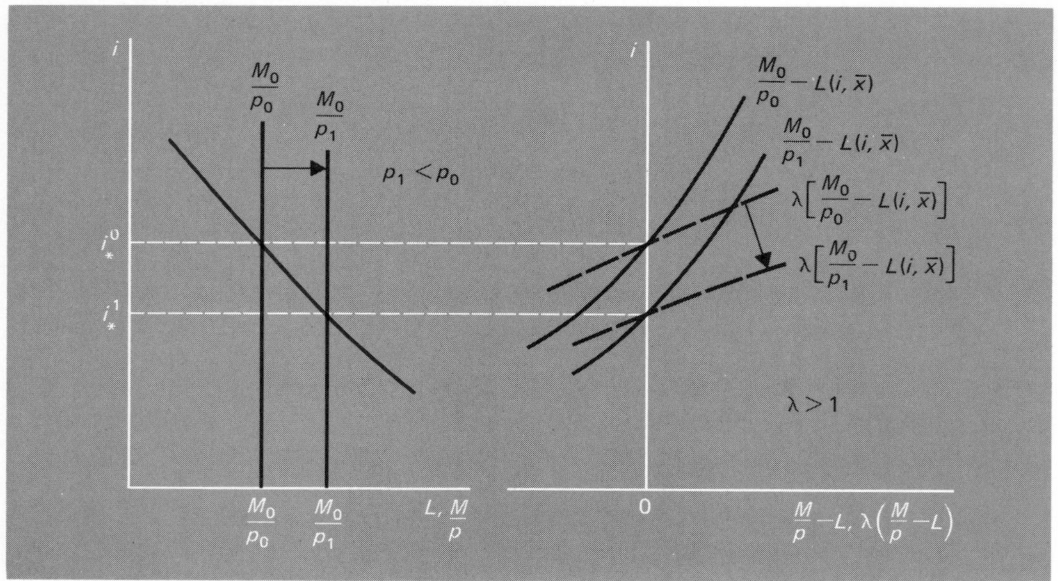

FIGURE 4-6

explanation is safely left to the reader. And it follows that a *rise* in p will shift the flow excess supply of money curve to the left.

We are now ready to depict graphically equation (18). In Figure 4-7 the market rate of interest, i_m, is determined at the point of intersection of the $I - S$ and the $\lambda[M/p - L(\cdot)]$ curves. And at point E, equation (18) is satisfied, and hence the loans market is cleared. This intersection, at point E, will be called a *temporary equilibrium* of this system, a term used to distinguish it from "full, general" equilib-

FIGURE 4-7

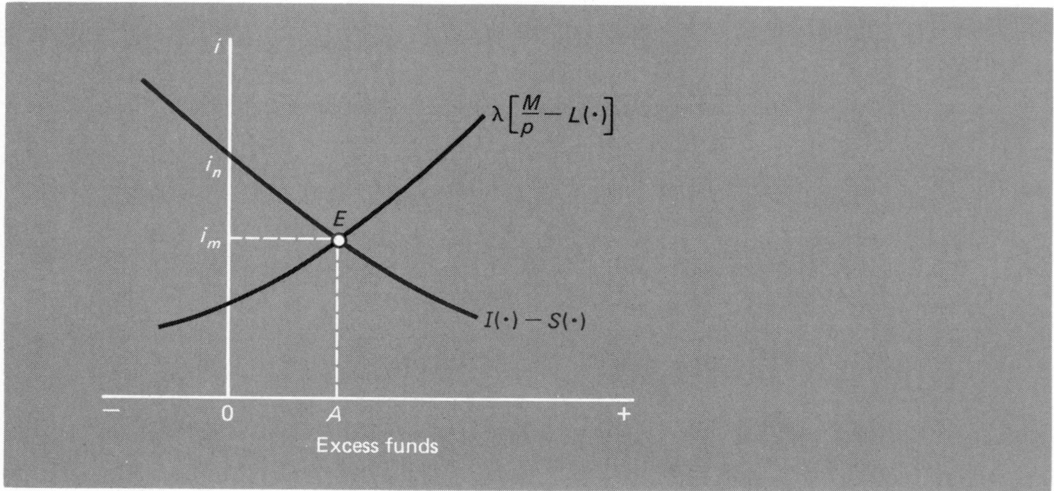

rium. Since, at point *E*, aggregate demand for loans is equal to aggregate supply of loans, one might think that, according to the "law of supply and demand," there is no tendency for the interest rate to change. This is possible, however, only if *other things are equal.* But other things will *not* remain equal. In particular, for the case depicted in Figure 4-7, at the market rate of interest, i_m, there is an excess demand for goods and services, which can be read off the $I - S$ curve and is equal to *OA*. But we know from (15a) that an excess demand for goods and services will induce a rise in the price level, which will shift the excess supply-of-money curve, $\lambda[M/p - L(\cdot)]$, to the left, a problem that we explore in the next section.

Since point *E* in Figure 4-7 also lies on the excess supply-of-money curve, $\lambda[M/p - L(\cdot)]$, we can say that, at the market rate of interest, there is excess supply of money, equal to *OA*. In other words, this excess supply of money materializes as excess demand for goods and services, which, in turn, engineers an increase in the price level. Therefore we have formally established this schema:

$$\frac{M}{p} - L(i,x) > 0 \rightarrow (I - S) > 0 \rightarrow \Delta p > 0$$

which is really Schema II of Chapter 3.

Figure 4-7 was deliberately constructed to depict the consequences of the case of excess supply of money. Now, Figure 4-8 is constructed to depict the case when, at the market rate of interest, i_m, there is excess demand for money. At point *F* we can read, from the $\lambda[M/p - L(\cdot)]$ curve, the *negative* distance *OB*, that is, negative excess supply of money, or the excess demand for money. But this same distance also represents excess demand for goods and services, $I - S$, but since it is negative, it follows that it also shows excess supply of goods and services. In summary, at the market rate of interest, i_m, the excess demand for money materializes as excess supply of goods and services. According to the law of supply and demand, summarized

FIGURE 4-8

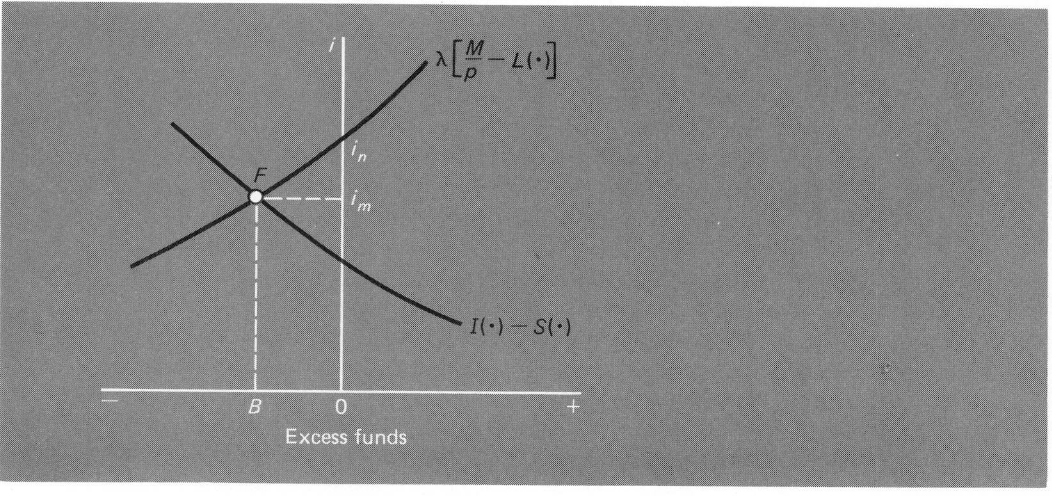

in (15b), the price level will fall. Again, it is a temporary equilibrium, since each fall in the price level will shift the excess supply-of-money curve to the right, which will produce yet a new interest rate.

Figure 4-9 depicts the case of full, general equilibrium. The intersection of the two curves occurs on the i-axis, which means that, at the market rate of interest, there is zero excess demand for goods and services (reading from the $I - S$ curve) and zero excess supply of money (reading from the $M/p - L(\cdot)$ curve). But according to the construction of this graph, the intersection always occurs for zero excess demand for loans, resulting in the clearance of all three markets, that for loans, for goods and services, and for money. There is no tendency for any of our endogenous variables to change. In particular, since the goods and services market is cleared, the price level will not change, which means, in turn, that there will be neither a shift of the excess supply-of-money curve nor a change in the interest rate.

Therefore we have established the following results:

$$\frac{M}{p} - L(\cdot) > 0 \rightarrow \Delta p > 0 \tag{I}$$

$$\frac{M}{p} - L(\cdot) < 0 \rightarrow \Delta p < 0 \tag{II}$$

$$\frac{M}{p} - L(\cdot) = 0 \rightarrow \Delta p = 0 \tag{III}$$

These are, of course, the same results claimed by the quantity theory of money. Ours, however, rely on the interest rate. In fact, following Wicksell, we can say that in (I), depicted by Figure 4-7, the excess supply of money causes the market rate of interest to be below the *natural rate.* And this discrepancy causes excess demand for goods and services, thereby raising the price level. The *natural rate* is defined as the level of interest rate for which there is zero excess demand for goods

FIGURE 4-9

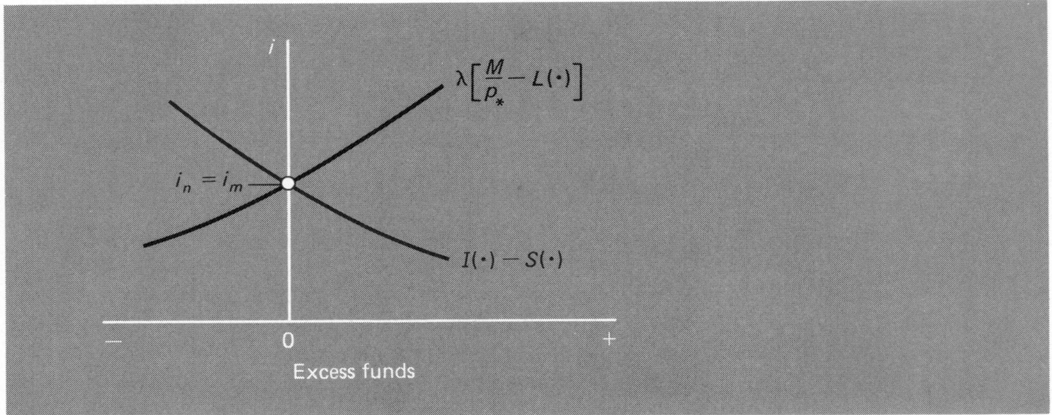

and services. In our graph the natural rate, i_n, is found where the $I - S$ curve intersects the i-axis. Similarly, in (II), illustrated by Figure 4-8, the market rate of interest is greater than the natural rate, causing an excess supply of goods and services, which, in turn, lowers the price level. Finally, in (III) and Figure 4-9 the market rate of interest is equal to the natural rate and there is clearance of all markets. Using this Wicksellian terminology, (I), (II), and (III) can be stated, respectively, as (I′), (II′), and (III′):

$$i_m < i_n \rightarrow \Delta p > 0 \tag{I'}$$

$$i_m > i_n \rightarrow \Delta p < 0 \tag{II'}$$

$$i_m = i_n \rightarrow \Delta p = 0 \tag{III'}$$

III. THE DYNAMIC BEHAVIOR OF THE MODEL: THE EQUILIBRATING MECHANISM

We recall that not all aspects of the cases depicted in Figures 4-7 and 4-8 were explored in our earlier analysis. In fact, we said earlier that these graphs represented temporary equilibria. It is now time, however, to complete that analysis.

Figure 4-7 assumed, at the outset, excess supply of real balances. For concreteness, with p_0 to denote the initial price level, the flow excess supply of real balances is represented as $\lambda[M/p_0 - L(\cdot)]$. Furthermore, we can reproduce the information of Figure 4-7 in Figure 4-10, with the original market rate of interest denoted as

FIGURE 4-10

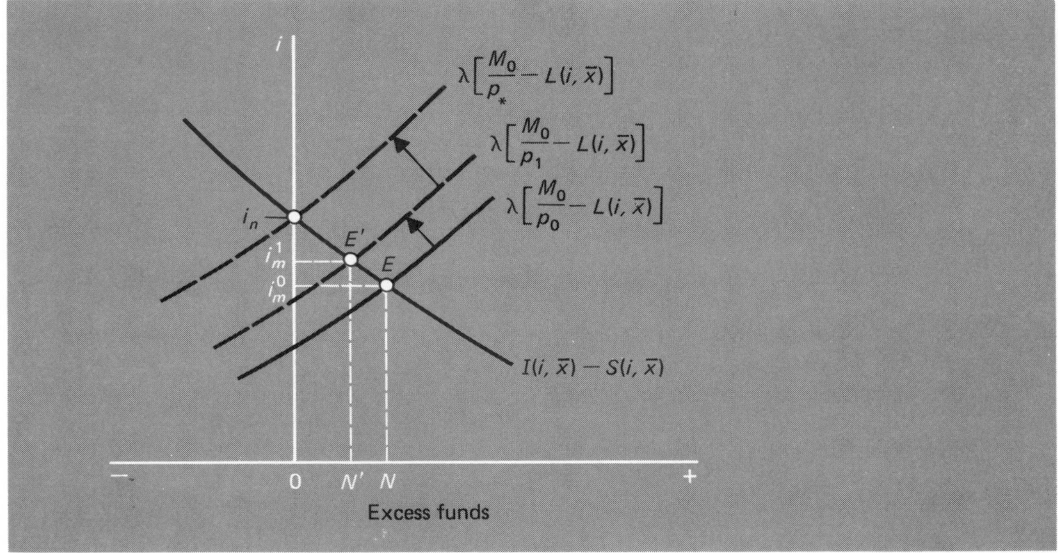

i_m^0 and determined at point E, the intersection of the $\lambda[M/p_0 - L(\cdot)]$ and the $I - S$ curves. Since $i_m^0 < i_n$, that is, since the market rate of interest is lower than the natural rate, there is excess demand for goods and services (equal to the flow excess supply of money, ON), which raises the price level higher than p_0, say to p_1. This increase in the price level shrinks the real supply of money, from M/p_0 to M/p_1 (where $M/p_1 < M/p_0$), thereby shifting the flow excess supply-of-money curve to the left. While the new temporary equilibrium at E' produces a higher market rate of interest, i_m^1, it still is lower than the natural rate of interest. In other words, despite the reduction in size of the excess supply of money, caused by the increase in the price level, some excess demand for goods and services remains. It follows, then, that the price level must rise again, say to p_2, shifting the excess supply-of-money curve farther to the left and forcing the market rate of interest upward, say to i_m^2. The price level will continue to rise, and thus the $\lambda[M/p - L(\cdot)]$ curve will continue to shift to the left, raising the market rate of interest, until the flow excess supply-of-money curve crosses the i-axis at i_n. This full equilibrium is represented in Figure 4-9.

We have examined this case in detail for several reasons. The primary one, of course, is that we now have a good grasp of the workings of the model. Specifically, we have seen what lies behind changes in the price level and in the interest rate; *how* these important variables change through time; and how the two markets (for loans and for goods and services) are interrelated, with one influencing the other. Of course, there is yet another important reason for our extensive treatment of this case: The interdependent markets provide a prime example of the methodology (and even the mentality) of *partial,* as compared with *general,* equilibrium analysis. Also, *within* the general equilibrium framework, our treatment distinguishes between *temporary* and *full* equilibria.

The mere fact that the loans market is cleared is not sufficient to persuade us that we can have equilibrium; this clearance cannot even guarantee absence of movements in the variable that this market determines, namely, the interest rate. As long as there is excess demand in the goods market, the supply side of the loans market will keep falling, thereby raising not only the price level but also the interest rate. A typical partial equilibrium examination of the problem assumes that *other things*—besides the market under examination, i.e., the loans market—remain the same, in particular, the goods market and the variable *this* market determines, that is, the price level. Thus the partial analysis predicts that the interest rate will remain the same, since the loans market is cleared!

We shall now complete briefly the case of Figure 4-8, where initially there is excess demand for real balances. In this case the market rate of interest is initially at i_m^0, above the natural rate of interest, thereby causing excess supply of goods and services, equal to OB. This is reproduced from Figure 4-8 in Figure 4-11. The excess supply of goods and services lowers the price level, say to $p_1 < p_0$, which enlarges the real balances, $M/p_1 > M/p_0$; decreases the excess flow demand for money; and thus enlarges the aggregate supply of loans. Hence the interest rate falls, say to $i_m^1 < i_m^0$. The way Figure 4-11 is drawn guarantees that although the interest rate falls and the demand for goods and services rises, the latter will not rise enough to

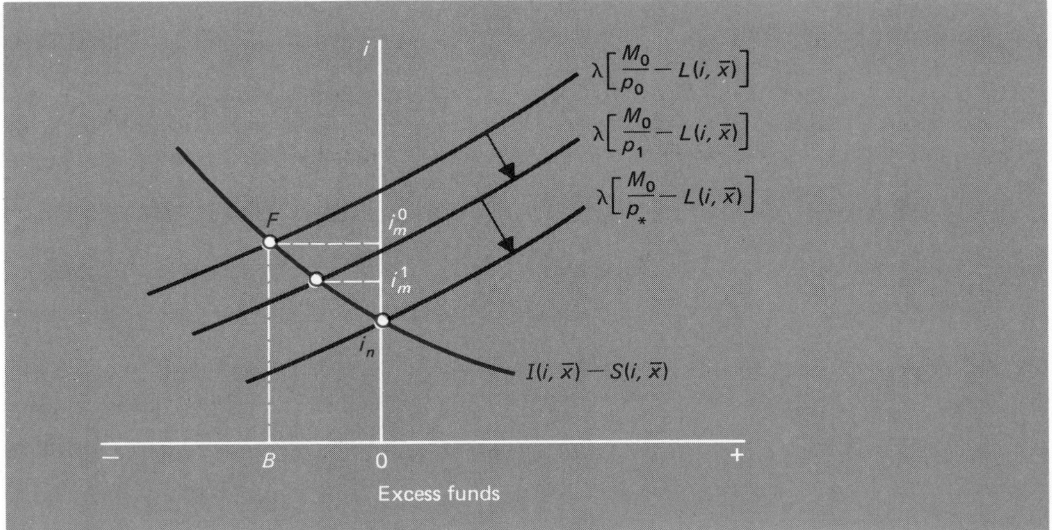

FIGURE 4-11

eliminate excess supply of goods and services. Thus the price level will keep falling, lowering the market rate of interest, i_m, until it becomes equal to the natural rate of interest—*where all markets clear and all motion stops.* This graph, again, will look like Figure 4-9.

We have seen above that as long as there is *disequilibrium,* the price level will continue to change until *full equilibrium* is reached. This suggests, first, that the equilibrium is stable; and, second, that changes in the price level are the key to the system's stability. In effect, the (short-run) system depends on only one variable, namely, the price level, and in this case the system is stable if the price level tends to fall when it is above its equilibrium value, and if it tends to rise when it is below equilibrium.

It is clear from Figure 4-12 that our system satisfies this stability test. Let us now suppose that the economy was originally at position *A,* with all markets cleared and the price level equal to p_*. Furthermore, let us suppose that the price level *falls* to p_1 (i.e., $p_1 < p_*$), which causes excess supply of money, which, in turn, is reflected as excess demand for goods and services, equal to *OK.* But the temporary equilibrium, established at point *B,* cannot be maintained, since the excess demand for goods and services will cause the price level to begin to rise (above p_1) and continue to rise until it becomes equal to p_*, thereby reestablishing equilibrium point *A.* Similarly, if the price level rises to $p_2 > p_*$, there will be excess demand for money and thus excess supply of goods and services, equal to *OL.* This will push the price level downward until it again becomes equal to p_*. (The reader should note that the above exercises were performed while keeping the nominal money supply fixed, at M_0.)

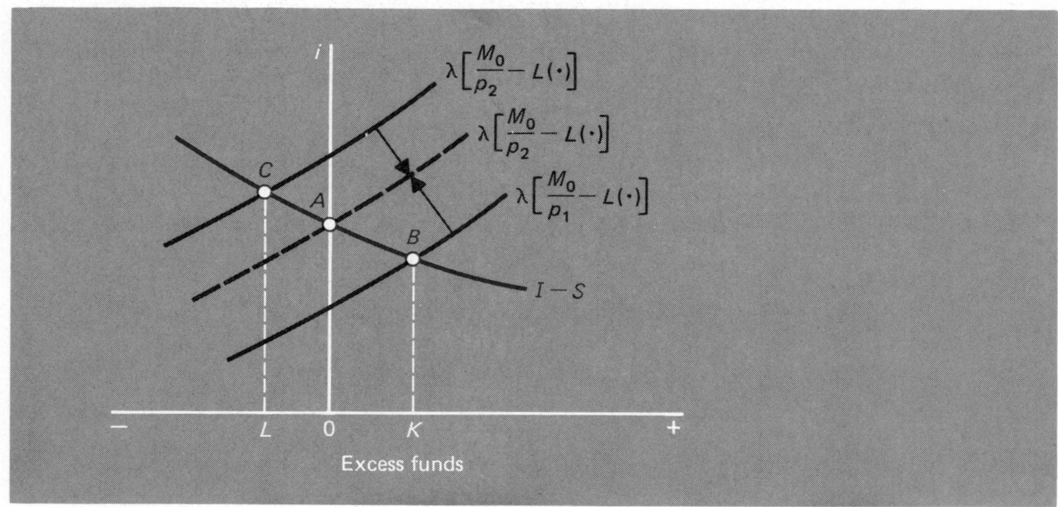

FIGURE 4-12

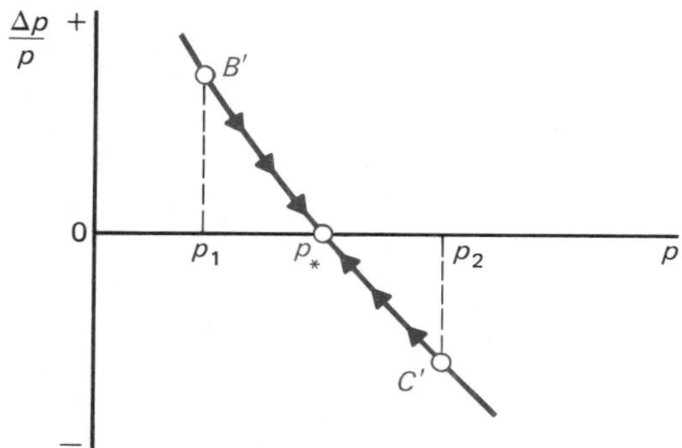

FIGURE 4-13

Schematically, we have established that

$$\left(\frac{\Delta p}{p}\right) \lesseqgtr 0 \text{ when } p \gtreqless p_*,$$

which is the standard definition of a stable price mechanism, as illustrated in Figure 4-13.

IV. CHANGES IN THE MONEY SUPPLY

We shall now examine the effects of a change in the money supply, *M,* on the interest rate and on the price level. We begin by examining the effects of a *one-shot* increase in the money supply and follow up by examining the effects of an increase in the *rate of growth* of the money supply.

1. EFFECTS OF A ONE-SHOT INCREASE IN M

Starting from a full-equilibrium position, such as that of Figure 4-9, incorporated into point H, Figure 4-14, let us imagine an increase, say a doubling, in the nominal quantity of money, from M_0 to M_1. Before this increase the market rate of interest coincided with the natural rate at i_n^0, and the price level was equal to p_0. However, this increase in M shifts the flow excess supply-of-money curve to the right. Thus we now have the curve labeled $\lambda[M_1/p_0 - L(i,\bar{x})]$ intersecting the excess demand-for-goods curve, $I - S$, at point F. At this temporary equilibrium, reminiscent of the situation depicted in Figure 4-7, there is an excess demand for goods and services (and thus excess supply of money) equal to the magnitude OA. Thus position F cannot be sustained without a *further* increase in the quantity of money, a case precluded by assumption. And the price level must rise, say to p_1, thus reaching a new temporary equilibrium at point G. At this point there is still excess demand for goods and services (albeit lower than before, $OA' < OA$), and the price level must rise further. This process will continue until the price level is raised to the point where the excess supply-of-money curve reverts to the original position, intersecting the $I - S$ curve on the interest axis at H. We see, then, that doubling the quantity of money leaves the (full) equilibrium rate of interest unchanged, at i_n^0.

The question remains, How much does the price level rise when the money supply rises? To begin with, we know that the price level will rise to the level p_*, which makes the real supply, M_1/p_*, exactly equal to the demand generated by $\bar{x}$ and i_n^0. But these two variables remain at their original level, the one prior to the increase in M. It follows, then, that the new real supply of money, M_1/p_*, must be equal to the old demand, which was exactly equal to M_0/p_0. Thus the "new" real supply must be equal to the "old" supply (i.e., $M_1/p_* = M_0/p_0$). And since the

FIGURE 4-14

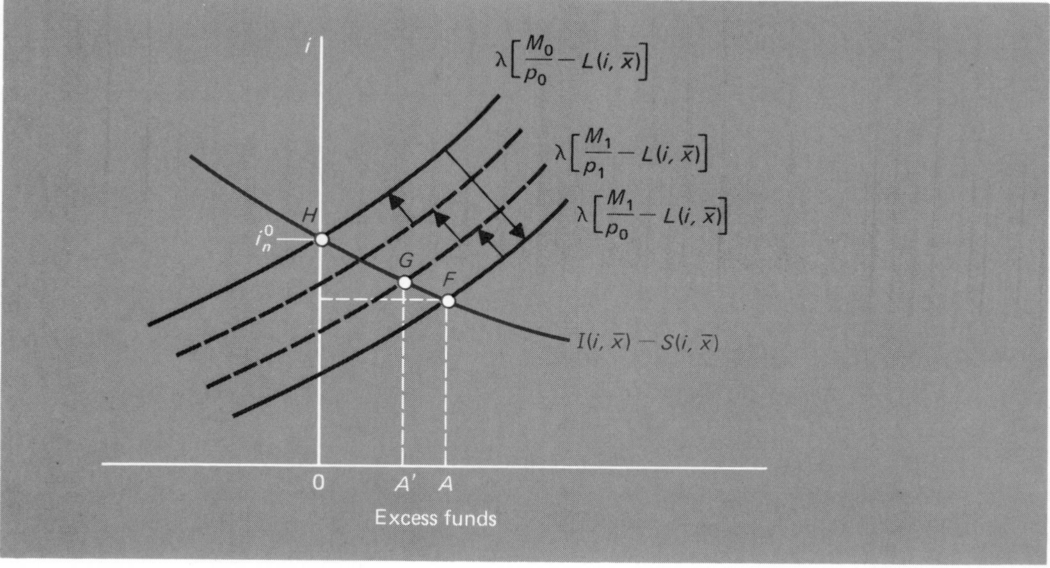

numerator on the left-hand side is twice as large as the numerator on the right-hand side (i.e., $M_1 = 2M_0$), it follows that the denominator on the left-hand side must also be twice as large as the denominator of the right-hand side (i.e., $p_* = 2p_0$).

In summary, we see that an *increase in the nominal quantity of money will increase the price level by the same proportion, but it will leave the interest rate unchanged.* These results are, of course, the standard quantity theory results, referred to in the literature as the *neutrality of money.*

Furthermore, it is interesting to trace the time paths of the price level and the interest rate that result from a one-shot increase in the money supply, from M_0 to M_1. In Figures 4-15a and 4-15b, t_0 represents the moment at which the money supply is increased. Until that time, it is assumed that the interest rate is equal to i^0_n, and the price level at p_0. As Figure 4-15b shows, this increase (at time t_0) in the money supply instantaneously (i.e., at time t_0) lowers the interst rate to i^1_m. This immediate reduction in the interest rate is what Friedman calls the "liquidity effect."[2] From there, the interest rate keeps rising through time until it reaches (asymptotically) its original level at i^c_n. This is what Friedman calls the "income-and-price level effect." In Figure 4-15a the price level starts rising at time t_0, and it keeps rising until it reaches twice its original level.

Comparing Figures 4-15a and 4-15b, we see that except for the instant t_0, the price level and the interest rate move in the same direction, a phenomenon that can explain what Keynes termed *Gibson's paradox.*[3] In the 1920s the British economist A. H. Gibson observed that over long periods of time the price level and the interest rate move together. And that as long as there is excess demand for goods and services, the price level will continue to rise, as will the interest rate. Here, in our analysis,

FIGURE 4-15

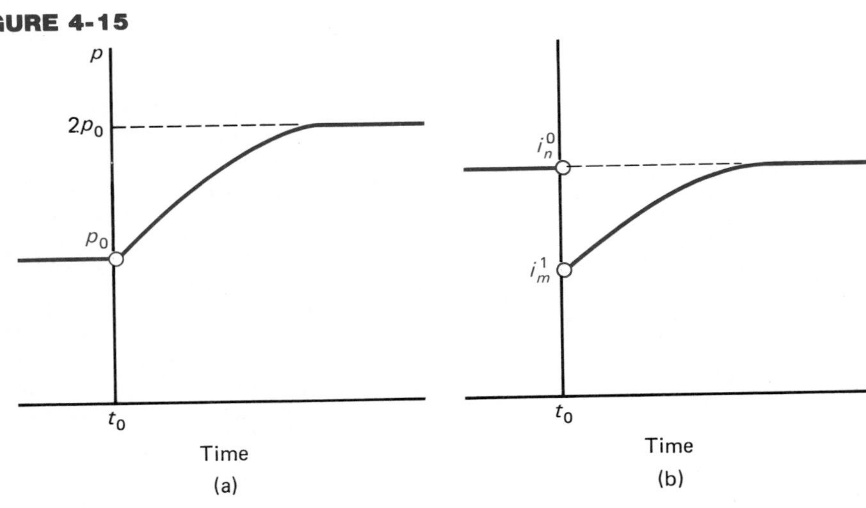

[2] Milton Friedman, "Factors Affecting the Interest Rates," in *Money and Finance: Readings in Theory, Policy, and Institutions,* ed. D. Carson (New York: John Wiley, 1972), pp. 319–30.

[3] J. M. Keynes, *A Treatise on Money* (London: Macmillan, 1930).

the excess demand for goods and services has been engineered by an increase in the nominal money supply, lowering temporarily the interest rate, which subsequently rises along with the price level. Keynes considered this analysis a possible explanation, but he rejected it because the Gibson paradox had been proved to hold over very long periods of time. Keynes maintained instead that over the long run both the natural and the market rate of interest move together, but that the market rate never quite catches up with the normal rate.

2. AN INCREASE IN THE RATE OF GROWTH, $\Delta M/M$

The self-liquidating nature of the excess supply of goods and services is apparent by now. Consider, once more, the familiar graph depicting an excess flow supply of money equal to OC and, therefore, identical excess demand for goods and services. As long as the nominal money supply is kept fixed at $\overline{M}$, the excess supply of real balances will continue to shrink, until it is eliminated completely, because the price level will continue to increase. Let us now suppose that the monetary authorities want to peg the market rate of interest at a level such as i_m^0, below the natural rate, i_n^0. It is clear that this commitment requires a continuous excess flow supply of money equal to OC, which, in turn, requires a real supply of money always equal to $\overline{M}/p_0$. Since the price level will keep rising (above p_0), the real supply of money, M/p, will remain equal to $\overline{M}/p_0$ only if the *nominal* money supply is being increased constantly and at precisely the rate of the price increase. However, the price level will be rising at a *constant* percentage rate, and thus the nominal quantity of money needs to increase at the same constant rate. This *constancy* of the percentage increase in the price level results from the usual assumption that it is proportional to excess demand for goods and services. But the latter, read from the $I - S$ curve, must be constant at the level OC if the interest rate is to be kept at i_m^0.

FIGURE 4-16

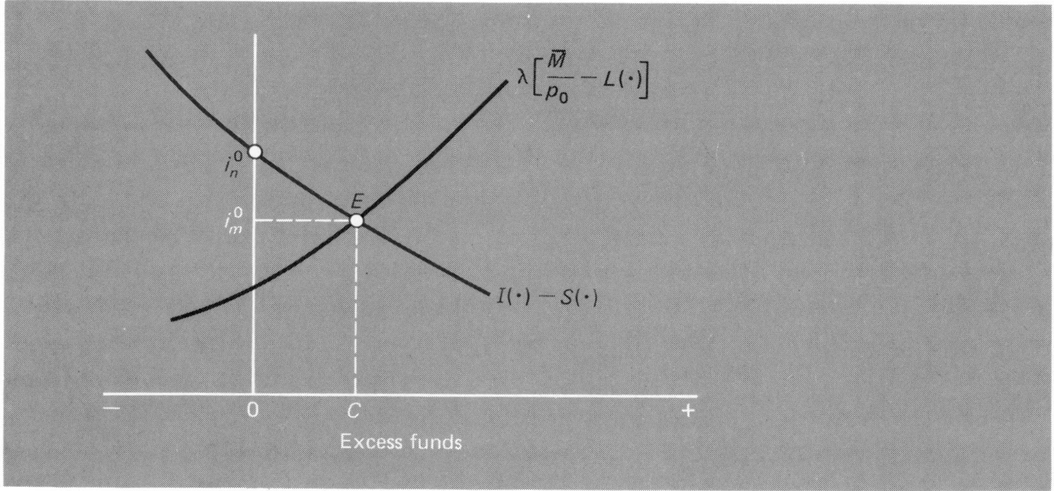

We have established, therefore, that if the monetary authority wants to keep the market rate of interest at a constant level below its normal rate, it must be prepared to impose on society a constant rate of inflation by increasing the quantity of money at that same constant rate. Or, conversely, the monetary authority must accept that a continuous, constant percentage increase in the nominal money supply will cause an equal (and also continuous) percentage increase in the price level.

We shall consider this result tentative, since it gives rise to two complications that must be resolved. First, it is implied that the rate of inflation, caused by a continuous equiproportionate increase in the money supply, requires *permanent excess demand* for goods and services (equal to *OC* in Figure 4-16). In other words, the system will be in a state of perpetual disequilibrium. While this is possible, it taxes our imagination. It would certainly be more appealing if we could show that the continuous increase in the money supply causes a continuous increase in the price level while the goods market, as well as the other markets, is cleared.

The second and more troublesome aspect of the above result is the implication that the rate of inflation is not, at least partly, anticipated by economic agents. On the contrary, it seems reasonable to assume that, after protracted periods of a constant rate of inflation, these agents, both firms and households, will start to count on this inflation; they start to expect it. This formation of inflationary expectations will alter behavior, the firms' demand for investment, and the households' demand for consumption (and thus their supply of savings). This observation leads us naturally to the material of the next section, which explores the effects of inflationary expectations on the agents' behavioral functions, namely, on households' savings and on firms' investment and, ultimately, on the equilibrium interest rates and actual rate of inflation.

V. INFLATIONARY EXPECTATIONS, NOMINAL VS. REAL RATE OF INTEREST, AND MONETARY POLICY

In the presence of inflationary expectations we must distinguish between the *nominal* rate of interest and its *real* rate, or, rather, the *expected real rate.* To find the expected real rate of interest, denoted here as i_r, we must correct the nominal rate for the expected rate of inflation, that is, subtract the expected rate of inflation, $(\Delta p/p)^e$, from the nominal rate:

$$i_r \equiv i - \left(\frac{\Delta p}{p}\right)^e$$

For economy of notation, we shall denote $(\Delta p/p)^e$ as q and hence $i_r \equiv i - q$.

This distinction between the nominal and the real rate of interest, first introduced by Irving Fisher,[4] is important because firms and households make their decisions to invest and to save, respectively, on the basis of the (expected) *real* rate. Until now we have implicitly assumed no expectations of inflation or deflation. There-

[4] Irving Fisher, *Theory of Interest* (New York: Macmillan, 1930).

fore the nominal and real rates coincided. In the above equation, if q is zero, $i_r = i$. For this reason we have always inserted i, and not i_r, in the I and S functions. We must now change all this and explicitly state the savings and investment functions as $I(i_r,x)$ and $S(i_r,x)$, with a graphical depiction, as in Figures 4-17a and 4-17b, respectively. Figure 4-17a illustrates the negative relation (derived earlier) between the *real* rate of interest and investment demand. Figure 4-17b illustrates the positive relation between i_r and savings (of course, under the assumption that the substitution effect outweighs the income effect).

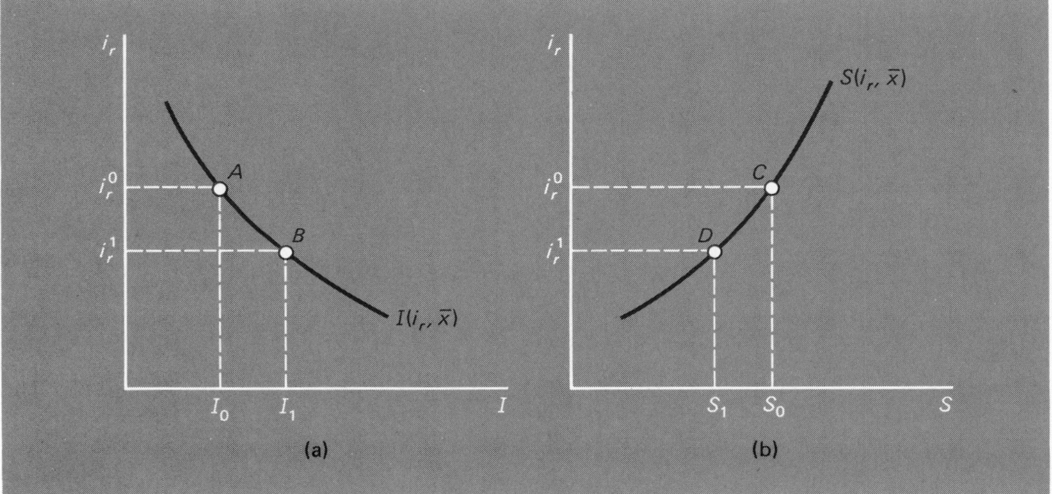

FIGURE 4-17

If we continue to depict the investment and savings schedules by graphs in which the vertical axis measures the nominal interest rate, i, there must be one investment curve and one savings curve for each assumed expected rate of inflation, q, since, for the same nominal interest rate, a different real rate of interest corresponds to each different expected rate of inflation. Symbolically, we see that

$$I(i_r,\bar{x}) = I(i - q,\bar{x})$$

$$S(i_r,\bar{x}) = S(i - q,\bar{x})$$

In other words, investment, and, similarly, savings, are a function of both the nominal interest rate, i, and of the expected rate of inflation (or deflation). We can therefore rewrite the above functions as

$$\tilde{I}(i,q,\bar{x}) \equiv I(i - q,\bar{x})$$

$$\tilde{S}(i,q,\bar{x}) \equiv S(i - q,\bar{x})$$

We can now derive the following result: In the $(i,\tilde{I})$-plane a higher rate of inflation shifts the investment curve to the right, that is, for each level of the nominal interest rate, investment demand increases. In Figure 4-18a, with the expected rate of inflation equal to q_0, we have the curve $\tilde{I}(i,q_0,\bar{x})$. Let us suppose, for concreteness, that $q_0 = 0$. Suppose further that the expected rate of inflation is now higher and equal to $q_1 > q_0$. Now, for the same nominal rate of interest, say i_0, the corresponding real rate is smaller, $i_r^1 \equiv i_0 - q_1$, as compared with the original one, $i_r^0 \equiv i_0 - q_0 = i_0$. If we depict the investment demand in the (i_r,I)-plane, we have a movement *along* the curve, as from point A to point B in Figure 4-17a. However, in the $(i,\tilde{I})$-plane, this must be shown as a shift of the $\tilde{I}$ curve. And since the increase in q lowers the real interest rate, which, in turn, increases investment demand, it follows that for the same level of nominal interest, i_0, investment must be greater than the original one at I_0; it must be, say, at I_1, which is shown as point B', as compared with point A' of Figure 4-18a. The shift from point A' to point B' in Figure 4-18a corresponds exactly to the movement along the I curve, from point A to point B, in Figure 4-17a. Repeating this same technique for all possible levels of the nominal interest rate in Figure 4-18a, we find that the new points will lie, as point B' does, to the right of points on the $\tilde{I}(i,q_0,\bar{x})$ curve. Connecting all these points, we find the investment curve corresponding to q_1, which lies uniformly to the right of the original one, as shown by curve $\tilde{I}(i,q_1,\bar{x})$ in Figure 4-18a. We have proved, therefore, that there is one I curve (in the (i,I)-plane) for each expected rate of inflation, and also that the higher the expected rate of inflation is, the farther to the right the I curve will lie.

Although we have mentioned only the expected rate of inflation, it should be clear that our analysis also covers the case of expected deflation. Or, in other words, we can speak, generally, of the expected rate of change in prices, q. If this rate is positive, we assume inflation, while a negative sign for q denotes deflation.

FIGURE 4-18

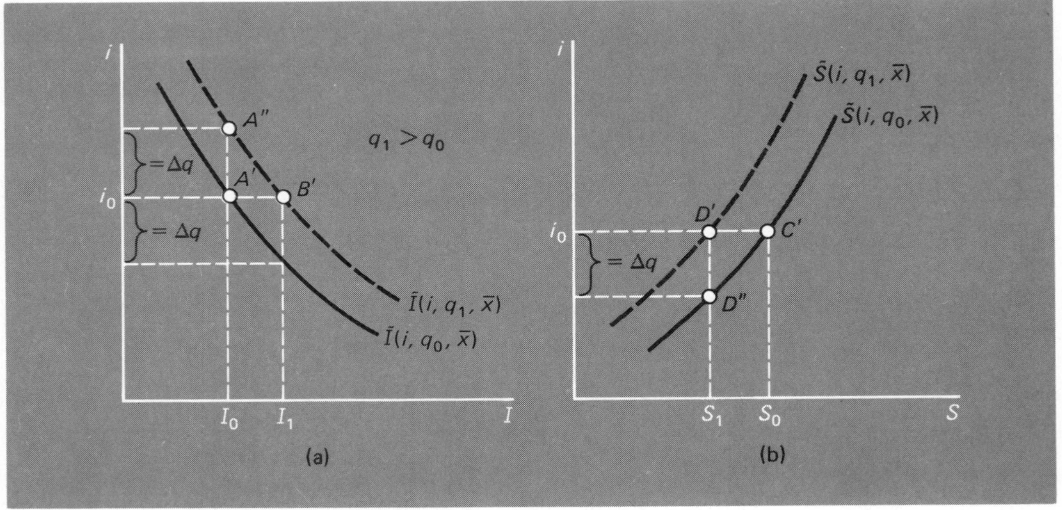

Our results are generalized in the following statement: *For each assumed expected rate of change in prices, there is a corresponding, different investment curve. And the higher (algebraically) the assumed expected rate of change in prices is, the farther to the right the investment curve lies.*

With the following experiment we shall see that when the expected rate of inflation rises by an amount equal to $\Delta q \equiv q_1 - q_0$, the investment curve shifts vertically upward by the same amount. Starting from point A' on the $\tilde{I}(i,q_0,\bar{x})$ curve in Figure 4-18a, let us suppose that we want to have the same investment, I_0, when the expected rate of inflation rises by Δq. Since investment depends only on the (expected) real rate of interest, I_0 will materialize only when the increase in the expected rate of inflation leaves the real rate unchanged. But the real rate remains unchanged only if the nominal rate rises by exactly Δq. Thus, for $I = I_0$, instead of A', we must have point A'', whose vertical distance from A' is Δq. Repeating this experiment for every level of investment, we derive the investment curve labeled $\tilde{I}(i,q_1,\bar{x})$, which lies above $\tilde{I}(i,q_0,\bar{x})$ at a vertical distance equal to Δq.

Restricting our attention to the case of a positive relation between the (real) rate of interest and savings, as in Figure 4-17b, a similar analysis applied to the savings function yields the following results: For the same i_0, an increase in the expected rate of inflation lowers the real rate of interest from i_r^0 to i_r^1 and thus lowers savings from S_0 to S_1. In Figure 4-17b this is shown as a movement (along the S curve) from point C to point D, while in Figure 4-18b this is shown as a shift from point C' to point D'. *Thus an increase in the expected rate of change in the price level will shift the (upward-sloping) savings curve to the left.* Moreover, employing an experiment analogous to the one in the preceding paragraph, we can show that the vertical downward shift is precisely equal to the increase, Δq, in the expected rate of inflation, as illustrated by the movement from point D' to point D'' in Figure 4-18b.

FIGURE 4-19

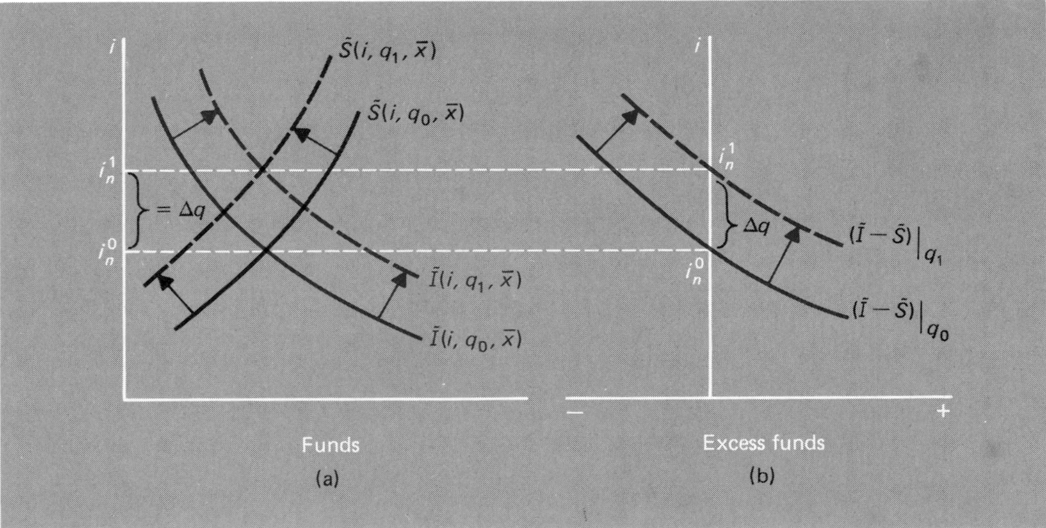

Summarizing our results in an alternative way, we can say that the increase in the expected rate of inflation, by Δq, from q_0 to q_1, shifts the $I - S$ curve upward by a vertical distance equal to Δq, as shown in Figure 4-19. This has an important implication: If a full equilibrium can be achieved, it will be characterized by a nominal natural rate of interest which must be increased by an amount equal to the rise in the expected rate of inflation. Of course, this also means that the real natural rate must remain unchanged as is depicted in Figure 4-20.

In other words, *the increase in the expected rate of inflation eventually increases the nominal rate of interest by an equal percentage, thus leaving the real rate unchanged.* In the literature this is called the *Fisher theorem,* the *Fisher hypothesis,* or the *Fisher effect.*

The question arises, Why did expectations change? A plausible answer is that people, who have experienced actual inflation in the recent past, have begun to anticipate future inflation and to incorporate it into their decision making. On the other hand, actual inflation occurs if the rate of growth in the money supply, $(\Delta M/M) \equiv \theta$, increases. We can say, then, that an increase from one particular constant rate of monetary expansion, θ_0, to another $\theta_1 > \theta_0$, increases the rate of inflation, $\Delta p/p$, which eventually becomes expected, that is, $(\Delta M/M) = (\Delta p/p) = (\Delta p/p)^e$, or $\theta = (\Delta p/p) = q$. In other words, the expectations of inflation are fulfilled and are ultimately engineered by an increase in the rate of growth of the money supply, θ. Note that with this explanation we can state the Fisher theorem in another way: *An increase in the rate of growth of the money supply will increase the (equilibrium) nominal interest rate by the same rate and thus leave the (equilibrium) real rate unchanged.*[5] Symbolically,

$$\frac{\Delta i}{\Delta \theta} = \frac{\Delta i}{\Delta(\Delta p/p)} = \frac{\Delta i}{\Delta q} = 1$$

$$\frac{\Delta i_r}{\Delta \theta} = \frac{\Delta i_r}{\Delta(\Delta p/p)} = \frac{\Delta i_r}{\Delta q} = 0$$

The equiproportionate increase in the nominal rate of interest, prompted by the expectations created when the rate of growth of money supply rises (i.e., by the Fisher effect), is the final and most important of the effects cited by Friedman in connection with monetary policy. He calls it the *price anticipation effect.*[6]

Recalling our earlier complications (mentioned on page 146), we see that we have already overcome one; we have shown that the increase in the rate of growth

[5] Thirty-three years later Robert A. Mundell showed that the Fisher theorem does not hold when savings is a function of real balances in addition to the real rate of interest; see his "Inflation and the Real Rate of Interest," *Journal of Political Economy,* June 1963, pp. 280–83. In M. G. Hadjimichalakis, "Expectations of the 'Myopic Perfect Foresight' Variety in Monetary Dynamics: Stability and Nonneutrality of Money," *Journal of Economic Dynamics and Control,* 3 (1981), we further question the stability of the system that yields the Fisher theorem.

[6] Friedman, "Factors Affecting the Interest Rates."

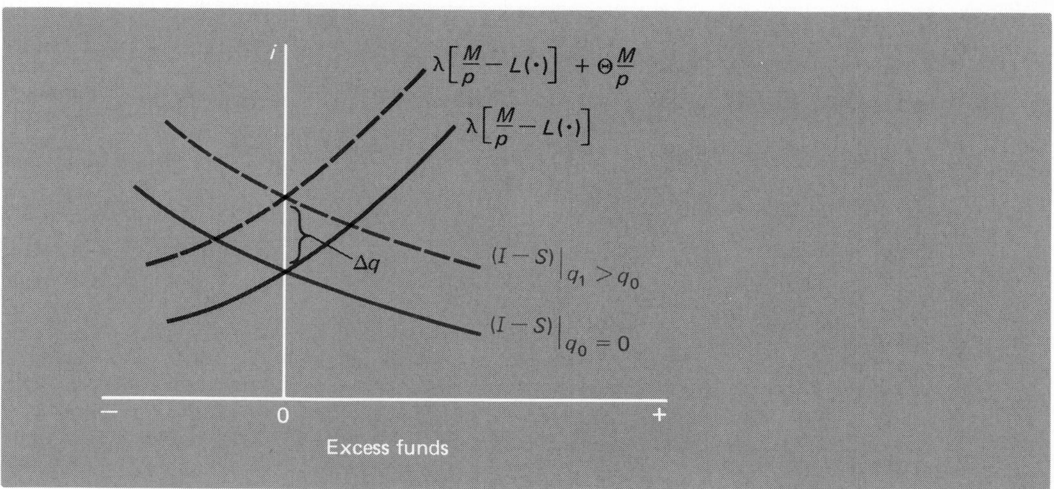

FIGURE 4-20

of the money supply does indeed increase actual (and expected) inflation, but *not* by creating permanent excess demand for goods and services. On the contrary, this increase in inflation is a property of *full* equilibrium when all markets, including the market for goods and services, are cleared.

We have also come a long way toward resolving the second complication, the problem of how to peg the nominal market interest rate below its natural rate. We saw earlier that this target required permanent and constant excess demand (for goods and services) and hence permanent and constant inflation, a result derived while assuming that no expectations were formed. But we now know that expectations will indeed be formed eventually and that households and firms will start considering them, respectively, in their savings and investment plans. This means that the $I - S$ curve will shift to the right, to the position $I(i,q_0) - S(i,q_0)$. Reproducing the information of Figure 4-16 in Figure 4-21, we see that in order to keep the nominal interest rate pegged at i_m^0, the authorities must now create a larger excess demand, $OD > OC$; but this also means that there must be excess supply of real balances in the same amount, *OD*, indicating that the authorities must be prepared to increase the money supply by a greater percentage than before, say by $\theta_1 > \theta_0$. (The intersection of the relevant curves will now occur at *F*.) But with a higher θ, that is, with θ_1, the rate of inflation will be higher, $(\Delta p/p)_1 = \theta_1$, and it will eventually be anticipated, q_1, that is, $\theta_1 = (\Delta p/p)_1 = q_1$. This again will shift the $I - S$ curve farther to the right, to the position $I(i,q_1) - S(i,q_1)$, requiring an intersection with an excess supply-of-money curve at point *G*. This, of course, means an even larger excess demand for goods, *OB*; an equal (to *OB*) excess supply of money; and an even higher inflation, say $(\Delta p/p)_2 > (\Delta p/p)_1$. This hyperinflation will continue until the economy breaks down, a process that Wicksell called the *cumulative* (inflationary) *process.*

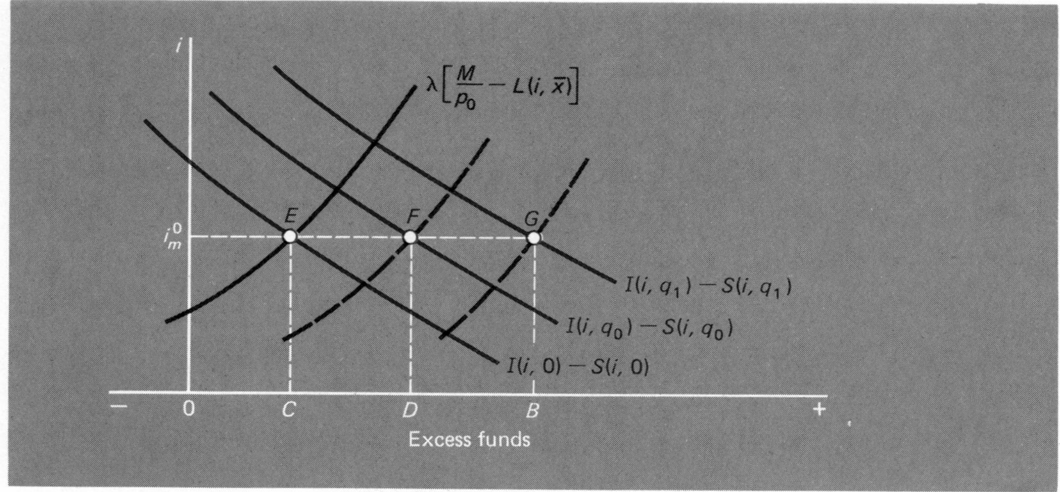

FIGURE 4-21

VI. AN HISTORICAL NOTE

The basic model used in this chapter was introduced by Knut Wicksell in 1898 and was popularized in the Anglo-Saxon literature by Keynes in the *Treatise* (1930). The distinction between nominal and (expected) real rate of interest was introduced by Irving Fisher (1930). But the reliance on this distinction is the cornerstone of much of modern monetary economics, especially of the neoclassical, or "monetarist," variety, which has been written since the mid-1960s. In fact, Milton Friedman's presidential address explicitly relies on this model.[7] The modern approach that we have used in this chapter owes much to Hugh Rose's work on modern (Wicksellian) monetary dynamics.[8]

The cumulative process was both introduced and explained extensively by Wicksell himself, who until recently was associated only with its "discovery." Wicksell examined a pure credit economy, that is, an economy in which all money was of the checking account variety. He emphasized that, in such an economy, it was easy for the banking sector to pursue, even unconsciously, a policy in which the market rate is lower than the natural rate of interest. This could happen, for example, because the banking sector fails to notice that the natural rate, for some underlying reason, increases, and that its members continue, as a matter of routine, to provide as much

---

[7] Milton Friedman, "The Role of Monetary Policy," *American Economic Review,* March 1968, pp. 1–17.

[8] See, for example, Hugh Rose, "Real and Monetary Factors in the Business Cycle," *Journal of Money, Credit and Banking,* May 1969, pp. 138–52; and "Effective Demand in the Long Run," in *Models of Economic Growth,* ed. J. A. Mirrlees and N. H. Stern (New York: John Wiley, 1973), pp. 25–47. Also see M. G. Hadjimichalakis, "The Rose-Wicksell Model: Inside Money, Stability, and Stabilization Policies," *Journal of Macroeconomics,* 1981.

credit as is demanded at the original market rate, i_m^0. In other words, this policy could become reality if the banking sector's supply of credit is perfectly elastic at the going market rate.

Keynes, who extended and popularized Wicksell's work, also believed that there was a lag in the reaction of the banking sector to changes in the natural rate of interest.[9] Thus it is conceivable, according to Keynes, for the market rate of interest to be chasing the natural rate, in an upward direction, without quite catching up with it. Under such circumstances, there will be continuous excess demand for goods and services and, therefore, continuous increases in the price level. In fact, this is Keynes' own explanation of the Gibson paradox.

Wicksell examined the deflationary cumulative process, but only as an addendum to his basic analysis; he showed the following symmetric result: As long as there is a conscious or unconscious commitment to keep the market rate of interest pegged at a level *above* the natural rate, deflation, leading to the formation of deflationary expectations, will occur. This formation of deflationary expectations would then lead to an ever-decreasing price level, the consequence of an ever-increasing excess supply of goods and services. We should note that Wicksell was examining, as we are here, an economy always fully employed. Thus it did not occur to him, while he was briefly examining this case, that a permanent or, even worse, an ever-increasing excess supply of goods and services could influence the level of production and thus the rate of employment.

While Keynes, examining this case in detail in 1930, would not fully understand its implications until six years later, he did, however, warn against the risk of creating a Gibson paradox (in the downward direction):

> That is to say, of a market rate of interest which is falling but never fast enough to catch up the natural rate of interest, so that there is a recurrent profit deflation leading to a recurrent income deflation and a sagging price level. If this occurs, our present régime of capitalistic individualism will assuredly be replaced by a far-reaching socialism.[10]

It is remarkable that Keynes made this statement, which referred to the Depression that had just begun, immediately after expressing the hope that he might not, once again, play Cassandra's role! Six years later his *General Theory* was designed to prevent that replacement of capitalism by socialism.

A final comment is in order here. Our analysis has shown that pegging the market rate of interest at a level below the natural rate of interest creates ever-accelerating inflation. Thirty-two years after the Keynesian revolution, Milton Friedman crowned his counterrevolution with a modification of the same analysis outlined here;[11] he claimed that, in addition to the natural rate of interest, there is a natural rate of unemployment toward which the economy gravitates, and, furthermore, that if the

---

[9] Keynes, *Treatise,* II, *The Applied Theory of Money,* pp. 177–86.

[10] Keynes, *Treatise,* II, *The Applied Theory of Money,* 346.

[11] Friedman, "Role of Monetary Policy."

monetary authority pegs the market rate of unemployment below its natural rate, an accelerating rate of inflation will result.

THE CONSEQUENCES OF THE INTEREST ELASTICITY OF THE DEMAND FOR MONEY

Most of Keynes' efforts to extend Wicksell's analysis concerned *applications* of the theory, for example, to issues of international economics. There were, however, some theoretical departures. The most fundamental difference between the theoretical analyses of these two economists centers on the form of the demand for real balances that each of their models incorporates. Wicksell, who did not set out to disprove the quantity theory but, rather, to make it immune from justified criticisms, used a demand for money of the quantity theory variety, that is, independent of the interest rate:

$$L = l \cdot Y = l \cdot f(x) \equiv L(x), \quad \frac{\Delta L}{\Delta x} > 0 \tag{19}$$

Keynes, however, recognized that l itself depends negatively on the interest rate, and hence he used the following demand for real balances:

$$L = l(i)f(x) = L(i,x), \quad \frac{\Delta L}{\Delta i} < 0, \quad \frac{\Delta L}{\Delta x} > 0 \tag{20}$$

We have seen that our results, so far, are independent of whether we use (19) or (20). In particular, an increase in the money supply will increase, by an equal percentage, the price level and leave the equilibrium real interest rate unchanged. Furthermore, our results on expectations and on the cumulative process are also invariant with respect to the particular form of the demand for real balances. There is, however, one important result that depends entirely on the form of the demand for money. This concerns the comparative statics of a shift in the investment and/or savings functions; in particular, whether it will change only the interest rate or whether it will also effect a change in the price level.

When the demand for real balances is independent of the interest rate, the excess flow supply curve is vertical, as in Figure 4-22a, while in full equilibrium it coincides with the i-axis, as in Figure 4-22b. Let us suppose, starting from a full-equilibrium position, such as point A in Figure 4-23a, either that investment rises because of an increase in the "animal spirits" of the entrepreneurs or that savings falls because of a change in household tastes, say a preference for present consumption. Either of these changes would shift the $I - S$ curve to the right, to the position $(I - S)'$, which implies that at the old market and natural rate, $i_n^0 = i_m^0$, there would be excess demand for loans equal to AC'. But this is not permitted by construction; the only market-determined interest rate can be found at the intersection of the relevant $I - S$ curve, that is, $(I - S)'$, and the excess supply-of-money curve. And since money has not changed, by assumption, we see that the excess supply-of-money curve continues to be the one that coincides with the i-axis. Thus the

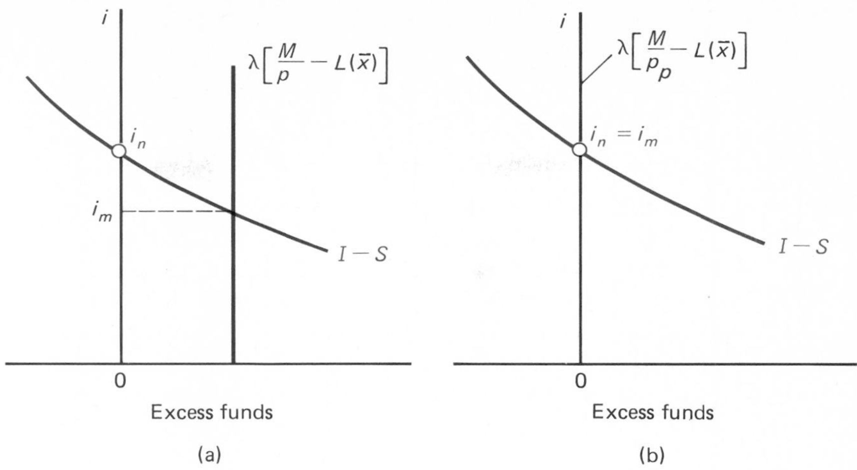

FIGURE 4-22

interest rate will rise instantaneously to point *B*, eliminating entirely the excess demand for loans, which is also excess demand for goods and services. Therefore no excess demand for goods and services remains to cause a change in the price level. And we can safely rely on the market and natural rate to clear all markets, including the goods and services market.

On the other hand, when the demand for money depends on the interest rate, the excess supply of money is upward sloping, as in Figure 4-23b, and when the $I - S$ curve shifts to the position $(I - S)'$, we have a *temporary* equilibrium at

FIGURE 4-23

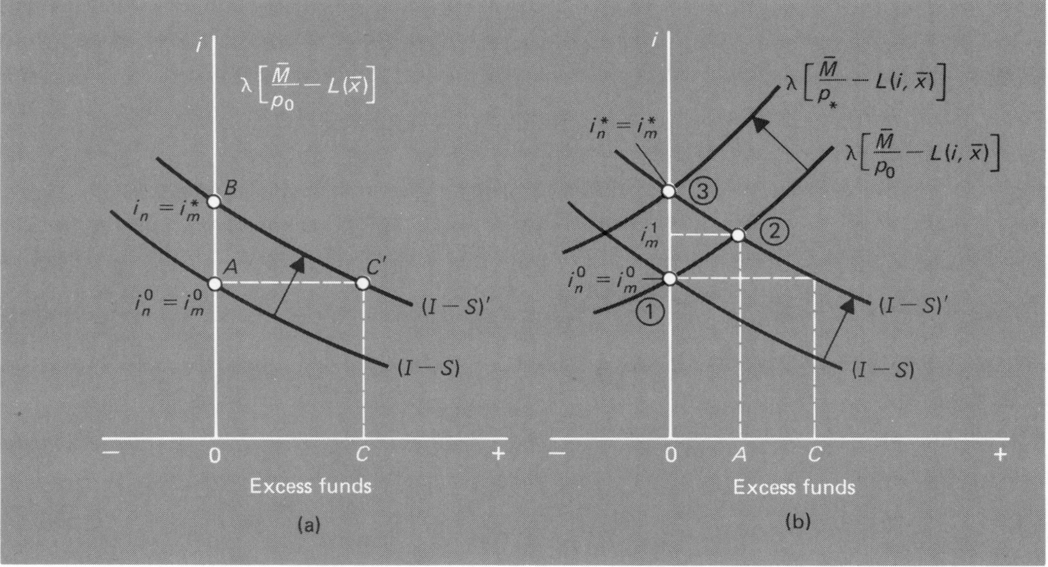

point ②, where the higher market rate, i_m^1, is still lower than the relevant natural rate, i_n^*. The excess demand for goods and services, *OC*, has not been eliminated entirely by the first rise in the market rate to i_m^1; at this level there is still excess demand for goods and services, equal to *OA*. From these data we see that the price level must rise and continue to rise, shifting the $\lambda\left[\frac{M}{p} - L(\cdot)\right]$ curve to the left until it intersects the $(I - S)'$ curve at the i-axis, that is, at position ③ in Figure 4-23b. The higher price level needed for and associated with this full-equilibrium position is denoted by $p_* > p_0$.

We have seen that when the demand for money depends on the interest rate, we cannot rely exclusively on the interest rate to eliminate, solely by its rise, all possible excess demand for goods and services. Since we have conducted this exercise on the assumption of a fixed nominal quantity of money, $\overline{M}$, we have proved that the price level can rise (fall) even if the money supply is not increased (decreased), *provided that the demand for money depends on the interest rate.*

We can now tie this result to our earlier one, that an increase (decrease) in the money supply will increase (decrease) the price level, whether the demand for money is interest-elastic or interest-inelastic. We can therefore state the following: While an increase in the money supply increases the price level, the converse is not generally true, since the price level may rise even with unchanged money supply. The converse is true only if the demand for money is interest-inelastic.

This means that the traditional neoclassical approach, of dichotomizing the model of an economy into a "real sector" and a "monetary sector" and examining the sectors separately, is valid only when the demand for money is interest-inelastic, that is, when it is of the quantity theory variety. In such a case, nothing that happens to the real sector affects the price level (which is the concern of the monetary sector) if the money supply is fixed. And, similarly, nothing happens to variables of the real sector, such as the interest rate, if the money supply changes; only the price level changes in this case. (Of course, the problem involving the consistency of the model and its ability to affect this price level remains, as we noted at the end of Chapter 3 and at the beginning of this chapter.) Alternatively, we can say that the price level rises (falls) if, and only if, the money supply increases (decreases), a statement that is valid only if the demand for money is independent of the interest rate.

Keynes' discovery, that the price level may change even when the money supply is kept fixed, disillusioned him, caused him to question his ideas, and induced him to launch his "revolution," as we shall see in the next chapter. In effect, he argued that if there is a connection between rising prices and rising employment, we are overlooking important aspects of the economy by simplifying, that is, by assuming that the demand for money does not depend on the interest rate.

QUESTIONS

1. Suppose that there is an increase in the risk estimate which is relevant for investment decisions.
   a. What will happen to the investment demand curve?

b. In a perpetually fully employed economy, what will happen to the interest rate and the price level? Does your answer depend on whether the demand for money is interest-elastic or not?

2. The creation of inflationary expectations increases both the price level and the interest rate. Why?

3. In a perpetually fully employed economy:

a. Why is it that the price level and the interest rate usually move in the same direction?

b. What will be the effect on both the interest rate and the price level when inflationary expectations are either created or increased?

4. What happens to the price level if the Central Bank decides to keep the interest rate at its original level? How might the Central Bank achieve this target?

5. "If the 'animal spirits' of entrepreneurs fall, the normal rate of interest will also fall, even if savings depends negatively on the interest rate." Why?

6. Prove that a doubling of the nominal money supply will ultimately double the price level—whether or not the demand for money depends on the interest rate.

7. What is the distinction between the market rate of interest and the natural rate of interest? How is this related to temporary equilibrium as opposed to full equilibrium?

8. Summarize the price adjustment mechanism in (a) the market for goods and services and (b) the loans market.

9. Show that Walras's law allows examination of only two of the three markets in the model.

10. Why is the distinction between a one-time increase in the money supply and an increase in the rate of growth of the money supply so important?

REFERENCES

FISHER, IRVING, *Theory of Interest.* New York: Macmillan, 1930.

FRIEDMAN, MILTON, "Factors Affecting the Interest Rates," in *Money and Finance: Readings in Theory, Policy and Institutions,* ed. D. Carson, pp. 319–30. New York: John Wiley, 1972.

———, "The Role of Monetary Policy," *American Economic Review,* March 1968, pp. 1–17.

———, "A Theoretical Framework for Monetary Analysis," *Journal of Political Economy,* March/April 1970, pp. 193–238.

HABERLER, GOTTFRIED, *Prosperity and Depression,* London: Allen & Unwin, 1958, 4th edition, Chap. 8.

HADJIMICHALAKIS, MICHAEL G., "Expectations of the 'Myopic Perfect Foresight' Variety in Monetary Dynamics: Stability and Nonneutrality of Money," *Journal of Economic Dynamics and Control,* pp. 391, 157–76, 1981.

HADJIMICHALAKIS, MICHAEL G., "The Rose-Wicksell Model: Inside Money, Stability, and Stabilization Policies," *Journal of Macroeconomics,* 1981.

———, "On the Effectiveness of Monetary Policy as a Stabilization Device," *Review of Economic Studies,* October 1973, pp. 561–70.

KEYNES, J. M., *A Treatise on Money.* London: Macmillan, 1930.

MUNDELL, ROBERT, "Inflation and the Real Rate of Interest," *Journal of Political Economy,* June 1963, pp. 280–83.

ROSE, HUGH, "Effective Demand in the Long Run," in *Models of Economic Growth,* eds. J. A. Mirrlees and N. H. Stern, pp. 25–47. New York: John Wiley, 1973.

———, "Real and Monetary Factors in the Business Cycle," *Journal of Money, Credit, and Banking,* May 1969, pp. 138–52.

WICKSELL, KNUT, *Interest and Prices,* 1898, trans. R. F. Kahn. London: Macmillan, 1936.

———, *Lectures on Political Economy,* Vol. II, *Money,* 1911, ed. Lionel Robbins. London: Routledge & Kegan Paul, 1934.

keynesian-neokeynesian macroeconomics and the neoclassical synthesis

Keynes' Break from the Classicists: the Keynesian Revolution

5

In Section I of this chapter we discover the reasons for Keynes' disillusionment with the prevailing orthodoxy. The two philosophies are, in fact, presented and contrasted in terms of their respective theorems. In effect, Keynes successfully demonstrated that in the neoclassical system both the interest rate and employment were indeterminate and that another crucial market, the money market, was necessary for a simultaneous determination of those two variables. Moreover, he proceeded to change the rules of the game, stating that investment and savings determine the employment level; they do not determine the interest rate. The interest rate is, then, assumed to be determined by the money market. We demonstrate that the "employment adjustment mechanism"—i.e., the statement that employment increases (falls) if, and only if, investment is greater (lower) than savings—is consistent with basic microeconomic considerations (i.e., the law of supply and demand) if the money wage is fixed. We also demonstrate that the "interest rate adjustment mechanism" based on liquidity preference—i.e., on the supply and demand for money—is consistent with the loanable funds theory established and used in Chapter 4.

Of course, investment being greater (less) than savings means that the goods market experiences excess demand (excess supply). Section II examines, in greater detail, the goods market and the role it plays to determine, *ceteris paribus,* the level of employment. Following the existing literature we first translate the *employment* adjustment mechanism into the *income* adjustment mechanism. In other words, the goods market determines—and changes—income. We then examine the role of particular components of aggregate demand in determining income. First, we consider the role of government demand as well as of taxation, both separately and as a net result, that is, as the *budget deficit* or *surplus*. Second, we examine the role of foreign trade and, in particular, beggar-thy-neighbor policies to increase a country's income. Finally, we introduce and examine a measure for the response of output to autonomous changes in aggregate demand. This measure of response is called a *multiplier*. Multipliers for different changes are derived in a simple fashion and are ranked according to their magnitudes.

I. KEYNES BREAKS AWAY FROM THE CLASSICISTS

At the end of Chapter 4 we discovered that the proposition "only money matters for changes in the price level" depends squarely on an assumption that neither the demand for nor the supply of money is influenced by the interest rate. We saw that an increase in the propensity to save (because of, say, the preachings of a modern-day Benjamin Franklin) will leave the price level unchanged *if* the excess supply of money is independent of the interest rate. In this case—depicted in Figure 5-1—a new equilibrium with a lower interest rate is achieved immediately. The higher savings rate is matched by a higher investment rate. No deficiency of demand for goods and services materializes; Say's Law holds, and thus there is no need for the price level to change.

For the case where the demand for (or supply of) money does depend on the interest rate, an increase in the propensity to save will influence the price level—namely, by lowering it—as the graph in Figure 5-2 shows. The increase in the propensity to save instantaneously decreases the interest rate. This brings us to position ② where, momentarily, the loans market is cleared. The market for goods and services, however, is not cleared; there is an excess supply of goods, which implies that the

FIGURE 5-1

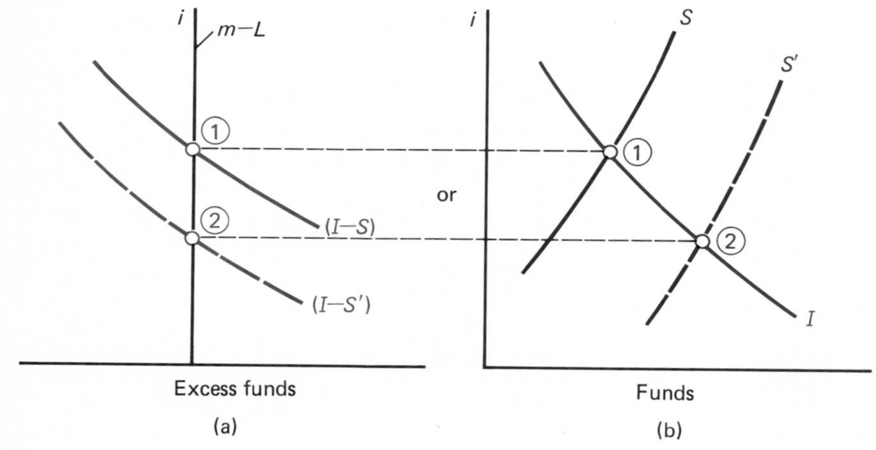

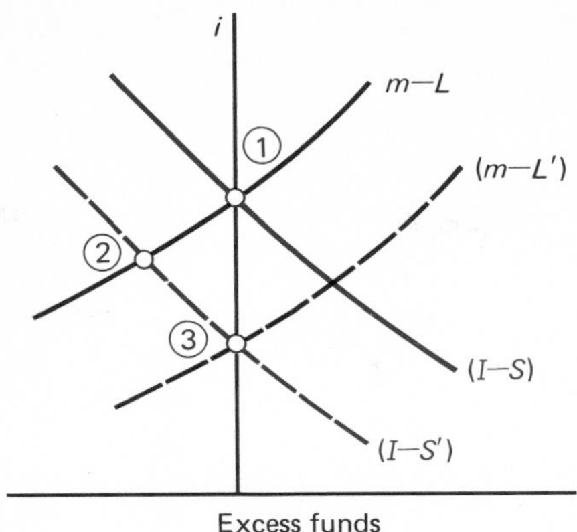

FIGURE 5-2

price level has to fall. This also means that at position ② there is excess demand for money. Of course, it is the fall of the interest rate that increases the demand for money. With a given price level, this means that the supply of real balances is given, and thus the increased demand causes excess demand for (i.e., negative excess supply of) money. Thus, for full equilibrium—position ③—the price level has to fall. (This fall in prices eliminates the excess supply of goods and services and, equivalently, enlarges the supply of real balances so that the market for money is also cleared.) We see that we cannot depend exclusively on the interest rate to instantaneously establish Say's Law. The price level also has to fall if the demand for money is interest-elastic. Now, if there is a relationship between changes in the price level and employment, we are in serious trouble. We are hiding crucial problems of the economy by assuming that the demand for money does not depend on the interest rate, that is, by accepting the quantity theory demand for money. We can therefore understand and appreciate why Keynes chose to begin his broadside attack on the neoclassical system by rejecting both the quantity theory and Say's Law.

We saw here that the price level, as well as the interest rate, falls. The employment level, x, does not change (fall), of course, because we have *assumed* full employment. If we did not have full employment, we would then expect x to vary. How could we, in principle, permit unemployment? We know that one way to definitely guarantee unemployment is to assume sufficiently high money wages, as did Keynes when he began his analysis. It should be clear at once that when employment is variable, graphs such as the ones we have been using are of no help, since there is one investment demand curve, one savings curve, and one demand-for-money curve for each x. This is what persuaded Keynes to part company with neoclassical macroeconomics to which he himself had been a major contributor.

To see how drastic a departure his has been, it is instructive to compare the major propositions of the old (neoclassical) with the new economics.

NEOCLASSICAL PROPOSITION ONE: The normal rate of interest can be relied upon to bring about Say's Law equality, thus goods and services market clearance, and, therefore, the absence of the possibility of unemployment.

For example, if i is below its equilibrium level, $\bar{i}$, as in Figure 5-3, the demand for loans (investment) is greater than the supply (i.e., savings), and thus there are forces increasing the interest rate until investment equals savings. But this also implies

FIGURE 5-3

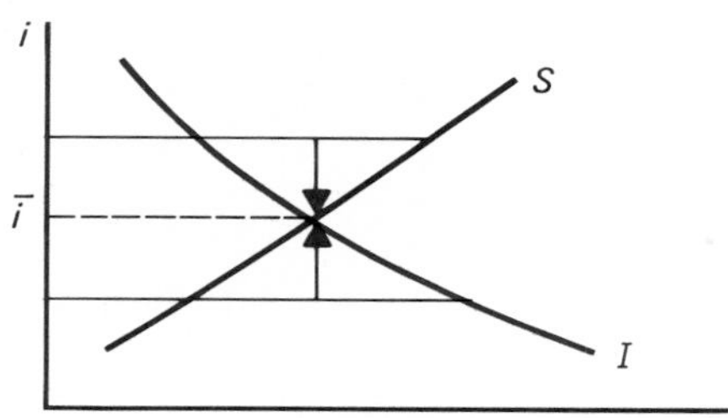

that the goods market is cleared. Since there is no deficiency in demand, it follows that we cannot have unemployment. A corollary to the above analysis is

> **NEOCLASSICAL PROPOSITION TWO:** The interest rate is determined by investment and savings only. Therefore, it is a real phenomenon.

Keynes rejected both propositions. He said that the first proposition is absurd. He pointed to the circularity of the argument. First, the neoclassicists assumed that x is given (at its full-employment level). This assumption permitted them to pick only one I and only one S curve out of an infinite number for each as shown in Figures 5-4 and 5-5. If, for example, x_2 is the full-employment level of x, they then use only the I and S curve corresponding to this level, as in Figure 5-6.

Second, the neoclassicists said that in case that investment is different from savings, the rate of interest moves to bring them to equality. Since they are now equal, the market for goods is cleared. Therefore there cannot be unemployment.

FIGURE 5-4

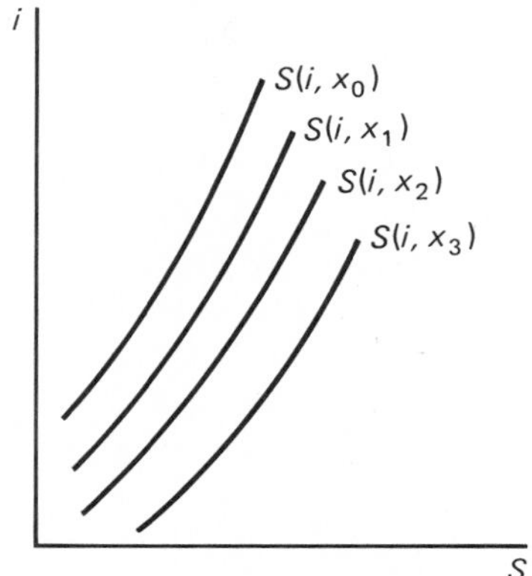

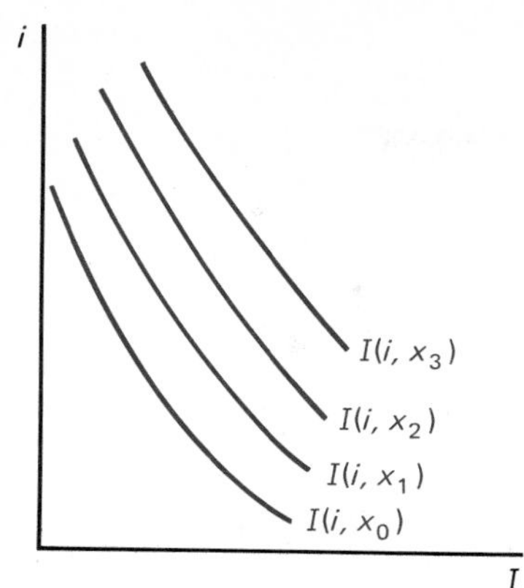

FIGURE 5-5

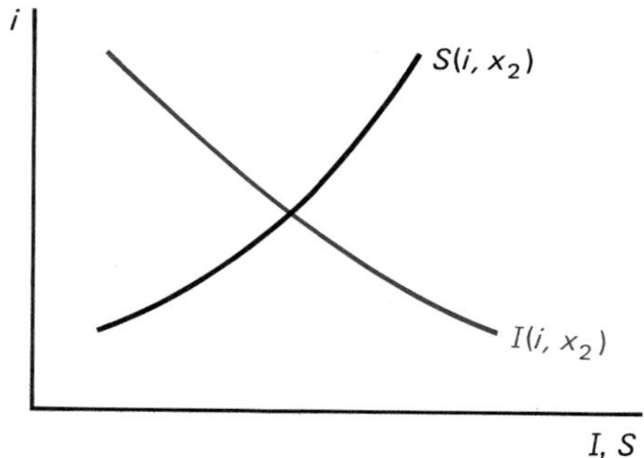

FIGURE 5-6

But they began by assuming that there is no unemployment! Keynes saw clearly that the classical position was tantamount to attempting to find the solution for two unknowns using only one equation:

$$I(i,x) - S(i,x) = 0$$

which is a function of two variables, i and x.

There are two ways out of this dilemma. The *first* is to assume knowledge of one of the two variables. The *second* is to add another equation in the same two unknowns, i and x. The first way is the one followed by the neoclassicists; the second is that of Keynes. The first approach assumed x as fixed (at its full-employment level) and, thereby, determining the interest rate. Thus the neoclassicists had a determinate theory of interest only in the *special case* of full employment. From this follows the first Keynesian proposition.

> **KEYNES' PROPOSITION ONE:** The neoclassicists had no theory of employment. They simply *assumed* full employment.

Of course, this is a most sympathetic treatment of the neoclassicists, who meant their theory to determine *both* the interest rate and the employment level. In

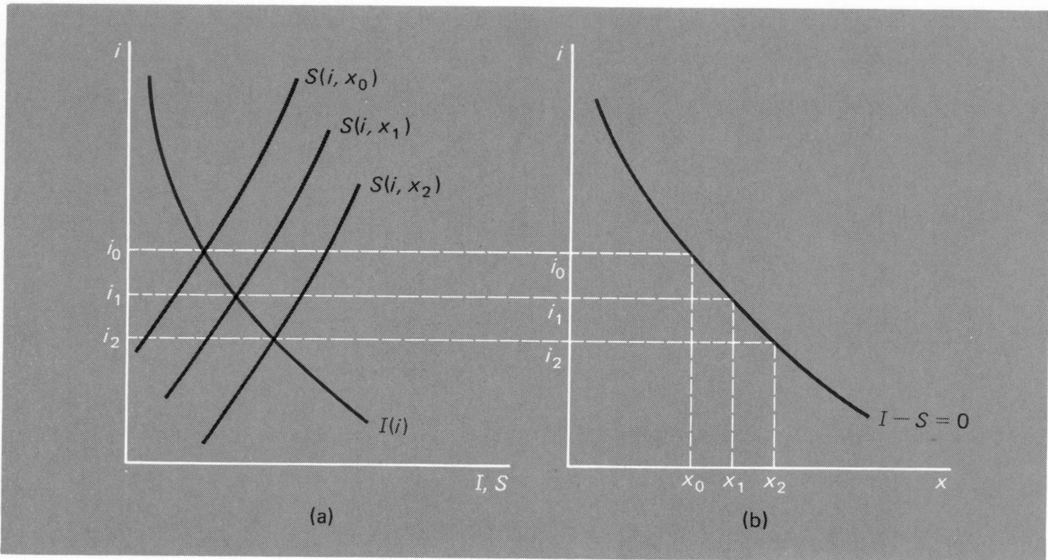

FIGURE 5-7

this case they are definitely wrong. Not only do they lack a theory of employment, but they also lack a determinate interest rate in their system. The equality of savings and investment gives us an infinity of interest rates, one for each level of employment, as shown in Figures 5-7a and 5-7b where, for simplicity of illustration, it is assumed that I is a function of i only.

Clearly, in order to determine both i and x we need another curve (equation), which is precisely the approach followed by Keynes (note the second method cited above). We know that at equilibrium, if it exists, all the markets are cleared. In particular, the excess demand for money must be zero. The $I - S = 0$ curve, like the one in Figure 5-7b, gives the set of all combinations of (i,x) such that the goods market is cleared. We also need the set of all (i,x) such that the existing stock of real balances is willingly held. Clearly, the equilibrium (or set of equilibria) is given by the intersection of these two sets. Since the money market is needed to determine the interest rate and, of course, the employment level, it follows that the second proposition of the neoclassicists does not hold. The interest rate is (also) a monetary phenomenon. We have thus established:

> **KEYNES' PROPOSITION TWO:** *In general,* the neoclassicists had no theory of interest. In their system, the interest rate was indeterminate.
>
> **KEYNES' PROPOSITION THREE:** The interest rate is not exclusively a real phenomenon. It is (also) a monetary phenomenon.

The establishment of these three propositions was enough to devastate the existing body of macroeconomics. It is remarkable that Keynes saw clearly that the system was an interdependent one, that is, general equilibrium, not partial equilibrium, problem. He proceeded to establish this system and went a long way toward solving its problems. And he did this despite lack of training in general equilibrium analysis and techniques. Whatever economics Keynes knew was of the Marshallian (i.e., partial equilibrium) variety, not of the Walrasian. Walrasian economics was banned from the British Isles!

Keynes did not stop with the three propositions established above. He proceeded to change completely the rules of the game. Before we consider that, however, it is instructive at this point to consider a schematic comparison of the classical and Keynesian systems. The pre-Keynesians started with the demand for and supply of labor. Perfect (real) wage flexibility gave the full-employment level of labor (Figure 5-8a). Given this level of labor, as well as the fact that in the short run the capital stock is fixed, we can determine from the production function what the level of output will be (Figure 5-8b). This output will be fully demanded (i.e., there cannot be a deficiency of demand), since the interest rate will be at the level that guarantees equality between savings and investment (i.e., $EG = I - S = 0$), as shown in Figure 5-8c. According to Keynes, the whole process is reversed. The clearance of the goods and money markets (in Figure 5-9a) gives us the effective (i.e., sustainable) employment (and income). We then examine whether this employment is equal to the supply of labor forthcoming at the established real wages. If it is less (as in Figure 5-9b), we have unemployment. Keynes maintained that unemployment is the general case, that is, the chance that the sustainable x is equal to $\bar{v}$ is one in an infinity. Thus, according to Keynes, full employment, as in the neoclassical system, is a *special* case, whereas unemployment is the general case.

FIGURE 5-8

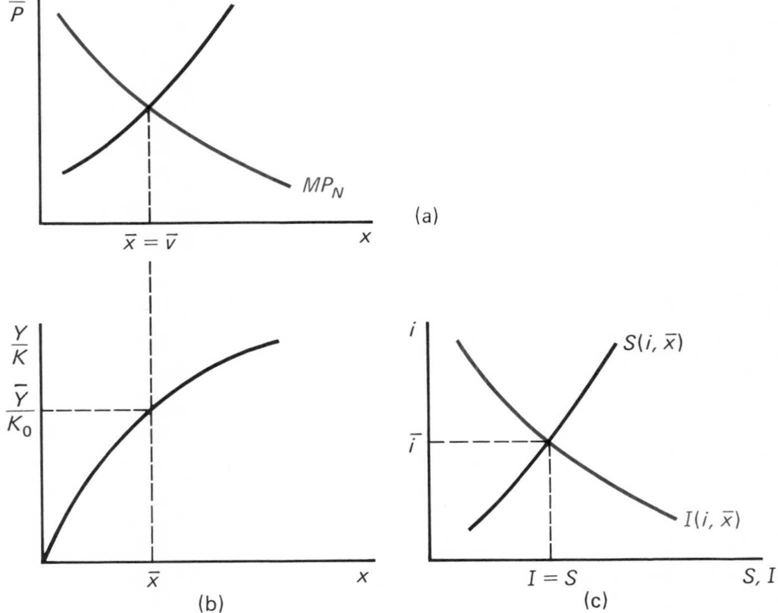

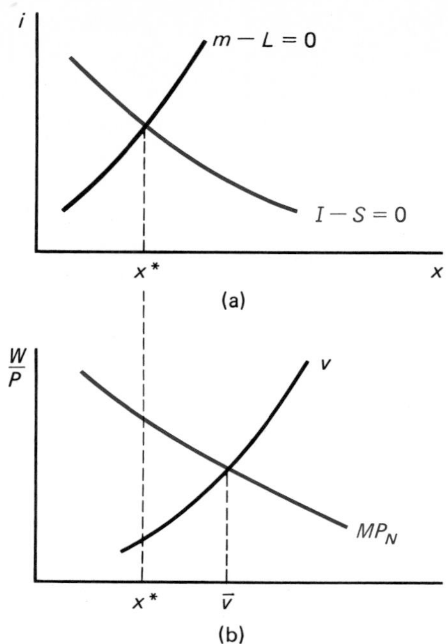

FIGURE 5-9

As we said earlier, Keynes did not stop here. He introduced two additional propositions:

> **KEYNES' PROPOSITION FOUR:** The equality of investment and savings determines employment (and thus income).

> **KEYNES' PROPOSITION FIVE:** The rate of interest is determined by the equality of the demand for and supply of money.

At first these two propositions might seem surprising, since we saw in Figure 5-9a that employment and the interest rate are determined simultaneously when the goods and money markets are cleared. In other words, in a general equilibrium system everything is interdependent, and it makes no sense to say, for example, that the interest rate is determined by the money market if the goods market is needed also. The answer to this puzzle is as follows. When, in general equilibrium, we say that a certain market *determines* a certain variable, we mean that if this market is not cleared, the variable in question moves in the appropriate direction to clear that market. For example, it is true that the price of peanuts is determined not only by the market for peanuts but also by the market for walnuts. When we say that the price of peanuts is determined by the market for peanuts, we mean that if there is excess demand for peanuts, the peanut price will rise, but if there is excess supply, the price will fall. In other words, when we say that a variable is *determined* by a certain market, we mean that we introduce an adjustment process of that variable on the basis of the *law of supply and demand.*

According to this interpretation, then, when Keynes says that the interest rate is *determined* by the demand for and supply of money, he means that the interest rate will rise if there is excess demand for money, and it will fall when there is excess supply of money. On the other hand, when Keynes says that the equality of investment and savings *determines* employment, x, he means that if there is an excess of investment over savings (i.e., excess demand for goods and services), employment rises, whereas an excess of savings over investment (i.e., an excess supply of goods and services) will cause employment to fall.

EMPLOYMENT ADJUSTMENT MECHANISM

Before we examine its consistency, let us see what Keynes said and compare his analysis with that of his predecessors. Assume that we start from equilibrium, and, therefore, according to both theories, investment is equal to savings at interest i_0 (point A in Figure 5-10). For simplicity of illustration, assume that investment demand depends only on the interest rate. Suppose further that the investment schedule shifts downward and to the left (e.g., because of an increase in the riskiness of investment or a fall in the "animal spirits" of the entrepreneurs). Now, for the same i, i_0, there is excess of savings over investment equal to BA. According to the neoclassical story, if the banking sector does not intervene to keep the interest rate at i_0 (by withdrawing money from the system), the excess supply of funds (i.e., the excess of savings over investment that is equivalent to excess supply of goods) will force the interest rate down to $\bar{i}$. The reduction of investment demand will be matched by a reduction of savings (i.e., an increase in consumption demand). The market for goods and services will be cleared with no change in the price level, since the money supply has not been changed and the demand for money is independent of the interest rate.

Keynes countered by saying that this is not the correct story. Rather, according to him, the excess saving, BA, (i.e., the excess supply of goods and services) can be eliminated even with the same interest rate i_0. The trick is that the savings

FIGURE 5-10

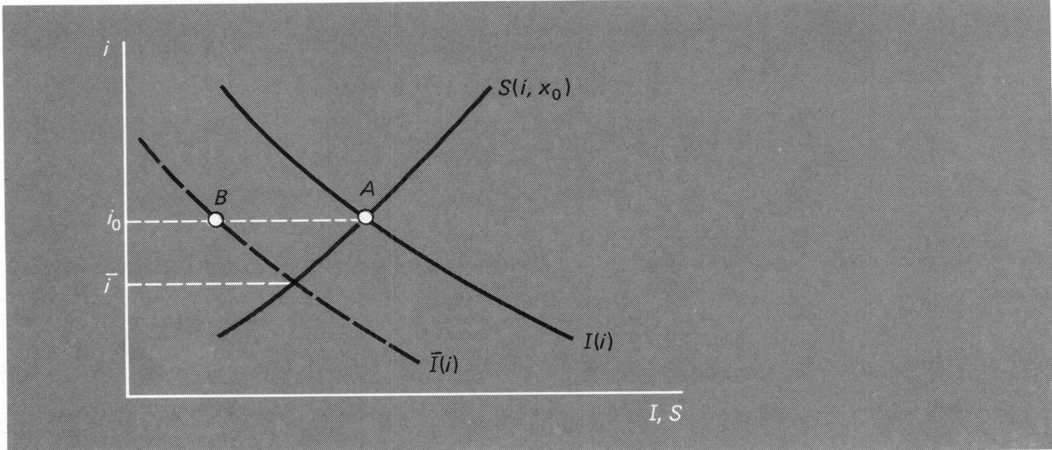

curve can shift inward. Recall that there is a positive relation between x and S, that is, in the (i,S)-plane, the S curve shifts to the right when x increases. Therefore, if there is a connection between the excess demand for goods $(I - S)$ and x, the discrepancy BA can be eliminated, even if i remains fixed. (In the classical system there is no such connection, since x is *assumed* fixed at full employment, x_0, in the Figure 5-10 graph.) Keynes introduced such a relation. He said that x increases when there is excess demand for goods and services, that is, when $I - S > 0$, and x decreases when $I - S < 0$. In our graph we have $I - S < 0$, and according to Keynes, x will fall, say to x_1. (Recall that for simplicity of exposition we are assuming, here, that I is independent of x.) This shifts the savings curve to the left, $S(i,x_1)$, as shown in Figure 5-11. From the way the graph in Figure 5-11 is drawn, we see that while a reduction in employment from x_0 to x_1 reduces the excess supply of goods by CA, there is still excess supply. Therefore x has to fall further, say to x_2. But there is still excess supply, which requires further reduction in x. The process will continue until x has fallen to x_e. The savings forthcoming from this employment (and income) is equal to the investment rate for the original level of the interest rate, i_0.

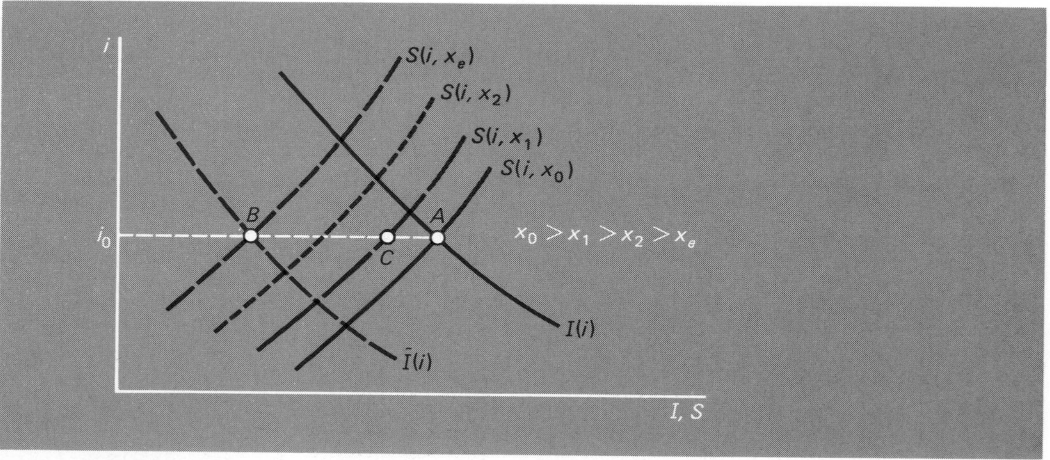

FIGURE 5-11

Of course, we can explicitly show the above process. Instead of using the (i,S) and (i,I)-plane and treating changes in x parametrically, we can utilize the (x,I) and (x,S)-plane and treat i parametrically as in Figure 5-12. (After all, i is kept fixed here.) This, naturally, has been the graphical approach followed by expositors of Keynes. For given i_0 and x_0, the reduction in investment causes excess supply of goods and services equal to BA. This reduces x, which narrows the gap between I and S until x falls to the level x_e.

The above graphical analysis was carried out under the simplifying assumption that investment does not depend on x. But we established in Chapter 1 that I is positively related to x. Introducing this realistic assumption does not negate our analysis. In Figure 5-11, when x falls, both the S curve and the I curve should

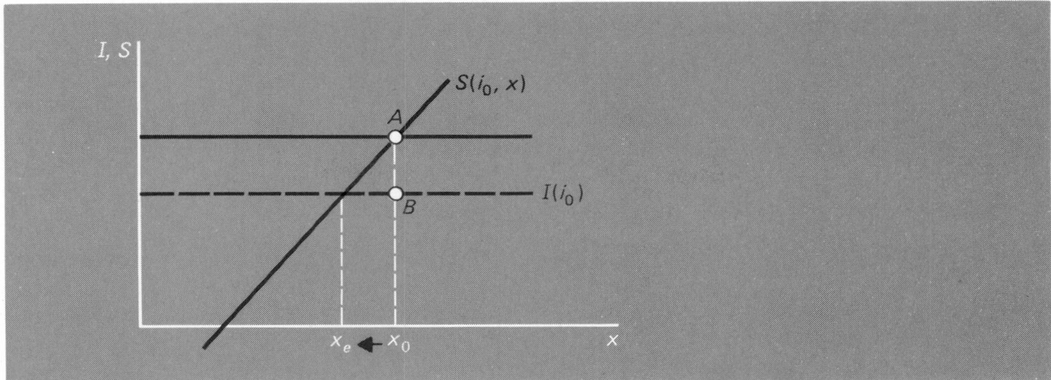

FIGURE 5-12

shift to the left. In Figure 5-13 the positive relation between I and x means that the I curve is upward sloping, not horizontal. Now, the story described earlier holds if the I curve in Figure 5-11 shifts to the left by less than the leftward shift of the S curve. In terms of Figure 5-13, this means that the I curve cuts the S curve from below, that is, the S curve is steeper than the I curve. As we saw earlier, this means that the marginal propensity to *spend* is less than *one*.

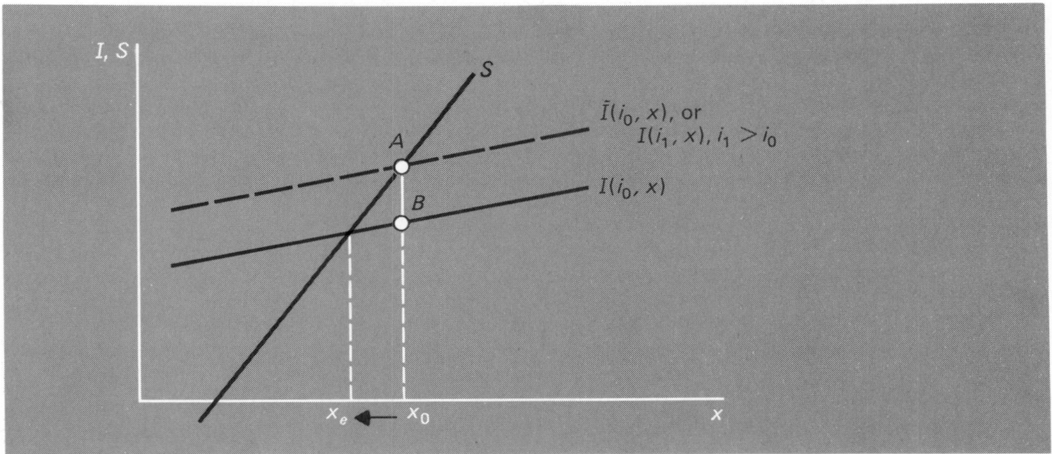

FIGURE 5-13

We can summarize the above employment adjustment mechanism with the following schema:

$$EG > 0 \rightarrow x \uparrow \text{ (i.e., } \Delta x > 0)$$
$$EG < 0 \rightarrow x \downarrow \text{ (i.e., } \Delta x < 0)$$
$$EG = 0 \rightarrow x \text{ unchanged (i.e., } \Delta x = 0)$$

More compactly, we can write

$$\Delta x \gtreqless 0 \quad \text{when} \quad EG \gtreqless 0 \tag{1}$$

All of this can be captured in the following simple equation:

$$\frac{\Delta x}{x} = \beta \cdot EG, \quad \beta > 0 \tag{1'}$$

In other words, the rate of change in employment is proportional to the excess demand for goods and services.

So much for the mechanics of the Keynesian assumption, that investment and savings *determine* employment; they do not determine the interest rate. The crucial economic questions are, Why is this so? and Is it consistent with basic economic principles? All the world knows (or stipulates) that the excess demand for goods and services *determines* the prices of those goods and services. (We have been using this stipulation for several chapters now.) If we accept this as an approximate, basic truth, we have to show that the Keynesian stipulation that excess demand for goods and services *determines* employment is consistent with the basic *law of supply and demand* (i.e., the price adjustment mechanism). Fortunately, this is very simple. Informally, the argument goes as follows: The excess demand for goods and services (which is registered as the running down of inventories, as established earlier in Chapter 4) causes a rise in prices. This rise in prices is a signal for entrepreneurs to make profits—"windfall profits," according to Keynes. Thus they have an incentive to increase their supply of goods and services. The increase in supply can come about only through an increase in production. According to our production function, since the capital stock is fixed in the short run, the only way to increase production is by hiring (employing) more workers. Thus, x increases. Similarly, with excess supply of goods and services, prices fall, causing "windfall losses." These losses can be avoided only by reducing production. Since the only variable input is labor, the reduction in production can only be accomplished by a fall in employment, x. We see, therefore, that the employment adjustment mechanism, or Keynes' assumption that excess demand for goods and services *determines* employment, is consistent with the price adjustment mechanism.

This issue requires more elaboration than the informal treatment given above because much confusion and controversy surrounds it in the professional literature. Friedman claimed that Keynes and the Keynesians assumed that prices and wages are fixed, and, in particular, they are *institutionally* given.[1] That is, according to Friedman, in this part of macroeconomics, the law of supply and demand is not utilized to determine prices and wages. The majority of economists who are nonspecialists in this field seem to hold similar views. It is also true that most, if not all, textbooks never mention prices or wages while examining the "Keynesian cross" or its mirror image, the *IS* curve. Since prices and wages are not mentioned, many

[1] See Milton Friedman, "A Theoretical Framework for Monetary Analysis," *Journal of Political Economy,* March/April 1970, pp. 193–238.

think that they do not enter into the picture because they are assumed fixed. But this does not follow. (In fact, if that were the case, the analysis would be inconsistent. More on this point a little later.) A carefully written textbook, while not mentioning prices and wages at this point, usually relies on the depletion of inventories and the need for replenishing them in order to establish the analogue of the employment adjustment mechanism. A moment's reflection will persuade the reader that this also implies a movement of prices. Recall that we relied on the *need* for *replenishing* the reduced inventories while establishing the price adjustment mechanism.

Let us first see whether Keynes and the Keynesians assumed absolute price *and* wage rigidity. Keynes, along with his predecessors and successors, including this book, assumes that the profit-maximizing firms hire labor up to the point where its marginal product is exactly equal to the real wage:

$$\frac{W}{P} = MP_N$$

Because of diminishing returns, the marginal productivity curve, MP_N, is downward sloping (as in Figure 5-14). It is clear that for employment to rise (fall), the real wage must fall (rise). Since the real wage is the ratio of money wages and prices only, if *both* wages and prices are assumed fixed, there is no way one can increase employment (unless the curve shifts, a point not at issue here). You may assume either one or the other as fixed, but not both. If Keynes did assume that both money wages and prices are fixed, he would be guilty not only of an unrealistic analysis but, worse, of a nonsensical analysis. But, of course, Keynes did no such thing.

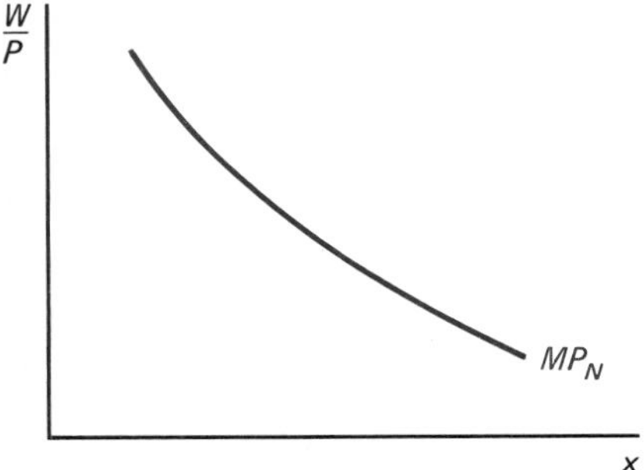

FIGURE 5-14

Let us put the pieces of the above reasoning together and formally derive the Keynesian employment adjustment mechanism. From the profit-maximizing rule, $MP_N = W/p$, we get the result that employment, x, rises (falls) if, and only if, the rate of change in prices, $\Delta p/p$, is algebraically greater (smaller) than the rate of change in money wages, $\Delta W/W$. Schematically, we have

$$\frac{\Delta p}{p} > \frac{\Delta W}{W} \rightarrow x \uparrow$$

$$\frac{\Delta p}{p} < \frac{\Delta W}{W} \rightarrow x \downarrow$$

and

$$\frac{\Delta p}{p} = \frac{\Delta W}{W} \rightarrow x \text{ unchanged}$$

More compactly, we can write this as

$$\left(\frac{\Delta x}{x}\right) \gtreqless 0 \quad \text{when} \quad \left(\frac{\Delta p}{p}\right) \gtreqless \left(\frac{\Delta W}{W}\right) \tag{2}$$

Keynes, operating under the dictum that "you had better learn to walk before you attempt to run," assumed, in the beginning of his analysis, and up to his Chapter 18, that money wages are fixed (i.e., that $\Delta W = 0$). This assumption drastically simplifies the above schema. We can now say that employment rises (falls) if, and only if, the price level rises (falls)—in other words, when $\Delta p > 0$ ($\Delta p < 0$). Schematically, and in compact form, we have

$$\Delta x \gtreqless 0 \quad \text{when} \quad \Delta p \gtreqless 0 \tag{3}$$

We now come to the final step. We stipulate, as we have repeatedly in this book, that the price of goods and services, p, rises (falls) if, and only if, there is positive (negative) excess demand for goods and services:

$$EG > 0 \rightarrow p\uparrow \text{ (i.e., } \Delta p > 0)$$
$$EG < 0 \rightarrow p\downarrow \text{ (i.e., } \Delta p < 0)$$
$$EG = 0 \rightarrow p \text{ unchanged (i.e., } \Delta p = 0)$$

This is written more compactly in the schema

$$\Delta p \gtreqless 0 \quad \text{when} \quad EG \gtreqless 0 \tag{4}$$

Combining (3) and (4), we have

$$\Delta x \gtreqless 0 \quad \text{when} \quad \Delta p \gtreqless 0 \quad \text{when} \quad EG \gtreqless 0 \tag{5}$$

Or simply,

$$\Delta x \gtreqless 0 \quad \text{when} \quad EG \gtreqless 0,$$

which is exactly (1), namely, the Keynesian employment adjustment mechanism. We have derived this mechanism by *assuming* that prices change according to the *law of supply and demand* for the goods and services market. Thus, far from assuming prices fixed, the Keynesian analysis says that employment increases (decreases) *because* the prices of goods and services increase (decrease). Recall that earlier, in our informal analysis, we stated that this rise (fall) in prices provides the incentive for entrepreneurs to increase their output by hiring more (less) labor.

In summary, the Keynesian employment adjustment mechanism is (a) consistent with the price adjustment mechanism and (b) far from assuming fixed prices, *relies* on price changes.

THE INTEREST ADJUSTMENT MECHANISM

Keynes' Proposition 5 states that the interest rate is determined by the excess demand for money. Of course, this contrasts sharply with the *non*-Wicksellian neoclassical proposition, which stipulates that the excess of investment over savings (i.e., excess demand for goods) engineers changes in the interest rate. The contrast between Keynes and Wicksell is not very sharp, however; both are "modern" in that they permit monetary phenomena to influence the interest rate (recall that the excess [flow] supply of money is a component of the supply of loanable funds). But their theories are different. Keynes stated that the interest rate rises when there is excess demand for money, it falls when there is excess supply of money, and it remains unchanged only when the demand for money is equal to its supply:

$$EM > 0 \rightarrow i\uparrow$$
$$EM < 0 \rightarrow i\downarrow$$
$$EM = 0 \rightarrow i \text{ unchanged}$$

This Keynesian interest rate adjustment can be represented by the following compact schema:

$$\Delta i \gtreqless 0 \quad \text{when} \quad EM \gtreqless 0 \qquad (6)$$

A simple equation that can capture the Keynesian stipulation is the following:

$$\Delta i = \delta_p \cdot EM \qquad (6')$$

Here, the positive number, δ_p, is the speed of adjustment of the money "market." Its inverse, $1/\delta_p$, is the time it takes for the demand for money to be made equal to the supply. Of course, this equality is brought about by appropriate changes in the interest rate. It hardly needs to be emphasized that in the simple form of (6′), it is assumed that the change in the interest rate is proportional to the excess demand or excess supply.

The Keynesian interest rate adjustment mechanism is usually called the "liquidity preference theory of interest," a name derived from Keynes' term for the demand for money, "liquidity preference." To this we can contrast the "loanable funds theory of interest" introduced by Wicksell and used even by Keynes in his earlier work. According to this theory (which we examined in Chapter 4), the interest rate rises when there is excess demand for loans (or loanable funds), it falls when there is excess supply, and it remains unchanged only when the loans market is cleared. Schematically,

$$EL > 0 \rightarrow i \uparrow \text{ (i.e., } \Delta i > 0)$$
$$EL < 0 \rightarrow i \downarrow \text{ (i.e., } \Delta i < 0)$$
$$EL = 0 \rightarrow i \text{ unchanged (i.e., } \Delta i = 0)$$

More compactly, we can write:

$$\Delta i \gtreqless 0 \quad \text{when} \quad EL \gtreqless 0 \tag{7}$$

Again, the spirit of this schema can be captured by a simple equation, (7′):

$$\Delta i = \delta_F \cdot EL \tag{7'}$$

where δ_F is the speed of adjustment in the loanable funds market, and $1/\delta_F$ is the time it takes to clear this market.[2]

Keynes' abandonment of the loanable funds theory of interest in favor of the liquidity preference theory of interest displeased several important economists, among them his close friend and colleague, Robertson, and Wicksell's disciple, Ohlin.[3] The debate between these three giants in the economics profession—Keynes, Robertson, and Ohlin—attracted other important names, such as Abba Lerner, J. R. Hicks, Harry G. Johnson, Hugh Rose, S. C. Tsiang, and Don Patinkin.[4] These economists debated not only the issue of where the interest rate is determined—in the loans or in the money market—but also whether the two theories of interest rate determination are consistent with each other, or even the same. In addition, the institutional aspects of the financial markets associated with each theory of interest were examined.

The debate, the loanable funds versus the liquidity preference determination of the interest rate, has historically been conducted under an agreement that the

---

[2] The subscripts p and F of δ are used to differentiate the market—"liquidity preference" and "loanable funds," respectively—to which the speed of adjustment is applied.

[3] See D. H. Robertson, "Mr. Keynes and the Rate of Interest," *Essays in Monetary Theory,* 1940, reprinted in *Readings in the Theory of Income Distribution* (London: Allen & Unwin, 1950), pp. 477–99; and Bertil Ohlin, "Some Notes on the Stockholm Theory of Saving and Investment II," *Economic Journal,* June 1937.

[4] Abba Lerner, "Alternative Formulations of the Rate of Interest," *Economic Journal,* 1938; J. M. Keynes, "Alternative Theories of the Rate of Interest," *Economic Journal,* June 1937, pp. 241–52; J. R. Hicks, *Value and Capital,* 2nd ed. (London: Oxford, 1946); H. G. Johnson, "Some Cambridge Controversies in Monetary Theory," *Review of Economic Studies,* 1951–52, pp. 90–110; H. Rose, "Liquidity Preference and Loanable Funds," *Review of Economic Studies,* February 1957; S. C. Tsiang, "Liquidity Preference and Loanable Funds Theories, Multiplier and Velocity Analyses: A Synthesis," *American Economic Review,* September 1956; and Don Patinkin, "Liquidity Preference and Loanable Funds, Stock and Flow Analysis," *Economica,* November 1958.

former is definitely the accepted one. This agreement imposed, upon the proponents of the liquidity preference theory, the burden of proof to show that either the two are the same or, at least, the latter is consistent with the former.

It is generally accepted that *at equilibrium* both theories are the same. In other words, whether one determines the interest rate as the solution to loans market clearance or as the solution to zero excess demand for money, that interest rate is the same. This, of course, does not come as a surprise to the reader of Chapter 4 in this book. We have seen that at full equilibrium, both the loans market and the market for goods and services are cleared. But as Figure 5-15 shows, this also implies that (at A) the money market is also cleared, that is, $EM = L(i,x) - M/p = 0$.

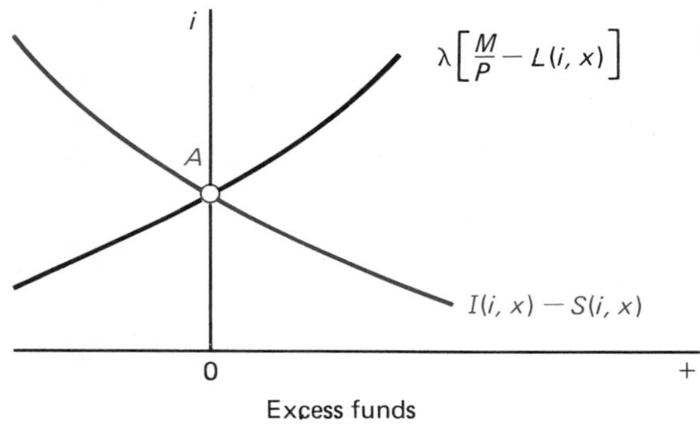

FIGURE 5-15

To determine whether the two theories are the same, or simply consistent with each other, we need to examine each component of the demand and supply sides of the two markets.

	DEMAND	SUPPLY
Money market:	$L(i,x)$	M/p
Loans market:	$I(i,x)$	$S(i,x) + \lambda\left[\frac{M}{p} - L(i,x)\right]$

It is clear from the above that the excess (flow) demand for money, EM, is

$$EM = \lambda[L(i,x) - M/p]$$

where the excess (again, flow) demand for loans, EL, is

$$EL = I(i,x) - S(i,x) + \lambda[L(i,x) - M/p]$$

Comparing EM and EL above, it appears that as long as investment $I(i,x)$ is different from savings, $S(i,x)$, that is, as long as the goods market is *not* cleared, excess demand for money is *not* the same thing as excess demand for loans. To demonstrate that an excess demand for money is tantamount to an excess demand for loans, it follows that we must find some way to eliminate the excess demand for goods, $I(\cdot) - S(\cdot)$, as a component of the excess demand for loans.

One such way was introduced by Hugh Rose in 1957.[5] His idea is simple: If there is excess demand for goods and services, which means $I(\cdot) - S(\cdot) > 0$, it must be that the plans of firms are not fulfilled. In particular, it must be that actual receipts are greater than the expected ones. The question here, in essence, is one of asking what firms do with these unexpected receipts. If firms lend these receipts, they should be considered another component of the supply of loanable funds. We thus have:

DEMAND	SUPPLY
$I(i,x)$	$S(i,x) + \lambda\left[\frac{M}{p} - L(i,x)\right] + I(i,x) - S(i,x)$

Thus the true excess demand for loans, EL, is

$$EL = I(i,x) - S(i,x) + \lambda\left[L(i,x) - \frac{M}{p}\right] - I(i,x) + S(i,x)$$
$$= \lambda\left[L(i,x) - \frac{M}{p}\right].$$

Similarly, if there is excess supply of goods and services, it means that firms have overestimated their expected receipts. The end result of an excess supply of goods and services is reflected in an accumulation of inventories that must be financed. This means that firms have to borrow in the loans market. Thus the excess supply of goods and services, $S(\cdot) - I(\cdot) > 0$, must be considered an additional component of the demand for loans:

DEMAND	SUPPLY
$I(i,x) + S(i,x) - I(i,x)$	$S(i,x) + \lambda\left[\frac{M}{p} - L(i,x)\right]$

The true excess demand for loans, again, is

$$\overline{EL} = I(i,x) + S(i,x) - I(i,x) - S(i,x) - \lambda\left[\frac{M}{p} - L(i,x)\right]$$
$$= \lambda\left[L(i,x) - \frac{M}{p}\right]$$

as earlier.

---

[5] Rose, "Liquidity Preference."

Hugh Rose concluded that the difference between the two theories arises in the assumptions made about the choices an agent has in financing an unintended accumulation of inventories (or in disposing of surplus from unintended decumulation). If we assume that firms enter the loans market and borrow to finance unintended accumulation of inventories and that they lend to dispose of unintended receipts associated with unplanned depletion of inventories, we have the Keynes liquidity preference theory of interest. On the other hand, if we require such firms to finance the accumulation of inventories by dishoarding and to dispose of their entire receipts by hoarding, then we have the traditional Wicksell-Robertson loanable funds theory of interest. Needless to say, Hugh Rose's explanation demonstrated that the two theories *are* consistent with each other.

To avoid any misunderstanding, it should be emphasized at this point that Keynes could just as well have carried his analysis using a loanable funds, rather than a liquidity preference, theory of interest, that is, using schema (7) rather than schema (6). It should also be pointed out that regardless of one's addition of either (6) or (7) to the employment adjustment mechanism (1), one is still identified as "Keynesian" and not as "neoclassical." It is mainly for this reason that we do not examine in greater detail the interesting views of more participants in the liquidity preference *versus* loanable funds debate. This is left to the more elaborate monograph on the topic.

II. THE "SIMPLE" KEYNESIAN SYSTEM: THE GOODS MARKET AND THE DETERMINATION OF INCOME AND EMPLOYMENT

In this section we examine in greater detail the role of the goods and services market in determining employment and income. In essence, this will be an elaboration of the Keynesian employment adjustment mechanism introduced earlier. As we saw in the preceding pages, this mechanism is merely one of several components of the Keynesian construction, a fact we should always keep in mind. Acknowledging this warning we can now embark safely upon a more detailed examination of the employment adjustment mechanism.

Keynes maintained that the goods market *determines* employment. More explicitly, he stated that employment, x, rises (i.e., $\Delta x > 0$) when there is excess demand for goods (i.e., when $EG > 0$) and falls (i.e., $\Delta x < 0$) when there is excess supply (i.e., $EG < 0$). It has no tendency to change (i.e., $\Delta x = 0$) only when this market is cleared ($EG = 0$). As we saw on page 172, we can merge all these statements into the following compact schema (1):

$$\Delta x \gtreqless 0 \quad \text{when} \quad EG \gtreqless 0 \tag{1}$$

Recall that we have already established that these changes in employment are induced by potential profits or losses caused by *changes in* prices. That the schema in (1) *relies* on changes in prices is another point that the reader should always keep in mind.

We have already established (e.g., in Chapter 1) that if the roles of the government and of foreign trade are ignored, intended aggregate demand is the sum of private consumption demand, C, and private investment demand, I. Intended aggregate supply, on the other hand, is the output currently produced, Y. Excess demand, EG, is $C + I - Y$ or, equivalently, $I - (Y - C)$. But we know that $Y - C$ is income not currently consumed, that is, it is savings, S. (Recall that $Y \equiv C + S$.) Thus we have established two equivalent formulas for EG:

$$EG = C + I - Y$$

$$EG = I - S$$

(We have also established that excess demand is reflected in the depletion of inventories and that excess supply, that is, negative EG, is reflected in the accumulation of inventories.) Using the two formulas above, we can rewrite (1) as either (8) or (9):

$$\Delta x \gtreqless 0 \quad \text{when} \quad C + I \gtreqless Y \tag{8}$$

$$\Delta x \gtreqless 0 \quad \text{when} \quad I - S \gtreqless 0 \tag{9}$$

It is (9) that Keynes suggested in his Proposition 4 when he insisted that investment and savings *determine* employment; it is this version we utilized in our graphical illustration of that proposition.

After adjusting to the shock inherent in novelty, economists liked Keynes' new gadget, embodied in the schema of (1). To their delight, this tool was very flexible and was applicable to a variety of problems. Only some modification or extension was needed to fit a particular purpose. Thus, not long after the *General Theory* was published, expositors of Keynes undertook *beautifications, extensions, modifications,* and, occasionally, *emasculations* of the *employment adjustment mechanism.* (These underlined words might well be used as the title of this section.)

1. INCOME DETERMINATION

The most significant modification transformed the mechanism from one of *employment* adjustment to one of *income* adjustment. Simultaneously, the national income accounts were being introduced by Kuznets, and income was regarded as the key indicator of ecnomic activity. In schematic form, the *income adjustment mechanism* can be represented by (10):

$$\Delta Y \gtreqless 0 \quad \text{when} \quad EG \gtreqless 0 \tag{10}$$

Because of the two formulas for *EG*, we have two equivalent explicit schemata, (11) and (12):

$$\Delta Y \gtreqless 0 \quad \text{when} \quad C + I \gtreqless Y \tag{11}$$

$$\Delta Y \gtreqless 0 \quad \text{when} \quad I - S \gtreqless 0 \tag{12}$$

At this point we should keep in mind that consumption, as well as savings, depends positively on income. Knowing the curve depicting consumption in the *(Y,C)*-plane, we can derive the savings curve in the *(Y,S)*-plane. Only the identity $C + S \equiv Y$ is needed for this. Recall that this identity merely states that income can be either consumed or saved. Suppose that the consumption function is depicted in the top panel of Figure 5-16 by the line $\overline{C}\overline{C}$. At the point that this curve intersects the 45° line, $C = Y$ (i.e., at an income level equal to Y_0), society does not save anything. All income is consumed. At income levels higher than Y_0, say Y_1, savings

FIGURE 5-16

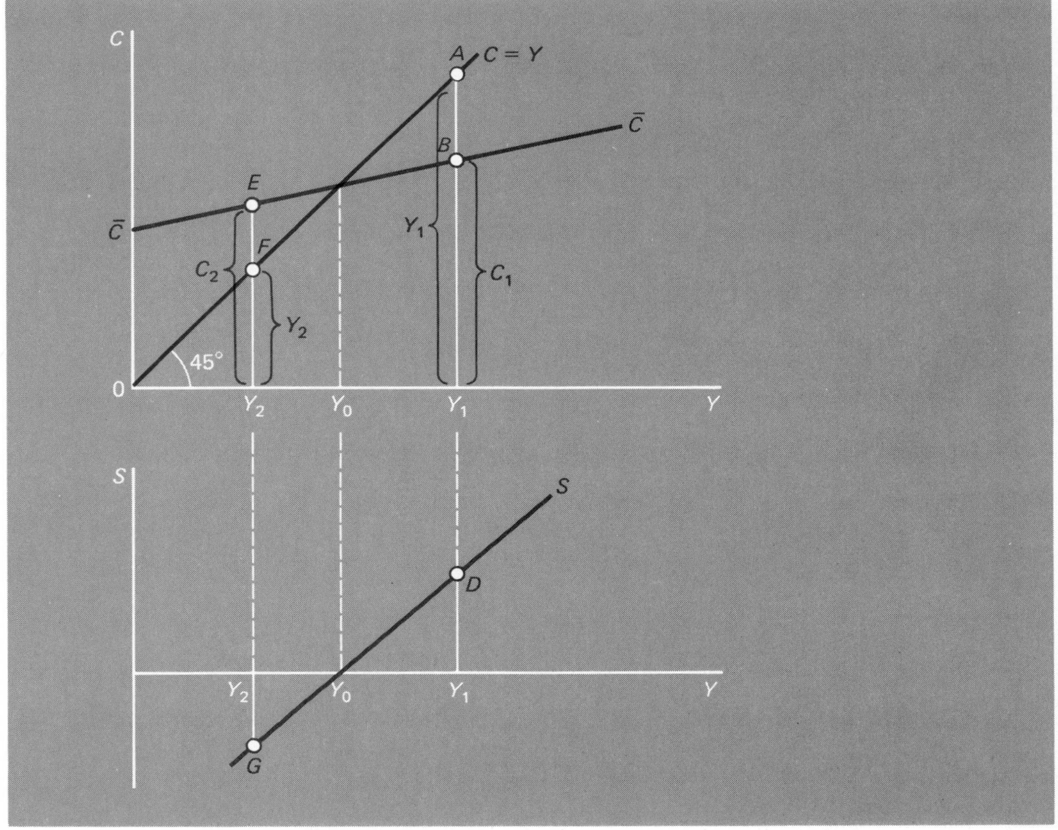

is found as the vertical difference between Y and C. Income, Y_1, is equal to the distance Y_1A; consumption is equal to Y_1B; and thus $S = Y - C = Y_1A - Y_1B = AB$. Note in the lower panel that the S curve has been drawn to show that for income equal to Y_1, savings, Y_1D, is equal to AB. Continuing, we find that at an income level equal to Y_2, there is dissaving: Society consumes more than its income, namely, $C_2 = Y_2E > Y_2F = Y_2$. Dissaving is equal to EF, which is precisely equal to Y_2G in the lower panel.

Whether we use schema (11) or schema (12) to *determine* income, we need the investment function. Our analysis in Chapter 2 revealed that investment depends positively on income. However, for purposes of illustration only, we must first assume that investment demand is a given number, independent of income, as in Figure 5-17.

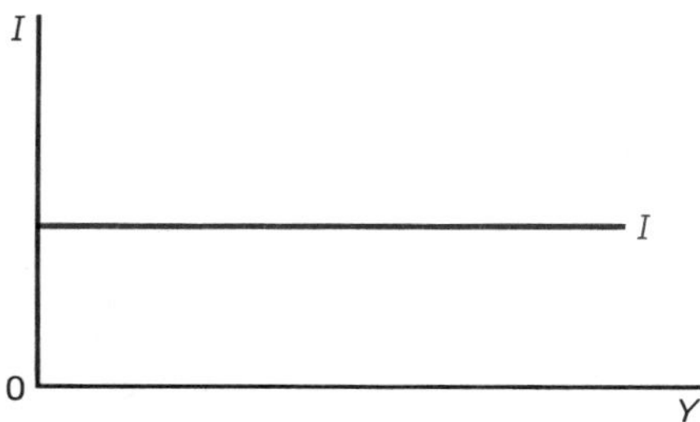

FIGURE 5-17

We now illustrate the income adjustment mechanism by utilizing simultaneously both of its versions, (11) and (12). In the upper panel of Figure 5-18 we depict separately the consumption function, C, and the investment function, I, as well as their sum, $C + I$. Since I is independent of Y, the curves $C + I$ and C are parallel, with a constant difference equal to the fixed level of investment demand. In the lower panel of Figure 5-18 we again depict the same horizontal investment curve, I, and also, using the technique of Figure 5-16, we derive and depict the implied savings curve, S.

We are now ready to illustrate the *income adjustment mechanism.* Let us suppose that the economy starts with income equal to Y_0. Concentrating on the upper panel, we see that aggregate demand (i.e., consumption plus investment) is equal to Y_0A. On the other hand, supply is Y_0, which is equal to Y_0B. Aggregate demand is greater than aggregate supply by an amount equal to AB. By the schema (11), it follows that income has to rise (i.e., since $C + I > Y$, it follows that $\Delta Y > 0$; in other words, Y must rise). Therefore we indicate a movement in the direction of higher income by placing an arrow pointing to the right.

The same result can be shown by concentrating on the lower panel and the schema in (12): At Y_0 investment is equal to Y_0E and savings is equal to Y_0F. The former is greater by an amount equal to EF, which is precisely equal to AB. Thus we find that $I - S > 0$. According to (12), it follows that $\Delta Y > 0$. And we have an arrow depicting a higher Y in the lower panel also. Similarly, we can show that if income is at *any* level below Y_e, it will always rise, since it will be accompanied

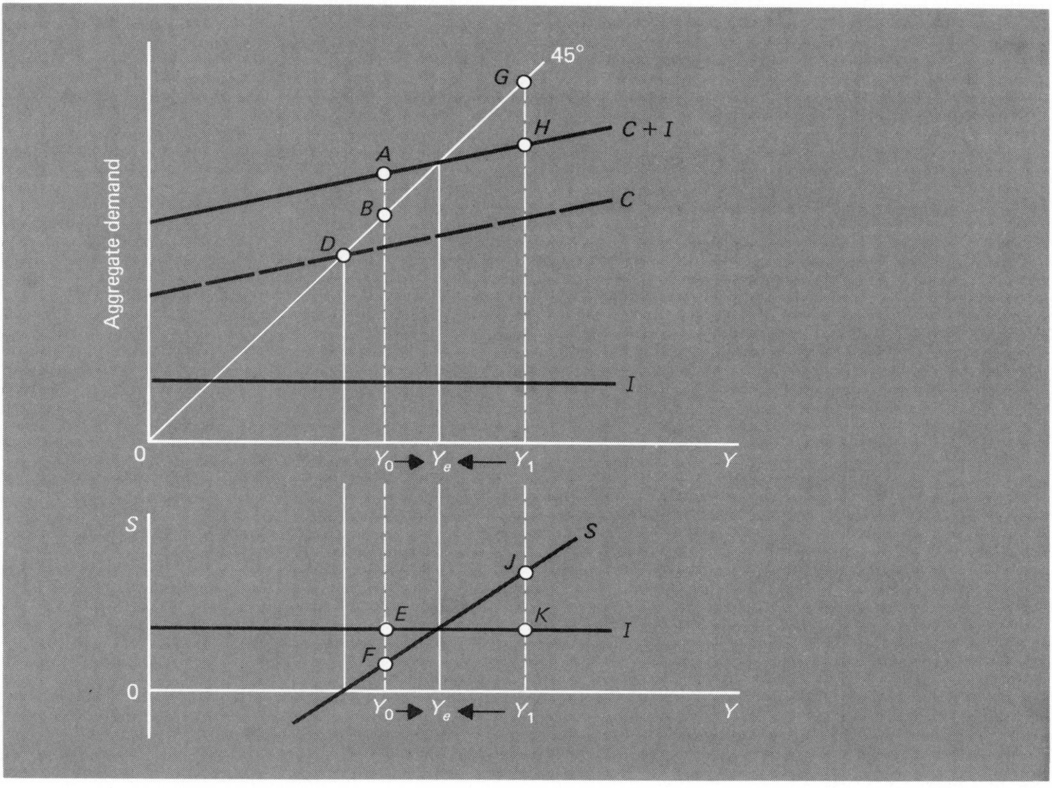

FIGURE 5-18

by excess demand, $C + I > Y$, or, equivalently, by a level of investment that is greater than savings, $I > S$.

Let us now examine a situation in which the income level is higher than Y_e, say at Y_1. In this case the upper panel shows that consumption plus investment falls short of aggregate supply, by an amount equal to *GH*. Since $C + I < Y$, it follows from (11) that $\Delta Y < 0$ (i.e., income has to fall). We have, therefore, an arrow pointing to the left. Concentrating on the lower panel, we see that at Y_1 investment is lower than savings, by an amount equal to *JK*, which is equal to *GH*. Since $I < S$, formula (12) dictates that Y falls (i.e., $\Delta Y < 0$).

We have seen that if income is lower than Y_e, there are economic forces to raise it; and if it is greater than Y_e, there are forces to lower it. The only level of income that can be sustained is Y_e. Note that with income at the level Y_e, aggregate demand, $C + I$, is equal to the aggregate supply, Y_e, because the $C + I$ curve intersects the 45° line at Y_e. By the formula in (11), $\Delta Y = 0$, and there is no tendency for income to change. The same result is derived from the lower panel. At Y_e the investment curve intersects the savings curve. Since $I - S = 0$, it follows from (12) that $\Delta Y = 0$ also.

We have established that income is determined at the level for which aggregate demand for goods and services is equal to aggregate supply. Moreover, there are forces that guarantee a rise in income when aggregate demand is greater than aggregate supply and, likewise, a fall in income when aggregate demand is lower than aggregate supply.

It was solely for expository purposes that we assumed, contrary to our knowledge, that investment is independent of income. But our results remain intact even when investment depends on income—as long as investment stays within some limits. Figure 5-19 examines the case that permits the dependence of investment on income but requires that the marginal propensity to spend (i.e., MPC + MPI) is less than one. Note that the slope of the investment schedule, $\Delta I/\Delta Y$, is less than the slope of the savings schedule, $\Delta S/\Delta Y$, as seen in the lower panel of Figure 5-19. Note that $\Delta I/\Delta Y < \Delta S/\Delta Y$. But $\Delta S/\Delta Y + \Delta C/\Delta Y \equiv 1$, from which it follows that $\Delta I/\Delta Y < 1 - \Delta C/\Delta Y$, or $\Delta C/\Delta Y + \Delta I/\Delta Y < 1$. The sum of the marginal propensity to consume and the marginal propensity to invest is termed the marginal propensity to spend.

It is not always necessary to draw both panels in graphs as we have done in Figures 5-18 and 5-19. Sometimes we shall concentrate on the upper panel, especially if we want to explicitly show consumption and aggregate demand. Incidentally, this sort of condensed graph is called the "Keynesian cross." At other times, when we have an interest in explicitly displaying savings, a graph like the lower panel of Figure 5-18 or Figure 5-19 is more suitable. It is obvious that in the preceding section

FIGURE 5-19

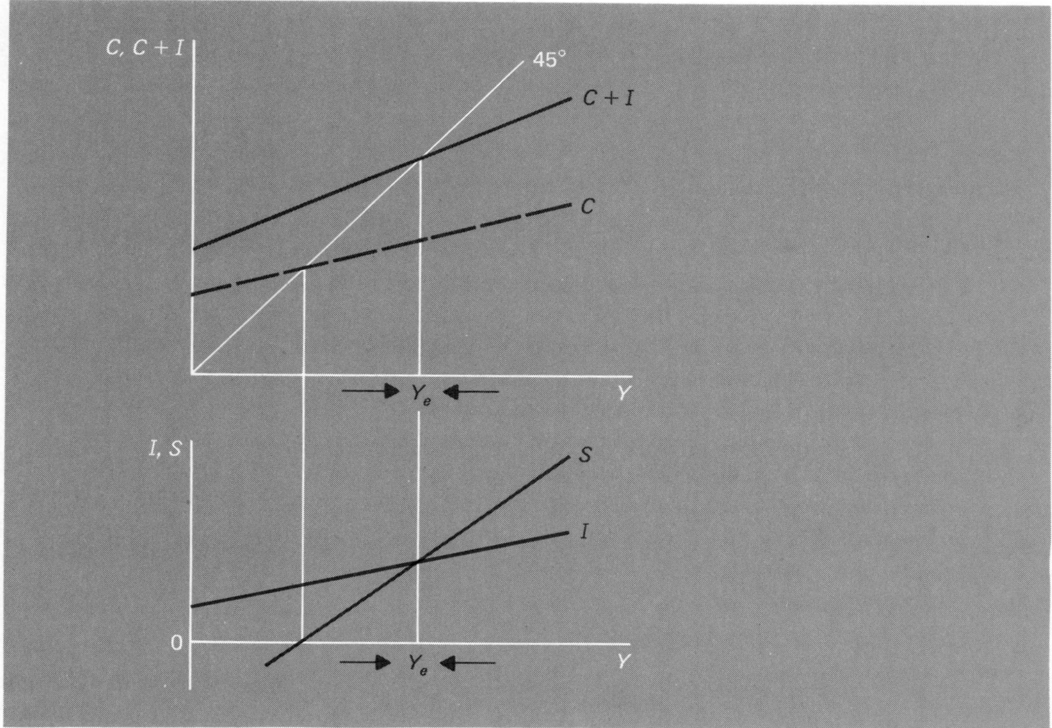

we concentrated on graphs of the latter variety—but to display employment rather than income.

Concentrating on a graph of the investment-savings variety, we can see that if the marginal propensity to spend is greater than one, then the movement is always away from equilibrium. We can see this is Figure 5-20, where a marginal propensity to spend greater than one is depicted by an investment schedule steeper than the savings schedule.

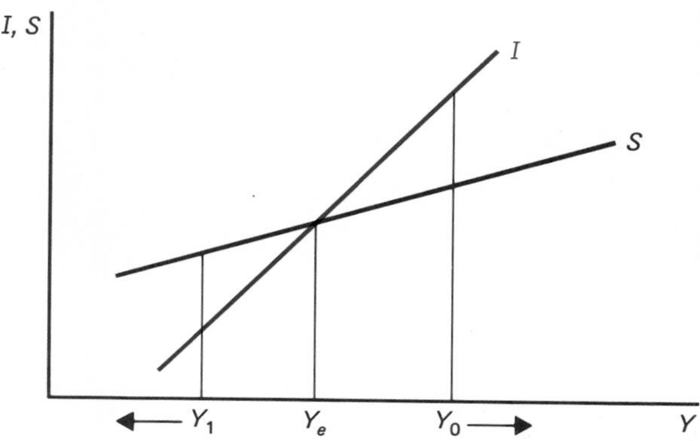

FIGURE 5-20

At an income level equal to Y_0, we see that investment is greater than savings, that is, there is excess demand for goods and services. Income, then, should rise, as the appropriate arrow indicates. On the other hand, when income is Y_1, that is, less than the equilibrium value Y_e, savings is greater than investment. This means that there is excess supply of goods and services, which implies that output must be reduced. And we note that when the marginal propensity to spend is greater than one, the *income adjustment mechanism is unstable.* We should emphasize that the instability refers to the mechanism and not to the economy as a whole, which may or may not be unstable as a consequence.

At this point it is instructive to clear up two common misconceptions. First, there is no *a priori* reason why the marginal propensity to spend should be less than one; it could easily be greater than one. Neither is there any *empirical* reason why it should be less than one. Yet there are textbooks that claim that the case of a marginal propensity to spend greater than one should be eliminated, either because it is unrealistic (i.e., for *a priori reasons*) or because it is empirically unsound. Neither reason is valid. These authors, it seems, feel that the *economy* will be unstable if the income adjustment mechanism is unstable. This is not the case. They seem to forget that this mechanism is only one component of the macroeconomic edifice, a system that can still be stable when all the components are put together.

Comparative statics

Changes in Savings Behavior: We shall examine the effects of a change in a particular underlying parameter on income, beginning with changes in savings behavior. Let us suppose that people are persuaded, say, by the preachings of a modern-

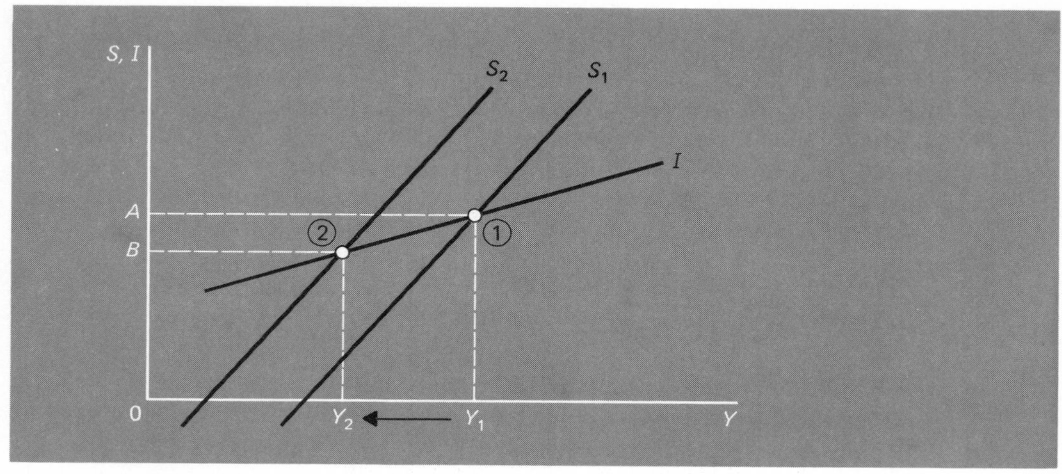

FIGURE 5-21

day Benjamin Franklin, to save more at each level of income. We are now examining a case that permits unemployment. Here we utilize the savings-investment graph which explicitly shows the increase in savings, although the "cross" diagram could also accommodate, but only implicitly, this exercise. In Figure 5-21 the original savings curve, S_1, intersects the investment schedule at point ①; this determines income level Y_1. The increase in savings at each level of income shifts the savings curve to the left of position S_1. The intersection of this new savings curve with the investment curve, assumed unchanged, occurs at point ② and determines a *lower* income, namely Y_2. We can now understand why neither workers nor firms would, in general, be in favor of such an increase in savings (i.e., a decrease in consumption demand); income falls, and they will both suffer. But the reduction in income will be accompanied by, and be a consequence of, a reduction in employment. We know that in the short

FIGURE 5-22

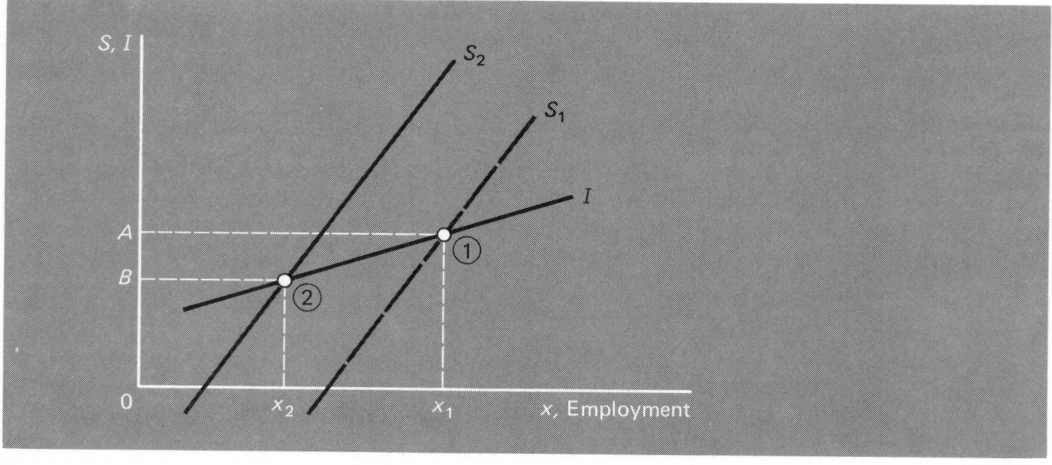

run the only variable factor is labor, which will bear the brunt of reduced income. (Later we shall also introduce unemployment of plant and equipment, a more realistic case.)

Of course, we can show the reduction in unemployment directly by using the investment-savings graph already introduced in the preceding section. In fact, this is what Keynes himself emphasized, since he was interested primarily in employment. We see in Figure 5-22 that the increase in savings lowers employment.

Figures 5-21 and 5-22 highlight another important result, namely, the self-defeating nature of the attempt to increase savings. The attempt to save more netted the economy *lower* savings; this is the *paradox of thrift.* The attempt to save more, and thus consume less, lowers income, and the total savings out of reduced income is less than before. In both Figures 5-21 and 5-22, OA was the quantity of original savings, while $OB < OA$ is the new total savings.

Changes in investment: public works

Suppose that the government increases its investment demand by building more highways and undertaking other public works projects. In fact, this is one of the methods Keynes recommended to extricate the economy from the Depression of the 1930s. In Figure 5-23 we shift the investment curve upward and to the left, to the position $I + I_g$, by an amount equal to this increased government investment. The original equilibrium was point ①, while the new one is point ②. In Figure 5-23 we see that the increased government investment has increased employment from x_1 to x_2.

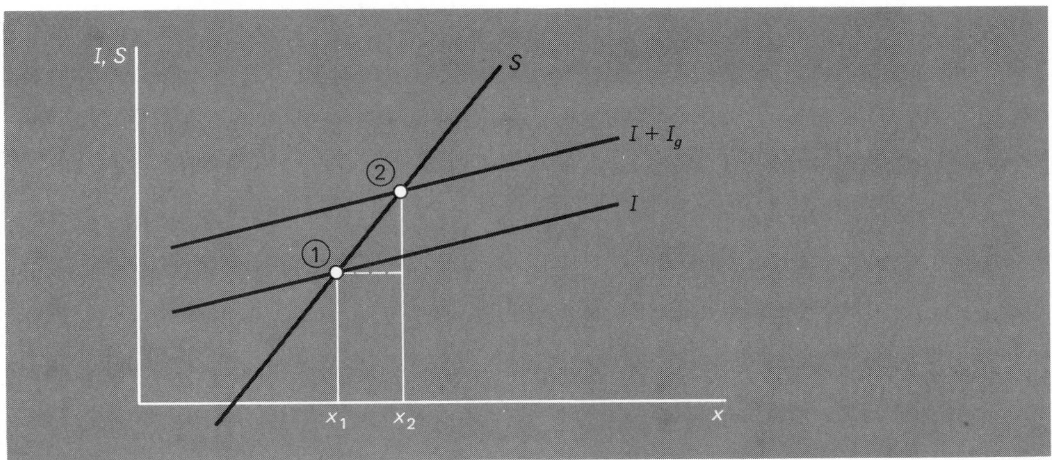

FIGURE 5-23

2. EXTENSIONS OF THE MECHANISM: FOREIGN TRADE

So far we have assumed that the economy under consideration is a closed one. In other words, we assumed that no trade was permitted between this economy and others. Actually, however, every economy engages in international trade. Foreigners demand a country's products, its exports. On the other hand, residents of this country demand goods produced in other countries; these are the country's imports. It is clear, then, that the demand side of the goods market has one additional component, namely, exports, χ. Similarly, on the supply side, we should add imports, μ. For simplicity we shall consider only the net result, the net *addition* to aggregate demand, $\chi - \mu$. This, of course, is the *trade surplus,* which will be denoted by ν. Allowing explicitly for international trade, the formulas for excess demand for goods, *EG,* are

$$EG = (C + I + \nu) - Y$$

$$EG = (I + \nu) - S$$

Here we are interested merely in showing how income (or employment) determination is influenced by foreign (net) demand; we are not interested in dealing with the intricacies of international trade. Although it should be obvious that each component of the trade surplus, exports as well as imports, is influenced by the level of the country's income, we shall assume in this exposition that this trade surplus is *exogenous,* or independent of income level. This simplifies the graphical presentation. Utilizing the above formulas for *EG,* we get schemata (13) and (14):

$$\Delta Y \gtreqless 0 \quad \text{when} \quad (C + I + \nu) \gtreqless Y \tag{13}$$

$$\Delta Y \gtreqless 0 \quad \text{when} \quad (I + \nu) \gtreqless S \tag{14}$$

In the "Keynesian cross" graph of Figure 5-24, which reproduces the schema in (13), the trade surplus, ν, is a horizontal line added to the two components of aggregate demand, *C* and *I.* Income is determined where aggregate demand, $C + I + \nu$, intersects the 45° line.

By means of the investment-savings graph, and utilizing schema (14), Figure 5-25 illustrates income determination in the presence of international demand. Equilibrium income Y_e, is determined where the curve depicting investment plus the trade surplus intersects the savings curve. (In both Figures 5-24 and 5-25, for simplicity, we assume that investment is also independent of the level of income.)

Comparative statics: an increase in the trade surplus

Let us suppose, for some reason, the trade surplus is increased, perhaps as the result of an increase in exports, a decrease in imports, or both, or even as the result of a greater increase in exports than in imports. It is clear from Figure 5-26 that an increase in the trade surplus raises the equilibrium level of income from Y_0 to Y_1.

Here, for expository purposes, we implicitly assume that the government has discretionary power to both choose and change the trade surplus. In the real

FIGURE 5-24

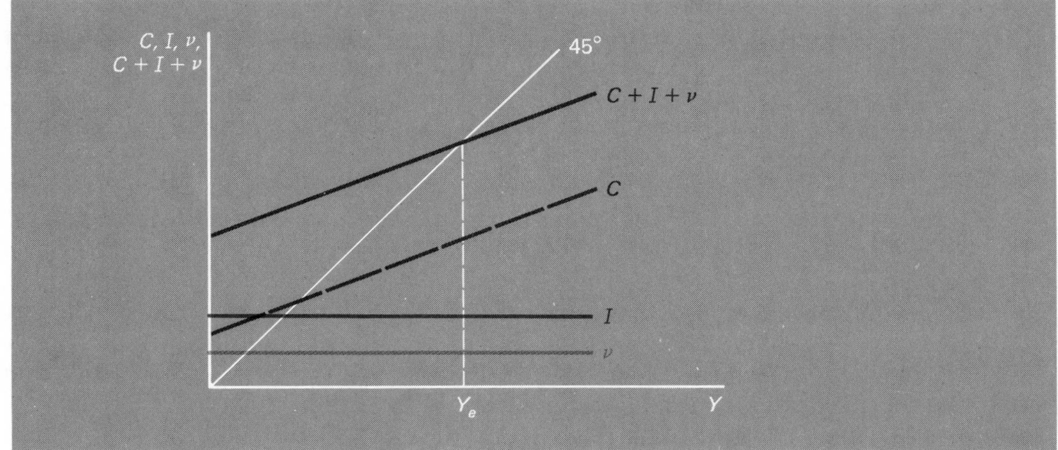

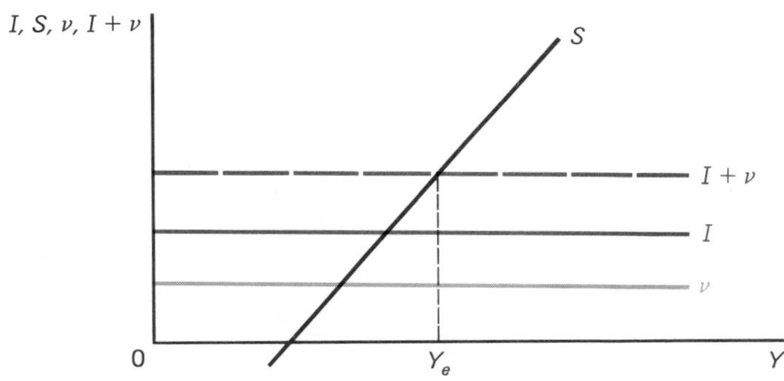

FIGURE 5-25

FIGURE 5-26

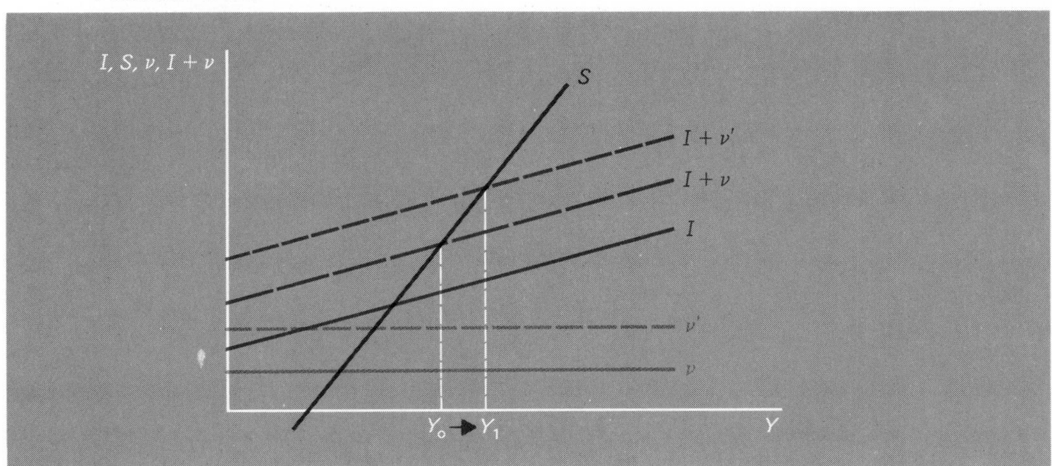

world, however, manipulation of the trade surplus (or deficit) is neither so simple nor so easy. At any rate, it is accomplished indirectly. For example, a devaluation of the country's currency might be used to raise the price of imports artificially and thus decrease them, and, simultaneously, to lower the price of exports artificially to increase foreign demand for a country's goods. Another method is by imposing, or increasing, import tariff rates. Still another method is by persuading foreign countries to reduce their exports to a country.[6]

This deliberate increase in the export surplus (or reduction of the export deficit) to raise a country's employment and income is called a "beggar-thy-neighbor" policy, presumably because it is at the expense of foreign countries that the employment is increased. No matter what this policy is called and no matter how it is engineered, we see that increases in the trade surplus do indeed increase employment. To stabilize their incomes different countries rely, in differing degrees, on manipulations of the trade surplus. Japan is one example of a country that relies heavily on its export surplus to stabilize national income, presumably at a high level.

3. EXTENSIONS OF THE MECHANISM: THE GOVERNMENT

It is now time to allow for government in our system. The government imposes taxes, T, and demands goods and services, G. If its expenditures on goods and services, G, are greater than its tax receipts, T, the government experiences a *deficit.* If tax receipts are greater than expenditures, there is a budget *surplus.* Finally, the budget is *balanced* when tax receipts are precisely equal to government expenditures. We shall use the symbol Z for the budget *deficit,* that is, $Z = G - T$. In the most general case, when both the government sector and foreign trade are explicit, the crucial national income identity, as we saw in Chapter 1, is

$$C + I + G + (\chi - \mu) \equiv Y \equiv C + S + T$$

In this case the formulas for EG, the excess demand for goods and services, are

$$EG = C + I + G + (\chi - \mu) - Y$$

$$EG = G + I + \chi - (S + T + \mu)$$

The latter formula can also be written as

$$EG = I + (G - T) + (\chi - \mu) - S$$

or as

$$EG = (I + Z + \nu) - S$$

[6] This method has been used recently; the United States has persuaded Japan to reduce her exports of automobiles to the U.S.

and, finally, as

$$EG = I + G + \nu - (S + T)$$

Depending on the particular formula used, we have different graphical tools.

In the remainder of this section we shall abstract from foreign trade (by setting $\chi - \mu = 0 = \nu$) to concentrate on the government sector. Even without trade, the situation will be complicated.

To begin with, we can use the two formulas for EG to introduce two general graphical approaches to income determination:[7]

$$\Delta Y \gtreqless 0 \quad \text{when} \quad C + I + G \gtreqless Y \tag{15}$$

$$\Delta Y \gtreqless 0 \quad \text{when} \quad I + G \gtreqless S + T \tag{16}$$

Figure 5-27 depicts the schema in (15), while Figure 5-28 depicts the schema in (16). These two graphs, and the schemata on which they are based, hide major difficulties which should be brought into the open. Before doing so, however, we

FIGURE 5-27

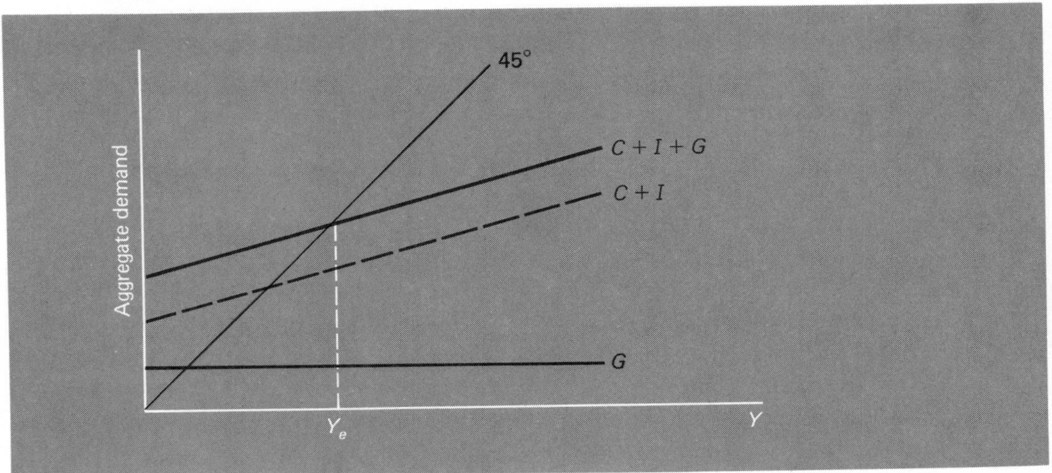

[7] Occasionally it is more convenient to work with schema (16′):

$$\Delta Y \gtreqless 0 \quad \text{when} \quad I + (G - T) \gtreqless S \tag{16′}$$

for which the net amount of the government budget deficit is added to investment demand. This latter approach is followed in the next chapter.

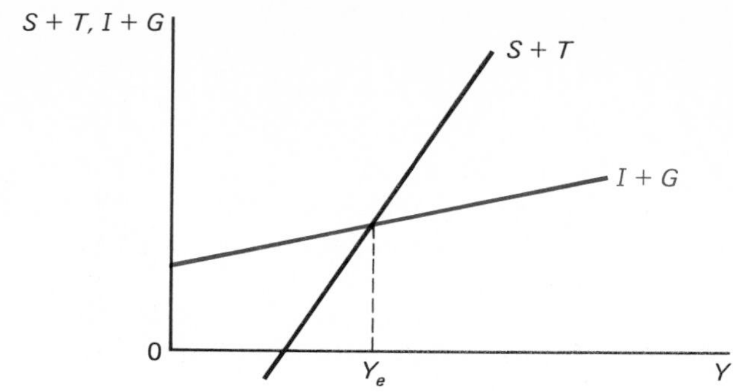

FIGURE 5-28

can extricate some results from these types of graphs. We note that in Figure 5-27 the government expenditure curve, G, is horizontal, implying that these expenditures are independent of the income level. The usual explanation for this assumption is that government demand for goods and services is predetermined and under the absolute control of the political process. Of course, this assumption does not preclude the government from using this quantity as a policy tool, as we shall see below.

In Figure 5-28 the $S + T$ curve is upward sloping, but the two curves, S and T, are not given separately. We know, of course, that the savings curve is upward sloping. Thus the upward-sloping $S + T$ curve is consistent with either lump-sum taxation or income taxation. In the former case, total taxation is considered a fixed quantity, independent of income. In the case of an income tax, total taxation increases with income. We shall return to the case of an explicit income tax shortly. Until then the reader is advised to consider the following as generally applicable to both cases, although it applies more to the case of lump-sum taxation than to income taxation.

Comparative statics: changes in total taxes, T

Assume that Congress decides to reduce the total amount of taxes by a specified amount. To determine the effect on income and output we shall use Figure 5-29, which is similar to Figure 5-28 and schema (16). The reduction in total savings shifts the $S + T$ curve downward from position $(S + T)_1$ to position $(S + T)_2$. In other words, for each level of income, the sum of savings and taxes is *lower* than before. Noting that the original equilibrium was point A, and given $(S + T)_2$ as the relevant $S + T$ curve, we see that at the original equilibrium income, Y_1, there is excess demand for goods and services equal to AC. This excess demand, according to schema (16), drives output (and thus income) upward, to level Y_2. The new equilibrium point is now point B. We see that a decrease in taxes, *if other things are equal,* will increase income. The caveat that other things must be equal is inserted here to emphasize that this schema (and graph) is only one component in the whole economic system. Later, however, we shall show that the result remains true, in general, even when we take into consideration the remaining components of the system. Having made this qualification, we can comment that the substantial tax cut in the United

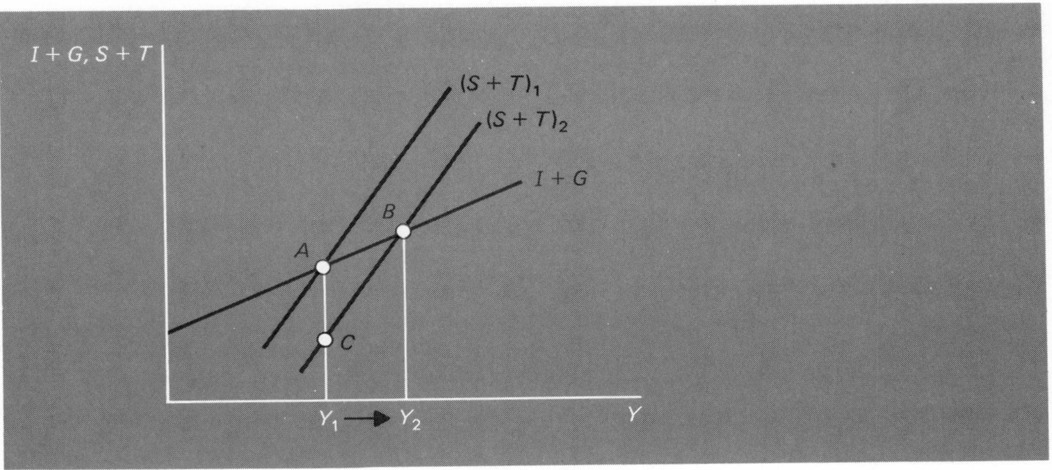

FIGURE 5-29

States in 1964 was designed specifically to increase the level of output. By all accounts, it was a successful economic policy.

Figure 5-29 considered the case of a tax *cut.* The reader can conduct the argument in reverse and show that a tax *increase* will, *ceteris paribus,* reduce output. For a disastrous example of an increase in taxes, we can cite the dramatic increase in taxation in 1931–32 recommended by the Hoover administration as an attempt to "balance the budget" in the misguided belief that this measure would drive the U.S. economy out of the Great Depression! But, of course, the *General Theory* had not yet been written.

Comparative statics: changes in government expenditure, G

In Figure 5-30 we illustrate the effects of an *increase* in government expenditure, G, on goods and services. The increase in G from G_0 to G_1 creates, at the original equilibrium output, Y_0, excess demand equal to the magnitude of the increase in government expenditure, *CA*. According to the income adjustment mechanism (15), this excess demand eventually raises output to Y_1. We see that, other things being equal, an increase in government expenditure will increase output. We can show the same result by utilizing the alternative graphical technique as in Figure 5-31, which is self-evident. With the qualification "other things being equal," we can again cite examples of successful, as well as detrimental, increases in government expenditures. Focusing first on the detrimental, we observe that the Hoover administration's attempt to balance the budget included a *decrease* in government expenditure. It is no wonder, then, that output and employment continued to fall during those years! As the U.S. economy prepared for World War II by increasing government expenditure on goods and services, output and employment continued to increase, as we have come to expect from our analysis here.

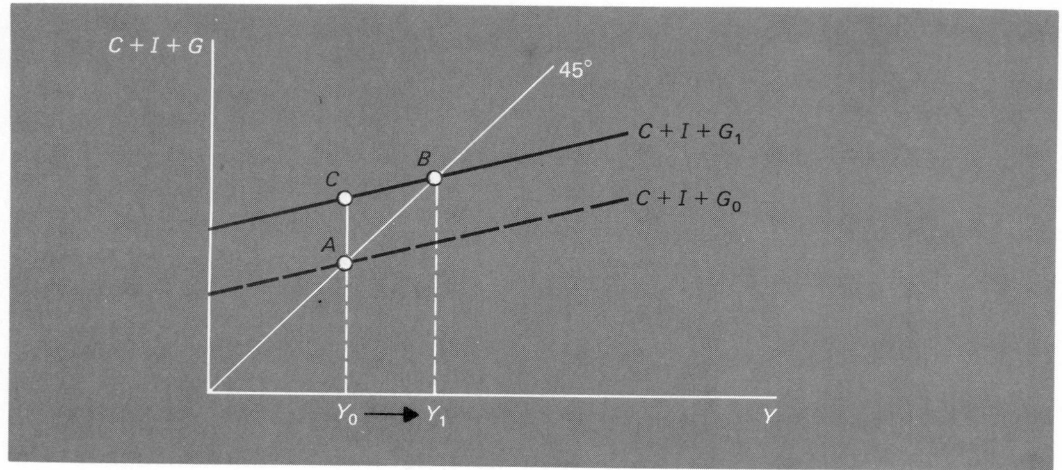

FIGURE 5-30

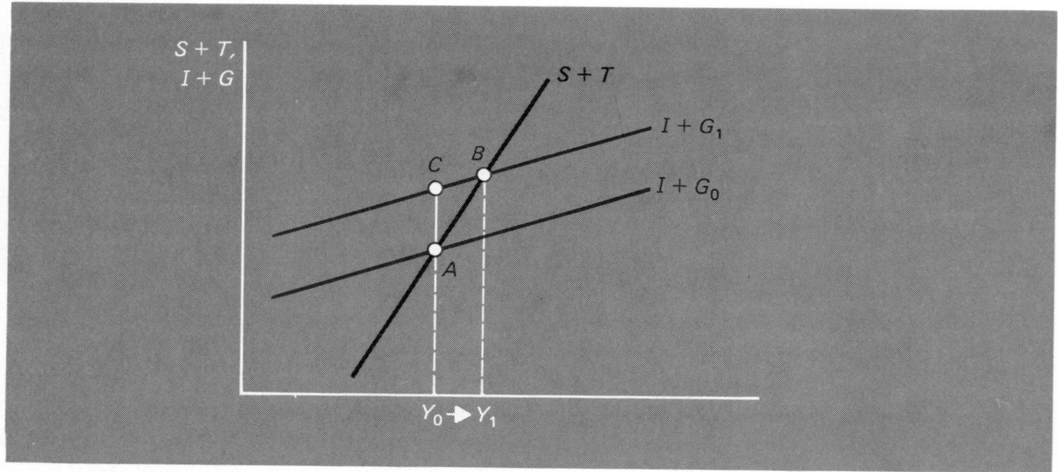

FIGURE 5-31

4. INCOME TAXATION AND DISPOSABLE INCOME

We mentioned earlier that our graphs and formulas were hiding important complications and that, in reality, they applied strictly only to the case of lump-sum taxation. The mere existence of taxes requires us to distinguish between *national income, Y,* and *disposable income,* Y_d.[8] The latter is found by subtracting total taxes from the former: $Y_d = Y - T$.

We now have to decide with which taxes we are dealing, lump-sum or income

[8] See, for example, Table 1-4 in Chapter 1.

taxes. Since we have already examined the former, we may now concentrate on income taxation. First, we see that if t denotes the fraction of income that goes to taxes, then total taxes are $T = t \cdot Y$. Disposable income is then $Y_d = Y - T = Y - t \cdot Y = (1 - t)\,Y$. From these calculations two results are clear: (a) with the same level of income, an increase in the tax rate *lowers* disposable income; and (b) with the same tax rate, an increase in national income increases disposable income. The crux of this matter is that consumption depends on disposable income rather than national income when the two differ: $C = C\,(Y_d, i, K)$. But since Y_d depends only on the level of national income, Y, and the tax rate, t, we can write consumption as $C = C\,(Y, t, i, K)$ with the following characteristics: First, $\Delta C/\Delta Y > 0$; thus an increase in Y increases Y_d, which, in turn, increases C. In schematic form: $Y \uparrow \rightarrow Y_d \uparrow \rightarrow C \uparrow$. And second, $\Delta C/\Delta t < 0$; thus an increase in the tax rate lowers disposable income, which, in turn, lowers consumption (i.e., $t \uparrow \rightarrow Y_d \downarrow \rightarrow C \downarrow$).

The outcome of all these manipulations is the knowledge that even when we are dealing with income taxation, we can distill consumption as a function of national income. However, this curve does not coincide with the consumption function that is derived in the absence of taxation. Moreover, this curve shifts downward when the tax rate rises. In Figure 5-32 the consumption curve labeled $C|_{t=t_0}$ corresponds to a higher tax rate than the curve labeled $C|_{t=t_1}$. In other words, it is assumed in Figure 5-32 that $t_1 < t_0$ (it is also assumed that tax receipts are zero when income is zero—no matter what the tax rate is). We can now use this information to examine the effect of tax-rate changes.

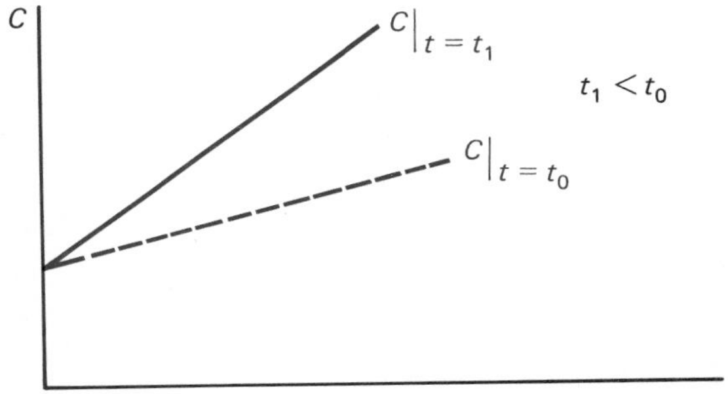

FIGURE 5-32

For concreteness, assume that Congress approves a *reduction* in the tax rate, say from t_0 to t_1. What will be the effects on output and income? The results are shown in Figure 5-33. With the original tax rate, t_0, aggregate demand intersects aggregate supply at point A, thereby yielding an output level Y_0. When the tax rate falls to t_1, the new aggregate demand curve shows excess demand, equal to CA, at the original level of output. Thus income has to rise—in fact, to the level Y_1. *We have shown that the decline in the income-tax rate increases output and income.*

The above result can also be derived by using the graph that relies on the equality between $I + G$ and $S + T$. The trick is to modify the $S + T$ curve. We now know that savings depends positively on disposable income, $S = S(Y_d, \ldots,)$,

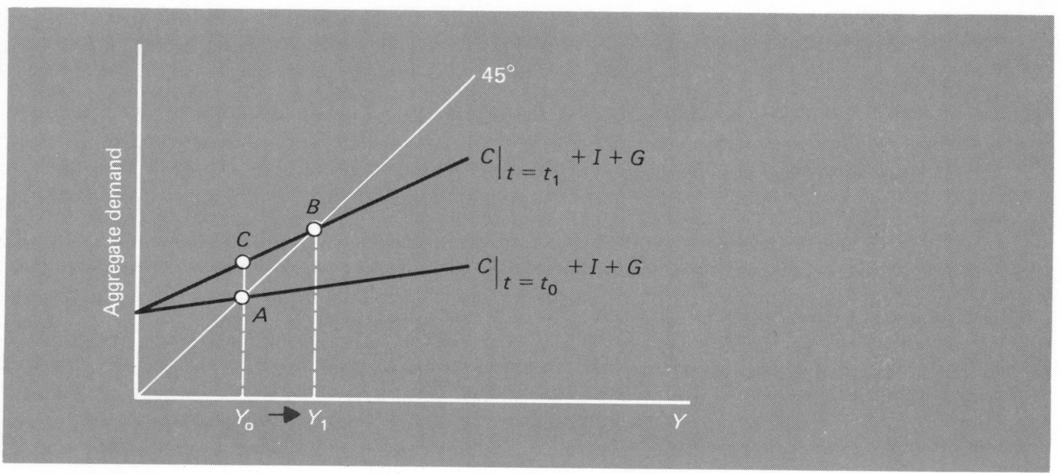

FIGURE 5-33

but Y_d depends positively on Y and negatively on t. We can thus write the savings function as $S = S(Y, t, \ldots,)$, with $\Delta S/\Delta Y > 0$, $\Delta S/\Delta t < 0$. An increase in income, with the tax rate fixed, raises disposable income and thus raises savings. On the other hand, with the level of income fixed, an increase in the tax rate lowers disposable income and thus lowers savings. The end result of this analysis is that the *savings curve is, as before, upward sloping. However, an increase in the tax rate shifts the S curve downward.* These results are shown in Figure 5-34a.

Tax receipts, tY, are increasing with income if income taxation is *proportional;* if t is independent of income, then tax receipts are a linear function of income, as curve T_1 in Figure 5-34b shows. If the tax is progressive (i.e., if t itself increases

FIGURE 5-34

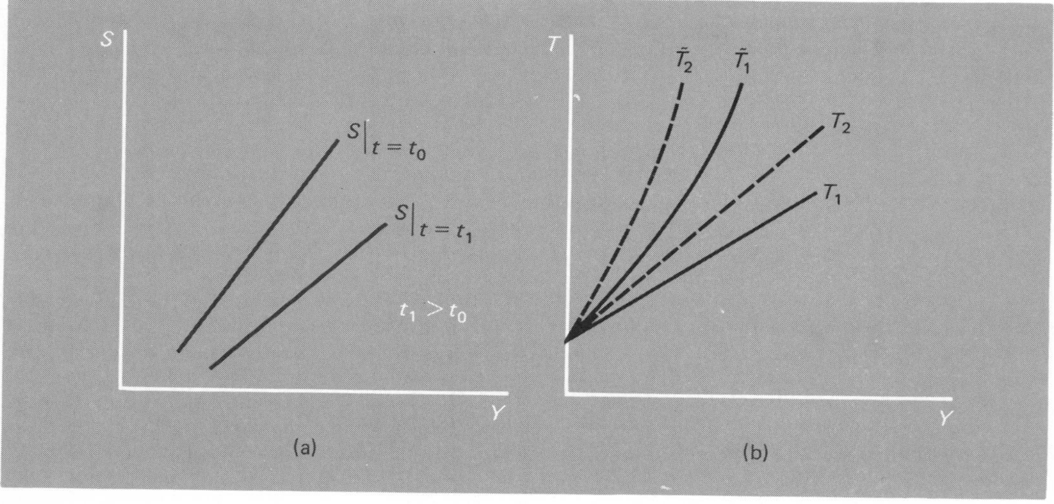

with income), then the tax revenue increases relatively more, as curve $\tilde{T}_1$ shows. Whichever income taxation we use, it should be clear that an increase in the tax rate (or rates in the case of progressive taxation) will shift the tax revenue curve upward. Thus in Figure 5-34b an increase in the proportional income-tax rate, t, shifts the curve from T_1 to T_2, while an increase in the progressive rates shifts the relevant curve from $\tilde{T}_1$ to $\tilde{T}_2$.

But we seem to be in a quandary now. We want the $S + T$ curve. But an increase in the tax rate(s) shifts the S curve *downward* while it shifts the T curve upward. What, then, will be the net effect? By a simple arithmetical example, we can show that the upward effect will dominate. Suppose that the tax rate is raised by 10 percent and also that income is \$100. This means that tax revenue rises by \$10 (i.e., $0.10 \times 100 = \$10$), and disposable income falls by the same amount. But the amount by which savings decrease depends on the marginal propensity to save, which is between zero and one, and usually around 0.20. Thus the fall in savings is \$2, for $0.20 \times \$10 = \$2$. This decrease would be equal to \$10 only if the MPS were equal to one, which is absurd. Thus we have seen that for this particular level of income, an increase of 10 percent in the tax rate raises tax revenue by \$10 and lowers savings by \$2. The *net rise* is \$8. Since we can perform the exercise for all levels of income and get similar results, we have established the following: *A rise in the income-tax rate shifts the $S + T$ curve upward and to the left, and a decrease in the tax rate shifts the curve downward and to the right.*

Equipped with this dictum, we can use this type of graph to determine output and income, as well as changes in these magnitudes when, for example, we *lower* the tax rate—the exercise we performed earlier. In Figure 5-35 the original equilibrium is shown as point A, the intersection of the $I + G$ curve and the $(S + T)_{t=t_0}$ curve. The latter is upward sloping because both components, S and T, separately rise with income. The original equilibrium is at the level Y_0. A fall in the income-tax rate from t_0 to t_1 lowers the $(S + T)$ curve immediately (i.e., for the original level of

FIGURE 5-35

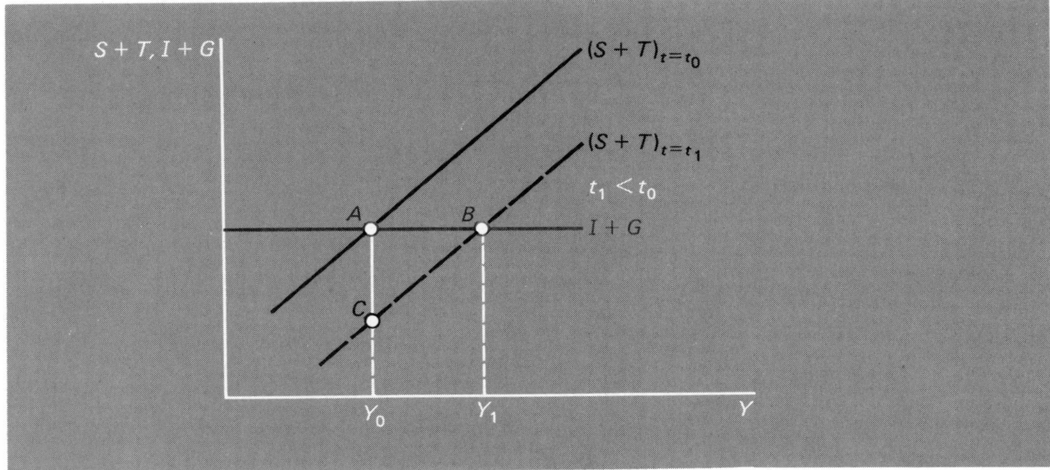

income, Y_0), causing excess demand (equal to AC). This engineers the increase in output and income to the level Y_1.

5. MULTIPLIERS

In this section we have performed several *comparative static* exercises; we changed parameters and examined the effects on output and employment. It is understandable that we are interested in the *relative* response of output to changes in alternative parameters. If these parameters are policy tools, we can then rank these tools in terms of their effectiveness in increasing, say, output. Or it may be that some of these parameters change irrespective of the will of the policy maker. If a particular economy is prone to these changes, or shocks, the policy maker may try to insulate the economy. In particular, the policy maker may prefer that output be *less* responsive to changes in these volatile parameters, an issue we examine in greater detail in Chapter 9. Here we shall concentrate briefly and exclusively on the degree of response.

Economists use a dimensionless number—a pure number—to measure the response of output to changes in aggregate demand that are produced by a change in a particular parameter. This dimensionless number, called the *multiplier,* is similar to, but not identical with, the concept of *elasticity,* which also measures response in terms of a pure number. Elasticity is the *percentage* change in the dependent variable created by a percentage change in another (independent) variable. The multiplier, on the other hand, measures the *absolute* change in output caused by an absolute change in an exogenous component of aggregate demand. But this change in an exogenous component should be measured in the same units as output itself is measured. We have, for example, the multiplier of changes in government expenditure, G, which is assumed exogenous. This multiplier is denoted as $\Delta Y/\Delta G$. Both the numerator and the denominator should be measured in the same units if we are going to obtain just a number.

In Figure 5-36 we find the number produced by a change in an unspecified exogenous component of aggregate demand, α. By using the "cross" diagram, which is particularly handy for such an exercise, we shall also see why this response of income to a change in a parameter is called a multiplier. Let us now assume that because of a change in a parameter, α, there is an increase in aggregate demand at the original income level, Y_0. In Figure 5-36 this change in demand is equal to CA. (Note that the same symbol, CA, was used in Figures 5-29, 5-30, 5-31, 5-33, and 5-35.) This, then, engineers an increase in output. The new equilibrium is at point B, with output (and income) at the level Y_1. The increase in output, ΔY, is equal to the difference $Y_1 - Y_0$, which, in turn, equals AD. Using the 45° line, we can translate the AD units into the equal number of units, DB. Thus the initial increase in aggregate demand by CA units has increased output by DB units. But CA is equal to DE, and this is less than DB. And the multiplier becomes $\Delta Y/\Delta\alpha = DB/DE$, which is clearly greater than one. Because it is greater than one, a *multiple* of the initial increase, this measurement of response is called a "multiplier."

But why does an exogenous increase in aggregate demand have a multiple effect on output? On what does the magnitude of a multiplier depend? Let us answer these by means of an example. Suppose that, for some reason, there is an increase

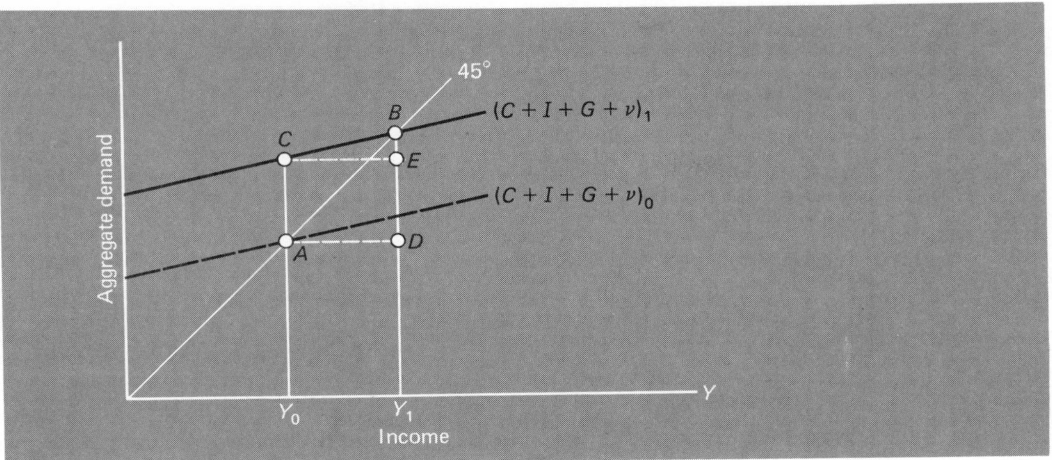

FIGURE 5-36

in aggregate demand equal to \$1 million. This unexpected increase in demand is met by depleting the economy's inventories, a signal to entrepreneurs for higher prices and profits. They, in turn, will produce this extra \$1 million worth of output in order to replenish their inventories. To increase production, they will hire labor and buy raw materials. The owners of these factors of production will experience a \$1 million increase in income. If the process stops here, we have a multiplier equal to one. But it does not; a part of this \$1 million in income will be spent on consumption of goods and services in an amount equal to the MPC times the increase in income, in general, $c \cdot \Delta\alpha$. If c is 0.8, \$800,000 will be spent (and \$200,000 saved). Again, inventories will be depleted by this amount—\$800,000—thereby inducing additional production of the same magnitude and creating new income of \$800,000. Eighty percent of these incomes (i.e., 0.8 × \$800,000 = \$640,000) will be spent on consumption, so new output and incomes of equal amount will eventually be created. The process will continue for many rounds. By adding up all the incomes created, we end up with a total increase in output and income equal to \$5 million. Clearly the multiplier is equal to 5. Each dollar spent created a total of \$5 in incomes. We see that the size of the multiplier depends on the magnitude of the MPC. If, in the above example, the MPC were 0.75, the total increase in output would be \$4 million and thus the multiplier would be 4. In general, the multiplier is equal to the inverse of the MPS:

$$\frac{\Delta Y}{\Delta\alpha} = \frac{1}{\text{MPS}} = \frac{1}{1 - c}$$

When taxes are introduced, however, the situation becomes more complex. The size of the relevant MPC changes depending on the tax structure of the economy. But the relevant size of the MPC for computing the multiplier is the MPC out of *national,* not disposable, income. Suppose that the MPC out of disposable income is 0.75 and that the income-tax rate is 0.2. Then disposable income is

$(1 - t)Y = 0.8Y$. Applying the MPC to this disposable income, we get consumption $C = 0.75 \times 0.8 \times Y$, and we clearly see that *the MPC out of national income is* $c(1 - t)$. In our example, the consumption function relating consumption to *national income,* Y, is $C = 0.6 \times Y$, which implies an MPC out of national income equal to 0.6. The true multiplier, in this case, is $1/(1 - 0.6) = 1/0.4 = 2.5$, not 4, as one might have hastily surmised. The lesson inherent in this example is that *the multiplier is smaller in the case of income taxation than in the case of no taxation or lump-sum taxation* (compare $1/[(1 - c) \cdot (1 - t)]$ with $1/(1 - c)$).

We can also find the multiplier for an *increase in the tax rate,* but we must be careful. To derive a dimensionless number, both the numerator and the denominator in $\Delta Y/\Delta\alpha$ must be in the same units. If α stands for the tax rate, t, this condition is not satisfied. Therefore $\Delta\alpha$ should be the initial decrease in aggregate demand when t rises. To find this decrease, we need initially the reduction in disposable income. But this is precisely the increase in tax revenue, which, in turn, is equal to the change in t (i.e., Δt times the original income). Thus the decrease in disposable income is $-Y\Delta t$. Now the *reduction* in aggregate demand, at the original income, is the MPC, c, times the reduction in disposable income (i.e, $\Delta\alpha = -cY\Delta t$). It follows, therefore, that the total change in income caused by a change, Δt, in the tax rate is

$$\Delta Y = -\frac{c \cdot Y \cdot \Delta t}{1 - c \cdot (1 - t)}$$

Of course, we can rewrite this as a relation between ΔY and Δt, as is usually done in the literature:

$$\frac{\Delta Y}{\Delta t} = -\frac{c \cdot Y}{1 - c(1 - t)}$$

While it looks as if it were a different multiplier, it is not.

When we examine the effects of an increase in government expenditure, G, matched exactly (i.e., financed by an equal increase in taxes, T), we must, obviously, determine the magnitude of the *balanced budget multiplier.* To do this using the technique we developed in this section, we must begin by determining the initial change in aggregate demand, $\Delta\alpha$, or the change in aggregate demand at the original income. This change has two components: first $\Delta\alpha_1 \equiv \Delta G$, the increase in government expenditures; and second, the decrease in aggregate demand, stemming from the reduction, at the original national income level, of the disposable income, which resulted from the increase in taxes, ΔT. Since this reduction in disposable income is $-\Delta T$, the reduction in consumption, at the original national income level, is $\Delta\alpha_2 \equiv -c\Delta T$. Therefore we have found the initial change, $\Delta\alpha$:

$$\Delta\alpha = \Delta\alpha_1 + \Delta\alpha_2$$

$$= \Delta G - c\Delta T$$

But the (dimensionless) multiplier in this lump-sum tax case is

$$\frac{\Delta Y}{\Delta \alpha}=\frac{1}{1-c},$$

from which it follows that

$$\Delta Y=\frac{1}{1-c}\cdot \Delta \alpha$$

or

$$\Delta Y=\frac{1}{1-c}(\Delta G-c\Delta T)$$

or

$$\Delta Y=\frac{1}{1-c}\cdot \Delta G(1-c).$$

And since

$$\Delta G=\Delta T,$$

it follows that

$$\Delta Y=\Delta G$$

or

$$\frac{\Delta Y}{\Delta G}=1.$$

We have shown, therefore, that the increase in income is equal to the increase in government expenditure and that the balanced budget multiplier is equal to one. For simplicity we employed the model with lump-sum taxation, but we can derive this same result even if we use the more complicated taxation systems and their implied multipliers.

However, some words of caution are in order here regarding multipliers in general and the balanced budget multiplier in particular. We have seen that multipliers, in general, show the response of output to changes in some (usually policy) parameter, *assuming that everything else remains the same.* But everything else does not remain the same; the output adjustment mechanism is only one of several components in the system. And we shall see that the magnitude of the multipliers, in general, diminishes in the complete model, a result occasionally forgotten by those who calculate multipliers in great detail, and by those who sometimes use them even to predict changes in the economy as a whole. We should note that this is an emasculation of the Keynesian system, and for this reason we shall not extend our discussion to cover some admittedly interesting issues.[9]

In addition, we are faced with the problem of "long run." In a complete model, which includes the government budget restraint (GBR),[10] the long-run, balanced budget multiplier turns out to be substantially greater than one. In a simple, proportional tax system where $T = t \cdot Y$, the long-run, balanced budget multiplier is $\Delta Y/\Delta G = 1/t$ because, in a true, long-run equilibrium, the budget must be balanced, $G = t \cdot Y$, from which it follows that $(\Delta Y/\Delta G) = 1/t$. However, the usefulness of this result as a guide to economic policy is even more limited than the partial and short-run, unitary balanced budget multiplier.

Furthermore, we should make a final point about Keynes' own use of the multiplier. His was an employment multiplier rather than the output multiplier we have been using so far. He compared the overall increase in employment, x, with the increase in employment caused by an exogenous increase in aggregate demand, called "primary employment." For the most part Keynes concentrated on the increase in employment emanating from an increase in investment, whether private or government, for projects such as public works. Here the influence of his disciple, R. F. Kahn, was instrumental both in Keynes' use of the multiplier and in his employment adjustment mechanism itself. Kahn was the author of "The Relation of Home Investment to Unemployment," which first introduced the concept of the multiplier.[11] We should note that in the above definition, the multiplier is again a dimensionless number.

In this section we examined, for the most part, output multipliers in order to equip the reader with enough knowledge to understand the existing literature, which deals almost exclusively with output multipliers. As we observed at the beginning of this section, output was considered, in the early post-Keynesian years, the key economic indicator. But the trend has been reversed since the publication of the *General Theory;* once again, employment, x, is the key variable. For this reason we shall conduct our analysis, beginning in the next chapter, by focusing mostly on employment, x, rather than on output, Y. But the reader can, of course, easily translate one into the other.

QUESTIONS

1. Evaluate: "The liquidity preference and loanable funds theories are the same at equilibrium but not away from equilibrium."

[9] We shall not discuss the separate effects on the budget deficit or on the budget surplus of an increase in government expenditure or of an increase in taxation. We shall, instead, leave these as exercises. However, the concept of the "full-employment surplus" is useful here. To explore this concept, see E. Cary Brown, "Fiscal Policy in the Thirties: A Reappraisal," *American Economic Review,* December 1956, pp. 857–79; and Arthur M. Okun and Nancy H. Teeters, "The Full Employment Surplus Revisited," *Brookings Papers on Economic Activity,* 1 (1970), 77–116.

[10] The government budget restraint is examined in Chapter 6.

[11] *Economic Journal,* June 1931.

2. In the neoclassical system both the interest rate and employment are indeterminate. What modification to economic theory did Keynes propose to remedy this?
3. Show and explain the equivalence of Keynes's stipulation that excess demand for goods and services determines employment with the basic law of supply and demand.
4. "If Keynes had assumed that both prices and wages are fixed, there would be no way of increasing employment." What does the Keynesian analysis actually imply concerning the role of price adjustment in increasing employment?
5. Compare and contrast the Keynesian interest rate adjustment mechanism with that utilized by Wicksell.
6. Suppose there is an increase in the risk estimate that is relevant for investment decisions. In an economy experiencing severe unemployment, what will happen to the employment? Contrast this result with the case of a perpetually fully employed economy.
7. Suppose that the typical household's tastes between present and future consumption change in such a way that the economy's propensity to save rises. What will happen to the interest rate and employment (both during the transition and at the new equilibrium)? Would your answer change if, instead, the government increases taxation?
8. Both elasticities and multipliers measure the responsiveness of economic variables. How are the two concepts different? Explain how the multiplier effect works. Relate the multiplier to the following:
    a. Marginal propensity to consume (MPC)
    b. Marginal propensity to save (MPS)
    c. Income taxes
    d. The consumption function
9. For economies that engage in international trade, what additional policies are available to increase employment?
10. Our derivation of labor demand implies that as long as the MP_N function remains unchanged, then employment will change only in response to changes in the real wage. What are some factors that might shift the MP_N function? Outline a scenario where employment changes even though the real wage is constant.

REFERENCES

BROWN, E. CARY, "Fiscal Policy in the Thirties: A Reappraisal," *American Economic Review,* December 1956, pp. 857–79.

CHRIST, CARL, "A Simple Macroeconomic Model with a Government Budget Restraint," *Journal of Political Economy,* January/February 1968, pp. 53–67.

HANSEN, ALVIN H., *Guide to Keynes.* New York: McGraw-Hill. 1953.

KAHN, R. F., "The Relation of Home Investment to Unemployment," *Economic Journal,* June 1931.

KEYNES, J. M., *The General Theory of Employment, Interest and Money.* New York: Harcourt, Brace & Co., 1936.

———, *A Treatise on Money.* London: Macmillan, 1930.

METZLER, LLOYD A., "Three Lags in the Circular Flow of Income," in *Income, Employment, and Public Policy.* New York: W. W. Norton & Co., Inc., 1948.

OKUN, ARTHUR, AND NANCY H. TEETERS, "The Full Employment Surplus Revisited," *Brookings Papers on Economic Activity,* 1 (1970), 77–116.

ROSE, HUGH, "Liquidity Preference and Loanable Funds," *Review of Economic Studies,* February 1957, pp. 111–19.

SAMUELSON, PAUL A., "The Simple Mathematics of Income Determination," in *Income, Employment, and Public Policy.* New York: W. W. Norton & Co., Inc., 1948.

6 The Incomplete Keynesian System: Determination of the interest rate, employment, and income

We saw in the preceding chapter that Keynes parted company with the neoclassicists when he realized that there is an infinity of combinations of interest rates and employment levels *(i,x)*, which permit clearance of the market for goods and services, and that an additional market clearance relation is needed, therefore, to determine the interest rate and employment level: the money market clearance. Thus the equilibrium employment level and interest rate are determined at the point where both the market for goods and the market for money are cleared. This simultaneous solution of the system is the province of general equilibrium analysis, introduced by Walras in 1874 and incorporated by him into a microeconomic framework, which is now accepted as our only microeconomic theory.[1] General equilibrium analysis was more or less the standard tool of micro in Continental Europe while Keynes was writing his book, but in Britain (and in all the Anglo-Saxon world) it was alien and almost literally forbidden; Marshall's influence was absolute. It was remarkable, therefore, that Keynes, the disciple and protegé of Marshall, saw the problem clearly and put forth a general equilibrium technique.

Chapter 14 of the *General Theory* provided the blueprint for the simultaneous determination of interest and employment. A year later, in 1937, J. R. Hicks formalized that approach in a simple model that has since been popularized as the *IS–LM*

[1] Léon Walras, *Elements of Pure Economics,* trans. William Jaffee (London: Allen & Unwin, 1954).

model.[2] It is noteworthy that prior to this endeavor, Hicks was involved in an effort to extend and popularize the Walrasian general equilibrium analysis. This effort culminated in the publication, in 1938, of his classic book, *Value and Capital*,[3] which outlines the techniques (especially in Chapter 5) that Hicks applied in his derivation of the *IS–LM* model. We shall use these Hicksian techniques here to determine simultaneously the interest rate and the employment (or income) level, to see how they move through time and how they are affected by economic policy.[4]

In Section I of this chapter we develop and describe the system that, according to Keynes, permits us to determine the interest rate, i, and employment, x, or, equivalently, income, Y. On the one hand, we introduce the interest adjustment mechanism, which states that the interest rate rises (falls) if, and only if, there is excess demand for (supply of) money. On the other hand, we have the employment adjustment mechanism, which states, assuming that money wages are constant, that employment rises (falls) if, and only if, there is excess demand for (supply of) goods and services, $EG > 0$, or $I - S > 0$ ($EG < 0$, or $I - S < 0$).

In Section II we derive all the combinations of interest rates, i, and employment, x (or income Y), that guarantee goods market clearance, that is, $EG = 0$, or $I - S = 0$; these combinations lie on a curve called the $EG = 0$ curve, or, more frequently, the *IS* curve. We shall also find all such combinations of (i,x) or (i,Y) that exhibit excess demand for goods and services, $EG > 0$, or $I - S > 0$, and those that exhibit excess supply of goods and services, $EG < 0$, or $I - S < 0$.

In Section III we derive similarly all the combinations of (i,x) or (i,Y) that guarantee clearance of the money market and form the $EM = 0$, or *LM* curve. Also, we find the combinations for which $EM > 0$ and $EM < 0$. And, finally, we see that there is an infinity of $EM = 0$ curves, one for each assumed price level.

Assuming that the price level is known, the intersection of the $EG = 0$ and $EM = 0$ curves determines, in Section IV, the interest rate, i, and employment, x (or income, Y), consistent with clearance of both markets. Furthermore, we not only establish the movements toward that equilibrium but also identify and exclude the unstable equilibria as inconsistent with a model that describes an economy capable of achieving equilibrium; such unstable equilibria are useless for comparative statics analysis.

In Section V we tentativeiy explore changes in the price level and introduce the *Keynesian real balance effect:* An increase in the price level diminishes real balances and induces a rise in the interest rate for each level of employment (or income); in other words, an increase in the price level shifts the *LM* curve to the left, which tends to decrease employment. The explicit consideration of all possible price levels also highlights the inadequacy of the $IS - LM$ apparatus, in the (i,x) or (i,Y)-planes, to determine all endogenous variables, including the interest rate and employment level.

---

[2] J. R. Hicks, "Mr. Keynes and the Classics," *Econometrica,* April 1937, pp. 147–59.

[3] J. R. Hicks, *Value and Capital,* 1st ed., 1938 (London: Oxford, 1946).

[4] The *IS–LM* technique was popularized by A. H. Hansen in his *Guide to Keynes* (New York: McGraw-Hill, 1953), and it is now referred to as the "Hicks-Hansen" analysis.

In Section VI we see how trade policy, fiscal policy, and monetary policy are, in general, effective in increasing employment (and income) when involuntary unemployment exists and is considered undesirable by the appropriate authorities.

In Section VII we compare the effects and the efficacy of monetary and fiscal policies. First, we discover that they have different sectoral effects, since they affect the interest rate differently, but that they have the same qualitative effects on employment. Second, we identify some extreme special cases when only monetary policy or only fiscal policy is effective. However, we also show that these special cases lack empirical support and should be rejected. And, finally, we examine the government budget restraint (GBR), which permits the explicit examination of alternative means of financing a government deficit, namely, by increasing the money supply and/or issuing new government bonds (i.e., by government borrowing in the open market). The current controversy over whether this government borrowing, needed to finance a given budget deficit, crowds out any and all effects of fiscal policy will be systematically explored.

I. DESCRIPTION OF INCOMPLETE KEYNESIAN SYSTEM

In the preceding chapter we established that Keynes insisted that a *general* theory of employment and interest forces us to solve simultaneously two equations, namely, market clearance for goods and services (which "determines" employment) and money market clearance (which "determines" the interest rate). The two equations are

$$\frac{\Delta x}{x} = \beta \cdot EG$$

$$\frac{\Delta x}{x} = \delta_p \cdot EM$$

In schematic form, we have, respectively,

$$\Delta x \gtreqless 0 \quad \text{when} \quad EG \gtreqless 0$$

$$\Delta i \gtreqless 0 \quad \text{when} \quad EM \gtreqless 0$$

(It is important to remember that the one-to-one relation between Δx and EG has been established in Chapter 5 under the assumption of money-wage rigidity, $\Delta W = 0$.) Equilibrium requires that there be no movement in either the employment level or the interest rate, that is, $\Delta x = 0$ and $\Delta i = 0$. Of course, this happens only if both excess demands are zero, $EG = 0$ and $EM = 0$.

We also saw in Chapter 5 that by substituting Y for x in the above equations and schemata, we have an income adjustment mechanism rather than an employment adjustment mechanism. Of course, we can substitute Y for x because in the short run, with the capital stock constant, there is a one-to-one positive relation between employment, x, and output, Y, which is always equal to income. And if we use Y rather than x, we are speaking of income determination rather than employment determination, with the respective pairs of equations and of schemata represented as follows:

$$\frac{\Delta Y}{Y} = \beta \cdot EG \quad \text{(i.e., } \Delta Y \gtreqless 0 \quad \text{when} \quad EG \gtreqless 0)$$

and

$$\Delta i = \delta_p \cdot EM \quad \text{(i.e., } \Delta i \gtreqless 0 \quad \text{when} \quad EM \gtreqless 0)$$

Early post-Keynesian economists made the substitution of Y for x in part because they considered income a key economic indicator and in part because they wanted to reenact the numbers in the national income accounts—which were also a novelty at that time. It now seems that the pendulum has swung back, and, once again, employment, x, is considered the key variable. Partly for this reason, we shall use mostly x in the following analysis and reserve Y for those parts of the book that are explicitly concerned with income. It should be understood that there is no change in the results and that the reader who so chooses may also consider x as being synonymous with income.

But whether we use x or Y, our approach is the following: Since one of our goals is the determination of the pair i and x (or i and Y), first we shall find all such pairs that clear the goods market, all (i,x) that guarantee that $EG = 0$. Then we shall find all pairs of the same variables (i,x) that guarantee that the money market is cleared, $EM = 0$. The intersection of the two sets, or curves, has both properties in common, that is, both markets are cleared. This is how i and x, or i and Y, are determined simultaneously. We shall also examine cases out of equilibrium, that is, when one or both markets are not cleared, to see how the interest rate and employment move through time. We shall start by deriving the $EG = 0$ curve.

II. THE *EG* = 0 (OR *IS*) CURVE

In the absence of a government sector and in the case of a closed economy (i.e., no international trade), the excess demand for goods and services is equal to the excess of investment over savings:

$$EG = I(i,x) - S(i,x) \equiv EG(i,x)$$

Thus EG is a function of (i,x). First, we shall derive the $EG = 0$ curve; in other words, we find all the combinations of (i,x) that clear the goods and services market. Since, in this special case, excess demand for goods and services is equal to zero if, and only if, investment equals savings, $I = S$, this curve has come to be known as the IS curve. We first derive this curve graphically for the special case when investment is independent of employment, as in Figure 6-1, and then we extend the analysis to include the case when investment depends positively on employment. Given the interest rate, at i_0, we can identify investment demand by the horizontal curve so denoted. We can also find the relevant savings curve. Their intersection (point A) determines the employment level (following the graphical exposition of Chapter 5) at x_0. (See the upper panel of Figure 6-2.) We chart this (i_0, x_0) combination in the (i,x)-plane (lower panel of Figure 6-2).

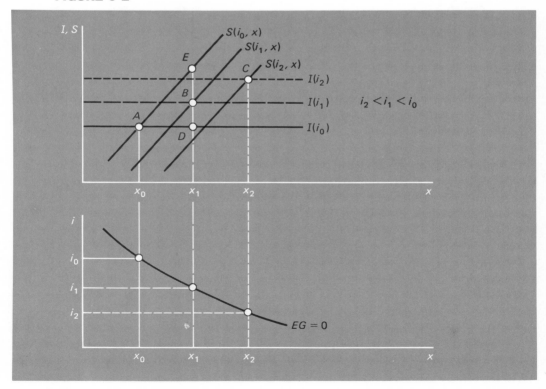

FIGURE 6-1

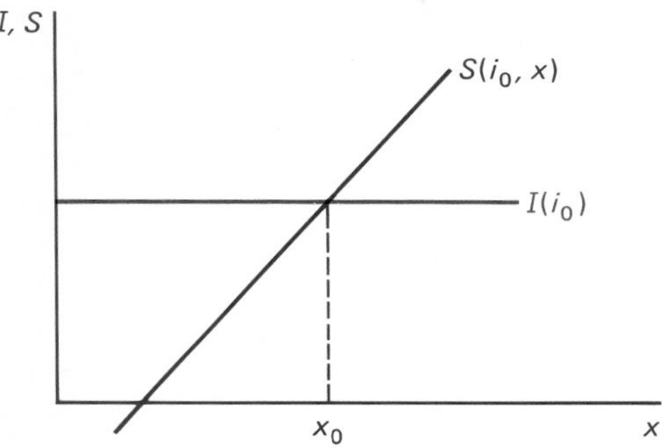

FIGURE 6-2

When i is lowered to i_1, the investment curve shifts upward (since there is a negative relation between investment and the interest rate), and the savings curve moves to the right. Now they intersect at B, giving a higher x, namely x_1. (In the graph it is assumed that savings and interest rate are positively related. But even if the relation were negative, meaning that the decrease in i would shift S to the left, the shift of I would overwhelm it, and again the end result would be an increase in x—somewhere between x_0 and x_1.) This new combination is plotted in the lower panel of Figure 6-2. Repeating this process for all i's, we derive the $EG = 0$ curve, that is, the so-called *IS* curve. The $EG = 0$ curve is definitely downward sloping in Figure 6-2 because it was assumed that investment is independent of employment. If, however, investment demand depends positively on employment, there are two possibilities. First, when the marginal propensity to spend is less than one—depicted by the requirement that the savings curve is steeper than the investment curve—the $EG = 0$ curve would still be downward sloping, as in Figure 6-3. Second, if the marginal propensity to spend is greater than one (i.e., when the investment curve is steeper than the savings curve), the $EG = 0$ curve would be upward sloping, as in Figure 6-4.

It can easily be demonstrated that the less sensitive both savings and investment are to changes in the interest rate, the steeper the derived $EG = 0$ curve is.

FIGURE 6-3

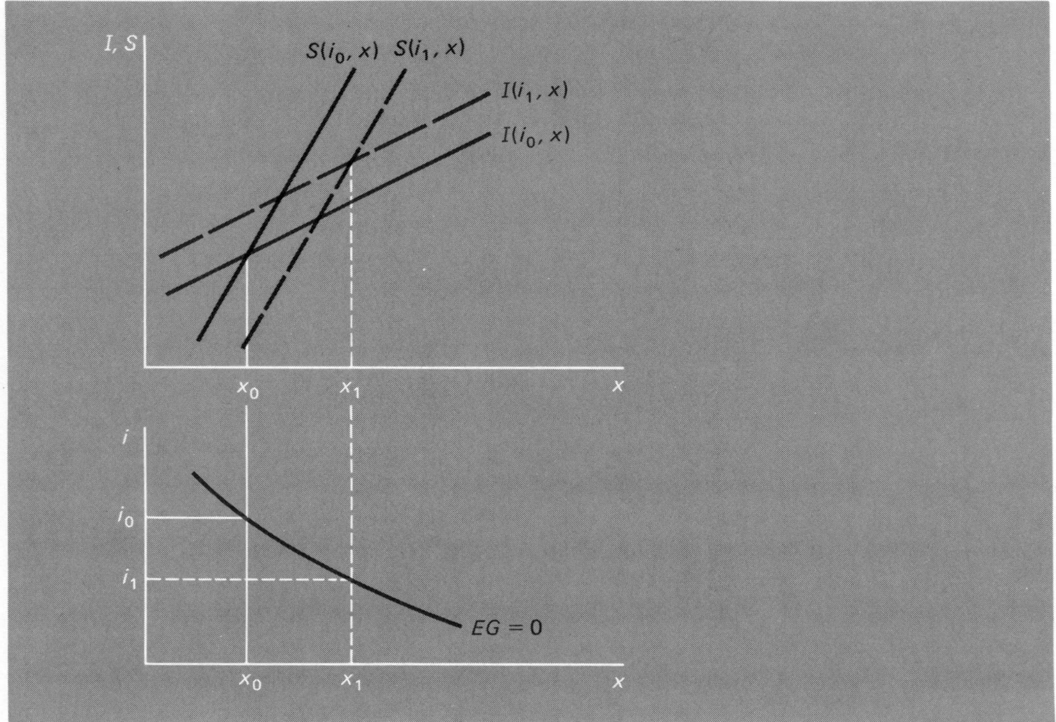

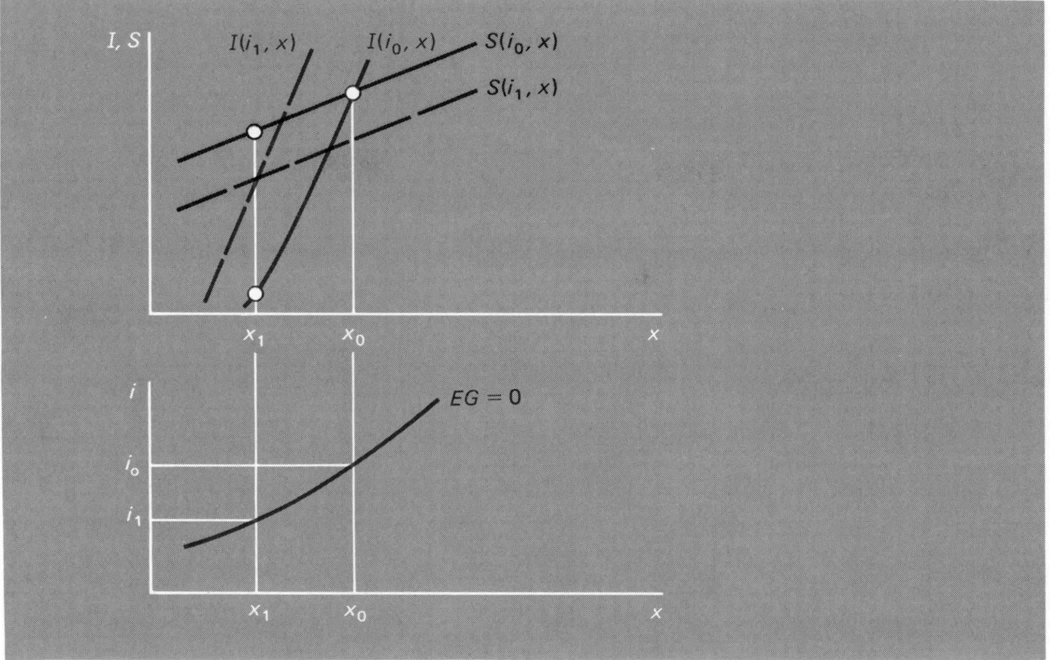

FIGURE 6-4

Figure 6-5a depicts the *extreme* case when neither investment nor savings depends on the interest rate. Equivalently, we can say that Figure 6-5a illustrates the case when the aggregate demand for goods and services is independent of the interest rate. On the other hand, Figure 6-5b depicts the *extreme opposite* case when aggregate demand is perfectly elastic with respect to the interest rate. The usual stipulation for this latter assumption is that investment (but not savings) be perfectly interest-elastic. These two extreme cases are introduced here not because of their realism, but because of the role they have played in some controversies.

FIGURE 6-5

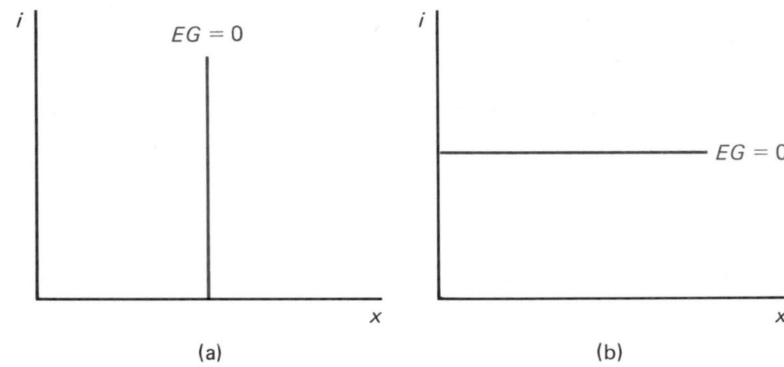

We have shown that the $EG = 0$ (or IS) curve captures all the combinations of interest rates and employment (i,x), such that the market for goods and services clears. When the marginal propensity to spend is less than one, a lower interest rate requires higher employment if the market for goods and services is to be kept cleared, because the lower interest rate increases aggregate demand (by increasing investment and, possibly, consumption—if savings and the interest rate are positively related). Something has to change in order to negate the excess demand, and the only candidate is x. While it is true that an increase in x increases one component of aggregate demand, namely investment, the other component, consumption, does not increase enough to fully spend (along with I) all the increase in income generated by the increase in x. This is the economic meaning of the assumption that the slope of the investment curve is smaller than that of the savings curve.

Let us now examine points off the $EG = 0$ curve, say to its right, as in Figure 6-6. Point A, to the right of the curve, can be considered a vertical upward movement from point C, which is on the curve. Thus A differs from C only in that the interest rate is higher $(i_0 > i_1)$. With this in mind, the question arises, If we start from a point for which the market for goods and services is cleared, what happens to this market if we keep the same x and increase the interest rate? The answer is straightforward: The increase in i decreases aggregate demand, since it lowers investment demand and, possibly, consumption (if savings and the interest rate are positively related). So point A shows a lower aggregate demand than point C and the same supply (since x is fixed). But at point C aggregate demand is equal to aggregate supply (i.e., $EG = 0$). Therefore there is excess supply of goods and services at A (i.e., $EG < 0$). The same result can be derived utilizing Figure 6-2. There the excess supply of goods and services is equal to DE, the distance between the savings and investment schedules, when both are drawn for the same interest rate, i_0, and evaluated at x equal to x_1.

The above arguments are for a downward-sloping $EG = 0$ curve. If it is

FIGURE 6-6

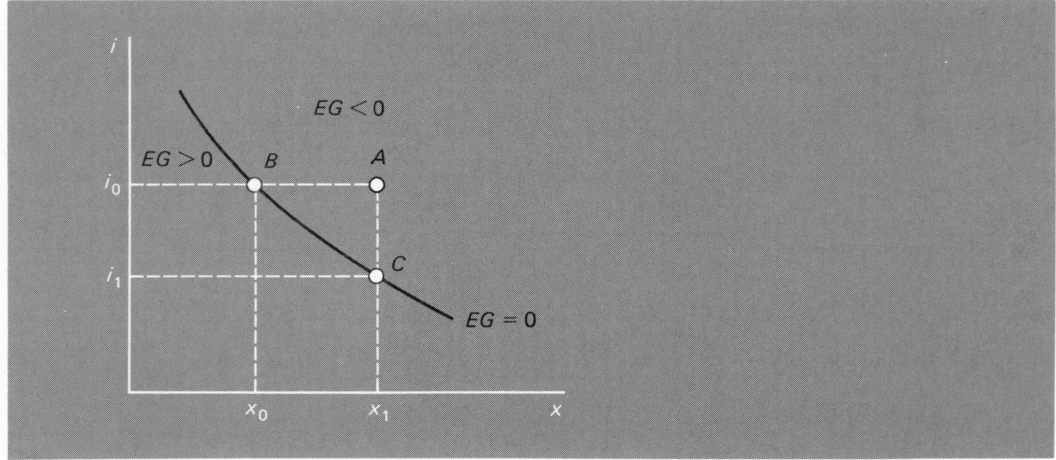

upward sloping, we find that to the right of the curve there is excess demand and that to the left there is excess supply, as in Figure 6-7. In that graph, consider a point H to the left of the $EG = 0$ curve. If we consider it as a *vertical* displacement of point G, we should inquire what happens to excess demand, starting from a zero value, when we increase the interest rate from i_1 to i_0 while keeping x fixed at x_1. Utilizing the information in Figure 6-4, we immediately see that this experiment produces an *excess supply* equal to FG. Thus, to the left of an upward-sloping $EG = 0$ curve, such as the one in Figure 6-7, we write $EG < 0$ and to its right we write $EG > 0$.

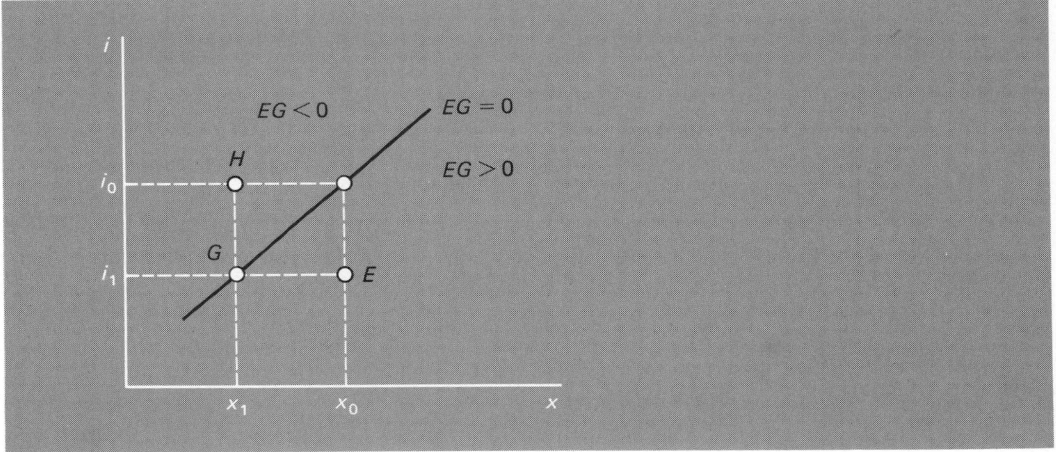

FIGURE 6-7

We can now complete the analysis by providing the dynamics of the market for goods and services. Because we assume at this stage that the money wage is fixed, we can derive a one-to-one relation between excess demand for (supply of) goods and services and *increases* (decreases) in the level of employment. We have already shown that

$$\Delta x \gtreqless 0 \quad \text{when} \quad \frac{\Delta p}{p} \gtreqless \frac{\Delta W}{W}$$

But if $\Delta W \equiv 0$, we have

$$\Delta x \gtreqless 0 \quad \text{when} \quad \frac{\Delta p}{p} \gtreqless 0$$

We know, however, that

$$\Delta p \gtreqless 0 \quad \text{when} \quad EG \gtreqless 0$$

And thus we have reestablished the "employment adjustment mechanism" of Keynes:

$$\Delta x \gtreqless 0 \quad \text{when} \quad EG \gtreqless 0$$

Employment remains constant (i.e., it does not move, $\Delta x = 0$) if, and only if, the excess demand for goods and services is zero, $EG = 0$. We can therefore relabel the $EG = 0$ curve as $\Delta x = 0$. Since employment rises, that is, $\Delta x > 0$ only if $EG > 0$, we see that to the right of the $\Delta x = 0$ curve we have $\Delta x < 0$, which can be shown with a horizontal arrow pointing toward *less* x. Similarly, to the left of the $\Delta x = 0$ curve, employment is rising, $\Delta x > 0$, and the horizontal arrow points toward more x. The "phase plane" is shown in Figure 6-8. If, however, the $\Delta x = 0$ curve is upward sloping, the movements are shown in Figure 6-9, which uses the information of Figure 6-7.

The $\Delta x = 0$ curve is called, in mathematical terms, the "singular" curve. Note that in the case depicted in Figure 6-9, the movements are away from the equilibrium curve. Nevertheless, this is not sufficient to cause instability, that is, a breakdown of the system. Whether the system is stable or unstable depends also on the movements of the interest rate, as we shall show later. If we choose to concentrate

FIGURE 6-8

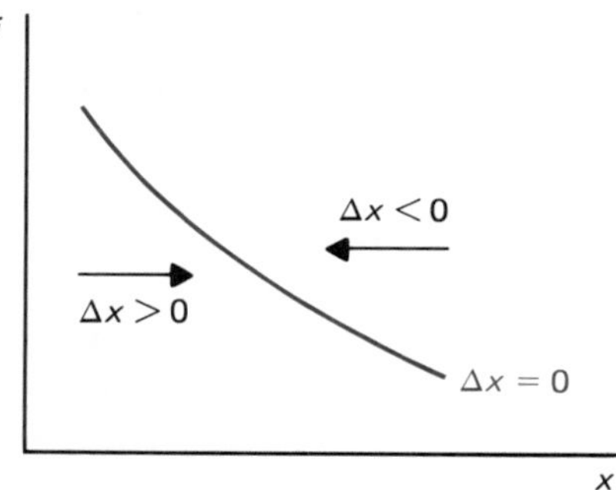

FIGURE 6-9

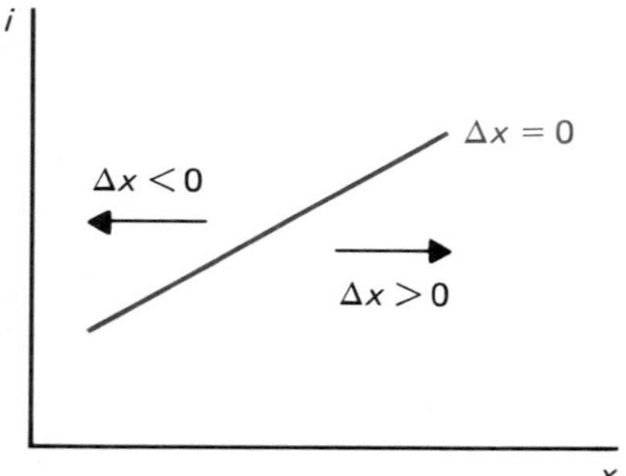

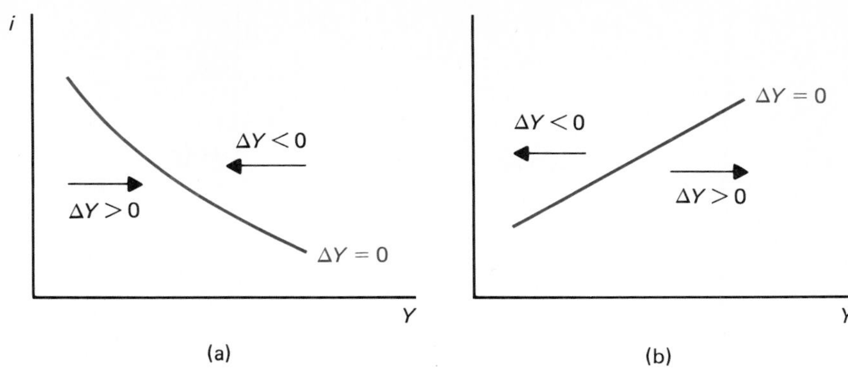

FIGURE 6-10

on income, Y, rather than employment, x, the counterparts of Figures 6-8 and 6-9 are shown in Figures 6-10a and 6-10b, respectively.

III. THE *EM* = 0 (OR *LM*) CURVE

The excess demand for money is written as

$$EM = L(i,x) - \frac{M}{p}$$

The supply of nominal money, M, is assumed to be under the absolute control of the monetary authority, and it can be regarded as exogenous at this stage. But the price level cannot be assumed exogenous, since it has to be determined within the system. Thus the excess demand for real balances is a function of three endogenous variables, a situation that will complicate our analysis a little. Clearance of the money market is represented by

$$EM\ (i,x,p) = L(i,x) - \frac{M}{p} = 0$$

Since we can realistically use only a two-dimensional graph, we cannot capture all the combinations of endogenous variables, the triplet (i,x,p), which guarantee that the market for money is cleared. If we use the (i,p)-plane, the derived curve is for a given x. If we use the (i,x)-plane, p must be assumed given. The LM curve introduced by Hicks, and used by a myriad of economists, is derived in the (i,x)-plane and thus is drawn for a given price level. We must, however, caution the reader that this does not mean that the price level is assumed fixed, as we shall make clear below. Let us now assume for the moment (tentatively) that we know the price level, p_0, and that, given this price level, we shall try to find all the combinations (i,x) that make the demand for money equal to the supply.

According to Keynes, the interest rate is determined at the point where the existing stock of real balances $(\overline{M}/p_0)$ is willingly held, that is, where the demand for money equals its supply. This gives us the interest rate $\bar{i}$ in Figure 6-11. However, in a graph where one axis (the vertical one) represents the interest rate and the other (the horizontal one) represents real balances (demanded and supplied), there is one demand curve for each x (the eliminated variable). Since there is a positive relation between employment x and the demand for real balances L, a higher x shifts the demand curve to the right.

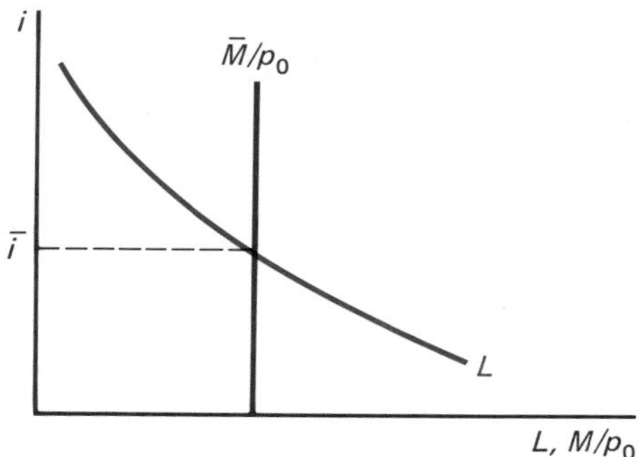

FIGURE 6-11

We are now ready to derive all the combinations *(i,x)* that clear the money market *(for a given price level).* From the left panel of Figure 6-12, we see that when $x = x_0$, the interest rate must be i_0 to make the demand equal to the supply. We plot this result in the right panel of Figure 6-12. When the employment level is higher, at x_1, the (money) market clearing interest rate is i_1, and again we plot it in the right panel. Similarly for x_2, we have i_2, and so forth, for all possible x's. Connecting all the points in the right-hand panel, we derive the $EM = 0$ (or so-called LM)

FIGURE 6-12

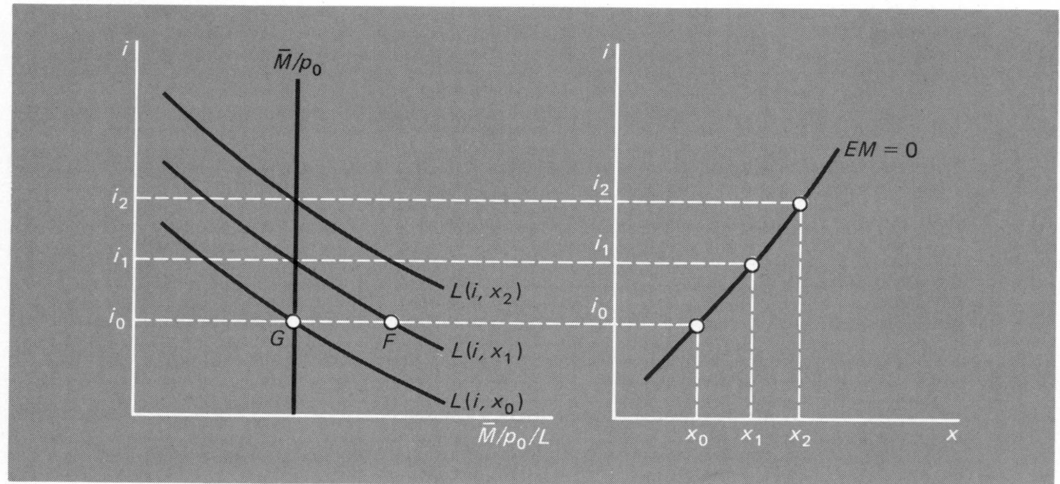

curve. We see that this curve is upward sloping. Summarizing in words, we see that if we start from an interest rate (and employment) that clears the money market, an increase in x will increase the demand, and since the supply is fixed, such an increase in x will increase the interest rate. Alternatively and equivalently, we can say that an increase in the interest rate will tend to decrease the demand for money. But since the supply is fixed and the rule says that the demand has to equal supply, there must be a change in some variable in order to increase demand by the same amount it would decrease if i increases. Of course, the only other variable is x, which is positively related to L. This necessitates a sufficient increase in x to keep the equality between demand and the (fixed) supply.

We have derived the $EM = 0$ curve for a *given* price level, but we shall see later that a different $EM = 0$ curve exists for each assumed price level. When we want to emphasize the particular price level used in the construction of the $EM = 0$ curve, we shall state it in its "nametag." For example, Figure 6-13 states that the LM curve was derived for a price level equal to p_0. Note that the LM curve is derived for a given M also. When this is crucial to our analysis, we shall underscore its importance by inserting the particular M, say M_0, in the nametag, such as

$$EM = 0 \Big|_{\substack{p = p_0 \\ M = M_0}}$$

At this point it seems advisable to introduce two special cases of the demand for real balances.

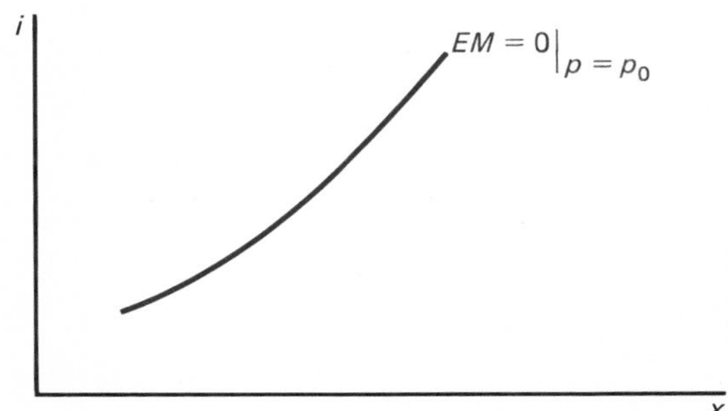

FIGURE 6-13

Case a

Zero interest elasticity of the demand for money. This, of course, is the *quantity theory* assumption and is depicted in Figure 6-14a.

Case b

Perfect (infinite) interest elasticity of the demand for money. This case is referred to in the literature as *liquidity trap* and is depicted in Figure 6-14b.

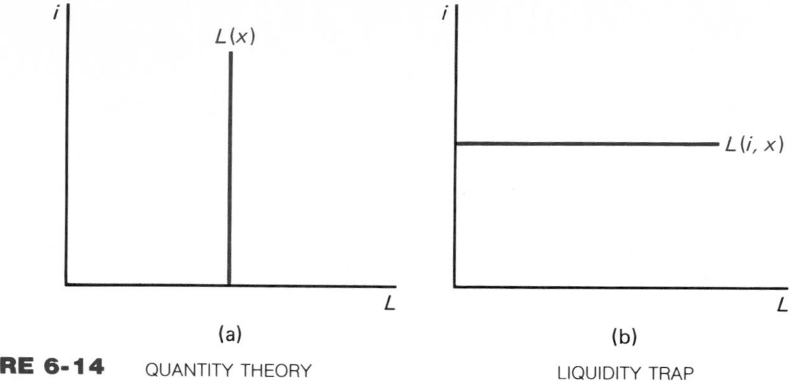

FIGURE 6-14 QUANTITY THEORY LIQUIDITY TRAP

Usually, however, it is stated in the literature that perfect elasticity occurs only at a sufficiently low (and critical) interest rate. For higher interest rates, the curve has its usual downward-sloping shape, as in Figure 6-15. There is one curve for each assumed level of x, but all curves converge at the same critical interest rate, i_0. We shall see later that several problems are associated with these two extreme cases. Moreover, many misconceptions are found in the literature regarding the liquidity trap. But we shall postpone examination of all these until later in this chapter. Sufficient for now is the observation that the term *trap* is appropriate, since the interest rate can never reach a level lower than i_0. The cases of quantity theory and liquidity trap are shown in Figures 6-16a and 6-16b, respectively.

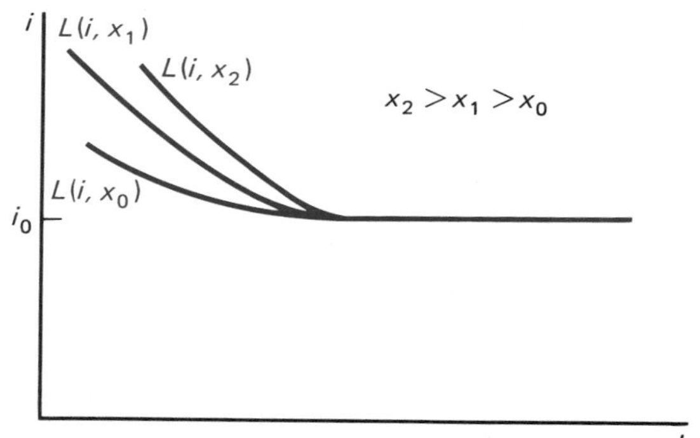

FIGURE 6-15

Let us derive some additional information regarding the $EM = 0$ curve for the case in which p and M are assumed at a particular level. A point, N, to the right of the particular LM curve (Figure 6-17), should exhibit excess demand for real balances, $EM > 0$; beginning from Q, a fall in the interest rate, with x given, increases the demand, and since the supply is fixed, this fall causes excess demand. This can be seen in the left panel of Figure 6-12, from which the LM curve of Figure 6-17 was derived. When $x = x_1$, the relevant demand curve is $L(i,x_1)$. We are at point F on this curve when $i = i_0$, which means that the quantity demanded

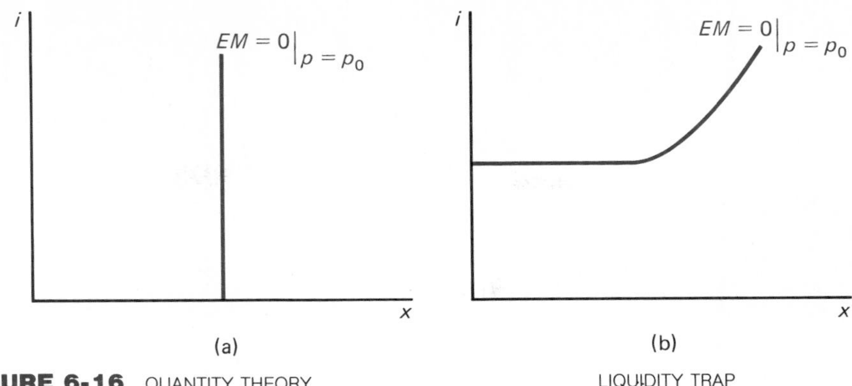

FIGURE 6-16 QUANTITY THEORY LIQUIDITY TRAP

is equal to i_0F, while the supply is the same as before, namely i_0G. And it follows that when $x = x_1$ and $i = i_0$, there is an excess demand for money equal to FG. Equivalently, beginning from point R in Figure 6-17, a rise in x, from x_0 to x_1, given i at the level i_1, increases the demand for money, thereby causing excess demand. Of course, using Figure 6-12 we can see that, again, the excess demand is equal to FG.

As before, we shall extend the analysis in order to provide the dynamics of interest "determination." Since, according to Keynes, the interest rate rises when there is excess demand, and it falls when there is excess supply of real balances, we use the adjustment mechanism:

$$\Delta i \gtreqless 0 \quad \text{when} \quad EM \gtreqless 0$$

It is clear that the $EM = 0$ curve can be renamed the "$\Delta i = 0$ curve." In the area below the curve, we have $\Delta i > 0$, since $EM > 0$; whereas above the curve, $\Delta i < 0$, since in this area $EM < 0$. All of these are shown in Figure 6-18 where

FIGURE 6-17

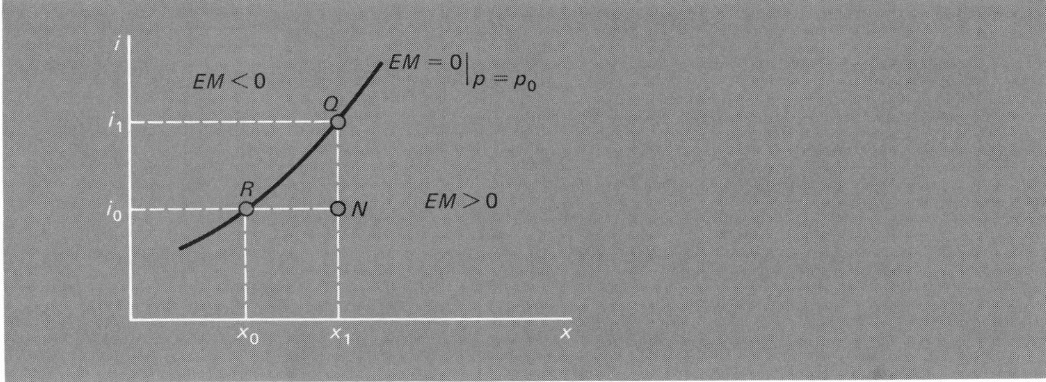

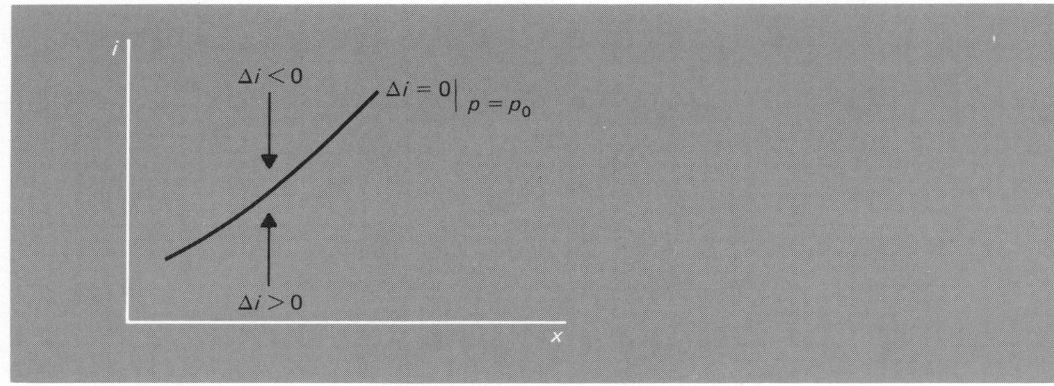

FIGURE 6-18

the arrows point to the appropriate directions. In the *(i, Y)*-plane the $EM = 0$ curve is similar, as in Figure 6-19.

We should note here that sometimes Keynes is interpreted as having said that the market for money is always cleared, in other words, that $EM = 0$ always. This means that the speed of adjustment of the money market, via the interest rate, is infinite. In such a case, of course, the economy is *always* on the *LM* curve. In fact, there is no room in the analysis for a point to occur off the curve.

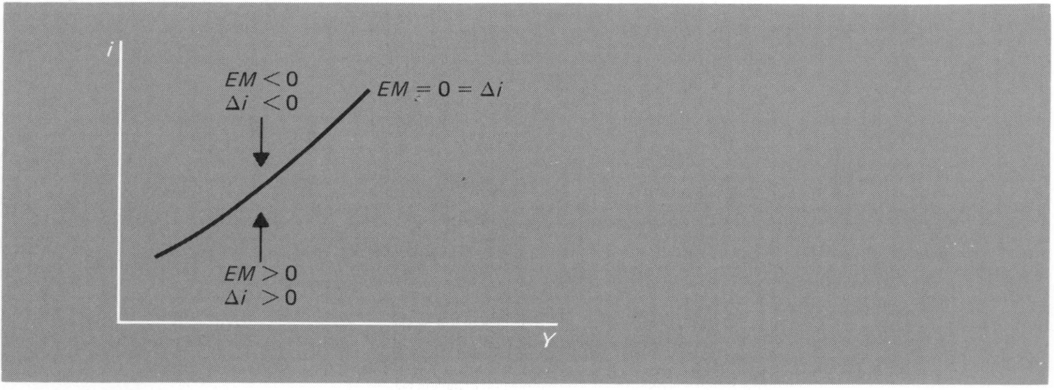

FIGURE 6-19

IV. DYNAMIC PROPERTIES OF THE INCOMPLETE GENERAL EQUILIBRIUM

We are now ready to provide a *tentative* determination of both the interest rate and employment. In equilibrium, the market for goods and services and the money market should be cleared. The $EG = 0$ curve provides us with all combinations of (i,x) that clear the goods and services market, while the $EM = 0$ curve yields all the combinations of the same variables that guarantee equality between demand for and supply of real balances. Thus the intersection of the two curves guarantees simultaneous clearance of both markets. This determination of interest and employment coincides with Keynes's insistence that the interest rate is also a monetary phenomenon, since the money market has a role to play. The employment theory implied here is *general,* as Keynes emphasized, since whatever employment level is determined results from interdependent forces operating in a framework that permits every possible level, not only the assumed full-employment level. Keynes, of course, went further by saying that unemployment is the *general case* and full employment is merely the *special case.* In other words, he said that the employment level determined by the intersection of the $EG = 0$ and $EM = 0$ curves, in all likelihood, would not be sufficient to employ exactly all those workers who are willing to offer their labor at the prevailing real wage. This is shown in Figure 6-20.

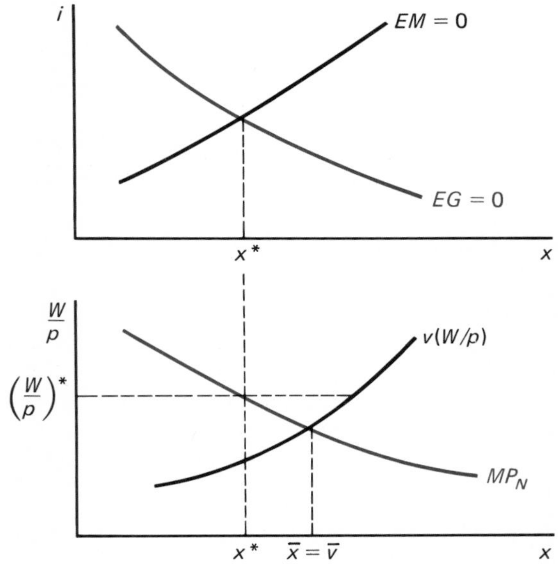

FIGURE 6-20

While it is true, of course, that one result, full employment, might emerge, as in the graph in Figure 6-21, this possibility, according to Keynes, is only one out of an infinity of possible outcomes. We are not yet ready, however, to take issue with this Keynesian contention. But we should emphasize here that even if we can eventually prove from our analysis that the case of full employment (i.e., Figure 6-21) will *always* emerge, Keynes' strong pronouncement, that his was a *general* theory of employment, cannot be dismissed. In other words, even if we disprove the major theorem of Keynes, that at equilibrium there will, in general, be involuntary unemployment, the Keynesian framework is useful. For this reason Keynesian analysis has still been used in recent times when unemployment has not been the major problem.

In a tentative way, we are also ready to examine the dynamics of employment (or income) and interest determination by assembling the information derived earlier

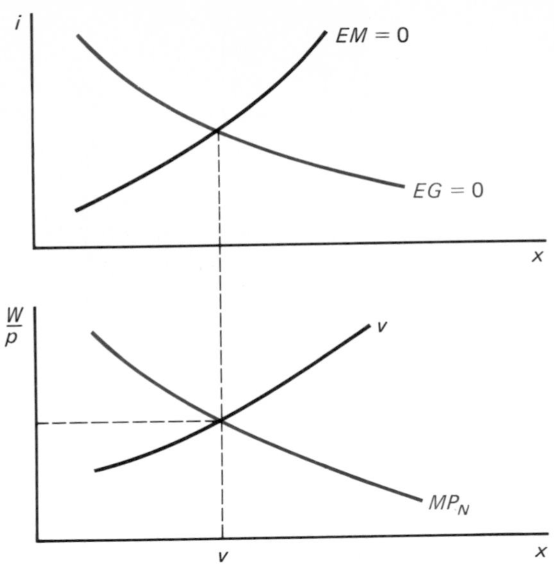

FIGURE 6-21

into a single graph, Figure 6-22, in which the "phase-plane" consists of four regions. In region A, both employment and interest are falling. One accustomed to thinking in "equilibrium" or "static" terms might consider a situation of falling interest and falling employment as peculiar. After all, it might be argued, doesn't a fall in interest stimulate aggregate demand, which would *increase* employment? Such a criticism disappears, however, when we recognize that any point in region A exhibits both excess supply of goods and services and excess supply of real balances. The excess supply of goods and services causes a fall in employment (because of the implied

FIGURE 6-22

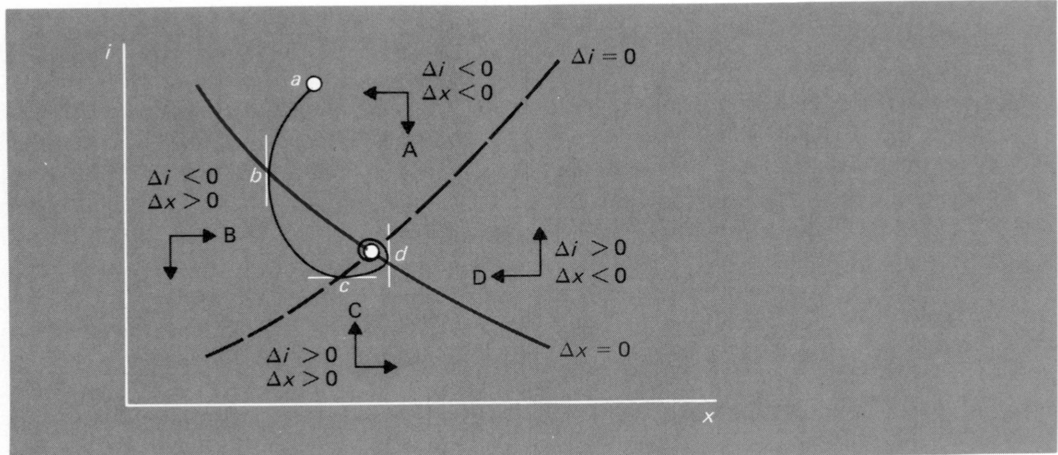

deficiency of aggregate demand), while the excess supply of real balances induces a fall in the interest rate.

Let us suppose that "history" begins at a point like *a* in region A. Both i and x will be falling until they reach the $\Delta x = 0$ curve, point *b*. Since at that point the market for goods and services is cleared, the drop in x stops. (Note that the tangent to the trajectory at that point is perpendicular to the x-axis.) But there is still an excess supply of money. Therefore the interest rate continues to fall and thus *b* is not an equilibrium point. The fall in the interest rate (which induces an increase in aggregate demand and, therefore, excess aggregate demand) brings the economy into region B in which there is excess demand for goods and services. Therefore employment starts to rise. But in this region there is still an excess supply of money; therefore the interest rate continues to fall, further increasing aggregate demand and thus employment. This process will continue until point *c* when the fall in the interest rate stops (note that the tangent to the trajectory at *c* is perpendicular to the i-axis) because the money market is cleared. However, there is still an excess demand for goods, and x will continue increasing, which, in turn, increases the demand for money, thereby causing excess demand for money. And the economy moves into region C where both markets experience excess demand, and therefore both interest and employment rise until point *d*. Employment stops rising, but the interest rate continues its upward movement because of excess demand for money. This increase in the interest rate causes deficiency in aggregate demand for goods and services, which takes us into region D where the interest rate rises but employment falls, a process that will continue until both markets are cleared and full equilibrium occurs.

The above convergence to equilibrium was established under the proviso that the $EG = 0$ curve is negatively sloped. Now suppose that the marginal propensity to spend is greater than one, which implies that the $EG = 0$ curve is positively sloped. Can we still establish stability, and, if so, under what conditions? Examine first the case when the (positive) slope of the $\Delta x = 0$ (i.e., the $EG = 0$) curve is greater than that of the $\Delta i = 0$ (or $EM = 0$) curve, as in Figure 6-23. We see that in this case the movements are, in general, away from equilibrium. Only two out of an infinity of possible paths lead the economy to equilibrium. The situation described in Figure 6-23 is one of a saddle-point equilibrium, which is, for all practical purposes, an unstable system. Since we are interested in providing a consistent and useful description of the economy, this situation should be excluded. We are left, then, with the case in which the *LM* curve is steeper than the *IS* curve, as in Figure 6-24. Obviously, the system can be consistent only if the slope of the $EM = 0$ curve is algebraically greater than that of the $EG = 0$ curve.

A special case of this dynamic analysis should be mentioned, namely, one in which the speed of adjustment in the money market is infinite. In this case the demand for money is always equal to its supply, a fact that restricts the paths that the economy might follow. This restriction can be seen in Figure 6-25a, which replaces Figure 6-22, and in Figure 6-25b, which replaces Figure 6-23. And, finally, in Figure 6-25c, which replaces Figure 6-24. In all three cases we see that there is only one path available to the economy. Of course, only the stable ones are legitimate, and the case of Figure 6-25b should be excluded. In the *(i-Y)*-plane, the analogue to Figure 6-22 would be Figure 6-26.

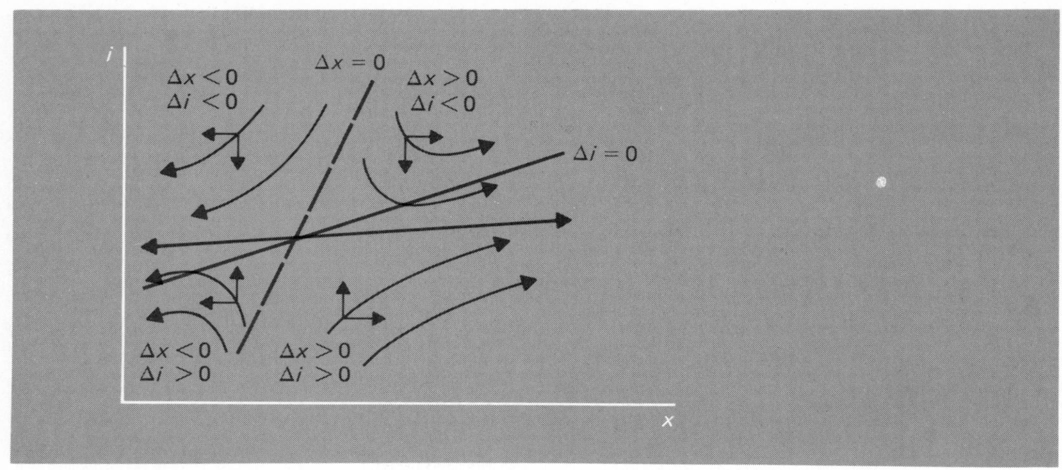

FIGURE 6-23

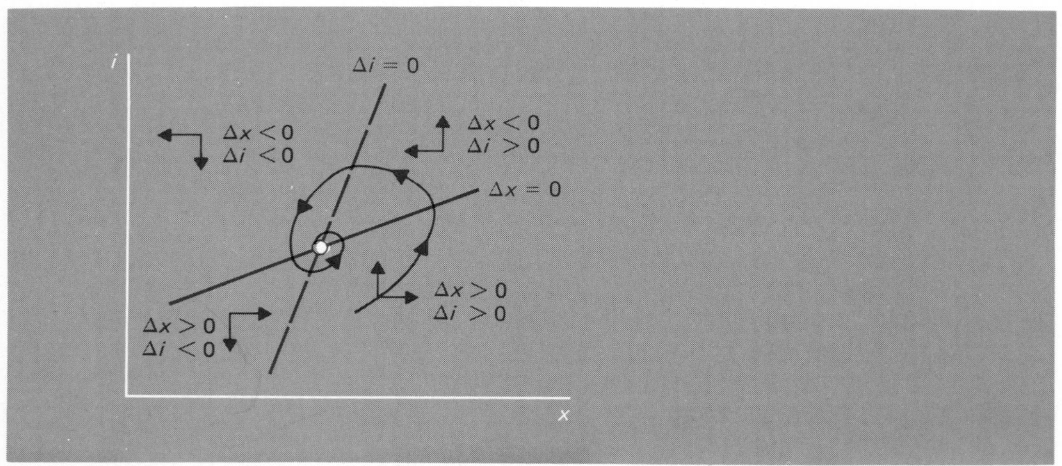

FIGURE 6-24

FIGURE 6-25

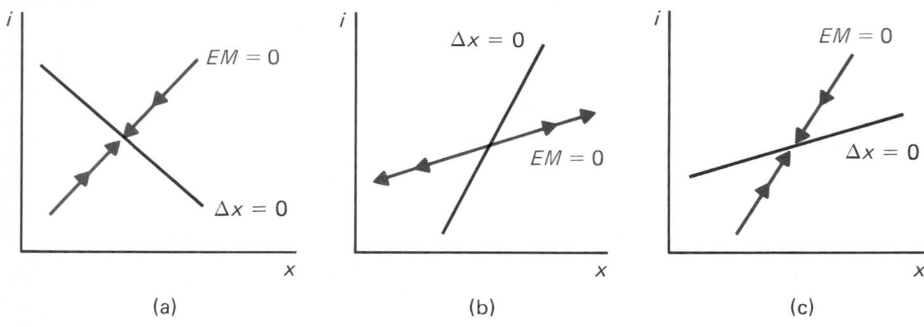

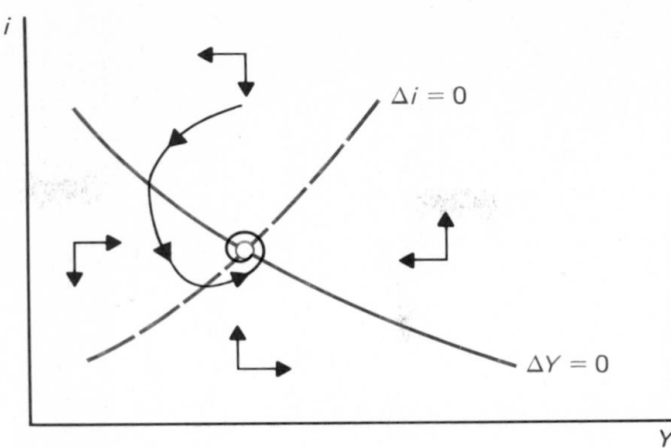

FIGURE 6-26

The determination of interest and employment has so far been referred to as "tentative." The same adjective has also been applied to the process by which the equilibrium is reached. The careful reader must have recognized the reason for this description, namely, that the analysis has not been complete. We observed earlier that interest and employment are not the only endogenous variables, or magnitudes, that must be simultaneously determined; the price level must also be determined. But we have not yet examined it because we restricted ourselves to a two-dimensional graphical analysis. In addition, we chose to utilize the *(i-x)*-plane or the *(i, Y)*-plane because of our interest in following the approach common in the literature since Hicks's original contribution. Now it is time to bring forth the shortcomings of the analysis and try to remedy them.

V. PRICE OR REAL BALANCE EFFECTS

We noticed earlier that the price level is an argument in the excess demand-for-money equation:

$$EM(i,x,p) = L(i,x) - \frac{M}{p}$$

When we examined the $EM = 0$ curve, we took care in emphasizing that this curve was derived for a particular price level, say p_0. Now suppose that we want to consider a higher price level, say $p_1 > p_0$. What will happen to our $EM = 0$ curve? We can find the answer by going behind the scenes and reexamining the way we derived the curve. First, since the price level is higher, the supply of real balances is lower, $\overline{M}/p_1 < \overline{M}/p_0$ for $p_1 > p_0$; and for each x, the interest rate that brings equality between the demand and the smaller supply is higher, as Figure 6-27 demonstrates.

We observe that when $x = x_0$ the interest rate that clears the market is now i_0', which is greater than i_0. Similarly, for x_1 the money-market-clearing interest rate is i_1', which is greater than i_1. Thus the $EM = 0$ curve shifts to the left when p increases, as the right panel of Figure 6-27 demonstrates.

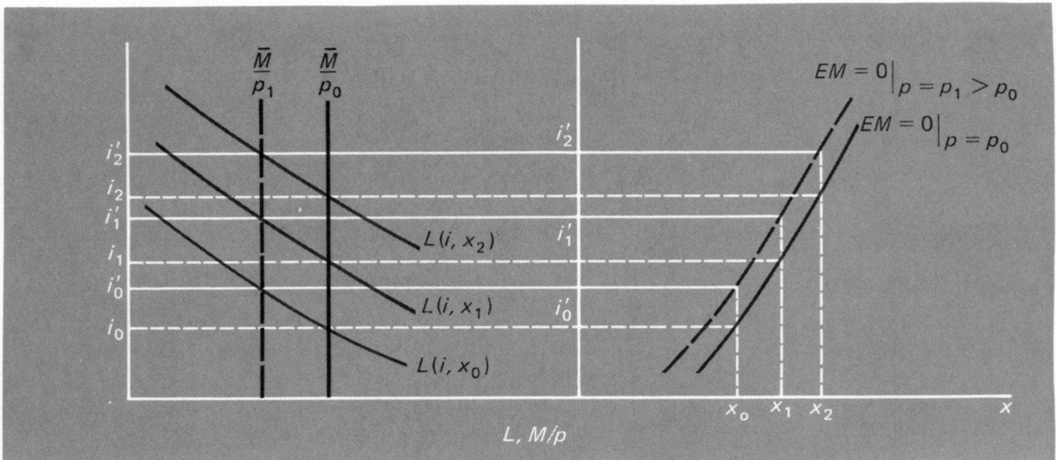

FIGURE 6-27

The leftward (rightward) shift of the $EM = 0$ curve when the price level increases (decreases) is a singularly Keynesian discovery, which in the literature is called the *Keynesian real balance effect.* Of course, the adjective "Keynesian" is meant to honor the discoverer. The term "real balance effect" is to identify and emphasize that the fall (say) in the price level enlarges (magnifies) the real balances, and this, in turn, lowers the interest rate if other things are equal, namely, if x is the same. Schematically, it is shown as

$$p\downarrow \longrightarrow \frac{M}{P}\uparrow \longrightarrow i\downarrow$$

Of course, other things are not equal when the price level falls; a fall in p, from p_0 to p_1, shifts the $EM = 0$ curve to the right, and since the $EG = 0$ curve remains the same (according to our analysis so far), the new intersection produces a higher x as well as a lower i, as shown in Figure 6-28. Schematically, this sequence of events is as follows:

$$p\downarrow \longrightarrow \frac{M}{P}\uparrow \longrightarrow i\downarrow \longrightarrow \begin{matrix} C\uparrow \\ I\uparrow \end{matrix} \longrightarrow EG\uparrow \longrightarrow x\uparrow$$

The first part of this schema, namely,

$$p\downarrow \longrightarrow \frac{M}{p}\uparrow \longrightarrow i\downarrow,$$

is shown in Figure 6-29 as a movement from point E to point F.

Since there is an infinity of possible price levels, it follows that the number of $EM = 0$ curves is also infinite. We can imagine the (i,x)-plane as being full of

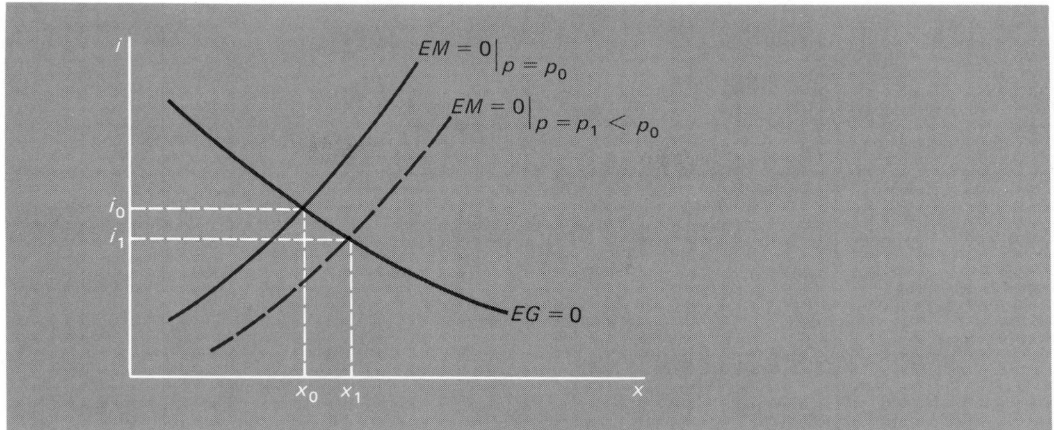

FIGURE 6-28

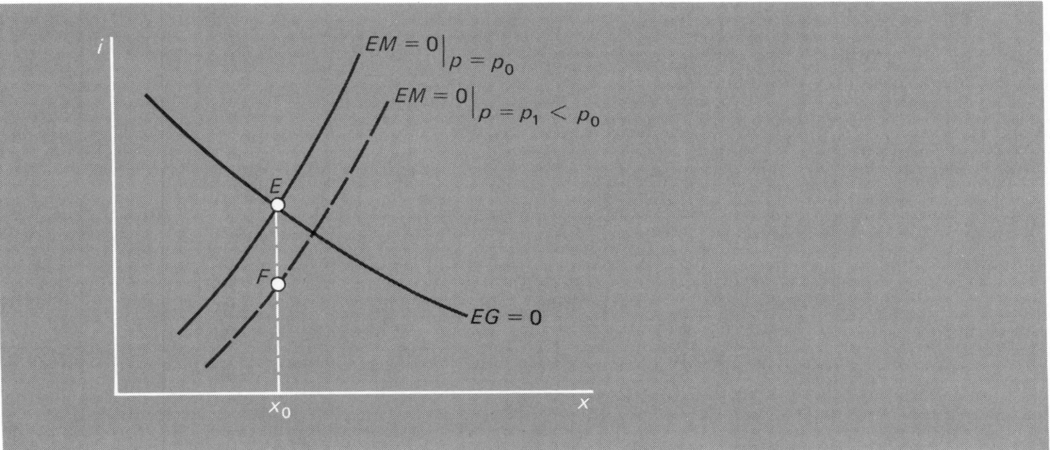

FIGURE 6-29

these $EM = 0$ curves, one for each price level. Five of them, all properly identified, are illustrated in Figure 6-30.

It is now clear that our analysis so far is incomplete. But how are our results influenced by this discovery? The most striking observation is that we have been able to determine neither the interest rate nor employment (not to mention the price level itself). We know that i and x are determined by the intersection of the $EG = 0$ and $EM = 0$ curves. But in order to find this intersection, we need to know the price level. Only then can we identify the relevant $EM = 0$ curve, which upon intersecting the (unique up to now) $EG = 0$ curve will give us the (i,x) point. The problem we are faced with is theoretically the same as that facing the partial equilibrium analyst who is attempting to determine the price of peanuts and needs to know the price of walnuts. Furthermore, the problem we are faced with is similar to the one discovered by Keynes himself, and one that permitted him to launch his

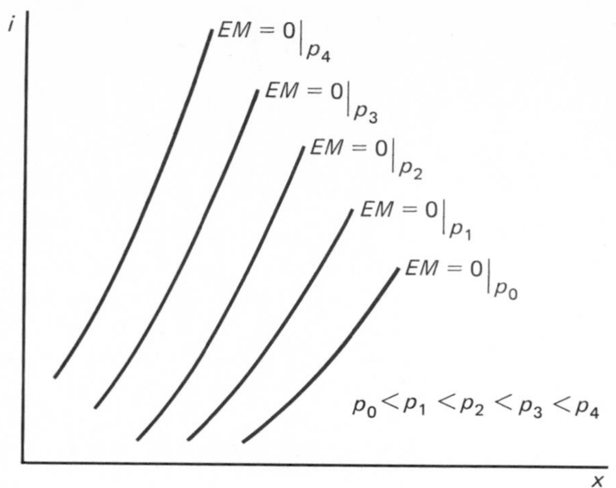

FIGURE 6-30

successful challenge to the neoclassicists. He discovered that they could not possibly have determined the interest rate within a general framework, since there is one interest rate for each employment level. Here we see that we could not possibly have determined *(i,x)* because there is one such pair for each price level, as in Figure 6-31.

In addition to our basic result, that we have not determined the interest rate and the level of employment, we are also confronted by a direct corollary to this result, that we have not established the Keynesian claim that unemployment equilibrium is the general case. For how can we claim such a result if we do not even know what level of employment will occur? Moreover, how do we know that the price level may not be such that it gives an $EM = 0$ curve that intersects the $EG = 0$ curve exactly at $x = v$? Such a price level is denoted as p^* in Figure 6-32. While the Keynesian thesis may or may not be correct, we have not yet established either result. But what we *have* established, even with our incomplete analysis, is that whatever equilibrium we get, it has to have the property that one (i.e., the

FIGURE 6-31

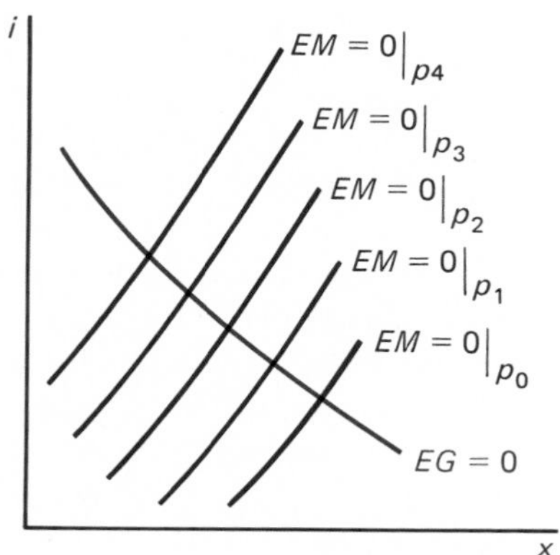

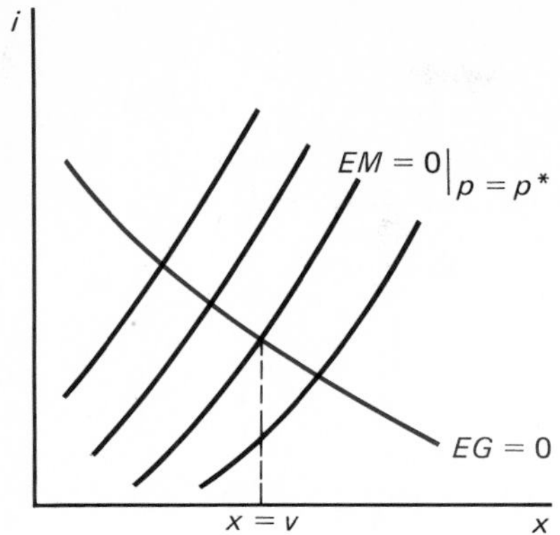

FIGURE 6-32

relevant) $EM = 0$ curve intersects the $EG = 0$ curve, since it is necessary for the equilibrium that (among other properties) the excess demand for money and the excess demand for goods and services must *both* be zero.

For now, we shall *assume* that the equilibrium price level p^* is such that it yields an $EM = 0$ curve guaranteeing $x^* < \bar{v}$, as in Figure 6-33. Under these circumstances, one might want to inquire whether there are any tools available to the policy maker aimed at reducing (or even eliminating) the involuntary unemployment, $\bar{v} - x^*$.

FIGURE 6-33

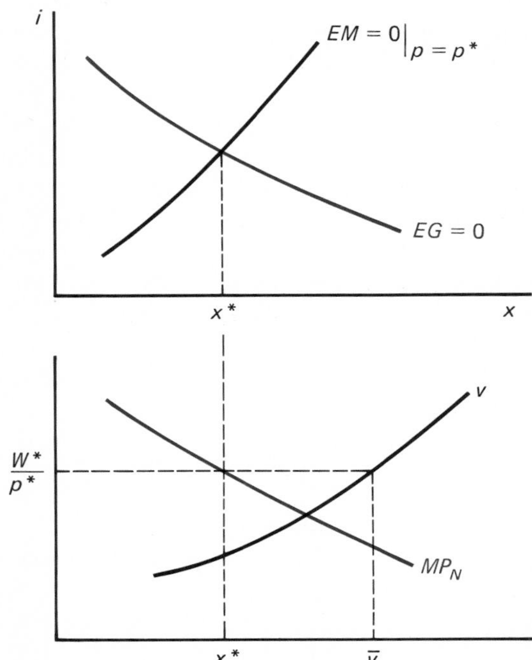

VI. ECONOMIC POLICY

Let us suppose that the government has decided that the involuntary unemployment, $x^* - v$ in Figure 6-33, is undesirable and that it must be reduced or eliminated. It is clear that this goal is possible only if the $EG = 0$ curve or the $EM = 0$ curve, or both, can deliberately be shifted.

SHIFTING THE $EG = 0$ CURVE

So far we have examined the case of a closed economy with a government that neither taxes nor provides services. If we relax these assumptions, we can see that the excess demand for goods and services has two more components. First, there is the budget deficit, Z (positive or negative), which is the difference between government expenditure, G, and tax revenues, T. Thus $Z = G - T$. The second additional component of aggregate demand is the trade surplus, υ, which is the difference between this country's exports, χ, and imports, μ. Thus $\upsilon = \chi - \mu$. The excess demand for goods and services is now

$$EG = I(i,x) - S(i,x) + Z + \upsilon$$

Now, $I - S$ is the domestic private excess demand, Z (if positive) is the excess demand of the government, and υ (if positive) is foreign excess demand (i.e., excess demand for our product originating from foreign nationals). It is clear, of course, that Z can increase either by increasing government expenditures while keeping tax revenue the same, or by decreasing tax revenue while keeping government expenditure the same, or, finally, by increasing government expenditure by more than the increase in tax revenue. Similarly, an increase in the trade surplus could come about by increasing exports, by decreasing imports, or by increasing exports by more than the increase in imports. For the time being, we shall examine the effects of a change in either the government budget deficit or the trade balance without inquiring about their components. Moreover, we shall assume that the government can change these magnitudes at will, as if they were true parameters. We must admit that this last assumption is very strong, since some of these components are not exogenous but endogenous (or depend on endogenous variables of the system). This is definitely the case with exports and imports and, given the tax system of this country, with tax revenues. We shall find occasion to relax this strong assumption later on. Changes in Z will be referred to as fiscal policy, and changes in υ as (foreign) trade (or commercial) policy.

FISCAL POLICY

An increase in the budget deficit will shift the $EG = 0$ curve to the right, which means that for each interest rate employment must be higher to clear the goods market. This can be seen by going back to a graph, similar to Figure 6-34, from which we can derive the $EG = 0$ curve. Keeping the interest rate the same, say at i_0, private investment demand is $I(i_0,x)$. To this we must add the increase in govern-

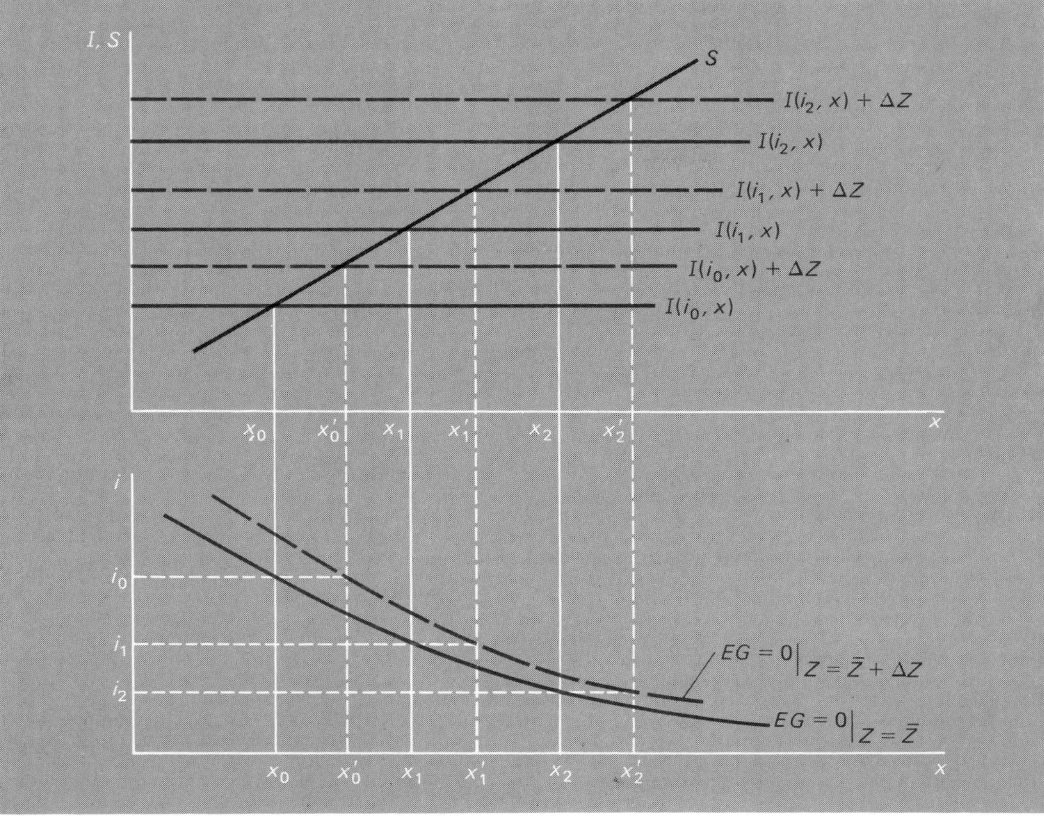

FIGURE 6-34

ment deficit, ΔZ. We see that for the same interest rate, i_0, the x that guarantees $I(\cdot) + \Delta Z = S$ (i.e., $EG = 0$) is now x_0', which is greater than x_0. Similarly, for a lower i, say i_1, we have $x = x_1'$, which is greater than x_1. The same is true of every level of the interest rate. These results are plotted in the lower panel of Figure 6-34, which shows that the new $EG = 0$ curve is located to the right of the previous one. (For simplicity of notation, in the graph in the lower panel of Figure 6-34 we depict the case of an increase in the budget deficit, beginning from a zero deficit. It should be clear, however, that the result would be the same even if we had started with a deficit different from zero. All we need to change in the graph in the lower panel is to label the curves as, say, $I(i_0,x) + Z$ and $I(i_0,x) + Z + \Delta Z$.)

TRADE POLICY

An increase in the trade surplus will shift the $EG = 0$ curve to the right for exactly the same reasons as the increase in the budget deficit does. To show this result, the reader merely has to substitute Δv for ΔZ in the graph in Figure 6-34.

Expressing this information in words, we see that an increase in either the budget deficit or the trade surplus will increase the aggregate demand for each level of the interest rate. This is so because, for the same interest rate, private investment demand will be the same, with or without the government deficit or trade surplus. And now the increase in aggregate demand can sustain a higher level of employment.

Equipped with the above results, we are now ready to examine, in a preliminary fashion, the first two ways by which the policy maker can reduce unemployment. It is clear that an increase in the budget deficit or an increase in the trade surplus will increase employment, as shown in Figure 6-35.

The reader may be surprised to learn that these policies can reduce unemployment even if the marginal propensity to spend is greater than one, that is, even if the $EG = 0$ curve is upward sloping. Some readers might think that since an increase in the budget deficit (or the trade surplus) shifts the $EG = 0$ curve to the left, what we need is the opposite of those policies. This is not the case, however, as Figure 6-36 shows. Other readers might think that the result is indeterminate because they suspect that the cards have been stacked in Figure 6-36. After all, if the $EG = 0$ curve is steeper than the $EM = 0$ curve, the increase in the budget deficit would *reduce* x, and not increase it, as shown in Figure 6-37.

This is where our earlier examination of stability comes in handy. The graph in Figure 6-37 notwithstanding, the result is illegitimate because the model is unstable. In the first place, the model described by Figure 6-37 is inconsistent. Moreover, we

FIGURE 6-35

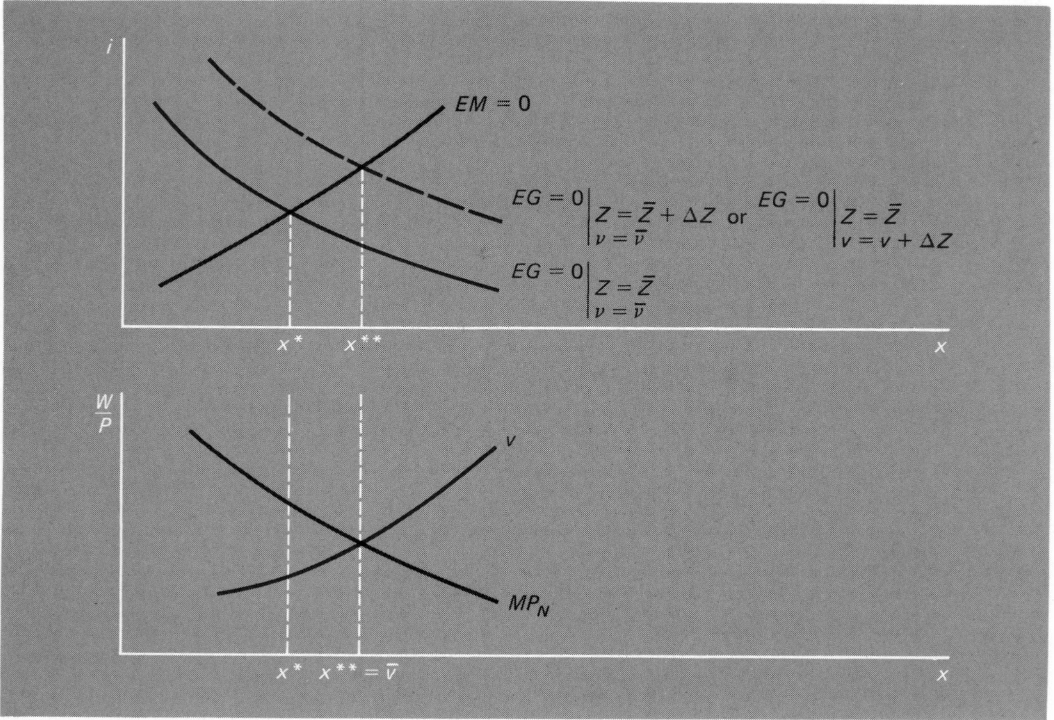

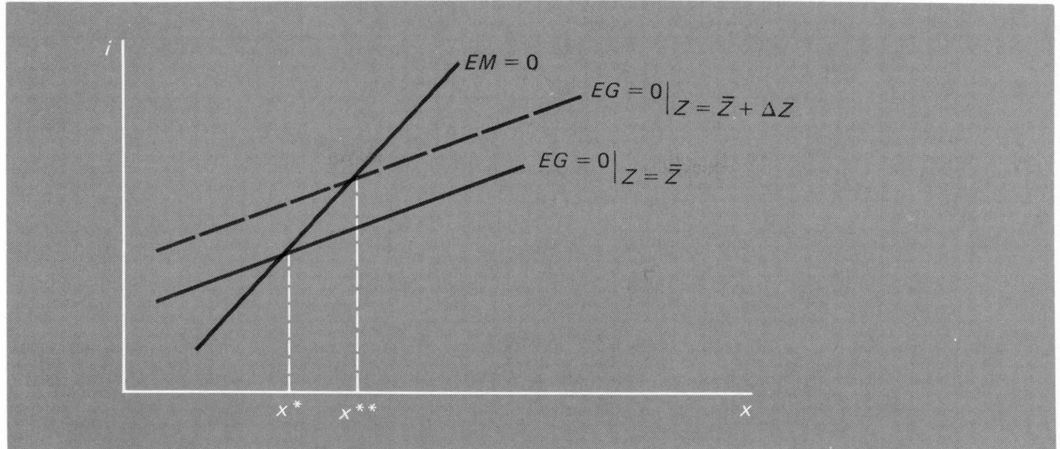

FIGURE 6-36

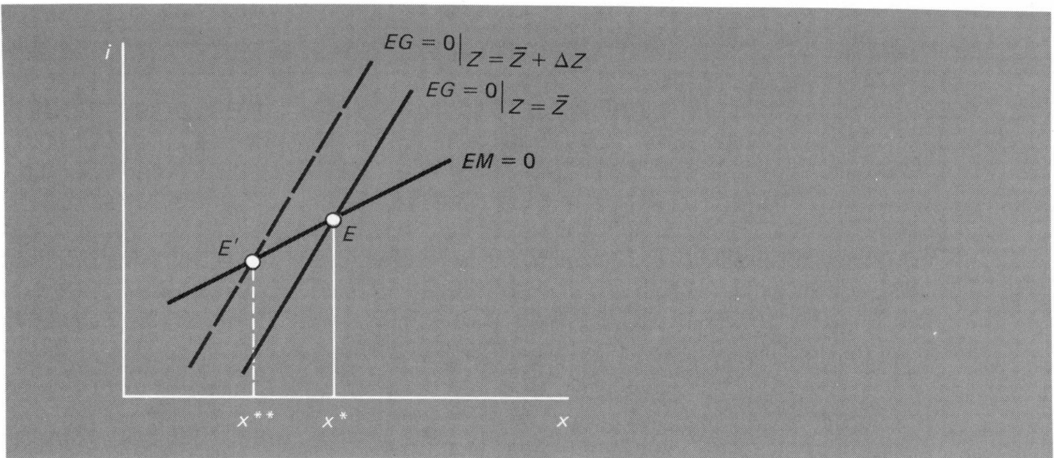

FIGURE 6-37

know that point E' (the new equilibrium) *cannot* be achieved. Why, then, should we aim at that point through policy if we know that we cannot reach it? Recognizing this impossibility, we can state that an increase in the budget deficit or an increase in the trade surplus shifts the $EG = 0$ curve toward a higher employment level, *subject to the limitations of our analysis.* Here is where there is a legitimate doubt. Our analysis has been conducted (tentatively) holding the price level fixed. But will it remain fixed? One naturally expects prices to rise when there is an increase in demand. But if the price level increases, the $EM = 0$ curve will shift to the left, thereby guaranteeing that the ultimate employment level can never be as high as x^{**}; it must be smaller. We identified the leftward shift of the $EM = 0$ curve caused by an increase in the price level as the "Keynesian real balance effect." This increase of the price level shrinks the supply of real balances, which, in turn, raises the interest rate for each given employment level x. The important question here is whether the increase in the price level will shift the $EM = 0$ curve so far to the left that the new equilibrium level of employment, x^{**}, will not be greater than x^{*}. It should be obvious that since Keynes—the discoverer of the "Keynesian real balance effect"—claimed that an increase in the budget deficit would definitely increase employment, he must have decided that the increase in p cannot shift the $EM = 0$ curve too far to the left.

It is clear that we have two opposing forces here, the direct increase in aggregate demand caused by the outright increase in the budget deficit and the indirect *decrease* in aggregate demand caused by the increase in the interest rate, which reduces private investment and consumption demand. This increase in the interest rate is the product of the reduction of real balances, which was engineered by the increase in the price level. Thus the question posed earlier amounts to our asking whether it is possible for the indirect decrease in aggregate demand (caused by a rise in prices) to negate all (or more) of the direct increase. If this is possible, then Keynes and the "Keynesians" were wrong in thinking that fiscal policy could be used as an antirecession weapon.

At this point, although we have not yet completed the model to accommodate the price level, it is possible to give a satisfactory answer to the above question. First, in economic theory we invariably find that indirect effects are not strong enough to outweigh direct effects. One should, therefore, expect the same here. Of course, this is not a "proof," since it is theoretically conceivable that this indirect effect might outweigh the direct effect. Therefore we need better reasons. Second, the indirect effect arises *because* the price level increases. But for the price level to increase, we have to have a *net increase* in aggregate demand. And if we did not, the indirect effect would be inoperative anyway. This proves conclusively (logically) that the price level could not have risen enough to completely negate the direct effect; it merely "arrests" a little the potential increase in employment. Third, there is a more direct answer to this question. We recall that, so far, we have followed Keynes in assuming

FIGURE 6-38

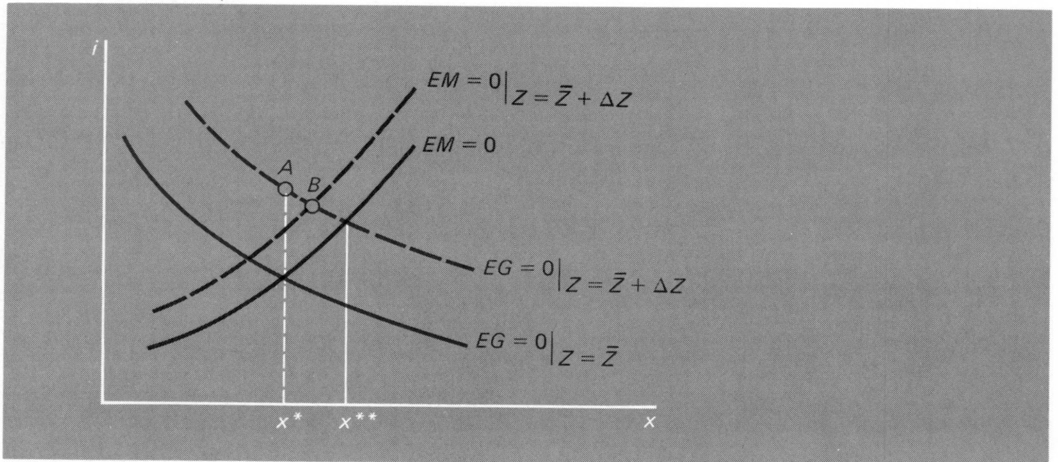

the money wage fixed. From this, it follows that the increase in the price level lowers the real wage, which, in turn, requires that the profit-maximizing firms increase their demand for employment. We can, therefore, legitimately proceed with our analysis which states that if unemployment exists, it can be reduced (or eliminated) by an increase in the budget deficit or by an increase in the trade surplus. A shift in the $EM = 0$ curve that might accompany the upward shift in the $EG = 0$ curve has to intersect this new $EG = 0$ curve to the right of point *A*, say at point *B* in Figure 6-38.

For the sake of completeness, we should mention another possible indirect decrease in aggregate demand, which involves the method by which the deficit might be financed. It has been argued that if this deficit is financed by issuing bonds, the interest rate would increase and would, therefore, further reduce private aggregate demand. However, we shall postpone until the end of this chapter the examination of this argument, since the model we have been using cannot handle this case.

SHIFTING THE $EM = 0$ CURVE—MONETARY POLICY

Another tool usually available to the policy maker is monetary policy. So far we have assumed that the nominal money supply is a fixed parameter, or that it is under the absolute control of the monetary authority, who may change the money supply if, by so doing, it can influence employment. We shall see that an increase in the nominal money supply will shift the $EM = 0$ curve to the right. In other words, the increase in the money supply will increase employment for each level of the interest rate, or, alternatively, for each employment level, it will decrease the interest rate.

Let us now go back to the basic components used in deriving the $EM = 0$ curve. Recall that "the" $EM = 0$ curve assumes a given price level, say p_0, and

FIGURE 6-39

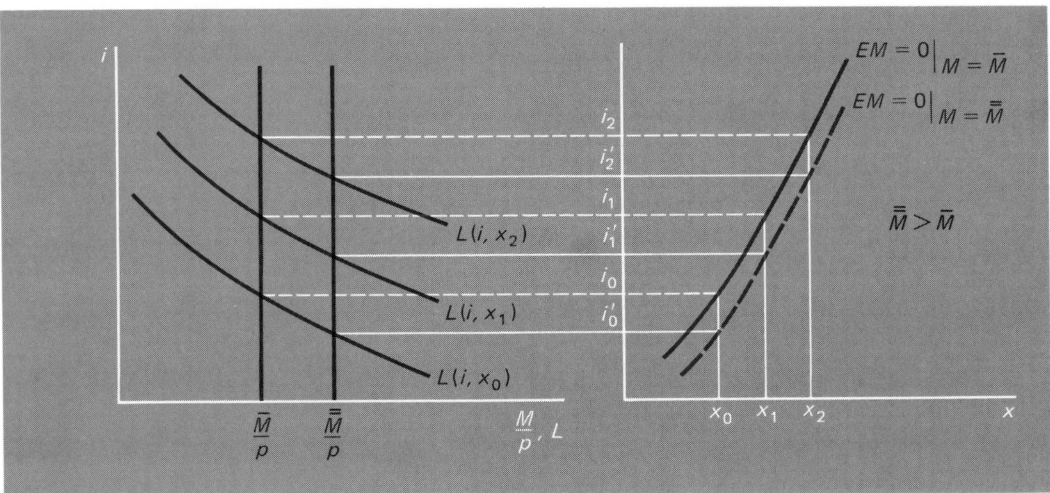

that an increase in M will therefore increase the real supply of money. Thus, for each level of x, the money-market-clearing interest rate will be lower, as shown in the left panel of Figure 6-39 on page 235. These results are assembled in the right panel, demonstrating a rightward shift of the $EM = 0$ curve (for the same p_0).

We are now ready to show that an increase in the nominal money supply will increase the employment level, as shown in Figure 6-40. Schematically and somewhat informally, we can say that an increase in the money supply lowers the interest rate, which induces an increase in private aggregate demand (i.e., in I and C), which, in turn, increases employment because of the rising price level. Note that the problem of price determination is present here. Since the price level increases, the new $EM = 0$ curve has to shift to the left, which prevents x^{**} from materializing. It has to be lower than x^{**}, but greater than x^*, for the same reasons we outlined in the preceding section.

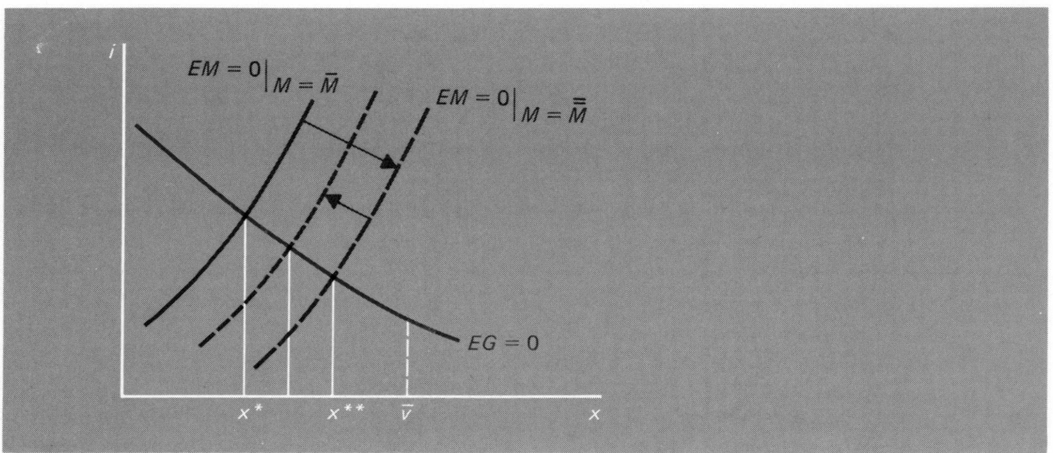

FIGURE 6-40

VII. COMPARISON OF FISCAL AND MONETARY POLICIES

We have seen that both monetary and fiscal policy can be used as antirecession tools. An increase in the nominal money supply can reduce unemployment, just as an increase in the budget deficit does. There is, however, a difference between the two, the most important being that an increase in the money supply increases employment but lowers the interest rate if the *IS* curve is downward sloping, whereas fiscal policy increases employment by *increasing* the interest rate. If fiscal policy is pursued, the increase in the interest rate occurs because the increase in economic activity is not accompanied by any increase in money; on the contrary, there is a decrease in the real supply because of the increase in the price level. This puts an extra strain on the financial market. On the other hand, if monetary policy is pursued, we have an increase in economic activity *because* the interest rate falls.

If the *IS* curve is upward sloping (i.e., when the marginal propensity to spend is greater than one), the interest rate increases, whether we use monetary or fiscal policy to increase economic activity. However, *for the same effect on x,* the increase in the interest rate is greater if we use fiscal policy than if we use monetary policy. This is shown in Figure 6-41. If we want to increase employment from x^* to v by fiscal policy, the interest rate will rise from i^* to i_F. On the other hand, if monetary policy is used, the interest rate will rise only to i_M.

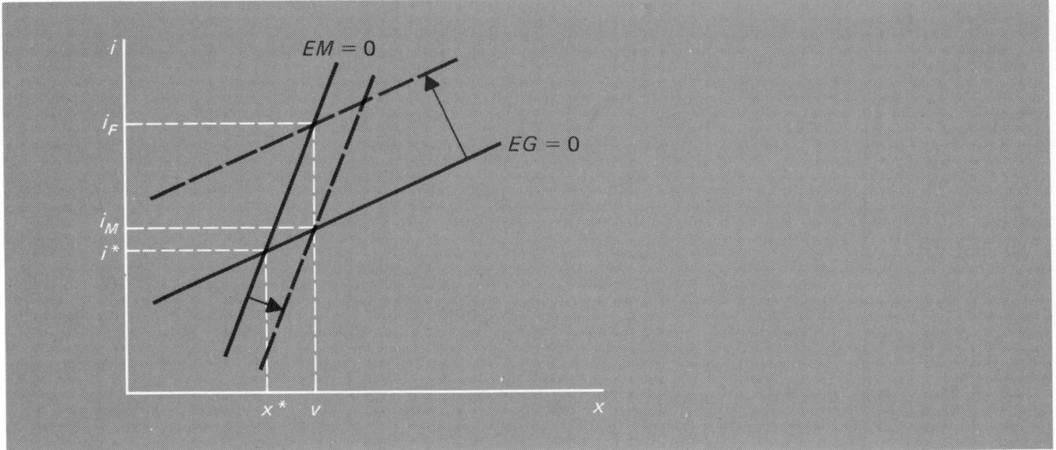

FIGURE 6-41

Because of the different effect of the two policies on the interest rate, there are different effects on the various sectors of the economy, even if employment rises under both policies. Thus the construction industry prefers the use of monetary policy for fighting unemployment, since this industry is very sensitive to changes in the interest rate. It is not surprising that the construction industry prefers the use of fiscal policy as a weapon against inflation. Under both circumstances, it expects to profit (or avoid losses) from interest rates lower than those that would result if fiscal policy were used to combat unemployment and if monetary policy were used to counteract inflation.

Knowledge of the various sectoral effects of alternative economic policy tools is important on purely economic, as well as political, grounds. If, for example, policy makers operate under the constraint of a five-year plan aimed at increasing the housing capacity of the economy, they must design an anti-inflation program favorable to the housing industry. We must also assume that in a democracy, the elected representatives are reluctant to support a policy that hurts the majority of their constituency. The policy maker responsible for, say, the reduction in unemployment is bound to try to design an effective antirecession policy that is acceptable to the legislative body.

In a sense, the policy maker's life is easier when there are alternative tools of achieving a specific target; the policy maker may use either one or a combination, a "mix," of policies that is considered the best under the circumstances, including political constraints.

It is not only the special-interest groups who disagree over the policy to be used. There are economists who claim (or are accused of claiming) that *only* fiscal policy can change employment. At the other extreme are those economists who insist that only monetary policy can influence employment, or that employment is determined by the Walrasian equations, independent of policy, and that we must be careful about monetary policy because of inflation. We shall examine the conditions under which each of these claims is correct and also inquire whether those conditions can be satisfied on theoretical and on empirical grounds.

THE ONLY-MONEY-MATTERS THESIS

We have seen (Section III) that when neither the demand for nor the supply of money depends on the interest rate, the excess demand for money is a function of employment and prices only: $EM(p,x)$. We have also seen that this gives a vertical $EM = 0$ curve in the (i,x)-plane. Under these circumstances, x cannot be changed by direct changes in the components of aggregate demand. An increase in the budget deficit, for example, will succeed in raising the interest rate for a given price level, but x will remain the same, as shown in Figures 6-42a and 6-42b.

Another implication of this analysis is that the price level will not change, an implication that follows indirectly from our assumption of fixed money wages. Since the marginal product of labor is known to remain constant (because x remains constant) and the money wage is constant (by assumption), it follows that the price level must remain constant, or we would have a contradiction. (Use the condition $\overline{W}/p = MP_N$; since Δx is zero, the result of Figure 6-42, the right-hand side does not change, and therefore the left-hand side must also remain unchanged. But since

FIGURE 6-42

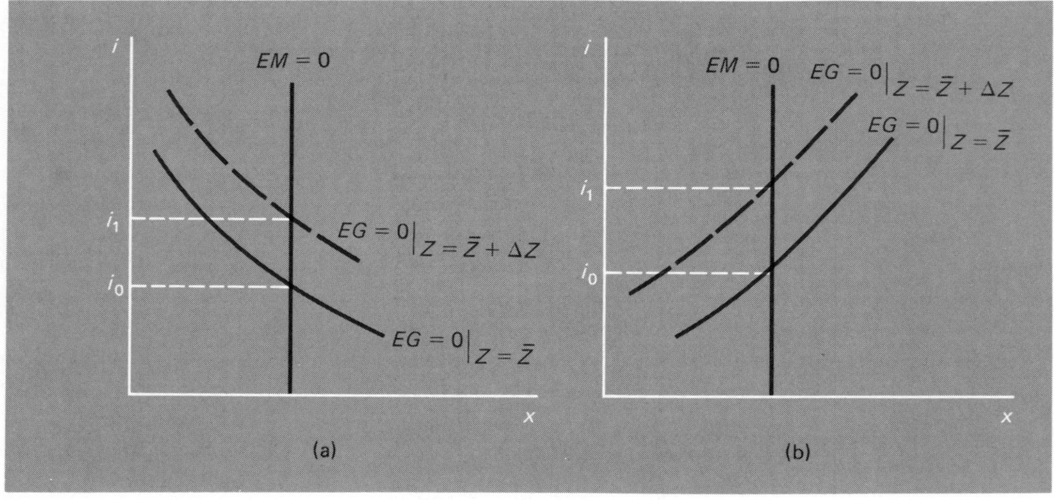

the numerator on the left-hand side is unchanged, the denominator, likewise, remains unchanged.)

It is clear that the only way to increase employment, under these circumstances, is to increase the nominal money supply. This would shift the $EM = 0$ curve to the right, as Figures 6-43a and 6-43b show. Whether the $EG = 0$ curve is downward sloping (as in Figure 6-43a) or upward sloping (as in Figure 6-43b), employment increases with an increase in the nominal money supply. (In the former case, however, the higher employment level is accompanied by a lower interest rate, whereas in the latter case, the interest rate is higher, neither of which is an issue here.)

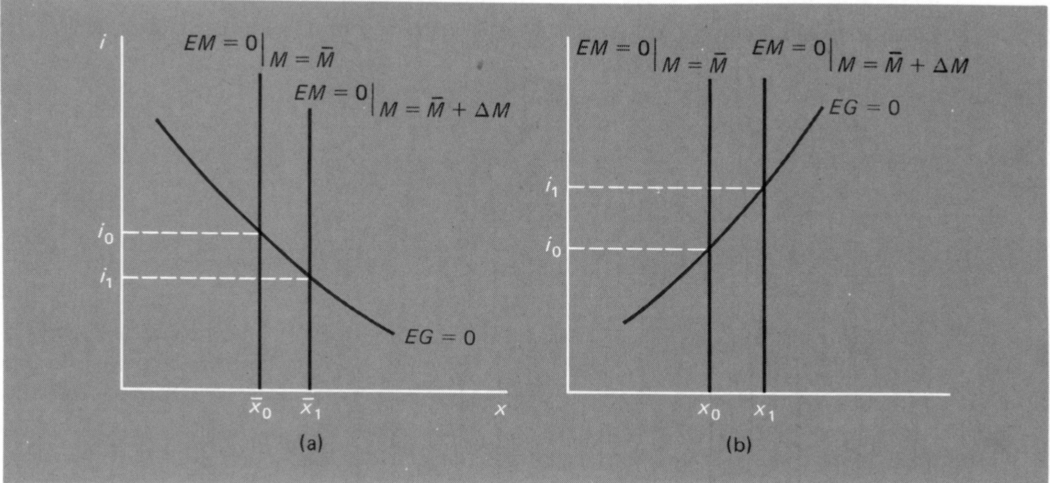

FIGURE 6-43

We see from the above analysis that the statement "Only an increase in the money supply can increase employment" is theoretically correct if one assumes that neither the demand for nor the supply of money is influenced by the interest rate. The reader should recall that in Chapter 4, in which we assumed full employment, we found that the statement "Only an increase in the money supply can increase the price level" was theoretically sound only under the same assumption regarding the interest sensitivity of the excess demand for money. Both statements are really versions of a more general statement attributed to the so-called *monetarists:* "Only money matters." We now know that the only-money-matters thesis is correct if, and only if, the interest rate does not influence the excess demand for money.

The first such claim, that only money matters, was made by Friedman, who in his attempt to resurrect the quantity theory, and the world of Say's law, confronted economists with an impressive piece of empirical work in which he claimed to have shown that there is no evidence of a negative relation between the demand for money and the interest rate. But on theoretical, as well as empirical, grounds, we do expect that both the demand for and the supply of money are influenced by the interest rate. Thus the only-money-matters thesis cannot be considered an operating rule for the policy maker.

THE ONLY-FISCAL-POLICY-MATTERS THESIS

It should be noted that the statement "Only money matters" was not the original monetarist thesis; their first position can be summarized as "Money matters, too," which was a reaction to views held, mostly unconsciously, by several economists in the 1940s and early 1950s. These economists claimed allegiance to Keynes, and they considered their views, whether they espoused that only fiscal policy matters or that money does not matter, as Keynesian. The late Harry G. Johnson called these views "vulgar Keynesianism" and those who subscribed to them "vulgar Keynesians." The vulgarity involves both the use of the adjective "Keynesian" and the application of their views to the real world. First, to attribute such views to Keynes does a grave injustice to the author of *A Tract on Monetary Reform, Treatise on Money, General Theory,* and numerous other works on money. It is generally agreed that no other economist has done more to enhance our understanding of the importance of money than Keynes. Second, the conditions necessary to prove theoretically that only fiscal policy matters are so strong that they are unlikely to be satisfied empirically.

Why, then, were such views held? We mentioned above that these views were held mostly unconsciously. Since most textbooks did not mention monetary policy as a tool for increasing employment (or reducing inflation), the reader could infer that the authors believed that money did not matter. This same phenomenon applied to expositions of economic policy in the press; even economists in important policy-making positions usually avoided mentioning the role of monetary policy. Milton Friedman cites some fascinating instances of this mentality. (With this, of course, we should contrast the paradoxical fact—at least for the United States—that the "new economics," that is, the deliberate use of fiscal policy as a tool for increasing employment, was introduced for the first time in the 1960s, according to James Tobin, one of its architects.[5]

Of course, there is an explanation for this preoccupation with fiscal policy so soon after Keynes' contribution. The idea that investment and savings (or consumption) "determine" employment, and not the interest rate, was novel. And the idea that an increase in the budget deficit could be beneficial was truly revolutionary. The moment that economists were converted to this view, they wanted to preach the new gospel to both their fellow economists and to the public. For, as Keynes said, "The difficulty lies, not in the new ideas, but in escaping from the old ones." Thus, at this early stage of the new religion, it was felt that there was no sense in mentioning what was old hat. After all, monetary policy had always been used as a policy tool. Thus the textbooks were filled with Keynesian cross diagrams. The emerging field of econometrics found a testing ground in empirical studies of consumption, savings, and investment and of other components of the developing national accounts. Therefore the complaint that monetary policy was not given "equal time" during that period was valid; only one part of the Keynesian system was considered.

Let us now suppose that one examines the Keynesian system as we have developed it so far. Are there any circumstances under which the only-fiscal-policy-

[5] See James Tobin, *The New Economics One Decade Older* (Princeton: Princeton University Press, 1974).

matters thesis is correct? We shall see that there are two. The first concerns a special case of the excess demand for goods and services, and the second concerns the famous liquidity trap. Now, if the excess demand for goods and services is independent of the interest rate, monetary policy cannot be effective in changing employment. We can see the reason in our earlier schema. We know that for money to be effective, no short-circuit should develop in the following network:

$$M\uparrow \rightarrow i\downarrow \rightarrow (C+I)\uparrow \rightarrow EG\uparrow \rightarrow p\uparrow \rightarrow x\uparrow$$

In this first case, despite the falling interest rate, the excess demand for goods and services does not increase, thereby ending this process. Since we cannot increase EG indirectly, we must do it directly through budget deficit. We can also see this by using the graphical apparatus in the (i,x)-plane. The interest inelasticity of the market for goods and services implies a vertical $EG = 0$ curve, as in Figure 6-44. An increase in the money supply decreases the interest rate, from i_0 to i_1, without any effect on x. However, an increase in the budget deficit, from $\bar{Z}$ to $\bar{Z} + \Delta Z$, with money supply given at $\bar{M}$, increases x to x_1 because it shifts the $EG = 0$ curve to the right.

We have just seen that when the market for goods and services does not respond to changes in the interest rate, the money-does-not-matter thesis is theoretically correct. But how realistic is this case? We see that it all depends on investment demand because consumption, and thus savings, are not responsive to the interest rate. In the 1940s and 1950s both econometric research and business surveys were conducted on this issue. For some time it was fashionable to say that changes in the interest rate were a minor concern to the entrepreneur, since other considerations, like uncertainty, were more important in the entrepreneur's decisions. But it was proved that at least one important component of investment demand, residential construction, was very sensitive to changes in the interest rate. That, of course, was enough to invalidate this special case. Better empirical research conducted later has

FIGURE 6-44

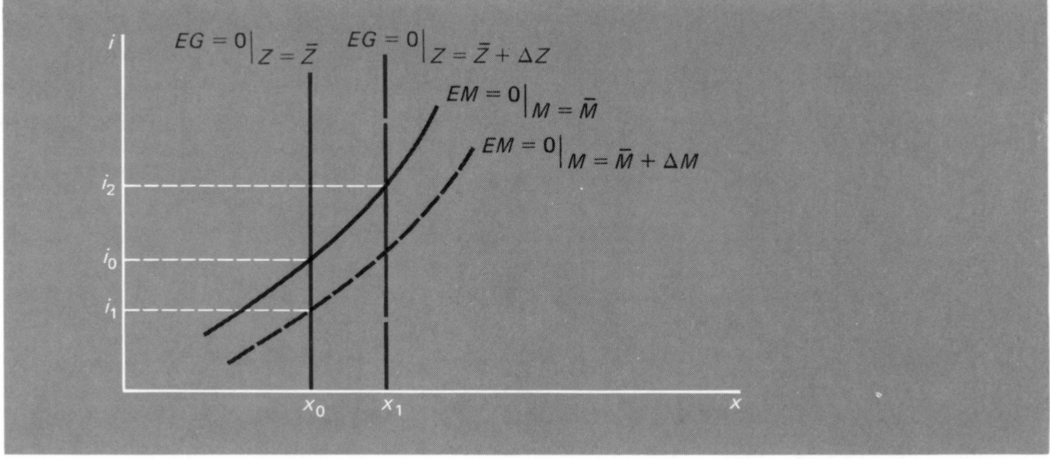

shown that nonresidential construction is also sensitive to the interest rate. Thus the special case above cannot be a guide to the policy maker as an operating rule; it is no more realistic than the interest inelasticity of the excess demand for money.

Another special case, the liquidity trap, produces the theoretical result that money does not matter. In this case an increase in the money supply fails to lower the interest rate and, therefore, effects an immediate short-circuit. With no change in the interest rate, there cannot be an increase in aggregate demand, even when it is responsive to the interest rate. In this case only the tail of the $EM = 0$ curve moves to the right, as shown in Figure 6-45. The result here is that only a shift in the $EG = 0$ curve can change x, as shown in Figure 6-46.

FIGURE 6-45

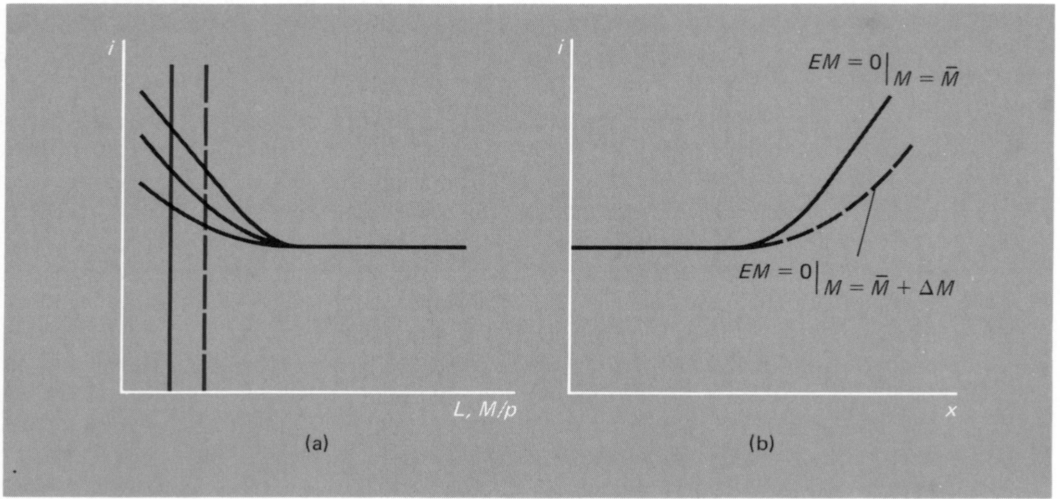

FIGURE 6-46

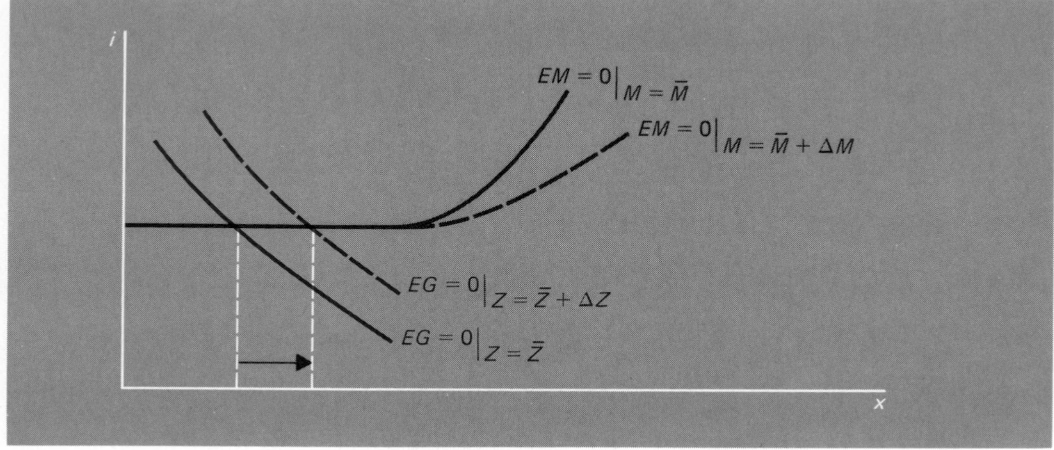

To understand the concept of the "liquidity trap," or "absolute liquidity preference," we must briefly sketch a theory of the demand for money, which we shall discuss in great detail in Chapter 13. According to the *General Theory,* money is an alternative to only one other asset, a (perpetual) government bond whose price, P_B, is the capitalized value of the perpetual "coupon," c, that it yields (i.e., $P_B = c/i$). It follows, therefore, that the price of a bond is inversely related to the interest rate: Higher bond prices correspond to lower interest rates and vice versa. Also, according to this theory, individual wealth holders (investors) form expectations about the (nominal) price level of bonds, which means that as the price reaches higher levels, more and more individuals expect it to fall. Of course, if the price of bonds falls, those who hold the bonds suffer capital losses. Therefore, as the price of bonds reaches sufficiently high levels and hence sufficiently low interest-rate levels, there is virtual unanimity that the bond price will fall. In this case all investors will want to hold all their wealth in the "safer" asset, namely, in money. In this sense the liquidity preference is absolute, that is, its elasticity is infinite.

This special and limiting case was introduced by Keynes solely to add scientific completeness to his analysis. However, he hastened to add in the same paragraph:

> But whilst this limiting case might become practically important in future, I know of no example of it hitherto. Indeed, owing to the unwillingness of most monetary authorities to deal boldly in debts of long term, there has not been much opportunity for a test. Moreover, if such a situation were to arise, it would mean that the public authority itself could borrow through the banking system on an unlimited scale at a nominal rate of interest.[6]

Because of this passage, the profession has not been willing to accept Friedman's assertion that Keynes examined *only* the case of "absolute liquidity preference" in his book.[7] It has become clear that Keynes dismissed the liquidity trap as unrealistic, since he placed so much importance on an activist *monetary* policy.

THE NEWEST VERSION OF ONLY-MONEY-MATTERS: CROWDING OUT

As we have seen, the claim that only money matters is true only when the demand for money is absolutely interest-inelastic. (Strictly speaking, only when both the demand for and the supply of money are absolutely inelastic.) In Chapter 13 we shall see that the empirical evidence is overwhelmingly in favor of the proposition that the demand for money is negatively related to the interest rate, a proposition that forces us to dismiss the only-money-matters thesis. On the other hand, the only-fiscal-policy-matters thesis is correct if either the aggregate demand for goods and

[6] J. M. Keynes, *The General Theory of Employment, Interest and Money* (New York: Harcourt, Brace & Co., 1936), p. 207.

[7] Milton Friedman, "A Theoretical Framework for Monetary Analysis," *Journal of Political Economy,* March/April 1970.

services is interest-inelastic or the demand for money is perfectly, or absolutely, elastic. But the empirical evidence (presented in Chapter 12) rejects the first condition. On the other hand, we shall see in Chapter 13 that the liquidity trap is not supported by the sophisticated empirical evidence of today, just as it was not supported by the casual empiricism of Keynes in 1936. Nonetheless, until the mid-1960s there was a controversy between "Keynesians" and "quantity theorists," or newly called monetarists, based precisely on the magnitudes of the interest elasticities. Since then, however, the monetarists have abandoned their reliance on the interest inelasticity of the demand for money, relying instead on the concept of "crowding out" and also claiming that Keynes and the Keynesians assume a perfectly elastic demand for money.

An early version of the crowding out argument, used mainly in the 1960s and since abandoned, relied on whether the increased government expenditure purchased goods that are valued by individuals or not. If they are valued by individuals, the private sector will diminish *its* expenditure by the same amount that the government increases its own. The following was a favorite example of that time: If the government buys one million dollars worth of toothpaste and distributes it, the population will decrease its own demand for toothpaste by the same amount, and there will be no net increase in aggregate demand. If, on the other hand, the government spends on items that are not valued by individuals or are useless, such as on war, the individuals will not, according to this argument, diminish their own wars by the same amount. Therefore, in this second case, there will be a net addition to aggregate demand for goods and services and hence an effect on income and employment.

In the late 1960s, during all of the 1970s, and into the 1980s the crowding out argument took a more sophisticated turn, relying on the government budget restraint (GBR), which was formally introduced in 1968 by Carl Christ.[8] The GBR states simply that all government expenditures, G, must be financed by taxes, T; or by issuing new money, which in real terms is $\Delta M/p$; or by issuing new government bonds, whose real value is $\Delta B/p$; or by a combination of all three:

$$G = T + \frac{\Delta M}{p} + \frac{\Delta B}{p}$$

To highlight the government budget deficit, $Z = G - T$, we can rewrite this equation as (1):

$$Z = \frac{\Delta M}{p} + \frac{\Delta B}{p} \tag{1}$$

It is clear from (1) that if the entire government budget deficit is financed by creating money (i.e., if $\Delta B \equiv 0$), we have

$$Z = \frac{\Delta M}{p} \tag{2}$$

[8] See Carl Christ, "On Fiscal and Monetary Policies and the Government Budget Restraint," *American Economic Review,* 1979, pp. 526–38.

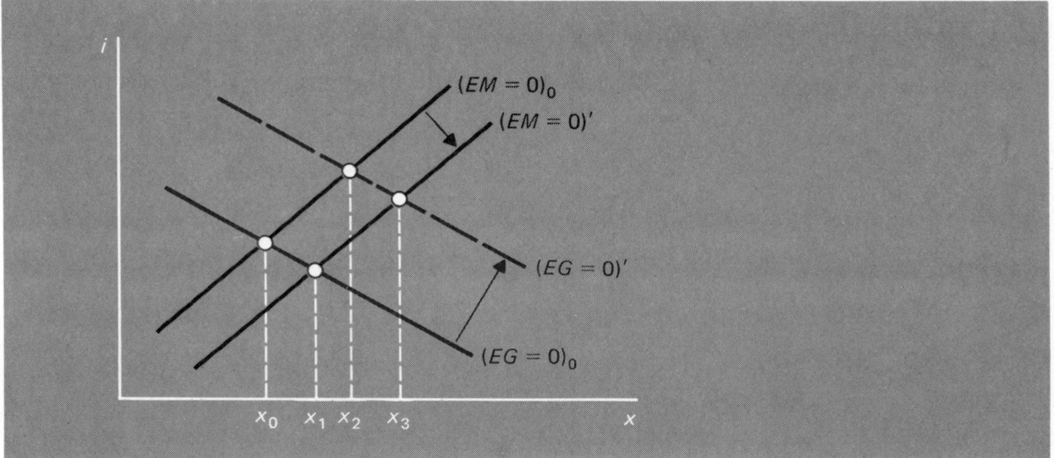

FIGURE 6-47

In this case, depicted in Figure 6-47, the change in the deficit shifts both the $EM = 0$ curve and the $EG = 0$ curve to the right. And it follows that this type of "fiscal policy" is more effective than the fiscal policy we examined previously. Instead of the employment level x_2, which is attained in the typical case, we now get x_3. Note that x_3 is higher than the employment level x_1, which emanates from a simple and pure monetary policy. These results are accepted universally. However, the monetarists claim that if the entire deficit is bond-financed, that is, if $\Delta M \equiv 0$, and hence if

$$Z = \frac{\Delta B}{p}, \tag{3}$$

government borrowing competes with private borrowing, thereby raising the interest rate enough to wipe out exactly the original increased government expenditure. It turns out that there is a circumstance under which this monetarist position is valid, namely, if the demand for (and supply of) money is independent of the interest rate. But since the demand for money is indeed interest-elastic, and since the monetarists themselves have abandoned such a claim,[9] it follows that the claim of crowding out must depend on some other argument.

This other argument, we shall see, relies on wealth effects: When new bonds are floated (created by the government), the wealth of individuals $(K + M/p + B/p)$, is increased, which, in turn, increases the demand for all assets, including money, thereby shifting the $EM = 0$ curve to the left, from $(EM = 0)_0$ to $(EM = 0)'$. Hence this bond-financed increase in the deficit has two effects: first, a shift of the $EG = 0$ curve to the right, say from $(EG = 0)_0$ to $(EG = 0)_1$, as in Figure 6-48;

[9] See Milton Friedman, *The Optimum Quantity of Money* (Chicago: Aldine, 1967), pp. 141–55.

and, second, a shift of the $EM = 0$ curve to the left, say from $(EM = 0)_0$ to $(EM = 0)_1$, as in Figure 6-48. In the case depicted in Figure 6-48 the crowding out is incomplete. The secondary effect merely reduces the original increase in x, from x_0 to x_1, by the distance x_1x_2, but it does not eliminate it entirely. Of course, the proponents of monetarism believe that the secondary effect is such that x_2 coincides with x_0, and that the secondary effect exactly negates the first-round effect, as in Figure 6-49.

In a seminal paper Blinder and Solow challenged this latest monetarist proposition.[10] In effect, they checkmated the monetarists by showing that the condi-

FIGURE 6-48

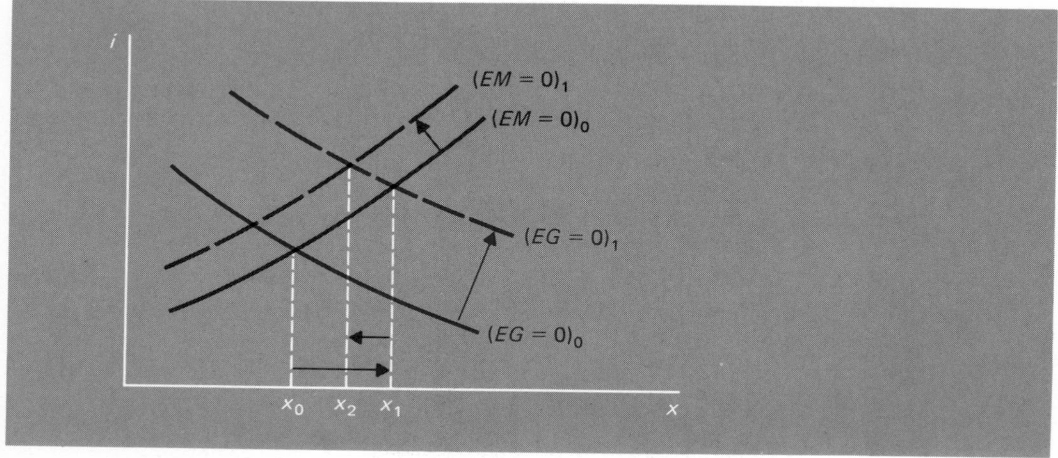

FIGURE 6-49

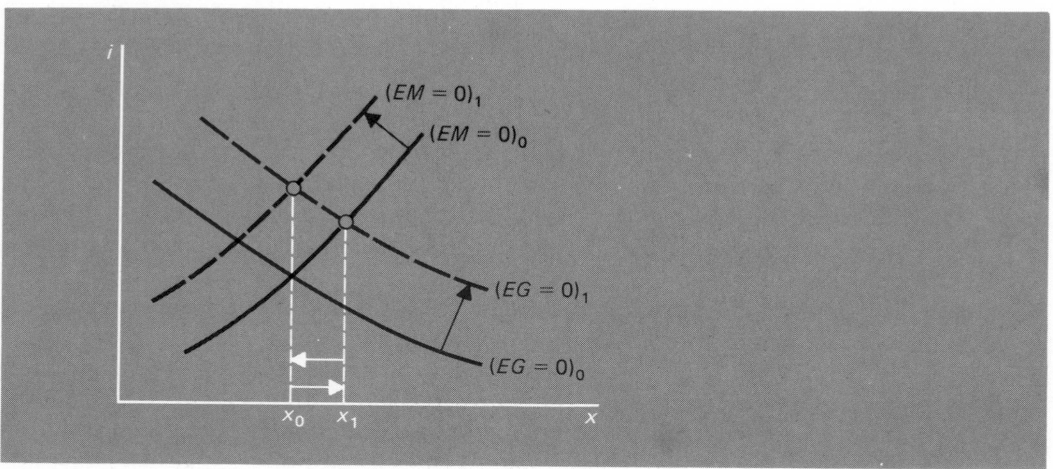

[10] A. S. Blinder and R. M. Solow, "Does Fiscal Policy Matter?" *Journal of Public Economics,* November 1973, pp. 319–37.

tions that guarantee complete crowding out will destabilize the economy; on the other hand, if the economy is indeed stable, as observed in the real world, complete crowding out cannot occur.

The reader of this section must have noticed that the $EG = 0$ and $EM = 0$ curves have been drawn under the tentative assumption of a given, a parametric price level. In fact, the Blinder-Solow paper, with its accompanying graphs, had this drawback. Subsequent work by many economists, which is dispassionately summarized (and extended) by Carl Christ,[11] has shown that this basic dilemma posed by Blinder and Solow still holds even when we allow for the full effects of an endogenously determined price level. On the other hand, a government deficit financed by other means, say by creation of money, does *not* destabilize the economic system.

QUESTIONS

1. Under what conditions is an increase in the budget deficit the only way to increase employment? Under what conditions will only an increase in the money supply do the job?
2. Rising interest rates can be the sign of either contractionary or expansionary policy or no deliberate policy at all. Explain.
3. How would you explain a situation where both the interest rate and employment were rising? How would your explanation change if both the interest rate and employment were falling?
4. Use the markets for automobiles and automobile tires (complements) to show graphically and explain verbally the distinction between partial and general equilibrium analysis.
5. Comment: "We know that the $\Delta x = 0$ curve (the *IS* curve) must be downward sloping in the $(i,x,)$-plane, since the system is unstable if this is not true."
6. On the one hand, by the "Keynesian real balance effect" a rise in the price level lowers employment. On the other hand, the "Keynesian employment adjustment mechanism" states that a rise in the price level induces an increase in employment. Explain the apparent paradox.
7. In using fiscal or trade policy to combat unemployment, how important is the marginal propensity to spend (in particular, whether it is less than or greater than one)?
8. Comment: "How can we expect to use fiscal or trade policy to combat unemployment when the direction of the policies' effect depends on the relative slopes of the $EG = 0$ and $EM = 0$ curves?"
9. Comment: "Whether we use expansionary monetary policy or expansionary fiscal policy doesn't really matter, since both increase employment." How do your comments change if the marginal propensity to spend is greater than one?

[11] See footnote 8.

10. Expansionary fiscal policy directly increases aggregate demand. But the fiscal policy also raises the interest rate, thereby reducing aggregate demand. Explain verbally why the direct effect of the policy on employment outweighs the indirect effect.

REFERENCES

BLINDER, A. S., AND R. M. SOLOW, "Does Fiscal Policy Matter?" *Journal of Public Economics,* November 1973, pp. 319–37.

CHRIST, CARL, "On Fiscal and Monetary Policies and the Government Budget Restraint," *American Economic Review,* 1979, pp. 526–38.

FRIEDMAN, MILTON, "The Demand for Money—Some Theoretical and Empirical Results," *Journal of Political Economy,* June 1959, pp. 327–51.

———, "A Theoretical Framework for Monetary Analysis," *Journal of Political Economy,* March/April 1970.

HANSEN, ALVIN H., *A Guide to Keynes.* New York: McGraw-Hill, 1953.

HICKS, J. R., *The Crisis in Keynesian Economics.* New York: Basic Books, 1974.

———, "Mr. Keynes and the Classics," *Econometrica,* April 1937, pp. 147–59.

———, *Value and Capital.* London: Oxford, 1938, 1946.

KEYNES, J. M., *The General Theory of Employment, Interest and Money,* Chaps. 14 and 16. Harcourt, Brace & Co., 1936.

MODIGLIANI, FRANCO, "Liquidity Preference and the Theory of Interest and Money," *Econometrica,* January 1944, pp. 45–88.

"A Symposium on Friedman's Theoretical Framework," *Journal of Political Economy,* September/October 1972, pp. 837–950.

Money Wages and Employment

7

In this chapter we examine the rationality of fixed money wages, noting that inelastic price expectations may be the underlying factor. Prolonged periods of unemployment may, however, modify these expectations and thus persuade workers to accept money-wage cuts. This chapter, which is patterned after and updates Keynes' Chapter 19, entitled "Changes in Money-Wages," shows that in the absence of deflationary expectations, money-wage flexibility will eventually lead the economy to full employment. However, if deflationary expectations are formed during this period, the whole system may collapse. This phenomenon explains Keynes' own fear of "depression psychology" and his advocacy of an *activist* monetary and fiscal policy over a do-nothing policy, that is, waiting for the emergence of money-wage flexibility as a tool to fight recessions. And it is this advocacy of activist economic policies that is the hallmark of Keynesian economics.

I. REALISM AND RATIONALITY OF MONEY-WAGE INFLEXIBILITY

In the preceding two chapters we assumed that the money wage is fixed. Keynes, up to his Chapter 18, made this same assumption. In Chapter 19, however, he relaxed this assumption by permitting money-wage cuts. We have already found two reasons for the preliminary assumption of fixed money wages. First, since Keynes wanted to permit, in principle, unemployment, he thought it natural to make an assumption that guaranteed just that. His second reason was based on convenience; by assuming fixed money wages, he argued, we can formally establish that excess demand for goods determines employment, that is, employment increases if, and only if, there is excess demand for goods and services. But now a question arises, Is the assumption of fixed money wages realistic? Do the facts show that workers resist money-wage cuts even if there is unemployment? There is strong evidence that workers do resist money-wage cuts. However, there is also evidence that they accept money-wage cuts after protracted periods of unemployment, but that when they do accept, or even advocate, them, they do so in a desperate effort to avoid the collapse of the business for which they work. During the first two years of the Great Depression, for example, the money wages did not fall even though unemployment escalated 700 percent.

Even if unemployment exists, there are several reasons for the observed downward inflexibility of the money wage; those already unemployed may find it beneficial to accept a money-wage cut, that is, lower wages than those earned by employed workers with similar qualifications. The issue of accepting a money-wage cut by an employed worker becomes operative only if, and when, the worker's employer demands it, because people outside the work force are willing to work for less. Employers are very reluctant, however, to impose wage cuts on these grounds, for the unemployed, who would be willing to work for less, are usually only a small fraction of the number of workers already employed. Why, then, should employers risk troubles with their work force, such as loss of morale, or intentional or unintentional reduction in efficiency?

Many more reasons can be found (and they have been cited by labor economists) for this downward inflexibility of money wages. Still, the economic theorist feels uneasy about the seeming reluctance of workers to accept a cut in their real wage produced by a cut in money wage, whereas they accept such cuts in real wages produced by an increase in the price level. Is this not a display of irrationality? After all, we have seen in the exercise of utility maximization by the worker that the worker's supply is a function of *real* wages, no matter how these real wages are determined or changed. The principle behind the downward inflexibility of the money wage is that the money wage is an independent determinant of the supply of labor. In other words, a worker prefers a real wage with a higher money wage (and price level) over an identical one with lower money wages and prices. For example, a worker may not be indifferent with regard to the following two offers: (a) $W = \$20$ per hour, $p = \$10$ per bushel of corn, and therefore the worker's real wage is $w = 20/10 = 2$ bushels of corn; or (b) $W = \$10$ per hour, $p = \$5$ per bushel of corn, and the worker's real wage is $w = 2$ bushels of corn. The worker will prefer offer (a) even though it yields the same real wage as offer (b). Symbolically, the supply of labor, N^s, can be written as

$$N^s = N^s(W/p, W) \tag{1}$$

with

$$\frac{W}{p}\uparrow \rightarrow N^s\uparrow \quad \text{and} \quad W\uparrow \rightarrow N^s\uparrow$$

Such a supply function of labor was introduced and examined by James Tobin[1] soon after Keynes' *General Theory.* Tobin showed that such behavior by workers is not necessarily irrational. On the contrary, there are circumstances under which the supply function $N^s(W/p, W)$ is rational, whereas $N^s(W/p)$ is not. One should recall that the utility maximization exercise was conducted under the assumption that the two components of real wages, W and p, are expected to remain the same. In fact, the exercise was conducted in the context of a barter economy, with no mention of money wages and prices. But in a monetary economy, the wage bargain—even if it is done for a *real wage*—is struck in terms of money wages. It is therefore in the interest of rational workers to make their money-wage bargain based upon what they expect the price level to be for the duration of the contract.

Suppose, said Tobin, that workers, on the basis of their past experience, expect a given (normal) price level. If it falls temporarily below that level, it will rise, and if it is above that, it will fall. Now, if the price level is below that normal level (presumably because of a slack in aggregate demand and thus in unemployment) and the workers agree to a lower money wage, they are irrational, for they will lose. When the price level rises (as they expect) to the normal level, they are stuck with a *lower* real wage for the duration of the contract. Moreover, if they save a part of their wage income, these savings will be reduced in real values. This behavior is hardly rational. On the contrary, workers should not allow the temporarily low price to confuse them into accepting a lower money wage. This, then, is the explanation, on rational grounds, of the downward inflexibility of the money wage.

In the above example we assumed that the expected (i.e., normal) price level is independent of the current price. In Hicks' terminology, a zero elasticity of price expectations was assumed. But this is not necessary, since the same result holds true as long as the (positive) elasticity of price expectations is less than one. (If $p^e = f[p]$, the elasticity, σ, of price expectations, p^e, is defined as $\sigma \equiv \Delta p^e/\Delta p \cdot p/p^e$.)

An arithmetical example that reproduces cases (a) and (b) above may help our understanding of this issue. Suppose that the money-wage rate was originally $W_0 = \$20$ per hour, the price level was $p_0 = \$10$ per bushel, and therefore the real wage was $w_0 = 2$ bushels (of corn) per hour. In other words, suppose that the original situation is case (a) above. Suppose also that in this original situation the expected price level, p_0^e, is equal to the actual price level, that is, $p_0^e = p_0 = \$10$. Now, suppose that the (actual) price level falls to $p_1 = \$5$. The question that we want to examine is, Will the workers accept a money-wage cut to $W_1 = \$10$, which will keep their real wage at the original level of 2 bushels per hour?

The answer depends on the workers' expectations about the price level. If they expect that the fall in the price level, from \$10 to \$5, is temporary and that in the next period, when the contract is still in operation, the price level will go back to \$10, in other words, if the expected price level *remains* at $p_1^e = \$10$, the workers will not accept *any* money-wage cut—let alone to \$10. In such a case the elasticity

[1] James Tobin, "Money Wage Rates and Unemployment," in *The New Economics,* ed. Seymour E. Harris (New York: Knopf, 1947), pp. 572–87.

of expectations is zero, since $\Delta p = p_1 - p_0 = 5 - 10 = -5$, $(\Delta p/p) = -5/10$, but $\Delta p^e = p_0^e - p_1^e = 10 - 10 = 0$; hence

$$\sigma = \left(\frac{\Delta p^e}{p^e} \Big/ \frac{\Delta p}{p}\right) = -\frac{0}{5/10} = 0$$

But suppose instead that workers do lower their expected price level (from $p_0^e = \$10$) to $p_1^e = \$7$. In this case the percentage reduction in expectations is 30 percent, or $\Delta p^e/p^e = (p_1^e - p_0^e)/p_0^e = (7 - 10)/10 = -3/10$, and the elasticity of expectations is $\sigma = (-3/10)/(-5/10) = 3/5$, which is, of course, less than one. In such a case the workers will accept *some* wage cut, but not a decrease to \$10 an hour—in fact, the decrease would hold at \$14 an hour, a total cut of \$6.

Only when their expected price level falls to $p_1^e = \$5$ will the elasticity of expectations be unity and the workers be willing to accept a money-wage cut to \$10. In other words, only then will they consider the above offers, (a) and (b), equivalent. For then $\Delta p^e/p^e = (5 - 10)/10 = -5/10$, and since $\Delta p/p = -5/10$,

$$\sigma = \left(\frac{\Delta p^e}{p^e} \Big/ \frac{\Delta p}{p}\right) = \frac{5/10}{5/10} = 1$$

In summary, we have seen that as long as workers hold inelastic price expectations, their reluctance to accept money-wage cuts is rational, for the level of the money wage exerts an independent influence on their decision to supply labor.

II. DIRECT VERSUS INDIRECT EFFECTS ON EMPLOYMENT OF MONEY-WAGE CUTS

We are now ready to relax the assumption of fixity of money wage. Suppose that workers do accept money-wage cuts. Will there be an increase in employment? This is the issue that Keynes examined, beginning with his Chapter 19. The issue is crucial. If we prove that the answer to the above question is yes, then we can tie money-wage cuts to unemployment. As long as there are unemployed workers, the money wage will be falling and continually reducing unemployment. Money wages will stop falling only when unemployment is eliminated. This concept has two implications. The first is theoretical: Keynes was able to show unemployment equilibrium only because he assumed money-wage inflexibility. The second implication gives rise to policy consideration: Since a money-wage cut will surely lead the economy to full employment, the policy maker has the option of not using a deliberate policy tool (money or deficit) to eliminate unemployment. In time the problem will correct itself. After all, we know that workers will eventually even volunteer a money-wage cut.

Keynes distinguished sharply between direct and indirect effects of money-wage cuts on employment. The former effect refers to the workers' own actions, that is, whether or not the workers can increase their own employment by accepting money-wage cuts. Keynes maintained that there was no method available to labor to increase employment; a fall in money wages does not, by itself, imply a fall in real wages. If real wages do not fall, the profit-maximizing firms will not increase their demand for labor. The indirect effects work through other markets via falling prices of goods and services.

DIRECT EFFECT

Keynes claimed that a fall in money wages will not directly increase employment because it will cause an equiproportionate fall in prices. Let us examine his explanation more carefully. Recall that Keynes went out of his way to attack the capitalistic system only on its own territory. The assumption of pure competition is, of course, a cornerstone of capitalism. It would have been easy for him to prove the existence of unemployment in the presence of imperfections in product and labor markets. Had he done so, however, his attack would have lost most of its effectiveness, and it might even have been dismissed. After all, most good economists blamed these imperfections for the existing unemployment. The assumption of pure competition guarantees that marginal cost equals marginal revenue, which, in turn, equals price. On the other hand, the *short run* is defined as a period during which the economy's capital stock is fixed. Thus we have only one variable factor of production. It follows that a fall in wages (the reward of the only variable factor) will cause an equiproportionate fall in marginal costs and thus the price level, that is, $\Delta W/W = \Delta p/p$. But we know that employers hire labor until its marginal product is equal to the real wage, $MP_N = W/p$, or

$$\Delta x \gtreqless 0 \quad \text{when} \quad \frac{\Delta p}{p} \gtreqless \frac{\Delta W}{W} \tag{2}$$

It follows that $\Delta x = 0$. Thus x cannot change because of the fall, $\Delta W/W$, in the money wage. The fall in money wages does not imply a fall in the real wage. Workers, then, are powerless in their effort to increase their employment by accepting money-wage cuts.

Tobin observed that when there are two or more variable factors of production, the above result may not hold. In particular, if these other factors did not accept cuts in their rewards while labor did, the unemployment of workers would be reduced because labor would be substituted for the other factors. The Keynesian result is valid only when the other factors competitively reduce their own rewards whenever labor accepts a wage cut. It should be pointed out, however, that this is a natural assumption to make; according to Tobin's own analysis, these other factors should behave like labor. If the workers move away from inelastic price expectations and, therefore, accept money-wage cuts, we should expect the other factors to behave similarly. So Tobin's point reinforces, rather than weakens, the Keynesian thesis. In summary, Keynes stated that if workers have inelastic price expectations, they are right in refusing money-wage cuts. On the other hand, if they do accept a cut, this, *by itself,* cannot reduce unemployment.

INDIRECT EFFECTS

Keynes was the first to notice that a fall in wages will, in general, increase employment indirectly. For this to happen, a way must be found to enable the price level to fall less than the wage level.

(i) Via trade

The fall in wages will tend to lower prices equiproportionately. But this fall in prices makes this country's goods more competitive in the international market. The balance of trade becomes more favorable, thereby increasing the aggregate demand for goods and services. This increase in aggregate demand will definitely arrest the fall in prices. Thus, if prices ultimately fall, they will not fall as much as wages. There will be a reduction in real wages, which will stimulate the demand by firms for labor and reduce unemployment. Keynes cautioned, however, that we cannot and should not rely on this method because other countries, at whose expense our employment increases, might retaliate by following a beggar-thy-neighbor policy of lowering *their* wages and prices. In such a case any gains in employment might be eradicated. This indirect trade effect, preceding such a retaliation, is shown graphically in Figure 7-1 with a shift of the *IS* curve to the right.

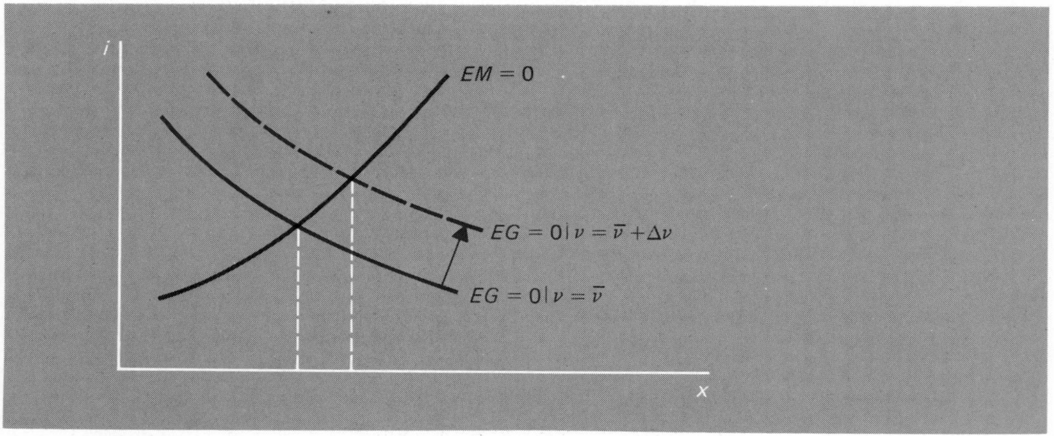

FIGURE 7-1

(ii) Via interest rate: Keynes' real balance effect

The fall in prices, caused by the money-wage cut, increases the real supply of money. This lowers the interest rate, which, in turn, stimulates aggregate demand by increasing both investment and consumption. This increase in aggregate demand arrests the decline in prices, that is, the price level cannot fall proportionately as much as the money wage. Therefore the real wage falls and encourages an increase in the demand for labor by the profit-maximizing firms. Schematically,

$$W\downarrow \rightarrow p\downarrow \rightarrow \frac{\overline{M}}{p}\uparrow \rightarrow i\downarrow \rightarrow (C+I)\uparrow \rightarrow EG\uparrow \rightarrow p\uparrow \rightarrow \frac{W}{p}\downarrow \rightarrow x\uparrow$$

This reduction in the interest rate caused by the fall in prices is uniquely Keynesian, and it has since been called the "Keynesian real balance effect." The term *Keynesian* is added to distinguish it from another real balance effect to be introduced later. We can show these results diagrammatically in the (i,x)-plane. Recall that there is one $EM = 0$ curve for each price level (for a given nominal money supply), and that the higher the price level, the farther to the left the curve lies. Thus the lower price level, induced by a wage cut, will shift the $EM = 0$ curve to the right, as shown in Figure 7-2. The end result is that x rises and i falls. (Of course, since we have not yet provided a way to determine prices, we cannot say at exactly what level prices will be, that is, which $EM = 0$ curve we shall finally end up with. Later in this chapter, we shall remedy this defect.)

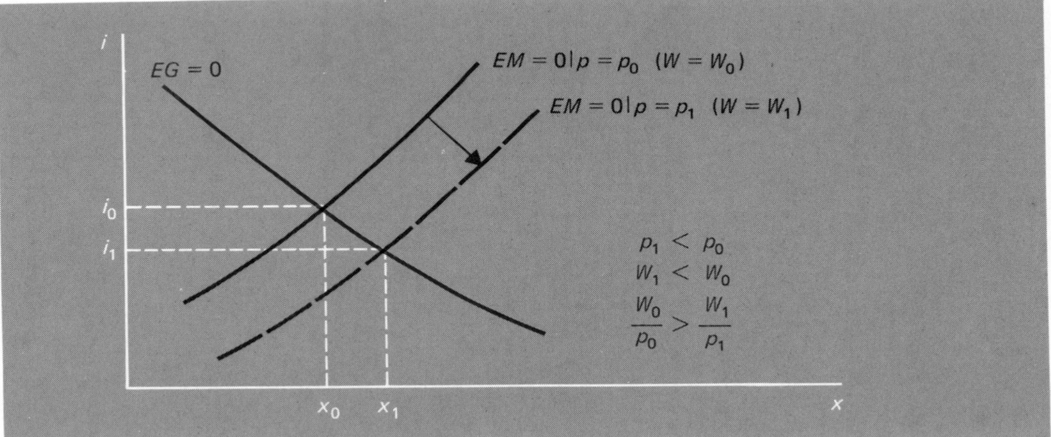

FIGURE 7-2

The above analysis shows that a fall in money wages will increase employment. What we need, then, is a mechanism capable of triggering such a fall in the money wage. We can achieve this by introducing the *money-wage adjustment mechanism,* according to which the money wage falls when there is excess supply of labor, $x - \bar{v} < 0$ (i.e., when there is unemployment); rises when there is excess demand for labor, $x - \bar{v} > 0$; and remains unchanged only when there is zero excess demand or excess supply of labor, $x - \bar{v} = 0$. Schematically, the money-wage adjustment mechanism is captured by (3):

$$\Delta W \gtreqless 0 \quad \text{when} \quad x - \bar{v} \gtreqless 0 \tag{3}$$

The information contained in (3) is embodied in Figure 7-3, where the horizontal axis denotes excess demand or excess supply of labor while the vertical axis measures the *percentage* rate of change in money wages, positive or negative, $\Delta W/W$.

It should now be clear that as long as the schema in (3), or its graphic representation, Figure 7-3, is operative, involuntary unemployment cannot exist *at*

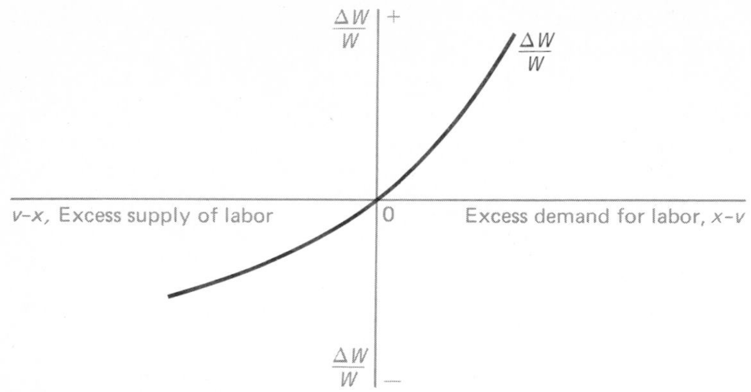

FIGURE 7-3

equilibrium. When there is involuntary unemployment, namely, when $x - \bar{v} < 0$, ΔW should be negative; in other words, as long as there is unemployment, the money wage, W, will be falling. But we have already shown that as long as this happens, the $EM = 0$ curve will, concurrently, keep shifting to the right. It will stop shifting only when $x = \bar{v}$, as shown in Figure 7-4.

As the reader may have guessed, there are two theoretical exceptions to this theoretical result: (a) the interest inelasticity of the excess demand for goods and services and (b) the liquidity trap.

a. *Interest inelasticity of EG.* In this case the Keynesian real balance effect is of no help. The fall in prices, resulting from the fall in money wages, increases real balances and thus lowers the interest rate, but with no increase in aggregate demand. A short circuit develops. Schematically, $W \downarrow \rightarrow p \downarrow \rightarrow M/p \uparrow \rightarrow i \downarrow \nrightarrow EG \uparrow$. This case is shown graphically in Figure 7-5.

FIGURE 7-4

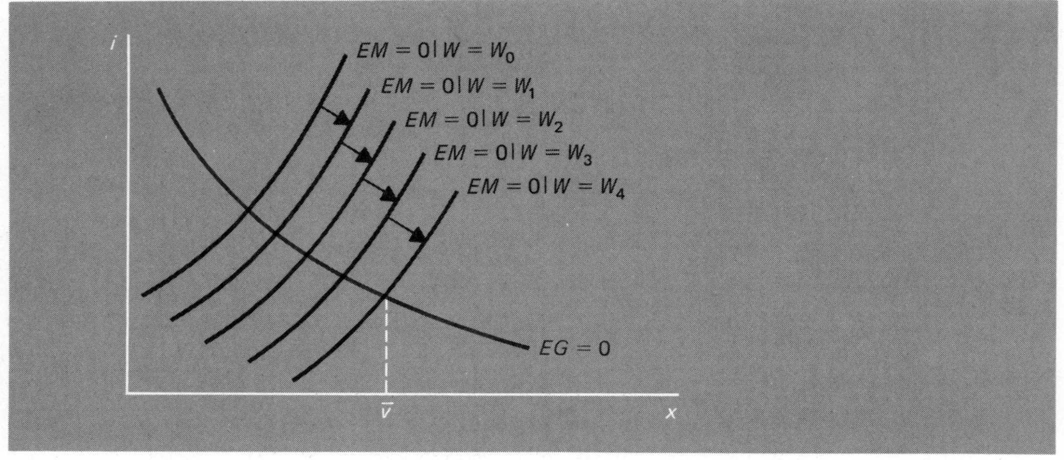

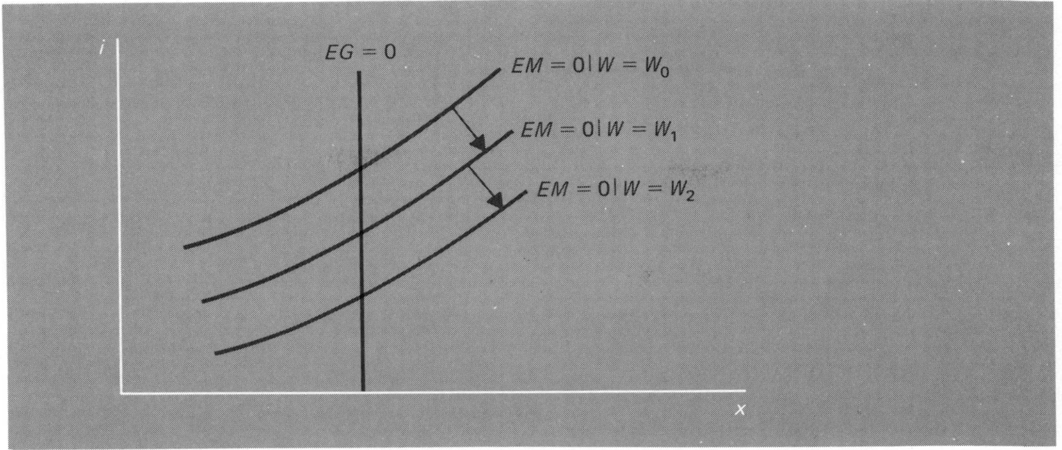

FIGURE 7-5

b. *Liquidity trap.* In this case the short circuit appears earlier. The money demanders absorb the increase in real balances without a fall in the interest rate: $W \downarrow \rightarrow p \downarrow \rightarrow M/p \uparrow \nrightarrow i \downarrow$. Keynes, naturally, discounted both these cases. They are theoretical *curiosa* and Keynes had no use for them, since he was mostly interested in developing operating rules for the policy maker. But if Keynes excluded these two cases, why did he stubbornly refuse to accept that full employment could be achieved without an activist monetary and fiscal policy? Why did he refuse to encourage money-wage flexibility, which, as we have seen, leads the economy to full employment? In fact, he seems to encourage downward inflexibility of money wages.[2]

(iii) Via the Pigou real balance effect

The two special theoretical cases, perfect elasticity of excess demand for money and zero elasticity of the excess demand for goods, prevent the system from attaining, in principle, a full-employment equilibrium. It is at this point, and for these reasons, that several economists sought another way by which a fall in prices from a money-wage cut could increase employment, even in the presence of the above two special cases. In our schematic presentation the question is, Since a short circuit may develop, either at stage ④ or stage ⑤, can we introduce another wire, as it were, to bypass the problem areas?

$$① \; W\downarrow \rightarrow ② \; p\downarrow \rightarrow ③ \; \frac{M}{p}\uparrow \nrightarrow ④ \; i\downarrow \nrightarrow ⑤ \; EG\uparrow \rightarrow ⑥ \; x\uparrow$$

In the above schema we connected stage ③ or ② with ⑤. A fall in prices (which implies an increase in real balances) increases aggregate demand, even if the interest

[2] Franco Modigliani emphasizes these two problems in his classic "Liquidity Preference and the Theory of Interest and Money," *Econometrica,* January 1944, pp. 45–88.

rate does not fall. This system is analogous to a standby generator, prepared to take over in case of a failure in either stage (4) or stage (5).

We must now try to establish a negative relationship between the price level and aggregate demand without relying upon its effects on the interest rate. One of the components of aggregate demand is consumption, and it is on this, or on its mirror image, savings, that economists have concentrated their efforts. There are at least two ways by which one can establish the negative relationship between consumption demand and the price level. Both modify the assumption underlying the consumption function. Recall that consumption was found to depend on the interest rate, output, and wealth. The country's real wealth is its physical capital. However, from the standpoint of individuals, wealth has two components, physical capital plus government assets, in particular, the quantity of money in real terms. Thus wealth is

$$\omega = K + \frac{M}{p}$$

The first component on the right-hand side is nonmonetary and the second is monetary wealth. If interest-bearing debt were examined, the monetary, or financial, component would include the real value of this debt. Thus the consumption function can be written as

$$C(Y, i, K + M/p)$$

or in per unit of physical capital (with the latter set equal to unity):

$$c(x, i, M/p)$$

An increase in wealth, *for a given output,* increases consumption. Therefore a fall in the price level increases real wealth by increasing its monetary component, and this, in turn, increases consumption demand. This is how the relationship is established.

Traditionally the relationship has been established using the savings function. In this case, what we need to show is an increase in savings if the price level increases for a given output:

$$S = \tilde{S}(Y, i, \omega) = \tilde{S}(Y, i, K + M/p)$$

or

$$\frac{S}{K} = \tilde{S}(Y/K,\ i,\ 1 + M/pK)$$

or, by setting $K = 1$:

$$S = S(i, x, M/p)$$

To establish a positive relationship between savings and the price level, we need a negative relationship between savings and wealth for a given level of output (i.e., $\omega\uparrow \rightarrow S\downarrow$). The scenario is as follows: Intertemporal maximization induces individuals to desire a target level of wealth. This same maximization tells them at what rate they should accumulate wealth to optimally reach the target. The closer they are to the target, the lower the rate of their accumulation. But other things being equal, they can accumulate wealth only by saving. This means that the closer they are to their target wealth, that is, the higher their level of wealth is, the lower their rate of saving. (This is precisely what we discovered in Chapter 2.) Now, if the price level rises, part of their wealth, namely the monetary component, shrinks, and they are forced to save at a higher level. This is how the positive relationship between savings and the price level is established. Several economists—Pigou, Haberler, Scitovsky, and Tobin—introduced this relationship at about the same time.[3] This effect is now called the *Pigou effect* partly because, at the theoretical level, Pigou is exonerated from the Keynesian accusations. Note that Pigou was considered the chief living victim of the Keynesian analysis.

It is worth sketching another approach briefly to prove the direct link between a fall in the price level and an increase in aggregate demand. This one is attributed to Tobin.[4] Recall (see equation (1)) that Keynes' analysis amounted to stipulating the labor supply function as

$$N^s(W/p, W), \quad \text{with} \quad \frac{W}{p}\uparrow \rightarrow N^s\uparrow \quad \text{and} \quad W\uparrow \rightarrow N^s\uparrow$$

Tobin also proved that this is consistent with an assumption that workers exhibit inelastic price expectations. Now it is natural to assume that workers, as demanders for goods and services, behave in a manner consistent with their attitudes as suppliers of labor. Of course, their real wages are their real income, and their money wages are their money income. Thus their consumption function is $C_w(W/p, W)$, where the subscript w is inserted to identify this as the consumption for workers. For the economy as a whole, whether or not the owners of other factors behave like the workers, the consumption function should be $C(Y, pY)$. The first argument is real income (output), and the second is money income. An increase in real income, given the price level, increases consumption, that is, $Y\uparrow \rightarrow C\uparrow$, as in the earlier analysis. But an increase in money income, given output, should *decrease* consumption, that is, $(pY)\uparrow \rightarrow C\downarrow$. Why? Because an increase in money income, with real income given, can come about only if the price level rises. But since inelastic expectations are assumed, the price level is expected either to fall or to rise less in the future. This induces consumers to curtail some of their consumption demand now in order to buy more later. Moreover,

[3] A. C. Pigou, "The Classical Stationary State," *Economic Journal,* December 1943, pp. 343–51; "Economic Progress in a Stable Environment," *Economica,* 1947, pp. 180–90; and G. Haberler, *Prosperity and Depression,* 3rd ed. (Geneva: League of Nations, 1941), pp. 242, 389, 403, 491–503.

[4] Tobin, "Money Wage Rates and Unemployment."

their real wealth is estimated at a lower level now than in the future because today's high price level shrinks their real balances.

Since consumption, as well as savings, depends on the price level, there is an infinity of savings curves in the (i,S)-plane, even with a given x, as shown in Figure 7-6. Similarly, there is an infinity of S curves in the (x,S)-plane, one for each p (with given i). As p increases, the S curve shifts to the left, as in Figure 7-7.

When we derived our $EG = 0$ curve, it was for a given price level. If the price level rises, the $EG = 0$ curve will shift to the left, if it is downward sloping, because for each different interest rate the S curves shift to the left, as shown in Figure 7-8. On the other hand, it can easily be shown that if the $EG = 0$ curve is positively sloped, the increase in p will shift the curve to the right, as in Figure 7-9. If $EG = 0$ is vertical, then it shifts to the left. (See Figure 7-10.)

We are now ready to show that even with interest inelasticity of aggregate demand for goods or with perfect elasticity of excess demand for money, a fall in prices, induced by a money-wage cut, will increase employment. The first case is shown in Figure 7-11. The case of liquidity trap is shown in Figure 7-12.

FIGURE 7-6

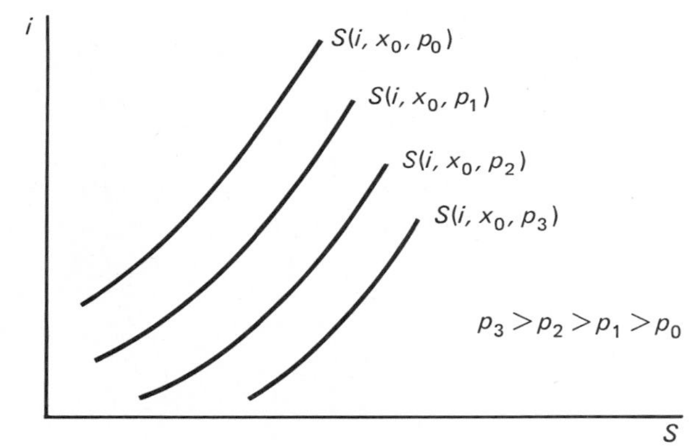

FIGURE 7-7

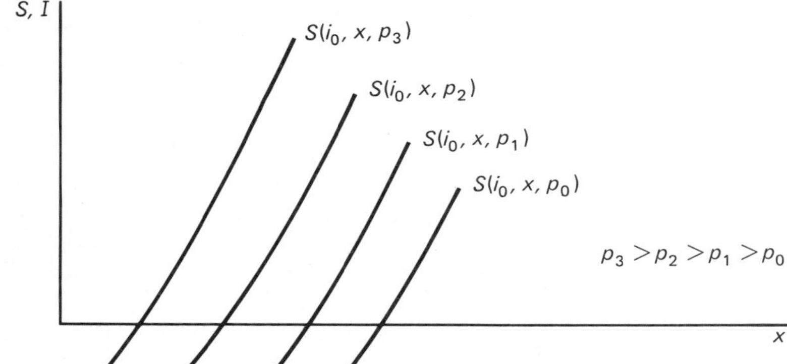

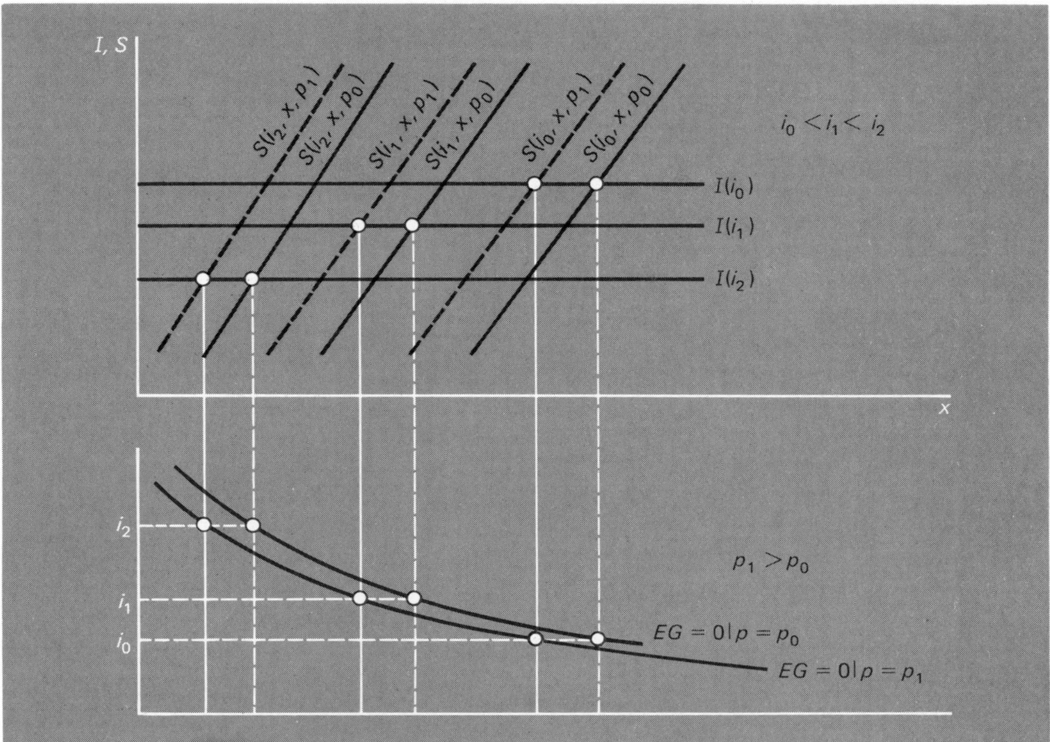

FIGURE 7-8

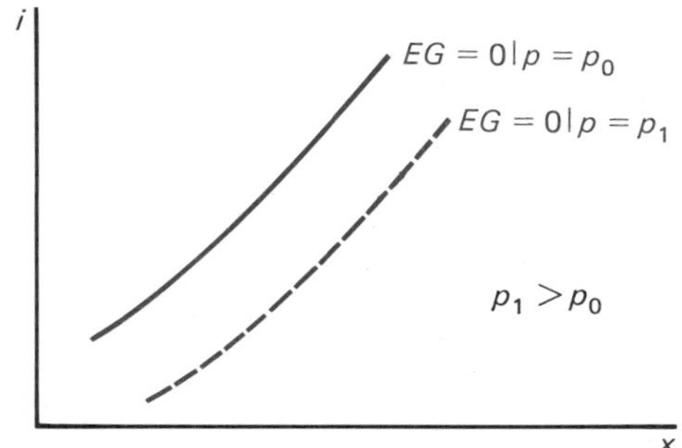

FIGURE 7-9

We can thus claim that as long as money-wage flexibility exists, full-employment equilibrium can be established whether or not liquidity trap or interest inelasticity of aggregate demand exists. It should be emphasized, however, that even the strongest proponents of the Pigou effect do not realistically expect it to make much difference. The fall in prices needed to raise wealth and aggregate demand sufficiently might be exorbitant. But as an answer to the special cases, it will do, since liquidity trap and interest inelasticity of aggregate demand are unrealistic cases also.

FIGURE 7-10

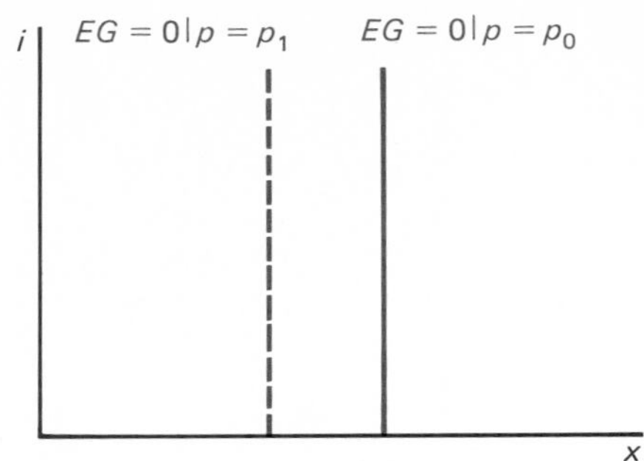

FIGURE 7-11

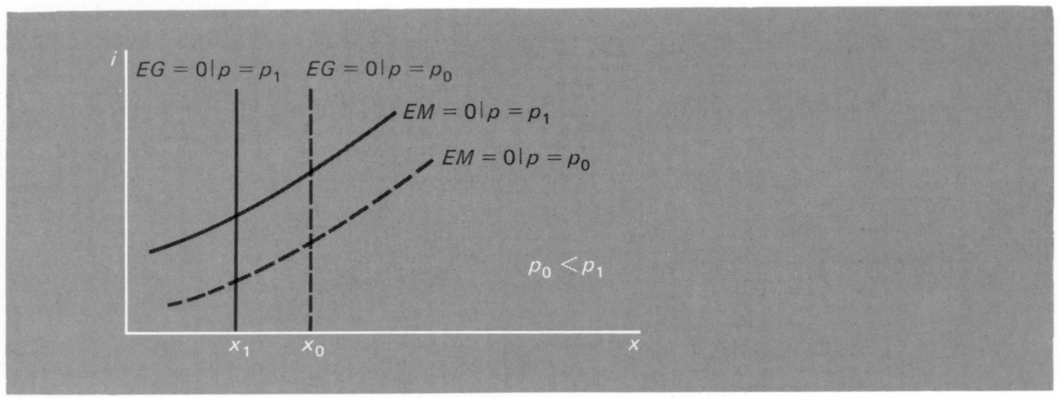

FIGURE 7-12

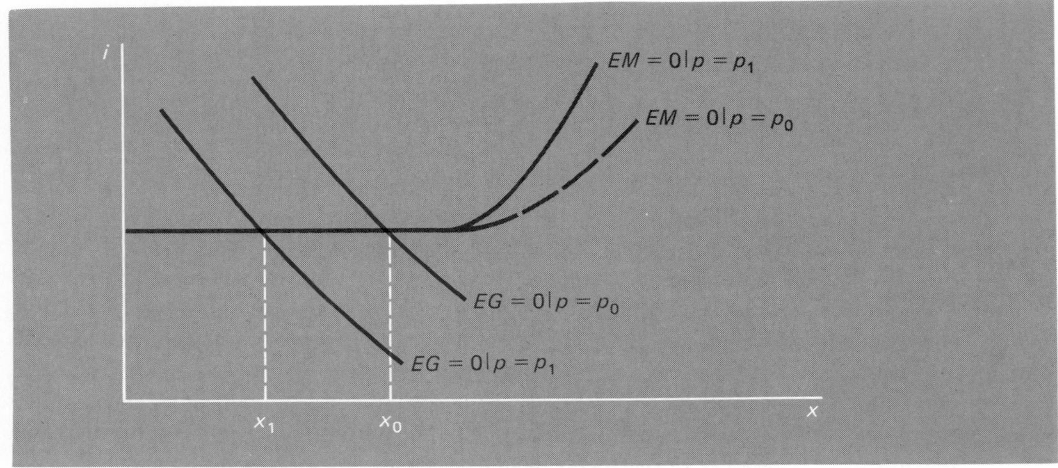

III. MONEY-WAGE FLEXIBILITY AS A POLICY TOOL?

We have established that, in general, money-wage flexibility will lead the economy to full employment. On the other hand, we know that even if workers initially refuse a money-wage cut, they eventually not only will accept it but also will even initiate it. After substantial and protracted unemployment, they face, on the one hand, stiffer competition by the unemployed, who are willing to work for less, and on the other, the possibility of cost-cutting measures by their employer, who is seeking to continue in business. Thus, in order to save their jobs, the workers themselves volunteer money-wage cuts. It follows that, given sufficient time, money-wage flexibility emerges.

The important question is whether we can, or should, rely on the emergence, sooner or later, of money-wage flexibility to safely lead the economy to full employment. If we can, then this is an option available to the policy maker, an option to do nothing rather than pursue an activist monetary and fiscal policy. We can call this a policy of benign neglect, or the let-them-bleed approach, or even the let-them-twist-slowly,-slowly-in-the-wind approach. Keynes argued strongly against such a policy. Is it because he had not examined the Pigou effect? Certainly not. Keynes could not be impressed by this argument. He himself discounted the special cases of liquidity trap and interest inelasticity of investment demand. He considered them irrelevant for the policy maker. He could hardly be impressed by an argument designed to eliminate these cases theoretically when he himself had already eliminated them on realistic grounds.

We must infer that Keynes discounted even his own real balance effect as a way of increasing employment. We can observe that a decrease in the price level shifts the $EM = 0$ curve to the right, in exactly the same way that an increase in the nominal money supply would, with a given price level. However, Keynes preferred the latter, the activist approach, to increasing employment. He said:

> While a flexible wage policy and a flexible money policy come, analytically, to the same thing, inasmuch as they are alternative means of changing the quantity of money in terms of wage-units (i.e., in real terms) in other respects there is, of course, *a world of difference between them.*[5]

In fact, he argues in favor of using both policies, fiscal as well as monetary, to make sure that we can get full employment.

For many reasons Keynes discouraged money-wage flexibility as a policy. First, he maintained, it will take time for workers to be persuaded, through their suffering, to accept money-wage cuts. In the beginning, they fight it and thereby cause social upheaval. This is hardly the environment for economic recovery. Is it not better to achieve the same increase in real balances by increasing the nominal money supply, rather than by cutting prices because of lower wages? Or as Keynes said:

[5] J. M. Keynes, *The General Theory of Employment, Interest and Money* (New York: Harcourt Brace & Co., 1936), p. 267, italics added.

Having regard to human nature and our institutions, it can only be a foolish person who would prefer a flexible wage policy to a flexible money policy, unless he can point to advantages from the former which are not obtainable from the latter.[6]

The major reason why Keynes did not accept money-wage flexibility as an implication of his own analysis is that the analysis itself is still incomplete. Substantial and prolonged wage and price cuts require a dynamic analysis, the crucial feature of which should be the formation of expectations. The analysis, so far, really assumes that the price cuts, caused by wage cuts, are unexpected.

But how long can they remain unexpected? Sooner or later people would begin taking them into consideration; they would start to count on them. If this is so, we have to distinguish between the real rate of interest and the nominal rate. It is the real rate of interest that enters the calculations of firms in their decisions to invest. The same is true of the decisions of savers. On the other hand, it is the nominal interest that matters in the demand for real balances because this is the opportunity cost of holding money. The real rate of interest, i_r, is determined by subtracting the expected rate of change in prices from the nominal rate. But the rate of change in prices is negative; thus the real rate is greater than the nominal rate:

$$i_r = i - (\Delta p/p)^e \quad \text{where} \quad (\Delta p/p)^e < 0$$

For the same nominal interest rate, it follows that there is an infinity of savings and investment schedules, one for each possible level of expectations. Thus, when price cuts come to be expected, the $EG = 0$ curve will shift to the left, possibly negating any beneficial effects that the rightward move of the $EM = 0$ curve might have as is illustrated in Figure 7–13.

This deflationary expectations effect was crucial in Keynes' calculations. It persuaded him to reject money-wage flexibility as a guide to policy. This deflationary expectations effect, it should be noted, could easily negate any beneficial Pigou effect. In other words, the potential shift of the $EG = 0$ curve to the right, because of the Pigou effect, is outweighed by a larger shift to the left. This appears to be why Keynes did not examine the Pigou effect in detail, although he mentioned it.

It is worth pursuing the deflationary expectations effect a little further at this moment. We can show that deflationary expectations, caused by downward wage flexibility, could *create* a liquidity trap where there was none. This is a devastating blow to wage flexibility as a policy tool. The argument can be shown more clearly when we use the real rate of interest, i_r, on the vertical axis, rather than the nominal i. We shall examine the case where neither liquidity trap nor interest inelasticity of aggregate demand exists, thereby precluding the introduction of the Pigou effect. Since excess demand for goods and services depends on the real rate of interest, a change in expectations does not shift the $EG = 0$ curve. On the other hand, since the demand for real balances depends on the nominal rate of interest, a fall in expecta-

[6] Ibid., p. 268.

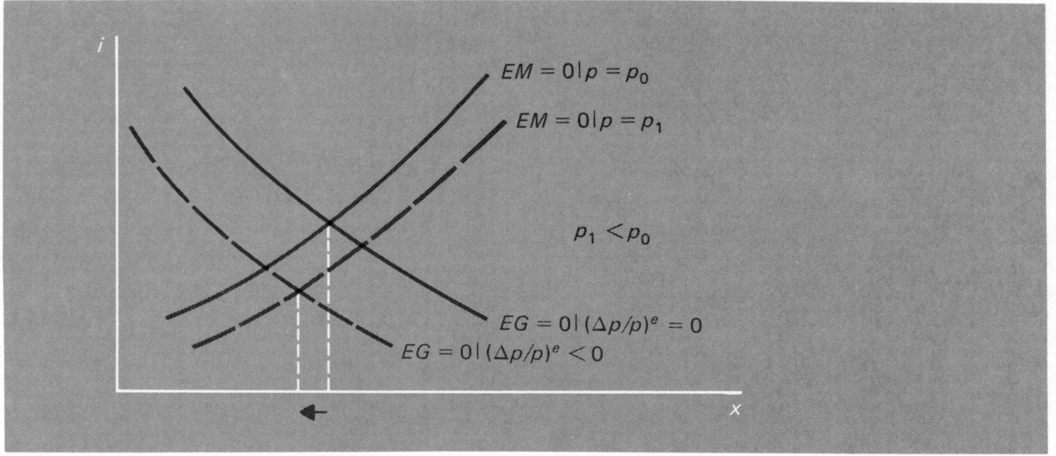

FIGURE 7-13

tions will shift the $EM = 0$ curve to the left, with a vertical displacement exactly equal to the fall in expectations. We already know that, assuming the absence of the special cases and given the absence of expectations, price-wage flexibility will guarantee full employment. Let us suppose that the wage and price level that ensures full employment gives us the $EM = 0|(\Delta p/p)^e = 0$ curve, as denoted in the graph in Figure 7-14. This curve is for zero expected deflation. Suppose now that deflation is equal to a certain negative number. The $EM = 0$ curve shifts to the left with a vertical distance exactly equal to the absolute value of that number. This formation of deflationary expectations lowers employment to $\bar{x}$. Of course, a further fall in prices could shift the $EM = 0|(\Delta p/p)^e < 0$ curve to the right. But it cannot shift enough to cut the $EG = 0$ curve at the point A, or further southeast. Thus there is an upper ceiling to employment equal to $\bar{\bar{x}}$. The curve cannot fall below point A

FIGURE 7-14

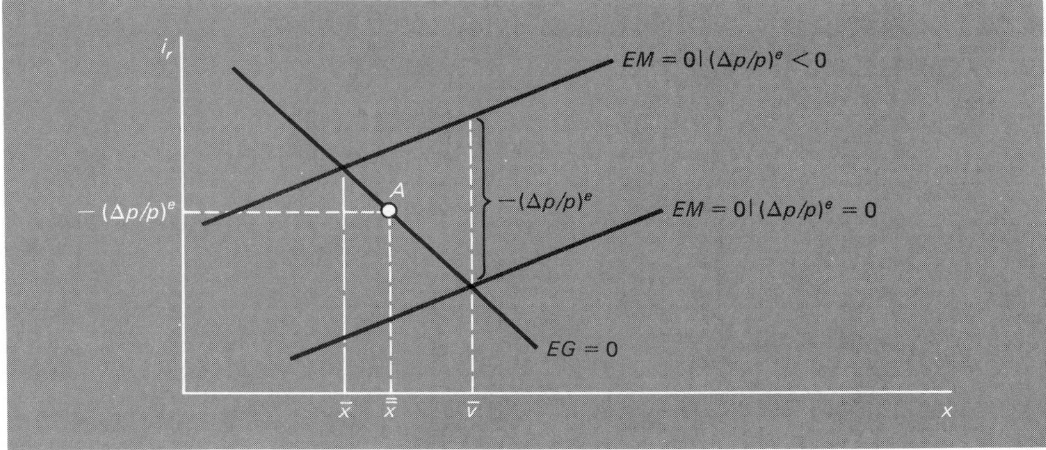

because, in a monetary economy, the nominal rate of interest cannot become zero, or negative. Thus

$$i = i_r + (\Delta p/p)^e > 0,$$

from which it follows that the real rate of interest cannot be less than the rate of *de*flation, $i_r > -(\Delta p/p)^e$. The ceiling on employment, $\bar{\bar{x}}$, is a reflection of the floor on the real rate of interest, $i_r = -(\Delta p/p)^e$. Of course, this is the essence of the liquidity trap: i_r, the rate of return on physical assets, is equal to the rate of return on real balances, $-(\Delta p/p)^e$. In other words, at this point the two assets are perfect substitutes. Note that, if prices *do* fall, the situation will become even worse because deflationary expectations will be reinforced.

In summary, we have seen that there are forces to bring the economy to full employment, just as the neoclassical economists had assumed, *provided* that no expectations are formed. If expectations are indeed formed, it is quite possible that increasing recession may ensue. It is the fear of such an eventuality that persuaded Keynes to advocate *activist* economic policies, be they fiscal or monetary policies. And the *hallmark* of *Keynesian* (or neo-Keynesian) economics is the advocacy of an activist economic policy. In Chapters 9 and 10 we shall see that monetarists are against the idea of an activist economic policy, be it monetary or fiscal. And we shall see that the controversy of whether to pursue an activist policy or not by far overshadows the controversy, which we explored in Chapter 6, of whether to use monetary as opposed to fiscal policy.

IV. MONEY-WAGE FLEXIBILITY AND THE PHILLIPS CURVE

In the early post-Keynesian literature, the eventually emerging money-wage flexibility, which is captured by the schema in (3) and Figure 7-3, was utilized to prove that the economy will gravitate toward full employment if we ignore expectations. A generation later, the same wage adjustment mechanism was utilized to explain the observed negative relation between money-wage inflation and the unemployment rate. The original explanation for this relationship also ignored expectations.

To see how the two issues are related, let us examine the money-wage adjustment mechanism of (3) in greater detail. First, we rewrite (3) in terms of percentage changes (rather than simply absolute changes) in money wages:

$$\frac{\Delta W}{W} \gtreqless 0 \quad \text{when} \quad x - v \gtreqless 0 \tag{4}$$

Now, unemployment, u, is the difference between the supply of labor, v, and the demand, x, that is, $u = v - x = -(x - v)$. We can utilize this definition to restate the mechanism of (4) in a way that highlights unemployment, u. This is achieved by rewriting (4) as (5):

$$\frac{\Delta W}{W} \gtreqless 0 \quad \text{when} \quad -u \gtreqless 0 \tag{5}$$

This schema states that when there is unemployment (i.e., $u > 0$), money-wage *de*flation results (i.e., $\Delta W/W < 0$), while money-wage *in*flation ($\Delta W/W > 0$) is the result of negative unemployment, $u < 0$. Only when unemployment is zero will money-wage inflation be zero.

Of course, zero involuntary unemployment does not mean zero actual, observed unemployment. From our earlier analysis (Chapter 1), we know that, depending on the prevailing wage, some people choose to be unemployed because they decide to consume their time as leisure. Moreover, others are unemployed because they are "between jobs"—even though there are enough unfilled vacancies to employ them all. The percentage of the work force that is unemployed even if there is zero involuntary unemployment is often called the "natural" rate of unemployment. Several other terms are used in the literature. Whatever the term used, we shall denote it by u_* and modify the schema of (5) accordingly:

$$\frac{\Delta W}{W} \gtreqless 0 \quad \text{when} \quad u_* - u \gtreqless 0 \tag{6}$$

Occasionally a single equation is used to capture the spirit of schema (6). Such an equation is (7):

$$\frac{\Delta W}{W} = \alpha \cdot (u_* - u) \tag{7}$$

The thrust of the schema in (6), as well as its explicit, algebraic formulation in (7), is that when the actual, observed rate of unemployment is lower than the natural rate, that is, when $u_* > u$, the money wage rises—we have money-wage *inflation.* In fact, (7) states that the percentage increase in money wages (i.e., money-wage inflation) is proportional to the excess of the natural over the actual unemployment rate. Similarly, the money wage falls when the actual rate is greater than the natural rate. This money-wage *deflation* is, according to (7), proportional to the excess of the actual over the natural unemployment rate. Finally, only when the actual rate of unemployment is equal to the natural one, which means $u_* = u$, is the money wage unchanged.

Diagrammatically, the relation between money-wage inflation or deflation, $\Delta W/W$, and actual, observed unemployment, u, captured by the schema in (6) or the equation in (7), is illustrated in Figure 7-15. The curve intersects the unemployment axis at the natural rate u_*, which signifies that when actual unemployment is at this rate, there is zero money-wage inflation. On the other hand, when observed unemployment is u_0, which is less than the natural rate (i.e., when $u_0 < u_*$), the relevant point on the curve is *A,* with the associated money-wage inflation equal to $(\Delta W/W)_0$. Similarly, we see that point *B* associates actual unemployment u_1 with a wage *de*flation equal to $(\Delta W/W)_1$, since the actual rate is greater than the natural rate (i.e., $u_1 > u_*$).

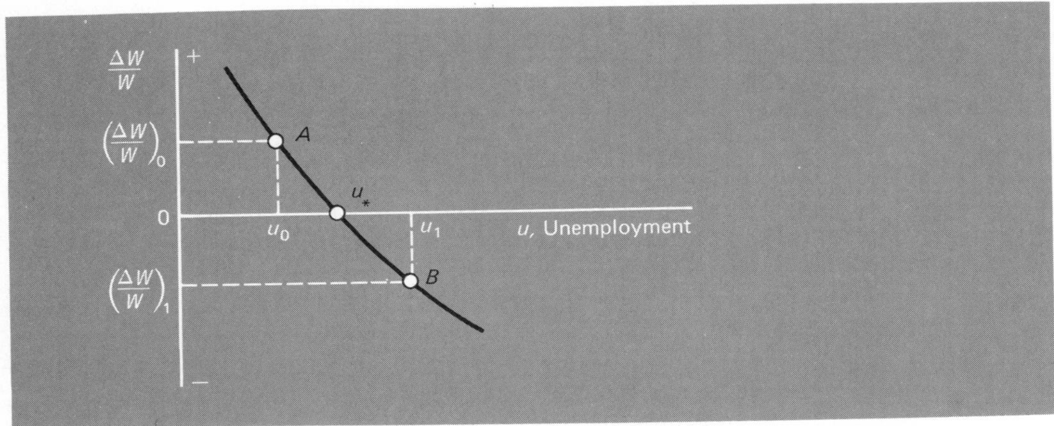

FIGURE 7-15

It is precisely the curve in Figure 7-15 that has been used to explain the negative relation between unemployment and money-wage inflation-deflation that was discovered empirically by A. W. Phillips.[7] Phillips, using British data for the period 1861–1957, concluded that there is such an empirical relation, but he did not provide a theory behind it. Other economists, however, were quick to point out that this relation is not surprising, since it is none other than the money-wage adjustment mechanism.[8] Thus they simply attributed the relation between observed inflation and observed unemployment, which is the end result of a complicated system, to the stipulation that the money wage rises (falls) if, and only if, there is excess demand for (excess supply of) labor. The curve of Figure 7-15 was even named the "Phillips curve" in honor of the presumed discoverer. It is supposed to theoretically generate the empirically observed negative relation between wage inflation and unemployment. This relation will be discussed in detail in Chapter 10.

QUESTIONS

1. Comment on the following:

a. "The introduction of a net Pigou effect precludes unemployment equilibrium due to a rigid money wage."

b. "Keynes and the modern Keynesians assume that both wages and prices are institutionally fixed . . ."

c. "Keynes assumed that the money wage is fixed. This permitted him

[7] A. W. Phillips, "The Relation between Unemployment and the Rate of Change of Money Wage Rates in the United Kingdom, 1861–1957," *Economica,* November 1958, pp. 283–99.

[8] R. G. Lipsey, "The Relationship between Unemployment and the Rate of Change of Money Wage Rates in the United Kingdom, 1862–1957: A Further Analysis," *Economica,* February 1960, pp. 1–41.

to say that employment rises (falls) whenever there is excess demand for (supply of) goods and services."

2. a. When is it true that the (sooner or later) emerging money-wage flexibility will lead the economy to full employment? Can this be used as a guide for economic policy?
   b. Comment on the following statement: "We can increase employment and the price level only if we increase the money supply."
3. Do you agree or disagree with the following statement? Explain. "Governments should not attempt to cure an observed recession. Recessions cure themselves because, in time, workers do accept lower money wages."
4. Distinguish between the direct and indirect effects of money-wage cuts.
5. On the one hand, Keynes emphasized that the interest rate and employment are determined, simultaneously, by both the goods market and the money market. On the other hand, he also emphasized that the goods market determines the employment level. Is there any contradiction in these statements? Explain.
6. Use Hicks' concept of the elasticity of price expectations to explain why workers might rationally refuse money-wage cuts.
7. How is the assumption of pure competition crucial to Keynes' conclusion that money-wage cuts will not directly increase employment? How is this argument changed if there are other variable factors of production?
8. Distinguish between the Pigou effect and the Keynesian real balance effect.
9. Why is the formation of expectations such a crucial element in evaluating the viability of money-wage cuts to increase employment? How is this connected to the argument over the existence of a liquidity trap?
10. Explain: "The empirically observed Phillips curve relationship is merely a reflection of the money-wage adjustment mechanism."

REFERENCES

FRIEDMAN, MILTON, "A Theoretical Framework for Monetary Analysis," *Journal of Political Economy,* March/April 1970, pp. 190–238.

HABERLER, GOTTFRIED, *Prosperity and Depression* (3rd ed.), pp. 242, 389, 403, 491–503. Geneva: League of Nations, 1941.

KEYNES, J. M. *The General Theory of Employment, Interest and Money,* Chap. 19. New York: Harcourt, Brace & Co., 1936.

LIPSEY, R. G., "The Relation between Unemployment and the Rate of Change in Money Wage Rates in the United Kingdom, 1862–1957: A Further Analysis," *Economica,* February 1960, pp. 1–41.

MODIGLIANI, FRANCO, "Liquidity Preference and the Theory of Interest and Money," *Econometrica,* January 1944, pp. 45–88.

PHILLIPS, A. W., "The Relation between Unemployment and the Rate of Change of Money Wage Rates in the United Kingdom, 1861–1957," *Economica,* November 1958, pp. 283–99.

PIGOU, A. C., "The Classical Stationary State," *Economic Journal,* December 1943, pp. 343–51.

———, "Economic Progress in a Stable Environment," *Economica,* 1947, pp. 180–90.

TOBIN, JAMES, "Money Wage Rates and Unemployment," in *The New Economics,* ed. Seymour E. Harris, pp. 572–87. New York: Knopf, 1947.

The Complete Macroeconomic System: determination of prices, employment, interest rate, and wages

In the complete macroeconomic system there are several endogenous variables, that is, magnitudes, that must be determined simultaneously by the system: the interest rate, i; employment (per unit of capital), x; the price level, p; and money wages, W. So far our analysis has been explicit only for the interest rate and employment (or income). Our focus on these two variables, with the concomitant use of the (i,x) or the (i,Y)-plane, was due in part to the importance of the interest rate and employment, and also because of our desire to accommodate the evolution of the standard literature.

Even while concentrating on the interest rate and employment, it became apparent early in the analysis (i.e., Chapter 6) that we not only lacked a framework capable of determining the price level but also were unable to determine the interest rate and employment themselves!

Utilizing Figure 8-1 we can briefly recapitulate the reasons for these shortcomings in our earlier analysis. We know that, among other things, a true equilibrium requires that both the market for goods and services and the market for money be cleared. Graphically, this means that an $EG = 0$, or IS, curve should intersect an $EM = 0$, or LM, curve. However, according to the Keynesian real balance effect, there is an infinity of $EM = 0$ curves, one for each price level, or the higher the price level, the farther to the left the relevant $EM = 0$ curve lies. Moreover, if a Pigou real balance effect is introduced, there is also an infinity of $EG = 0$ curves, or the higher the price level, the farther to the left the relevant $EG = 0$ curve lies.

It follows, therefore, that each assumed price level has a different pair of

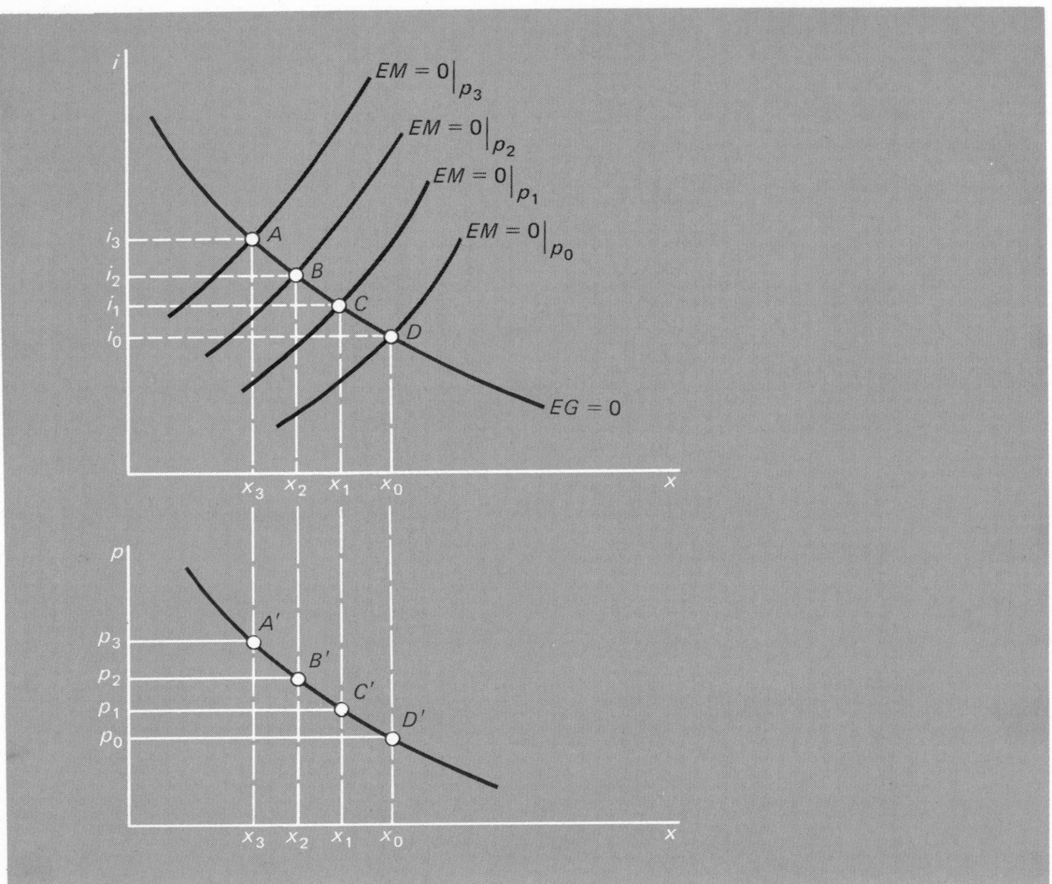

FIGURE 8-1

relevant $EG = 0$ and $EM = 0$ curves, the intersection of which gives a different pair (i,x). For simplicity of exposition, Figure 8-1 excludes a Pigou real balance effect, which, in turn, implies the existence of only one $EG = 0$ curve. However, there are still an infinite number of $EM = 0$ curves because of the Keynes real balance effect. Thus we see in the upper panel of Figure 8-1 that when the price level is equal to p_0, the "equilibrium" levels of i and x are i_0 and x_0, respectively. But when $p = p_1$, the levels are i_1, x_1, and so forth. Therefore, unless we know the price level, we cannot determine the levels of the interest rate and employment. But the price level is one of the unknowns that must be determined. It is imperative, therefore, that we determine the price level if we hope to ever determine all the other variables.

There are other reasons for our interest in actually determining the price level. The first is historical; it has always been accepted that one of the crucial tasks of macroeconomics in general and of monetary theory in particular is to determine the price level. Recall that in the pre-Keynesian period, determination of the price level was the *only* task of macroeconomics, that is, of Volume II of economic theory.

The second important reason for the determination of the price level is its connection with the role of supply; since p is *directly* dependent upon the demand for and supply of goods and services, its determination brings to focus the role of *supply* in the whole macroeconomic scheme. There have been complaints, sometimes justified, that supply has been ignored in the modern macroeconomic structure and in the policy implications of that structure.

And, finally, in modern times the rising price level (i.e., inflation) has been a problem of major concern for governments, as well as for economists. Unless we are able to determine the price level, we cannot possibly monitor its change, that is, we cannot theoretically trace inflation, and we cannot design remedies for inflation.

In what follows we shall establish and then utilize a framework capable of simultaneously determining all endogenous macroeconomic variables, with emphasis on the price level, p; employment, x (and income, Y); the interest rate, i; and money wage, W. While we are still interested in monitoring employment, x (or income, Y), we shall give "equal time," so to speak, to the price level by assigning an axis to it. In other words, we shall examine the whole system in the (p,x)-plane and in the (p, Y)-plane.

In Section I we introduce the general framework. First we derive the "effective demand curve," which depicts all the combinations of prices, p, and employment, x, or income, Y, that the market system can support. Next we introduce the supply, or marginal cost, or productivity, curve, which is consistent with the profit-maximizing behavior of firms. In addition, we identify several "supply-side" factors, such as changes in factor (money) prices, in productivity, and in capacity utilization, as well as changes in tax rates, which are capable of shifting this marginal cost curve.

In Section II we examine the special case of fixed money wages in order to familiarize ourselves with this new technique and also to relate our results to those previously derived. With money wages given, we can determine the other three endogenous variables, a goal we were not able to achieve with our earlier framework. In Section III we determine the price level and *income*, along with the interest rate, in an analysis reminiscent of and consistent with standard price theory, in fact the theory of both the firm and the industry. And, finally, in Section IV we determine all four endogenous variables and also describe their equilibrating mechanism, tracing their dynamic behavior. Furthermore, we confirm our earlier results, especially those in Chapter 7.

I. THE GENERAL FRAMEWORK: EFFECTIVE DEMAND AND SUPPLY

We are searching for an equilibrium that will determine the four endogenous variables, p, x, i, and W. This equilibrium must be full, so that these variables should not exhibit any tendency to move; schematically we should have $\Delta p = 0$, $\Delta x = 0$, $\Delta i = 0$, and $\Delta W = 0$. To keep our analysis from being unnecessarily complicated, we shall continue our earlier assumption that the money market is continuously cleared (i.e., that $EM = 0$), so that we will not have to account for $\Delta i = 0$. We start by deriving a curve that consists of all combinations of prices, p, and employment, x (or prices, p, and income, Y), with zero excess demand for goods and services (and with zero excess demand for money). This curve will be called "the effective demand curve," and it has the property that $\Delta p = 0$.

1. THE EFFECTIVE DEMAND CURVE

We shall employ Figure 8-1 for our derivation of this curve. The upper panel of Figure 8-1 has been drawn under the simplifying assumption of no Pigou effect, which implies that in the (i,x)-plane there is only one $EG = 0$ curve while there is an infinity of $EM = 0$ curves, one for each level of p. Four such curves, corresponding to four different price levels, were drawn in this panel. To translate this information into the (p,x)-plane of the lower panel of Figure 8-1, we proceed as follows: If the price level is p_3, we find the appropriate $EM = 0$ curve. Its intersection with the $EG = 0$ curve at A determines the interest rate at i_3 and employment at x_3. In other words, *if* $p = p_3$, employment is $x = x_3$ and interest is $i = i_3$. And since we are not explicitly concerned with the interest rate, we shall "store" it in our "memory bank" for possible future use. But we do want to *display* x. Thus we translate the information at A into a point A' in the lower panel of Figure 8-1, which gives $x = x_3$ if $p = p_3$.

Note what we have done. Point A gives the information (i_3,x_3,p_3) with (i_3,x_3) displayed explicitly on the two axes and with p_3 implicitly. Point A' gives the same information (i_3,x_3,p_3), but we display explicitly (x_3,p_3) while i_3 is implicit. If at any time in the future we need i_3 (corresponding to $[x_3,p_3]$), we can go back and resurrect it. Note that the use of the expressions "memory bank," "display," and "storing" was deliberate; our approach is analogous to that of the small calculators (or computers for that matter) with memory (storage). What we display on the front panel is not all the information we have, but rather what we need at the moment. We "store" i in the "memory bank" and display (p,x), whereas earlier we stored p and displayed (i,x).

Now, if the price level is lower, say $p = p_2$, we know that the appropriate $EM = 0$ curve must lie to the right of the earlier one. We must find it from its

FIGURE 8-2

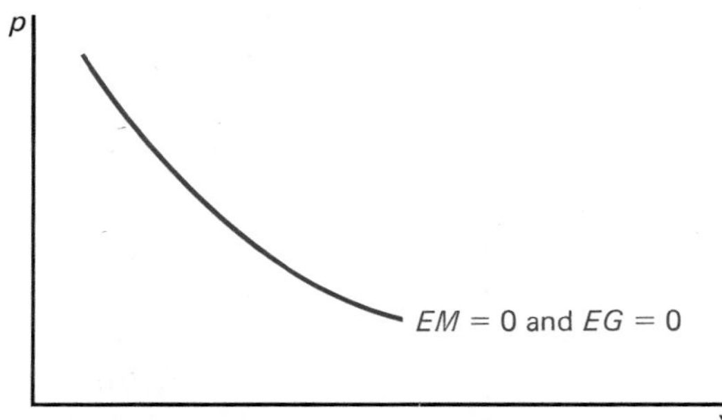

nametag. Its intersection with $EG = 0$ occurs at point *B*, giving the information (i_2, x_2, p_2). We retain (or discard) i_2 and display the information (x_2, p_2) as point *B′* in the lower panel. We repeat the process for all possible price levels and connect the points, such as *A′*, *B′*, *C′*, and *D′*. Thus we have the curve in the lower panel of Figure 8-1.

It is important to know exactly what this curve shows: all the combinations of (p,x) (and, in the background also i) that guarantee that *both* the market for goods and services and the money market are cleared. Therefore we can name the curve the "$EM = 0$ *and* $EG = 0$" curve, as in Figure 8-2. In words, this curve shows, for each price level, what level of employment is allowed by the *market system*. It is truly the *effective demand* curve, which Keynes must have envisioned but never developed. This relation is negative (here) solely because of Keynes' real balance effect, which states that a fall in the price level increases the real balances, thereby decreasing the (money) market-clearing interest rate. The lower interest rate, in turn,

FIGURE 8-3

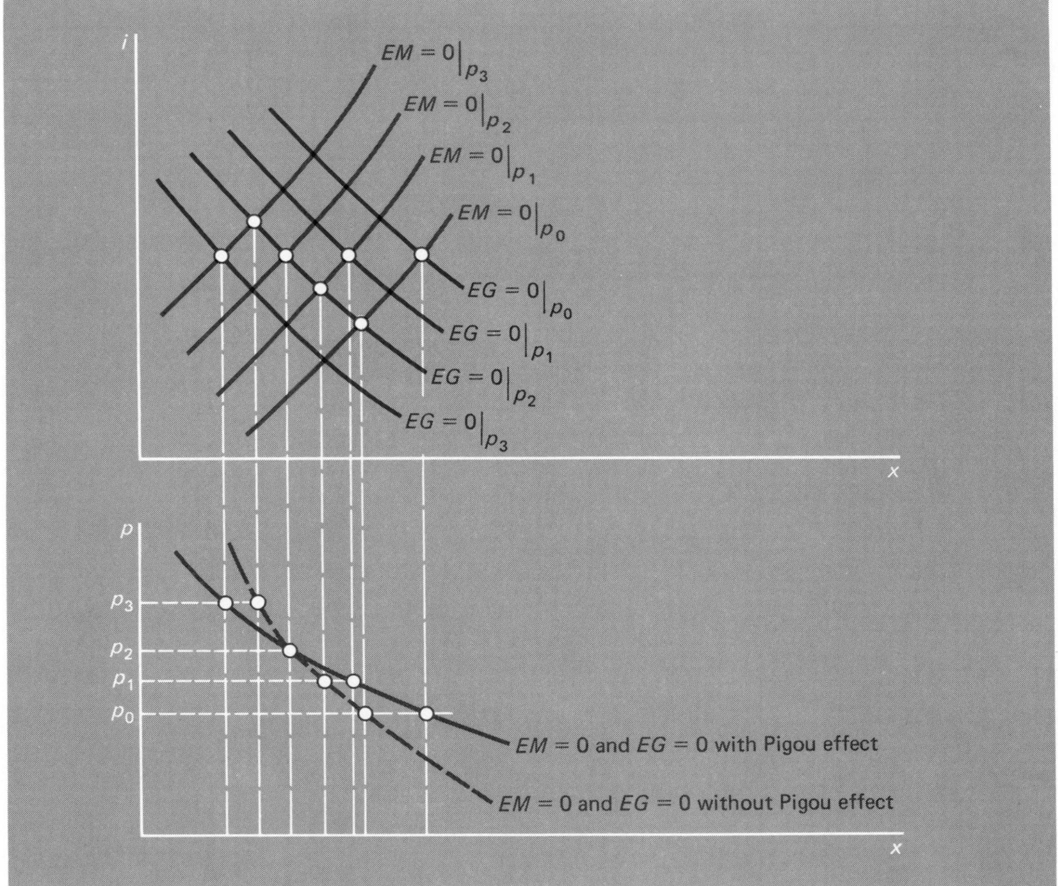

increases the aggregate demand for goods and services, which can be satisfied only by an increase in employment.

Now that we are used to the technique, we may incorporate a "Pigou real balance effect," which means that there is one $EG = 0$, or *IS*, curve for each *p*, and, moreover, that the higher the price level, the farther to the left the relevant $EG = 0$ curve will be. Given a price level, say p_2, we check the nametags and find the appropriate "$EM = 0$ and $EG = 0$" curve, and thus their intersection. We then translate this information in the (p,x)-plane, as we did earlier. We see from Figure 8-3 that the "$EM = 0$ and $EG = 0$" curve, or the effective demand curve, is also downward sloping, the only difference being that, in this case, the curve is flatter than it would be if the Pigou effect were absent. This is also shown in Figure 8-3.

As one would expect, the introduction of a Pigou effect when it is not needed should not make any qualitative difference. A sharp difference, however, occurs when we compare the effective demand curve in the presence and in the absence of a Pigou effect in the two extreme "Keynesian" cases. We examine first the case of interest inelasticity of the $EG = 0$ curve. The derivation of the effective demand curve is depicted in Figure 8-4, which shows that this curve is vertical in the (p,x)-plane, that is, employment is the same, namely $\bar{x}$, no matter what the price level is. The introduction of a Pigou effect transforms this same curve into a downward-sloping one, as shown in Figure 8-5.

The corresponding results in the presence of a liquidity trap are shown in Figures 8-6 and 8-7. First, without a Pigou effect we again get a vertical effective

FIGURE 8-4 INTEREST INELASTICITY OF AGGREGATE DEMAND *WITHOUT* PIGOU EFFECT

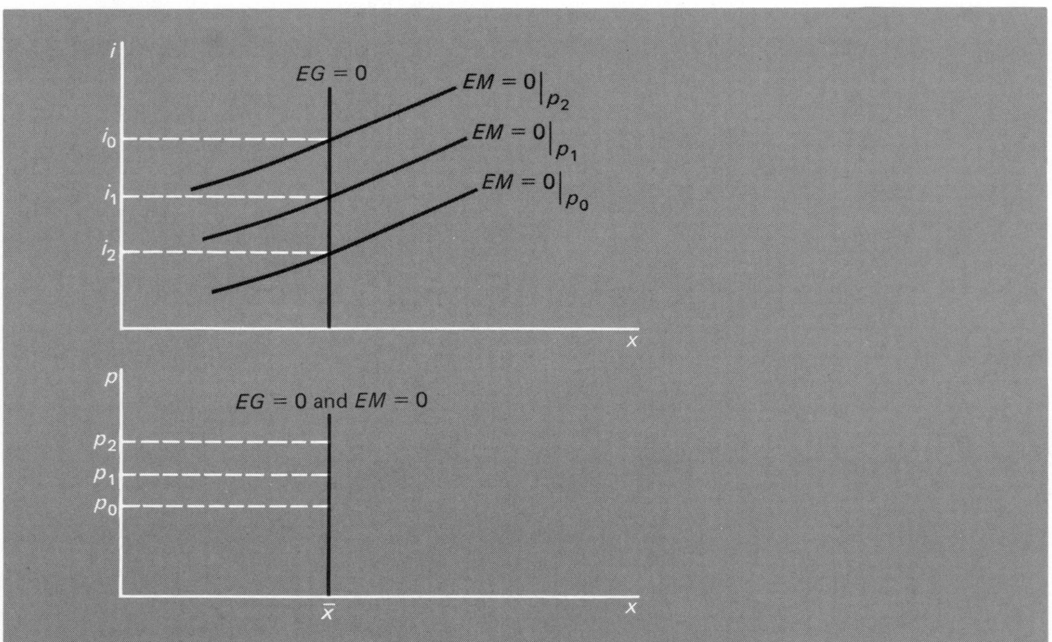

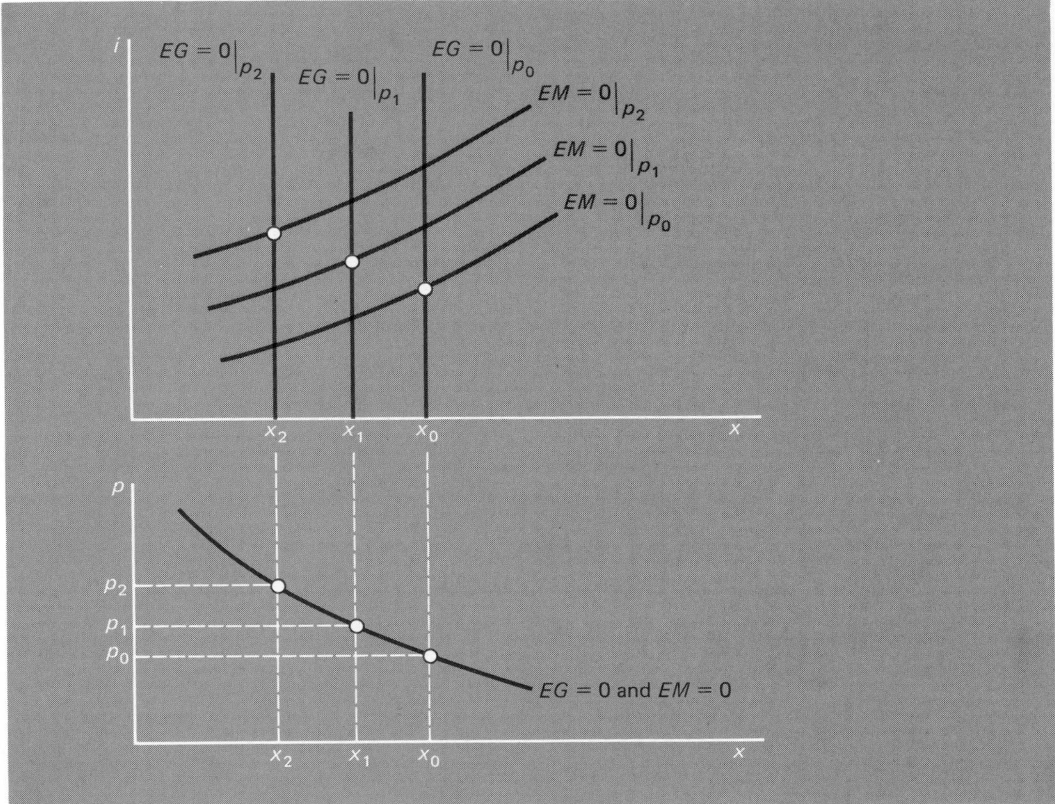

FIGURE 8-5 INTEREST INELASTICITY WITH PIGOU EFFECT

demand curve. A decrease in the price level, even though it increases the supply of real balances, does not lower the interest rate. Thus aggregate demand remains the same and employment cannot increase. However, as in the previous special case, the curve becomes downward sloping when we introduce a Pigou effect. As expected, a reduction in the price level increases real balances, which directly increase consumption and, therefore, increase aggregate demand and employment.[1]

Note also that the extreme "monetarist case" produces a downward-sloping effective demand curve, as shown in Figure 8-8.

Of course, we have another "special" case, namely, that which occurs when the $EG = 0$ curve is upward sloping. This is a far more interesting case than that of the liquidity trap or of the interest inelasticity of the aggregate demand for goods, both of which have little, if any, chance of occurring; on the other hand, marginal

[1] The effective demand curve is downward sloping for an additional reason, even though this reason lies outside our formal analysis: A higher price level increases the nominal income and drives individuals into higher income-tax brackets; this, in turn, reduces their disposable income and, hence, their consumption demand. For more on this issue, see Chapter 10.

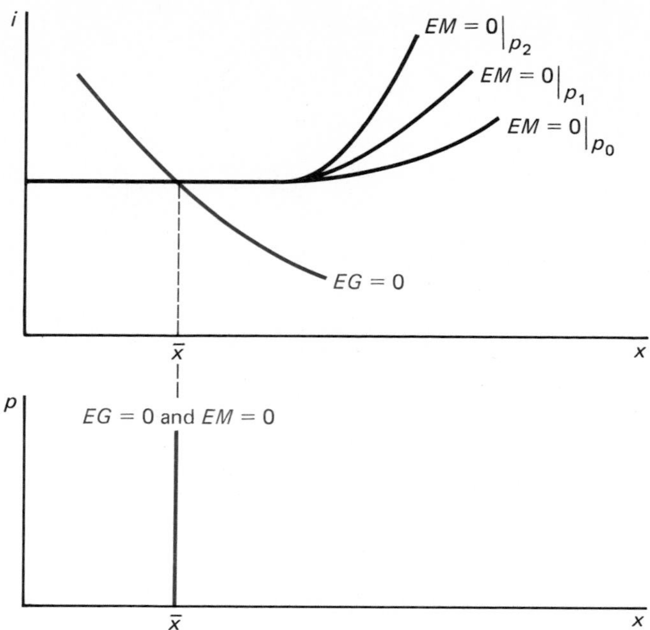

FIGURE 8-6 LIQUIDITY TRAP WITHOUT PIGOU EFFECT

propensity to spend greater than one, the condition for an upward-sloping $EG = 0$ curve, could easily be realized. We see in Figure 8-9 that whether we have a Pigou effect or not, the effective demand curve is downward sloping. Again, when a Pigou effect is permitted, the curve is flatter. Note that Figure 8-9 incorporates only the stable case, that is, when the $EM = 0$ curve is steeper than the $EG = 0$ curve. Also note that an increase in p shifts the $EG = 0$ curve to the right, as was proved earlier. (It is left for the reader to show that the effective demand curve is *upward sloping* when the $EG = 0$ curve is steeper than the $EM = 0$ curve in the $[i,x]$-plane.)

Points off the effective demand curve

We have established that the effective demand curve depicts all the combinations of prices and employment consistent with zero excess demand for goods and services and with zero excess demand for real balances. Now, the question arises, What happens in the two markets if the economy finds itself with a combination of prices and employment giving a point off this curve, in particular a point above and to the right?

Our diagrammatic analysis will be simplified drastically if we assume that one of the two markets clears instantaneously. As we explained in Chapter 4, the speed of adjustment of any market depends on the availability and cost of information. Of course, information is more plentiful and less costly in the highly organized "financial," or money, market than in the goods market, since the goods "market" is really a proxy for a myriad of diverse markets. This is why, in the real world, the money market clears a lot faster than the goods market. We shall go to the extreme, however,

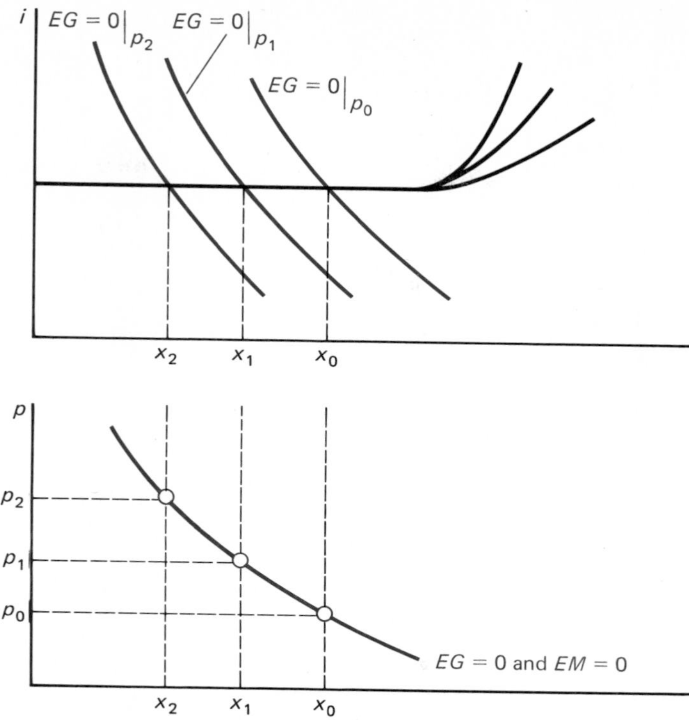

FIGURE 8-7 LIQUIDITY TRAP WITH PIGOU EFFECT

in assuming that the money market not only clears faster than the goods market but, in fact, clears instantaneously. In other words, we shall assume that the interest rate is always at whatever level guarantees clearance of the money market. Graphically, this means that in the *(i,x)*-plane, the economy is *always* on the $EM = 0$ curve. With the above assumption, we shall now prove that to the right of (and above) the "$EM = 0$ and $EG = 0$" curve there is excess supply of goods and services (i.e., $EG < 0$), and that to the left there is excess demand (i.e., $EG > 0$). We should point out that without this assumption of instantaneous clearance of the money market, we would have a situation in which no essential difference in the results would occur, but our analysis would become excessively complicated.

With these assumptions in mind, we begin by taking a point such as *A* in Figure 8-10, which can be reconstructed either as a vertical displacement of point *B* on the curve or as a horizontal movement from *C*. Considering the former, the question reduces itself to one of determining whether excess supply of or excess demand for goods will arise if we increase the price level from p_0 to p_1 while keeping employment the same, at x_0. In order to answer this question, we have to go back to our "memory bank," that is, to the graph from which we have derived our "$EM=0$ and $EG = 0$" curve. This is shown in Figure 8-11, which was drawn without a Pigou effect or any of the special cases.

First, find the point that corresponds to *B*. It must be an intersection of

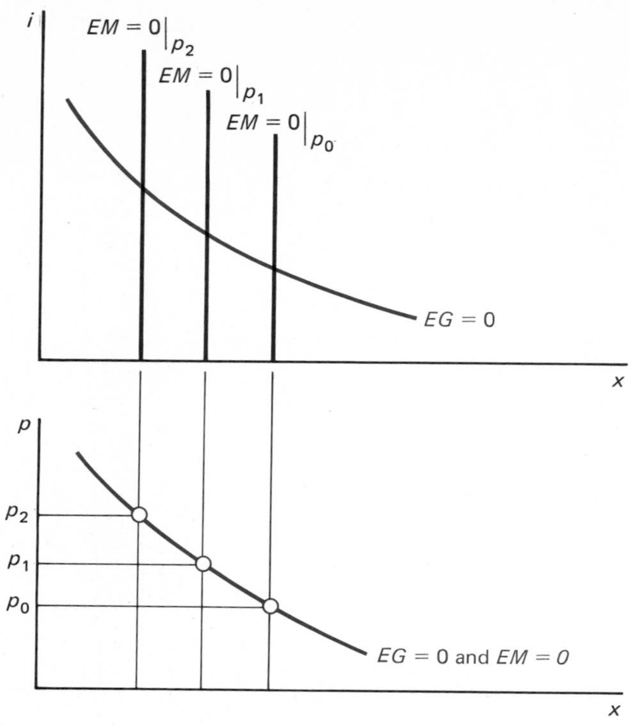

FIGURE 8-8

the $EG = 0$ curve and the $EM = 0|_{p_0}$ curve corresponding to the price level equal to p_0. It is point B' in Figure 8-11. In order to begin to answer the question we posed, we must increase p to p_1 while keeping x equal to x_0. This increase in p shifts the $EM = 0$ curve to the left, giving us the curve labeled $EM = 0|_{p_1}$. And since the money market is always cleared, an increase in p, keeping x constant, takes us to point A'. But point A' is above the $EG = 0$ curve, and we know from our earlier analysis that in this region there is excess supply of goods and services, $EG < 0$. Thus A, which is the mirror image of A', has to show excess supply of goods and services.

With a similar analysis, we can show that below the "$EM = 0$ and $EG = 0$," or effective demand curve, there must be excess demand for goods and services, $EG > 0$. Of course, this result is not surprising; it makes a lot of sense. Starting from a situation with equilibrium in the goods and money markets, an increase in the price level reduces the supply of real balances, thereby raising the interest rate. The increase in the rate of interest reduces aggregate demand for goods and services. Since we started from a situation where aggregate demand was equal to aggregate supply, and the demand fell while the supply remained the same (because x remained the same), it follows that we will end up with excess supply. Of course, if a Pigou effect is present, there is an additional reason for excess supply: The decrease in real balances reduces wealth, which induces increased savings and, therefore, reduced

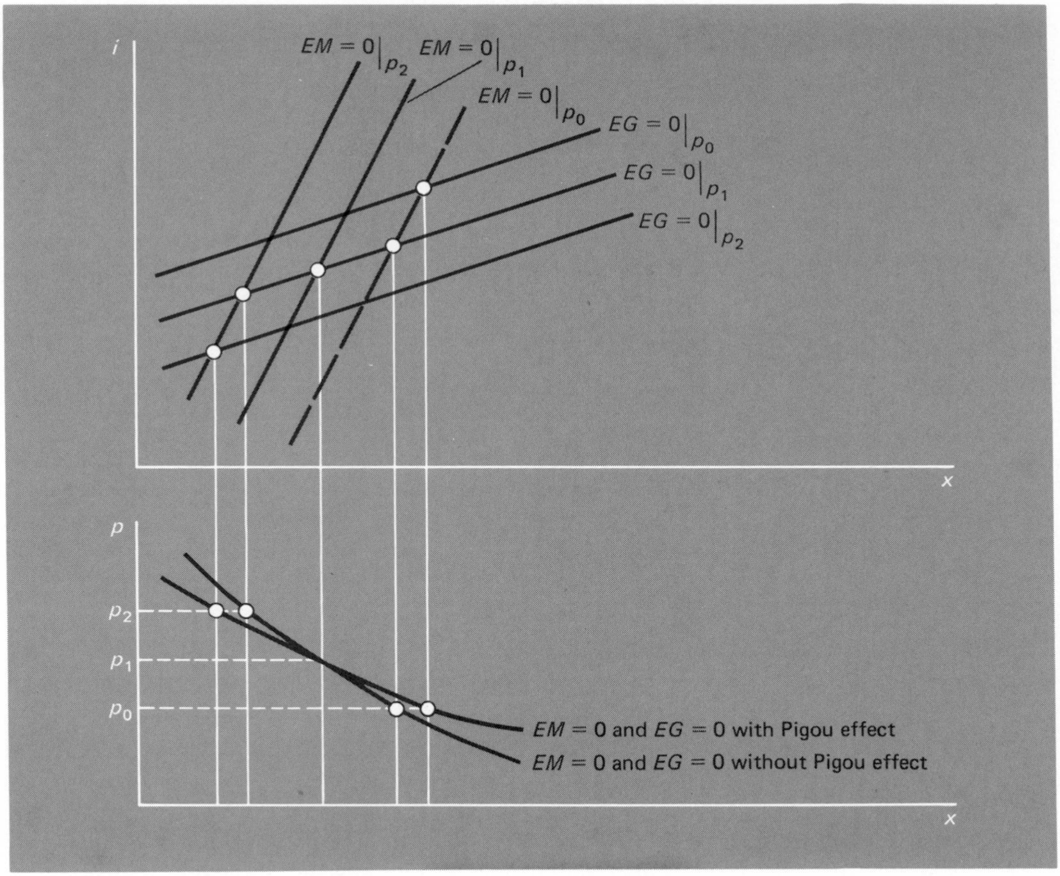

FIGURE 8-9 MARGINAL PROPENSITY TO SPEND GREATER THAN ONE WITH OR WITHOUT PIGOU EFFECT

FIGURE 8-10

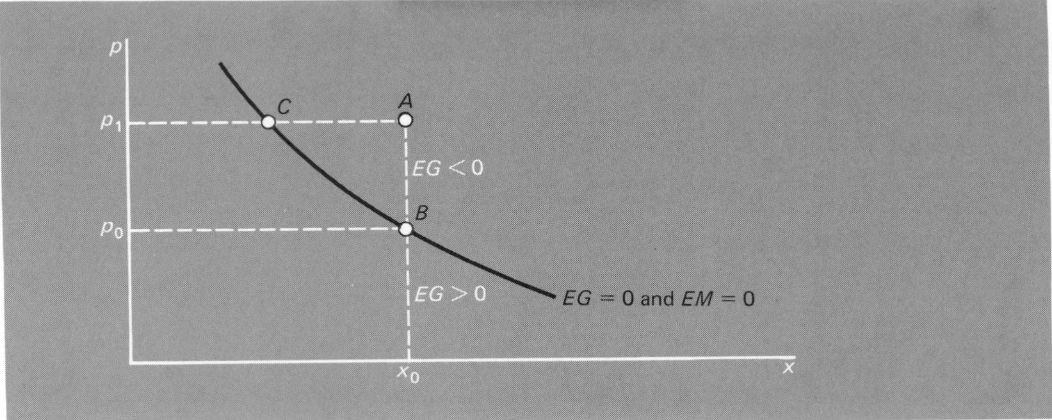

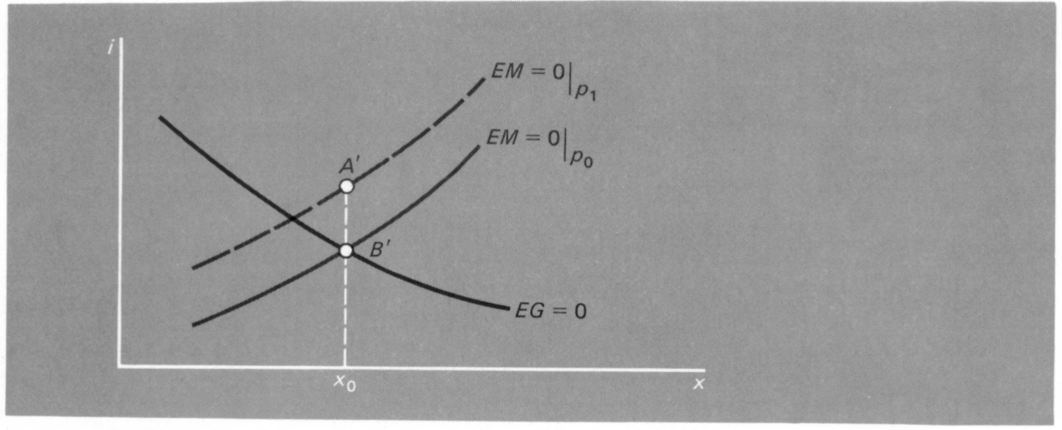

FIGURE 8-11

consumption demand. Thus the excess supply must be even greater than in the absence of a Pigou effect, as shown in Figure 8-12. The increase in p, to p_1, shifts the $EG = 0$ curve in addition to the $EM = 0$ curve. Thus the relevant curve, from which A' is considered to have been displaced, is $EG = 0|_{p_1}$, and the relevant point is E and not B'.

It is left for the reader to show that the special cases (without a Pigou effect) also show similar behavior, that to the right of the vertical curve there is excess supply of goods and services and to the left there is excess demand. Figure 8-13 depicts these special cases. The reader can also show that to the right of an *upward-sloping* "$EM = 0$ and $EG = 0$" curve, $EG > 0$, and to its left, $EG < 0$, as in Figure 8-14.

We are now ready to examine the dynamic behavior of our system. As we stated earlier, the cornerstone of dynamics is the "law of supply and demand," in

FIGURE 8-12 PIGOU EFFECT

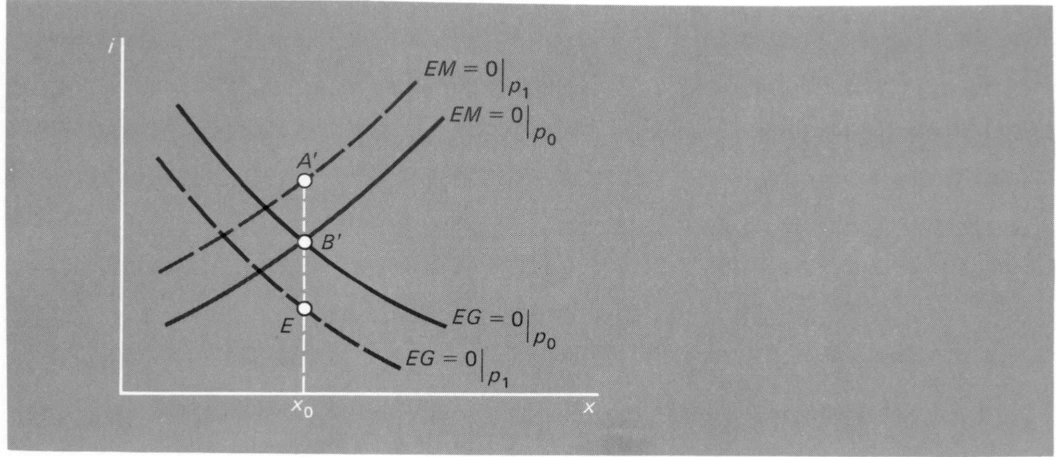

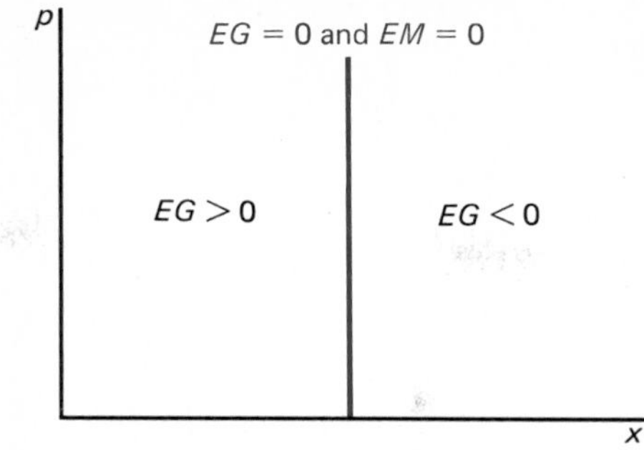

FIGURE 8-13 LIQUIDITY TRAP OR INTEREST INELASTICITY OF EG

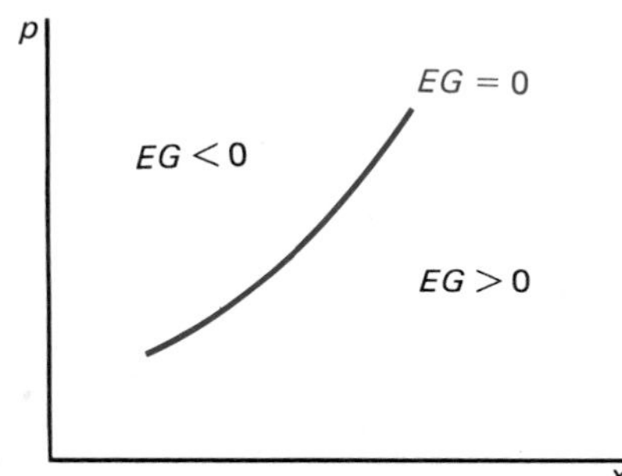

FIGURE 8-14

particular, the requirement that the price level will rise when there is excess demand for goods and services, fall when there is excess supply, and remain constant only when there is zero excess demand for or supply of goods and services. Schematically, we have

$$\Delta p \gtreqless 0 \quad \text{when} \quad EG \gtreqless 0$$

Applying this law of supply and demand, we see that above and to the right of the "$EM = 0$ and $EG = 0$" curve (where $EG < 0$) the price level is falling (i.e., $\Delta p < 0$). And to the left, since $EG > 0$, the price is rising (i.e., $\Delta p > 0$). Since the price level does not change only when the economy is on the curve, we can rename (relabel) the effective demand curve as the "$\Delta p = 0$" curve. The general case of a downward-sloping $\Delta p = 0$ curve, the phase plane, with the appropriate arrows, is shown in Figure 8-15a. The special case is depicted in 8-15b.

2. THE SUPPLY SIDE: MARGINAL COST, OR MARGINAL PRODUCTIVITY, CURVES

So far we have derived all the combinations of (p,x) that guarantee clearance of both the market for goods and services and the money market. We saw that there is an infinity of such combinations, all located on the $\Delta p = 0$ (or "$EM = 0$ and

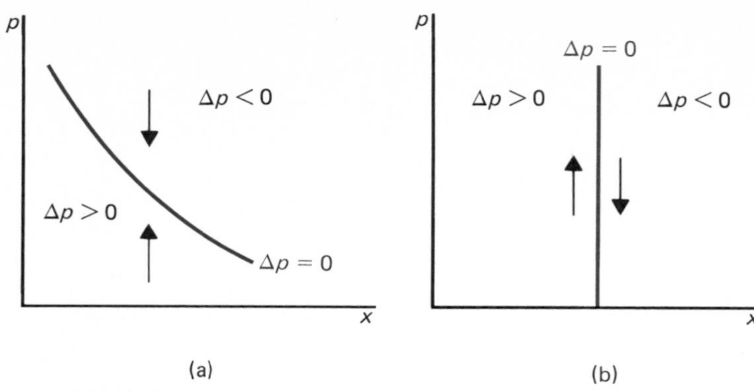

FIGURE 8-15 PHASE PLANE OF GENERAL CASE PHASE PLANE OF SPECIAL CASE

$EG = 0$") curve. It should be evident by now that in order to find exactly which combination of price and employment levels will actually materialize, we must introduce at least another curve, otherwise the system might be indeterminate.

The problem we are faced with here is reminiscent of the one discovered by Keynes, who saw that the interest rate was indeterminate in the classical system, which relied only on the intersection of the investment and savings curves. Keynes saw that there was one such pair of curves for each employment level, which implied that there was one level of interest rate for each employment level. Here we see that there is, in general, a different employment level for each different price level, because in the (i,x)-plane there is a different pair of $EM = 0$ and $EG = 0$ curves for each assumed price level.

This dilemma of indeterminancy is avoided if we utilize all the information in the economic system. We begin by using another cornerstone of our system, that firms are rational agents. In the present case this means that firms hire labor until its (labor's) marginal product is equal to the real wage:

$$\frac{W}{p} = MP_N, \quad \text{i.e., when} \quad p = \frac{W}{MP_N}$$

Of course, this fundamental relation involves three variables: p, x, and W. If we want to depict it in the (p,x)-plane, we must treat the omitted variable, W, parametrically. First, let us find the relation between prices and employment for a given money wage, W. We see from $p = W/MP_N$ that when W is given, p must rise in order to increase x. This increase in x decreases MP_N and therefore increases the right-hand side (RHS), W/MP_N, of the above equation. Therefore the LHS, p, must also rise. Paraphrasing, we can state that for employment to rise, given the money wage, the price level must rise. Only then will the real wage fall, and we know that only a fall in the real wage will induce firms to hire more labor. This positive relation between prices, p, and employment, x (for a given money wage), is shown in Figure 8-16 and will be referred to as the "marginal productivity curve," or "marginal cost curve."

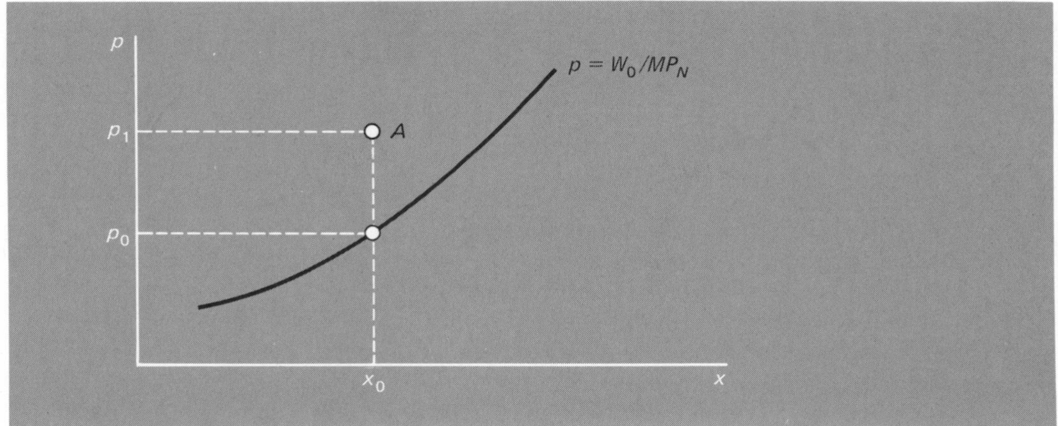

FIGURE 8-16

Now, there must be one such curve for each level of the money wage, and a higher money wage will shift the curve to the left. We can conduct the experiment for a given *x*, say x_0. If we increase the money wage from W_0 to W_1, in order for employment to remain the same, at x_0, the real wage must remain the same, at MP_N. But this can happen only if the price level *increases* at the same proportion. Therefore let us suppose that this increase in *p* gives us p_1, and thus point *A* in Figure 8-16, which proves conclusively that an increase in the money wage shifts the marginal cost curve upward (and to the left). In the case of flexible money wages, any money-wage rate is conceivable. We must therefore imagine the *(p,x)*-plane filled with $p = W_i/MP_N$ curves, five of which are shown in Figure 8-17. Note that it is

FIGURE 8-17

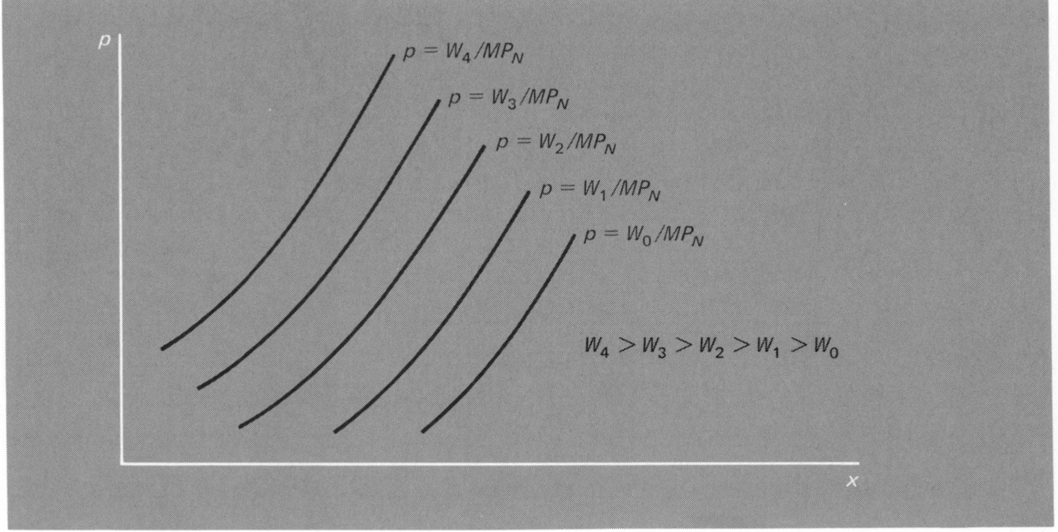

sufficient to know one point *(p,x)* in this plane in order to deduce the money wage, since through such a point there must pass a marginal productivity curve for a money wage consistent with the known p and x.

We have seen above that an increase in the money wage shifts the marginal cost (or productivity, or supply) curve upward and to the left. In our simplified economy the money wage is, of course, a proxy for the (money) price of all variable inputs. This means that a similar shift will occur when the money price of any input rises. Of particular importance, in recent times, have been changes in the prices of such inputs as grain, energy in general, and oil in particular, and other imported materials. An increase in the price of any (or all) of these factors of production will shift the marginal cost curve upward and to the left.

But even with the money wage fixed, in the abstract case (and in the general case, with the money price of every input fixed), the marginal cost curve shifts to the left when the productivity (either in general or of a particular factor) falls. If for the same level of capital, the average unit of labor produces less than before, we can say that the *productivity has fallen or has deteriorated.* This can be attributed to any one (or more) of several factors: to less-efficient labor; to less capital; to outmoded, or obsolete, capital; to inept organization; and even to other factors. Two of these reasons, "less capital" and "obsolete capital," are, of course, related; a lower rate of capital accumulation (i.e., lower investment) reduces the capital/labor ratio, which directly reduces the productivity of labor. And this lower investment also decreases productivity because new capital goods usually "embody" any advances in technology. Thus it is clear that the entire capital stock of the economy becomes relatively more obsolete and, therefore, less efficient whenever capital formation slows down.

Whatever its origin, we can represent this fall in productivity by a rise (to

FIGURE 8-18

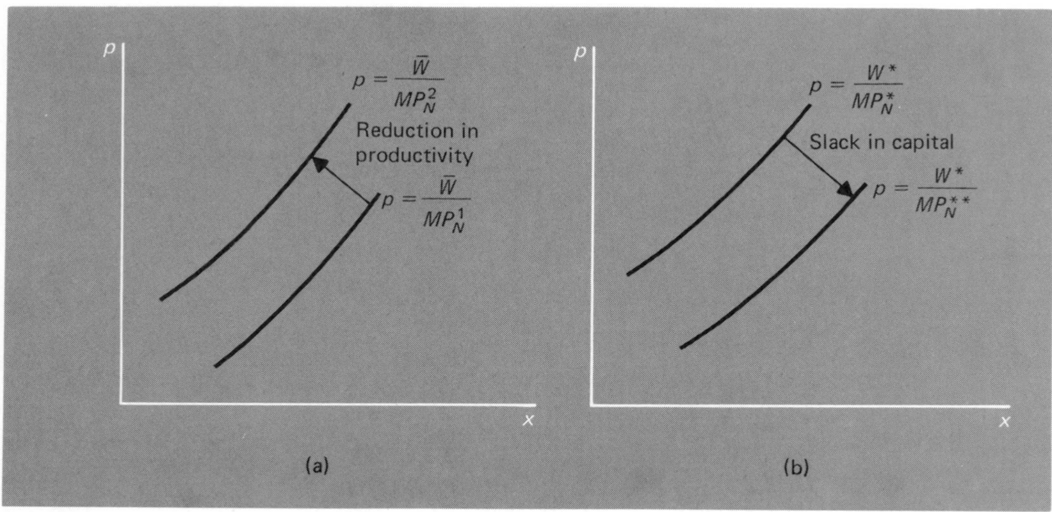

the left) of the marginal cost curve in the manner of Figure 8-18a, where $\overline{W}/MP_N^2$ represents the fallen productivity (risen costs) as compared with the original one, $\overline{W}/MP_N^1$. Of course, the converse is also true. An improvement in productivity lowers the marginal cost curve (i.e., shifts it to the right). Measured productivity also increases and the marginal cost curve falls whenever production is increased while there is nonutilized plant capacity, or, in other words, whenever there is a "slack" in the capital stock of the economy. This case is illustrated in Figure 8-18b.

Finally, an *increase in tax rates* raises the marginal cost curve, usually through the reduction in productivity, as we outlined above. An increase, say, in corporate tax rates reduces the profitability of investment and hence reduces capital formation, which, as we know, lowers the productivity of labor and raises marginal cost. To further illustrate these cases we shall cite and examine, mainly in Chapter 9 but also in Chapter 10, examples from recent U.S. history.

3. THE $\Delta W = 0$ CURVE

We can now take into consideration the stipulation introduced in Chapter 7, that the money wage increases when there is excess demand for labor and falls when there is excess supply. This information is embodied in the following schema:

$$\Delta W \gtreqless 0 \quad \text{when} \quad x - v \gtreqless 0$$

Of course, x is consistent with $MP_N = W/p$, and this is the demand for labor. The money wage stops changing only when the demand for labor, x, equals the supply, v. Because we assume that the supply, v, is fixed at $\bar{v}$, it follows that when $x < \bar{v}$, the money wage falls (i.e., $\Delta W < 0$), and when $x > \bar{v}$, the money wage rises (i.e.,

FIGURE 8-19

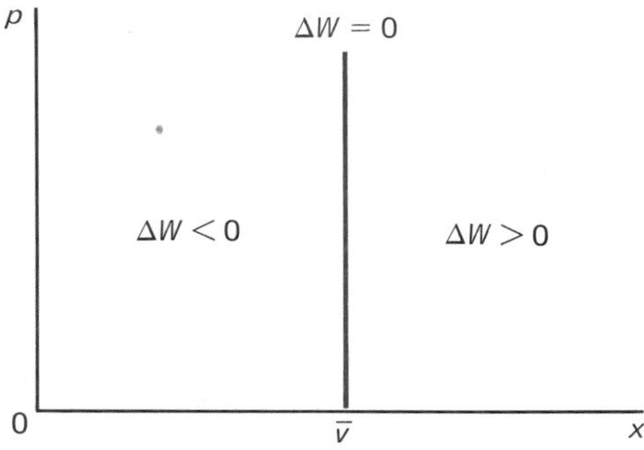

$\Delta W > 0$). This information is illustrated in Figure 8-19, where we have not used arrows, since the money wage is not represented on either axis. A fall in money wages (i.e., $\Delta W < 0$) can be represented only by a movement that takes the economy on a productivity curve corresponding to a lower money wage W.

4. THE EMPLOYMENT-ADJUSTMENT MECHANISM, Δx

To complete our analysis, we need to provide a rule for change (or for constancy) in x. We can derive this from the marginal productivity rule. We know that employment, x, can increase only if the real wage falls. But a fall in the real wage can come about in several ways, such as a rise in the price level while the money wage remains constant; or a fall in the money wage while the price level remains constant. The real wage could rise even if both W and p are rising, or if both are falling. In general,

$$\Delta x \gtreqless 0 \quad \text{when} \quad \frac{\Delta p}{p} \gtreqless \frac{\Delta W}{W}$$

We note that in order for x to rise, if both p and W are rising, p should be rising proportionately more than W. If both are falling, p should be falling proportionately less.

We shall utilize this rule to find all the points (x,p) for which x does not change (i.e., for which $\Delta x = 0$). These points will lie on the "singular" curve, labeled $\Delta x = 0$. On one side of this curve will lie all the points for which $\Delta x > 0$, and on the other side all the points for which $\Delta x < 0$.

II. A SPECIAL CASE: FIXED MONEY WAGES

We shall first examine a special case in order to familiarize ourselves with the new technique and also to relate our results to those previously derived. We recall that earlier we were unable to determine the price level even (or especially) when the money-wage rate was fixed. It is this special case of fixed money wages that we shall examine in this section. Symbolically, we shall assume $\Delta W \equiv 0$.

The fixity of money wages, of course, gives us a result that we have used repeatedly, namely, that employment rises if, and only if, the price level rises. This result simplifies considerably the rules of motion in x, outlined above. By substituting zero for ΔW in the above formula, these rules are now

$$\Delta x \gtreqless 0 \quad \text{when} \quad \Delta p \gtreqless 0$$

Because the law of supply and demand links changes in p to excess demand for or excess supply of goods and services, these rules can be written as

$$\Delta x \gtreqless 0 \quad \text{when} \quad \Delta p \gtreqless 0 \quad \text{when} \quad EG \gtreqless 0$$

It is clear that our task of finding all the points for which $\Delta x = 0$, all the points for which $\Delta x > 0$, and all the points for which $\Delta x < 0$ has become much simpler in the case of fixed money wages. The singular curve $\Delta x = 0$ *coincides* with the "$EM = 0$ and $EG = 0$" curve, which, in turn, coincides with the $\Delta p = 0$ curve. Similarly, the region for which $EG > 0$ (and thus $\Delta p > 0$) is also the region in which $\Delta x > 0$. Also, $\Delta x < 0$ in the region where $EG < 0$ (and thus $\Delta p < 0$). The $\Delta x = 0$ curve, as well as the regions $\Delta x < 0$ and $\Delta x > 0$, complete with the appropriate arrows, are shown in Figure 8-20. Since the same "$EM = 0$ and $EG = 0$" curve has been called both the $\Delta p = 0$ curve and the $\Delta x = 0$ curve, we can relabel it the "$\Delta p = 0$ and $\Delta x = 0$" curve (or sometimes merely $\Delta p = 0 = \Delta x$). It is the locus of all combinations of prices and employment levels that guarantee that all motion in these two variables will cease. The phase plane of Figure 8-21 identifies the "$\Delta p = 0$ and $\Delta x = 0$" curve, the region in which $\Delta p > 0$ and $\Delta x > 0$, as well as the region in which $\Delta p < 0$ and $\Delta x < 0$. The arrows pointing toward increasing and decreasing p, as well as toward increasing and decreasing x, are inserted in the same graph.

We can now see how the equilibrium values of (p,x) are determined. Given the money wage, say $W = W_3$, we know that the price and employment level must

FIGURE 8-20

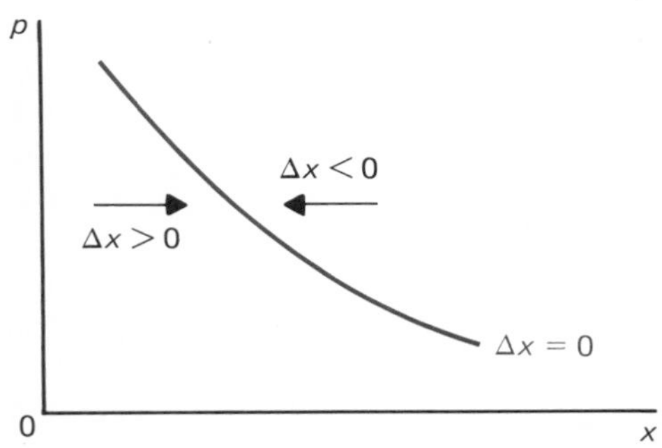

FIGURE 8-21 PHASE PLANE WHEN W IS FIXED

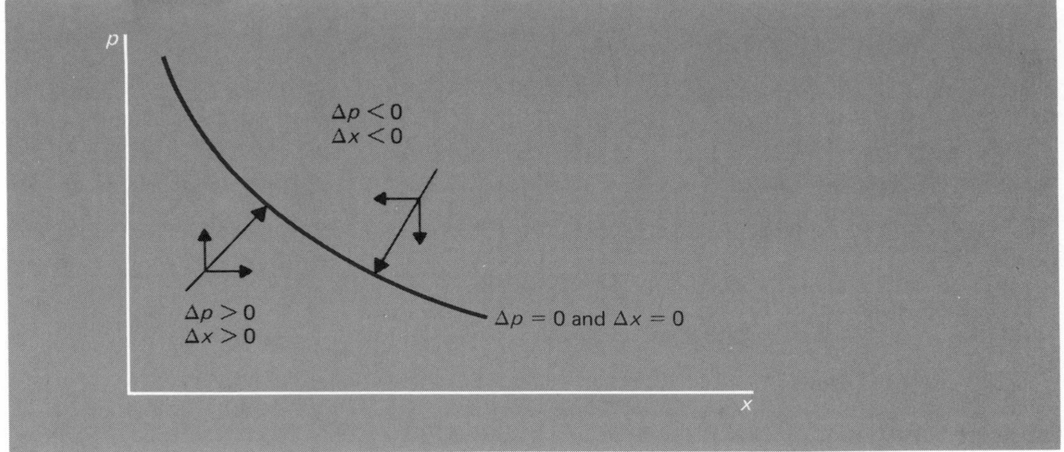

be on the productivity curve corresponding to W_3. On the other hand, we cannot have an equilibrium unless employment and prices are at "rest" (i.e., not changing). This happens at the intersection, E, of the productivity curve and the "$\Delta p = 0$ and $\Delta x = 0$" curve, as shown in Figure 8-22.

Figure 8-22 also shows that an "unemployment equilibrium" is possible. If the money wage that can clear the labor market is lower than W_3, say $W = W_1$, the economy will come to rest exhibiting involuntary unemployment. It is also clear from Figure 8-22 that the equilibrium point E is stable, that is, there are forces in the economy to bring it about. For suppose that the economy finds itself with prices and wages below those of the equilibrium, say at point A, which indicates an excess demand for goods and services. The price level will now rise and cause an increase in employment because of the falling real wage. This process will continue until the market is cleared. At this point the price level will stop rising, and thus the real wage will stop falling, thereby exhausting profit opportunities for hiring additional labor. Opposite forces are in operation, however, when there is excess supply of goods and services (point B). *Note that with a fixed money wage there is only one path for the economy (p and x) to follow, namely, the economy must move on the relevant productivity curve* (W_3 in Figure 8-22).

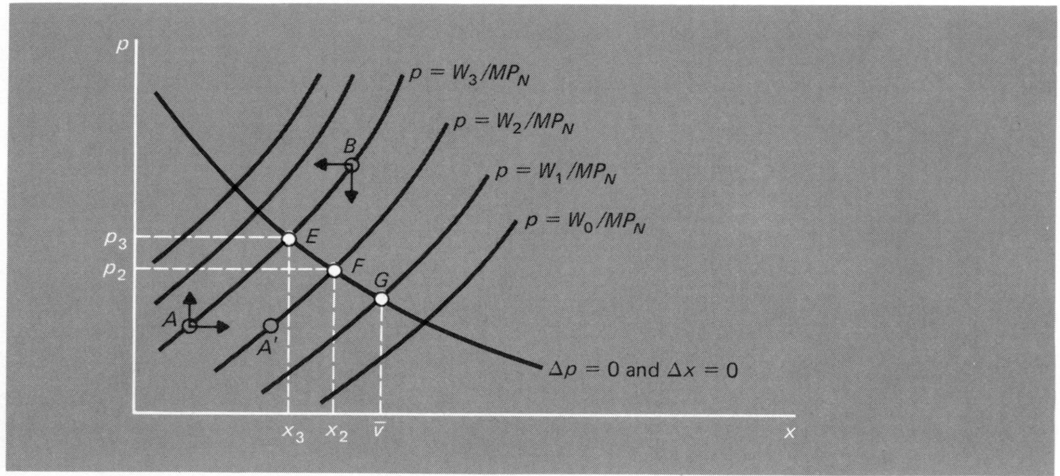

FIGURE 8-22

In this case of a fixed money wage, the marginal productivity curve was utilized in two ways. First, it provided the full-equilibrium position of the economy, as at point E in Figure 8-22. Second, it gave the exact path of (p,x) that the economy will follow toward equilibrium: from B to E if the economy started with excess supply of goods and services, and from A to E with excess demand. The economy is constrained to move along this path (as long as the money wage is fixed at W_3) because of the profit maximization rule for firms.

WAGE CUTS

We can now see that, *once and for all,* money-wage cuts can increase employment. This is shown in Figure 8-22. If, for example, a new wage level, W_2, is agreed upon, the economy will *eventually* reach point F with employment $x_2 > x_3$. Three points are in order regarding this statement. The first refers to paths that the economy will follow in order to reach F. If the money-wage cut were introduced while the economy was in disequilibrium, say at point A, the money-wage cut would take us immediately to point A', and from there the price and employment levels would steadily rise until we reached equilibrium. The immediate jump from point A to point A' is a reflection of the assumption that employers instantaneously (and always) hire labor up to the point that equates its marginal product to the real wage. With the price level equal to the one given by point A, a cut in W immediately lowers the real wage, and, by assumption, employment should immediately rise to the level implied by point A'. Suppose, instead, that the money-wage cut is introduced after the economy has rested for some time, at point E (and the society considered this unemployment undesirable). The money-wage cut "fools" firms into hiring more people (point H in Figure 8-23). To be sure, point H is profit maximizing, but only if the price level remains the same. But the price level cannot remain this high because the greater quantity of goods being produced will create excess supply, causing prices to fall and inducing firms to start firing workers.

The second point concerns the proviso of *once and for all* wage cuts. This requires emphasis; if we introduce money-wage flexibility and changes in W through time, then $\Delta W \neq 0$. This type of graph cannot handle this case because the $\Delta x = 0$ curve will *not* coincide with $\Delta p = 0$. Therefore the policy of changing money wages *through time* will be examined later when the general model will permit it.

Finally, we should point out that in some well-known extreme cases, a policy of money-wage cuts may not be effective in increasing employment. The $\Delta p = 0$,

FIGURE 8-23 MONEY WAGE CUTS STARTING FROM EQUILIBRIUM

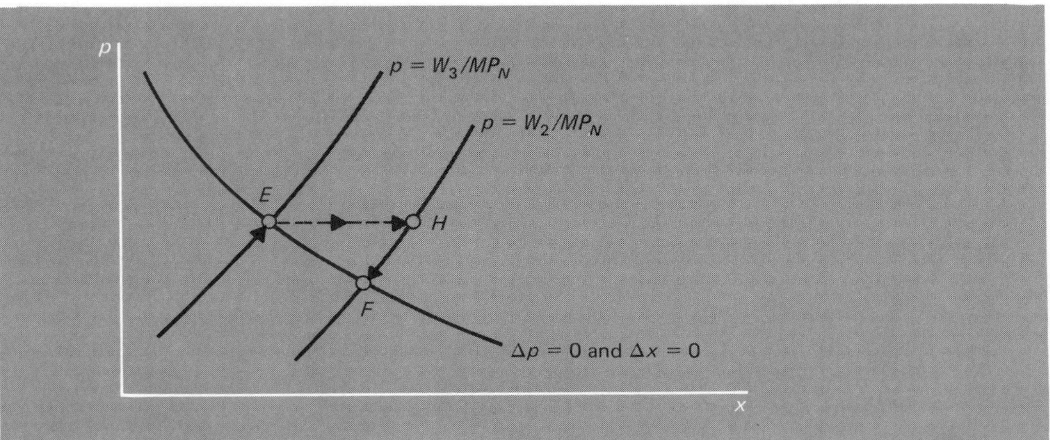

$\Delta x = 0$ curve of Figure 8-23 is drawn under the assumption that the two special cases are absent, either by a direct assumption or indirectly by incorporating a Pigou effect. (Recall that even if there is a liquidity trap or interest inelasticity of *EG*, the $\Delta p = 0$, $\Delta x = 0$ curve is still downward sloping if a Pigou effect is present.) Let us suppose, instead, that a liquidity trap, for example, is present but that there is no Pigou effect. In this case the $\Delta p = 0$, $\Delta x = 0$ curve is vertical, as in Figure 8-24, and a money-wage cut will lower the price level without increasing employment. This also implies that the price falls by the same percentage as the wage is cut. Of course, in this case the indirect ways of increasing employment are absent, and, as Keynes emphasized, the money-wage cut by itself will not (directly) increase employment.

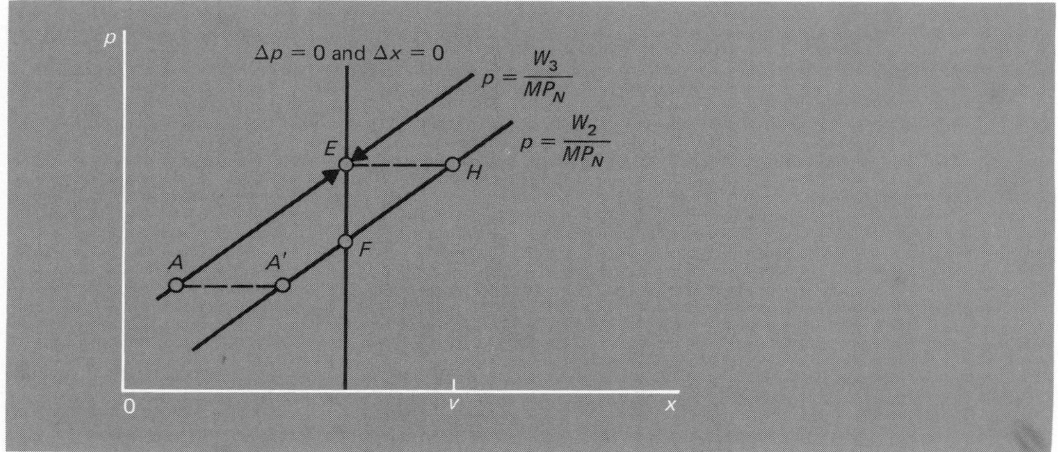

FIGURE 8-24 MONEY WAGE CUT IN THE SPECIAL CASES

III. PRICES AND OUTPUT, EFFECTIVE DEMAND AND SUPPLY, AND THE THEORY OF THE FIRM

The rule we have utilized so far (that the marginal product of labor is equal to its real wage) is, of course, *a rule for hiring labor.* Now, using the more familiar (but equivalent) rule—marginal cost (of output), *MC*, equals marginal revenue, *MR*—which is *a rule for supply of output,* we shall translate our analysis into more traditional jargon. Since we deal with pure competition, the rule $MC = MR$ becomes $MC = p$. But we know that when labor is the only variable factor, the *MC* (of one unit of output) is equal to W/MP_N. (The reader is reminded that the proof is as follows: One unit of labor costs *W* dollars. But one unit of labor produces, at the margin, MP_N units of output. Therefore each of the MP_N units costs W/MP_N dollars.) Thus the $MC = p$ rule becomes $p = W/MP_N$, that is, it is the same as the equation depicted by the "marginal productivity" curve. We could, therefore, call this curve the "marginal cost" curve, or, since firms supply along their *MC* curve (this is the meaning of the rule $p = MC$), the "supply curve." Of course, a true marginal cost or supply curve should have output, not labor, on the horizontal axis. Fortunately, there is a one-to-one increasing relation between employment, x, and output, Y, because of the production function, $Y = Kf(x)$, and the fixity of the economy's capital stock, K. Thus it is an easy matter to translate any point (p,x) on this supply curve into a point (p, Y). Similarly, we can translate any point (p,x) on the "$EG = 0$ and $EM = 0$" curve into a point (p, Y).

Diagrammatically, we need to add another panel relating x and Y. In Figure 8-25 we see how we can transform the supply curve (for a given $W = W_0$) from one displaying labor, x, into one displaying output, Y. Knowing W_0 permits us to identify the "supply" curve, $p = W_0/MP_N$. If prices now equal p_0, the profit-maximizing firms will want to hire x_0 units of labor. Using the lower panel, we can find that the firms combine x_0 units of labor with their fixed capital in order to produce and supply Y_0^s units of output. (The superscript s is inserted to denote supply.) Similarly, if $p = p_1$, we find that firms will hire x_1 units of labor in order to produce and supply Y_1^s units of output.

Thus we know all the supply possibilities, one for each assumed price level, p. Of course, we need to know which pair (p, Y) can be sustained. This is where the notion of *effective aggregate demand* comes into play. In other words, we need our "$EG = 0$ and $EM = 0$" (or $\Delta p = 0$ and $\Delta x = 0$) curve in the (p, Y)-plane, which is now truly a demand curve. It shows the output that can be supported by the market system, that is, the output that is "effectively demanded."

FIGURE 8-25

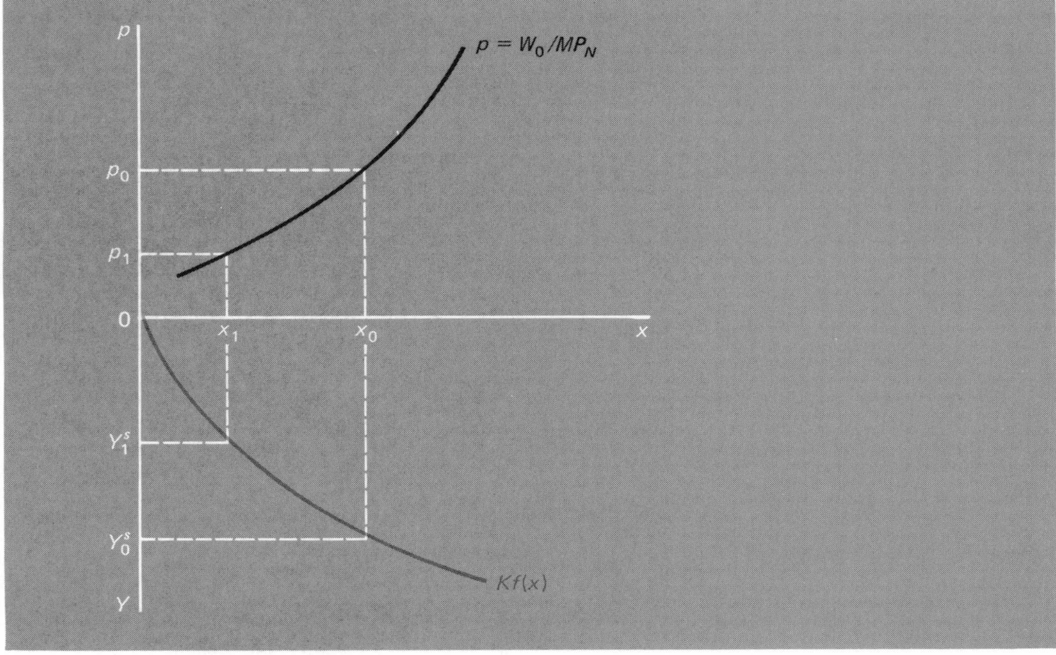

Figure 8-26 shows the interaction of the two curves. Let us suppose that $p = p_0$ and, therefore, that the profit-maximizing firms want to be at point A. This means, utilizing the lower panel, that they want to supply Y_0^s units of output. However, if $p = p_0$, the relevant $EM = 0|_{p=p_0}$ curve and the relevant $EG = 0|_{p=p_0}$ curve (neither shown here) give us a point B on the "$EM = 0$ and $EG = 0$" curve. This is translated into Y_0^d units of output in the lower panel. And we see that our exercise has this economic meaning: For p_0 to be an equilibrium price level (i.e., if p_0 is to permit clearance of both the money and the output markets), the level of output should be equal to Y_0^d. In this sense the market can absorb, or "demand," only Y_0^d units. Since the market can absorb less than what the firms want to supply, there is excess supply of goods and services, $Y_0^s - Y_0^d$. The law of supply and demand comes into play bringing the prices down, say, to the level p_1. At this new level the excess supply is lower, $Y_1^s - Y_1^d$, but still positive, causing a further decline of prices until they become equal to p_*. At p_*, the supply Y^s is equal to the "demand," Y^d. The firms (collectively) produce exactly the amount that the market can absorb.

In this book we have been explicitly interested in the employment level rather than in output. Most post-Keynesian expositions emphasize the latter. It is, however, a very simple matter to relate our exposition to theirs. For example, the supply curve, Y^s, in the (p, Y)-plane of Figure 8-27b is derived from the familiar ones on Figure 8-27a. Figure 8-28 utilizes the "$EG = 0$ and $EM = 0$" curve and the production

FIGURE 8-26

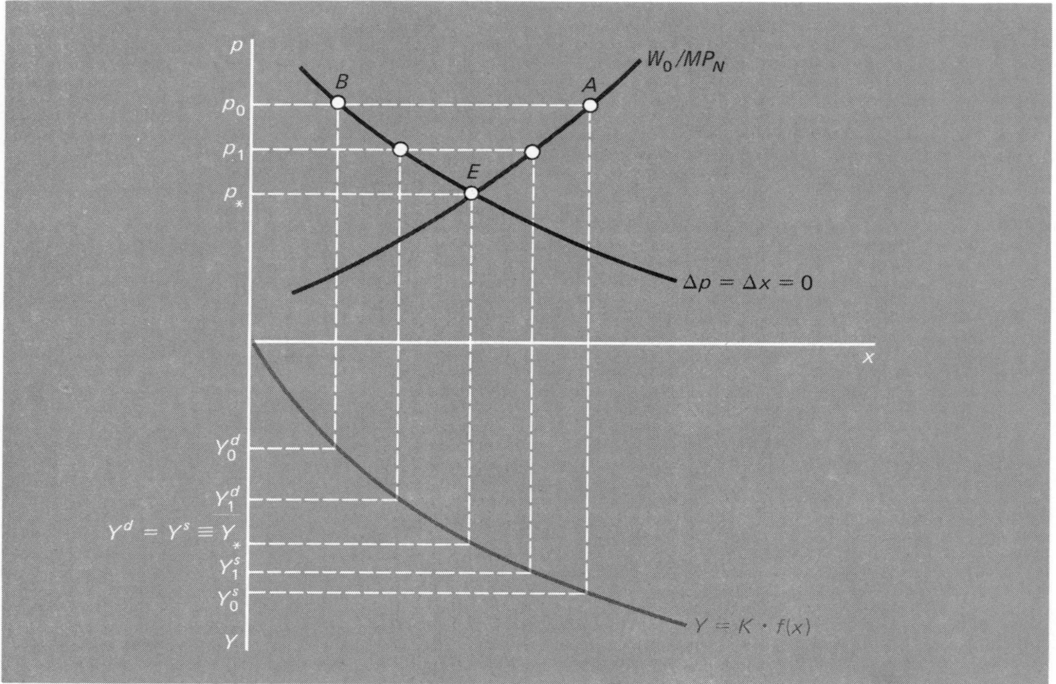

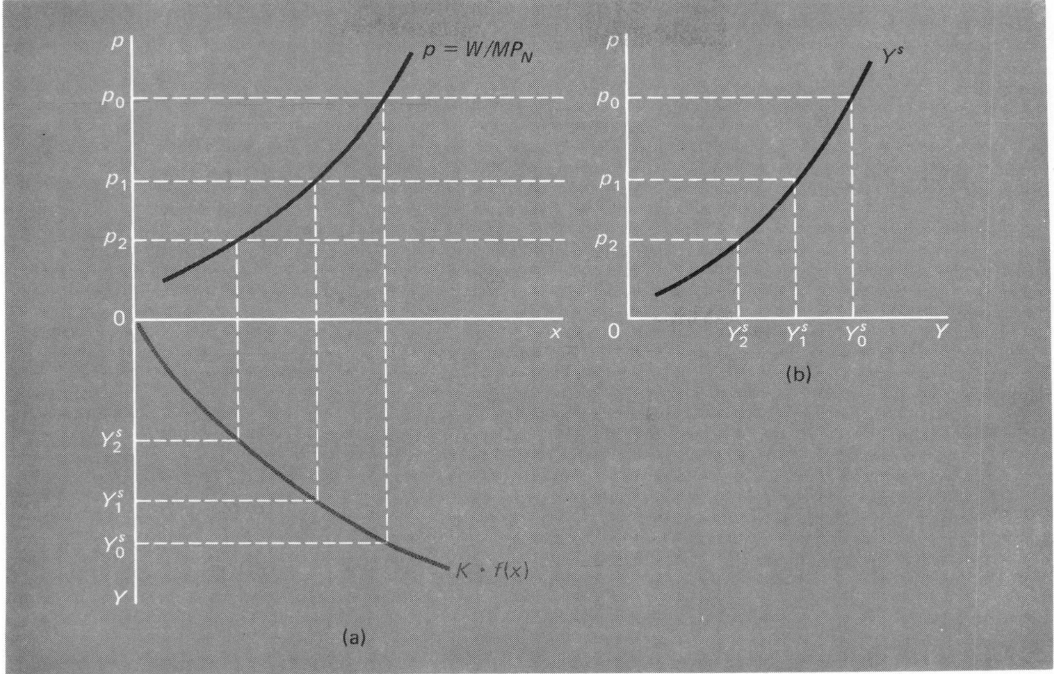

FIGURE 8-27

function (Figure 8-28a) in order to give the effective aggregate demand, Y^d, in the (p, Y)-plane (Figure 8-28b).

Finally, Figure 8-29 summarizes the analysis and information of Figure 8-25. Of course, the unique path that the economy now follows toward the equilibrium point, E, is the supply curve, Y^s. Our insistence that the firms always operate on their MC or supply curve is analogous to a similar problem in general economic theory. Consider the case of one industry, say that of producing peanuts. Given the market price, whether it is a peanut market-clearing price or not, the typical firm is faced with a horizontal marginal revenue curve, as in the right panel of Figure 8-30. Its intersection with the MC curve determines the firm's supply. If $p = p_0$, the firms collectively supply more peanuts than the consumers demand. Thus the price will fall, say to p_1, where an excess supply still exists. The price will continue falling until p_* is reached and the market is cleared. The point is, however, that during this disequilibrium process the firms always operate on their MC curve.

IV. FLEXIBLE MONEY WAGES

In the preceding section we saw that when money wages are fixed, unemployment equilibrium is possible. The assumption of fixed money wages was introduced, beginning with Keynes, partly because it greatly simplified the technical analysis and partly

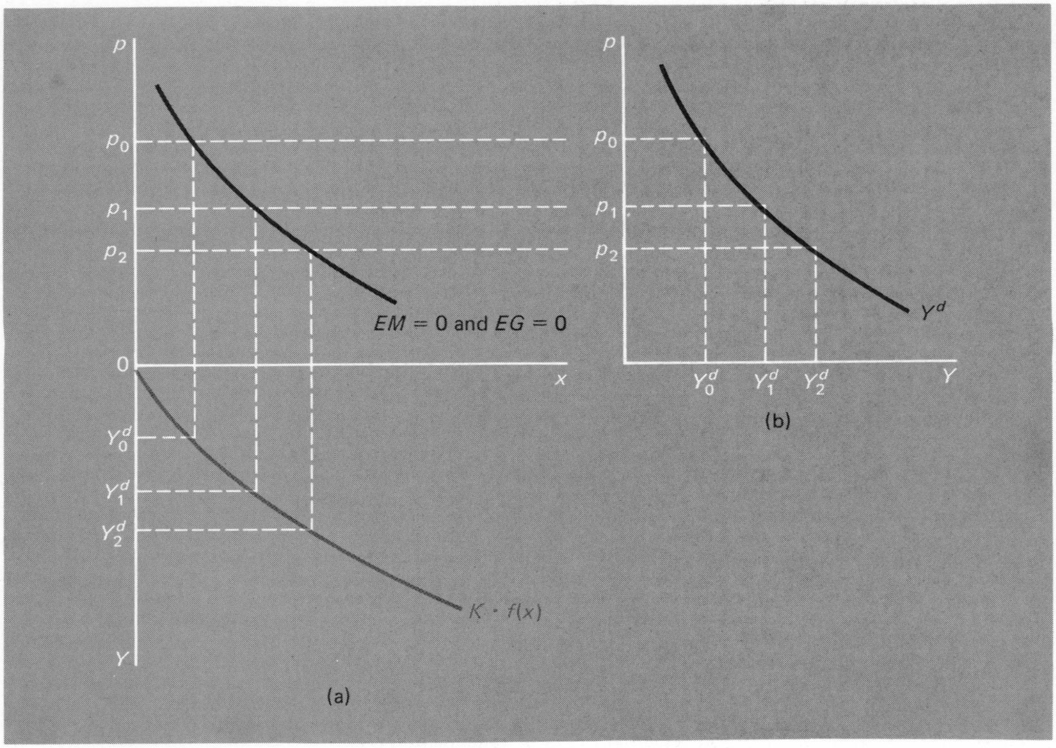

FIGURE 8-28

FIGURE 8-29

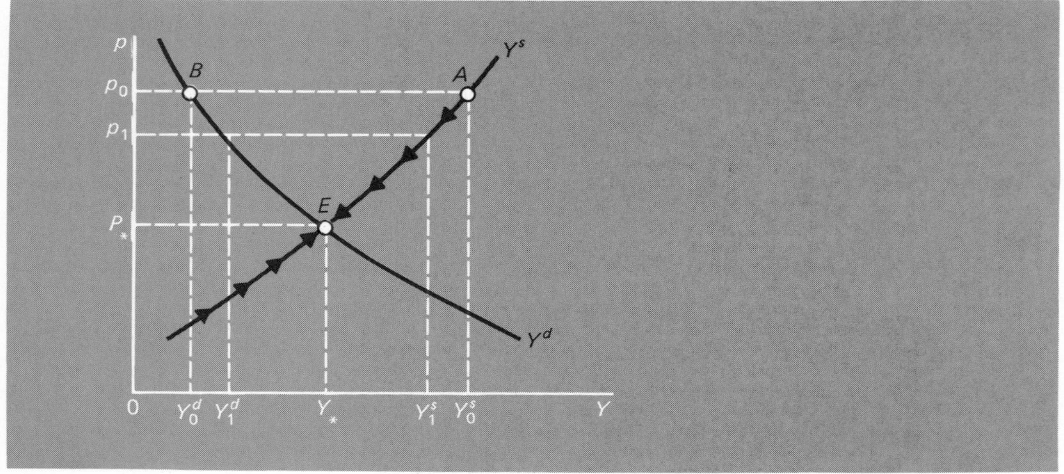

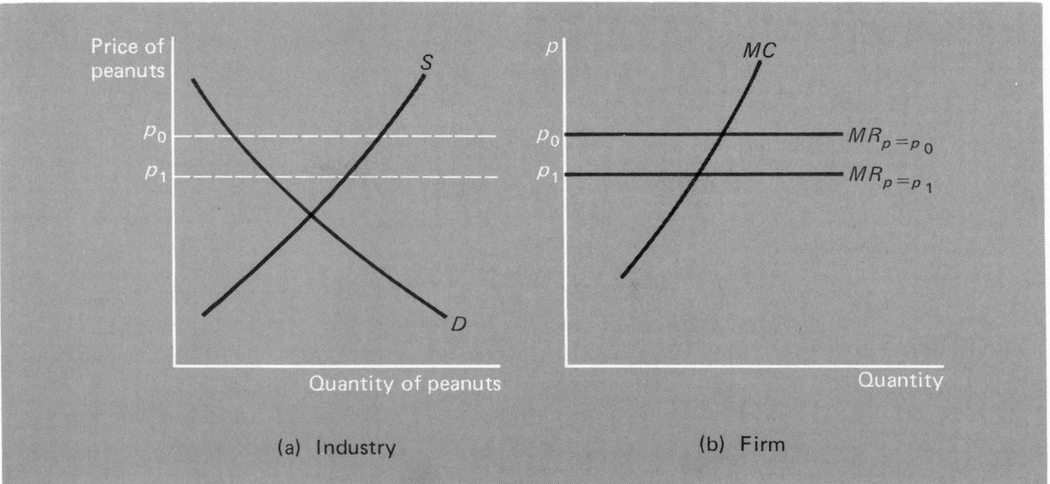

FIGURE 8-30

because it reflected the truth of the statement that workers, *in the beginning,* do resist money-wage cuts enacted solely because of unemployment. And we saw the reasons why even employers are reluctant to cut money wages on that ground. However, as we indicated in Chapter 7, history shows that after protracted periods of unemployment, workers not only will accept money-wage cuts but may actually initiate the cuts.

We must, therefore, extend our analysis to cover the case of flexible money wages. For this, we shall resurrect the following rule: The money wage rises when there is excess demand for labor (i.e., $x - v > 0$), falls when there is excess supply of labor (i.e., unemployment, $x - v < 0$), and remains the same only if there is zero excess demand or excess supply of labor (i.e., full employment):

$$\Delta W \gtreqless 0 \quad \text{when} \quad x - v \gtreqless 0$$

With our extended model, the money wage, *W,* will be endogenously determined, as will be the price level, employment, the interest rate, and all the other variables, such as income, that lurk in the background. We shall again be explicit in the determination and movements of both the price level and employment. Thus we need to develop the $\Delta p = 0$ and $\Delta x = 0$ curves. With the money wage flexible, obeying the above rule, the major complication occurs regarding the $\Delta x = 0$ curve. In the special case of fixed money wages, we saw that the $\Delta x = 0$ curve coincides with the $\Delta p = 0$ curve (which is also the "$EM = 0$ and $EG = 0$" curve), since a fixed money wage causes employment to rise (fall) if, and only if, the price level rises (falls); and, similarly, employment remains unchanged if, and only if, the price level remains unchanged.

In the general case, however, we saw that employment rises (falls) if, and only if, the rate of change in prices is algebraically greater (smaller) than the rate of change in money wages. We have, in other words, the familiar rule:

$$\Delta x \overset{>}{\underset{<}{=}} 0 \quad \text{when} \quad \frac{\Delta p}{p} \overset{>}{\underset{<}{=}} \frac{\Delta W}{W}$$

THE $\Delta x = 0$ CURVE

Let us now concentrate on the $\Delta x = 0$ curve. We want to find all the combinations of the price level and employment that satisfy the requirement that $\Delta p/p = \Delta W/W$. This, of course, implies that the *real* wage will remain constant and, therefore, employment will stay unchanged.

It should be clear why the $\Delta x = 0$ curve does not coincide with the $\Delta p = 0$ curve in this case. The latter curve requires that the price level not change. The $\Delta x = 0$ curve, on the other hand, requires that the percentage change in prices be equal to the percentage change in money wages. However, the latter change could be positive, negative, or zero. Only when the percentage change in money wages (equal to the percentage change in prices) is equal to zero do the two curves coincide. This helps us discover the characteristics of the intersection of the two curves, $\Delta x = 0$ and $\Delta p = 0$. Their intersection gives us the equilibrium point (or points). (A true equilibrium has the property that, among other things, neither employment nor the price level moves.)

At the point(s) of intersection of the two curves, the percentage change in money wages, $\Delta W/W$, is equal to the percentage change in prices, $\Delta p/p$, by virtue of its lying on the $\Delta x = 0$ curve. On the other hand, this same point lies on the $\Delta p = 0$ curve, which implies that the percentage change in prices (which is equal to the percentage change in money wages) is equal to zero. It follows, therefore, that at equilibrium the percentage change in money wages is zero. But we know, by our earlier rule, that the rate of change in money wages is zero if, and only if, there is zero excess demand or excess supply of labor, that is, if, and only if, $x = \bar{v}$. *We have proved, therefore, that the two curves intersect at a point that guarantees equilibrium with full employment.*

While we have found one point on the unknown $\Delta x = 0$ curve, namely, point E at $x = \bar{v}$, we should now consider another point, with abscissa x lower than v and equal, say, to $\tilde{x}$ in Figure 8-31. For this level of x there is, of course, unemployment. By our earlier rule, this implies that for $x = \tilde{x}$, the money wage, W, will be falling (i.e., $\Delta W < 0$). But on the $\Delta x = 0$ curve, $\Delta W/W$ should be equal to $\Delta p/p$. Hence, for $x = \tilde{x}$, $\Delta p/p$ should be negative (i.e., Δp should also be negative). We know that to the right and above the $\Delta p = 0$ curve, Δp is negative. Therefore, for $x = \tilde{x}$, the point on the $\Delta x = 0$ curve should lie to the right of the $\Delta p = 0$ curve. Point A in Figure 8-31 is such a point. We can repeat our analysis for any level of x less than $\bar{v}$ and find that points on the $\Delta x = 0$ curve should lie *above* the $\Delta p = 0$ curve.

Now examine any point with abscissa greater than $\bar{v}$, say a point with $x = \bar{x} > \bar{v}$. It follows that if it lies on the $\Delta x = 0$ curve, the point must satisfy

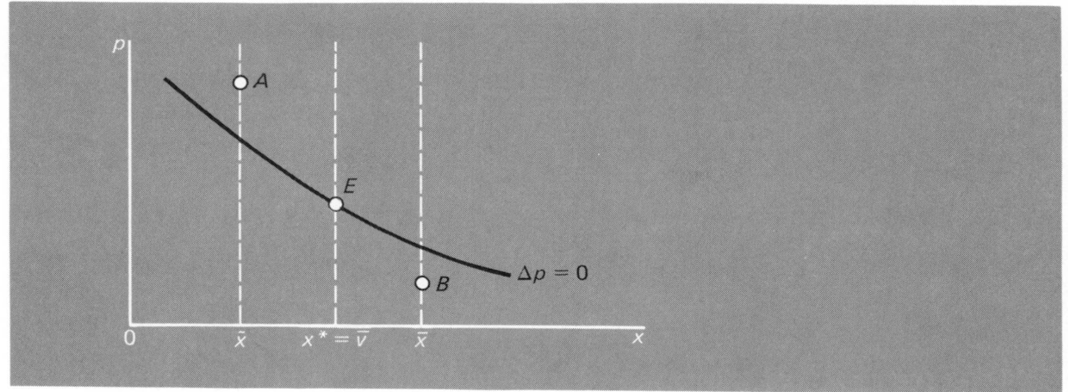

FIGURE 8-31

$\Delta p/p = \Delta W/W > 0$ (since $\bar{x} > \bar{v}$). In other words, $\Delta p > 0$. Thus, for $x > \bar{v}$, we have to be in the region $\Delta p > 0$, that is, *below* the $\Delta p = 0$ curve, at a point like B in Figure 8-31.

We have found that the $\Delta x = 0$ curve lies above the $\Delta p = 0$ curve when $x < \bar{v}$, and below it when $x > \bar{v}$. But we have examined the case of a negatively sloped $\Delta p = 0$ curve. It follows, then, that *when the $\Delta p = 0$ curve is downward sloping, the $\Delta x = 0$ curve is also downward sloping with (absolute) slope greater than that of the $\Delta p = 0$ curve,* as shown in Figure 8-32. It is left for the reader to show that if the $\Delta p = 0$ curve is upward sloping, the $\Delta x = 0$ curve is also upward sloping, but not so steep as the $\Delta p = 0$ curve, as in Figure 8-33.

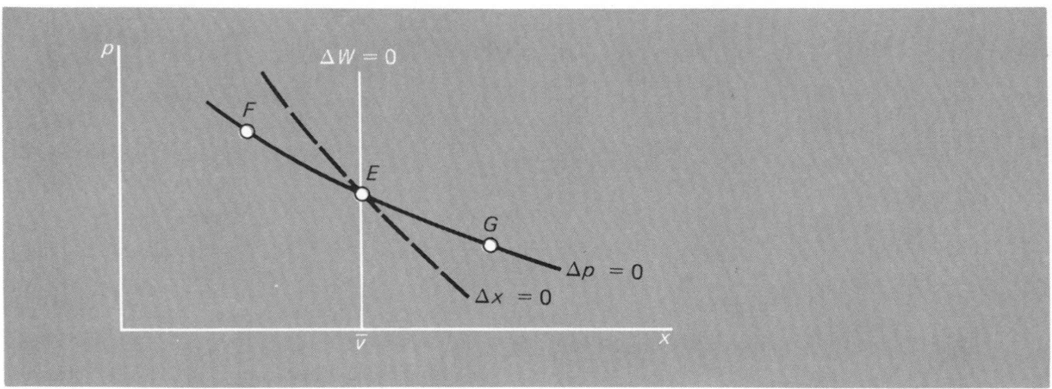

FIGURE 8-32

POINTS OFF THE $\Delta x = 0$ CURVE

We now want to identify the regions in which $\Delta x > 0$ and $\Delta x < 0$. The former must occur when the real wage is falling, whereas a falling employment, according to our rules, can come about only if the real wage is rising. By now it should be

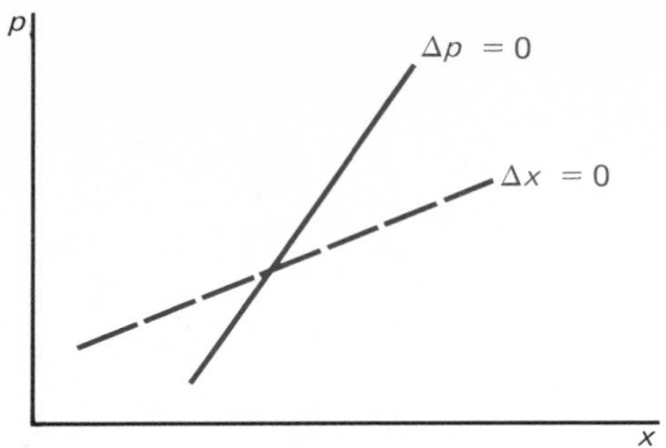

FIGURE 8-33

clear that on one side of the $\Delta x = 0$ singular curve $\Delta x > 0$, and on the other side $\Delta x < 0$. The question is, Which is which? To answer this question, begin by taking a point to the left of the $\Delta x = 0$ curve in Figure 8-32. In particular, choose the point strategically so that it will lie on the $\Delta p = 0$ curve, as does point *F*. This guarantees that at such a point the rate of change in prices, $\Delta p/p$, is zero. However, this point lies to the left of the full-employment level, $\bar{v}$; it follows, then, that the money wage should be falling. With unchanging price level and falling money wage, the real wage is falling: $\Delta p/p = 0 > \Delta W/W$. Thus x will be rising at this point (i.e., $\Delta x > 0$). It follows that *to the left of the* $\Delta x = 0$ *curve,* $\Delta x > 0$, since the real wage is falling in this region.

In a similar fashion, a point such as G to the right of the $\Delta x = 0$ curve, but *on* the $\Delta p = 0$ curve, reveals a rising real wage, which implies a falling employment (i.e., $\Delta p/p = 0 < \Delta W/W$, inducing $\Delta x < 0$). This information is shown in the phase plane of Figure 8-34a.

Note that in the case in which the $\Delta x = 0$ curve is upward sloping, to its right $\Delta x > 0$ and to its left $\Delta x < 0$, as Figure 8-34b shows.

We have established everything we need to know regarding points on and off the singular curve $\Delta x = 0$. On the other hand, the characteristics of the $\Delta p = 0$ singular curve remain identical with the ones established in the preceding section, which, for convenience, are reproduced in Figure 8-35.

FIGURE 8-34

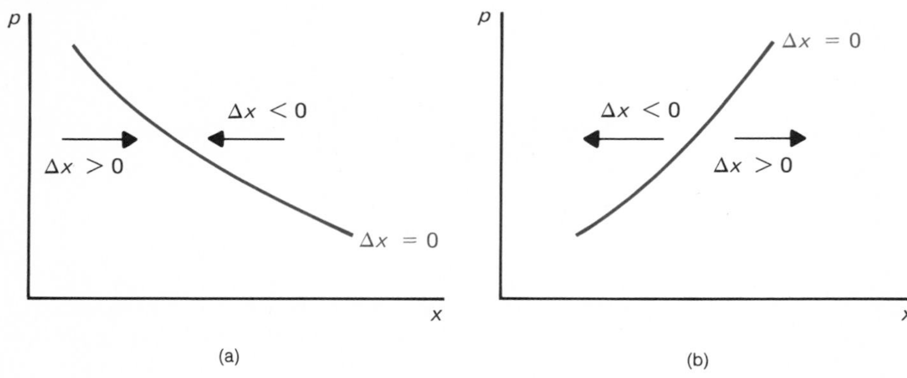

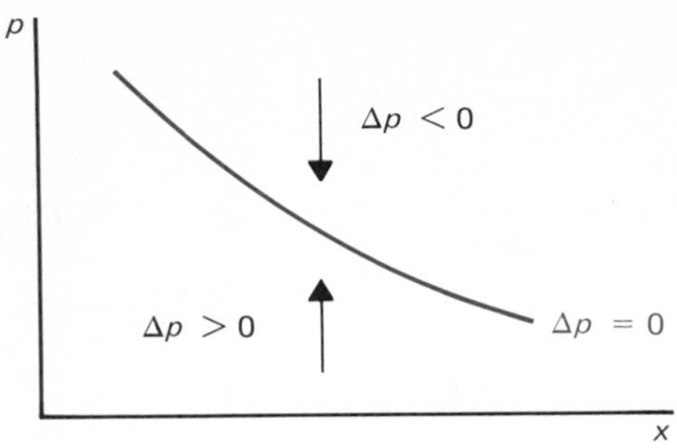

FIGURE 8-35

FULL EQUILIBRIUM AND DYNAMICS OF THE SYSTEM

At a true equilibrium all motion stops. In particular, employment and the price level, among other things, should remain constant. (For employment to remain constant, the real wage must not change, which, in turn, implies that the money wage and the price level must change at the same rate.) This happens at the intersection of the $\Delta p = 0$ and the $\Delta x = 0$ curves. We have already seen that the intersection occurs at full employment, that is, when the equilibrium value of x, call it x^*, is equal to $\bar{v}$. Briefly, we can see that employment will remain constant if the real wage does not change, a situation that occurs only when money wages and the price level change at the same rate. However, since the market for goods and services also clears at equilibrium, the price level does not change. It follows, therefore, that the rate of change in money wages (which should be equal to that of prices) must also be zero. But this happens, in this wage flexibility case, only if the labor market is cleared. Thus the equilibrium occurs at full employment, as shown in Figure 8-36, which determines point E with values (p^*,x^*) where $x^* = \bar{v}$.

FIGURE 8-36

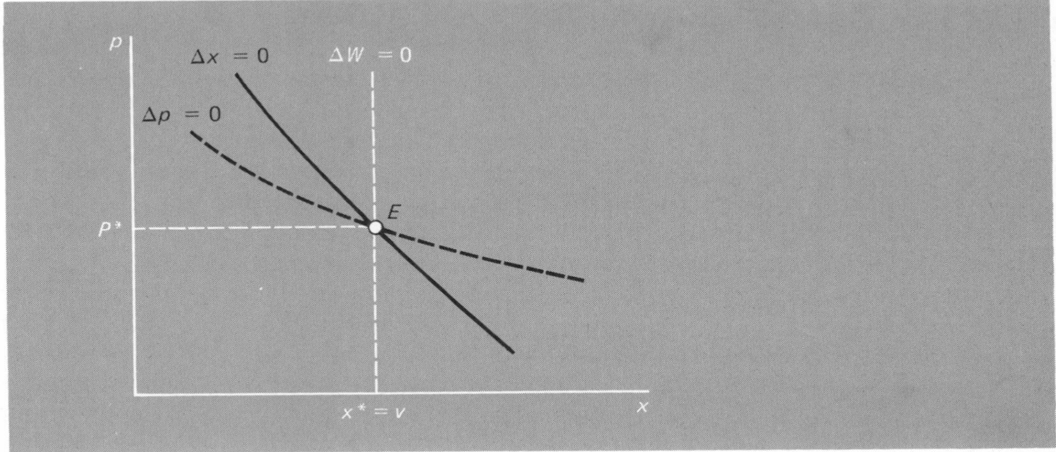

But what about the third endogenous variable of the system, namely, W? Its equilibrium value is easy to determine once we know p^* and $x^* = v$. From the marginal productivity condition, it follows that $W^* = p \cdot \text{MP}\bar{v}$ (where we inserted $\bar{v}$ for N in order to denote the marginal product of labor at full employment, $\bar{v}$). We can even present it diagrammatically in the (p,x)-plane, a representation that must, of course, be implicit. Recall that there is one productivity line passing through each point (see Figure 8-17). Such a line passes through point E with a nametag, W^*, as reproduced in Figure 8-37.

FIGURE 8-37 DETERMINATION OF p^*, x^*, W^*

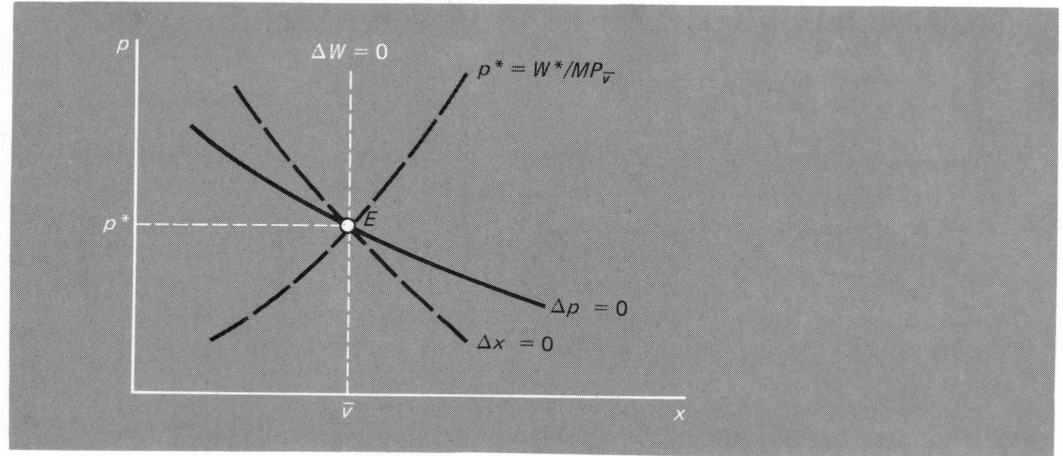

We shall now examine whether the equilibrium point will materialize. We begin by supposing that the economy finds itself with prices and employment different from the equilibrium ones, either because it is the beginning of "history" or because there was a displacement of equilibrium. But are there forces in operation to bring the economy back to equilibrium?

First, we examine the phase plane incorporating the information of both the $\Delta x = 0$ and the $\Delta p = 0$ curves. We see in Figure 8-38 that no matter where the economy may find itself temporarily, all the motions are toward equilibrium. For example, point A reflects excess supply of goods and services, which will cause the price level to fall. On the other hand, at that point there is excess supply of labor causing a fall in money wages. In fact, there is so much excess supply of labor that the fall in money wages is proportionately greater than the fall in prices. This implies that the real wage falls and that there is, therefore, increased hiring of labor even if the prices of goods produced are falling. At a point like B there is excess demand for goods and services; thus the price level will rise. But since there is unemployment, the money wage will fall. And with the real wage falling on both counts, employment will increase. Note that at a point like C, lying above both curves but to the left of the imagined $\Delta W = 0$ curve, the price level falls proportionately more than the money wage does, so that the real wage rises and, therefore, employment falls.

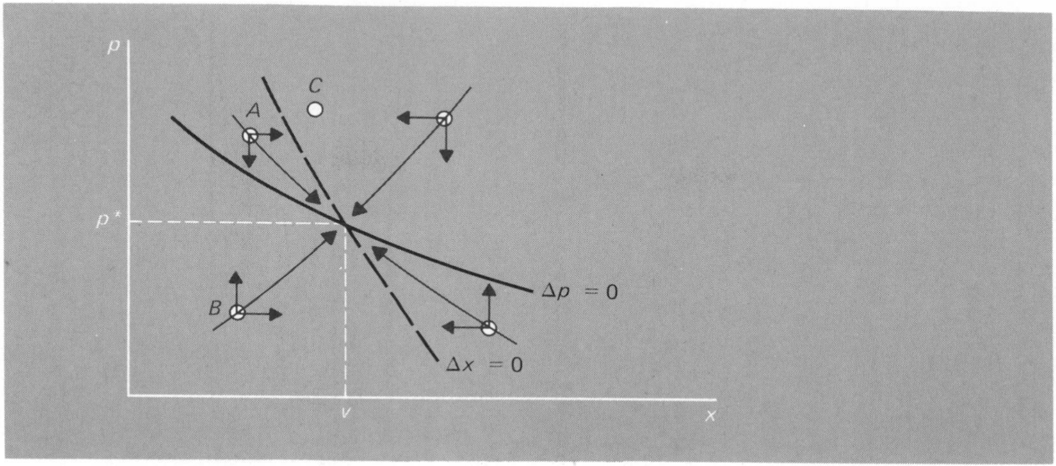

FIGURE 8-38 STABILITY

What we have just proved is that when the marginal propensity to spend is less than one, the economic system is definitely stable. Moreover, the system is stable even if the marginal propensity to spend is greater than one, as long as it is not so great that it makes the (positive) *IS* curve steeper than the *LM* curve (in the [*i*,*x*] plane). However, stability may or may not occur if the marginal propensity to spend is so great that the *IS* curve is steeper than the *LM* curve. Figure 8-39 describes the case of a stable, even though oscillating, system, while Figure 8-40 shows the case of unstable oscillations.

It is reassuring to know that even if the marginal propensity to spend is greater than one, the system can still be stable and, therefore, usable. This statement is important, since there is no *a priori* reason why the marginal propensity to spend should be either less than one or even merely small.

FIGURE 8-39

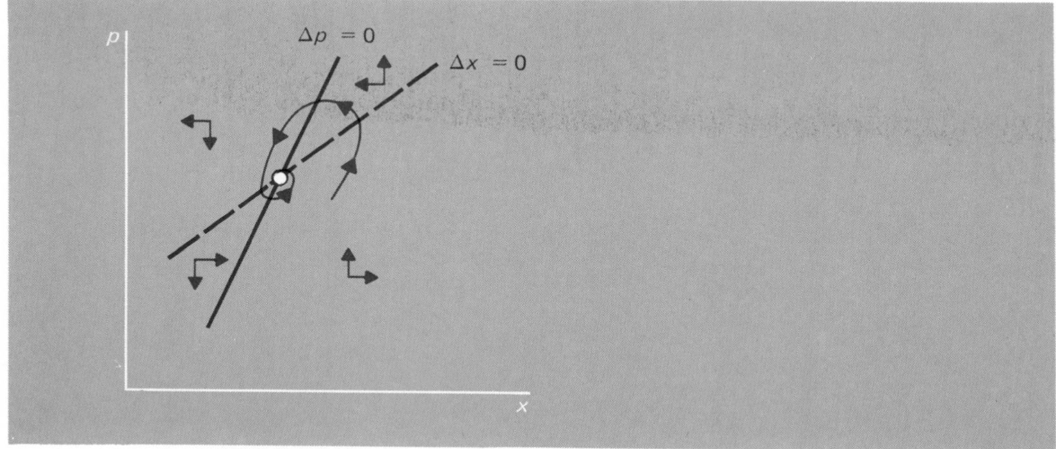

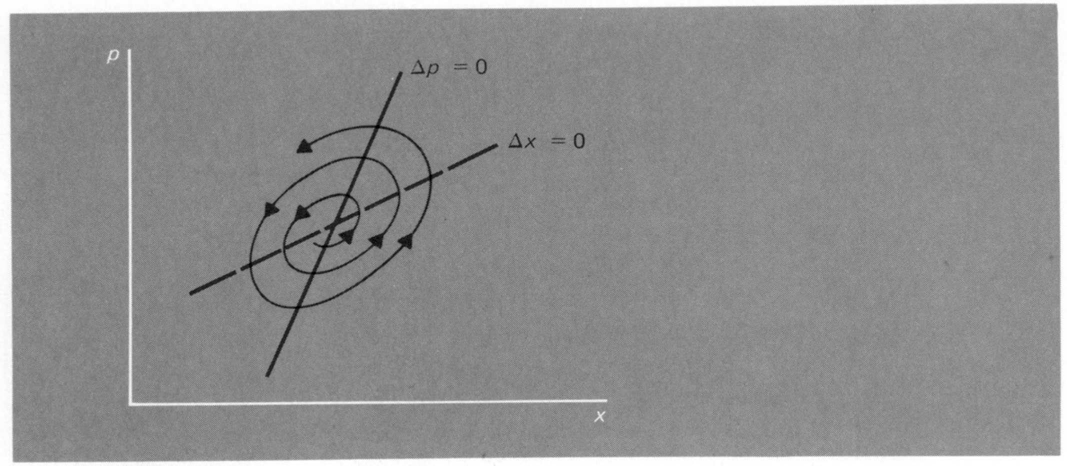

FIGURE 8-40

The extreme Keynesian cases are represented in Figure 8-41. It is clear that in the extreme cases, of a liquidity trap or of interest inelasticity of aggregate demand for goods, money-wage flexibility is no remedy for increasing employment. In fact, there is the tendency for a collapse of the system, that is, for the price level to fall to zero! It is, then, a relief that these cases are not expected to materialize. Otherwise we would face a total collapse of the economic system, and not just chronic unemployment.

We saw earlier that *at equilibrium* we can determine the wage rate W^*, as well as prices, p^*, and employment, $x^* = \nu$. The same holds true even for points outside equilibrium; we use the same reasoning as when we determined W^*. Recall that through every point in the *(p,x)*-plane a productivity line, implying a specific money wage, passes. That money wage is the one consistent with the specified p

FIGURE 8-41

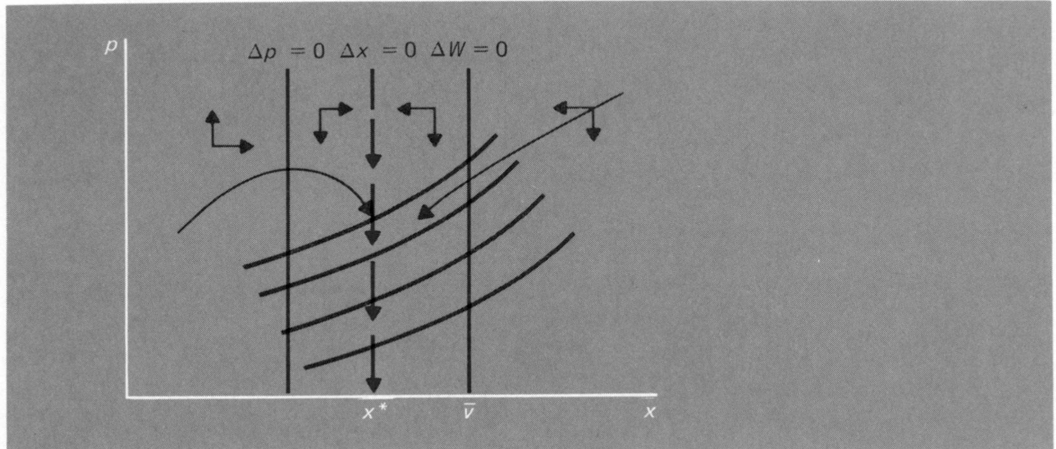

and x, as we can see from Figure 8-42. Moreover, as the economy moves along the trajectory AE, we can, in a similar way, read from the appropriate productivity line the movements of the money wage. For example, when the economy is at point A' with $p = p_1$ and $x = x_1$, the money wage has fallen to W_1.

Another important point should be emphasized here. The trajectories emanating from any point should be consistent with the information provided by the $\Delta W = 0$ curve. This is especially important for a point like B in Figure 8-43, where

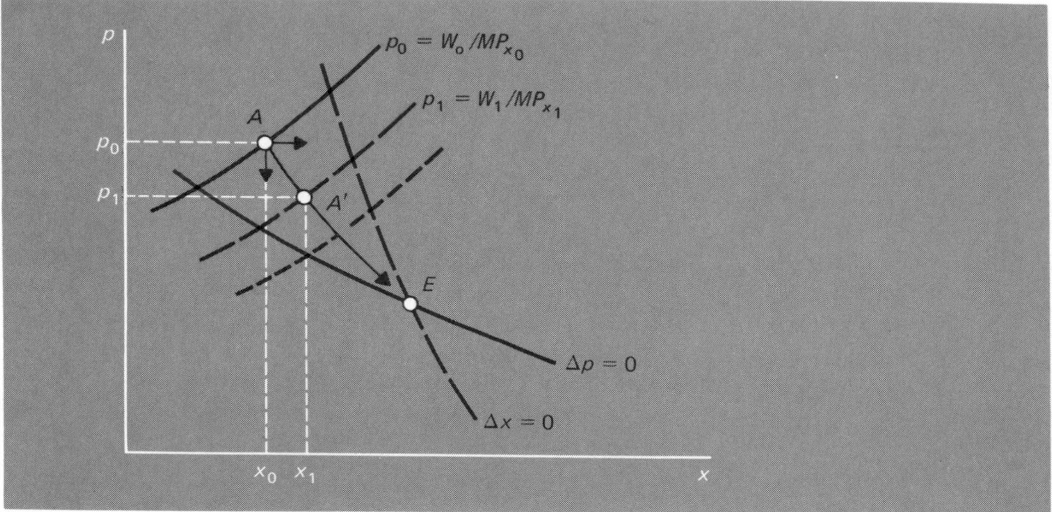

FIGURE 8-42

FIGURE 8-43

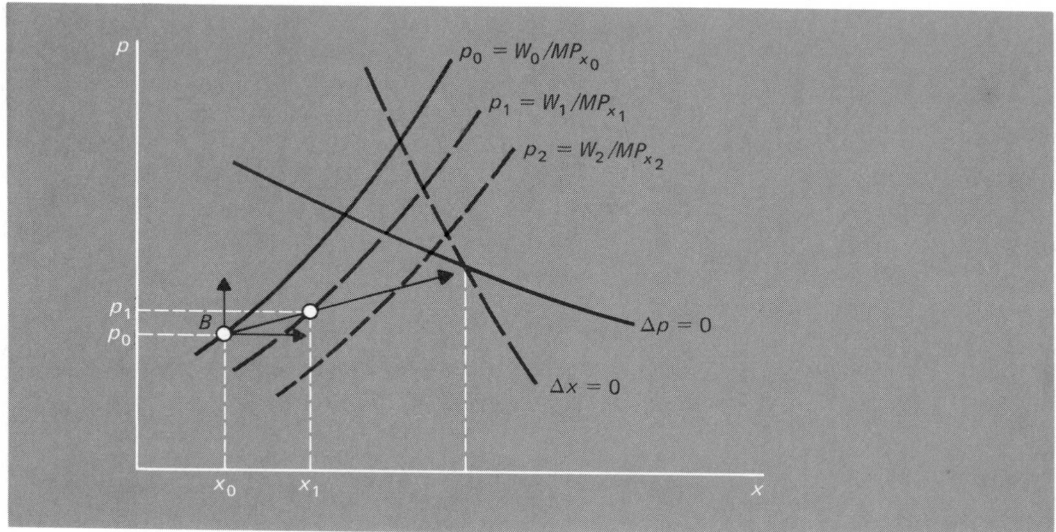

the upward movement of prices and employment should be consistent with the fact that there is unemployment and, therefore, a fall in the money wage. But a fall in money wages can be shown with a productivity line farther to the right. Thus the slope of the trajectory must be smaller than the slope of the family of productivity curves here.

The analysis of this section can be extended in several directions. It can be shown that an expansionary (monetary or fiscal) policy will shift both the $\Delta x = 0$ and the $\Delta p = 0$ curves upward so that they will intersect at the original employment level. In this case both monetary policy and fiscal policy are neutral—provided the assumptions of the model, especially the assumptions of no expectation formation and of money-wage flexibility, hold. In such a case the implication of this exercise is that both the price level and the money wage increase by the same percentage, leaving real wages and, therefore, employment unchanged. As with the model of this section, the result of this exercise is clearly a long-run one. In fact, by repeating this policy and tracing the equilibrium points, one can get the true long-run supply curve, which is vertical in the (p,x)-plane and, therefore, in the (p, Y)-plane.

One may wonder why expansionary economic policy is even attempted in an economy that exhibits full employment, such as the one described in this section. For this reason we shall examine "stabilization policies" only when they may be needed; namely, when money wages are temporarily fixed or when the system exhibits oscillations, stable or unstable. These are topics taken up in the next chapter.

QUESTIONS

1. Under what conditions is the following statement correct? "We can increase the price level and employment only if we increase the money supply." Are these conditions likely to be satisfied?
2. In deciding whether it is profitable to expand their plants, firms (or their creditors) take into consideration an element of risk. On the other hand, in deciding whether to invest their wealth in bonds or money, the public is faced with the risk of capital gains or losses.

   Suppose the relevant estimates of risk decrease. What will happen to the prices of goods and services and the employment level? Trace the effects through the markets and explain each step fully.
3. Suppose that, due to the preaching of a modern-day Ben Franklin, people save more at each level of their income. What will happen to the price level, the interest rates, and the level of employment? (Assume that the economy is initially at equilibrium with less than full employment.)
4. Is the following statement true or false? Why? "We know that prices rise (fall) if, and only if, there is excess demand for (excess supply of) goods and services. Therefore Keynes must have been wrong when he asserted that employment rises (falls) if, and only if, there is excess demand for (excess supply of) goods and services."

5. Derive the "$EM = 0$ and $EG = 0$" curve in the case when the $EG = 0$ curve is steeper than the $EM = 0$ curve in the (i,x)-plane. Assuming that the money market clears instantaneously, in which areas does the goods market exhibit excess demand? Excess supply?
6. Given profit maximization by firms and an assumption of fixed money wages, trace the movement of the economy toward equilibrium from a position of excess supply in the goods market.
7. Prove that when money wages are flexible, the $\Delta x = 0$ curve intersects the $\Delta p = 0$ curve at full employment. Why is this result important to the overall results of the model?
8. Show that if the $\Delta p = 0$ curve is upward sloping in the (p,x)-plane, then the $\Delta x = 0$ curve is also upward sloping but less steep than the $\Delta p = 0$ curve. Also show that to the right of the $\Delta x = 0$ curve $\Delta x > 0$ and to its left $\Delta x < 0$.
9. Explain verbally why full equilibrium in this model must occur at full employment.
10. What restrictions on the marginal propensity to spend are *sufficient* to guarantee that the system is stable? What restrictions are *necessary* for the system to be stable?
11. It is claimed that the modern macroeconomic framework cannot examine the "supply side" of the economy, and therefore it concentrates exclusively on the "demand side." As a proof, it is pointed out that policy makers rely on demand management, such as manipulating the money supply and the government budget. Evaluate this thesis.
12. Evaluate: "Since only money matters, we should not worry about the recent slowdown in productivity; nor should we worry about market power, whether domestic (trade unions, monopolies) or foreign (oil cartels), whether natural (utilities) or government-induced (minimum wages, agricultural price supports)."

REFERENCES

(See Also the References for Chapter 7)

KEYNES, J. M., *The General Theory of Employment, Interest and Money.* New York: Harcourt, Brace & Co., 1936.

KLEIN, LAWRENCE R., "The Supply Side," *American Economic Review,* March 1978, pp. 1–7.

PATINKIN, DON, "Price Flexibility and Full Employment," *American Economic Review,* 1948, pp. 543–64.

U.S. DEPARTMENT OF COMMERCE, *Growth Policy for the Eighties* (Proceedings of a Workshop on Supply-Side Economics, Washington, D.C., February 14, 1980).

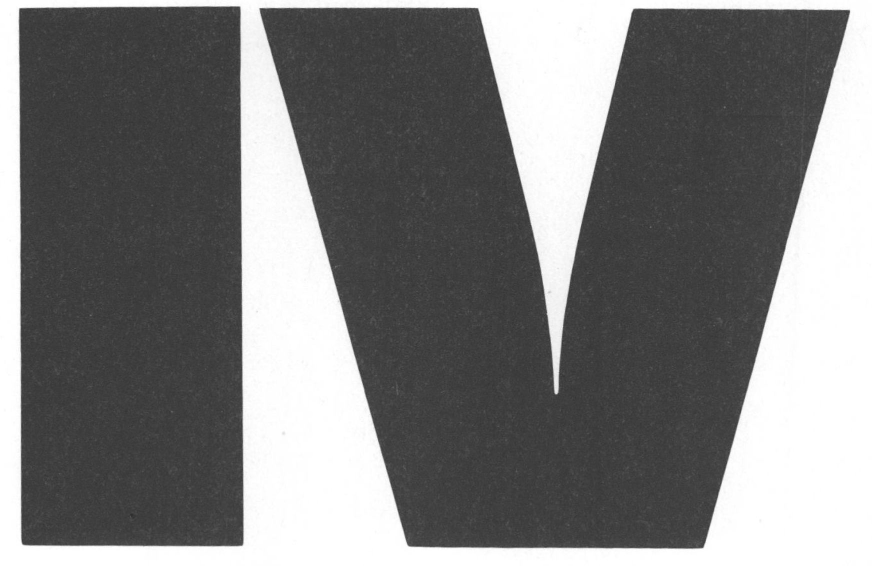

IV economic stabilization, inflation, and unemployment

9 The Role of Monetary and Fiscal Policy in Economic Stabilization

The complete macroeconomic model developed in Chapter 8 will now be applied to real-world situations. We shall utilize this model in examining how monetary and fiscal policies really work, an exposition that will be complemented with historical illustrations.

In Section I we examine how the proper authorities, by manipulating the money supply or the budget deficit, can achieve a new alternative equilibrium with a permanently higher level of employment. We shall refer to this sort of economic policy as *comparative static* stabilization. Of course, achieving a *permanently higher equilibrium* level of employment implies that the economy exhibited *unemployment equilibrium* in the first place. For this reason we shall utilize in this section the *fixed money-wage model,* which we know is capable of establishing unemployment equilibrium. The major result of this section, barring the unrealistic special cases, is that both monetary and fiscal policy are capable of increasing employment, but at the expense of a higher price level. Examples from modern U.S. history, spanning the period from the Great Depression to the present, will then be provided. In this historical journey we shall witness both correct and incorrect—even disastrous—implementations of monetary and fiscal policy.

Some real-world implications of a situation in which more employment is achieved only in combination with higher prices provide the theme of Section II. Two politico-economic philosophies are introduced and examined there. The first philosophy objects to *price stability* if it is achieved at the expense of jobs. In other words, the party espousing this philosophy cares more about *employment* than about price stability. This is why we call this the *Employment Stability party,* or the *ES party.* The second philosophy objects to more jobs if they are achieved at the expense of higher prices. This party, which obviously cares more about price stability than about employment stability, is called the *Price Stability party,* or the *PS party.*

In this section, however, we see that single-mindedness in the pursuit of either of these goals, price stability or employment stability, could lead to catastrophic results. For example, in the face of a particular outside disturbance, such as an increase in "market power" that adversely affects *supply,* single-minded pursuit of employment stability (or "pegging") could produce inflation. On the other hand, the same disturbance could produce severe recessions if the PS party is in power and attempts to stick to the goal of price stability.

Although shades of these two philosophies exist in political parties all over the world, we shall examine real-world situations taken from modern American history. In fact, the *great recession* of 1974–75 is explained as the natural outcome of a relentless pursuit of the PS party philosophy. We shall find that the roots of this recession were disturbances on the supply side, such as (a) crop failure and the rise in grain prices, (b) devaluation of the dollar, (c) quadrupling of oil prices by OPEC, and (d) drastic wage increases that followed the lifting of wage and price controls.

It is interesting to see that the 1978–80 recession, almost as severe as the one in 1974–75, also has its roots in supply-side shocks, such as (a) the doubling of oil prices, (b) inflationary expectations caused by the belief that the imposition of wage-price controls was imminent, and (c) a drastic productivity slowdown. We shall also note that the (new) administration and the Fed responded to these supply shocks in a manner reminiscent of the response by the earlier administration in 1974–75.

In Section II we also examine several ways to favorably influence the supply side, by reversing the effects of the shocks. One way is to provide incentives, mainly for capital formation, to improve the economy's productivity. A second way is the reduction in tax rates, which, by increasing after-tax wages and profits, improves the efficiency of both labor and capital. This is a modification, as well as a generalization, of the idea associated with the "Laffer curve." A third way is the deliberate reduction in market power, whether this power is attributed to natural monopolies or to government regulations. It should be mentioned that the outcome of these three measures, namely, the decrease in prices and the rise in employment, meets with the approval of both political philosophies.

Section III examines the issues and problems associated with the use of *dynamic stabilization* policies, a term that refers to the manipulation of the money supply and of the budget deficit in order to reduce, or possibly eliminate, oscillations in key economic magnitudes, especially employment and the price level (or the rate of inflation). In the real world the most frequently used stabilization policies are of this dynamic variety, and for this reason this use of economic policy is controversial. Some economists argue that this conduct of economic policy should not be left to the *discretion* of *authorities,* but that the latter should follow a set of predetermined *rules.* (This is the famous rules *versus* authorities debate.) Some of these same economists also argue that the *only* rule to be followed is a fixed rate of growth in the money supply, a prescription that is recommended in the belief that the economy is basically stable; in fact, it is asserted that if it were not for "bad" monetary policies, the economy would never experience any oscillations at all. The merits or demerits of all these assertions will also be explained in this section.

I. MONETARY AND FISCAL POLICY: COMPARATIVE STATIC STABILIZATION

We shall first examine how monetary and fiscal policy can *permanently* increase employment. A permanent increase in employment can come about only if an *alternative* equilibrium is reached. For this reason we shall call these policies comparative static stabilization policies. (As is well known, the examination of alternative equilibria is the province of comparative statics.) And we know that an equilibrium exhibiting unemployment can materialize in the case of fixed money wages—at a sufficiently high level. Therefore this is the model we shall now utilize.

1. THE MECHANICS OF MONETARY AND FISCAL POLICY

We begin by assuming that the equilibrium level of employment, $\bar{x}$ in Figure 9-1, is considered too low by the government. This equilibrium is achieved by the intersection, at E, of the "$\Delta p = 0$ and $\Delta x = 0$" curve, with the "productivity" or "supply" curve depicting a fixed money wage equal to W_3. An increase in employment can be accomplished by either fiscal or monetary policy and without having to force a money-wage cut; what we need is a shift of the $\Delta p = 0$, $\Delta x = 0$ curve to the right. If, for example, the central government wants to increase employment from $\bar{x}$ to v (in Figure 9-1) without changing the money wage, it must shift the $\Delta p = 0$, $\Delta x = 0$ curve sufficiently to the right (i.e., to the position $[\Delta p = 0, \Delta x = 0]'$), so that it

FIGURE 9-1

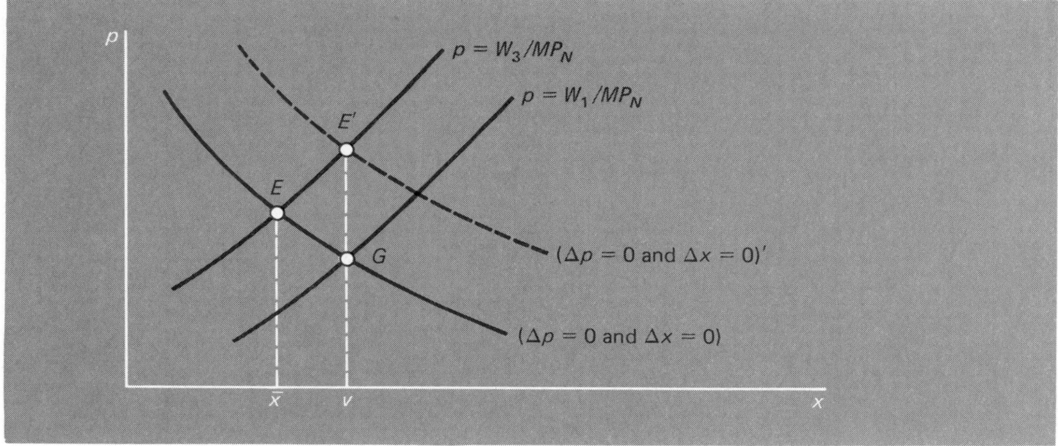

will intersect the same productivity $(p = W_3/MP_N)$ curve at $x = v$ (i.e., point E' in Figure 9-1). What we need to show, then, is that monetary and fiscal policy can indeed shift the $\Delta p = 0$, $\Delta x = 0$ curve.

1.A. Monetary policy

Beginning with monetary policy, let us suppose that the nominal money supply is increased by the monetary authority. But how will this increase affect the $\Delta p = 0$, $\Delta x = 0$ curve? To answer this question, we must go back to the components from which we constructed the curve, for example, Figure 8-1 in Chapter 8. Recall that all the $EM = 0$ curves in the upper panel of that figure were drawn for the same stock of nominal money, say M_0. Since we know that an increase in M shifts *an* $EM = 0$ curve to the right, it follows that *each* of the $EM = 0$ curves in the upper panel of that graph will shift to the right. This is explicitly shown in Figure 9-2. Each of the curves in the upper panel is now identified with respect to both

FIGURE 9-2 MONETARY POLICY: INCREASE IN M FROM M_0 to M_1

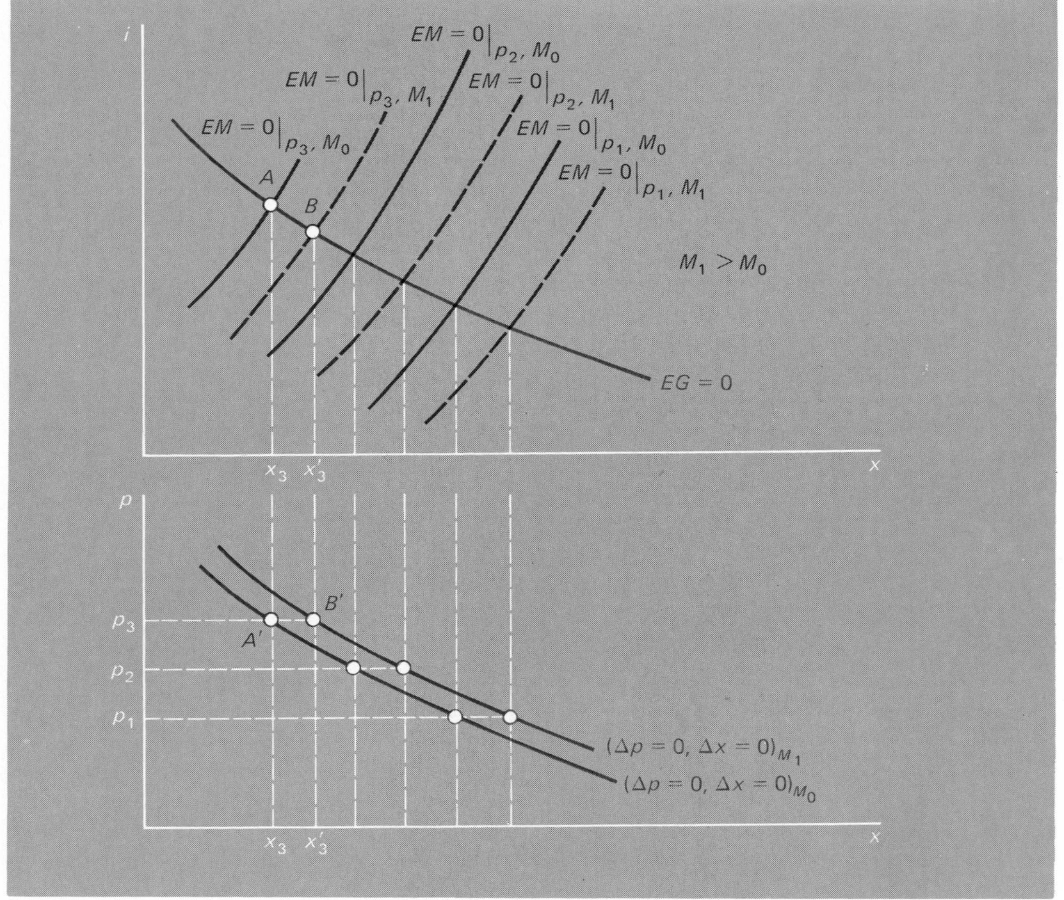

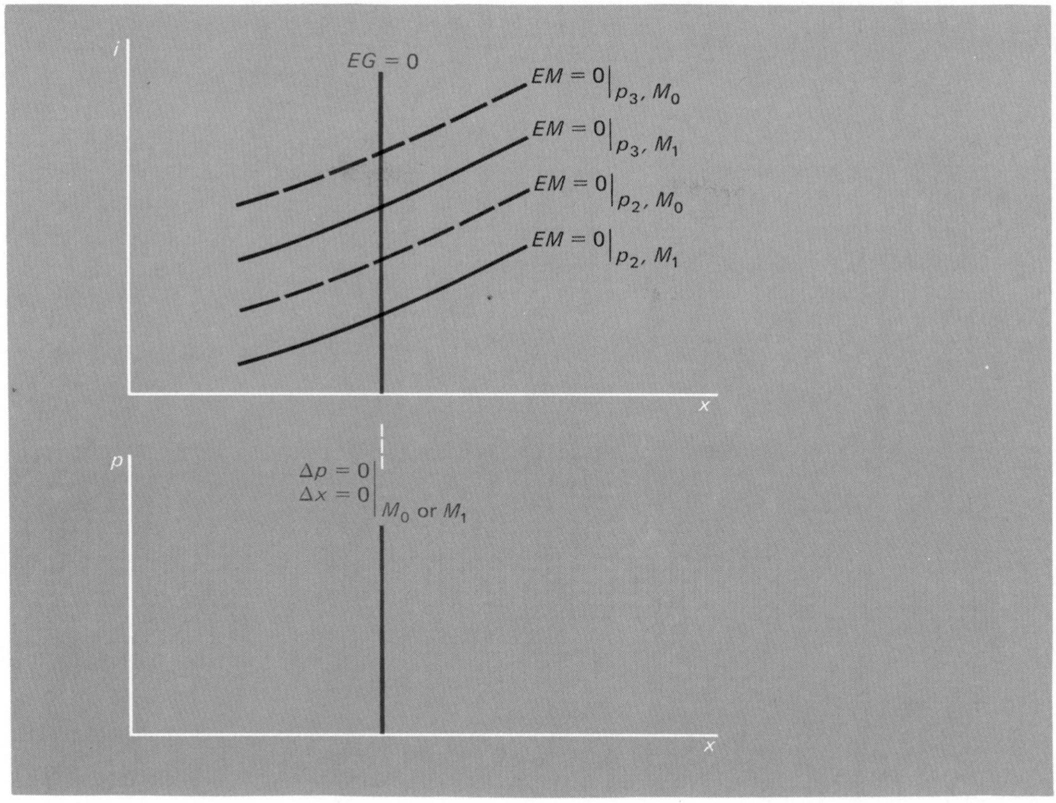

FIGURE 9-3 MONETARY POLICY WITH INTEREST INELASTICITY OF EG WITHOUT A PIGOU EFFECT

the price level and the quantity of money for which it is relevant. For the same price level, an increase in M increases x. This holds for each p, and therefore the $\Delta p = 0$, $\Delta x = 0$ curve shifts to the right (and above). With $p = p_3$, for example, the increase in M from M_0 to M_1 gives us point B instead of A in the upper panel. These can be translated as points B' and A', respectively, in the lower panel of Figure 9-2. Thus, for $p = p_3$, an increase in M increases x from x_3 to x_3'. We can now observe a similar increase for every other value of p. The graph in Figure 9-2 was constructed ignoring the special cases *and* the Pigou effect. In the presence either of a liquidity trap or of interest inelasticity of aggregate demand, monetary policy cannot shift the $\Delta p = 0$, $\Delta x = 0$ curve, and thus it cannot increase employment. This is shown in Figure 9-3, which examines the case of interest inelasticity of aggregate demand.

We know that when a Pigou effect is introduced in this case, the $\Delta p = 0$, $\Delta x = 0$ curve becomes negatively sloped. In such a case, of course, monetary policy will shift the curve, so that it can indeed increase employment, as seen in Figure 9-4. Of course, the same is true of the monetarist case depicted in Figure 9-5. Therefore we have proved the proposition that, in general, an increase in the nominal money

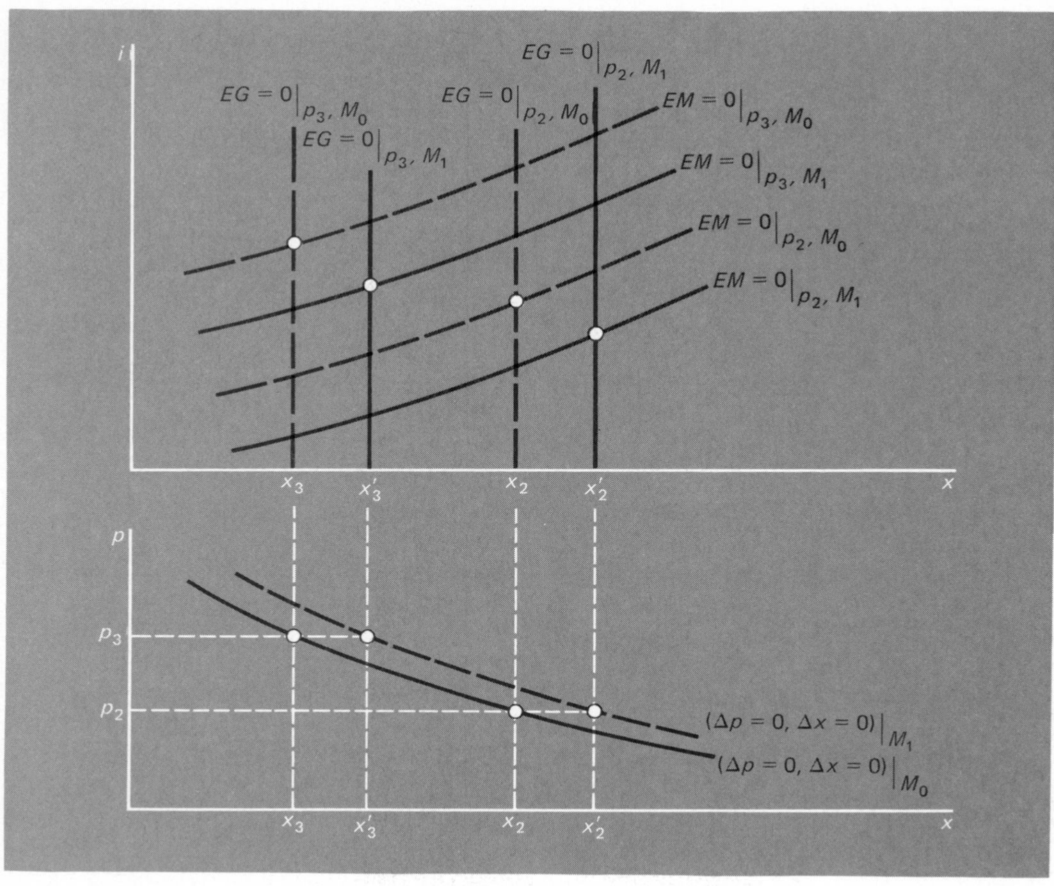

FIGURE 9-4 MONETARY POLICY WITH INTEREST INELASTICITY OF EG *AND* A PIGOU EFFECT

supply will increase employment *and* the price level. However, the only exceptions are the unrealistic special cases without a Pigou effect.

1.B. Fiscal policy

We can easily see that an increase in the budget deficit will, in general, shift the $\Delta p = 0$, $\Delta x = 0$ curve to the right. The usual case is described in Figure 9-6, where an increase in the budget deficit from z_0 to z_1 shifts the $EG = 0$ curve to the right in the upper panel, since this implies that for the same price level, employment will be higher. Since this is true of *every* price level, the $\Delta p = 0$, $\Delta x = 0$ curve shifts to the right in the lower panel of Figure 9-6. If the $\Delta p = 0$, $\Delta x = 0$ curve is vertical (reflecting one of the two special cases and the absence of a Pigou effect), it will also shift to the right when the budget deficit increases, a case shown in Figure 9-7.

In the extreme monetarist case, that is, when the excess demand for money is independent of the interest rate, fiscal policy is incapable of shifting the $\Delta p = 0$,

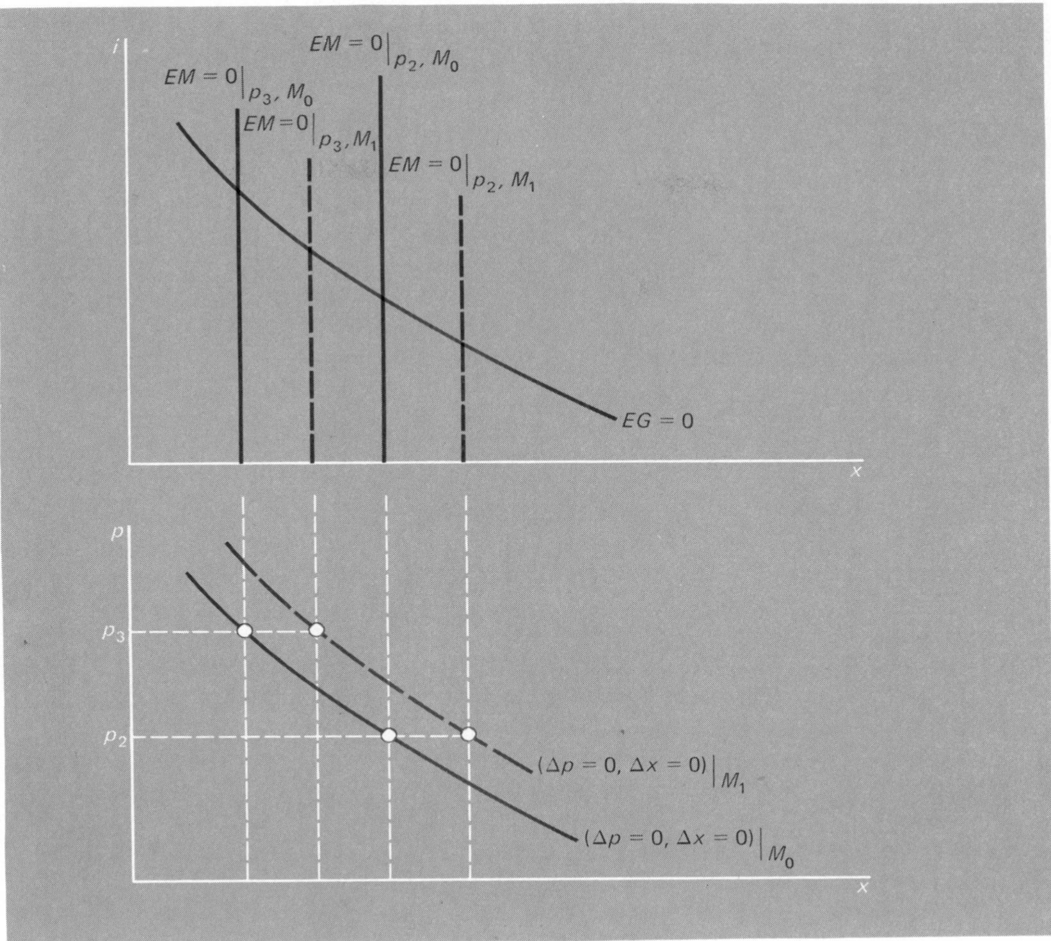

FIGURE 9-5 MONETARY POLICY IN THE MONETARIST CASE

$\Delta x = 0$ curve, and thus fiscal policy cannot be used as a weapon against unemployment. Figure 9-8 depicts this case. The upper panel shows that even when the budget deficit increases, employment remains the same for every price level. The only change will be in the interest rate, a variable not displayed in the lower panel. Thus the $\Delta p = 0$, $\Delta x = 0$ curve does not shift, and we see that commercial policy aimed at increasing the trade surplus has precisely the same effects as an increase in the budget deficit. What is needed, therefore, is the substitution of the term "trade surplus" for "budget deficit," or the symbol v for z.

In summary, we see that monetary policy is an effective tool in the fight against unemployment that is accompanied by wage rigidity. It fails only in the unrealistic cases of a liquidity trap or interest inelasticity of aggregate demand for goods when each of them is combined with the absence of a Pigou effect. Similarly, fiscal policy is effective barring the unrealistic case of interest insensitivity of the

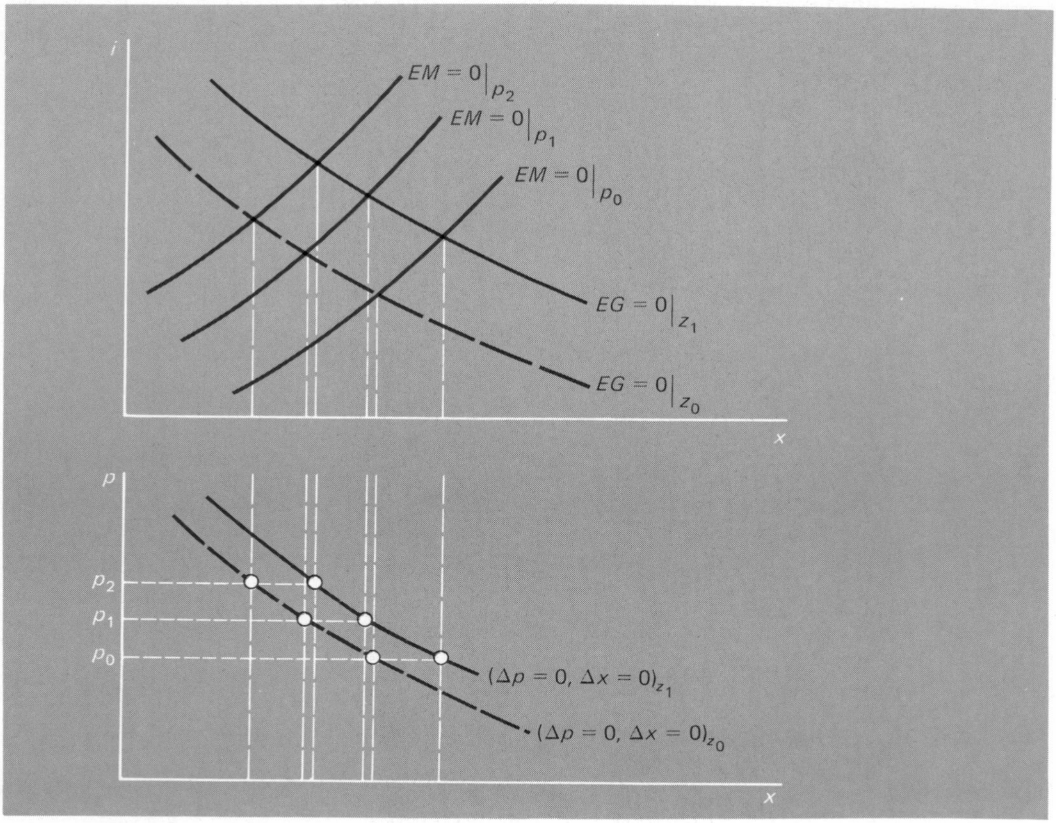

FIGURE 9-6 FISCAL POLICY: $z_1 > z_0$

FIGURE 9-7

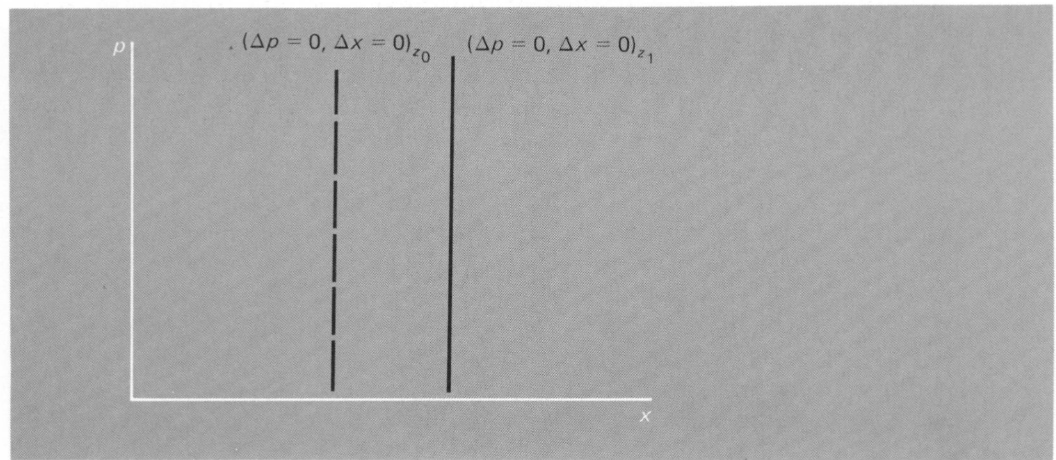

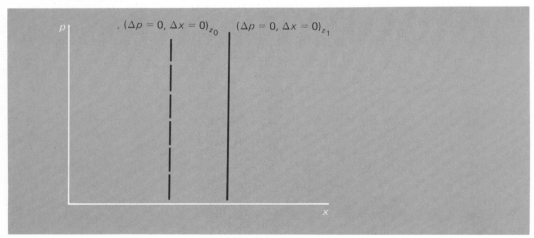

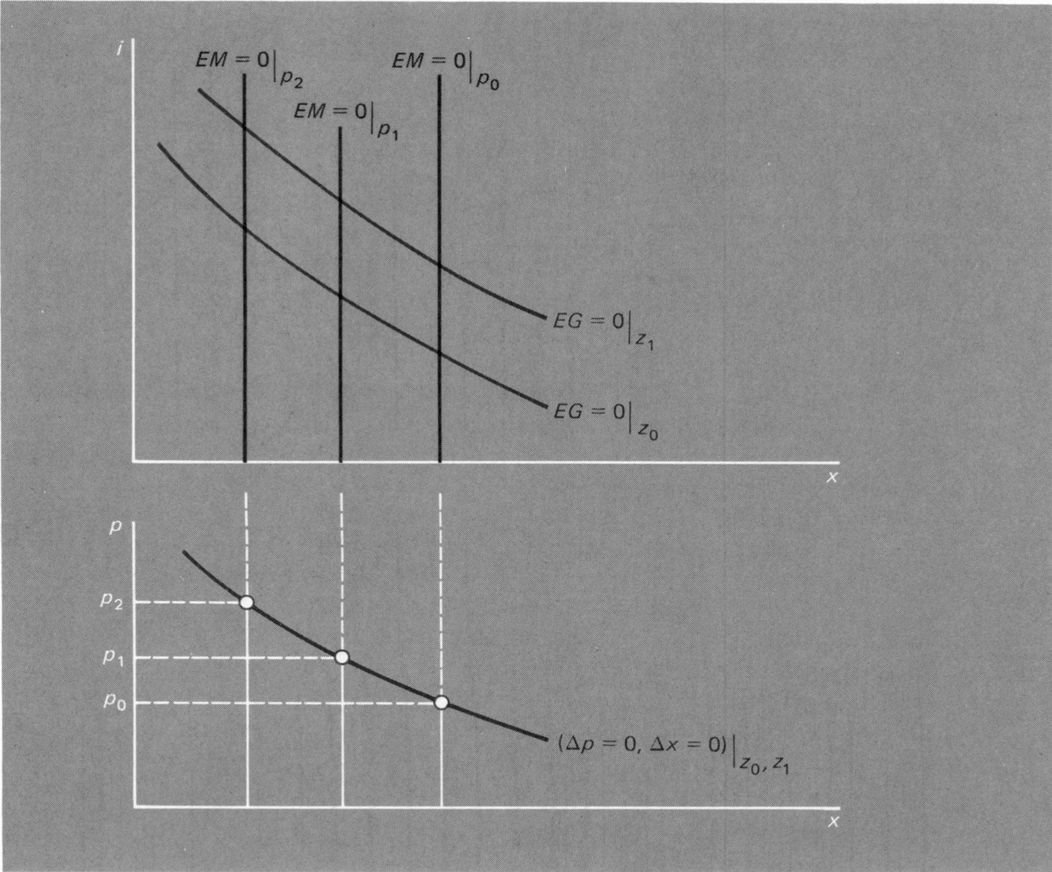

FIGURE 9-8 FISCAL POLICY IN THE MONETARIST CASE

excess demand for money. Yet another important conclusion in this section concerns the price level: *Whether we use monetary or fiscal policy to fight unemployment, the price level will rise. The price level will not rise only when the policy used (be it monetary or fiscal) fails in its assigned task to increase employment.* This needs to be emphasized in view of the confusion in the literature. Some economists have claimed that fiscal policy increases employment without raising the price level, whereas monetary policy increases employment only at the expense of higher prices. That argument ignores the fact that the only way to increase employment is by lowering the *real* wage. But with fixed money wages, the only way to lower the real wage is by increasing the price level. Therefore we see that both policies, monetary and fiscal, have similar qualitative effects on the price level. They do differ, however, in their effects on the interest rate; barring the special cases, the combinations *(p,x)* reflect a higher interest rate when fiscal policy is used.

2. HISTORICAL EXAMPLES

We have established that the price level rises when monetary or fiscal policy is effective in increasing employment. This happened even in the 1930s when the economy was coming out of the Great Depression and 25 percent of the labor force was unemployed. (Between 1933 and 1936 prices were rising at the rate of 2.8 percent per year.) During those years, both monetary and fiscal policy were being applied as antirecession tools. Of course, their application was not based on a well-thought-out analysis, and for this reason it was not methodical. During World War II, again, employment and prices rose together, this time mainly because of increased government expenditure associated with the war effort. (It is generally accepted that because of wartime price controls, the officially recorded prices understated the "true" prices.) Because a part of the government deficit was financed by creating (printing) money, monetary policy was also being used during those years. What we should note here is that prices will rise whether we are at high or low employment levels. We shall discuss later the magnitudes of the rates of change in prices (see Chapter 10). By the end of the war, unemployment was not one of the problems facing the American economy.

So much for the successful—though painful and prolonged—battle against the Great Depression. However, there is no agreement in the profession about its causes. Monetarists argue that it was caused exclusively by monetary mismanagement.[1] But there is agreement that once the Great Depression began, "bad" monetary policy, such as that which led to the banking crisis of 1930 and to the subsequent fall in the money supply, definitely contributed toward making the situation worse. In addition, bad fiscal policy played its role in the Great Depression; in the midst of the Depression (1931–32), in order to balance the budget, the Hoover administration recommended, and Congress approved, a dramatic increase in taxes and a reduction in government spending! No matter how the Depression started, there is no doubt that this aggravated the situation; it lowered both prices and employment.

Fiscal policy in modern times

In more recent times, once again, every deliberately engineered fiscal policy, as well as every expansionary monetary policy, has been effective. The years 1961–65 deserve special note, since that was the one period in American history during which fiscal policy was used both *deliberately* and *methodically* to stimulate economic activity. The 1961–65 experiment provides a success story that economists recall fondly. During the first two to three years of this period, the Kennedy administration designed a policy of gradual expansion, which resulted in an actual, gradual increase in prosperity. (It should be noted that the Kennedy administration took over in the midst of the 1960–61 recession.) By 1963 the administration (and its advisers) had become bolder; they actually aimed at full employment. Their recommendation for a substantial tax cut—both for individuals and for business—was approved in 1964. This tax cut was innovative in these respects: It included not only corporate tax deductions but also an equal amount of tax incentives for investment in plant and

[1] For the classic monetarist position, see the impressive *A Monetary History of the United States 1867–1960,* by Milton Friedman and Anna J. Schwartz (Princeton, N.J.: Princeton University Press, 1963), especially Chap. 7, "The Great Contraction 1929–1933."

equipment; in addition, the tax cut was recommended while the economy was still expanding. This careful guidance of the economy achieved its target; by 1966 unemployment was down to 4 percent, the accepted "full-employment" unemployment rate at the time! In terms of strength and length of the growth process, the economy's performance during the 1960s was unprecedented, at least during peacetime. Also it should be noted that the rate of inflation during 1961–65 was about equal to what it had been during 1955–60.

The period from 1965 on, while again confirming the efficacy of fiscal policy, also underscores the lesson that the conduct of economic policy ultimately rests on political considerations. The year 1965 marked the beginning of a substantial U.S. involvement in the Vietnam War, with drastically higher government spending for that war. President Johnson, because of a variety of political considerations, did not heed his economic advisers' recommendation for a tax increase. This recommended tax hike was designed to reduce the expansionary (inflationary) impact of the increased government spending. With no tax increase, the predictions of economic theory were confirmed when the price level kept rising and unemployment falling, the latter to 3.5 percent in 1969, a figure that was below the 4 percent full-employment figure accepted then.

During 1969 and 1970 the new (Nixon) administration followed a restrictive fiscal policy, prompted by design and by chance, the latter aspect resulting from the beginning of U.S. disengagement from the war in Southeast Asia. Predictably, there was a drastic increase in unemployment, the price society had to pay for the lower inflation.

After the imposition of (peacetime) wage and price controls in August 1971, the Nixon administration followed a wide-scale expansionary policy in 1972 (which was accompanied, as we shall see below, by an equally expansionary monetary policy). Of course, the wage and price controls hid the inflationary pressures on wages and prices, and the expected increase in employment and GNP soon followed. The Nixon administration changed gears immediately after the election and adhered to a very restrictive policy (which was also accompanied by a very restrictive monetary policy). Partly because of this restrictive fiscal (and monetary) policy, the seeds of the "great recession" were sown. Many economists agree that the 1972 fiscal policy was too expansionary, whereas the one that followed, in 1973, was too contractionary. In the midst of the great recession, in 1974, fiscal policy was considered only mildly restrictive, but in view of the great redistribution of income (because of the rising oil prices, and rising grain and food prices), which further reduced aggregate demand, in effect and by default, it was too restrictive. Therefore it did very little to help the economy out of the recession.

The early part of 1975 provides us with an example of ineffective fiscal policy. The Tax Reduction Act of 1975 was designed to lead the economy out of the recession. However, it suffered from a major flaw. All these rebates, tax cuts for individuals and corporations, were only temporary ones, to be used, or given, one time only. As many economists predicted, the rebates had only a minor effect (increase) on consumption and, therefore, on aggregate demand. For the remainder of 1975 and during 1976, fiscal policy was slightly more expansionary, but the economy was already on its way to a slow recovery.

On assuming the presidency, Jimmy Carter suggested another temporary package of tax rebates, but he later withdrew this proposal when it became apparent that the economy was recovering very well and that there was now the danger of severe inflation. A recent example of an effective, but painful, fiscal policy is seen in the years 1978–80, years of extreme inflationary pressures (coming from the supply side). The fiscal policy that was followed, to counter these inflationary pressures, was very restrictive and the economy was almost at a point of another great recession; unemployment reached the 8 percent mark, and, of course, inflation subsided. (Of course, we should add that monetary policy was even more restrictive during this period.) Finally, the substantial reduction in the growth rate of government expenditure and in the tax rates, engineered by the Reagan Administration, have not yet had sufficient time to have their effects felt.

Monetary policy in recent times

Turning now to *examples of effectiveness of monetary policy,* we shall start with the years 1969 and 1970. Beginning in 1969, the year Richard M. Nixon became president, monetarism came into prominence in policy making. Nixon's administration relied mainly on monetarists, who served as advisers and architects of economic policy. Consequently, despite the restrictive nature of fiscal policy, it was monetary policy, beginning in 1969, as we saw above, that provided the main weapon for deflating the economy. This design in policy worked very well to bring inflation down. Unfortunately, the administration and its advisers, believers in the "religion of zero inflation," were not content when a rate of inflation as low as 4 percent (down from over 6 percent) was achieved and at a considerable sacrifice to employment and output. The Federal Reserve, with the administration's active encouragement and full support, pushed for its real target, zero inflation. There was a negative reaction in the profession to the administration's target. It was labeled "unreasonable price stability" by Phelps, who, citing the appalling loss of output and employment, reminded the policy makers that "there is no immaculate connection between money (or fiscal variables) and the price level."[2]

Inflation was very much under control when the administration decided in 1971 to change gears and attempt, instead, to increase employment. Because of its fears of rekindling inflation, the administration imposed wage and price controls in August 1971. According to this program, money wages were frozen, but prices were permitted to vary within bounds. This program had the immediate effect of lowering the real wage and, thereby, inducing profit-maximizing firms to hire more labor.[3] The program also increased aggregate demand from abroad, since the allowable official

---

[2] See Edmund Phelps, "Unreasonable Price Stability: The Pyrrhic Victory over Inflation," in *The Battle against Unemployment,* rev. ed., ed. Arthur M. Okun (New York: W. W. Norton & Co., Inc., 1972). The quotation is from page 215.

[3] It was shown later that price controls were more effective than wage controls. See R. J. Gordon, "The Response of Wages and Prices to the First Two Years of Controls," *Brookings Papers on Economic Activity,* 3 (1973), 765–78; and Charles L. Schultze, "Falling Profits, Rising Profit Margins and the Full Employment Profit Rate," *Brookings Papers on Economic Activity,* 2 (1975), 449–69.

rate of inflation for the United States was lower than the foreign one. Thus employment rose for this reason also. More important, however, was the presence of a very expansionary monetary policy, which was pursued during the various phases (I, II, III, etc.) of the controls. This policy had the expected result: reduction in unemployment. But the consequent rise in prices was hidden behind the controls. And as soon as these controls were lifted, the rate of inflation skyrocketed. (Of course, several other factors, totally unrelated to the increase in the money supply, produced the dramatic increase in inflation in 1973–74: the newly formed oil cartel that quadrupled oil prices, the drastic increase in foreign demand, the lifting of wage-price controls, and the worst U.S. grain crop in more than a decade.)

In 1973 and in 1974 there was a massive monetary effort to lower inflation, which had by then reached the 10 percent mark. As a result, unemployment almost doubled—from 5 percent to over 9 percent. This was stabilization with a vengeance! Unemployment had reached the highest rate since the Great Depression. It can be said that this magnitude is the modern-day analogue to the 1930 Depression. It is interesting that the "great recession" of 1974–75 followed the famous Economic Summit Conference of 1974, convened by the new president, Gerald Ford, to reach a consensus about the economic policies his administration should follow. Although some of the summit's recommendations will be examined in the next section, we can mention here that the economists agreed that the administration should follow moderation in pursuing its policies. This recommendation, as well as others, was ignored by the administration. But did the next administration learn the lessons of the 1973–75 period? We shall see below.

During the recovery period of 1975–76, monetary policy *seemed* to be moderately expansionary. But actually it was more expansionary than it appeared; the *demand* function for money started falling—as we shall see, in greater detail, in both Chapters 13 and 14—which implied that a smaller rate of growth in the money supply could go a lot further toward influencing the economy positively. Moreover, this shifting, or "instability," of the demand for money induced the Fed to pay attention to instruments other than the money aggregates.[4] The Fed deserves (and needs) this acknowledgment, especially in view of widespread criticism of its actions at that time.

We come now to the final episode of a very effective contractionary monetary policy. This episode begins in 1978–79 when inflationary pressures, fueled mainly by shocks on the supply side (but also aided by the hitherto expansionary demand management policies), were increased substantially. These pressures were reminiscent of the ones experienced in 1973–75: rises in food prices and in oil prices, the devaluation of the U.S. currency, and a great productivity slowdown. In fact, the restrictive monetary policy was originally designed primarily to raise the interest rates and support the dollar and only secondarily to fight inflation. This policy was moderately

[4] Because of the alertness of some members of the Fed staff, the instability of the demand function for money was pointed out and a change in policy occurred. See Jared Enzler, Lewis Johnson, and John Paulus, "Some Problems of Money Demand," *Brookings Papers on Economic Activity* 1 (1976), 261–80. See also Stephen M. Goldfeld, "The Case of Missing Money," *Brookings Papers on Economic Activity,* 3 (1976), 683–730.

successful. But as the oil prices skyrocketed and "voluntary" wage-price guidelines were introduced, inflationary expectation drove the actual inflation rate into the double-digit region. (These inflationary expectations were mostly based on the belief that mandatory wage-price controls were imminent.) The Fed's response was a very restrictive policy, which drove interest rates to the 20 percent level for about three months in 1980. This and other policies eventually created a severe recession, with the rate of unemployment at 8 percent, but they reduced inflation, from about 18 to about 10 percent. There has been widespread criticism of the Fed's actions (and, of course, the administration's) for engineering another great recession; the Fed simply "did not learn the lesson" of the 1973–75 recession. However, it must be pointed out that this time the inflationary pressures were considerably stronger and the fears of a runaway inflation very real, as far as the Federal Reserve was concerned. But whether the policy that the Fed followed was the best one is a different matter. In view of this issue, we shall continue examining this episode in the section devoted to supply-side shocks.

However, this last episode had an interesting sequel. The "other policies," referred to above, which were used to combat inflation included *credit controls* enacted for the first time under a Presidential authorization (which has since expired). These credit controls were held at least partly responsible for the dramatic fall in the quantity of money to a level lower than intended by the Federal Reserve for the second quarter of 1980. When the controls were lifted, by July 1980, the quantity of money skyrocketed. To keep the rate of growth in the money supply for the entire year of 1980 within the targeted range, the Federal Reserve was forced to reduce drastically the money supply from October to December 1980 and into January 1981, with the consequence that the interest rates exceeded the 20 percent mark (in fact, 22 percent). A more important reason for the volatility of monetary aggregates (as well as the volatility of interest rates) can be directly attributed to the Federal Reserve's switch in operating procedures. As we shall see in greater detail in Chapter 14, beginning October 6, 1979, to achieve its monetary targets, the Fed has been manipulating reserves rather than the federal funds interest rate. This switch in operating procedures magnified the role of borrowed reserves, something that was inadvertently ignored by the Fed. Moreover, compounding the difficulties, the switch rendered the existing monetary statistical data useless as a guide to monetary policy under the new monetary regime.[5]

II. TWO POLITICO-ECONOMIC PHILOSOPHIES

In the preceding section we established that an increase in employment, brought about by expansionary (monetary or fiscal) policy, is always accompanied by an increase in the price level. It is natural, then, that those who believe that they would gain from an increase in employment would favor this policy. On the other hand,

[5] See Michael G. Hadjimichalakis, "Reserves *vs* Federal Funds Operating Procedures: A General Equilibrium Analysis," *Economics Letters,* vol. 7, 1981, and references cited there.

those who believe that they would lose from the accompanying increase in the price level would be against expansionary policy.

In the former category, we naturally expect to find labor unions. Also in this category are members of minority groups, whether they are labor union members or not, who usually are most vulnerable to unemployment; they are the most likely to be "the last hired and first fired." Members of this first category would be interested in employment stability—of course, at a fairly high level.

Against higher price levels (and the accompanying higher employment levels) must be all of those who are not faced with the possibility of unemployment. Tenured faculty would largely fall into this category! Fixed-income groups are usually in this category, although some pensions and social security benefits are adjusted for price rises. Mostly, however, it is those whose income is primarily from monetary assets (i.e., those who do not depend largely on income from present employment) that are members of this second category. All these people favor price stability. We should emphasize that the distinguishing characteristic of the former group is that they *object to price stability if it is achieved at the expense of jobs.* Similarly, the second group *objects to more jobs if they are achieved at the expense of higher prices.* Everybody (except, perhaps, the large net borrower) is against price increases. But when they are faced with the alternative, they reveal their true preference.

Here we shall examine two politico-economic philosophies, each associated with the special interests of the above-mentioned groups. For concreteness, we shall assume that there are two political parties adhering to those two philosophies and that each intends to pursue domestic economic policies according to the interests of its constituency. As mentioned earlier, the party aiming at employment stability will occasionally be referred to as the ES party; the party interested in achieving price stability will be referred to as the PS party.

We shall assume here that the ES party is committed to using whatever monetary and fiscal policies are needed to peg the employment level at a predetermined (high) level. Similarly, the PS party stands ready to use deliberate economic policy to guarantee a constant price level.

Our analysis will aim at finding the economic consequences of pursuing (separately, of course) each of the two philosophies in the face of a disturbance that moves the economy away from the goal of each party. Again we shall utilize the fixed money-wage model for two reasons. First, we want to examine a situation that permits unemployment equilibrium and thus permits a meaningful economic policy. Second, we want to choose a disturbance linked to one of the reasons behind fixed money wages (as well as fixed monetary rewards of other factors of production), namely, market power.

1. THE PARTY FOR EMPLOYMENT STABILITY—THE ES PARTY

We start the analysis by assuming that the prevailing equilibrium employment level, equal to x_*, is the one desired by the ES party. This equilibrium is labeled ① in Figure 9-9; it is the intersection of the "effective demand" curve and the "productivity," or "supply," curve, consistent with the assumed fixed wage, W_1.

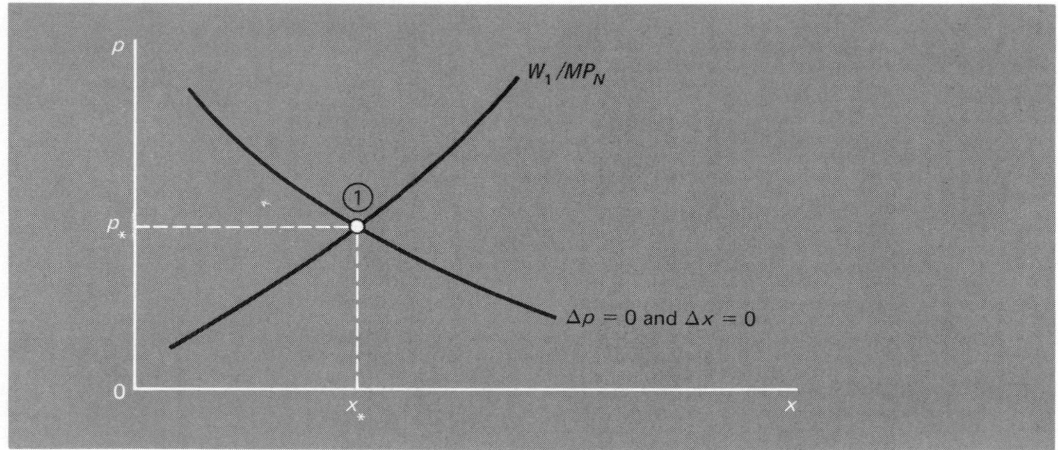

FIGURE 9-9

Let us now suppose that workers, because of newly acquired, additional market power, are able to negotiate a new fixed money wage, higher than before, say equal to W_2. The economy will eventually reach a new equilibrium, namely point ②, at the intersection of the same "effective demand" curve and the new relevant "productivity," or "supply," curve appropriate for the higher wage; this supply curve is labeled W_2/MP_N and is shown in Figure 9-10.

The end result of the higher money wage is both a higher price level and a lower employment level, x_2. (Note: This is one of several cases in which a higher price level is *not* associated with higher employment. This is the reason extra care was taken above to state that higher employment is accompanied by higher prices in the case of an *increase* in effective demand (through policy).) The party for employ-

FIGURE 9-10

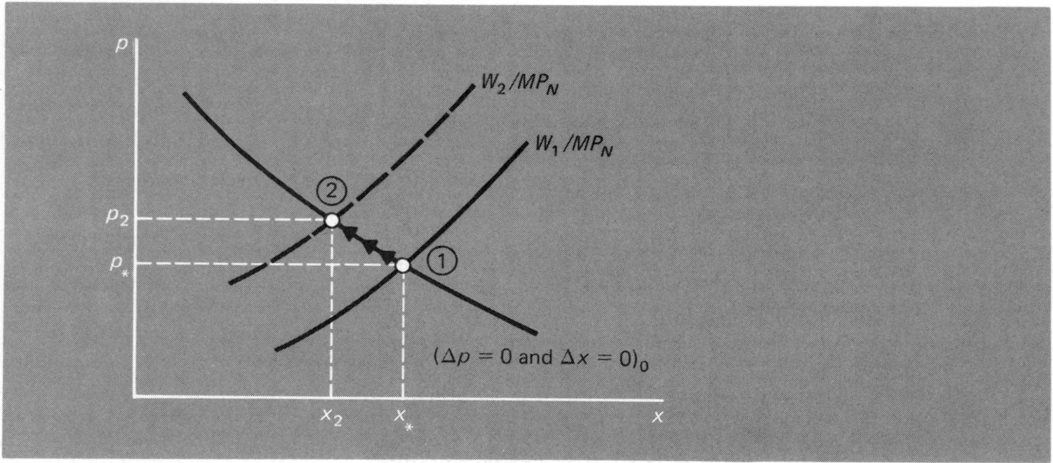

ment stability will obviously react to this reduction in employment, from its desired level, x_*.

Two options are open to the policy maker of the ES party. One is to persuade workers to accept the previous lower money wage, W_1, by pointing out to them that their newly discovered market power was self-defeating; it led to a lower employment level. If workers are not persuaded by this argument in view of, say, inelastic price expectations,[6] it is unlikely that the ES party will then fight with its natural constituents to force them to give up the higher money wage, W_2, already negotiated. The only choice available to the policy maker committed to achieving the employment level x_* is to increase aggregate demand, by either expansionary fiscal or expansionary monetary policy. This expansionary (monetary or fiscal) policy will shift the "effective demand" curve sufficiently to the right, so that it will intersect the supply curve appropriate for the higher wage, labeled W_2/MP_N, precisely at an employment level equal to x_*. This is shown in Figure 9-11 by point ③ at the intersection of the (new) "effective demand" curve, consistent with the expansionary policy; this new "effective demand" curve is labeled $(\Delta p = 0 \text{ and } \Delta x = 0)_1$, as compared with the old one labeled $(\Delta p = 0 \text{ and } \Delta x = 0)_0$.

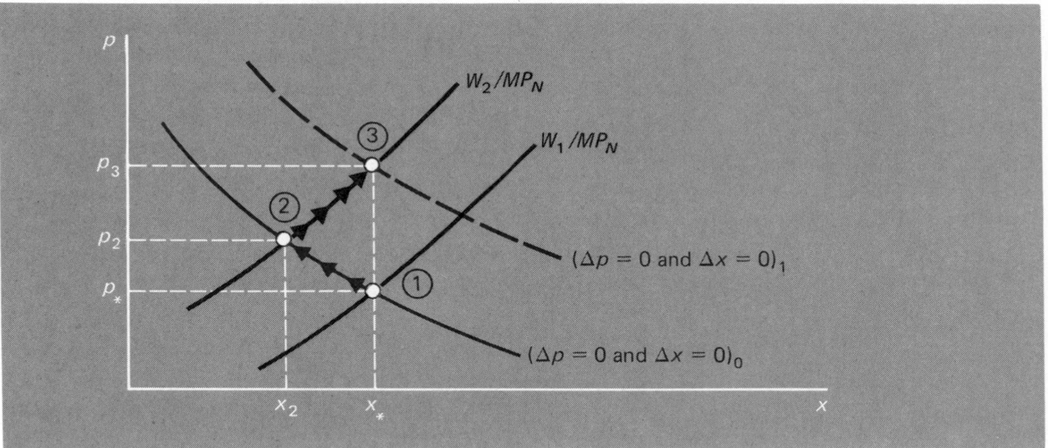

FIGURE 9-11

It is clear now that (comparing point ③ with point ②) the ES party has been able to keep its commitment to maintain employment at x_*. But this was achieved only by imposing a higher price level on the economy. For the interest of our scenario, the story does not end with position ③, since workers now find that their market power was for naught; the higher price level evaporated their higher incomes. Let us now suppose that they are determined to use their power to raise the money wage, say to W_3. The intersection of the new supply curve W_3/MP_N, with the relevant "effective demand" curve, $(\Delta p = 0 \text{ and } \Delta x = 0)_1$, leads the economy to position ④, with both lower employment and a higher price level, p_4. (See Figure 9-12.)

[6] See Chapter 7.

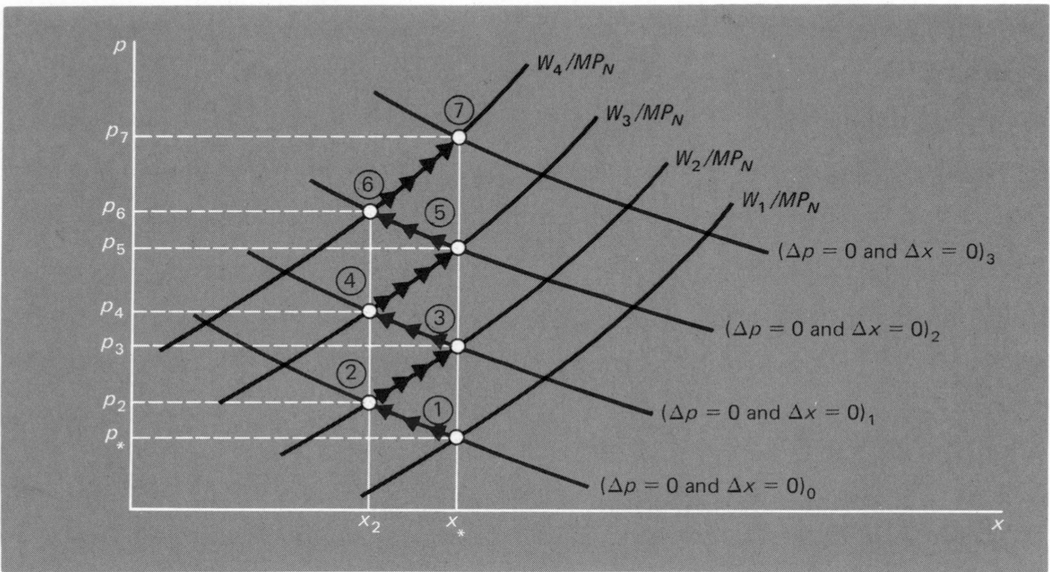

FIGURE 9-12

This leads the ES party administration to an expansionary policy, which, in turn, leads the economy to position ⑤, with the desired employment level, x_*, but with a still higher price level at p_5. The workers would then lead the economy to position ⑥ (with lower employment and a still higher price level p_6), but the government, in turn, would take the economy to position ⑦, and so forth.

One important result is clear from the above exercise. When the government pegs employment *at any level* in the presence of (especially increasing) market power, a continuous increase in the price level results.

The emphasis on the words "at any level" is meant to differentiate this result from another (which will be explored in detail in Chapter 10), namely, one that states that "accelerating inflation occurs when the *un*employment rate is pegged below *its* 'natural' or 'normal' rate."

Another important result should be emphasized: Changes in the "supply," or "productivity," curve brought about by increases in the wages of labor, because of (increases in) market power, can adversely affect both the price level and the employment level. This result is more general. As we know from Chapter 8, when the model is extended to include more than one variable factor of production (labor, here), a *parametric* change in the nominal (monetary) remuneration of *any* such factor will have exactly the same effects on prices and employment. For example, the recent drastic increase in the price of oil, because of the newly discovered market power of the OPEC countries, would have the same effect on prices and employment as the increase in money wages. And, finally, it should be recalled that there are additional reasons for upward shifts in the supply curve, such as a deterioration in productivity or an increase in tax rates, which may solicit a similar response by the ES party.

2. THE PARTY FOR PRICE STABILITY—THE PS PARTY

We have already stipulated that the PS party is committed to using whatever monetary or fiscal policies are needed to guarantee price stability. Instead of the ES party's monitoring of only the x-axis, we now have the monitoring of only the p-axis!

Let us examine the same problem as before. We are interested in the consequences of the pursuit of price stability, given a disturbance in the system, such as an increase in labor market power, which shifts the supply curve. Again we start from a position of equilibrium, that is, point ① in Figure 9-13, where the price level, p_*, is the one desired by the PS party.

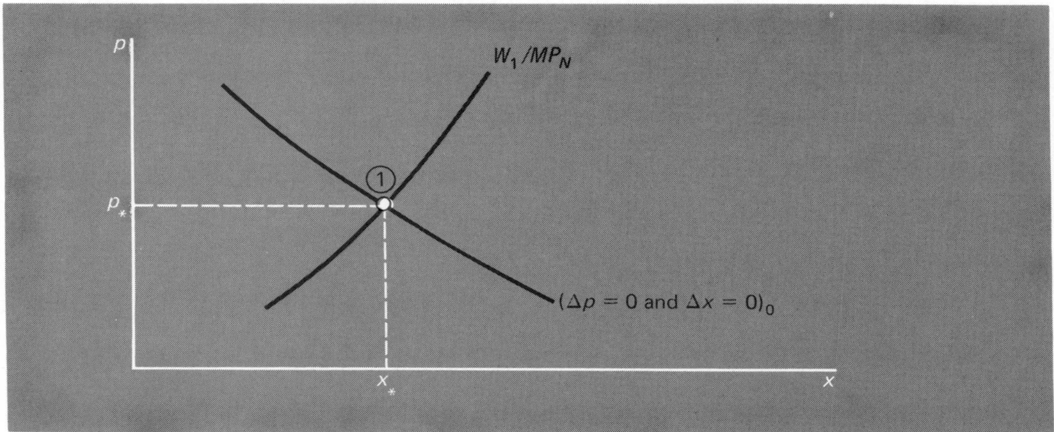

FIGURE 9-13

Assume, as before, that labor unions are successful in negotiating a higher money wage, W_2. This parametric increase in wages shifts the supply curve to the left. The relevant supply curve is the one labeled W_2/MP_N in Figure 9-14. Its intersection with the same effective demand curve, $(\Delta p = 0 \text{ and } \Delta x = 0)_0$, denotes the new equilibrium position, ②. The result of the higher money wages is, as before, a higher price level, p_2, and a lower employment level, x_2, that is, a recession. But now the administration's reaction will be different. The administration sees that the price level, p_2, is higher than the desired one, p_*. To achieve this (lower) desired price level, it will initiate *contractionary* monetary and fiscal policies, thereby lowering the effective demand curve. In Figure 9-14 this new effective demand curve is labeled $(\Delta p = 0 \text{ and } \Delta x = 0)_1$, and it intersects the relevant supply curve, W_2/MP_N, at point ③ At this position the price level is brought down to the desired one, p_*, but at the expense of employment, which falls even further, to the level equal to x_3. So that, in its attempt to maintain the desired price level, the PS party administration imposed a reduction in employment, that is, a further recession.

We have now identified the crucial difference between the two stylized parties: With increased market power possessed by the owners of any factor of production, the ES party is willing to get rid of the accompanying recession by raising the prices

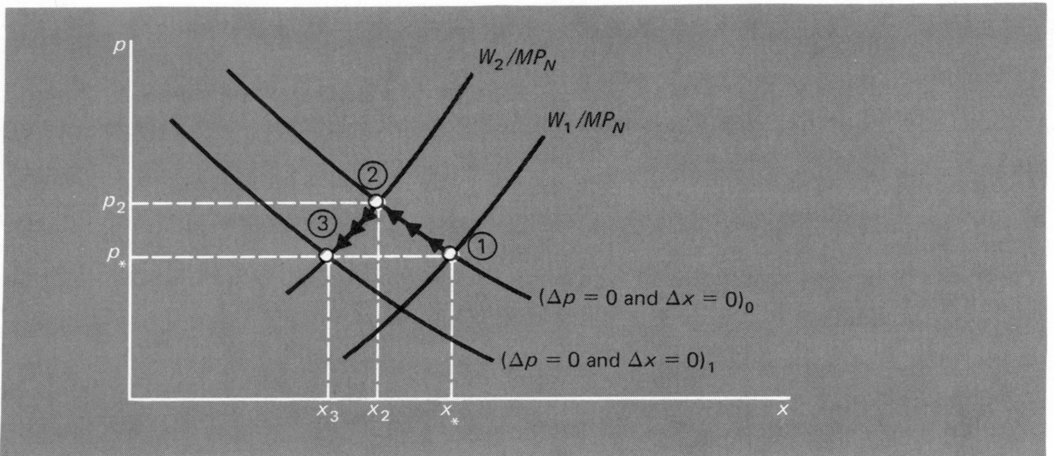

FIGURE 9-14

of goods and services; the PS party, on the other hand, is willing to initiate a further, deeper recession in order to achieve price stability.

It hardly needs reemphasizing that the original disturbance, shock, in the supply curve might be caused by the increased market power of the owners of factors other than labor, or by any of the other supply-side reasons. Most of the examples in the next section will deal with these other factors.

3. SUPPLY SHOCKS: SOME EXAMPLES FROM RECENT U.S. HISTORY

Most countries have parties that roughly correspond to the two abstract, caricatured parties examined above. In the United States, for example, it is widely accepted that the Democratic party is more sensitive to recession (reduction in employment) than to inflation. On the other hand, the Republican party is thought to be more sensitive to inflation than to employment, since, it is pointed out, five out of the six postwar recessions occurred during Republican administrations. It is also pointed out that two severe inflations began during Democratic administrations (both during wars, the Korean and Vietnam wars).

This section will not provide a detailed examination and evaluation of the economic policies of the two American parties. Rather, we shall provide some illustrations from recent history to see how real-life policy makers have responded to supply shocks. We shall associate the ES party with the Democrats and the PS party with the Republicans. Of course, this distinction is too sharp, but our abstract parties are, after all, only caricatures of real parties.

The Republican administrations from 1969 to 1976 provide us with some substantial examples of a PS party behavior. Beginning in 1969, the Nixon administration demonstrated its determination to eliminate the high inflation rate (this high rate was caused, for the most part, by large government spending on the Vietnam War, beginning in 1966, and not by the increased market power of the owners of factors of production, although some evidence to support the latter case developed in 1968). During 1969 and 1970 there was a deliberate contractionary economic policy, both fiscal and monetary, that lowered effective demand, slowed down inflation, and increased unemployment. This was the recession of 1969–70. Unemployment reached its peak in 1971 while the administration was pushing for a zero inflation rate, a target that one economist termed "unreasonable price stability."

In August 1971 wage and price controls were introduced. In reality, they were meant to be more wage and less price controls (because prices were permitted to vary to cover costs).[7] With the fixing of money wage by controls, the economic situation of 1971 corresponded precisely to the model presented in this section. Hence its application is almost exact. The economic policy pursued during the next two years was not, of course, truly characteristic of the PS party. On the one hand, there were the peacetime controls. On the other, there was an unrelenting increase in the money supply, which was aimed at increasing employment.

We come next to the 1973–75 period, which provides us with a classic example of the economics of a true PS party philosophy. The first disturbance, a rise in the price of grains—which are factors of production for several other goods—was caused by a dismal crop in 1972. This helped shift the supply curve upward, as shown in Figure 9-15. Naturally, this increased the price level to p_1 and reduced employment to x_1. There was then debate in the profession about the causes of that inflation (as the price level was *moving* from p_* to p_1). Most economists subscribed to the above explanation, citing the effect of the grain crop failure. (Simultaneously, there was

FIGURE 9-15

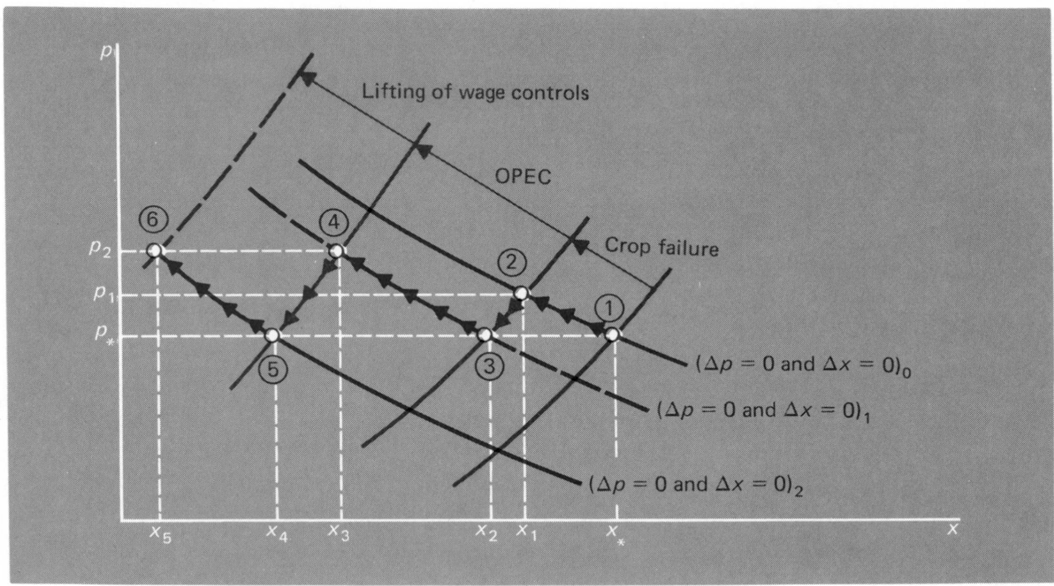

[7] See, however, footnote 3.

an increased demand for our exports. To avoid complications, this is not shown in the graph.) For one reason or another, the administration decided to follow contractionary policy, despite the many who urged caution, emphasizing that the supply-induced "inflation" would come to an end as soon as the price *level* reached p_1. For inflation to continue, they argued, next year's crop would have to again fail (shifting the supply curve upward).

The contractionary policy, as a reaction to the crop failure, shifted the effective demand curve to position $(\Delta p = 0 \text{ and } \Delta x = 0)_1$, thereby producing the lower employment level x_2. This is precisely when the second major disturbance occurred. The newly formed oil cartel, OPEC, started to raise the price of oil, quadrupling it within a short period. This, of course, raised the price level and worsened the recession by bringing employment all the way down to x_3. Still the administration was unwilling to permit the higher price level p_2. And once more it applied contractionary policy, lowering effective demand to $(\Delta p = 0 \text{ and } \Delta x = 0)_2$ and lowering employment to x_4. In 1974 yet another supply-side shock followed, namely, the lifting of wage and price controls. Wages had a lot of catching up to do; in fact, they rose by 9 percent, up from 6 percent in 1972. This shifted the supply curve farther to the left and to the new "equilibrium" position ⑥. The resulting lower employment, x_5, produced the worst recession since the Great Depression, namely, an unemployment rate in excess of 9 percent.[8]

In the 1976 presidential campaign, the strong labor support for the Democratic party was widely debated. It was argued that a Democratic victory would open the door to worse inflation, which was about 5.4 percent at the time. The argument followed closely the analysis given above under "The ES Party." A Democratic ascent to the presidency, it was asserted, would increase labor's market power because of the imminent passage of the bill repealing the "right-to-work" laws. (That bill could not survive a veto by a Republican administration.) The resulting increase in market power would be followed by higher negotiated money wages, thereby shifting the supply curve upward. Furthermore, the increase would be even higher because of expected drastic increases in the minimum wage—another pet bill of labor unions. It should be mentioned that labor has achieved only the second of these goals—the increase in the minimum wage. This may mean, of course, that there are several shades of ES parties!

Until 1978, the third year of the Carter presidency, no important supply shocks occurred. But beginning with that year, there were several shocks on the supply side, changes very similar to the ones that beset the Nixon-Ford presidencies in the period 1973–75. These shocks included (a) the substantial devaluation of the dollar, (b) a substantial slowdown in labor productivity, and (c) a rise in oil prices first by OPEC and then by domestic suppliers. On top of these "exogenous" supply shocks, there were two of the Carter administration's own doing, namely, (d) increases in social security and other payroll taxes and (e) increases in the minimum wage.

---

[8] For a most readable monograph devoted to the 1971–76 episodes, see Alan S. Blinder, *Economic Policy and the Great Stagflation* (New York: Academic Press, 1979).

Shocks (d) and (e) were applied twice, on January 1, 1978, and again on January 1 of the following year. The first three crept along during 1978, but the third, the oil-price shock, was further aggravated in 1979 by the events following the revolution in Iran.

It is interesting to see how the Carter administration responded to these supply shocks. In the fall of 1978 more restrictive fiscal and monetary policies were pursued. There was an immediate increase in the discount rate by a full percentage point, which was followed by an announcement of a tight fiscal policy to take effect in January 1979. These measures were taken primarily to support the dollar, and only secondarily to fight inflation. For this fight the Carter administration introduced voluntary wage-price guidelines. But these guidelines produced effects opposite to those intended; instead of reducing inflation, they aggravated it. The guidelines created expectations of mandatory controls, which were quickly translated into further inflationary expectations as both unions and businesses tried to avoid getting caught with lower wages and prices. This was another supply shock, the most severe yet. As employment was falling, prices kept rising. The tight monetary and fiscal policies had an effect (a negative one) on employment, but no effect on prices; these policies were simply overwhelmed by the supply shocks, and especially by the inflationary expectations. In October 1979, with the concurrence of the administration, a more restrictive monetary policy was announced by the Fed. A restrictive fiscal policy was further recommended by the president in his Budget Message of January 1980.

But the most drastic monetary and fiscal restrictions were yet to come. In March 1980 further reductions in the budget, including a hiring freeze by the federal government, were announced. At the same time the Fed restricted the growth of money so much that several key interest rates, including the prime rate and the Treasury Bill rate, approached or even exceeded the 15 to 20 percent bracket. This finally did it! Within three months these interest rates were halved, and, for the first time in several months, inflation was reduced. However, as predicted by our theory, the end result was a considerable increase in unemployment, which approached the 8 percent mark.

All this history is illustrated compactly in Figure 9-16, where only major changes in either the supply side or policy are recorded. The first shift in the supply curve is the result of these 1978 events: devaluation, productivity slowdown, OPEC oil price increases, payroll taxes, and minimum wage increases. This moved the economy from position ① to position ②. Prices rose, and employment fell from x_1 to x_2. The mildly contractionary monetary and fiscal policies of 1978 brought the economy to position ③, with a small reduction in employment, to x_3. The productivity slowdown continued into 1979 and, in conjunction with the expectations of wage and price controls, provided a considerable shift in the supply curve, to a new position at ④. The consequent increase in price (inflation) and fall in employment, to x_4, is not surprising. This elicited the further contractionary policy, which shifted the effective demand curve inward and to position ⑤. Of course, the result of this reduction in demand and in price (inflation) was the further increase in unemployment (reduction in employment to x_5).

Even a cursory glance at Figure 9-16 reveals that the response of the Carter

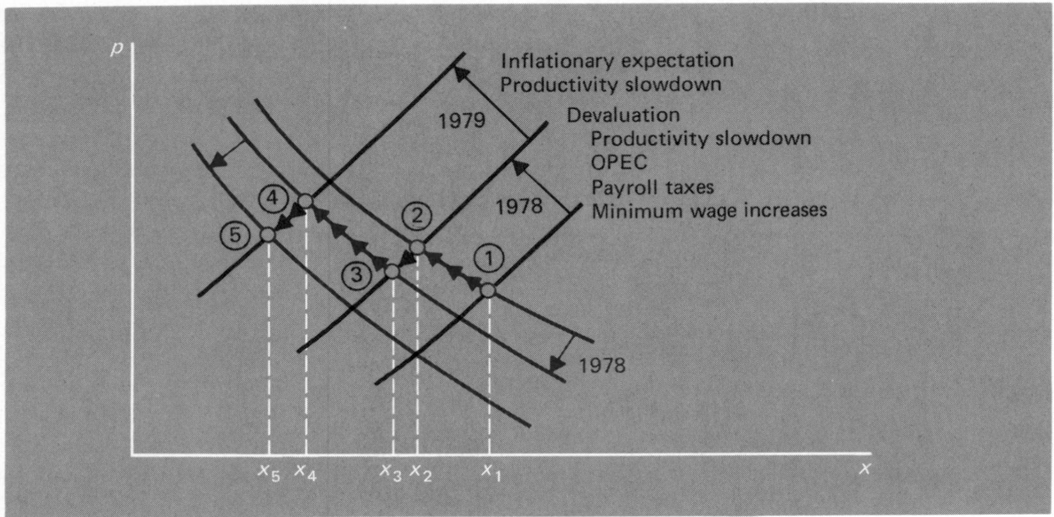

FIGURE 9-16

administration (and the Fed) to the supply shocks was very similar to that of the Nixon-Ford administrations. It is not surprising, then, that the "true" Democrats, the "true ES party members," labeled the Carter policies "Republican" policies, a complaint that did, of course, mark the Democratic primaries of 1980. Naturally, the Carter administration responded by stressing the differences between the 1973–75 and the 1979–80 recessions. The former, it argued, was created because the Nixon-Ford administration was not satisfied with the speed at which the inflation rate was *falling,* while the Carter recession was created to stop an *increasing* inflation rate, which was threatening to get out of control.

4: SUPPLY SHOCKS: SUGGESTED REMEDIES

The great recessions of 1973–75 and of 1979–80 have the common characteristic that they were engineered in order to either speed up the reduction of the existing inflation rate or reverse its direction. There has been, and still is, a heated debate among both academic economists and policy makers over whether this slowdown of inflation was worth the considerable cost to the society in the form of these recessions. Some economists argue that the inflation we experienced in both episodes was temporary and would have run its course, negating the need to create a recession. It is argued, in other words, that the recessions were preventable by simply accommodating the supply-induced inflation; that is to say, there was no need for a deliberate contractionary economic policy in the form of an inward shift of the effective demand curve.

Here we shall examine some suggested remedies for inflation, as alternatives to creating a recession. In fact, if these remedies work, they have even more pleasant outcomes: They increase, rather than decrease, employment while lowering prices.

The common characteristic of all these policies is that they operate by influencing (i.e., shifting) the supply curve.

Reduction in market power

One way of reducing the price level while increasing employment is to reduce market power, whether this power is held by labor unions or by monopolies. A reduction in money wages, W, for example, reduces the marginal cost W/MP_N, which directly shifts the supply curve to the right, as in Figure 9-17a. The simultaneous reduction in both prices and unemployment is certainly welcomed by both the ES and the PS parties. It should not be surprising, then, that efforts to increase supply invariably meet with strong bipartisan support. In their 1980 Presidential campaigns, both Jimmy Carter and Ronald Reagan advocated supply side remedies. It is in this spirit that the economists participating in the 1974 Economic Summit Conference *unanimously recommended that measures be taken to reduce market power.*

The 1974 Economic Summit Conference made the observation that market power may be possessed not only by owners of factors of production (labor unions, oil producers, etc.) but also by producers of final goods and services; the latter, by themselves, could create inflationary bias. (For this new definition of "inflationary bias" and the role of market power by producers of final output, see Chapter 10.) Moreover, market power may be the unfortunate outcome of the government's own actions, as well as the result of natural monopolies of oligopolies.

There are several ways in which governmental actions can contribute to a worsening of market power. Here we shall touch on one. To begin with, let us consider an industry that already exhibits oligopolistic characteristics. A good example is civil aviation. In this case, to protect the consumer from artificially high air fares, the government creates a watchdog, a regulatory body. This agency, the Civil Aeronautics Board, was established to protect the consumer. Whether or not the consumer is protected will not be examined here. However, it must be stressed that, by restricting entry, the CAB ended up as the protector of the existing firms in the industry. This is certainly an increase in market power.

The participants in the Economic Summit Conference identified twelve governmental regulatory bodies, including the CAB, that are contributors to the increase in market power. That conference resolved unanimously that these culprits should be marked for extinction. In the jargon of the conference, these "sacred cows" should be sacrificed at the altar of economical stability! In addition to the elimination of those agencies, the participants recommended that the antitrust laws be vigorously implemented to increase competition in all industries. Since then the CAB has, in effect, been dismantled. Furthermore, the trucking industry has been deregulated considerably.

Increase in productivity

Another means to decrease both prices and unemployment is by improving productivity. In Chapter 8 we saw that a deterioration in productivity will have the opposite effect. If, then, we can find a way to improve productivity, the supply curve will shift to the right, the price level will fall, and employment will rise, as in Figure 9-17a. To design such a policy to improve productivity, we need to know how pro-

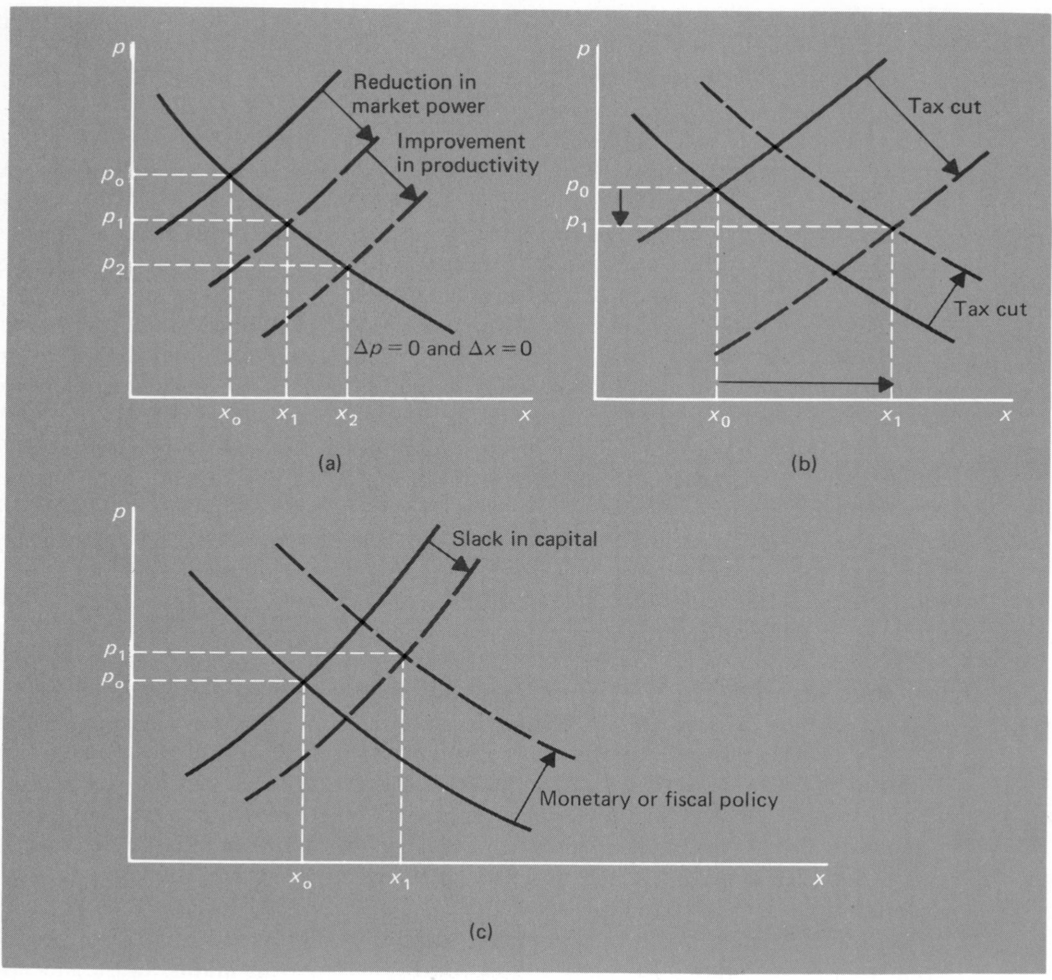

FIGURE 9-17

ductivity changes occur. The recent U.S. experience is useful in this endeavor. It has been documented by Norsworthy, Harper, and Kunze,[9] for example, that in the U.S. private, nonfarm business sector, the average annual growth of productivity fell from 2.8 percent in 1948–65 to 2.0 percent in 1965–73 and to 1.1 percent in 1973–78. Although there is not full agreement about all the reasons for the slowdown, and although some pieces of the puzzle are still missing, there is considerable agreement that the 1973–78 productivity slowdown was dominated by the effects of diminished

[9] See J. R. Norsworthy, M. J. Harper, and K. Kunze, "The Slowdown in Productivity Growth: Analysis of Some Contributing Factors," *Brookings Papers on Economic Activity,* 2 (1979), 387–421; and Peter K. Clark, "Issues in the Analysis of Capital Formation and Productivity Growth," *Brookings Papers on Economic Activity,* 2 (1979), 424–31.

capital formation. This is, of course, consistent with our observations, in Chapter 8, that investment in new capital goods not only increases directly the capital/labor ratio and, therefore, productivity, but that it also encompasses, or embodies, technological advances. This means that a slowdown in capital formation has the opposite effects. It was also suggested that capital and energy are "complementary" factors, which means that the reduction in the use of energy (because of its higher price) also reduced capital use, further aggravating the productivity slowdown. A popular belief that environmental restrictions, in the form of required investment in pollution abatement, are the reason for the *observed* lower productivity seems to be wrong. Only 0.1 percentage point was attributable to these restrictions. The research on the puzzle of the productivity slowdown implies that any inducement to increase capital formation will improve productivity. Hence, tax incentives for investment in new plant and equipment are recommended. But tax reductions, in general, are recommended as a supply-side remedy, a topic to which we turn.

Tax reductions

The recommendation for a tax reduction, in its crudest form, is stated as the "Laffer curve," which stipulates that a decrease in tax rates will actually increase tax revenues because a given percentage decrease in tax rates will increase output, and taxable income, by a greater percentage. This curve was named after Arthur Laffer, one of President Reagan's economic advisers. The popular interpretation of this proposition relies on the demand side; hence the usual reference to President Kennedy's tax cut. However, such a reliance on the demand side will also imply that the increase in income (and employment) will definitely be accompanied by higher prices. But the proponents of the view that a tax cut will benefit the economy rely explicitly on the supply side. One such version stipulates that the reduction in tax rates will increase the *after-tax wage,* which will increase the *supply* of labor. (According to the production function, the increased labor, if *utilized,* even with the same quantity of capital, will increase output.) Of course, the key question here is whether the increased supply of labor will be demanded by the firms or, equivalently, whether the increased output will be absorbed in the market system. To assume that it will is tantamount to relying on the *long run,* when full employment is always guaranteed. One way of incorporating this idea is in a growth model (see Chapter 16). But we can extend the analysis by retaining the spirit of the above proposal so that it can be useful even without the full-employment stipulation.

We can achieve this extension by stipulating that the reduction in tax rates, which increases *after-tax* wages, provides the incentive for workers, and especially for highly paid executives, to work harder and more efficiently, since they now retain more of their incomes. This idea can be generalized further when we note that the reduction in *corporate taxes* will increase the incentives for capital accumulation, that is, for investment in new plant and equipment, which increases productivity along the lines discussed in the preceding section. In summary, we can see that the reduction in taxes increases the efficiency of both labor and capital, which shifts the supply curve to the right. Of course, the increased incomes will also increase aggregate demand, which will shift the effective demand to the right. However, this increase in aggregate demand is not as inflationary as it was hitherto thought, since the supply curve also shifts. In fact, Figure 9-17b, which illustrates this suggestion, was designed to depict the case in which the net result is a *reduction* in the price level, even though there is a substantial increase in employment. Obviously, in this case, the supply side outweighs the demand side, so the price level falls rather than rises. In general, anything is possible, but even if the price level rises, it will not rise by as much as in the case of a pure demand-management policy. This result is similar to the case of an increase in aggregate demand in the presence of "slack in the capital," that is, in the presence of unemployment in capital, as well as in labor, which is the usual case. In such a situation, an expansionary monetary or fiscal policy can increase employment without a substantial increase in prices, as shown in Figure 9-17c.

During the recession of 1978–80, several economists urged the administration to cancel or postpone the 1978 and 1979 increases in the social security taxes. That recommendation, which went unheeded, was merely an application of this analysis. Another recommendation, which also was not adopted by the Carter administration, was the abandonment or postponement of the increase in minimum wages. Had this recommendation been adopted, it would have slightly reduced both the inflationary pressures and the unemployment rate.

It should now be clear that most of these supply-side measures are *long-term* rather than *short-term* goals, and that some of them may be politically nonfeasible. Demand management policies, on the other hand, can be applied quickly, which explains why we observe the use of these policies almost exclusively.[10]

III. DYNAMIC STABILIZATION POLICIES

1. THE ISSUES

The concept of stabilization policies discussed in the previous sections dealt exclusively with the displacing of one equilibrium position by another. This is the standard use of the term *stabilization policy,* a concept introduced in the early post-Keynesian years. The interest was in the *comparison* of alternative equilibria, rather than in the *path* that an economy would follow toward a new equilibrium.

Of course, economists, as well as policy makers, are interested in the path that key economic variables follow. The statistical monitoring of these variables through time is the province of *time series.* Even very early analyses of economic time series revealed *cyclical* movements in important variables, especially employment. On the other hand, we have already observed *theoretical* cases capable of generating cycles in employment and the price level. In particular, a marginal propensity to spend sufficiently greater than one is capable of producing either stable or unstable oscillations, as in Figures 9-18a and 9-18b, respectively.

We can record the information on employment separately from that on price level. Utilizing the information in Figure 9-18a, we see that Figure 9-19a monitors

---

[10] However, supply-side economics are a characteristic of the late 1970s and the 1980s. For a discussion of these issues, see U.S. Department of Commerce, *Growth Policy for the Eighties* (Proceedings of a Workshop on Supply-Side Economics, February 14, 1980).

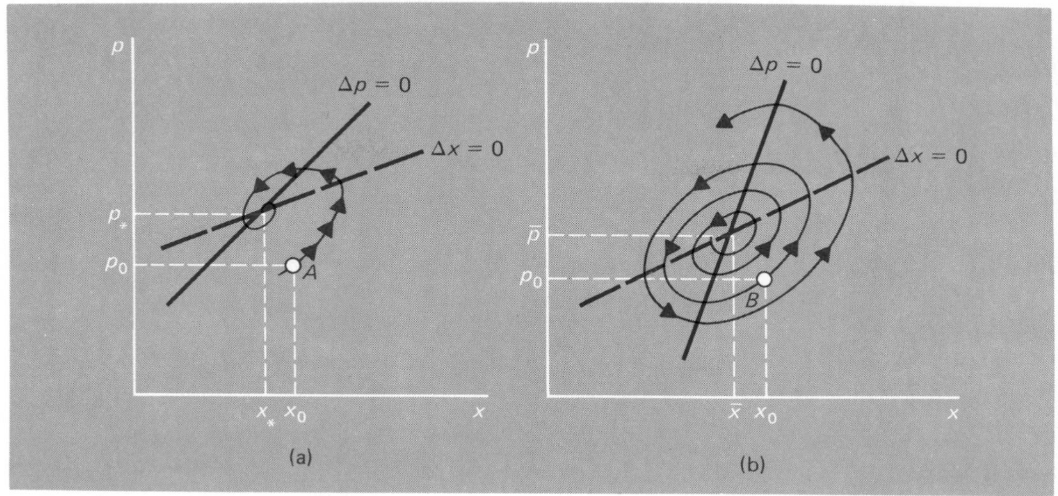

FIGURE 9-18 STABLE OSCILLATIONS UNSTABLE OSCILLATIONS

employment through time, whereas Figure 9-19b monitors the price level through time. In the construction of these two graphs, it has been assumed, for illustrative purposes, that at time t_0 the economy starts at point A in Figure 9-18a, that is, at an employment level, x_0, above the equilibrium and with a price level, p_0, below equilibrium. These two figures (and the underlying information) purport to reenact theoretically the real-world case of stable oscillations in employment and prices. In other words, because of the reasons underlying Figures 9-19a and 9-19b, we statistically observe *oscillations that tend to disappear through time.* On the other hand, Figures 9-20a and 9-20b record, separately for each variable through time, the information

FIGURE 9-19

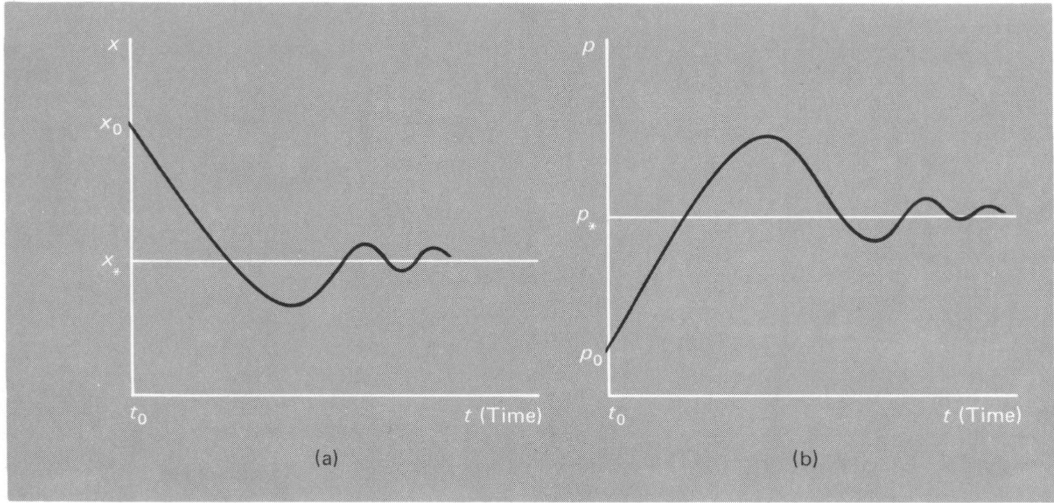

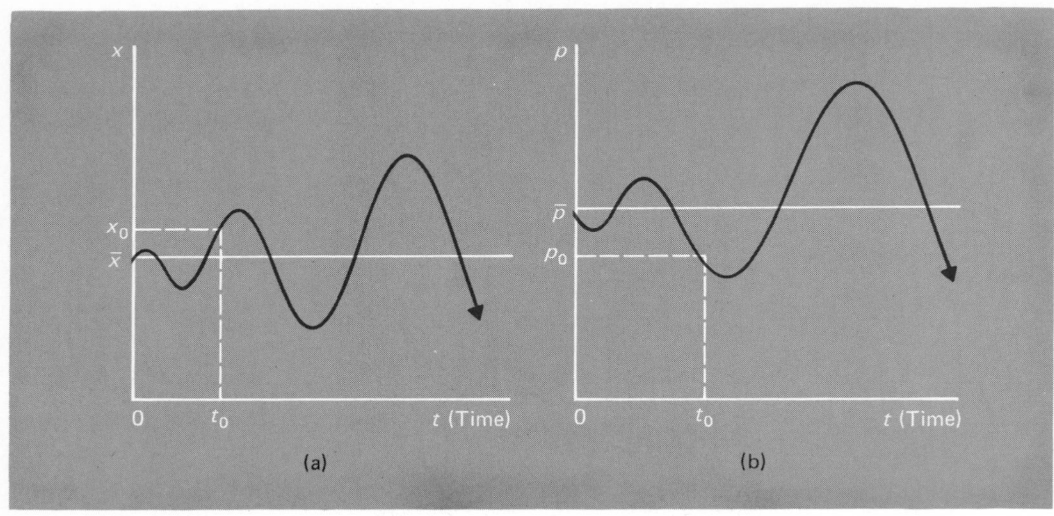

FIGURE 9-20

embodied in Figure 9-18b. The implication here is that, if *ever-increasing cycles* are observed in the movements of the price level and employment, they can be attributed to the reasons lurking behind the model captured by Figure 9-18b. (The "story" begins at time t_0 when the economy is at point *B* in Figure 9-18b.)

Despite the *stable* oscillations, such as the ones described in Figure 9-19, it is accepted in the profession that the economy would be better off had they not existed or had they been smaller. In Figure 9-21, path (b) is considered superior to path (a). In examining why this is so, we shall concentrate only on employment.

Oscillations in employment would mean that the economy will alternate between unemployment and overfull employment. We know that unemployment is a

FIGURE 9-21

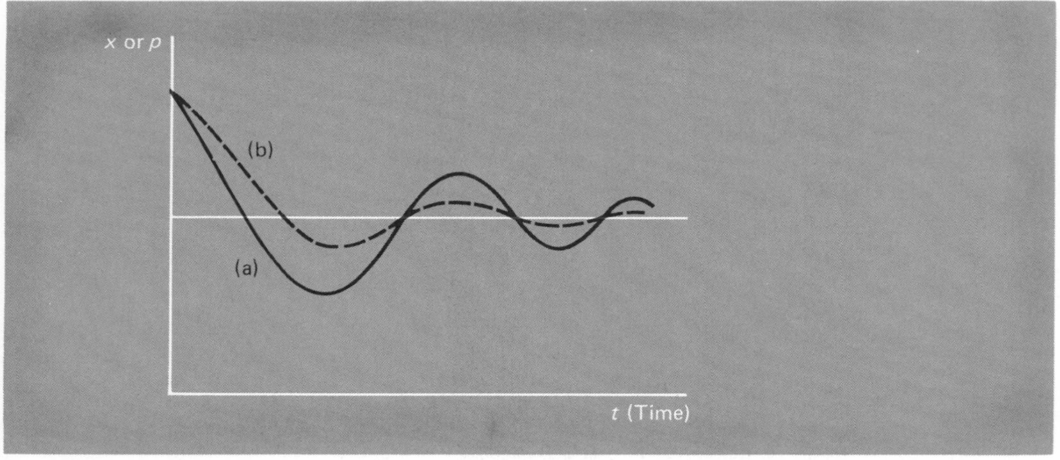

bad thing, but so is overfull employment. Unemployment means the loss of output, and hence a lowering of the standard of living. Overfull employment creates distortions; it strains the capacity (human as well as physical) of the economy. It is therefore better to smooth out these cycles, that is, to reduce the difference between the troughs and the peaks. This brings us to the second meaning of the term *stabilization policy: the use of monetary and fiscal policy to reduce, or possibly eliminate, the oscillations in key economic variables.* We shall call these efforts *dynamic* stabilization policies.

Because the economy is seldom at equilibrium, for all practical purposes, economic policy is primarily of the dynamic, and not of the comparative static, variety. It should not surprise us then when we see, in the following pages, that the conduct of dynamic stabilization policies is the subject of intense controversy. Not only is there disagreement about which policy instrument(s) (monetary vs. fiscal) should be used, but also whether policy makers ("authorities") may use discretion, or whether they should follow, like automata, preset rules. Further controversy then surrounds which rules should be followed, or if, ultimately, there should be policy at all.

2. AUTOMATIC OR BUILT-IN STABILIZERS

To reduce, or even to eliminate, observed oscillations in the economic system and to hasten its convergence to equilibrium, several proposals for economic stability were introduced in the 1940s. Proposals of this sort, in both Europe and the United States, had one element in common: They utilized either existing or newly designed, *built-in, automatic* stabilizers for the job. Most of those automatic stabilizers were fiscal instruments, reflecting the new fashion of the times and the influence of the Keynesian revolution.

A fiscal built-in stabilizer operates by automatically triggering an increase in the size of the budget deficit (or a reduction of surplus) whenever economic conditions threaten a downswing in economic activity. This automatic expansionary change in the deficit is aimed at reducing both the magnitude and the duration of a recession. Similarly, in inflationary times, pressure on the economy is alleviated by automatically reducing the budget deficit or increasing the surplus.

In our modern economy the fiscal stabilizers operate especially through (a) government transfer payments, such as unemployment compensation and welfare payments, which rise during recessions and fall during prosperity; and (b) taxation, which is lighter during recessions (because of loss of income from increases in unemployment) and much higher during a heated economy. In addition, most modern governments depend for their revenues on progressive taxation, which increases the potency of the fiscal built-in stabilizer.

An interesting complication arises here. Since progressive taxation lowers the multiplier's magnitude, the increase in the potency of the *dynamic* stabilizer is achieved at the expense of the *comparative static* stabilizer. In a sense this is a good development; it also explains why the dynamic stabilizer becomes more potent. If, for example, a contractionary shock, such as a reduction in the trade balance, occurs, the fall in employment will be smaller. This is why oscillations are of a smaller magnitude with progressive rather than proportional taxation. Of course, a question arises about whether a conflict might develop between the goals of comparative static and dynamic stabilization. In the abstract, one might argue that it does not matter that the potency of the medicine used for comparative static stabilization diminishes. This implies that the policy maker should use larger quantities of the diluted medicine. In other words, to achieve a new equilibrium with, say, permanently higher employment, the policy maker has to increase government expenditure by larger amounts. In the real world, however, problems might arise because of political constraints. For example, it may be difficult for politicians to approve a larger rather than a smaller deficit. If these political constraints are important, there will be a trade-off between dynamic and comparative static stabilization. Which one should be favored depends on the economy. If, for instance, an economy is prone to prolonged periods of unemployment—this is the real-world analogue to unemployment *equilibrium*—and, on frequent occasions, comparative static stabilization is called for, it may be useful to have very potent comparative static stabilizers. Proportional taxation is one way of achieving this potency. On the other hand, progressive taxation is better suited for an economy in which the main and usual problem is oscillations around *the* full-employment equilibrium.

There is diversity of opinion regarding the recommended use of fiscal built-in stabilizers. Some economists believe that the *rates* of taxes and unemployment contributions and payments should be tied to the level of economic activity and thus be variable. In the United States the Commission on Money and Credit, presumably agreeing with this view, recommended that the task of *manipulating the rates* be assigned to the president. Others believe that manipulation of rates is inadvisable, because it is either unnecessary or dangerous. Still others believe that this manipulation of rates is politically nonfeasible (for some countries).

This difference of opinion is not limited to *fiscal* stabilizers, but to stabilizers in general, whether fiscal or monetary. Whether we should use only automatic stabilizers or whether we should supplement these stabilizers with discretionary policies is hotly debated in the profession. Political and philosophical, as well as economic, considerations have entered into this debate.

3. MILTON FRIEDMAN AND HENRY SIMONS—RULES VS. AUTHORITIES

One of the early and stronger supporters of the view that we should rely *exclusively* on automatic stabilizers was Milton Friedman, who proposed "a Monetary and Fiscal Framework for Economic Stability."[11] Friedman's proposal contained four main recommendations: (1) fixed rates of transfer payments; (2) fixed rates of *progressive* taxation; (3) total elimination of the Federal Reserve Board's authority to engage in open market operations and the elimination of the private sector's ability to create money by forcing on banks a 100 percent reserve requirement (money should be created only to finance budget deficits, and it should be retired only when there is a budgetary surplus—money creation or destruction should be the only means to finance the deficit and to keep the surplus, respectively); and (4) no deliberate change in government purchases of goods and services for stabilization purposes.

[11] *American Economic Review,* 1948.

A crucial characteristic of the original Friedman proposal is the underlying stipulation that the budget deficit is the reflection of a recession (or at least an undesirable downswing), which requires an activist expansionary monetary policy. Similarly, a budget surplus is the symptom of a heated economy, and it requires an activist contractionary monetary policy. Thus this proposal guarantees the continuous use of corrective monetary policy, as long as the economy is out of a full-employment equilibrium. Through the years, Friedman introduced a succession of proposals. In these new proposals the chief victim has been the *activist* monetary policy found in the original proposal. As we shall see (primarily in Chapter 10), Friedman has now abandoned it and settled down to the belief that we do *not* need *even an activist monetary* policy; he now recommends a steady growth in the money supply, preferably at about 2 percent.

One key characteristic of the 1948 proposal that survived in all subsequent ones is the exclusive reliance on automatic, built-in stabilizers. In Friedman's words, "The framework should operate under *'the rule of law'* rather than the discretionary *authority* of administrators."[12] In the general philosophy, as well as in some of the specific components of his proposal, Friedman was expounding the views of his mentor, Henry Simons, whose chief aim was to provide

> bold schemes for restoring the free enterprise system to a securely workable basis. The requisite measures, radical in the money field and more radical elsewhere, will become possible politically only with the revival or development of *a real religion of freedom,* of a strong middle-class movement, and of values (and revulsions) of a rather intense sort.[13]

Thus, according to Simons:

> . . . we need to design and establish with the greatest intelligence a monetary system good enough so that, hereafter, we may hold to it irrationally—on faith—as a *religion,* if you please.[14]

This system should be

> clear enough and reasonable enough to provide the basis for a new *"religion of money,"* around which might be regimented strong sentiments against tinkering with currency.[15]

Thus Henry Simons proposed that the "religion of freedom" should be achieved by following a "religion of money": The conduct of monetary policy should

---

[12] Ibid., p. 370, italics added.

[13] Henry C. Simons, "Rules versus Authorities in Monetary Policy," *Journal of Political Economy* (1936). Reprinted in American Economic Association, *Readings in Monetary Theory* (London: Allen & Unwin, 1952), pp. 337–68. All references are from this reprint. The above quotation is from page 355.

[14] Ibid., p. 350, italics added.

[15] Ibid., p. 341, italics added.

be spelled out as a rule of law, with the force of a "constitutional amendment."[16] The conduct of monetary policy should not be left to the *discretion* of monetary *authorities.* In this way Simons declared himself in favor of rules and against authorities in the conduct of monetary policy.

Friedman was, and is, in favor of automatic stabilizers not solely for philosophical and political reasons. He argues that, even on economic grounds alone, automatic stabilizers are superior to discretionary policy. His criterion of superiority rests on stability, namely, on the assertion that the economy's path is "more stable" if automatic rules rather than discretionary policies are followed. In fact, his assertion is stronger: (His) automatic rules will increase the stability of the economy, whereas (any) discretionary policy may destabilize an (inherently stable) economy. His position can be illustrated in Figure 9-22 where curve (a) depicts employment's path in the absence of any policy. It is shown to exhibit stable oscillations. If automatic stabilizers are used, Friedman asserts that the path of the economy will be similar to the one depicted by curve (b), that is, with smaller oscillations. This is what the term *more stable* economy means. On the other hand, Friedman fears that a discretionary policy will create a path like curve (c), that is, it will turn the stable oscillations into unstable ones.

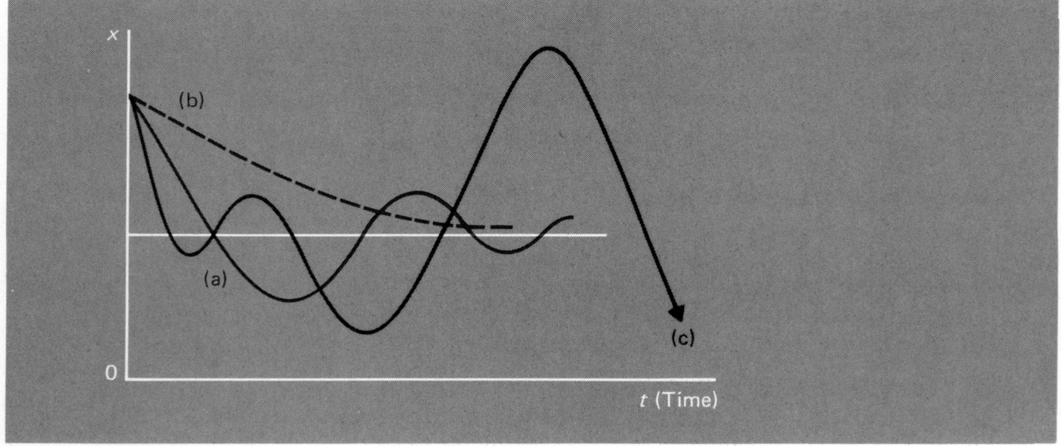

FIGURE 9-22

Friedman attributes the greater effectiveness of automatic rules in stabilizing the economy to the time lags (i.e., delays) inherent in the use of economic policy. He has provided an analysis of the role of time lags in economic policy, which, although brief and heuristic, is masterly. The continuous interest in this topic during the last thirty years can be attributed largely to Friedman's original 1948 work.

In the original Friedman proposal, for expository purposes, the total time lag was subdivided into three parts: "(1) the lag between the need for action and the recognition of this need; (2) the lag between recognition of the need for action

[16] Ibid., p. 362.

and the taking of action; and (3) the lag between the actions and its effects."[17] Now, with good economic forecasting, the first lag can be negative under discretionary policy, but it would be positive under an automatic rule. Thus, under ideal conditions, the first time lag can be smaller under discretionary policy. Not trusting the ability of economists to forecast, Friedman asserts that the difference, if any, is negligible. Similarly, he asserts that the third lag is slightly in favor of automatic rules. However, mainly because of political difficulties (at least for a presidential democracy like the U.S.), the second lag, which can be called a *governmental lag,* is substantially longer under discretionary policy. In this way, Friedman establishes the

> strong presumption that these discretionary actions will in general be subject to longer lags than the automatic reactions *and hence will be destabilizing even more frequently.*[18]

Friedman's argument, however, is not general. Establishing that the time lag of discretionary actions is longer than that of automatic rules is tantamount to proving that discretionary policies are more destabilizing only when the two policies, discretionary and automatic, are identical. If they are not, the opposite result is possible. Thus Friedman's argument is correct only when there is some prior reason necessitating that the two policies should be the same. But why should a discretionary policy merely duplicate the automatic rule which is available anyway?

Other economists, following Friedman's lead, relied on our *ignorance* of the length of the time lag. Knowledge of the exact length of the time lags is the *sine qua non* for the proper *timing* of policy. And without timing, discretionary policy may backfire. It may turn out, for example, that when the "authorities" apply expansionary policy, the opposite policy may be needed; by that time the economy may be overheated. The expansionary policy would thus aggravate inflation and thereby enlarge the oscillation.

4. PHILLIPS AND THE MODERNS

Since the appearance of another seminal work by A. W. Phillips, "Stabilization Policy in a Closed Economy,"[19] extensive research has been devoted to studying the effectiveness of fiscal and monetary policies as stabilization devices *in the presence of time lags.* Using increasingly more complex models, Phillips introduced advanced techniques to derive and examine the actual path that the economy would follow, both in the presence and in the absence of deliberate stabilization policies. We shall capture the basic results of these efforts by examining two adverse situations in which an economy might find itself, situations that might suggest the use of stabilization policies. The first case involves tracing the path that the economy will follow when the authorities attempt to reach a new (presumably better) equilibrium; the second case examines cycles and, in particular, methods of reducing the magnitude of oscillations.

---

[17] Friedman, *A Monetary and Fiscal Framework,* p. 382.

[18] Ibid., p. 381, italics added.

[19] *Economic Journal,* 1954.

Case 1. Achieving a new position

Suppose that an *outside shock,* say a reduction in foreign demand for our products, causes aggregate demand to decrease. What is the actual path that the economy will follow in the absence of a stabilization policy? Can a deliberate policy correct the adverse effects of the outside shock and bring the economy to the original position? If the answer is yes, what is the exact path that the economy will follow? Are there any dangers of destabilizing the economy?

In the (p,x)-plane, the reduction in the trade surplus shifts the $\Delta p = 0$, $\Delta x = 0$ curve inward with the ultimate effect of reducing both the price level and employment from $(\bar{x},\bar{p})$ to $(\bar{\bar{x}},\bar{\bar{p}})$, as shown in Figure 9-23a. In the same graph we also depict the path that both prices and employment will follow. We know that this path is the relevant productivity line, $p = \overline{W}/MP_N$. Concentrating on employment, curve (a) in Figure 9-23b depicts the latter's path *through time.*

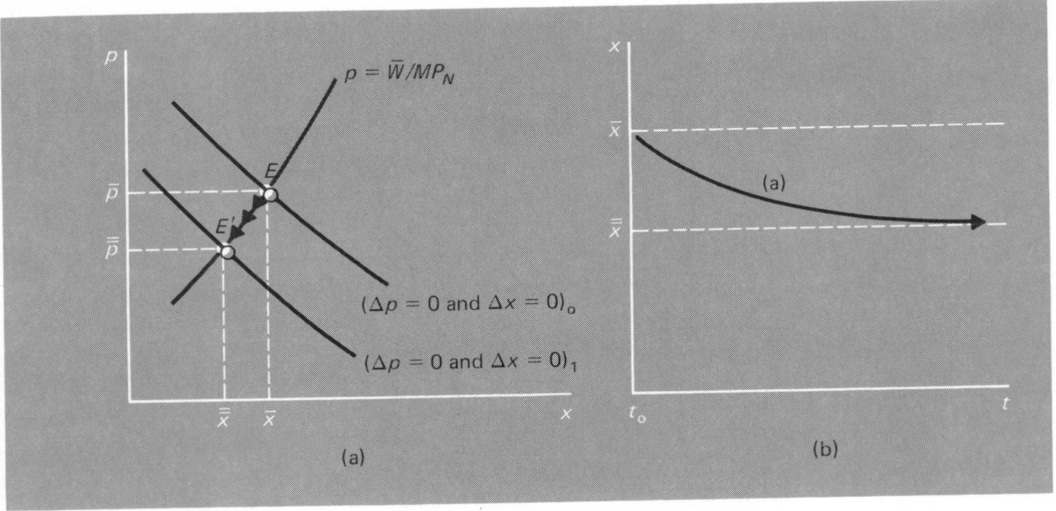

FIGURE 9-23

Phillips and others have shown that a deliberate stabilization policy could generate any one of the trajectories (b), (c), or (d) in Figure 9-24. In other words, the economy can be brought back to the original position without oscillations (trajectory (b)); it can be brought back with damped oscillations (curve (c)), or it may never be brought back because the stabilization policy actually destabilizes the system by creating explosive cycles (curve (d)).

The curve that will be observed depends upon (1) the time lags, especially the governmental lag (the lag between the intended and actual increase in government expenditure); (2) the variable that triggers the policy pursued (e.g., the level of employment, x, or the difference between the intended level, $\bar{x}$, and the actual level, x, or, further still, the cumulative loss of employment); (3) the vigor by which the policy is pursued; and, finally, (4) the various elasticities of the behavioral functions (e.g., marginal propensity to consume or interest elasticity of investment demand, etc).

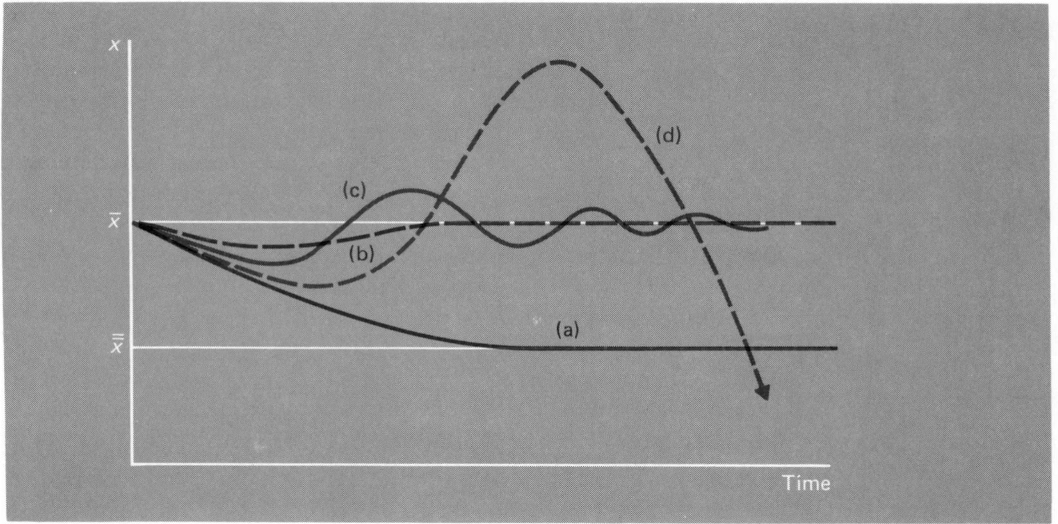

FIGURE 9-24

An important result of this analysis is that other things being equal, the smaller the governmental lag, the easier it is to stabilize the economy, that is, to bring it back to its original position with no oscillations or as few as possible. On the other hand, with a given governmental lag, there may be an upper limit in the vigor with which the policy should be pursued if instability is to be avoided.

This result is not troublesome for a parliamentary democracy. In such a political system, the government in power, by definition, has the votes to immediately change the taxation and/or transfer payments necessary for an effective stabilization policy.

In a presidential democracy like the United States, the above result complicates the conduct of economic policy. The policy maker's life becomes much more difficult because a more exact knowledge of several parameters is needed for successful stabilization. For this reason the economic advisers should occasionally recommend abandoning a policy, previously suggested, if passage of that necessary legislation is so delayed that it violates the upper limit of a permissible governmental lag. It is primarily because of the delay in passing the necessary legislation through Congress that the Carter administration withdrew its recommendation for tax rebates. It was felt that by the time Congress was ready to pass the legislation, the economy would be so heated up that the additional demand for goods and services coming from the tax cut would actually be inflationary.

A second example of the theorem (that the smaller the governmental lag, the more stabilizing a given policy is) can be found in one of the recommendations of the Commission on Money and Credit in 1960. The commission felt that the governmental lag could be shortened by passing a law granting the president of the United States power to manipulate taxation rates according to the needs for stabilization. It should be added, however, that the U.S. Congress was unwilling to relinquish its constitutional right to set and change the country's taxation system. Had Congress approved the commission's recommendation, the Johnson administration, in 1965, might have heeded the advice of its CEA to raise taxes and cool off the heated economy, a result of the drastically increased expenditure needed to finance the escalating Vietnam War. As it happened, President Johnson kept the tax rates fixed, and the expected result of increased inflation followed.

For still another example, we recall the Nixon administration's impounding of funds already appropriated for government expenditure. President Nixon's advisers felt that these expenditures were destabilizing (i.e., further increasing a high rate of inflation). For this reason, President Nixon impounded the funds. (The Supreme Court later determined that the impounding was illegal, since that authority rested with the Congress of the United States.)

Case 2. Oscillations around equilibrium

Let us suppose that the economy oscillates around a specific value. There are two cases to be examined here. The first is one of stable oscillations, as we have already shown in Figure 9-19. We have already established that our own complete model is capable of generating such cycles. Phillips was also able to generate oscillations in his model, in the absence of policy, either by using a particular investment function (relying on the acceleration principle) or by explicitly introducing expectations of inflation.

In the case of stable oscillations, the relevant questions are whether monetary and fiscal policy can narrow or eliminate these oscillations, and if so, whether they should be used for such a purpose. Phillips and others have shown that policy could reduce or eliminate the oscillations. Of course, deliberate policy, if not well designed, could destabilize the system by actually turning the oscillations from stable to unstable.

We turn now to the unstable case. It has been shown by Phillips and others that monetary or fiscal policy can stabilize the economy, even if it were unstable to begin with.[20] Of course, in this case there cannot be any disagreement about whether deliberate policy should be used. The whole economic system would collapse if authorities insisted on doing nothing. There is debate, however, about whether the actual economy exhibits such instability. Many monetarists, like Friedman, *assume* that the economy is inherently stable. In fact, they go as far as stipulating that all the observed cycles exist only because of faulty use of monetary policy. Friedman's 1948 proposal was explicitly designed for "a world in which cyclical movements, other than those introduced by 'bad' monetary and fiscal arrangements, were of no consequence."[21]

Because of this belief Friedman and his associates now argue that neither fiscal nor monetary policy should be used as (dynamic) stabilization devices. According to them, the only way to stabilize an economy is to *not* use monetary policy. They argue that the monetary authorities should follow the rule of increasing the nominal

---

[20] See Michael G. Hadjimichalakis, "The Rose-Wicksell Model: Inside Money, Stability, and Stabilization Policies," *Journal of Macroeconomics,* vol. 3, No. 3, 1981 and M. G. Hadjimichalakis, "On the Effectiveness of Monetary Policy as a Stabilization Device," *Review of Economic Studies,* October, 1973, pp. 561–70.

[21] Friedman, *A Monetary and Fiscal Framework,* p. 370.

money supply at a constant rate (around 2 percent). They argue that the rate of change in the money supply should not be altered for the purpose of dynamic stabilization. Moreover, interest rates should not be a tool to be manipulated for economic stability. On this latter issue, Friedman and others started by arguing that the monetary authority should not attempt to manipulate interest rates, but only the rate of change in the money supply, and ended up by comparing their policy of a fixed rate of change in the money supply with a fixed interest rate, a somewhat fictitious target! Of course, we know from our Wicksellian model that trying to keep the interest rate fixed at a rate different from the natural one might destabilize a stable system.

It is an historical fact, however, that for years the U.S. government pegged the interest rates on government securities. But this "stabilization" of interest rates was not done for "dynamic stabilization" purposes. It was done exclusively because the U.S. Treasury, in promoting U.S. securities to potential buyers, had guaranteed that the prices of those securities would not fall. Those, however, were *expansionary* years, and thus there was upward pressure on interest rates (i.e., downward pressure on the prices of securities). To keep the prices up, the government had to intervene in the open market and buy securities by *creating money.* In other words, the Federal Reserve lost control of the money supply in much the same way that it had lost control when it was committed to keep a fixed exchange rate. The end result was an increase in inflation.

The above historical experience highlights how dangerous it is to establish "rules" for bureaucracies. They may diligently apply these rules when rules are needed, but they may also stick to them when circumstances no longer require such treatment. This is a crucial reason why the "new religion of money" as a rule for a fixed rate of growth in the money supply may be dangerous. Once this rule becomes the habit of bureaucracies and the "religion" of the public, it may be impossible to later convince them of the need for a change—even if there is the danger of another Great Depression!

The preference of monetarists for a rule of fixed rate of growth in the money supply rests entirely on their stipulation that, in the absence of manipulation of the money supply, there can be no cyclical movements in economic activity. According to Friedman and his associates, these cyclical movements in aggregate demand are generated because of lags in the response of aggregate demand to monetary policy. Variable rates of growth in the money supply might then compound these cyclical movements. For this reason they advocate a rule for a *fixed* rate of growth of money. (Friedman decides on exactly *which* fixed rate on other grounds, as we shall see in Chapter 10.)

It should be noted here that neither Friedman nor anybody else has offered any convincing evidence that the economy is inherently stable, let alone without "cycles of any consequence." They accept, merely on faith, that the economy is stable in the absence of policy. The conventional wisdom in the profession is that there are circumstances, other than "bad" monetary and fiscal policies, that create the economy's inherent tendency for either stable or unstable oscillations that must be reckoned with in a discretionary manner. In the words of Paul Samuelson:

> At the present time an automatic gyropilot can keep an airplane pretty stable while the pilot catches a nap; but when something unusual comes

up, the human pilot must still take over. No one has yet found a gadget with all the flexibility of man. Similarly in the social field: we have not yet arrived at a stage where any nation is likely to create for itself a set of constitutional procedures displacing the need for discretionary policy formation and responsible human intelligence.[22]

QUESTIONS

1. *Statement A:* "We can have full equilibrium without full employment only if money wages are held constant."
Statement B: "Since workers will sooner or later accept money-wage cuts, it follows from statement A that the government should not use monetary or fiscal policies in order to bring about full employment. The economy will cure unemployment by itself if left alone. This approach has the advantage of achieving full employment with lower prices than if we use deliberate policies."
a. Is statement A correct? Explain why workers sometimes refuse money-wage cuts.
b. Is statement B correct? With which sentences do you agree; with which do you disagree and why?
c. Explain what will happen if the government does use monetary or fiscal policy.

2. Show under what conditions each of the following statements is correct with regard to efforts to increase GNP and employment:
a. "Money matters."
b. "Fiscal policy matters."
c. "Only money matters."
d. "Only fiscal policy matters."

3. What will happen to the price level and employment if people decide to save more at each level of income? Show that the government can eliminate the above effects by using either monetary or fiscal policy. What considerations might persuade the government to use (say) monetary policy but not fiscal policy? What about the opposite?

4. If some people favor budget deficits for increasing employment but do not favor increases in the money supply for that purpose because they do not want price increases, how would you advise them? (Address the price increase aspects.)

5. How can monetary or fiscal policy counteract the effect of a change in the typical household's tastes for present and future consumption? Trace the effects through the price level, interest rate, and employment. Would your answer change if, instead, the risk premium of doing business is

---

[22] Paul A. Samuelson, *Economics,* 7th ed. (New York: McGraw-Hill, 1967), p. 339.

increased? (Hint: Assume the economy's propensity to consume present goods rises. What policy would counteract this?)

6. Comment: "Since both monetary and fiscal policy can raise employment and since both also result in higher prices, all the debate about which policy is appropriate is unnecessary."
7. Comment: "We have established that both monetary and fiscal policy result in movements of prices and employment in the same direction. But in the real world, we sometimes observe rising prices and falling employment. Therefore the model must be wrong."
8. Under what conditions will a reduction of tax rates on wages increase the supply of labor? When and under what conditions will this increased labor supply find employment?
9. The recent increase in both unemployment and inflation has been attributed to the substantial reduction in productivity growth. Explain whether this can be so; also state and explain an economic policy designed to increase productivity.
10. Demand-management policies increase employment at the expense of higher prices. On the other hand, supply-side management, say a reduction in market power or an increase in productivity, increases employment while reducing prices. Why, then, are demand-management policies favored by policy makers?
11. It is claimed that a rule for a fixed rate of growth of the money supply will stabilize the economy:
    a. Examine this view in the face of supply-side shocks, such as crop failures, earthquakes, or the creation of oil cartels.
    b. Alternatively, examine the same view in the face of instability of the money demand function.
12. Are the following statements true or false? Explain.
    a. "Because of timing and time lags, an activist economic policy *will* destabilize the economy."
    b. "Because of timing and time lags, an activist economic policy *may* destabilize the economy."
    c. "The economy is 'superstable'; in fact, cyclical movements are the results of 'bad' monetary policy."
    d. "The economy is inherently unstable; hence an activist economic policy is always a 'must.'"
13. Is a tax cut inflationary or deflationary?

REFERENCES

BLINDER, ALAN S., *Economic Policy and the Great Stagflation.* New York: Academic Press, 1979.

ENZLER, JARED, LEWIS JOHNSON, AND JOHN PAULUS, "Some Problems of Money Demand," *Brookings Papers on Economic Activity,* 1 (1976), 261–80.

FRIEDMAN, MILTON, "A Monetary and Fiscal Framework for Economic Stability," *American Economic Review,* June 1948, pp. 245–64. Also reprinted in American Economic Association, *Readings in Monetary Economics.* London: Allen & Unwin, 1952. Quotations are from this reprint.

———, *A Program for Monetary Stability.* New York: Fordham University Press, 1960.

FRIEDMAN, MILTON, AND ANNA J. SCHWARTZ, *A Monetary History of the United States, 1867–1960.* Princeton, N.J.: Princeton University Press, 1963.

GOLDFELD, STEPHEN M., "The Case of Missing Money," *Brookings Papers on Economic Activity,* 3 (1976), 683–730.

GORDON, ROBERT J., "The Response of Wages and Prices to the First Two Years of Controls," *Brookings Papers on Economic Activity,* 3 (1973), 765–78.

HADJIMICHALAKIS, MICHAEL G., "Reserves *vs* Federal Funds Operating Procedures: A General Equilibrium Analysis," *Economics Letters,* vol. 7, 1981.

———, "The Rose-Wicksell Model: Inside Money, Stability, and Stabilization Policies," *Journal of Macroeconomics,* vol. 3, No. 3,1981.

———, "On the Effectiveness of Monetary Policy as a Stabilization Device," *Review of Economic Studies,* October 1973, pp. 561–70.

NORSWORTHY, J. R., M. J. HARPER, AND K. KUNZE, "The Slowdown in Productivity Growth: Analysis of Some Contributing Factors," *Brookings Papers on Economic Activity,* 2 (1979), 387–421.

PHELPS, EDMUND S., "Unreasonable Price Stability—The Pyrrhic Victory over Inflation," in *The Battle against Unemployment* (rev. ed.), ed. Arthur M. Okun, pp. 44–53. New York: W. W. Norton & Co., Inc., 1972.

PHILLIPS, A. W., "Stabilization Policy in a Closed Economy," *Economic Journal,* 1954, pp. 290–323.

SCHULTZE, CHARLES L., "Falling Profits, Rising Profit Margins and the Full Employment Profit Rate," *Brookings Papers on Economic Activity,* 2 (1975), 449–69.

SIMON, HENRY C., "Rules versus Authorities in Monetary Policy," *Journal of Political Economy,* 1936. Reprinted in American Economic Association, *Readings in Monetary Theory,* pp. 337–68. London: Allen & Unwin, 1952. All references are from this reprint.

Inflation and Unemployment

10

In this chapter we examine the problem of the coexistence of inflation and unemployment, and the "cruel dilemma" it poses for the policy maker. We consider both wage and price inflation in the long run as well as the short run. Furthermore, we examine the coexistence of unfilled vacancies and unemployment, as well as the influence of expectations on inflation in the presence of unemployment. Instead of summarizing this chapter, we can simply record its table of contents:

I. DEMAND PULL INFLATION

In Section I of Chapter 9 we established that an expansionary economic policy increases both the price level and employment. The particular policy could be an increase in the nominal money supply (monetary policy) or an increase in the budget deficit (fiscal policy), or even an increase in the trade surplus (commercial policy). All these instruments produce increasing prices and employment by raising *effective demand,* as shown in Figure 10-1. The new equilibrium point, *B,* exhibits a higher price level ($p_1 > p_0$) and higher employment. This increase in the price level caused by expansionary economic policies is called *demand pull inflation* because it results from increasing effective demand.

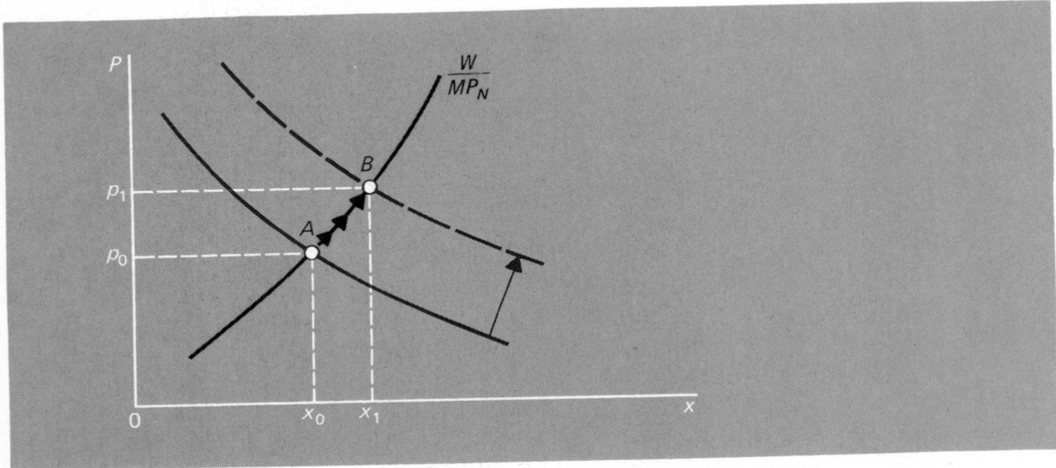

FIGURE 10-1

Keynes is the modern intellectual father of the concept of "demand pull inflation," not only because he provided the general macroeconomic framework needed to examine all kinds of expansionary policy but also because he was the first to apply it to analyze the inflationary period of World War II.[1]

Two points should be emphasized in our reexamination of the (Keynesian) demand pull inflation. First, as is clear from Figure 10-1, a permanent increase in the money supply, in the budget deficit, or in the trade surplus will cause inflation as the economy moves from the original equilibrium (point *A*) to the new one (point *B*). When the new equilibrium is reached, *inflation,* which is defined as the rate of *increase* in the price level, will cease. Only when an expansionary policy is applied continuously will there be a persistent rise in prices (i.e., inflation).

Second, Figure 10-1 establishes that increases in prices are associated with increases in employment, and decreases in prices with decreases in employment. We can restate this relationship as follows: Increases (decreases) in prices are associated

[1] J. M. Keynes, *How to Pay for the War* (New York: Harcourt, Brace & Co., 1940).

with decreases (increases) in *un*employment. Schematically we can write this compactly:

$$\left(\frac{\Delta p}{p}\right) \begin{matrix} > \\ = \\ < \end{matrix} 0 \quad \text{when} \quad \Delta u \begin{matrix} < \\ = \\ > \end{matrix} 0$$

where u is defined as the unemployment rate, $u = N^s/K - N^d/K = v - x$. This schema is depicted graphically in Figure 10-2.

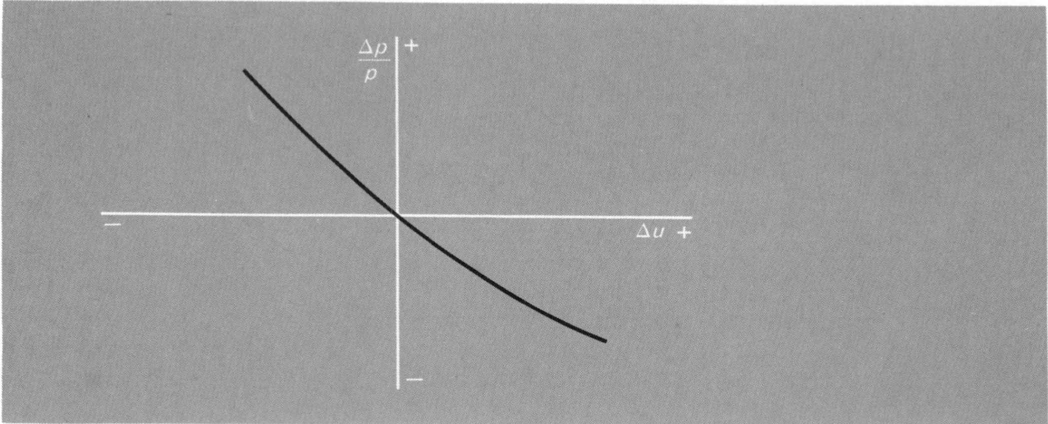

FIGURE 10-2

A generation after Keynes this view was resurrected by several economists who claimed that inflation depends *not* so much on the *level* but on the rate of *change* in unemployment.

II. COST PUSH INFLATION: THE "CRUEL DILEMMA"

In Section II of Chapter 9 we saw that an exogenous increase in cost—for a variety of reasons—increases the price level but decreases employment. This is shown again in Figure 10-3. The increase in costs, represented by a shift of the cost curve to the left, produces higher prices and lower employment. Note that as the economy moves from the original equilibrium (point ①) to the final one (point ②), the price level rises and employment falls (i.e., unemployment rises).

The rise in the price level brought about by a rise in costs has been called *cost push inflation.* Cost push figured prominently in the literature of the 1950s, which concentrated exclusively on *market power of firms and labor unions* as the reason for a rise in cost. Moreover, it was claimed that cost push poses a cruel dilemma for the policy maker because it can be eliminated only by a reduction in employment. This reduction in employment (and in prices) will result from pursuing

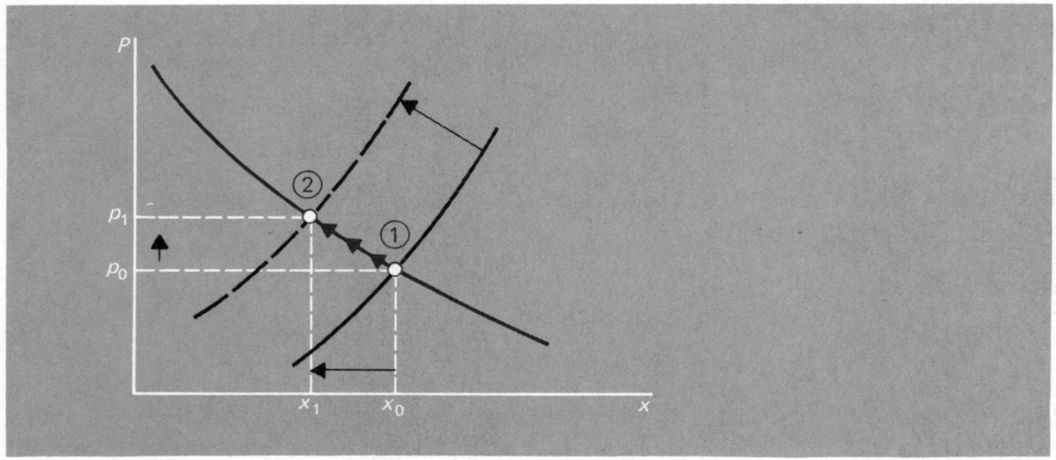

FIGURE 10-3

a restrictive economic policy. This is shown in Figure 10-4 where the increase in market power (say by labor unions) raises prices to p_1 and lowers employment to x_1. According to this view, the only way to bring the price level back to p_0 is to follow a restrictive monetary or fiscal policy and thereby lower effective demand (shift the curve inward). But this policy would, of course, further lower employment to x_2.

In Section II of Chapter 9 we saw that if the Price Stability (PS) party were in power, this is precisely how it would react to an increase in market power. On the other hand, if the Employment Stability (ES) party were in power, the reaction would be an *expansionary* (rather than a contractionary) policy. This is shown in Figure 10-5 where points ① and ② are as in Figure 10-4, but where point ③ is

FIGURE 10-4

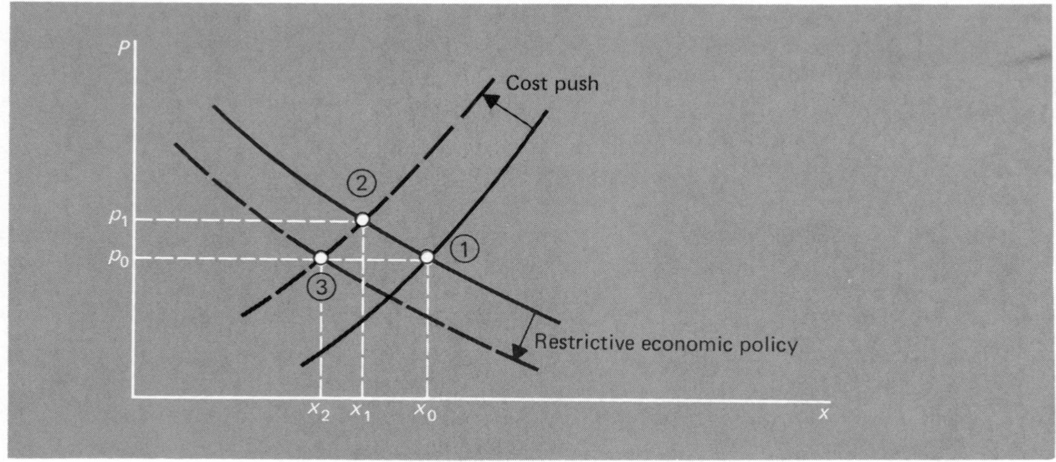

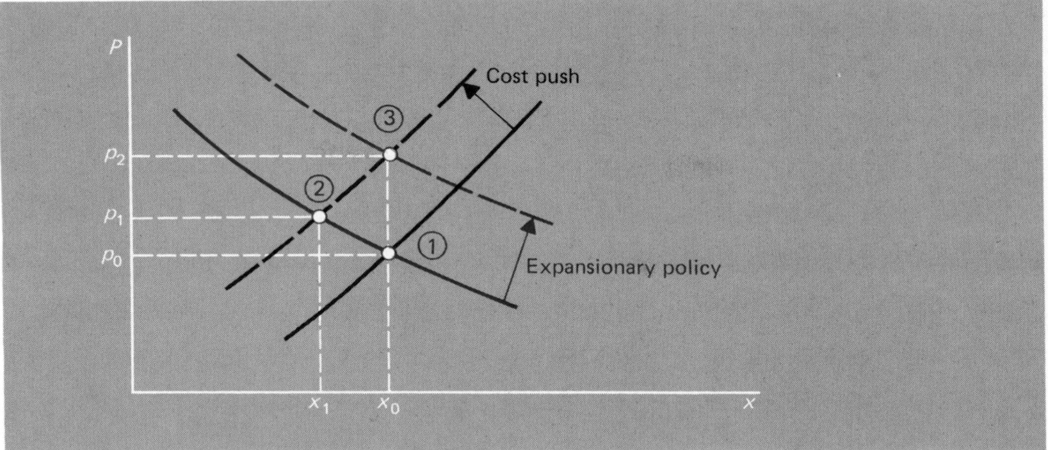

FIGURE 10-5

achieved as the intersection of the higher cost curve with a higher effective demand curve.

We see now that Figures 10-4 and 10-5 depict the policy maker's dilemma. If society wants the old price level, it has to pay dearly by drastically reducing employment—from x_0 to x_2 in Figure 10-4. On the other hand, the original employment level x_0 can be maintained only with a substantial increase in the price level—from p_0 to p_2 in Figure 10-5.

Figures 10-4 and 10-5 also illustrate a basic misconception in the literature of the 1950s. Invariably there was a confusion between *high* prices and *rising* prices. Of course, only the latter is inflation. It is true that during the transition period, when the economy moves from a lower price level (such as p_0) to a higher price level (such as p_1), the price level is rising. However, the mere introduction or existence of market power is not sufficient to cause prices to perpetually rise. When point ② is reached, that is, when the new equilibrium is achieved, the rise in prices will stop. This is precisely what we should expect from the basic theory of the firm. We know that monopolistic or oligopolistic, profit-maximizing firms will charge a higher price than perfectly competitive firms, but when they achieve maximum profit with a particular price, they will adhere to it until there is a change in some underlying parameter.

To have continually rising prices, market power has to be ever-increasing, thereby continuously shifting the cost curve to the left and definitely producing a rise in prices. This increase in prices is magnified when the increasing market power of firms and labor unions combines with the efforts of an Employment Stability (ES) party. In this case we will have an ever-increasing price level, oscillating between increases caused by cost push and those caused by demand pull. This is illustrated in Figure 10-6, which is a reproduction of Figure 9-12. The wage-price spiral of the last ten years cannot be attributed to increasing market power of industry and labor unions; there simply was not enough increase in their market power to explain the oscillations in inflation.

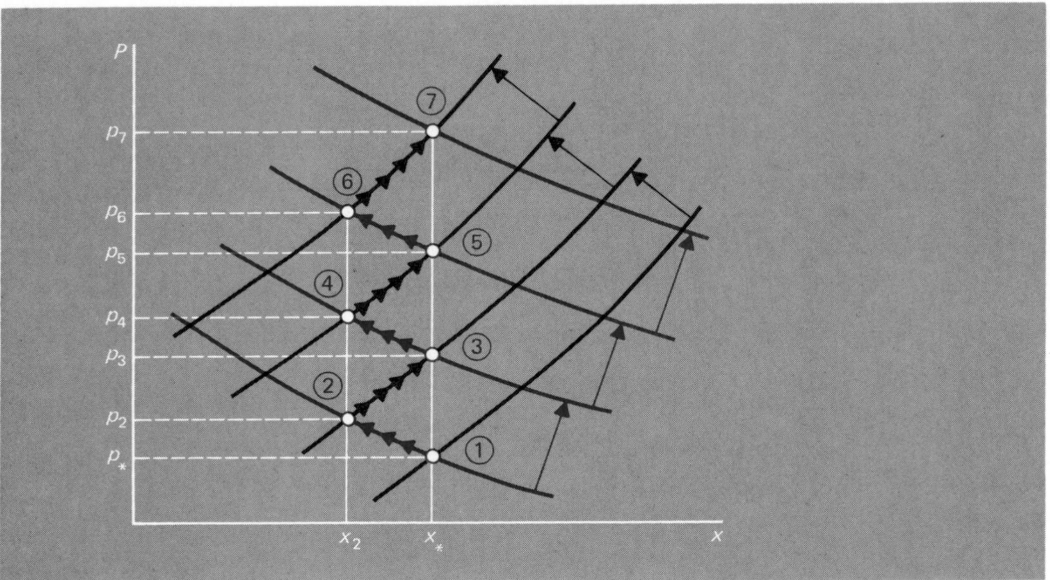

FIGURE 10-6

It is clear, then, that market power cannot be relied on to explain inflation. But, as Tobin points out, it can explain the *inflationary bias* that modern economies are experiencing. Let us, then, briefly examine what "inflationary bias" is and how it can result from market power. We can say that an economy experiences inflationary bias when there is inflation even in the absence of excess demand for goods and services in the aggregate. We know, of course, that the price of any good rises when there is excess demand, falls when there is excess supply, and remains the same when demand is equal to supply. The key, however, is how responsive the price is to excess demand and excess supply. This is where market power is relevant.

In the absence of market power, the speed at which the price of a good rises in response to excess demand is equal to the speed at which the price falls in response to excess supply. The response, in other words, is the same whether we have excess demand or excess supply. For example, if an *excess demand* of \$1 million causes a 10 percent *rise* in price, it must follow that a \$1 million excess supply induces a 10 percent *decline* in price.

In the presence of market power, the response is *asymmetric:* The price of a good rises faster in response to excess demand than it falls in response to excess supply. In terms of our example, although excess demand of \$1 million causes a 10 percent rise in price, excess supply of an equal magnitude causes a smaller decline, of, say, 5 percent.

Equipped with this concept, we can easily show how market power causes inflationary bias. We can first examine the case of the absence of market power. Let us suppose that a change in tastes influences people to demand an additional \$1 million worth of good 1 and to decrease their demand for good 2 by the same amount. In this example, aggregate demand for goods has remained the same. The price of good 1 rises by 10 percent and the price of good 2 falls by 10 percent in the absence of market power. In this case it follows that the change in price is, on the average, equal to zero. If we compare this with the case of market power, we see that there will be an increase in the price of good 1 by 10 percent and a fall of 5 percent in the price of good 2. To determine the average price change, we add the two percentage changes and divide by 2. Thus

$$\frac{10\% + (-5\%)}{2} = \frac{5\%}{2} = 2.5\%$$

We see that even though the aggregate demand for goods and services has not changed, market power causes the prices to rise on the average.

It can actually be shown that for prices to remain unchanged, on the average, there has to be *net excess supply*. This, of course, means that there is insufficient aggregate demand, which, in turn, causes unemployment. This is another way to establish the "cruel dilemma."

III. MONEY-WAGE INFLATION AND UNEMPLOYMENT: THE PHILLIPS CURVE

Cost push was introduced in the 1950s in an attempt to explain the prevailing inflation that existed even in the presence of substantial unemployment of both labor and capital. In 1958 A. W. Phillips published his empirical study of British data about the relation between unemployment and the rate of change of money-wage rates.[2] As the study's title indicates, Phillips examined the relationship between money-wage inflation and unemployment and not between price inflation and unemployment. Figure 10-7 is a reproduction of Phillips' Figure 1, which summarized the central result of his study, namely, that money-wage inflation is inversely related to the *level* of unemployment.

Later we shall see how to derive the relation between *price* inflation and unemployment by starting from the relation between money-wage inflation and unemployment. Of course, the relation between price inflation and unemployment strikingly shows the policy maker's dilemma. Lower inflation can be achieved only by higher unemployment and its accompanying loss of output, and, similarly, lower unemployment can be achieved only by accepting a higher rate of inflation. It is this relation, with its cruel dilemma, that economists of the early 1950s were seeking. It should therefore not be surprising that the first attempts to explain Phillips' relation, later known as the Phillips curve, relied on *cost push* caused by market power, an explanation quickly challenged and rejected.

Richard Lipsey, who further analyzed the Phillips curve, stipulated that the negative relationship between money-wage inflation and unemployment can be ex-

---

[2] A. W. Phillips, "The Relation between Unemployment and the Rate of Change of Money Wage Rates in the United Kingdom, 1861–1957," *Economica,* November 1958, pp. 283–99.

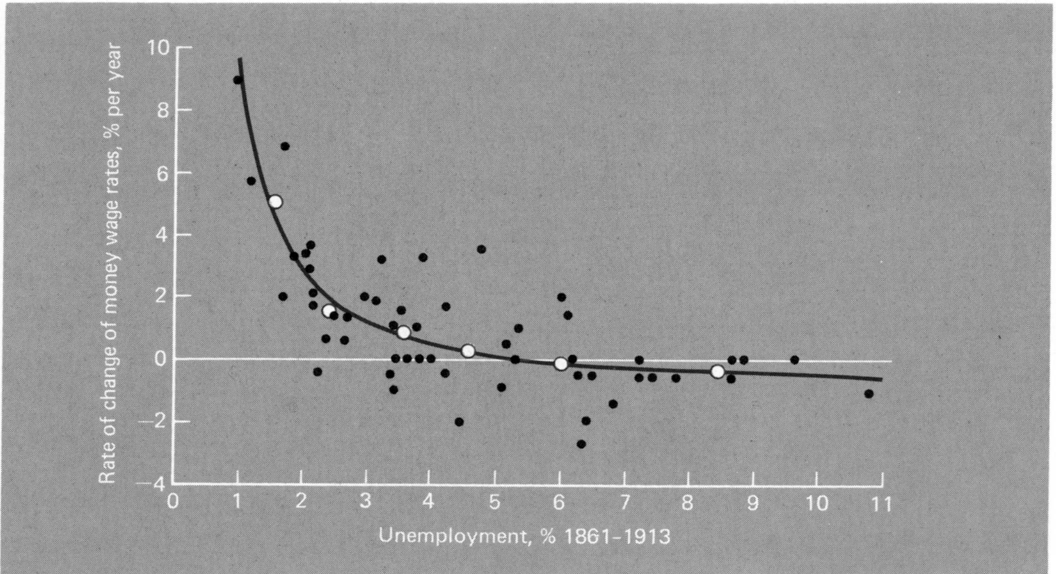

FIGURE 10-7

plained better by applying the law of supply and demand to the labor market.[3] Of course, this law is the money-wage adjustment mechanism which states that the money wage rises when there is excess demand for labor, falls when there is excess supply of labor, and remains unchanged when the labor market is cleared:

$$\Delta W \gtreqless 0 \quad \text{when } x - v \gtreqless 0$$

In addition, we can further modify this mechanism by rewriting it in terms of percentage changes in money wages:

$$\frac{\Delta W}{W} \gtreqless 0 \quad \text{when } x - v \gtreqless 0 \qquad (1)$$

Or we can reproduce this mechanism as Figure 10-8.

We can also rewrite the money-wage adjustment mechanism and its graphical representation to highlight unemployment, u, as the difference between supply of labor, v, and demand, x, that is, $u = v - x$. From this, it follows that $u = -(x - v)$. Thus we can rewrite schema (1) as (2):

$$\frac{\Delta W}{W} \gtreqless 0 \quad \text{when } -u \gtreqless 0 \qquad (2)$$

[3] Richard G. Lipsey, "The Relationship between Unemployment and the Rate of Change of Money Wage Rates in the United Kingdom, 1862–1957: A Further Analysis," *Economica,* February 1960, pp. 1–41.

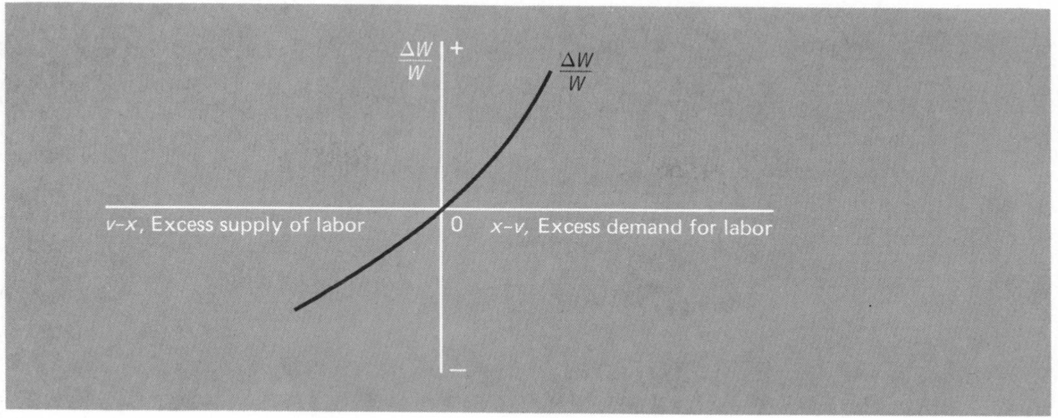

FIGURE 10-8

And the spirit of schema (2) is embodied in the simple equation, (3):

$$\frac{\Delta W}{W} = \alpha \cdot (-u) \quad \text{where } \alpha > 0 \tag{3}$$

Schema (2) or equation (3) is now depcited in Figure 10-9.

Although Figure 10-9 illustrates the negative relation between money-wage inflation and unemployment, it is still inadequate because it does not show inflation coexisting with unemployment. Money-wage inflation is zero when unemployment is zero. The cruel dilemma does not yet present itself: One additional factor is needed to establish it, namely, that zero involuntary unemployment does not mean zero actual unemployment. We know from our earlier analysis that, depending on the existing wage, some people may choose to be unemployed, that is, to "consume their time as leisure." Moreover, others may be unemployed because they are "between

FIGURE 10-9

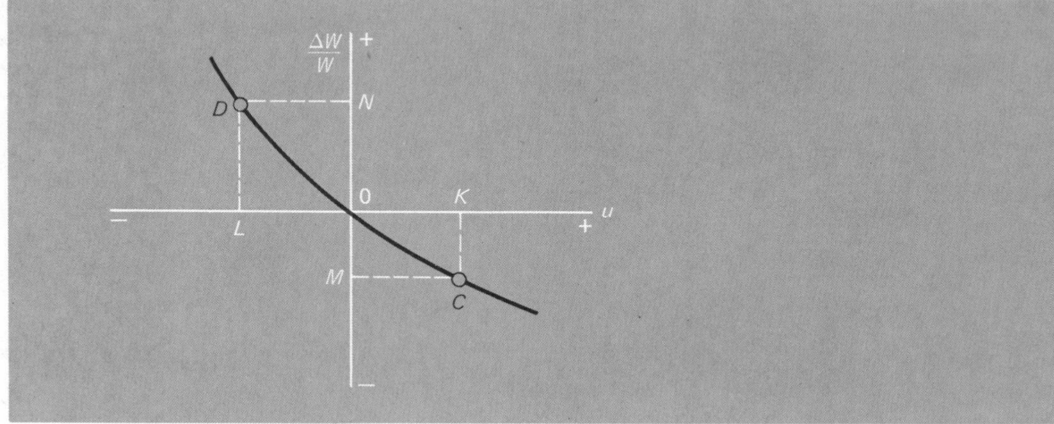

jobs" despite sufficient vacancies elsewhere. The percentage of the work force that is unemployed even with zero involuntary unemployment is often called the "natural" rate of unemployment, or an alternative term such as "full employment rate of unemployment," "frictional," "normal," "warranted rate," or "voluntary." Whatever the term, we shall denote it by the symbol u_* and modify (2) and (3) accordingly. In place of the former, we now have (4); and in place of the latter, we have (5):

$$\Delta W \gtreqless 0 \quad \text{when } u_* - u \gtreqless 0 \tag{4}$$

$$\frac{\Delta W}{W} = \alpha(u_* - u) \tag{5}$$

The essence of the schema in (4), or of its explicit formulation in (5), is that even when the actual, or observed, rate of unemployment is lower than the natural rate (i.e., when $u_* - u > 0$), the money wage rises and we have money-wage inflation. In fact, (5) states that the percentage increase in money wages (i.e., money-wage inflation) is proportional to the excess of the natural over the actual unemployment rate. Similarly, the money wage falls when the actual rate is greater than the natural rate and we experience money-wage *deflation.* Only when actual unemployment is equal to the natural rate (i.e., $u_* = u$) is the money wage unchanged.

Diagrammatically, the relation between money-wage inflation or deflation, $\Delta W/W$, and actual observed unemployment, u, is illustrated in Figure 10-10. The curve intersects the unemployment axis at the natural rate u_*, signifying that when observed unemployment is at this rate, there is zero money-wage inflation. On the other hand, when observed unemployment is u_0, which is less than the natural rate, $u_0 < u_*$, the relevant point on the curve is A with the associated money-wage inflation equal to $(\Delta W/W)_0$. Similarly, we see that point B associates actual unemployment

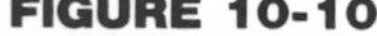

FIGURE 10-10

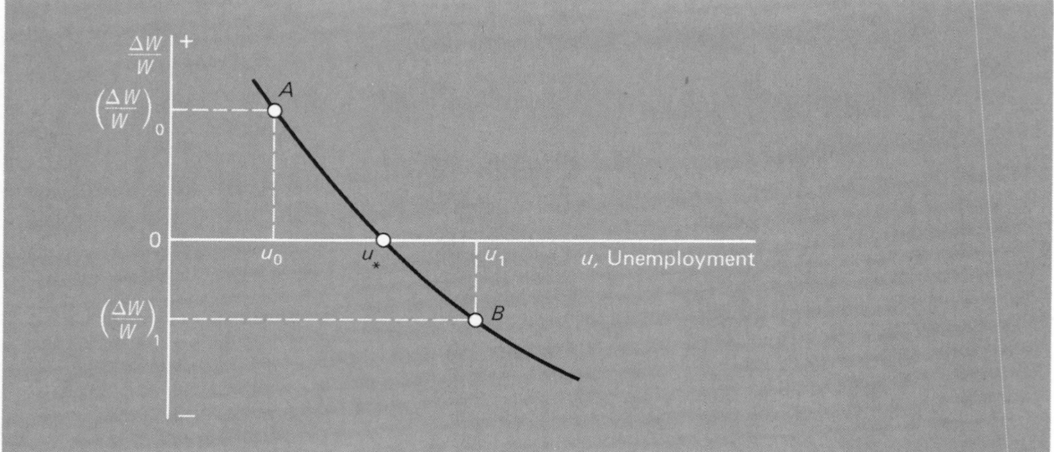

u_1 with a wage *de*flation equal to $(\Delta W/W)_1$, since the actual rate is greater than the natural rate, that is, $u_1 > u_*$.

We see that the curve of Figure 10-10, as well as its schematic and algebraic formulations, (4) and (5), not only depicts the negative relation between money-wage inflation and unemployment but also illustrates the policy maker's dilemma. In fact, the curve of Figure 10-10 looks very much like Phillips' own, reproduced earlier in Figure 10-7.

It is important to stress that we generated this curve relying only on the "law of supply and demand" (for the labor market) as it is reflected by the "money-wage adjustment mechanism." In particular, we avoided dubious theorizing about cost push based on market power. This reliance on the law of supply and demand to theoretically derive the empirical Phillips curve was introduced by Lipsey and adopted by Edmund Phelps, another major figure in the literature on inflation and unemployment, who rejected the cost push explanation on two additional grounds.[4] First, he noted that in many countries, especially in the United States, only a small proportion of the civilian labor force belongs to labor unions. Phelps further noted that while Phillips and Lipsey were able to find the relation between money-wage inflation and unemployment using only nineteenth-century or twentieth-century data, labor unionism was much weaker in the nineteenth century.

We have been able to distill the Phillips curve from the money-wage adjustment mechanism. Now a new problem, which has attracted much attention in the literature, arises, Can we derive the money-wage adjustment mechanism itself from the rational behavior of the agents of the economy, namely, households and firms? If we can do this, we shall have unearthed the microeconomic foundations of the Phillips curve. This has been the subject of intense research during the last decade, and although the money-wage adjustment mechanism has been established by a variety of approaches, or maybe because this mechanism has been established by a variety of approaches, the issue and the controversies are by no means settled.

The standard reference on the subject is the Phelps volume entitled *Microeconomic Foundations of Employment and Inflation Theory,* which incorporates several early contributions.[5] Of special interest are the Phelps, Mortensen, and Holt papers in that volume. We shall not pursue the issue of establishing the wage adjustment mechanism from the rational behavior of individual agents until the end of the chapter where an approach, based upon Tobin's work, but similar to that of Phelps, is examined.

EARLY EMPIRICAL WORK: PHILLIPS AND LIPSEY

In his original contribution Phillips postulated the following relation between unemployment, u_t, and the rate of change in money wages, $\Delta W/W_t$ (where t denotes the

[4] Edmund Phelps, "Money Wage Dynamics and Labor Market Equilibrium," in *Microeconomic Foundations of Employment and Inflation Theory,* ed. Edmund Phelps (New York: W. W. Norton & Co., Inc., 1970).

[5] Phelps, ed., *Microeconomic Foundations of Employment and Inflation Theory.*

time period, and a, b, c are constants to be estimated from the data, and ϵ_t is an "error" term):

$$\log\left(\frac{\Delta W_t}{W_t} + a\right) = b + c \log u_t + \epsilon_t \tag{I}$$

Using the method of "ordinary least squares" [6] in his study of the United Kingdom from 1861 to 1913, Phillips found that a 1.0 percent rise in the unemployment rate was associated with a 1.4 percent fall in the rate of change in money wages:

$$\log\left(\frac{\Delta W_t}{W_t} + 0.90\right) = 0.984 - 1.394 \log u_t + \epsilon_t \tag{I'}$$

Phillips observed that the correlation between $\Delta W/W$ and u changed with different subsamples. This fact became important, as we shall see, when researchers attempted to measure the "expectations-ridden" Phillips curves in the late 1960s and early 1970s. It should be pointed out, however, that although Phillips did not explicitly attempt to measure the effect of changes in inflation, $\Delta p/p$, on $\Delta W/W$, he used $\Delta p/p$ to explore the possibility that during the sample period, 1929–37, $\Delta W/W$ was above the level predicted by equation (I'). (Like most authors writing during this period, Phillips had only a vague notion of the role of price expectations.)

Figure 10-11 reproduces a graph from Phillips' original article, with equation (I') plotted in the $(\Delta W/W, u)$-plane. Note that when $\Delta W/W$ is rising, the scatter of points from 1886 to 1889 lies above the fitted curve; and when $\Delta W/W$ is falling, the data points for the years 1890 to 1893 lie below the curve. Since this phenomenon was evident from other sample periods, it prompted Phillips to conclude that the data are governed by counterclockwise *loops*.

To account for the counterclockwise "loops" suggested by Phillips, Lipsey introduced both the rate of change in unemployment and the level of unemployment, reasoning that when the unemployment rate is rising, $\Delta W/W$ should fall below the rate suggested by the use of the level of unemployment alone.[7] His idea was to capture the negative relation between (Keynesian) demand pull inflation and *changes* in unemployment. Lipsey's results are summarized in equation (II) where, as predicted, the coefficient of $\Delta u/u$ is negative. We should also note that the functional form of this regression differs from Phillips' and that Lipsey chose this form to stress the particular nonlinearity of the relationship:

---

[6] Ordinary least squares is an appealing technique used to find the statistical relation between two variables. The error term ϵ_t is the difference between an actual observation of $\Delta W/W$ and the predicted value of $\Delta W/W$, obtained from the equation. The researcher finds the "best" fit by selecting values of the coefficients, in this case of a, b, and c, so that the error terms are as small as possible. Actually, the criterion is to select values of the coefficients so that the sum of the errors squared is minimized.

[7] Lipsey, "Relationship between Unemployment and Rate of Change of Money Wage Rates."

$$\frac{\Delta W_t}{W_t} = -1.52 + 7.60\, u_t^{-1} + 1.61\, u_t^{-2} - 0.023 \frac{\Delta u_t}{u_t} + \epsilon_t \qquad \text{(II)}$$

In addition to $\Delta u/u$, Lipsey added the actual rate of inflation to measure the cost of living. Note that a rise in the rate of inflation by 1 percent raises money wages by only 0.21 of 1 percent, far less than the amount required to maintain constant real wages during inflationary periods:

$$\frac{\Delta W}{W} = -1.21 + 6.45\, u^{-1} + 2.26\, u^{-2} - .019 \frac{\Delta u}{u} + .21 \frac{\Delta p}{p}$$

with $(\Delta W/W)/(\Delta p/p) = 21$ percent.

Lipsey remarked, along with Phillips, that the regression equations were sensitive to the sample period examined. This result may suggest that variables, excluded from the regressions, could improve the fit of the relationship, helping to make it more stable over time.

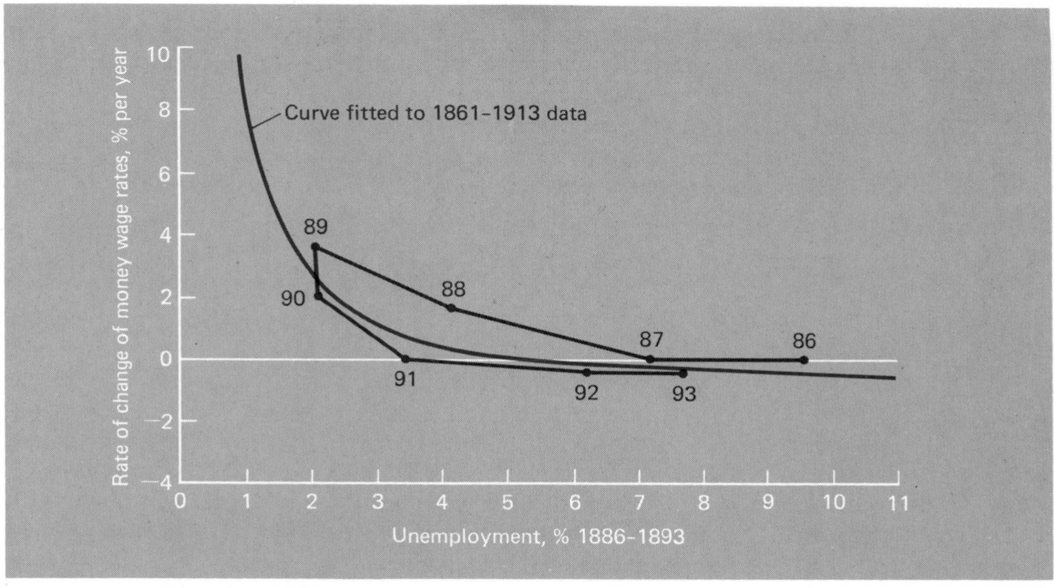

FIGURE 10-11

IV. PRICE INFLATION AND UNEMPLOYMENT: WAGE-PRICE GUIDELINES

More often than not, the Phillips curve that is used relates the rate of price inflation, $\Delta p/p$, rather than wage inflation, $\Delta W/W$, to the unemployment level, u. Given the relation between money-wage inflation and unemployment, this other relationship, between price inflation and unemployment, is easily found. We can start from the profit-maximizing rule for hiring labor, namely, that the real wage, W/p, is equal to the marginal product of labor, MP_N. Since this latter symbol is awkward, we use another:

$$\zeta \equiv MP_N$$

And from the equality

$$\frac{W}{p} = \zeta,$$

we have the result that

$$\frac{\Delta W}{W} - \frac{\Delta p}{p} = \frac{\Delta \zeta}{\zeta} \tag{6}$$

By (6), the difference between money-wage inflation and price inflation is equal to the rate of change in productivity. The latter is usually assumed constant, although for the U.S. economy, as we have seen in Chapter 9, there has been considerable slowdown of productivity in recent years.

It is clear, then, that all we must do to find the relation between the rate of price inflation and unemployment is to subtract the rate of change in productivity:

$$\frac{\Delta p}{p} = \frac{\Delta W}{W} - \frac{\Delta \zeta}{\zeta}$$

or

$$\frac{\Delta p}{p} = \alpha\,(u_* - u) - \frac{\Delta \zeta}{\zeta} \tag{7}$$

This relation is shown in Figure 10-12 where the rate of change in productivity is assumed to be 1.5 percent, which is more consistent with the recent U.S. experience. In Figure 10-13 we illustrate this relation separately.

At this point we should stress that the relation we have just derived is between inflation and the *level* of unemployment. In Section I we derived a relation between inflation and the rate of *change* in unemployment, a relation used by early post-Keynesian economists and referred to occasionally as "Keynesian." Even now, in the 1980s, many economists believe that the rate of inflation is a function of both the level and the rate of change in unemployment, as Lipsey stipulated earlier.

A number of researchers have taken productivity into account when attempting to estimate the Phillips curve. We have seen in (6) that nominal wages, adjusted for inflation, should grow with productivity. John Vanderkamp, for example, estimated

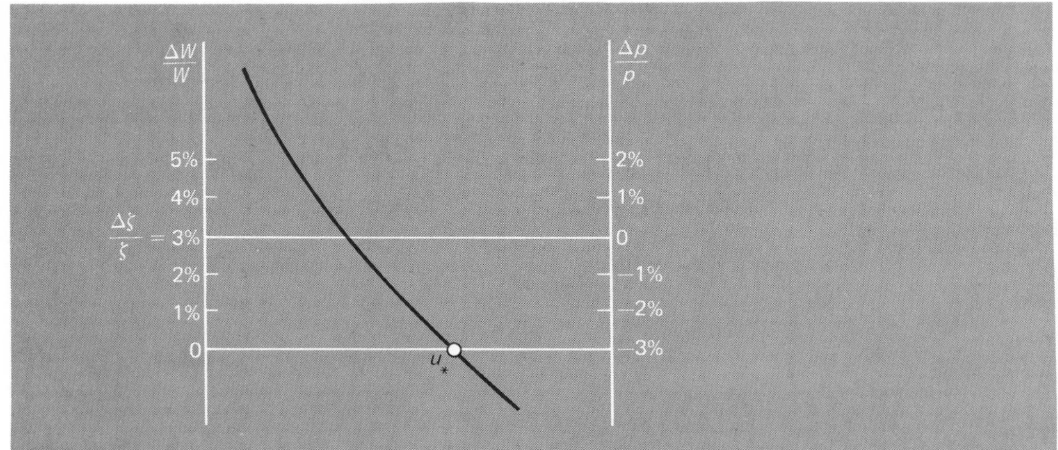

FIGURE 10-12

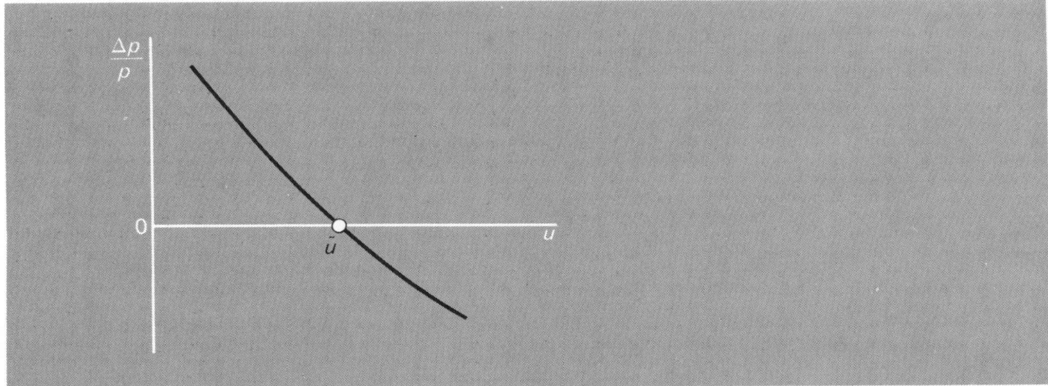

FIGURE 10-13

an equation defining $\Delta\zeta/\zeta$ as the deviation from trend of aggregate labor productivity.[8] His results confirmed that increasing productivity will raise the rate of wage changes:

$$\frac{\Delta W_t}{W_t} = 1.90 + 2.88\ u_t^{-1} + 16.02\ (\Delta u_t/u_t)^{-1} + 0.36\frac{\Delta\zeta_t}{\zeta_t} + 0.76\frac{\Delta p_t^e}{p_t} + \epsilon_t$$

And Vanderkamp's results were confirmed by Kuh,[9] who found that a 1 percent increase in labor's productivity will increase money wages by 0.19 of 1 percent:

[8] John Vanderkamp, "Wage Adjustment, Productivity, and Price Change Expectations," *Review of Economic Studies,* January 1972, pp. 61–72.

[9] E. Kuh, "A Productivity Theory of Wage Levels—An Alternative to the Phillips Curve," *Review of Economic Studies,* October 1967, pp. 333–60.

$$\left(\frac{\Delta W}{W}\right)_t = -0.10 - 0.20\left(\frac{\Delta W}{W}\right)_{t-1} + 0.19\left(\frac{\Delta \zeta_t}{\zeta_t}\right)_t + 0.11\left(\frac{\Delta p}{p}\right)_t + 0.0021\left(\frac{\Delta u}{u}\right)_t + \epsilon_t$$

(He defined $\Delta\zeta/\zeta$ slightly differently here, as the two-quarter-moving-average of labor productivity.)

The relation between price inflation and unemployment highlights dramatically the policy maker's dilemma. To lower unemployment below the value $\tilde{u}$, the policy maker must be willing to impose price inflation on society. Moreover, the policy maker is confronted with an array of price inflation rates and their corresponding levels of unemployment, and the question arises, Which of these combinations is the *best*, the *optimal* choice for society? We shall, however, postpone our attempt to answer this question. In the meantime we shall use the relation between money-wage inflation and price inflation to examine some issues of economic policy that have been prominent recently, especially during the 1960s.

Since, by (6),

$$\frac{\Delta p}{p} = \frac{\Delta W}{W} - \frac{\Delta \zeta}{\zeta}, \tag{8}$$

it follows that the rate of price inflation is zero when the percentage increase in money wages is precisely equal to the rate of productivity growth:

$$\frac{\Delta p}{p} = 0 \quad \text{when} \quad \frac{\Delta W}{W} = \frac{\Delta \zeta}{\zeta}$$

Early in the presidency of John F. Kennedy, the Council of Economic Advisers used this simple rule to design "guideposts for noninflationary wage and price behavior." In designing these wage-price guidelines, the council chose a rate of increase in productivity equal to 3 percent. Of course, this rate was economywide. Doubtless there were some industries with more rapid productivity growth, as well as others with very slow or even negative productivity change. But the council maintained that wages in *every* industry should increase by 3 percent per year, whether the particular industry experienced rapid technological progress or remained stagnant. This rule implied, furthermore, that industries with technological progress greater than 3 percent should actually lower their prices. (For example, an industry with a 5 percent rate of technological progress required a fall in prices equal to 2 percent, as the arithmetic of formula (8) implies: −2 percent = 3 percent − 5 percent.) Of course, industries with productivity increases lower than 3 percent should raise their prices, while the ones with a rate of progress equal to 3 percent should keep their prices constant. Applying this rule, the council hoped that some prices would fall, some would rise, and some would remain unchanged. The end result, however, would be that on the average, the price level would remain unchanged. In other words, the CEA's target was a zero rate of price inflation.

The CEA could have designed another rule; it could have aimed at zero changes in prices for every industry. This, of course, would mean that money wages would rise in industries with rapid technological progress and fall in those with slow technological progress. It was felt, however, that the guidelines would sell better if they gave the appearance of impartiality, that is, of not favoring a particular labor union over another, or favoring workers over employers. Since the guidelines were voluntary, the appearance of fairness was crucial. In fact, not only did the guidelines have the appearance of fairness but they were indeed fair. If they were followed to the letter, the relative shares of labor and capital would remain unchanged. The appearance of fairness, however, created a problem of enforcement. Presumably, a violation of the guidelines called for the president, either directly or through the CEA, to identify the violators and bring pressure on them by using the prestige of the office to create unfavorable public opinion. However, it was easier to create public pressure against an industry that raised its prices than against one that failed to lower them. But an industry that does not lower its prices when it experiences rapid productivity growth (i.e., greater than 3 percent) is capable of raising its wages by more than 3 percent. This capability, of course, evokes discontent in labor unions dealing with these industries, and it prompts requests for higher wages.

Beginning in 1966, violations of the *price* guidelines, either by failing to lower prices when they were required to or by raising them beyond the prescribed guidelines, were more frequent as the economy became overstimulated by large expenditures for the Vietnam War. Of course, price increases are the expected consequence of an increase in effective demand. Thus the wage-price guidelines that seemed to be working fairly well between 1961 and 1965, a period with excess capacity and substantial unemployment, became less and less enforceable as unemployment and excess capacity of plant and equipment diminished. Finally, on assuming the presidency, Richard M. Nixon announced that his administration was abandoning all wage-price guidelines. As we have seen in Chapter 9, President Carter reintroduced wage-price guidelines during the second half of his presidency. They were not successful, however, probably in light of the experience with President Nixon's *controls* in 1971. If anything, President Carter's guidelines fueled inflationary expectations in anticipation that the guidelines would then be upgraded to full-fledged controls. Once again, the incoming Republican, President Reagan, abolished the guidelines.

V. THE EXPECTATIONS-RIDDEN PHILLIPS CURVE

Our analysis in this chapter has utilized the money-wage adjustment mechanism to explain the negative relationship between inflation and unemployment. More specifically, it utilized the "law" that stipulates that involuntary unemployment lowers money wages while excess demand for labor (i.e., unfilled vacancies) raises the money wage. Only when excess demand for or excess supply of labor is zero will the money wage remain constant.

It is important to recall that it is this law, the money-wage adjustment mechanism, on which we relied in Chapter 7 to show that, in the *absence of expectations*, the economy will eventually gravitate toward full employment. In particular, we saw that when there is involuntary unemployment, the money wage will continue to fall, thereby causing the prices of goods and services to fall, real balances to increase, and the interest rate to fall. The end result will be an increase in both aggregate demand and employment, which will continue until full employment is reached. Keynes, who introduced the above process, noticed that sooner or later workers and firms would start anticipating the money wage and price deflation, and that this would have a negative effect on employment. In Chapter 7 we saw that these deflationary expectations may lead the economy to ever-increasing unemployment rather than to full employment. Keynes' idea, stated simply, was that households and firms could not observe wages and prices falling, period after period, (a) without starting to anticipate these reductions and (b) without including them in their decision making.

An analogous idea was introduced with the application of the money-wage adjustment mechanism to the Phillips curve. In this context we can say that actual inflation, whether in wages or in prices, depends not only on the difference between the actual and natural rate of unemployment but also on the expected rate of inflation—again, either in price or in wage-expected inflation. (Please note that two issues regarding expectations will again be important: (a) how these expectations are formed, and (b) how they influence the actual rate of inflation.) In other words, actual inflation is a function of two variables. It follows, then, that there is a whole family, an infinity, of Phillips curves, one for each assumed expected rate of inflation. The question now is, How does a Phillips curve shift when an increase in the expected rate of inflation occurs?

Let us suppose that the expected rate of inflation is equal to $(\Delta p/p)^e_0$, and that the relevant curve is so identified in Figure 10-14. To see how this curve will shift when we assume a higher expected rate of inflation, say $(\Delta p/p)^e_1 > (\Delta p/p)^e_0$, we proceed as follows: At the original expected rate of inflation equal to $(\Delta p/p)^e_0$, the actual inflation rate, *OA*, accompanies the unemployment level, u_0. But with the new, higher expected rate of inflation, $(\Delta p/p)^e_1$, at what actual rate of inflation can the same level of unemployment, u_0, be achieved? If it can be achieved with an inflation rate higher than *OA*, it means that the Phillips curve shifts to the right,

FIGURE 10-14

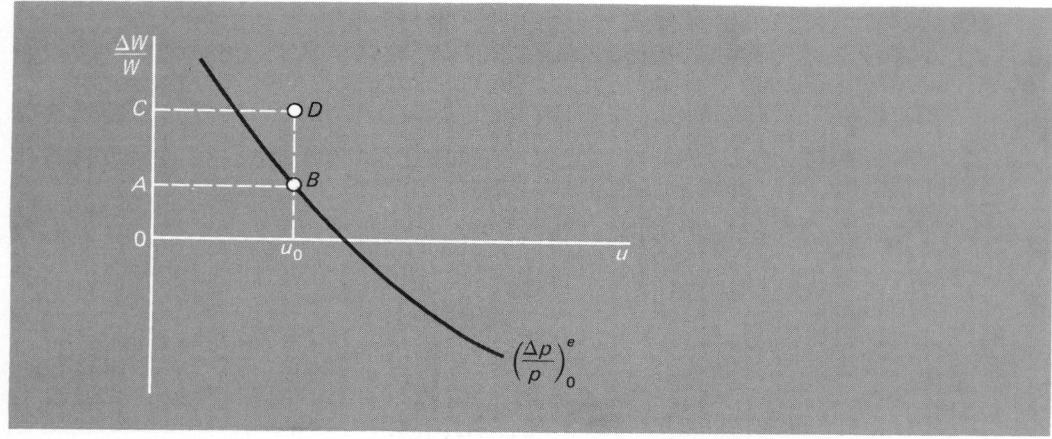

whereas if it can be achieved at a rate lower than *OA,* the curve shifts to the left. It is clear, however, that the employment level, u_0, can be achieved only at a higher actual rate of inflation when the expected rate rises: A higher expected rate of inflation will erode some of the workers' money-wage increases; they will then attempt to restore them by demanding higher wage increases. On the other hand, employers who expect to enjoy higher prices for their products will gladly pay the extra labor costs. It follows that when the expected rate of inflation is greater than $(\Delta p/p)_0^e$, the actual rate of inflation has to be greater than *OA,* say *OC.* This means that *D* is a point on the Phillips curve associated with the expected rate of inflation, $(\Delta p/p)_1^e$. Repeating this process for *all possible levels of unemployment,* we can find all the points of the Phillips curve designated $(\Delta p/p)_1^e$, which is shown in Figure 10-15.

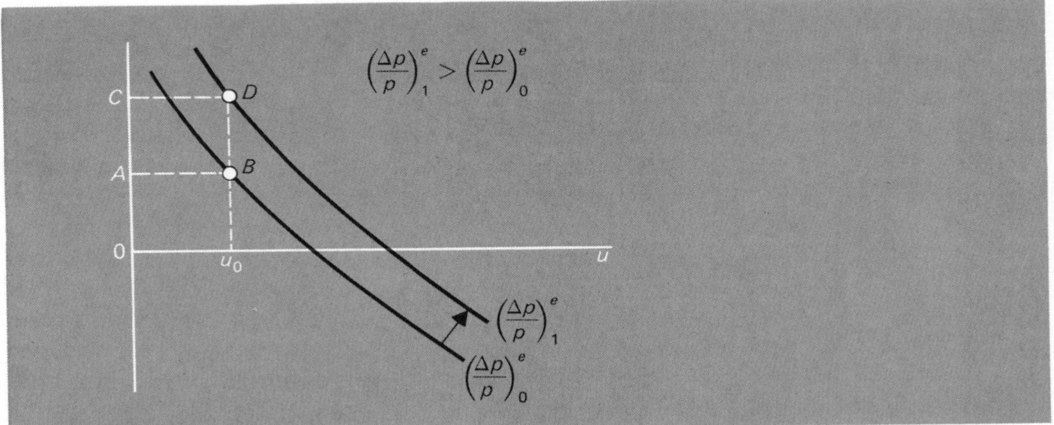

FIGURE 10-15

We have just demonstrated that as the expected rate of inflation rises, the Phillips curve shifts to the right. Precisely how much the curve will shift is controversial and will be examined in the next section. For the present we shall summarize schematically our two results that (a) the greater the difference between the natural and actual rates of unemployment, the higher the actual rate of inflation, and (b) the greater the expected rate of inflation, the higher the actual rate of inflation.

$$(u_* - u)\uparrow \rightarrow \frac{\Delta p}{p}\uparrow \tag{9a}$$

$$\left(\frac{\Delta p}{p}\right)^e \uparrow \rightarrow \frac{\Delta p}{p}\uparrow \tag{9b}$$

The former schema (9a) depicts a northwest movement, upward and to the left, *along* the same Phillips curve, while the second (9b) represents a northeast *shift,* upward and to the right, of the Phillips curve itself. The essence of (9a) and (9b) can be captured by the following simple equation:

$$\frac{\Delta p}{p} = \alpha\ (u_* - u) + \beta \cdot \left(\frac{\Delta p}{p}\right)^e \tag{10}$$

We have noted that there is an infinity of Phillips curves, one for each possible expected rate of inflation. Five, all appropriately identified, are depicted in Figure 10-16. Of course, this greatly complicates the life of the policy maker; true enough, there is a trade-off between inflation and unemployment, but how does the policy maker select a curve on which to operate? The apparent answer is that the policy maker should first determine the rate of inflation that the economy expects and then operate on the Phillips curve that bears that identification tag. This procedure, however, turns out to be more complicated; it is applicable only when expectations do not change. But expectations do change, and this is why we have difficulties.

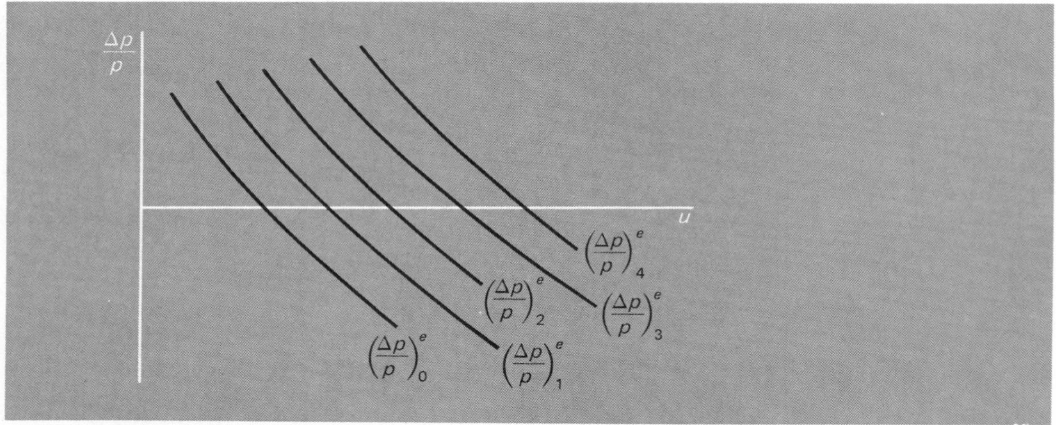

FIGURE 10-16

Assume, for example, that the economy had experienced zero actual inflation for some time and that this zero inflation had been expected. This means that the economy was at point *A* in Figure 10-17 on the Phillips curve with the identification tag $(\Delta p/p)^e = 0$. Now, assume further that an expansionary policy raises the rate of inflation to *OB*, say 3 percent. This obviously lowers the unemployment rate to less than *OA*.

Initially, a society accustomed to a zero percent inflation will consider the 3 percent inflation an aberration, a temporary phenomenon; people will, therefore, not change their expectations of zero inflation. But as the 3 percent inflation persists, they will start to modify their expectations, first, say, to 1.0 percent, then to 1.5 percent, until, in the long-run, their percentage will equal the actual one. Note, however, that as soon as an expected rate of inflation different from zero occurs, the particular Phillips curve of Figure 10-17 is of no help. We have to operate on the

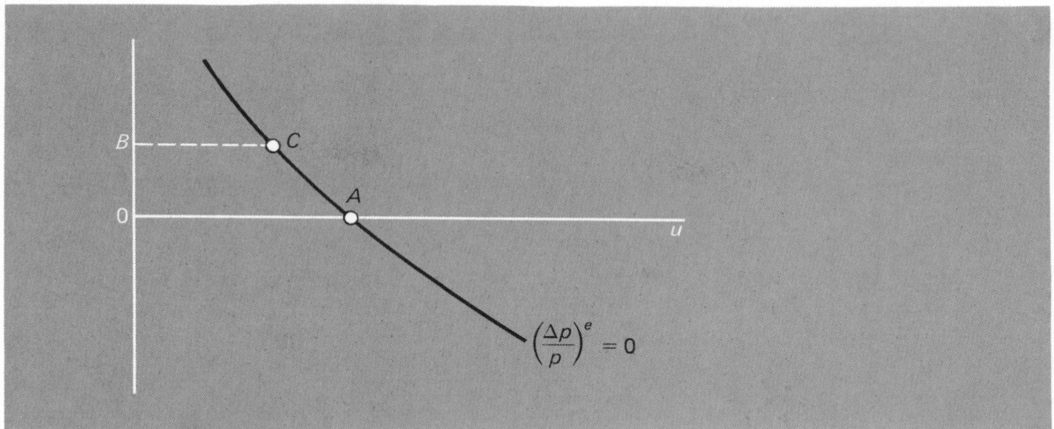

FIGURE 10-17

curve with an identification tag corresponding precisely to the expected inflation rate.

The exact path that inflation and unemployment will follow depends obviously on the particular expectations adjustment mechanism assumed. One such mechanism, which has been used extensively since its introduction in 1956, assumes that at any moment the expected rate of inflation is the weighted average of past actual rates of inflation, with the more recent rates weighted more heavily. These weights and the speed of adjustment of expectations that these weights determine should obviously depend, among other things, on the availability and cost of information. Here, we shall not pursue this matter further. We do want to emphasize, however, that no matter which expectations formation and adjustment mechanism we adopt, the expected rate of inflation, as well as other variables, will be changing, as long as the actual and expected rates of inflation differ. Equilibrium requires, therefore, that the expected and actual rates of inflation be equal: $\Delta p/p = (\Delta p/p)^e$.

This necessary condition for equilibrium turns out to be helpful in deriving the *equilibrium* Phillips curve, which is consistent with equilibrium and takes into consideration the two variables on which the actual rate of inflation depends. Since this actual rate is a function of unemployment and the expected rate of inflation, and since the expected rate is equal to the actual rate, it follows that the actual rate of inflation depends on unemployment and on the actual rate of inflation itself. In other words, we can distill the ultimate relation between actual inflation and actual unemployment.

We can now achieve this graphically by drawing the family of Phillips curves and identifying them by the *actual* rather than by the expected rate of inflation, since the two are equal, as in Figure 10-18. For each rate of inflation, we find the relevant Phillips curve. But only one point on each curve is viable—the one corresponding to the ordinate equal to the nametag of the curve. For example, in Figure 10-18, only point *A* of the Phillips curve, drawn for an expected and actual rate of inflation equal to 1 percent, can be a point on the equilibrium curve. Similarly,

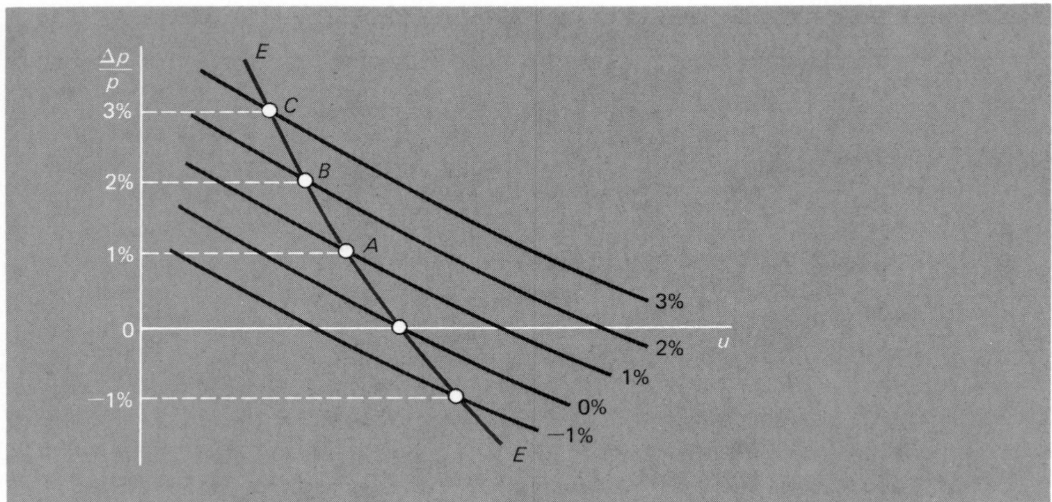

FIGURE 10-18

for the curve with the nametag of 2 percent, only point B is viable. Connecting all such points, we have the equilibrium Phillips curve, labeled EE. This curve is downward sloping, signifying that even when expectations are formed and taken into consideration, there is still a trade-off between inflation and unemployment.

The foregoing analysis was meant only to describe the technique by which we can derive the equilibrium Phillips curve. Its exact form is an entirely different, and controversial, matter. It can, for example, be derived as in Figure 10-19, that is, as a vertical line, signifying *no* trade-off between inflation and unemployment.

FIGURE 10-19

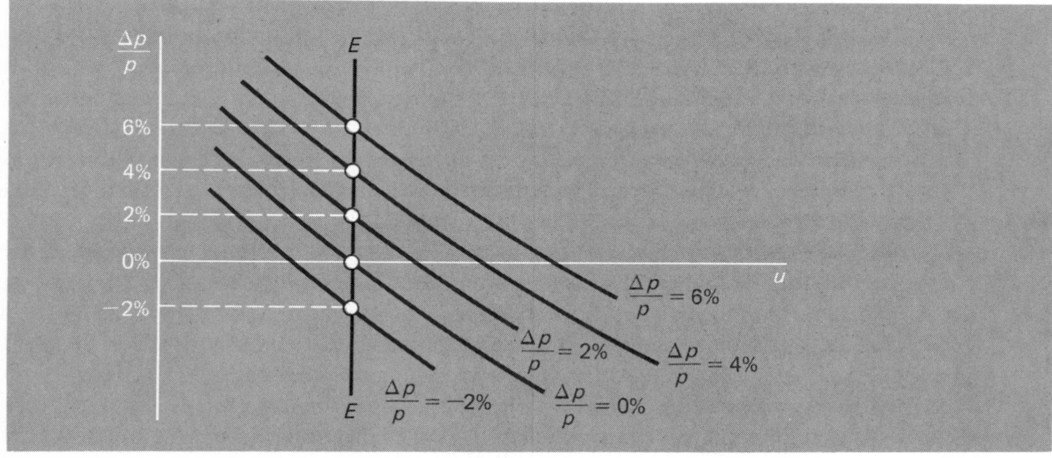

VI. THE VERTICALITY OF THE PHILLIPS CURVE DEBATE

Whether the form of the *equilibrium* Phillips curve is that of Figure 10-18 or of Figure 10-19 is a matter of great importance to the policy maker. Concentrating first on the form in Figure 10-18, we can reach two conclusions. First, the *momentary* Phillips curves are flatter than the equilibrium curve. This means that, initially, the policy maker can reduce unemployment without substantially increasing the inflation rate. But as time passes, and people start anticipating inflation and including it in their decision making, a reduction in unemployment is much more costly; an equal reduction in unemployment will now necessitate a much higher increase in inflation. Our second conclusion shows that despite the anticipation of inflation and its inclusion in decision making, there is still a trade-off between inflation and unemployment, a trade-off that the policy maker can utilize.

More troublesome—and substantially more controversial—is the case inherent in Figure 10-19. Like the previous case, it admits that, initially, the policy maker can reduce unemployment with only a moderate increase in inflation. But, in contrast to the former case, as people anticipate inflation, they become accustomed to it and include it in the wage and other bargains and thereby preclude a lasting trade-off between inflation and unemployment. In fact, Figure 10-19 stipulates that the economy will *eventually converge to the natural rate of unemployment.* And this unemployment rate is consistent with any rate of inflation, be it +10 percent, +20 percent, or a rate of *deflation* equal to 20 percent. Therefore, according to this view, the policy maker's dilemma is not the choice between inflation and unemployment but the choice among the infinite numbers of inflation or deflation rates. (Which of these is *optimal,* according to this view, will be examined in Section IX.)

An important corollary to the "natural rate" stipulation is the "acceleration" proposition: *Accelerating inflation results when the unemployment rate is pegged below its natural rate.* It is easy to find the reason. Since the natural rate is the only sustainable rate, a lower unemployment rate requires continuous expansionary policy. Using Figure 10-20 let us suppose that, initially, the economy is at the natural rate, u_*, with zero inflation. The policy maker who desires u_1 instead of u_*, can achieve it, at first, by using expansionary policy to inflate the economy to 2 percent (point *A*). However, when people get accustomed to the 2 percent inflation, the gain in employment will have dissipated, since the relevant Phillips curve is the one with the tag $\Delta p/p = 2$ percent. Operating on this Phillips curve, the policy maker needs to inflate the economy to 4 percent, that is, reaching point *B*. Again unemployment will move to u_* when the economy adjusts to 4 percent, and the operational Phillips curve is now the one with a tag of 4 percent. Using this curve, the policy maker can achieve the unemployment rate u_1 only when inflation is equal to 6 percent, that is, at point *C*, and so on.

At this point it is instructive to relate this reason for accelerating inflation to the Wicksellian view. Here, an attempt to peg the actual rate of unemployment below its natural, or normal, rate produces accelerating inflation. Wicksell, on the other hand, taught us, as we saw in Chapter 4, that an attempt to peg the *interest*

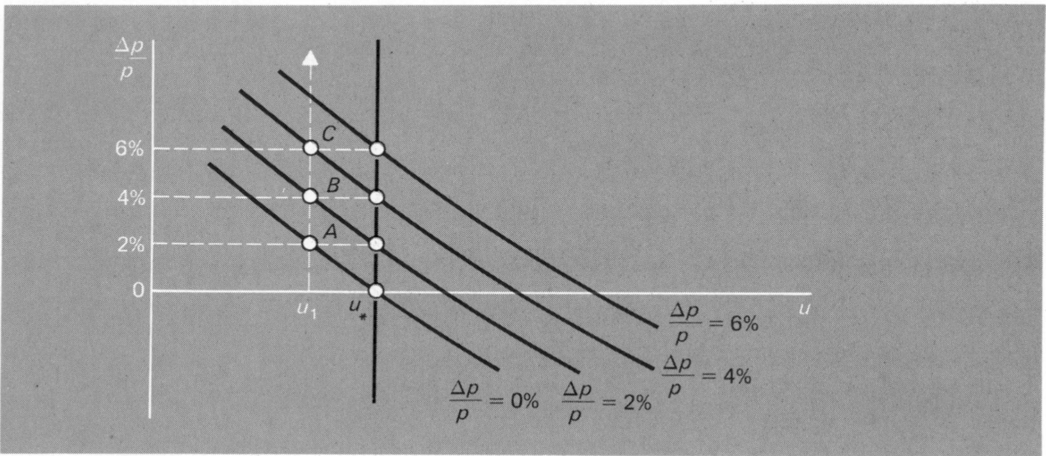

FIGURE 10-20

rate below its natural, or normal, rate will create an ever-increasing, or accelerating, inflation. The accelerationist view in this chapter should not be confused with that in Chapter 9, where we saw that pegging *employment* (not unemployment) at *any* level, in the face of continually rising costs, would require an ever-increasing *price level.*

The natural rate hypothesis, with its accelerationist implications, was introduced by Milton Friedman and Edmund Phelps in the late 1960s.[10] Friedman also emphasized that because of the accelerationist implications, the policy maker is not faced with a dilemma between lower unemployment and higher inflation, but, instead, with a dilemma between unemployment today and unemployment in the future.

Friedman's idea seems to be twofold. First, the reduction of unemployment, in the present, from u_* to u_0, will be reversed in the future; that is, it will be increased from u_0 to u_* when people adjust to the higher rate of inflation (see Figure 10-21). Second, a reduction in unemployment, below the natural rate, requires an accelerating inflation, which will eventually become so costly that the policy maker, at a future date, will be forced to reverse it by pursuing a restrictive monetary and fiscal policy. This, of course, will increase unemployment. In fact, for some time unemployment will be even greater than the natural rate. All these conclusions can be deduced by using a graph similar to that in Figure 10-20.

Whether the Phillips curve is vertical or whether it is downward sloping has strong policy implications. It is imperative, therefore, that we inquire in greater detail whether, and under what conditions, the curve is vertical. It should be clear from the outset that there is full agreement in the profession that the *momentary* (sometimes called short-run) Phillips curve is downward sloping and fairly flat. Every-

[10] Milton Friedman, "The Role of Monetary Policy," *American Economic Review,* March 1968, pp. 1–17; and Edmund S. Phelps, "Phillips Curve, Expectations of Inflation and Optimal Unemployment over Time," *Economica,* August 1967, pp. 254–81.

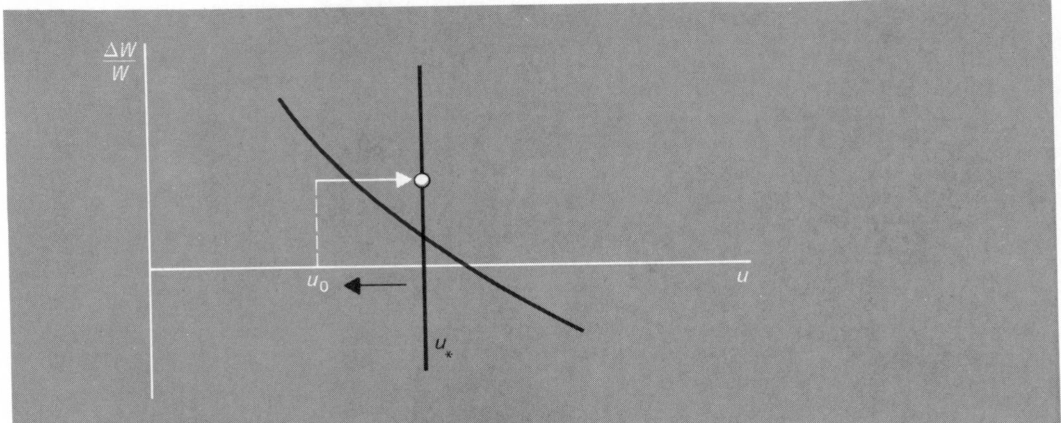

FIGURE 10-21

one agrees that unemployment can be decreased through expansionary policy. They disagree about whether this reduction in unemployment will last. For this reason we shall inquire whether, *at equilibrium,* there is a trade-off between inflation and unemployment.

For some unexplainable reason, the literature on the Phillips curve uses the terms *equilibrium* and *long run* synonymously and reserves the term *short run* for the momentary Phillips curve. Although we shall follow this tradition, we must emphasize that in all other branches of economics, the *short run* is defined as a period during which we can assume that the capital intensity of the economy is fixed. The *long run,* on the other hand, treats the capital intensity as variable, a point that will come up later in this section.

The expectations-ridden Phillips curve was described earlier (p. 372) by the single equation

$$\frac{\Delta p}{p} = \alpha(u_* - u) + \beta \cdot \left(\frac{\Delta p}{p}\right)^e, \tag{10}$$

which captures the schema of (9a) and of (9b): It says, first, that inflation rises if actual employment is less than the natural rate; and, second, that even if the two rates of unemployment are equal, inflation rises when the expected rate of inflation rises. Two important questions now arise, What generates changes in expectations? and How much does actual inflation rise when expected inflation rises, say, by 1 percent? The answers to these two questions will help us find the slope of the equilibrium Phillips curve.

The economics profession does not know precisely how expectations are formed or how they change. And while working rules of thumb have been introduced during the last two decades, serious work still lies ahead. However, one certainty does exist: We know that we cannot have equilibrium if the expected rate of inflation is different from the actual rate of inflation. This, in turn, means that further changes will occur, such as a change in the expected rate of inflation. Symbolically, we can show that a condition for equilibrium is as follows:

$$\frac{\Delta p}{p} = \left(\frac{\Delta p}{p}\right)^e \tag{11}$$

In our previous graphical analysis we have already assumed the condition for equilibrium presented in (11); Figures 10-18 and 10-19 used the actual rather than the expected rate of inflation as nametags for the momentary Phillips curves. Although we shall see later in our analysis why (11) is *necessary* for equilibrium, we can say even now that it is *not* the violation of (11) that causes the equilibrium Phillips curve of Figure 10-18 to be downward sloping. This statement brings us to the second question posed above, How much does the actual rate of inflation increase when there is, say, a 1 percent increase in the expected rate of inflation? If the increase in the actual rate is less than 1 percent, the equilibrium Phillips curve will be downward sloping. If, on the other hand, a 1 percent increase in the expected rate of inflation increases the actual rate by precisely 1 percent, the equilibrium Phillips curve will be vertical.

This issue can be handled symbolically. Recall the simple equation representing the expectations-ridden Phillips curve, equation (10), which we repeat here for convenience:

$$\frac{\Delta p}{p} = \alpha(u_* - u) + \beta \cdot \left(\frac{\Delta p}{p}\right)^e \tag{10}$$

The essence of this issue is whether β in equation (10) is less than one or equal to one. If it is equal to one, an increase of a certain percentage in the expected inflation rate will vertically shift the Phillips curve by the same percentage. The end result will be a vertical equilibrium Phillips curve. If, however, β is less than one, the vertical displacement of the expectations-ridden Phillips curve will be less than the assumed percentage increase in expectations, which, in turn, will produce a downward-sloping equilibrium Phillips curve.

There are two schools of thought on this issue. First, Milton Friedman and Edmund Phelps argue that, *at equilibrium*, β has to be equal to one, $\beta = 1$. Substituting this into (10), we arrive at (12):

$$\frac{\Delta p}{p} = \alpha(u_* - u) + \left(\frac{\Delta p}{p}\right)^e \tag{12}$$

According to this school of thought, this is the correct expectations-ridden price Phillips curve. Except for a correction for the change in productivity, the money-wage Phillips curve is

$$\frac{\Delta W}{W} = \alpha(u_* - u) + \left(\frac{\Delta p}{p}\right)^e \tag{12a}$$

This simply states that the actual rate of (price or money-wage) inflation is determined by taking the expected inflation rate and increasing it if there is excess demand and decreasing it if there is excess supply. This also implies that when there is zero excess demand or excess supply, the rate of inflation is precisely the expected one. Whether the proponents of this view agree unanimously that (12) or (12a) is the correct adjustment mechanism *for all periods of time* (i.e., both outside of equilibrium and at equilibrium) is a matter of interpretation. The proponents do agree, however, that it holds at equilibrium; otherwise, they maintain, people would suffer from "money illusion," which would contradict what we saw in Chapter 7, namely, that workers make their plans on the basis of real wages expected to prevail for the duration of the contract. At equilibrium, by (11), the expected rate of inflation is equal to the actual rate. Substituting this into (12a) and rearranging, we get

$$\frac{\Delta W}{W} - \frac{\Delta p}{p} = \alpha(u_* - u) \tag{12b}$$

This merely describes what was just said, that the changes in real wages, or the left-hand side, depend on excess demand for or excess supply of labor, or the right-hand side. We can now rewrite the above equation in the following equivalent form:

$$\frac{\Delta\left(\frac{W}{p}\right)}{\frac{W}{p}} = \alpha(u_* - u) \tag{12c}$$

It is simple to show arithmetically why the assumption of $\beta = 1$ implies a vertical equilibrium Phillips curve. Using (11), we can write (10) as

$$\frac{\Delta p}{p}(1 - \beta) = \alpha(u_* - u) \tag{13}$$

If $\beta = 1$, the left-hand side of (13) is zero, requiring that the right-hand side also be zero. But since α is not zero, the term in parenthesis, $(u_* - u)$, has to be zero, that is, $u = u_*$. In other words, at equilibrium, actual employment should be equal to the natural rate. This is the natural rate theory. It is important to repeat that expectations must also be realized if a vertical equilibrium Phillips curve is to materialize. We can show this by assuming that $\beta = 1$, which permits us to use (12) as follows:

$$\frac{\Delta p}{p} = \alpha(u_* - u) + \left(\frac{\Delta p}{p}\right)^e$$

or

$$\frac{\Delta p}{p} - \left(\frac{\Delta p}{p}\right)^e = \alpha(u_* - u)$$

If it were possible to have an expected rate of inflation always less than the actual rate, the left-hand side would be positive, implying that the right-hand side would also be positive, and that actual unemployment would therefore be less than the natural rate, $u_* > u$. In this case, even though money-wage, and price, changes *fully* reflect expectations, that is, even though $\beta \equiv 1$, unemployment can be different from the natural rate when people forecast incorrectly the actually realized inflation rate.

On the other side of the issue are economists, including Robert Solow and James Tobin, who argue, first, that a β less than one is a fact of life; it is confirmed empirically. Second, they argue that a β less than one does not necessarily imply irrationality on the part of workers and firms; our world is complicated, comprised of several markets for heterogeneous labor as well as several markets for goods and services. Frictions arise for many reasons, including the lack of costless, plentiful, information. Because of the heterogeneity of labor, money wages themselves, or their rate of change, acquire independent importance. Both labor unions and firms compare money wages and money-wage increases achieved by different groups of workers. Firms do this to compare costs. In addition, as we shall see in more detail later, the existence of different markets for labor implies that some of them will exhibit excess demand while others exhibit excess supply. But in the markets with excess supply, money wages either fall little or do not fall at all. This creates an asymmetrical response, which in many cases is sufficient to prevent a real-wage adjustment mechanism (i.e., equation (12b)). It is argued that employers undertake explicit or implicit long-term contracts when they hire workers. These contracts create wage rigidity; the changes in money wages will not fully reflect expected inflation and, especially, not expected *deflation.*

Occasionally these same economists, while willing to agree in principle that in the long run all these impediments to a real-wage adjustment mechanism are transient, will stress that this long run is indeed very long and that the implication of the natural rate stipulation offers no useful guide to economic policy. And this is what really counts. In the words of the late Harry G. Johnson:

> Practically, however, if people learn about inflation and adjust slowly, then Friedman's argument may not be important: people will behave as if there were no inflation or deflation.[11]

Or in the words of Franco Modigliani:

> In any event, what is really important for practical purposes is not the long-run equilibrium relation as such, but the speed with which it is approached. Both the model sketched out and the empirical evidence suggest that the process of acceleration or deceleration of wages when unemploy-

---

[11] Harry G. Johnson, *Macroeconomics and Monetary Theory* (Chicago: Aldine, 1972), p. 158.

ment differs from the [natural] rate will have more nearly the character of a crawl than of a gallop.[12]

For these nonmonetarist economists, a vertical equilibrium Phillips curve is of no practical significance: It cannot be used for policy considerations. It may show that in the long run the economy will converge to the natural, or full-employment, rate, but the speed will be horrendously slow. Thus it is argued that stabilization policies can and should be used. The verticality of the equilibrium Phillips curve is the same old neoclassical proposition that the economy will gravitate toward full employment. But as we saw in Chapter 7, we cannot rely on money-wage flexibility to achieve full employment because the approach is painfully slow.

THE TRUE LONG-RUN PHILLIPS CURVE

The natural rate hypothesis relies on the long run for the assumption that expectations are fulfilled (i.e., $\Delta p/p = (\Delta p/p)^e$) and that they are *fully* reflected in actual money-wage changes (i.e., $\beta \equiv 1$). It is surprising, however, that this long run does not permit changes in the economy's capital intensity! We can now show that a long-run trade-off between inflation and unemployment is possible, *even if* expectations are realized and *fully* reflected in money-wage and price changes.

Friedman's natural rate of unemployment, u_*, is the outcome of the labor-leisure choice, the one we used in Chapter 1. In other words, the percentage of the work force, u_*, that is unemployed is so by choice. This assumption permits Friedman to claim that a temporary reduction of unemployment, resulting when $u < u_*$, is unfavorable because workers are *fooled* into consuming less of their time as leisure. However, he implicitly assumes that this rate, u_*, is *independent* of expected and actual inflation. In a true long run this is not correct. Let us see why.

Assume that the rate of a steady monetary expansion rises, say from $(\Delta M/M)_0$ to $(\Delta M/M)_1$. This will increase the rate of inflation, and this increased inflation will eventually be expected. In other words, when we had $(\Delta M/M)_0$, $(\Delta p/p)_0 = (\Delta p/p)_0^e$. But when $(\Delta M/M)_1 > (\Delta M/M)_0$, we get $(\Delta p/p)_1 = (\Delta p/p)_1^e$ where $(\Delta p/p)_1 > (\Delta p/p)_0$. This increase in the inflation rate makes money less desirable, since its yield falls from $-(\Delta p/p)_0$ to $-(\Delta p/p)_1$. More of society's wealth is channeled into real capital assets than into monetary assets. The end result is an increase in the (full-employment) capital intensity, K/N, in other words, a fall in $x \equiv N/K$. But we know that this lowers the rate of profit and increases the real wage. And this increase in the real wage will increase the supply of labor by *decreasing* the consumption of leisure.

In other words, the increased inflation increases the natural rate, u_*. Thus we see that there is a different u_* for each actual (and expected) inflation rate. The only way that this can be avoided is if money is "superneutral," that is, if the rate of monetary expansion and the consequent inflation, which is fully expected, cannot

---

[12] Page 8 in Franco Modigliani, "The Monetarist Controversy or, Should We Foresake Stabilization Policies?" *American Economic Review,* March 1977, pp. 1–19.

affect the capital intensity. Nobody, not even Friedman, argues such a case. Phelps, on the other hand, explicitly admits this outcome.

We can show this result graphically. It means that we have a vertical Phillips curve, which shifts because the natural rate keeps changing and thereby traces a downward-sloping, long-run Phillips curve, as in Figure 10-22. Note that $u_*(\Delta p/p)$ is inserted to show the negative dependence of the natural rate on the rate of inflation.

The careful reader must have noticed that the above construction, as well as the preceding arguments, relied on the assumption that the supply curve of labor is an increasing function of the real wage. But we know from the analysis in Chapter 1 that rational household behavior may produce a completely inelastic supply curve of labor. (Such is the case, for example, with homothetic preferences exhibiting unitary elasticity of substitution.) In such a case there is only one natural rate, u_*. But Friedman's analysis will not hold here, either, as Modigliani has pointed out.[13]

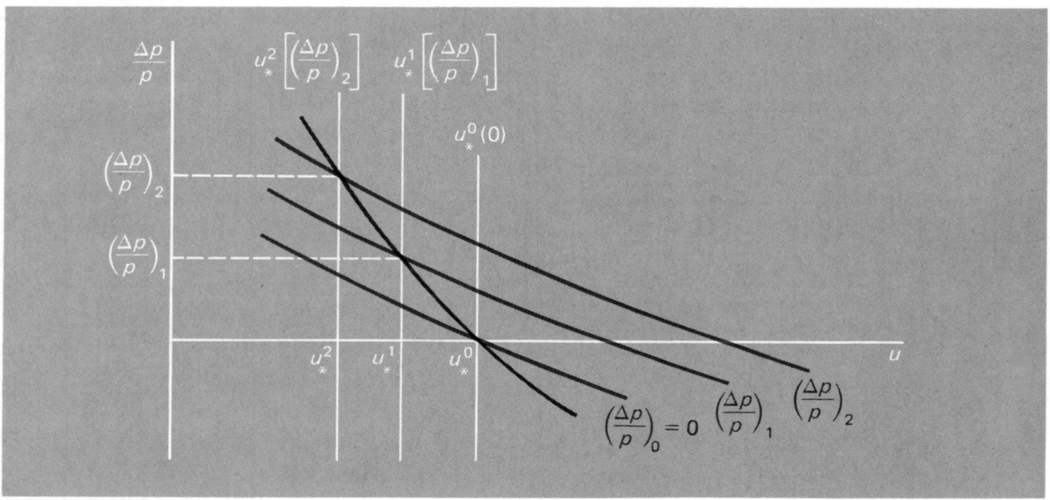

FIGURE 10-22

There remains the question of whether this long-run trade-off between inflation and unemployment is useful. It may be that this result is not useful to the day-to-day manager of the economy for many of the reasons that the natural rate hypothesis is not. On the other hand, for the student of history it may be very useful. After all, a Phillips curve has repeatedly been fitted, with success, for the long-run data.

EMPIRICAL WORK ON THE EXPECTATIONS-RIDDEN PHILLIPS CURVE

We have seen that whether the "long-run" equilibrium Phillips curve is vertical depends on the magnitude of β in equation (10), in particular on whether β is equal

[13] Ibid., pp. 6–7. See also Chapter 1.

to one. To estimate this equation empirically, we must rewrite it in a form that is amenable to empirical testing, namely (III):

$$\left(\frac{\Delta p}{p}\right)_t = \alpha\ (u_t^* - u_t) + \beta \cdot \left(\frac{\Delta p}{p}\right)_t^e + \epsilon_t \qquad \text{(III)}$$

where $(\Delta p/p)_t$ is the rate of change in prices in period t, and $(\Delta p/p)_t^e$ is the expected rate of inflation, from period $t-1$ to period t.

Now a new problem arises: To estimate (III), we need to know the changes in expected prices. This, in turn, means that we must have a "theory" about the formation and movements of expected inflation, that is, about $(\Delta p/p)_t^e$ and $\Delta[(\Delta p/p)_t^e]$. In other words, in order to test the natural rate hypothesis, we must formulate (and test) a joint hypothesis: First, for a given deviation in unemployment from its natural rate, will a rise in inflationary expectations be accompanied by an equiproportionate rise in the actual rate of inflation, that is, will $\beta = 1$? And, second, how are these expectations of the rate of inflation formed?

Although we know that at an equilibrium actual inflation, $\Delta p/p$, must be equal to expected inflation, $(\Delta p/p)^e$, in general, we do not know how these expectations are formed. One of the earlier theories is that of Philip Cagan,[14] who stipulated that when the actual rate of inflation turns out to be greater than the expected, $(\Delta p/p)^e$, the latter increases; and, similarly, when actual inflation is lower than the (previously) expected rate, expected inflation falls:

$$\Delta[(\Delta p/p)^e] \gtreqless 0 \quad \text{when} \quad \Delta p/p \gtreqless (\Delta p/p)^e$$

Cagan suggested the following equation as the exact form that captures the spirit of the above schema:

$$\Delta[(\Delta p/p)^e] = \gamma[(\Delta p/p) - (\Delta p/p)^e], \ \gamma > 0$$

For purposes of estimation we use the following equation:

$$\Delta[(\Delta p/p)_t^e] = \Gamma \cdot [(\Delta p/p)_{t-1} - (\Delta p/p)_{t-1}^e] \qquad \text{(IV)}$$

Now, rewriting (IV) we see immediately that the expectation of the rate of inflation for this period is a weighted average (with weights Γ, and $1 - \Gamma$) of the actual inflation rate for the last period and of its previous expectation:

$$(\Delta p/p)_t^e = \Gamma \cdot (\Delta p/p)_{t-1} + (1 - \Gamma)(\Delta p/p)_{t-1}^e$$

By successively substituting $(\Delta p/p)_{t-1}^e$, $(\Delta p/p)_{t-2}^e$, and so forth, into equation (IV), we can establish that the expected inflation rate is a weighted average, or a "distributed lag" of *all* past inflation rates, as in (V):

---

[14] Philip Cagan, "The Monetary Dynamics of Hyperinflation," in *Studies in the Quantity Theory of Money,* ed. M. Friedman (Chicago: University of Chicago Press, 1956), pp. 25–117.

$$(\Delta p/p)^e_t = \Gamma \cdot (\Delta p/p)_{t-1} + \Gamma \cdot (1-\Gamma)(\Delta p/p)_{t-2} + \Gamma \cdot (1-\Gamma)^2 (\Delta p/p)_{t-3} + \ldots \quad \text{(V)}$$

Note that Γ can take values between zero and unity; and that the closer the values of Γ are to unity, the more weight individuals place on current rates of inflation in forming their expectations. In the limit (i.e., when Γ is unity), $(\Delta p/p)^e_t = (\Delta p/p)_t$, and the best prediction of the future (i.e., next period's) rate of inflation is the currently *observed* rate of inflation. Alternatively, we can see that the smaller the value of Γ is, the greater will be the effect that inflation rates in the remote past have on the formation of expectations about the rate of inflation in the next period.

In our attempts to categorize and compare the existing empirical evidence on the slope of the long-run equilibrium Phillips curve, we have discovered that no meaningful comparison of the existing studies is possible, as different studies use different periods of time, different data, and even different estimation techniques. For this reason we shall test the above-mentioned joint hypothesis ourselves in order to make sure that the various results are comparable.

To gain a better understanding of the behavior of prices through the postwar period, we divide our sample into four overlapping periods, and we report the results of our estimations of (V) in Table 10-1. Note that during the earlier subsamples, from 1950:2 to 1965:4 and from 1955:2 to 1970:4, revisions in inflationary expectations were relatively unresponsive to the error in forecasting the previous period's rate of inflation. When this is the case, individuals will be less likely to abandon earlier forecasts of the average rate of inflation when new information in the form of the actual rate of inflation becomes available. These results suggest that the actual rate of inflation observed last period constitutes only 40 percent of the input into the formation of expectations. The remaining 60 percent is attributed to the previous forecast of the inflation rate. However, the roles are reversed as we proceed through the postwar period. From 1964:2 to 1979:4 individuals were far more responsive to changes in the inflationary environment, attributing 60 percent to the actual rate of inflation in their formation of expectations. In the later subsamples we see that individuals demonstrate a greater tendency to ignore evidence concerning the expected inflation rate from past observations.

Armed with our values of inflationary expectations, which can be generated from our respective estimates of Γ and $(1-\Gamma)$, we are ready to estimate the "expectations-ridden Phillips curve," (III). The results are reported in Table 10-2.

TABLE 10-1 CAGAN'S ADAPTIVE EXPECTATIONS $(\Delta p/p)^e_t = \Gamma(\Delta p/p)_{t-1} + (1-\Gamma)(\Delta p/p)^e_{t-1}$

SAMPLE PERIOD	Γ	$1-\Gamma$
50:2–65:4	.364	.636
55:2–70:4	.259	.741
60:2–75:4	.565	.435
64:2–79:4	.569	.431
50:2–79:4	.487	.513

TABLE 10-2 EXPECTATIONS-RIDDEN PHILLIPS CURVES
$(\Delta p/p)_t = \alpha_0 + \alpha_1 u_t + \beta(\Delta p/p)^e_t + \epsilon_1$

SAMPLE PERIOD	α_0	α_1	β	$\alpha_1/(1-\beta)$
50:4–65:4	.308	−.022	.537*	−.048
55:4–70:4	.814*	−.143*	.825*	−.817
60:4–75:4	.532*	−.089*	.937*†	−1.413
64:4–79:4	.458	−.073	.958*†	−1.739
50:4–79:4	.175	−.016	.909*†	−.176

* Indicates that the coefficient is twice its standard error.
† Indicates rejection of the hypothesis that the coefficient differs from unity at a 95% confidence level.

Even though the coefficients for α_1, the relation between the unemployment rate and the inflation rate, do not withstand standard tests for statistical significance for all subsamples, the results tend to support our theory. For the entire postwar period, 1950:4 to 1979:4, for example, a fall in the unemployment rate of 1 percent below its natural rate is associated with an additional .02 percent actual quarterly rate of change in prices. These coefficients provide us with an estimate of the movement along the momentary Phillips curve for a given anticipated rate of inflation. In the very short run, before individuals begin to revise expectations, the potential arises for policy makers to exploit the trade-off by reducing unemployment with relatively minor consequences to the inflation rate. As anticipations change, however, the trade-off becomes less pronounced. Whether or not a permanent trade-off exists, in the absence of changes in the capital stock, depends on the magnitude of β. Recall that in equilibrium $(\Delta p/p)_t = (\Delta p/p)^e_t$ and from our estimated equation we get

$$(\Delta p/p)(1-\beta) = \alpha_0 + \alpha_1 u_t + \epsilon_t$$

Rearranging terms, we find that the slope of the equilibrium Phillips curve is given by $\alpha_1/(1-\beta)$:

$$(\Delta p/p) = \frac{\alpha_0}{1-\beta} + \frac{\alpha_1}{1-\beta}\, u_t$$

As β approaches unity, our choice between lower levels of unemployment and higher inflation rates becomes less appealing. With $\beta = 1$, the equilibrium Phillips curve is vertical and the natural rate of unemployment may be associated with any inflation rate.

The results in Table 10-2 suggest that as we proceed through the postwar period, the slope of the equilibrium Phillips curve becomes increasingly vertical, ranging from −0.06 to −1.48. From a statistical point of view, we are unable to reject the hypothesis that β is unity for the latter two subsamples and the entire sample period. During the years prior to 1970 our results tend to reject the natural rate hypothesis, but through the 1970s when the economy experienced an era of unprecedented inflation, β appears to have approached unity.

It is important to reiterate the assumptions, both implicit and explicit, that we have used in deriving our results. We have performed estimations and tests that involve a joint hypothesis. So our estimates of β, and any implications that we draw from those estimates, must remain conditional on the correctness of the underlying hypothesis—that expectations of the price level and its movements are formed adaptively.

VII. FORMATION OF EXPECTATIONS—RATIONAL EXPECTATIONS

In the theoretical part of the preceding section we examined the equilibrium Phillips curve. We relied heavily on one of the properties of a true equilibrium, namely, that the expected rate of inflation was equal to the actually realized rate:

$$\left(\frac{\Delta p}{p}\right) = \left(\frac{\Delta p}{p}\right)^e$$

No serious effort was made to determine the actual path that inflation and unemployment will follow. Obviously, this path depends on the way expectations are formed and change through time.

As we mentioned earlier, the economics profession does not have precise formulas by which expectations are formed. One fact, however, is clear: If the actual rate of inflation is different from the expected rate, this expected rate will eventually change. In particular, when the actual rate of inflation is greater than the expected rate, the latter increases. On the other hand, expected inflation falls if the actual rate turns out to be less than the expected one. Only when the two rates are equal will the expected rate of inflation remain unchanged. As we saw in the last part of the preceding section, this stipulation can be written in the following compact form:

$$\Delta[(\Delta p/p)^e] \gtreqless 0 \quad \text{when} \quad \Delta p/p \gtreqless (\Delta p/p)^e$$

An equation capturing the essence of the above schema is the following:

$$\Delta[(\Delta p/p)^e] = \gamma\,[(\Delta p/p) - (\Delta p/p)^e], \ \gamma > 0 \qquad (14)$$

The positive number, γ, is the speed by which expectations are revised. This means, of course, that $1/\gamma$ is the time it takes for expected inflation to become equal to the actual rate. If, for example, γ is infinitely large, expected inflation is instantly revised and becomes equal to the actual rate. This case is usually referred to in the literature as *myopic perfect foresight.* This should be contrasted, however, with the case of *true perfect foresight* that will be introduced below.

Equation (14) is called the *adaptive expectations* equation, a name derived from its ability to show, at any point in time, that the expected rate of inflation is equal to the *weighted* average of past actual rates of inflation, with inflation rates from the more recent past weighted more heavily.

The adaptive expectations mechanism was introduced in 1956 by Philip Cagan, a former student of Friedman.[15] Friedman himself, like dozens of economists, used this mechanism extensively, both in his theoretical and in his empirical work. Its appeal lies in the assumption that the agents of the economy learn from the past and, therefore, continually change their expectations in the light of new information. In addition, this mechanism is easy to handle, both theoretically and empirically.

The next important contribution in the theory of expectations came five years after Cagan's when John Muth stipulated that not all expectations adjustment mechanisms are rational. Expectations are rational, in the Muth sense, if they are consistent with the model itself.[16] This has been taken to mean different things by different people. One such interpretation is that the agents, in forming their expectations about the future, make the most efficient use of the information available to them at the time. A variant of this view asserts that expectations are rational only if they are the same as the predictions of the model used. In other words, we must assume, in the present context, that the typical agent knows the precise evolution of these relevant variables of the economy.

For the problem we are examining, rational expectations have been taken to mean that people correctly anticipate the actually realized rate of inflation. This is the assumption of a *true perfect foresight.*

The marriage of the natural rate hypothesis (NRH) and the rational expectations hypothesis (REH), in this extreme form, yields the not-too-surprising result that the authorities cannot "fool" workers or firms even for an instant. Therefore the proponents of this view maintain that there is no room—even for the short run, and thus for a succession of short runs—for stabilization policies. Neither fiscal nor monetary policy, they argue, will have any effect on the path that the economy will follow. In the words of Thomas Sargent and Neil Wallace, the leading exponents of this view:

> In this system, there is no sense in which the authority has the option to conduct countercyclical policy. To exploit the Phillips curve, it must somehow trick the public. But by virtue of the assumption that expectations are rational, there is no feedback rule that the authority can employ and expect to be able systematically to fool the public. *This means that the authority cannot expect to exploit the Phillips curve even for one period.*[17]

---

[15] The adaptive expectations equation was the first important contribution in two decades. Until then, the standard references were Keynes' *General Theory,* Chap. 12, and J. R. Hicks' *Value and Capital* (London: Oxford, 1939 and 1946).

[16] John Muth, "Rational Expectations and the Theory of Price Movements," *Econometrica,* July 1961, pp. 315–33.

[17] Federal Reserve Bank of Minneapolis, p. 6, italics added.

But is there any added importance to this result? According to the proponents of a marriage between NRH and REH, this result eliminates all justifications for stabilization policies. The result here is much stronger than that of a vertical Phillips curve. We saw, there, that despite one's acceptance that in the "long run" no trade-off between inflation and unemployment exists, still—as a *practical* matter—the authority can utilize a meaningful trade-off. But under the Sargent-Wallace system no trade-off exists "even for one period," an implication of euthanasia for anticyclical policy makers!

Of course, the proponents of this view admit that if the economic agents are unaware of or do not anticipate changes in the money supply and/or the budget deficit, then, and only then, will there be any effect on the rate of unemployment. And this effect will be merely temporary. Once the element of surprise disappears, the ability of the authority to influence the economy also disappears. For this reason the proponents of this view argue that authorities should preannounce the path of these variables, especially that of the money supply. (A fashionable topic of research nowadays is the relation between unanticipated changes in the money supply and changes in unemployment.)

The same attitude is shown toward any expected shock; as long as it is expected, economic agents will discount it. Such discounting amounts to incorporating into prices all the relevant information concerning the anticipated shock. The authority can do better only if it has better information, a situation that is impossible by the very definition of rational expectations. Of course, there still remains the case of *unanticipated shocks,* say, on the supply side. This kind of shock has plagued the U.S., as well as other economies, in the 1970s, as Modigliani noted in his presidential address. According to the proponents of the NRH-REH combination, these shocks are similar to unexpected changes in the money supply and in the government deficit. In other words, although they have an effect, it is only temporary. This amounts to a situation where economic agents *cannot* incorporate the relevant information from a future shock into current prices (since the shock is by definition unanticipated). But as soon as the shock actually occurs, the information *is* built into prices, ruling out continuing but not temporary real output effects. Yet Modigliani and Blinder, who analyzed the supply shocks of the 1973–75 period, claim that they have had profound destabilizing effects on the American economy.[18] Moreover, both maintain that this instability was aggravated by the hands-off policy of the administration, which was advised mostly by proponents of the NRH–REH school.

But how extensive is the influence of the NRH–REH school of thought? Here we must distinguish between the NRH school, the REH school, and the NRH–REH school. We have seen that even those economists willing to accept, in principle, the NRH are still unimpressed by its policy implications. The REH, by itself, is gaining support in the profession, but mainly to explain the working of single, specialized markets. Especially promising is the version that states that expectations in a market are rational when the agents rely on the data actually available to them at the time of their decision making.

---

[18] Modigliani, "Monetarist Controversy,"; and Alan S. Blinder, *Economic Policy and the Great Stagflation* (New York: Academic Press, 1979).

We come now to the NRH–REH combination itself. This is an application of rational expectations to the whole economy—and a special version of that economy at that. The influence of this view has increased recently, since the results of NRH–REH have been accepted by several economists of the monetarist persuasion. However, criticisms have also emerged, attacking the NRH–REH combination on its own ground. As for reactions of nonmonetarists, the following evaluation from Modigliani is typical:

> But the most glaring flaw of [NRH–REH] is its inconsistency with the evidence: if it were valid, deviations of unemployment from the natural rate would be small and transitory—in which case *The General Theory* would not have been written and neither would this paper. Sargent (1976) has attempted to remedy this fatal flaw by hypothesizing that the persistent and large fluctuations in unemployment reflect merely corresponding swings in the natural rate itself. In other words, what happened to the United States in the 1930s was a severe attack of contagious laziness! I can only say that, despite Sargent's ingenuity, neither I nor, I expect, most others at least of the nonmonetarists' persuasion are quite ready yet to turn over the field of economic fluctuations to the social psychologist![19]

We shall not embark, here, upon a detailed analysis and critique of the REH as it has been applied to the economy as a whole. And it is the examination of the economy as a whole that concerns us in this book. We shall, instead, highlight some analytical weaknesses that make it unacceptable to the student of general interdependent analysis.[20] In the next subsection, after constructing a typical NRH–REH model, we shall highlight some of its crucial flaws.

RATIONAL EXPECTATIONS AND GENERAL INTERDEPENDENT ANALYSIS

In our opinion, the crucial element Muth introduced is the requirement that the assumptions of the model, *in particular that of expectations formation,* should be consistent. We should not merely tack on to a model an expectation formation mechanism—*whatever it may be*—without inquiring whether this mechanism is consistent with *intertemporal equilibrium.* And how do we define this last concept? Intertemporal equilibrium satisfies two conditions: (a) that markets are cleared and (b) that expectations are fulfilled. This is the dynamic analogue of the static competitive equilbrium. Now we test the consistency of the model by proving the *existence* and *stability* of this intertemporal equilibrium. Both tests are necessary. In this view, the assumptions that markets are cleared (i.e., perfect competition) and that expectations are fulfilled (i.e., perfect foresight) should not be interpreted as a description of the state of the

[19] Modigliani, "Monetarist Controversy," p. 6.

[20] We prefer this latter term to the traditional *general equilibrium analysis,* which implies mistakenly that it deals only with equilibrium situations.

system at every moment, but rather as the *target* toward which the system is drawn over time. In other words, the intertemporal equilibrium path should not be taken as the path the economy will actually follow, but, instead, as a benchmark with which the actual path should be compared, a *criterion path.* If one shows that the actual path diverges from this target, the model does not make any sense; it is inconsistent. We can also apply this criterion to the expectations formation. Given the other adjustment mechanisms of the system, for example, those of prices, the expectation formation mechanism is "irrational" (i.e., inconsistent) if the path derived does not lead to the intertemporal equilibrium. (Recall that one of the two conditions for this intertemporal equilibrium is that expectations be fulfilled. Thus the test means that if the path diverges, fulfillment of expectations cannot materialize.) This test has to be passed whether expectations are formed adaptively, à la Cagan, or by utilizing the idea of minimizing the cost of information, à la Stigler, something that has not yet been formally derived.

Since the literature lacks a theory of expectations formation based on maximizing (or minimizing) behavior of the individual (or average) agent, our natural *first step* is to assume that the agents possess knowledge of the actual evolution of the system in the future, that is, *assume* fulfillment of the second of the two conditions of intertemporal equilibrium. With this assumption we are at least guaranteed that expectations are "rational." We can term this first step the "naive view" of "rational" expectations. (Despite its naiveté, this view can be useful, for example, in comparative "dynamics.") This is what the proponents of REH mean when they say that "all that the agents have to learn are the properties of the model itself." How is this done? Like a science-fiction tale, these average agents, while contemplating their future actions, are assumed to close their eyes while a scientist (economist?) hypnotizes them, makes them see the future *as it will actually happen,* and programs them to follow this course when they wake up! Of course, in this case there is no stability problem or, in general, any legitimate dynamics, since the actual evolution of the system is not only predetermined, by programming the agents, but also known by everyone.

In fact, this predetermined system was achieved more elegantly even *before* the appearance of the Muth paper by the masters of general equilibrium analysis, especially by Malinvaud and by Arrow-Debreu, by means of a *complete set of futures markets.* In their system all the transactions for the future are concluded in the beginning of the temporal sequence, leaving only the carrying out of prearranged deliveries. That this is equivalent to the plot of our science-fiction parable is seen by the proof (e.g., in Arrow-Hahn's book) that the assumption of a complete set of futures markets implies the perfect foresight requirement (the converse is also true).

The idea of perfect foresight—or its equivalent, perfect futures markets—is acceptable when we examine, like Malinvaud, Arrow-Debreu, and others, a nonmonetary, *real* economy, but it is *fatal* when introduced into a monetary model as a formation of expectations hypothesis. It is the essence of a realistic (i.e., monetary) economy that perfect futures markets do not exist; this is the reason why people need to hold money. Looked at from the other side, we see that *if there is a complete set of futures markets, there is no reason for money to exist;* this is why this assumption is good for a real model, which *avoids* problems associated with money. This is also why this assumption implies the "real-wage" adjustment mechanism for every instant of time. No wonder there is no room for stabilization policies! In other words, studies that use this assumption claim, in effect, that *in a non-monetary economy money does not matter!*

But this "empty box" is not what we envisioned for the dynamic analysis in this book. We are examining a *monetary economy* where time is taken seriously and where, of course, the agents, in their plans, look forward. To do justice to both the Muth concept of "rational" expectations (i.e., consistency) and the concept of a "monetary economy," we must check whether the assumptions of the model, including that of "expectations formation," are mutually consistent *in the absence of perfect futures markets.* That is to say, we must show that the assumptions of the model permit the economy to converge to the "intertemporal equilibrium," in which "the markets are cleared and expectations fulfilled." This is why several economists consider the assumption of perfect foresight, in the above sense, *inferior* to the assumption of adaptive expectations. The assumption of "perfect foresight"—among other things—precludes a monetary economy, whereas the assumption of "adaptive expectations" permits it *and* can be consistent with the requirement of "rational expectations," in our sense of the concept. If "perfect foresight" is to pass the above requirements, it must be the concept of "perfect *myopic* foresight," which was explained earlier. This concept permits, *in principle,* nonfulfillment of expectations.

We stated above that the "adaptive expectations" assumption *can* pass the criterion of "rationality," or "consistency": what is needed is some restriction (sometimes nonbinding) on its speed of adjustment. *Example:* If the speed of adjustment, ϵ, in the goods market tends to infinity, "adaptive expectations" are "rational" only if γ is bounded below some number, as in the Cagan condition. However, if ϵ is bounded by some positive number, the restriction on γ is not binding; γ can tend to infinity, and the rationality is still guaranteed.[21]

For a critique at a higher, analytical and philosophical level we should cite an important recent contribution by Swamy, Barth and Tinsley,[22] who have shown that a conflict exists between the Muth-Lucas-Sargent rational expectations hypothesis and the Bayesian definition of rationality. According to these authors, the source of this conflict is that the rational expectations hypothesis requires the coincidence of subjective and objective (however one defines this term) probabilities of events, whereas the subjective Bayesian definition of rationality uses only subjective probabilities without equating them to any objective probabilities. These authors argue furthermore that the rational expectations hypothesis, which may be regarded as a linguistic axiom, is too restrictive to be very useful in practice. To eliminate this conflict, these authors develop an alternative, logically consistent microeconomic model, based on a Bayesian model of subjective expectations which, when aggregated across individuals, results

---

[21] See Michael G. Hadjimichalakis, "Equilibrium and Disequilibrium Growth with Money: The Tobin Models," *Review of Economic Studies,* October 1971, pp. 457–79; and M. G. Hadjimichalakis, "Money, Expectations, and Dynamics: An Alternative View," *International Economic Review,* October 1971, pp. 381–402.

[22] See P. A. V. B. Swamy, J. R. Barth and P. A. Tinsley, "The Rational Expectations Approach to Economic Modelling," *Special Studies Paper* No. 143, Federal Reserve Board, July, 1980.

in a macroeconomic model with stochastic coefficients. Finally, they demonstrate that the time series models which form an integral part of rational expectations models are as difficult to identify as conventional macro-econometric models.

A SIMPLE RATIONAL EXPECTATIONS MODEL, ITS IMPLICATIONS AND ITS WEAKNESSES

We shall first develop a very simple, but frequently used, model of the REH to see its strengths and its weaknesses.

We start with a basic cornerstone of the model, the supply function

$$y_t - \bar{y}_F = b_1(p_t - {}_{t-1}p_t^e) + \epsilon_t \tag{15}$$

where

y_t = real output in period t
$\bar{y}_F$ = full-employment level of output (fixed)
p_t = price level in period t
${}_{t-1}p_t^e$ = expectation of price level for period t but formed at the end of period $t-1$
ϵ_t = deviations of output from the full-employment level which are unexplained by unanticipated price changes (its expectation, ϵ_t^e, is zero)

The "structure" of this single economy is captured by this quantity theory determination of price level:

$$p_t = \alpha M_t + v_t \tag{16}$$

where M_t is the stock of nominal balances, and v_t is a proxy for all other variables that may affect the price level. But, invariably, its expectation is assumed zero, $v_t^e \doteq 0$, which means that those other factors have no systematic effect on prices. In perfect quantity theory fashion, only money stock matters in influencing the price level.

According to the REH, expectations are rational if they are the predictions based on the structure of the model. And since here the "structure" says that prices depend only on the money stock, expectations of the price level are rational only if they depend on the expectations of the money stock: Taking the expectation of (16), we have

$$ {}_{t-1}p_t^e = \alpha\, {}_{t-1}M_t^e \tag{17}$$

Now, substituting rational expectations, that is, (17) into (15), along with the structure itself, (16), we have[23]

---

[23] $y_t - \bar{y}_F = b_1(p_t - {}_{t-1}p_t^e) + \epsilon_t$
$= b_1p_t - b_1\, {}_{t-1}p_t^e + \epsilon_t$ (multiplying through)
$= b_1(M_t + v_t) - b_1\, {}_{t-1}p_t^e + \epsilon_t$ (by (16))
$= \alpha b_1 M_t + b_1 v_t - b_1\, {}_{t-1}M_t^e + \epsilon_t$ (by (17))
$= \alpha b_1(M_t - {}_{t-1}M_t^e) + b_1 v_t + \epsilon_t$ (collecting terms)

$$y_t - \bar{y}_F = \alpha b_1 (M_t - {}_{t-1}M_t^e) + b_1 v_t + \epsilon_t \tag{18}$$

This is a crucial equation. It says that any deviation, $y_t - \bar{y}_F$, of actual output from full-employment output, has two components: first the "noise" in the relation between prices and money, $b_1 v_t$, and second, unanticipated changes in the money supply, $M_t - {}_{t-1}M_t^e$. Now the noise, on the average, is zero, since its "expectation," $b_1 v_t^e$, is zero, and hence only unanticipated money changes can matter. If, on the other hand, people know the policy rule that the Fed follows, that is, if they know M_t, then on average the actual money stock is anticipated correctly and hence $M_t - {}_{t-1}M_t^e = 0$ and $y_t - \bar{y}_F = 0$. In other words, if the path of the money stock is correctly forecasted, the economy will always be at full employment, and moreover no economic policy can systematically influence actual economic activity (output, y_t).

Next, writers of the REH school contrast equation (18) and its implication to those derived by using a nonrational expectation formation. They single out adaptive expectations, such as the one depicted by (14), but here, for illustration, we shall use even a simpler, and more vulnerable, version. In particular, we shall assume that expectations are formed extrapolatively, that is, the expectation of period t's price level is a proportion, λ, of last period's observed price level:

$${}_{t-1}p_t^e = \lambda p_{t-1}, \quad 0 < \lambda \leqq 1 \tag{19}$$

The expectations formed by (19) are said to be nonrational because, in forming these expectations, individuals ignore the "structure" of the model (i.e., equation (16)) and the "true" price expectation derived from this structure (i.e., (17)).

Now, substituting (19) and (16) (but not (17)) into (15), we have

$$y_t - \bar{y}_F = \alpha b_1 (M_t - \lambda M_{t-1}) + b_1 (v_t - \lambda v_{t-1}) + \epsilon_t \tag{20}$$

Of course, (20) says that monetary policy can have an effect on the difference $y_t - \bar{y}_F$ and, therefore, on current output, y_t; but some claim that this ability is attributed to the use of the nonrational expectations of (19) rather than the rational expectations of (17).

Now to make the REH, as depicted by (15), (16), (17), or by its end result, equation (18), consistent with the postwar data, several rational expectations writers add to the right-hand side of (15) (i.e., to the supply function) the variable y_{t-1}, last period's output. We now have (15′) and (18′) in place of (15) and (18):

$$y_t - \bar{y}_F = b_1 (p_t - {}_{t-1}p_t^e) + b_2 y_{t-1} + \epsilon_t \tag{15′}$$

$$y_t - y_F = b_1 (M_t - {}_{t-1}M_t^e) + b_2 y_{t-1} + b_1 (v_t - v_{t-1}) + \epsilon_t \tag{18′}$$

This modification is introduced in a *totally ad hoc* manner; and while it helps the model to be consistent with postwar observations of output, it seems to negate, in effect, what some writers have seen as the essence of rational expectations. For a key characteristic of the REH is that deviations of output, y, or employment, x, from their natural rates should not be correlated through time (i.e., serially correlated). Strong correlation through time implies that *output is responsive to errors made in expectations of prices in the remote past,* and this response violates the premise of "rational expectations." And yet the introduction of y_{t-1}, y_{t-2}, and so forth, in the supply function accomplishes, in effect, just that. Do adaptive expectations slip in through the back door? And is the fit better for just this reason?

On the topic of empirical testing of the REH, another point is noteworthy. Suppose that the government (Fed) uses the following (anticyclical) stabilization policy rule: Increase the money stock in the next period if, at the end of this period, output is less than its full-employment level; and reduce the money supply if output is greater than its full-employment level. Schematically, the rule is

$$\Delta M_t \gtreqless 0 \quad \text{when} \quad y_{t-1} - \bar{y}_F \lesseqgtr 0$$

Suppose that the exact rule is given by the equation

$$M_t = h_0 - h_1 \cdot (y_{t-1} - \bar{y}_F) + u_t \tag{21}$$

Furthermore, suppose that people indeed know this rule, that is, ${}_{t-1}M_t^e = M_t$. Then it can be shown that equation (18′) can be reduced to the form of equation (20). In other words, it can be shown that data are generated in a similar manner and, as it is usually stated, the two theories are *observationally equivalent.* We cannot test directly which one is supported by the evidence. For this reason several economists undertook indirect tests, but it seems that they still cannot answer the question that was posed.

Of course, the writers who have worked in the REH area differ among themselves in terms of the assumptions used and in terms of the emphasis on particular points. Four writers—Thomas Sargent, Neil Wallace, Robert Barro, and Robert Lucas—have been on the forefront of this work. For the student who is interested in pursuing these notions further, we will contrast the focus of each of these writers' work. Thomas Sargent and Neil Wallace have been largely responsible for the development of a mathematical as well as a logical methodology that clarifies the meaning of the statement that "economic agents form their expectations of economic variables based on the structure of the relevant model."[24] The development of this methodology has occurred in a body of literature that involves some highly restrictive assumptions—in particular, that economic agents can, without cost, determine the structure of the model.

Robert Barro is best known for his efforts to empirically test the implication of REH that "only surprises matter."[25] He has found that anticipated money growth

[24] Thomas Sargent and N. Wallace, "Rational Expectations and the Theory of Economic Policy," *Journal of Monetary Economics,* April 1976, pp. 169–84; "Rational Expectations and the Optimal Money Supply Rule," *Journal of Political Economy,* April 1975, pp. 241–54.

[25] Robert J. Barro, "Unanticipated Money Growth and Unemployment in the United States," *American Economic Review,* March 1977, pp. 101–15; "Unanticipated Money, Output and the Price Level in the United States," *Journal of Political Economy,* August 1978, pp. 549–80.

has no real effects, whereas unanticipated money growth does have real effects. Barro's work suffers from a problem shared by all empirical work (including ours) that involves a role for expectations. Any empirical test essentially tests a joint hypothesis, not only one involving the implications of REH, but also one to see whether the expectations have been correctly specified. Barro's work has been especially useful in highlighting this difficulty, since some other researchers (in particular Small)[26] have been able to significantly alter Barro's results by a modification to the expectation formation specification.

Lucas's best-known contribution investigates whether the ability of the monetary authority to produce real effects tends to deteriorate as such policy is being used.[27] The tests are based on a supply equation similar to (15) (often referred to as the Lucas supply equation). His study found that in countries where the use of monetary policy in the past has resulted in a highly volatile price level, monetary policy appears to be unable to produce significant real effects even in the short run but merely results in immediate price-level changes. However, in countries that have experienced a history of relatively stable price levels, monetary policy is able to affect output in the short run. While this study is a relaxation of the strictest form of the REH, it is still not very encouraging for the use of anticyclical activist policy, since the results of that policy show a tendency to deteriorate as the policy is being used.

Leaving empirical testing aside, there are some additional theoretical weaknesses of the REH on its own ground.

First, labor contracts are usually specified in terms of a fixed money wage and for periods longer than it takes the monetary authority to adjust (or readjust) its targets for monetary growth. This allows a certain degree of "stickiness" in real wages, even though both sides of a labor contract are aware of changing targets by the monetary authority (and of the impact of these changes upon prices.) And even though these changes in monetary targets are perfectly anticipated, long-term contracts do indeed allow the monetary authority to use an effective activist (anticyclical) policy.[28] Several authors have pointed out that in this case we should expect to see contract terms becoming endogenous—in particular, in efforts to set contracts in real rather than nominal terms or to shorten contract periods to reduce potential ex post losses.

Second, although it seems sensible to assert that individuals form expectations from the true underlying structure of the economy, rational expectations, at least in the existing literature, have little to say about how this structure comes to be known, what information costs are involved, or how quickly individuals can acquire knowledge of this structure. Two avenues can be followed here. One approach is to assume that individuals learn the structure of the economy immediately and costlessly. But

---

[26] David H. Small, "A Comment on Robert Barro's Unanticipated Money Growth and Employment in the United States" (Paper 7908, University of Wisconsin, March 1979).

[27] Robert E. Lucas, Jr., "Some International Evidence on Output-Inflation Tradeoff," *American Economic Review,* June 1973, pp. 326–34.

[28] Edmund S. Phelps and John B. Taylor, "Stabilizing Powers of Monetary Policy under Rational Expectations," *Journal of Political Economy,* February 1977, pp. 163–90.

this is unrealistic. The other approach is to realize that the period over which the REH is applicable is a true long run, a steady state. It takes a long time for individuals to learn the structure of the economy and to form their expectations. Suppose a change in the structure occurs during the period of transition (toward the long run). It seems sensible to stipulate that this knowledge is costly and is acquired *adaptively*;[29] and in such a case an activist policy will indeed be effective in influencing real output (or employment).

In order for the REH to preserve the neutrality of money, it must assume a steady-state, long-run model, in which expectations have already converged to their long-run values. In fact, most advocates of the REH define the period of expectations formation to be long enough to allow individuals to acquire sufficient information regarding the outcome of future prices, thereby ensuring that expectations are always fulfilled. In effect, real time is abstracted from, so that, as we saw earlier, it is not surprising that only unanticipated shocks matter!

Even this last point, the long-run insensitivity of output (and employment) to changes in the money stock, is true only because of restrictive special assumptions regarding the supply function (15). In particular, $\bar{y}_F$, the full-employment level of output, is *assumed* fixed; and this is why money does not matter in the long run. But this "assumption" can be the implication of the model only if we assume that money is "superneutral," that is, only if we assume that a change in the rate of growth in the money supply does not have any real effects. However, it is known that a perfectly anticipated increase in the rate of growth of the money supply will increase the (perfectly anticipated) rate of inflation, which, in turn, will increase the capital stock (or capital intensity of the economy) as individuals substitute capital for real balances in their portfolios.[30] And this will have real effects on $\bar{y}_F$ and employment, as we saw in the preceding section.

In summary, the idea of consistent or "rational" expectations is a welcome addition to macroeconomic theory (as it has already been in microeconomics). The concept is promising and is proving particularly useful in highlighting the incentives that economic agents face in forecasting economic variables (including policy variables), thereby discounting future shocks and causing those shocks to be embodied in current prices. But in evaluating the implications of REH, it is important to keep in mind the strong assumptions upon which it is based. A long list of potential violations of these assumptions includes nominally based contracts, costly information, and shifts in the structure of the model to be learned, as well as the possibility of changes over time in the full-employment level of output.

---

[29] Benjamin Friedman, "Optimal Expectations and the Extreme Information Assumption of 'Rational Expectations' Macromodels," *Journal of Monetary Economics,* 1979, pp. 23–41; and E. L. Feige and D. K. Pierce, "Economically Rational Expectations," *Journal of Political Economy,* June 1976, pp. 499–522.

[30] See James Tobin, "Money and Economic Growth," *Econometrica,* October 1965, pp. 671–84; Michael G. Hadjimichalakis, "Money, Expectations, and Dynamics: An Alternative View," *International Economic Review,* October 1971, pp. 381–402; and Lewis O. Johnson, "The Level of Unemployment in a Growing Monetary Economy" (Ph.D. dissertation, University of Washington, 1972).

VIII. HETEROGENEOUS LABOR (MULTIPLE LABOR MARKETS) AND THE PHILLIPS CURVE

So far we have conducted our analysis under the simplifying assumption of homogeneous labor. In the last section of Chapter 7, and especially in this chapter, we translated the "money-wage adjustment mechanism" for the single market into the (momentary) Phillips curve. It is a fact, however, that many different labor markets exist, by virtue of both different quality and different geographic location. Here we explicitly want to permit heterogeneous labor. Two essential questions will be asked. First, can we extend our analysis in this case? In particular, can we derive the Phillips curve in the presence of more than one market for labor? And, second, does the introduction of heterogeneous labor have peculiarities of its own? That is, does a change in this particular assumption modify the results we previously derived?

The first thing we notice is that the analysis is capable of handling simultaneously both unemployment and unfilled vacancies. Previously we could have *either* the case of Figure 10-23a (unfilled vacancies) or the case of Figure 10-23b (unemployment), but not both.

We can now have some markets showing excess demand (unfilled vacancies) and some having excess supply (unemployment), a desired property for a model. In the real world, unemployment and unfilled vacancies coexist (and the Bureau of Labor Statistics monitors both).

One thing is clear from the statistics—in prosperous times, markets of the form of Figure 10-23a predominate. In other words, during prosperity there are more unfilled vacancies than there are unemployed workers. Recessions, on the other hand, are characterized by more unemployed people than unfilled vacancies. The British economist Lord William Beveridge, who was an occasional collaborator of Keynes,

FIGURE 10-23

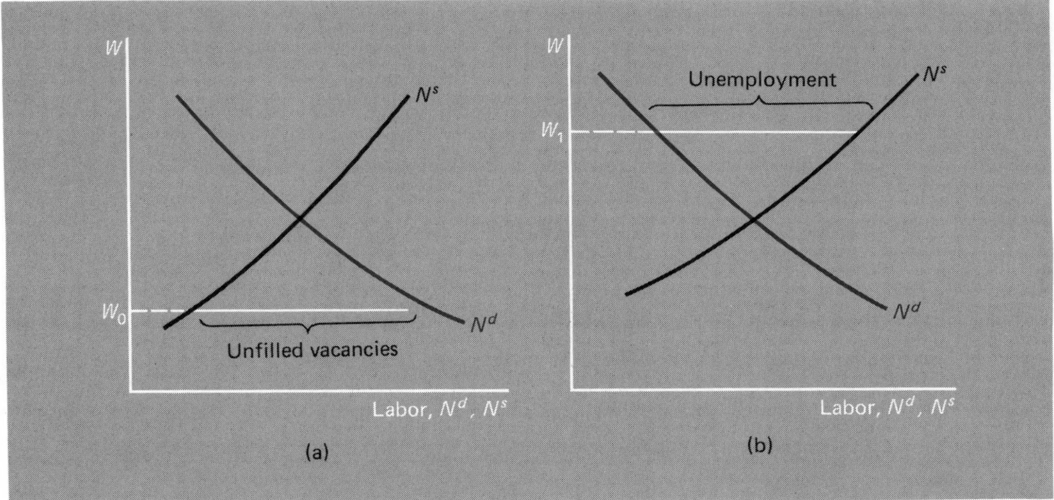

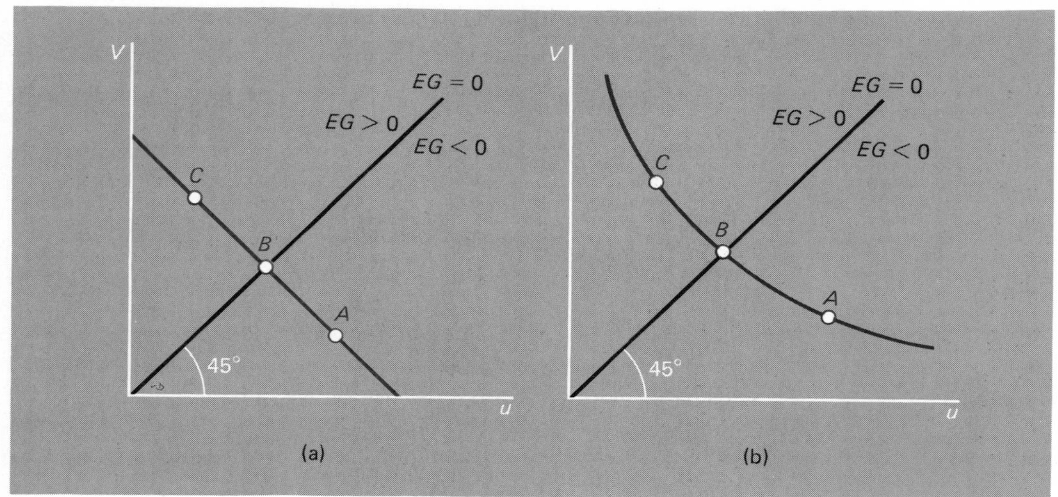

FIGURE 10-24

examined the relationship between unemployment and unfilled vacancies and ventured to define *full employment* as the state of the economy in which the number of unfilled vacancies is equal to the number of unemployed.

In the 1970s James Tobin carefully examined the relation between the two and derived the Phillips curve in their presence. In this section we shall mainly follow Tobin's analysis.[31] First we shall introduce the *Beveridge curve,* named by Tobin to honor Lord Beveridge. This curve plots unemployment against unfilled vacancies as aggregate excess demand varies. This is shown as a downward relation. In the true two-labor-market economy, the Beveridge curve is a straight line, as in Figure 10-24a. In the general case of many markets, its form is that of Figure 10-24b. Tobin calls a point such as *B,* where a Beveridge curve and the 45° line intersect, a Beveridge (full-employment) point. Points to the right and downward on the Beveridge curve, such as *A,* depict a situation where labor markets with excess supply predominate, that is, a situation of recession. Points to the left of the 45° line depict a heated economy with more markets experiencing excess demand than excess supply.

A question now arises, How can we move the economy *along* a Beveridge curve? The answer is, By manipulating aggregate demand. In fact, the 45° line is assumed to exhibit zero excess demand for goods and services, $EG = 0$. Points to the right exhibit excess supply, $EG < 0$, and points to the left exhibit excess demand, $EG > 0$. Thus, increases in aggregate demand move the economy northwest on the Beveridge curve. If we start at point *A,* we decrease unemployment by creating increas-

[31] James Tobin, "Inflation and Unemployment," *American Economic Review,* March 1972, pp. 1–18. I am greatly indebted to Professor Tobin for the contents of this section. Not only did he explain orally this approach to me and my class at the University of Washington, but he also graciously made available to me his classnotes, "J. Tobin, Economics 12, Spring Term, 1972," to compare my exposition to his.

ingly more vacancies. Beyond point *B,* we have an overheated economy with more unfilled vacancies than unemployment.

Next, we should realize that there are many, in fact, an infinity of, Beveridge curves, as in Figure 10-25. Which particular curve is the relevant one depends on the *structure* of the economy, that is, the degree of heterogeneity of labor in the economy under consideration. In general, the more heterogeneous the economy, the higher the appropriate Beveridge curve will be, and, in particular, the higher the corresponding "full-employment" rate of unemployment. For example, if the skills are geographically and qualitatively dispersed, we may observe a lot more unemployed people, as well as unfilled vacancies, even if they coincide in numbers, at point *B′* as compared with point B in Figure 10-25. It is little help for an unemployed logger in Sappho, Washington, to hear that there is an unfilled vacancy for a nuclear engineer in Boston, Massachusetts. First, it would take time for him to learn about the opening; second, he would need training in this new line of work, and he would have to relocate. Obviously, the child of the logger has a better chance of becoming a future nuclear engineer in Boston than his or her father does.

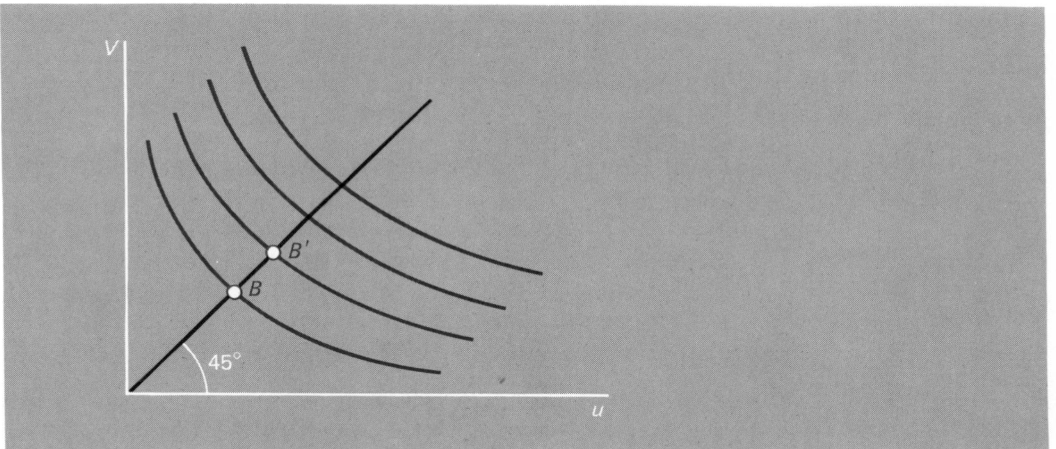

FIGURE 10-25

Even the above example, however, opens our eyes to the fact that the Beveridge curve moves. As time passes, there are several forces that push the curve inward! Information about openings is transmitted to unemployed people, and information about unemployed people to employers. As time passes, unemployed people change their skills through training or retraining programs. Of course, changes in wages are instrumental in inducing people to develop new skills or to relocate. Therefore one way to push the Beveridge curve inward is to use the market system with free movements in wages.

But what prevents the Beveridge curve from moving so far downward that it will coincide with the axes? The *structural* change in the economy is responsible. This change causes disequilibria in different markets for goods and in different labor markets as new products are introduced, or as others stop being fashionable, or as new production techniques are introduced, and so forth. The culmination of all these upward and downward movements produces the observed Beveridge curve. In other words, the position of the curve represents a balance between these opposing forces.

It is easy to surmise that the policy maker is capable of deliberately shifting the Beveridge curve inward—or, inadvertently, outward. Efforts to match the unemployed with unfilled vacancies aim precisely at this goal, to shift the curve inward. The techniques include more rapid dissemination of information about existing vacancies. Similarly, retraining unemployed persons to acquire skills for which vacancies exist also lowers the Beveridge curve. In fact, the Manpower Development and Training Act of 1962 was designed specifically for this purpose. To this list, we can add efforts to increase price and wage flexibility, usually by more vigorous enforcement of antitrust laws to increase competition in the economy. (It is assumed that markets in excess supply show sluggish response when the participants possess market power.)

Graphically, a shift in the Beveridge curve with a given level of excess demand, be it zero, positive, or negative, is depicted as a movement along a line with a slope equal to that of the 45° line, that is, the 45° line itself, or a line parallel to it, as shown in Figure 10-26.

As we noted earlier, there are labor markets exhibiting excess demand (i.e., unfilled vacancies) while, *simultaneously,* there are others with excess supply (i.e., unemployment). The money wage in the former markets will be rising while that in the latter will be falling. In this context, Tobin pointed out that there is an *asymmetry* of wage response between the case of excess demand and the case of excess supply. For the same amount of excess demand and excess supply, money wages rise proportionately more in the former case than in the latter. When the response is symmetric, the money-wage response line is a straight line through the origin, such as line *ROR* in Figure 10-27. In the asymmetric response, we have a kink at the origin, as in line *ROR'*. This means that if the unfilled vacancies, say *OK,* are precisely equal to the unemployed, *OL,* the money-wage *in*flation resulting from the former is much higher than the money-wage *de*flation resulting from the latter (i.e., $OA > OB$).

FIGURE 10-26

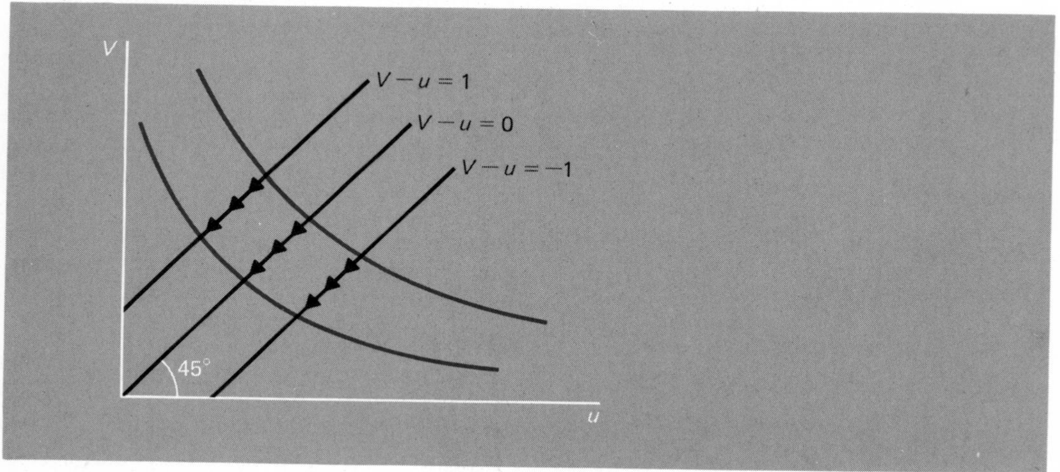

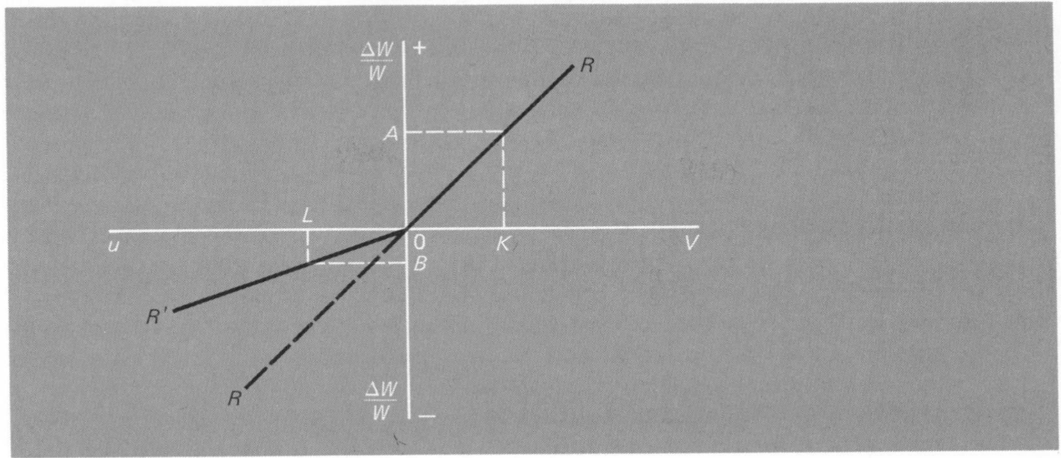

FIGURE 10-27

The reasons cited by Tobin for the sluggish response of the money wage in the sectors with excess supply are the same ones we analyzed in the beginning of Chapter 7 and earlier in this chapter.[32]

Employers do not force the employed workers to accept lower wages merely because there are some (unemployed) people who are willing to work for less. Employers are afraid of the loss of morale and the consequent fall in productivity that will accompany such money-wage cuts. The existence of explicit or implicit contracts for hiring workers at specific wages also contributes to the downward inflexibility of money wages. Also, and this is very important in this extended model, with heterogeneous labor, money-wage cuts will imply a loss of status for some workers as compared with others. As far as they are concerned, this is their *relative* wage, namely, their money wage relative to that achieved by workers in other industries.

Why do money wages rise almost immediately when there is excess demand? Obviously, the workers are in favor of such increases. And employers, faced with shortages (unfilled vacancies), would have every reason to offer higher wages to attract workers from other industries. These, in brief, are the reasons for the asymmetry in the wage response, which produces a nonlinear, in fact, a kinked, overall money-wage adjustment mechanism.

There are two important implications of the asymmetric response of money wages. First, it causes an *inflationary bias.* To see this, suppose that each market was originally at equilibrium and, because of taste changes, there was a reshuffling in aggregate demand, which, in turn, created in one market excess demand for labor (unfilled vacancies) and, in the other, an equal amount of excess supply (unemploy-

---

[32] Compare, for example, Tobin's papers: "Money Wage Rates and Employment," *The New Economics,* ed. S. Harris (New York: Knopf, 1947), pp. 572–87; "The Cruel Dilemma," in *The Battle against Unemployment,* rev. ed., ed. Arthur M. Okun (New York: W. W. Norton & Co., Inc., 1972), pp. 44–53; and "Inflation and Unemployment," *American Economic Review,* March 1972, pp. 147–60.

ment), or $OK = OL$, as in Figure 10-28. We see that although a vacancy exists for every unemployed worker and, therefore, full employment in the Beveridge sense, there is overall inflation in the economy because the *OK* unfilled vacancies cause inflation equal to *OA*, while an equal number of unemployed persons, *OL*, cause a deflation of only *OB*. The weighted average is, then, not zero, but positive, and equal to *OC*. Graphically this is found by connecting points *X* and *Y* on the relevant, kinked, wage adjustment curve *ROR'* with a straight line and finding its midpoint, *C*, which lies on the vertical axis. This positive inflation in the presence of zero excess demand for labor, in aggregate, is the inflationary bias. (Note that if we had a symmetric wage response function such as *ROR*, and if we connected points *X* and *Z* and found its midpoint, we would end up with the origin *O*.) A corollary to this result states that to have zero inflation, the economy must experience excess supply, as Figure 10-29 shows. Zero inflation materializes (at point *C*) only when unemployment, *OB*, is greater than unfilled vacancies, *OA*.

The second important implication of this analysis concerns the magnitude of the inflationary bias: The greater the dispersion of excess demand and excess supply, the greater the inflationary bias. This can be shown on our graph in Figure 10-28. The midpoint of the line connecting points *X'* and *Y'* is *C'*, with an inflation rate equal to *OC'*, greater than *OC*, which, in turn, is the midpoint of the line connecting *X* and *Y*. Points *X'* and *Y'* correspond to higher unemployment and (equal) unfilled vacancies than do points *X* and *Y*. In other words, the higher the "full-employment" level of unemployment, the higher the inflation rate. (This will have important implications for the Phillips curve.)

We are now ready to derive the Phillips curve by combining the Beveridge curve and the (asymmetric) money-wage adjustment mechanism. Let us suppose that the Beveridge curve for the economy is the one labeled #1 in Figure 10-30. If the

FIGURE 10-28

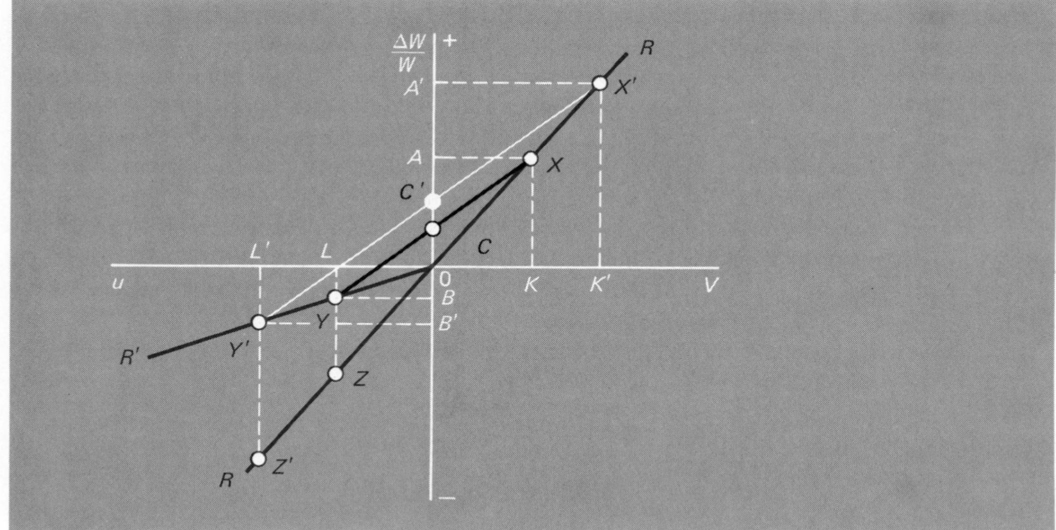

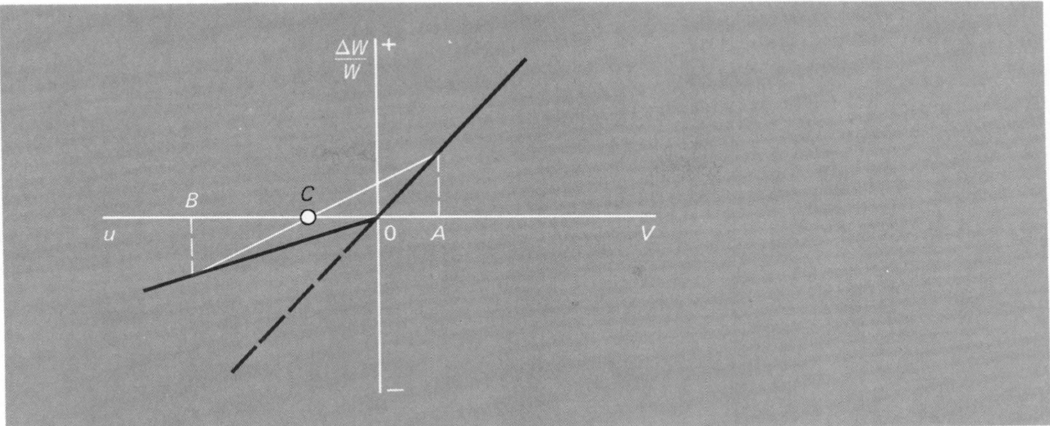

FIGURE 10-29

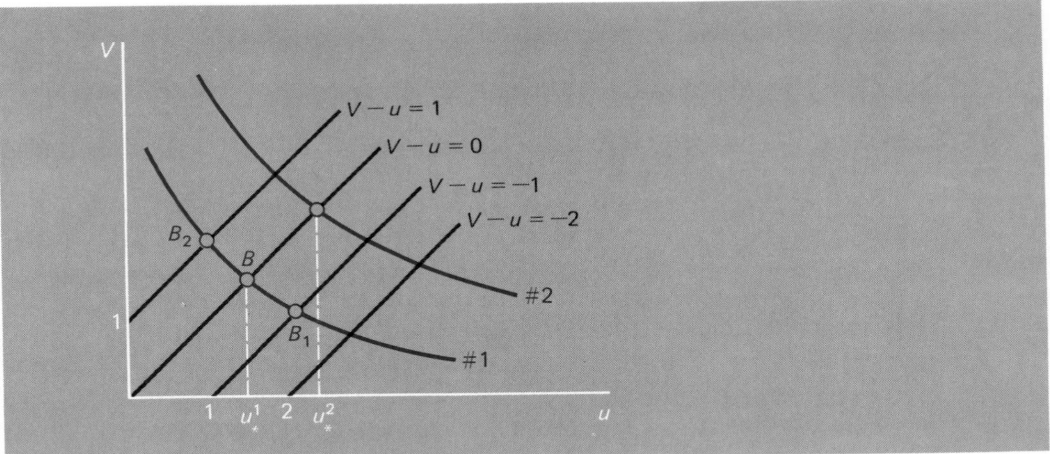

FIGURE 10-30

money-wage adjustment mechanism is symmetric, point B (the Beveridge point) is associated with zero inflation. The implied Phillips curve will intersect the unemployment axis at u_*^1, as Figure 10-31 shows. For higher levels of unemployment, along the same Beveridge curve, say at point B_1, which illustrates a case of excess supply of labor, the economy experiences money-wage deflation. On the other hand, a point like B_2, which exhibits excess demand for labor, will produce money-wage inflation. Repeating the process for all points on the Beveridge curve #1, we have the Phillips curve called AA. It is now easy to see that the Phillips curve will shift to the right of AA when the money-wage adjustment mechanism of the economy is the asymmetric one. It suffices to recall that with zero excess supply or demand for labor (i.e., at the Beveridge point), there will be positive money-wage inflation, say equal to OC in Figures 10-28 and 10-31. The relevant Phillips curve will then show this, and it

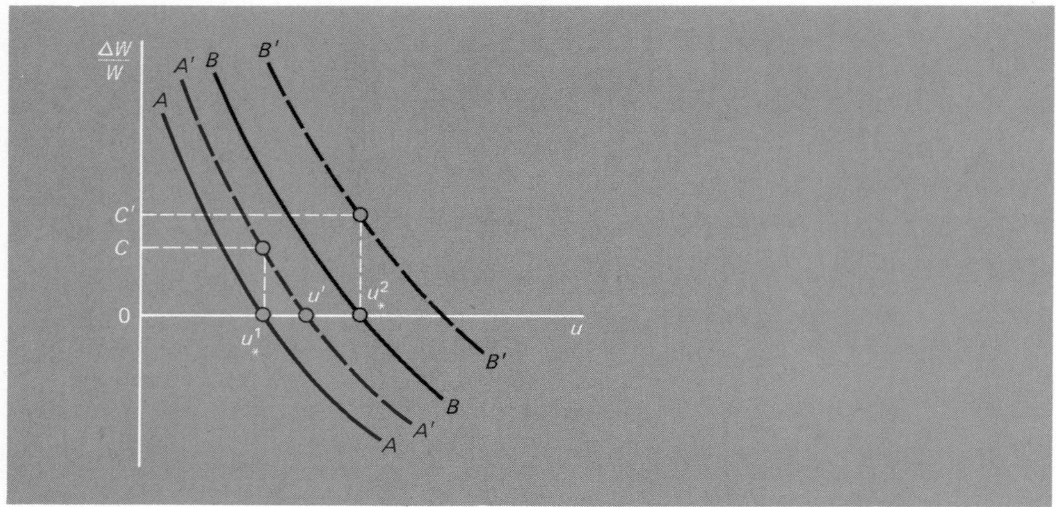

FIGURE 10-31

is labeled $A'A'$. Note also that in this case inflation will be zero only if employment is u', which is greater than u^1_*.

Now, suppose for reasons explained earlier that the Beveridge curve shifts upward and to the right. How will this affect the two Phillips curves we have derived? The second result we derived earlier is useful here. Beginning with the symmetric money-wage adjustment mechanism, zero inflation will correspond to the higher full-employment, unemployment level, u^2_*. With Beveridge curve #2 and the symmetric mechanism, we have the Phillips curve labeled *BB*. With the same Beveridge curve #2 and the asymmetric adjustment mechanism, we get Phillips curve $B'B'$. Note that the inflationary bias is now greater, $OC' > OC$. To this newly derived Phillips curve we can add expectations, as in the preceding section.

IX. THE COSTS OF INFLATION AND UNEMPLOYMENT AND SOME REMEDIES

We have already discovered that, as a practical matter, there is a trade-off between inflation and unemployment, which poses a "cruel dilemma" for the policy maker, who must, in accord with the tastes of society, decide upon the right combination of inflation and unemployment. A society that is sensitive about unemployment will have indifference curves such as those in Figure 10-32a, and it will choose a high rate of inflation and a low level of unemployment. A society more fearful of inflation than of unemployment has tastes such as those in Figure 10-32b, with a consequent higher level of unemployment and a lower level of inflation.

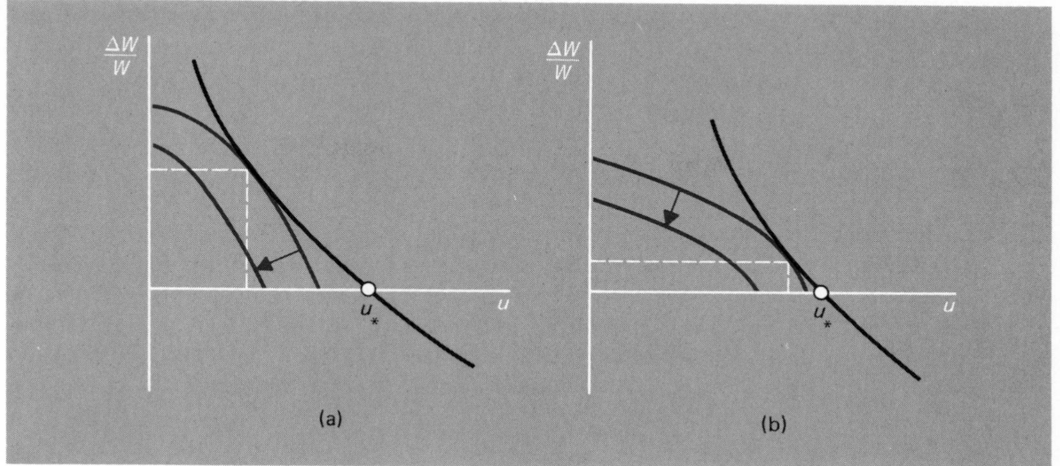

FIGURE 10-32

In the Figure 10-32 graphs we have considered both inflation and unemployment as "evils," or "bads." But why are they? What are the *costs* associated with a 1 percent increase in unemployment? In inflation? We shall examine these questions in turn.

1. COSTS OF UNEMPLOYMENT

The most obvious cost of unemployment is the loss of income to the unemployed. How important is this loss? Economists have been using a simple but fairly accurate rule to measure the loss of income caused by unemployment, *Okun's law,* which states that a reduction in unemployment by 1 percent increases real GNP by about 3 percent. More explicitly, Okun's law relates the *GNP gap* to the difference between the actual and "natural" rates of unemployment. The gap is the difference between potential output, Y_p, and actual output, Y, divided by actual output:

$$\text{GNP gap} = \frac{Y_p - Y}{Y}$$

Okun's law relates this gap to the difference $(u - u_*)$:

$$\text{GNP gap} = \eta \cdot (u - u_*)$$

Arthur M. Okun, who introduced this relation in 1961, found that η was equal to 3.15 percent.[33] Twelve years later he found it to be about 3 percent. If the

[33] Arthur M. Okun, "Potential GNP: Its Measurements and Significance" (American Statistical Association, Proceedings of the Business and Economic Statistics Section, 1962).

natural rate is 4 percent, a reduction of unemployment from 5 to 4 percent increases GNP by 3 percent. This surprisingly high response of output to changes in *un*employment can be explained by examining its components.

First, a 1 percent reduction in unemployment increases jobs for the unemployed by roughly 1 percent, in fact by 1.05 percent. Second, it lengthens the workweek because of less part-time and more overtime employment. The 1 percent decrease in unemployment was found to lengthen the workweek by 0.40 percent. Third, the labor force itself increases. It was found that when the economy worsens, many unemployed people who cannot find jobs get discouraged and drop out of the labor force, that is, they do *not* actively seek employment. When the economy improves, however, these "hidden unemployed" reenter the labor force and take jobs when they become available. Most studies estimate this increase at 0.65 percent. As Table 10-3 shows, a decrease in unemployment from 5 to 4 percent (the natural rate, u_*) adds 2.1 percent labor input to the economy.

TABLE 10-3

COMPONENT	PERCENT
Jobs for the unemployed	1.05
Lengthened work week	0.40
Increased labor force participation	0.65
Total addition to labor input	2.10

SOURCE: Arthur M. Okun, "Upward Mobility in a High-Pressure Economy," *Brookings Papers on Economic Activity,* 1(1973), 211.

Now, how does an increase of 2.1 percent in labor input affect output? One would expect, simply from basic considerations of diminishing returns, that the percentage increase in output would be less than 2.1 percent, say 1.5 percent. This would give a value of η, in the Okun's law formula, equal to 1.5 percent, not 3 percent. Why, then, is η equal to 3 percent? The answer is that productivity increases, rather than diminishes, with improvement in the economic environment. This has been confirmed empirically numerous times and is explained by Okun:

> The empirical finding becomes comprehensible once it is recognized that, for a substantial period of time, much of labor input is essentially a fixed cost, reflecting contractual commitments, indivisibilities or complementarity with capital, transaction costs of hiring and firing, and the value of skills that workers have acquired on the job. Thus, in periods of recession or slack, the amount of labor kept on the payroll is greater than the amount technologically required to produce the prevailing depressed level of output. *Given the initial presence of such on-the-job underemployment, when*

demand strengthens, output can be expanded without a commensurate expansion in labor input and a spurt of productivity results.[34]

Okun estimated the *increase* in productivity resulting from the assumed reduction in unemployment from 5 to 4 percent for two periods of time. For the first year of rising employment, he found that the elasticity of output with respect to the increased labor input of 2.1 percent was equal to 1.5, thus yielding an Okun elasticity, η, equal to 3.15. Over the longer horizon of three years, the former elasticity is 1⅓, yielding η equal to 2.8 percent.

The above observation makes it imperative for us to stress that Okun's law, and fiscal policy. In terms of the terminology of Section VIII, it applies to movements in the northwest direction *along* the Beveridge curve. As we know, reduction in unemployment caused by microeconomic policy measures would increase output only according to the production function.

This is the right place to introduce some negative aspects of reducing unemployment. Of course, we do not refer to the increase in inflation, which will be examined below. A reduction in unemployment reduces the amount of leisure. So, in Friedman's analysis, when workers are "fooled" into accepting a decrease in their consumption of leisure as inflation rises, we should subtract this loss of leisure from the benefits of increased output. But this is correct only to the extent that unemployment is voluntary. If it is voluntary, the value of lost leisure is almost equal to the new wage, which implies that society's loss is substantially less than the output loss. Since we are dealing with involuntary unemployment, however, this loss is negligible.

Other economists, following Alchian, claim that unemployment is caused by search that is beneficial to the economy because it produces information.[35] Thus, when we reduce this search activity, there is a loss that we should subtract from the benefit of increased production. However, one should be careful here; the production aspect of search is important only in the case of long-run analysis for which the search model was designed and is applicable. In other words, unemployment caused by search explains the natural rate, u_*, or, in the Tobin model, it determines the Beveridge point, in general, the movements of the Beveridge curve itself.

The above analysis concentrated on the benefits of a reduction in unemployment for the *economy as a whole.* But this hides some very disturbing aspects of *distribution.* Even a casual look at the unemployment statistics reveals that unemployment is *unevenly distributed* among various groups. When unemployment increases, minorities and unskilled laborers are the first to lose their jobs. The same is true of teen-agers, especially black and other minority teen-agers. It follows that when unemployment decreases, these groups will benefit. This decrease may also further indirectly other administrative goals. In particular, the "war on poverty" is helped by reducing unemployment. Certainly this has some value which must be included in our calculations of the benefits of decreasing unemployment.

---

[34] Arthur M. Okun, "Upward Mobility in a High-Pressure Economy," *Brookings Papers on Economic Activity,* 1(1973), 212, italics added.

[35] A. Alchian, "Information Costs, Pricing and Resource Unemployment," in *Microeconomic Foundations of Employment and Inflation Theory,* ed. Phelps, pp. 27–52.

2. COST OF INFLATION

As with unemployment, we shall distinguish between distributional and overall costs of inflation. In addition, we shall distinguish between an anticipated and an unanticipated rise in the rate of inflation.

Unanticipated inflation

Unforeseen, unanticipated inflation has substantial *redistributive effects.* The transfer of wealth in such cases can be very substantial—ranging into the billions. Those who both borrow and repay in nominal terms will gain at the expense of their creditors. Homeowners who bought their homes by undertaking mortgages—which usually require regular payments in fixed money terms—are the principal gainers. Savings and loan associations and their depositors, who financed all those mortgages, are among the losers. Since the typical family in the United States owns its home, it gains from inflation. But it also loses because its portfolio contains some monetary assets, such as currency and deposits. To the extent that the typical person's portfolio contains both assets that gain in value from inflation and assets that lose in value from inflation, the per person *net distributive* effects are much smaller than is generally thought. It appears that most people are likely to exaggerate their losses caused by inflation and ignore their gains. This may explain why people seem to be truly frightened of inflation.

G. L. Bach estimates that if all inflation between 1946 and 1972 had been unanticipated, the total transfer of wealth from creditors to debtors would have been \$1.5 trillion.[36] However, he also estimates that only one-half to two-thirds of that period's inflation was unanticipated, and hence the net transfer of wealth was roughly two-thirds of a trillion dollars. Of all sectors of the U.S. economy, the only net creditor is the household sector. The entire government sector (national, state, and local) is the chief debtor, accounting for up to 50 percent of the net debt, while unincorporated businesses, nonfinancial corporations, and financial corporations account, roughly evenly, for the rest. These last four sectors are the gainers, and, of course, the household sector is the loser.

Even within the household sector, the net loser, there are gainers and losers. Bach shows that the ones hit hardest by inflation are the very poor and the very rich. The poor are not debtors, since very few will lend to them. The rich do not need to borrow. Both groups have most of their wealth in monetary assets, the poor in money and the rich in bonds. On the other hand, the middle and upper-middle classes are debtors and also hold their wealth mainly in houses and durable goods. The effect of inflation on the household sector has also been examined by age groups. It has been found that unexpected inflation redistributes wealth from the elderly to the young. The elderly are net creditors and also hold their wealth mainly in liquid, monetary, assets, while the young are net debtors and their wealth is invested in houses and durable goods, like the middle and upper-middle classes.

Even though the business sector, as a whole, gains from inflation, there are

---

[36] G. L. Bach, "Inflation: Who Gains and Who Loses?" *Challenge,* July/August 1974, pp. 48–55.

still gainers and losers within this sector, just as there is redistribution of wealth among households. This redistribution depends not only on whether a firm is a creditor or a debtor but also on the depreciation allowances for capital. Inflation raises the price of capital goods, but depreciation allowances are usually based on the old, lower, price. As Bach points out, net creditor firms with large depreciations are highly vulnerable to inflation, while net debtors with small depreciation accounts are much less so. Hence the net gainers are those firms with very high debtor positions and very low depreciation losses.

Turning to the government sector, we noted that this sector gains from inflation, since it is a net debtor. But its gain from inflation is much larger than that, because of the tax structure. Inflation is justifiably criticized as a hidden tax, a means by which Congress can surreptitiously appropriate revenues without explicit legislation. As their pretax income rises proportionately with inflation, individuals are forced into a higher marginal tax bracket. For example, a worker with a pretax income of $15,000 would, after five years and a 10 percent inflation rate, earn approximately $\$24,000 = 15,000 \times (1.10)^5$. If the marginal tax rate were 20 and 30 percent, respectively, the worker's after-tax, *real* income would have fallen from $\$15,000(1 - .20) = \$12,000$ to approximately $\$10,000 = \$24,000(1 - .30)/(1.10)^5$. This reduction in after-tax income occurs whether the income is from labor, from profits, or from interest. The reduction of after-tax profits of business has recently attracted attention, since it discourages capital formation, which in turn lowers productivity, thereby further aggravating inflation. Feldstein and Summers, for example, estimate that inflation increased the 1977 tax burden on corporate income by more than $32 billion, raising the total effective tax rate by 50 percent.[37]

Some economists have argued that the tax system should be indexed to inflation, so that marginal tax brackets would adjust with inflation to maintain a constant real level of revenues. They argue that such indexation would eliminate the incentive for Congress to expand the role of government, using a tax base for which no member of Congress must claim responsibility. On the other hand, the current tax system provides the economy with an automatic stabilizer: Since the marginal tax rate rises with inflation, the marginal propensity to consume, from after-tax income, will of course fall. We should point out, however, that progressive taxation provides a "built-in stabilizer" only against inflation that emanates from demand management. In the case of supply-side shocks, it could become destabilizing.[38]

There are other misconceptions regarding inflation. It was once thought that when inflation is unanticipated, wages lag systematically behind prices. But this is contrary to the findings of empirical work. Furthermore, according to conventional wisdom, the teachers, civil servants, and social security recipients lose from unanticipated inflation because they have fixed salaries. Payments to social security recipients, however, are indexed for inflation and, for all practical purposes, so are the salaries of teachers and civil servants. But it is true that retired people who depend on private pension schemes are losers.

---

[37] Martin Feldstein and Lawrence Summers, "Inflation and the Taxation of Capital Income in the Corporate Sector," *National Tax Journal,* December 1979, pp. 445–70.

[38] Blinder, *Economic Policy and the Great Stagflation.*

Let us now examine the *overall* costs of unexpected inflation. We should recall that, in general, unexpected inflation is the result of expansionary policy, which, as we know from our earlier analysis, increases employment. The overall costs of inflation are compared with the benefits from this increase in employment. (This is proved by the equation $\Delta p/p - [\Delta p/p]^e = \alpha[u_* - u]$. When the left-hand side is positive, the right-hand side must also be positive. This means that $u_* > u$.) Two *overall* costs of unanticipated inflation are usually mentioned. First, unanticipated inflation distorts relative prices, which, in turn, causes a misallocation of resources. Even when there is no distortion, firms incur extra costs by continuously changing price tags, printing new catalogs, and so forth. Second—and this is true whether this increase is correctly or incorrectly anticipated—the increase in inflation raises the opportunity cost of holding money. This increase in opportunity cost induces people to economize on money by holding less of it and by making more frequent trips between savings banks and commercial banks, or between their businesses (or homes) and commercial banks. The resources devoted to these extra trips constitute the cost of inflation.[39]

Fully anticipated inflation

It is easy to see why there are no *distributive effects* when inflation is fully and correctly anticipated. If the actual rate of inflation is, say, 6 percent, and everybody expects that prices will continue to rise by 6 percent, this inflation will be built into every contract: Lenders will demand it, and borrowers will gladly accept it. Workers will demand it, and firms will offer it, and so forth. Nobody will gain, and nobody will lose except the holders of currency, as we saw above.

Let us now turn to the overall effects of a fully and correctly anticipated rate of inflation. Of the two costs mentioned above, the first disappears. No misallocation of resources will occur because there will be *no* changes in relative prices. We end up with only the cost of the extra trips between financial institutions. (James Tobin calculated that an *outside estimate* of the social cost of an increase in the rate of inflation by five percentage points is only 1 percent of GNP. This also means that a reduction of inflation by 1 percent increases GNP by 0.20 of 1 percent.)

Using the social cost of fully anticipated inflation, Milton Friedman designed his *optimum quantity of money rule.*[40] Recall that in Chapter 9 we saw that Friedman favors a constant rate of monetary expansion. Earlier in this chapter we also saw that Friedman believes in the natural rate hypothesis—that unemployment will always gravitate toward its (unique) natural rate. According to Friedman, the choice of the particular constant rate of monetary expansion is made easy by the natural rate hypothesis. The authorities should aim at making the social cost of fully anticipated

---

[39] If i_m is the nominal rate of return on money—currency and demand deposits—the real rate of money is $i_m - (\Delta p/p)^e$. Denoting the real rate of return on an alternative asset as i_r, we can find the opportunity cost of holding money by the difference: $i_r - [i_m - (\Delta p/p)^e]$ or $i_r - i_m + (\Delta p/p)^e$. Usually i_m is zero. Whether it is zero or not, an increase in the expected rate of inflation increases the opportunity cost of holding money.

[40] Milton Friedman, *The Optimum Quantity of Money and Other Essays* (Chicago: Aldine, 1969), pp. 1–50.

inflation equal to zero. Friedman argues that the cost of money creation is zero. We should therefore aim at making the opportunity cost of holding money equal to zero. If we have a situation like that in the United States where no interest is paid on money, $i_m = 0$, it means that the opportunity costs, $i_r + \Delta p/p$, should be equal to zero. In other words, we should have deflation equal to the negative of the real rate of return on real assets: $\Delta p/p = -i_r$. We note here that we do not have to choose deflation or zero inflation. We can achieve zero social cost by merely paying interest on money.[41]

The majority of the economics profession accepts neither the fixed monetary expansion rule nor the zero inflation (or actually deflationary) rule. For example, Edmund Phelps (the same Phelps of the vertical Phillips curve) argues in favor of a constant rate of inflation, around 4 or 5 percent. He argues that even if the costs, in terms of reduced employment and production, are completely temporary, the benefits of lowering inflation will come later and thus should be discounted. Hence inflation should be positive. In Phelps's words, "We have to live in the present as well as the future." Incidentally, Phelps does not accept a constant rule, or "ritual price stability," either.[42]

3. RECOMMENDED MEASURES

Recommended measures against inflation and unemployment include not only short-run, anticyclical, stabilization policies but also policies aimed at improving the trade-off. In addition, there are measures unrelated to stabilization policy that are aimed directly at inflation and unemployment—mostly measures to ameliorate their ill effects.

There are three ways by which we can lower the trade-off, that is, lower the Phillips curve. The first is by shifting the Beveridge curve. The second is by reducing or even eliminating the inflationary bias caused by the asymmetry of response in prices and wages between excess supply and excess demand situations. The third is by lowering inflationary expectations.

A shift of the Beveridge curve is favorable only if it is in the inward direction: For the same level of aggregate demand, both unemployment and unfilled vacancies are lower. The Phillips curve derived from a lower Beveridge curve is also lower, as we know from Section VIII. Now, faster spreading of information about unfilled vacancies shifts the Beveridge curve in the desired direction. Assistance in relocating unemployed workers to areas with unfilled vacancies also has the same effect. Perhaps the most effective way of shifting the Beveridge curve is to retrain the unemployed so they may acquire new skills. All these labor policies lay behind the recommendations that culminated in the Manpower Development and Training Act of 1962.

To reduce the inflationary bias, and thus shift the Phillips curve inward, the policy maker needs to cope with the reasons behind such bias, mainly market power by both labor unions and industry, and the unfortunate effects of government regulation. We know that labor unions create downward inflexibility in wages when

[41] Interest on demand deposits is permitted as of December 31, 1980.

[42] Edmund S. Phelps, "Unreasonable Price Stability," in *The Battle against Unemployment*, ed. Okun, p. 223.

they do not care as much about their unemployed or their potential members as they do about their senior members. We know that downward wage inflexibility can materialize even in nonunionized, unskilled labor markets because of minimum wage laws.

The possession of market power by producers also creates downward price inflexibility and, therefore, inflationary bias. Even industries without market power, like agriculture, exhibit downward price inflexibility because of government price supports. And, finally, we have some unfortunate side effects from the actions of government regulatory bodies, which, as we saw in Chapter 9, create downward price inflexibility, either directly or indirectly by increasing the market power of the industry they are supposed to regulate in the public interest. Most economists agree that the policy maker should attempt to break, or at least reduce, the market power of labor and industry, and to eliminate either the government agencies or the regulations that have so drastically raised the inflationary bias of the economy. While this is easier said than done, it may at least pave the way for more vigorous enforcement of antitrust regulations and for the enactment of sunset laws.

The above measures are clearly long run. It will take time for the labor policies to have a significant effect. Similarly, reducing the inflationary bias attributed to the concentration of market power is, if anything, a long-term goal. In the short run, the only way to shift the Phillips curve inward is to attempt to reduce inflationary expectations. In 1961 the wage-price guideposts, or "incomes policy," were introduced for this reason. As we saw earlier, they were helpful in the earlier stages, but by 1966, when the economy was overheated, they were falling apart; President Nixon officially abandoned them in January 1969. The architects of these voluntary guideposts emphasized that they were meant to guide the government in dealing with wage and price negotiations among industries with substantial power. They stressed, first, that nonmarket remedies are for industries in which the market system does not work competitively to begin with. And, second, in the words of Tobin:

> For a variety of reasons unconnected with macroeconomic policy, the government is involved in the setting of certain prices and wages. . . . The guideposts set standards of public interest in the terms of the settlement. Too often, previously, the government—aided and abetted by the industrial relations fraternity and their mystique that the results of collective bargaining is always good because the process is good—was interested solely in the fact of settlement, not of the content. Under the guideposts, the government seeks peace but not peace at any price level.[43]

In August 1971 President Nixon introduced a mandatory wage-price *freeze,* an extreme measure designed to, among other things, reduce inflationary expectations. This measure failed. But there is disagreement about whether it also failed to reduce inflationary expectations, and if it did, whether the failure was caused by premature lifting of those controls.

---

[43] Tobin, "Cruel Dilemma," p. 52.

Since there will always be occasions for a battle against cyclical unemployment and, therefore, increases in unanticipated inflation, it seems prudent that the government try to ameliorate some of its ill effects. The major problem in this instance is the redistribution of wealth from creditors to debtors—a situation that usually wipes out the life-long savings of many people. An important remedy, here, is the recommendation, almost unanimous in the profession, that the government create *real assets,* say a real bond, an asset with guaranteed purchasing power. And savers and pension funds could buy this asset to avoid the ills of unanticipated inflation.

A proposal aimed at reducing the distributional aspects of unemployment espouses the creation of public service jobs for the "hard-core," minority unemployed. Usually these workers are the "last hired, first fired." It makes sense to hire these workers directly rather than to overheat the economy in the hope that these people may be hired.

QUESTIONS

1. It is claimed that "market power" by unions or industry causes inflation. What are the requirements for making such a claim?

2. If the AFL–CIO drastically increases its membership thereby giving itself market power, why is there a general rise in money wages even though the economy remains at full employment (as defined by Beveridge)?

3. Suppose that there is greater heterogeneity in the labor force as a result of some structural change. Assuming full employment, how would your answer to question 2 change? (What happens to the rate of change of money wages?)

4. Comment on the following: "You can have a downward-sloping long-run Phillips curve even when expectations are fulfilled and are fully reflected in actual money-wage changes." Trace the effects carefully.

5. It has been argued that market power creates inflationary bias. What is meant by this? Under what conditions is this statement true? Are there any conditions where the statement could be false? Explain.

6. Compare the Wicksellian analysis of pegging market interest rates with Friedman's accelerationist hypothesis.

7. What are the costs of inflation? In answering this question, why is it important to distinguish between anticipated and unanticipated inflation?

8. What policies might allow the Phillips curve to be shifted inward?

9. Show that the Phillips curve is downward sloping when $\beta < 1$ and/or $(\Delta p/p)^e < (\Delta p/p)$.

10. Why is $(\Delta p/p)^e = (\Delta p/p)$ a requirement for equilibrium?

11. Both the monetarists and the rational expectations advocates argue against the use of activist monetary and other economic policies. Is there any fundamental difference in their explanations?

12. Evidence from the postwar data suggests that price setters add to the current inflation rate a larger portion of expected inflation. Why?

13. Money must be "superneutral" for the Phillips curve to be vertical. Explain.
14. Even though money is "neutral" (i.e., money does not matter in the long run), it is not "superneutral" (i.e., its rate of change matters). Explain.

REFERENCES

BACH, G. L., "Inflation: Who Gains and Who Loses?" *Challenge,* July/August 1974, pp. 48–55.

BARRO, ROBERT J., "Unanticipated Money Growth and Unemployment in the United States," *American Economic Review,* March 1977, pp. 101–15.

BLINDER, ALAN S., *Economic Policy and the Great Stagflation.* New York: Academic Press, 1979.

CAGAN, PHILIP, "The Monetary Dynamics of Hyperinflation," in *Studies in the Quantity Theory of Money,* ed. M. Friedman, pp. 25–117. Chicago: University of Chicago Press, 1956.

FRIEDMAN, BENJAMIN M., "Optimal Expectations and the Extreme Information Assumption of 'Rational Expectations' Macromodels," *Journal of Monetary Economics,* 1979, pp. 23–41.

FRIEDMAN, MILTON, *The Optimum Quantity of Money,* pp. 1–50. Chicago: Aldine, 1969.

———, "The Role of Monetary Policy," *American Economic Review,* March 1968, pp. 1–17.

HADJIMICHALAKIS, MICHAEL G., "Money, Expectations, and Dynamics: An Alternative View," *International Economic Review,* October 1971, pp. 381–402.

KEYNES, J. M., *How to Pay for the War.* New York: Harcourt, Brace & Co., 1940.

LIPSEY, RICHARD G., "The Relationship between Unemployment and the Rate of Change of the Money Wage Rates in the United Kingdom, 1862–1957: A Further Analysis," *Economica,* February 1960, pp. 1–41.

LUCAS, ROBERT E., JR., "Some International Evidence on Output-Inflation Tradeoffs," *American Economic Review,* June 1973, pp. 326–34.

MODIGLIANI, FRANCO, "The Monetarist Controversy or, Should We Foresake Stabilization Policies?" *American Economic Review,* March 1977, pp. 1–19.

MUTH, JOHN, "Rational Expectations and the Theory of Price Movements," *Econometrica,* July 1961, pp. 315–33.

OKUN, ARTHUR M., "Upward Mobility in a High-Pressure Economy," *Brookings Papers on Economic Activity,* 1 (1973).

PHELPS, EDMUND S., ed., *Microeconomic Foundations of Employment and Inflation Theory.* New York: W. W. Norton & Co., Inc., 1970.

PHELPS, EDMUND S., "Phillips Curve, Expectations of Inflation and Optimal Unemployment over Time," *Economica,* August 1967, pp. 254–81.

PHELPS, E. S., and J. B. TAYLOR, "Stabilization Power of Monetary Policy under Rational Expectations," *Journal of Political Economy,* February 1977, pp. 163–90.

PHILLIPS, A. W., "The Relation between Unemployment and the Rate of Change of Money Wage Rates in the United Kingdom, 1861–1957," *Economica,* November 1958, pp. 282–99.

SARGENT, T. J., and N. WALLACE, " 'Rational' Expectations, the Optimal Monetary Instrument and the Optimal Money Supply Rule," *Journal of Political Economy,* April 1975, pp. 241–54.

TOBIN, JAMES, "Inflation and Unemployment," *American Economic Review,* March 1972, pp. 1–18.

The behavioral functions

The Consumption and Savings functions

11

In Chapter 2 we briefly examined the consumption-savings behavior of the average household. We shall now examine this same issue in greater detail, and, employing standard household choice theory, we shall derive the household's consumption and hence its savings function.

Starting with the special case of given, *fixed,* endowments of each period's income, in Section I we show that when the substitution effect outweighs the income effect, there is a negative relation between consumption and the interest rate; and with the same assumption there is a positive relation between the interest rate and savings. But in Section II we see that when each period's endowment is *variable,* it is possible to have a positive relation between savings and the interest rate even if the relation between consumption and interest rate is also positive.

Finally, by employing the assumption of homothetic preferences, in Section III we derive exact forms of the consumption and savings functions, forms that are useful for empirical research. Here we concentrate on the *life-cycle* and the *permanent-income* hypotheses, associated, respectively, with the names of Franco Modigliani and Milton Friedman, but we also examine briefly the earlier *relative-income* hypothesis of James Duesenberry.

I. A TWO-PERIOD MODEL

Let us consider the case of an individual who knows his endowment of corn for period 1 (today) and of corn for period 2 (tomorrow), y_1 and y_2, respectively. How much corn will he consume in each period? The answer depends on whether or not borrowing and lending are permitted. If they are not, the individual will consume, at most, y_1 units of corn in period 1 and, at most, y_2 units in period 2. (If he is not satiated with y_1 and y_2 for the respective periods, he will consume precisely these quantities.) If borrowing and lending are permitted, then, there is the possibility of intertemporal exchange, that is, trade, between the two periods. Depending on the terms of such a trade, the individual may be a net borrower or a net lender, or even not a trader at all.

If P_1 denotes the relative price of corn today and P_2 the relative price of corn tomorrow, we know that $P_1 = 1/P_2$. Obviously, P_1 denotes the number of units of corn tomorrow which one gets if he gives up one unit of corn today. Or, equivalently, P_1 is the number of units of corn tomorrow that the individual will give up if he gets one unit of corn today.

Similarly, P_2, the relative price of corn tomorrow, shows the number of units of corn today that one individual will get if he gives up one unit of corn tomorrow. Equivalently, P_2 is the number of units of corn the individual has to give up today in order to secure one unit of corn tomorrow. And if one knows the relative price of the one good, he automatically knows the relative price of the other good.

Figure 11-1 depicts the individual's endowment and the relative prices. The slope of the downward-sloping straight line through E, the endowment point, is equal to (minus) the relative price of the good depicted on the horizontal axis, that is, of corn today. The shaded area in Figure 11-1 depicts all the baskets of corn today and corn tomorrow that the individual can afford to consume in the absence of borrowing and lending. When borrowing and lending are permitted, the individual

FIGURE 11-1

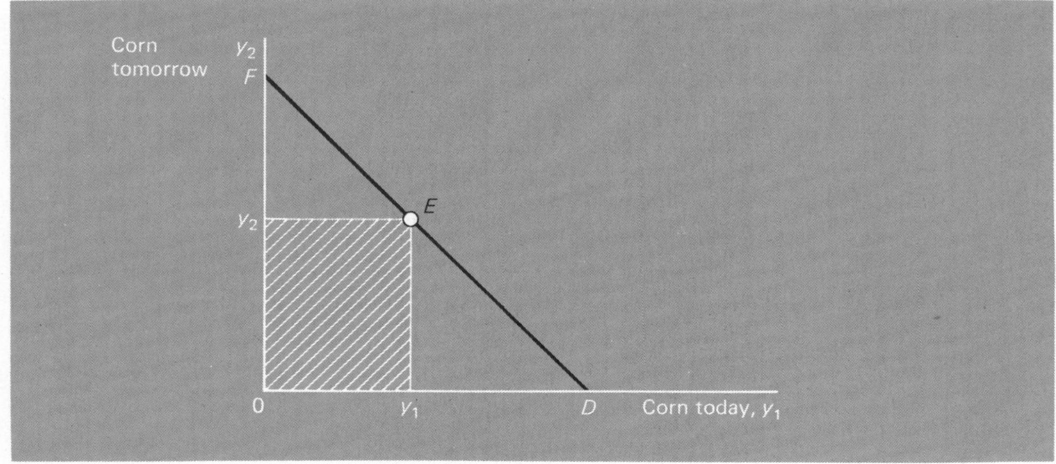

can consume any basket in the triangle *OFED.* We shall assume that the individual will never be satiated and thus will consume only on the line *FED,* which can now be called the *consumption possibilities line,* or simply the budget line.

We have already denoted the endowments of corn today and corn tomorrow by y_1 and y_2, respectively. Now, C_1 and C_2 will denote the quantities of corn today and corn tomorrow, respectively, that the individual consumes. Recalling the notation of Chapter 1, (y_1, y_2) corresponds to (a,b), while (C_1, C_2) corresponds to (A,B). Using this notation, we can measure the pair (y_1, y_2) in terms of one number denoting the individual's wealth. In units of corn today, individual wealth is equal to

$$I_1 = y_1 + P_2 y_2 \tag{1'}$$

Note that P_2, the relative price of corn tomorrow, is an operator transforming units of corn tomorrow into units of corn today: $P_2 y_2$ are units of corn today; thus we can safely add them to y_1, which are units of corn today. Similarly, multiplying y_1 by P_1, the relative price of corn today, translates the y_1 units of corn today into $P_1 y_1$ units of corn tomorrow. And adding this to y_2, we get the individual's wealth in units of tomorrow's corn:

$$I_2 = P_1 y_1 + y_2 \tag{2'}$$

The intercept of the consumption possibilities line on the horizontal axis measures I_1, the value of the endowment point (y_1, y_2) in units of corn today. The intercept on the vertical axis measures I_2, as shown in Figure 11-2. Note that by dividing I_2 by I_1, we can find the slope of the consumption possibilities line:

$$\frac{I_2}{I_1} = \frac{P_1 y_1 + y_2}{y_1 + P_2 y_2} = \frac{P_1 y_1 + y_2}{y_1 + \dfrac{1}{P_1} \cdot y_2} = \frac{P_1 y_1 + y_2}{\dfrac{P_1 y_1 + y_2}{P_1}} = \frac{1}{\dfrac{1}{P_1}} = P_1 \tag{3'}$$

FIGURE 11-2

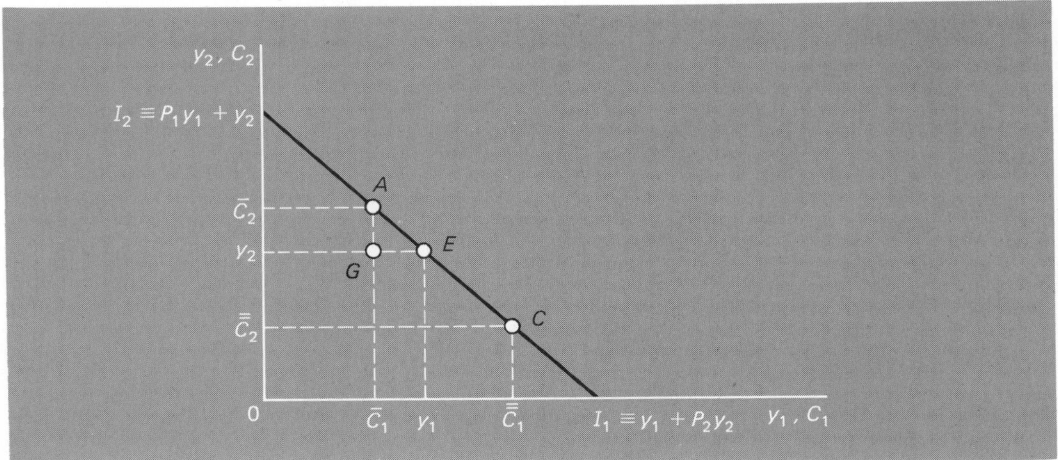

Of course, in units of corn today, the algebraic form of the consumption possibilities line is

$$C_1 + P_2C_2 = I_1 \equiv y_1 + P_2y_2 \tag{4'}$$

and in units of corn tomorrow,

$$P_1C_1 + C_2 = I_2 \equiv P_1y_1 + y_2 \tag{5'}$$

Now, if the individual decides to consume a point such as *A*, located northwest of *E* (on the consumption possibilities line, of course), it is clear that the individual consumes less than the endowment of corn today, $\overline{C}_1 < y_1$. We say, then, that the individual *saves* the difference, $y_1 - \overline{C}_1$, and trades, exchanges, or lends this quantity of corn today for $\overline{AG}$ units of corn tomorrow. Note that since the ratio $\overline{AG}/\overline{GE}$ is precisely the relative price P_1, the individual will have $\overline{C}_2 - y_2 = AG$ extra units of corn to consume tomorrow. By extra, we mean in addition to the endowment, y_2. Similarly, if the individual decides to consume at a point like *C*, we say that this individual dissaves an amount equal to $\overline{\overline{C}}_1 - y_1$; the individual borrows this amount promising to pay $y_2 - \overline{\overline{C}}_2$ units of corn tomorrow.

Given the endowment point and the relative prices (i.e., given the consumption possibilities line), where, precisely, the individual will consume depends on his preferences in ranking baskets of goods. The indifference map shown in Figure 11-3 is the same as that in Chapters 1 and 2. The indifference curves are downward sloping, convex (exhibiting diminishing marginal rate of substitution), and nonintersecting, such that a curve to the right and northeast of another denotes more preferred baskets.

As in Chapters 1 and 2, individuals will choose the most preferred basket they can afford, which is shown by the tangency of an indifference curve and the budget line, as in Figure 11-4. This graph depicts the case of a saver, or lender, since we are assuming that the average household is a net saver, or lender.

FIGURE 11-3

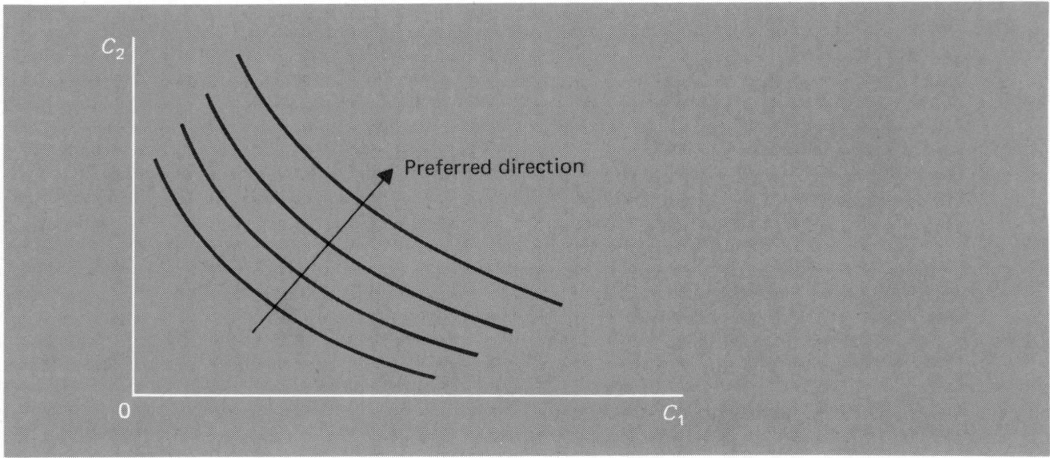

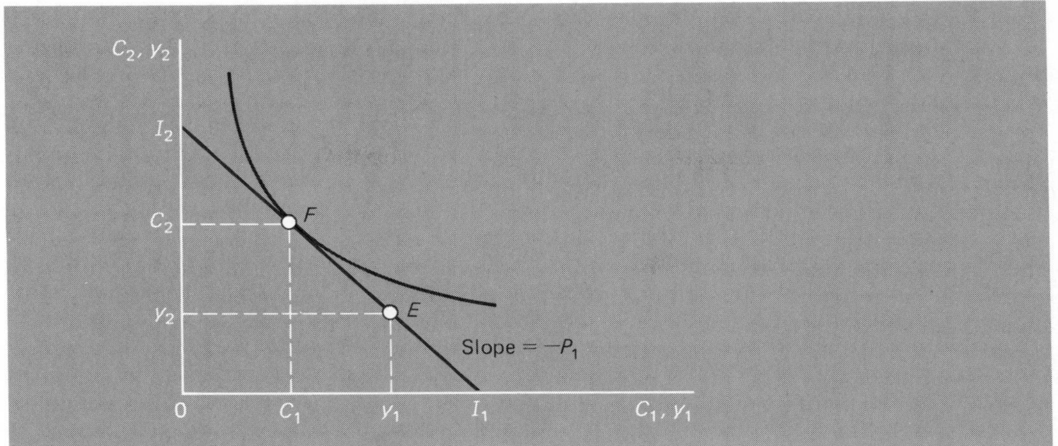

FIGURE 11-4

We stated before that P_1 is the number of units of corn that will be delivered to individuals in the next period if they give up one unit of corn today. Obviously, this quantity has to be more than one unit. *This excess over unity we define as the interest rate,* which we shall denote by *i.* Thus $P_1 - 1 = i$, or

$$P_1 = 1 + i \tag{6}$$

Since the relative price of corn tomorrow, P_2, is the number of units of corn individuals give up in order to have one unit of corn delivered to them tomorrow, it is clear that the quantity, P_2, has to be less than one. Working from a different perspective, we can see this immediately, since we know that P_2 is the inverse of P_1 and, therefore, $P_2 = 1/P_1$, or

$$P_2 = \frac{1}{1 + i} \tag{7}$$

And, since i is positive, it follows that P_2 is less than one. Furthermore, people frequently refer to P_2 as the present value of one unit of corn available tomorrow.

It is clear that when we are given the interest rate, we immediately know P_2 and P_1, and thus we immediately know the slope of the budget line. Of course, we also know the value of the endowment bundle (or any basket for that matter) measured in units of the good available in period 1 or in period 2. All of these are shown in Figure 11-5, which reproduces the information of Figure 11-4. Note that now the value of the endowment point (y_1, y_2) measured in units of corn in period 1—and equal to the intercept on the horizontal axis—is labeled $y_1 + [1/(1 + i)] \cdot y_2$, which necessitates a change in our algebraic expressions. Substituting (7) into (1′), we get

$$I_1 \equiv y_1 + \frac{1}{1 + i} \cdot y_2 \tag{1}$$

We shall be referring to this as the *present value* of the endowment basket. Similarly, substituting (6) into (2′), we get

$$I_2 = (1 + i)\, y_1 + y_2 \tag{2}$$

which is depicted in Figure 11-5 as the intercept of the budget line on the vertical axis. Sometimes we shall call this the *future value* of the endowment point.

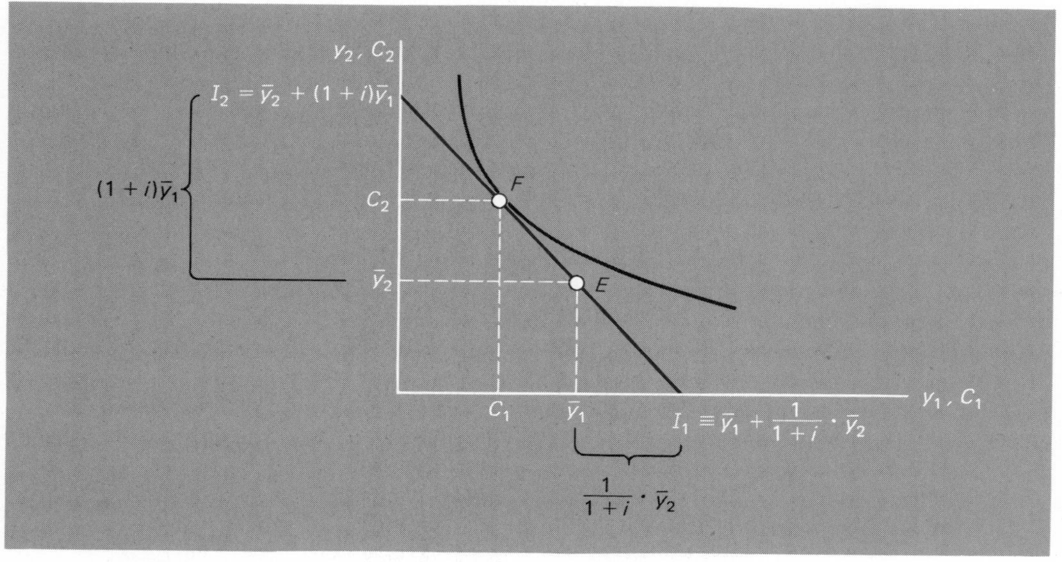

FIGURE 11-5

We know from Chapters 1 and 2 that, given the relative prices, we can find the value of *any* basket in units of any good. Utilizing our present terminology we can say that, given the interest rate, we can immediately find the relative price of the good available in period one; it is equal to $1 + i$. Now draw a line passing through the point representing the basket in question with slope equal to $1 + i$. Extending this line until it meets the good in period 1 axis, we see that this intercept is the present value of the basket. On the other hand, the intercept on the axis representing the good in period 2 gives the future value of the basket. Apply this result and technique on basket F, that is, find the value of the individual's preferred (and "consumed") basket. Of course, it gives the present value and future value as precisely equal to the present value and future value, respectively, of the endowment point E. This is another way of saying that the preferred point F lies on the consumption possibilities (or budget) line. Similarly, we can say that the consumption point $F = (C_1, C_2)$ satisfies constraints (4) and (5), which are the modified versions of (4′) and (5′) after we substitute (7) and (6), respectively:

$$C_1 + \frac{1}{1+i} \cdot C_2 = y_1 + \frac{1}{1+i} \cdot y_2 \tag{4}$$

$$(1 + i)\, C_1 + C_2 = (1 + i)\, y_1 + y_2 \tag{5}$$

For the sake of thoroughness, we can modify (3′) into (3) by the appropriate substitutions:

$$\frac{I_2}{I_1} = \frac{(1 + i)\, y_1 + y_2}{y_1 + \dfrac{1}{1 + i} \cdot y_2} = 1 + i \tag{3}$$

We can summarize the implications of Figure 11-5 as follows: Given the interest rate, i, and given the individual's endowment of today's and tomorrow's corn, y_1 and y_2, respectively, we can find the consumption possibilities line; we know that the preferred (i.e., realized) point, $F = (C_1, C_2)$, will lie on this line. Therefore consumption of corn today, C_1, depends on i and y_1, y_2. We can use the shorthand notation:

$$C_1 = C(i\,;\, y_1, y_2) \tag{8}$$

On the other hand, savings has been defined as corn today that has not been consumed, $S \equiv y_1 - C_1$. Thus we can write:

$$S = y_1 - C(i\,;\, y_1, y_2) = S(i\,;\, y_1, y_2) \tag{9}$$

We have established, therefore, that current consumption and savings (current income not presently consumed) depend on (a) the interest rate, i; (b) current income, y_1; and (c) future income, y_2. Of course, we can safely say that future income depends on wealth. Here we are examining the average household whose wealth represents society's wealth, which, in turn, is society's capital stock, K. In the preceding chapters we used the notation Y for current income and C for current consumption. There we specified that consumption depends on Y and K, that is, $C = C(Y, K)$, as does savings, $S = S(Y, K)$. Utilizing this earlier notation, the results so far in this chapter not only confirm this dependence of S and C on Y and K but also show that, in general, a third variable, namely, the interest rate, i, also influences consumption and savings. In later analysis we shall utilize the following specification of C and S:

$$C = C(i, Y, K) \tag{10}$$

$$S = S(i, Y, K) \tag{11}$$

CHANGES IN CURRENT INCOME, y_1

To see how savings and consumption are influenced by changes in their three determinants, y_1, y_2, and i, we shall begin with y_1. Let us suppose that the individual's original situation can be depicted with a graph like Figure 11-5, with endowments of the two goods equal to $\bar{y}_1$ and $\bar{y}_2$. Let us suppose further that, for some reason, the individual's endowment of corn today increases to $\bar{\bar{y}}_1$, but that everything else remains the same, in particular, i remains at i_1 and corn tomorrow remains at $\bar{y}_2$. Given these assumptions, we want to see what will happen to current consumption, C_1, and to savings, S.

In Figure 11-6 we reproduce the information for this initial situation with endowment point E and most preferred point F. Now the new endowment point is E', a horizontal displacement of E. We see that the value of the individual's endowment increases, whether we measure it in units of corn today or corn tomorrow. Originally it was OD units of today's corn, whereas now it is OL units of today's corn. Similarly, we see that in units of tomorrow's corn, it increased from OC to OK units. We recall that our goods are normal, that is, an increase in the individual's income will increase the demand for each good. Because of this assumption, the new most preferred basket will lie on the new budget line, *below point A and above point B.* (Note that if it lies below point B, corn tomorrow has to be an inferior good. On the other hand, if the preferred point lies above point A, corn today would be an inferior good.)

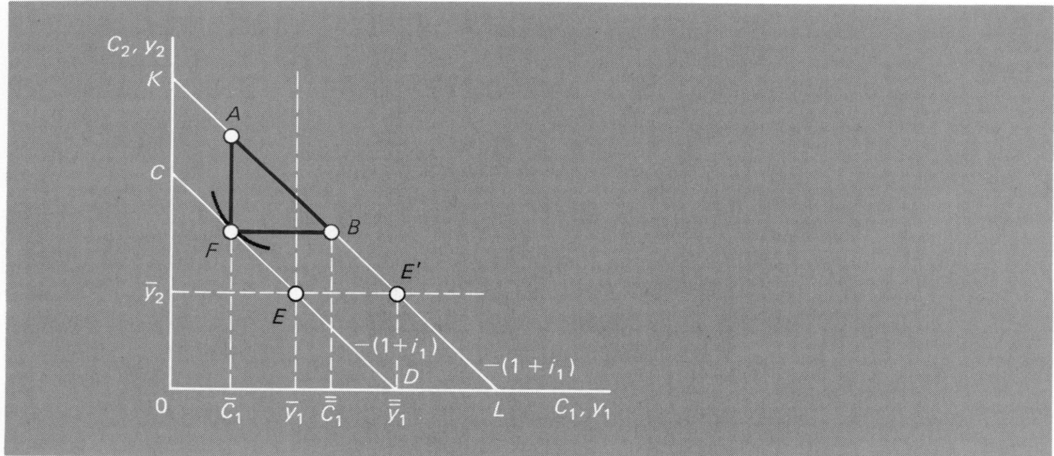

FIGURE 11-6

Because the new most preferred point will lie on the segment AB, two crucial results are derived immediately. First, the increase in y_1 will cause an increase in the current consumption demand, which will clearly be greater than the original one, $\bar{C}_1$. Second, the increase in current income, y_1, will increase savings. But one might suspect that there is ambiguity regarding this effect; after all, savings is current income not presently consumed, $S = y_1 - C_1$. But since both y_1 and C_1 rise, we do not know the final result. And this is where the additional information we derived above proves useful.

Suppose that the new most preferred point is point B itself. In such a case, because $EFBE'$ is a parallelogram, FB would be equal to EE', which implies that current consumption has increased by an amount (FB) precisely equal to the increase EE' in y_1, that is, $\bar{\bar{C}}_1 - \bar{C}_1 = \bar{\bar{y}}_1 - \bar{y}_1$. It would follow, then, that savings remained the same: $S = \bar{\bar{y}}_1 - \bar{\bar{C}}_1 = \bar{y}_1 - \bar{C}_1$. Of course, if the new most preferred point lies even lower than B, there would be a *decrease* in savings caused by the increase in y_1. But we have seen above that neither B nor any other point southeast of it can materialize as a new most preferred point, proving conclusively that S will increase.

We have just proved that an increase in current income, y_1, will increase both current consumption and savings. Or, using mathematical shorthand symbols, we have proved that $(\Delta S/\Delta y_1) > 0$ and $(\Delta C/\Delta y_1) > 0$.

Usually the assumption of homothetic preferences is introduced in this context. In such circumstances, the increase in C_1 and S is such that the original ratio, $\overline{C}_2$ over $\overline{C}_1$, is preserved. In other words, the new most preferred point, call it G, will lie at the intersection of segment AB and a straight line through the origin and the original most preferred point F. This is shown clearly in Figure 11-7.

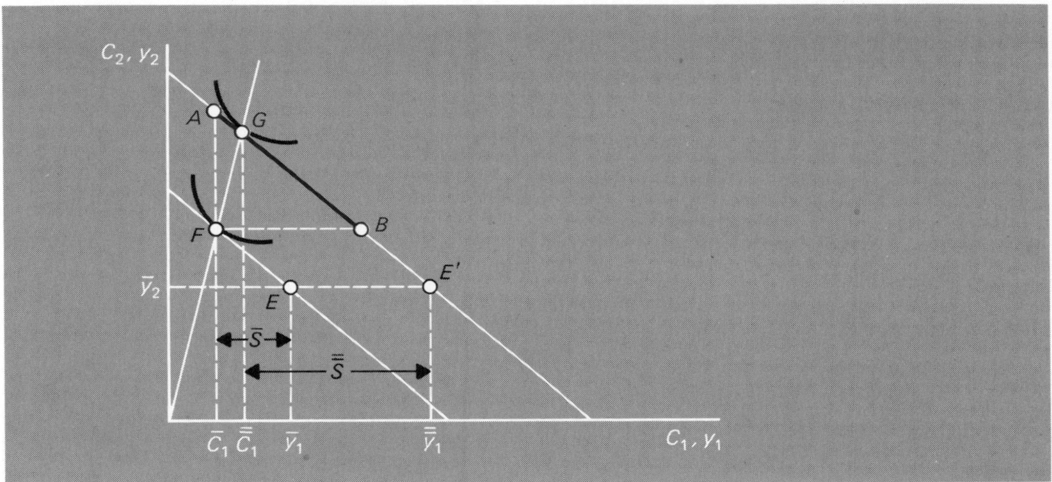

FIGURE 11-7

CHANGES IN FUTURE INCOME, y_2, OR CAPITAL STOCK K

Assume that the individual who was originally endowed with $\overline{y}_1$ units of corn today and $\overline{y}_2$ units of corn tomorrow, and who was faced with interest rate i_1, chose basket F in Figure 11-8. Now suppose this individual's endowment point is vertically displaced to the position E', that is, y_1 remains the same but y_2 rises to $\overline{\overline{y}}_2$. We see immediately that the value of the individual's new endowment is higher than that of the old and that this result is independent of the units of measurement, corn today or corn tomorrow. As in the preceding exercise, the new most preferred point will lie on the segment AB, excluding the endpoints A and B. It follows immediately that current consumption demand will increase; it has to be greater than its original level, $\overline{C}_1$. The effect of the increase in y_2 on savings is even easier to derive than in the preceding exercise because savings is out of current income y_1, that is, corn today that is *not* currently consumed. But in this exercise, C_1 has *increased* from $\overline{C}_1$ to $\overline{\overline{C}}_1$ while y_1

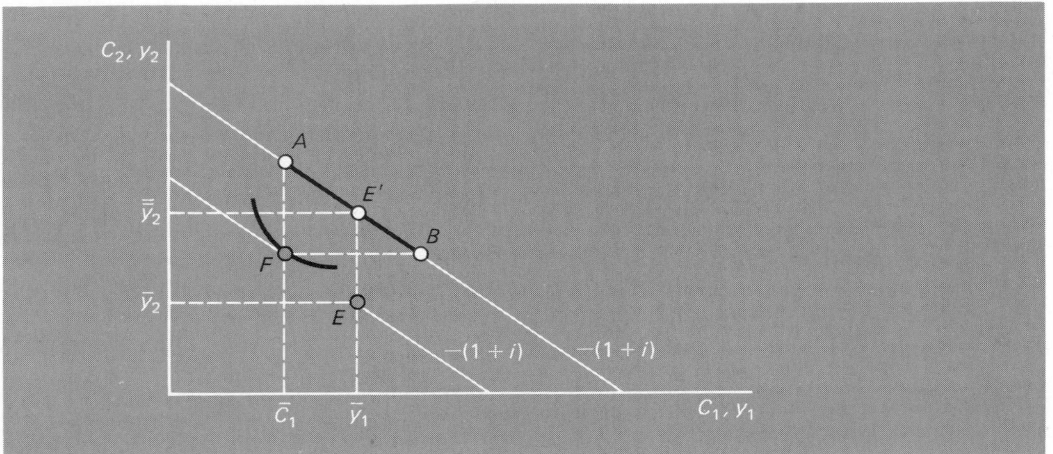

FIGURE 11-8

remained the same, at $\bar{y}_1$. It follows, then, that $\bar{\bar{S}} \equiv \bar{y}_1 - \bar{\bar{C}}_1$ is less than $\bar{S} \equiv \bar{y}_1 - \bar{C}_1$.

While we can give several explanations for this rise in savings produced by the rise of y_2, we prefer the most direct: Individuals save in order to guarantee future income greater than their endowment, $\bar{y}_2$. But since y_2 has increased above $\bar{y}_2$ (and their preferences have not changed), they have every reason *not* to save as much as before. (We should recall this interpretation later when the situations become more complicated.) We stated earlier that occasionally economists identify y_2 with society's *capital*. The results just derived can then be restated as follows: An increase in the capital stock K will increase current consumption, C, and *decrease* savings (out of current income), S. For the latter result, the following interpretation is given: Individuals save in order to achieve a specified stock of capital. But since capital has increased, they can slow down their rate of capital accumulation (i.e., their saving).

The symbolical shorthand for both versions of our results is

a. For $C_1 = C(i, y_1, y_2)$ and $S = y_1 - C_1(\cdot) = S(i, y_1, y_2)$, we have

$$\frac{\Delta C}{\Delta y_2} > 0, \frac{\Delta S}{\Delta y_2} < 0.$$

b. For $C = C(i, Y, K)$ and $S = S(i, Y, K)$ we have

$$\frac{\Delta C}{\Delta K} > 0, \frac{\Delta S}{\Delta K} < 0.$$

INTEREST RATE EFFECT

Let us start with a situation similar to that in Figure 11-5. More explicitly, let us assume that originally the interest rate was equal to i_0. The corresponding budget line, *AEB*, and the most preferred point, *F* (determined by the highest achievable indifference curve not shown in the graph), are shown in Figure 11-9, which is drawn to depict the case of a *net saver.* Now suppose that the interest rate rises to i_1. To find the new budget line, we first find its slope, equal (in absolute value) to $(1+i_1)$, which is greater than that of the budget line *AEB.* The new budget line, then, is derived by drawing a straight line through the (unchanged) endowment point, *E,* with slope equal to $(1+i_1)$. In Figure 11-9 this is line *A′ EB′*.

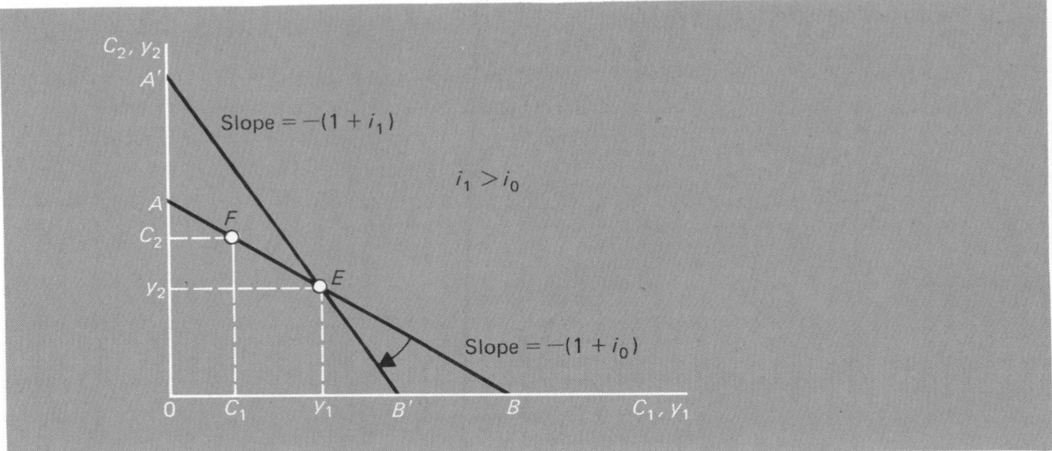

FIGURE 11-9

The first important result is that an increase in the interest rate will lower the present value of the endowment, (y_1,y_2), and for a simple reason. The increase in the interest rate will lower the relative price (and thus the present value) of each unit of corn tomorrow. Therefore the y_2 units of corn tomorrow command fewer total units of corn today, that is, $[1/(1+i_1)] < [1/(1+i_0)]$, and thus $[1/(1+i_1)] \cdot y_2 < [1/(1+i_0)] \cdot y_2$. It is this smaller quantity that we add to the same quantity of corn today, y_1, in order to find the present value of the basket (y_1,y_2). In Figure 11-9 the new present value is *OB′*, whereas the old was *OB.* A similar explanation proves that *an increase in the interest rate will increase the future value (i.e., in units of corn tomorrow) of the endowment (y_1,y_2).*

Of course, we have seen both of these results in the analysis of Chapters 1 and 2, which also proved that if the relative price of the good for which each of the individuals is a *net supplier* increases, the individuals become better off; their *real income* rises, that is, they can achieve a higher indifference curve than before. This is the case we are examining here. The increase in *i* increases the relative price of corn today. But individuals do not consume all of their corn today, that is, $y_1 - C_1 > 0$; each individual is a net saver, a net lender. (In this application, this term is the analogue to the abstract term *net supplier.*) Since these individuals are better off, they demand more of every normal good. Here we assume that both corn today and corn tomorrow are normal, and that individuals, therefore, will demand more of each, in particular more of corn today. But there is a substitution effect working in the opposite direction for this good: The price of corn today has risen, and thus one would want to demand less. *If the substitution effect wins out, the increase in the interest rate will lower consumption of corn today, that is,* $\Delta C_1/\Delta i < 0$. Since y_1 is the same, it would then mean that savings, which is $y_1 - C_1$, will increase. It follows, therefore, that *if the substitution effect (for corn today) outweighs the income effect, an increase in the interest rate will increase savings (i.e., the quantity of today's corn that is not currently consumed).* The opposite results, of course, will hold if the income effect wins out.

Note that for C_2, the demand for corn tomorrow, such an ambiguity does not occur; the income effect for the good in excess demand is of the same direction as that of the substitution effect: The increase in i lowers the relative price of corn tomorrow. Therefore the individual would want to substitute corn tomorrow for corn today (substitution effect, implying an increase in C_2). But since he is better off, he wants to consume more of every normal good and, in particular, more of C_2. This is the income effect. Both effects show, then, an increase in C_2, and there is no ambiguity here.

In Figure 11-10 we show the case in which the substitution effect wins out for corn today. The movement from F to Q represents the substitution effect. The increase in the interest rate increases the relative price of corn today. If at the higher price $(1+i_1)$ the individual is forced to consume a basket equivalent to F (i.e., lying on the same indifference curve), he would want to consume less corn today. This is the substitution effect, and it is precisely equal to KR. The movement from Q to G represents the income effects. Note that the lines tangent to the two points Q and G are parallel. The one passing through G represents a higher income—measured at the given prices in either corn today or corn tomorrow—than the one passing through Q. This increase in income induces individuals to consume *more* of each of the two goods than is consumed at Q. (Note that G lies northeast of point Q.) In

FIGURE 11-10

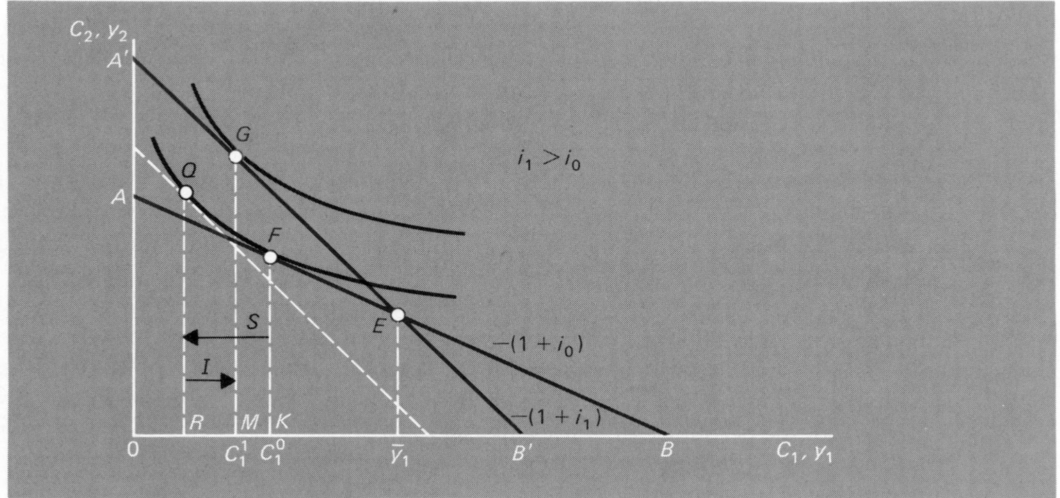

particular, each individual would consume precisely *RM* units *more* of corn today. This is the *income effect,* and it is in the opposite direction from the substitution effect. However, the absolute value of the (negative) substitution effect is greater than the (positive) income effect, from which it follows that the increase in the interest rate, from i_0 to i_1, will lower current consumption from C_1^0 to C_1^1. Similarly, savings now rises from $\bar{y}_1 - C_1^0$ to $\bar{y}_1 - C_1^1$.

Figure 11-11 depicts the case in which the income effect outweighs the substitution effect. The increase in the interest rate, and thus of the relative price of corn today, would induce the individual, on substitution grounds, to consume *RK* fewer units of corn today than previously. But this is outweighed by a greater increase in the consumption of corn today because of the increase in income. The net result is that the increase in the interest rate, from i_0 to i_1, will *increase the consumption demand* for corn today, from C_1^0 to C_1^1, and will thus *decrease savings,* from $\bar{y}_1 - C_1^0$ to $\bar{y}_1 - C_1^1$.

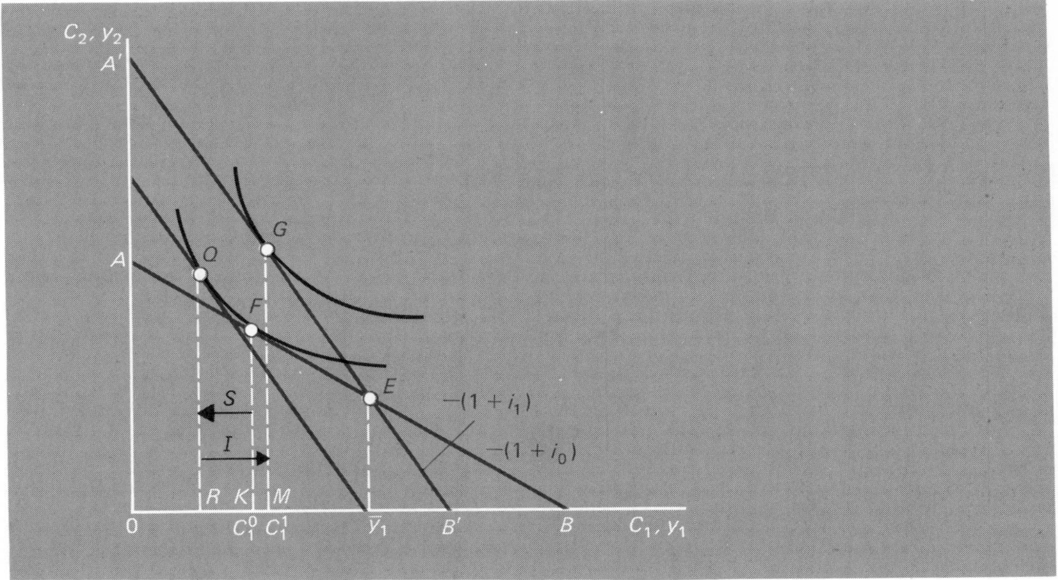

FIGURE 11-11

In summary, we have found that *an increase in the interest rate will decrease current consumption and increase savings if, and only if, the substitution effect outweighs the income effect.* In the literature, one usually sees upward-sloping savings curves with respect to the interest rate, as in Figure 11-12. It should be clear that an implicit assumption is present: For the average household, the substitution effect outweighs the income effect. We should note here that, until 1936, the conventional wisdom held that the interest rate was the *only* determinant of savings and consumption and that the relation was positive between S and i and negative between C and i. In 1936 Keynes, for the first time, said that the interest rate was neither the only determinant nor the most important one.[1] A more important determinant, according to Keynes, was current income, y_1 in this chapter's notation. He emphasized that it is conceivable that the increase in the interest rate may decrease savings or leave savings unchanged. Although he did not explicitly introduce a theory such as the present one, we know now that this can happen, the former situation if the substitution effect is outweighed by the income effect and the latter when they cancel each other.

FIGURE 11-12

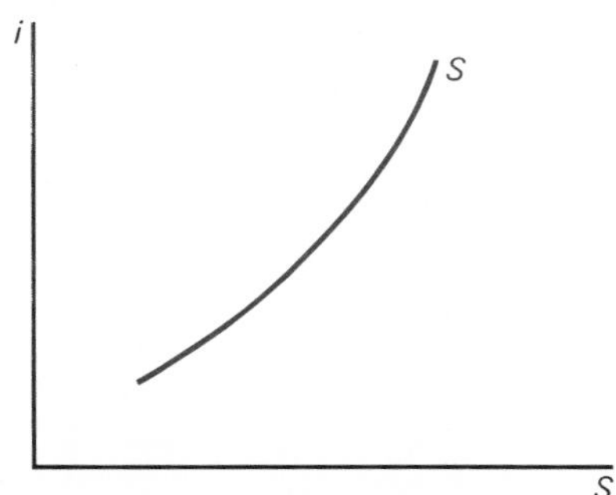

II. THE INTERTEMPORAL PRODUCTION POSSIBILITY CURVE, IPPC

Until now we have conducted our analysis under the assumption that the individual is endowed with a given quantity of income (corn) in each period, that is, $(\bar{y}_1, \bar{y}_2)$ for periods 1 and 2, respectively. The endowment point, however, is itself a matter of economic decision making. In other words, the magnitudes y_1 and y_2 are not exogenously given but are, instead, economic variables that must be endogenously determined in a complete analysis. In the rest of this section we shall inquire about their origins, how they are determined, and whether our earlier results must be modified.

We now extend our analysis by assuming that the economy has an infinite number of possible endowment baskets, (y_1, y_2), rather than just one, and that these are produced by the economy's basic resources, according to the usual assumption of a constant returns-to-scale technology. *It is the endowment of these basic resources that we now assume fixed* (in the short run). The infinity of possible baskets (y_1, y_2) is shown by the line $Y_2 Y_1$ in Figure 11-13, where we see that this curve is downward sloping, which means that society can have more corn today only if it has less corn tomorrow, and vice versa.

This curve is the two-period analogue of the familiar two-good production possibility curve. We shall be referring to it as the intertemporal production possibility curve, or IPPC. More precisely, this curve depicts, for each specified amount of the

---

[1] J. M. Keynes, *The General Theory of Employment, Interest and Money* (New York: Harcourt, Brace & Co., 1936), Chaps. 8–10.

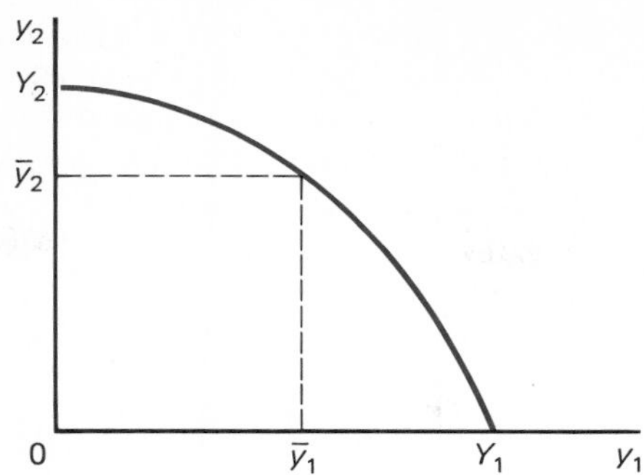

FIGURE 11-13

good in one period, the maximum amount of the good, in another period, that can be produced. For example, if we want to produce $\bar{y}_1$ units of corn today, the maximum amount of tomorrow's corn we can produce is $\bar{y}_2$. On the other hand, if we produce Y_1 units of y_1, no units of y_2 can be produced.

Let us now examine the shape of the IPPC more carefully. Not only is this curve downward sloping but it is also bowed out. This means that if we keep increasing the production of the one good by equal amounts, we have to decrease the production of the other by increasingly more units. In Figure 11-14 the segments *KL, LM,* and *MN* are all equal to one unit of corn today. Therefore if we begin with *OK* units of today's corn (and thus *OA* units of tomorrow's), and we want to increase it by one unit (to *OL*), we need to give up *AB* units of y_2. On the other hand, the increase by one unit, from *OL* to *OM,* requires us to give up $BC > AB$ units of y_2, and so forth.

The number of units of tomorrow's corn, y_2, that individuals must give up in order to produce one more unit of corn today we call the *relative cost,* or *opportunity cost,* of y_1. Similarly, the relative cost of y_2 is the number of units of today's corn individuals must give up in order to produce one more unit of corn tomorrow. Employ-

FIGURE 11-14

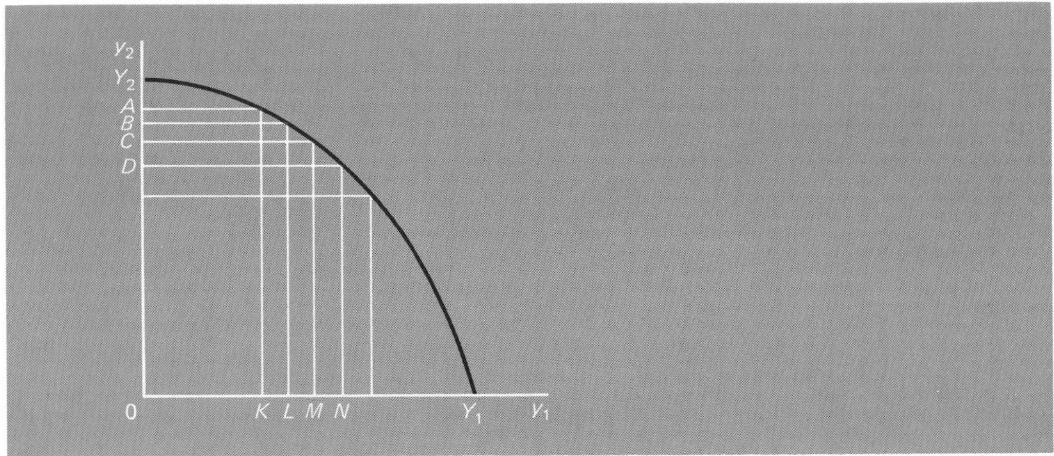

ing these definitions, we can say that the bowed-out IPPC reflects the fact that both corn today and corn tomorrow are produced at increasing cost. More precisely, in the (y_1, y_2)-plane, with the horizontal axis depicting y_1 and the vertical one depicting y_2, the relative cost of y_1 is given by the slope of the tangent to the IPPC. In the same plane the relative cost of y_2 is measured by the inverse of the slope of the same tangent. Note that in order to increase the production of y_1 we move clockwise along the IPPC, say from point A to point B in Figure 11-15. Such a movement increases the slope of the tangent, exemplifying the statement that y_1 is produced at increasing (relative) cost. Similarly, a counterclockwise movement, in order to increase y_2, reduces the slope of the tangent, thereby increasing its inverse, which represents the relative cost of y_2.

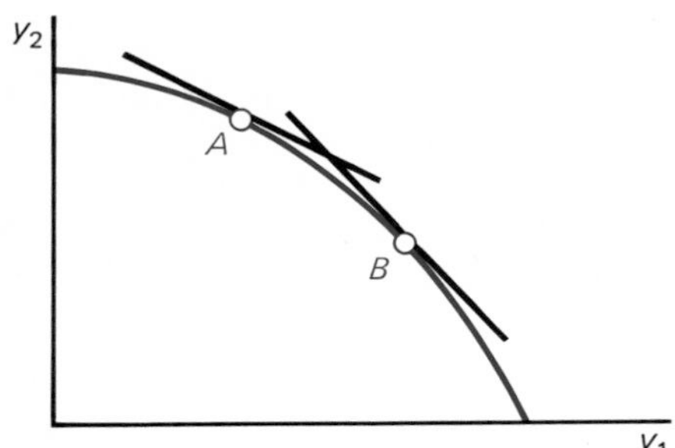

FIGURE 11-15

The reader must have already noticed the similarity between this chapter's definition of *relative,* or *opportunity, cost* and our previous definition of *relative price.* For good y_1, the relative cost denotes the number of units of y_2 we give up in order to produce, that is, *to acquire through production,* one more unit of good y_1. The relative price of y_1, on the other hand, denotes the number of units of y_2 that we give up *in order to acquire one unit of y_1 through the market.* Both of them are operators transforming units of corn today in units of corn tomorrow. The only, and crucial, difference is that the relative price performs the transformation in the market, whereas the relative cost transforms y_1 into y_2 through production. This is why the term *marginal rate of transformation* is sometimes used instead of *relative cost.*

THE DETERMINATION OF THE ENDOWMENT POINT

The problem of determining the economy's endowment of corn today and corn tomorrow is analytically the same as that of finding the production of two goods, corn and barley, or of A and B, in the same period. We shall denote the quantities of the two goods that are produced by a and b. The production possibility curve, PPC, for these goods is shown in Figure 11-16. We recall that production is carried out by *profit-maximizing* firms that are *price takers* with respect to both the goods they sell and the goods they buy. And if P denotes the relative price of B, it follows

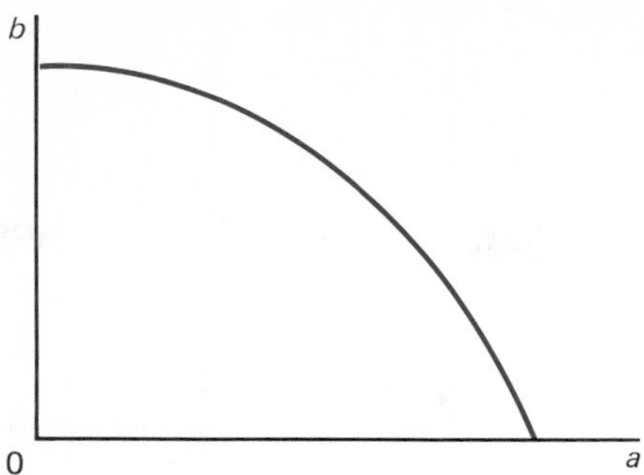

FIGURE 11-16

that $1/P$ denotes the relative price of *A*. Now, given the market prices, say at P^0, let us find the amounts of *a* and *b* that will maximize the profits of the firms.

In Figure 11-17 the slope of the straight line closest to the origin denotes the given relative price of *A*, $1/P_0$. We shall show that the maximum profit production point is *E*, which is the point of tangency of the PPC and a line with a slope equal to $1/P_0$. Note that the value of point *E* is equal to *OK* units of good *A* (or *OQ* units of good *B*), which is the amount that the firm will receive by producing basket *E* and selling it in the market at the relative price of *B* equal to P_0. From this we have to subtract the cost of resources used. But no matter which point on the PPC is produced, it will use the same amount of given resources (assumed in deriving the PPC). The value of these resources can be measured in either units of *A* or units of *B*, and it will be a given fixed number, whether we produce at point *E*, *E'*,

FIGURE 11-17

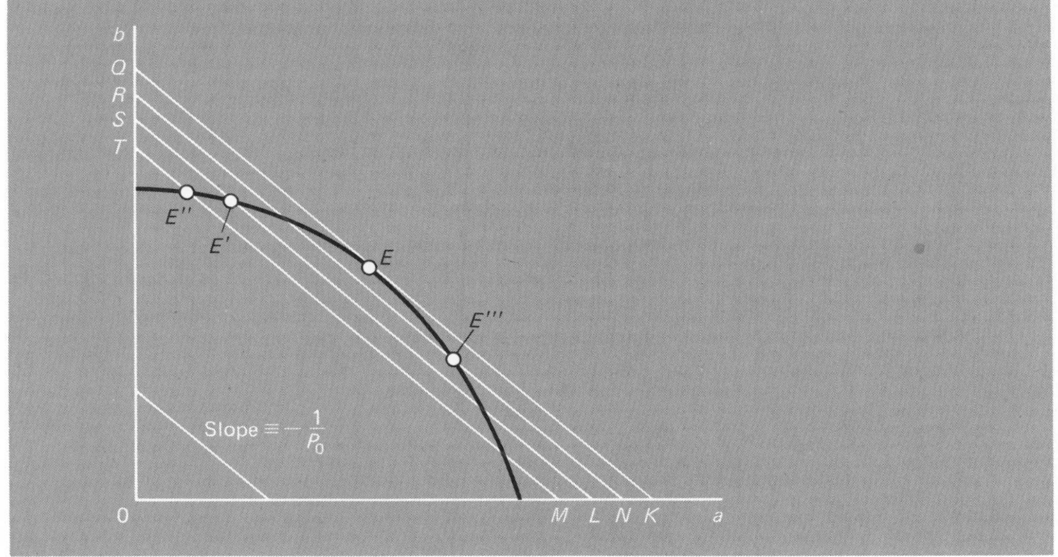

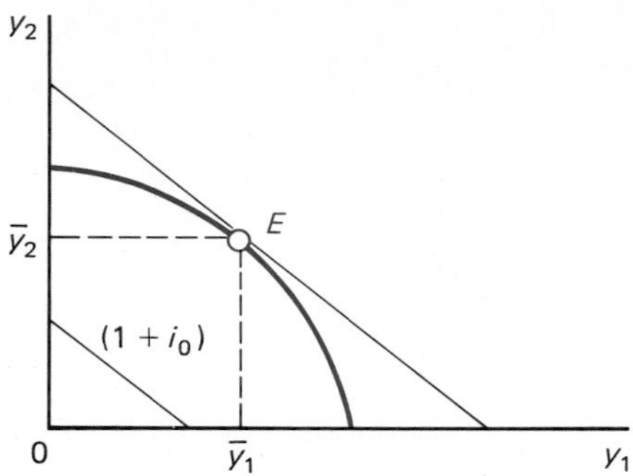

FIGURE 11-18

E''', or at any other point. Thus the *profit-maximizing point* is the *revenue-maximizing point.*

It is easy to see why point E is the revenue-maximizing point; the value of any other point on the PPC is less than that of point E. For example, point E' gives revenue equal to OL units of A, which, of course, is less than the OK units of revenue that point E yields. Similarly, for points E'' and E''' the revenue is OM and ON units, respectively, which are both less than OK. Moreover, we can show that this result holds true even when we measure revenue in units of B. It is clear that the OQ units of B that basket E yields as revenue is greater than the OR, OS, and OT units that baskets E''', E$'$, and E'', respectively, yield.

In summary, we have shown that the maximum profit point, E, is found where a line with slope equal to the assumed relative price of good A, $1/P_0$, is tangent to the PPC. But we know that the slope of the tangent to the PPC is the relative cost of A. We also observe that the inverse of the relative price of A is the relative price of B, and, similarly, that the inverse of the slope of the tangent to the PPC is the relative cost of B. Thus we have established the firm's profit-maximizing formula: *Produce (and supply) quantities of each of the goods up to the point where the relative cost of each of the goods is equal to its relative price.*

This is the method by which the economy's endowments of each good are determined. It is this theory we shall apply to find the economy's endowment of current and future income (corn today and corn tomorrow). We begin by assuming that the market interest rate is equal to i_0, which implies that the relative price of corn today is $1 + i_0$ units of corn tomorrow. We now draw a line with slope $-(1 + i_0)$ and move it in a parallel fashion until it becomes tangent to the IPPC, as in Figure 11-18. The point of tangency, E, is the economy's endowment point, possessing the characteristic that the relative price of today's corn is equal to its relative cost. Similarly, at E, the relative price (i.e., the present value) of tomorrow's corn is equal to its relative cost.

CONSUMPTION-SAVINGS DECISIONS

Having determined, as in the preceding paragraph, the endowment point E, we proceed more or less as in the earlier sections of this chapter. Figure 11-19 superimposes the average household's preferences in the graph with the IPPC. Recall that firms

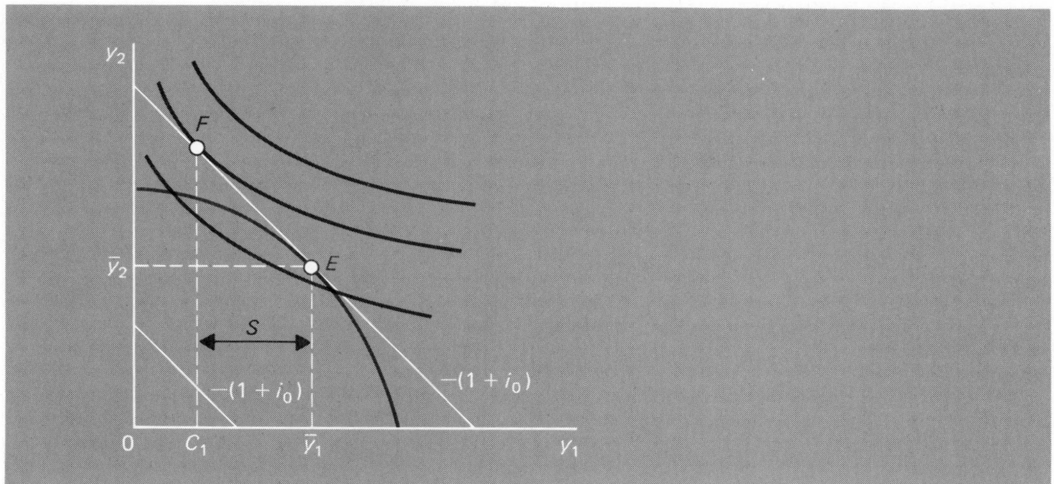

FIGURE 11-19

are owned by households, and, therefore, given the interest rate, at i_0, the firms produce at point E in order to maximize the owners' (i.e., the households') profits. The value of the endowment point E in units of y_1, y_2, or in combinations thereof, is shown by the line tangent to the IPPC at E. This is, of course, the consumption possibility line, or budget line. The individual's most preferred basket, F, is found at the tangency of this line and an indifference curve. Figure 11-19 represents the (typical) case in which the average consumer is a net saver. With the interest rate equal to i_0, this consumer's current income is $\bar{y}_1$, of which C_1 units are consumed and $S \equiv y_1 - C_1$ units are saved. The only difference, so far, in our analysis is that the endowment point, as well as consumption and savings, is determined by knowledge of the interest rate.

Let us now assume that the interest rate rises from i_0 to i_1. In Figure 11-20 we see that the new endowment point E' consists of more current corn, $y_1^1 > y_1^0$ (and, of course, less of tomorrow's corn). The increase in the interest rate increases the relative price of today's corn, making it possible to cover the higher relative cost that an increase in y_1 requires. We also see that the increase in the interest rate lowers the present value of the (new) endowment, from OK to OL units. Thus the extension of our analysis to make the endowment endogenous did not change this basic result. This is important because the higher interest rate increases the "corn today" component, y_1, of the endowment point. (Obviously, the increase in y_1 is more than outweighed by the decreased value, in y_1 units, of y_2, i.e., $|[1/(1 + i_1)] \cdot y_2^1 - [1/(1 + i_0)] \cdot y_2^0| > y_1^1 - y_1^0$.) Note, however, that even though the present value of the endowment OL is lower, it is still higher than the OM it would have been if the endowment remained fixed at E.

We now examine the effect of an increase in the interest rate on the preferred point F. Current consumption of the average household is less than current income, y_1, which is, therefore, identified as the good in excess supply. The increase in the

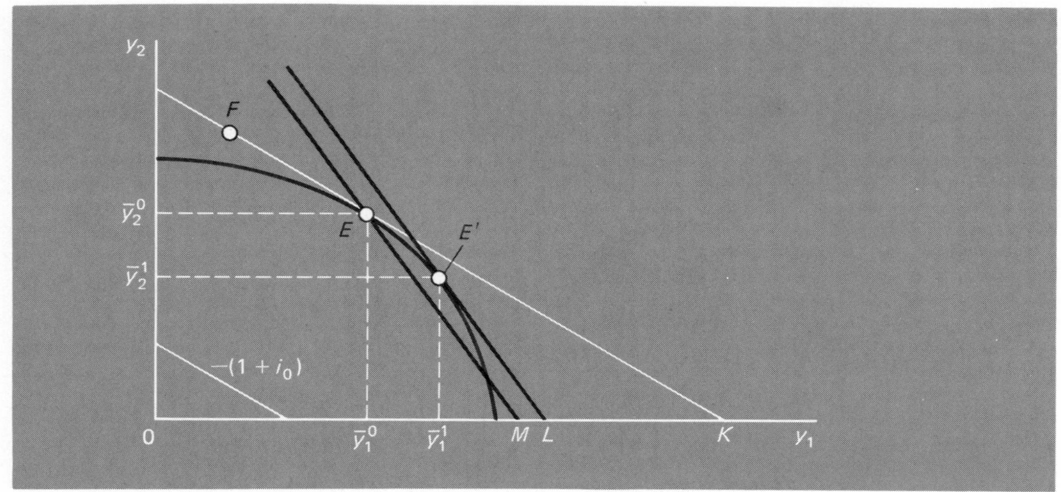

FIGURE 11-20

interest rate raises the relative price of this good. In the fixed endowment case, we saw that the increase in price makes individuals wealthier, in the sense that they can now reach a higher indifference curve. In the present variable-endowment-case, this is true *a fortiori.*

Figure 11-21, which reproduces the information of Figure 11-20, permits a comparison of the two cases. *With the endowment fixed* at point E, the preferred point moved from F to G when i increased. This movement was divided into a

FIGURE 11-21

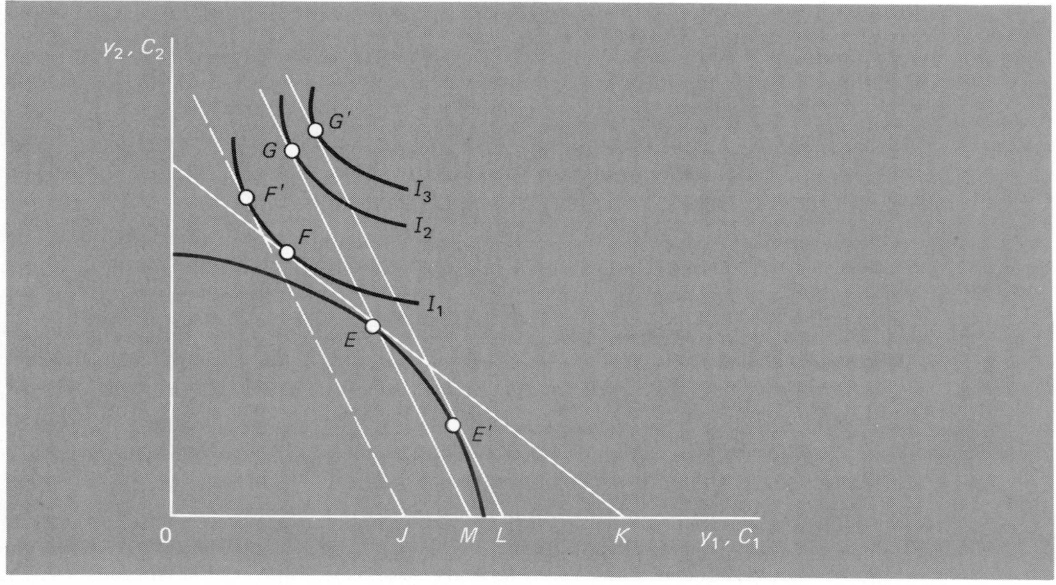

substitution effect (movement from F to F') and an income effect (movement from F' to G). The motivating force behind the income effect was that an increase in i increased the individual's real income, since this individual was a net lender (a net supplier of loans). Measuring this change in income at the new interest rate, i_1, the present value of income increased by JM. Now, with endowment variable, the endowment point moves from E to E', so that there is an additional increase in the present value of income equal to ML. As a result, in the variable endowment model, in terms of the new prices, income changes by $JM + ML = JL$, so that the income effect is given by the movement from F' to G'.

It follows from this analysis that the increase in the interest rate will again create the two opposing tendencies with regard to current consumption demand, C_1: The income effect induces individuals to consume *more* and the substitution effect induces them to consume *less*. *However, in the variable endowment case, the income effect is greater, and thus it is more likely that the income effect will outweigh the substitution effect.* The two opposing tendencies are shown clearly in Figures 11-22 and 11-23. The former assumes that the substitution effect wins out and, therefore, that the higher interest rate, $i_1 > i_0$, implies lower consumption demand, $C_1^1 < C_1^0$. On the other hand, Figure 11-23 depicts the situation when the income effect of the rise in the interest rate outweighs the substitution effect. In this case the increase in the interest rate *increases* consumption demand.

We now come to the only truly important difference between the fixed endowment and the variable endowment cases. It involves the savings rate, $y_1 - C_1$. When the endowment of current income, y_1, is fixed, savings increases if, and only if, consumption, C_1, decreases. It follows, then, that in such a case an increase in the

FIGURE 11-22

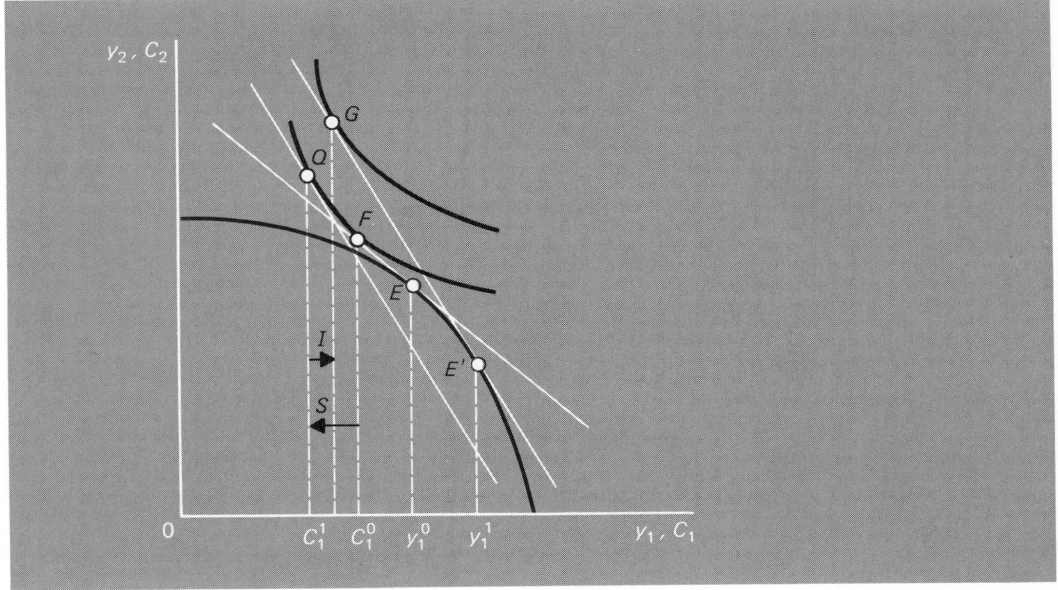

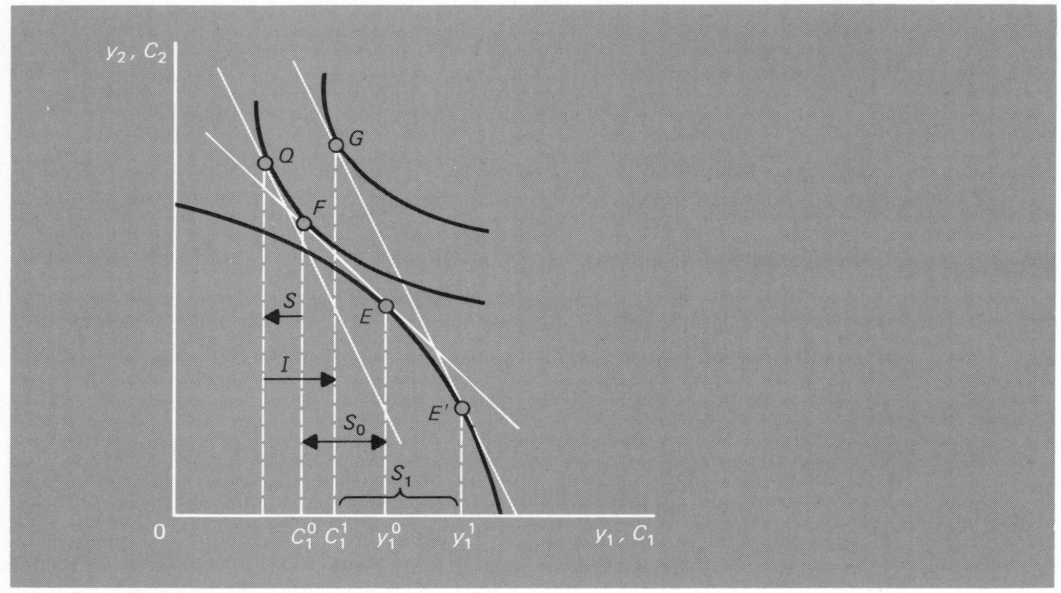

FIGURE 11-23

interest rate increases savings if, and only if, the substitution effect outweighs the income effect. This is so because only then will consumption demand fall. In the variable endowment case, an increase in the interest rate increases y_1. *It follows, then, that the assumption that the substitution effect outweighs the income effect is only a sufficient condition and not a necessary one for the increase in the interest rate to increase savings.* Even if this condition does not hold, implying that an increase in the interest rate *increases* consumption C_1, the change in $y_1 - C_1$ may still be positive, which happens when the increase in current consumption demand is more than outweighed by the increase in current income. It is this case that we depicted in Figure 11-23.

III. EXACT FORMS OF CONSUMPTION FUNCTIONS

The assumption of homotheticity of preferences figured prominently in the postwar literature on consumption and savings. The main target of this literature was the derivation, both theoretically and empirically, of the exact form of the production and savings functions.

We recall that homotheticity of preferences means that indifference curves have the same slope along a ray from the origin,[2] as shown in Figure 11-24. Along the ray *OA*, all indifference curves have tangents with the same slope. Since these

[2] See Chapter 1.

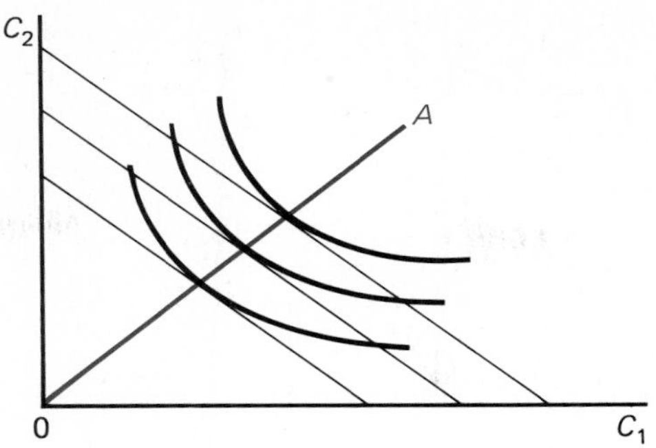

FIGURE 11-24

tangents can be regarded as budget lines (with slope equal to $[1 + i]$), it follows that when preferences are homothetic the ratio of the quantities consumed, C_2 and C_1 (which is depicted by the slope of the ray OA), depends only on the relative price $(1 + i)$. As long as i is given, $(1 + i)$ is given, and thus the ratio C_2/C_1 is given. Moreover, because of the shape of an indifference curve, the higher $(1 + i)$ is, the higher the ratio C_2/C_1 is, as shown in Figure 11-25.

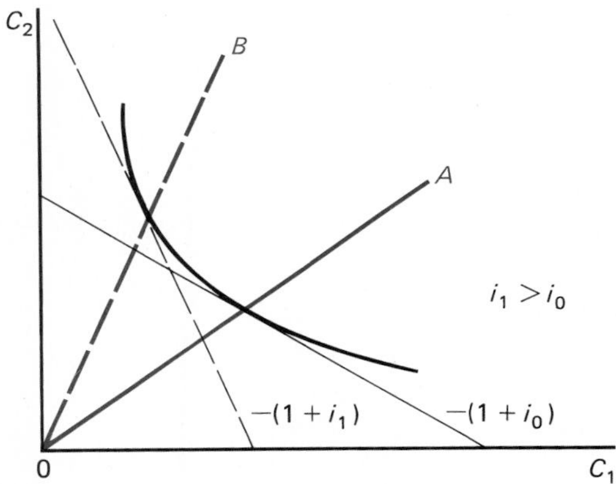

FIGURE 11-25

We can summarize by saying that, with homothetic preferences, the ratio C_2/C_1 is an increasing function, ψ, of the relative price of C_1, $1 + i$:

$$\frac{C_2}{C_1} = \psi(1 + i) \tag{12}$$

Graphically, we have Figure 11-26. A special case is when ψ is a straight line through the origin, as in Figure 11-27. Its algebraic expression is given by (13), where λ is the slope of this straight line:

$$\frac{C_2}{C_1} = \lambda \cdot (1 + i) \tag{13}$$

FIGURE 11-26

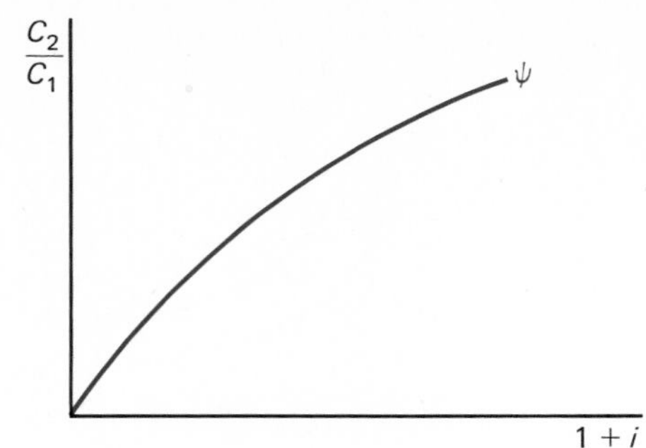

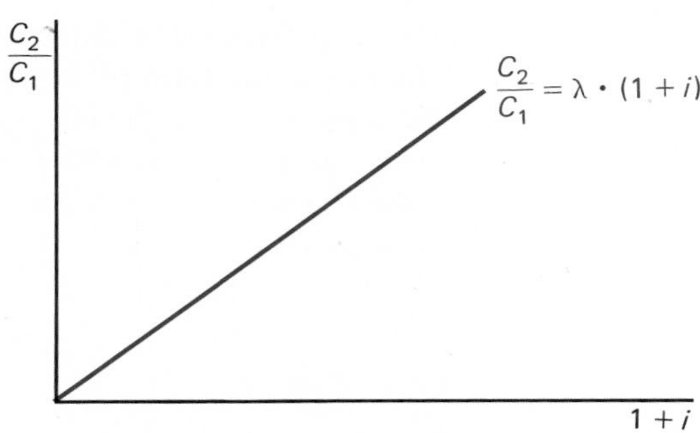

FIGURE 11-27

Of course, the budget constraint also has to be satisfied:

$$C_1 + \frac{C_2}{1+i} = y_1 + \frac{y_2}{1+i} \equiv \bar{I}_1 \tag{14}$$

Solving this equation for C_2, we have

$$C_2 = -(1+i)\ C_1 + y_1\ (1+i) + y_2$$

Solving (12) for C_2, we have

$$C_2 = C_1 \cdot \psi\,(1+i) \tag{15}$$

The LHSs are the same, and thus the RHSs are the same:

$$C_1 \cdot \psi(1+i) = -(1+i)\ C_1 + y_1\ (1+i) + y_2$$

Collecting terms and solving for C_1, we have

$$C_1 = \frac{(1+i)\ [y_1 + y_2/(1+i)]}{\psi + (1+i)} \tag{16}$$

Substituting (16) into (15), we get

$$C_2 = \frac{\psi}{\psi + (1+i)} \cdot [(1+i)\, y_1 + y_2] \tag{17}$$

Since $y_1 + y_2/(1 + i) = I_1$ and $(1 + i)\, y_1 + y_2 = I_2$, defining

$$\alpha_1(i) = \frac{1+i}{\psi(\,\cdot\,) + (1+i)} \tag{18}$$

$$\alpha_2(i) = \frac{\psi(\cdot)}{\psi(\cdot) + (1+i)} \tag{19}$$

We can rewrite (16) and (17) as

$$C_1 = \alpha_1(i)\, I_1 \tag{20}$$

$$C_2 = \alpha_2(\cdot)\, I_2 \tag{21}$$

where

$$\alpha_1 + \alpha_2 = \frac{1+i}{\psi + (1+i)} + \frac{\psi}{\psi + (1+i)} = \frac{\psi + (1+i)}{\psi + (1+i)} = 1$$

Let us now concentrate on current consumption. Graphically, it is shown in Figure 11-28. The slope α_1 is both the *MPC and the APC of the present value of the income stream,* as long as the interest rate remains the same. It should not surprise us to find that, *ceteris paribus,* an increase in the interest rate may, in general, have an ambiguous effect on C_1. Note that an increase in the interest rate *decreases* I_1. However, by (18), α_1 may increase, decrease, or remain unchanged. Of course, if the increase in i decreases α_1, then C_1 will definitely fall. (Note that for this result it is *not necessary* that α_1 fall; it is only sufficient.) It can be shown that an increase in the interest rate will decrease α_1 if, and only if, the elasticity of substitution, σ,

FIGURE 11-28

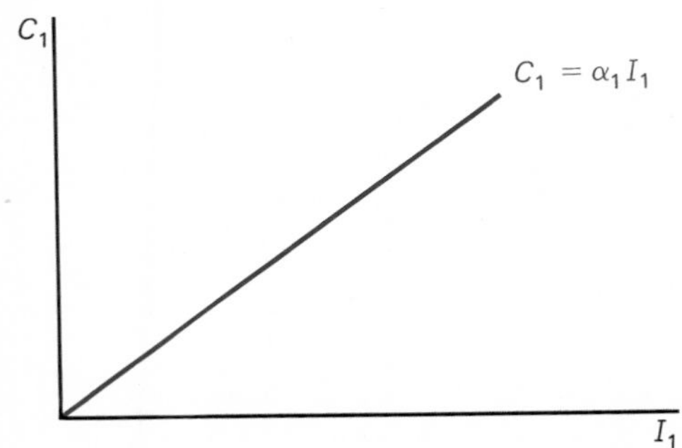

is greater than one; it will increase it if, and only if, σ is less than one; and α will remain constant if, and only if, σ is equal to one.

It should be clear that the simple case of (13), $C_2/C_1 = \lambda \cdot (1 + i)$, exhibits unitary elasticity of substitution. With this kind of homothetic preferences, then, we have constant α's, α_1 and α_2, independent of the interest rate and consumption demands:

$$C_1 = \bar{\alpha}_1 I_1 \tag{20a}$$

$$C_2 = \bar{\alpha}_2 I_2 \tag{21a}$$

where

$$\bar{\alpha}_1 = \frac{1}{1+\lambda}, \ \bar{\alpha}_2 = \frac{\lambda}{1+\lambda} \text{ and } \bar{\alpha}_1 + \bar{\alpha}_2 = 1$$

The bar over the α's symbolizes their fixed values.

Concentrating on C_1, we see that when $\sigma = 1$, an increase in the interest rate decreases C_1 because it lowers I_1 while keeping $\bar{\alpha}_1$ the same. Thus $\bar{\alpha}_1 I_1$, which is C_1, falls. Moreover, if $y_2 \equiv 0$, that is, if the individual is endowed with only corn today, the present value, I_1, is y_1, which is independent of the interest rate. Thus, for the case where $\sigma \equiv 1$ and $y_2 \equiv 0$, C_1 is independent of the interest rate. A change in i changes neither $\bar{\alpha}_1$ nor I_1. Current consumption is a constant number:

$$C_1 = \bar{\alpha}_1 I_1 = \bar{\alpha}_1 y_1$$

FIGURE 11-29

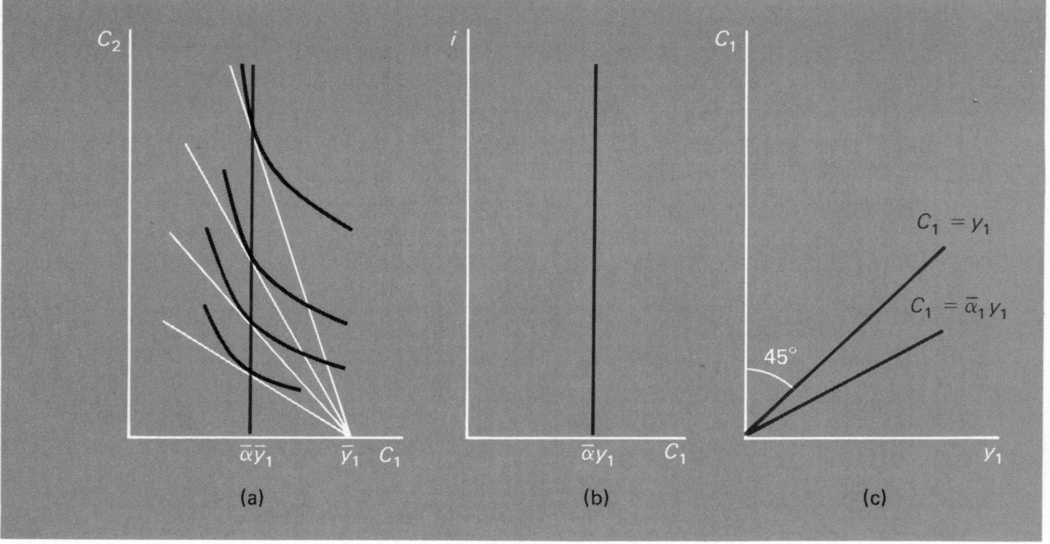

The "offer curve" for this case is vertical, as shown in Figure 11-29a. The consumption function is shown in Figure 11-29b in the (C_1,i)-plane, and in Figure 11-29c in the (y_1,C_1)-plane. In this special case, then, current consumption depends only on current income, y_1. Moreover, the ratio of current consumption to current income, C_1/y_1, is fixed. This is the APC out of current income, which coincides with the MPC out of current income. The savings function for this case is shown in Figures 11-30a and 11-30b.

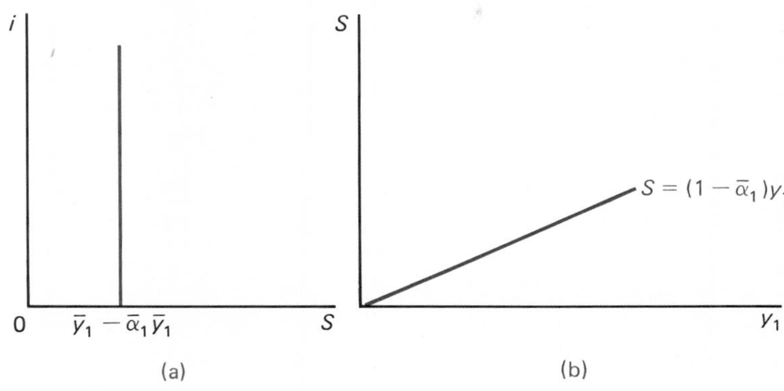

FIGURE 11-30

The above results can be extended to cover the multiperiod case. Thus, in the general case of homothetic preferences alone, we have

$$
\begin{aligned}
C_1 &= \alpha_1(i)\, I_1 \\
C_2 &= \alpha_2(i)\, I_2 \\
&\vdots \\
C_t &= \alpha_t(i)\, I_t
\end{aligned}
\tag{22}
$$

with $\sum_t \alpha_t \equiv 1$.
In the special case, we have

$$
\begin{aligned}
C_1 &= \bar{\alpha}_1 I_1 \\
C_2 &= \bar{\alpha}_2 I_2 \\
&\vdots \\
C_t &= \bar{\alpha}_t I_t
\end{aligned}
\tag{23}
$$

and $\sum_t \alpha_t \equiv 1$.

The two most important, and certainly most influential, postwar contributions in the literature on consumption-savings were made by Franco Modigliani and his associates—most notably Richard Brumberg and A. Ando[3] on the one hand and Milton Friedman[4] on the other. The former introduced the "life-cycle hypothesis," whereas the latter introduced the "permanent income hypothesis." Both contributions examine households' behavior in an intertemporal setting and both assume homothetic preferences. Therefore they work with the (current) consumption function of the form $C_1 = \alpha_1 I_1$. In their effort to derive further theoretical and empirical results, they derive equivalent formulations of the I_1 component. In this effort, their approaches differ. We begin our analysis with the "permanent income hypothesis" because the theory involved is more abstract and, therefore, less specific, despite its later introduction (1957 cf. with 1954).[5]

PERMANENT INCOME HYPOTHESIS

Perhaps the best way of explaining the transformation of I_1 into "permanent income" is the following. Using the same interest rate that transforms the income stream y_1, $y_2, \cdots$, into the present value I_1, let us find the equivalent level of *constant* income flow over time. This *constant* income is what we call *permanent* income.

We first illustrate it in the two-period model with assumed endowments, $\bar{y}_1$ and $\bar{y}_2$. Given the interest rate, the present value of the stream $\bar{y}_1$ and $\bar{y}_2$ is found to be I_1:

$$I_1 = \bar{y}_1 + \frac{\bar{y}_2}{1+i} \tag{24}$$

The level of constant income over time, $\bar{y}$, which is equivalent to I_1, is the solution to the equation

$$I_1 = \bar{y} + \frac{\bar{y}}{1+i}$$

Factoring out, we have

$$I_1 = \bar{y}\left(1 + \frac{1}{1+i}\right)$$

[3] See Franco Modigliani and Richard Brumberg, "Utility Analysis and the Consumption Function: An Interpretation of Cross Section Data," in *Post Keynesian Economics,* ed. K. Kurihara (New Brunswick, N.J.: Rutgers University Press, 1954); and Albert Ando and Franco Modigliani, "The 'Life Cycle' Hypothesis of Saving: Aggregate Implications and Tests," *American Economic Review,* March 1963, pp. 55–84.

[4] Milton Friedman, *A Theory of the Consumption Function* (Princeton: National Bureau of Economic Research, 1957).

[5] Note: The rest of this chapter may be too esoteric for a reader who does not intend to specialize in these issues.

Taking the common denominator, we have

$$I_1 = \bar{y} \cdot \frac{1+i+1}{1+i}$$

or

$$I_1 = \bar{y} \cdot \frac{2+i}{1+i} \tag{25}$$

Solving this equation for $\bar{y}$ and denoting this solution as y^p (the superscript p stands for the word *permanent*), we have the following expression for "permanent income":

$$y^p = \frac{1+i}{2+i} \cdot I_1 \tag{26}$$

The assumption of homothetic preferences gave us the consumption function

$$C_1 = \alpha_1 I_1 \tag{20}$$

Substituting for I_1, we have

$$C_1 = \alpha_1 \cdot \frac{2+i}{1+i} y^p$$

or

$$C_1 = \beta \cdot y^p \tag{27}$$

where

$$\beta \equiv \alpha_1 \cdot \frac{2+i}{1+i} \tag{28}$$

We now turn to the multiperiod model for which the permanent income hypothesis was really designed. This case can be simplified drastically if an infinity of periods is assumed, for then the uniform flow of income over time is

$$y^p = i \cdot I_1 \tag{29}$$

This y^p is the permanent income. Equation (29) can be rewritten as

$$I_1 = \frac{1}{i} \cdot y^p \tag{30}$$

Note that this transformation of I_1 into permanent income, y^p, necessitates knowledge not only of the actual *incomes over time (i.e., $\bar{y}_1$, $\bar{y}_2$, $\bar{y}_3$, $\cdots$, etc.) but also of the fact that the interest rate is expected to remain the same.*

Now, as before, we tie (30) with the consumption function derived from homothetic preferences. We thus have the consumption function

$$C_1 = \beta^* y^p \tag{27'}$$

where

$$\beta^* = \frac{\alpha_1}{i} \tag{28'}$$

Note that whether we are examining the two-period case (and thus (27)) or the multiperiod model (and thus (27')), given the interest rate, consumption is a constant proportion of permanent income. We shall use the symbol C^p for this consumption and β for the proportion without specifying it as coming out of the two-period or out of the multiperiod model:

$$C^p = \beta \cdot y^p \tag{31}$$

Diagrammatically, this implies that the consumption function is a straight line through the origin, as in Figure 11-31. The proportion β is, of course, both the average propensity to consume (APC) and the marginal propensity to consume (MPC) out of permanent income.

In summary, under the assumptions that lie behind the permanent income hypothesis and under the assumption of homothetic preferences, current consumption is a constant proportion of permanent income.

These assumptions should always be recalled when we try to apply the results of this theory to the real world. In particular, there are occasions for which *observed* income is not an unbiased estimate of permanent income. We shall show that even though the "true" consumption function is as we derived it above (i.e., (31), with its graphical version Figure 11-31), the observed consumption function derived by

FIGURE 11-31

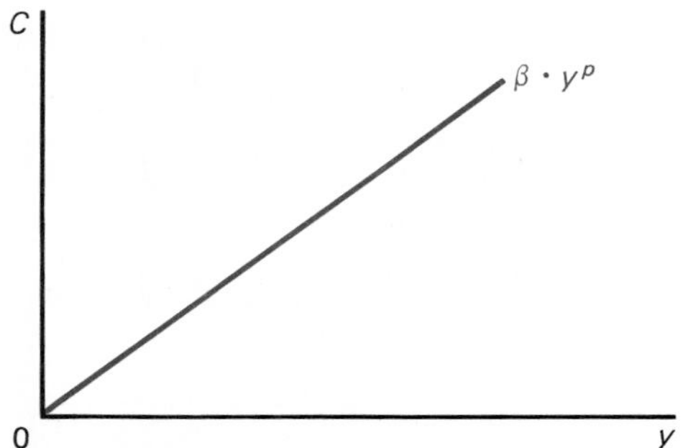

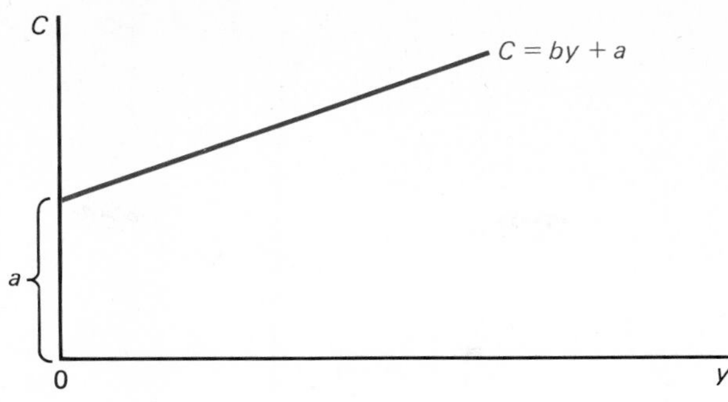

FIGURE 11-32

using either *cross-section* data or *short time-series* data is of the form $C = by + a$, which is depicted in Figure 11-32.

Let us first examine the consumption function derived from *cross-section* budget studies. Families with high current income, y's, have average income, $\bar{y}$, greater than permanent income. The difference, in this case positive, between current (average) income $\bar{y}$ and permanent income, $\bar{y} - \bar{y}^p$, is transitory income, $\bar{y}^t$. Similarly, households with low current income have average current income $\bar{y}$ lower than their permanent income, $\bar{y}^p$. In this case the transitory income is negative, $\bar{y} - y^p = y^t < 0$. This transitory income, whether positive or negative, is assumed to be a truly transitory *random* fluctuation in income: There is no correlation between transitory and permanent income.

Similarly, observed consumption also has transitory and permanent components, $C = C^p + C^t$. Again the transitory component of consumption is truly a random variable, that is, there is no correlation between C^p and C^t. Moreover, and this is important, there is no correlation between transitory income, y^t, and transitory consumption, C_t. (Thus, if an individual's current income has increased because of an unexpected gift, this individual is assumed to save all the increase.)

These assumptions imply that families with high incomes, and, therefore, positive transitory income, will have lower APC than the average family. Figure 11-33 illustrates this case. Take income group m_1 with average income $\bar{y}_{m_1}$ greater than the population's average y^*. For this group, the transitory income, $y^t_{m_1}$, is shown in the graph to be positive, that is, $\bar{y}_{m_1} - \bar{y}^p_{m_1} \equiv y^t_{m_1} > 0$. This income group m_1 will consume *as if* it had income equal to $y^p_{m_1}$. But with income equal to $y^p_{m_1}$, this group consumes $C^p_{m_1}$. Therefore this group will consume *below* the βy curve, in particular, at point B (which is the horizontal displacement of point A relevant for $y^p_{m_1}$).

An income group m_2, whose average current income is below that of the whole population, will have a negative transitory income, $\bar{y}_{m_2} - \bar{y}^p_{m_2} = \bar{y}^t_{m_2} < 0$, and it will consume more than βy, in particular, at point D. A straight line connecting the origin and point D has a slope greater than β. This means that low-income groups have a higher APC than high-income groups whose APC (the slope of a line connecting O and B) is lower than β. If we repeat this process for all examined income groups, we shall derive a curve that has a positive intercept and is flatter than the βy curve, as in Figure 11-34.

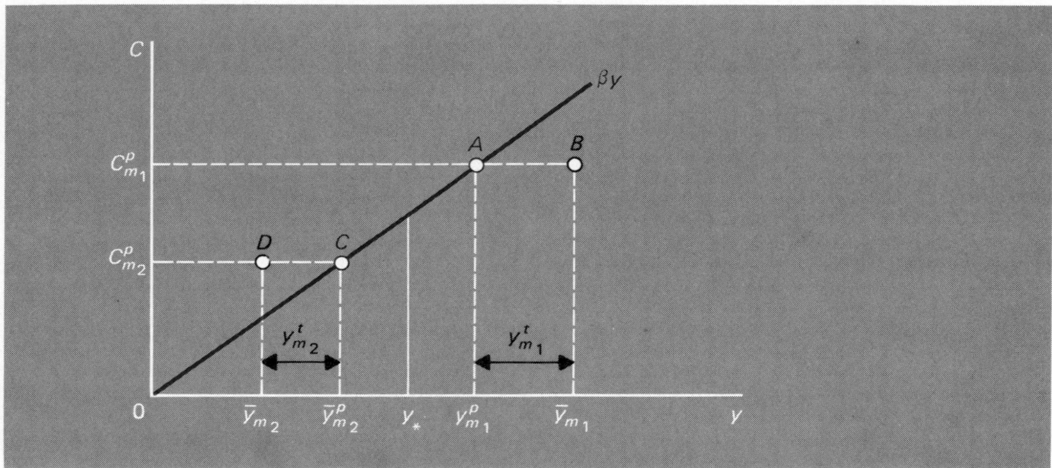

FIGURE 11-33

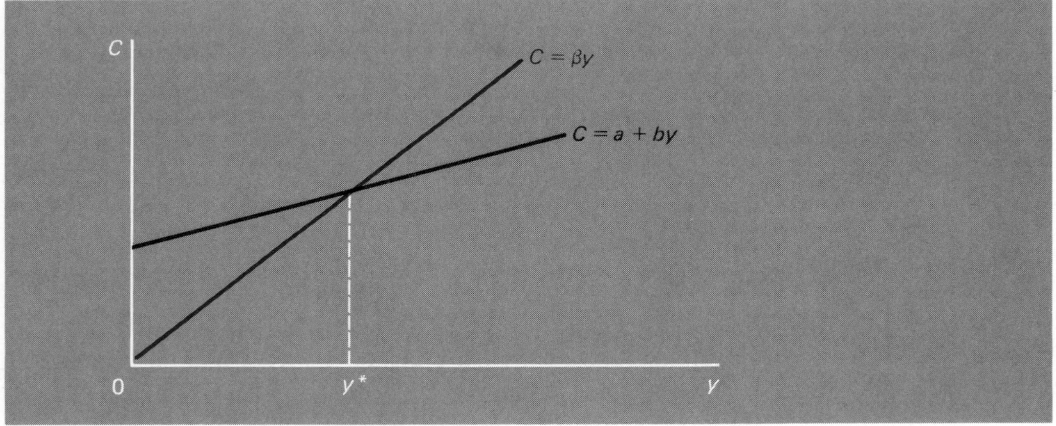

FIGURE 11-34

Turning now to short time series, we only need to change the language slightly; short time series involves the taking of data from a period equal in length to that of a business cycle. Now, for a cyclical trough, the bulk of the data comes from households with $\bar{y} < \bar{y}^p$; and for the peak of the cycle, it comes from households with $\bar{y} > \bar{y}^p$. For the former period, consumption will be greater than βy; and for the peak period, consumption will be less than βy, thereby rendering the same statistical illusion as with cross-section data. Thus the consumption function is also of the form $by + a$, as in Figure 11-34.

We now come to the *long time series* for which the permanent income hypothesis has been designed. Any household (or income group for that matter) has approximately as many income observations *above* its permanent income as below it. Thus, over the long run, the transitory effects approximately cancel out, and current income, in the long run, *is* an unbiased estimate of permanent income, thereby allowing the consumption-income ratio (APC) to remain constant.

LIFE-CYCLE HYPOTHESIS

The life-cycle hypothesis gives *theoretical* results similar to those of the permanent income hypothesis. In particular, it shows that in the long run, consumption is roughly proportional to income. Also, consumption functions derived from cross-section or short time-series data have positive intercepts and are flatter than the long-run relations.

There are, however, some important differences. First, while Friedman's contribution is abstract and sufficiently general to apply to any income stream without inquiring about the origins of this stream, Modigliani and his associates assume a life-cycle origin of this income stream. In particular, they make the realistic assumption that the income of an average individual is low, or even zero, at the early stages of his life (e.g., until graduation), and that it peaks in his middle age and starts to fall thereafter. However, there can be different versions depending on whether the individual intends to end his life with a bequest to his heirs. At any rate, this hypothesis regarding the working years of individuals can be (and has been) tested. Now, returning to the theoretical analysis, the very fact that the individuals' middle years are the most productive (with the [usual] assumption that he wants to spread his income stream into a smooth consumption stream, usually increasing over time) accounts for the usual explanation of consumption functions derived from cross-section budget studies. During these middle years, the individual is a net saver (lender), whereas during the remaining years he is a net dissaver. Thus the individuals in high-income groups are usually in the middle of their life and, therefore, consume a smaller proportion of their income, whereas the opposite is true of individuals in low-income groups. (Note the similarity between the two explanations. Friedman's states that families with higher incomes have positive transitory incomes and, therefore, consume a lower proportion of their incomes. Modigliani goes one step further and says that these higher incomes are earned primarily by people in the middle of their life who, therefore, consume a lower proportion of their incomes because they are net savers.)

The second difference between the life-cycle and permanent income hypotheses is found in the way that the contributors transformed the present value I_1 into equivalent expressions. Whereas Friedman reduces this into permanent income, Modigliani and associates (here, especially Ando) reduce I_1 to income from labor and income from property. In the general case, the income stream $y_1, y_2, y_3, \cdots, y_n$ is split into an income stream generated by labor, $y_1^N, y_2^N, \cdots, y_n^N$, and an income stream generated by *assets*, $y_1^a, y_2^a, \cdots, y_n^a$. Thus the present value is

$$I_1 = \left(y_1^N + \frac{y_2^N}{1+i} + \frac{y_3^N}{(1+i)^2} + \cdots + \frac{y_n^N}{(1+i)^{n-1}}\right) + \left(y_1^A + \frac{y_2^A}{1+i} + \cdots + \frac{y_n^A}{(1+i)^{n-1}}\right)$$

or

$$I_1 = I_1^N + I_1^A$$

It is now reasonable to assume that I_1^A, the present value of income from assets, is the value of the assets themselves; their market makes sure that this is approximately true. Call this value A, that is, $A \equiv I_1^A$. Using the consumption function derived from homothetic preferences, equation (20),

$$C_1 = \alpha_1 I_1, \tag{20}$$

we have

$$C_1 = \alpha_1 I_1^N + \alpha_1 A \tag{32}$$

Plotting this consumption function against present value of labor income I_1^N, we get Figure 11-35.

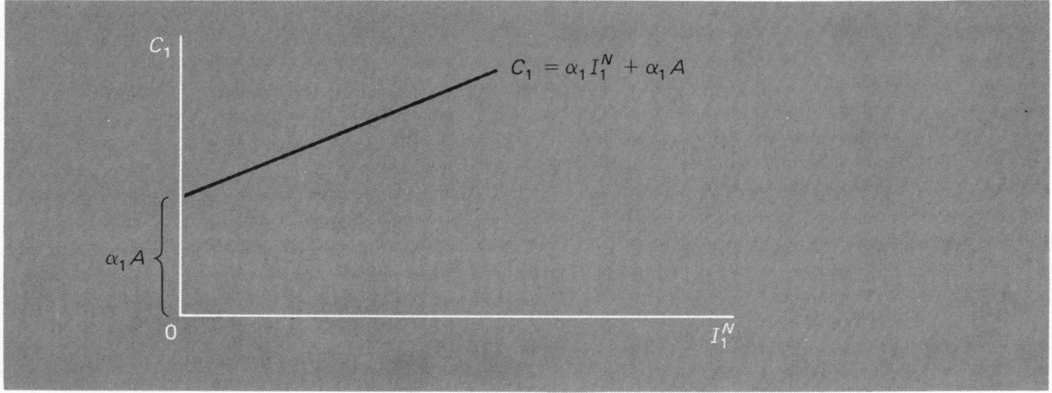

FIGURE 11-35

The slope of the curve in Figure 11-35 is α_1, which is the MPC out of present value of labor income. The intercept is positive, reflecting the fact that average individuals possess property a part of which (equal to the intercept, $\alpha_1 A$) they can consume even if they have zero I_1^N. Note that the higher the I_1^N, the lower the APC, and also that the MPC is always less than the APC. The curve in Figure 11-35 is the short-run consumption function, which, as time passes, shifts upward, keeping the same slope, α_1, because property, A, increases. This is shown in Figure 11-36.

The long-run consumption function is also plotted in the same graph. This is a straight line through the origin, implying that in the long run, consumption is a constant proportion of the present value of labor income. But to what is this constant proportion equal? To find out, we take equation (32) and rewrite it as

$$C = \alpha_1 I_1^N + \alpha_1 A = \alpha_1 I_1^N \cdot (1 + A/I_1^N)$$

or

$$C = \alpha_1 (1 + A/I_1^N) \cdot I_1^N$$

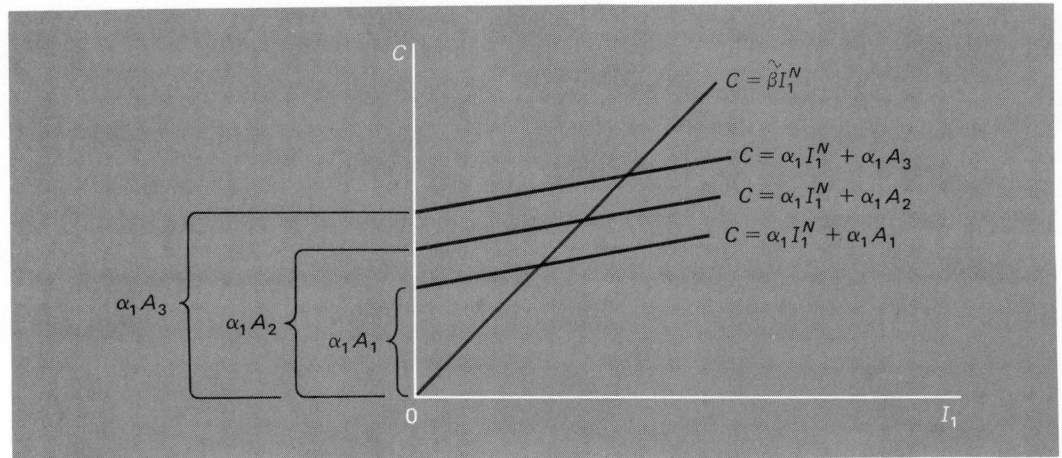

FIGURE 11-36

or

$$C = \tilde{\beta} \cdot I_1^N \tag{33}$$

where

$$\tilde{\beta} \equiv \alpha_1(1 + A/I_1^N) \tag{34}$$

Empirically, the theory is (and has been) confirmed by showing that the ratio of property to labor income, A/I_1^N, is constant over the long run. The constancy of the MPC = APC can also be shown by dividing both sides of (32) by current income, y_1:

$$\frac{C_1}{y_1} = \alpha_1 \frac{I_1^N}{y_1} + \alpha_1 \frac{A}{y_1} \tag{35}$$

It has been proved that the share of labor in current income, that is, I_1^N/y_1, and the property-output, or capital-output, ratio, A/y_1, remain constant over long periods of time. Thus the RHS of (35) is constant, implying that its LHS is also constant.

It is clear that the life-cycle approach has the distinct advantage that these magnitudes, cited above, are observable. Moreover, assets (property) are explicitly introduced in the consumption function.

EXPECTATIONS AND LIFE-CYCLE, PERMANENT INCOME HYPOTHESES

Since both the life-cycle and permanent income theories use I_1 as a starting point, it should be clear by now that expectations about the future play a crucial role. Expectations about the interest rate have already been introduced; specifically, the interest rate is expected to remain the same. The crucial magnitudes, however, seem to be $y_2, y_3, \cdots, y_n$. In the life-cycle model, only the expectations regarding the *labor component* of these values, $y_2^N, y_3^N, \cdots, y_n^N$ are of great importance; the asset markets roughly confirm expectations regarding property income.

Ando and Modigliani tie future labor incomes, $y_2^N, y_3^N, \cdots y_n^N$, to *present* labor income.[6] Moreover, they assume that when present labor income rises, expectations regarding future labor income are revised upward:

$$I_1^N - y_1^N = \delta(y_1^N) \quad \text{where} \quad (y_1^N)\uparrow \rightarrow \delta\uparrow$$

or

$$I_1^N = y_1^N + \delta(y_1^N) \equiv \Omega(y_1^N) \quad \text{where} \quad (\Delta\Omega/\Delta y_1^N) > 0$$

It follows that the present value of the labor income *stream* I_1 is an increasing function of *current* labor income, y_1^N. Substituting in (32), we get the short-run consumption function in terms of current labor income, y_1^N, and not I_1^N:

$$C = \alpha_1 I_1^N + \alpha_1 A$$

or

$$C = \alpha_1 \Omega\,(y_1^N) + \alpha_1 A$$

Now, assuming that $(\Delta\Omega/\Delta y_1^N)$ is fixed, we have

$$C = \hat{\alpha} \cdot y_1^N + \alpha_1 A \tag{36}$$

where

$$\hat{\alpha} = \alpha_1 \cdot (\Delta\Omega/\Delta y_1^N) \tag{37}$$

Of course, we can also derive the long-run consumption function by substituting into (33):

$$C = \tilde{\beta} \cdot I_1^N$$
$$= \tilde{\beta} \cdot \Omega(y_1^N)$$

Assuming that $(\Delta\Omega/\Delta y_1^N)$ is approximately a fixed number equal to μ, we have

$$C = \tilde{\beta} \cdot \mu y_1^N$$

[6] See Ando and Modigliani, "The 'Life Cycle' Hypothesis of Saving."

or

$$C = \hat{\beta} \cdot y_1^N \tag{38}$$

where

$$\hat{\beta} = \tilde{\beta} \cdot \mu \tag{39}$$

Figure 11-37 plots both the short-run and the long-run consumption functions against *current labor income,* y_1^N.

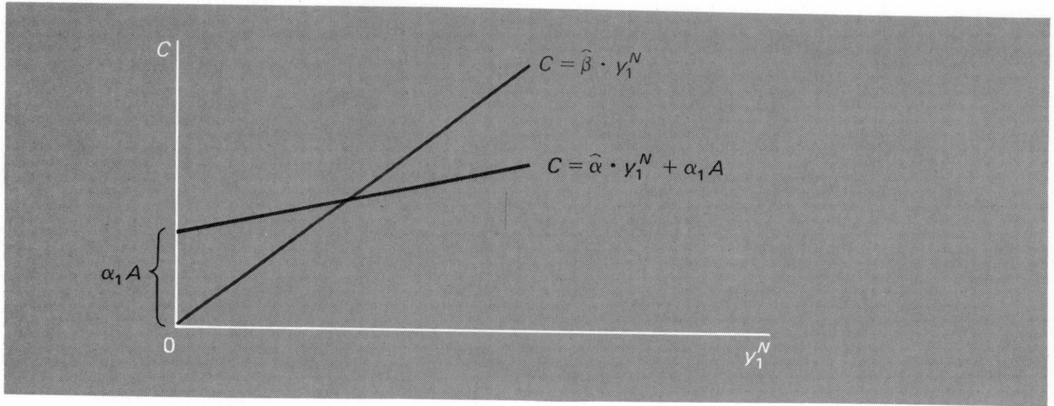

FIGURE 11-37

Turning now to Friedman's theory, it is also clear that "permanent income" is not observable, since it depends on expectations about the future. Here Friedman used a more sophisticated expectations formula than Modigliani did. (He was writing immediately after the introduction of this formula, the adaptive expectations one.) In particular, he assumed that the estimate of permanent income is constructed as a weighted average of observed past levels of the average individual's income.

The formula used is

$$Y^p = \sum_{i=0}^{\infty} \delta_i Y_{t-i} \tag{40}$$

where

$$\sum_{i=0}^{\infty} \delta_i = 1,$$

that is, the sum of the weights add up to 100 percent and the weight is decreasing as we move further into the past (i.e., the weight is exponentially decreasing with i). Here the subscript denotes the current time period, *not* transitory income.

First, we see that the expectations formula used by the life-cycle contributors

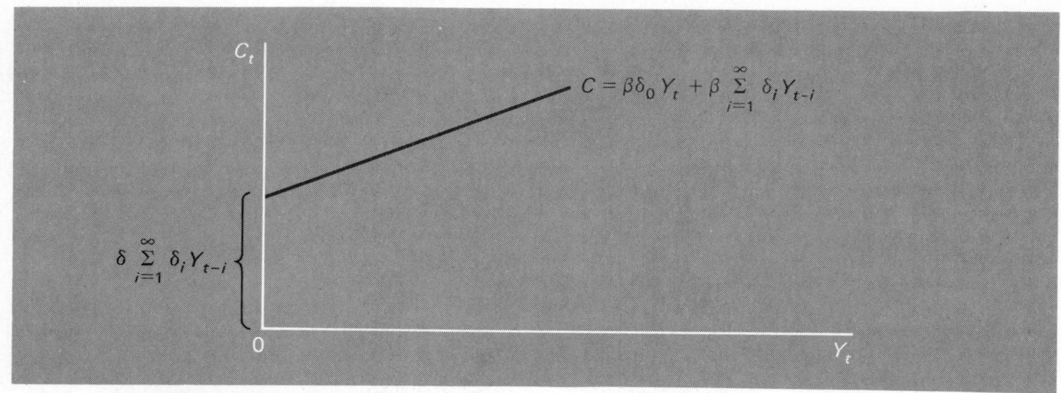

FIGURE 11-38

is a special case, a variation of the one used by Friedman. Modigliani and others assigned a weight only to Y_t (and, possibly, to a few other lagged earlier values) as compared with Friedman, who assigned weights to all previous values of Y.

Second, we see that the expectations formula (40) permits us to formally derive a short-run consumption function of the form $C = a + bY$ as in Figure 11-38. Using Friedman's equation (31),

$$C = \beta \cdot Y^p = \beta \sum_{i=0}^{\infty} \delta_i Y_{t-i} = \beta\delta_0 Y_t$$

$$+ \beta \sum_{i=1}^{\infty} \delta_i Y_{t-i} \qquad \text{by (40)}$$

or

$$C = bY_t + a$$

where

$$b = \beta\delta_0$$

$$a = \beta \sum_{i=1}^{\infty} \delta_i Y_{t-i}$$

Note that all the information embodied in a is given from the past.

HISTORICAL NOTE

The investigations into the exact shape of the consumption and savings functions began with Keynes himself, who volunteered the speculation that the consumption function, when plotted against current income, is of the form $C = bY + a$, that is, APC decreases with income "*especially* [*in*] *the case where we have short periods in view, as in the case of the so-called cyclical fluctuations.*"[7] Of course, this shape of the consumption function was neither necessary nor essential for his analysis, and he actually made little use of it.

At about the same time, the national income accounts made their initial appearance. Early econometric studies making use of these early data confirmed Keynes' conjecture. Using short time-series data, the derived consumption function was, in fact, in the predicted shape, which also appeared when derived from cross-section data. These early results convinced several economists that this was the actual consumption function, so much so that they were prepared to use it for forecasts. (It should be noted, however, that econometric knowledge was minimal at the time.) It was just such a consumption function—with current income the sole determinant of consumption and the APC decreasing with this income—that was used by several economists during World War II to predict that private consumption demand, after the war, would be too low. Of course, private consumption demand did not fall, indicating that something was amiss.

Concurrently, however, the father of national income accounts, Simon Kuznets, determined that although the cross-section and short time-series consumption functions are of the $C = bY + a$ form, over the long run (in fact, all the way back to 1869) the APC is fairly constant.[8]

By the late 1940s it was fairly obvious that the short-run consumption function has the property that MPC $<$ APC (from which it follows that APC falls with Y) but that, in the long run, the MPC is equal to APC (and is constant). The profession was therefore challenged to provide a theoretical explanation for these empirical results.

In 1949 James Duesenberry was among the first to attempt such an explanation with his *relative income hypothesis.*[9] According to this view, it is not so much the *absolute* but the *relative* current income that influences a household's consumption. The relative position that the household occupies in the distribution of income among all households is the determinant of consumption. While testing this hypothesis in 1951, James Tobin found that when *wealth* is included in the consumption function, the *absolute* income hypothesis is superior to the relative income hypothesis.[10] In effect, the early postwar econometricians failed in their predictions because they ignored wealth as an argument in the consumption function. Eventually the *life-cycle* and *permanent income* hypotheses further elaborated the concept of wealth.

---

[7] Keynes, *General Theory,* p. 97, italics added.

[8] Simon Kuznets, *National Product since 1869* (New York: National Bureau of Economic Research, 1946).

[9] James Duesenberry, *Income, Saving, and the Theory of Consumer Behavior* (Cambridge, Mass.: Harvard University Press, 1949).

[10] James Tobin, "Relative Income, Absolute Income and Saving," in *Money, Trade, and Economic Growth: Essays in Honor of J. H. Williams* (New York: Macmillan, 1951).

IV. EMPIRICAL EVIDENCE

In 1963 Daniel Suits summarized the state of knowledge concerning consumption behavior.[11] His major conclusions were as follows:

1. Consumption is related to long-run, as well as short-run, variables. Therefore the reaction of consumption does not appear to occur on a daily basis.
2. Most studies agree that an additional dollar of disposable personal income results in about sixty-five cents of additional consumption expenditures, with the remaining thirty-five cents going to savings.
3. Consumption spending is more autonomous than the early theories assumed. Access to consumer credit and the possibility of working longer hours or of taking on secondary employment reduce the effect of the income constraint.
4. Variables such as liquidity and the availability of consumer credit have important effects on consumption. The effects of monetary policy on expenditure come primarily through these channels, rather than directly through interest rates.
5. The responsiveness of consumer expenditures is asymmetrical. The effect of an increase in income is, in general, not the same as that of a decrease in income.

Most early studies of the consumption function used a form that Keynes had introduced and had used as an example:

$$C_t = a + bY_t$$

This formula has been referred to as the income-constrained consumption function, or the *absolute income hypothesis* (since it posits current consumption as some constant fraction of current income). Estimates of this equation were based on Kuznets' empirical work, and they generally found that $a > 0$ (i.e., a positive level of current consumption even if current income is zero); a short-run marginal propensity to consume (i.e., b, of about 0.7); and a long-run marginal propensity to consume (i.e., β, of about 0.9). The absolute income hypothesis implied that consumption follows the same time pattern as does income. But, as we have seen earlier, the evidence suggested some conflict between the long-run and the short-run findings.

The work that followed consisted primarily of the theoretical development and empirical testing of various hypotheses designed to reconcile the short-run and long-run empirical findings. First, we shall briefly mention Duesenberry's relative income hypothesis and then move on to consider the permanent income and life-cycle theories of consumption behavior.

---

[11] Daniel B. Suits, "The Determinants of Consumer Expenditure: A Review of Present Knowledge," in Commission on Money and Credit, *Impacts of Monetary Policy* (Englewood Cliffs, N.J.: Prentice-Hall, Inc., 1963).

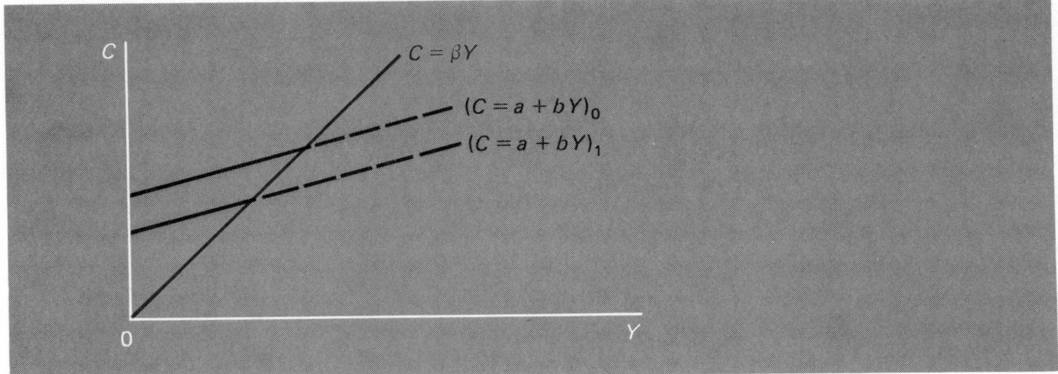

FIGURE 11-39

The *relative income hypothesis,* introduced by Duesenberry,[12] accepts that long-run behavior can be well represented by the traditional consumption function:

$$C_t = a + bY_t$$

But short-run behavior involves some rigidities or slowness of adjustment of consumption to changes in income. Duesenberry explained these rigidities in terms of consumption habits that introduce a "ratchet" effect, illustrated in Figure 11-39. For example, a family may cling to the consumption level to which it is accustomed despite a short-run decline in income; or a family whose income is suddenly increased may be slow to adjust its consumption pattern. Therefore the result is a short-run MPC that is smaller than the long-run MPC. Duesenberry attempted to capture this phenomenon by estimating the following equation:

$$\frac{C_t}{Y_t} = 1.20 - 0.25\frac{Y_t}{Y_{max}}$$

where Y_{max} is the highest level of income attained in the past. So the long-run MPC (when $Y_t = Y_{max}$) is approximately 0.95; and the short-run MPC becomes larger (smaller) as Y_t becomes smaller (larger) relative to Y_{max}.

The *permanent income theory* proposed by Milton Friedman asserts that individuals try to consume the maximum amount possible while leaving their level of wealth unchanged. Clearly, such behavior requires that individuals form some notion of their expected future, or permanent, income. Most empirical studies assume that permanent income is a geometrically declining distributed lag of current and past income, since these quantities are directly observable.

$$Y^p = \gamma Y_t + \gamma(1-\gamma)Y_{t-1} + \gamma(1-\gamma)^2 Y_{t-2} + \cdot\cdot\cdot$$

[12] Duesenberry, *Income, Saving, and the Theory of Consumer Behavior.*

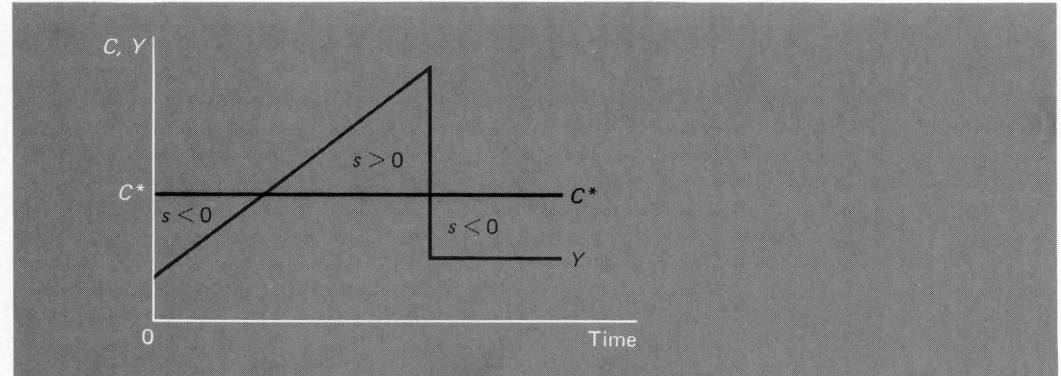

FIGURE 11-40

In practice, the weights attached to past values of income die out, so that only the past three to five years are empirically important.

In his own extensive empirical work on the consumption function, Friedman finds the results to be consistent with the permanent income hypothesis. In particular, he finds that

$$C^p = 0.88\ Y^p,$$

so that the ratio of aggregate consumption to aggregate permanent income for the United States is about 0.88. This measure, according to Friedman's estimates, has been roughly constant for the past half-century.[13]

The other major theory of the determination of consumption behavior is the *life-cycle hypothesis,* associated primarily with the work of Ando and Modigliani.[14] According to this theory, individuals maximize utility over their life span, which involves saving and dissaving in order to smooth consumption over time, as illustrated in Figure 11-40. The implication of this maximization is that consumption in each period depends not only on income in that period but also on income (or expected income) in all periods. The intertemporal constraint requires that the present value of the income stream be equal to the present value of the consumption stream.

The early test of this hypothesis by Ando and Modigliani used a simplifying assumption, that expected future labor income will be proportional to current labor income. Using our notation, we can summarize their results:

$$C_t = 0.7\mathbf{I}_t^N + 0.06A_t$$

Although later studies have relaxed the simplifying assumption and made expected labor income a function of both current and recent past incomes, the coefficient estimates remain basically unchanged.

---

[13] See Friedman, *Theory of the Consumption Function,* p. 228.

[14] Ando and Modigliani, "The 'Life Cycle' Hypothesis of Saving."

QUESTIONS

1. What are relative prices?
   a. Express the price of current consumption in terms of the interest rate.
   b. Express the price of future consumption in terms of the interest rate.
2. Prove that an increase in current income increases both consumption and savings. What additional results are known if preferences are assumed to be homothetic?
3. Prove that an increase in future income increases consumption and decreases savings.
4. How does the effect of interest rate changes on consumption and savings differ for net borrowers and net lenders?
5. What is the distinction between relative costs and relative prices? What relationship between the two must hold at the profit-maximizing point?
6. What is permanent income?
7. How does the permanent income hypothesis explain the empirical finding that the consumption function has a positive rather than a zero intercept?
8. Compare the assumptions and implications of the life-cycle hypothesis with those of the permanent income hypothesis.
9. Suppose that the average household is endowed with 500 bushels of today's corn and zero bushels of tomorrow's corn. If preferences between present and future corn are homothetic and of the form $C_2/C_1 = .5(1 + i)$, find the exact form of the savings curve both with respect to current income and with respect to the interest rate. What are the APC and MPC today's corn?
10. Comment: "With fixed endowment, if an increase in i increases current consumption, then current consumption must be an inferior good."
11. Advocates of "supply-side" economics recommend a reduction of tax rates on interest so that the resultant increase in the "after tax" interest rate may stimulate savings and, hence, growth. Construct an arithmetical example which supports this view and another which rejects it.
12. Using the permanent income hypothesis, examine the effects on consumption demand of:
    a. a temporary 10 percent tax reduction
    b. a permanent 10 percent tax cut in the first year, with a promise for two further such cuts in the two succeeding years
    c. a preannounced permanent tax cut of 10 percent for each of three years

REFERENCES

ANDO, ALBERT, and FRANCO MODIGLIANI, "The 'Life Cycle' Hypothesis of Saving: Aggregate Implications and Tests," *American Economic Review,* March 1963.

DUESENBERRY, JAMES S., *Income, Saving, and the Theory of Consumer Behavior.* Cambridge, Mass.: Harvard University Press, 1949.

FISHER, IRVING, *Theory of Interest.* New York: Macmillan, 1930.

FRIEDMAN, MILTON, *A Theory of the Consumption Function.* Princeton, N.J.: Princeton University Press, 1957.

KEYNES, J. M., *The General Theory of Employment, Interest and Money,* Chaps. 8–10. New York: Harcourt, Brace & Co., 1936.

KUZNETS, SIMON, "National Product since 1869." New York: National Bureau of Economic Research, 1946.

MALINUAND, E., *Lectures on Microeconomic Theory,* Chap. 10. Amsterdam: North-Holland Press, 1972.

MODIGLIANI, FRANCO, and RICHARD BRUMBERG, "A Utility Analysis and the Consumption Function: An Interpretation of Cross-Section Data," in *Post-Keynesian Economics,* ed. K. Kurihara. New Brunswick, N.J.: Rutgers University Press, 1954.

RAMSEY, FRANK P., "A Mathematical Theory of Saving," *Economic Journal,* 1928.

TOBIN, JAMES, "Relative Income, Absolute Income, and Saving," *Money, Trade, and Economic Growth: Essays in Honor of John H. Williams.* New York: Macmillan, 1951.

The Investment function

12

In this chapter we examine several theories that yield the investment function. In Section I we employ the basic Fisherian two-period production model as a convenient vehicle for illustrating all the existing approaches to deriving the investment function—the *present value* approach, the *marginal efficiency of investment* approach, and the approaches based on the *increasing cost* of investment. In Section II the present value criterion is used at an elementary level in order to derive the investment function. Section III derives the investment function from the marginal efficiency of investment viewpoint, and it highlights basic shortcomings of this approach as well as that of the preceding section. Section IV highlights the importance of increasing cost of investing at the firm level and actually derives investment demand based on increasing subjective costs. This utilizes Kalecki's *principle of increasing risk* and proceeds to motivate the modern mathematical theories of increasing adjustment costs. Section V examines two approaches that view investment as a supply function and not as a demand function based on demand for capital by firms independent of households. The first of these relies almost exclusively on the implications of efficient production, namely, factor price equalization, the Stolper-Samuelson theorem, and the Rybczynski theorem, while the second embeds the two-sector model in a stock-flow formulation. Section VI examines the empirical evidence, with an emphasis on Jorgenson's work.

I. THE IMPLICATIONS OF THE FISHERIAN MODEL[1]

With the intertemporal production possibility curve (IPPC) and the method used to derive the economy's endowment point—both introduced in the chapter on consumption—we shall begin our exploration of the theory of investment.

It is assumed, as before, that the (average) firm has the ability to transform present output (today's corn) into future output (tomorrow's corn) and vice versa, at increasing cost, as shown in Figure 12-1. Future output, y_2, is used as a *proxy* for investment today, that is, for the *addition* to the economy's capital stock for the following reason: If all other resources are held fixed, the only way to produce more output tomorrow is to have more capital tomorrow, that is, by *investing today.* Thus there is a one-to-one relationship between future output, y_2, and investment today. The assumed constancy of all other factors is also responsible for the convexity of the IPPC: With a constant returns-to-scale technology and with all other factors constant, an increase in capital will increase output, but not by the same proportion. The increase in future output will be proportionately less than the increase in capital. Thus, future output is produced at increasing cost.

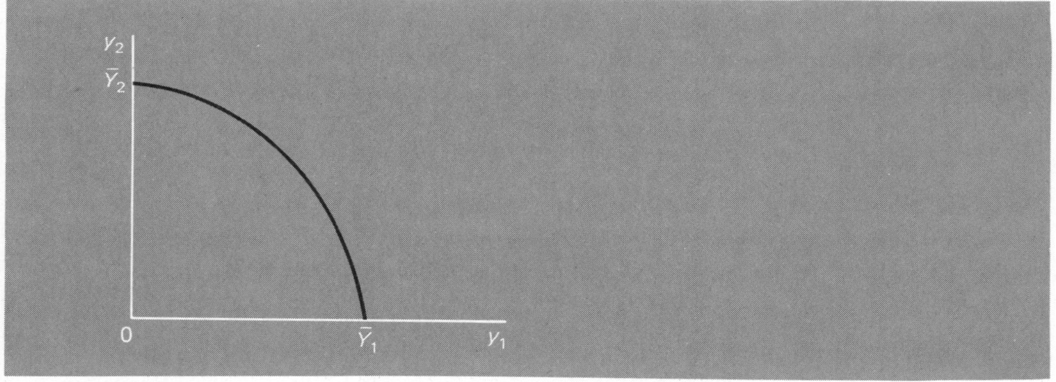

FIGURE 12-1

We already know that the profit-maximizing firm will produce that combination (y_1,y_2) which equates the relative price and relative (opportunity) costs of the respective goods. The relative prices are given by the market. In particular, the relative price of today's output, y_1, is $(1 + i)$ units of y_2, and the relative price of tomorrow's output is $1/(1 + i)$ units of y_1, where i is the rate of interest. In Figure 12-2, when the interest rate is equal to i_0, the firm will produce at point E_0, that is, y_1^0 units of today's output and y_2^0 units of tomorrow's output. When the interest rate is higher, at i_1, profit is maximized if the firm produces at E_1. In other words, the firm produces less y_2, namely, $y_2^1 < y_2^0$, and more y_1, that is, $y_1^1 > y_1^0$. The reason is obvious; the increase in the interest rate increases the relative price of y_1, making it possible to

[1] See Irving Fisher, *Theory of Interest* (New York: Macmillan, 1930).

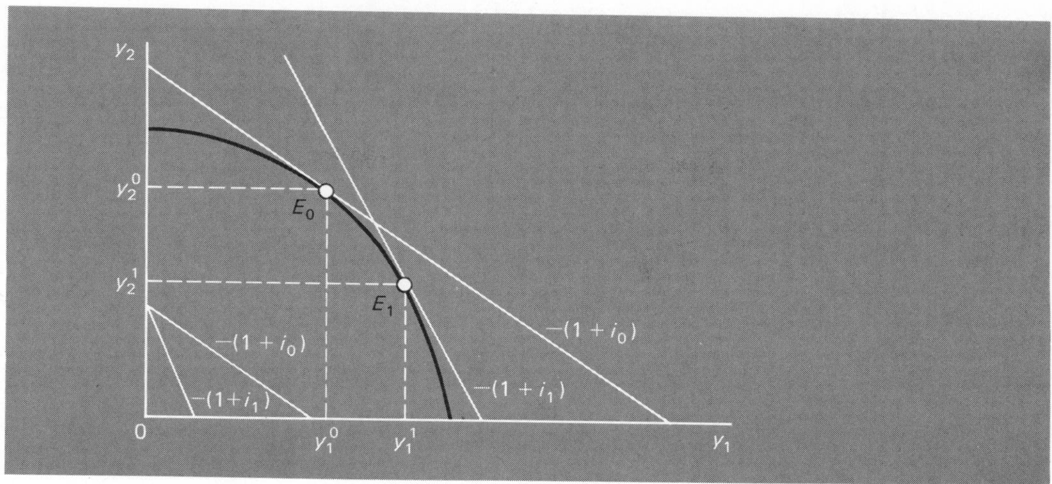

FIGURE 12-2

cover the higher cost that an increase in the production of y_1 requires. On the other hand, the increase in i lowers the relative price, $1/(1 + i)$, of y_2, which can no longer cover the relative cost. The production of y_2 will have to be reduced, thus lowering its relative cost until it is covered by the reduced relative price $1/(1 + i)$, as depicted by the upward-sloping supply curve of y_2 with respect to its price, $1/(1 + i)$, (= costs), in Figure 12-3.

The result of the above analysis is that an increase in the interest rate *lowers* future output, a result we can depict by the curve in Figure 12-4. But according to the stipulations of our analysis, an increase in future output, y_2, can come about only if there is an *increase* in the capital stock, thereby establishing a negative relation between the interest rate and the increase in the capital stock, ΔK. The latter, of course, is called investment, I. And in Figure 12-5 we draw the investment schedule, showing this negative relation between the interest rate and investment.

The (Fisherian) two-period analysis has just given us a primitive, yet important, theory of investment. But even more important is the observation that almost all modern (and more definitive) theories of investment can be derived as extensions

FIGURE 12-3

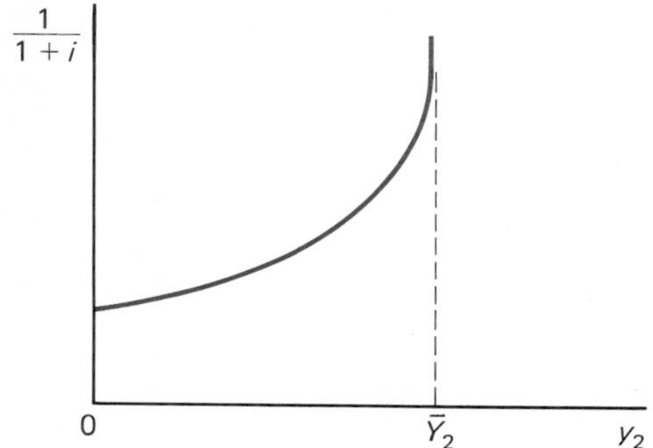

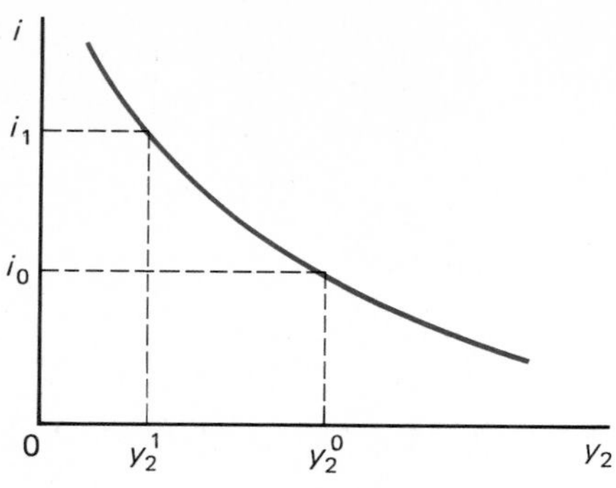

FIGURE 12-4

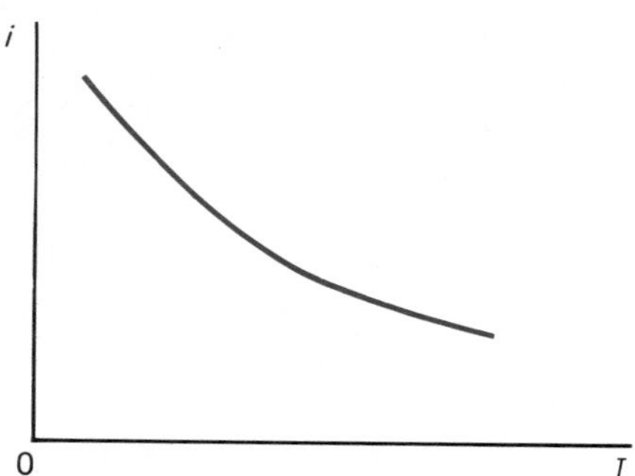

FIGURE 12-5

of either the analysis itself or the spirit of the analysis. Here we shall briefly examine how these modern theories are related to the one just sketched, and in the sections that follow, we shall examine these theories in greater detail.

First, we should note that the spirit of this analysis is that the given resources of an economy can produce either goods that can be consumed today, y_1, or goods that can be consumed tomorrow, y_2, or combinations of both. But since more goods tomorrow can be produced only if we add to the capital stock today (i.e., if we invest), the spirit of the analysis implies that the given resources can produce either consumption goods (this is the true meaning of y_1) or investment (capital) goods (this is the true meaning of y_2). It is not surprising, then, that some economists analyzed the problem directly by examining a two-sector (consumption goods and investment goods) model. The given resources and technology of the economy provide us with the transformation curve, giving all the combinations of consumption and investment goods that can be produced, as in Figure 12-6. This approach is discussed in detail in Section V.

Next we observe that in order to maximize its profits, the firm produces a "basket" whose value is maximized, whether it is measured in terms of future goods or present goods. In Figure 12-7, when the interest rate is i_0, point *E* yields the highest value. It is *OB* units in terms of future goods and *OA* in terms of today's goods. Of course, *OA* is the *present value* of basket *E*. Note that if we maximize the one value, we also maximize the other. Economists naturally concentrated on

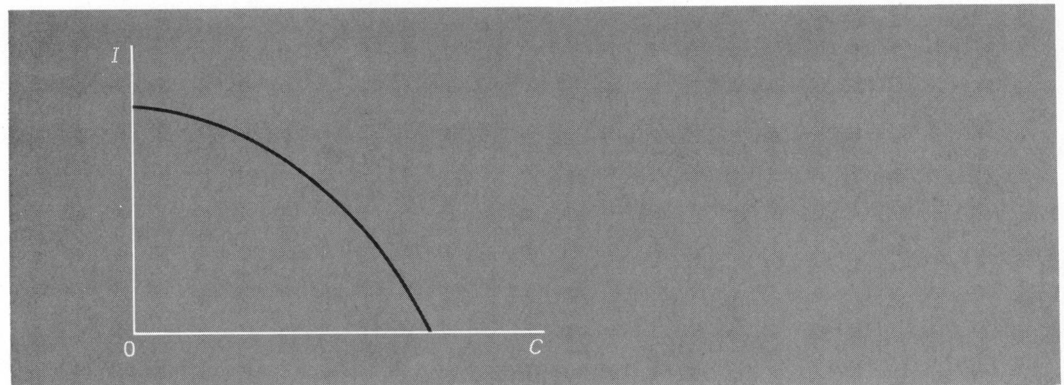

FIGURE 12-6

the *maximization of the present value.* In this two-period model, the present value, *PV,* of basket $(\bar{y}_1, \bar{y}_2)$ is

$$PV = \bar{y}_1 + \frac{1}{1+i} \cdot \bar{y}_2$$

This can be generalized, of course, for many periods. The present value criterion is analyzed in Section II.

Finally, we observe that the profit-maximizing point (such as E of Figure 12-7) has the following property: For each good, the relative price is equal to the opportunity (relative) cost. Let us now concentrate on present output, y_1, whose relative price is $(1 + i)$, that is, the units of future output, y_2, that we get if we *give up* one unit of present output. But what is the opportunity cost of y_1?

FIGURE 12-7

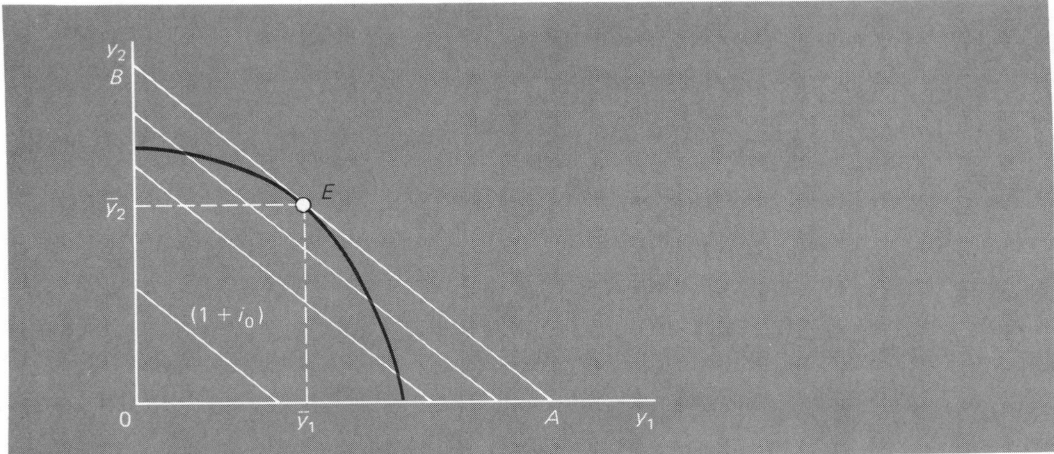

In this setting we give up one unit of y_1 in order to increase our capital. Thus, in the next period we shall have the remainder of this unit of capital, $(1 - \delta)$, plus whatever this extra unit of capital can produce, that is, the marginal product of capital, MP_K (where δ is the rate of depreciation). Thus, if we avoid consuming one unit of present output in order to add it to our capital stock, in the future we shall get $[(1 - \delta) + MP_K]$ units of future output. It follows, then, that for y_1, relative-price-equals-opportunity-cost can be expressed by the following equality:

$$\text{Relative price} = (1 + i) = (1 - \delta) + MP_K = \text{Opportunity cost}$$

Subtracting unity from both sides, we have

$$i = MP_K - \delta \tag{1}$$

that is, the profit-maximizing addition to capital (investment) is carried to the point where the net marginal product is equal to the (assumed) market rate of interest.

Because this net marginal product of the firm is derived from within the firm, it is sometimes called the *internal rate of return.* More often, it is called the *marginal efficiency of investment,* MEI. Thus we have the criterion that investment is carried to the point where the MEI is made equal to the interest rate. This criterion will be examined in Section III. Here we shall make only two additional points. First, that the criterion captured by equation (1) is broad enough to generate several cases. For example, if capital is indestructible (i.e., $\delta \equiv 0$), the marginal product of capital and the interest rate coincide. But, at the other extreme, if capital lasts only one period and then disappears, the net marginal product of capital is equal to $MP_K - 1$, and this, in turn, is equal to the interest rate. The second point involves critical extensions of this criterion to be undertaken in Section IV, where we shall see that, in general, the condition is, as here, that $i =$ MEI, but that the MEI is less than the net marginal product, that is, MEI $< MP_K - \delta$. And that, generally, $i < MP_K - \delta$.

II. THE PRESENT VALUE CRITERION

In Section I we saw that in an intertemporal setting, maximizing profits is equivalent to maximizing the present value of all the future net receipts that will arise from the decision under consideration. Let us now see how the present value criterion has been applied to investment decisions.

Suppose that a firm is considering whether it is worth undertaking an investment project, such as building a new factory. Assume that the life of the factory is $(n + 1)$ years and its cost is P_I units of today's output. The firm should first estimate the net return in each of the periods of the project's life. Of course, we must assume that to operate the factory, the firm must hire labor and buy raw materials from which to produce finished goods. The finished goods will be sold at the price prevailing in each of the periods. From these receipts, then, we subtract the cost of labor and raw materials. We denote *net* receipts in period j by R_j, where j assumes the values 0, 1, 2, 3, . . . , n. Thus the investment project gives rise to the following stream of net receipts:

$$R_0, R_1, R_2, \ldots, R_n$$

The value of this stream, in units of goods in period 0, is what we call the present value, PV:

$$\text{PV} = R_0 + \frac{R_1}{1+i} + \frac{R_2}{(1+i)^2} + \ldots + \frac{R_n}{(1+i)^n}$$

This formula is therefore the generalization of the one dealing with two periods. Note that if we had only two periods, our formula would be reduced to the familiar one:

$$\text{PV} = R_0 + \frac{R_1}{1+i}$$

And, furthermore, that *the present value criterion states that if the PV is greater than the cost, P_I, of buying the investment good, the project is worth undertaking.*

We can now rank all candidate investment projects according to their PV, as in Figure 12-8a. We can approximate this information by a smooth curve, as in Figure 12-8b.

Without any loss of generality, we rank (according to their PV) all projects costing P_I. It is clear from Figure 12-9 that A is the last investment project worth undertaking. For project A, P_I = PV. It is clear from the formula of PV that the higher the interest rate, i, by which we discount the stream of future net receipts, the lower the PV of every investment project will be. Thus, when we draw the PV curve, we should specify the interest rate used in our calculations. For example, in Figure 12-10 the PV ($i = i_0$) curve uses i_0 for discounting. When i is greater, say i_1,

FIGURE 12-8

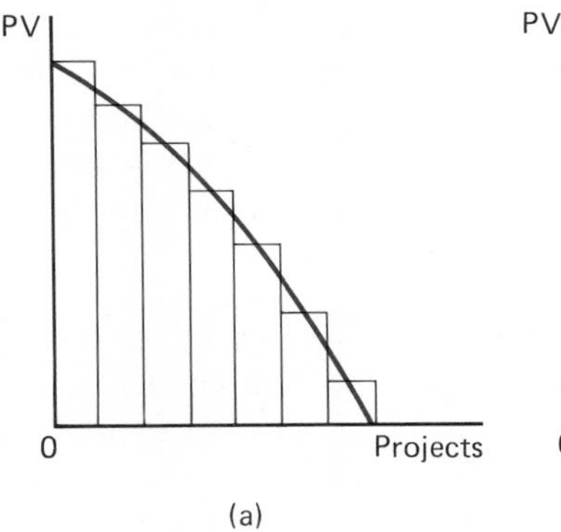

(a)

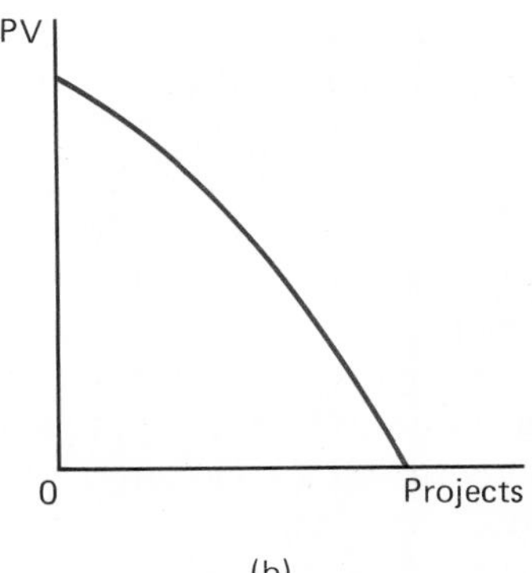

(b)

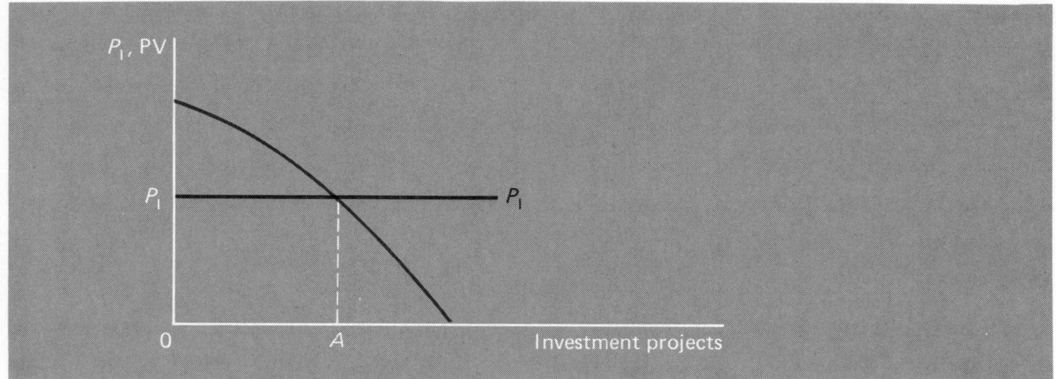

FIGURE 12-9

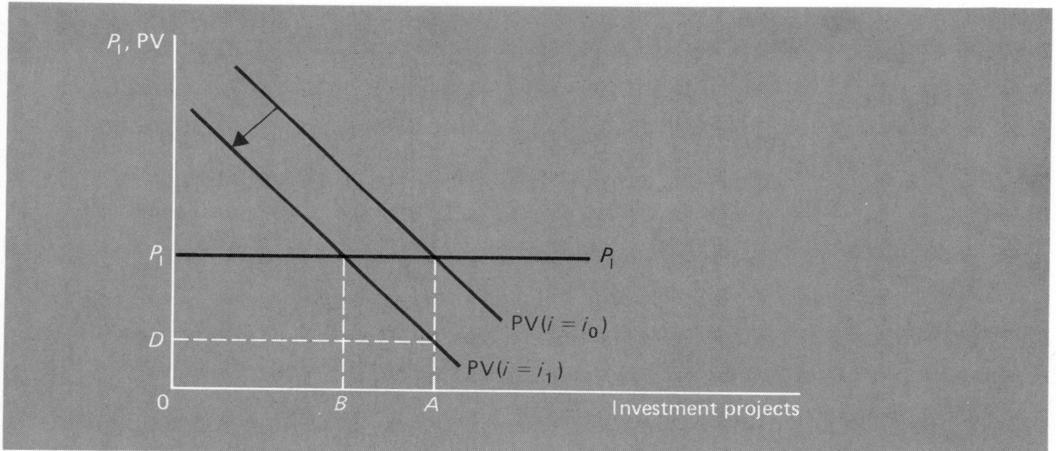

FIGURE 12-10

the present value of *each* project falls, and thus the PV($i = i_1$) curve is lower than the PV($i = i_0$) curve. From this it immediately follows that the higher interest rate, i_1, makes some hitherto worthwhile projects unprofitable. Note, in particular, that the investment project labeled *A* is not profitable any more; its PV is equal to *OD,* while its cost is OP_I. The same is true of all projects between *B* and *A*. Since some projects become unprofitable and will never be undertaken when the interest rate rises, economists state that the higher the interest rate, the lower the investment demand.

Now, if the interest rate remains the same but one or more *R*'s increase, the PV curve will shift to the right; each project will achieve a higher PV, as shown in Figure 12-11. The higher *R*'s increased the PVs so that all projects between *F* and *G* become profitable. Higher *R*'s are associated with increased economic activity, which is usually represented by higher income or (equivalently) higher employment (per unit of capital).

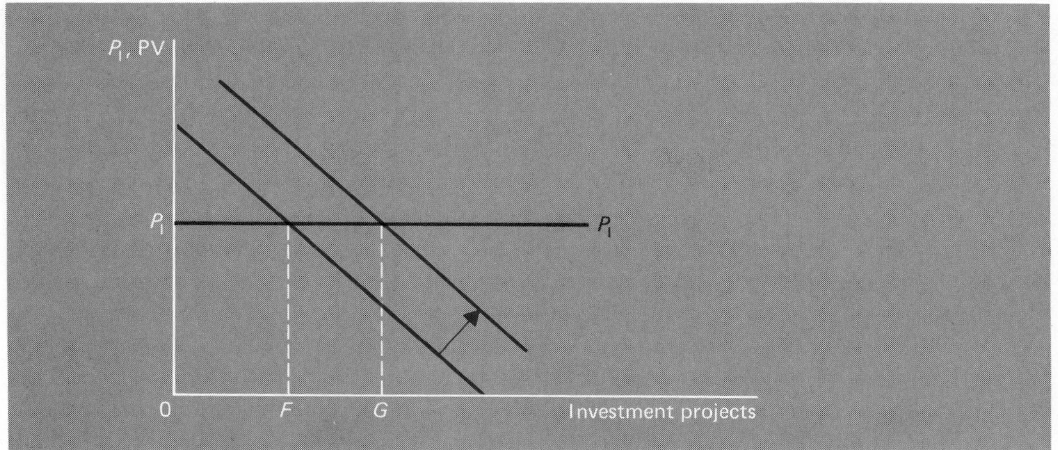

FIGURE 12-11

We can summarize our results by saying that investment, *I*, is a decreasing function of the interest rate and an increasing function of income or employment:

$$I = I(i, Y), \text{ with } i\uparrow \rightarrow I\downarrow \text{ (i.e., } \frac{\Delta I}{\Delta i} < 0)$$

$$\text{and } Y\uparrow \rightarrow I\uparrow \text{ (i.e., } \frac{\Delta I}{\Delta Y} > 0)$$

or

$$I = I(i, x), \text{ with } i\uparrow \rightarrow I\downarrow \text{ (i.e., } \frac{\Delta I}{\Delta i} < 0)$$

$$\text{and } x\uparrow \rightarrow I\uparrow \text{ (i.e., } \frac{\Delta I}{\Delta x} > 0)$$

III. THE MARGINAL EFFICIENCY OF INVESTMENT

In the preceding section we saw that the present value criterion stipulates the following: *Using the market rate of interest as the discount rate,* find the present value of the stream $R_0, R_1, R_2, \ldots, R_n$. *And if this PV is greater than the market price of the investment project, P_I, undertake the investment project.* Profit maximization will then induce the firm to invest up to the point where the PV of the marginal project is equal to its market price, P_I.

In Section I we briefly introduced the criterion by which investment is undertaken up to the point where the internal rate of return of the project is equal to the market rate of interest. Let us now examine this criterion, in our multiperiod setting, which stipulates the following: *Find the discount rate, d, that makes the PV of the stream $R_0, R_1, R_2, \ldots, R_n$ exactly equal to the market price of the project, P_I,* that is, find d such that

$$PV \equiv R_0 + \frac{R_1}{1+d} + \frac{R_2}{(1+d)^2} + \ldots + \frac{R_n}{(1+d)^n} = P_I$$

(I.e., solve the above equation for its only unknown, d.) *If the solved-for d is greater than or equal to the market rate of interest, i, then buy the investment good.* Profit maximization will push the firm to the margin where the last undertaken project has d equal to i. Of course, this d is the *internal rate of return* of the investment project. Keynes named it the marginal efficiency of capital, but we shall call it the *marginal efficiency of investment* (MEI).

As earlier, we can rank all prospective investment projects according to their profitability, but this time using the MEI as the criterion. The curve in Figure 12-12 describes this ranking. If the interest rate is equal to i_0, all projects from zero to I_0 will be undertaken, the last one being I_0. If the interest rate falls to i_1, all projects between I_0 and I_1 will *also* be undertaken. (For this reason, it is agreed that investment demand increases when the interest rate falls.) If any or all net receipts, R_j, increase (because, say, of brisker economic activity), the MEI of every project increases, and thus the curve shifts to the right. This implies that for the same interest rate, more investment projects will be undertaken than before. For example, in Figure 12-13, with the same interest rate i_0, we stop at project I_0' as opposed to I_0. Similarly, if the interest rate is equal to i_1, we stop at project I_1'. (It is agreed, therefore, that the higher the economic activity [i.e., the higher the income, Y, or the employment/capital ratio, x], the higher the investment demand.)

We have seen that the MEI criterion yielded the same results as the PV criterion, namely, that a fall in the interest rate makes some investment projects, previously unprofitable, now profitable. The same result occurs when there is a rise in the level of economic activity, represented by either the level of income, Y, or the employment/capital ratio x. These results are usually summarized as before: Invest-

FIGURE 12-12

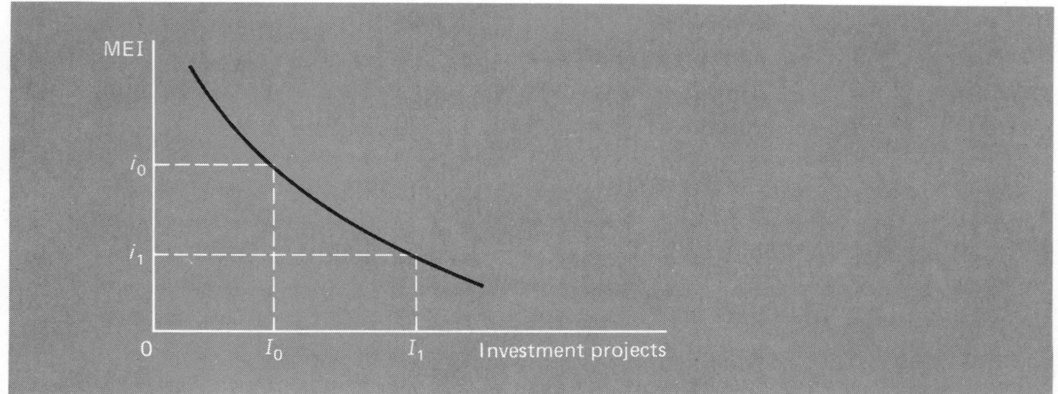

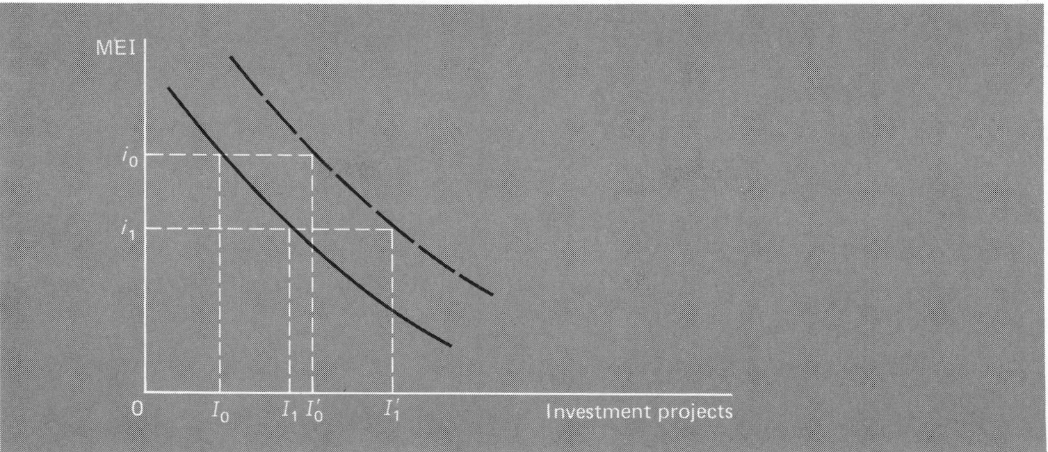

FIGURE 12-13

ment I is a decreasing function of the interest rate i and an increasing function of x. Symbolically:

$$I = I(i,x), \quad \text{with} \quad \frac{\Delta I}{\Delta i} < 0, \frac{\Delta I}{\Delta x} > 0$$

Our analysis has been very informal, and its conclusions, using the PV and MEI criteria, are meant to be merely suggestive; they provide a motivation for a theory of investment—but only that. We have yet to prove whether *there is* an investment function and whether it is of the form stipulated above. We shall see below that the interpretation of the preceding results, namely, that they provide an investment function, has been hasty. To see this, let us now take a critical look at our results, concentrating only on those derived via the MEI criterion.

First, investment will be carried to the point where its MEI is equal to the (existing) interest rate, i, and, thereby, allowing MEI and interest rate, i, to be used interchangeably. It follows that the relation between the interest rate and the amount of investment is exactly that which exists between the MEI and the amount of investment. It is clear, then, that if we want to establish a negative relation between the level of investment and the interest rate, we must prove a negative relation between investment and the MEI.

Second, inspection of the formula used in the derivation of the MEI reveals that a rise in the price of the investment goods lowers the MEI. Similarly, a fall in the "prospective yield," R_0, R_1, . . . , R_n, again lowers the MEI. Thus, if we can establish a negative relation between prospective yield and the amount of investment and/or a positive relation between the price of investment goods and the amount of investment, we can also establish that the MEI is a decreasing function of the amount of investment (from which it would follow that there is a negative relation between the amount of investment and the interest rate). This was the approach followed by Keynes, who examined directly the investment function for the *entire economy* rather than for a *single firm.* In the words of Keynes, "the marginal efficiency of . . . capital will diminish as the investment in it is increased, partly because the prospective yield will fall as the supply of capital is increased, and partly because, as a rule, pressure on the facilities for producing . . . capital will cause its supply price to increase."[2]

According to Keynes, the price of investment goods rises because they are produced at increasing costs. Obviously, he envisions an economy with consumption and investment goods produced in separate industries by distinct technologies, as shown in Figure 12-14a. The cost, and thus the price of the investment goods, in terms of the consumption goods, increase when the production of investment goods increases, as shown in Figure 12-14b. Note that if we have a one-sector economy whose output can be used either for consumption or for investment purposes (as depicted in Figure 12-15a), the cost of investment goods will be constant, as shown in Figure 12-15b. In such a case, then, the falling MEI cannot be attributed to the rising supply price of investment goods; it can be attributed only to falling prospective yield.

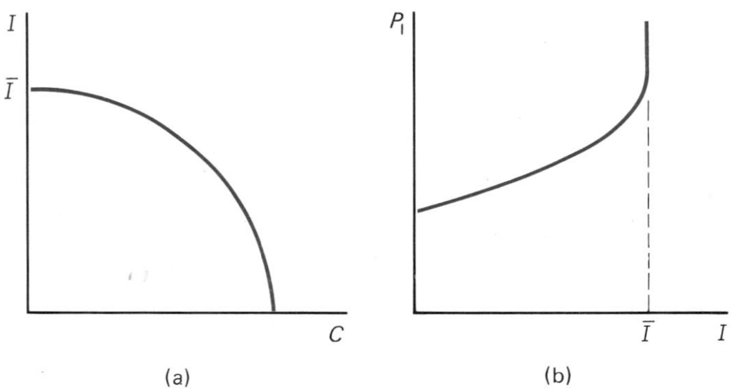

FIGURE 12-14

Keynes attributed the falling prospective yield to entrepreneurial expectations, to which he devoted a most impressive chapter (Chapter 12). Unfortunately, to date, no formal derivation of the investment function has successfully incorporated expectations, and we shall not attempt one here.

It is clear that if entrepreneurial expectations are assumed away, and if output can be transformed into investment, either without cost or at fixed cost, the MEI schedule is not downward sloping but rather horizontal at the current rate of profit, *r*, as shown in Figure 12-16. In such a case, however, there are two problems. First, we have indeterminancy of the level of investment; and, second, a fall, say, in the interest rate would prompt an infinite increase in investment demand. This latter characteristic, however, cannot be supported by the facts. In the real world, a fall in the interest rate increases investment, but not at an infinite rate. For these reasons

[2] See J. M. Keynes, *The General Theory of Employment, Interest and Money* (New York: Harcourt, Brace & Co., 1936), p. 136.

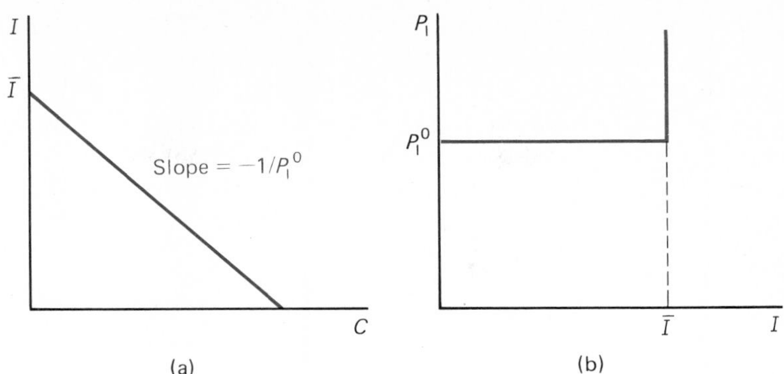

FIGURE 12-15

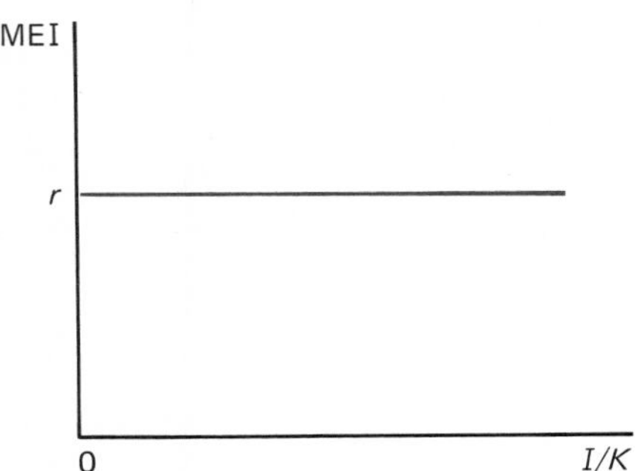

FIGURE 12-16

the literature of the last few years has concentrated its efforts on the derivation of the investment function under the assumption of increasing cost of investment goods.

There are two basic approaches. The first derives the investment function at the firm level. The second approach is similar to Keynes', for it derives the investment function directly at the industry level or the entire economy level. However, it differs from Keynes' approach because it considers the investment function a *supply* function of investment goods and not a *demand* function based on the demand for new capital by firms, independently from households. In this aspect it is the first approach that is similar to that of Keynes. In the following section we examine the first approach, and in Section V we examine the second.

IV. INCREASING COSTS AT THE FIRM LEVEL

Let us examine a firm that is a price taker in everything it buys and in everything it sells. Using the formula from which we derive the MEI,

$$R_0 + \frac{R_1}{1+d} + \ldots + \frac{R_n}{(1+d)^n} = P_I$$

(where P_I denotes the price of investment goods), it is clear immediately that *d*, the MEI, is independent of the level of investment that the firm undertakes. And the reasons are simple.

First, if the firm is a price taker, the price it pays for buying the investment good cannot be influenced by the number of investment goods that the firm purchases, regardless of whether the investment goods industry operates at increasing or constant costs.

Second, each period's net profit, *R*, is also independent of the size of investment. Recall that each *R* is of the form

$$R = py - wl$$

where *y* is the output of the project, *p* is the output's price, *l* is the firm's demand for inputs (labor, raw materials, etc.), and *w* is the price of the input. But if the firm is truly a price taker, neither the price it charges for its product, *p*, nor the price it is charged for inputs, *w*, will be influenced by the quantities. Moreover, because of constant returns to scale, if the number of investment goods purchased is, say, doubled, the units of output, *y*, as well as the inputs, *l*, will double. Thus net receipts will double—from which it follows that the rate of return, *d, per investment good,* will remain the same. Thus the MEI will be the same whether the firm buys one, two, or a hundred units of the investment good. This is shown in Figure 12-17.

It is clear that if the market rate of interest is equal to i_0, the firm's investment demand is zero. On the other hand, if the interest rate is even slightly less than the fixed MEI, such as i_1, demand is infinitely high. But if the interest rate is equal to the MEI, the actual level of investment demand will be indeterminate. On reflection, this is a confirmation of a standard result in the theory of the firm, namely, that with constant returns to scale, the *size* and number of firms is indeterminate. Furthermore, this result is consistent with a basic proposition regarding portfolio behavior: With bonds and capital considered perfect substitutes, their returns should be equal if both are to be held.

The indeterminancy of investment demand by a price-taking firm operating under constant returns to scale was noticed by Michael Kalecki as early as 1937.[3] Had he been willing to move outside the realm of pure competition, he could have derived a downward-sloping MEI schedule, and thus a downward-sloping investment demand. If, for example, the firm is a monopolist (i.e., a price maker for the goods it sells), it is clear that the "prospective yield" will fall when the level of investment increases. Similarly, if the firm is a monopsonist (i.e., a price maker for the goods it buys), the prospective yield will once again fall when investment increases. In the former case, the price of output, *p*, will fall, whereas in the second case, the prices of inputs, *w*, and the price of the investment good, P_I, will rise.

Kalecki was interested in deriving a determinate (and downward-sloping) demand for investment, still assuming pure competition. On the other hand, Abba Lerner asserted that capital is actually heterogeneous and that a firm would have

[3] Michael Kalecki, "The Principle of Increasing Risk," *Economica,* November 1937, pp. 440–47.

FIGURE 12-17

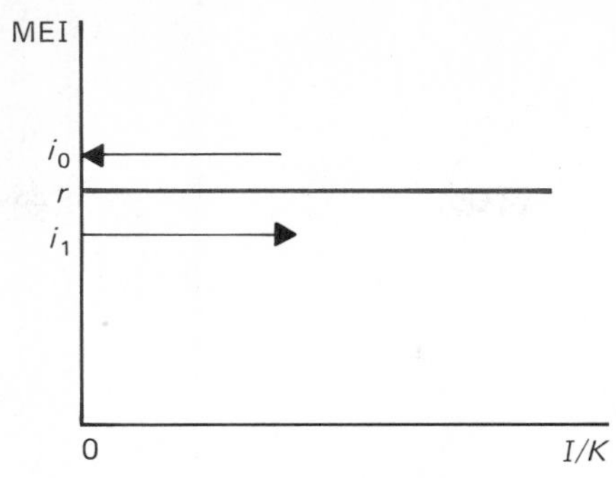

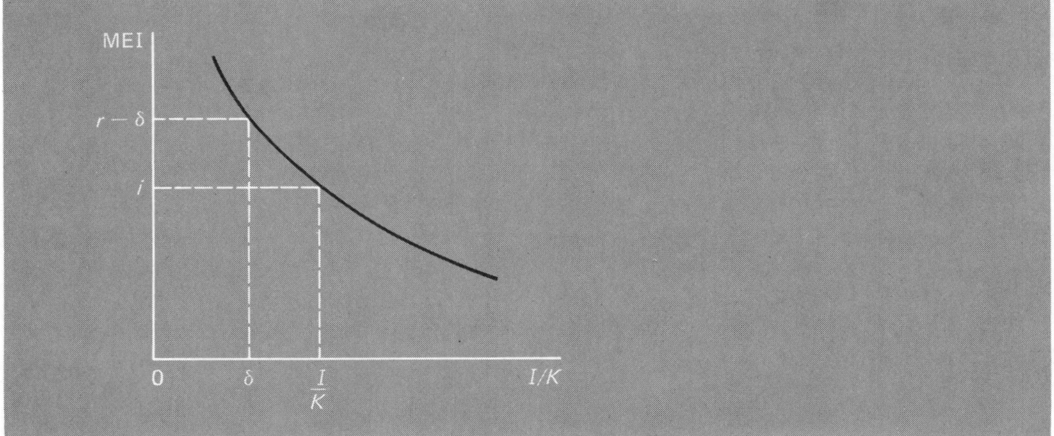

FIGURE 12-18

some monopsony power in the market for the investment good it purchases.[4] Thus the firm would be facing a rising marginal cost of investment goods, from which Lerner was able to derive a diminishing MEI schedule, as shown in Figure 12-18.

Lerner is also credited with making the crucial distinction between the net marginal product of capital, $r - \delta$, and the marginal efficiency of investment, MEI, where each is a percentage rate of return. Of course, capital, K, is a *stock*, while investment, I/K, is a *flow*. According to Lerner, the two rates of return, $r - \delta$ and MEI, are equal when *net* investment is zero (i.e., when gross investment is equal to the rate of depreciation, δ). As investment increases beyond δ, the MEI falls. Of course, I/K is determined when marginal profitability, (MEI $- i$), falls to zero (i.e., when the MEI falls to i). (Figure 12-18 illustrates all these conclusions.) If, however, we want to assume a nondepreciating capital (i.e., with $\delta = 0$), the MEI axis can be drawn through δ in Figure 12-18, giving us the case in Figure 12-19. A similar graph could be used if we wanted to operate with *net* rather than *gross* investment.

[4] Abba P. Lerner, *The Economics of Control* (New York: Macmillan, 1944), Chap. 25.

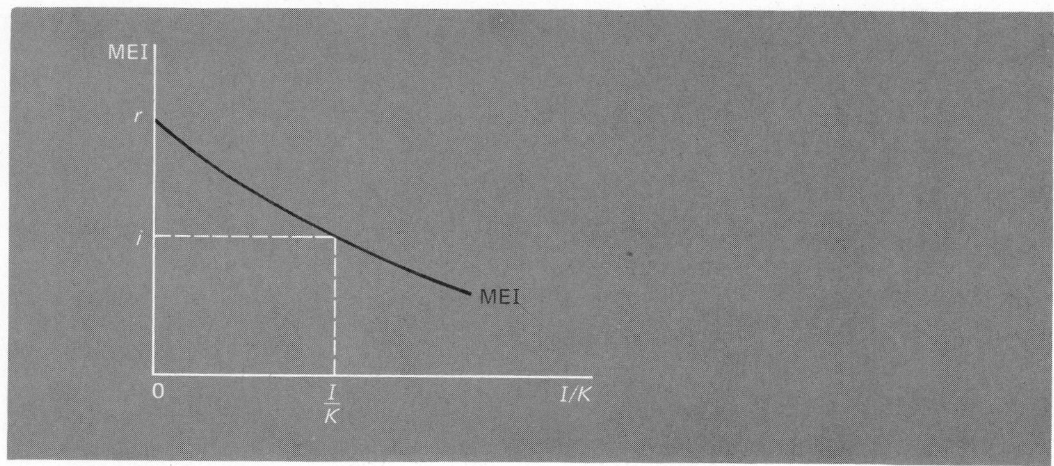

FIGURE 12-19

In such a case the MEI schedule would cut the vertical axis at $r - \delta$ rather than at r.

Kalecki was not as willing as Lerner to move outside the realm of pure competition. This is why he introduced the *principle of increasing risk;* according to Kalecki, there is an increasing risk premium required by the lenders of funds. Presumably the risk premium involves uncertainty about the possibility of default and about future need for funds held in liquid form. Of course, this is in addition to the riskless interest rate, which, in keeping with the assumptions of pure competition, is independent of investment demand, and thus of the demand for funds.

In Figure 12-20 the market interest rate is assumed to remain fixed at i_0, regardless of the level of investment demand. However, an increasing premium, σ, is *added* to i_0 as I/K increases, thereby increasing the marginal cost of funds according to the $i_0 + \sigma$ curve. The rate of investment is determined at the point where the marginal cost of (financing the) investment, $i_0 + \sigma$, is equal to its marginal profit, r. The same result can be derived if the risk premium is *subtracted* from r, instead of being added to the interest rate, as in Figure 12-21. In this case $r - \sigma$ is the perceived or true rate of profit for the firm. In either case the firm is confronted with increasing costs of adjusting its capital stock. In the case of a risk premium, we are referring to *increasing* subjective costs. The results, however, would remain the same even if the increasing costs were *objective.*

Changes in the interest rate: Let us suppose that the interest rate increases from i_0 to i_1, with everything else remaining the same. What will happen to the rate of investment? We can see that if at each level of I/K we add to the higher interest rate, i_1, the same risk premium we added before, the marginal cost curve shifts bodily upward, intersecting the rr curve at a lower rate of investment, $[(I/K)_1 < (I/K)_0]$, as in Figure 12-22. It follows, therefore, that *an increase in the interest rate will lower the firm's investment demand, I/K.* Of course, the same result can be derived if, instead of adding the risk premium to the interest rate, we subtract the premium from the rate of profit, r, as in Figure 12-23.

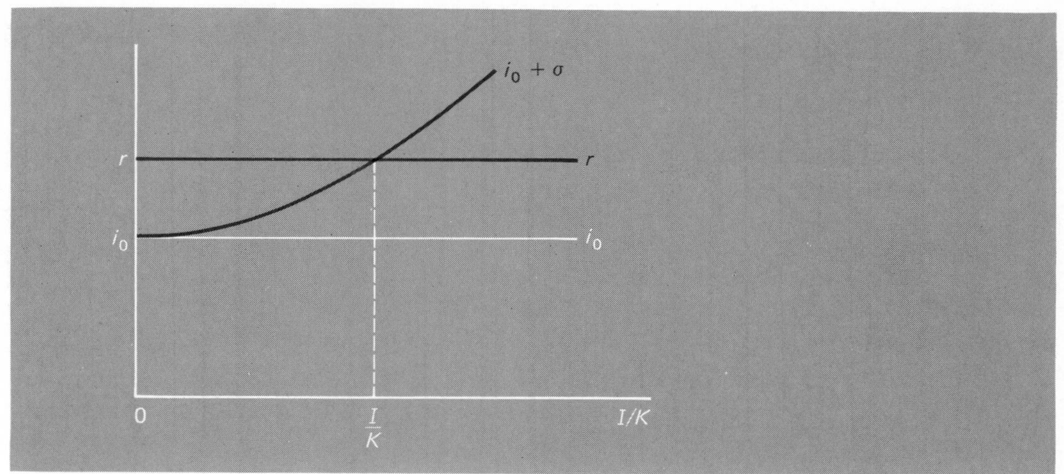

FIGURE 12-20

Changes in r: An increase in the (net) rate of profit, from r_0 to r_1, shifts the *rr* curve upward, as in Figure 12-24. This increase in r permits a higher rate of investment because it can cover the resulting higher-risk premium. And *it follows that the higher the rate of profit, r, the higher the firm's investment demand.*

We can summarize both results by stating that investment demand, I/K, is a function, ϕ, increasing in the rate of profit, r, and decreasing in the interest rate, i:

$$\frac{I}{K} = \phi(r,i), \quad \frac{\Delta(I/K)}{\Delta r} > 0, \quad \frac{\Delta(I/K)}{\Delta i} < 0$$

We know, of course, that the rate of profit r is an increasing function of the employment/capital ratio x. Thus the higher the x, the higher the r, and, finally, the higher

FIGURE 12-21

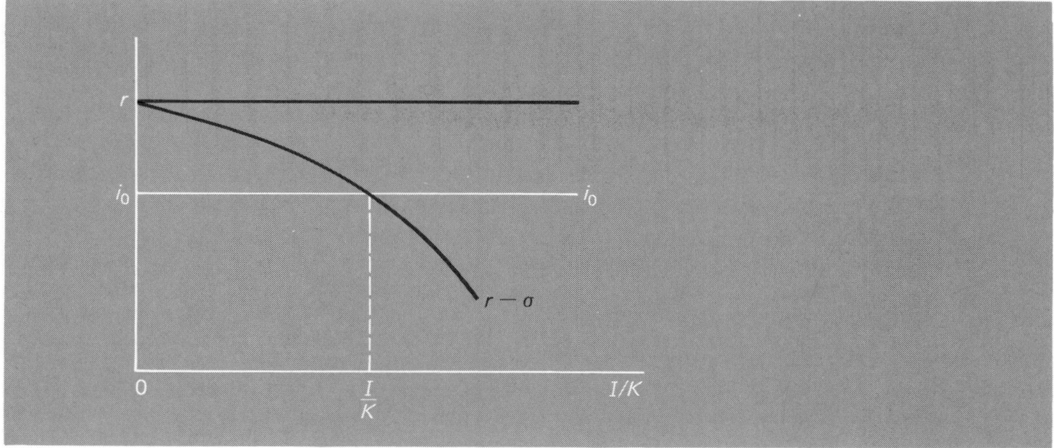

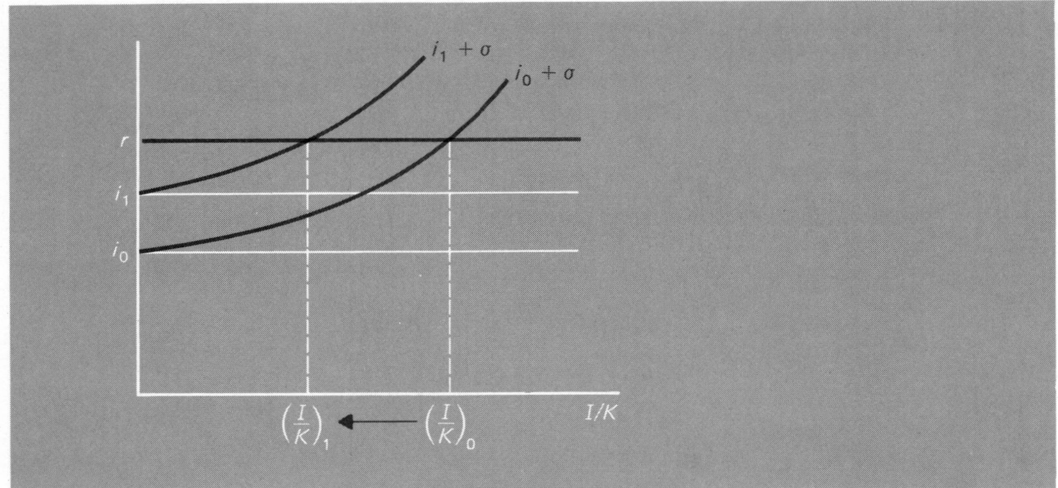

FIGURE 12-22

the rate of investment, I/K. We can therefore denote the investment demand function, I/K, as an increasing function of x and a decreasing function of i:

$$\frac{I}{K} = I(i,x), \quad \frac{\Delta I}{\Delta i} < 0, \quad \frac{\Delta I}{\Delta x} > 0$$

The investment function derived above is the one used extensively by Hugh Rose,[5] and the one adopted in this book. This same function can be derived by relying on increasing *objective*, rather than *subjective*, costs of adjustment. The seminal modern work is that of Eisner and Strotz.[6] Important extensions, as well as more advanced mathematical formulations, have been undertaken by Lucas, Treadway, Gould, Uzawa, and Bradford.[7] The unifying principle in all of this literature is the authors' contention that *some* notion of increasing costs of adjustment is necessary

[5] See, for example, Hugh Rose, "Unemployment in a Theory of Growth," *International Economic Review,* September 1966; and Hugh Rose, "Effective Demand in the Long Run," in *Models of Economic Growth,* ed. J. A. Mirrlees and N. H. Stern (New York: Wiley, 1973), pp. 25–47.

[6] R. Eisner and R. H. Strotz, "Determinants of Business Investment," in Commission on Money and Credit, *Impacts of Monetary Policy* (Englewood Cliffs, N.J.: Prentice-Hall, 1963), pp. 59–337.

[7] Robert E. Lucas, Jr., "Adjustment Costs and the Theory of Supply," *Journal of Political Economy,* August 1967, pp. 321–34; J. Gould, "Adjustment Costs in the Theory of Investment of the Firm," *Review of Economic Studies,* January 1968, pp. 47–56; Arthur Treadway, "On Rational Entrepreneurial Behavior and the Demand for Investment," *Review of Economic Studies,* April 1969, pp. 227–39; H. Uzawa, "The Penrose Effect and Optimum Growth," *Economic Studies Quarterly,* September 1968, pp. 1–14; and Eliot B. Bradford, "Implications of Rational Behavior for the Foundations of Economic Dynamics" (Ph.D. dissertation, University of Washington, 1975).

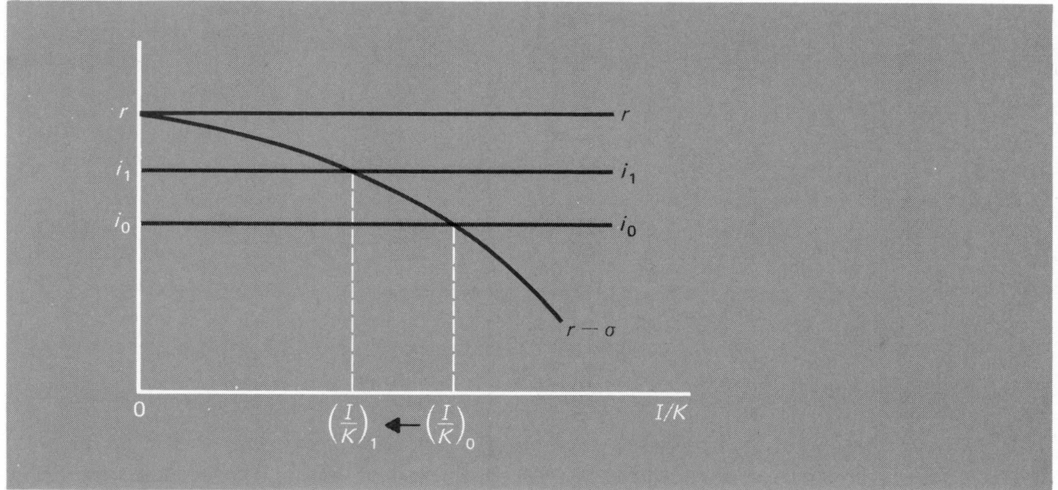

FIGURE 12-23

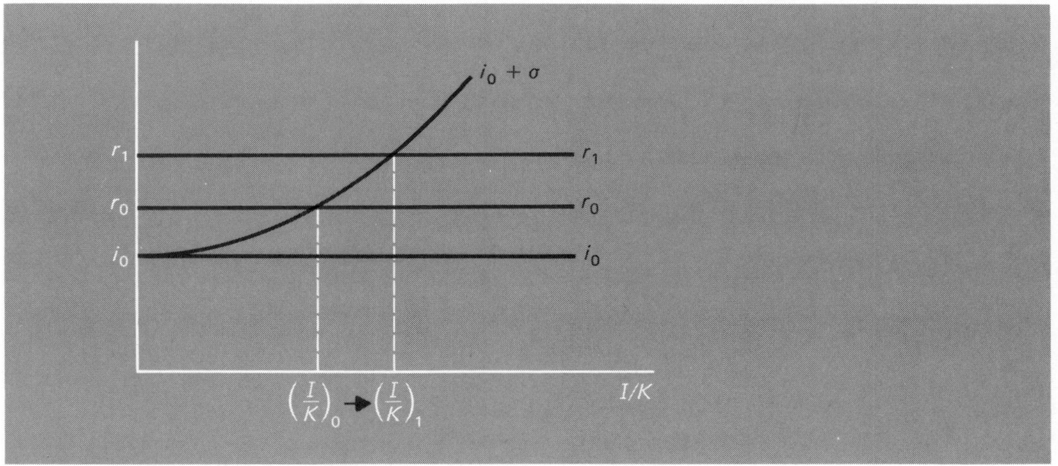

FIGURE 12-24

to effectively impede sudden large changes in the firm's stock of capital, their basis for deriving a finite rate of investment in the form of the above function.

V. THE TWO-SECTOR MODEL AND THE STOCK-FLOW APPROACH TO INVESTMENT

As noted earlier, the two-period Fisherian model can be transformed into a two-sector production model. Investment goods, *I*, replace corn tomorrow (y_2); and consumption goods, *C*, replace corn today (y_1). These two goods are producible by the

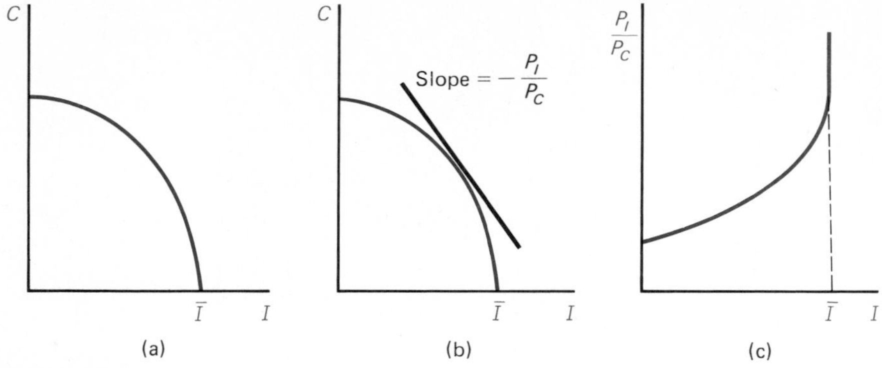

FIGURE 12-25

two factors of production—labor and capital—according to linear homogeneous production functions. Since the economy's endowments of factors of production are fixed in a given period, it follows that the two goods, C and I, are produced at increasing costs, that is, the production possibilities curve is concave, as in Figure 12-25a. Since production (and thus supply) occurs at the point where the opportunity costs are equal to relative prices, as in Figure 12-25b, it follows that the supply curve for investment goods is upward sloping, as in Figure 12-25c.

Thus, one of the two characteristically Keynesian elements, namely, the rising supply price of capital, is achieved at the aggregate level merely by assuming two separate goods (investment goods and consumption goods) produced by different (constant returns to scale) technologies. We shall employ this two-sector model in deriving the investment function, $I/K = I(i,x)$, $(\Delta I/\Delta i) < 0$, $(\Delta I/\Delta x) > 0$, in two slightly different ways.

The first of these relies almost exclusively on the properties of efficient production in this two-good setting. As is well known, the production possibility curve in the $(I/K, C/K)$-plane is the mirror image of the "contract curve" in the employment, capital plane; points on the one curve correspond to points on the other and vice versa.

In the Edgeworth box of Figure 12-26, the contract curve is derived as the locus of all tangency points of isoquants for goods I/K and C/K using origins O_I and O_C, respectively. Of course, the dimensions of the Edgeworth box represent the fixed quantities of labor and capital. The contract curve is the locus of all *efficient* production points, since it is obviously impossible to increase the output of the one industry without decreasing the output of the other.

The contract curve in Figure 12-26 has been drawn with the assumption that for all wage-rental ratios, w/r, the investment goods industry is labor intensive, that is, the labor/capital ratio for the investment goods industry, $x_I \equiv N_I/K_I$, is greater than that for the consumption goods industry, $x_C \equiv N_C/K_C$. Of course, this also means that the consumption goods industry is capital intensive. Because the factor intensities in the two industries are different, and because of the assumption of constant returns to scale, there is a one-to-one relation between the relative prices of produced goods and the prices of factors of production. (Obviously, the latter

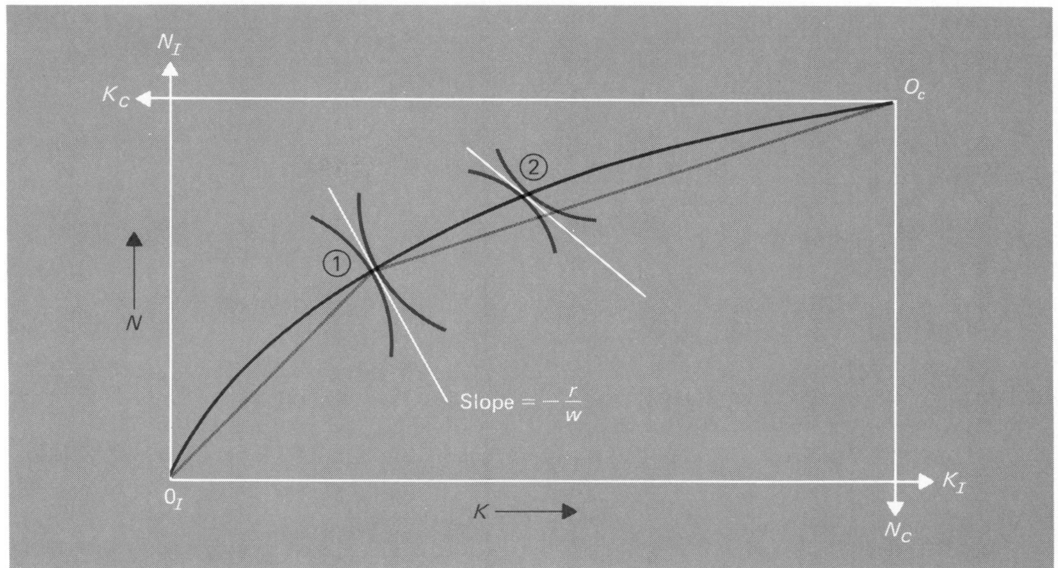

FIGURE 12-26

depend only on the labor/capital intensity because of the constant returns-to-scale technologies.) Moreover, factor prices w and r do not depend on factor supplies. This is the well-known *factor price equalization theorem,* which we shall apply in this section.

It is clear from either Figure 12-25a or Figure 12-25b that I/K depends on the relative price of capital, P_I/P_C. In Figure 12-27, in order to produce the quantity $(I/K)_1$, its relative price has to be equal to (minus) the slope of the tangent at point

FIGURE 12-27

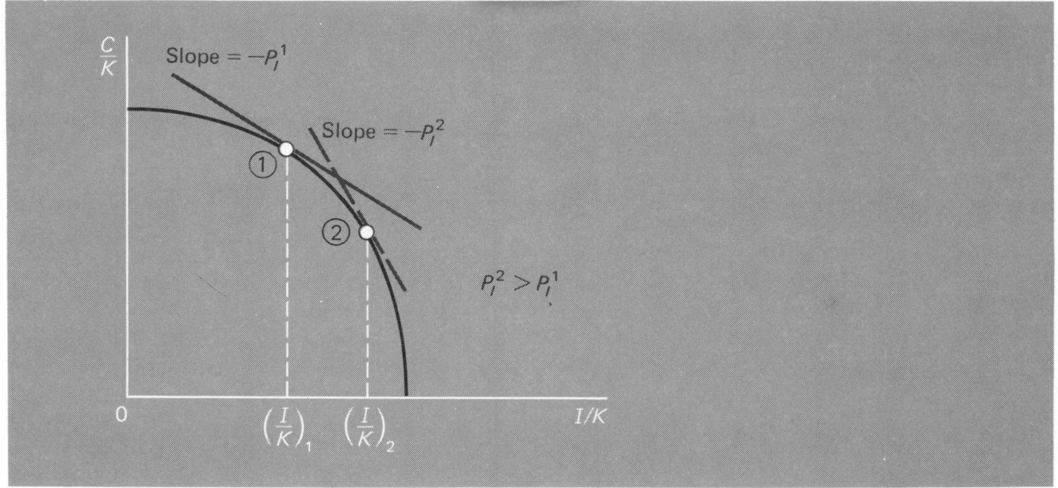

①. Thus, knowing P_I/P_C, we know I/K—but that is not all we know; point ① in Figure 12-27 is the mirror image of point ① in Figure 12-26. But at this latter point, we now know x_I and x_C. Since w and r depend only on these x's, we also know the factor prices. In fact, the slope of the tangent at ① in Figure 12-26 is equal to r/w. Using the consumption good as the numeraire (i.e., setting $P_C \equiv 1$), it is clear that by knowing P_I, we also know w and r. Thus, saying that I/K is a function of P_I is equivalent to saying that I/K is a function of w and r. However, not both w and r are needed, because if we know the one we also know the other. We can say, therefore, that I/K is a function of r.

Next, we shall examine whether I/K increases or decreases with r. We know that the higher the relative price of capital, the higher is I/K. For example, when the relative price of capital increases from a magnitude equal to the slope at point ① to a magnitude equal to the slope at point ② in Figure 12-27, I/K increases from $(I/K)_1$ to $(I/K)_2$. This exercise corresponds to a movement from point ① to point ② in Figure 12-26. In this latter graph, the labor/capital ratio, x, decreases for both industries as we move from ① to ②. This necessitates a fall in r and a rise in w, as is shown by the flatter common tangent at ②. Thus we have shown that there is a negative relation between the rental r and I/K. This, of course, is the essence of the *Stolper-Samuelson theorem:* An increase in the price of the good in one industry, with the price of the other remaining the same, will increase the reward to the factor used more intensively in the production of the good whose price has risen and will lower the reward to the factor used more intensively in the production of the good whose price remains constant.

We next examine the relation between I/K and the economy's labor/capital ratio with the prices of goods remaining constant. For concreteness, let us suppose that the economy's labor force, N, increases while its capital stock remains the same. This will change the dimensions of the Edgeworth box, as in Figure 12-28. The origin for the consumption good moves upward from O_C to O_C'. Now, assume that

FIGURE 12-28

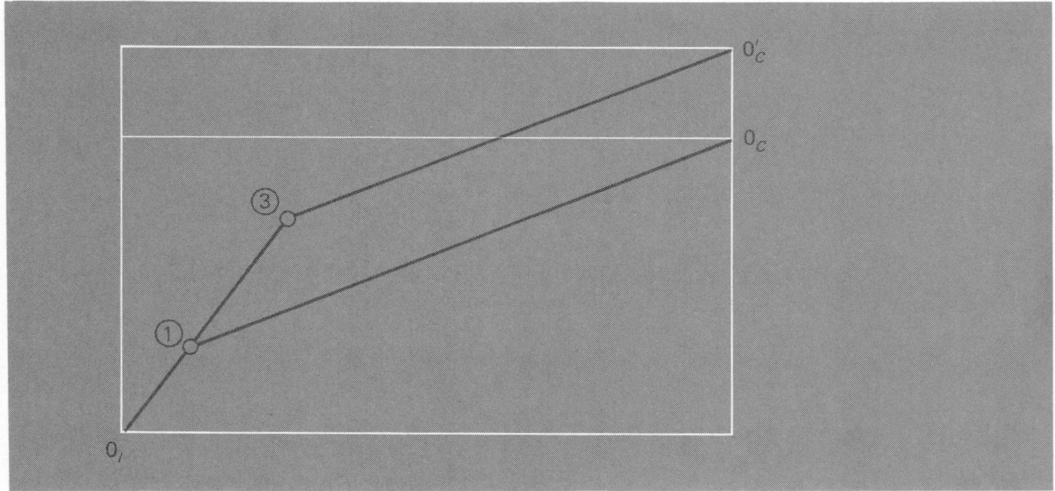

originally the economy produced at point ① on the contract curve. (Note that only a single point, namely, point ① of the contract curve, is shown in Figure 12-28.) Since w and r depend solely on P_I and P_C (and, therefore, not on the supply of N and K), and since x_I and x_C, in turn, depend only on w and r, it follows that with goods prices fixed, the labor/capital intensities of both goods will remain the same. This is shown in Figure 12-28 where the expansion path for I/K remains the same while that of C/K is parallel to the original one to accommodate the new origin. The new production point has to be ③; it has the aforementioned property of constancy of x_I and x_C, and both resources are fully employed.

These results can be shown in the $(I/K, C/K)$-plane. The new production possibilities curve moves out and to the right. Moreover, point ③—corresponding to point ③ in Figure 12-28—displays the following property, that for the same prices of I and C, the increase in N (while K is kept constant) results in higher production of I and lower production of C. This is a reflection of the *Rybczynski theorem:* An increase in one factor, while the other factor and the prices of the two goods produced remain the same, will increase the output of that industry which uses the increased factor more intensively and will actually decrease the output of that which uses the constant factor more intensively.

As has been shown by R. W. Jones, the result can be generalized to cover the case of an increase in both factors, but one in which, say N, is increased proportionately more than the other, K.[8] In this case the labor intensive good, I, will increase by a greater percentage than N did, while the capital intensive good will increase proportionately less than K:

$$\% \Delta I > \% \Delta N > \% \Delta K > \% \Delta C$$

The upshot of this generalized Rybczynski theorem is that *an increase in x will increase the rate of investment, I/K.*

We can summarize our results, so far, by stating that I/K is a function of r and x:

$$\frac{I}{K} = I(r,x) \tag{2}$$

with

$$\frac{\Delta I}{\Delta r} < 0, \ \frac{\Delta I}{\Delta x} > 0$$

The property $(\Delta I/\Delta r) < 0$ can be isolated conceptually as the *position on* PPC (e.g., point ① as compared with ②) while property $(\Delta I/\Delta x) > 0$ represents the *location* of the PPC (e.g., an increase in x shifts the curve out and to the right, and thus we have point ③ instead of ① in Figure 12-29).

[8] R. W. Jones, "The Structure of Simple General Equilibrium Models," *Journal of Political Economy,* December 1965, pp. 557–72.

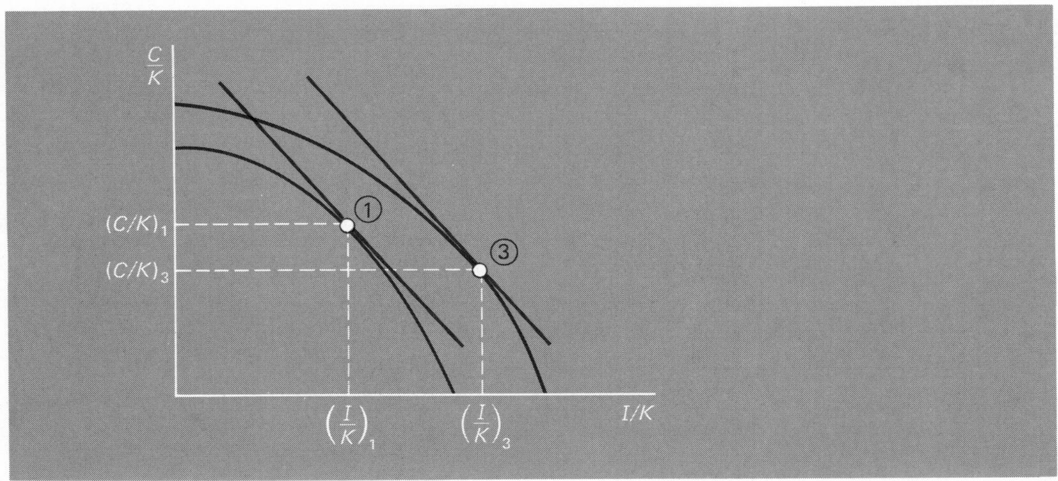

FIGURE 12-29

It is clear, of course, that there has to be a different supply curve for I/K with respect to P_I for each different x. The higher x is, the farther to the right this supply curve will be, that is, for the same P_I, the rate of investment, I/K, is greater when x is greater—another way of depicting the Rybczynski theorem, as shown in Figure 12-30.

We can now guarantee that, at the market level, the interest rate, i, is equal to the rate of return on capital, r. This result is possible if we assume that the two assets, "bonds" and "capital goods," are perfect substitutes. Thus, for both of them to be held, it must be the case that $i = r$. Otherwise, infinite flows would be desired. Substituting i for r in (2), we have the familiar investment function:

$$\frac{I}{K} = I(i,x), \quad \frac{\Delta I}{\Delta i} < 0, \quad \frac{\Delta I}{\Delta x} > 0 \tag{3}$$

Note that the equality $i = r$ is a characteristic of the Fisherian model, and in this respect it differs from the Keynesian one where, in general, $i < r$.

A second noteworthy point is that both the investment function, (3), and its partial derivatives are implications of efficient production. Thus investment here is a supply function for new capital goods, not a demand function based on the optimal capital policies of firms. Keynes, on the other hand, emphasized the latter, especially since he wanted to show that different agents are behind savings and investment decisions.

Perhaps the most important criticism of this approach attacks the assumptions used to derive the signs of properties $(\Delta I/\Delta i) < 0$ and $(\Delta I/\Delta x) > 0$, both of which are squarely dependent on the arbitrary assumption that the capital goods industry is labor intensive while the consumption goods industry is capital intensive. Of course, the signs of these partials would be reversed if the opposite assumption were made.

We see that the use of a two-sector model to achieve a rising supply price

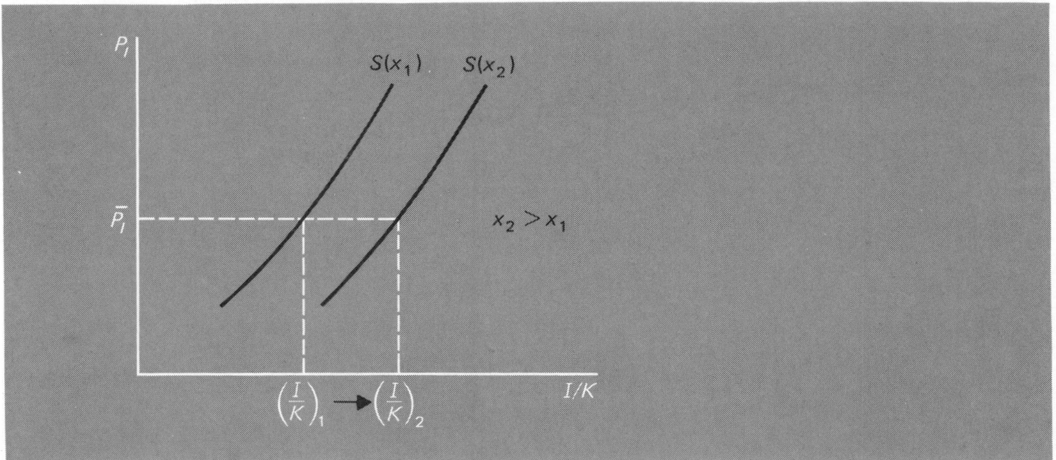

FIGURE 12-30

of capital goods imposed a relatively heavy price on us. On the other hand, the investment function of the preceding section implies a rising supply price because of increasing adjustment cost. At this point it may be interesting to keep in mind that, as Hugh Rose has said: *The use for which output is destined is a much more definitive characteristic than the techniques by which it is produced.*

There is a second way by which we can derive the investment function and still employ the implications of a two-sector model. This differs from the one above in the way it introduces the dependence of I/K on the interest rate. It also carefully distinguishes between the stock of capital and investment, the latter of which is a flow. It is the interaction of stocks and flows that yields the investment function.

According to this approach, there is a demand for the stock of capital, which is a decreasing function of both the relative price of capital and the interest rate, that is, $D_K(i, P_I)$. Given the interest rate, say at i_0, we draw the downward-sloping demand curve for capital as a function of its relative price, P_I, as in Figure 12-31. Since the supply of capital is fixed at a point in time, P_I is determined instantaneously by the supply and demand for capital stock. In other words, *at any moment in time, the relative price of capital, P_I, is at the level that makes the existing stock of capital willingly held.*

The flow of investment is the production (and thus supply) of investment goods, which can be derived from the production possibility curve. Thus there is an upward-sloping supply curve of investment goods (per unit of capital), as in Figure 12-32. Since an increase in x shifts the production possibility curve to the right, as in the Rybczynski theorem, it follows that this increase in x will shift the supply curve to the right. Thus there is an infinity of S curves, one for each assumed x.

Having carefully distinguished between the *stock* of capital and the *flow* of investment, we can see how, according to this theory, their interaction determines the level of investment as a function of i and x. We can see this in terms of Figure 12-33. The stocks are shown in the left-hand panel. When the interest rate is i_0, the

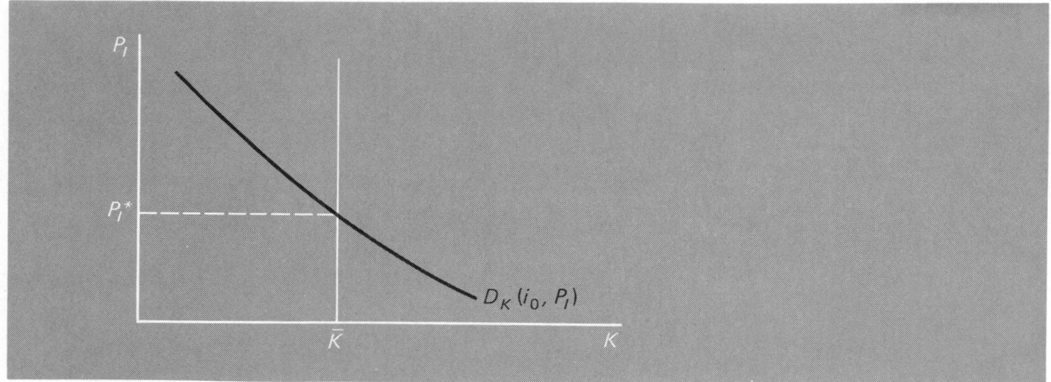

FIGURE 12-31

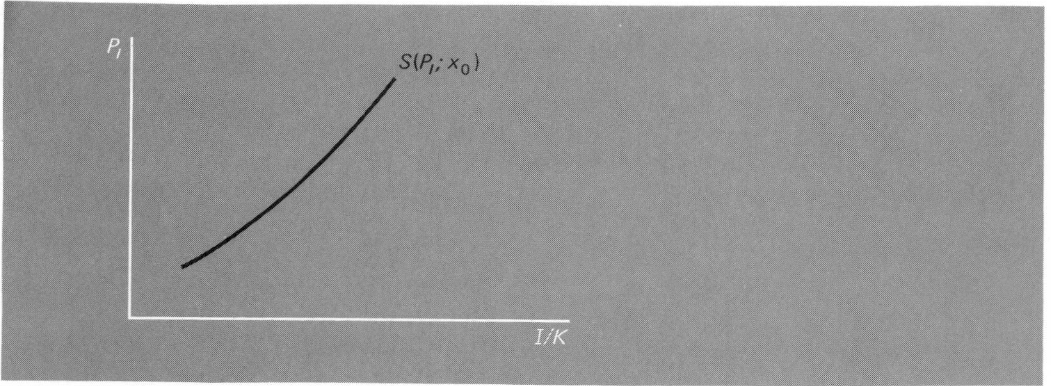

FIGURE 12-32

relevant demand curve for capital is $D_K(i_0, P_I)$. Its intersection with the stock of existing capital, K_0, gives P_I^0 as the market relative price of capital. But at this market relative price of capital, producers are willing to produce $(I/K)_0$. Thus when $i = i_0$, investment per unit of capital is $(I/K)_0$.

Let us now suppose that the interest rate is lower, namely $i_1 < i_0$. The relevant demand curve for capital moves upward to $D_K(i_1, P_I)$. Since the stock of capital is independent of i, the new market price of capital is P_I^1. At this higher relative price, investment per unit of capital will be higher, namely $(I/K)_1$. Therefore we have *established that a lower interest rate, i, will induce a higher rate of investment, (I/K).*

Assume further that we start with an interest rate equal to i_0, with the capital stock equal to K_0, and employment per unit of capital equal to x_0. Given these conditions, the market relative price of capital would equal P_I^0, and thus the implied rate of investment would be equal to $(I/K)_0$, as in Figure 12-34. Now suppose that x rises to x_1. (To avoid unnecessary complications, we assume that the rise in x is due solely to a rise in N, and not to any change in K.) According to the familiar Rybczynski theorem, this rise in x shifts the supply curve of investment to the right.

With the same price of capital (and interest rate), we have a higher *(I/K)*, that is, $(I/K)_1$. It is clear, then, that, *ceteris paribus, an increase in x will increase I/K.*

We can summarize both the above results with the familiar investment function:

$$\frac{I}{K} = I(i,x), \quad \frac{\Delta I}{\Delta i} < 0, \quad \frac{\Delta I}{\Delta x} > 0 \tag{3}$$

Obviously, this approach, inasmuch as it relies on the two-sector assumptions, is vulnerable to the criticisms already noted.

FIGURE 12-33

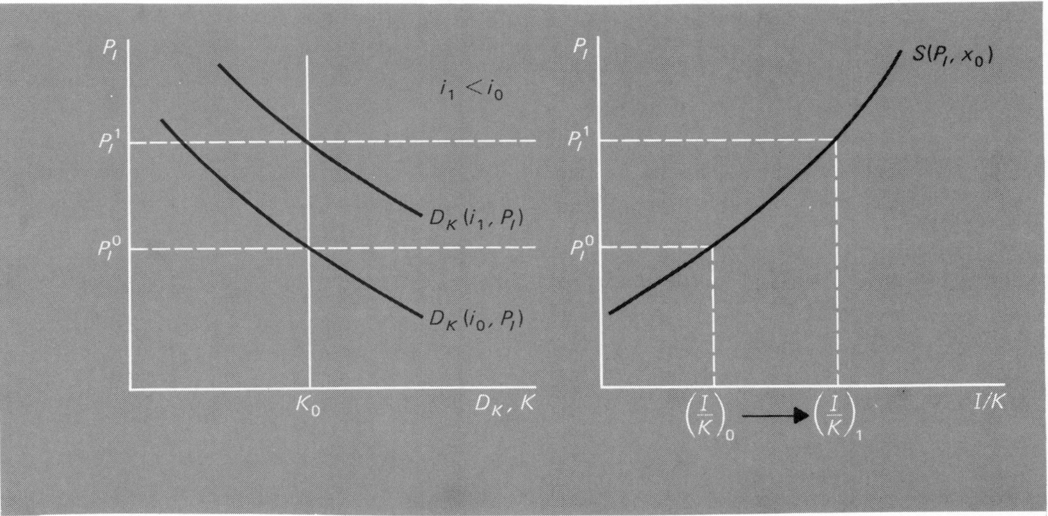

FIGURE 12-34

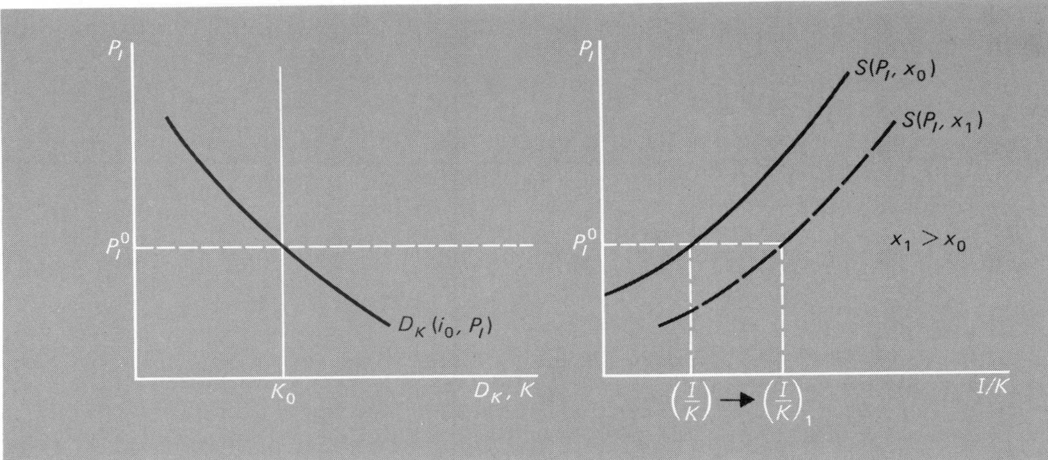

Variants of the above method of deriving the investment function have been used by several economists during the last few years. J. G. Witte assumed both the negative relation between D_K and P_I and the positive relation between the supply of investment and its relative price.[9] However, he did not follow the assumptions (and thus the implications) of linear homogeneous technologies. In fact, he did not even use a two-sector model. His analysis is, essentially, partial equilibrium analysis for an industry producing one particular capital good. The demand curve for capital slopes downward (with respect to P_I) because firms in the industry face a number of increasing costs as output expands from greater use of capital: fixed entrepreneurial capacity, falling demand price for the output of the industry, and rising supply price of some inputs for the industry. On the other hand, the demand for capital *shifts* downward as the parametric rate of interest rises, since further returns from capital are discounted more heavily in view of the alternative possibility of holding bonds.

Witte's article voiced his reaction to the tendency of confusing stocks and flows—in particular, that economists often considered the marginal product of capital curve as the demand for investment, in the same way that we consider the marginal product of labor curve as the labor demand curve. However, the marginal product of capital depicts demand for capital services. If we then assume that there is a one-to-one relation between the capital stock and its services, it follows that the marginal product of capital curve depicts demand for the capital stock—and not demand for investment flows. It is this demand for capital that Witte's $D_K(\cdot)$ represents.

Foley and Sidrauski applied the two-sector aspect of the rising supply of investment goods, but they did not adhere to the assumption of certainty.[10] In their explanation of $D_K(\cdot)$, desired portfolio items depend on relative rates of return. In particular, both physical capital and bonds are held because of differential liquidity characteristics or risk aversion. Finally, F. Brechling has made the above model dynamic by introducing expectations.[11]

The instantaneous determination of the price of capital goods, P_I, at the level that makes the existing stock of capital willingly held, is reminiscent of Keynes' liquidity preference theory of interest. It is this same determination of P_I that underlies James Tobin's capital-account approach to macroeconomics,[12] although his theory of investment is not dependent upon a rising supply price of investment.

Tobin's theory, often called Tobin's "q" theory of investment, is appealing both for its simplicity and its realism. According to Tobin, investment is an increasing

---

[9] J. G. Witte, Jr., "The Micro-Foundations of the Social Investment Function," *Journal of Political Economy,* October 1963, pp. 441–56.

[10] D. K. Foley and M. Sidrauski, *Monetary and Fiscal Policy in a Growing Economy* (New York: Macmillan, 1971), Chap. 6.

[11] Frank P. Brechling, *Investment and Employment Decisions* (Manchester, Ind.: University of Manchester Press, 1975).

[12] James Tobin, "A General Equilibrium Approach to Monetary Theory," *Journal of Money, Credit and Banking,* 1 (February 1969), 15–29; James Tobin and William C. Brainard, "Asset Markets and the Cost of Capital," in *Economic Progress, Private Values, and Public Policy, Essays in Honor of William Fellner,* ed. B. Balassa and R. Nelson (Amsterdam: North Holland, 1977), pp. 236–62.

function of q where q is the ratio of two valuations of capital. The numerator is the equity value of capital (in the stock, or assets market) and the denominator is the replacement cost of the same physical capital. Hence, the higher the equity value of capital as compared to its replacement cost, the greater the incentive to invest (in physical capital). On the other hand, the lower the valuation of capital in the stock market, as compared to its replacement cost, the greater the incentive to buy equity of already installed capital rather than undertake its new installation. It turns out that q is also equal to the ratio of expected rate of profit, r, and the required rate of return on capital in the stock market, r_K, which can be identified with the interest rate. It follows then, that investment is an increasing function of the profit rate, r, and hence, of x, and a decreasing function of the interest rate, i, exactly as our analysis above has established. The importance of Tobin's theory lies in the fact that the empirical investigator does not have to compute r and r_K separately, but instead can find, more easily, the market valuation and the replacement cost of capital.

VI. JORGENSON'S WORK: EMPIRICAL INVESTIGATIONS

The gross national product accounts subdivide investment into three main categories: business fixed investment, changes in business inventories, and residential construction. We can see from Table 1-1 of Chapter 1 that the total investment expenditure of \$395.3 billion in 1980 was divided into \$296.0 billion for business fixed investment, −\$5.9 billion for changes in business inventories, and \$105.3 billion for residential construction. Each of these three categories has peculiarities of its own, and a complete examination of investment should provide an overview and a delineation of each. Our approach has been to examine the determinants of investment as a whole. Strictly speaking, we have analyzed only the determinants of business fixed investment on the grounds that this investment is the prototype for investment in general; only minor modifications are needed in order to apply the analysis to the other two categories of investment. However, the empirical work examines both investment as a whole and its three categories separately. Here we shall concentrate on investment in general and on fixed business investment, although we shall make brief mention of inventories and of residential construction.

In the early post-Keynesian, postwar literature, economists claimed that the interest rate played little or no role in the calculations of business firms deciding whether to increase their fixed capital. The "evidence" was provided by surveys of business firms, both in the United States and in Europe, especially Britain.[13] For this reason models of investment that do not rely on the interest rate were designed and eventually tested. Such a prominent model is the (fixed) "accelerator" view of

---

[13] See T. Wilson and P. W. S. Andrews, eds., *Oxford Studies in the Price Mechanism* (London: Oxford, 1951); and John R. Meyer and Edwin Kuh, *The Investment Decision: An Empirical Study* (Cambridge, Mass.: Harvard University Press, 1957).

investment, which is based on the stipulation that there is a fixed desired capital/output ratio, α, that is, $K_t^*/Y_t = \alpha$, which can be written as

$$K_t^* = \alpha Y_t \tag{4}$$

and which can be interpreted as the demand for capital (or desired capital). From this demand for capital, which is a *stock*, we can derive the demand for investment, which is a *flow*, by noting that a relation similar to (4) must hold for every period, say $t - 1$: $K_{t-1} = \alpha Y_{t-1}$. Subtracting this from (4), we get $K_t^* - K_{t-1} = \alpha (Y_t - Y_{t-1})$. But $K_t^* - K_{t-1}$ is ΔK, which is the addition to the capital stock, that is, investment, I_t:

$$I_t = \alpha \Delta Y_t \tag{5}$$

This is the traditional (fixed) accelerator, which has been used by the economists Samuelson, Hicks, and others.[14] One unsatisfactory aspect of the fixed, or simple, accelerator is its assumption that the entire discrepancy, $K_t^* - K_{t-1}$, between desired capital stock and the capital stock that existed at the end of the previous period, is eliminated by investment in a single period. For this reason both Chenery and Koyck introduced the "flexible accelerator" model, which stipulates that the discrepancy between desired capital stock, K_t^*, and actual, K_{t-1}, is eliminated over several periods of time.[15] This model permits the possibility that desired and actual capital stock may differ at any point in time. The flexible accelerator can be captured by the following equation:

$$I_t = K_t - K_{t-1} = (1 - \lambda)\,(K_t^* - K_{t-1}) \tag{6}$$

which says that the addition to the capital stock, $K_t - K_{t-1} = \Delta K_t = I_t$, is a proportion of the discrepancy between desired and actual capital stock. When $\lambda = 0$ in (6), we have the simple, fixed, accelerator, (5).

It should be noted here that although the mechanism of lagged adjustment of (6) is realistic, it was introduced in a totally *ad hoc* manner, with no basis on theory. It was only in the late 1960s that several economists derived it from a theory that relies on increasing costs of adjustment.[16] It should also be noted that the early flexible accelerator literature considered K_t^*, the (desired) demand for capital, as independent of the interest rate, as in (5). In fact, in (5), not only is the interest rate

---

[14] See Paul A. Samuelson, "A Synthesis of the Principle of Acceleration and the Multiplier," *Journal of Political Economy,* December 1939, pp. 786–97; J. R. Hicks, *A Contribution to the Theory of the Trade Cycle* (London: Oxford at the Clarendon Press, 1950); and J. R. Meyer and E. Kuh, "Accelerator and Related Theories of Investment: An Empirical Inquiry," *Review of Economics and Statistics,* August 1955, pp. 217–300.

[15] H. B. Chenery, "Overcapacity and the Acceleration Principle," *Econometrica,* January 1952, pp. 200–11; and L. M. Koyck, *Distributed Lags and Investment Analysis* (Amsterdam: North-Holland Press, 1954).

[16] See footnotes 6 and 7.

missing as a direct determinant of desired capital stock but so are changes in the price of capital, depreciation rates, tax rates, tax structure, and price of output. Reacting to this approach, Dale Jorgenson introduced what he called the "neoclassical" approach to investment behavior.[17]

Jorgenson's influence has been so great that no account of investment decisions is complete if we do not mention his work, which was mostly empirical. This work, done principally in the 1960s, is aimed at deriving and estimating investment, which is a flow, from the demand for capital, which is a stock. His demand for capital is a demand for capital services, which is derived from maximizing behavior by using a neoclassical production function. This demand for capital services depends negatively on the rental of capital, e, if renting capital is a choice, or negatively on the "user cost" of capital if buying it is a choice. The rental of capital is, of course, the marginal product of capital, MP_K, and we already know what the latter is. The user cost consists of the real interest payments, $i \cdot P_I$ (where i is the real interest rate and P_I, as earlier, is the price of the investment good), plus depreciation expenses, $\delta \cdot P_I$ (where δ is the depreciation rate) minus the expected capital gains, ΔP_I, which would materialize from a (potential) resale of the capital good.

In a perfect resale market, the rental (or the marginal product of capital) must be equal to the user cost of capital:

$$(i+\delta)\, P_I - \Delta P_I = MP_K \equiv e \tag{7}$$

or

$$i+\delta-\frac{\Delta P_I}{P_I}=\frac{MP_K}{P_I}=\frac{e}{P_I}=r \tag{7'}$$

This equation merely states that, at the margin, a firm would be indifferent between buying and renting its capital, provided that we have such perfect markets. This equality, and the underlying concept of user cost, can be generalized to account for taxation of the firm's profits, but we shall not pursue this avenue here.

From an equation similar to (7) and from the rational behavior of firms, Jorgenson derived the demand for capital services as a decreasing function of the user cost of capital (or the real rate of interest) and as an increasing function (in fact, a constant proportion) of a scale variable, namely, the value of output, pY:

$$K=\gamma\frac{pY}{e} \tag{8'}$$

Because he relies on maximization (of profits) and on the production function, both neoclassical concepts, Jorgenson calls his theory "neoclassical." This should

[17] Dale W. Jorgenson, "Capital Theory and Investment," *American Economic Review*, May 1963, pp. 247–59.

not be taken to mean that it must be contrasted with the "Keynesian" theory. Another reason why Jorgenson's theory is neoclassical is the equality of MP_K and user cost. A quick comparison with the analysis of our first section shows that the user cost can be made consistent with Keynes' MEC; as it is, it is a slightly different MEC, again a Keynesian concept. More fundamentally, Jorgenson's theory is neoclassical in the sense that it is a demand for the services of capital, which, like the demand for any other factor, is the marginal productivity curve.

Because there is a one-to-one relation between capital and its services, the demand for capital services *is* the demand for capital, so we can write the demand for (i.e., desired) capital, K^*, as

$$K_t^* = \gamma \cdot \frac{pY_t}{e} \tag{8}$$

But the demand for capital, or "desired" capital, is not the demand for investment, because the former is a stock and the latter a flow concept. To derive the demand for investment, which is the addition to the existing capital stock, Jorgenson assumed that any discrepancy between the desired capital stock, K_t^* (which, he assumed, is finite), and the actual stock, K_t, is eliminated, *via* investment, with a lag, say, of several periods. Therefore a fraction (not necessarily constant) of the stock discrepancy materializes as flow investment demand. In other words, Jorgenson adopted the lagged adjustment stipulation, which was used by the early flexible accelerator writers and represented by (6). Although his derivation of K_t^* is an improvement over (4), in the sense that it is derived from the maximizing behavior of firms, Jorgenson's adoption of (6) makes his model vulnerable to the charge that it is at least partly *ad hoc.* Of course, nobody had derived, by the early 1960s, the mechanism (6) from maximizing behavior. Furthermore, several quite different models, in addition to the ones already mentioned, adopted this realistic, although then an *ad hoc,* mechanism.

Jorgenson, both alone and with associates, empirically tested his model and estimated the investment function. Moreover, he computed the response of investment to changes in the interest rate, which is the chief determinant of the user cost, with changes in the price of goods and services and in the price of capital goods. He also extended the analysis by introducing and estimating the effects of taxation on investment.

To complete a model of investment based on the flexible accelerator, it is necessary to specify a model of capital replacement, since the model's theoretical implications apply to actual changes in the capital stock (i.e., *net* investment) rather than to gross investment. Most studies use a geometric distribution in which replacement is proportional to the actual capital stock. This approach is simple compared with alternative approaches, but it has received support from the results of numerous empirical tests. Therefore the specified model is

$$I_t = K_t - K_{t-1} = (1 - \lambda)\,(K_t^* - K_{t-1}) + \delta K_{t-1} \tag{9}$$

We shall now focus on a study by Jorgenson and Siebert that tests the performance of four basic investment models: the accelerator model, the expected profits model, the liquidity model, and the neoclassical model.[18] We have already specified the first and the last of these models, and we shall specify the other two shortly. All of the tests employ the geometric distribution for replacement capital; they differ only in their specification of the desired level of capital, K_t^*. This study investigates the investment behavior of individual firms in order to avoid the possible biases involved in aggregation across firms.

The first of these models, the *simple accelerator theory* of investment, uses equation (4) for K_t^*. Using this, along with the basic specification of the "distributed lag" function, Jorgenson and Siebert estimate the investment function for the General Motors Corporation for the period 1949–63:

$$I_t = .20 + \underset{(.03)}{.07}(Y_{t-1} - Y_{t-2}) + \underset{(.21)}{.48}(I_{t-1} - \delta K_{t-2}) + \underset{(.06)}{.19}K_{t-1}.$$

$$R^2 = .62,\ \text{S.E.} = .19,\ \text{D.W.} = 2.21$$

The model successfully accounts for about 62 percent of the variation in investment, using the lagged change in desired capital and lagged net investment. The particular distributed lag structure was chosen on the basis of its empirical goodness of fit. All three explanatory variables play a statistically significant role in explaining investment behavior. This can be seen by comparing each coefficient with its standard error, which is reported in parentheses. The ratio (coefficient/standard error) is called the "t" ratio and can be compared with values found in statistical tables in order to determine the probability with which the actual true coefficient is nonzero. Here investment shows a significant positive relation to both the lagged change in desired capital and the lagged net investment.

The *liquidity theory* of investment asserts that the supply of funds schedule for investment becomes very steep at the level of investment that exhausts the supply of internal funds, that is,

$$K_t^* = \beta L_t, \tag{10}$$

where L is a measure of the liquidity position of the firm. Firms are viewed as being reluctant to undertake investment projects that must be financed by borrowing. This model again addresses the effect of interest rates only implicitly, insofar as they affect the allocation of internal funds and the degree of reluctance of the firm to borrow in order to undertake investment projects. The results (again for General Motors) are summarized by the following:

$$I_t = .23 + \underset{(.27)}{.30}(L_t - L_{t-1}) + \underset{(.27)}{.49}(L_{t-1} - L_{t-2}) + \underset{(.23)}{.40}(I_{t-1} - \delta K_{t-2}) + \underset{(.06)}{.17}K_{t-1}.$$

$$R^2 = .61,\ \text{S.E.} = .20,\ \text{D.W.} = 2.29 \tag{11}$$

[18] Dale W. Jorgenson and C. D. Siebert, "A Comparison of Alternative Econometric Models of Corporate Investment Behavior," *American Economic Review*, September 1968, pp. 681–712.

Using the best-fitting lag for this model, investment is positively related to current and lagged changes in desired capital and to lagged net investment. The model performs somewhat less well than does the accelerator model, as shown by the slightly lower R^2 and the higher standard error.

Another possible determinant of the desired capital stock is *expected profits.* Investment is undertaken not in response to production that has been profitable in the past, but in response to expected profits in the future, which make future output (and therefore investment) desirable. Jorgenson and Siebert use the market value *(MV)* of the firm to measure expected profits; when a firm is expected to earn profits in the future, it would be expected to show a higher current market value today as the expected future profits are capitalized:

$$K_t^* = \epsilon MV_t \tag{12}$$

The resulting investment function is

$$\begin{aligned} I_t = .28 + &\underset{(.03)}{.09}(MV_t - MV_{t-1}) + \underset{(.03)}{.06}(MV_{t-1} - MV_{t-2}) + \underset{(.06)}{.15}K_{t-1}. \\ &R^2 = .64, \text{ S.E.} = .19, \text{ D.W.} = 1.36 \end{aligned} \tag{13}$$

Finally, as we have seen, the neoclassical theory suggests a desired capital stock proportional to the value of output divided by the cost of capital services. The form of the neoclassical model is derived from profit maximization by the firm and is often based on the use of a Cobb-Douglas form for the production function. The cost of capital, which is fundamental to the neoclassical model, is viewed as an increasing function of the interest rate and of depreciation, and as *independent of the liquidity position of the firm,* as in (8) above. Now, defining $NC_t = p_t Y_t / e$, we get (8′):

$$K_t^* = \gamma \frac{p_t Y_t}{e} = \gamma NC_t \tag{8′}$$

Hence the estimated relationship is

$$\begin{aligned} I_t = .24 + &\underset{(.01)}{.02}(NC_t - NC_{t-1}) + \underset{(.01)}{.02}(NC_{t-1} - NC_{t-2}) \\ &+ \underset{(.21)}{.34}(I_{t-1} - K_{t-2}) + \underset{(.05)}{.18}K_{t-1}. \\ &R^2 = .70, \text{ S.E.} = .18, \text{ D.W.} = 2.03 \end{aligned} \tag{14}$$

While the estimates reported here are for General Motors Corporation alone, similar estimates are made by Jorgenson and Siebert for fourteen other Fortune 500 corporations. Based on several measures of performance, the rankings of the models in terms of explanatory ability is: best fit, the neoclassical model; next best, the expected profits model; then the accelerator model; and, finally, the liquidity model.

Because it has been so influential, Jorgenson's work has attracted criticism on both empirical and theoretical grounds. Brechling summarizes the criticisms, which center on Jorgenson's empirical implementation of the noeclassical model.[19] First, the use of equation (8′), above, allows the estimation of only one parameter, γ, of the underlying Cobb-Douglas production function. Brechling points out that, especially in the interest of policy applications, estimation of *all* the relevant parameters is highly desirable. Second, if output differs from desired output (i.e., $Y_t \neq Y_t^*$), because of either entrepreneurial errors or adjustment lags, potentially serious estimation biases are introduced into the ordinary least squares estimates. And, finally, the constraints of the production function require that lagged adjustment of one factor (capital) to its desired level be accompanied by either lagged adjustment of the other factor (labor) *or* underutilization of some factor. Jorgenson's work, it is argued, with its narrow focus on the investment function, does not account for deviations of actual from desired output or for the implications of lagged capital adjustment in decisions involving the other factors of production.

Furthermore, there are theoretical shortcomings in Jorgenson's work, especially because it was carried out, almost in its entirety, before the advent of crucial new theoretical developments that have relied on increasing costs of adjustment. The first criticism, then, concerns Jorgenson's adoption of the *ad hoc* lagged response by the firms. However, we know now that the essence of that mechanism can be derived theoretically by means of increasing adjustment costs. An alternative way of deriving the lagged response is by assuming a decreasing returns-to-scale technology, rather than the constant returns to scale inherent in the Jorgenson Cobb-Douglas function.

This brings us to a second shortcoming of Jorgenson's work: He stipulates that there is a *finite* level of desired capital, K_t^*, derived from the demand-for-capital curve. His stipulation means that the demand for capital services (which is then identified as the demand for capital) must be downward sloping with respect to the user cost. But the *firm's* demand curve is downward sloping only if the production function exhibits decreasing returns to scale. This is the same problem we encountered and resolved, by means of increasing adjustment costs, in Section IV.

Returning to the positive side of things, we see that, of the four competing theories tested by Jorgenson, the only one that relies on the interest rate is his, and thus it is not surprising that this model performed the best. Of course, in (14) the interest rate enters only implicitly, via the user cost which determines NC_t. But even in his first examination Jorgenson derived explicitly the response of investment to changes in the interest rate (as well as to changes in the price level, the price of capital goods, and taxation).[20]

---

[19] Brechling, *Investment and Employment Decisions.*

[20] Jorgenson, "Capital Theory and Investment."

Other empirical investigations followed, which examined the *time pattern* of the response of investment to changes in the interest rate.[21] Most of these investigations suggest small initial changes in investment when interest rates change, followed by larger investment changes, and then successively smaller adjustments, until the desired capital stock is reached. Somewhere between 10 and 30 percent of the total response of investment to changes in the interest rate appears to occur within one year. Separate components of investment exhibit a different sensitivity to interest rate moves, with residential construction quite sensitive and inventory investment much less so. When all components of investment are considered together, elasticity estimates from most studies cluster in the −0.3 to −0.9 range. There is no doubt, however, that we are on firm ground in this book when we rely on the interest elasticity of investment demand. And, of course, the greater the sensitivity of investment to the interest rate, the more potent is monetary policy as a stabilization tool.

Most ongoing research, both theoretical and empirical, revolves around Tobin's "q theory," Jorgenson's "neoclassical theory," and the Kalecki-Eisner-Strotz "increasing adjustment cost theory." Martin S. Feldstein and several of his students at Harvard are making substantial contributions on supply-side issues involving the effects of taxation and inflation on investment.[22]

QUESTIONS

1. Explain in words how the negative relation between the interest rate and investment is established in the Fisherian model.
2. Using the present value maximization approach to investment, show graphically the relationship between investment and the interest rate and between investment and income or employment. How do these results compare with the MEI approach?
3. What problems are presented by the notion of a horizontal MEI curve? What two approaches get around these problems? Outline the contributions of Kalecki and Lerner in this area.
4. Show graphically the use of the concept of increasing adjustment costs to solve the horizontal MEI problem. What is the effect of change in *i*? Changes in the rate of profit?
5. State and show graphically the factor price equalization theorem.
6. State and show graphically the Stolper-Samuelson theorem.
7. State and show graphically the Rybczynski theorem.

---

[21] C. W. Bischoff, "Business Investment in the 1970s: A Comparison of Models," *Brookings Papers on Economic Activity,* 1971; M. K. Evans, "A Study of Industry Investment Decisions," *Review of Economics and Statistics,* May 1967, pp. 151–64; Robert E. Hall, "Investment, Interest Rates, and the Effects of Stabilization Policy," *Brookings Papers on Economic Activity,* 1977; and D. W. Jorgenson, "Econometric Studies of Investment Behavior: A Survey," *Journal of Economic Literature,* December 1971, pp. 1111–47.

[22] See, for example, Martin S. Feldstein and Lawrence Summers, "Inflation, Tax Rules, and the Long Term Interest Rate," *Brookings Papers on Economic Activity,* 1 (1978).

8. Explain how the investment function can be viewed alternatively as a demand or as a supply function.
9. Using the Stolper-Samuelson theorem, what assumptions must be made about factor intensities to generate an inverse relationship between the price of investment goods and the user cost of capital?
10. What does the Rybczynski theorem imply about the relationship between x and investment? What are some possible criticisms of this approach?
11. Why is Jorgenson's concept of user cost useful in deriving interest elasticity of investment?
12. Using any model of your choice, examine the effect on investment of a reduction in the corporate income tax.

REFERENCES

BISCHOFF, G. W., "Business Investment in the 1970s: A Comparison of Models," *Brookings Papers on Economic Activity,* 1 (1971).

BRECHLING, FRANK, *Investment and Employment Decisions.* Manchester, Ind.: Manchester University Press, 1975.

EISNER, R., and R. H. STROTZ, "Determinants of Business Investment," Commission on Money and Credit, *Impacts of Monetary Policies,* pp. 59–337. Englewood Cliffs, N.J.: Prentice-Hall, 1963.

FELDSTEIN, MARTIN S., and LAWRENCE SUMMERS, "Inflation, Tax Rules, and the Long Term Interest Rate," *Brookings Papers on Economic Activity,* 1 (1978).

FISHER, IRVING, *Theory of Interest.* New York: Macmillan, 1930.

FOLEY, D., and M. SIDRAUSKI, *Monetary Policy and Fiscal Policy in a Growing Economy,* Chap. 6. New York: Macmillan, 1971.

GOULD, J. P., "Adjustment Costs in the Theory of Investment of the Firm," *Review of Economic Studies,* January 1968, pp. 47–56.

JONES, R. W., "The Structure of Simple General Equilibrium Models, *Journal of Political Economy,* December 1965, pp. 557–72.

JORGENSON, DALE W., "Capital Theory and Investment Behavior," *American Economic Review,* May 1963, pp. 247–59.

———, "Econometric Studies of Investment Behavior: A Survey," *Journal of Economic Literature,* December 1971, pp. 1111–47.

JORGENSON, DALE W., and C. D. SIEBERT, "A Comparison of Alternative Theories of Investment," *American Economic Review,* September 1968, pp. 681–712.

KALECKI, MICHAEL, "The Principle of Increasing Risk," *Economica,* November 1937, pp. 440–47.

KEYNES, J. M., *The General Theory of Employment, Interest, and Money,* Chaps. 11 and 12. New York: Harcourt, Brace & Co., 1935.

LERNER, ABBA P., *The Economics of Control,* Chap. 25. New York: Macmillan, 1944.

LUCAS, ROBERT E., JR., "Adjustment Costs and the Theory of Supply," *Journal of Political Economy,* August 1967, pp. 321–34.

ROSE, HUGH, "Effective Demand in the Long Run," in *Models of Economic Growth,* ed. J. Mirrlees and N. H. Stern, pp. 25–47. New York: Wiley, 1973.

TOBIN, JAMES, "A General Equilibrium Approach to Monetary Theory," *Journal of Money, Credit and Banking,* February 1969, pp. 15–29.

TOBIN, JAMES, and WILLIAM C. BRAINARD, "Asset Markets and the Cost of Capital," in *Economic Progress, Private Values, and Public Policy. Essays in Honor of William Fellner,* ed. B. Balassa and R. Nelson, pp. 236–62. Amsterdam: North Holland, 1977.

TREADWAY, ARTHUR, "On Rational Entrepreneurial Behavior and the Demand for Investment," *Review of Economic Studies,* April 1969, pp. 227–39.

UZAWA, H., "The Penrose Effect and Optimum Growth," *Economic Studies Quarterly,* September 1968, pp. 1–16.

WITTE, JAMES G., JR., "The Microfoundations of the Social Investment Function," *Journal of Political Economy,* October 1963, pp. 441–56.

13 The Demand for Money

In this chapter we establish a negative relation between the interest rate and the demand for money. (This relation is in addition to the positive one between the demand for money and the level of income.) We shall examine four alternative theories, one in each of the first four sections. First, in the Tobin-Baumol manner, we show that even the transactions demand for money is dependent upon the interest rate. Second, we establish, along the lines of Keynes and Tobin, a negative relation between the demand for money and the interest rate, the case when wealth holders have *certain* but *inelastic expectations* of bond prices (or interest rates) that are *different.* Among the shortcomings of this approach is the implication that investors hold either bonds or cash, but not both. The third theory, examined in Section III, is designed to derive the demand for money and for a diversified portfolio. The theory is based on *uncertainty* of expectations and is modeled after Tobin. The fourth theory, the topic of Section IV, also considers money as one of several alternative assets available to the wealth holder. The demand for these assets is derived by using standard microeconomic tools, such as utility maximization, which is subject to the wealth constraint. We find that the resulting demands for all assets are functions of all the assumed parameters, that is, wealth and the prices or yields of the assets. We see, once again, that the demand for money depends on the interest rate. This fourth approach is the one espoused by Friedman. In Section V we examine the empirical evidence, which shows, contrary to some earlier work, that there is substantial interest elasticity of the demand for money. The recently observed instability (or shift) of the demand function for money is also examined and its impact on the conduct of economic policy explained.

I. THE TRANSACTIONS DEMAND FOR MONEY AND THE INTEREST RATE

The demand for money that we derived in Chapter 3 was based solely on the *transactions motive.* Symbolically, and in nominal terms, the stock demand was represented by $l \cdot pY$; in real terms, this demand was $l \cdot Y$. It was clear, therefore, that the transactions demand for real balances depends on the level of output (income), Y, and on the determinants of l, the fraction of income held in money, which, in turn, is the inverse of the velocity, V. In Chapter 3 we saw that V, as well as its inverse, l, was determined by the payments habits of society. We saw, for example, that if the average worker is paid more often, say, once a week rather than once a month, the demand for money falls. We stressed the traditional belief that the payments habits of society change very slowly, and thus, for all practical purposes, can be assumed fixed. And this, in turn, implies that the velocity and its inverse are fixed.

Keynes was willing to go along with this view, admitting that the transactions demand for money is independent of the interest rate. Given this tenet, he had to rely on two other motives, the *speculative* and the *precautionary,* to establish a negative relation between the demand for money and the interest rate. Two decades later, however, William Baumol and James Tobin challenged that view; they proved that even the transactions demand for money depends on the interest rate.[1]

Let us now reexamine our earlier example, reproduced in Figure 13-1. We saw that a person who is paid \$300 once a month, and who spends \$10 a day until the thirtieth of the month, has to hold, on the average, \$150 in cash, that is, one-half of his spendable income. But more careful examination of this example reveals that we were hasty in our conclusions, which conclusions are valid only if the (average) individual is *obliged* to hold his transactions balances in cash.

The issue can perhaps be best illustrated by means of the following extreme example. Suppose that an individual receiving his payroll check of \$300 deposits all of it into his savings account. (Henceforth we shall consider this sum as bonds.) And each day as he returns from work, he stops at the bank to withdraw \$10, which he immediately spends at the grocery next door. It is clear that, for all practical purposes, this individual does not hold any cash. Yet it is also true that he holds, on the average, \$150 worth of *transactions balances*—but in bonds and not in cash.

The difference between the two extreme examples lies in the number of times the individual is willing to move his transactions balances between cash and bonds. In the first case, none; and in the second, thirty times in thirty days. In fact, we can show that the demand for cash diminishes as the average person increases the

---

[1] William J. Baumol, "The Transactions Demand for Cash: An Inventory Theoretic Approach," *Quarterly Journal of Economics,* November 1952, pp. 545–56; and James Tobin, "The Interest-Elasticity of Transaction Demand for Cash," *Review of Economics and Statistics,* September 1956, pp. 241–47.

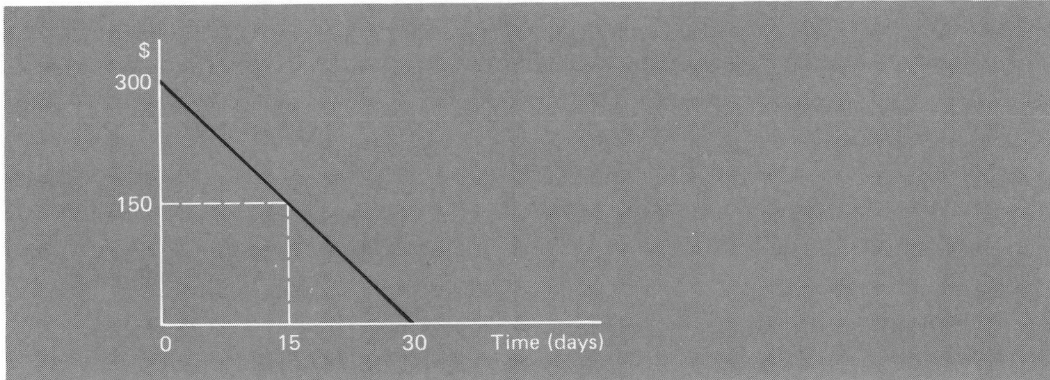

FIGURE 13-1

number of moves between money and bonds. We have already seen that with no trips to the bank, the individual will hold one-half of his spendable income in cash. Examine now the case of an individual who wants to make only one trip, in addition to payday, during the month. On payday this individual deposits \$150 in interest-bearing bonds and keeps \$150 in cash. He spends \$10 per day until the fifteenth of the month when he runs out of cash. For these first fifteen days this individual holds, on the average \$75. Now, on the fifteenth of the month, he withdraws from his savings account the remaining \$150, which he spends, again, at the rate of \$10 per day until it is exhausted on the thirtieth of the month. Now, between the fifteenth and the thirtieth of the month, he again holds, on the average, \$75. The average of the average is the same, that is, \$75. We see that with one trip to the bank this individual reduced his demand for cash from \$150 to \$75. This is illustrated in Figure 13-2. (In this case the individual will earn interest equal to $150 \times (i/2)$, where i is the *monthly* interest rate. In general, he earns $(Y/2) \times (i/2)$, where Y is his monthly spendable income.)

FIGURE 13-2 ONE TRIP

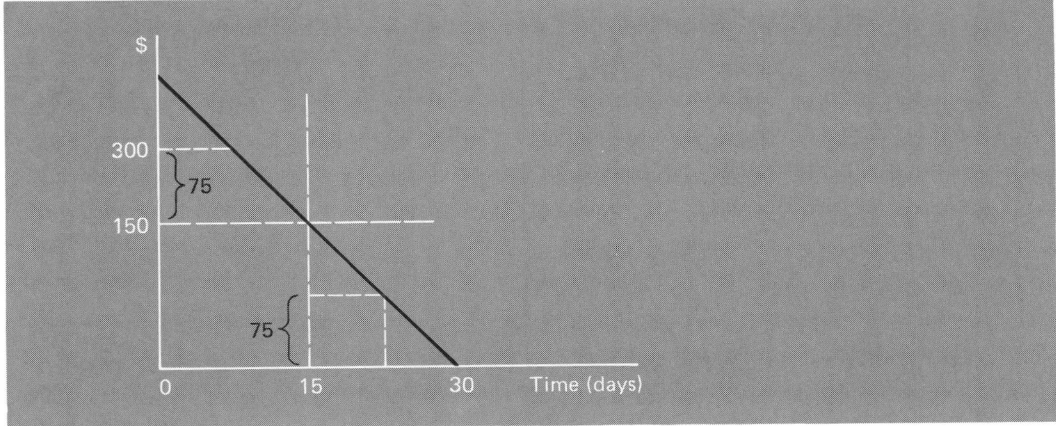

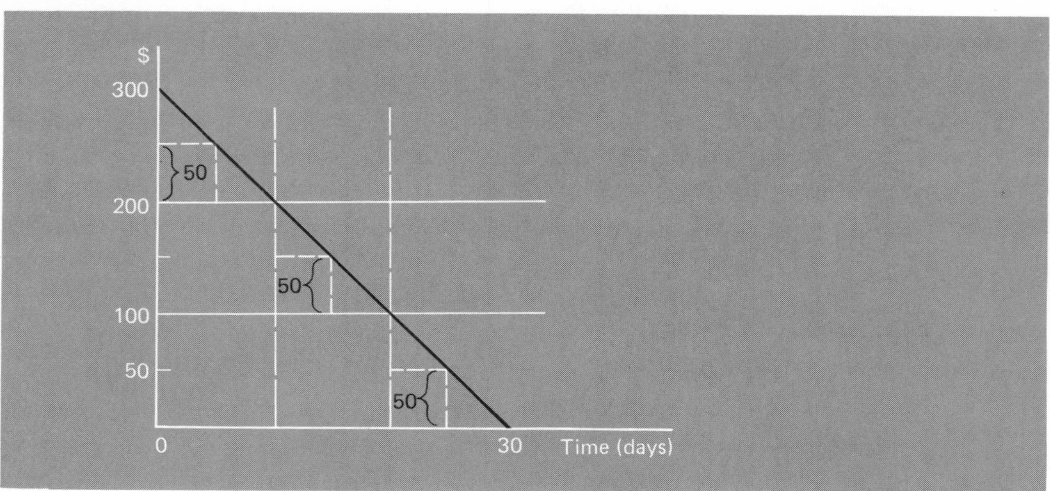

FIGURE 13-3 TWO TRIPS

In Figure 13-3 we depict the case of two trips for the purpose of withdrawing funds from one's savings account. On payday, two-thirds of his income (i.e., \$200 and, in general, $[2/3] \cdot Y$) is deposited and one-third (i.e., \$100) is kept in cash and spent within ten days. During the first ten days, this individual holds, on the average, \$50. He also holds \$50 between the tenth and the twentieth of the month, and between the twentieth and the thirtieth. On the tenth, he makes his first trip to the bank and withdraws \$100. Similarly, on the twentieth of the month, he makes his second trip to withdraw the last \$100, which he spends by payday. We see that in the two-trip case, the individual holds less money than in the one-trip case, namely \$50, or $(Y/2) \times (1/3)$, and that he earns interest equal to $100 \times (i/3) + 100 \times (2i/3) = 100 \times i$. In general, he earns

$$\frac{Y}{3} \cdot \frac{i}{3} + \frac{Y}{3} \cdot \frac{2i}{3} = \frac{3iY}{9} = \frac{iY}{3}$$

Similarly, we can show that with three trips, this individual will hold, on the average, only \$37.50, or, in general, $(Y/2) \cdot (1/4)$, in cash. They will earn

$$75 \times \frac{i}{4} + 75 \times \frac{2i}{4} + 75 \times \frac{3i}{4} = 112.50 \times i$$

In general, they will earn

$$\frac{Y}{4} \cdot \frac{i}{4} + \frac{Y}{4} \cdot \frac{2i}{4} + \frac{Y}{4} \cdot \frac{3i}{4} = \frac{iY}{16} \cdot (1 + 2 + 3) = \frac{3iY}{8}$$

Table 13-1 summarizes our information about the demand for cash and the earnings in the cases of zero, one, two, three, and n trips. We distinguish between total and marginal earnings for reasons that will shortly become obvious.

TABLE 13-1

NUMBER OF TRIPS	DEMAND FOR CASH	TOTAL REVENUE	MARGINAL REVENUE
0	\$150, $\frac{Y}{2}$	—	—
1	\$75, $\frac{Y}{2} \cdot \frac{1}{2}$	$75 \times i, \frac{iY}{4}$	$75 \times i, \frac{iY}{4}$
2	\$50, $\frac{Y}{2} \cdot \frac{1}{3}$	$100 \times i, \frac{iY}{3}$	$25 \times i, \frac{iY}{3} - \frac{iY}{4} = \frac{iY}{12}$
3	\$37.50, $\frac{Y}{2} \cdot \frac{1}{4}$	$112.50 \times i, \frac{3}{8} iY$	$12.50 \times i, \frac{9}{24} iY - \frac{8}{24} iY = \frac{iY}{24}$
.	.		
.	.		
.	.		
.	.		
n	$\frac{Y}{2} \cdot \frac{1}{(n+1)}$	$\frac{niY}{2(n+1)}$	0

From now on we shall substitute the term *transactions* (between bonds and cash) for those *trips* to the bank to withdraw from the savings account. Using this term, we can summarize our result as follows: *The demand for money is determined by the number of transactions between money and bonds. The higher the number of these transactions, the lower the demand for money will be.*

The question arises, How is the number of transactions (between money and bonds) determined? Of course, the standard criterion of rationality is profit, or net revenue-maximization. Now, *revenue* comes from interest earnings. *Costs,* which must be subtracted from revenue, are both monetary and nonmonetary. For example, actual costs of going to the bank belong to the former category. (Enduring the condescension of tellers may be a nonmonetary cost for a person who goes too frequently to the bank for withdrawals.)

According to Table 13-1, *total revenue* is accruing at a decreasing rate as the number of transactions increases, that is, a decreasing *marginal revenue* exists for each additional transaction, as shown in the last column of Table 13-1. The former relation is depicted in the upper panel of Figure 13-4, and the latter in the lower panel. For simplicity, we assume here that the *marginal cost* of each transaction is constant. This means that the *total cost* of transactions increases at a fixed rate with the number of transactions. In Figure 13-4 the optimum number of transactions is n_*. At this number, total *net* revenue is at its maximum and equal to *AB,* a state achieved when the marginal revenue of the last transaction is equal to the marginal cost. In the upper panel, *marginal revenue* is represented by the slope of the tangent to the total revenue curve, *TR,* and the marginal cost by the slope of the total cost curve, *TC.* Marginal cost, marginal revenue, and the optimum point are shown in the lower panel of Figure 13-4.

We need only one additional step to establish a relation between the interest

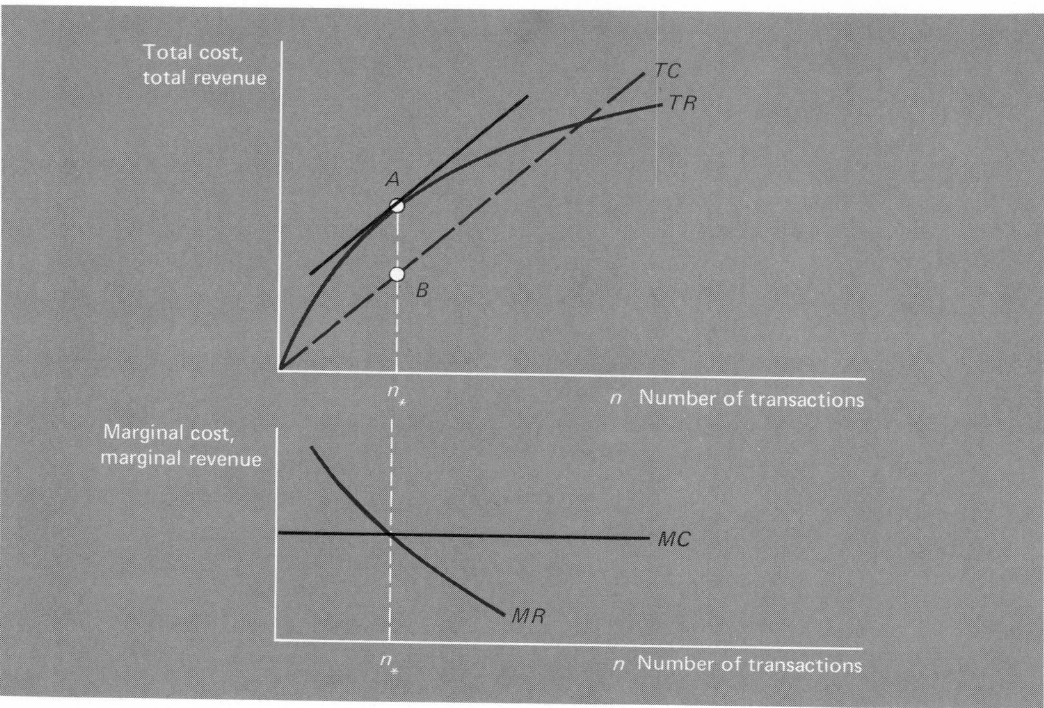

FIGURE 13-4

rate and the demand for money. In particular, we need to show that a change in the interest rate will change the number of transactions. (The change in the number of transactions will, in turn, induce a change in the demand for money.) But this is easily shown. The total revenue curve and the marginal revenue curve have been drawn for a *particular* level of the interest rate. Let us concentrate only on the marginal revenue curve, *MR;* there must be one such curve for each assumed level of the interest rate. Moreover, simple inspection of Table 13-1 can convince the reader that the higher the interest rate, the farther to the right the *MR* curve will lie. In other words, for the same number of transactions the corresponding marginal revenue will be higher when the interest rate is greater. In Figure 13-5 the curve labeled $MR(i_0)$ corresponds to an interest rate, i_0, lower than that assumed in the construction curve $MR(i_1)$, that is, $i_1 > i_0$. It is clear that when the interest rate rises from i_0 to i_1, the optimal number of transactions rises from n_*^0 to n_*^1.

We have, therefore, established the link between the interest rate and the number of transactions. In particular, we can see that *an increase (decline) in the interest rate increases (reduces) the number of transactions (between money and bonds).* Since we know that an increase (decrease) in the number of transactions reduces (increases) the demand for money, we have established this result: *An increase in the interest rate lowers the demand for money, and, similarly, a reduction in the interest rate increases the demand for money.* This is shown graphically in Figure 13-6, where D_M is the demand for money.

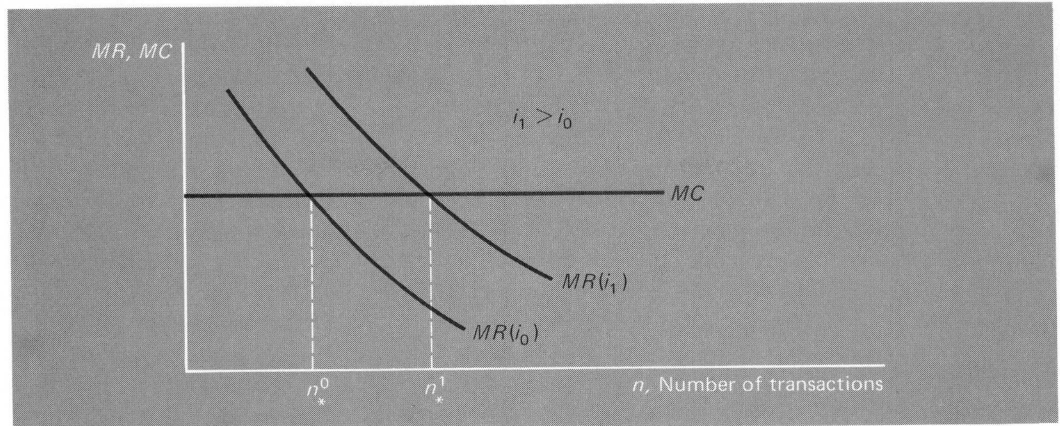

FIGURE 13-5

FIGURE 13-6

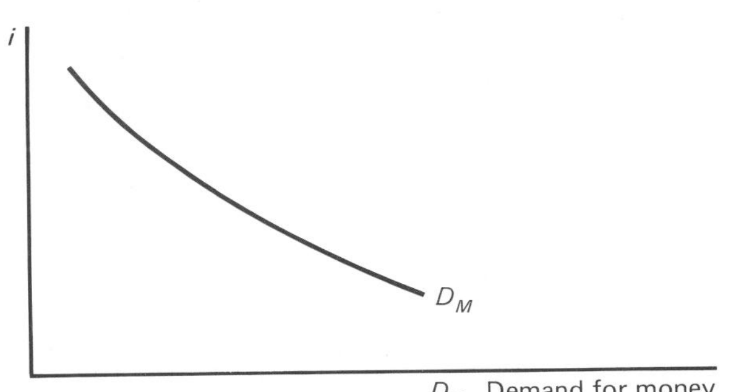

FIGURE 13-7

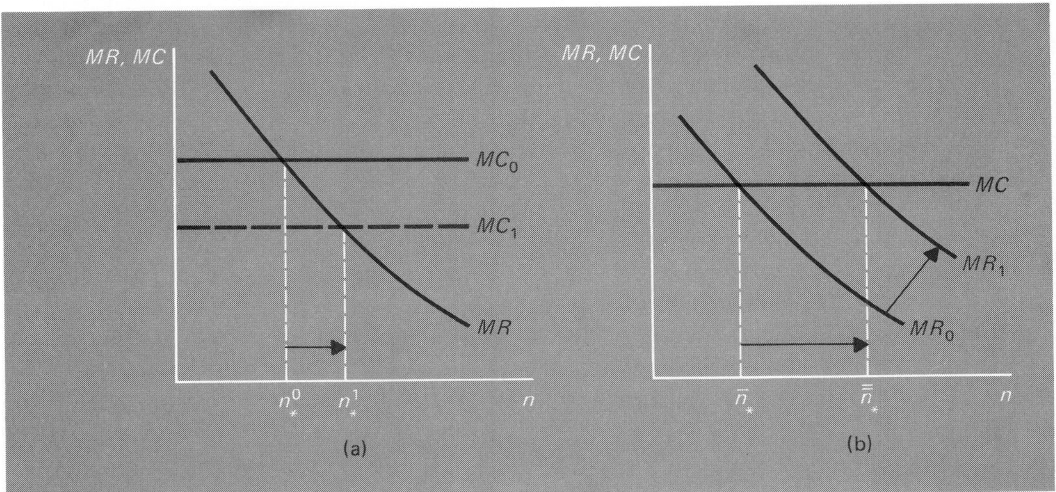

Although here we are interested only in establishing the negative relation between the interest rate and the demand for money, we should mention that graphs similar to Figures 13-4 and 13-5 can also be used to explain the implications behind certain banking practices. When, for example, some banks make the transactions less costly, say, by permitting transfers from savings to checking accounts, and vice versa, by telephone, the *MC* curve shifts downward, as in Figure 13-7a, thereby increasing the optimal number of transactions; this, in turn, reduces the demand for money. Similarly, more pleasant bank lobbies, music, or lollipops increase the in kind marginal revenue, thereby shifting the *MR* curve to the right. This is shown in Figure 13-7b, which has the same implications that Figure 13-7a does.

II. SPECULATIVE DEMAND FOR MONEY: CERTAIN EXPECTATIONS

Keynes adopted the classical view that the transactions demand for money depends only on the payments habits of society, and not on the interest rate. He pointed out, however, that because money is a *store of value,* people want to hold it even though they may not need it during the period for transactions purposes. But what makes people hold some of their wealth in cash, which does not pay interest, rather than in another asset, such as a bond, which yields interest? Keynes suggested that people forgo interest by holding cash, rather than bonds, because of the *uncertainty* and *risk* that surround bond holdings. Bonds are traded in the market and their price fluctuates. It is possible that the capital losses, because of a fall in the price of bonds, may outweigh the interest accrued. In such a case it is better to hold one's wealth in cash rather than in bonds. Zero return is better than a negative return! Of course, one has to estimate the future price of bonds before he can decide in what form to keep his wealth. But the expected price of bonds is *uncertain,* while the nominal return on money is certain, namely zero. This uncertainty of expectations may persuade an individual to hold some of the *certain* asset, money, in his portfolio.

Although Keynes emphasized the risk and uncertainty of expectations as reasons for holding money, as well as the reasons for establishing a relation between the interest rate and the demand for money, his formal analysis dealt with risk emanating from *certain,* but different, expectations among different (groups of) individuals. It was Tobin who provided the formal and definitive analysis of uncertainty. Here we shall establish the dependence of the demand for money on the interest rate, first by relying on *certain* expectations of future bond prices and, second, on the *uncertainty* of such expectations. The former is Keynes' way; the second is Tobin's. We shall, however, present both approaches by relying on Tobin's modern exposition, the classic "Liquidity Preference as Behavior toward Risk."[2]

Tobin's *portfolio choice theory* will be presented in its simplest form; we shall assume, along with Keynes, that there are only two assets, money and bonds. Here a bond is a perpetuity yielding the fixed amount of c dollars each period, with

[2] See *Review of Economic Studies,* February 1958, pp. 65–86.

c representing *coupon.* Knowing the coupon and the prevailing interest rate, we can find the market price of the bond; it is simply the capitalized value of the coupon. With interest rate, *i,* the coupon, *c,* the price of bonds *P,* is

$$P = \frac{c}{i}$$

We shall apply this formula to find the price of bonds in any period. We shall denote the current period with the subscript 0, and the future period by the subscript 1. The term *expected* will occasionally be used in place of *future.* Thus the current and expected prices of bonds, P_0 and P_1, are respectively

$$P_0 = \frac{c}{i_0} \tag{1a}$$

$$P_1 = \frac{c}{i_1} \tag{1b}$$

Using (1a) and (1b), we can find formulas for *capital gains* (or *losses*). If a bond is bought now for P_0 dollars, and sold in the next period for P_1 dollars, the *absolute* capital gains are $(P_1 - P_0)$. The capital gains in *percentage terms* will be denoted by *g* and are found by using (1a) and (1b). (We are using Tobin's symbols.)

$$g \equiv \frac{P_1 - P_0}{P_0}$$

$$= \frac{P_1}{P_0} - 1$$

$$= \frac{c/i_1}{c/i_0} - 1 \text{ by (1a) and (1b).}$$

Thus

$$g = \frac{i_0}{i_1} - 1 \tag{2}$$

Equipped with these simple tools, we are now ready to examine the approach that relies on certainty of expectations. We are considering an individual who has the problem of deciding whether to hold his wealth, between now and the next period, in bonds, in cash, or in both. The individual knows that if he keeps his wealth in cash, his return will be zero. It is clear, then, that if he expects with certainty that bonds will give a net return greater than zero, he will hold *all* his wealth in bonds. If, on the other hand, he expects with certainty that the net return on bonds is negative, he will hold all his wealth in cash. Finally, if the net return on bonds is exactly zero, that is, if he merely breaks even, he will be indifferent between bonds and cash. Symbolically, this *portfolio criterion* is given by the following schema, (3):

$$\text{If} \quad c + P_1 - P_0 \gtreqless 0, \quad \text{then} \quad \begin{array}{l}\text{all wealth in bonds}\\ \text{indifferent}\\ \text{all wealth in cash}\end{array} \tag{3}$$

The left-hand side of schema (3) states that in the next period, the individual who has now invested P_0 dollars will receive the coupon payment, c, plus the selling price, P_1. Subtracting P_0, the price he now pays to buy the bond, we can find the net return in dollars. Note that if the price rises above what he pays now (i.e., if $P_1 > P_0$), he reaps both the coupon, c, and capital gains. Since his net return is positive, he will invest all his wealth in bonds. He will do the same even if the price of bonds remains the same (i.e., $P_1 = P_0$), or even if it falls, *provided that it falls by less than the value of the coupon.* On the other hand, if the bond price falls by more than the value of the coupon, the capital loss outweighs the interest accrued. The net return in dollars is negative, that is, the return on bonds is lower than the return on money, which is zero, thereby inducing the individual to keep all his wealth in cash.

Now, if we divide the left-hand side of (3) by today's price of bonds, P_0, we get

$$\text{If} \quad \frac{c}{P_0} + \frac{P_1}{P_0} - 1 \gtreqless 0, \quad \text{then} \quad \begin{array}{l}\text{all wealth in bonds}\\ \text{indifferent}\\ \text{all wealth in cash}\end{array}$$

which, by using (1a) and (1b), becomes:

$$\text{If} \quad i_0 + \frac{i_0}{i_1} - 1 \gtreqless 0, \quad \text{then} \quad \begin{array}{l}\text{all wealth in bonds}\\ \text{indifferent}\\ \text{all wealth in cash}\end{array} \tag{4}$$

Using the criterion in (3), it is obvious that the individual can decide in what form to keep his wealth only if he knows today's price, P_0, and tomorrow's price, P_1. (It is taken for granted that the coupon is always known.) Equivalently, using (4), the decision can be made with the knowledge of today's and tomorrow's interest rates, i_0 and i_1, respectively. It is clear that when today's price is known, the holdings of bonds and money are functions of the expected, or tomorrow's, price. This is the same as saying that with today's interest rate, i_0, known, the holdings of or demands for money and bonds depend on the expected interest rate, i_1. Two examples will help illustrate the issues.

Example 1

Known: $c = \$5$, $P_0 = \$100$. Unknown: $P_1 = ?$ Applying the criterion in (3), we have:

$$\text{If} \quad P_1 \begin{matrix} > \\ = \\ < \end{matrix} \$95, \quad \text{then} \quad \begin{matrix} \text{all wealth in bonds} \\ \text{indifferent} \\ \text{all wealth in cash} \end{matrix} \tag{3'}$$

This schema establishes the demands for bonds and for money as functions of the expected price of bonds. Figure 13-8a depicts the demand for bonds, D_B, and Figure 13-8b represents the demand for money, D_M, with both as functions of the expected price of bonds. Figure 13-8a shows that if the expected price of bonds is less than \$95, the demand for bonds is zero, since all wealth is kept in cash; the demand curve coincides with the vertical axis. If, on the other hand, the expected price of bonds is greater than \$95, the demand for bonds is a constant, equal to total wealth (assumed to be equal to the distance OA). If the expected price is exactly equal to \$95, there is indeterminancy. Figure 13-8a, in other words, shows that *the demand for bonds is a nondecreasing function of the expected price of bonds.*

Figure 13-8b depicts the *demand for money as a nonincreasing function of the expected price of bonds.* It is the mirror image of Figure 13-8a, from which it can be derived as an implication. When the expected bond price is less than \$95, the demand for money is always equal to the individual's total wealth, OA. When the price is greater than \$95, since everything is kept in bonds, the demand for money is zero and the curve coincides with the vertical axis.

Formula (3′) and its diagrammatic representation in Figures 13-8a and 13-8b highlight the *critical level of the expected price of bonds;* in our example, this critical value is \$95. Utilizing equations (1a) and (1b), or (4), we can find a *critical level of the expected interest rate.* With a coupon of \$5, an expected price equal to \$95 implies an expected interest rate equal to 5/95. Of course, an expected price *greater* than \$95 implies an expected interest rate *lower* than 5/95. Thus, for an

FIGURE 13-8

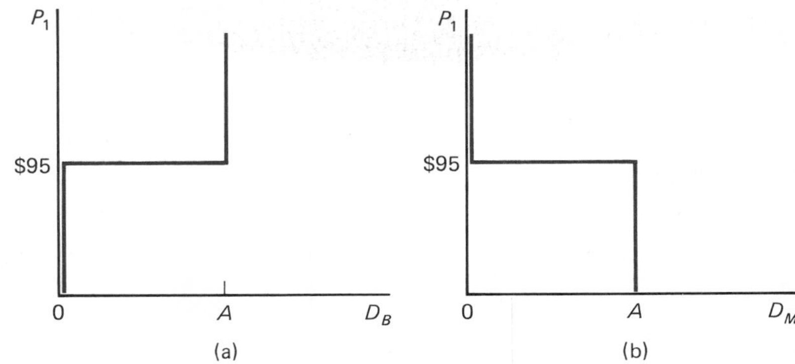

interest rate lower than 5/95, the demand for bonds is equal to the individual's wealth and the demand for money is zero. On the other hand, an expected interest rate *greater* than 5/95 implies a demand for bonds equal to zero and a demand for money equal to the individual's wealth, OA. These statements can be written compactly in (4′):

$$\text{If} \quad i_1 \begin{matrix} < \\ = \\ > \end{matrix} (5/95), \quad \text{then} \quad \begin{matrix} \text{all wealth in bonds} \\ \text{indifferent} \\ \text{all wealth in cash} \end{matrix} \tag{4′}$$

All of these are, in turn, summarized in Figures 13-9a and 13-9b. The former illustrates that the demand for bonds is a nonincreasing function of the expected interest rate, i_1, while Figure 13-9b illustrates that the demand for money is a nondecreasing function of i_1.

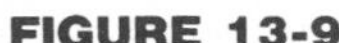

FIGURE 13-9

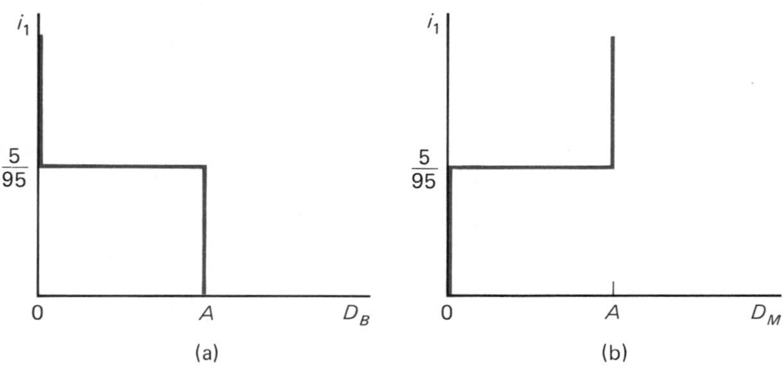

Example 1 assumed knowledge of one of the two variables, in particular, the present price of bonds. This assumption helped us derive the demands for the two assets as functions of the remaining variable. The role of the variables is reversed in example 2, which assumes knowledge of the other variable, the future price of bonds.

Example 2

Known: $c = \$5$, $P_1 = \$100$. Unknown: $P_0 = ?$ Applying. directly, formula (3), we get the results:

$$\text{If} \quad P_0 \begin{matrix} < \\ = \\ > \end{matrix} \$105, \quad \text{then} \quad \begin{matrix} \text{all wealth in bonds} \\ \text{indifferent} \\ \text{all wealth in cash} \end{matrix} \tag{3″}$$

Formula (3″) highlights the critical value of the present price of bonds. Above this price, the demand for bonds is zero, while the demand for money is equal to the individual's wealth. Below it, the demand for bonds is equal to the individual's wealth and the demand for money is zero. In other words, *the demand for bonds is a nonincreasing function and the demand for money a nondecreasing function of the present price of bonds.* These are shown in Figures 13-10a and 13-10b, which are, by now, self-explanatory.

FIGURE 13-10

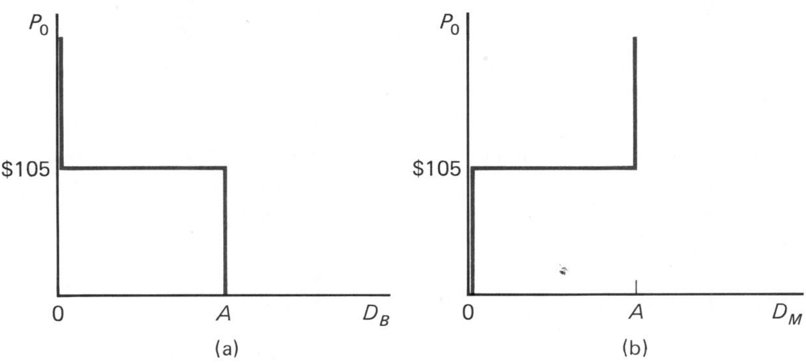

Again applying formula (1a), or, directly, formula (4), we can focus on the *critical value of the present interest rate;* in this example the critical present interest rate, i_0, is equal to 5/105. This is shown explicitly in formula (4″) and its diagrammatic representations, Figures 13-11a and 13-11b.

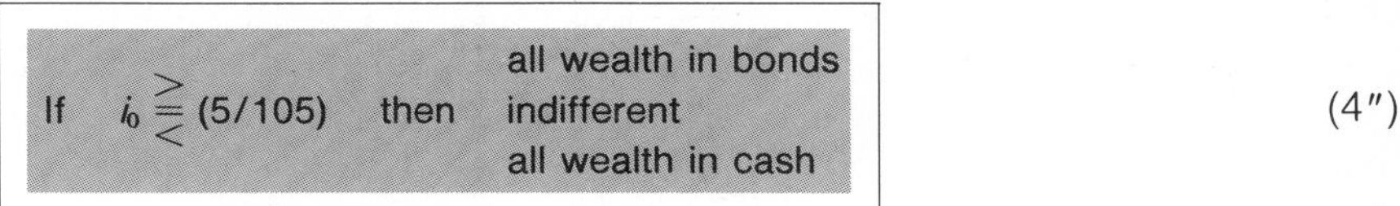

$$\text{If} \quad i_0 \begin{matrix} > \\ = \\ < \end{matrix} (5/105) \quad \text{then} \quad \begin{matrix} \text{all wealth in bonds} \\ \text{indifferent} \\ \text{all wealth in cash} \end{matrix} \qquad (4'')$$

FIGURE 13-11

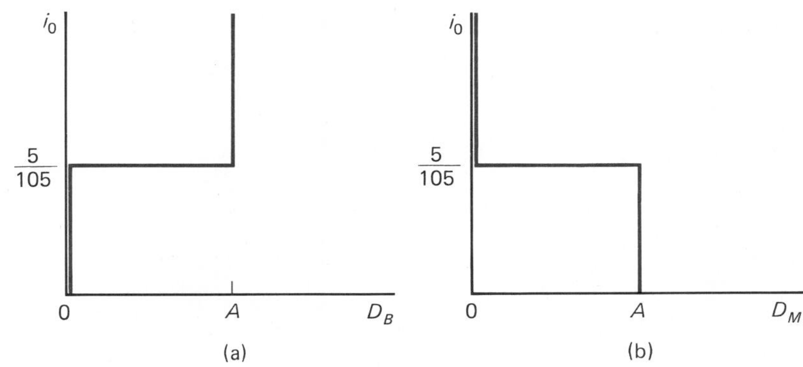

Of particular interest to us in this chapter is Figure 13-11b, which illustrates that the demand for money is a *nonincreasing* function of the *current* interest rate. This is close to saying that the demand for money is a *decreasing* function of the current interest rate. We shall see how we actually derive such a decreasing function, that is, a downward-sloping demand curve for money. First, however, we shall derive a graph in the form of Figure 13-11b by a general analysis rather than by specific examples.

THE ZERO PROFITABILITY LINE, ZPL

We already know that the portfolio decision of an individual agent depends on the magnitudes of two variables, namely, the present price of bonds, P_0, and the future price of bonds, P_1. Equivalently, this decision depends on the current interest rate, i_0, and on the future, expected, interest rate, i_1. Here we shall emphasize the latter. First, we shall concentrate on the equation that makes the individual investor indifferent between holding his wealth in money or in bonds. This is the middle of the three statements in (4):

If $i_0 - i_0/i_1 - 1 = 0$, then indifferent (between money and bonds). Solving this equation for i_1, we get:

$$\text{If } i_1 = \frac{i_0}{1 - i_0}, \quad \text{then indifferent} \tag{5}$$

In Figure 13-12 we depict this equation in the (i_0, i_1)-plane. The curve is upward sloping. It is important to know exactly what this curve depicts. It shows all the combinations of present and expected interest rates that yield zero profit to the portfolio holder and thus make him indifferent between money and bonds. We shall call this curve the *zero profitability line,* ZPL. For each level of the current

FIGURE 13-12

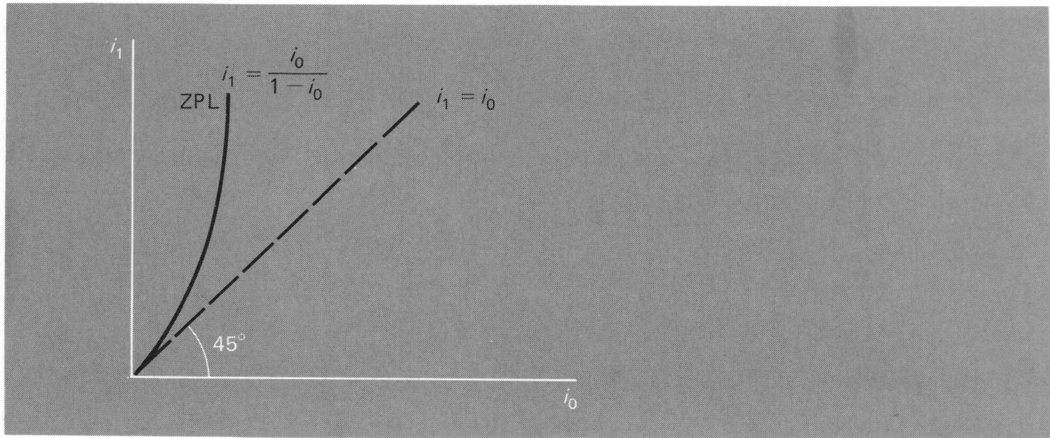

rate of interest, the ZPL shows the level of the expected interest rate that creates sufficient capital losses to negate exactly the current interest rate. Note that this expected interest rate must be *greater* than the assumed current one. This is why the zero profitability line lies uniformly *above* the 45° line whose equation is $i_1 = i_0$. The left-hand side (LHS) of the equation is the same as the LHS of (5). But the RHS of (5) is $i_0 \cdot [1/(1-i_0)]$, that is, greater than i_0, because $1/(1-i_0)$ is greater than one.

Because the zero profitability line is upward sloping, it follows that if the current interest rate is higher, the individual investors can still break even—but only if the expected interest rate is even higher. (The reader should be able to translate this statement into terms applicable to present and expected bond prices rather than to interest rates.)

We have just found all the combinations of present and expected interest rates that make the investors indifferent between money and bonds. All these combinations lie on the zero profitability line, $i_1 = i_0/(1-i_0)$. We now need to find what happens when a combination lies to the left or to the right of this curve. Let us suppose that the current and expected interest rates are captured by point *A* in Figure 13-13, that is, to the *right* of and *below* the ZPL. This means that if the present interest rate is at the level *OK*, the expected rate is at a level *lower* than that needed to guarantee zero profitability. For zero profitability a level equal to *KC* is needed, but point *A* represents a level of only *KA* (i.e., $KA < KC$).

To see what happens at point *A*, let us conduct the following mental experiment. Suppose that at the current interest rate of *OK* percent some individual had expected tomorrow's interest rate to equal *KC* percent. This means that for this combination, the capital loss of investing in bonds is exactly equal to the interest earnings. The individual is, therefore, indifferent between money and bonds. Suppose, now, that the individual's estimate of future interest rate *falls* from *KC* percent to *KA* percent. This means that he now expects the bond price to be even greater than his original estimate. But the original estimate gave losses equal to the current interest

FIGURE 13-13

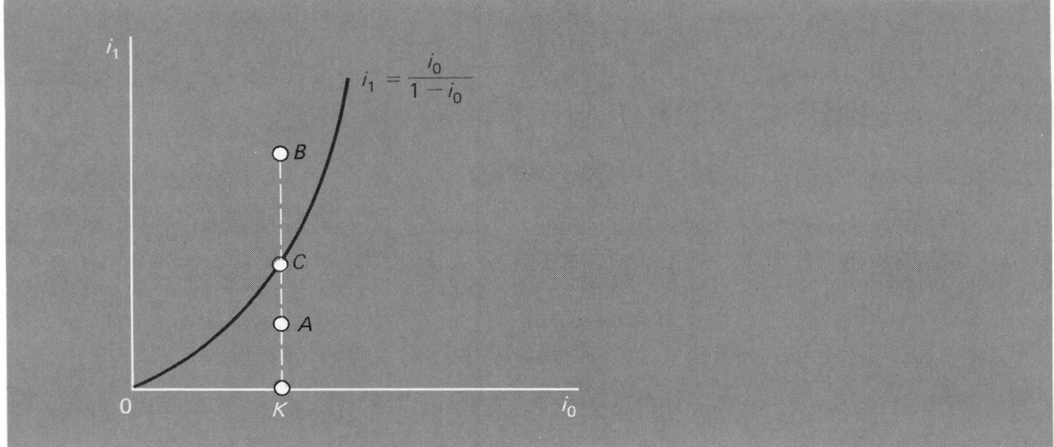

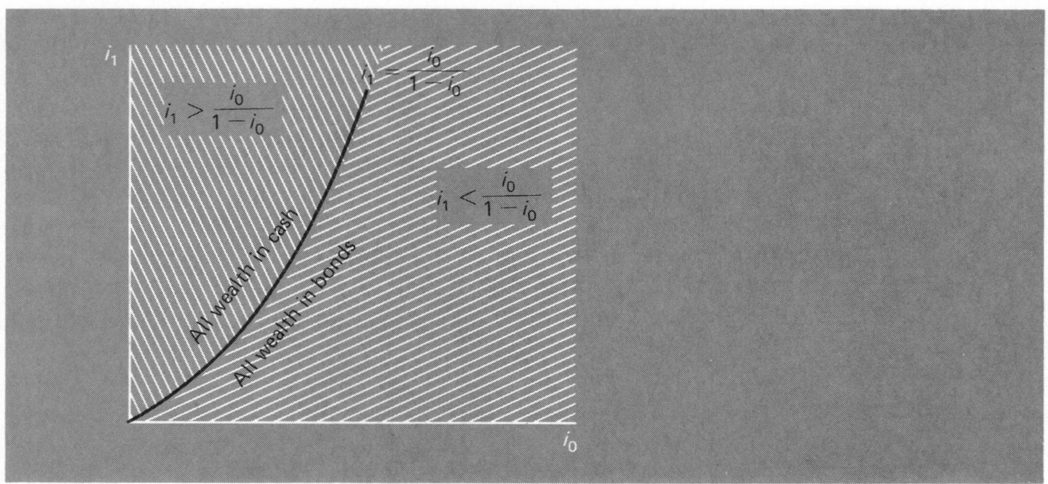

FIGURE 13-14

rate. With a higher expected bond price, the capital losses *must be less* than before. In fact, the losses may turn out to be *gains*. Hence there will be a positive net return, making it profitable for the investor to put all his wealth into bonds. We can repeat this analysis for any point to the right of and below the ZPL, and we can reverse the argument for any point to the left of and above the ZPL. We have thus established this result:

> The investor will hold his entire wealth in bonds if the combination representing current and expected interest rates lies to the right and below the ZPL. All his wealth will be held in cash if the combination lies to the left and above the ZPL.

The above results can be shown by simple arithmetic. We can see from (4) that the statement "if $i_0 - i_0/i_1 - 1 > 0$, then all in bonds," can be written "if $i_1 < i_0/(1-i_0)$, then all in bonds." Similarly, the inequality $i_0 - i_0/i_1 - 1 < 0$ can be written as $i_1 > i_0/(1-i_0)$, which implies that all wealth should then be in cash. All these statements are captured in Figure 13-14.

EXPECTATIONS

Our analysis still requires knowledge of the current and the expected rates of interest. Of course, the current rate is given in each period by the bonds market. Up-to-the-last-minute reports on Wall Street are regularly, and continuously, available. But what about the future rate of interest? The absence of these data makes portfolio choice difficult. Recall that we are examining the case of expectations held with *certainty*. We shall examine two situations. First, one in which the investor has in mind a specific interest rate as the expected one, a level independent of the current rate. The implication here is that if the current interest rate is greater than the expected one, the investor expects it to fall. On the other hand, he expects the interest rate to rise if it currently happens to be lower than the expected one. This is shown by the horizontal line, $\bar{i}_1\bar{i}_1$, depicting an assumed expected rate equal to $\bar{i}_1$.

The intersection of the ZPL and the expectations line, $\bar{i}_1\bar{i}_1$, is of critical importance. In fact, it gives us the *critical* level of the current rate of interest. At this interest rate, equal to *OC* in Figure 13-15, the investor is indifferent between money and bonds. If the current rate is lower than the critical value, say equal to *OA,* the combination of current and expected interest rates is represented by point *B,* clearly to the left of and above the ZPL, the region that dictates that all the wealth should be kept in cash. If, on the other hand, the current rate is greater than the critical value, say *OD,* the combination is point *E,* which lies in the region requiring that all should be kept in bonds. We can concentrate on money only and state that above the critical level of the current interest rate, the investor holds zero money, while his demand for money is equal to his entire wealth when the current rate is below the critical value. Finally, his demand for money is indeterminate when the current rate is at the critical level. All these statements are shown graphically in Figure 13-16, which is similar to Figure 13-11b. (Here, $O\omega$ represents the individual investor's total wealth.)

We shall now show that this demand curve for money can be derived even if the expected interest rate depends positively on the current rate. In other words, suppose that the investor revises his estimate of future interest rates on the basis of current rates: the higher the current interest rate, the higher is the expected rate. This is shown by an upward-sloping expectations curve, such as line $i_1 = h(i_0)$ in Figure 13-17. In this graph we see that the intersection of the expectations curve and the ZPL again produces a critical level of the current interest rate with the same properties as those in Figure 13-15. For this reason the notation of the two graphs was kept identical. If the current interest rate is less than *OC,* wealth is kept in cash. But wealth will all be held in bonds when the current rate is greater than *OC.*

In Figure 13-17 we see that the dependence of the expected interest rate on the current rate does not modify our earlier result, because of the way the two curves intersect. Suppose, instead, that, as in Figure 13-18, the expectations line is steeper than the ZPL. Then, when the current interest rate is greater than the critical rate, OC', say $OD' > OC'$, the implied expected interest rate is such that the combination of the two rates, point E', lies to the *left* of the ZPL, or in the "all in cash" region. On the other hand, when the current interest rate is lower than the critical value OC', say $OA' < OC'$, the relevant point, B', lies in the "all in bonds" region. The case of Figure 13-18 yields a demand-for-money curve that is nondecreasing (i.e, increasing) with the current interest rate, as in Figure 13-19. Since this is contrary to what empirical work has taught us, we should exclude it. Thus we shall assume that the expectations line has a smaller slope than the ZPL. It can be shown that this assumption is tantamount to requiring that the *elasticity of expectations is roughly less than one.* The slope of the ZPL is

$$\left.\frac{\Delta i_1}{\Delta i_0}\right|_{\text{ZPL}} = \frac{1}{(1 - i_0)^2} \tag{I}$$

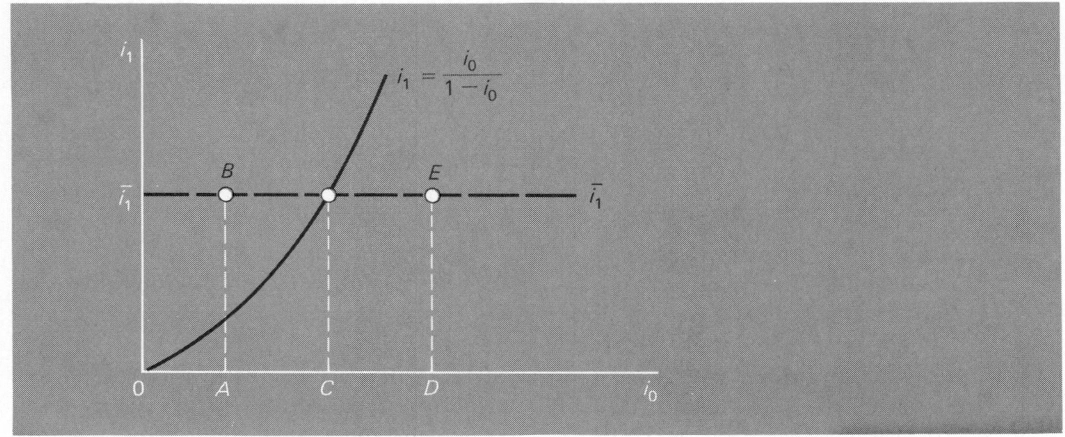

FIGURE 13-15

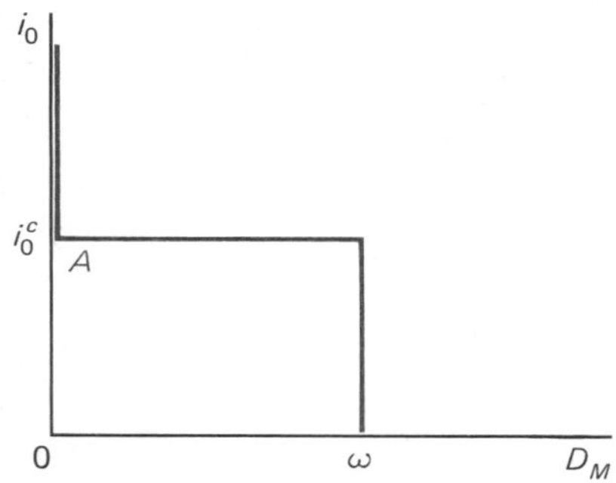

FIGURE 13-16

FIGURE 13-17

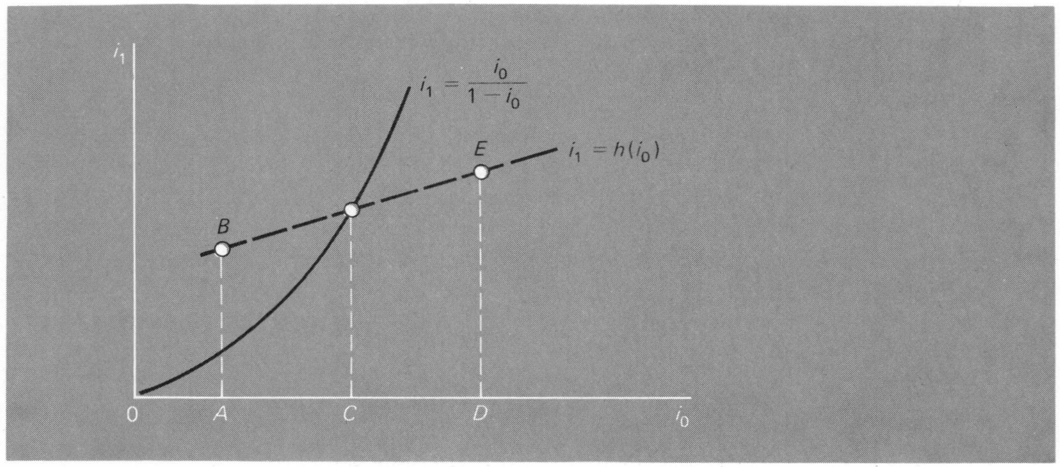

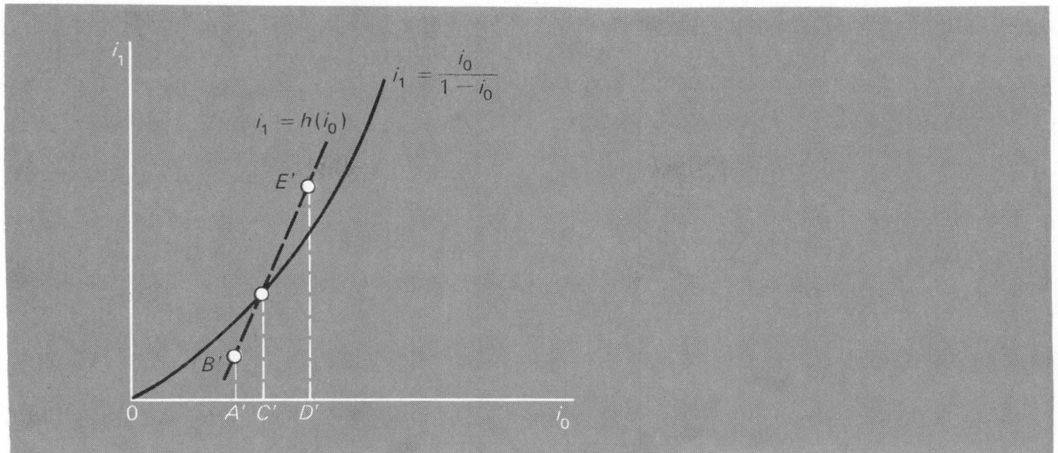

FIGURE 13-18

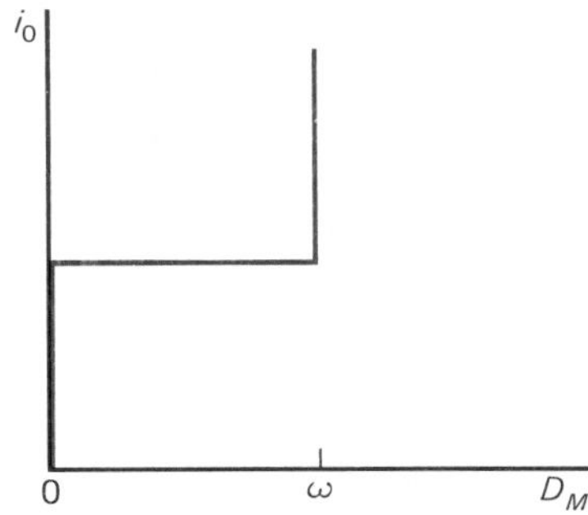

FIGURE 13-19

The slope of the expectations line, EL, is

$$\left.\frac{\Delta i_1}{\Delta i_0}\right|_{\mathrm{EL}} = \frac{\Delta h}{\Delta i_0} \tag{II}$$

The requirement that the slope of the expectations line be less than the slope of the ZPL can be written as

$$\frac{\Delta h}{\Delta i_0} < \frac{1}{(1 - i_0)^2}$$

or

$$\frac{\Delta h}{\Delta i_0} < \frac{1}{(1 - i_0)} \cdot \frac{1}{(1 - i_0)} \tag{III}$$

The slopes are evaluated at the point of intersection, that is, when

$$h(i_0) = \frac{i_0}{1 - i_0} \tag{IV}$$

From this equation, we can get

$$\frac{h(i_0)}{i_0} = \frac{1}{1 - i_0}$$

Substituting this into (III), we get

$$\frac{\Delta h}{\Delta i_0} < \frac{1}{1 - i_0} \cdot \frac{h(i_0)}{i_0},$$

and rearranging, we establish that

$$\frac{\Delta h}{\Delta i_0} \cdot \frac{i_0}{h(i_0)} < \frac{1}{1 - i_0} \tag{V}$$

The LHS of (V) is, of course, the elasticity of expectations, or the ratio of the percentage change in the expected rate of interest and the percentage change in the current interest, that is, $(\Delta i_1/i_1)/(\Delta i_0/i_0)$, using the relation $i_1 = h(i_0)$. Note that the RHS of (V) is a number *greater* than one. Thus (V) says that the elasticity of expectations has to be less than a number that is (slightly) greater than one. It follows that this inequality is indeed satisfied if the elasticity of expectations is equal to or less than one. We see that *when the elasticity of expectations is less than one, we can derive the demand for money as a decreasing function of the current interest rate.* This fact was noticed as early as 1939 by Nicholas Kaldor, who stated that "it is . . . not so much the uncertainty concerning future interest rates as the *inelasticity of interest expectations* which is responsible for Mr. Keynes' 'liquidity preference function' . . ."[3]

In summary, we have seen that when an individual possesses *certain* but *inelastic* expectations of the interest rate, he can ascertain the critical value of the current rate; if the current rate of interest exceeds the critical value, his demand for money is zero. On the other hand, his demand for money is equal to his entire wealth when the current rate of interest is lower than its critical level.

The next step is to assume that people differ in their expectations and, therefore, in their estimations of the critical values of the current interest rate. Given this assumption, we can plot the aggregate demand for cash. By aggregating over individuals or groups of individuals with identical critical values, we get a curve like the one in Figure 13-20a. At interest rates *above the maximum critical* one, the

[3] Nicholas Kaldor, "Speculation and Economic Stability," *Review of Economic Studies,* 1939, italics added.

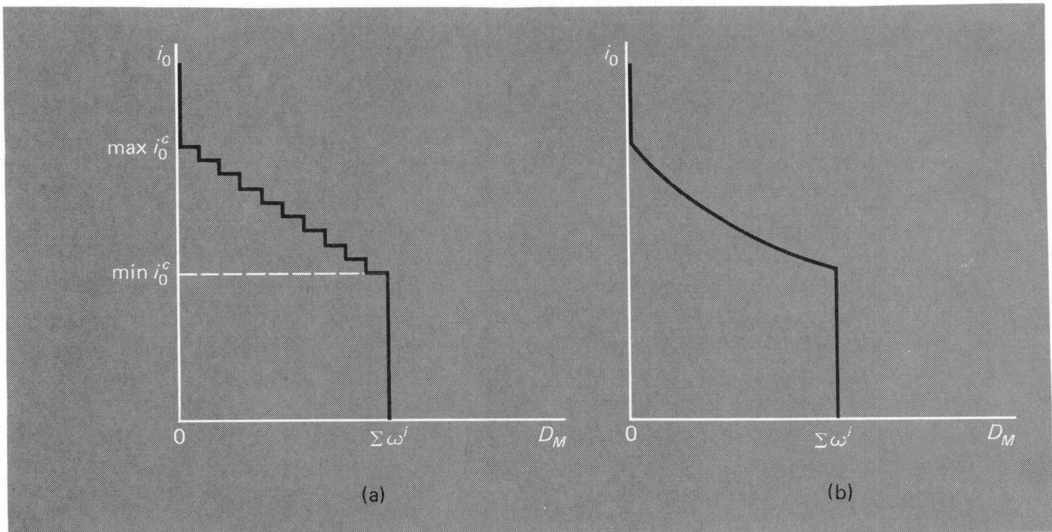

FIGURE 13-20

aggregate demand for cash is zero. As the interest rate becomes lower, more and more individuals demand cash until the *minimum critical* interest rate is reached. Below that level, everybody will want to hold their entire wealth in cash. We can then smooth out the curve, as in Figure 13-20b. In this way we end up with a *truly downward-sloping* demand curve for money.

Example 3

Let us now derive the aggregate demand for money by means of an arithmetical example. Suppose that the coupon, *c*, on a perpetual bond is \$5. Also, suppose that in the society under consideration there are three groups of wealth holders, 1, 2, and 3, whose *certain* expected bond prices are \$95, \$120, and \$145, respectively, and that the wealth of each group is equal to \$100 million. Simple arithmetic reveals that the critical present bond prices are \$100 for group 1, \$125 for group 2, and \$150 for group 3. Since the coupon is \$5, these are translated, respectively, into the critical current interest rates of 0.05, 0.04, and 0.033. Figures 13-21a, 13-21b, and 13-21c depict, respectively, the demand for money by groups 1, 2, and 3. The aggregate demand for money is depicted in Figure 13-22.

Two elements of this approach must be emphasized. First, to obtain a truly downward-sloping demand curve for cash, we need different expectations among different groups of people. If everybody holds the same expectation of the interest rate, the curve will be horizontal at the *common* critical interest rate implied by the common expectations, as in Figure 13-23.

The second element exposes the limitation of this approach as a *general* theory of the demand for money; it implies that *almost everybody* holds only one asset—either money or bonds, but not both. This theory stipulates that investors whose critical interest rates are lower than the prevailing one in the market will

FIGURE 13-21

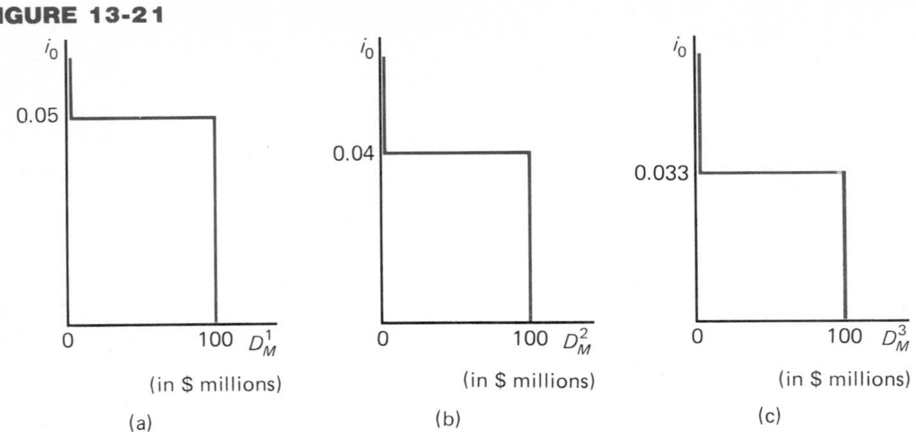

FIGURE 13-22

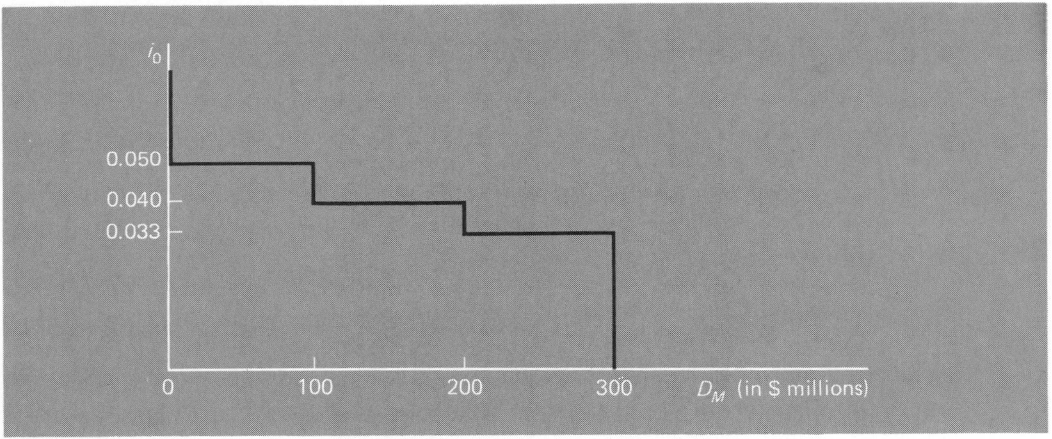

FIGURE 13-23

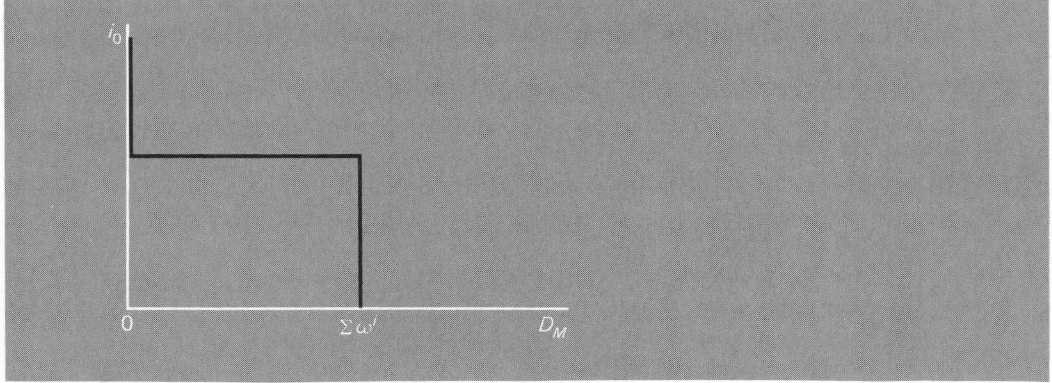

hold only bonds, while those with critical values greater than the market interest rate will hold only cash. No doubt, *some* people hold only one or the other, but a typical investor is a *diversifier,* that is, this investor holds both assets. Our theory here cannot explain this behavior, except of course for those whose critical value happens to coincide with the market rate of interest. Partly for this reason, Tobin introduced formally the case of uncertainty—to explain theoretically why the typical investor holds both assets.

Before we embark upon the uncertainty approach, we shall conclude our present analysis. We saw that as long as people hold *certain* expectations that are *inelastic* and *different* among groups, the demand for money depends negatively on the interest rate. However, the interest rate is not the only argument in the demand function. The demand for money is a function of wealth as well as of the interest rate, that is, $D_M = D_M(i, \omega)$. Thus, in the interest-rate–demand-for-money plane, there must be one demand curve for each assumed level of wealth; the greater the wealth is, the farther to the right the demand curve lies, as in Figure 13-24.

Next, it is worth noting that wealth itself depends on the interest rate because part of wealth consists of bonds, which increase in value when the interest rate falls, as we know from formula (1a). Thus the demand for money ultimately depends only on the interest rate. How can we show this graphically? We first identify the interest rate that corresponds to a particular level of wealth. For example, in Figure 13-25, when the interest rate is equal to $\bar{i}$, wealth is equal to $\bar{\omega}$. But with this level of wealth, the demand-for-money curve is labeled $D_M(i,\bar{\omega})$. It is clear, then, that only one point on this latter curve belongs to the true demand-for-money curve, and this is point *A*. When the interest rate is lower, say $\bar{\bar{i}}$, wealth is greater, say $\bar{\bar{\omega}}$, and the relevant demand curve is the one labeled $D_M(i,\bar{\bar{\omega}})$. But only point *B* on this curve is relevant for the true demand-for-money curve. Similarly, when the interest rate is still lower, at $\bar{\bar{\bar{i}}}$, wealth is greater, $\bar{\bar{\bar{\omega}}}$. With this wealth, the demand for money is labeled $D_M(i,\bar{\bar{\bar{\omega}}})$, yielding a sustainable point *C*. We can continue this process of associating levels of the interest rate with the corresponding levels of wealth, finding

FIGURE 13-24

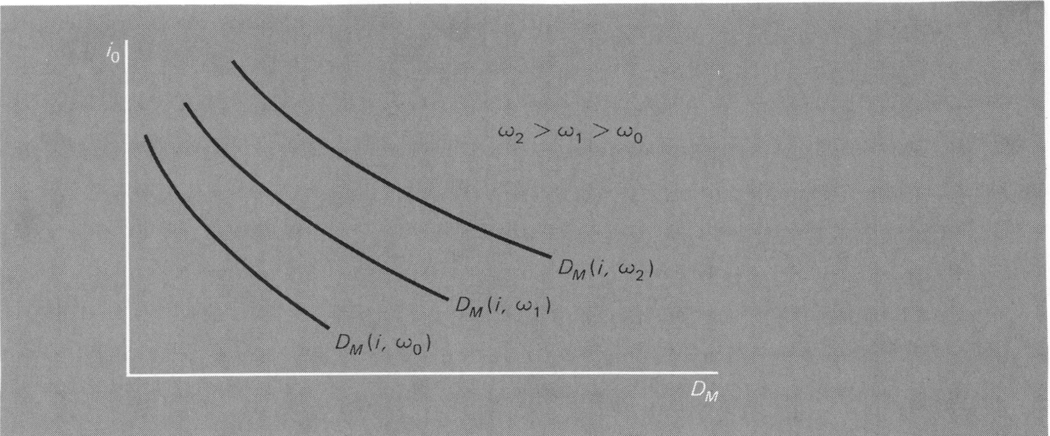

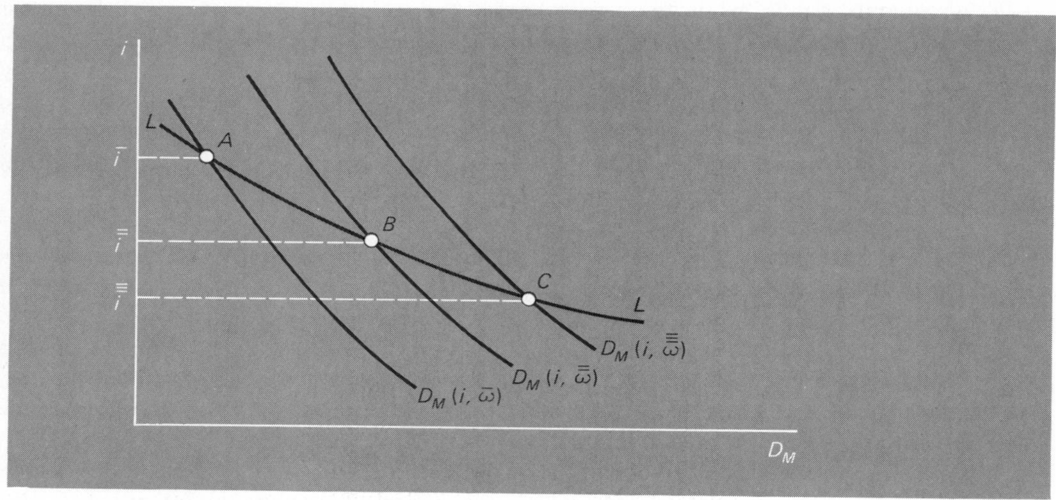

FIGURE 13-25

the demand curve so labeled, and the only relevant point on such a curve. Connecting all such points, *A, B, C,* and so forth, we derive the true demand-for-money curve, *LL,* which, as we see in Figure 13-25, is substantially more responsive to the interest rate (i.e., more interest-elastic).

III. THE SPECULATIVE DEMAND FOR MONEY UNDER UNCERTAINTY

In the preceding section we assumed that investors hold expectations about future prices and, therefore, future interest rates, with complete certainty. We shall now make the analysis more realistic by assuming that investors are uncertain about these interest rates. All outcomes are possible—each is assigned with a probability of its occurrence. Instead of working with the expected interest rate, we shall work with a magnitude that the expected and current interest rate together determine, namely, capital gains, *g,* which, by (2), is $g = i_0/i_1 - 1$.

We shall assume that the investor knows the probability (or frequency) distribution of capital gains, *g.* This is shown in Figure 13-26 by the familiar bell-shaped curve, or normal probability distribution. This curve should read as follows: A level of capital gains equal to or less than, say, g_0, has a probability of occurrence equal to the area under the curve to the left of this particular level. Similarly, capital gains equal to or greater than g_0 have a probability equal to the area under the curve to the right of g_0. The entire area under the curve is 1, reflecting 100 percent probability (i.e., certainty).

The important characteristics of a probability distribution are called *moments.* The first moment is the *mean,* $\bar{g}$. This is the average capital gain that is expected. The mean, by itself, is not important; it has to be supplemented by the second moment,

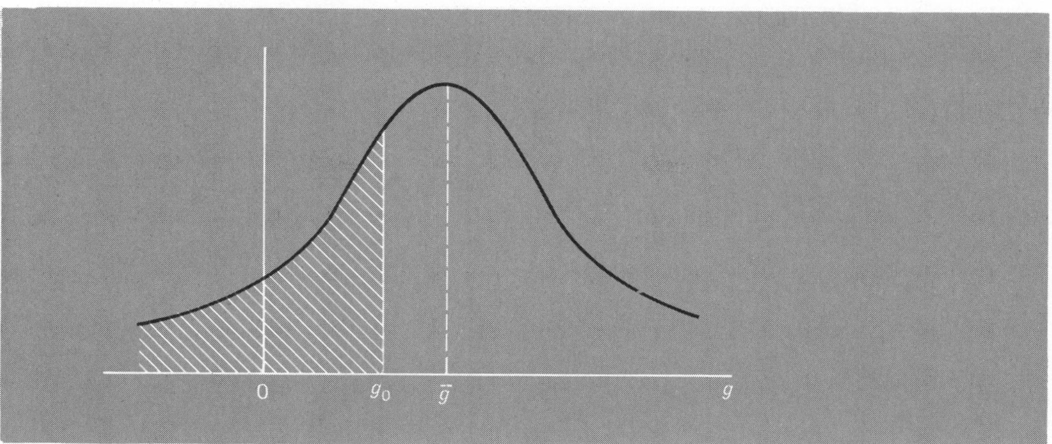

FIGURE 13-26

the *standard deviation,* σ_g, which measures the degree of dispersion around the mean. The standard deviation affects the "skinniness" or the "fatness" of the bell-shaped curve. To see its importance, examine two probability distributions with the same mean, but with the first skinnier than the second. The skinnier one illustrates less uncertainty, less risk than the fatter one does. A fatter probability distribution is a reflection of a higher standard deviation. We can say, then, that when two probability distributions have the same mean capital gain, $\bar{g}$, the one with the higher standard deviation represents more uncertainty, more risk. Graphically, the standard deviation, σ_g, of the bell-shaped curve is found by the distance, on the abscissa, between one of the points of inflection and the mean. Still another measure is given by the property that $\bar{g} \pm \sigma_g$ is two-thirds of the area under the curve. Thus the skinny curve, 1, in Figure 13-27, has about a 67 percent chance that the actual capital gains will lie between $\bar{g} + (\sigma_g)_1$ and $\bar{g} - (\sigma_g)_1$. Curve 2, on the other hand, has the same chance of yielding an actual capital gain between $\bar{g} + (\sigma_g)_2$ and $\bar{g} - (\sigma_g)_2$. The person with the former probability distribution is less uncertain about the capital gains than the person with the second, the fatter probability distribution.

Following Tobin, we shall examine the rational behavior of an individual who must decide under uncertainty. In particular, we shall assume that the individual has a (subjective) probability distribution with a given mean, $\bar{g}$, and a given standard deviation, σ_g. He is faced with the problem of allocating his given wealth, ω, between money, M, and bonds, B, that is,

$$D_M + D_B = \omega$$

We shall find it useful to work with percentages of wealth held in the respective asset. Dividing both sides of the above constraint by ω, we get

$$\frac{D_M}{\omega} + \frac{D_B}{\omega} = 1$$

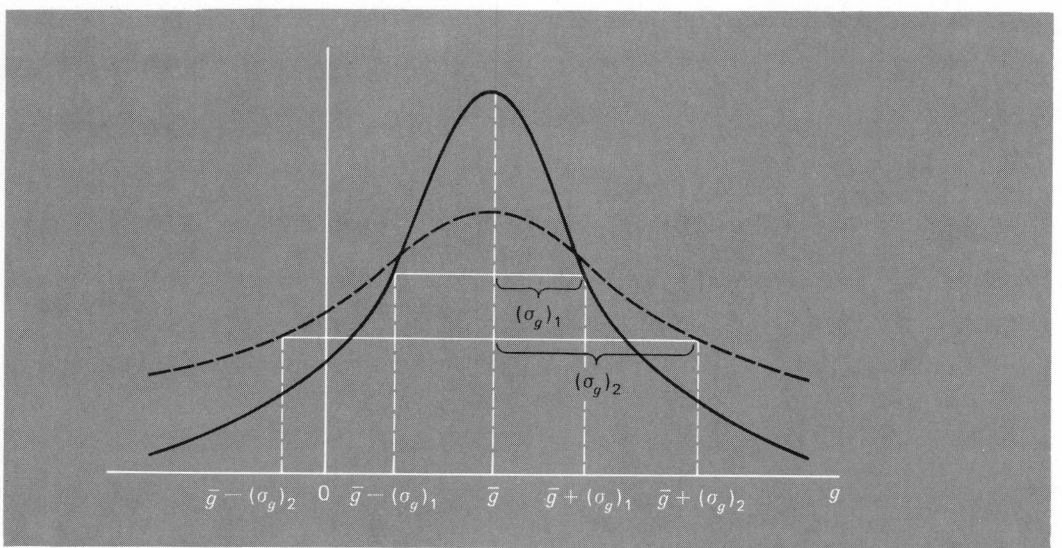

FIGURE 13-27

We shall define $D_M/\omega = A_1$ (i.e., the percentage of wealth held in cash), and $D_B/\omega = A_2$ (i.e., the percentage of wealth held in bonds). Here we shall restrict our analysis to two assets, whereas Tobin extended his to n assets where, of course, $\Sigma A_i = 1$.

The expression e_i will represent the (percentage) return of the ith asset. Here, e_1 is the return on cash, and e_2 is the return on bonds. Since, until recently in the United States, no interest was paid on demand deposits or on notes if we assume zero inflation, the return on cash is zero, or $e_1 = 0$. The return on bonds consists of interest accrued, i_0, plus (or minus) capital gains (or losses), g. We know from the analysis of the preceding section that $e_2 = i_0 + i_0/i_1 - 1 = i_0 + g$. The present interest rate, i_0, is given by the market. On the other hand, g depends on the expected interest rate, i_1, and is thus a random variable having a probability distribution as described earlier. (From now on we shall drop the subscript 0 from the current interest rate. Also the analysis can be generalized easily if $e_1 > 0$.)

If A_1 percent of the individual's wealth is invested in cash and A_2 percent is invested in bonds, then the average dollar in the portfolio earns

$$R = A_1 \cdot e_1 + A_2 \cdot e_2$$

$$= A_1 \cdot 0 + A_2 \cdot (i + g)$$

$$= A_2 \cdot (i + g)$$

Since the mean of $(i + g)$ is $(i + \bar{g})$, the mean return, μ_R, is

$$\mu_R = A_2 \cdot (i + \bar{g}) \tag{6}$$

Example

If $A_1 = 25\%$ and $A_2 = 75\%$, $i = 7\%$ and $\bar{g} = 3\%$, the average dollar in the portfolio earns $.75 \times 10\% = 7.5\%$, and not 10%, because 25 cents of each dollar is invested in a zero-yielding asset (i.e., in cash).

The mean return of the portfolio, μ_R, was found to be proportional to the mean $(i + \bar{g})$, the factor of proportionality being A_2. Similarly, the standard deviation of the portfolio, σ_R, is proportional to the standard deviation, σ_g:

$$\sigma_R = A_2 \cdot \sigma_g \tag{7}$$

Solving each of the equations (6) and (7) for A_2, we get, respectively,

$$A_2 = \frac{1}{(i + \bar{g})} \cdot \mu_R \tag{6'}$$

$$A_2 = \frac{1}{\sigma_g} \cdot \sigma_R \tag{7'}$$

In Figure 13-28, which consists of four parts, we depict equation (6′) by the line in the northwest quadrant. Similarly, (7′) is depicted by the line in the southeast quadrant. (The reader should be careful to avoid confusion between dependent and independent variables. In case of doubt, it is suggested that the reader reproduce each of these parts separately by always reserving the vertical axis for A_2 and the horizontal axis for the independent variables, μ_R and σ_R.)

Proceeding with our analysis, we see that the LHSs of (6′) and (7′) are

FIGURE 13-28

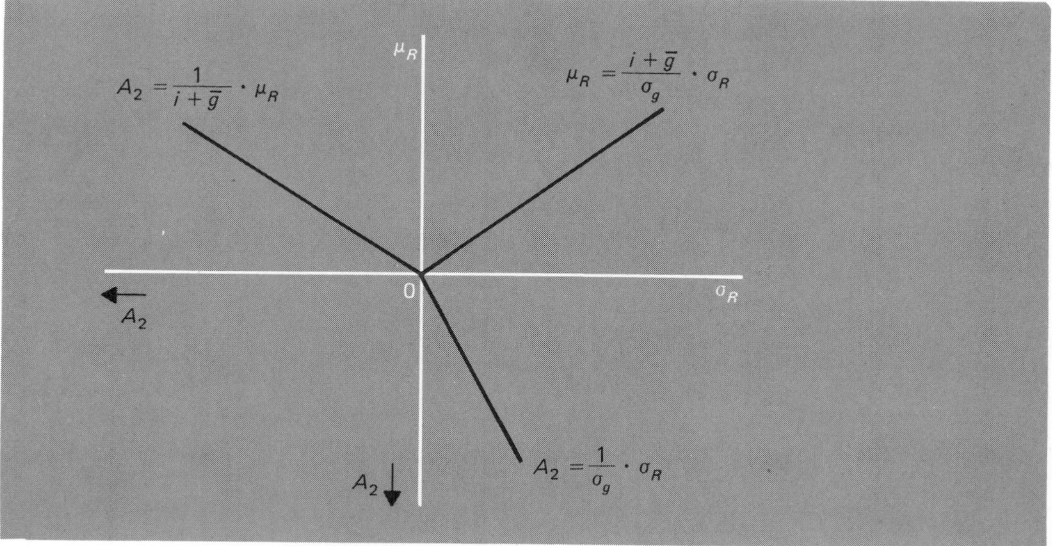

equal. This necessitates that the RHSs should be equal, that is, $(1/(i + \bar{g})) \cdot \mu_R = (1/\sigma_g) \cdot \sigma_R$. This can be rewritten as (8):

$$\mu_R = \frac{i + \bar{g}}{\sigma_g} \cdot \sigma_R \tag{8}$$

This equation is depicted in the northeast part of Figure 13-28. The line has, of course, a slope equal to $(i + \bar{g})/\sigma_g$. This line and its slope are of crucial importance for our theory. The slope $(i + \bar{g})/\sigma_g$ is a *relative price*, an *opportunity cost.* It shows how much return, μ_R, the individual will reap if he undertakes one more unit of risk, σ_R. This can also be stated as the units of return, μ_R, that one must *forgo* if he wants to reduce his risk by one unit. Here, return is a "good," or a commodity, and risk is a "bad," or a discommodity. Moving toward the right along the σ_R-axis increases the bad (i.e., decreases the good). If we define the opposite of *risk* as "security" or "insurance," a reduction in σ_R (i.e., a leftward movement along the σ_R-axis), will denote an increase of the good "security" or "insurance."

The line itself in the northeast quadrant is like a "budget" line. It shows the maximum return, μ_R, that the individual will get for each specified undertaken risk, σ_R. Or, equivalently, for each level of return, μ_R, it shows the minimum risk that the individual would have to undertake. Now, suppose that we know how much risk, σ_R, and how much return, μ_R, the individual has decided to assume. In other words, suppose that the individual has decided to "consume" basket B on his budget line, as in Figure 13-29. We have several ways by which we can find our two unknowns, A_1 and A_2. The abscissa of B is $\bar{\sigma}_R$. But, utilizing the southeast portion of the graph, we know that $\bar{\sigma}_R$ corresponds to $\bar{A}_2$ percent. Since $A_1 = 1 - A_2$, we can find that unknown as well. In fact, in Figure 13-29, A_1 is measured from point K moving upward, since the distance OK is 1, or 100 percent.

FIGURE 13-29

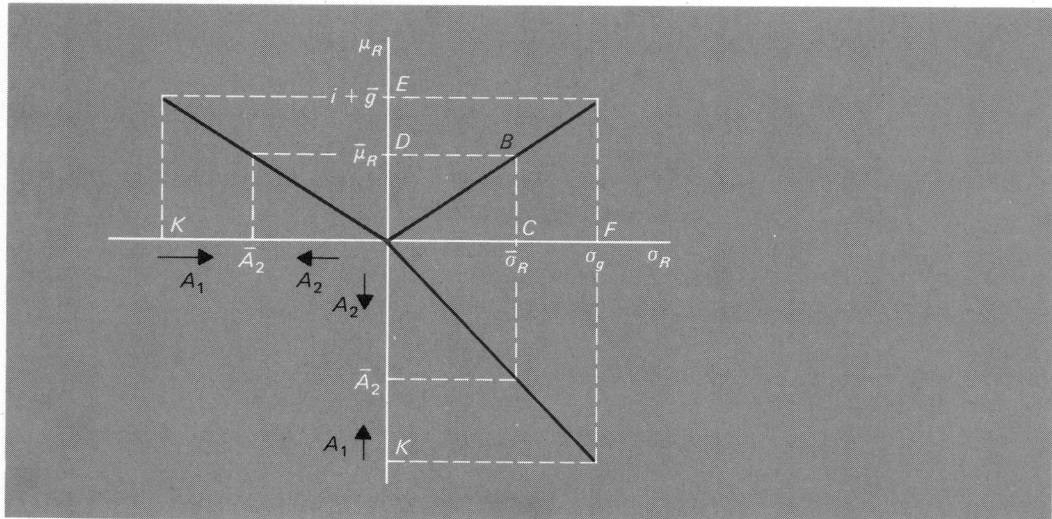

A second way is to utilize the μ_R-axis and the line in the northwest part of the graph. Point B gives return equal to $\bar{\mu}_R$, which, in turn, gives $\bar{A}_2$ and $1 - \bar{A}_2 = \bar{A}_1$. There are two other graphical techniques that do not even need the northwest and southeast portions of the graph. These techniques utilize the assumed known parameters σ_g and $i + \bar{g}$. From (6′) we know that A_2 is equal to $\bar{\mu}_R$ divided by $i + \bar{g}$, that is, OD/OE (on the vertical axis). Note that the denominator is greater than the numerator, thereby giving a value of less than one for A_2. On the other hand, utilizing (7′) and the σ_R-axis, we find $\bar{A}_2 = (\bar{\sigma}_R/\sigma_g) = (OC/OF)$. Note also that

$$A_1 + A_2 = (DE/OE) + (OD/OE) = 1, \text{ and}$$

$$A_1 + A_2 = (CF/OF) + (OC/OF) = 1$$

The next step is to find a way to determine the "basket" of risk and return, on the budget restraint, that individuals will "consume." The problem is simply an application of the usual one faced by a household. The only difference is that we are dealing with one commodity, namely, return, and one discommodity, namely, risk, rather than the usual case of two commodities. In such a situation a household's *convex* preferences are shown by upward-sloping indifference curves of the form depicted in Figure 13-30a. Since we are always assuming that individuals prefer more good rather than less, and since more risk is less "security," it follows that the indifference curve should be upward sloping, as in Figure 13-30a.

In Figure 13-30a note that a movement from A to B implies that the individual is willing to give up return equal to $A'B'$ in order to gain "security" (i.e., less risk) equal to $A''B''$ and still retain an equivalent combination of the two. The curve in Figure 13-30a is *convex* for the same reason that in the two-*commodity* case the downward-sloping indifference curves are convex, as in Figure 13-30b. Convexity of indifference curves is a reflection, in general, of the *principle of diminishing marginal rate of substitution:* the individual is willing to give up increasingly less of one good when he wants to keep getting one more unit of the other good and still have equivalent baskets. In the present context this is called the *principle of increasing risk aversion:* if the individual wants to keep increasing his return by the same amount, say, by

FIGURE 13-30

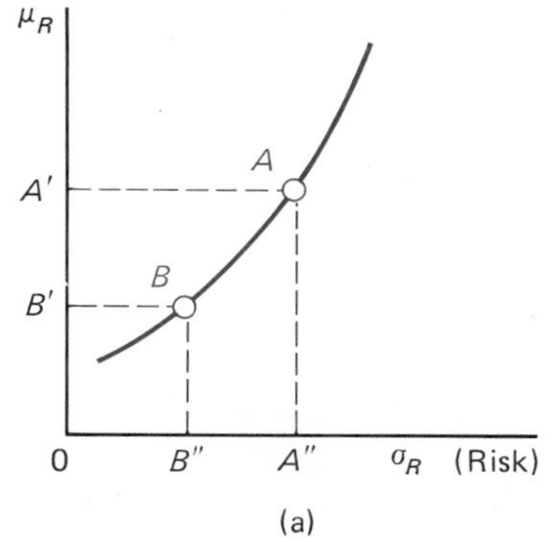

(a)

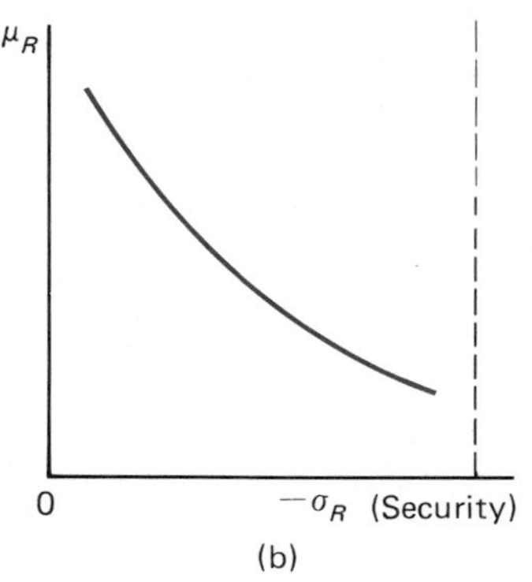

(b)

one unit, to get equivalent combinations, he would want to undertake increasingly less risk. This is indeed increasing risk aversion. We can also state it as follows: In order to keep undertaking one more unit of risk, the individual would want to be compensated by increasingly higher return.

We can now imagine the risk-return plane as containing an infinite number of indifference curves of the form depicted in Figure 13-30a. Obviously, the next step is to rank indifference curves. Remember our criterion for such ranking: If an indifference curve includes even one basket that contains more of each of the two *goods* than does a basket belonging to another indifference curve, the first curve is preferred to the other. In the present case, this means that northwest is the preferred direction. Of the two indifference curves in Figure 13-31, I_2I_2 is preferred to I_1I_1. We simply observe that basket D on I_2I_2 contains more of return, μ_R, that is, $OD' > OC'$, and less of risk (i.e., more of "security"), $OD'' < OC''$, than basket C lying on I_1I_1.

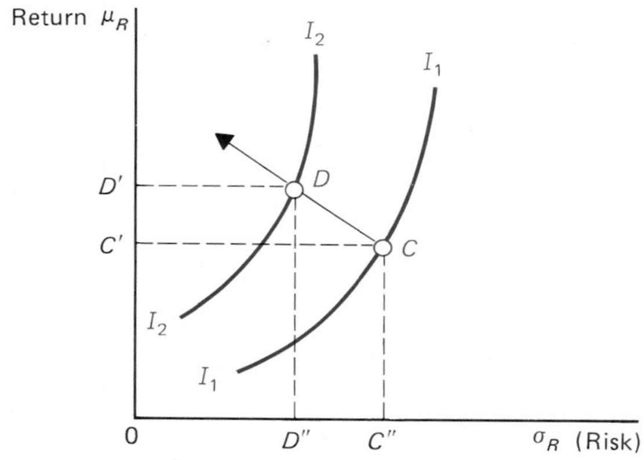

FIGURE 13-31

As with the usual analysis of household choice, the rational investor's problem is one of finding the point(s) where an indifference curve is tangent to the budget line. This indifference curve is clearly the highest that can be reached, and the precise combination of risk and return represented by the tangency point is, therefore, the most preferred among all the combinations attainable. Point E in Figure 13-32 is such a point, the investor's optimum point. Knowing point E we can proceed, as earlier, to find the exact percentages of wealth held in the form of bonds and cash, A_2 and A_1, respectively. These are OL and $1 - OL$, respectively, or $OM/ON = OR/OQ = A_2$ and $MN/ON = RQ/OQ = A_1$.

COMPARATIVE STATICS: CHANGES IN THE INTEREST RATE

We have found the optimum combination of bonds and money that an investor will hold, given his probability distribution of capital gains, his preferences of the two moments of this distribution, and the interest rate. We shall now undertake compara-

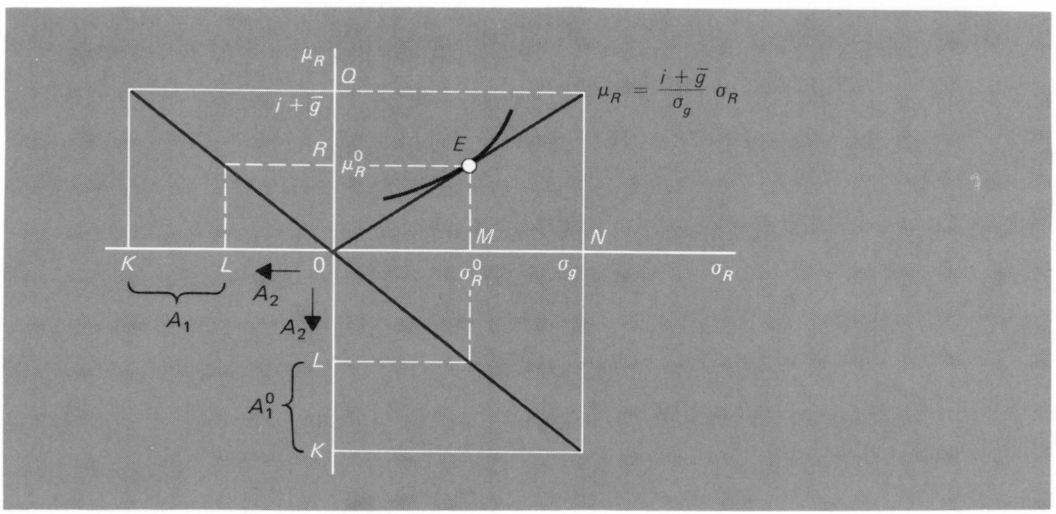

FIGURE 13-32

tive statics, beginning with the examination of the effects of a change, say, of an increase in the interest rate when the other parameters remain the same. Since the interest rate is a component of the slope of the budget line, this line will shift with a change in the interest rate. If the interest rate increases from i_0 to i_1, the slope rises from $(i_0 + \bar{g}_0)/(\sigma_g)_0$ to $(i_1 + \bar{g}_0)/(\sigma_g)_0$, as shown in Figure 13-33a. Now the optimum point is *F*. This means that the fraction of wealth held in bonds, A_2, *rises* from *OM*/*ON* to *OM'*/*ON*. On the other hand, the fraction A_1, held in cash, falls from *MN*/*ON* to *M'N*/*ON*. In other words, we have proved that the demand for

FIGURE 13-33

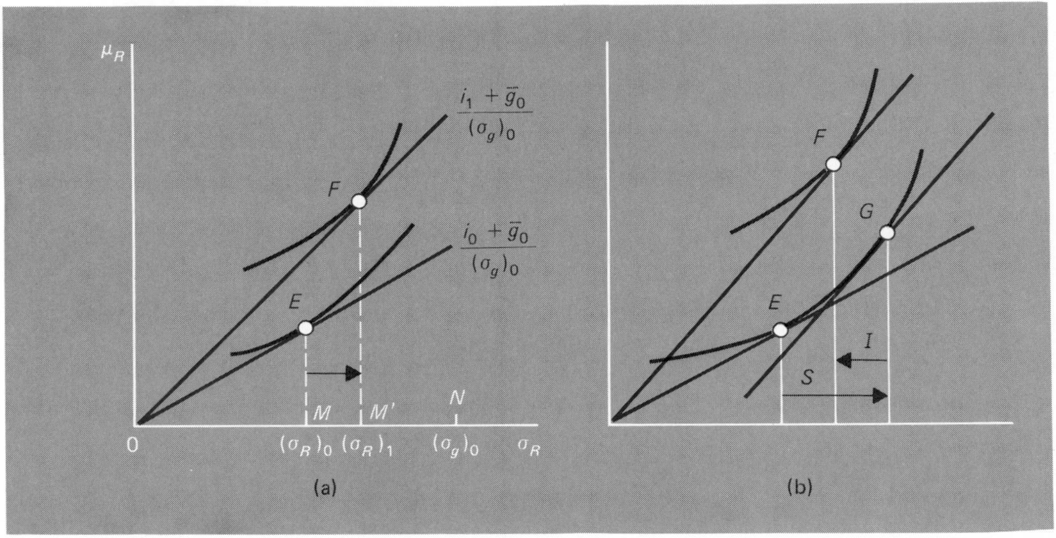

bonds increases with an increase in the interest rate, and, more important for our present goal, that an increase in the interest rate reduces the demand for money.

The reader should realize that this result is not airtight. Figure 13-34a illustrates the case of an increase in the interest rate that implies a rise in the demand for money (and a fall in the demand for bonds). Originally A_2 was equal to OM/ON, and A_1 was MN/ON. After the increase in the interest rate, A_2 fell to OM'/ON, and A_1 rose to $M'N/ON$.

Since we endeavor to derive a negative relation between the interest rate and the demand for money, we naturally want to eliminate the case of Figure 13-34a. What is the reason for such a result? Why is the *interest rate effect* positive in Figure 13-34a and negative in Figure 13-33a? The interest rate effect is the result of two other effects: the substitution effect and the income, or wealth, effect. An increase in the interest rate raises the (relative) price of the good called "security." If we force the individual to choose a combination (of the two goods) that is equivalent to his original choice, he will want to "consume" less of the good whose relative price has risen and more of the good whose price has fallen. Thus he will want to consume less of "security" (i.e., to undertake more risk). This is called the *substitution effect* and is represented by a move on the original indifference curve.

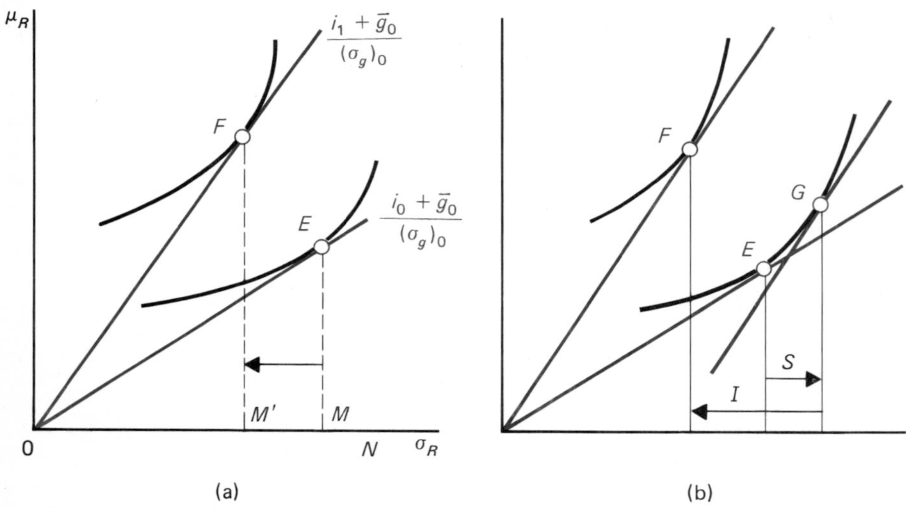

FIGURE 13-34

On the other hand, the increase in the interest rate makes the individual *wealthier,* and he will want to consume more of every good that is normal. In particular, he will want to consume more of "security" (i.e., less of risk). This is called the *income,* or *wealth, effect.* Note that it is in the opposite direction from the substitution effect.

If the substitution effect is greater than the income effect, the interest rate effect is negative, that is, the increase in the interest rate will increase the amount of risk undertaken, with the ultimate result that more bonds and less money are now demanded. When the income effect outweighs the substitution effect, however, the interest rate effect is positive.

Figure 13-33b reproduces Figure 13-33a and also illustrates that, here, the substitution effect is greater than the income effect. The interest rate effect, which is the *observed* movement from E to F, is considered as a movement from E to G, or the substitution effect, and a movement from G to F, or the income effect. We see that the two effects are in opposite directions, as the arrows show, and that the former outweighs the latter. Figure 13-34b reproduces the information of Figure 13-34a and shows that, in this case, the income effect wins out.

It is clear, then, that the negative relation between the interest rate and the demand for money can be established only when we *assume* that the substitution effect (of a change in the interest rate) is greater than the income effect. We can summarize by stating:

> The demand for money is a decreasing function of the interest rate if, and only if, the substitution effect outweighs the income effect.

Under that assumption, the demand-for-money curve is like the one depicted in Figure 13-35.

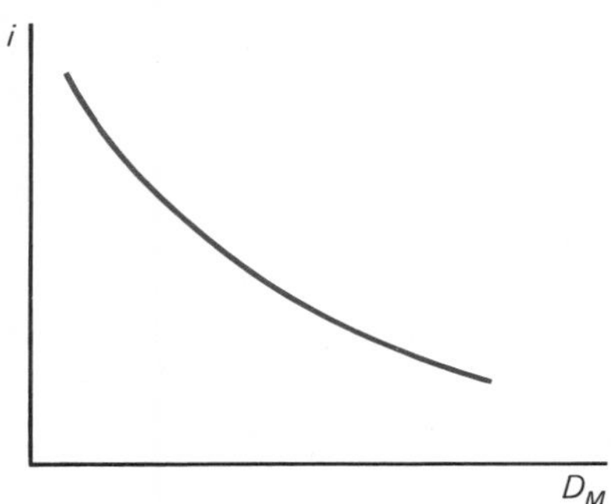

FIGURE 13-35

COMPARATIVE STATICS: CHANGES IN THE MEAN CAPITAL GAINS

Suppose, again, that we start from a position like point E in Figure 13-32, and that the mean capital gains increase. In other words, we assume that there is a change in one of the two moments of the subjective probability distribution; the standard deviation, σ_g, remains the same, but the mean, $\bar{g}$, *rises.* This is seen graphically as a rightward movement of the same probability distribution. In Figure 13-36 the dashed line is the new probability distribution with mean equal to $\bar{g}_1$, while the original one is the solid line with mean $\bar{g}_0$.

Assuming that the substitution effect outweighs the income effect—a prerequisite for the law of demand for money—the result of this change is similar to that of Figure 13-33a. The increase in $\bar{g}$ makes the budget line steeper just as the increase

FIGURE 13-36

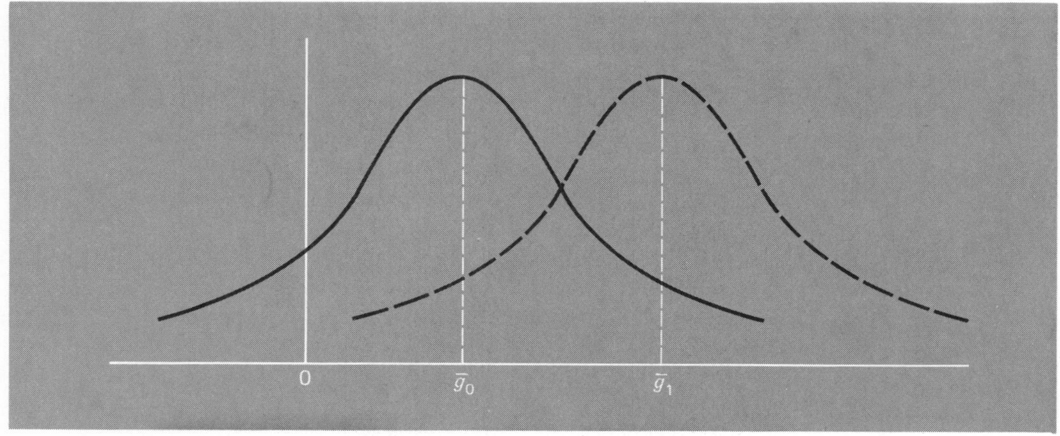

FIGURE 13-37

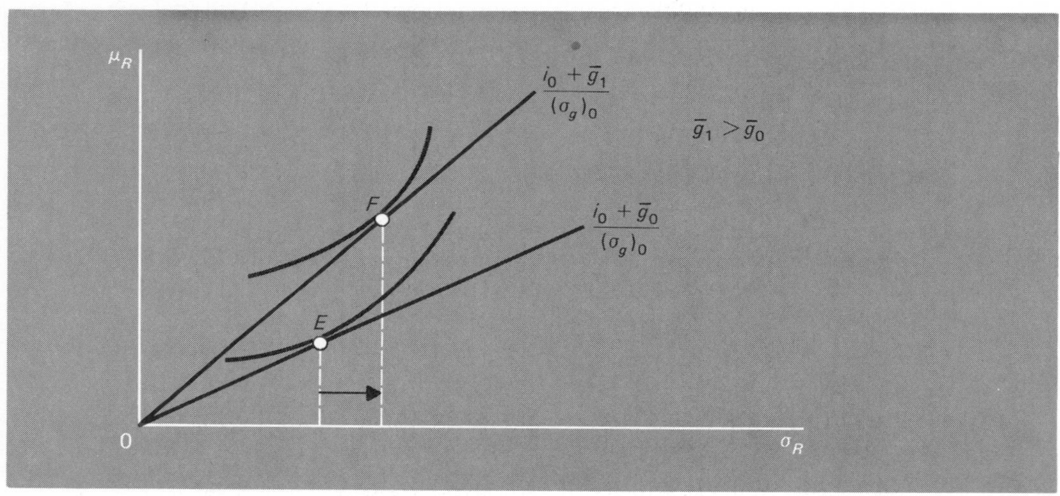

FIGURE 13-38

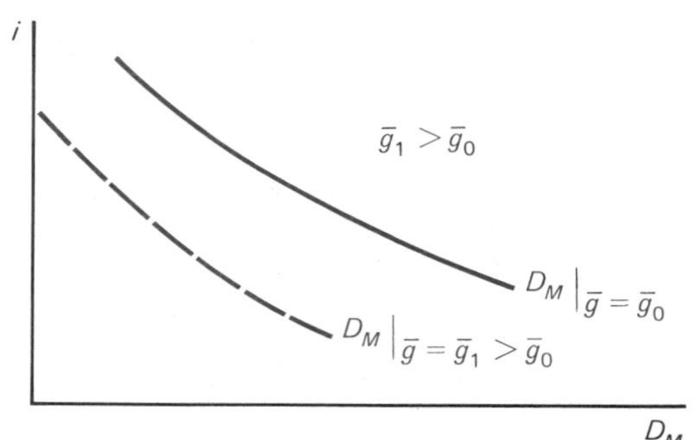

in the interest rate, i, does. This is shown in Figure 13-37. Note that the only difference between Figures 13-37 and 13-33a is in the label of the respective budget line.

Our result shows that if people expect higher capital gains in bonds, the demand for bonds will, naturally, increase at the expense of the demand for money. This means that for the same interest rate, people will demand less money. In other words, the demand for money will shift inward. In Figure 13-38 the demand-for-money curve shifts from position $D_M\big|_{\bar{g}=\bar{g}_0}$ to position $D_M\big|_{\bar{g}=\bar{g}_1>\bar{g}_0}$.

COMPARATIVE STATICS: AN INCREASE IN RISK

Again starting from position E, depicting the optimum combination of money and bonds, assume that there is a change in the estimate of the second moment, the standard deviation, σ_g. In particular, suppose that the standard deviation is now greater, that is, $(\sigma_g)_1 > (\sigma_g)_0$. Since we associate this standard deviation with risk (or uncertainty), we now assume that there is an increase in the investors' estimate of uncertainty, or risk of investing in bonds. This is shown graphically in Figure 13-39, where the probability distribution becomes "fatter" (the dashed line), while the mean, $\bar{g}$, remains the same. Since σ_g enters into the denominator of the formula for the slope of the budget line, $(i_0 + \bar{g})/\sigma_g$, this slope is now smaller (i.e., the budget line becomes flatter). In terms of economics, this means that the relative price of "security" *falls*, or, equivalently, the relative price of return *rises*.

To see the effect of this increase on the riskiness of bonds, it is easier to concentrate on the vertical axis (or the graph that relies on the northwest quadrant) in deriving the values of A_1 and A_2. Before the change in σ_g, the optimum point E implied a value of A_2 equal to OR/OQ and a value of A_1 equal to RQ/OQ. With the increase in risk, that is, with $(\sigma_g)_1 > (\sigma_g)_0$, the new optimum is point G, which yields

FIGURE 13-39

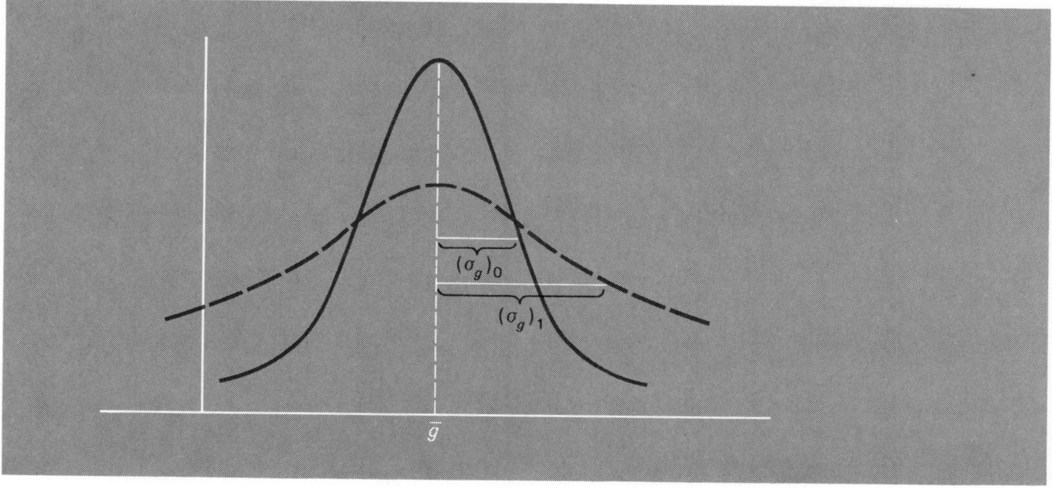

$$A_2 = (OR'/OQ) < (OR/OQ)$$

and

$$A_1 = (R'Q/OQ) > (RQ/OQ)$$

As expected, the greater risk of bonds induces investors to switch some of their wealth from bonds to cash. We therefore obtain this result:

> Greater risk (or uncertainty) in bonds increases the demand for money and diminishes the demand for bonds.

FIGURE 13-40

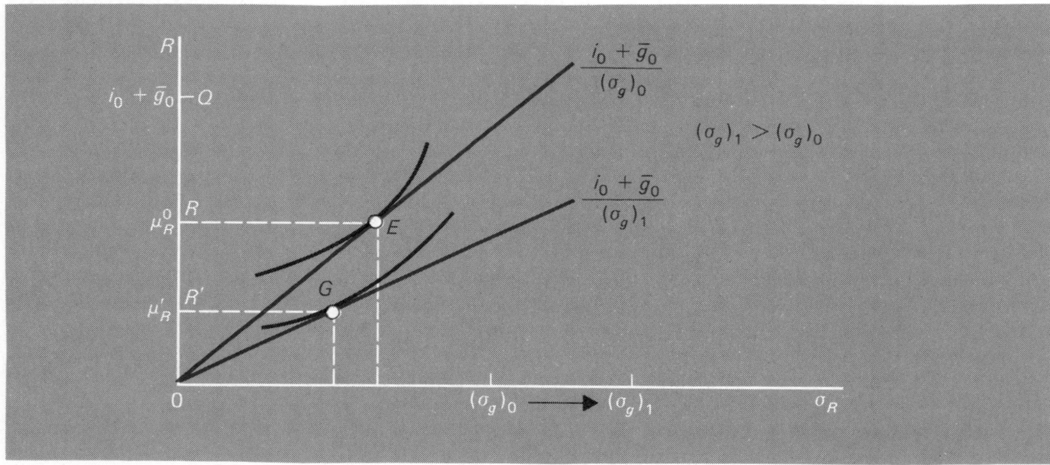

FIGURE 13-41

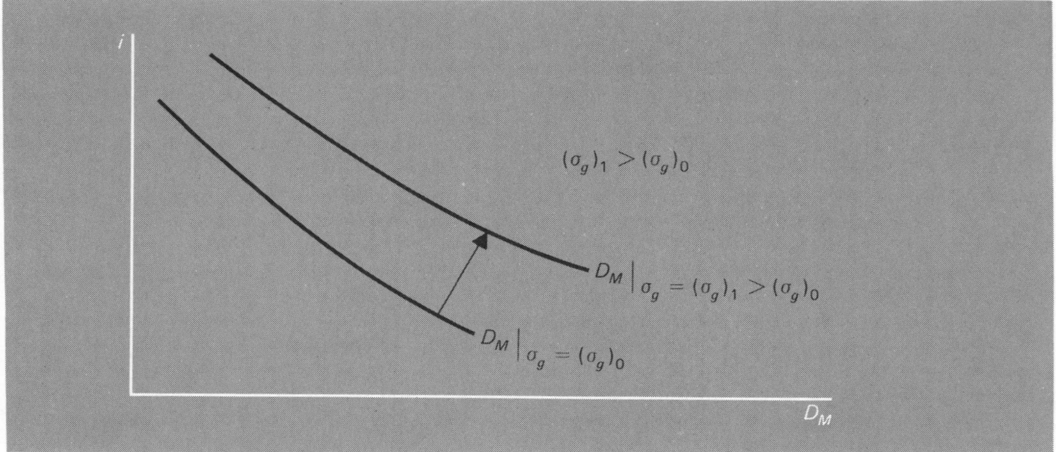

This result is, of course, true of *every* level of the interest rate. This means that the increase in risk shifts the demand for money upward and to the right, as in Figure 13-41.

IV. FRIEDMAN'S DEMAND FOR MONEY

The fourth way of deriving the demand for money is based upon the work of Milton Friedman, who considers money one of four assets in which an investor can hold his wealth: money, goods, bonds, and equity shares.[4] We should recall here that in his *Tract,* Keynes examined money as an alternative to goods, while in his *Treatise* he examined it as an alternative to bonds and equity shares. And, finally, in his *General Theory,* he examined money as an alternative to bonds only. In a sense, Friedman combines the analyses of the *Tract* and the *Treatise.*

Friedman begins by stating that we can use standard household-choice theoretic techniques—which he never specifies—to derive the demand for money of, say, a household that obeys its wealth constraint. As with the standard theory, the derived demand for each asset must be a function of all the "prices" of these assets, as well as of the wealth; all of these are assumed as parameters in the choice-theoretic problem. Prices here are the *rates of return,* or *yields,* of the four assets. Friedman maintains that the rate of return on money is simply its *value,* $1/p$. He chooses to write the return on bonds as the interest rate *minus* the rate of change in the interest rate, $i - \Delta i/i$. (Of course, capital gains, $-\Delta i/i$, are equivalent to our earlier $g = i_0/i_e - 1$.) Similarly, the rate of return on equities is equal to the equity rate, r_e, plus capital gains in equities, which are written as $(\Delta r_e/r_e)$, *plus* whatever inflation is expected, that is, $r_e - (\Delta r_e/r_e) + \Delta p/p$. (The latter component arises because equities are not fixed in nominal money values.) Finally, the rate of return on any (physical) good is simply its rate of price change, $\Delta p/p$. Here, of course, Friedman assumes that the asset "goods" is the same "basket" for which the Consumer Price Index, CPI, is calculated. All these parameters, along with wealth, are arguments in Friedman's most general demand-for-money function:

$$M = f\left(p,\ i - \frac{\Delta i}{i},\ r_e - \frac{\Delta r_e}{r_e} + \frac{\Delta p}{p},\ \frac{\Delta p}{p},\ \omega\right) \tag{9}$$

Next, Friedman assumes that bonds and equities are perfect substitutes and that their returns are, therefore, equalized:

$$i - \frac{\Delta i}{i} = r_e - \frac{\Delta r_e}{r_e} + \frac{\Delta p}{p} \tag{10}$$

---

[4] Milton Friedman, "The Quantity Theory of Money—A Restatement," in *Studies in the Quantity Theory of Money,* ed. Milton Friedman (Chicago: University of Chicago Press, 1956), pp. 3–21.

Moreover, for simplicity, he assumes that the interest rate and the equity rate will not change (i.e., that the bond and equity prices will remain unchanged), or that $\Delta i/i = \Delta r_e/r_e = 0$. On the other hand, he still permits changes in the price level. With all these simplifications, (10) becomes

$$i = r_e + \frac{\Delta p}{p} \tag{10'}$$

Since, in general, wealth, ω, is the capitalized value of income, we can rewrite it as Y_m/r, where r is the economywide return and Y_m is money income. But since return, r, must be some weighted average of the other returns, i, r_e, and $\Delta p/p$, which are already accounted for in (9), we can replace ω by Y_m. Because of (10) and (10′), the third argument in (9) disappears and the final form is (11):

$$M_d = f(p, i, \frac{\Delta p}{p}, Y_m) \tag{11}$$

Since Friedman assumes that (11) is derived from utility maximization, and since this technique yields *real* demands, it follows that M_d is homogeneous of the first degree in all the variables that are expressed in money terms, that is, in p and Y_m. In other words, if we multiply p and Y_m by the same positive number, M_d must also be multiplied by the same positive constant. If this constant is chosen to be equal to $1/p$, we can get from (11):

$$\frac{1}{p} \cdot M_d = f\left(\frac{p}{p}, i, \frac{\Delta p}{p}, \frac{Y_m}{p}\right)$$

Since $Y = Y_m/p$, this can be rewritten as (12):

$$\frac{M_d}{p} = g(i, \frac{\Delta p}{p}, Y) \tag{12}$$

This is the demand for *real* balances; it is a function of the interest rate and of real income, which we have already been using, as well as a function of the rate of inflation, since we now permit changes in the price level.

Friedman also shows how we can express the above demand function for money in the familiar quantity theory form, that of either the Cambridge or the Fisher variety.[5] If we multiply the variables p and Y_m of (11) by $1/Y_m$, we get

$$\frac{M_d}{Y_m} = f\left(\frac{p}{Y_m}, i, \frac{\Delta p}{p}, \frac{Y_m}{Y_m}\right),$$

[5] See Chapter 3.

which can be rewritten as

$$\frac{M_d}{Y_m} = l\left(i, \frac{1}{Y}, \frac{\Delta p}{p}\right) \tag{13}$$

This l is the one we used in Chapter 3, that is, the "Cambridge k." Of course, we can write the nominal money demand, M_d, as

$$M_d = l\left(i, \frac{1}{Y}, \frac{\Delta p}{p}\right) \cdot Y_m$$

and, since $l(\cdot) = 1/V$ and $Y_m = p \cdot Y$,

$$M_d \cdot V = p \cdot Y \tag{14}$$

Immediately we notice the similarity between (14) and the "traditional" quantity theory equation. It should be emphasized, however, that velocity, V, is variable depending on i, Y, and $\Delta p/p$:

$$i\uparrow \rightarrow V\uparrow, \quad Y\uparrow \rightarrow V\downarrow, \quad \text{and} \quad \frac{\Delta p}{p}\uparrow \rightarrow V\uparrow$$

Friedman's derivation of the demand for money was presented in an unnecessarily controversial way. Friedman claimed that the quantity theory was not meant to be a theory of price (or income) determination, that it was simply a theory of the demand for money. This claim was deliberately designed to make the quantity theory immune from Keynesian criticism. But this immediately created controversy. If the quantity theory were merely a theory of the demand for money, the *General Theory* would not have been written. In a sense, Friedman's theory was a *refutation* rather than a *restatement* of the quantity theory!

And this was not all. Friedman asserted that his version of the quantity theory was based on Chicago's oral tradition and, in particular, on the teachings of Henry Simons, Lloyd Mints, Frank Knight, and Jacob Viner. Don Patinkin, himself a student of these economists, disputed this claim.[6] So did the late Harry G. Johnson, a colleague of Friedman's at Chicago.[7] Both of these economists claimed not only that Friedman's restatement was of his own making but also that "Friedman's quantity theory is Keynesian economics written in another language."[8]

It is fair to say that Friedman's is another way to derive the demand for money from rational behavior. Compared with Tobin's method, it has the disadvantage of not being formal; it does not even permit expectations or changes in bond and

---

[6] Don Patinkin, "The Chicago Tradition, the Quantity Theory, and Friedman," *Journal of Money, Credit and Banking,* February 1969.

[7] Harry G. Johnson, *Macroeconomics and Monetary Theory* (Chicago: Aldine, 1972).

[8] Ibid. p. 96

equity prices—let alone uncertainty. It has the advantage that the (expected) rate of inflation is an explicit argument in the demand function for money. Friedman's theory was presented as a foreword to several studies in the quantity theory of money. Foremost among these was Phillip Cagan's paper "The Monetary Dynamics of Hyperinflation," which seems to have been instrumental in Friedman's decision to permit changes in the price level, even though he assumed that changes in bond and share prices do not occur.

V. EVIDENCE IN SUPPORT OF THEORY

Although several distinct theories for deriving the demand for money have been discussed in this chapter, all of these share at least one common characteristic: They indicate the existence of a relationship between the stock of money demanded and a few basic economic variables. These theories vary, however, in their emphasis on interest rates and on income, or wealth, as determinants of money demand. In this section we briefly examine some of the empirical evidence on the demand for money. Following earlier sections of the chapter, our examination centers on the evidence concerning the relationship between interest rates and the demand for money.

A huge body of literature has been generated in an attempt to quantify the relationship between interest rates and the demand for money. Controversies have developed concerning the proper way to define the variables; and the actual numerical results have varied. But Laidler finds that the results are clear:

> . . . whether one thinks of the demand-for-money function as being constrained by income, wealth, or expected income, whether one defines money to include time deposits or exclude them, whether one ignores the identification problem or deals with it, whether one uses a short rate of interest, a long one, or the return on financial intermediaries' liabilities, or whether one ignores the own rate of return on money or takes explicit account of it, there is an overwhelming body of evidence in favor of the proposition that the demand for money is negatively related to the rate of interest. Of all the issues in monetary economics, this is the one that appears to have been settled most decisively.[9]

Within this context, several additional questions can be addressed:

1. If we agree that the interest rate is important in the determination of money demand, in what range does the interest elasticity lie?
2. Does money demand appear to be more closely related to long-term or to short-term interest rates?

---

[9] David E. W. Laidler, *The Demand for Money: Theories and Evidence,* 2nd ed. (New York: Dun-Donnelley, 1977), p. 130.

3. Does the empirical evidence support the existence of a liquidity trap?

Numerous studies demonstrate strongly consistent estimates of the interest elasticity of money demand—usually in the range between -0.1 and -0.8. Simultaneous equation models, which attempt to deal with the supply of as well as the demand for money, confirm the range of estimates from the simpler, single-equation models. Furthermore, these elasticity estimates gain support from their stability over various sample periods. For example, a well-known study by Laidler estimates an elasticity of -0.18 to -0.20 for the period 1919–60.[10] A later study by Goldfeld produced an elasticity estimate of -0.15 for the period 1952–72.[11]

The numerical ranges of elasticity estimates become even narrower when studies are divided into categories according to the nature of the interest rate definition used. Some authors have argued that the close substitutes for money are other highly liquid assets, such as the liabilities of savings and loan associations; from this perspective the appropriate rate would be interest on those assets. Other researchers have viewed the substitute for money as a whole portfolio, making a collection of long- and short-term rates appropriate. A firm conclusion has not been reached on this issue. In general, studies that use a long-term rate of interest tend to indicate higher interest-elasticity measures, in the -0.5 to -0.9 range, while studies that use a short-term rate produce estimates in the -0.1 to -0.5 range.

One single-equation model, estimated by Stephen Goldfeld, takes the following form:

$$m = \ln \frac{M}{p} = \alpha + \epsilon_{Lr_{cp}} \ln r_{cp} + \epsilon_{Lr_{td}} \ln r_{td} + \epsilon_{Lx} \ln \text{GNP} + \epsilon_{Lm}\, m_{-1}$$

where r_{cp} is the interest rate on commercial paper; r_{td} is the interest rate on commercial bank time deposits; and ϵ_{Li} is the elasticity of money demand, with respect to variable "*i.*" Goldfeld's estimates of the elasticities can be summarized:[12]

$$\epsilon_{Lr_{cp}} = -0.07$$

$$\epsilon_{Lr_{td}} = -0.16$$

$$\epsilon_{Lx} = 0.68$$

Other single-equation models are summarized in Table 13-2.

[10] David Laidler, "The Rate of Interest and the Demand for Money—Some Empirical Evidence," *Journal of Political Economy,* December 1966, pp. 545–55.

[11] Stephen M. Goldfeld, "The Demand for Money Revisited," *Brookings Papers on Economic Activity,* 3(1973), 577–638.

[12] Ibid.

TABLE 13-2 SINGLE-EQUATION ESTIMATES OF THE DEMAND FOR MONEY

REFERENCE	INTEREST ELASTICITY	INTEREST RATE USED (L = LONG, S = SHORT RATE)	SCALE VARIABLE	TIME PERIOD
Chow (1966)	−0.08	L	Permanent income	1897–1958
Goldfeld (1973)	−0.07	S	GNP	1952–1972
Laidler (1966)	−0.19	S	Permanent income	1919–1960
	−0.70	L	Permanent income	1919–1960
Latané (1954)	−0.70	L	GNP	1919–1952
Meltzer (1963)	−0.80	L	Wealth	1900–1958

As we saw earlier, in 1936 Keynes made a brief reference to the possibility of a liquidity trap, a situation in which the money demand function becomes perfectly elastic at very low rates of interest. While his remarks have inspired numerous tests designed to prove the actual existence of such a trap, no such evidence has been unearthed. We must be content, therefore, with the knowledge that the interest elasticity of money demand does not appear to fall as the interest rate falls.

We should mention briefly the single major study with findings counter to our conclusion about the interest elasticity of money demand, Milton Friedman's study, which states that there is no statistically significant link between these two variables.[13] This study has been criticized by numerous economists, among them Laidler, Meltzer, and Johnson.[14] The most frequent criticisms refer to improperly defined variables, to the omission of variables from regressions, and to other more technical issues. Although the Friedman study is often cited, the bulk of the evidence certainly supports the other conclusion.

After the interest rate, the second explanatory variable in most money demand studies is a "scale" variable such as income, wealth, or expected wealth. Early studies emphasized the transactions demand for money and assumed that transactions were proportional to income. But gradually the emphasis shifted to measures of wealth as money came to be viewed as merely one asset within a portfolio. The empirical evidence appears to support a measure of wealth rather than current income as the scale variable determining the long-run equilibrium amount of money balances that individuals desire to hold. But in recent years, income has made a reappearance in

[13] Milton Friedman, "The Demand for Money—Some Theoretical and Empirical Results," *Journal of Political Economy,* June 1959, pp. 327–51.

[14] Laidler, "Rate of Interest"; Allan H. Meltzer, "The Demand for Money: The Evidence from the Time Series," *Journal of Political Economy,* June 1963, pp. 219–46; and Johnson, *Macroeconomics and Monetary Theory.*

money demand functions, as a determinant of the speed with which individuals move toward their equilibrium level of desired money balances.

In summary, the empirical evidence supports overwhelmingly the theoretical implication that a negative relation exists between money demand and the rate of

TABLE 13-3 ACTUAL AND PREDICTED VALUES AND ERRORS FROM A DYNAMIC SIMULATION OF AN M_1 DEMAND EQUATION, 1974:3–1979:1

YEAR AND QUARTER, AND SUMMARY STATISTIC	ANNUALIZED RATE OF GROWTH (PERCENT OR PERCENTAGE POINTS)			LEVEL (BILLIONS OF DOLLARS OR PERCENT)			
	ACTUAL	PREDICTED	ERROR	ACTUAL	PREDICTED	CUMULATIVE ERROR	CUMULATIVE PERCENTAGE ERROR*
Year and Quarter							
1974:3	4.0	7.9	−4.0	279.0	284.0	−5.0	−1.8
4	4.6	8.6	−4.0	282.1	290.1	−8.0	−2.8
1975:1	2.1	8.5	−6.4	283.6	296.3	−12.6	−4.5
2	5.7	8.9	−3.2	287.7	302.9	−15.2	−5.3
3	7.3	9.2	−1.9	292.9	309.9	−16.9	−5.8
4	3.0	9.2	−6.2	295.1	317.0	−21.9	−7.4
1976:1	4.6	9.6	−5.1	298.5	324.6	−26.1	−8.8
2	6.4	8.6	−2.2	303.3	331.6	−28.3	−9.3
3	4.2	7.8	−3.6	306.5	338.1	−31.6	−10.3
4	7.4	8.0	−0.5	312.1	344.8	−32.7	−10.5
1977:1	7.4	8.6	−1.2	317.9	352.2	−34.3	−10.8
2	7.4	9.0	−1.6	323.8	360.1	−36.3	−11.2
3	8.7	8.2	0.5	330.8	367.5	−36.7	−11.1
4	7.4	7.4	−0.0	336.9	374.3	−37.4	−11.1
1978:1	6.7	7.0	−0.3	342.5	380.8	−38.3	−11.2
2	9.2	9.4	−0.2	350.4	389.7	−39.4	−11.2
3	8.2	8.5	−0.3	357.5	398.0	−40.5	−11.3
4	4.3	8.6	−4.3	361.4	406.5	−45.1	−12.5
1979:1	−2.4	8.2	−10.6	359.2	414.9	−55.7	−15.5
Summary statistic							
Mean error			−2.9			−29.6	
Mean absolute error			3.0			29.6	
Root-mean-square error			4.0			32.3	

Note: Actual values are from the Board of Governors of the Federal Reserve System. Predicted values are from a dynamic simulation of the M_1 equation. This equation uses the same specification and sample period (1960:4 to 1974:2) as the equation for M_1 reported in "A Proposal for Redefining Monetary Aggregates," *Federal Reserve Bulletin,* 65 (January 1979), 26. Figures are rounded.

* Cumulative error as a percent of actual level.

SOURCE: R. D. Porter, T. D. Simpson, and E. Mauskopf, "Financial Innovation and the Monetary Aggregates," *Brookings Papers on Economic Activity,* 1 (1979), 214.

interest. Estimates of the elasticity cluster in the −0.1 to −0.9 range, depending, in part, on the particular interest rate used. But no evidence has been found that indicates the actual existence of a liquidity trap. And the controversy remains over the proper choice of a scale variable that affects money demand. The evidence does tend, however, to imply a role for wealth in determining the long-run equilibrium level of desired money balances, as well as a role for current income in determining the speed with which individuals choose to move toward this equilibrium. Although, for simplicity of exposition, in the preceding pages we have relied exclusively on single-equation estimates, we should emphasize that similar conclusions are derived from the more complicated "simultaneous equations" estimates.[15]

INSTABILITY OF MONEY DEMAND

The earlier version of our quotation from Laidler, dated 1969, emphasized that the demand function for money is "stable," which means simply that this function does not shift, so that one can predict the demand for real balances from the (assumed or actual) levels of the interest rate and of GNP. However, there is now considerable evidence that since mid-1974 the demand for money has been persistently and increasingly overpredicted. Until the second quarter of 1974 the forecasting error has been rising steadily, from 1.8 percent or $5 billion, to 15.5 percent, or $55.7 billion. Apparently the demand-for-money curve has been shifting.

This instability, according to its discoverers, is attributable to "innovations and regulations changes that have reduced the cost of converting assets between money and interest-bearing instruments or developments that have reduced the value of transactions per dollar of GNP."[16] Over the years, however, several writers have examined an array of innovations and regulation changes. For example, regulations were changed to permit negotiable-orders-of-withdrawal (NOW) accounts at commercial banks and at other financial institutions; these accounts permit, in effect, payment of interest on checkable balances, competing directly with (checkable) demand deposits (which are money and do not pay interest). Innovations have included the issuance of certificates of deposit (CDs), Eurodollars, and bank-related commercial paper. In addition, we now have automatic transfer services (ATS), which encourage the switching of funds from demand deposits to savings accounts. Another financial instrument that has emerged recently is the security repurchase agreement (RPs) and checkable money-market mutual funds. A repurchase agreement denotes a sale (by a bank) of government securities in exchange for immediately available funds, with an agreement for the securities to be repurchased and the funds returned at a future date, usually the next day.

---

[15] For the work of the other authors mentioned in Table 13-2, see H. A. Latané, "Cash Balances and the Interest Rate—A Pragmatic Approach," *Review of Economics and Statistics,* November 1954, pp. 456–60; and Gregory Chow, "On the Short-Run and Long-Run Demand for Money," *Journal of Political Economy,* April 1966, pp. 111–31.

[16] See Jared Enzler, Lewis Johnson, and John Paulus, "Some Problems of Money Demand," *Brookings Papers on Economic Activity,* 1(1976), 279.

While most economists now agree that the demand-for-money function has been shifting and that this shift is caused by financial innovations, which appear continually, they differ in their explanations.[17]

The apparent instability of the demand for money has had two serious repercussions, both associated with the conduct of monetary policy. First, it has caused a change in the definitions of the various measures of money. For example, *M*-1 used to include only currency and demand deposits with the commercial banks. Now this measure is called M-1A, while M-1B includes the components of M-1A plus other checkable deposits, or other transactions accounts, at all depository institutions. Transactions accounts are essentially any accounts on which checks can be written. These issues are examined extensively in the next Chapter.

The second consequence of the instability of money demand is the apparent weakness in the argument that the Federal Reserve should control the monetary aggregates. This argument relies on a stable money demand.[18] Besides, it is difficult to control a magnitude that is difficult to define, or requires continual changes in its definition, whenever it seems that new financial instruments and, hence, new measures of money supply will be forthcoming.[19]

QUESTIONS

1. Suppose that the economy consists of only three groups of individuals, who expect with *certainty* different future prices for a perpetual bond carrying a coupon of $10. Group A expects the price to be $90; group B, $100; and group C, $120. Derive the aggregate *demand for money* as a function of the interest rate. Be exact with the numbers on the interest rate axis.

---

[17] See, for example, Enzler, Johnson, and Paulus, "Some Problems of Money Demand"; S. M. Goldfeld, "The Case of Missing Money," *Brookings Papers on Economic Activity,* 3(1976), 683–739; P. A. Tinsley and Bonnie Garrett with M. E. Friar, "The Measurement of Money Demand" (*Special Studies Paper,* No. 133, Federal Reserve Board, October 1978); and R. D. Porter, T. D. Simpson, and E. Mauskopf, "Financial Innovation and the Monetary Aggregates," *Brookings Papers on Economic Activity,* 1(1979), 214. There are, of course, economists who do not believe that the demand-for-money curve has shifted; they attribute this recent weakness in the monetary aggregates to monetary policy that was too tight, a reflection, they argue, on the methods by which the Federal Reserve Board conducts economic policy. See William Poole, "The Monetary Deceleration: What Does It Mean and Why Is It Happening?" *Brookings Papers on Economic* Activity, 1(1979), 231–38. For another view, see M. Hamburger, "Behavior of the Money Stock, Is There a Puzzle?" *Journal of Monetary Economics,* July 1977, pp. 265–88.

[18] See William Poole, "Optimal Choice of Monetary Instruments in a Simple Stochastic Macro Model," *Quarterly Journal of Economics* vol. 84(1970), pp. 197–216.

[19] For an extensive discussion of this topic, see the papers in *Controlling Monetary Aggregates III,* proceedings of a conference sponsored by the Federal Reserve Bank of Boston, October 1980.

2. "If the substitution effect outweighs the income effect, then we can derive the law of demand for money from rational behavior toward *uncertainty*." Prove this.
3. If for each present rate of interest people expect a higher future interest rate than before, what will happen to the demand curve for money derived from a theory of inelastic interest expectations and certainty?
4. Assume that the coupon on a perpetual bond is $5. Assume also that there are three groups of wealth holders, A, B, and C, for which the *certain* expected bond prices are, respectively, $95, $145, and $120.
   a. Find the aggregate demand for money giving exact numbers on the interest rate axis.
   b. If the expected bond prices change to $45, $70, and $57.50 for A, B, and C, respectively, find the new aggregate demand for money.
   c. What happens to the rate of interest, price level, and employment when expectations change from $95, $145, and $120 to $45, $70, and $57.50?
5. Why does a rise in the interest rate lower the transactions demand for money? How would longer lines at the bank affect the transactions demand for money?
6. Draw and explain the zero profitability line in terms of current and expected bond prices.
7. Show the connection between the elasticity of price expectations and the relationship between money demand and the interest rate.
8. What are some of the limitations of the money demand derivation from certainty?
9. Explain the role of income and substitution effects in deriving the demand for money from uncertainty.
10. Why does expected inflation affect the demand for money?
11. What does instability of money demand mean? What are its implications for the conduct of monetary policy? For the monetary instruments used?

REFERENCES

BAUMOL, WILLIAM J., "The Transactions Demand for Cash: An Inventory Theoretic Approach," *Quarterly Journal of Economics,* November 1952, pp. 545–56.

ENZLER, JARED, LEWIS JOHNSON, and JOHN PAULUS, "Some Problems of Money Demand," *Brookings Papers on Economic Activity,* 1(1976), 261–80.

FRIEDMAN, MILTON, "The Demand for Money—Some Theoretical and Empirical Results," *Journal of Political Economy,* June 1959, pp. 327–51.

———, "The Quantity Theory of Money—A Restatement," in *Studies in the Quantity Theory of Money,* ed. M. Friedman. Chicago: University of Chicago Press, 1956.

GOLDFELD, STEPHEN M., "The Case of the Missing Money," *Brookings Papers on Economic Activity,* 3(1976), 683–739.

———, "The Demand for Money Revisited," *Brookings Papers on Economic Activity,* 3(1973), 577–638.

HICKS, J. R., "A Suggestion for Simplifying the Theory of Money," *Economica,* February 1935, pp. 1–19.

JOHNSON, HARRY G., *Macroeconomics and Monetary Theory,* Chap. 16. Chicago: Aldine, 1972.

KEYNES, J. M., *The General Theory of Employment, Interest and Money,* Chaps. 13 and 15. New York: Harcourt, Brace & Co., 1936.

———, *A Tract for Monetary Reform.* London: Macmillan, 1923.

———, *A Treatise on Money.* London: Macmillan, 1930.

MILLER, M. H., and D. ORR, "A Model of Demand for Money by Firms," *Quarterly Journal of Economics,* August 1966.

PATINKIN, DON, "The Chicago Tradition, the Quantity Theory, and Friedman," *Journal of Money, Credit and Banking,* February 1969, pp. 46–70.

TOBIN, JAMES, "The Interest-Elasticity of the Transactions Demand for Cash," *Review of Economics and Statistics,* September 1956, pp. 241–47.

———, "Liquidity Preference, as Behavior toward Risk," *Review of Economic Studies,* February 1958, pp. 65–86.

———, "Money, Capital, and Other Stores of Value," *American Economic Review,* May 1961.

———, "The Theory of Portfolio Selection," in *The Theory of Interest Rates,* ed. F. Hahn and F. Brechling, Chap. 1. New York: Macmillan, 1965.

14 The Supply of Money and Monetary Control

In this chapter we examine the intricacies of money supply: what it is, who or what creates it, and how it can be changed; and we discuss in detail the main instruments for conducting monetary policy: open market operations (OMO), the discount rate policy, and the reserve requirement policy, exactly as they are currently implemented. That is, we incorporate the fundamental change in operating procedures that occurred in October 1979.

All of these aspects will be examined in the context of the "new," or "modern," view of money, which relies on the rational behavior of banks, in fact, of financial institutions in general and of households (the nonbank public). The money supply is therefore an endogenous variable, the end result of the combined decisions of banks and households, as well as of the Federal Reserve System. Actually this new view is not so "new"; it was introduced in the early 1960s by James Tobin and further advanced by his associates at Yale, especially William Brainard.[1] This view

[1] See James Tobin, "Commercial Banks as Creators of 'Money,' " in *Banking and Monetary Studies,* ed. Deane Carson (Homewood, Ill.: Richard D. Irwin, 1963), pp. 408–19; James Tobin, "An Essay on the Principles of Debt Management," in *Fiscal and Debt Management Policies* (Englewood Cliffs, N.J.: Prentice-Hall, 1963), pp. 143–218; J. Tobin and W. C. Brainard, "Financial Intermediaries and the Effectiveness of Monetary Controls," *American Economic Review,* May 1963, pp. 383–400; W. C. Brainard and J. Tobin, "Pitfalls in Financial Model Building," *American Economic Review,* May 1968, pp. 352–77; and James Tobin, "A General Equilibrium Approach to Monetary Theory," *Journal of Money, Credit and Banking,* February 1969, pp. 15–29.

differs from the "old," or "traditional," view, which excludes any rational behavior of individual agents but, instead, applies the money multiplier mechanically, thereby treating money supply as an exogenous variable, or a true parameter.

We examine two versions of the new view in this chapter. In Section I we cast our analysis in a five-asset economy, while in Section II we simplify by assuming explicitly only one asset as an alternative to money. As a byproduct of our analysis in both sections, we shed light on the old debate about whether banks *create* money or whether they merely lend whatever money is deposited with them. A second byproduct, derived exclusively from our analysis in Section I, will be our determination of an *array* (or vector) of interest rates rather than of "the" interest rate; from this analysis we can see how the Treasury Bill (T-bill) rate, the Treasury Bond rate, the loan rate, the rate of return on capital, and other rates are determined, and how they, in turn, are influenced by the various instruments of monetary policy.

So far we have avoided stating exactly what money is and how its supply can be altered. We have merely assumed that the money supply, whatever that is, can be changed at will by the "monetary authority." In general, the monetary authority is the country's Central Bank—in the United States it is the Federal Reserve System, known as the Fed.[2]

Until recently there have always been two popular definitions of money supply, the *narrower* one and the *broader* one. The narrower one was simply M-1, which included cash, C, outside of banks (i.e., coins and notes in the possession of the nonbank public) plus demand deposits at commercial banks. In addition, there were two broader measures of money, M-2, which included the components of M-1 plus savings and time deposits at commercial banks, other than negotiable certificates of deposit; and M-3, which included M-2 plus savings and time deposits at thrift institutions. The narrower version, M-1, satisfied the strictest requirement of money as a medium of exchange, whereas the other measures satisfied it to a lesser degree. The idea behind these definitions of money aggregates was that time deposits did not directly serve as a medium of exchange and that deposits at thrift institutions were less liquid than were similar deposits at commercial banks. For years sharp distinctions among types of deposits and depository institutions made the three basic definitions of monetary aggregates satisfactory.

But as we saw at the end of Chapter 13, in recent years financial innovations and regulatory changes have blurred the once-clear lines between the various types of deposits. For example, regulations have changed to permit NOW (negotiable order of withdrawal) accounts, which are similar to checking accounts but bear interest; credit union share drafts; and demand deposits at savings banks, which also provide checking-type services. Similarly, financial innovations were introduced, such as ATS (automatic transfer services), RPs (repurchase agreements), and CDs (certificates of deposit).

Concurrently, and probably because of these changes, models that attempt to estimate and forecast the demand for money have experienced increasing problems,

[2] See the latest edition of *The Federal Reserve System, Purposes and Functions* for an authoritative account of the institutional aspects of the Fed.

as we saw in Section V of Chapter 13. One of the Federal Reserve's responses was the introduction of new monetary aggregate measures, which attempt, at least as a stopgap measure, to take account of the innovations in financial markets.

The narrowest of the new measures is M-1A, which includes currency, C, and demand deposits, D_{1A}, at commercial banks (excluding those held by official institutions and foreign banks). M-1B includes the components of M-1A plus "other checkable deposits," D_{1B}, that is, interest-bearing checkable deposits at all depository institutions and demand deposits at mutual savings banks. Measure M-2 includes M-1B plus D_2; D_2 includes savings and small time deposits at banks and thrift institutions plus some other financial instruments including overnight repurchase agreements at commercial banks, overnight Eurodollars held by U.S. residents, and money market mutual fund shares. The broadest measure of M, M-3, includes M-2 plus large time deposits at all institutions and term repurchase agreements.

For the purposes of our book we shall define the money supply, M, in general terms as

$$M = C + D; \tag{1}$$

of course, if $D = D_{1A}$ we are using the narrowest definition, M-1A, and if $D = D_{1A} + D_{1B}$ we are using M-1B, and so forth, for D_2 and D_3.

In Section I we shall determine the money supply, M, and see how it can be influenced by the standard tools of monetary policy. As a byproduct, we shall also determine an entire array of interest rates and rates of return. In Section II we see how the money supply is determined and influenced, using a very simple model that still retains the flavor of the "new view" of money. In Section III we examine the actual conduct of monetary policy, emphasizing its occasional reliance on monetary aggregates, on the Federal Funds rate, and on the recent move toward a direct control of the reserve, or monetary, base. And, finally, in Section IV we examine the empirical investigations, concentrating on the size of the interest elasticity of the supply of money.

I. THE NEW VIEW OF MONEY SUPPLY IN A FIVE-ASSET ECONOMY

1. DETERMINATION OF MONEY SUPPLY ALONG WITH THE RATES OF RETURN

From our above explanation and from (1) we notice immediately that whether we use the broader or the narrower definition, the money supply consists of liabilities of the Fed, that is, C, and of liabilities of the banks and other financial institutions, D. While the Fed and the financial institutions must be willing to create these liabilities in order for the money supply to reach any given level, their willingness, by itself, is not sufficient; the nonbank public must also be willing to hold these liabilities. Why is it, for example, that the public wants to hold the amount C even though it does not yield any return as compared with other items, such as T-bills, in the average household's portfolio? Any analysis of money should be able to answer questions like this.

Of course, there are additional questions. For example, in the United States the (nominal) yield on demand deposits is the same as that on currency, namely, zero. What, then, determines the quantities of these two assets held by the public? Searching for this answer can complicate the analysis. But, in what follows, we simplify the analysis by assuming that the demand for currency, C, is a constant, that is, it depends on *exogenous* factors, such as the payments habits of society or the degree of crime, and not on endogenous variables. For our purposes, however, this assumption is realistic, even though it is not realistic for the persons responsible for predicting and manipulating the money supply on a day-to-day basis.

With this assumption, we know one of the two components of M, namely, C. Let us now find a way to determine the other component, D. Fortunately, a real-world assumption can easily come to our help; the Fed is allowed (and required) by law to fix the return on several assets, *including* those on demand and time deposits. Traditionally, these returns have been set so low that they are binding. In other words, these returns are so low (in fact, sometimes zero) that banks (and other financial institutions) will gladly accept any amount of deposits. *This means that the level of deposits, D, is whatever the public wants it to be.* It is clear, then, that the determinants of D are also the determinants of the money supply.

But how is D determined? How can we say that this D, which reflects the households' decisions, is under the control of the Fed? And how is it that banks *create* money?

To show the ability of the Central Bank to determine and control the total money supply and to demonstrate the ability of the banking sector to "create" money, economists have traditionally relied on a very simple, mechanistic approach, which we shall call the *traditional,* or *old,* view. To illustrate this view we must merely show that the (demand) deposits, D, are a *constant* multiple of some entity under the absolute control of the Fed.

The Fed regulations require commercial banks (and other financial institutions) to keep a certain percentage of deposits in *reserves.* This percentage, which we shall denote by κ, is called the *reserve requirement,* which is satisfied mainly by accounts with a Federal Reserve Bank, although currency in the commercial banks themselves, the *vault cash,* is also considered part of a bank's reserves. With deposits equal to D, the entire banking sector's required reserves, R_R, are

$$R_R = \kappa D \tag{2}$$

This equation is true by definition. Also true by definition is the relation

$$D = \frac{1}{\kappa} \cdot R_R \tag{3}$$

which states that (demand) deposits are a multiple, $1/\kappa$, of the required reserves. If, for example, $\kappa = 0.20$, $1/\kappa$ is five, which means that for every single dollar in required reserves there are five dollars in deposits. Moreover, it means that for every one-dollar *increase* (decrease) in required reserves, there will be a five-dollar increase (decrease) in deposits. Therefore the magnitude $1/\kappa$ is called the *money multiplier.*

The traditional view assumes that the amount of required reserves is under the *direct* (and absolute) control of the Central Bank, that is, it is a parameter, as in (4), where the bar over R_R is meant to denote its fixed value:

$$D = \frac{1}{\kappa} \cdot \overline{R}_R \tag{4}$$

By fixing this amount, $\overline{R}_R$, the Central Bank also fixes the amount of deposits, D. If, for example, $\overline{R}_R$ = \$100 billion, with a reserve requirement, κ, equal to 0.20 and hence a money multiplier equal to 5, the amount of deposits, D, will be equal to \$500 billion.[3]

According to the traditional view, the Central Bank controls (fixes) the amount of required reserves, R_R. But how does it achieve this? It does so by fixing the amount of nonborrowed reserves, R^*, which is defined as *total reserves, TR,* minus the amount of *borrowed reserves,* R_B, which are reserves borrowed by commercial banks from any one of the twelve Federal Reserve Banks:

$$R^* = TR - R_B \tag{5}$$

We shall use the term *nonborrowed reserve base,* or simply, *reserve base,* to denote nonborrowed reserves.

Our use of the concept and magnitude, reserve base, rather than the more familiar *monetary base,* stems partly from our simplifying assumption that the public's currency holding, C, is fixed. In general, the *nonborrowed monetary base,* B^*, consists of nonborrowed reserves, R^*, plus currency holdings by the public:

$$B^* = R^* + C \tag{5'}$$

The *total monetary base,* then, is the nonborrowed monetary base, B^*, plus borrowed reserves, R_B. The monetary base is sometimes called *high-powered money.* (The reader should note eventually, however, that our high-powered money, R^*, is more high powered than B^*, since part of any increase in unborrowed reserves will find its way to the pockets of individuals rather than in bank reserves.)

The banks may use the *total reserves, TR* (made available by the Fed), in two alternative ways: as *required reserves,* R_R, in the sense that they support a multiple amount of deposits, or as *excess reserves,* R_E, in the sense that they are idle balances. Hence

$$R_R + R_E = TR \tag{6}$$

Now, (5) becomes

$$R^* = R_R + R_E - R_B$$

---

[3] To avoid repetition, we shall postpone a more detailed analysis of money creation until Section II, where the traditional view will be considered as an *extreme, special* case of the modern view.

Finally, we define *free reserves,* R_F, as the difference between excess and borrowed reserves:

$$R_F \equiv R_E - R_B \gtreqless 0 \tag{7}$$

so

$$R_R + R_F = R^* \tag{8}$$

If we use the more general formula (5′), we get the more familiar (8′):

$$R_R + R_F + C = B^* \tag{8'}$$

(Equation (8) will be derived, below, as a market-clearing equilibrium condition.) In effect, then, the traditional view presumes either that the reserve base is the same thing as required reserves or, at least, that changes in the reserve base are reflected in equal changes in required reserves; in other words, the change in free reserves is zero.

The modern, or new, view regards R^* but not R_R as a parameter. Instead, R_R is an endogenous variable determined by the interaction—in the market system—of the profit-maximizing behavior of banks and of the rational behavior of the nonbank public. Similarly, whether we employ the narrow (*M*-1) or the broad (*M*-2) definition of the money supply, its total must be the end result of the combined decisions of (a) the banks, (b) the nonbank public, and (c) the Fed. Since the components of the total money supply (and some of its determinants) are items, or entries—either as assets or as liabilities—in the balance sheets of those three entities, these items must be considered as results of their conscious portfolio decisions. Understanding the money supply, then, requires an examination of the portfolio behavior of the banks and of the nonbank public, as well as of the instruments of monetary control possessed by the Central Bank.

Tables 14-1a, 14-2a, and 14-3a illustrate simplified, hypothetical balance sheets of the nonbank public, the banks, and the Federal Reserve System, respectively. In

TABLE 14-1a CASE 1 (ALL NUMBERS ARE BILLIONS OF DOLLARS)

PUBLIC			
Assets		Liabilities	
Currency	150	Net Worth	950
Deposits	500	Loans	250
Government Securities	350		
Common Stock	200		
	1,200		1,200

Table 14-1a we see that the total money supply is equal to $650 billion, $150 billion of which is currency in the public's possession and the rest, $500 billion, is deposits. Both of these items are entered as assets in the balance sheet of the nonbank public. On the other hand, the $500 billion in deposits is also a liability of the banking industry, as shown in Table 14-2a. This same table shows that $100 billion of the banking industry's assets counts as reserves, $15 billion of which is currency (or *vault cash*) and $85 billion of which is deposited with the Fed system—the twelve Federal Reserve Banks. Of course, this last item appears in Table 14-3a as a liability of the Federal Reserve System. Another liability of the Fed is the currency in the (commercial) banks' vaults, $15 billion, and the currency in the hands of the nonbank public, $150 billion, for a total of $165 billion.

The reader should note that the tables of Case 1 have been constructed so that they may be consistent with the old view. Since, in this case, there are no *borrowed reserves,* the *total reserves* are also the *reserve base,* $100 billion, an amount that is exactly equal to the *required reserves,* R_R—assuming, as earlier, that the reserve requirement, κ, is equal ot 0.20 (i.e., $R_R = 0.20 \times \$500 = \$100$ billion). There is no compelling reason, however, for the tables to be as they are in 14-1a, 14-2a, and 14-3a. When the appropriate circumstances warrant it, Tables 14-1b and 14-2b can represent the balance sheets of the public and the banks, respectively, while Table 14-3a (but reproduced here as Table 14-3b) still depicts the balance sheet of the Central Bank. Alterna-

TABLE 14-2a CASE 1 (Continued)

BANKS			
Assets		Liabilities	
Currency	15	Deposits	500
Reserves with Fed	85	Net Worth	50
Government Securities	200		
Loans	250		
	550		550

TABLE 14-3a CASE 1 (Continued)

FEDERAL RESERVE SYSTEM			
Assets		Liabilities	
Government Securities	250	Federal Reserve Notes	165
		Deposits: Member Bank Reserve Accounts	85
	250		250

TABLE 14-1b CASE 2 (ALL NUMBERS ARE BILLIONS OF DOLLARS)

PUBLIC			
Assets		**Liabilities**	
Currency	150	Net Worth	950
Deposits	400	Loans	200
Government Securities	400		
Common Stock	200		
	1,150		1,150

TABLE 14-2b CASE 2 (Continued)

BANKS			
Assets		**Liabilities**	
Currency	15	Deposits	400
Reserves with Fed	85	Net Worth	50
Government Securities	150		
Loans	200		
	450		450

TABLE 14-3b CASE 2 (Continued)
(SAME AS 14-3a)

FEDERAL RESERVE SYSTEM			
Assets		**Liabilities**	
Government Securities	250	Federal Reserve Notes	165
		Deposits: Member Bank Reserve Accounts	85
	250		250

tively, the balance sheets of these three sectors can be represented by Tables 14-1c, 14-2c, and 14-3c.

Let us denote the configuration of Tables 14-1a, 14-2a, and 14-3a as Case 1; the configuration of Tables 14-1b, 14-2b, and 14-3b as Case 2; and that of Tables 14-1c, 14-2c, and 14-3c as Case 3. *In all these cases the reserve base is the same,* and it is equal to $100 billion. As mentioned earlier, in Case 1 the required reserves and the reserve base coincide, since there are no borrowed reserves (and no free

TABLE 14-1c CASE 3 (ALL NUMBERS ARE BILLIONS OF DOLLARS)

PUBLIC			
Assets		Liabilities	
Currency	150	Net Worth	950
Deposits	550	Loans	280
Government Securities	330		
Common Stock	200		
	1,230		1,230

TABLE 14-2c CASE 3 (Continued)

BANKS			
Assets		Liabilities	
Currency	15	Deposits	550
Reserves with Fed	95	Loans from Fed	10
Government Securities	220	Net Worth	50
Loans	280		
	610		610

TABLE 14-3c CASE 3 (Continued)

FEDERAL RESERVE SYSTEM			
Assets		Liabilities	
Government Securities	250	Federal Reserve Notes	165
Loans to Member Banks	10	Deposits: Member Bank Reserve Accounts	95
	260		260

reserves). In Case 2 the reserve base of \$100 billion is divided between \$80 billion as required reserves (i.e., 0.20 × \$400 = \$80) and \$20 billion as free reserves. Finally, in Case 3 we have a (nonborrowed) reserve base of \$100 billion, since we subtract the \$10 billion of borrowed reserves from the \$110 billion of total reserves. In this case the free reserves are negative (i.e., minus \$10 billion). And the required reserves of \$110 billion (= 0.20 × \$550) exceed the (nonborrowed) reserve base (of \$100 billion).

The crucial question then arises, Why does the same amount of reserve base support different amounts of deposits and, therefore, different amounts of total money supply? In particular—employing the terminology that the reserve base is called *high-powered* money—why is the reserve base of $100 billion more high powered in Case 3 than in Case 1? And why is it more high powered in Case 1 than in Case 2? Questions like this can easily be answered when we rely on the new, or modern, view. According to this view, the items in the portfolios of the public and of the banking sectors depend on the *rates of return* on these items. Moreover, in true *general* (or *interdependent*) equilibrium fashion, these returns are determined simultaneously by supply and demand. In the simplified examples of our tables there are five assets: (1) government demand debt, that is, currency and reserves (as one item); (2) (interest-bearing) government securities; (3) loans (from the banks to the nonbank public); (4) deposits; and (5) equity capital (or common stock).

Now, let r_M denote the rate on currency and reserves, r_B the rate on government securities (bills or bonds), r_L the loan rate, r_D the rate on deposits, and r_K the rate on equity capital. The nonbank public decides in what form to hold its wealth (as augmented by loans from the banks) on the basis of the levels of the rates $(r_M, r_B, r_L, r_K, r_D)$; this array (or vector) of the rates of return, which are relevant for the portfolio decisions of the public, we shall occasionally denote with one symbol, r^P, where the superscript P stands for the word *public.* On the other hand, the banks can borrow from the Central Bank at the going *discount rate,* denoted by d. Hence the level of d must also be a determinant of the assets held and of the liabilities incurred by the banks. In our simplified scheme we shall assume that the banks do not hold equity capital and that its return, r_K, is not among the decision variables relevant for the banks; this array of returns, denoted by r^B, is (r_M, r_B, r_L, r_D, d).

We shall now specify how the demand for each asset by the relevant sector, whether by the banks or by the nonbank public, is influenced by the rates of return. In general, both the nonbank public and the banking sector increase (decrease) their demand for an asset when its rate rises (falls). For example, the higher the rate of return on government securities—say of the T-bill—the higher the proportion of their disposable wealth held (invested) in these securities. On the other hand, the higher the rate of return on a competing asset, the smaller the proportion of wealth invested in another asset. For example, the higher the return on capital, the smaller the proportion of wealth held (invested) in government securities. In other words, we are assuming that all these assets are *gross substitutes.*

In our simplified economy there are six rates of return and interest rates: $r_M, r_B, r_L, r_D, r_K, d$. Some of these returns are determined in the market system, that is, at the levels that clear the markets. The securities (i.e., T-bill) rate, r_B, the loan rate, r_L, and the rate on equity capital, r_K, belong in this category. The remaining three rates may or may not be allowed to be market determined. Two of these, however, namely, r_M and d, are fixed (and manipulated) in every country by the Central Bank. In the United States r_M is fixed at zero: The rate on currency is, obviously, zero and so is the rate on reserves with the Fed—although on several occasions proposals have been made to pay interest on reserves held at Federal Reserve Banks. In some countries the deposit rate r_D, is market determined, but in the United States the Fed fixes this rate, at the level zero for demand deposits but now at a positive level for some transactions deposits such as NOW accounts. In general, the Fed fixes the deposit rate at a *sufficiently low* level so that it is *binding;* at this low rate the banks willingly accept any and all deposits. In this case the amount of the deposits, D, is at whatever level the public wants it to be. The exact amount of deposits, then, depends on the rates that competing assets can earn. The higher the other rates are, say, the higher the T-bill rate is, the lower the proportion of its wealth that the public will be willing to hold in deposits that earn zero interest. On the other hand, deposits become more attractive, even though they earn zero interest, when the returns on competing assets fall. It is clear, then, that a particular policy can influence the amount of deposits and, therefore, total money supply *only to the extent* that this policy can influence these competing rates of return.

The *endogenous* rates of return, namely, r_B, r_L, and r_K, are determined at whatever level is necessary to make the demand for each asset equal to its supply. The supply of capital (equities) is equal to its past accumulation, while the demand for capital emanates (only) from the nonbank public. And the demand for the *asset* called loans is the amount of IOUs, and it emanates from the lenders (i.e., the banks). The supply of this asset originates with the borrowers (i.e., the nonbank public). (Note, in this context, that in Table 14-1a loans enter as liabilities of the public, and in Table 14-2a, as assets of the banks.) As noted above, the deposit rate, r_D, is so low (say, at zero) that the supply, furnished by the banks, is whatever the demanders, the nonbank public, want.

The remaining two assets constitute government debt. Currency and reserves, as a single asset, are called *demand debt;* the other asset, government securities, is *interest-bearing debt.* (In the real world, they correspond to several government issues of differing maturity, for example, 13-week T-bills, 26-week T-bills, 5-year bonds, 10-year bonds, perpetuities, etc.) The total government debt—demand debt, as well as (interest-bearing) government securities—reflects the sum of past governmental deficits. In other words, *all previous budget deficits have been financed by issuing either demand debt or (interest-bearing) government securities.* Although, in essence, this statement is true, in practice—because the U.S. Treasury and the Fed are two separate entities—the budget deficit is financed only by issuing (interest-bearing) government securities. The Fed, in turn, may *monetize* some of this debt; in other words, by buying some of these securities from the banks and the public, and by issuing *its* debt, currency, and reserves (i.e., the demand debt), the Fed, in essence, finances some of the deficit by "printing" money. In fact, the Fed is not constrained in the amount of the debt it can monetize. For example, it can monetize more than the period's deficit by buying some of the accumulated debt of earlier periods.

If we chose to consider this purchase by the Fed as a component of the demand for securities, we would have, along with those emanating from the nonbank public and from the banks, *three* components of demand. Furthermore, the supply of (interest-bearing) government securities would be the cumulative amount issued by the Treasury to date. However, we choose, instead, to consider this demand as emanating from only *two* sources, from the banks and from the nonbank public. With this approach the relevant supply is the amount of (interest-bearing) securities available to the nongovernmental sector, that is, the total sum of government securities already issued by the Treasury *minus* the amount in the possession of (i.e., monetized by) the Fed. (We prefer this approach because the demands emanating from the banks and the nonbank public are based on typical rational behavior, whereas the "demand" by the Fed is based on other considerations.)

At this point it is helpful to introduce the balance sheet of the U.S. Treasury and the implied *consolidated balance sheet* of the joint governmental sector, the Fed-Treasury. Thus, for Case 1 we have—in addition to Tables 14-1a, 14-2a, and 14-3a—Tables 14-4a and 14-5a. From Table 14-5a we see that the *net total* government debt is $800 billion. From Tables 14-3a or 14-5a we also see that of this $800 billion, $550 billion is interest-bearing debt and $250 billion is (interest-free) demand debt. The most frequently used tool of monetary policy is the manipulation of the *composition of the total government debt* effected by the Fed through a purchase of or a sale of government securities. This tool, called *open market operation* (OMO), will be examined in detail below.

TABLE 14-4a CASE 1 (Continued)

U.S. TREASURY			
Assets		Liabilities	
Net Worth (Negative)	800	Government Securities	800
	800		800

TABLE 14-5a CASE 1 (Continued)

CONSOLIDATED BALANCE SHEET OF FED AND U.S. TREASURY			
Assets		Liabilities	
Loans to Member Banks	0	Notes (Currency)	165
Net Worth (Negative)	800	Deposits: Member Bank Reserve Accounts	85
		Government Securities (Net = 800 − 250)	550
	800		800

We turn now to the asset "demand debt," which consists of currency plus reserves. Since we are assuming that the public's demand for currency is a constant, we can subtract this amount from the total amount of demand debt already issued by the Fed and determine the *supply of reserves,* or *reserve base.* What is left on the demand side is the banking sector's demand for currency (i.e., *vault cash*) and its demand for reserves to be deposited at the Fed. This demand can be written as the *demand for required reserves,* κD, plus the *demand for free reserves,* R_F (i.e., $\kappa D + R_F$). Denoting the total amount of demand debt as G^D, the relevant *supply of reserves* is, then, $G^D - C$, which is the (nonborrowed) reserve base, R^*. Thus the market-for-reserves-clearing equation is

$$\kappa D + R_F = R^* \tag{9}$$

We can now see that the traditional view of money supply is an *extreme, special* case of the new view. First, it concentrates only on this equation, ignoring the other four market-clearing equations, which we have examined verbally. Second, and more important in this *partial* format, the traditional view assumes that the free reserves, R_F, are fixed, which implies that changes in the reserve base, R^*, in turn, imply equal changes in the deposits, D, according to the (fixed) multiplier, $1/\kappa$. Note that $\kappa D = R^* - R_F$, or

$$D = \frac{1}{\kappa} \cdot (R^* - R_F) \tag{10}$$

and when R_F is assumed fixed (i.e., $\Delta R_F = 0$), it follows that

$$\Delta D = \frac{1}{\kappa} (\Delta R^* - \Delta R_F) \tag{11}$$

or

$$\Delta D = \frac{1}{\kappa} \cdot \Delta R^* \tag{12}$$

2. THE TOOLS OF MONETARY POLICY

We have already mentioned that one of the tools of monetary control available to the Fed is the *OMO.* Other instruments include manipulation of the other parameters, of which only two, *discount rate* and the *reserve requirements* manipulations, are used relatively often. Of course, the manipulation of the deposit rate, r_D, can serve as an instrument of monetary policy, although it has not yet been used in the United States. In the real world there are several forms of deposits, such as bank or savings and loan association time deposits, whose rates have indeed been manipulated by the Fed, which can modify the Regulation Q ceilings on these rates. In the remainder of this section we illustrate the three most frequently used tools of monetary policy, beginning with open market operations, OMO.

The monetary authority manipulates these three tools in order to control, that is, to set the amount of *effective reserves,* $R^* - R_F$, at whatever level is necessary at whatever level is necessary to achieve a predetermined quantity of deposits, D, and hence of money, M. The exact method used depends upon the particular operating procedure. Until October 1979, the Fed used to attempt to achieve its objectives by manipulating (controlling) the federal funds rate, r_F, which is the rate banks charge for overnight lending of reserves to each other. In earlier years the

Fed controlled the T-bill rate, r_B, itself. For simplicity, and without any loss of realism, we can identify the federal funds rate with the T-bill rate. Thus, under the federal funds operating regime, r_B was a policy parameter while R^* was endogenous. However, on October 6, 1979 the Fed introduced a new operating procedure, the reserves operating target, which attempts to control the effective reserve base by manipulating the amount of nonborrowed reserves, or nonborrowed reserve base, R^*.

The key difference between the two regimes is the switch in the roles played by R^* and r_B. Under the old federal funds operating regime, the Fed set the path (or level) of r_B, as a policy parameter, and then, R^* was transformed into an endogenous variable. In other words, under the old regime R^* is at whatever level is consistent with the preset path of r_B and with clearance of the reserves market as well as the other markets. On the other hand, the new regime reestablishes the bill rate, r_B, as a market-clearing, endogenous variable and treats the nonborrowed reserve base, R^*, as a true policy parameter. It is this latter regime that we are examining explicitly in this chapter.

In summary, schematically, under a reserves operating target, the *instruments* of monetary control (or "parameters," or "exogenous" variables) determine the endogenous variables r_B, r_L, r_K. Given the levels of these variables, we can determine additional endogenous variables, such as the (demand) deposits, *D*, and hence, various concepts of the money supply, *M*, the level of borrowed and free reserves, and the level of total reserves:

INSTRUMENTS		ENDOGENOUS VARIABLES
$\left.\begin{matrix} R^* \\ d \\ \kappa \\ r_D \end{matrix}\right\}$	$\Longrightarrow$	r_B, r_L, r_K, D, R_F, M

Under the earlier federal funds operating target, we have the schema:

INSTRUMENTS		ENDOGENOUS VARIABLES
$\left.\begin{matrix} r_B \\ d \\ \kappa \\ r_D \end{matrix}\right\}$	$\Longrightarrow$	R^*, r_L, r_K, D, R_F, M

(Note that r_B and R^* change positions when the operating target changes.)

Open market operations, OMO

Let us assume, starting from an initial position depicted in Case 1 and by Tables 14-1a, 14-2a, 14-3a, 14-4a, and 14-5a, that the Central Bank buys \$50 billion worth of (interest-bearing) government securities. The effects of this action are represented by Case 4, that is, by Tables 14-1d, 14-2d, 14-3d, 14-4d, and 14-5d. Comparing 14-5d with 14-5a, we can see that the *size* of the net total government debt has remained the same, namely \$800 billion, while only its *composition* has changed: The demand debt *rose* by \$50 billion (from 165 + 85 = \$250 billion to 165 + 135 = \$300 billion). The essence of this OMO is that it has *decreased* the supply of government securities available to the banks and to the nonbank public from \$550 to \$500 billion. Similarly, the reserve base has been raised from 250 − 150 = \$100 billion to 300 − 150 = \$150 billion. Hence, at the original rates of return, call them r_B^0, r_L^0, r_K^0, there is *excess demand* for government securities and *excess supply* of reserves.

TABLE 14-1d CASE 4 (ALL NUMBERS ARE BILLIONS OF DOLLARS)

PUBLIC			
Assets		Liabilities	
Currency	150	Net Worth	950
Deposits	700	Loans	350
Government Securities	250		
Common Stock	200		
	1,300		1,300

TABLE 14-2d CASE 4 (Continued)

BANKS			
Assets		Liabilities	
Currency	15	Deposits	700
Reserves with Fed	135	Net Worth	50
Government Securities	250		
Loans	350		
	750		750

TABLE 14-3d CASE 4 (Continued)

FEDERAL RESERVE SYSTEM			
Assets		Liabilities	
Government Securities	300	Federal Reserve Notes	165
		Deposits: Member Bank Reserve Accounts	135
	300		300

TABLE 14-4d CASE 4 (Continued

U.S. TREASURY			
Assets		**Liabilities**	
Net Worth (Negative)	800	Government Securities	800
	800		800

TABLE 14-5d CASE 4 (Continued)

CONSOLIDATED BALANCE SHEET OF FED AND U.S. TREASURY			
Assets		**Liabilities**	
Loans to Member Banks	0	Notes (Currency)	165
Net Worth (Negative)	800	Deposits: Member Bank Reserve Accounts	135
		Government Securities (Net = 800 − 300)	500
	800		800

This creation of an excess supply of reserves means that the banks (and the public) need an incentive to increase their demand for reserves (and currency) in order to make the demand equal to the larger supply. If the return on (currency and) reserves, r_M, were variable, or market determined, an increase in its level would provide such an incentive. But since it is fixed (at zero) the incentive must come from elsewhere, in particular, from *a decrease in the rates of competing assets.* The excess demand for securities engineers such a decrease; this excess demand can be eliminated by a fall in the securities rate, r_B, from r_B^0 to r_B^1. But now, given the original loan rate, r_L^0, the difference $r_L^0 - r_B^1$ is greater than before. This difference is, for the banks, the opportunity cost of holding securities, an increase that induces the banks to offer more loans, thereby causing *excess demand* for the asset loans. But the public will be willing to borrow more (i.e., supply more assets called loans) if the loan rate *falls,* say, to r_L^1. Hence $r_L^1 < r_L^0$.

Because of the increase in loans, the disposable wealth of the nonbank public rises, causing an increase in the public's demand for equity capital. But the supply of this capital is fixed (at $200 billion in our example), which implies a tendency for *excess demand for* equity capital. This potential excess demand is eliminated, however, when the public, because of competition, is willing to accept a lower rate on capital, $r_K^1 < r_K^0$.

We have just established that *all three rates of return will fall* from their original levels, $r_B^1 < r_B^0$; $r_L^1 < r_L^0$; and $r_K^1 < r_K^0$; which induces the nonbank public to hold more of its disposable assets in the form of interest-free assets, namely, in demand deposits, and less in interest-bearing government securities. (Recall that we are assuming that the public's demand for currency is fixed, independent of rates of return; without our assumption this component of interest-free assets will also rise.)

The reduction in these three rates of return is also what induces the banks to hold more interest-free assets, more reserves—in addition to required reserves—or, in other words, to hold more free reserves. But in Case 1, our starting point, there were zero free reserves, which implies that we shall now have a positive amount of free reserves, namely, $150 - \kappa D = 150 - \frac{1}{5} \cdot 700 = 150 - 140 =$ \$10 billion. This is *a general result:* An open market purchase of government securities lowers all the rates of return and increases (algebraically) the amount of free reserves, which means that if free reserves already existed, they would be increased. If free reserves were negative, that is, if there were *net borrowed reserves* to start with, these net borrowed reserves would be reduced.

This increase in free reserves, which accompanies an open market increase in the reserve base, is responsible for the *variable* and *lower* money multiplier than the simple-minded, traditional view asserted. In our example the traditional view would predict that the increase of \$50 billion in the reserve base would increase money supply by \$250 billion rather than by the actual \$200 billion. In other words, the effective multiplier (the ratio of deposits to the reserve base) has fallen from 5 to 4, although it is still true that the reserve requirement is 0.20.

Changes in the discount rate, d

Again we shall consider Case 1 as the initial position of the economy, with market-determined rates of return, r_B^0, r_L^0, r_K^0, and an initial discount rate fixed at d^0. Let us now suppose that the Fed, while leaving both the size and the composition of the total government debt unchanged, raises the discount rate to d^1, that is, $d^1 > d^0$. As mentioned earlier, the discount rate is one of the (direct) decision variables of banks but not of the nonbank public; the banks can borrow from the Fed at the prevailing level of the discount rate, whereas the "discount window" is not open to the public.

Government securities and loans (with returns r_B and r_L, respectively) are assets competing with the asset "free reserves" for a place in the portfolios of banks, thereby establishing a negative relation between the demand for free reserves and r_B and r_L: The higher any one of these rates is, given the level of the other *and given the level of the discount rate,* the higher the opportunity cost of free reserves will be, and, therefore, the lower the demand for free reserves. For example, the difference, $r_L - d$, is the opportunity cost (of free reserves), since this is the (profit) rate that banks forgo when they keep free reserves instead of lending. Therefore an increase in r_L (with d fixed) increases the opportunity cost and reduces the demand for free reserves. A similar reasoning, applied to the difference $r_B - d$, establishes a negative relation between free reserves and r_B.

We now turn to the behavioral relation between the discount rate and the demand for free reserves. We see that an increase in d decreases the difference $r_L - d$, that is, it decreases the opportunity cost of keeping free reserves. And since it is less costly now to keep free reserves, their demand will increase. Of course, this increase is algebraic. If we start from a position with a negative amount of free reserves (i.e., with net *borrowed* reserves), the aforementioned increase is, in fact, a *reduction* in borrowed reserves, a result one would expect when the discount rate rises.[4]

We are now ready to examine the effects on free reserves and, therefore, on the supply of money caused by an increase in the discount rate from d^0 to d^1, starting from the position depicted by the tables of Case 1. The tables of Case 2 were constructed to reflect the consequences of an increase in d from an initial position depicted by Case 1. We should note from the outset that Case 2 represents an equilibrium position, with all markets cleared, as does Case 1. In Case 2 the total demand for currency is the same as it was in Case 1, namely, \$165 billion and equal to the supply. The aggregate demand for government securities is 400 + 150 = \$550 billion and equal to the net supply (i.e., the amount of government securities outside the governmental sectors), as in Case 1. (Note, however, that the distribution between banks and the nonbank public is different.) The demand for equity capital, \$200 billion, is the same as in Case 1 and equal to the (fixed) supply. And, finally, the demand for *deposits* is equal to the supply, but this amount, \$400 billion, is \$100 billion less than in Case 1. Since the size of the *reserve base* is the same as in Case 1, equal to \$100 billion, and since the amount of *required reserves* has fallen from $\frac{1}{5} \times 500 = \$100$ billion to $\frac{1}{5} \times 400 = \$80$ billion, the end result is the creation—that is, the *increase* from zero—of free reserves, now equal to \$20 billion. *This increase in free reserves is responsible for the dilution of the money-making power of the same size of reserve base.* Now, in Case 2 the total money supply is $C + D = 150 + 400 = \$550$ billion, as compared with 150 + 500 = \$650 billion in Case 1.

The explanation of these results is as follows: The sequence of events originates in the "market" for reserves. The increase in the discount rate, which reduces the opportunity cost of carrying free reserves, increases the demand for these reserves at the expense of *all other* assets, or, in other words, it decreases the demand for government securities and the demand for loans. Hence the increase in the discount rate causes excess demand for reserves, as well as excess supply of government securities and of the asset called loans. The excess demand for reserves could be eliminated by an appropriate fall in their rate of return, r_M, but since r_M is fixed and cannot fall, the elimination of this excess demand can be accomplished by an *increase* in the rates of return of the competing assets. The next question, then, arises, Are there forces that accomplish this increase in returns? The answer is yes; the excess supply of government securities will increase the bill rate, r_B. In fact, the bill rate must rise sufficiently to induce the public to increase its holdings of these securities—from \$350 billion to \$400 billion. Similarly, the excess supply of the asset loans necessitates an increase in the loan rate, r_L, which brings down the supply of loans (by the public) and increases their demand (by the banks). This increase in both the bill and the loan rates, r_B and r_L, respectively, induces the public to switch from deposits (\$400 billion as compared with \$500 billion) that do not yield any return

[4] The positive relation between the banking sector's demand for free reserves and the discount rate can be seen in another way: To the extent that they are net borrowers from the Fed, the banks can earn the discount rate by simply repaying loans to the Fed, and as this rate of return rises they will want to repay more loans. But this reduction in net borrowing is tantamount to an increase in free reserves.

to government securities ($400 billion as compared with $350 billion) and to more loans (algebraically, from −$250 billion to −$200 billion). Note that the *disposable* assets of the nonbank public fall from $1,200 billion to $1,150 billion, which tends to *decrease* the public's demand for capital. But the potential excess supply of capital is eliminated only if the rate of return on capital, r_K, increases.

Similarly, the reduction in deposits (consistent with the decrease of required reserves, which is caused by the increase of free reserves) reduces the banking sector's disposable assets, that is, the sum (net worth *plus* deposits *minus* required reserves), $50 + 400 - \frac{1}{5} \times 400 = \$370$ billion, which is allocated to holdings of (a) free reserves ($20 billion), (b) government securities ($150 billion), and (c) loans ($200 billion).

In summary, the increase (by the Fed) of the discount rate, *d*, decreases the supply of money because it increases the amount of free reserves and because it increases all the endogenously determined rates of return, r_B, r_L, and r_K. Moreover, these increases encourage the public to reduce its deposits by switching to all other assets.

Case 3—Tables 14-1c, 14-2c, and 14-3c—has been constructed to depict the consequences of a *reduction* in the discount rate, *d*, from the initial position, Case 1. The reduction in *d* increases the opportunity cost, $r_L - d$, or $r_B - d$, of carrying free reserves, thereby lowering these holdings. Since we started, in Case 1, from a position of zero free reserves, we must end up with *negative* free reserves, that is, with *borrowed* reserves—in fact, with $10 billion. Note that the new equilibrium position produces a larger size of required reserves because of the larger size of deposits, $\frac{1}{5} \times 550 = \$110$ billion, even though the reserve base is the same: Reserve base = Total reserves *minus* Borrowed reserves = 110 − 10 = $100 billion. What is not shown explicitly in Tables 14-1c, 14-2c, and 14-3c is the effect on the rates of return, r_B, r_L, and r_K. Reversing the reasoning of the previous exercise, that is, Case 2, we can show that all these rates fall, encouraging the public to reduce, or attempt to reduce, the holdings of these assets and to substitute interest-free deposits in their place.

Changes in the reserve requirement, κ

An increase in the reserve requirement, κ, say from $\frac{1}{5}$ to $\frac{1}{4}$, initially creates an excess demand for reserves (i.e., demand greater than the reserve base). This excess could be eliminated by a sufficient *reduction* in the rate of return on currency and reserves, r_M. But since this rate is fixed, an *increase* in the rates of return of the competing assets—government securities, loans, and capital—can accomplish the same purpose, since it would increase the opportunity cost of holding reserves.

Briefly, this increase in the rates of return is accomplished as follows. The increase in the reserve requirement, from κ_0 to κ_1, for the initial amount of deposits decreases the disposable wealth of banks, net worth *minus* $\kappa_1 \cdot D$, thereby reducing the banks' demand for every asset that can enter their portfolios. This causes *excess supply* for government securities and for loans which must be eliminated by a rise in the nonbank public's demand, which, in turn, can happen only if the rates of return (on these assets) rise. The increase in all these rates, including the return on capital, is necessary to induce the public to switch from the interest-free deposits to every remaining asset. In addition to the higher rates, r_B, r_L, and r_K, the final position, as compared with Case 1, exhibits a *lower money supply;* even though the amount of required reserves increases because of the decrease (from zero) in free reserves, caused by the increase in their opportunity cost, this is overwhelmed by the increase needed by the change in the reserve requirement. All this is captured by Case 5 in Tables 14-1e through 14-5e, which show the effects of increasing the reserve requirement from ⅕, as in Case 1, to ¼.

TABLE 14-1e CASE 5 (ALL NUMBERS ARE BILLIONS OF DOLLARS)

PUBLIC			
Assets		Liabilities	
Currency	150	Net Worth	950
Deposits	420	Loans	220
Government Securities	400		
Common Stock	200		
	1,170		1,170

TABLE 14-2e CASE 5 (Continued)

BANKS			
Assets		Liabilities	
Currency	15	Deposits	420
Reserves with Fed	90	Net Worth	50
Government Securities	150	Loans from Fed	5
Loans	220		
	475		475

TABLE 14-3e CASE 5 (Continued)

FEDERAL RESERVE SYSTEM			
Assets		Liabilities	
Government Securities	250	Federal Reserve Notes	165
Loans to Member Banks	10	Deposits: Member Bank Reserve Accounts	95
	260		260

TABLE 14-4e CASE 5 (Continued)

U.S. TREASURY			
Assets		Liabilities	
Net Worth (Negative)	800	Government Securities	800
	800		800

TABLE 14-5e CASE 5 (Continued)

CONSOLIDATED BALANCE SHEET OF FED AND U.S. TREASURY			
Assets		Liabilities	
Loans to Member Banks	5	Notes (Currency)	165
Net Worth (Negative)	800	Deposits: Member Bank Reserve Accounts	90
		Government Securities	550
	805		805

II. THE MONEY SUPPLY IN A SIMPLE MODEL

In this section we examine a simpler model for generating the supply of money, by restricting both the number of markets and the number of interest rates. First we concentrate exclusively on only one market, that for currency and reserves, and on its equation, (9). We then simplify our model by concentrating on one interest rate, or rate of return, i, with the assumption, either implicit or explicit, that all assets, except currency and reserves, are perfect substitutes. Therefore i is the interest paid on Treasury securities and on private loans, and the rate of return on capital. The model we are presenting here captures the spirit of the "new view" and considers the "old view" as a special case, and yet it has been adopted by such monetarists as Brunner, Meltzer, and Rasche, and such nonmonetarists as Teigen; Modigliani, and Cooper; and De Leeuw and Gramlich.[5]

[5] K. Brunner and A. H. Meltzer, "A Monetarist Framework for Aggregative Analysis," *Kredit and Kapital,* 1972; K. Brunner and A. H. Meltzer, "Money, Debt, and Economic Activity," *Journal of Political Economy,* September/October 1972, pp. 951–77; R. Teigen, "Demand and Supply Functions for Money in the United States: Some Structural Estimates," *Econometrica,* October 1964, pp. 476–509; Franco Modigliani, Robert H. Rasche, and J. Philip Cooper, "Central Bank Policy, Money Supply and the Short-Term Rate of Interest," *Journal of Money, Credit and Banking,* May 1970, pp. 166–218; and F. De Leeuw and E. Gramlich, "The Channels of Monetary Policy: A Further Report on Federal Reserve MIT Model," *Journal of Finance,* May 1969, pp. 265–90.

Let us first consider the market for currency and reserves, and its equation (9):

$$\kappa D + R_F = R^* \tag{9}$$

or

$$D = \frac{1}{\kappa}(R^* - R_F) \tag{10}$$

As we saw earlier, R^*, the reserve base, is under the absolute control of the Fed. However, free reserves, R_F, are an endogenous variable, the result of rational decisions by commercial banks and dependent on the interest rate vector. Here, of course, we have only one market-determined interest rate, namely, i, in addition to the discount rate, d, which is fixed by the Fed.

With an explanation similar to our earlier one, we can see that, in general, free reserves, whether positive or negative, depend negatively on the interest rate, i, and positively on the discount rate, d; this is denoted by $R_F(i,d)$ and shown in Figure 14-1. The demand for free reserves is negatively related to the interest rate, since, as we observed earlier, for a given discount rate, say at the level d_0, an increase in the interest rate increases the opportunity cost, $i - d$, of barren free reserves. This, in turn, prompts banks to reduce their free reserves and to increase their holding of other assets, such as Treasury Bills and IOUs. In fact, the decrease in free reserves may be such that they now hold negative free reserves (i.e., net borrowed reserves), as we see in Figure 14-1, where the interest rate is higher than i_* while the discount rate remains fixed at d_0.

A special, extreme, case is the one that lies behind the explanation of the "old," or "traditional," view, that is, when the demand for free reserves is independent of the interest rate, with the usual assumption that the fixed free reserves are zero.

FIGURE 14-1

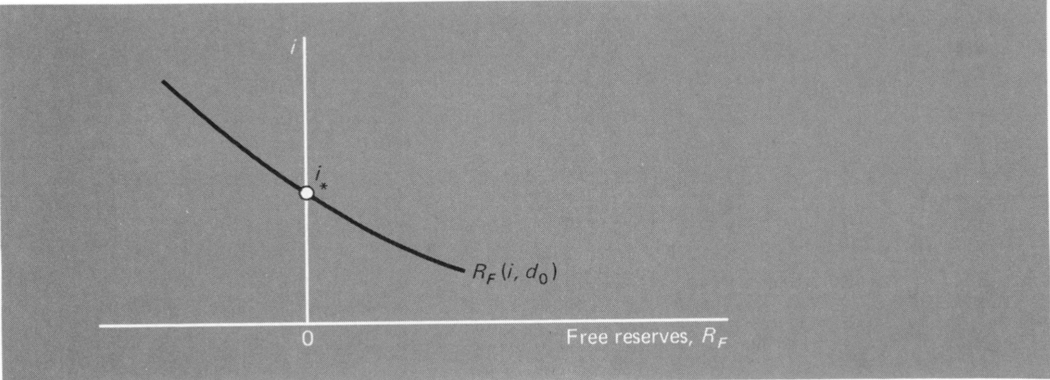

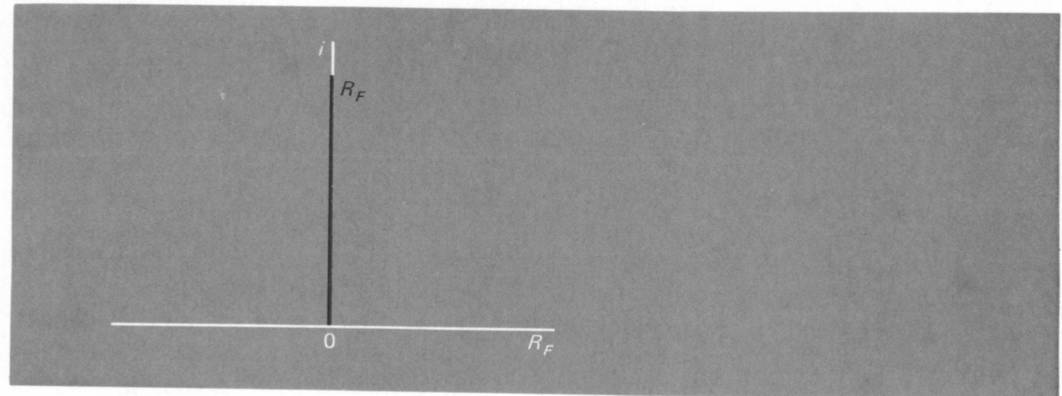

FIGURE 14-2

However, the old view of money can be valid whether free reserves are zero, positive, or negative, as long as they are independent of the interest rate, as in Figure 14-2.

We shall examine the consequences of both the old and new views for the most frequently used and most important policy instrument, the open market operations, or OMO. In so doing, we shall emphasize the actual process by which the money supply increases. And we shall again simplify by assuming that one of the two components of the money supply, namely, currency, is fixed so that an increase in the money supply is identical with an increase in deposits, D (i.e., so that $\Delta M = \Delta D$). Therefore, to explore the problem of increasing the money supply, we must examine the effect on deposits of a change in the Fed's policy.

1. THE OLD VIEW

To examine the effects of expansionary OMO when the demand for free reserves is a constant, say zero, let us consider the following hypothetical example:[6] The Fed buys \$1,000 million worth of government securities from the nonbank public (i.e., $\Delta R^* =$ \$1,000 million). If we assume that the (given) reserve requirement, κ, is 0.20, it follows that the money (or deposit) multiplier is equal to 5 (i.e., $1/\kappa = 5$), and that the increase in deposits should be equal to \$5,000 million:

$$\begin{aligned} \Delta M = \Delta D &= \frac{1}{\kappa} \cdot \Delta R^* \\ &= 5 \cdot 1{,}000 \\ &= \$5{,}000 \text{ million} \end{aligned}$$

We can see that the arithmetic is simple; it says that deposits, and hence money, will increase by \$5,000 million. But how is this initial purchase by the Fed of \$1,000 million worth of securities transformed into \$5,000 million worth of deposits? Let us examine this process.

[6] For a simple explanation of the following process of monetary expansion, see Dorothy M. Nichols, *Modern Money Mechanics* (Federal Reserve Bank of Chicago, June 1975).

In exchange for the securities purchased, the Fed signs checks of $1,000 million in total to the nonbank public. Since we assume that the public's demand for currency is constant, the entire $1,000 million will be deposited in (commercial) banks and end up as a change in bank reserves (with the Fed). In other words, the nonbank public, in place of its government securities, now acquires an alternative asset, namely (demand) deposits of $1,000 million, which are the liability of banks and are matched by their asset, reserves at the Fed. All of this is shown as the initial changes that take place in the balance sheets of the Fed and of the consolidated banking sector, as indicated in Tables 14-6 and 14-7.

TABLE 14-6 (MILLIONS OF DOLLARS)

FEDERAL RESERVE SYSTEM			
Assets		Liabilities	
Government Securities	+1,000	Reserve Accounts of Member Banks	+1,000

TABLE 14-7 (MILLIONS OF DOLLARS)

ALL COMMERCIAL BANKS			
Assets		Liabilities	
Reserves with Fed	+1,000	Deposits: Member Bank Reserve Accounts	+1,000

Now, since the public's deposits with commercial banks have increased by $1,000 million, required reserves have increased by $200 million, or $R_R = \kappa \cdot \Delta R_*$, and, therefore, free reserves have increased by $800 million, or $\Delta R_F = (1 - \kappa)\Delta R_*$. But since we assume that in equilibrium free reserves are equal to zero, this clearly represents a disequilibrium position for banks. Equilibrium will be reached only when every dollar change in the reserve base is converted into a dollar change in required reserves, so that free reserves are again zero. This can be accomplished when the public is persuaded to hold more deposits and when the commercial banks, using a portion of these deposits, acquire additional earning assets, such as IOUs and T-bills. The final, or net, result, as we stated earlier, is that the banks' assets and liabilities both increase by a total of $5,000 million, as shown in Table 14-8.

Now, free reserves are again zero; the entire change in the reserve base has been transformed into required reserves, that is, those required to support the enlarged volume of deposits (i.e., 1,000 = 0.20 × 5,000). Of course, this result, that the change

TABLE 14-8 (MILLIONS OF DOLLARS)

CONSOLIDATED BALANCE SHEET OF ALL BANKS			
Assets		Liabilities	
Reserves		Deposits:	+5,000
with Fed	+1,000	Member Bank	
Loans and T-bills	+4,000	Reserve Accounts	
	5,000		5,000

in deposits is a fixed multiple of the change in the reserve base alone, rests squarely on the stipulation that the demand for free reserves is fixed (at zero) and is, therefore, independent of the interest rate. We shall see that this stipulation is untenable in the real world. In addition, we must emphasize that the entire banking system is able to "create" money, in fact, \$4,000 million, in addition to the \$1,000 million created by the Fed. And we shall see below how we can reconcile this ability to "create money" with the claim by bankers that they do not create money, but that they, instead, merely invest (a portion of) what is deposited with them.

So far we have examined the net effect of expansionary OMO on *all* banks taken together. Now we can disaggregate this process and explain it as a step-by-step expansion by a myriad of independent banks, *all of which want to hold zero free reserves in equilibrium.* The banks in which the public deposits the checks received from the Fed are called Stage 1 banks. And since their demand deposits have increased by \$1,000 million, required reserves have increased by \$200 million, leaving \$800 million as free reserves, which these Stage 1 banks use to acquire additional loans and T-bills from the nonbank public and, therefore, to create an equal amount, of \$800 million, in demand deposits.

As the individuals who have borrowed from Stage 1 banks run down their demand deposits and spend the proceeds, the funds are transferred to Stage 2 banks, which now experience an increase of \$800 million in their deposits. (Note that as funds are being transferred among banks, so is "ownership" of the reserve accounts with the Fed.) Of these \$800 million worth of reserves, 0.20(800) = \$160 million are required and 0.80(800) = \$640 million are free reserves. Stage 2 banks will now alter their portfolios by making additional loans and by purchasing additional T-bills, in the amount of \$640 million, and thereby create an equivalent amount of deposits. As the borrowers from Stage 2 banks run down their deposit accounts and spend their proceeds, the funds are transferred to Stage 3 banks, and so forth. The process continues until all free reserves are squeezed out of the system, as shown by

$$\Delta D = (1 + 0.8 + 0.8^2 + 0.8^3 + \ldots)1{,}000$$
$$= \frac{1}{1 - 0.8}\,1{,}000 = \frac{1}{0.2}\,1{,}000 = 5{,}000$$

and, in general,

$$\Delta D = \frac{1}{\kappa} \cdot \Delta R^* \quad \text{when} \quad R_F \equiv 0$$

Note that in the above process all that any *single* bank does is lend out a portion of the change in its reserves. By doing this, it acquires additional assets and creates an equivalent amount of liabilities against itself. While this bank does not create the liability without first having the asset, the system, as a whole, does nevertheless effect a multiple expansion of total liabilities, that is, of demand deposits!

2. THE NEW VIEW

Until now we have ignored the interest rate effect on the demand for free reserves and, therefore, on deposit creation caused by expansionary OMO. This deliberate neglect was justified by our behavioral assumptions, that (a) the public's demand for currency is a constant, and that (b) the banks' demand for free reserves is a constant, namely, zero. Next, let us relax assumption (b) and assume that the banks' demand for free reserves is, as explained earlier, inversely related to the interest rate.

Now, as before, when the Fed engages in expansionary OMO, the reserve base, R^*, increases by an amount equal in value to the Fed's purchases of government securities. However, the mere act of purchasing these securities raises their prices, thereby lowering the interest rate. Moreover, the increase in loans by the banks further lowers the interest rate. We should emphasize that this reduction in the interest rate is necessary to persuade the nonbank public to substitute in its portfolio barren demand deposits for interest-bearing securities. Now, of course, the fall in the interest rate(s) will have profound effects on the magnitude of the increase in deposits. In particular, the lower interest rate will increase the amount of free reserves in the banks, thereby lowering the amount of required reserves. Therefore a change in the reserve base is not converted, dollar-for-dollar, into a change in required reserves; rather, part of the dollar goes into free reserves because of the decrease in the interest rate. This leakage in the "effective reserve base," as the required reserves can be called, has the ultimate effect of dampening the increase in the volume of deposits to an amount less than $(1/\kappa) \cdot \Delta R^* =$ \$5,000 million. For example, the fall in the interest rate may induce an increase of \$200 million in free reserves, leaving an increase of only \$800 million in required reserves. In such a case the increase in deposits will be only \$4,000 million and not \$5,000 million, so that, in general, we have

$$\Delta D = \frac{1}{\kappa}(\Delta R^* - \Delta R_F) < \frac{1}{\kappa} \cdot \Delta R^*$$

At this point we should emphasize that our earlier division of banks into Stage 1 banks, Stage 2 banks, and so forth, is applicable to this general case and, therefore, to the claim that an individual bank merely lends out what is deposited with it. However, the banking system, as a whole, creates fewer deposits than the old view would lead us to believe. The more interest-elastic the demand for free reserves is, the smaller the change in the volume of deposits, for any given change in the reserve base, will be.

In summary, the change in the money supply brought about by OMO has an exogenous component, $(1/\kappa) \cdot \Delta R^*$, and an endogenous component, $(1/\kappa)(-\Delta R_F)$, which pull in opposite directions. Therefore the case where $\Delta F_R = 0$ when $\Delta R^* > 0$ is only one possibility among many; at the other end of the spectrum is the case where $\Delta R_F = \Delta R^*$. However, this could happen only in an extreme situation where economic conditions were so depressed and the interest rate were so low that banks would choose, because of a lack of profitable investment opportunities, to hold the entire amount of any change in the reserve base in the form of free reserves. This situation would therefore constitute a form of liquidity trap, since the monetary authority would be unable to increase the money supply.

III. THE CONDUCT OF MONETARY POLICY

Whether one uses the complicated (and more realistic) model of Section I or the simplified model of Section II, an important implication of the new view of money is that the money multiplier is variable: As the Central Bank increases reserves, the multiplier falls. This is a reflection of the fact that the money supply is partly endogenous. It is still true, of course, that, barring an extreme case, namely, when $\Delta R^* = \Delta R_F$ (i.e., when the entire increase in unborrowed reserves is held by the banks as free reserves), exogenous, deliberate increases in the reserve base will increase the supply of money. For greater precision we must recognize that an increase in free reserves is the natural consequence of an increase in the reserve base.

At the Fed, of course, those responsible for the manipulation of the money supply will say that this is easier said than done. With this in mind, let us now consider the manner in which the Fed manipulates the money supply. Until early in 1970 the Fed increased or decreased the money supply according to the level of interest rates. If the interest rates were above the Fed's target, the money supply was increased; if the interest rates were below the target, the money supply was decreased. This was a relatively easy task, since interest rates can be directly manipulated. In 1970, mostly because of empirical results indicating that the demand for money is a stable function of a few variables, and because of the increased influence of the monetarists, it was decided that the Fed should pay more attention to the monetary aggregates, both M-1 and M-2. In particular, the Fed decided to adopt an "intermediate target strategy" where the objective was to maintain a given (short-run) path for these monetary aggregates. Of course, this intermediate targeting of monetary aggregates did not require the Fed to adopt the impossible task of always increasing, for example, the money supply by the *exact* percentage required in each period. It was only required to operate in a "band" of percentages, say between a 5 and a 8 percent increase in M-1 for the fourth quarter of 1973.

In its efforts to regulate the monetary aggregates, the Fed discovered a "direct target," namely, the "Federal Funds" rate, which is the interest rate at which commercial banks borrow reserves, overnight, from each other. These are reserves that are "free," not needed by some banks, and, therefore, able to be loaned to those banks short of reserves. The emergence of this market (since the 1950s) made it easier for the Fed to manipulate the money supply. It established "bands" for the Federal Funds rate and it intervened with open market operations whenever this rate was outside these bands. The question arises, Why did the Fed not increase or decrease *M*-1 directly? We see that the Fed did not directly alter *M*-1 because it is partly endogenous and, therefore, not a direct policy parameter; it is the end result of a change of some other parameter.

As we implied at the end of Chapter 13, in the mid-1970s the Fed decided not to rely exclusively on monetary aggregates, especially because of the instability, or the shifting, of the demand-for-money function. Other interest rates, in addition to the Federal Funds rate, were monitored as barometers of the economy's health. Nevertheless, empirical studies have proved definitely that during the 1970s, as opposed to the 1960s, the Fed did indeed follow the intermediate target strategy of manipulating the monetary aggregates. The Fed, however, found it difficult to follow precisely the predetermined path of the monetary aggregates, especially that of *M*-1, but also that of *M*-2. For this reason, in late 1979 the Fed decided to manipulate a family of reserve aggregates such as the reserve base, R^*, and, to a lesser degree, the monetary base, B^*, directly, in the hope that it would have better control over *M*-1 and *M*-2.

But we know from the preceding analysis that although the nonborrowed reserve base is an exogenous magnitude, a true policy parameter, the money supply is not. This is also true, in fact more so, of the monetary base. What matters for the money supply is the *effective reserve base,* or the *effective monetary base,* which are endogenous, since one of their components, namely, free reserves, is endogenous, the result of rational decision making by the banks. In addition, changes in economic activity or changes in "tastes" for assets can change the interest rate(s) and, therefore, the effective reserve base and the money supply. In other words, moving from a target based on the Federal Funds rate to a target based on the reserve (or monetary) base is not a guarantee that the targets of rates of growth in the money supply, of *M*-1 or *M*-2, *M*-1*A,* or *M*-1*B,* will be achieved any easier.

The above observations are true whether one uses the complicated model of Section I or the simple model of Section II. Why, then, not rely exclusively on the simpler model? Of course, the simpler model has its advantages, and this is undoubtedly the reason why so many prominent monetary economists and macroeconomists use it. Nevertheless, the reliance on only one asset, alternative to money, and hence on only one interest rate, deprives us of several important complications. For example, the financial innovations of the 1970s made other assets more desirable than demand deposits, thereby blurring the distinction between *M*-1 and *M*-2, among other things, which contributed to the observed, continuous, overprediction of *M*-1 in the late 1970s. Because of the recognition that there are several assets that are alternatives to money—i.e., because of the implicit acceptance of the model of Section I—the Fed moved to redefine the measures of money, as indicated at the beginning of this chapter. Another advantage of that model is that it helps us determine an entire array of interest rates and not merely "the" interest rate.

As has been mentioned several times already, on October 6, 1979, the Federal Reserve changed its operating procedure from one of targeting a federal funds interest rate to one of a nonborrowed reserves operating target. We have already seen that this switch in procedures reversed the role played by the federal funds rate and nonborrowed reserves. The new procedure reestablished nonborrowed reserves as an instrument of control while reassigning to the federal funds rate the role of a market-clearing, endogenous variable. It is instructive to compare the effects of this change in operating procedures on monetary control; in particular, how each instrument affects interest rates and monetary aggregates.

We have already examined the new procedure in great detail in Section I. In comparing that procedure with the old, federal funds operating regime, we shall avoid relying on the concept of free reserves. We can, instead, examine separately the components of free reserves, that is, excess reserves and borrowed reserves. We shall assume, for simplicity, that the amount of excess reserves is constant (as it has been in recent years), which implies that a change in free reserves is equal to minus the change in borrowed reserves. In other words, an increase in free reserves is (primarily) a reflection of a reduction in borrowed reserves. In Table 14-9, which summarizes the results that we have derived so far, we decompose the effects on free reserves, and concentrate instead on borrowed reserves (without even recording the effects on excess reserves).[7]

This table (as well as Table 14-10) should be read as follows: for each *row* the instrument on the lefthand side is increased. The signs refer to the change, + for increase, − for decrease in the endogenous variable depicted by the column. For example, in Table 14-9 the first row indicates that an increase in unborrowed reserves, R^*, reduces the bill or federal funds rate, r_B; decreases the loan rate, r_L; reduces the capital rate, r_K; reduces borrowed reserves, R_B; increases total reserves, *TR;* increases demand deposits, *D;* and increases the money supply, *M.*

In the remainder of this section we merely summarize (Table 14-10) the respective results that can be derived if the Fed follows a federal funds (or bill-rate) operating target and compares them to those of the new regime. Comparing the first rows in each table, we see that the two operating targets amount, analytically, to the same thing—they yield the same qualitative results. In particular, whichever operating target is followed, an increase (decrease) in nonborrowed reserves is always associated with a fall (rise) in all three rates of return, with a fall (rise) in borrowed reserves, and with a rise (fall) in total reserves, demand deposits and the money supply.

Closer examination reveals that there are important differences between the two regimes when the effects on the same variables of other instruments of monetary policy, such as the discount rate and reserve requirement ratios are compared. In particular, under a reserves operating target, an increase in the discount rate, *while the other instruments of monetary policy are fixed,* is accompanied by the same (fixed) amount of nonborrowed reserves. Under the federal funds regime, the same monetary policy (i.e., the same increase in the discount rate) *requires* an *increase* in nonborrowed

[7] For a detailed, nonmathematical, treatment of these issues, see M. G. Hadjimichalakis, "Precision of Monetary Control and Volatility of Rates: A Comparative Analysis of the Reserves and the Federal Funds Operating Targets." Federal Reserve Special Studies Paper No. 150, January 1981.

reserves, since we need, for a pure discount rate policy, to keep the level of all instruments fixed. With a federal funds operating target, this means that the level of the federal funds rate must be kept fixed. (For thoroughness, we should add that under both operating targets, the remaining endogenous variables move in the same direction: the loan rate and the capital rate both rise, while borrowed reserves, total reserves, demand deposits, and the money supply all fall.) Similarly, a pure reserve-requirement-ratio increase requires—and is accompanied by—an increase in nonborrowed reserves under a federal funds target, while it leaves the amount of nonborrowed reserves unchanged under a reserves operating target. (Again, we should add that, with the exception of the federal funds rate, the increase in reserve requirement ratios changes all the other variables in the same direction: It increases the loans and capital rates, it increases both borrowed and total reserves, while it lowers demand deposits and the money supply.)

We see that under a federal funds operating target the Fed loses some control of the discount rate and the reserve requirement ratio as instruments of monetary policy. Or what amounts to the same thing, nonborrowed and other measures of reserves are not reliable indicators of an expansionary or a contractionary policy. This is one reason why some economists have been arguing for years for the adoption of a (nonborrowed) reserves operating target. Of course, the Fed adopted the new operating procedure because it believed that this procedure is better than the older one, even (or especially), in the case of the open market operations. One such reason was the new operating procedure's ability to provide more precise monetary control. We can illustrate the use of the new procedure, in terms of our framework, as follows. The Federal Reserve decides on a target for the money supply. But the money supply is related, through one or more multipliers, to reserves. Using the old technique the Federal Reserve attempted to control reserves by varying the bill or the federal funds rate. But the relation between reserves and this rate is not known precisely and is subject to some uncertainty (or shocks), as is the relation between reserves and the money supply. Thus, under the old operating target there were at least two links subject to uncertainty and, of course, to error. The new technique, however, should eliminate one of them, and thus, reduce the sources of error. If we directly attempt to control reserves, we have only the uncontrolled elements of the multiplier relation (from reserves to money) with which to contend.

The nonborrowed reserves operating procedure was introduced to achieve better precision of monetary control, that is, attainment of targeted monetary aggregates. However, during the first year of its implementation there were violent gyrations in the monetary aggregates as well as in interest rates. As an example, Chart 1 shows the actual path that M-1B followed during the first year of the new procedure, and, for comparison, its targeted growth range of 4 to 6 percent. The reasons for these violent gyrations were the subject of extensive research both within and outside the Federal Reserve System. Surely the unusual conditions prevailing in 1980, especially the imposition of credit controls, were partly responsible. But also the change in the procedure itself played a crucial role. The structure of the financial system changed, rendering the data generated by the old regime almost useless as a guide. To the extent that one uses these data to estimate multipliers and other relations, one is bound to miss the target. Moreover, with the new regime the role of borrowed

TABLE 14-9 NONBORROWED RESERVES OPERATING TARGET

		EFFECT ON ENDOGENOUS VARIABLE						
		Federal Funds, or Bill Rate, r_B	Loan Rate, r_L	Equity Capital Rate, r_K	Borrowed Reserves, R_B	Total Reserves, TR	Demand Deposits, D	Money Supply, M
INCREASE IN INSTRUMENT	Nonborrowed Reserves, R^*	−	−	−	−	+	+	+
	Discount Rate, d	+	+	+	−	−	−	−
	Reserve Requirement Ratio, κ	+	+	+	+	+	−	−

NOTE: The table should be read as follows: For each row, the left-hand side instrument is increased. The signs refer to the change, + for increase and − for decrease, in the endogenous variable depicted by the column. For example, the first row states that an increase in nonborrowed reserves reduces the federal funds rate, reduces the loan rate, reduces the equity capital rate, and reduces the amount of borrowed reserves, but it increases total reserves, demand deposits, and the money supply.

(and hence of free) reserves was magnified since borrowed reserves depend on differences between interest rates and the discount rate. But the essence of the new (reserves) regime is to permit substantial variation in interest rates.[8] With the knowledge acquired as a result of the passage of time and of intensive research, the Federal Reserve has been able to reduce the range of volatility in the monetary aggregates.

IV. EMPIRICAL EVIDENCE

We should make a final point about the implications of the interest sensitivity of the supply of money. We have seen repeatedly in this book, especially in Chapters 4, 6, 7, 8, and 9, that if neither the demand for nor the supply of money depends on the interest rate, then only money matters and fiscal policy is irrelevant. We have seen, *a priori,* that the supply of money does indeed depend positively on the interest rate(s). It follows, therefore, that even if the demand for money were interest-

CHART 14-1

GROWTH RANGES AND ACTUAL MONETARY GROWTH

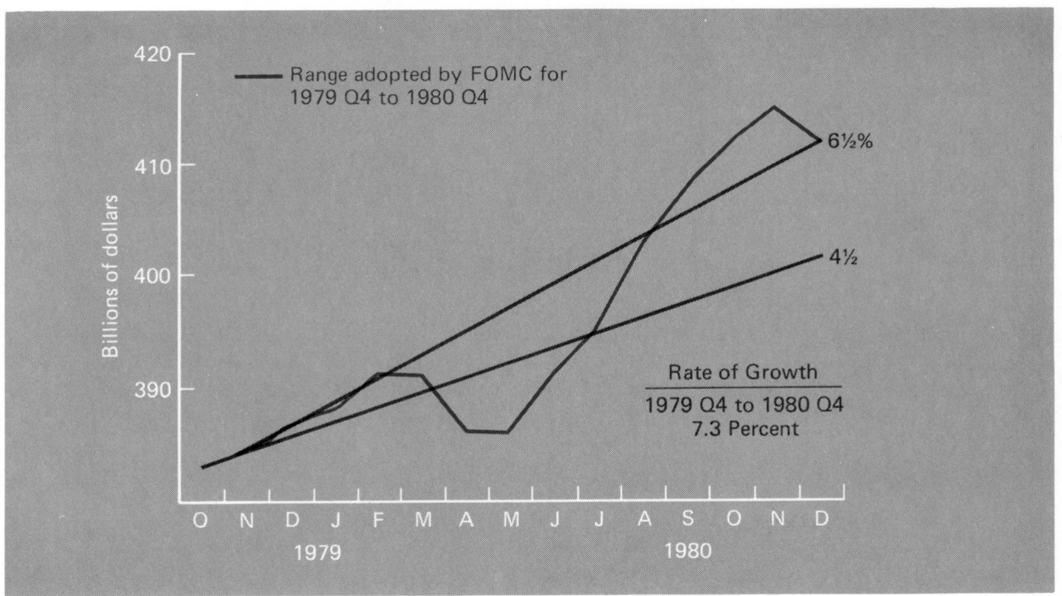

SOURCE: *New Monetary Control Procedures,* Federal Reserve Staff Study, Board of Governors, Washington, D.C., February 1981.

---

[8] See Federal Reserve Staff Study, *New Monetary Control Procedures,* Volumes I and II, Washington D.C. Board of Governors, February 1981, M. G. Hadjimichalakis, "Reserves *vs* Federal Funds Operating Monetary Procedures: A General Equilibrium Analysis," *Economics Letters,* Vol. 6, 1981 and M. G. Hadjimichalakis, "Monetary Control: The Role of the Discount Rate and other Supplemental Monetary Instruments," *Economics Letters,* Vol. 6, 1981.

TABLE 14-10 FEDERAL FUNDS OPERATING TARGET

		EFFECT ON ENDOGENOUS VARIABLE						
		Nonborrowed Reserves, R^*	Loan Rate, r_L	Equity Capital Rate, r_K	Borrowed Reserves, R_B	Total Reserves, TR	Demand Deposits, D	Money Supply, M
INCREASE IN INSTRUMENT	Federal Funds or Bill Rate, r_B	−	+	+	+	−	−	−
	Discount Rate, d	+	+	+	−	−	−	−
	Reserve Requirement Ratio, κ	+	+	+	+	+	−	−

NOTE: The table should be read as follows: For each row, the left-hand side instrument is increased. The signs refer to the change, + for increase and − for decrease, in the endogenous variable depicted by the column. For example, the first row states that an increase in the federal funds rate will reduce the amount of nonborrowed reserves, that it will increase the loan rate, the capital rate, and borrowed reserves, and that it will reduce total reserves, demand deposits, and the money supply.

inelastic, fiscal policy would still matter. In this, the final section of this chapter we examine the empirical research on this issue.

The central question in empirical studies on the supply of money is the impact of moves in the various interest rates on the behavioral parameters that taken together make up the "money multiplier." A secondary question deals with the time pattern of response of the multiplier to interest rate changes. The results of several studies of these issues can be summarized, as in tables such as 14-11.

TABLE 14-11

INTEREST ELASTICITY ESTIMATES FOR FUNCTIONS AFFECTING THE SUPPLY OF MONEY

Reference	Impact Elasticity	Total Elasticity
Teigen (1964)		
Unborrowed Reserves		
r_k	0.20	0.20
d	−0.17	−0.17
De Leeuw (1965)		
Currency		
r_k	−0.03	−0.36
Rate on time deposits	−0.01	−0.14
Time Deposits		
r_b	−0.04	−0.37
Rate on time deposits	0.07	0.68
Bank Borrowings		
r_b	−0.13	0.50
d	−0.19	−0.70
Goldfeld (1966)		
Currency		
r_b	−0.01	−0.07
Rate on time deposits	−0.02	−0.14
Time Deposits		
r_b	−0.13	−1.62
Rate on time deposits	0.03	0.37
Bank Borrowings		
d	−0.98	−2.38
r_b	0.88	2.13
Excess Reserves		
r_b	−0.38	−0.35
FRB–MIT–PENN		
Free Reserves		
r_b	−3.95	−8.47
d	3.48	7.46

SOURCES: Ronald Teigen, "Demand and Supply Functions for Money in the United States: Some Structural Estimates," *Econometrica,* 32 (October 1964), 476–509; Frank De Leeuw, "A Model of Financial Behavior," in *The Brookings Quarterly Econometric Model of the United States,* ed. James Duesenberry, Gary Fromm, Lawrence Klein, and Edwin Kuh (Chicago: Rand McNally, 1965), Chap. 13; and Stephen Goldfeld, *Commercial Bank Behavior and Economic Activity* (Amsterdam: North-Holland Press, 1966).

In general, the interest elasticity of the supply of money appears to be relatively low, although estimates are not as consistent across studies as are the estimates for money demand.

The negative relation between the rate of interest and free reserves, which forms the foundation of open market operations, is supported by the empirical evidence. As we see in Chart 14-2, the relation between reserves and deposits varies over time,

CHART 14-2

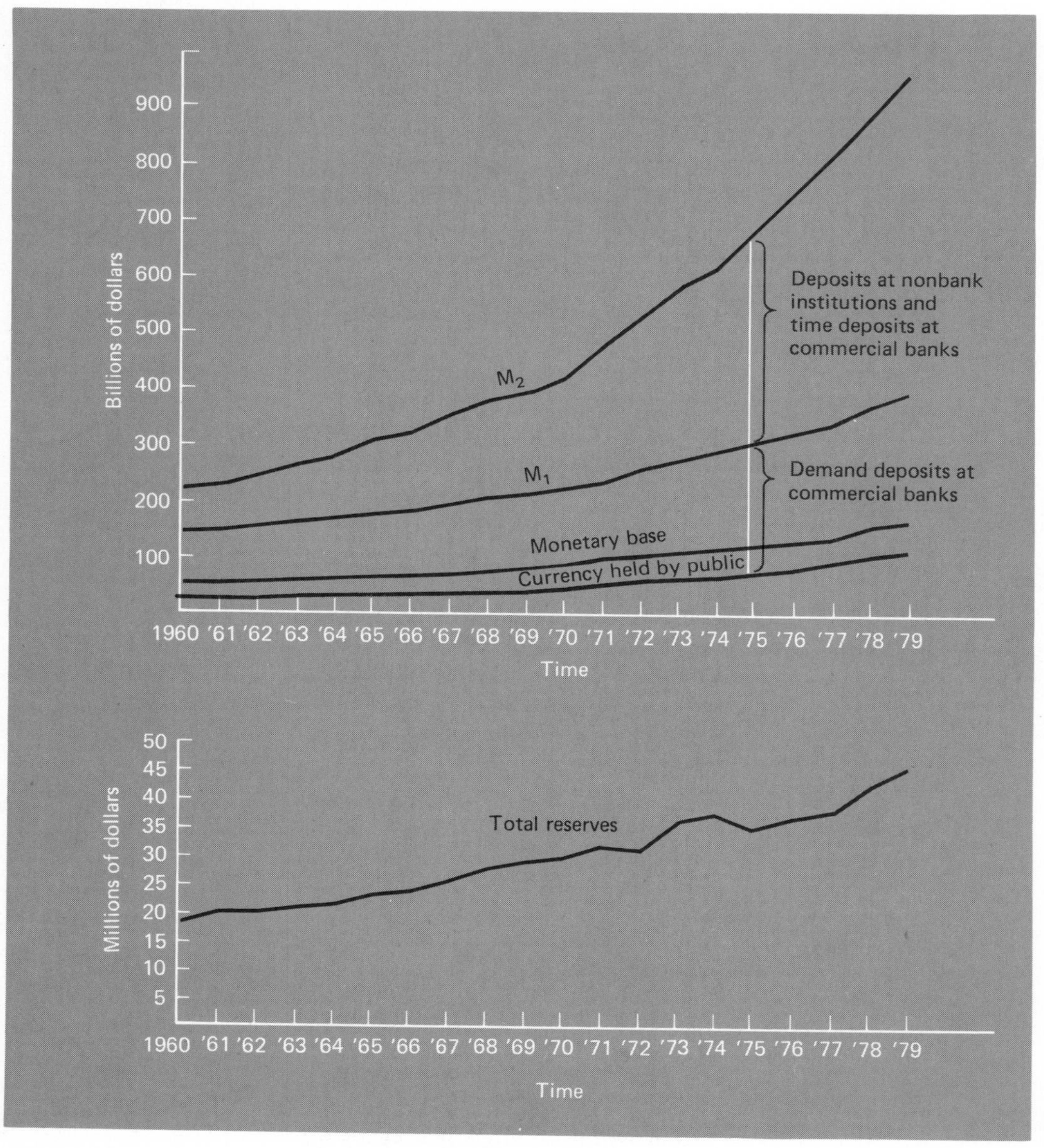

showing the importance of the newer approach to money supply determination as opposed to the older, fixed multiplier, approach. And the FRB–MIT–PENN model results strongly support the notion of a positive relation between the discount rate and free reserves, a relation whose basis in theory we have examined.

QUESTIONS

1. What is the primary difference between the "traditional" view of money supply determination and the "modern" view? Why is the modern view an improvement?
2. Why is the level of demand deposits whatever level the public desires? Is this always true? Why is it important? If individuals maximize wealth, what must policy affect in order to affect the money supply?
3. What are *reserves?* Why are banks required to hold reserves? Do banks ever hold reserves in excess of those required? Why? How are reserves related to the money multiplier?
4. Who determines the money supply?
5. If the Central Bank sells $10 billion worth of government securities, what is the (direction of) effect on the rate of return on capital, the loan rate, and the bond rate? How are free reserves affected?
6. What is the discount rate? If the discount rate is lowered, say from 10 to 9 percent, what is the effect on free reserves? What happens to the rate of return on each asset in the model?
7. According to the traditional view, how much would the money supply change in response to a $25 billion purchase of government securities by the Central Bank if the required reserve ratio is 0.2?
8. According to the modern view, would the money supply change in question 7 be larger or smaller?
9. Explain the results in questions 7 and 8 in terms of the money multiplier.
10. How important do you think the distinction between the two views would be in actually conducting monetary policy?

REFERENCES

BRAINARD, WILLIAM C., and JAMES TOBIN, "Pitfalls in Financial Model Building," *American Economic Review,* May 1968, pp. 352–77.

BRUNNER, KARL, and ALLAN H. MELTZER, "Money, Debt and Economic Activity," *Journal of Political Economy,* September/October 1972, pp. 951–77.

DE LEEUW, FRANK, and EDWARD GRAMLICH, "The Channels of Monetary Policy: A Further Report on the Federal Reserve MIT Model," *Journal of Finance,* May 1969, pp. 265–90.

FEDERAL RESERVE BOARD, *Federal Reserve Bulletin,* any issue.

FEDERAL RESERVE STAFF STUDY, *New Monetary Control Procedures,* Vols. I and II, Washington D.C. Board of Governors of the Federal Reserve System, February 1981.

HADJIMICHALAKIS, MICHAEL G., "Precision of Monetary Control and Volatility of Rates: A Comparative Analysis of the Reserves and the Federal Funds Operating Targets," *Special Studies* No. 150, Federal Reserve Board, Washington, D.C., January 1981.

———, "Reserves *vs* Federal Funds Operating Monetary Procedures: A General Equilibrium Analysis," *Economics Letters,* Vol. 7, 1981.

———, "Monetary Control: The Role of the Discount Rate and other Supplemental Monetary Instruments," *Economics Letters,* Vol. 7, 1981.

MODIGLIANI, FRANCO, ROBERT H. RASCHE, and J. PHILIP COOPER, "Central Bank Policy, Money Supply, and the Short-Term Rate of Interest," *Journal of Money, Credit and Banking,* May 1970, pp. 166–218.

TEIGEN, RONALD, "Demand and Supply Functions for Money in the United States: Some Structural Estimates," *Econometrica,* October 1964, pp. 476–509.

TOBIN, JAMES, "Commercial Banks as Creators of 'Money,' " in *Banking and Monetary Studies,* ed. Deane Carson, pp. 408–19. Homewood, Ill.: Richard D. Irwin, 1963.

———, "An Essay on the Principles of Debt Management," in *Fiscal and Debt Management Policies,* pp. 143–218. Englewood Cliffs, N.J.: Prentice-Hall, 1963.

———, "A General Equilibrium Approach to Monetary Theory," *Journal of Money, Credit and Banking,* February 1969, pp. 15–29.

TOBIN, JAMES, and WILLIAM C. BRAINARD, "Financial Intermediaries and the Effectiveness of Monetary Controls," *American Economic Review,* May 1963, pp. 383–400.

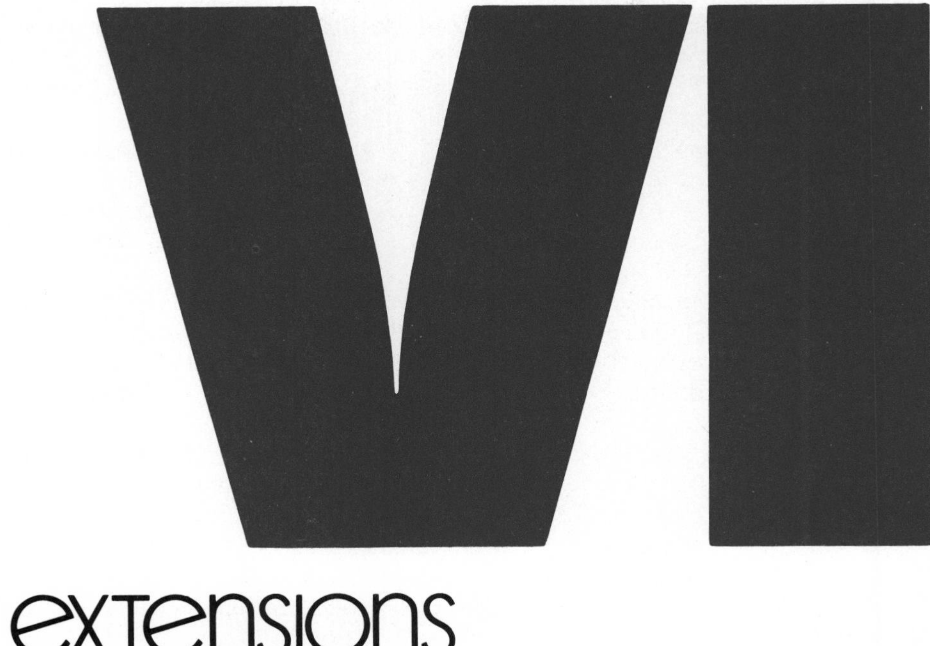

extensions

The Open Economy

15

In this chapter we shall cast our analysis on a world economy that consists of only two countries—"ours," or the domestic economy, and the rest of the world. Each of these countries has its own currency, say dollars ($) for our country and pounds (£) for the rest of the world. The foreign currency is called foreign exchange. To proceed with our analysis, we need an operator to transform foreign currency (or exchange) into domestic currency and vice versa. This duty is performed by the *exchange rate,* which is the relative price of foreign currency; specifically, the exchange rate, e, is the number of units (dollars) of the domestic currency we need to spend (or we get) when we buy (sell) one unit of foreign currency; it has the dimension in number of units of dollars per unit of pounds, that is, $e = \$/£$.

It is easy to see how we can transform pounds into dollars and vice versa. To begin, let us suppose that the domestic price of good A is denoted by p_a and its foreign price by p_a^*. Multiplying p_a^* by the foreign exchange rate gives the price of good A in terms of domestic currency: $p_a = e \cdot p_a^*$. Note that p_a = dollars/units of A, p_a^* = pounds/units of A, and e = dollars/pounds:

$$e \cdot p_a^* = \frac{\text{Dollars}}{\text{Pounds}} \cdot \frac{\text{Pounds}}{\text{Units of } A} = \frac{\text{Dollars}}{\text{Units of } A}$$

Thus $e \cdot p_a^*$ is dollars per unit of good A, which is the price of good A in dollars.

In this chapter, which purports to give only the flavor of an open economy, we shall abstract from issues of growth and of unemployment. Although this will deprive us of the opportunity to examine such issues as the potential conflict of internal *versus* external balance, we can still examine a variety of other important topics. The assumption of the short-run coupled with full employment implies that employment per unit of capital, x, is fixed at $\bar{x}$. Under these assumptions, the appropriate model is an extension of the model used in Chapter 4.

The introduction of economic interaction between this country and other countries necessitates substantial modification of the model. The most important modification is the increase in the number of markets we need to examine. In the corresponding closed economy, we had only three markets—the market for goods and services, the market for loans (bonds), and the market for money. By Walras' Law, we needed to examine only two of these—the goods and services market and the loans market. Now we also have the market for foreign exchange. It is in this last market that the two currencies are traded and their relative price, the exchange rate, e, is determined.

Only three of these four markets need to be examined explicitly. We shall choose to examine the same two we examined earlier, namely, the market for goods and services and the market for loans, plus the new one, namely, the market for foreign exchange. And next we must specify the demand and supply side for each of these markets in an open economy.

THE MARKET FOR GOODS AND SERVICES

The demand for goods and services consists of domestic consumption, C; plus domestic investment, I; plus government demand, G; plus demand from foreign countries (i.e., *exports*), χ. The supply of goods and services consists of domestic production (i.e., supply from domestic sources), Y; plus supply from foreign sources (i.e., imports), μ. Schematically:

$$\text{Demand} = C + I + G + \chi$$

$$\text{Supply} = Y + \mu$$

Excess demand for goods and services, EG, is found by subtracting supply from demand:

$$EG = C + I + G + (\chi - \mu) - Y$$

But, by definition, we have $Y \equiv C + S + T$, where S and T are, respectively, savings and taxes. Hence

$$EG = C + I + G + (\chi - \mu) - (C + S + T)$$

or

$$EG = (I - S) + (G - T) + (\chi - \mu)$$

The first component on the right emanates from the domestic private sector, the second from the government sector, and the third from the foreign sector. Since we are not examining fiscal policy, we assume that the government budget deficit, $G - T$, is always zero. However, we can no longer ignore the *balance of trade*, $\chi - \mu$. We denote this, as earlier, by ν and refer to it as the trade surplus, with the understanding that when it is negative we have a trade deficit. Excess demand for goods and services is then

$$EG = I - S + \chi - \mu \tag{1}$$

or

$$EG = I - S + \nu \tag{1'}$$

As earlier, investment per unit of capital, I, depends negatively on the domestic interest rate, i. It also depends positively on employment per unit of capital, x, but for simplicity of notation we eventually suppress this dependence, since we assume a fixed $\bar{x}$. Thus

$$I = I(i, \bar{x}), \quad \frac{\Delta I}{\Delta i} < 0, \quad \frac{\Delta I}{\Delta x} > 0 \tag{2}$$

Similarly,

$$S = S(i, \bar{x}), \quad \frac{\Delta S}{\Delta i} \gtreqless 0, \quad \frac{\Delta S}{\Delta x} > 0 \tag{3}$$

In the earlier chapters, whenever we examined the trade surplus, ν, we treated it as a parameter, but now it is time to consider it as a behavioral relation and find its ultimate determinants. First, we assume that our country exports good Y, the only good produced, and imports from the rest of the world good Y_*. The prices of the two goods are p and p_*, each of which is expressed in terms of the currency of the respective country of origin. Household choice theory tells us that imports and exports depend on relative prices. Specifically, imports, or our demand for the foreign good, Y_*, depends *negatively* on the relative price of Y_*. But the relative price of Y_* (in this Y, Y_* world) is the number of units of Y we give up to obtain (from abroad) one unit of Y_*. This is called the *terms of trade* and can be written as T:

$$T = \frac{e \cdot p_*}{p} \tag{4}$$

(Note that the numerator is the price of Y_* translated into dollars, since $e \cdot p_*$ transforms the pound price of a unit of Y_* into the dollar price of one unit of the same good; hence the numerator has the dimensions of dollars/units of Y_*. The denominator has the dimensions of dollars/units of Y.

Therefore

$$T = \frac{\text{Dollars}}{\text{Units of } Y_*} \Big/ \frac{\text{Dollars}}{\text{Units of } Y} = \frac{\text{Units of } Y}{\text{Units of } Y_*};$$

That is T is indeed the number of units of Y we give up per unit of Y. In other words, we specify that

$$\mu = \mu(T), \quad \frac{\Delta\mu}{\Delta T} < 0 \tag{5}$$

Similarly, exports, χ, which are the demand for our good, Y, by foreigners, depend negatively on the relative price of good Y. But the relative price of Y is the inverse of the relative price of Y_*. Thus exports depend *positively* on the relative price of Y_*, that is, on T:

$$\chi = \chi(T), \quad \frac{\Delta\chi}{\Delta T} > 0 \tag{6}$$

We shall assume directly that the trade surplus, ν, depends positively on the terms of trade, T:

$$\nu = \nu(T), \quad \frac{\Delta\nu}{\Delta T} > 0 \tag{7}$$

(Actually the sign $\Delta\nu/\Delta T > 0$ can be derived by making certain assumptions about the elasticity of each country's demand for imports.) But the terms of trade, T, (t.o.t.), depend on e, p_*, and p. We shall assume that p_* is a given parameter, perhaps because our country cannot influence foreign prices, and we shall therefore suppress its notation. Of the remaining two variables, an increase in e increases the t.o.t. and hence raises the trade surplus. In other words, an increase in e means a devaluation of the dollar, which makes foreign goods less competitive and our goods more competitive. Exports rise and imports fall, thus raising their difference, ν. And it follows that $\Delta\nu/\Delta e > 0$. On the other hand, with a given exchange rate, e, an increase in our price level, p, increases the relative price of our good, that is, it reduces the relative price of the foreign good, which induces an increase in our imports and a fall in our exports; hence an increase in p will, ceteris paribus, reduce ν (i.e., $\Delta\nu/\Delta p < 0$).

In summary, we have

$$\nu = \nu(p,e), \frac{\Delta\nu}{\Delta p} < 0, \frac{\Delta\nu}{\Delta e} > 0 \tag{8}$$

Excess demand for goods, then, depends on the triplet (i,p,e). We can represent this compactly by

$$EG = EG(i,p,e), \frac{\Delta EG}{\Delta i} = \frac{\Delta I}{\Delta i} - \frac{\Delta S}{\Delta i} < 0, \frac{\Delta EG}{\Delta p} = \frac{\Delta\nu}{\Delta p} < 0, \frac{\Delta EG}{\Delta e} = \frac{\Delta\nu}{\Delta e} > 0 \tag{9}$$

THE LOANS MARKET

On the demand side of the loans market we have three components: investment demand, hoarding, and capital outflows. We are already familiar with the first two components. Domestic investment demand gives rise to demand for loans, since it is assumed that firms demand loans to finance their domestic investments. Hoarding enters as a component of demand for loans because it emanates from individuals who have fewer real balances than they need, and therefore they borrow to finance these additions to their balances, that is, they borrow to keep it in cash. The third item is characteristic of an open economy. *Capital outflows,* C.O., can come from more than one source, from residents of this country who borrow here to make direct investments abroad, such as the building of a factory abroad, or from short-term movements of capital, lent to foreigners because of more favorable terms. Or, finally, from residents of foreign countries who wish to borrow in the United States and, therefore, demand loans in the United States.

On the supply side, we also have three components: savings, dishoarding, and capital inflows. As earlier, one source of the supply of loans comes from current domestic savings. The second component, dishoarding, comes from individuals who hold more money than they need, and therefore they lend part or all of it. However, the final component of supply, *capital inflows,* C.I., is symmetric to the corresponding component of demand, and it comes from the opposite set of circumstances, for example, from residents of foreign countries who wish to lend in the United States because of what they perceive as being more favorable terms than they can find in their own countries.

In summary, we have

$$\text{Demand} = I + \text{Hoarding} + \text{C.O.}$$

$$\text{Supply} = S + \text{Dishoarding} + \text{C.I.}$$

Moreover, we can rearrange the terms on the demand and supply sides with the aim of expressing hoarding and dishoarding and capital inflows and outflows in *net* terms. By subtracting C.I. and hoarding from both the demand and supply side, we get

$$\text{Demand} = I + (\text{C.O.} - \text{C.I.})$$

$$\text{Supply} = S + (\text{Dishoarding} - \text{Hoarding})$$

We define net capital *out*flows as the difference between C.O. and C.I.:

$$c \equiv \text{C.O.} - \text{C.I.}$$

Of course, if $c < 0$, we have net capital *in*flows. Also, we define *net* dishoarding as $\lambda(M/p - L)$, where $M/p - L$ is the stock excess supply of money. The letter λ is an operator that transforms stocks into flows; it has a dimension of a pure number per unit of time, for example, $\lambda = 1/4$/per year. This means that each year the agents add one-fourth of their excess supply of money to the supply of loans, so that in four years they eliminate the difference. On the other hand, by defining the period in our example as equal to four years, λ becomes equal to one.

The excess demand for loans, *EL* (which is found by subtracting supply from demand), is

$$EL = I(\cdot) - S(\cdot) + c(\cdot) - \lambda\left[\frac{M}{p} - L(\cdot)\right] \tag{10}$$

We recall that the demand for real balances,[1] L, depends negatively on the domestic interest rate and positively on employment per unit of capital, x. However this last element is fixed at $\bar{x}$.

$$L = L(i, \bar{x}), \quad \frac{\Delta L}{\Delta i} < 0 \tag{11}$$

The final behavioral relation in this market is for capital outflows, c. We assume that capital outflows depend negatively on the domestic interest rate and positively on the foreign interest rate: A higher domestic interest rate induces more *in*flows (i.e., foreign capital to be lent here), and it discourages domestic funds from leaving the country. The opposite effects result from a rise in the *foreign* interest rate, i_*. However, i_* is assumed to be a given parameter and it will be suppressed. Capital outflows also depend negatively on x, $\Delta c/\Delta x < 0$: An increase in x raises the domestic rate of profit, which encourages inflows and discourages outflows. This characteristic is also suppressed, since we assume a fixed $\bar{x}$. In summary:

$$c = c(i, i_*, \bar{x}), \frac{\Delta c}{\Delta i} < 0, \frac{\Delta c}{\Delta i_*} > 0, \frac{\Delta c}{\Delta x} < 0 \tag{12}$$

Of course, capital outflows can be positive or negative. There is a pivotal domestic interest rate, call it $\hat{i}$, which makes these net flows zero. A lower domestic interest rate encourages net outflows and a higher one causes negative outflows, that is, inflows, as in Figure 15-1. Presumably the pivotal interest rate, $\hat{i}$, is related (for example, it may be equal) to the riskless foreign interest rate. The elasticity of the capital outflows curve, c, increases as capital mobility between countries increases. In the case of perfect capital mobility, this curve is horizontal, as shown in Figure 15-1. (Note: In the analysis above, we specified that capital flows depend on *levels* of the interest rate. An alternative theory relies on *changes* in interest rates. This latter one is the portfolio, or capital asset, approach. For the short-run period we are examining, our approach seems realistic.)

In summary, excess demand for loans depends on the endogenous variables, i and p, and on the exogenous variable, M (x is omitted):

$$EL = EL(i, p; M), \frac{\Delta EL}{\Delta i} < 0, \frac{\Delta EL}{\Delta p} > 0, \frac{\Delta EL}{\Delta M} < 0 \tag{13}$$

---

[1] The demand for real balances depends also on the terms of trade, T. We exclude it, however, to simplify our graphical analysis; but it should be noted that nothing of substance is involved.

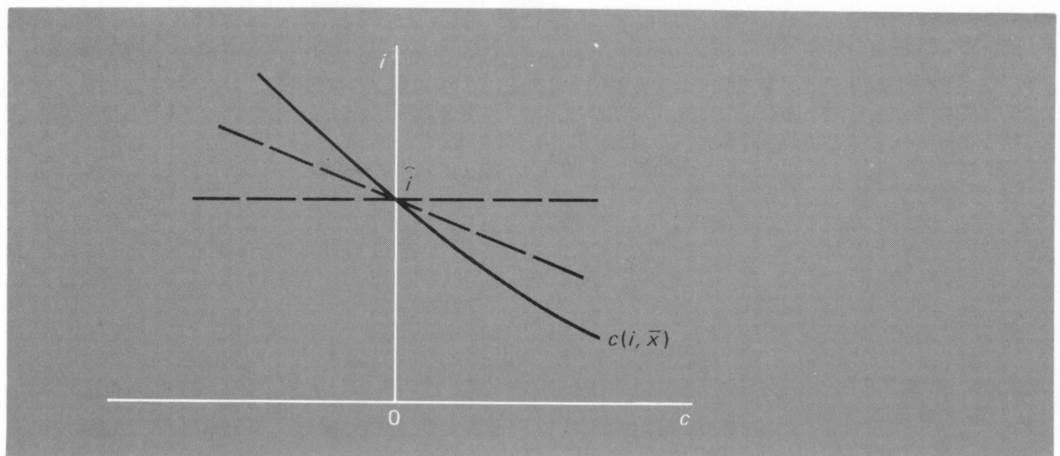

FIGURE 15-1

THE FOREIGN EXCHANGE MARKET

In the home country individuals demand foreign exchange (pounds) to pay for imports, μ, and for capital outflows. On the other hand, the supply of foreign exchange emanates from exports, χ (that is, from the sale of pounds, or the receipts of exports, for dollars), and from capital inflows (that is, from funds, denominated in pounds and brought into this country to be loaned, but which were first *sold* in the foreign exchange market for dollars):

$$\text{Demand} = \mu - \text{C.O.}$$

$$\text{Supply} = \chi = \text{C.I.}$$

Or, rearranging terms, and denoting $c = \text{C.O.} - \text{C.I.}$ and $\nu = \chi - \mu$, we have

$$\text{Demand} = c = \text{C.O.} - \text{C.I.}$$

$$\text{Supply} = \nu = \chi - \mu$$

Therefore, excess demand for foreign exchange, *EF,* is (keeping foreign i_* fixed):

$$EF = c(i,\bar{x}) - \nu(e,p) \tag{14}$$

or

$$EF = EF(i,e,p), \text{ with } \frac{\Delta EF}{\Delta i} = \frac{\Delta c}{\Delta i} < 0, \frac{\Delta EF}{\Delta e} = -\frac{\Delta \nu}{\Delta e} < 0, \frac{\Delta EF}{\Delta p} = -\frac{\Delta \nu}{\Delta p} > 0 \tag{14'}$$

Walras' Law provides a minimum test of consistency for our specification of the model. It states that the sum of the excess (flow) demands for all goods and financial claims must be equal to zero. Recalling that demand for loans means supply of bonds and vice versa, and denoting the excess demand for bonds as *EB,* we need

$$EB + EG + EM + EF = 0$$

or

$$EL = -EB = EG + EM + EF$$

or

$$EL = (I - S + \nu) - \lambda\left(\frac{M}{p} - L\right) + c - \nu,$$

that is,

$$EL = I - S + c - \lambda\left(\frac{M}{p} - L\right)$$

This is precisely what we specified earlier in (10). Now, by Walras' Law, we must examine explicitly only three of the four markets: the goods and services market, the loans market, and the foreign exchange market. Of these, the first represents the "real" sector, while the loans and foreign exchange markets represent the "financial" sector.

We must now specify the law of supply and demand for each market. For the goods and services market, this means that the price of goods and services rises (falls) if, and only if, there is positive (negative) excess demand. In schematic form:

$$\Delta p \gtreqless 0 \quad \text{when} \quad EG \gtreqless 0 \tag{15}$$

A specific equation that captures the above schema of supply and demand is

$$\frac{\Delta p}{p} = \epsilon \cdot EG, \quad \epsilon > 0 \tag{15a}$$

Applying the law of supply and demand to the loans market, we have, compactly,

$$\Delta i \gtreqless 0 \quad \text{when} \quad EL \gtreqless 0 \tag{16}$$

or, algebraically,

$$\Delta i = \delta \cdot EL, \quad \delta > 0 \tag{16a}$$

And, finally, the law of supply and demand for the foreign exchange market states that

$$\Delta e \gtreqless 0 \quad \text{when} \quad EF \gtreqless 0 \tag{17}$$

or, algebraically,

$$\Delta e = \gamma \cdot EF, \quad \gamma > 0 \tag{17a}$$

Thus the entire model of an open economy is captured simultaneously by the following three schemata:

$$\Delta p \gtreqless 0 \quad \text{when} \quad EG \gtreqless 0 \tag{15}$$

$$\Delta i \gtreqless 0 \quad \text{when} \quad EL \gtreqless 0 \tag{16}$$

$$\Delta e \gtreqless 0 \quad \text{when} \quad EF \gtreqless 0 \tag{17}$$

or by following the three equations:

$$\frac{\Delta p}{p} = \epsilon \cdot EG \tag{15a}$$

$$\Delta i = \delta \cdot EL \tag{16a}$$

$$\Delta e = \gamma \cdot EF \tag{17a}$$

The positive numbers, ϵ, δ, and γ, are the speeds of adjustment of the goods, the loans, and the foreign exchange markets. The inverse of any speed, say $1/\gamma$, is the time it takes to clear the respective market. For any market, the speed of adjustment, and thus the time it takes for market clearance, depend on the availability and cost of information: The more costly (and less easily accessible) the information regarding a market, the slower the clearance of the market. Of the three markets, the goods market has the slowest speed; the next slowest speed is shown in the foreign exchange market; and the fastest-clearing market, because of its superior organization, is the loans market. While the Bretton Woods Agreement was in effect, the exchange rate was fixed, set by the International Monetary Fund, IMF, rather than directly by the foreign exchange market. That situation can be explained by setting γ equal to zero. Currently, with a flexible exchange system, γ is very high. One of the cases we shall examine below is that of perfect exchange rate flexibility (i.e., when $\gamma \to \infty$ or $1/\gamma \to 0$).

One of our main interests below is to describe the full equilibrium of the system. This obviously occurs when *all* markets are cleared (i.e., when $EG = 0$, $EL = 0$, and $EF = 0$). By Walras' Law, it follows that the remaining market, the money market, is then also cleared (i.e., $EM = 0$). Finding the full equilibrium means finding the three endogenous variables, i, e, and p. Note that the three equations $EG = 0$, $EL = 0$, and $EF = 0$ are functions of the three unknowns. We can directly apply some simple arithmetical techniques to solve these three equations for the three unknowns—provided, of course, that we know their exact form. In general, however, we do not know their exact form, so we must rely on qualitative analysis. One method of solution is to solve one of the three equations for the one unknown in terms of the remaining two. Then we can substitute this solution in the remaining two equations and solve them for the final two unknowns. Going back to the first solution, we can then solve for that variable as well. Another method for solving the system is to first solve two of the equations for two unknowns in terms of the remaining unknown and then substitute these solutions into the remaining equation to find the remaining unknown.

If we are only interested in the equilibrium values (or solutions) of (i,e,p), it does not matter which method or which equation(s) we use first. But if we are interested in the properties of the equilibrium, such as the exact paths that the endogenous variables will follow, and whether the equilibrium is stable or not, then the choice of the method of solution is crucial for the result, and it has economic significance.

We shall explain two methods of solution, each relying on different institutional arrangements and, therefore, applicable whenever those arrangements are valid.

METHOD 1

We assume that the loans market clears instantaneously, that $\delta \to \infty$, while the other two markets do not clear as fast. But when $\delta \to \infty$, $EL = 0$, regardless of whether the other markets are cleared. On the other hand, EL depends on $(i,p;M)$. Since the instantaneous clearance of the loans market determines, instantaneously, the interest rate, we can solve the equation $EL(i,p;M) = 0$ for i as a function of the remaining variables, p and M. We can write this solution as $i = i_*(p;M)$ and proceed to determine how i changes when p and M change. We then substitute this solution into the equations (14′) and (9), which at equilibrium become

$$EF[i_*(p;M),p,e] = 0$$

$$EG[i_*(p;M),e,p] = 0$$

Note that these two equations are functions of only two variables, e and p, given the value of the parameter M. We can, therefore, solve them (for the given M) and find the equilibrium values of e and p. If we are also interested in the value of i, we can insert the solution for p (and the given value of M) into i_* and find the exact level of the interest rate at equilibrium. Continuing in this fashion, we can also find how e and p approach the equilibrium, and so forth.

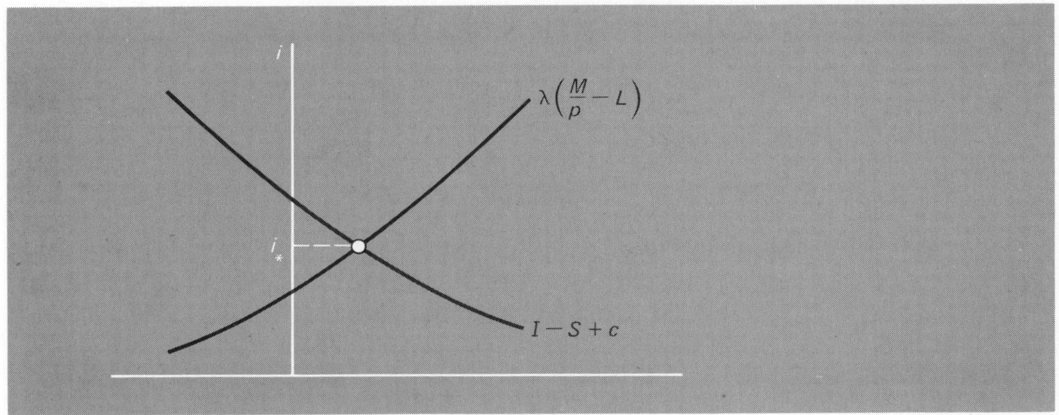

FIGURE 15-2

We recall that this is precisely the approach that we followed in Chapter 4, that is, $EL = 0$ if, and only if,

$$I(i) - S(i) + c(i) = \lambda\left[\frac{M}{p} - L(i)\right] \tag{18}$$

The solution is found graphically by the intersection of the $I(i) - S(i) + c(i)$ curve and the $\lambda[M/p - L(i)]$ curve, as in Figure 15-2. Figure 15-3 shows the effect on i_* when the price level rises. This increase in the price level lowers the amount of real balances, thus shifting the $\lambda(M/p - L)$ curve to the left; hence, for the given money supply (M_0), the interest rate rises (i.e., $\Delta i_*/\Delta p > 0$). We found this same result for the closed economy model of Chapter 4. Similarly, in Figure 15-4, the increase in

FIGURE 15-3

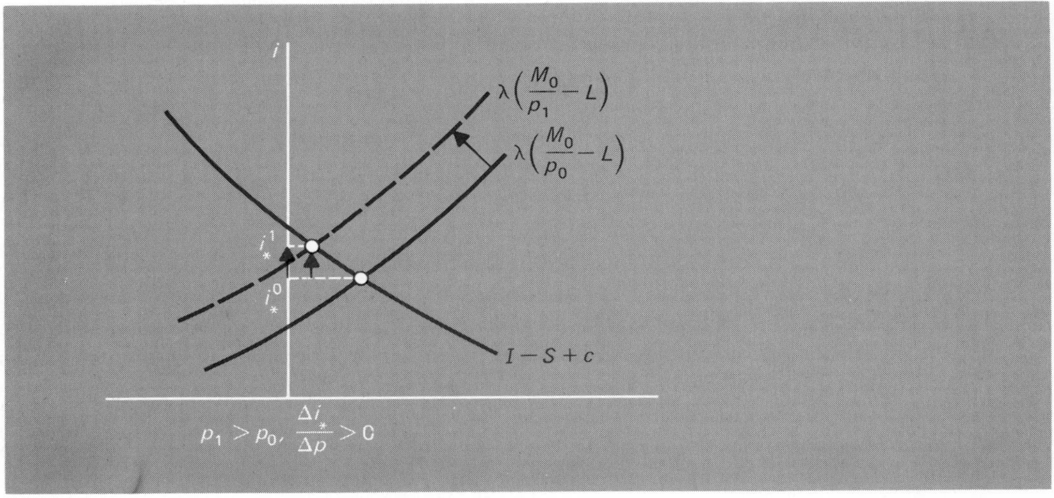

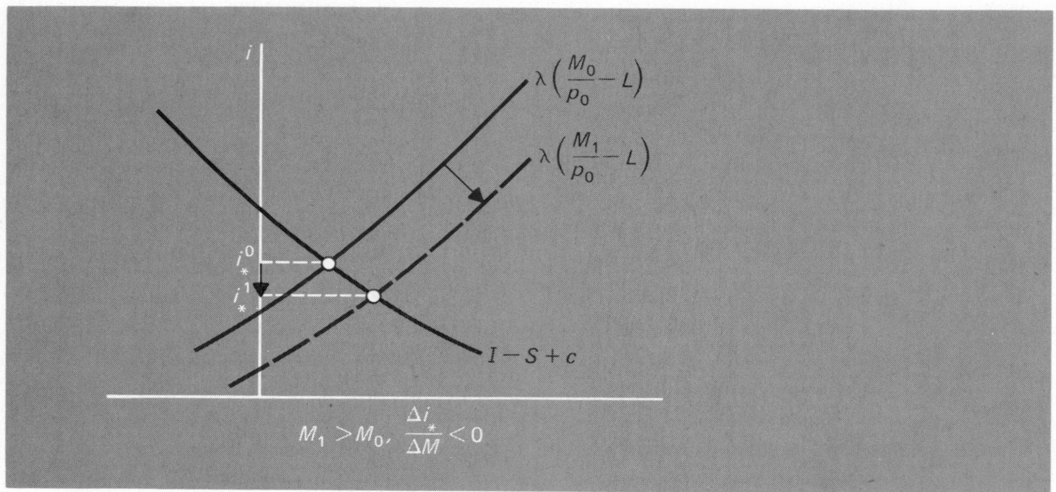

FIGURE 15-4

M (from M_0 to M_1) increases real balances, shifting the $\lambda(M/p - L)$ curve to the right and causing the interest rate to fall (i.e., $\Delta i_*/\Delta M < 0$).

The equation $EL = 0$ is entirely described by its solution, $i = i_*(p;M)$, with $\Delta i_*/\Delta p > 0$ and $\Delta i_*/\Delta M < 0$. Substituting this solution (and its characteristics) into the remaining two equations, $\Delta e = \gamma \cdot EF$ and $\Delta p = \epsilon \cdot EG$, we have

$$\Delta e = \gamma\{c[i_*(p;M)] - \nu(e,p)\} \tag{19}$$

$$\Delta p = \epsilon\{I[i_*(p;M)] - S[i_*(p;M)] + \nu(e,p)\} \tag{20}$$

These two equations, in two unknowns, describe the motion of these two variables, e and p (and by implication the laws of motion of $i = i_*[p;M]$). Furthermore, at full equilibrium, which occurs only when both Δe and Δp (i.e., the changes in these variables) are zero, the RHS of these equations must be zero:

$$c[i_*(p;M)] - \nu(e,p) = 0 \tag{19'}$$

$$I[i_*(p;M)] - S[i_*(p;M)] + \nu(e,p) = 0 \tag{20'}$$

Using the techniques learned in this book, the reader can find all the combinations of p and e that satisfy the first equation, as well as all the combinations of p and e that satisfy the second. Having found these combinations, the reader will note that the intersection of these two curves gives the equilibrium values of p and e, as in Figures 15-5 and 15-6. The reader can also find the signs of Δe and Δp for points that lie off these curves, and, therefore, off the equilibrium point, all of which will describe graphically the laws of motion as depicted by the arrows and will enable the economist to find the stable solution, that is, to exclude the case of Figure 15-7.

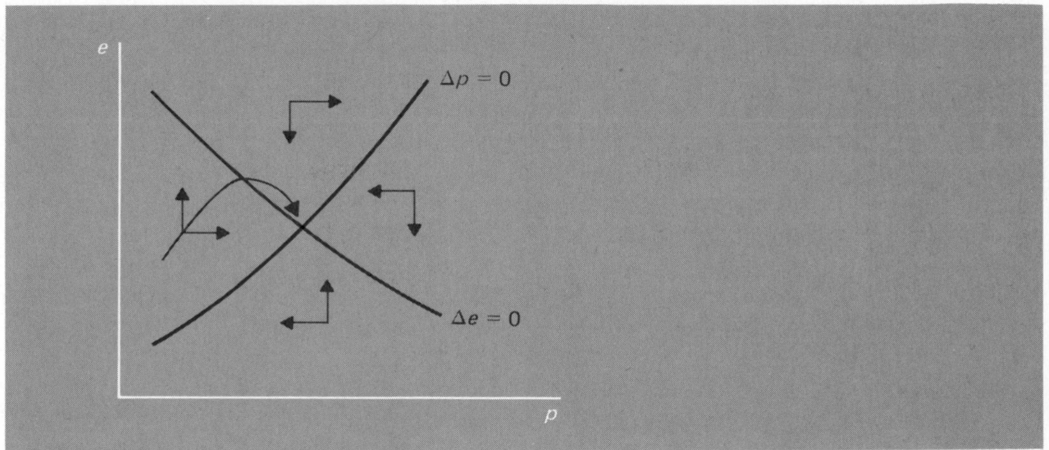

FIGURE 15-5

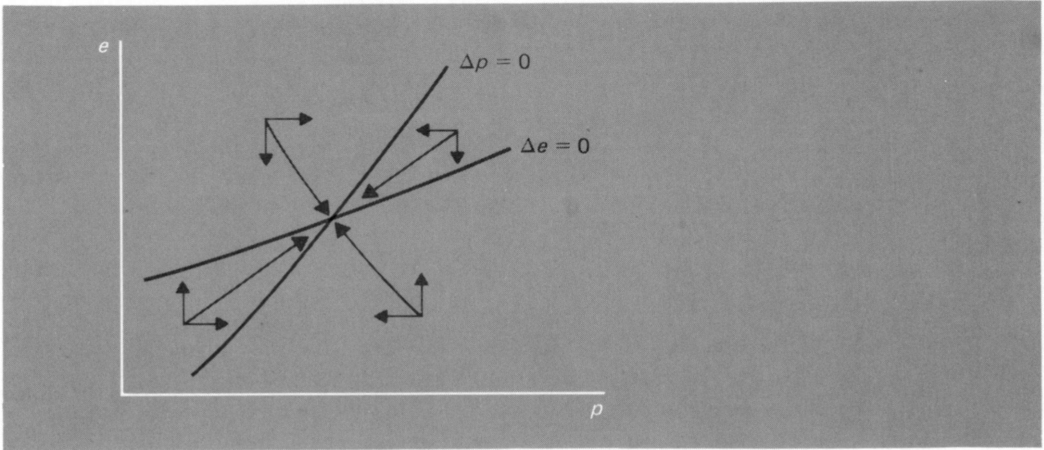

FIGURE 15-6

METHOD 2

Method 2 assumes that both "financial" markets (i.e., both the loans market and the foreign exchange market) clear a lot faster than the single market that describes the "real" sector (i.e., the goods and services market). This approach allows us to be more realistic, inasmuch as current institutional arrangements reflect this assumption. Moreover, this approach permits us to dichotomize (tentatively) the entire system into a real sector and a financial sector, so that we can examine first the financial sector, separating it from the real sector, and then combine the two.

Here we assume not only that the financial markets, as they are described by (16a) and (17a) above, clear faster than the goods and services market, (15a), but that they clear infinitely fast: The speeds of adjustment δ and γ, respectively,

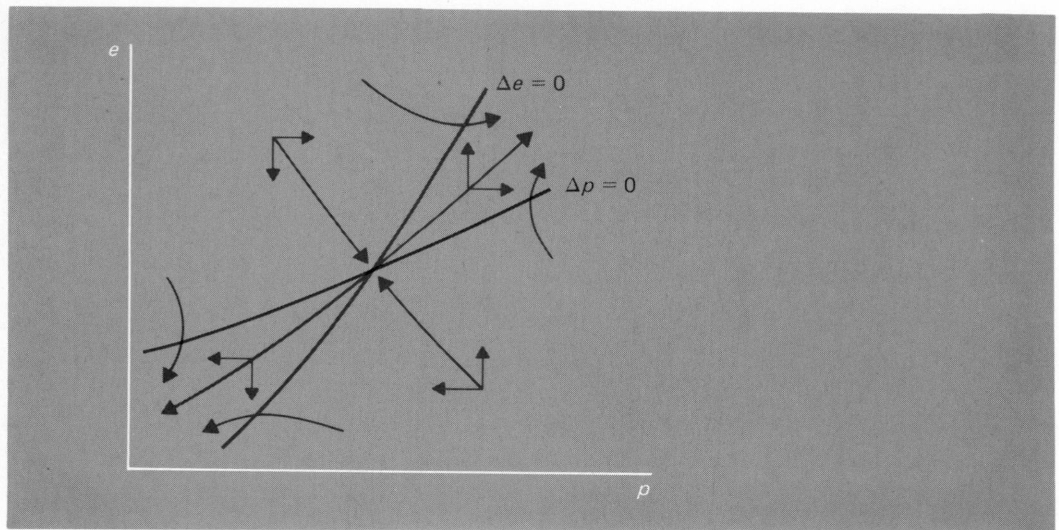

FIGURE 15-7 UNSTABLE

of the loans market and of the market for foreign exchange are infinite. In such a case both markets are instantaneously and always cleared, that is, we always have

$$EL = I(i) - S(i) + c(i) - \lambda\left[\frac{M}{p} - L(i)\right] = 0 \tag{21}$$

$$EF = c(i) - \nu(e,p) = 0 \tag{22}$$

The approach is to solve these two equations for the "financial" variables, i and e, and also to see how these solutions are affected by other magnitudes, regardless of whether these magnitudes are endogenous variables, p; or exogenous parameters such as the money supply, M; or the foreign interest rate, i_*; or still different magnitudes. With this in mind, we shall solve these two equations graphically for i and e. (If we know the exact form of these equations, we can solve arithmetically for these two unknowns.) We shall use the (e,i)-plane, with the horizontal axis denoting e and the vertical axis denoting i.

First we find all the combinations of e and i that clear the loans market, that is, all the combinations that satisfy $EL = 0$, equation (21). This is an equation in i, p, and M, but not in e. Hence all the (e,i) combinations lie on a horizontal line to emphasize the fact that $EL = 0$ does not depend on e. The curve intersects the i-axis at i_0, which is the solution of (21) when we fix (i.e., when we know) the values of p and M. We can denote these values, respectively, by p_0 and M_0 and specify them in the name-tag of the $EL = 0$ curve, $EL = 0\Big|_{\substack{M=M_0 \\ p=p_0}}$, as shown in Figure 15-8. On the other hand, if we assume a higher M, say $M_1 > M_0$, the $EL = 0$ curve shifts downward because an increase in M—with p still assumed fixed at p_0—

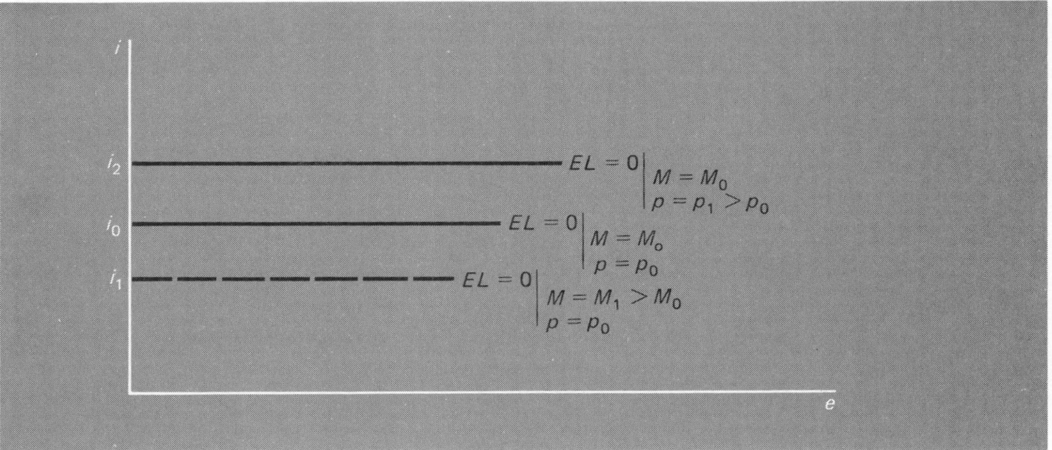

FIGURE 15-8

increases real balances, from M_0/p_0 to M_1/p_0, and therefore increases the supply of loans, which, in turn, lowers the interest rate, as seen in the solution of (21) for i when $M = M_1$ and $p = p_0$. However, the opposite happens if we increase p while keeping M fixed. In Figure 15-8 the $EL = 0$ curve intersects the i-axis at i_2, which is higher than i_0, when p rises from p_0 to p_1. An increase in p, with M constant, decreases real balances and, in turn, the supply of loans, which ultimately raises the interest rate.

Next we want to find all the combinations of i and e that clear the foreign exchange market, that is, all the combinations that satisfy $EF = 0$, equation (22). To do this we should note that EF is a function of i, e, and p, and that the combinations, therefore, are found for a given assumed p. Let us write (22) as

$$c(i) = \nu(e,p) \tag{23}$$

Suppose that with $p = p_0$, the pair (i_0,e_0) is one combination of i and e such that $EF = 0$. Now consider the following conceptual exercise: Suppose i increases to $i_1 > i_0$. Then the left-hand side, LHS, of (23) will decrease, since net capital outflows decrease. Now, if e remains at the original level, e_0, there will be excess supply of foreign exchange, $EF < 0$, since the RHS will remain at the original level. Thus ν has to fall to maintain the equality $c = \nu$ (i.e., $EF = 0$). But with p fixed, ν falls only if e falls, that is, the trade surplus falls only if the dollar is revalued. Therefore we see that all the combinations (i,e) that clear the foreign exchange market lie on a downward-sloping curve labeled $EF = 0|_{p = p_0}$, as in Figure 15-9.

At this point we want to find how the $EF = 0$ curve will shift when we assume a higher price level. Let us suppose that starting from a combination (i_0,e_0) satisfying the equation $EF = 0$, we increase p, from p_0 to p_1. In other words, starting from point A in Figure 15-10, we raise p to p_1. Now, if we show that e must rise, say to B, to preserve the equation $c = \nu$, this means that the curve shifts to the

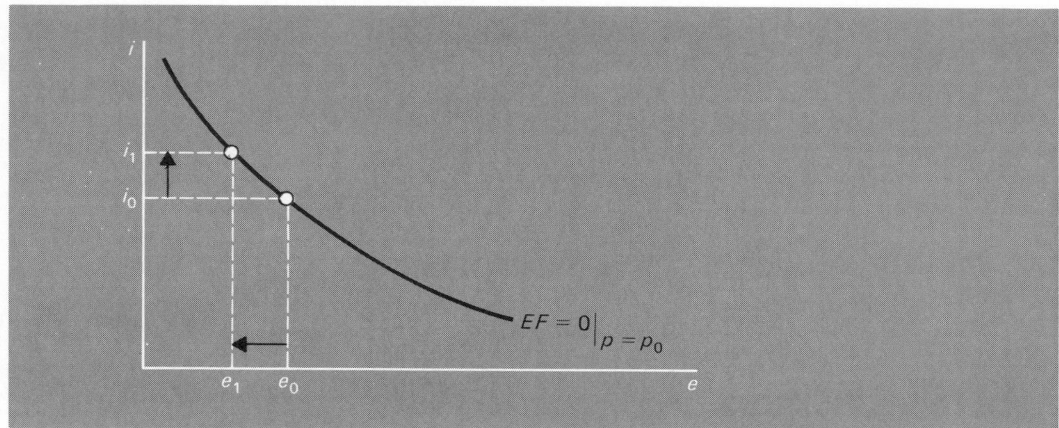

FIGURE 15-9

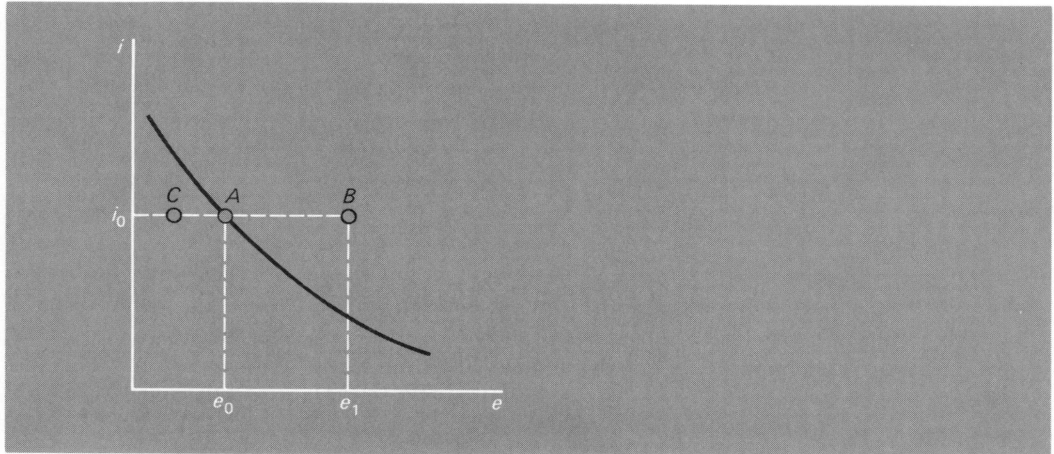

FIGURE 15-10

right (passing through B). If, on the other hand, e must fall, say to point C, to preserve $EF = 0$, this means that the $EF = 0$ curve shifts to the left (passing through C). Concentrating on equation (23), we see that if we fix i at i_0 (as in Figure 15-10) and increase p from p_0 to p_1, the LHS of (23) remains the same because capital outflows, c, depend only on i. On the other hand, with e fixed at e_0, the increase in p decreases v, the trade surplus. Thus if e remains the same (at e_0), there will be a tendency for $c > v$ (i.e., for $EF > 0$). But this excess demand for foreign exchange will disappear only if e rises, say to e_1 (i.e., only if the dollar is devalued). We have seen that an increase in p to p_1, while keeping i at i_0, requires an increase in e to e_1 if the equality $c = v$ is to be preserved. In other words, we shall have point B. Repeating this exercise for all possible levels of i, we find that the new points will always lie to the right (as at B). Connecting these points, we have the curve labeled $EF = 0|_{p = p_1 > p_0}$, which lies to the right of the $EF = 0|_{p = p_0}$ curve, as in Figure 15-11.

We should emphasize an important property of the $EF = 0$ curve. Since the equation $EF = 0$, that is, $c(i) = v(e,p)$, does *not* depend on M, it follows that any change in this important parameter will have no effect on the $EF = 0$ curve. In other words, for a given price there is only one $EF = 0$ curve, no matter what the money supply is; a change in M does not shift the $EF = 0$ curve, whereas we have shown that it does shift the $EL = 0$ curve (downward).

In summary, we have found all the combinations of (i,e) that clear the loans market, that is, when $EL = 0$, and we noted that they lie on a horizontal line. We have also found all the combinations of (i,e) that clear the foreign exchange market, that is, when $EF = 0$. They lie on a downward-sloping curve. Now, the intersection of these two curves satisfies both $EL = 0$ and $EF = 0$, which is the solution of the two equations (21) and (22) and represents the solution of the financial sector for i and e for given values of M and p. This solution is denoted as $i(p;M)$ and $e(p;M)$ and is illustrated in Figure 15-12. According to Figure 15-12, we see that, ignoring the real sector (that is, assuming a given price level) and assuming a certain nominal quantity of money, M_0, the interest rate and the exchange rate that clear simultaneously (and instantaneously) both financial markets—the loans and foreign exchange markets—are, respectively, i_0 and e_0. We can call this the *temporary* equilibrium.

Again ignoring the real sector, let us examine how the (temporary) equilibrium values of i and e are affected by a change, say an increase, in the nominal money supply, M. We know that the $EF = 0$ curve will not shift but that the $EL = 0$ curve will shift downward, producing the immediate result, illustrated in Figure 15-13, that the interest rate will fall and that the relative price of foreign exchange, e, will rise, that is, the country's currency will be devalued. The economic explanation of these results is straight-forward; we can say that, *ignoring its effects on the price*

FIGURE 15-11

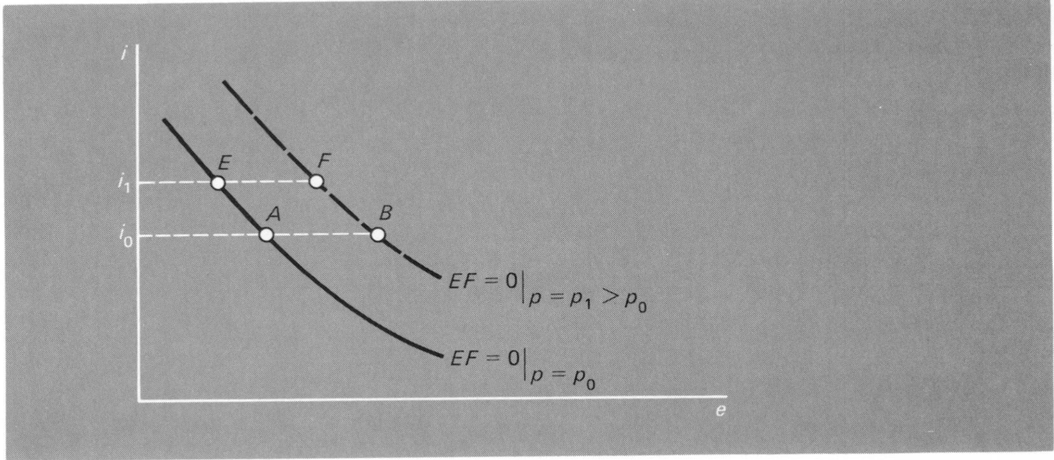

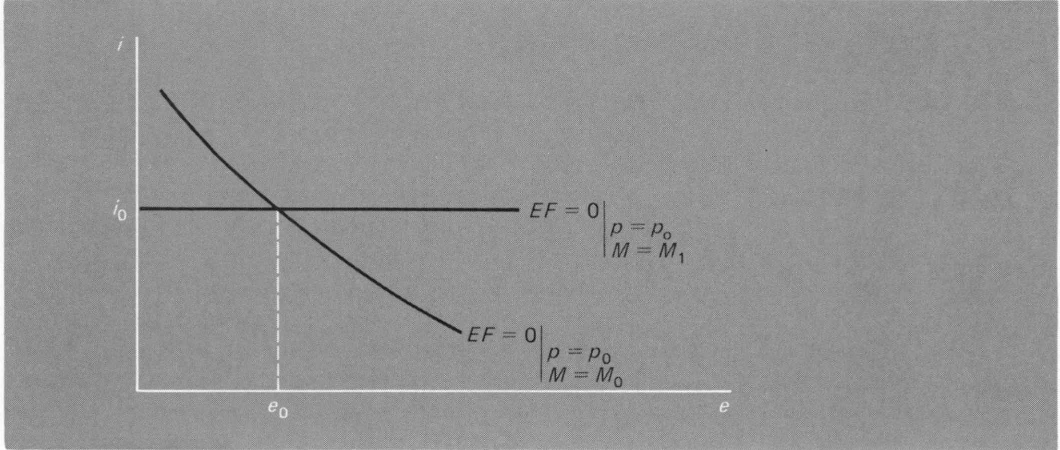

FIGURE 15-12

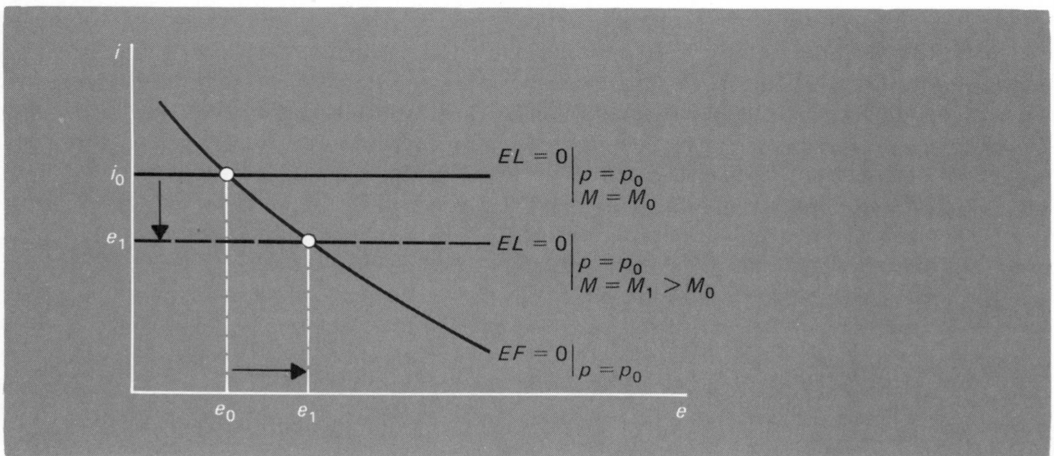

FIGURE 15-13

level, an increase in the nominal money supply, M, increases the supply of loans, thereby lowering the interest rate. The lower interest rate, on the other hand, induces an increase in capital outflows and a decrease in capital inflows, thereby increasing *net* capital outflows, a situation that tends to cause excess demand for foreign exchange. To prevent this excess demand for foreign exchange, *its* relative price, the exchange rate, e, rises, that is, the country's own currency is devalued. Schematically, the solutions for i and e have the properties, respectively,

$$\left.\frac{\Delta i}{\Delta M}\right|_{\bar{p}} < 0 \quad \text{and} \quad \left.\frac{\Delta e}{\Delta M}\right|_{\bar{p}} > 0$$

So far we have carried out our analysis under the tentative assumption that we shall ignore the real sector, that is, the goods and services market, and hence the price level. Of course, the price level, p, is not a datum in an economic system like ours; it is market determined, and it can be at whatever level is consistent with our model. In the next section, however, we examine the entire system inclusive of the market for goods and services and, therefore, determine the price level in addition to i and e. As a prelude to that, let us now examine the effect on the (temporary) equilibrium levels of i and e of an increase in the price level. (For example, this increase in the price level may become necessary because of an excess demand for goods and services [in the ignored market] while the market for foreign exchange and the loans markets are cleared.)

We know that an increase in the price level (while, of course, the money supply is fixed at $\overline{M}$) shifts the $EL = 0$ curve upward and the $EF = 0$ curve to the right, as in Figure 15-14. In this case we see that an increase in the price level increases the interest rate and devalues the country's currency (i.e., it increases e). This seems reasonable enough, since an increase in the price level reduces the real supply of money and hence the supply of loans, thereby raising the interest rate. The increase in the interest rate attracts capital inflows and discourages outflows, which improves the value of the domestic currency (i.e., it reduces the relative price of foreign exchange).

However, the effect on the exchange rate, e, is neither as clear-cut as the above explanation implies nor as clear-cut as Figure 15-14 depicts. The increase in the price level raises the interest rate, causing a decrease in the outflows, which is a favorable effect (to the dollar). However, another effect from the increase in the price level, one that results in a reduction in the trade surplus, is an unfavorable effect. Figure 15-14 depicts the case when the favorable effect outweighs the unfavorable effect, a case in which the *indirect* (and favorable) effect of a rise in the price level,

FIGURE 15-14

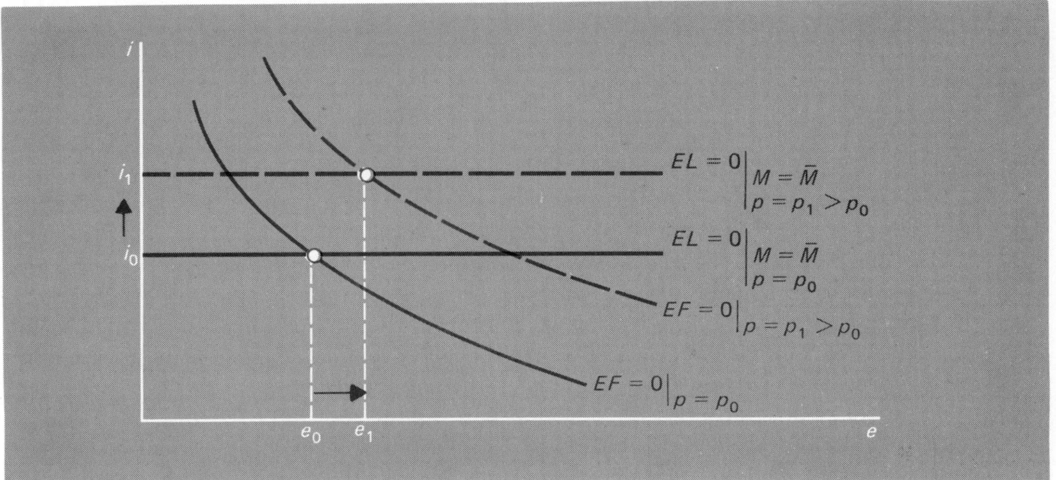

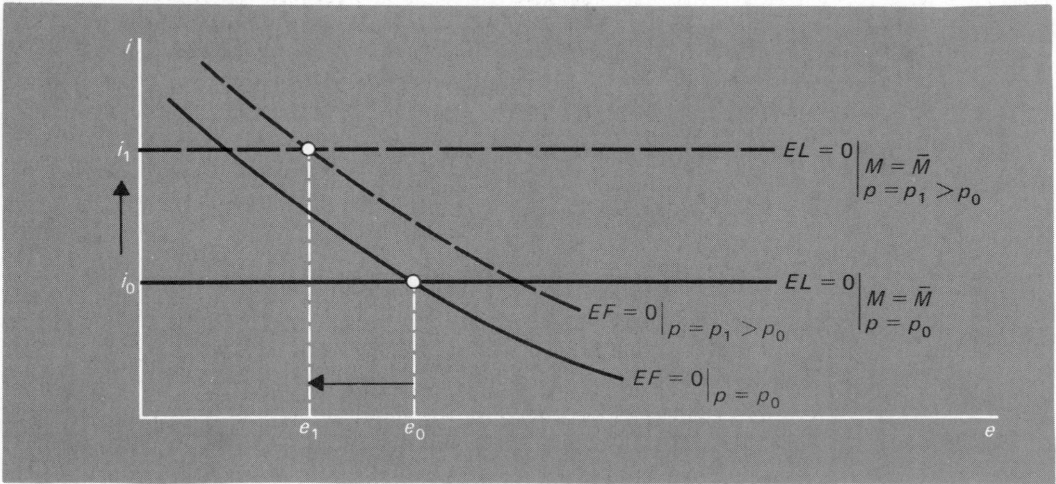

FIGURE 15-15

caused by the rise in the interest rate, outweighs the *direct* and unfavorable effect on the balance of trade. However, the opposite result is possible, as shown in Figure 15-15. In this case the direct, or balance-of-trade, effect outweighs the indirect, or capital account, effect.

In summary, the instantaneous clearance of the loans and foreign exchange markets provides the solutions for *i* and *e*, which depend on the price level, *p*, and on the money supply, *M*. Of course, the former is an endogenous variable while the money supply is assumed to be an exogenous parameter. We can write the solutions, with their characteristics, as

$$i = i(p;M), \quad \text{with} \quad \frac{\Delta i}{\Delta p} > 0, \ \frac{\Delta i}{\Delta M} < 0 \tag{24}$$

$$e = e(p;M), \quad \text{with} \quad \frac{\Delta e}{\Delta p} \gtreqless 0, \ \frac{\Delta e}{\Delta M} > 0 \tag{25}$$

One interesting implication of the above result, regarding the effect of a change in the price level on the interest rate and on the exchange rate, is that despite the clearance of both the foreign exchange and the loans markets, the variables they determine may vary depending on what is happening in the goods market. For example, if there is excess demand for goods and services, the price level will rise, thereby increasing the interest rate and also raising the foreign exchange rate if the capital account effect outweighs the trade surplus effect, or lowering the foreign exchange rate if the trade surplus effect dominates the capital account effect. Only when the market for goods and services is cleared will the interest and exchange rates remain unchanged. In this case, of course, all endogenous variables—the interest rate, the exchange rate, and the price level—will be unchanged. This is *full* equilibrium, as compared with the *temporary* equilibrium, in which only the foreign exchange and the loans markets are cleared. This brings us to the second stage of our "two-stage" solution.

We shall now incorporate into our analysis the real sector which has been ignored until now. This sector is described by the price adjustment mechanism. In schematic form we have

$$\frac{\Delta p}{p} \gtreqless 0 \quad \text{when} \quad EG \gtreqless 0 \tag{15}$$

In algebraic form we have

$$\frac{\Delta p}{p} = \epsilon \cdot EG \tag{15a}$$

or, explicitly,

$$\frac{\Delta p}{p} = \epsilon \cdot [I(i) - S(i) + \nu(e,p)] \tag{15b}$$

If we incorporate the distilled information from the financial sector, that is, (24) and (25) into (15b), we have

$$\frac{\Delta p}{p} = \epsilon\{I[i(p;M)] - S[i(p;M)] + \nu[e(p;M),p]\} \tag{26}$$

The only variables in (26) are p and M. But only the former is endogenous, yielding one equation in one unknown, p. For a given level of the parameter, M, we can find the equilibrium value of p, that is, we can find the level of p for which $\Delta p = 0$, which occurs when the RHS of (26) is zero. This means that the goods market is cleared, $EG = 0$, and that, *in addition,* the loans and foreign exchange markets are cleared. (And, lurking in the background is the money market, which is also cleared.)

The ultimate one equation in one unknown, p, can be written in two additional ways besides (26). In (26) we emphasize that the price of goods and services rises if, and only if, there is excess demand for goods and services. But since the foreign exchange market always and instantaneously clears, that is, $EF = 0$ always, which means that $c[i(p;M)] \equiv \nu[e(p;M),p]$, we can replace ν by c in (26) to get

$$\frac{\Delta p}{p} = \epsilon\{I[i(p;M)] - S[i(p;M)] + c[i(p;M)]\} \tag{27}$$

Moreover, since $EL = 0$ always, we have

$$I[i(p;M)] - S[i(p;M)] + c[i(p;M)] \equiv \frac{M}{p} - L[i(p;M)]$$

Thus (26) or (27) can be written as

$$\frac{\Delta p}{p} = \epsilon\left\{\frac{M}{p} - L[i(p;M)]\right\} \tag{28}$$

This latter equation states that the price of goods and services rises (falls) if, and only if, there is excess supply of (excess demand for) money, which is the usual quantity theory of money statement. The reader, however, should not fail to see the roundabout way in which this statement has been formulated and how many "secrets," the results of interdependencies, it hides, or at least incorporates!

Using any of the following, (26), (27), or (28), we can now show that the system converges to full equilibrium (i.e., when $\Delta p = 0$), where *all* markets are cleared. This is shown in Figure 15-16 where p_0 is the solution to

$$I - S + v = 0, \quad \text{or} \quad I - S + c = 0, \quad \text{or} \quad \frac{M}{p} - L = 0$$

after we set $\Delta p = 0$ in (26), or (27), or (28), respectively. Of course, given our assumptions, these are alternative but equivalent methods of solution.

Using, say, formulation (26), we can easily show that when $p < p_0$, $EG > 0$, and that when $p > p_0$, $EG < 0$. What Figure 15-16 shows is that for $p < p_0$, $(\Delta p/p) = \epsilon \cdot EG > 0$. Furthermore, since an increase in p reduces the magnitude of EG, as p increases, EG and, therefore, $\Delta p/p$ will get smaller, so that the system converges to equilibrium. The opposite explanation applies for $p > p_0$.

Finally, knowing the full-equilibrium price level, p_0 (and, of course, the value of the parameter M), we can go back to the (tentative) solutions, (24) and (25), to determine the full-equilibrium values of i and e, respectively. Diagrammatically, we

FIGURE 15-16

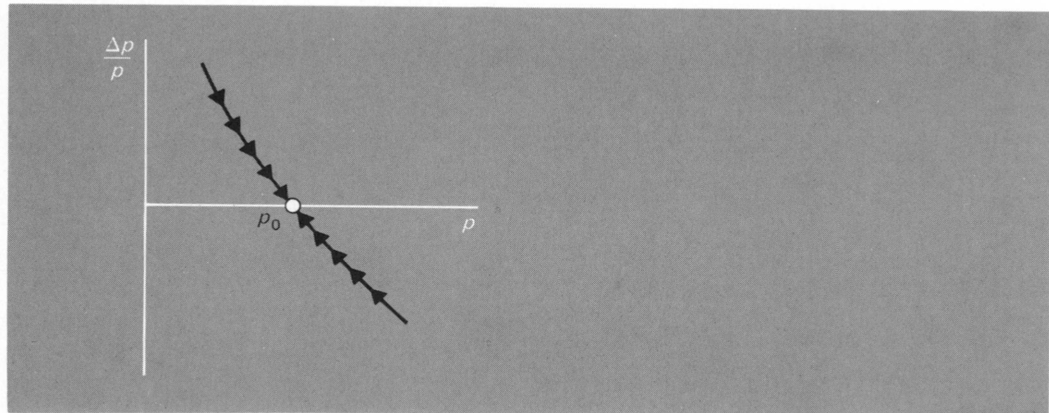

can go to the graphs where the $EL = 0$ and $EF = 0$ curves bear identification tags $M = \overline{M}$ and $p = p_0$.

COMPARATIVE STATICS: CHANGES IN THE MONEY SUPPLY, *M*

An increase in the nominal money supply, *M*, increases the price level by the same percentage:

$$\frac{\Delta M}{M} = \frac{\Delta p}{p} \tag{29}$$

This is, of course, the quantity theory result. Graphically, the $\Delta p/p$ curve shifts to the right in such a way that it intersects the p-axis at a distance from p_0 equal to the percentage change in *M*. In Figure 15-17 a doubling of the money supply doubles the price level. This result can be derived algebraically, whether we use equation (26), (27), or (28).

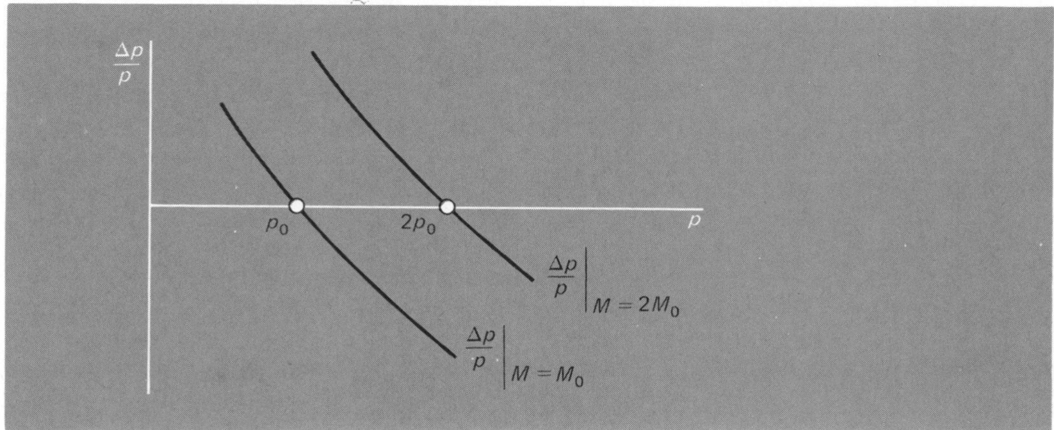

FIGURE 15-17

Let us now examine the effect of the rise in *M* on the interest rate, *i*. This issue can be illustrated with a graph similar to Figure 15-12, after incorporating the information in Figures 15-13 and 15-14. The increase in *M*, from M_0 to $2M_0$, ultimately leaves the $EL = 0$ curves in the same position. While this increase in *M* (i.e., doubling of M_0) shifts the $EL = 0$ curve downward, the equiproportionate (i.e., doubling) rise in the price level shifts it back to its previous position. On the other hand, the $EF = 0$ curve will shift to the right because of the increase in *p* (and not because of the increase in *M*). The end result is shown in Figure 15-18, where we see that there is no change in the interest rate, which is, of course, the neoclassical

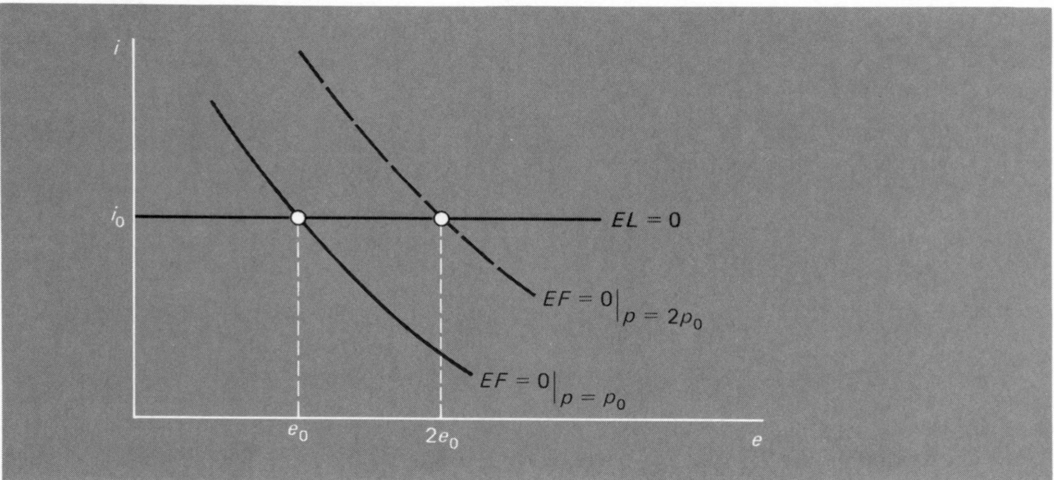

FIGURE 15-18

result of neutrality of money. On the other hand, the exchange rate rises, in fact, by the same percentage as the increase in money and prices. This is the purchasing power parity (PPP) result, usually associated with the quantity theory.

We can see why the interest rate remains, ultimately, at the original level by examining the loans market clearance:

$$I(i) - S(i) + c(i) = \frac{M}{p} - L(i) \tag{21}$$

When $M = M_0$ and $p = p_0$, solving this one equation in one unknown, we get the result $i = i_0$. When $M = 2M_0$ and $p = 2p_0$, the real balances remain the same and nothing changes, that is, the solution is the same, $i = i_0$.

The effect on the exchange rate, e, is best illustrated by concentrating on clearance of the foreign exchange market, $EF = 0$:

$$c(i) = \nu(e,p) \tag{23}$$

The increase in the money supply leaves the interest rate unchanged (at i_0). Therefore the LHS, or net capital outflows, remains unchanged. On the other hand, the increase in the money supply increases the price level by an equal percentage (doubling, $2p_0$), thereby decreasing the trade surplus and, in turn, causing excess demand for foreign exchange. This potential excess demand for foreign exchange, $EF = c - \nu > 0$, can be eliminated only if the currency is devalued, that is, if the value of foreign exchange, e, rises. By how much will the foreign exchange rate rise? As long as the trade balance depends only on the t.o.t., T, which is equal to $(e \cdot p_*)/p$, and as long as the foreign price level is maintained fixed, e must rise at precisely the same rate as the price level. This is the only way in which the t.o.t., T, will remain unchanged, which, in turn, will leave the trade balance, ν, unchanged and equal to the unchanged c. It follows that under these assumptions we shall have the purchasing power parity result:

$$\frac{\Delta e}{e} = \frac{\Delta p}{p} \quad \left(\text{since } \frac{\Delta T}{T} = \frac{\Delta e}{e} + \frac{\Delta p_*}{p_*} - \frac{\Delta p}{p}; \quad \text{but} \right.$$

$$\left. \frac{\Delta T}{T} = 0 \quad \text{and} \quad \frac{\Delta p_*}{p_*} = 0, \quad \text{hence } \frac{\Delta e}{e} - \frac{\Delta p}{p} = 0 \right).$$

FIGURE 15-19

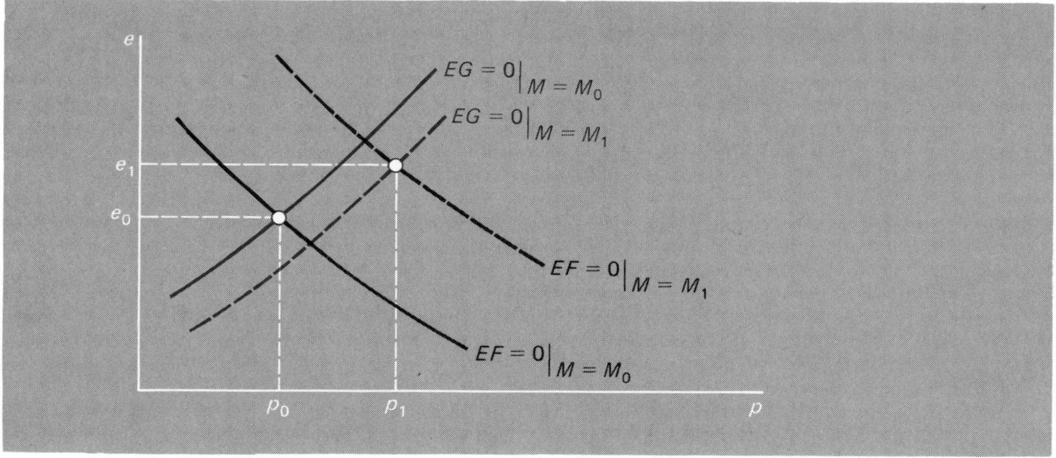

FIGURE 15-20

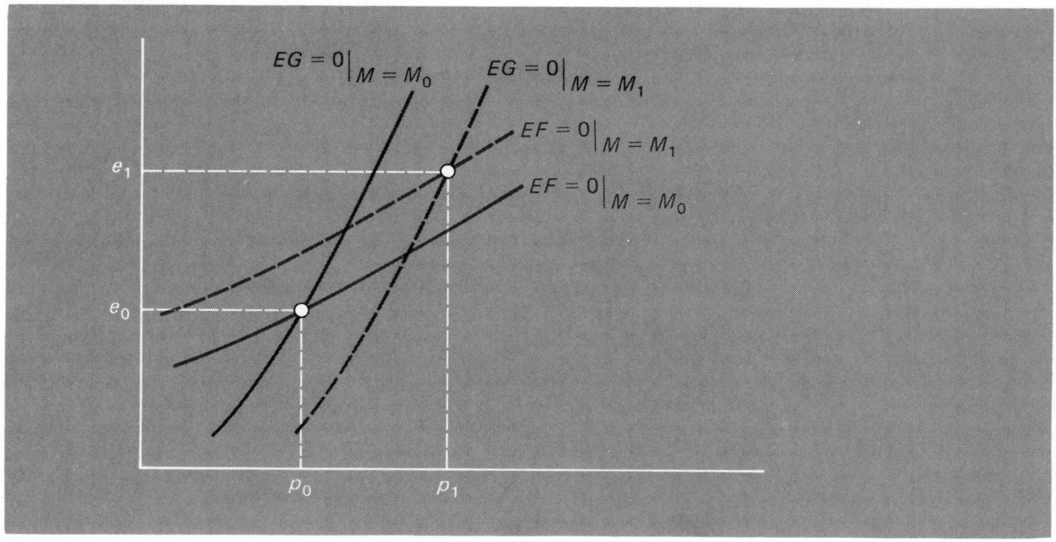

A given percentage increase in the money supply will raise the price level by the same percentage, and it will devalue the relative price of this currency (vis-à-vis the currency of the rest of the world) by the same percentage.

In summary, an increase in the money supply will increase the price level, p, and the exchange rate, e, by the same percentage, but it will leave the interest rate unchanged. It should be emphasized that these results are true whenever our assumptions, in particular, full employment and the absence of expectations formation, hold.

The reader should be able to derive the same results by using the first method of solution. In particular, the reader should be able to show, for example, that the $EF = 0$ and $EG = 0$ curves (for a graph similar to Figure 15-5) will shift, as in Figure 15-19 or Figure 15-20.

CONCLUDING COMMENTS

We have shown that when all four markets (goods, loans, foreign exchange, and money) are considered, an increase in the nominal supply of money will cause a proportional increase in both the price level and the exchange rate, with no change in the interest rate. These neutral results depend on our assumptions, in particular, full-employment and no inflationary expectations. The assumptions have allowed us to analyze a simple open economy while making only minor additions to our basic model. Of course, we have been able to address only a few of the many interesting questions that arise in the area of international economics.

For students who are interested in further reading and study about open economies, we will briefly mention a few of the classic works of interest. An excellent text by Caves and Jones covers both the pure theory of international trade (a microeconomic perspective) and applications of macroeconomics to the world economy. Much of the early work in analyzing the potential of stabilization policy in an open economy was done by James Meade. Robert Mundell continued this tradition of policy analysis and is best known for his work on the feasibility of pursuing simultaneously both domestic goals (full employment and/or price stability) and external goals (balance-of-payments equilibrium). In recent years the late Harry G. Johnson was a prodigious source of insightful analysis and new ideas in the field of international economics. His work on the "monetary approach to the balance of payments" inspired a whole new body of literature, which focuses on the nature and causes of balance-of-payments disequilibria. Of course, our approach in this chapter is in the same spirit. Recent advances in the theory of an open economy have begun to utilize a portfolio, or capital account, approach to capital inflows and outflows. These advances, also following the suggestions of Johnson, are reminiscent of the analyses of our chapters 13 and 14. The Allen-Kenen and McMahon works are good examples of this approach.[2]

[2] The analysis of this chapter is based on the short-run section of Hadjimichalakis, "Domestic and Foreign Capital Accumulation in a Monetary Economy."

QUESTIONS

1. It has been observed that the price level and the interest rate move in the same direction. Show that this is so both in a closed economy and in an open economy with always full employment. Also in a closed economy that permits variable employment.

2. Examine an economy that exhibits continuous clearance of the labor, loans, and foreign exchange markets.

a. Ignoring the goods market (and thus the price level), explain verbally and illustrate graphically why an increase in the nominal money supply will definitely lower the interest rate and devalue the currency.

b. If the goods market is also considered, how will your results in part *a* be modified?

3. In a fully employed economy, what will be the effects of a reduction in the rate of growth of the money supply on the exchange rate and inflation?

4. In a flexible exchange rate regime, with full employment always prevailing:

a. Examining only the "financial" markets, i.e., the loans and foreign exchange markets, what effect does a rise in the price level have on the exchange rate? What effect does an increase in the money supply have on the exchange rate?

b. Examining *all* relevant markets, why is it that the exchange rate and the price level sometimes move in the *same* and sometimes in the *opposite* directions?

5. What is the exchange rate? How is it related to the terms of trade?

6. How do changes in the domestic and foreign interest rate affect net capital outflows? Why? How do the changes in net capital outflows affect the market for foreign exchange?

7. Show that Walras' Law allows examination of only three of the four markets in the model.

8. What is a "speed of adjustment"? What factors might affect speeds of adjustment in various markets? Why are speeds of adjustment important?

9. When the loans and foreign exchange markets clear instantaneously, the whole system can be reduced to one equation for clearance of the goods market. This equation can be written in several forms, including:

$$\Delta p/p = \epsilon\{I[i(p;M)] - S[i(p;M)] + c[i(p;M)]\} \tag{a}$$

$$I[i(p;M)] - S[i(p;M)] + c[i(p;M)] = M/p - L[i(p;M)] \tag{b}$$

$$\Delta p/p = \epsilon\{M/p - L[i(p;M)]\} \tag{c}$$

Carefully explain why each of these statements is equivalent to the others given the assumptions.

10. Equation (c) in question 9 has been called a version of the quantity theory. Why?

11. What is purchasing-power-parity? What specific feature of our analysis is responsible for this result?

REFERENCES

ALLEN, POLLY R. and PETER B. KENEN, *Asset Markets, Exchange Rates And Economic Integration: A Synthesis.* New York: Cambridge University, 1980.

CAVES, RICHARD E., and RONALD W. JONES, *World Trade and Payments: An Introduction* (2nd ed.). Boston: Little, Brown, 1977.

FRENKEL, JACOB A., and HARRY G. JOHNSON, eds., *The Monetary Approach to the Balance of Payments.* University of Toronto: Toronto, 1976.

HADJIMICHALAKIS, MICHAEL G., "Domestic and Foreign Capital Accumulation in a Monetary Economy," University of Washington, Institute for Economic Research, Discussion Paper No. 7217, October 1972.

MCMAHON, MICHAEL R., "The Capital Account Approach To International Monetary Analysis" (Ph.D. Dissertation, University of Washington, 1978).

MEADE, J. E., *The Balance of Payments.* London: Oxford, 1951.

MUNDELL, R. A., *International Economics.* New York: Macmillan, 1968.

———, *Monetary Theory.* Pacific Palisades, Calif.: Goodyear, 1971.

The Growing Economy

16

So far our emphasis has been on the short run, a period short enough to let us treat the capital stock, K, as a given, fixed, magnitude. We have examined two cases. First we concentrated on full employment, a case in which the real wage is at whatever level is necessary to equate the demand for labor, N^d, with the supply of labor, N^s, which is the entire labor force. And we found that $N^d = N^s = N$, at a fixed level. Furthermore, since our key magnitude, x, was defined as employment per unit of capital, that is, $x = N/K$, and since both the numerator and the denominator were fixed, it followed that x itself was fixed when we assumed both *full employment* and the *short run*. This is the procedure we followed in Chapters 2–4 and 15.

In Chapters 5–10 we examined the case of variable employment (or variable "utilization") of the given labor force in the short run, a case in which the demand for labor, N^d, can be different from the supply of labor, that is, the labor force, N^s. In general, then, since $x = N^d/K$, or employment, per unit of (the fixed) capital, is variable, and since the fixed capital stock is assumed to be fully utilized, we were able to interpret a rise (fall) in x as a rise (fall) in employment. (Although we occasionally considered the case of underutilized capital stock, $K^d < \overline{K}$, this case was not fully integrated in our analysis.)

In this final chapter we shall permit the growth of both productive factors: population and capital. Population, and hence the labor force, grow at a "natural" rate, while capital grows by the additions that are undertaken as "investment." Thus both the numerator, N, and the denominator, K, of the magnitude, x, will be allowed to vary. Moreover, for several reasons we shall concentrate only on the case of full employment. The first reason is its simplicity, especially since we merely intend to introduce growth analysis, which is relatively new in the literature. In fact, with only a few exceptions, this literature focuses entirely on full employment.

Besides simplicity, there are other reasons why full employment is a reasonable hypothesis when we are examining growth, for we are, in effect, looking at the long-run *trend* of the economy and observing in some periods unemployment and in others overfull employment. Now, if we *define* the employment observed in the trend as *the* full employment, then unemployment and overfull employment become deviations from the trend, and they cancel each other out statistically.

Yet another justification for the assumption of full employment relies on the following interpretation about government policy: We assume, and rightly so, that many governments have a long-run commitment to full employment and that, in fact, they achieve it by an appropriate use of monetary and fiscal policy. Adhering to this view, we can examine only the end result, that is, full employment. This interpretation is what Samuelson called the "neoclassical synthesis." In other words, by using "Keynesian" activist policies we do indeed achieve what the "neoclassicists" assumed as being the usual case. Or, paraphrasing Lloyd Metzler, we see that the more we use Keynesian remedies, the less we need them.

While assuming full employment, we shall examine only two cases: first, when no borrowing or lending is permitted; and second, when borrowing and lending are permitted in a nonmonetary, or barter, economy. This sequence follows, of course, the format of Chapter 2. But we shall stop short of relaxing the assumption of barter; we shall not introduce money, as the reader of Chapters 3 and 4 might expect. This treatment is left for the more specialized or for the more advanced text. Here we simply summarize the recent advances on that topic.

The most important contribution to this literature, and, in fact, one of the most important contributions to macroeconomics in general, is the extension of the basic growth model by James Tobin to incorporate money.[1] Tobin showed that an increase in the rate of monetary expansion will raise permanently the capital intensity (i.e., the capital/labor ratio) of an economy. Further investigation revealed that the original Tobin model was unstable and, therefore, useless for economic policy—the main reason for its introduction.[2] In particular it was proved that the model was unstable because it was inconsistent in the first place: Tobin's stipulations that "in each period of time, the markets are cleared and expectations are fulfilled" fail to materialize because the *short run* of the system is unstable. And it was shown that when this system is unstable in the short run, it will remain unstable in the long, or growth, run. It soon became apparent that when expectations (of inflation) are present, even "innocent" stipulations, such as continuous clearance of markets, may

---

[1] James Tobin, "Money and Economic Growth," *Econometrica,* October 1965, pp. 671–84.

[2] See Keizo Nagatani, "A Note on Professor Tobin's Money and Economic Growth," *Econometrica,* January 1970; Michael G. Hadjimichalakis, "Equilibrium and Disequilibrium Growth with Money: The Tobin Models," *Review of Economic Studies,* October 1971, pp. 457–79; and Michael G. Hadjimichalakis, "Money Expectations and Dynamics: An Alternative View," *International Economic Review,* October 1971, pp. 381–402.

render the model inconsistent. Hence, more work was needed to specify both the price adjustment mechanism (which presumably brings about the market clearance) and the formation and movement of expectations (which leads to their fulfillment). Subsequent research, which included the development of such concepts as "rational expectations," had its roots in the efforts to stabilize the Tobin growth model. Most of the "money and growth" literature assumes full employment, although there have been some notable attempts to permit unemployment.[3]

I. GROWTH IN THE SIMPLE BARTER MODEL

To develop a self-contained analysis, we shall briefly describe the economy we are examining—even at the cost of some repetition. (Nevertheless, the reader will benefit by rereading Chapter 2, which offers a more elaborate description of this economy.)

THE MODEL[4]

We assume that the two factors of production, labor, N, and capital, K, produce one homogeneous good, Y, according to the production function, (1),

$$Y = F(N,K) \tag{1}$$

which exhibits constant returns to scale. In other words, if we multiply both magnitudes, N and K, by any positive constant number, say λ, the quantity of output Y is also multiplied by the same number:

$$\lambda Y = F(\lambda N, \lambda K)$$

This characteristic allows us to rewrite the production function in its "intensive" forms as (1a) and (1b):

$$\frac{Y}{K} = f(x) \tag{1a}$$

[3] See Hugh Rose, "Unemployment in a Theory of Growth," *International Economic Review,* September 1966; Keizo Nagatani, "A Monetary Growth Model with Variable Employment," *Journal of Money, Credit and Banking,* May 1969, pp. 188–206; Lewis O. Johnson, "The Level of Unemployment in a Growing Monetary Economy" (Ph.D. dissertation, University of Washington, 1972); and Lewis O. Johnson, "Alternative Adjustment Mechanisms and The Long Run Phillips Relation," Special Studies Paper No. 40, Federal Reserve Board, January 1974.

[4] The classic references for the neoclassical growth model are Robert M. Solow, "A Contribution to the Theory of Economic Growth," *Quarterly Journal of Economics,* February 1956, pp. 65–94; and T. Swan, "Economic Growth and Capital Accumulation," *Economic Record,* November 1956, pp. 334–61. James Tobin, "A Dynamic Aggregative Model," *Journal of Political Economy,* April 1955, examined briefly the same model. A more extensive and easy-to-read treatment can be found in R. M. Solow, *Growth Theory An Exposition.* New York: Oxford University Press, 1970.

$$Y = K \cdot f(x) \tag{1b}$$

where x is, of course, N/K. The average product of capital, Y/K, and output, Y, are, respectively, of the forms shown in Figures 16-1a and 16-1b.

Production is carried out by the agents called "firms," which maximize their profits by demanding labor up to the point where the marginal product of labor, MP_N, is equal to the real wage, w. This maximum profit, r, turns out to be equal to the marginal product of capital, MP_K. And the profit-maximizing rule, $MP_N = w$, gives us the demand-for-labor schedule, N^d/K, or MP_N, as shown in the top panel of Figure 16-2.

In the growth literature the assumption is usually made that, in a given (short) period, the supply of labor is a fixed magnitude independent of the level of the real wage. (This supply of labor, per unit of capital, is also shown in the top panel of Figure 16-2.) But we know that a vertical supply of labor is consistent with rational behavior of households; in fact, such a curve is derived when household tastes are homothetic with unitary elasticity of substitution. Usually, this fixed supply of labor (the labor force) is assumed to be the same thing as the population. But even if we make the more realistic assumption that there is a one-to-one relation between the size of population and the labor force, we can still have a vertical supply of labor. We can, therefore, use the terms *supply of labor, labor force,* and *population* interchangeably.

Continuous full employment is guaranteed by an assumption of perfect wage flexibility. In other words, it is assumed that in each instant of time, the real wage, w, is at whatever level is needed to make the demand for labor (per unit of capital), N^d/K—denoted by x—equal to the supply of labor (per unit of capital), which is denoted by $v \equiv N^s/K$. The assumption of full employment is illustrated in the top panel of Figure 16-2. The real wage is instantaneously determined as $\bar{w}$, and the given labor force (per unit of capital), $\bar{v}$, is demanded (by firms); in other words, at $w = \bar{w}$, we have $x = \bar{v} = \bar{x}$. This full employment $\bar{x}$ yields output (and income)

FIGURE 16-1

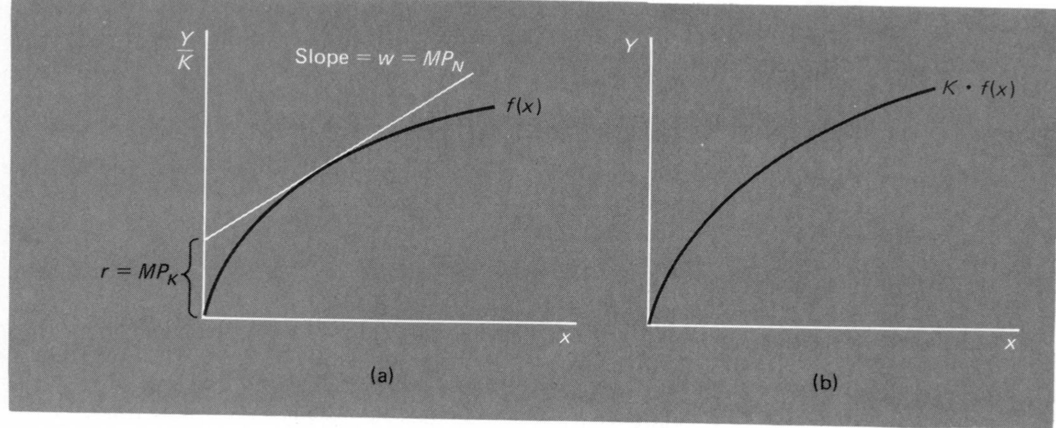

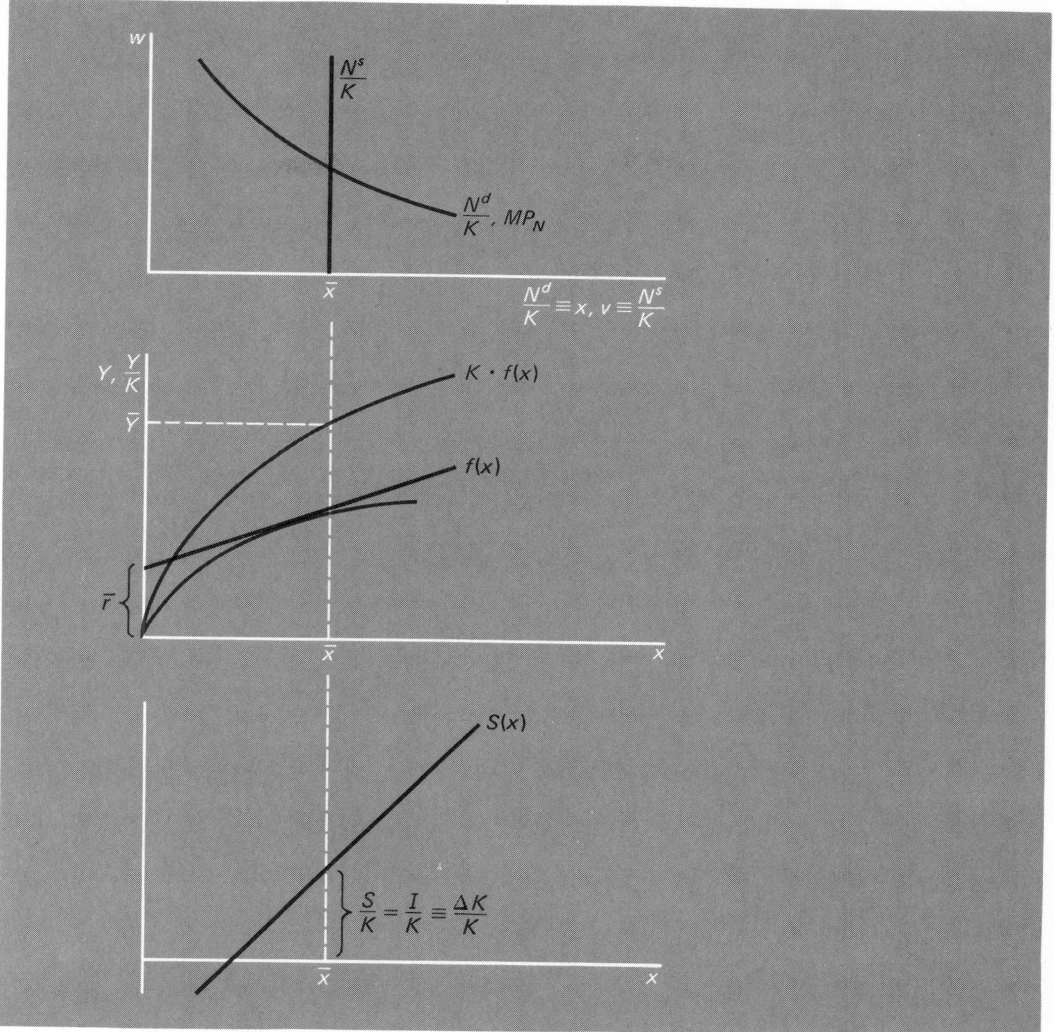

FIGURE 16-2

equal to $\bar{Y}$, as shown in the middle panel of Figure 16-2. In the same panel we can also find the profit rate, $\bar{r}$.

All other magnitudes of interest can be determined once we know the level of x; for example, in the lowest panel of Figure 16-2 we can see that the savings rate, S/K, which is an increasing function, S, of x, as in (2), is $S(\bar{x})$. This in turn, is equal to the rate of investment, I/K, that is, the rate of capital accumulation, $\Delta K/K$, because of the assumption of no borrowing or lending incorporated in (3):

$$\frac{S}{K} = S(x), \tag{2}$$

$$S \equiv I \tag{3}$$

In summary, we can say that in each (short) period of time, the instantaneous clearance of the labor market—brought about by appropriate movements of the real wage—determines employment per unit of capital, x. And knowing x, we can determine all the other important economic magnitudes. Ultimately, then, it is the size of x that matters and requires monitoring through time. Although x is defined as $x \equiv N^d/K$, we can take advantage of the continuous market clearance, $N^d = N^s$, to write

$$x = \frac{N^s}{K} \tag{4}$$

It is also clear that x may change as time passes, since the numerator N^s usually changes because of population growth. On the other hand, the denominator changes primarily because of accumulation of capital through investment. Since we endeavor here to trace the path that the economy may follow, we need only to find the path that x will take; knowing x will permit us to find all the other unknowns. But how will x change? We see that since $x = N^s/K$, there are several reasons why x may increase: The population N^s may grow, for example, while the capital stock K remains the same; K may fall while N^s remains the same; or both may fall, but with K falling proportionately more than N^s. Similarly, x increases if both N^s and K increase, but N^s increases proportionately more than K.

In general, we can write

% change in x = % change in N^s *minus* % change in K

Or, using symbols,

$$\%\Delta x = \%\Delta N^s - \%\Delta K$$

But the percentage change in x is $\Delta x/x$; similarly, $\%\Delta N^s = \Delta N^s/N^s$ and $\%\Delta K = \Delta K/K$. Thus we have the basic *fundamental equation of change:*

$$\frac{\Delta x}{x} = \frac{\Delta N^s}{N^s} - \frac{\Delta K}{K} \tag{5}$$

Notice that equation (5) is applicable to both positive and negative changes. Suppose, for example, that both N^s and K decrease. If $\Delta K/K$ is *absolutely* smaller than $\Delta N^s/N^s$, x will *fall* at the rate $\Delta x/x$. Now, assuming, for example, that $\Delta N^s/N^s = -5\%$ and $\Delta K/K = -3\%$, it follows that $\Delta x/x = -5\% - (-3\%) = -2\%$.

We know that $\Delta N^s/N^s$ is, of course, the rate of population growth. And we shall assume, until further notice, that population grows at a constant rate, n percent per period:

$$\frac{\Delta N^s}{N^s} = n \tag{6}$$

This is a realistic assumption derived from experience. It says, more or less, that population grows as compound interest does:

$$N(t) = N_0(1 + n)^t \tag{7}$$

The population, and thus the labor force, at time t are equal to what originally was N_0 times $(1 + n)$ raised to the power of t. This is the familiar compound interest formula where the "interest rate" is, of course, equal to n.

Let us now take the rate of capital growth, or, as it is called, the rate of capital accumulation, $\Delta K/K$. We note that the change in capital, ΔK, can come about only through investment, I (i.e., $\Delta K = I$). But since we are examining a simple economy, one without borrowing or lending, investment is identically equal to saving, $I \equiv S$ by (3). Dividing both sides by K we get $I/K \equiv S/K$, and thus we have $\Delta K/K = S/K$. Using, then, equation (2) we finally derive

$$\frac{\Delta K}{K} = \frac{S}{K} = S(x) \tag{8}$$

In the literature a particularly simple savings function has been used extensively, namely, it is assumed that savings is a constant fraction of national income:

$$S = s \cdot Y \tag{9}$$

Note that s is, of course, the marginal propensity to save, a number between 0 and 1. If we divide both sides of (9) by K and recall that the average product of capital, Y/K, is $f(x)$, we find that the savings rate is

$$\frac{S}{K} = s \cdot f(x) = S(x) \tag{10}$$

While we shall find occasions to use this special equation (10), we shall start with the general case of (8).

Now, substituting n for $\Delta N^s/N^s$ and $S(x)$ for $\Delta K/K$ in the fundamental equation (5), we have

$$\frac{\Delta x}{x} = n - S(x) \tag{11}$$

This equation will be used extensively below to indicate both the path that the economy will follow and the long-run equilibrium.

CHARACTERISTICS OF EQUILIBRIUM

Long-run equilibrium is found when the employment/capital ratio, x, remains unchanged (i.e., when $\Delta x = 0$). However, it follows from (11) that

$$\Delta x = 0 \quad \text{if, and only if,} \quad n = S(x),$$

that is, the employment/capital ratio (or its inverse, the capital/labor ratio) remains unchanged when the rate of savings (and thus capital accumulation) is equal to the (natural) rate of population growth. The reason is clear; if each potential worker is equipped from infancy with the same amount of capital as are all other workers, the capital per worker (or its inverse) will not change.

Let us now see what happens to the other economic magnitudes when the rate of savings is equal to the rate of population growth. First, both capital and labor change at the same rate, n. Since our production function, $Y = F(K,N)$, exhibits constant returns to scale, it follows that output will be changing at the same rate, n:

$$(1 + n)Y = F[(1 + n)K, (1 + n)N]$$

Moreover, with the national output, Y, equal to national income, the latter will also be changing at the same rate. And since savings, S, is homogeneous of degree one and both income and capital grow at the rate n, savings should also grow at this rate. But what is not saved, that is, consumption, C, must also grow at the same rate. Thus, at long-run equilibrium the following magnitudes grow at the same natural rate, n: population, and thus labor force N^s; capital (K); output (Y); and, in turn, income, consumption (C), and savings (S). This is why economists call this long-run equilibrium *balanced* growth. However, it is sometimes called a *golden age* and often a *steady state.* This latter name is derived from the fact that the labor/capital ratio, x, and thus its inverse, the capital/labor ratio, remain unchanged. Since x remains unchanged, the marginal product of capital (which is equal to the rate of profit, r) and the marginal product of labor (which is equal to the real wage, w) also remain unchanged. (Of course, total wages, wN, and total profits, rK, grow at the rate n.) Moreover, since consumption and population grow at the same rate, it follows that *per capita* consumption remains unchanged, as do *per capita* GNP, income, and savings.

The diagrammatic description of the steady state is very simple, as seen in Figure 16-3, where the horizontal axis depicts x while the vertical axis measures rates of growth (i.e., n and S). Since, at this stage, the population growth rate is

FIGURE 16-3

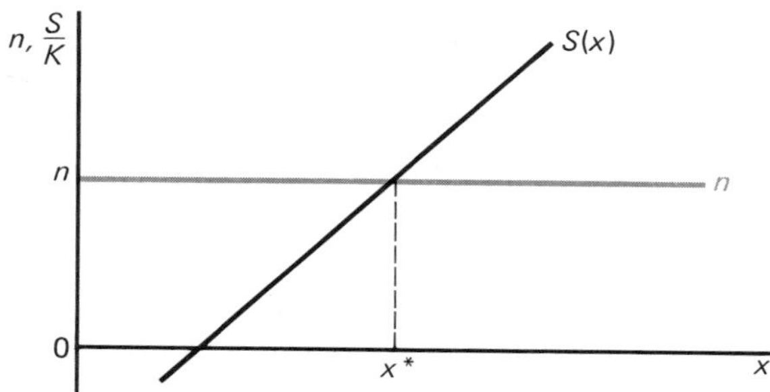

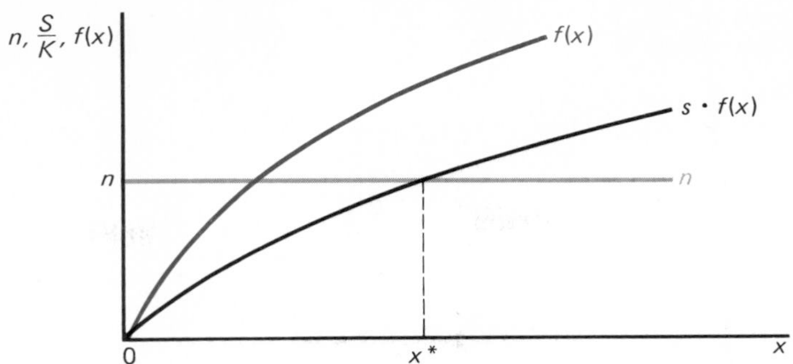

FIGURE 16-4

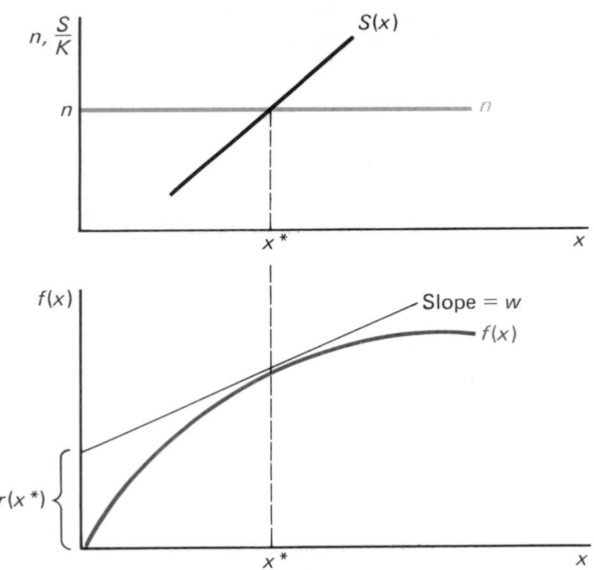

FIGURE 16-5

fixed, independent of x, the curve depicting it is horizontal. On the other hand, savings per unit of capital, S, is an increasing function of x. The intersection of the two curves gives us the steady state, x^*. If we use the special savings function of (10), we have the case depicted in Figure 16-4. Figure 16-5 shows how we can determine the steady-state distribution of income. The upper panel helps us determine, as before, x^*, and the lower panel depicts real-wage and profit rates. Of course, we could present all the information in one graph, but we shall reserve this for the special savings function, $S = s \cdot f(x)$, as in Figure 16-6.

All the preceding results can be derived using the inverse of x, that is, the capital/labor ratio, $k \equiv 1/x = K/N$. If we also use the special savings function, $S = s \cdot Y$, we can find *per capita* savings. Dividing both sides of

$$S = s \cdot F(K,N)$$

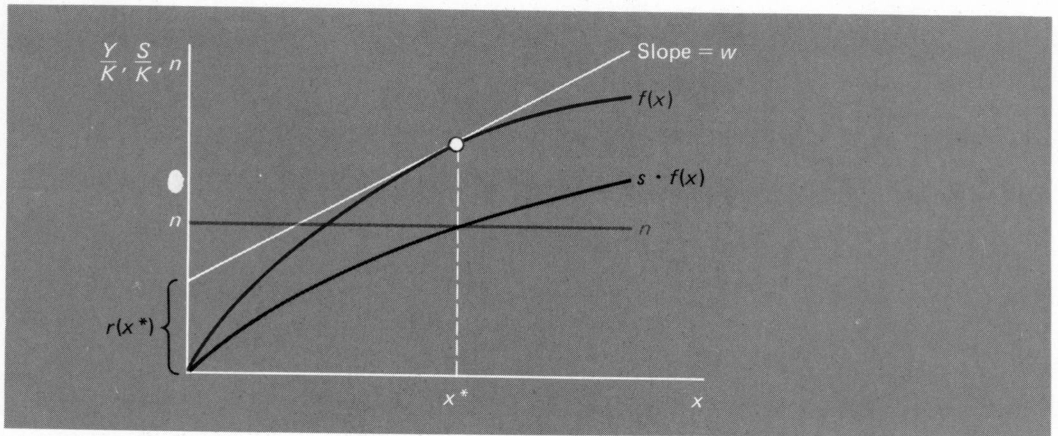

FIGURE 16-6

by N, we have

$$\frac{S}{N} = s \cdot F\left(\frac{K}{N}, 1\right) = s \cdot F(k, 1)$$

by the homogeneity of the production function. Defining $F(k,1) \equiv \phi(k)$, we have the *per capita* savings:

$$\frac{S}{N} = s \cdot \phi(k) \tag{12}$$

Since $S + C \equiv Y$, we know that the marginal propensity to consume, $(\Delta C/\Delta Y) \equiv c$, plus the marginal propensity to save, $(\Delta S/\Delta Y) \equiv s$, is equal to 1, that is, $s + c = 1$. Writing $C = cY$ for total consumption, the *per capita* consumption is given by

$$\frac{C}{N} = c \cdot \phi(k) \tag{13}$$

We are interested in tracing the path that the capital/labor will follow. Since $k \equiv K/N^s$, the rate of change in k is given by (14):

$$\frac{\Delta k}{k} = \frac{\Delta K}{K} - \frac{\Delta N^s}{N^s} \tag{14}$$

As before, at equilibrium, the capital/labor ratio must remain unchanged (i.e., $\Delta k = 0$). But this can only happen if

$$\frac{\Delta K}{K} = \frac{\Delta N^s}{N^s}$$

This, of course, is the same condition we discovered earlier, and we can utilize the same graphical technique as before. However, we shall explicitly examine k. Multiplying both sides of (14) by $k \equiv K/N^s$, we get

$$\Delta k = k \cdot \frac{\Delta K}{K} - \frac{\Delta N^s}{N^s} \cdot \frac{K}{N^s}$$

$$= \frac{K}{N^s} \cdot \frac{\Delta K}{K} - n\frac{K}{N^s}, \quad \text{since} \quad \frac{\Delta N^s}{N^s} \equiv n$$

or

$$k = \frac{\Delta K}{N} - nk$$

But $\Delta K \equiv I \equiv S$. Therefore $(\Delta K/N) \equiv (S/N) = s \cdot \phi(k)$. Substituting in the above equation, we derive as fundamental equation (in k):

$$\Delta k = s \cdot \phi(k) - nk \tag{15}$$

To show the steady-state equilibrium, we use the output-per-head graph derived and examined earlier. Knowing the *per capita* output (for each level of k) and the MPS, s, we can immediately find the $s \cdot \phi(k)$ curve, as in Figure 16-7. On the other hand, it is clear from (15) that $\Delta k = 0$ if, and only if, $s \cdot \phi(k) = nk$. In the same graph we construct the nk line, which is a straight line through the origin with slope equal to n. The intersection of nk and the $s \cdot \phi(k)$ curve gives us the steady-state capital/labor ratio, k^*, which is, of course, exactly equal to the inverse of x^*. And, finally, the steady-state real-wage and profit rates can be shown in the same graph, where the slope of the tangent to $\phi(k)$ at k^* is the profit rate and the

FIGURE 16-7

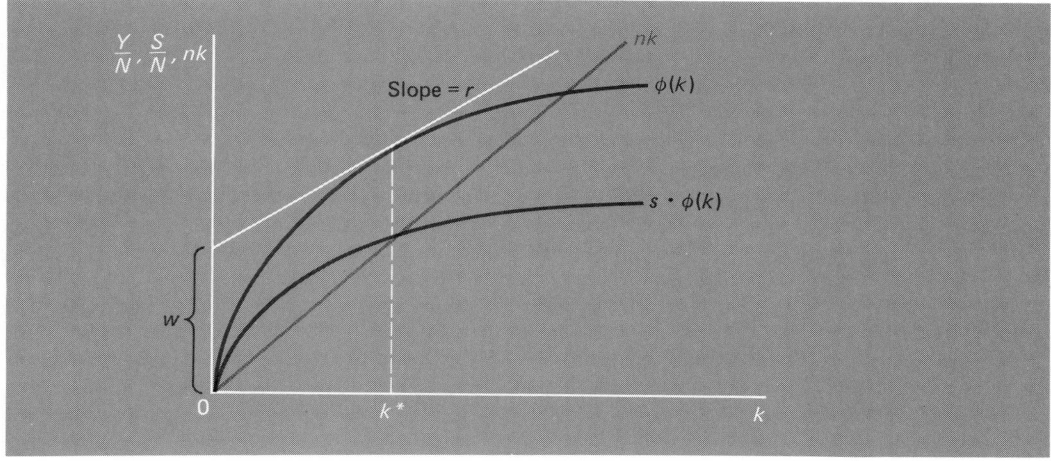

intercept of this line on the vertical axis is the real-wage rate. We shall return to this graph later in this analysis.

STABILITY OF EQUILIBRIUM

We have seen the properties of the steady state. Now a new question arises in the reader's mind, How do we know that the economy will actually reach the equilibrium point? That is, if we suppose that our analysis begins when x is not x^*, are there forces in the economy to lead it to x^*? Let us examine this issue by using Figure 16-8. Assume that the economy starts with a labor/capital ratio equal to x_0. At this x the savings rate, $S(x_0)$, is greater than the population growth rate, n, and the percentage increase in capital is greater than the percentage increase in population (labor force), which raises the capital/labor ratio, that is, it *lowers* x. (Note the arrow pointing toward a lower x and thus in the direction of x^*.) We can verify this result by using the fundamental equation (11):

$$\frac{\Delta x}{x} = n - S(x) \tag{11}$$

At $x = x_0$, $S(x_0) > n$. Therefore the RHS of (11) is negative, and its equal, the LHS of (11), must also be negative (i.e., $\Delta x/x$ must be negative). And since x is always positive, it follows that $\Delta x/x < 0$ implies that $\Delta x < 0$ (i.e., that x *falls*).

Note that as long as x is greater than x^*, the forces we have just described will still exist, and thus x will be falling. Now, if x were to start at a level lower than x^*, say at x_1, we see that S would be lower than the fixed n. (Recall that S falls when x falls.) Now the RHS of (11) is positive, implying that its LHS is positive, which means that x is rising, as indicated by the arrow that now points toward a higher x, toward x^*. Therefore we have proved that in the case of Figure 16-8 the equilibrium will eventually be reached and that the system is stable.

FIGURE 16-8

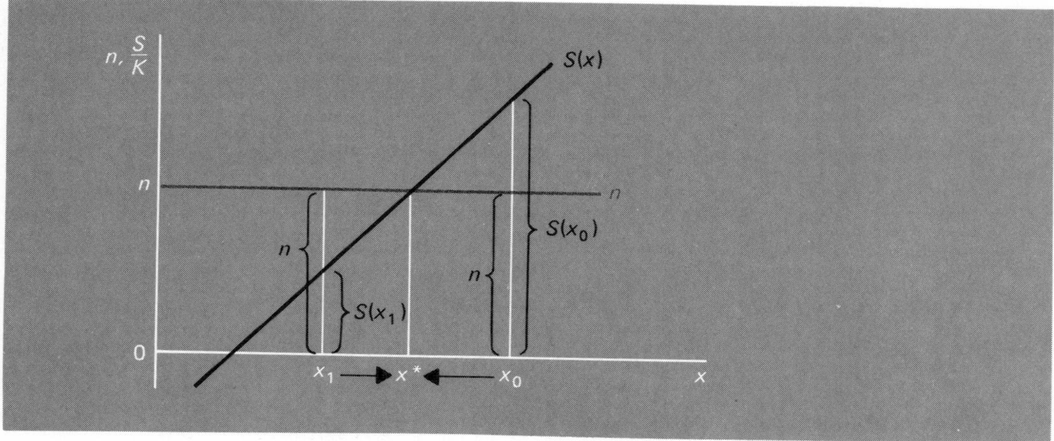

This issue, whether the system is stable or unstable, has been associated with the economic prospects of capitalism, which (capitalism) the model is purported to represent. If the system is stable, capitalism is in good shape. If the system is unstable, capitalism needs a "shot in the arm." Otherwise it is doomed. This interpretation of the issue of stability is attributed to the original work on the topic by Harrod and Domar, who claimed that the system exhibited instability (or "knife-edge stability").[5]

There are other more important reasons why we should inquire into the stability of the system. First, stability is needed to show the consistency of the various assumptions that we made in setting up the model; it is the logical consistency of the *model* we are testing by examining stability and not primarily the stability of the *real world!* We observe that the real world does not exhibit a galloping (upward or downward) employment/capital ratio, but our model must show this if it is going to be consistent.

A few more words about the logical consistency of any model are in order here. With a model we have the audacity to represent the actual, complicated world. But before we even attempt to empirically test our model, we must make sure that the array of assumptions we have made are not mutually inconsistent. There are two tests of consistency, namely, the existence test and the stability test, both of which have to be performed by the economist. First, since we examine equilibrium, we must make sure that an equilibrium actually *exists* in our model. If it does not exist, it means that our assumptions are inconsistent. This is the existence test. Next we must inquire whether the equilibrium can be reached; if it cannot be reached, it is the same as if it does not exist. This is the stability test. We should mention here that the existence of an equilibrium is guaranteed in *our* model above, because of the way the n and S curves are drawn, one is horizontal and the other upward sloping. Sooner or later they will cross each other for a *positive* level of x.

Furthermore, we want a model that can be used for comparative statics, or dynamics. We want to examine alternative equilibria that correspond to different policies or to different circumstances. We may want to achieve, for example, a different equilibrium by shifting either the S or the n curve. If the equilibrium is stable, the new equilibrium is achievable. If it is unstable in the first place, it will never be reached. In the latter case, why, then, would we try for a new equilibrium, say, through a deliberate economic policy, if we know that we can never reach it? This crucial relation between stability and policy-induced, alternative equilibria forces us to make sure that the system is stable. (Note: There are, of course, cases for which the real world shows instability. In those cases the economist's aim is twofold: first, to design a model exhibiting instability; and second, to design policies that can turn the model from an unstable to a stable one.)

We have already seen that the model represented by Figure 16-8 is stable. Suppose, instead, that savings per unit of capital S were a decreasing function of x. It is an easy matter, then, to show that the resulting model would be unstable. Take

---

[5] See R. F. Harrod, "An Essay in Dynamic Theory," *Economic Journal,* March 1939; and "Lecture Three" in *Towards a Dynamic Economics.* London: Macmillan, 1948. Also E. Domar, "Capital Expansion, Rate of Growth and Employment," *Econometrica,* 1946.

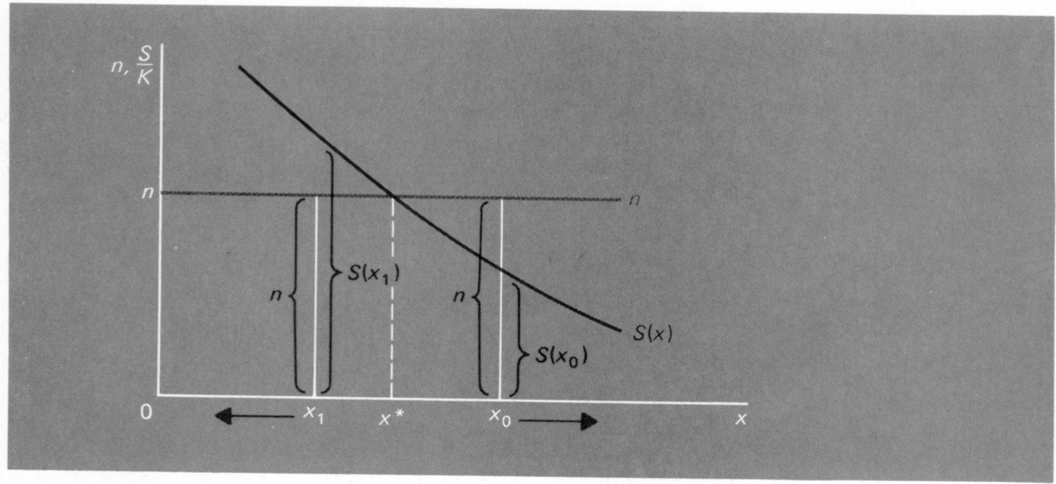

FIGURE 16-9

Figure 16-9 and suppose that initially the employment/capital ratio is higher than the equilibrium one, say $x = x_0 > x^*$. At x_0 the population growth rate, n, is greater than S. The economy "produces" more workers than capital, and thus the labor/capital ratio will increase. The movement, therefore, is away from, and not toward, the equilibrium point x^*, as shown by the arrow in the graph. If, on the other hand, x is initially below x^*, say at x_1, S would be greater than n, and thus x would be falling. Again the movement would be *away* from the equilibrium point. And we see that the equilibrium cannot be reached and that the system is unstable.

We saw that the case depicted in Figure 16-8 is stable and that the case depicted in Figure 16-9 is unstable. But how likely is this latter case? Not very; savings per unit of capital can be a decreasing function of x only if the MPS is negative, which is impossible.

STABILITY AND UNDERDEVELOPED COUNTRIES

Still we are not out of the woods; suppose that the rate of population growth is an increasing function of x rather than a fixed rate. Some neo-Malthusian theory of population, for example, might lie behind such a stipulation. In this case the system is stable if, when x increases, the savings rate, S, increases more than the population growth rate, n, does. If, on the other hand, when x increases, the population growth rate, n, increases more than the savings rate, S, the system is unstable. Figure 16-10 shows the stable case. At the equilibrium point x^*, the S curve is steeper than the n curve. Note that if, initially, x is equal to x_0, S is greater than n, and thus x tends to fall toward the equilibrium point x^*. If, on the other hand, x was lower than x^*, say at x_1, the population growth rate would be greater than the savings rate, inducing an increase in x. Thus, everywhere the movement is toward equilibrium.

Figure 16-11 depicts the case when the population growth rate increases

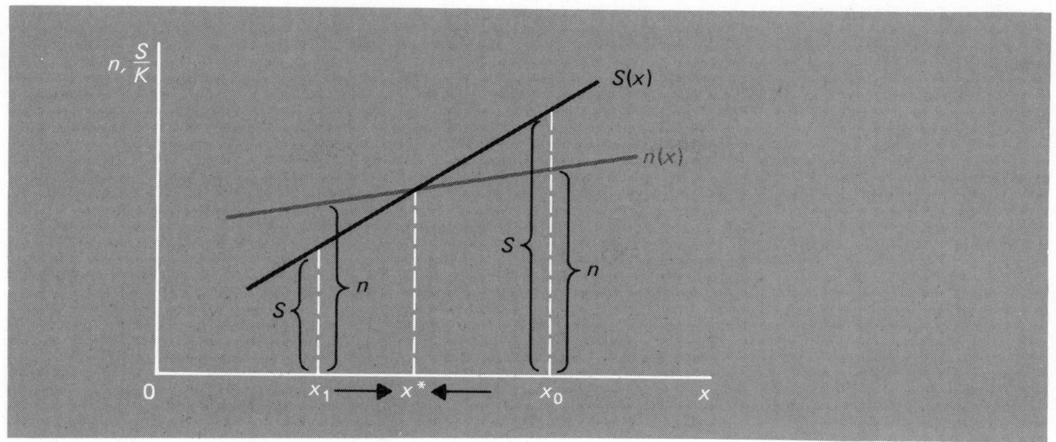

FIGURE 16-10

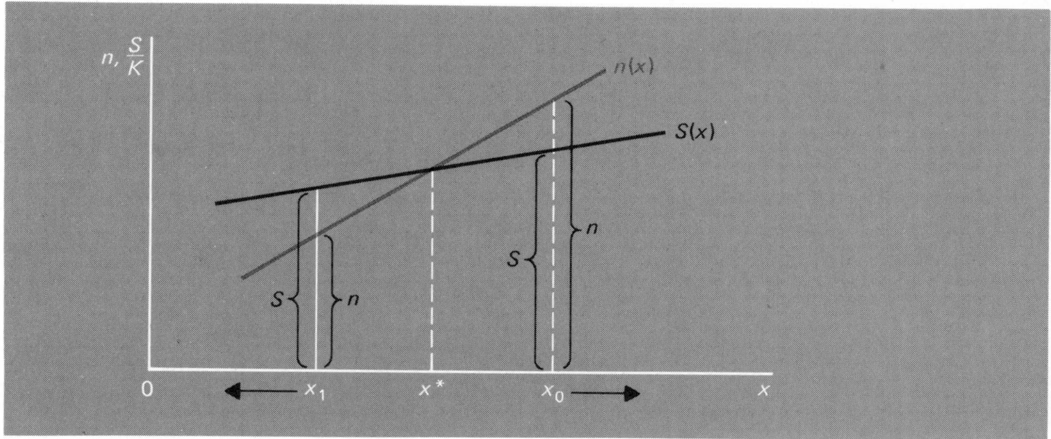

FIGURE 16-11

more than the rate of capital growth. The system is unstable. This case can help explain the predicament of countries with very high rates of population growth. Of course, it is conceivable that the system may have more than one equilibrium, such as the one in Figure 16-12, which depicts a case with two steady-state equilibria: Point *A* giving x^* is a stable equilibrium, whereas point *B* is an unstable one. If a country has an employment/capital ratio greater than x^{**} (i.e., a *very low* capital/labor ratio), we say that the country is in a *low capital trap.*[6] The term *trap* is used to point out that the country cannot increase its capital intensity (i.e., it cannot *lower* its employment/capital ratio). With $x = x_0$, for example, n is greater than S, which implies that x will *rise,* say to x_1. At the new level, x_1, again n is greater

[6] See R. R. Nelson, "A Theory of the Low Level Equilibrium Trap in Underdeveloped Economies," *American Economic Review,* December 1956.

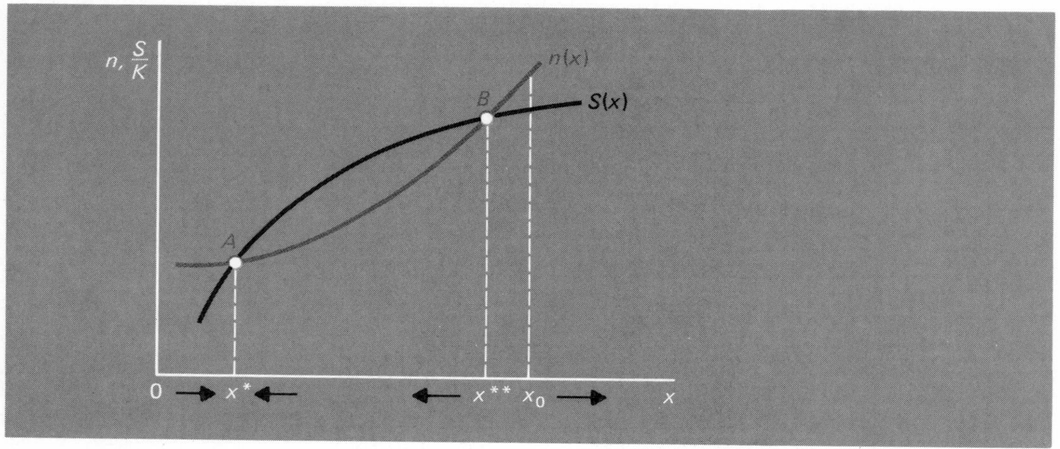

FIGURE 16-12

than S, causing a further rise in x. An unstable equilibrium, like point B of Figure 16-12, can explain the "low capital trap," a characteristic of underdeveloped countries. But such countries have additional characteristics, *per capita* GNP and *per capita* national income are very low and continue to fall. This is referred to in the literature as a "low income trap," which can also be explained by an unstable equilibrium like B. When x keeps increasing away from x^{**}, its inverse ($k \equiv 1/x$) keeps falling. But we know that output and income *per capita*, Y/N, are positively related to the capital/labor ratio, k. Thus, as k continues to fall, the *per capita* income also is falling, as shown in Figure 16-13. Moreover, since *per capita* consumption is an increasing function of *per capita* income, that is, $C/N = c \cdot \phi(k)$, *per capita* consumption also continues to fall.

Furthermore, we observe that in such underdeveloped countries the wage rate is low and keeps falling while the rate of profit is high and keeps rising, characteristics that can also be explained by an unstable equilibrium. When x continues to rise (to the right of x^{**} of Figure 16-12), the marginal product of labor, which

FIGURE 16-13

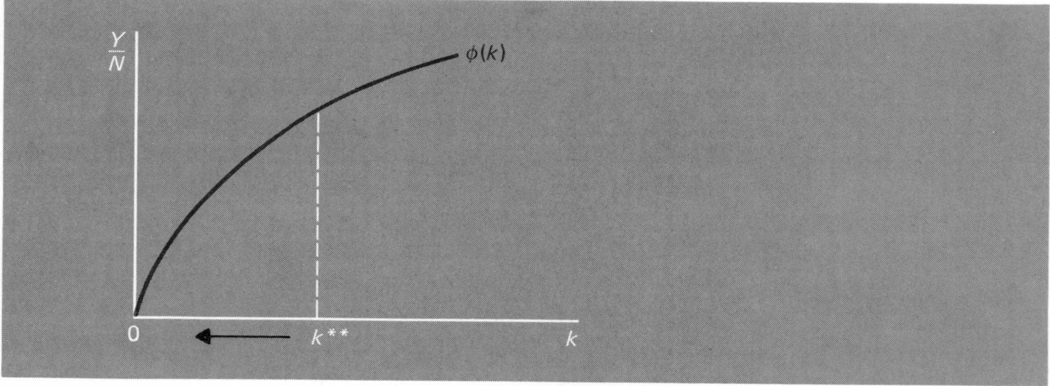

equals the real wage, continues to fall and the marginal product of capital, which is the profit rate, continues to rise. Capital is scarce and becomes even scarcer, thereby commanding ever higher reward. While the society's capital stock is small, those few who own it become extremely wealthy. This is why, in the midst of misery, one can see some very wealthy individuals. Of course, this display of wealth, in the midst of misery, breeds discontent and political instability, which, in turn, prevents foreign capital from flowing into the country to take advantage of a higher rate of profit than the one in the developed countries. The political instability makes foreign investment a very risky business.

The many remedies usually recommended, and sometimes even attempted, will not be examined, since they are outside of the scope of this book. Nevertheless we shall mention one, foreign aid, since it is directly related to our discussion of stability. If foreign aid is given to a country, say, in the form of capital, then $x = N/K$ falls (because the denominator, K, rises). If sufficient aid is given to this country, so that x falls *below* x^{**}, the economy will be driven (by itself) to the "good," the stable equilibrium A of Figure 16-12.

In summary, if we want our model to exhibit stability (as we do here), we must assume that an increase in x increases savings per unit of capital, S, to a greater degree than it increases the rate of population growth, n. In what follows we assume that n is independent of x, which guarantees the satisfaction of this condition for stability.

COMPARATIVE DYNAMICS

We now return to the simple world of a fixed rate of population growth. Suppose, for concreteness, that, at the outset, the given rate of population growth is n_0, as in the upper panel of Figure 16-14. The steady-state x is then equal to x_0. In the lower panel we find the profit rate r_0 and wage rate w_0. Now suppose that the rate of population growth is permanently reduced to a new fixed level, such as n_1, say, because of the efforts of the "zero population growth" advocates. The new steady state, which is achievable because the system is stable, will have a permanently lower employment/capital ratio, x_1 in Figure 16-14. But we cannot say yet whether the new steady-state is preferable to (i.e., better than) the old one giving x_0. However, we do have a strong basis for saying which people will get hurt and which will benefit from the change. It is clear from the lower panel of Figure 16-14 that the new steady-state labor intensity, x_1, will yield lower profits and a higher wage rate. Presumably, other things being equal (and if the assumptions and stipulations of our model are satisfied), the labor unions would be in favor of such a reduction of the rate of population growth, but members of the Chamber of Commerce would be against it.

Suppose, again, that we start with n at n_0 and that, consequently, the steady state, x, is at x_0. Now suppose that people are persuaded, say, by a modern-day Benjamin Franklin, to consume less for each level of x and thus of income. This has the effect of shifting the S curve to the left (because saving is higher for each x) —from $S_0(x)$ to $S_1(x)$ in Figure 16-15. These results are similar in all respects to those of the preceding exercise, the lowering of n. In particular, the steady-state x

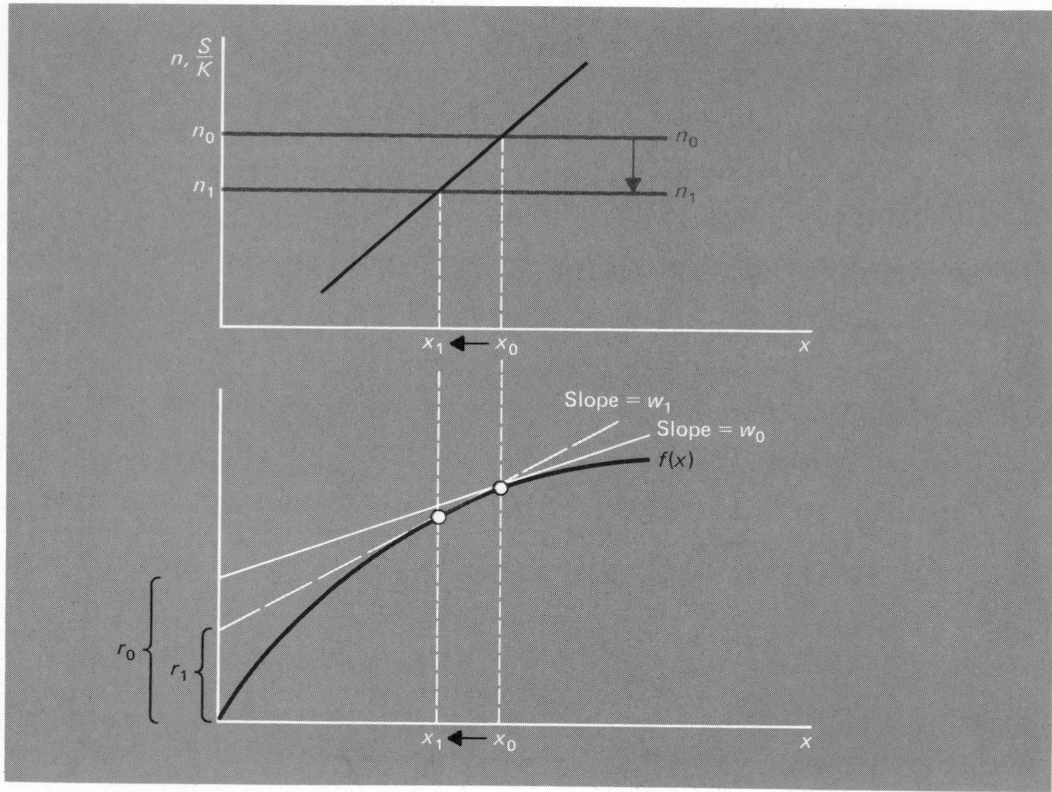

FIGURE 16-14

is lower at x_1, and thus the profit falls (to r_1) while the wage rate rises (to w_1) permanently. Again, presumably the owners of capital would be against such a move, whereas workers would favor it. Here the caution regarding fulfillment of the assumptions of the model is even more pertinent than in the preceding exercise. Most important is the assumption that the economy guarantees full employment of its labor force. *When we relax this assumption, we see that workers will not, in general, be in favor of an increase in the propensity to save.* We have already devoted a good deal of this book to examining this latter result, which revolutionized economic theory in the 1930s.

We can show the results above in the graph that uses the capital/labor ratio, k. We assume, in this case, that s, the MPS, increases from s_0 to s_1, which shifts the savings-per-head curve from $s_0 \cdot \phi(k)$ to $s_1 \cdot \phi(k)$ in Figure 16-16.

OPTIMAL GROWTH

The second of the two comparative dynamic exercises above suggests that the government can influence the steady-state capital/labor ratio, as well as the distribution of income. For example, it can modify the tax structure of the economy, thereby changing

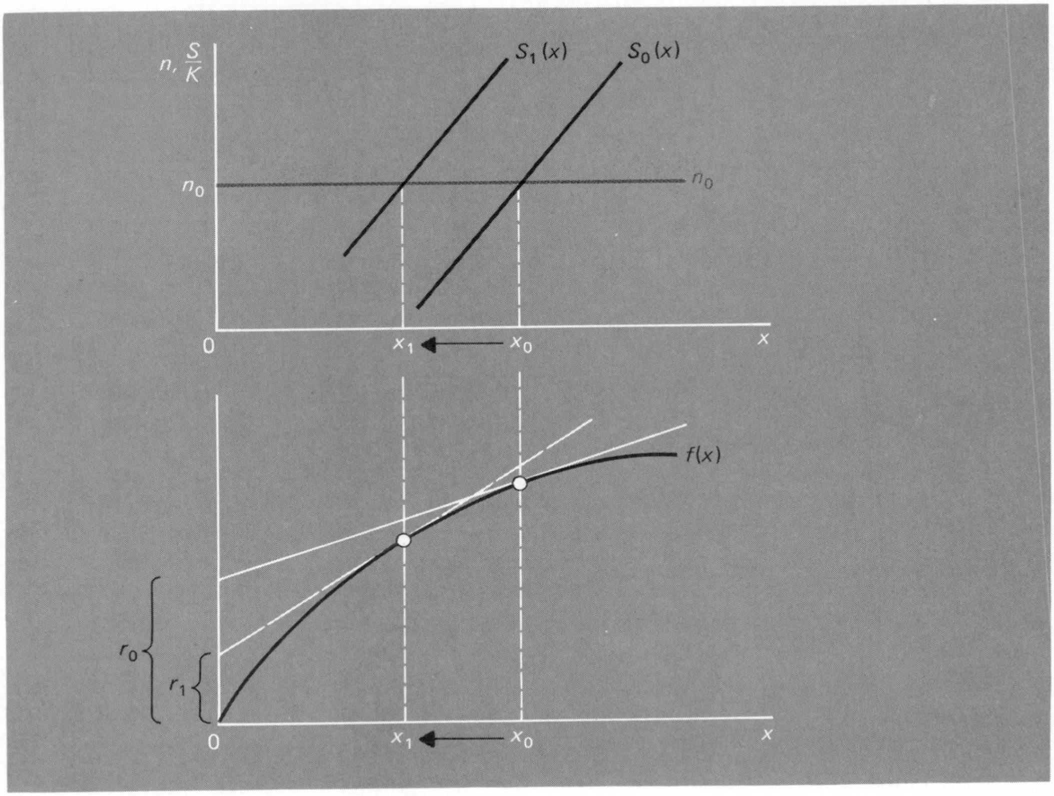

FIGURE 16-15

FIGURE 16-16

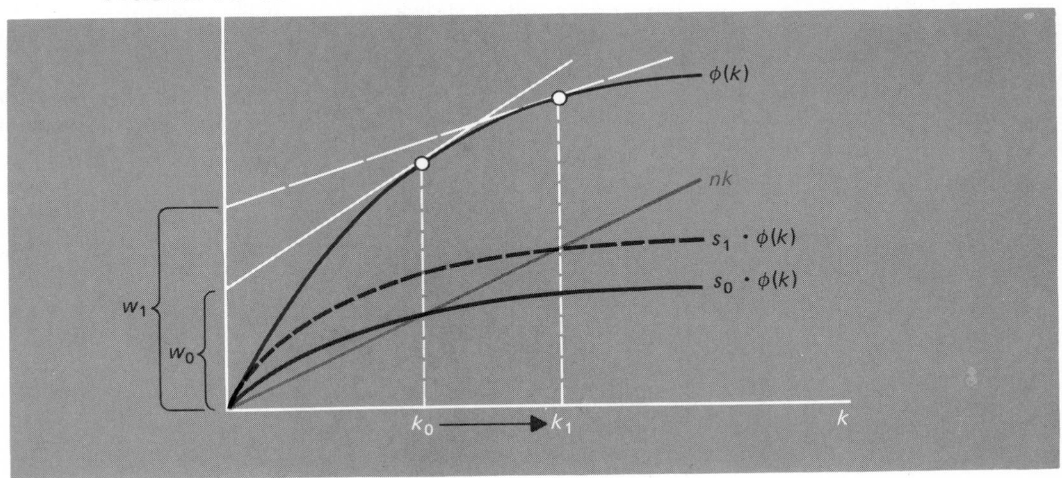

s, which shifts the S curve. But if the government can influence the steady state, k, it can also influence *per capita* income and *per capita* consumption. Now, since it is clear that there is an infinity of possible k's, one for each assumed governmental policy, the obvious question arises, Which one k is the *best?* This is a question for which the policy maker would surely like an answer. But, in order to provide such an answer, we need to know the criterion used for ranking possible steady-state paths. If the accepted criterion is consumption per head—presumably because it provides a measure of the individual's (and thus the society's) welfare—it is fairly easy to find the answer to this question; we simply must find that path that yields the highest consumption per head, C/N.

The answer can be found a lot faster if we use the model in terms of k rather than its inverse, x. We want to find the steady state that gives the highest C/N. But the steady state has the characteristic, according to (15), that $s \cdot \phi(k) = nk$, which can be rewritten as $(1 - c)\phi(k) = nk$ (since $s + c \equiv 1$). Rearranging, we have $c \cdot \phi(k) = \phi(k) - nk$. But the LHS of this last equation is equal to C/N, as we have already seen in equation (13). It follows, then that the RHS is also equal to C/N and that we have just derived the formula for *per capita* consumption:

$$\frac{C}{N} = \phi(k) - nk \tag{16}$$

We can also find C/N graphically, as in Figure 16-17. We begin by drawing a straight line through the origin with slope equal to the rate of population growth, n. We then draw the production function as output per head, $Y/N = \phi(k)$. It is now easy to find C/N for a given k; all we have to do is vertically subtract nk from $\phi(k)$. For example, if $k = k_0 = OA$, we subtract $AB \equiv nk_0$ from $AC \equiv \phi(k_0)$. According to (16), this difference, equal to CB, is precisely the consumption per head, C/N, if $k = k_0$. Repeating this process, we see that as k increases, starting from zero, consumption per head, C/N, increases up to a point, and that it then decreases, becoming zero when $k = \bar{k}$. If we like, we can depict this information in a separate graph, as in Figure 16-18, which shows all the possible levels of *per capita* consumption that can last indefinitely. It is clear that the highest steady state,

FIGURE 16-17

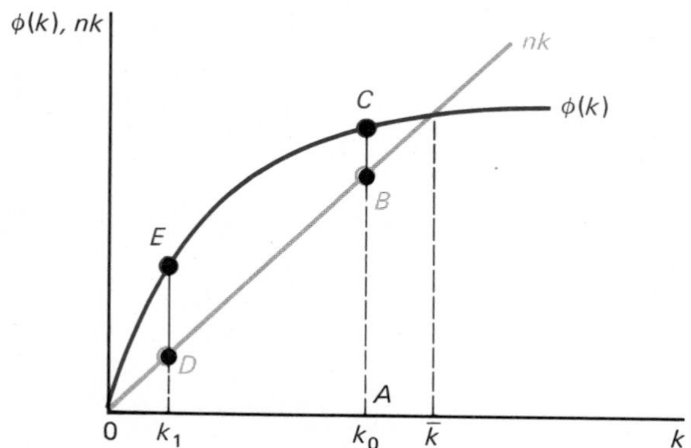

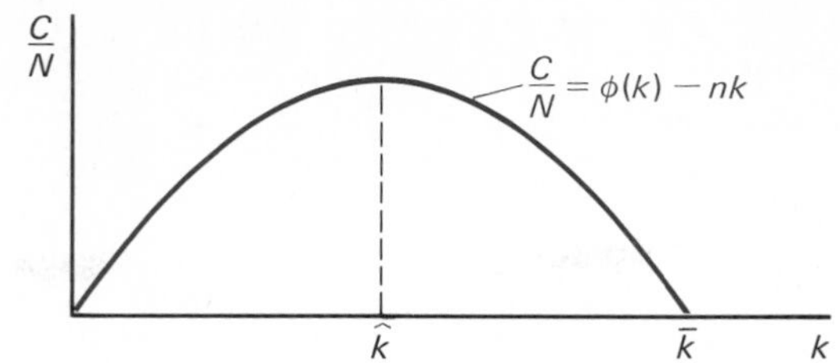

FIGURE 16-18

C/N, occurs when $k = \hat{k}$, as in Figure 16-18. This capital/labor ratio, the one that gives the highest *per capita* consumption, can be found in a graph similar to Figure 16-17, where we must find the highest vertical difference between $\phi(k)$ and nk. According to the familiar graphical rule, this occurs when k is such that the slope of $\phi(k)$ is equal to the slope of nk, as shown in Figure 16-19. When $k = \hat{k}$, FG is the highest possible permanent consumption per head.

The graphical rule gives us the crucial characteristic of this "best" steady state. For this $\hat{k}$, the slope of $\phi(k)$, which is, of course, the rate of profit, must equal the slope of nk, which is the rate of population growth. It follows, then, that the steady state with the highest C/N occurs when *the rate of profit is equal to the rate of population growth,* $MP_k = n$.

However, we still must guarantee that $\hat{k}$ will be derived by an intersection of the nk curve and an $s \cdot \phi(k)$ curve in the manner, say, of Figure 16-7. This necessitates finding an s, call it $\hat{s}$, such that $\hat{s} \cdot \phi(\hat{k}) = n\hat{k}$. In other words, knowing $\hat{k}$, the government must design its taxation, say, in such a manner that the resulting s will give us an $s \cdot \phi(k)$ curve that crosses the nk curve at precisely the level $\hat{k}$, as shown in Figure 16-20.

We can describe the same results with a graph that uses the employment/capital ratio, x. First, call the x that yields the maximum C/N, $\hat{x}$. Since it is a steady-state x, it must be derived from the intersection of an nn curve and an $S(x) \equiv s \cdot f(x)$ curve, in a manner similar to that of Figure 16-6. On the other hand, the rate of profit is represented by the intercept (on the vertical axis) of a tangent

FIGURE 16-19

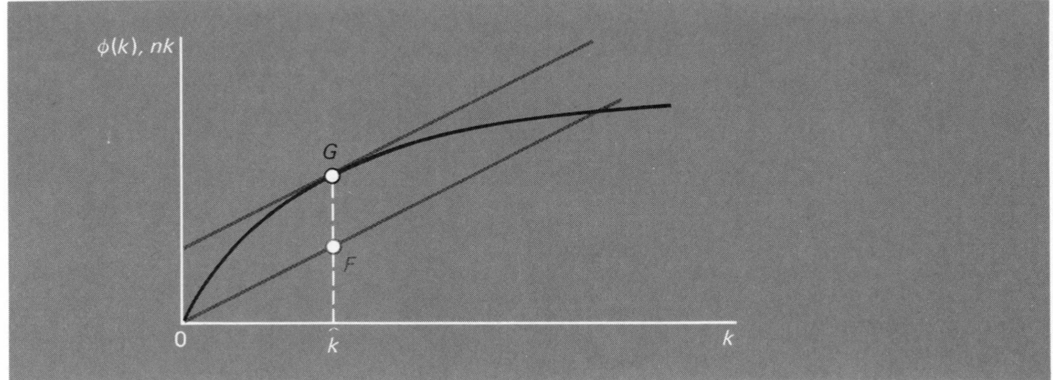

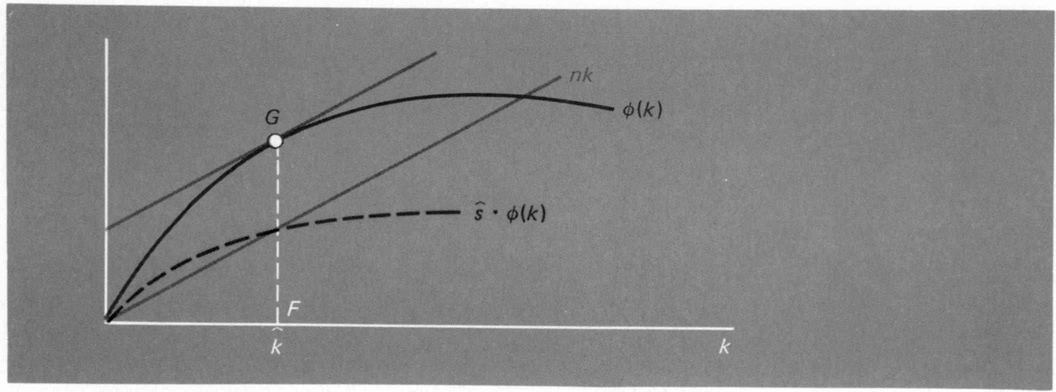

FIGURE 16-20

to the $f(x)$ curve. And this rate of profit must be equal to n. It follows, then, that the intersection of the $\hat{s} \cdot f(x)$ and the nn curves should occur at $\hat{x}$, which has the following property, that the tangent of $f(\hat{x})$ has an intercept on the vertical axis equal to n. This is shown in Figure 16-21.

The steady state with the highest consumption per head has been labeled the *golden rule* steady state.[7] The golden rule itself maintains that the rate of profit should be made equal to the rate of population growth. (Note: One should not confuse the "golden rule" steady state with the "golden age".)

Let us now suppose that an economy has reached a steady state in which k is *greater* than $\hat{k}$. Such an economy was shown (by Phelps and Koopmans) to be *dynamically inefficient.*[8] To make it *dynamically efficient* the policy maker must lower s, thus shifting the $s \cdot \phi(k)$ curve inward (toward the k-axis) so that a lower k may be achieved, as shown in Figure 16-22. This is a movement in the optimal direction.

But we are now faced with another problem. When k is reduced (from k_0 to $\hat{k}$ in Figure 16-22), the rate of profit increases while the real wage falls. And, obviously, the owners of capital will benefit while workers will lose. Knowing this, how can we say, then, that this steady state is preferred over the earlier one? Do we consider workers "second-class citizens?" Since we do not, we are saying that the movement from k_0 to $\hat{k}$ is in the optimal direction in the sense that if the capitalists compensate the workers for their losses, the capitalists will still be better off than before. It is in this sense that the golden rule steady state is "optimal." (Note: If $k < \hat{k}$, the steady state may not be dynamically *inefficient* in the *general case.*)[9]

---

[7] See E. S. Phelps, "The Golden Rule of Accumulation: A Fable for Growthmen," *American Economic Review,* September 1961, pp. 638–43; Joan Robinson, "A Neoclassical Theorem," *Review of Economic Studies,* June 1962, pp. 219–26; and C. C. von Weizsacker, *Wachstum, Zins und Optimale Investifionsquote* (Basel: Kyklos-Verlag, 1962).

[8] See E. S. Phelps, "Second Essay on the Golden Rule of Accumulation," *American Economic Review,* September 1965, pp. 793–814.

[9] See, for example, F. P. Ramsey, "A Mathematical Theory of Saving," *Economic Journal,* December 1978, pp. 543–59. Also T. C. Koopmans, "On the Concept of Optimal Economic Growth," in *Scripta Varia,* pp. 225–87. Vatican City: Pontifical Academy of Sciences, 1965.

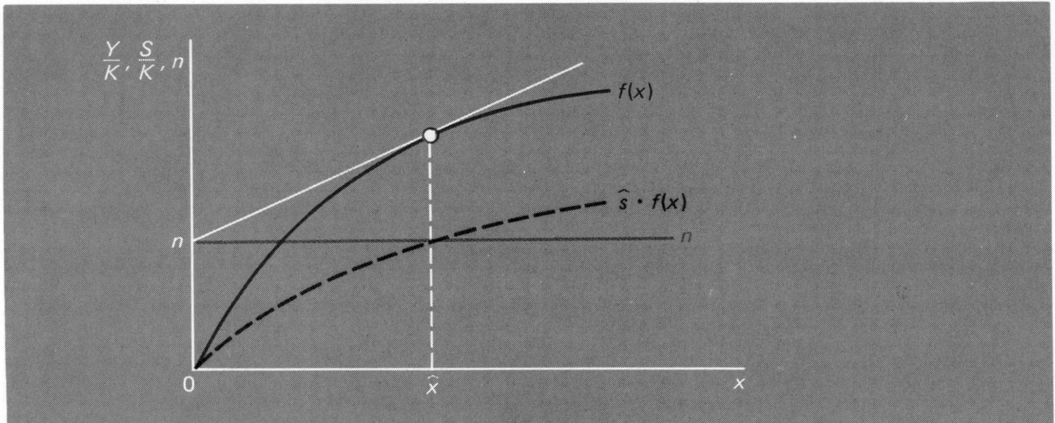

FIGURE 16-21

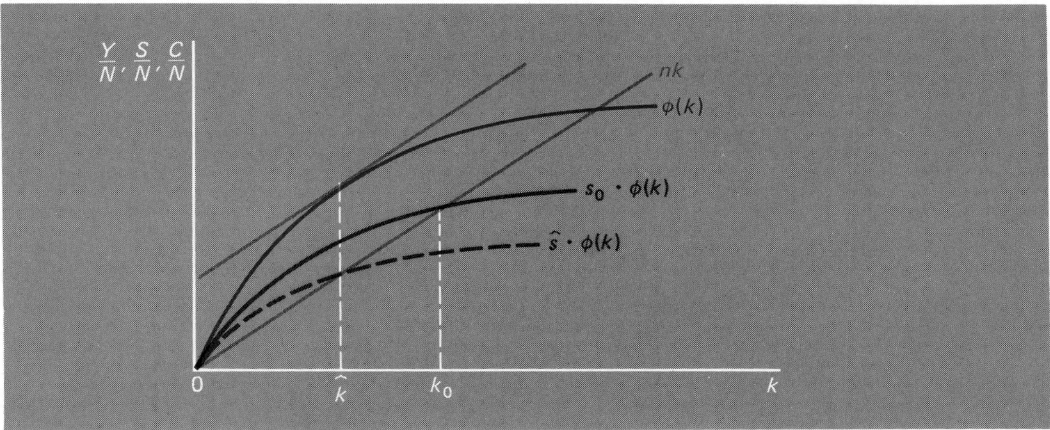

FIGURE 16-22

II. GROWTH WITH BORROWING AND LENDING

We shall now explicitly introduce borrowing and lending to see what modifications, if any, our analysis and results need. The first implication of borrowing and lending is the possible dependence of the savings rate, S/K, on the interest rate as well as on the employment, per unit of capital, x, as in (17):

$$\frac{S}{K} = S(i,x), \quad \frac{\Delta S}{\Delta i} \gtreqless 0, \quad \frac{\Delta S}{\Delta x} > 0 \tag{17}$$

In the most frequently mentioned case, there is a positive relation between savings and the interest rate. Of course, our earlier result, that the savings rate depends

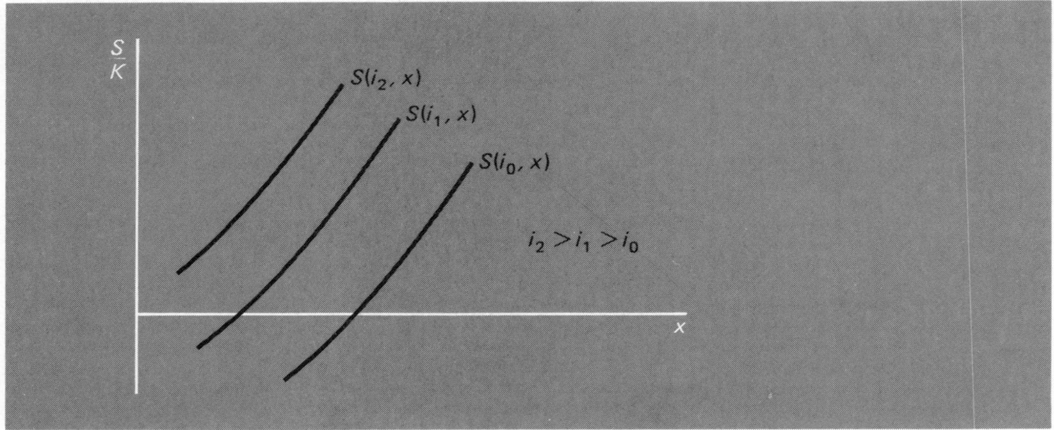

FIGURE 16-23

positively on x, still holds. We can depict (17) graphically, as in Figure 16-23: Given the interest rate, the S curve is upward sloping with respect to x. Moreover, there are an infinite number of S curves, one for each assumed level of i; the higher i is, the farther to the left the S curve will lie.

There is another way to depict (17) graphically. It is exemplified in Figure 16-24, where the explicit independent variable is now i, while x enters implicitly, parametrically. Given x, there is (normally) a positive relation between S/K and i. Moreover, there is an infinity of S curves, one for each assumed level of x; the higher x is, the farther to the right the S curve will lie.

The introduction of borrowing and lending separates the decisions (by the firms) to invest from the decisions (by the households) to save: One can invest more than one saves (by borrowing the difference); and vice versa, one can invest less

FIGURE 16-24

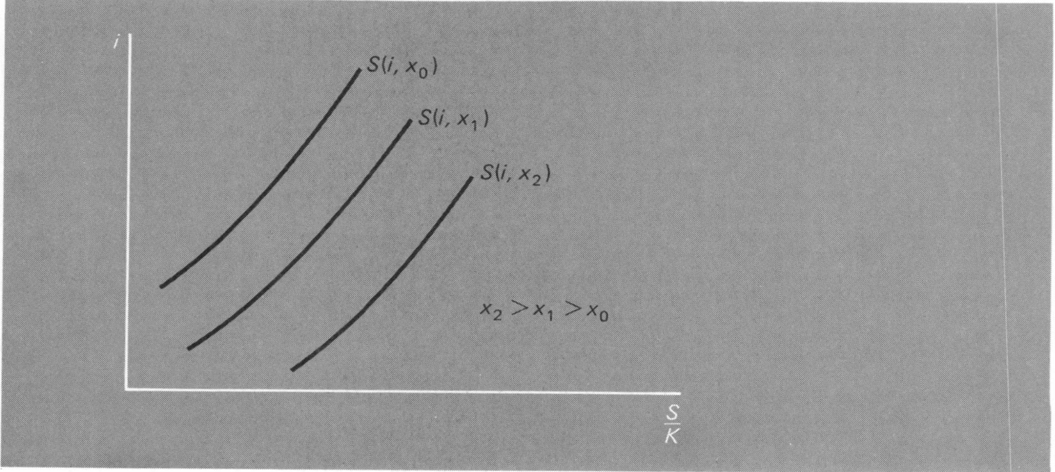

than one saves (by lending the difference). Investment is undertaken by firms that are assumed to finance it by borrowing. Investment is, therefore, negatively related to the interest rate—which is the cost of borrowing—and positively related to the rate of (prospective) profit and, therefore, positively related to x. Furthermore, an exogenous parameter, the risk premium, σ, influences investment negatively. In summary, we have investment, per unit of capital:

$$\frac{I}{K} = I(i,x;\sigma), \quad \frac{\Delta I}{\Delta i} < 0, \quad \frac{\Delta I}{\Delta x} > 0, \quad \frac{\Delta I}{\Delta \sigma} < 0 \tag{18}$$

In the (i,I)-plane—i.e., when i is the explicit independent variable—the investment curve is downward sloping, as in Figure 16-25, and when x rises the curve

FIGURE 16-25

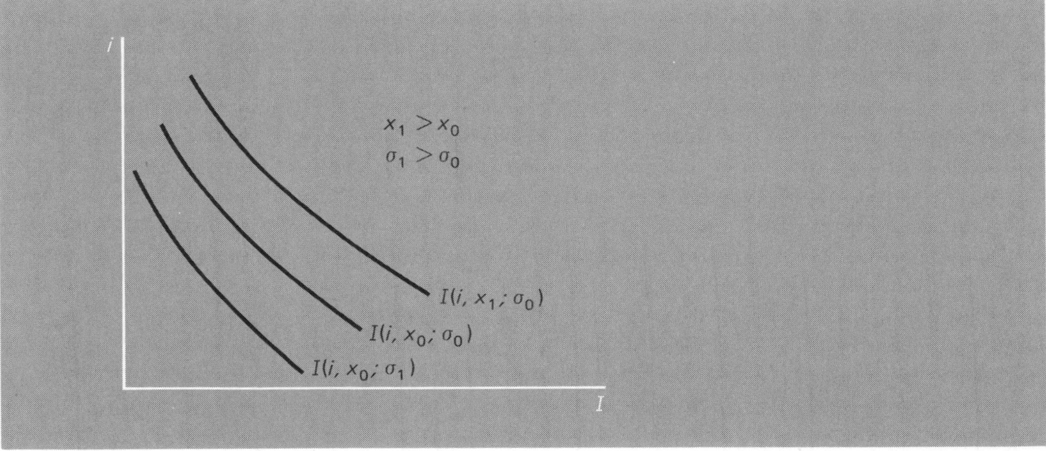

FIGURE 16-26

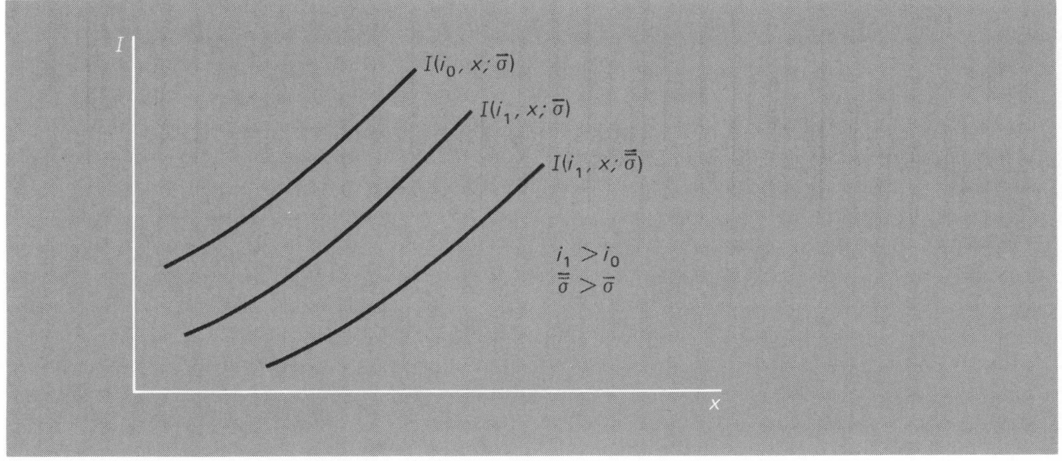

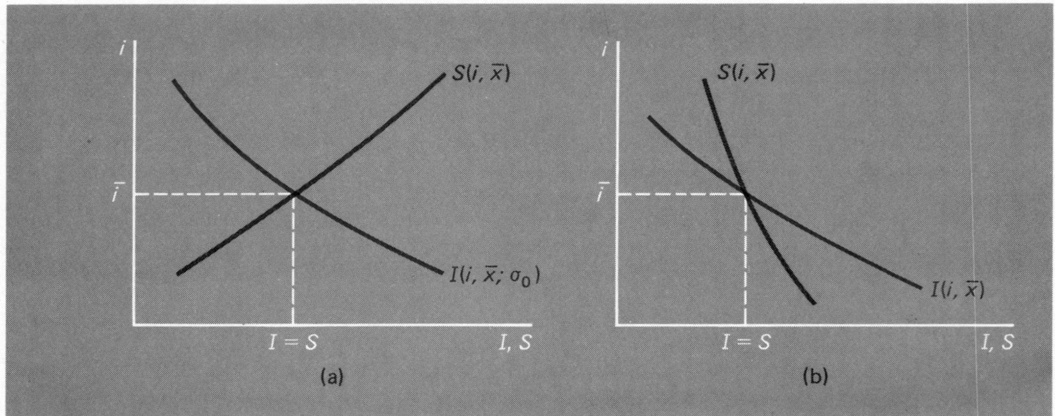

FIGURE 16-27

shifts to the right; when the risk premium rises, the I curve shifts to the left. In the (x,I)-plane, the I curve is upward sloping; the curve shifts to the right when either i or σ rises, as in Figure 16-26. In other words, there is an infinity of I curves, one for each implicitly taken variable.

Another implication of borrowing and lending is the existence of a loans (or credit) market that determines the interest rate. In each period of time, given the full-employment level of x, say $\bar{x}$, we can find (from graphs similar to Figures 16-24 and 16-26, respectively) the relevant pair of S and I curves. The I curve is the demand for loans, and the S curve is the supply of loans (as functions of the rate of interest). By an extreme version of the "law of supply and demand," it is assumed that the interest rate moves rapidly to clear the loans market instantaneously, that is, to bring about equality (19). In Figure 16-27a this clearance of the loans

$$I(i,\bar{x};\sigma) = S(i,\bar{x}) \tag{19}$$

market is achieved at an interest rate equal to $\bar{i}$. This equality can be achieved even with a downward-sloping S curve, provided that it is steeper than the I curve, as in Figure 16-27b. This restriction can be written as

$$\frac{\Delta I}{\Delta i} < \frac{\Delta S}{\Delta i}$$

Of course, equality between investment and savings implies also that aggregate demand for goods and services is equal to aggregate supply, Y. In other words, the clearance of the loans market implies clearance of the goods and services market. Since the labor market is also cleared instantaneously—by an appropriate movement of the real wage—it follows that, in our model, all three markets are continuously cleared in each period of time.

We are now ready to allow x to vary through time as population (and thus the labor force) grows and as capital accumulates with investing. As earlier, we use the equality $x = N^s/K$ and derive the percentage change of x as

$$\frac{\Delta x}{x} = \frac{\Delta N^s}{N^s} - \frac{\Delta K}{K} \tag{5}$$

Also, as earlier, we assume that the population (and thus the labor force) rises at the exponential rate n, that is, we assume that $\Delta N^s/N^s = n$. On the other hand, the change in capital, ΔK equals investment, I:

$$\frac{\Delta K}{K} = \frac{I}{K} \equiv I(i,x)$$

However, we know that in every period of time all markets are cleared. In particular, the loans market is cleared, which implies that always

$$I(i,x) = S(i,x)$$

Substituting in the above equation of change, we have

$$\frac{\Delta x}{x} = n - S(i,x) \tag{20}$$

Now, comparing our fundamental equation of change, (20), with the similar equation in the preceding section, equation (11):

$$\frac{\Delta x}{x} = n - S(x) \tag{11}$$

one might think that relaxing our assumptions, by permitting borrowing and lending, complicates the system (by adding another variable, namely, i) to the point where the dynamic system becomes indeterminate. After all, formula (20) is one equation in two unknowns, i and x. However, when we use all the information available to us, our system is not indeterminate.

At this point we recall that when we know x, we also know the relevant pair of I and S curves in the loans market. Thus, given x, we can find the interest rate that clears the loans market. In Figure 16-28, when x is equal to x_0, the interest rate implied by the equality $I(i,x_0) = S(i,x_0)$ is equal to i_0. Now, suppose that x is higher, namely, equal to x_1, and that the relevant I and S curves are the ones labeled $I(i,x_1)$ and $S(i,x_1)$. Their intersection gives an interest rate equal to i_1, lower than i_0. Two results evolve from the above exercise. First, that we can find a relation between x and i, or, in other words, that since $I(i,x) = S(i,x)$ always, the (market) interest rate that guarantees this equality is a function of the employment/capital ratio, x. Second, and this follows from the above graph, that the higher x is, the lower the interest rate will be.

The above results, unfortunately, are not unqualified, since we can show just as easily that an increase in x may increase the rate of interest, i, as seen in Figure 16-29. Comparison of Figures 16-28 and 16-29 reveals that whether i will

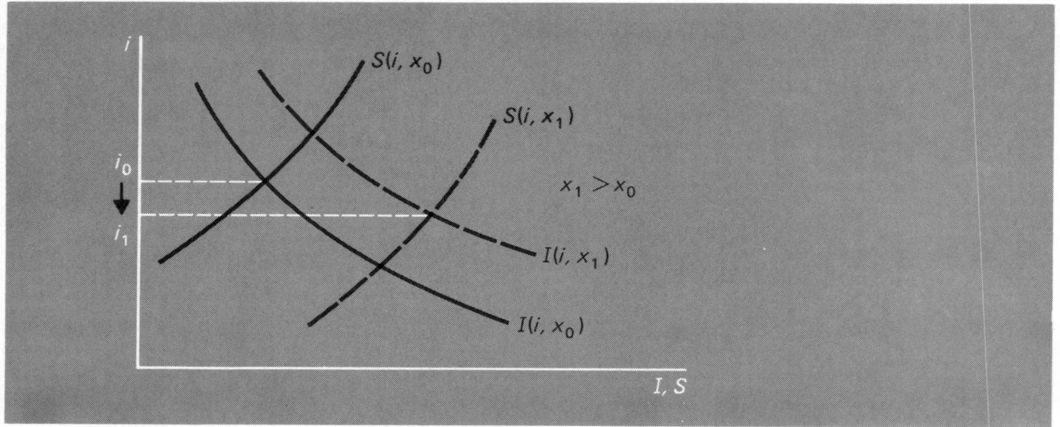

FIGURE 16-28

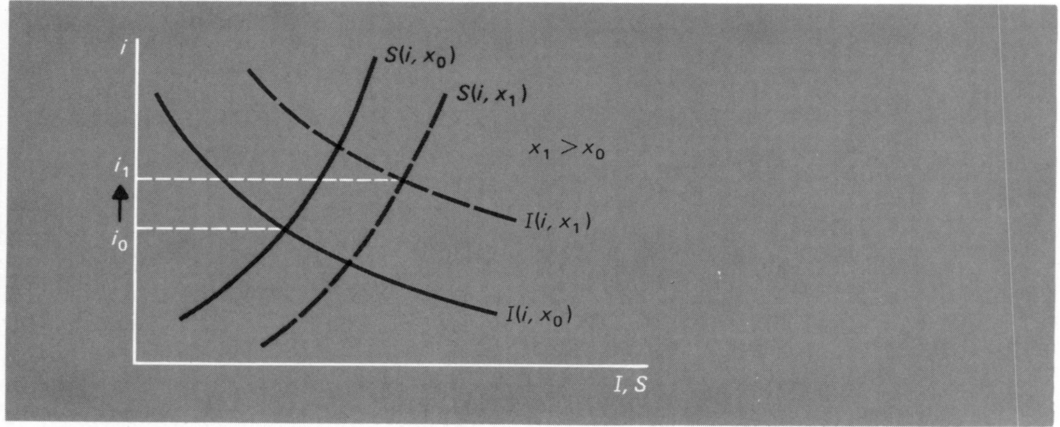

FIGURE 16-29

increase or decrease (because of a rise in x) depends on whether the outward shift of the I curve is greater than the outward shift of the S curve, or whether the opposite is true. When the former occurs, the interest rate will increase, but when the latter occurs, the interest rate will fall.

It seems, then, that when the effect of an increase in x on investment is less than it is on savings, the interest rate will fall, and when it is greater, the interest rate will rise. We can confirm this directly in Figure 16-30, which plots I and S against x. In this graph the interest rate enters parametrically (i.e., there is one I and S curve for each assumed i). In both parts of the graph, when i *falls* to $i_1 < i_0$, the investment schedule shifts upward (because investment is a decreasing function of i) and the savings curve shifts downward (because of the assumption, here, that S increases with i). Now, in Figure 16-30a, when i equals i_0, the x for which $I = S$ must be at the level x_0. When the interest rate is *lower* (i.e., $i_1 < i_0$), x *rises* to $x_1 > x_0$.

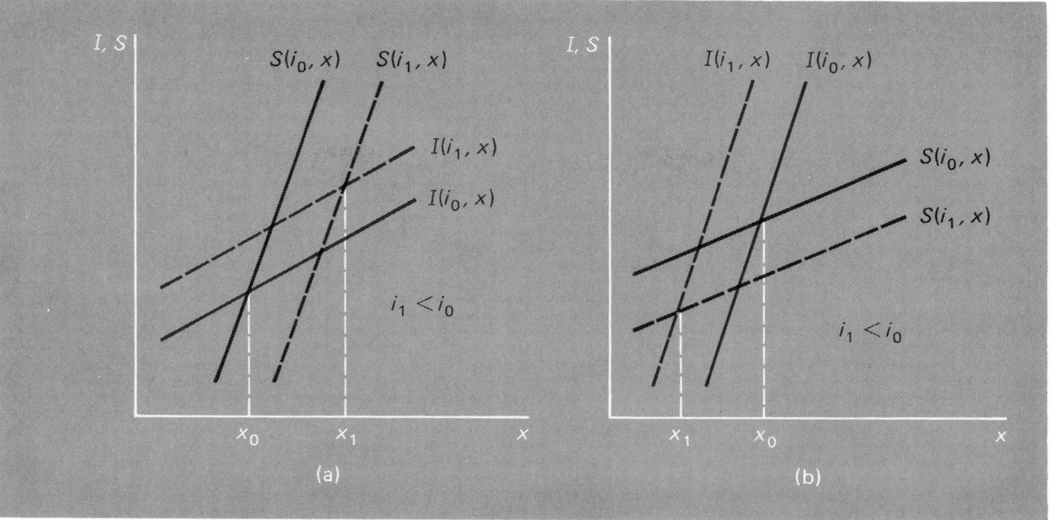

FIGURE 16-30

In Figure 16-30b, when $i = i_0$, x is again equal to x_0. But when *i falls* (to i_1), x also *falls* (to x_1).

It is clear, then, that in Figure 16-30b i and x move in the same direction, whereas in Figure 16-30a i and x move in opposite directions. The only difference between the two graphs involves the slope of the I and S curves: In Figure 16-30a the slope of the I curve is smaller than the slope of the S curve (i.e., $\Delta I/\Delta x < \Delta S/\Delta x$); in Figure 16-30b the opposite is true (i.e., $\Delta I/\Delta x > \Delta S/\Delta x$). The condition $\Delta I/\Delta x < \Delta S/\Delta x$ can be manipulated to show that it corresponds to the condition that the *marginal propensity to spend* (i.e., that the sum of the marginal propensity to consume and the marginal propensity to invest) is less than one.

This follows from the fact that $C + S \equiv Y$ and thus $\Delta C/\Delta Y + \Delta S/\Delta Y \equiv 1$. Hence $\Delta S/\Delta Y = 1 - \Delta C/\Delta Y$. Now $\Delta I/\Delta x < \Delta S/\Delta x$ holds if, and only if, $\Delta I/\Delta Y < \Delta S/\Delta Y$. Substituting in this last inequality for $\Delta S/\Delta Y$, we get $\Delta I/\Delta Y < 1 - \Delta C/\Delta Y$, or $\Delta C/\Delta Y + \Delta I/\Delta Y < 1$. In other words, the condition $\Delta I/\Delta x < \Delta S/\Delta x$ implies that the marginal propensity to spend is less than one.

As was noted in earlier chapters, there seems to be neither an *a priori* nor an empirical reason why the marginal propensity to spend should be less than or greater than one. Therefore, in order that our analysis may have wider applicability, we have not followed the convention that *assumes* that the marginal propensity to spend is less than one. Instead, in our analysis this magnitude has been permitted to be even greater than one.

Let us now summarize the thoughts of the last few pages in which we have been trying to find the relation between the interest rate and employment per unit of capital that is implied by continuous clearance of the loans market. We see that one thing is certain: As long as the response of investment demand to changes in the interest rate is smaller than the response of savings to a similar change (i.e., as

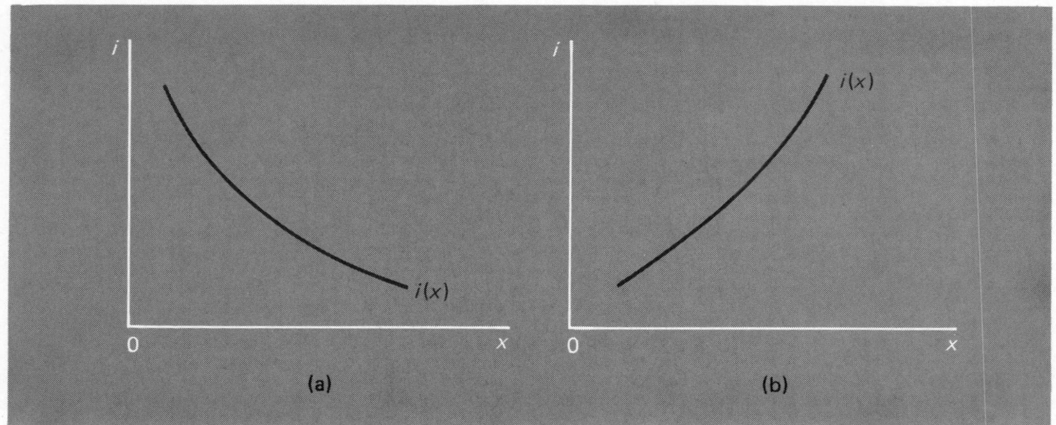

FIGURE 16-31

long as $\Delta I/\Delta i < \Delta S/\Delta i$), we have the right to say that in each period the loans market is cleared. Thus we can determine the level of the interest rate by knowing the level of x for this period. Moreover, we have just established the following result: In the (i,x)-plane the curve depicting the market-clearing interest rate is downward sloping when the marginal propensity to spend is less than one, as in Figure 16-31a, and upward sloping when the marginal propensity to spend is greater than one, as in Figure 16-31b.

We are now ready to continue our long-run analysis. In the fundamental equation of change:

$$\frac{\Delta x}{x} = n - S(i,x) \tag{20}$$

we can replace the interest rate with the general solution for the loans market, $I - S = 0$, that is, with $i(x)$. Thus, savings per unit of capital is *solely* a function of x. We denote this as $G(x)$:

$$S(i,x) = S[i(x),x] \equiv G(x) \tag{21}$$

It follows that our fundamental equation of change is only a function of x:

$$\frac{\Delta x}{x} = n - G(x) \tag{22}$$

Note that (22) is of the same form as the fundamental equation of change for the barter model without borrowing and lending:

$$\frac{\Delta x}{x} = n - S(x) \tag{11}$$

Thus we can reexamine all the issues we have already examined in the earlier model. But here we shall concentrate our efforts solely on differences between the two models.

We know that we can graphically depict the equilibrium of this system. As in the simpler model, the economy will come to rest only when x remains constant, that is, when $\Delta x = 0$. This, in turn, happens only when the rate of savings, $G(x)$, is equal to the rate of population growth:

$$G(x) = n \tag{23}$$

This is precisely the condition we derived from the simpler model.

In our attempt to depict this steady state graphically, we note that we do not even know how the savings rate, G, reacts to changes in x. In the simpler model, as long as the marginal propensity to save, MPS, is positive, the savings rate increases when x rises. Here the assumption of positive MPS is not enough for G to be an increasing function of x. By (21), we have

$$G(x) = S[i(x),x]$$

We see that an increase in x will have two effects. First, it has the tendency to increase S, as long as the MPS is positive, an effect captured by the second argument in $S[\cdot]$. However, there is also a second effect that operates through the loans market, and this is embodied in the first argument of $S[\cdot]$, namely $i(x)$. This effect is even indeterminate in sign. We know that an increase in x may either increase or decrease the interest rate, or even leave it unchanged. If, for example, the marginal propensity to spend is less than one (the typical assumption made in the literature), i will fall and this, in turn, will lower savings (assuming, along with the standard literature, that $\Delta S/\Delta i > 0$). In this case an increase in x will increase G only if the direct effect will outweigh the indirect, that is, the market-for-loans effect. On the other hand, when the relation between i and x is positive (i.e., when the marginal propensity to spend is greater than one), both effects point toward a higher G when x rises—provided that there is a positive relation between savings and the interest rate.

In summary, we have seen that the introduction of borrowing and lending forces us to cope with the determination of the interest rate and that this, in turn, requires additional restrictions on our model. We have seen that without additional assumptions we cannot determine the effect on G of an increase in x. Yet we know from our simple model that we need a positive relation between G and x if we are going to guarantee stability of the steady state.

In Figure 16-32a G is an increasing function of x. It intersects the population growth rate curve nn (which is independent of x) where x equals x_*. This steady-state employment/capital ratio is stable. In other words, if the economy starts at a point different from x_*, there are forces moving the economy *toward* x_*. In Figure 16-32b, however, the downward-sloping G curve results in an unstable steady state.

It is clear that if we are going to have a model that represents a stable economy, and, moreover, a system that can be used for comparative dynamics—say through policy—we need to guarantee that the direct effect (of an increase in x)

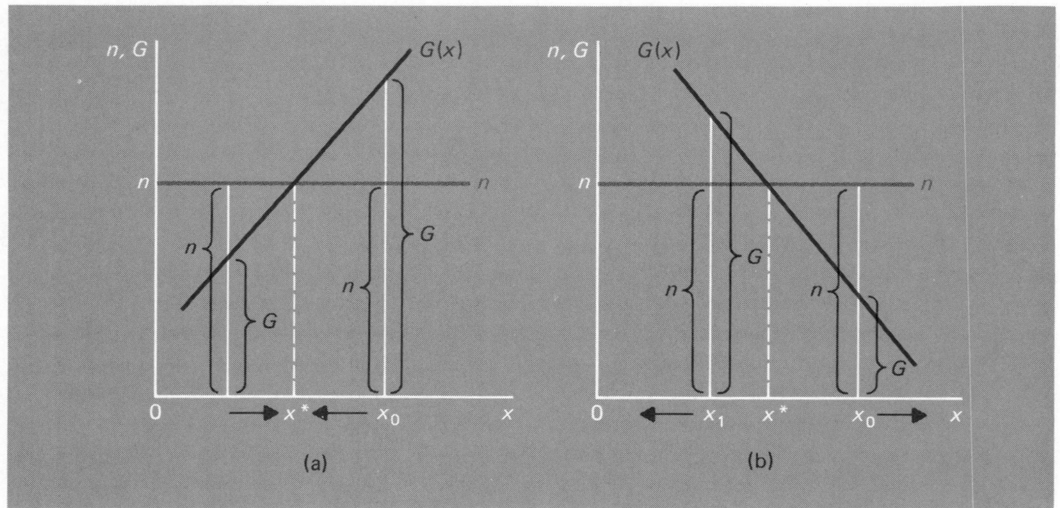

FIGURE 16-32

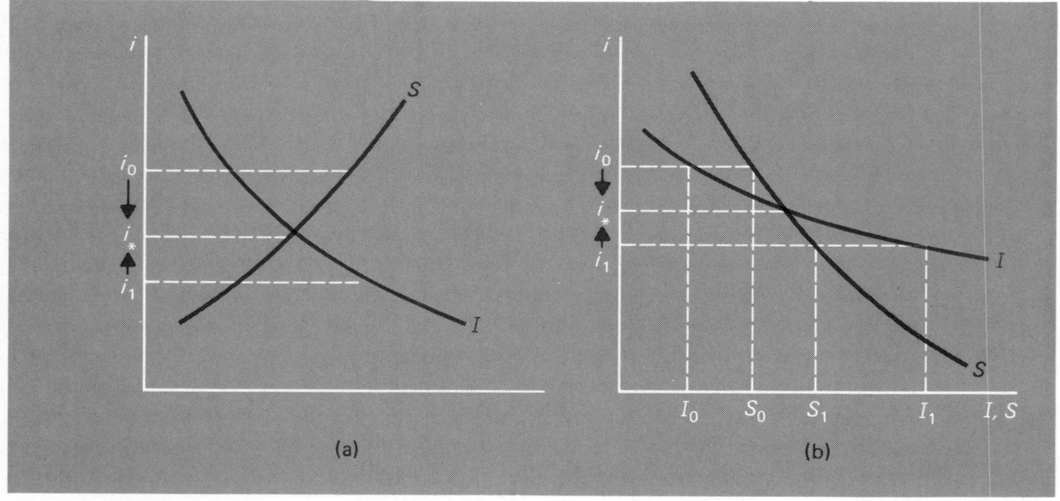

FIGURE 16-33

outweighs the loans market effect if the latter is negative. (The precise algebraic conditions are left for more advanced texts.)

As we mentioned above, we can perform the same exercises as in Section I. These, however, will be left to the reader. Instead, we shall show the usefulness of this richer model by solving a problem that could not even be formulated when we used the simple barter model.

Let us begin by supposing that the Kalecki-type risk premium is lowered for each level of investment. If so, what will its effect be on the steady-state labor/capital ratio and, therefore, on all other variables derived from x, such as w, r, and

C/K? We know from our earlier analysis, in Chapter 2, that the decrease in the risk premium will shift the investment schedule to the right. This will raise the interest rate, whether the savings curve increases or decreases with the interest rate, as shown in Figures 16-33a and 16-33b. Of course, these graphs are for a given x. But there are infinitely many I curves, one for each x. Therefore each one of these curves will shift to the right, which means that *for each* x the interest rate will rise, which, in turn, implies that savings per unit of capital G will rise for each x. This is the definition of a shift of the $G(x)$ curve to the left, namely, that for each x, G is greater than before. The change in the parameter, σ, the risk premium, is what engineers the shift in the G curve, as shown in Figure 16-34. This shift of the G curve decreases the steady state, x, from x_* to x_{**}, as shown in Figure 16-35.

FIGURE 16-34

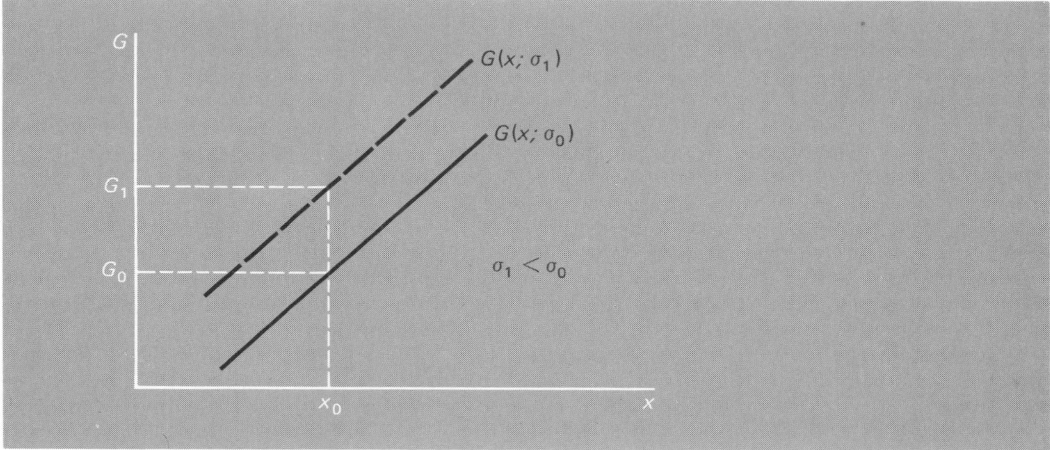

FIGURE 16-35

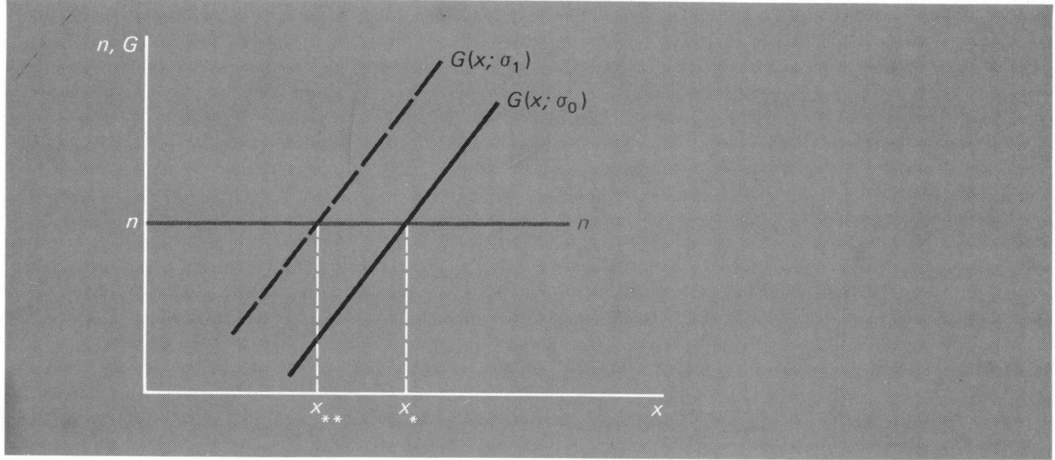

In summary, the introduction of borrowing and lending into the basic barter model enriches our understanding of the growth process. Among other things, it permits more plausible explanations of the data. This important extension of the Solow-Swan-Tobin growth model was achieved by Hugh Rose.[10]

QUESTIONS

1. Suppose that the rate of population growth of a capitalist economy falls. What will happen to the new steady-state wages and rate of return on capital? Explain fully.

2. Suppose that the economy becomes "thriftier." What would be the effect on the steady-state capital intensity, real wages, and rate of profit?

3. Suppose that an economy is at a steady state. Suppose also that the population grows at 2 percent and that the rate of profit is also 2 percent.
   a. Consumption, savings, output, and capital all grow at 2 percent. Why?
   b. Suppose that the society decides to save a higher percentage of its income. What will happen to the capital/labor ratio, the rate of profit, and the real wage in the new steady state?
   c. Will the economy *as a whole* gain or lose by the increase in savings propensity in part *b?* What is your criterion?

4. a. A crucial characteristic of many underdeveloped countries is that income per capita and consumption per capita are low and *keep falling.* Why is this so?
   b. Another characteristic is that they experience political and social unrest because a particular group of people enjoy very high incomes, which keep increasing while the rest of society as well as the average of society experience the opposite. Why is this so?

5. In the situations described in question 4, would foreign direct investment help? Would it be likely to occur? Why? Would foreign aid help? What would be an important determinant of the success of a foreign aid program?

6. a. If you are a labor union leader (or a worker), would you favor an increase in society's propensity to consume? Why?
   b. Would you favor the above increase in the propensity to consume if you were the president of the U.S. and in addition you were informed that the rate of profit is equal to 1 percent while the rate of population growth is equal to 2 percent? Would this move be consistent with your administration's goal to reduce poverty?

7. Suppose that it is agreed by everyone that the economy is at a steady state with the population growing at 4 percent per year and the rate of profit equal to 2 percent. Politician # 1 claims that he can improve *everybody's* welfare by lowering taxation and thereby lowering the marginal

[10] Hugh Rose, "Unemployment in a Theory of Growth," *International Economic Review,* September 1966.

and average propensities to save. Politician #2 claims that Politician #1 is a demagogue, since it is impossible to improve the country's position. As a proof, he points to the very small rate of profit. Comment on the respective merits of their positions.

8. Why does knowledge of x allow all the other variables of the model to be determined?

9. What is the "golden age"? What is the "golden rule"? What is the relationship between the two?

10. How are the results of the growth model altered when borrowing and lending are introduced?

REFERENCES

DOMAR, E., "Capital Expansion, Rate of Growth and Employment," *Econometrica,* 1946.

HADJIMICHALAKIS, M. G., "Equilibrium and Disequilibrium Growth with Money: The Tobin Models," *Review of Economic Studies,* October 1971, pp. 457–79.

HARROD, R. F. *Towards a Dynamic Economics,* "Lecture Three." London: Macmillan, 1948.

NELSON, R. R., "A Theory of the Low Level Equilibrium Trap in Underdeveloped Economics," *American Economic Review,* December 1956.

PHELPS, E. S., "Second Essay on the Golden Rule of Accumulation," *American Economic Review,* September 1965.

RAMSEY, F. P., "A Mathematical Theory of Saving," *Economic Journal,* December 1928, pp. 543–59.

ROBINSON, J., "A Neoclassical Theorem," *Review of Economic Studies,* June 1962, pp. 219–26.

ROSE, H., "Unemployment in a Theory of Growth," *International Economic Review,* September 1966.

SOLOW, R. M., "A Contribution to the Theory of Economic Growth," *Quarterly Journal of Economics,* February 1956, pp. 65–94.

SWAN, T., "Economic Growth and Capital Accumulation," *Economic Record,* November 1956, pp. 334–61.

TOBIN, J., "A Dynamic Aggregative Model," *Journal of Political Economy,* April 1955.

———, "Money and Economic Growth," *Econometrica,* October 1965.

Author Index